Lecture Notes in Computer Science

T0190027

Lecture Notes in Computer Science

Lecture Notes in Computer Science

Edited by G. Goos and J. Hartmanis

497

F. Dehne   F. Fiala
W.W. Koczkodaj (Eds.)

Advances in Computing and Information – ICCI '91

International Conference on Computing and Information
Ottawa, Canada, May 27–29, 1991
Proceedings

Springer-Verlag
Berlin Heidelberg New York London Paris
Tokyo Hong Kong Barcelona Budapest

Volume Editors

Frank Dehne
Frantisek Fiala
School of Computer Science
Carleton University
Ottawa, Canada K1S 5B6

Waldemar W. Koczkodaj
Department of Mathematics and Computer Science
Laurentian University
Sudbury, Canada P3E 2C6

CR Subject Classification (1991): D.1–2, E.2–4, F.0–2, H, I.2

ISBN 3-540-54029-6 Springer-Verlag Berlin Heidelberg New York
ISBN 0-387-54029-6 Springer-Verlag New York Berlin Heidelberg

Printing and binding: Druckhaus Beltz, Hemsbach/Bergstr.
2145/3140-543210 – Printed on acid-free paper

Preface

This volume contains papers presented at the *Third International Conference on Computing and Information*, ICCI'91, held at Carleton University in Ottawa, Canada, May 27-29, 1991. The conference was organized by the School of Computer Science at Carleton University, and was sponsored by the Natural Sciences and Engineering Research Council of Canada (NSERC) and Carleton University.

In response to the program committee's call for papers, 166 papers were submitted out of which 71 were selected for presentation, 60 as regular papers, 11 as short papers. In addition, 3 invited papers were presented.

ICCI'91 was an international forum for the presentation of original results in research, development, and applications in computing and information processing. The conference was aimed at both practitioners and theoreticians. It was organized along five streams:

- A Algorithms and Complexity,
- B Databases and Information Systems,
- C Parallel Processing and Systems,
- D Distributed Computing and Systems,
- E Expert Systems, Artificial Intelligence.

May 1991

F. Dehne
F. Fiala
W.W. Koczkodaj

General Chair: W. W. Koczkodaj (Laurentian U.)

Program Committee:

F. Dehne (Carleton U.), Chair

Stream A: Algorithms and Complexity

H. Alt (Freie U. Berlin)
T. Asano (Osaka Elec.-Comm. U.)
S. K. Das (U. of North Texas)
I. Gargantini (U. of Western Ontario)
K. Hinrichs (U. Gesamthochschule Siegen)
H. Jürgensen (U. of Western Ontario)
R. Klein (U. Gesamthochschule Essen)
B. Simons (IBM Almaden Research Centre)

Stream B: Databases and Information Systems

T. Merrett (McGill U.)
J. Orenstein (Object Design)
E. Otoo (Carleton U.)
J. Slonim (IBM Canada Laboratory)

Stream C: Parallel Processing and Systems

S. Akl (Queen's U.)
M. Cosnard (Ecole Normale Superieure de Lyon)
G.R. Gao (McGill U.)
M.A. Langston (U. of Tennessee)
R. Miller (State U. of New York)

Stream D: Distributed Computing and Systems

J.E. Burns (Georgia Institute of Technology)
Y.H. Chin (National Tsing-Hua U.)
G. Karam (Carleton U.)
N. Santoro (Carleton U.)
H. Wedde (Wayne State U.)

Stream E: Expert Systems, AI

F. Bacchus (U. of Waterloo)
N. Cercone (Simon Fraser U.)
M. Gini (U. of Minnesota)
J.I. Glasgow (Queen's U.)
T.A. Marsland (U. of Alberta)
D. Peacock (Bell-Northern Research)
D. Scuse (U. of Manitoba)

Organizing Committee:

F. Fiala (Carleton U.), Chair
R. Carter (Carleton U.)
J. Chinneck (Carleton U.)
L. Nel (Carleton U.)
J. Oommen (Carleton U.)

List of Referees

Ahamad, M.
Ajtai, M.
Akl, S.
Akyildiz, I.
Alt, H.
Asano, T.
Bacchus, F.
Baron, R.
Bloemer, J
Burns, J.E.
Cercone, N.
Chin, Y.H.
Cosnard, M.
Das, S. K.
Dehne, F.
Deugo, D.
Elcock, E.W.
Fars, D.
Fiala, F.

Gao, G.R.
Gargantini, I.
Gini, M.
Glasgow, J.I.
Godau, M.
Groeneboer, C.
Haber, F.
Hall, G.
Hinrichs, K.
Iwanowski, S.
Jürgensen, H.
Karam, G.
Klein, R.
Koczkodaj, W.W.
Lakshmanan, L.V.S.
Langston, M.A.
Marsland, T.A.
McFetridge, P.
Merrett, T.

Miller, R.
Orenstein, J.
Osborne, R.
Otoo, E.
Peacock, D.
Popowich, F.
Schaeffer, S.
Scuse, D.
Shilling, J.
Simons, B.
Slonim, J.
Szafron, D.
van Beek, P.
Vogel, C.
Webber, R.E.
Wedde, H.
Wu, X.
Yu, S.
Zhang, K.

Table of Contents

4. Parallel Processing and Systems   299

5. Distributed Computing and Systems   509

6. Expert Systems, Artificial Intelligence   641

Author Index   745

1. Invited Papers

What's Wrong With Formal Programming Methods?

Eric C.R. Hehner

Department of Computer Science, University of Toronto, Toronto M5S 1A4 Canada

The January 1991 issue of *Computing Research News* includes the headline **Formal Software Design Methods Next Step In Improving Quality**, with an excellent article by Dick Kieburtz [0] explaining the advantage to industry of taking this step. The trouble is: it's been the next step for ten years! In May 1982 Tony Hoare [1] made the same argument very persuasively: software engineering is not worthy of the name, certainly is not a profession, until it is based on scientific principles and is practiced with the same degree of precision as other professional engineering. Since then, formal methods have been learned and used by a few companies in Europe, though it is not yet known how successfully (people are always ready to claim success for their latest efforts). In North America, formal methods have hardly made a start. Why such a poor showing for something so highly recommended?

Before answering, I should say what is meant by formal programming methods. There is a widespread misconception that "formal" means careful and detailed, and "informal" means either sloppy or sketchy. Even authors of mathematical texts, who should know better, sometimes make a statement (in English), followed by the word "Formally", followed by a more careful and detailed statement (in English). By "formal" we mean using a mathematical formalism. A mathematical formalism is a notation (set of formulas) intended to aid in the precise and concise expression of some limited discourse. A theory is a formalism together with some rules of proof or calculation so that we can say what observations to expect. We can have a theory of almost anything, from a theory of matter, to a theory of motion, to a theory of computation, to a theory of theories.

What good is a theory of programming? Who wants it? Thousands of programmers program every day without it. Why should they bother to learn it? The answer is the same as for any other theory. For example, why should anyone learn a theory of motion? You can move around perfectly well without it. You can throw a ball without it. Yet we think it important enough to teach a theory of motion in high school.

What's Right

One answer is that a mathematical theory gives a much greater degree of precision by providing a method of calculation. It is unlikely that we could send a rocket to Jupiter without a mathematical theory of motion. And even baseball pitchers are finding that their pitch can be improved by hiring an expert who knows some theory. Similarly a lot of mundane programming can be done without the aid of a theory of programming, but the more difficult programming is very unlikely to be done correctly without a good theory. The software industry has an overwhelming experience of buggy programs to support that statement. And even mundane programming can be improved by the use of a theory.

Another answer is that a theory provides a kind of understanding. Our ability to control and predict motion changes from an art to a science when we learn a mathematical theory. Similarly programming changes from an art to a science when we learn to understand programs in the same way we understand mathematical theorems. With a scientific outlook, we change our view of how the world works and what is possible. It is a valuable part of education for anyone.

Formal programming methods allows us to prove that a computation does what its specification says it should do. More importantly, formal methods help us to write specifications, and to design programs so that their computations will provably satisfy a specification. This is analogous to the use of mathematics in all professional engineering: civil engineers must know and apply the theories of geometry and material stress; electrical engineers must know and apply electromagnetic theory. So why don't software engineers know and apply a theory of programming?

What's Wrong

The reason most often cited is lack of programmer education. Even programmers with a degree in computer science from a respectable university are unlikely to know any formal programming methods, because only a small fraction of universities teach that subject, and where it is taught it is probably an optional course taken by a small fraction of the students there. It is usually placed late in the curriculum, after students have been taught to program, and so implicitly taught that formal methods are not necessary.

Education may be part of the reason, but I think there is another reason that the software industry has not yet adopted formal methods. The methods offered by academia so far have been clumsy, unwieldy, awkward methods. They slow down the process of software production without increasing the quality. It is just as easy to make mistakes in the use of the formalism and in proofs as it is to make mistakes in programming. The typical result at present is a buggy program together with a buggy proof resulting in the erroneous conclusion: program proved correct.

Formal methods with proofs potentially offer a far more powerful means of finding errors in programs than testing, because a proof considers all possible computations at once, whereas testing considers only one computation at a time. To realize this potential, we must be able to do proofs accurately. Verification of a finished program against the original specification has been justifiably criticized as next to impossible. But proofs of programming steps, during program construction, have been shown to be quite do-able. Typically they are not too deep, but they involve a lot of detail, and that's where the errors occur. That's exactly the sort of task that computers should be helping us with. It is reasonable to hope that some day a prover will be as common and helpful a part of programming systems as a syntax checker and type checker are today. If history is any guide, the first ones will be usable only by their own designers, and they may confirm negative feeling about formal methods. But later, polished provers will be able to say "bug on line 123", with an indication of what's wrong, as reliably as syntax checkers and type checkers do now.

Three formalisms

Let us examine some of the formal methods academia has offered industry. The first usable theory was outlined by Hoare [2] in 1969 (based on earlier work by Floyd); it is still probably the most widely known. In it, a specification is a pair of predicates of the state, called the precondition and the postcondition. To say that a program or program fragment S satisfies the specification given by precondition P and postcondition R we write

$$\{P\}\ S\ \{R\}$$

meaning: if P is true at the start of execution of S, then execution will terminate and R will be true at the end. (The notation here is not the original one, but it is the one universally used now; the meaning here is total correctness, not the original partial correctness.) Let's try it on a trivial example. Informally, the specification is to increase the value of integer variable x. Formally, we face a problem: we are given no way to relate the final value of a variable to its initial value. We have to use a trick: introduce an extra variable, not part of the state space, to carry the relation. We write

$$\forall X \cdot \{x = X\}\ S\ \{x > X\}$$

meaning: whatever x may have been equal to at the start, it is greater than that at the end. For S we might propose the assignment $x := x+1$. To prove it correct, we must use the assignment rule

$$\{\text{substitute } e \text{ for } x \text{ in } R\ \}\ x := e\ \{R\}$$

In the example, this means

$$\{x+1 > X\}\ x := x+1\ \{x > X\}$$

The precondition is not what we want, so we now use the consequence rule

$$(\forall \sigma \cdot A \Rightarrow P) \wedge \{P\}\ S\ \{R\} \wedge (\forall \sigma \cdot R \Rightarrow Z) \Rightarrow \{A\}\ S\ \{Z\}$$

where σ (the state) stands for all variables. In the example, this means we must prove

$$\forall x \cdot (x = X) \Rightarrow (x+1 > X)$$

which is now a simple theorem of ordinary logic. All that, just to prove the obvious! Perhaps the example is unfair precisely because it is so obvious; the formalism is meant to help with problems that are not obvious. On the other hand, we fear that if trivial problems are this difficult, nontrivial ones will be impossible. We'll try a slightly bigger example later. Also, a sequence of proof steps can be collapsed into one step by the use of derived rules. There is a trade-off: fewer steps, but more rules to learn.

Dijkstra [3] designed a formalism in 1976 that defines the semantics of programs explicitly by a function instead of implicitly by axioms. This formalism is probably the most studied one, certainly the one used by most textbooks on formal methods (including one by me). For program (fragment) S and postcondition R, $wp(S, R)$ is the necessary and sufficient precondition for execution of S to end in postcondition R. As before, we use a pair of predicates of the state as specification. To say that a program or program fragment S satisfies the specification given by precondition P and postcondition R we write

$$\forall \sigma \cdot P \Rightarrow wp(S, R)$$

To say "increase x", we still face the problem of relating final values to initial values. We write

$$\forall x, X \cdot (x = X) \Rightarrow wp(S, x > X)$$

As before, we can try the assignment $x := x+1$ for S. wp applied to an assignment is defined as

$$wp(x := e, R) = (\text{substitute } e \text{ for } x \text{ in } R)$$

so we must prove, as before,

$$\forall x, X \cdot (x = X) \Rightarrow (x+1 > X)$$

The formalism that has been used most by industry (in Europe) is Jones's VDM [4]. As in the previous two, a specification is a pair of predicates, but the second predicate is a relation between the initial and final states. The formalism automatically gives us a way to refer to the initial values of variables within the second predicate: the initial value of x is an x with a left-pointing arrow over it. My word processor lacks that typographic ability, so I shall use $\overleftarrow{x}$, which we can pronounce "pre x". The semantics of programs is given implicitly by axioms, as in Hoare logic, and the Hoare triple notation is used. The problem of increasing x

becomes

$$\{true\}\ S\ \{x > \grave{}x\}$$

The precondition *true* means that we want x increased under all initial conditions. Once again, let's take $x := x+1$ for S. One of the two rules for assignment is

$$\{true\}\ x := e\ \{x = \grave{}e\}$$

In our example, that gives us

$$\{true\}\ x := x+1\ \{x = \grave{}x+1\}$$

The postcondition is not what we want so we need to use the consequence rule

$$(\forall \sigma \cdot A \Rightarrow P)\ \wedge\ \{P\}\ S\ \{R\}\ \wedge\ (\forall \grave{}\sigma, \sigma \cdot R \Rightarrow Z)\ \Rightarrow\ \{A\}\ S\ \{Z\}$$

This means proving

$$\forall \grave{}x, x \cdot (x = \grave{}x+1) \Rightarrow (x > \grave{}x)$$

as before.

A New View

People often confuse programs with computer behavior. They talk about what a program "does"; of course it just sits there on the page or screen; it is the computer that "does" something. They ask whether a program "terminates"; of course it does; it is the execution that may not terminate. A program is not computer behavior, but a description or specification of computer behavior. Furthermore, a computer may not behave as specified by a program for a variety of reasons: a disk head may crash, a compiler may have a bug, or a resource may become exhausted (stack overflow, number overflow), to mention a few. Then the difference between a program and computer behavior is obvious.

As we shall see, this small confusion has been a large hindrance in the development of formal methods. We have always talked about "the specification of programs", and "a program satisfies a specification". We have always had two languages: the specification language (usually ordinary logic), and the programming language. But we are *not* specifying programs; we are specifying computation. A program *is* a specification. We need *one* language.

A program is a specification, but not every specification is a program. A program is an implemented specification, one that a computer can execute. To be so, it must be written in a subset of the specification language, called the programming language.

A specification serves as a contract between a client who wants a computer to behave a certain way and a programmer who customizes a computer to behave as desired. For this purpose, a specification must be written as clearly, as understandably, as possible. The programmer then refines the specification to obtain a program, which a computer can execute. Sometimes the clearest, most understandable specification is already a program. When that is so, there is no need for any other specification, and no need for refinement. However, the programming notations are only part of the specification notations: those that happen to be implemented. Specifiers should use whatever notations help to make their specifications clear, including but not limited to programming notations.

A New Formalism

To go with the change in view, I offer a new formalism, described in [5] and in a forthcoming book [6]. In it, a specification is a single predicate in the initial and final values of the variables. The initial value of x is undecorated, and the final value is x'. To say that x is to be increased, we write simply

$$x' > x$$

That is surely the clearest and simplest form of specification. As we will see later, the reduction to a single predicate is no loss of information. Since a program is a specification, a program must also be a predicate in the initial and final values of the variables. For example, an assignment $x := e$ is a predicate that could be written in conventional logic notation as

$$(x := e) = (x' = e \wedge y' = y \wedge \ldots)$$

saying that $x' = e$ and all other variables are are unchanged. Semantics is explicit, as in Dijkstra's formalism, using initial and final values of variables as in Jones's formalism.

Given a specification S, the programmer's problem is to find a program P such that computer behavior satisfying P also satisfies S. In logic terms, that means

$$P \Rightarrow S$$

With specification $x' > x$ and program $x := x+1$ we must prove

$$(x' = x+1) \Rightarrow (x' > x)$$

This is the same as in the previous formalisms, but we arrive here directly.

Multiplication, Hoare-style

A more reasonable comparison of these formal methods can be made with a slightly larger example. Let x and y be integer variables; when x and y are initially nonnegative, we want their product $x \times y$ to be the final value of variable x. The program could be just

$$x := x \times y$$

except that we disallow multiplication, allowing only addition, multiplication by 2, division by 2, testing for even or odd, and testing for zero. This is exactly the situation of the designer of a multplier in a binary computer, and our program will be the standard binary multiplication.

First let us use Hoare Logic. The most convenient way to use it is not to quote rules explicitly, but implicitly by the placement of the predicates. Predicates surrounding an assignment must be according to the assignment rule.

> {substitute e for x in R }
>
> $x := e$
>
> {R}

The sequential composition rule

$$\{P\}\ A\ \{Q\}\ \wedge\ \{Q\}\ B\ \{R\} \ \Rightarrow\ \{P\}\ A;B\ \{R\}$$

simply places the intermediate predicate between the statements.

> $\{P\}$
>
> $A;$
>
> $\{Q\}$
>
> B
>
> $\{R\}$

Predicates placed next to one another must be according to the consequence rule, the first implying the second. A predicate before an **if**-statement must be copied to the start of each branch, in one case conjoined with the condition, and in the other conjoined with its negation. The predicate after the entire **if**-statement must be the disjunction of the predicates at the ends of the two branches.

> $\{P\}$
>
> **if** c **then** $\{P \wedge c\}$ A $\{Q\}$ **else** $\{P \wedge \neg c\}$ B $\{R\}$
>
> $\{Q \vee R\}$

The predicate before a **while**-loop must be of a particular form: $I \wedge 0 \le v$ where I is called the invariant, and v is an integer expression called the variant. The predicate after the loop must be the invariant conjoined with the negation of the condition. Using V as an extra variable to stand for the initial value of the variant, the body of the loop must satisfy the specification shown below.

> $\{I \wedge 0 \le v\}$
>
> **while** c **do** $\{I \wedge 0 \le v = V \wedge c\}$ B $\{I \wedge 0 \le v < V\}$
>
> $\{I \wedge \neg c\}$

Here it all is in action.

> $\forall X, Y \cdot$ $\{0 \le x = X \wedge 0 \le y = Y\}$
>
> $s := 0$
>
> $\{0 \le x = X \wedge 0 \le y = Y \wedge s = 0\};$

$\{s + x \times y = X \times Y \wedge 0 \leq y\}$

while $y \neq 0$ **do**

    $\{s + x \times y = X \times Y \wedge 0 < y = Y\}$

    if *even*(y) **then begin**

        $\{s + x \times y = X \times Y \wedge 0 < y = Y \wedge even(y)\}$

        $\{s + x \times 2 \times y/2 = X \times Y \wedge 0 \leq y/2 < Y\}$

        $x := x \times 2;$

        $\{s + x \times y/2 = X \times Y \wedge 0 \leq y/2 < Y\}$

        $y := y/2$

        $\{s + x \times y = X \times Y \wedge 0 \leq y < Y\}$ **end**

    else begin

        $\{s + x \times y = X \times Y \wedge 0 < y = Y \wedge \neg even(y)\}$

        $\{s + x + x \times (y-1) = X \times Y \wedge 0 \leq (y-1)/2 < Y\}$

        $s := s + x;$

        $\{s + x \times 2 \times (y-1)/2 = X \times Y \wedge 0 \leq (y-1)/2 < Y\}$

        $x := x \times 2;$

        $\{s + x \times (y-1)/2 = X \times Y \wedge 0 \leq (y-1)/2 < Y\}$

        $y := (y-1)/2$

        $\{s + x \times y = X \times Y \wedge 0 \leq y < Y \}$ **end**

    $\{s + x \times y = X \times Y \wedge 0 \leq y < Y\}$

$\{s + x \times y = X \times Y \wedge y = 0\};$

$\{s = X \times Y\}$

$x := s$

$\{x = X \times Y\}$

Multiplication, Dijkstra-style

To use Dijkstra's formalism for the multiplication problem we will need to apply wp to **if**, **while**, and sequential composition, in addition to assignment. Two of them are reasonably easy:

$$wp(\textbf{if } c \textbf{ then } A \textbf{ else } B, R) = (c \Rightarrow wp(A, R)) \wedge (\neg c \Rightarrow wp(B, R))$$

$$wp(A; B, R) = wp(A, wp(B, R))$$

The treatment of loops is more difficult. We must define $wp(W, R)$ where W is the loop **while** c **do** B. We do so as the limit of a sequence of approximations. We define $W_0, W_1, W_2, \ldots$ as follows:

$$wp(W_0, R) = \textit{false}$$

$$wp(W_{n+1}, R) = wp(\textbf{if } c \textbf{ then begin } B; W_n \textbf{ end}, R)$$

From this recurrence we can calculate $wp(W_n, R)$ for any natural n. Then

$$wp(W, R) = \exists n \cdot wp(W_n, R)$$

Unfortunately, this is not directly usable for the development and practical proving of programs. Instead, we use it to prove a theorem similar to the **while** rule in Hoare Logic.

$$I \wedge 0 \leq v \wedge (I \wedge 0 \leq v = V \wedge c \Rightarrow wp(B, I \wedge 0 \leq v < V)) \Rightarrow wp(W, I \wedge \neg c)$$

It says roughly: if the invariant is true before the start of the loop, and the body maintains the invariant and decreases the variant but not below zero, then the loop execution terminates and results in the invariant and the negation of the loop condition.

Most users of Dijkstra's formalism do not state their proof obligations explicitly in terms of wp; instead they present them implicitly by the placement of assertions in the program text, exactly as do the user's of the Hoare formalism. In practice, the two formalisms are used the same way.

Multiplication, Jones-style

Jones offers two formats for the use of VDM. One is to name every piece of a program, and to state separately the pre- and postcondition for each name. The other is to place them in the program text as in the Hoare style. But there is a difference: for Jones, a predicate cannot serve as both the postcondition for one statement and the precondition for the sequentially following statement because a precondition is a predicate of one state and a postcondition is a predicate of two states. The rule for sequential composition is

$$\{P\}\ A\ \{Q\}\ \wedge\ (\forall\ `\sigma, \sigma\cdot Q \Rightarrow R)\ \wedge\ \{R\}\ B\ \{S\}\ \Rightarrow\ \{P\}\ A;B\ \{Q;S\}$$

where $Q;S$ is relational composition, defined as

$$(Q;S)(`\sigma, \sigma) = \exists\sigma''\cdot Q(`\sigma, \sigma')\wedge S(\sigma'', \sigma)$$

The VDM book suggests that these predicates be placed in the program in the following format:

$$\{P\}$$

$$\{P\}$$
$$A$$
$$\{Q\}$$

$$;$$

$$\{R\}$$
$$B$$
$$\{S\}$$

$$\{Q;S\}$$

It seems we must pay for the convenience of having initial values given to us in the formalism by making the sequential composition rule more complicated. We pay even more for the **while** rule.

$$\{I \wedge 0 \leq v\}$$

while c **do** $\{I \wedge 0 \leq v \wedge c\}\ B\ \{I \wedge 0 \leq v < `v \wedge R\}$

$$\{I \wedge \neg c \wedge (R \vee ok)\}$$

where R must be a transitive relation, and ok is the identity relation. The rule for **if** is unchanged from Hoare logic.

Putting it all together, we get the following.

$\{0 \le x \wedge 0 \le y\}$

$\quad\{0 \le y\}$

$\quad s := 0$

$\quad\{x = \grave{}x \wedge 0 \le y = \grave{}y \wedge s = 0\}$

$;$

$\quad\{0 \le y\}$

while $y \ne 0$ **do**

$\quad\{0 < y\}$

if *even(y)* **then begin**

$\quad\{0 < y \wedge even(y)\}$

$\quad\quad\{0 < y \wedge even(y)\}$

$\quad\quad x := x \times 2$

$\quad\quad\{x = \grave{}x/2 \wedge 0 < y = \grave{}y \wedge even(\grave{}y) \wedge s = \grave{}s\}$

$\quad ;$

$\quad\quad\{0 < y \wedge even(y)\}$

$\quad\quad y := y/2$

$\quad\quad\{x = \grave{}x \wedge y = \grave{}y/2 \wedge 0 < \grave{}y \wedge even(\grave{}y) \wedge s = \grave{}s\}$

$\quad\{0 \le y < \grave{}y \wedge s + x \times y = \grave{}s + \grave{}x \times \grave{}y\}$ **end**

else begin

$\quad\{0 < y \wedge \neg even(y)\}$

$\quad\quad\{0 < y \wedge \neg even(y)\}$

$\quad\quad s := s + x$

$\quad\quad\{x = \grave{}x \wedge 0 < y = \grave{}y \wedge \neg even(\grave{}y) \wedge s = \grave{}s + \grave{}x\}$

$\quad ;$

$\quad\quad\{0 < y \wedge \neg even(y)\}$

$\quad\quad x := x \times 2$

$$\{x=`x{\times}2 \wedge 0{<}y=`y \wedge \neg even(`y) \wedge s=`s\}$$

;

$$\{0{<}y \wedge \neg even(y)\}$$

$$y := (y-1)/2$$

$$\{x=`x \wedge y=(`y-1)/2 \wedge 0{<}`y \wedge \neg even(`y) \wedge s=`s\}$$

$$\{0{\leq}y{<}`y \wedge s+x{\times}y = `s+`x{\times}`y\} \textbf{ end}$$

$$\{0{\leq}y{<}`y \wedge s+x{\times}y = `s+`x{\times}`y\}$$

$$\{y=0 \wedge (s+x{\times}y = `s+`x{\times}`y \vee x=`x \wedge y=`x \wedge s=`s))\}$$

$$\{s = `s + `x{\times}`y\}$$

;

$$\{true\}$$

$$x := s$$

$$\{x = `s\}$$

$$\{x = `x{\times}`y\}$$

Multiplication, new way

In order to use a formalism for program construction, not just for after-the-fact verification, a programmer has to be able to progress from specification to program in small steps. In general, one may need to form a sequence of specifications $S_0\, S_1$ $S_2\, ...\, S_n$ starting with the given specification S_0 and ending with a program S_n. Each specification is said to be "refined" by the next. Intermediate specifications, and even the original specification, may be partly in programming notation and partly in nonprogramming notation waiting to be refined. Refinement relates two specifications, not necessarily a specification and a program. We say specification S is refined by specification R, written $S{\cdot}: R$, if all computer behavior satisfying R also satisfies S. We define it formally as

$$(S{\cdot}: R) = (\forall \sigma, \sigma'{\cdot}\ S \Leftarrow R)$$

where $\Leftarrow$ is "is implied by".

In this formalism, a program is a predicate, and it could be written in traditional predicate noations. The empty (do nothing) program ok is the identity relation:

$$ok \quad = \quad (x'{=}x \wedge y'{=}y \wedge s'{=}s)$$

We saw assignment previously. For example,

$$(x{:=}\, x{\times}2) \quad = \quad (x' = x{\times}2 \wedge y'{=}y \wedge s'{=}s)$$

Specifications P and Q can be composed by relational composition $P;Q$. And **if then else** is just a ternary boolean operator that can be defined by a truth table or by equating to other boolean operators.

$$\textbf{if } c \textbf{ then } a \textbf{ else } b \quad = \quad c \wedge a \vee \neg c \wedge b$$

We simplify our lives enormously by leaving out the **while** loop in favor of recursion.

Here is the multiplication example.

$$x' = x{\times}y\cdot: \quad s{:=}\, 0; \quad s' = s + x{\times}y; \quad x{:=}\, s$$

$$s' = s + x{\times}y\cdot: \quad \textbf{if } y{=}0 \textbf{ then } ok$$
$$\textbf{else if } even(y) \textbf{ then } (x{:=}\, x{\times}2; \quad y{:=}\, y/2; \quad s' = s + x{\times}y)$$
$$\textbf{else } (s{:=}\, s{+}x; \quad x{:=}\, x{\times}2; \quad y{:=}\, (y{-}1)/2; \quad s' = s + x{\times}y)$$

Each of these refinements is a theorem of ordinary logic. The first says that the specification $x' = x{\times}y$ is implied by the relational composition of three predicates. This relational composition is now a new specification, most of which is already in programming notation. We just need to refine the middle part. There are no special inference rules for programming. We can make them look like traditional logic by making the translations we have given, then prove them in the ordinary way. Or better yet, we can prove some laws about programming notations and use them to prove these theorems more directly. For example, the Substitution Law says

$$(x:= e; P) \quad = \quad (\text{substitute } e \text{ for } x \text{ in } P)$$

This is not an axiom or postulate, but an easily proven law. Using it to simplify the $y{\neq}0 \wedge even(y)$ case, we get

$$x:= x{\times}2; \quad y:= y/2; \quad s' = s + x{\times}y$$

$$= \quad x:= x{\times}2; \quad s' = s + x{\times}y/2$$

$$= \quad s' = s + x{\times}2{\times}y/2$$

$$= \quad s' = s + x{\times}y$$

Similarly in the $y{\neq}0 \wedge \neg even(y)$ case, making all three substitutions at once,

$$s:= s{+}x; \quad x:= x{\times}2; \quad y:= (y{-}1)/2; \quad s' = s + x{\times}y$$

$$= \quad s' = s{+}x + x{\times}2{\times}(y{-}1)/2$$

$$= \quad s' = s + x{\times}y$$

Each of these cases implies (in fact, equals) the specification being refined. All that remains is

$$y{=}0 \wedge ok$$

$$= \quad y{=}0 \wedge x'{=}x \wedge y'{=}y \wedge s'{=}s$$

$$\Rightarrow \quad s' = s + x{\times}y$$

Clearly these proofs are completely trivial, and can be carried out automatically and silently by a prover.

To a prover, the programming notations are predicates. To a compiler, the nonprogramming notations are just identifiers. To a compiler, the above refinements look like this:

$$P{\cdot}: \quad s:= 0; \quad Q; \quad x:= s$$

$$Q{\cdot}: \quad \textbf{if } y{=}0 \textbf{ then } ok$$

$$\textbf{else if } even(y) \textbf{ then } (x:= x{\times}2; \quad y:= y/2; \quad Q)$$

$$\textbf{else } (s:= s{+}x; \quad x:= x{\times}2; \quad y:= (y{-}1)/2; \quad Q)$$

The occurrence of Q in the first line can be compiled as an inline "macro". The occurrences of Q at the ends of the last two lines can be compiled as branches back to the labelling Q , and that is the loop.

Execution Time

In one respect, we have been cheating. If the specification were really as we have said, we could have written a simpler program, say one that runs in linear time. We wanted logarithmic time, but we never said so, and never proved that we have achieved it. This criticism applies to all developments so far.

The problem is easily solved: we just add a time variable t , and increase its value to represent the passage of time. We can use the formalism we already have, without change, to reason about the final value of t and thus find the execution time. The time variable is ignored by the compiler; it is there for the prover.

In the multiplication example, we place an assignment $t := t+$something in each of the two parts of the **if** that take time. If we know enough about the compiler and the hardware to know exactly how long each part takes, we can increase t by that amount and find the real-time of execution. If not, let's just increase t by 1 .

$P\colon\quad s := 0;\ Q;\ x := s$

$Q\colon$ **if** $y=0$ **then** ok

        else if $even(y)$ **then** $(x := x \times 2;\ y := y/2;\ t := t+1;\ Q)$

        else $(s := s+x;\ x := x \times 2;\ y := (y-1)/2;\ t := t+1;\ Q)$

Each of these refinements is a theorem when we replace P and Q by

if $y<0$ **then** $t'-t = \infty$ **else if** $y=0$ **then** $t'-t = 0$ **else** $t'-t \le 1 + log_2 y$

This says that if y starts negative, exection time is infinite; if y starts at 0, execution time is 0; if y starts positive, execution time is bounded by $1 + log_2y$.

The proof proceeds by cases; we'll look at the case $y>0 \wedge even(y)$. In this case, we have

$$x:= x\times2; \; y:= y/2; \; t:= t+1; \; t'-t \le 1 + log_2y$$

$$= \quad t'-(t+1) \le 1 + log_2(y/2)$$

$$= \quad t'-t \le 1 + log_2y$$

In the previous formalisms, we proved termination by finding a variant. A variant is really a time bound, though we did not call it that; the variant we used proved that execution time was at most linear in y. We then threw away the bound, and concluded only that execution time was finite. To conclude that execution terminates (without stating a bound) is of no practical use, for it gives no clue how long one must wait for a result. If a program is claimed to have finite execution time, but in fact has infinite execution time, there is no time at which a complaint can be made that execution has taken too long.

It is sometimes important to be able to say and prove that execution will not terminate. If we refine $P\cdot: P$, we have an infinite loop. Charging time 1 for each iteration, we can prove

$$t'-t = \infty\cdot: \; t:= t+1; \; t'-t = \infty$$

The right side of this refinement can be simplified according to the Substitution Law as follows:

$$t:= t+1; \; t'-t = \infty$$

$$= \quad t'-(t+1) = \infty$$

$$= \quad t'-t = \infty+1$$

$$= \quad t'-t = \infty$$

which implies (and equals) the left side.

Multiplication, one more time

Here is another solution to the multiplication problem, one that does not use an extra variable s to accumulate a sum. Since multplication is not allowed, $x:= x\times y$ is not a program, but it is still a perfectly good specification of what is wanted (ignoring time). It can be refined as follows.

$$x:= x\times y\cdot: \quad \textbf{if } x=0 \textbf{ then } ok$$
$$\textbf{else if } even(x) \textbf{ then } (x:= x/2; \ x:= x\times y; \ x:= x\times 2)$$
$$\textbf{else } (x:= (x-1)/2; \ x:= x\times y; \ x:= x\times 2; \ x:= x+y)$$

The uses of $x:= x\times y$ on the right are compiled as calls. The proof is very easy, and we leave it as an exercise.

Data Representation

The formal definition of data types has followed a well-established mathematical tradition: we define a space of values of the type, and functions (operations) on these values. Here is the well-worn stack example. We introduce the syntax *stack* as a new type in terms of some already known type X. We also introduce *empty*, *push*, *pop*, and *top* of the following types.

    empty: *stack*

    push: *stack*$\times X \rightarrow$*stack*

    pop: *stack*$\rightarrow$*stack*

    top: *stack*$\rightarrow X$

And we can compare stacks for equality and inequality. The type *stack* can be defined by a domain axiom and an induction axiom

    stack = *empty* + *stack* $\times X$

    $(\forall s\cdot P(s)) \ = \ P(empty) \wedge \forall s, x\cdot (P(s) \Rightarrow P(push(s, x)))$

where $P: stack \rightarrow bool$. Consequently we can say that all stacks are formed either as the empty stack or by pushing something onto a stack. Let $s, t: stack$ and $x, y: X$; then

$$push(s, x) \neq empty$$

$$(push(s, x) = push(t, y)) = (s=t) \wedge (x=y)$$

$$pop(push(s, x)) = s$$

$$top(push(s, x)) = x$$

These axioms are modelled on the Peano axioms for the natural numbers, and they provide us with a powerful formal apparatus for the investigation of stacks. We have defined *push* and *pop* as functions, but most programming is not functional; it is imperative. We program *push* and *pop* as procedures with the result that the theory is not applicable. And a programmer has no need to prove anything about all possible stacks by induction. All we want is some way to prove that data placed in the stack will be found there later when needed. Here is a simple imperative stack theory.

We introduce three names: *push* (a procedure with parameter of type X), *pop* (a parameterless procedure), and *top* (an expression of type X) with the axioms

$$top'=x \cdot: push(x)$$

$$ok \cdot: push(x); pop$$

where $x: X$.

The first axiom says that $push(x)$ makes the *top* equal x . The second axiom says that a *pop* undoes a *push* . To illustrate their use, we begin with the first axiom, and sequentially compose the *push* with two occurrences of the empty action ok .

$$top'=x \cdot: push(x); ok; ok$$

Next we use the second axiom to refine each of the occurrences of ok .

$$top'=x \cdot: push(x); push(y); pop; push(z); pop$$

Let's throw in one more occurrence of the empty action

$$top'=x \cdot: push(x); push(y); ok; pop; push(z); pop$$

and refine it

$top'=x$·: *push*(x); *push*(y); *push*(w); *pop*; *pop*; *push*(z); *pop*

We see that properly balanced *push*es and *pop*s will never disturb data from an earlier *push* ; it will be there when wanted, and that's all a programmer needs to prove.

Conclusion

What's wrong with formal programming methods? They are not yet ready for general use. I have tried to illustrate, with a few examples, that formal methods of program development can be greatly simplified without loss, and thereby greatly improved, over the methods found currently in textbooks. If I had more space, I could show that the opportunities for simplification are even greater for programming with interaction, with parallelism, with communicating processes. It is reasonable and necessary for us to go through a period of exploration; least fixed points and continuity, temporal logic, and sets of interleaved communication sequences are all good academic research, but they are not the tools that industry needs.

Can programmers learn formal methods? Every programmer has learned a formalism: a programming language is a formal language. But programmers are naturally reluctant to learn a formalism that seems to be too complicated for its benefits. When industry was offered the first usable high-level programming language (Fortran), they jumped at it; when something much better came along shortly afterward (Algol), they were already committed. This time, they are not making the same mistake.

With the new, simplified methods outlined in this paper and elsewhere [5, 6], I am optimistic that Kieburtz is right, that the use of formal design methods is just around the corner.

References

[0] R.B.Kieburtz: "Formal Software Design Methods Next Step In Improving Quality", *Computing Research News*, January 1991 p14.

[1] C.A.R.Hoare: "Programming is an engineering profession", PRG-27, Oxford University, May 1982. Also published in P.J.L. Wallis (ed.): *Software Engineering* State of the art report, Pergamon, 1983v11 n3 p77-84. Also published as "Programming: Sorcery or Science", *IEEE Software*, April 1984 p5-16. Also published in Hoare & Jones (ed.): *Essays in Computing Science*, Prentice-Hall, 1989 p315-324.

[2] C.A.R.Hoare: "An axiomatic basis for computer programming", *CACM* October 1969 v12 n10 p576-580, 583. Also published in Hoare & Jones (ed.): *Essays in Computing Science*, Prentice-Hall, 1989 p45-58.

[3] E.W.Dijkstra: *A Discipline of Programming*, Prentice-Hall, 1976.

[4] C.B.Jones: *Systematic Software Development Using VDM*, Prentice-Hall, 1986, second ed. 1990.

[5] E.C.R.Hehner: "A Practical Theory of Programming", *Science of Computer Programming*, North-Holland, 1990, v14 p133-158.

[6] E.C.R.Hehner: *A Practical Theory of Programming*, (to be published) 1991.

COMPUTER SCIENCE AND COMMUNICATIONS PROTOCOLS: RESEARCH RELATIONSHIPS

Robert L. Probert

Protocols/Software Engineering Research Group
Department of Computer Science
University of Ottawa
Ottawa, Ontario K1N 6N5
Fax: (613) 564-9486 Tel: (613) 564-5425
E-Mail: rlpsl@acadvm1.uottawa.ca

Abstract

Many of the interesting problems in Computer Science related to Software Engineering have yielded only to partial solutions or not at all. In the related areas of research denoted Communications Software Engineering and Protocols, most corresponding problems are on their way to a solution. In this presentation, we will explore some similarities and differences between these research areas by giving examples of problems which appear to be tractable in one area and not the other, and conclude with some ideas for building conceptual bridges.

1.   Introduction

One of the central problems in both theoretical and applied computer science is the problem we will denote the **conformance problem**, namely (in simplest terms):

Given a specification S of desirable process behaviours, and an implementation I derived from S, verify that I exhibits only behaviours which exactly correspond to behaviours included in S.

A difficulty with such a definition is of course the ambiguity of many of the key terms such as "derived from", "verify", "exhibits", and "exactly corresponds". This ambiguity is long-standing in mainstream computer science despite valiant attempts by both theoretical computer scientists and software engineers to develop a "pragmatically rigorous" foundation for software engineering. Such a foundation would provide cost-effective tools and engineering techniques based on realistic, yet mathematically precise models.

In the area of communications protocols, however, substantive progress has been made towards what might be termed "foundations of protocol engineering". An abstraction of the protocol engineering process is given in Figure 1.

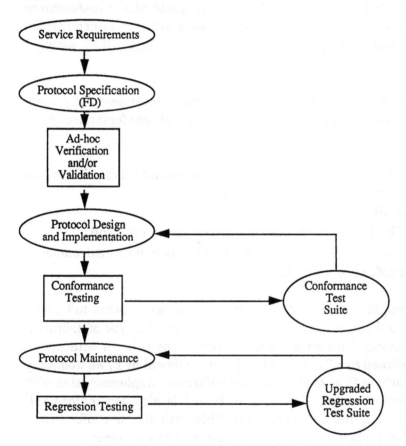

Figure 1. Current Protocol Engineering Process

A major contribution towards this progress has been the development of a number of standardized specification languages intended for communication protocols and services, called **formal description techniques or FDTs**. [Bo89] These FDTs vary from FSM-based (SDL and Estelle) to process algebraic LOTOS, a derivation of Milner's CCS combined with ACT ONE, a notation for abstract data types. [Mi80]

In this domain, the **protocol conformance problem** has been further refined as follows:

Given a formal description (FD) F of a protocol P which has been validated or verified as cooperating correctly with other protocol entities to provide a service S, and an implementation I of the protocol, the conformance problem is to determine whether for all mandatory (deterministic) behaviours B of F and for all possible executions E of I, B⊇E. If so, we say I **simply conforms** to F.

Again, this is a simplification of both theoretical treatments of process equivalence and more applied interpretations of conformance to a specification.

To illustrate this, observe that a more abstract definition of conformance is (assuming P is formally specified as E) [Br91]:
I conforms to P **iff**
∀ t ∈ Traces (F) (the set of all legal interaction sequences) **and**
∀ e (interaction events between the protocol entity and its environment)
   I after t **refuses** e ⇒ P after t **refuses** e

The reader might observe that simple conformance appears to be only indirectly related to theoretical conformance. However, this type of definition is based on observing failures of conformance. Thus, if an interaction sequence t•e ("t followed by e") is refused by I, but is allowed by P, we would say that I fails to conform to P, or that I is a non-conformant implementation of P. However, if I accepts t•e, but P refused it, then I is also non-conformant. Thus, the theoretical definition is not compatible with simple conformance. Rather, refusal non-conformance implies simple non-conformance.

Refinements of this approach are possible, but the fundamental problem is that behaviours of concurrent processes are best described as stimulus/response sequences and not as simply offers and refusals. Thus, the theoretical model needs to be expanded. In addition, real protocols contain options, and are therefore properly represented by either comprehensive formal descriptions or improperly represented by non-deterministic abstractions.

In a complementary way, a pragmatic formulation of conformance must consider mandatory and optional behaviours. This is handled in communications protocols by constructs in international standard languages for specifying abstract conformance test suites, such as TTCN (Tree and Tabular Combined Notation) and ASN.1 (Abstract Syntax Notation). [PrMo91]

2. An Example of a Difficult Problem in Computer Science

Proving conformance of an implementation I to a specification S can be theoretically accomplished by a finite number of finite tests, provided that S halts on all inputs in the domain of I:

Let S(x), I(x) denote the behaviours exhibited by the specification and the implementation, respectively, on being presented x.

Lemma 1 (Existence of a complete test suite given S and I):

For all S, I such that Dom (S) $\supseteq$ Dom (I), there exists
at least one (finite) test suite T of inputs (test data) such that:

[$\forall t \in T$, P(t) = S(t)] iff P conforms to S

Lemma 2: There exists no uniform recursive (algorithmic) procedure to determine such a set T given S and P.

The first result offers encouragement in that a complete and sound test suite always exists to solve the conformance for a program P and a specification S. The second result then renders the first result useless in practice, since it shows there can be no uniform (automated) test generation technique for producing such test suites.

A common difficulty in the pragmatically rigorous specification of concurrent systems was observed by Lamport [Lam89], namely the impossibility of implementing a system that functions properly in the presence of arbitrary behaviour by the environment. Any method to overcome this difficulty involves either placing constraints on the environment (user) formally or by means of convention. Again in the protocols world, concepts of interaction points and points of control and observation [PrMo91] provide a degree of pragmatic rigor.

3. Related Problems in Communications Protocols

Two key related subproblems of the conformance problem in the domain of communications protocols are:

i) specification and design of conformance test suites

and

ii) assessment of the completeness of a conformance test suite with respect to the specification.

While extremely difficult and interesting problems in their own right, the global requirement for interoperability of open communications systems has turned the attention of the industrial world towards developing pragmatic solutions to these problems. As senior protocols research Harry Rudin recently stated, conformance testing research has been the most successful area in protocol engineering in transferring research results, methods, and tools into the industrial sector. This is likely related to the successful collaboration between researchers and practitioners in the development of a comprehensive precise conformance testing framework. [ISO9646] In turn, a requirement for pragmatic rigor in specifications necessitated by conformance testing methods has helped to build new bridges between formalists and practitioners in communications software engineering.

Communications protocols are often specified using an extended state/transition model in which externally observable interactions are represented by the input/output sequences associated with the transition labels. This type of representation allows the protocol behaviour to be represented as sets of paths through the specification. These individual paths are clearly identified when the specification is presented as a digraph. Most existing protocol test design techniques are based only on structural or syntactic coverage, i.e., covering the edges of the digraph, without regard to the degree of test coverage of various functions provided by the protocol specification. In many instances, these test design techniques select meaningless test paths, i.e., paths which would never appear in practice as an actual execution trace of the protocol. Moreover, selected paths may include infeasible paths which can never be executed. A similar problem can occur for data-flow coverge criteria. [Ur87]

This infeasible path problem appears to be much more serious in general computer science than in the area of communications protocols. A novel approach to this coverage problem was proposed, called mutation testing [DeLi78, DeGu88, Off89, WoHa88] and modified for protocol test coverage measurement [GuPr90] where it appears to be much more effective.

A complementary test design approach has been developed which may lead to the selection of realistic and *meaningful* test paths [BoPr89]. The approach is summarized in Figure 1. First, the protocol specification is represented in simplified EFSM form (a straightforward, though presently manual translation for existing protocols described in either Estelle or SDL). Secondly, the test designer partially identifies key semantic units or functional components of the protocol, called *phases*. These phases are represented by either Directed Behaviour Modules (**DBM**s) or Error/Recovery Modules (**ERM**s). Both types of modules can be manually derived from the specification by first choosing the sets S (start states) and T (goal states) for each phase, and then finding all paths which are made up of the appropriate type of transitions as specified in the next section. This is of course a tedious procedure for the more complex **DBM**s.

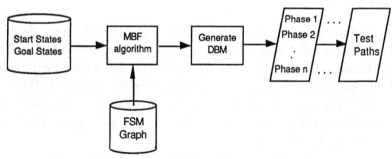

Figure 1: Overview of Phase Decomposition Process

To enhance the efficiency of the test case generation process, and also to make it easier to determine the coverage of a given test suite, it is necessary to automate the phase decomposition process. It has been found that by assigning certain 'label numbers' to the nodes of the specification after choosing the sets S and T for each phase, it is possible to automatically generate all the paths between S and T that are made up only of the appropriate transition types. These paths then comprise the phase represented by the **DBM** with sets S and T. Thus it is possible to semi-automatically produce a phase decomposition of the protocol.

The above assignment of labels to nodes is accomplished by the Reverse Breadth First (RBF) labelling algorithm. [BoPr89] This labelling algorithm is quite different in its intention from many existing numbering algorithms, and has been shown to be useful for achieving an effective phase decomposition of real protocols. [BGPU89]

4. Conclusions

This abstract is intended to very briefly point out differences and similarities between research in traditional software engineering (if "traditional" can be applied to such a young discipline) and the particularly challenging domain of protocol engineering. The interested reader is encouraged to refer to an ongoing series of annual monographs describing work in this area. [IFIP] A number of indirectly related references are listed as well.

Acknowledgements

The author is grateful to the Natural Science and Engineering Research Council of Canada, and the Telecommunications Research Institute of Ontario for their support. In addition, discussions with colleagues and students in the Protocols/Software Engineering Research Group at the University of Ottawa and Professor David Parnas of Queen's University and Murray Woodside of Carleton University helped to inspire the high-level observations in the presentation.

References

[BGPU89]   Boyce, T.T., T. Grenier, R.L. Probert and H. Ural, "Formalization of ISDN LAPD for conformance testing", IEEE INFOCOM'89, IEEE Computer Society, 1989, pp. 234-246.

[Bo89]   Bochmann, G.v., "Specifications of a Simplified Transport Protocol Using Different Formal Description Techniques", Comp. Nedtworks and ISDN Systems, 18 (1989/90) 335-377.

[BoPr89]   Boyce, T.T. and Probert, R.L., "A polynomial-Time Labelling Algorithm for Functional Decomposition of Communications Protocols", University of Ottawa Technical Report 91-06, 1991.

[Br91]   Brinksma, E., "A Formal Approach to Testing Distributed Systems", personal communication, 1991.

[DeGu88]   DeMillo, R.A., D.S. Guindi, W.M. McCracken, A.J. Offutt and K.N. King, "An Extended Overview of the Mothra Software Testing Environment", Proceedings of Second Workshop on Software Testing, Verification, and Analysis, Computer Society Press, 1988, pp. 142-151.

[DeLi78]   DeMillo, R.A., R.J. Lipton and F.G. Sayward, "Hints on test data selection: help for the practising programmer", IEEE Computer, Vol. 11, No. 4, pp. 34-41, April 1978.

[GMMP90]   Geldrez, C., S. Matwin, J. Morin, and R. Probert, "An Application of explanation-based learning to protocol conformance testing", IEEE Expert, October 1990, Volume 5, Number 5, pp. 45-60.

[H85]   Hoare, C.A.R., Communicating Sequential Processes, Prentice-Hall, New Jersey, 1985.

[GuPr90]   Guo, F. and Probert, R.L., "Mutation Testing of Communication Protocols: Methodology and Assessment of Coverage", University of Ottawa Technical Report 91-5, 1991.

[GHW85]   Guttag, J.V., Horning, J.J., and Wing, J.M., "The Larch Family of Specification Language", IEEE Software, Vol. 2, No. 5, Sept. 1985, pp. 24-36.

[Ha88]   Harel, D. et al., "Statemate: A Working Environment for the Development of Complex Reactive Systems", in Proc. 10th IEEE Int'l, Conf. Software Eng., Apr. 1988, CS Press, Los Alamitos, Calif., Order No. 849.

[Howd82]   Howden, W.E., "Weak Mutation Testing and Completeness of Test Sets", IEEE Transactions on Software Engineering 8, 2, July 1982.

[IFIP]   Protocol Specification, Testing, and Verification, Volumes I-X, North Holland (1981-1990).

[ISO9074] International Organization for Standardization, IS 9074, Information Processing Systems -- Open Systems Interconnection -- Estelle -- A Formal Description Technique Based on an Extended State Transition Model, May 1989.

[ISO9646]   International Organization for Standardization, IS 9646-2, OSI
            Conformance Testing Methodology and Framework, especially Part 2:
            Abstract Test Suite Specification, 1990.

[Jo86]   Jones, C.B., Systematic Software Development Using VDM, Prentice Hall
            Int'l. 1986.

[Lam89]   Lamport, L., "A Simple Approach to Specifying Concurrent Systems",
            Comm. ACM, Vol. 32, No. 1, Jan. 1989, pp. 32-45.

[MaMi89]   Manas, J.A., T.de Miguel, H. van Thienen, "The Implementation of a
            Specification Language for OSI Systems", in The Formal Description
            Technique LOTOS, P.H.J. van Eijk, C.A. Vissers and M. Diaz (Editors), pp.
            409-421, North-Holland, 1989.

[McG83]   McMullin, P.R. and J.D. Gannon, "Combining Testing with Formal
            Specifications: A Case Study", IEEE Trans. Software Eng., Vol. 9, No. 3,
            May 1983.

[Mi80]   Milner, A.I.R.G., A Calculus of Communicating Systems, Lecture Notes in
            Computer Science 92, Springer-Verlag, 1980.

[Off89]   Offutt, A.J., "The Coupling Effect: Fact or Fiction?", Proceedings of the
            ACM SIGSOFT '89 Third Symposium on Software Testing Analysis, and
            Verification (TAV3), December 13-15, 1989.

[PrMo91]   Probert, R.L. and O. Monkewich, "TTCN - The International Notation for
            Conformance Testing of Communications Systems, J. of Computer
            Networks and ISDN (to appear).

[SaP90]   Saleh, K. and R. Probert, "A service-based method for the synthesis of
            communication protocols", International Journal of Mini and
            Microcomputers, Volume 12, Issue 3, 1990, pp. 97-103.

[SaP90]   Saleh, K. and R. Probert, "Synthesis of communication protocols: Survey
            and assessment", accepted September 28, 1990 for publication in IEEE
            Transactions on Computers, Special Issue on Protocol Engineering.

[Ur87]   Ural, H., "Test Sequence Selection Based on Static Data Flow Analysis",
            Computer Communications, Vol. 10, No. 5, October 1987, pp. 234-242.

[West87]   West, C.H., "Protocol Validation by Random State Exploration", Protocol
            Specification, Testing and Verification, VI, 1987, pp. 233-242.

[WoHa88]   Woodward, M.R. and K. Halewood, "From Weak to Strong, Dead or Alive?
            An Analysis of Some Mutation Testing Issues". Proceedings of Second
            Workshop on Software Testing, Verification, and Analysis, Computer
            Society Press, 1988, pp. 152-158.

REAPING THE BENEFITS OF MASS PRODUCTION
WITH MASSIVELY PARALLEL COMPUTING
- Four Example Applications -

Stephen J. Smith

Thinking Machines Corporation

245 First Street Cambridge, MA 02142

(617) 234-1000, smith@think.com

Abstract

Mass production, as an idea, has had a long and successful history. First recognized and distilled in the early 19th century by such men as Adam Smith and Charles Babbage, it has since been successfully applied to virtually every manufacturing process, from farming to automobile manufacture [1][2][3]. Strangely, though, these methods have not generally been considered to be applicable to the development (manufacture) of computer software. It is the thesis of this paper that not only would this be a good idea but that, in fact, such techniques are already being employed with high degrees of success. Four example applications, implemented on a massively parallel supercomputer, are presented to illustrate this point.

Introduction

It may at first seem that the normal images of mass production (car parts moving along a conveyor belt or mechanical robots designed to repeatedly tighten a single bolt) have nothing to do with software engineering or computer programming. Consider, however, that any programmer or group of programmers in a research lab seeking to solve a problem are producing a product. The product is the solution to the problem, and as with any industrial factory it is desired that this product be built as inexpensively and as efficiently as possible.

This paper describes how one of the rules of mass production - the use of powerful yet sometimes crude tools and processes - can be applied successfully to a variety of computer applications. The results allow for high quality solutions with a minimum of expense in person-years of development costs. This is accomplished through the use of simple, powerful but computationally expensive software methods such as simulated annealing [4], memory-based reasoning [5] and genetic optimization [6]; and is enabled by a computationally powerful massively parallel supercomputer [7].

The Rules of Mass Production

Mass production could be described as consisting of just the following two basic rules:

1. Tasks are specialized so that they can be carried out repeatedly in simple processes that require a minimum of wasted motion (either physical or computational).

2. Tasks and processes are modified to match the available tools.

For instance, farming has benefited greatly from the application of mass production techniques. Initially crops were cultivated by hand and farmers could sustain crops on small plots of land. Then a new tool, the hoe, was invented. It was crude, but it was a simple tool of wood and metal and readily available. Because it was cruder than doing things by hand, the process of farming changed to accommodate this new tool. Crops now had to be planted in long straight rows wide enough for the hoe (thereby using more land than was normally required to grow just the plants) and weeding and cultivating could only be performed within these rows – it was no longer possible to weed and till precisely between individual plants. Of course, now a single farmer could support several acres of crops.

There were many further stages in this evolution of farming tools, culminating in the large diesel powered backhoes and combines of today that enable a single farmer to cultivate hundreds of acres. Note that there are some general trends:

1). The precision of the tools decreased as waste from the process increased (not all the weeds were pulled, not all the soil was tilled).

2). The specialization of the tools increased (hands are very general tools, capable of playing the piano or opening jars, hoes are much more limited).

3). The power of the tools increased.

4). The process changed (farming now was accomplished in long, wide, straight rows).

5). The total production increased (from a fraction of an acre per day to many more).

Computer program development is in many ways like tending a farm. Here farming by hand is analogous to the programmer who makes use of few tools except perhaps the computer language he or she is writing in. The eventual product is very efficient, wastes no memory or CPU cycles, and is perfectly tailored to the task it was designed for. It is, however, very brittle in that small changes may require massive redesigns, and it may have required many person-years of effort to develop.

The mass production approach to computer program development attacks problems differently. Here a very powerful hardware tool is applied (a massively parallel supercomputer) and very computationally expensive software tools (genetic optimization, simulated annealing, and memory-based reasoning) are used to produce a system that performs well. Optimal use of computer memory and CPU cycles is not guaranteed but the system is built from generic tools and is not brittle. Small changes may be tried in order to optimize the system with little programmer cost; and the power of the hardware compensates for the losses of program efficiency. A tradeoff can, thus, be made between coarse, high level programming tools and program development time. This seems to be a smart trade considering the relative changes in price-performance between computer hardware and computer programmers.

The following sections of this paper describe four applications, their algorithms, and their implementations that demonstrate these qualities of mass production. The applications include: 1) A Census return classification task that is solved with a Memory-Based Reasoning (MBR) system. 2) A handwritten character recognition task that is also solved with an MBR system. 3) A market segmentation problem that is optimized with a simulated annealing approach. and 4) A sorting network task which is performed with a genetic optimization system.

The Connection Machine Supercomputer

The Connection Machine CM-2 Supercomputer [7] was used to carry out all the experiments on the four presented applications. It is a SIMD (Single Instruction Multiple Data) parallel computer containing up to 65,536 single bit processors, each of which contains a maximum of 128K bytes of local memory. The single bit processors are grouped into sets of 32 and each group shares a single or double precision floating point accelerator. Interprocessor communication is accomplished via a 12 dimensional hypercube network, and indirect memory access is enabled with specialized hardware. The machine is capable of peak performance in excess of 25 gigaflops and has run in excess of 10 gigaflops on production code. The total memory of the system can be 8 gigabytes.

Census Return Classification

The Problem

Every ten years the U.S. Bureau of the Census sends out forms to the households of the United States. One of every six of these forms, 28 million in all, are the long form that seeks to categorize the occupation and industry segment of the respondents. The returns consist of free text responses to questions such as: "What kind of work is this person doing?" and numerical or multiple choice responses to question such as: "What is this person's age?" The Census takes these responses and then categorizes them into one of a possible 504 occupation categories and one of a possible 232 industry categories. An example industry category might be "Beverage Industries" (code 120), and an example occupation category might be "Real Estate Sales Occupations" (code 254). The cost of coding these responses by hand approaches 15 million dollars.

Algorithm and Implementation

Two automated systems were built to perform this classification; one was based on expert system technology [8], the other utilized an empirical learning method called Memory-Based Reasoning

(MBR) [9] and was implemented on the Connection Machine. The MBR technique is a variant of nearest neighbor classification methods. The intent is to use a large database of previously classified training examples and to assign the category of whichever training example most nearly matches the unclassified test example. On a serial computer this match phase can be computationally $O(N)$ (where N = number of training examples). On a massively parallel computer, where the number of processors equals the number of training examples, the problem reduces to constant time where one training example is stored per processor, and the test example can be broadcast and matched in parallel. This is how the algorithm was implemented on the Connection Machine.

The power of the algorithm lies in its simplicity. It requires no elaborate preformatting of the training data, which allows experiments to be performed quickly and additions, deletions or modifications to the database can be accomplished dynamically. One of the key modifications over simple nearest neighbor is that the MBR system weights the fields being matched so that, for example, the presence or absence of the word "computer" would bear more weight in determining a close match than would common, non-discriminating words like "the" or "of." These words and other numeric fields are weighted by the probability of category occurrence conditional to the occurrence of the field [P("category=901"|"field=computer")]. This calculation, though simple, is computationally expensive when carried out on the over 130,000 example training database available from the Census. On the Connection Machine, however, the probabilities of each field and conjunction of fields in a given test example can be calculated over the entire database in under 200 milliseconds. These fields and conjunctions of fields can also be precalculated and stored. When this is done, the over 4.5 million features of the database and their conditional probabilities can be calculated and stored in less than ten minutes.

Results

The Census classification system using MBR was able to process 63% and 57% of the returns at human levels of accuracy for the industry and occupation codes respectively. Human coders achieve levels of accuracy of 90% correct on industry coding and 86% correct on the occupation coding and are able to perform 94% of the industry and 95% of the occupation classifications without referring the return to a human expert. Thus the automated MBR system could accurately handle approximately 60% of the work load now performed by human coders.

The expert based system solution to this problem was able to process 57% of the industry classifications and 37% of the occupation classifications - an average of 13% fewer returns than the MBR system. More importantly, perhaps, is the fact that the development and optimization of the MBR system required only four person-months while the expert based system required over sixteen person-years - almost 50 times greater.

Handwritten Character Recognition

The Problem

Translating handwritten character images to machine readable form (ascii) is an important problem found in a variety of domains; from the banking industry, where such a system could be used to read the dollar amounts on bank checks and credit card receipts, to the Postal service, where it could be used to read the addresses and postal codes on mail envelopes [10]. Typically this problem is attacked by scanning in the image, performing segmentation (where the original image is broken up into smaller images which each contain an individual character), normalization of the resulting character images and then searching the image for discriminating features that identify the image.

Determining the optimal defining features for each character is a human intensive, time consuming process that often results in a system of general features that achieve moderate levels of accuracy but requires the addition of an ever increasing numbers of "special case" features to continue to incrementally improve the performance. Statistical approaches similar to MBR, called template matching, have also been considered but have often been dismissed as being too computationally costly.

Algorithm and Implementation

A set of 2,000 scanned images of the postal codes from U.S. mail envelopes was segmented and size normalized to result in 5,000 32x32 pixel array images of individual numerals. These images were then classified by hand and used as a training database.

A variety of empirical learning methods, including a back propagation neural network [11], an ID3 like system [12], and MBR variants were used with the training database to build classification systems. The MBR system was implemented on the Connection Machine in a manner similar to that employed for the Census classification system - one pre-classified character image per processor. The system was tested with an n-way cross validation approach (n equal to the number of training examples) where a single training image was removed from the database and used as a test example. Two successful match techniques were used. The first was a simple hamming distance metric that summed the number of mismatching pixels between the test example and each training example. The second distance metric attempted to incorporate the degree of mismatch between two mismatching pixels by measuring the euclidean distance between the given pixel location and the nearest pixel location with the same state (on/off). This second metric effected a "rubber-band" match where the character images are viewed as physically deformable with some energy depending on how far a test image must be "stretched" in order to exactly correspond to a given training image. Normally these methods are computationally expensive [13]. The Connection Machine implementation, however, allowed the precomputation of pixel to pixel distance maps and the metric could be computed by a simple table lookup and summation for each pixel.

Results

The performance of the neural network and ID3 systems was inferior to even the simple hamming distance MBR method. This simple match technique achieved 90.4% correct classifications in the n-way cross validation tests. The improved euclidean distance metric achieved 96.6% correct classifications for the system. It appears also that a larger training database, which is now available, could significantly improve these numbers. The simple hamming metric showed the following performance changes as database size was varied:

Training Examples	Percent Correct
582	81.0%
2851	88.5%
4462	89.9%
5365	90.4%

Market Segmentation Optimization

The Problem

Mass mailings of catalogs and advertisements are an expensive yet effective way for many companies to sell their product. The expense is accrued from the printing and mailing costs of the catalogs, and the design costs of offering multiple catalogs each targeted at a different subpopulation of customers. Profit is accrued when the recipient of the catalog purchases product which in turn is in direct proportion to how well the catalog matches the interests and needs of the recipient.

Today, via data on individual buying habits collected from credit and demographic information sources, it is often possible to tailor a catalog to an individual such that their purchases are maximized. An interesting optimization problem now arises in that the set of catalogs and mailings that maximizes purchases also maximizes expenses (the cost of designing and printing personalized catalogs for each individual is prohibitive) - similarly minimizing costs also minimizes purchases [14].

Algorithm and Implementation

This problem was attacked by first determining an equation for the overall profit or loss of a given catalog mailing. This included a measure of the design costs of multiple catalogs, printing and mailing costs, and an estimate of customer purchases based on how well a given catalog matched his or her interests. A population of customers with specific preferences and a set of several different catalogs was simulated on the Connection Machine. The profit or loss of the system could then be evaluated by summing the individual profit or loss from each different catalog mailing and its targeted customers. This profit or loss could be evaluated locally and a simulated annealing approach was used to optimize the system, using the local change in profit as an energy function that governed the probability of a given customer receiving one catalog or another. The set of catalogs that optimized the system could then be determined.

Each customer was simulated on an individual processor and the system was initiated with an optimal personalized catalog for each customer. The system proceeded by attempting to find pairs or groups of customers that could share the same catalog with a minimal loss of purchase dollars. As the system progressed through the annealing schedule the temperature was decreased giving higher probability of acceptance to any transition of a customer from a catalog of small circulation to one of larger circulation such that the total number of catalogs decreased with time.

Results

The number of catalogs at the beginning of the annealing schedule was typically 8,000 and as the temperature was lowered the system converged to approximately 30 catalogs; conveniently, nearly the same set of optimal catalogs was determined independent of the optimization run. The system required four person-months to develop. It is, however, difficult to compare this with the development times of other methods as no other approaches are currently known. This lack of other methods may well be due to the large size of the search space of the problem - on the order of 10^{87} possible solutions.

Sorting Network Optimization

The Problem

Sorting networks are representations of a series of two element comparisons and exchanges necessary to sort a set of numbers. Batcher's bitonic sort, for instance, could be represented in this way as a network with a set of inputs connected by links representing the comparisons between two elements [15]. The order of the comparison-exchange steps is constrained by moving through the network in a consistent direction. Each comparison and exchange corresponds to a computation step; thus the fewer exchanges that are made the more quickly the sort can be accomplished. There is, currently, no way of determining the minimum number of comparison/exchange steps that would be necessary for a given number of elements. Because of this, determining sorting networks with minimal numbers of comparison/exchange steps has been a topic of interest in computer science for some time [16].

Algorithm and Implementation

A sixteen element sorting network was optimized on the Connection Machine with a process called "genetic algorithms" or more generally "simulated evolution". The intent of the method is to encode possible solutions to the given problem into the genetic material of simulated organisms in a large population. By then applying several of the operators of evolution (competition, reproduction, genetic crossover, and genetic mutation) and equating fitness with the performance of the solution contained in the genetic material of the organism, an improved solution is discovered with proceeding generations.

Such a system was implemented on the Connection Machine by encoding sixteen element sorting networks into simulated chromosomes and storing one in each processor. The evolutionary operators can then be carried out in parallel and large populations of hundreds of thousands of simulated organisms can be maintained.

A sorting network can be fully evaluated by testing whether or not it is able to sort all sequences of zeros and ones. It is not necessary to test all possible numeric inputs. For a sixteen element network this would correspond to 2^{16} or 65,536 required test cases to evaluate one network. To effect this evaluation within the simulated evolution paradigm, simulated parasites are evolved alongside each sorting network host such that the parasites gain fitness and reproductive advantage at the expense of the host by presenting test sequences that the host is unable to sort correctly. Normally the parasite will contain from 10-20 test sequences.

Results

The system was able to evolve a functional sixteen element sorting network of 61 comparison/exchange steps [17]. This compares favorably with the best known human solution of 60 steps. It is again, however, difficult to compare the person-hours expended developing the simulated evolution system with the person-hours expended analyzing the problem by hand. Some indication of the human effort expended and the difficulty of the problem is given, though, by looking at the history of the decreases in what was thought to be the optimal solution. In 1962 the optimal solution was determined to be 65 comparison/exchange steps. This number dropped to 63 in 1964, to 62 in early 1969 and then to 60 only later in 1969. Thus the topic was of active interest to researchers in computer science for at least seven years.

Conclusion

The four applications presented in this paper come from the diverse areas of computer science, marketing, database classification, and image analysis, yet all have responded favorably to the application of mass production techniques. All four applications were successfully adapted to use available massively parallel hardware and software tools which resulted in simplified code and decreased development time:

1). The optical character recognition system achieved up to 96.6% correct performance on presegmented and normalized characters, and required only five person-months to produce.

2). The market segmentation application, though not tested in a production environment, realized a substantial profit on "paper" and required four person-months to produce.

3). The evolved sorting network achieved a minimum of 61 exchanges, which while no longer the best, would nonetheless have been the optimal solution (beating the best human solution) for the seven years from 1962 to 1969, when the optimization of sorting networks was an important research issue in computer science.

4). The census classification system could accurately process 17% more of the census returns than an expert system and required almost 50 times fewer person-months to develop.

These tasks responded well to the application of general purpose software tools such as simulated annealing, genetic optimization and Memory-Based Reasoning and it was possible to adapt them to take advantage of the computational power of the Connection Machine Supercomputer. It might be argued, however, that these are special cases that were easily adapted to fit the new tools available and that other tasks would still need to be "handcrafted" with more precision and less power. This may be true in some cases, but it is encouraging to realize that all of the above examples were being solved with human, labor-intensive approaches (expert systems, image feature construction) before these new "mass production" techniques were made available. It is thus conceivable that in the future many more tasks can be adapted to take advantage of the powerful new tools that massively parallel supercomputing provides.

Acknowledgements

Thanks to Danny Hillis who originally suggested this idea, and to Debbie Widener, Noel Smith, Gary Drescher, Dave Waltz, and Anand Bodapati for their help in the review and production of this paper. Some of the work reported here but previously unpublished was performed by Alex Singer, Brewster Kahle, Donna Fritzsche and Jim Hutchinson.

References

[1] *Descriptions des arts et metiers, faites ou approuvees par messieurs de l'Academie royale des science*, 45. (1761-89).

[2] Adam Smith. *An Inquiry into the Nature and Causes of the Wealth of Nations* (1776).

[3] Charles Babbage. *On the Economy of Machinery and Manufacture* (1832).

[4] S. Kirkpatrick, C. D. Gelatt, M. P. Vecchi. "Optimization by Simulated Annealing". *Science*, 220, 4598, 671-680, 13 May 1983.

[5] Craig Stanfill, David Waltz. "Toward Memory-Based Reasoning". *Communications of the ACM* 29, 12, 1213-1228.

[6] John Holland. *Adaptation in Natural and Artificial Systems*. Ann Arbor: The University of Michigan Press. 1975.

[7] W. Daniel Hillis. *The Connection Machine*. MIT Press. Cambridge, MA. 1985.

[8] M. Appel, E. Hellerman. "Census Bureau Experiments With Automated Industry and Occupation Coding". *Proc. Amer. Statistical Assoc*, (1983), 32-40.

[9] Robert H. Creecy, Brij M. Masand, Stephen J. Smith, David Waltz. "Trading Mips and Memory for Knowledge Engineering: Automatic Classification of Census Returns on a Massively Parallel Supercomputer". Submitted to *Communications of the ACM* (1991).

[10] Pervez Ahmed, C. Y. Suen. "Computer Recognition of Totally Unconstrained Handwritten Zip Codes". *Internation Journal of Pattern Recognition and Artificial Intelligence* 1, 1 (1987).

[11] C. Rummelhart, J. McClelland et al. *Parallel Distributed Processing*. MIT Press, Cambridge, MA (1986).

[12] R. Quinlan. "Learning Efficient Classification Procedures And Their Applications To Chess End Games". In R. Michalski, J. Carbonell, T. Mitchell (eds.), *Machine Learning: An Artificial Intelligence Approach*, Tioga Publishing, Los Angeles, CA (1983), 463-482.

[13] D. J. Burr. "Elastic Matching of Line Drawings". *IEEE Transactions on Pattern Analysis and Machine Intelligence*, PAMI-3, 6, 708-713 (November 1981).

[14] David Waltz." Massively Parallel AI". *Proc. National Conf. AI*, (AAAI '90), Boston, (August 1990))

[15] K. E. Batcher, "A New Internal Sorting Method". *Goodyear Aerospace Report GER-11759* (1964).

[16] D. Knuth. *Sorting and Searching, Vol. 3. The Art of Computer Programming* (Addison-Wesley, New York, 1973).

[17] W. Daniel Hillis. "Co-Evolving Parasites Improve Simulated Evolution as an Optimization Procedure". *Physica D* 42, 228-234. North-Holland (1990).

2. Algorithms and Complexity

ON THE QUICKEST PATH PROBLEM
(Extended Abstract)

Yung-Chen Hung   Gen-Huey Chen
Department of Computer Science and Information Engineering
National Taiwan University, Taipei, Taiwan
Fax: (886)-(2)-3628167

Abstract--In this paper, we propose an $O(mn^2)$ time algorithm that finds all-pairs quickest paths in a given network N, where n and m are the numbers of nodes and arcs, respectively, in N. Besides, the quickest path between any two nodes can be determined in $O(\log m)$ time, provided $O(mn^2)$ time preprocessing is made.

1. Introduction

The quickest path problem, originally proposed by Chen and Chin [1], is a variant of the shortest path problem. Given a network N and an amount of data, the problem is to find the quickest paths to transmit these data in N.

Let $N=(V, A, C, L)$ be a network, where $|V|=n$, $|A|=m$, $G=(V, A)$ is a directed graph without self loops and without multiple arcs between any two nodes, and $C(u, v)\geq0$ and $L(u, v)\geq0$ are the capacity and the lead time, respectively, of an arc $(u, v)\in A$. Suppose $P=(u_1, u_2, ..., u_k)$ is a path from node u_1 to node u_k. The lead time of P is defined as $L(P) = \Sigma_{1\leq i\leq k-1}L(u_i, u_{i+1})$. The capacity of P is defined as $C(P) = \min_{1\leq i\leq k-1}C(u_i, u_{i+1})$. The total transmission time to send σ units of data from u_1 to u_k through path P is defined as $T(P, \sigma) =$ (the lead time of P + σ/the capacity of P)$= L(P) + \sigma/C(P)$. The quickest path to send σ units of data from a node s to another node t, denoted by $QP(s, t, \sigma)$, is the path P satisfying $T(P, \sigma) = \min\{ T(P_i, \sigma) \mid \forall P_i=(u_{i1}, u_{i2}, ..., u_{ik})$, where $s=u_{i1}$ and $t=u_{ik} \}$. Also, denote by $MP(s, t)$ the path from s to t with the minimal lead time; namely, $MP(s, t)$ is the path P satisfying $L(P)$ $= \min\{ L(P_i) \mid \forall P_i=(u_{i1}, u_{i2}, ..., u_{ik})$, where $s=u_{i1}$ and $t=u_{ik} \}$.

Chen and Chin [1] have solved the one-source quickest path problem (1_QSP for short) in $O(m^2 + nm\log m)$ time, where n and m are the numbers of nodes and arcs, respectively, in N. Chen and Chin also showed that the quickest path between two specified nodes can be found in $O(\log m)$ time, provided $O(m^2 + nm\log m)$ preprocessing time is spent. In this paper, we propose an $O(mn^2)$ time algorithm to solve the all-pairs quickest paths problem (A_QSP for short). Besides, we show that the quickest path between any two nodes can be found in $O(\log m)$ time, provided $O(mn^2)$ preprocessing time is spent. Our result generalizes Chen and Chin's result.

A more complete version of this paper appears in [2].

2. An $O(mn^2)$ time Algorithm to Solve the A_QSP

In the algorithm, N is regarded as empty (containing no arcs) at first. The arcs of the input network are sorted into nonincreasing order of capacities and then inserted into N one by one. Since new paths may be established from a node s to another node t when an arc is added to N. Many new paths from s to t may be generated after an arc (assuming (v, w)) was added to N, only one path that consists of the minimal lead time path from s to v, the arc (v, w), and the minimal lead time path from w to t is needed to be considered. The reason is that the arcs are added to N in nonincreasing sequence of their capacities and as a result, the capacities of these newly generated paths (all through (v, w)) are dominated by the capacity of (v, w). Therefore, the minimal lead time path and the minimal transmission time path from s to t through the arc (v, w) are the same one that consists of the minimal lead time path from s to v, the arc (v, w), and the minimal lead time path from w to t. It is easy to check that the time complexity of the algorithm is $O(mn^2)$.

3. Solve the A_QSP with Preprocessing Allowed

Consider the range $(0, \infty)$ of possible values of σ. In [1], Chen and Chin have proposed an $O(m^2 + mn\log m)$ time algorithm that finds the intervals of σ for a given pair of nodes such that the quickest paths between this pair of nodes are the same for each interval of σ. As a generalization of Chen and Chin's result, we have designed an $O(mn^2)$ time algorithm that finds the intervals of σ for all pairs of nodes. Since there are at most m intervals for each pair of nodes, our result is optimal. After these intervals have been found, the quickest path between any pair of nodes for any value of σ can be determined in $O(\log m)$ time.

The algorithm to find intervals consists of four stages. The first three stages are almost the same as the algorithm of Section 2. As in Section 2, N is regarded as empty at first. The arcs of the input network are sorted into nonicreasing order of capacities and then inserted into N one by one. For convenience, let $MP_i(s, t)$ be the minimal lead time path after inserting i arcs into N. The fourth stage constructs the intervals of σ for all pairs of nodes in $O(mn^2)$ time. Now we explain how to construct intervals for one pair of nodes s and t. Suppose $(v_1, w_1), (v_2, w_2), ..., (v_m, w_m)$ are the arcs of N and $C(v_1, w_1) > C(v_2, w_2) > ... > C(v_m, w_m)$. Since the transmission time of each path $MP_j(s, t)$, $1 \leq j \leq m$, is a function of σ, we have $y = MP_j(s, t) + x/C(v_j, w_j)$, where $y = T(MP_j(s, t), \sigma)$ and $x = \sigma$. It is easy to see that the minimal transmission time for each value of σ is determined as $\min\{ MP_j(s, t) + x/C(v_j, w_j) \mid j=1,...,m \}$. Equivalently, the lower portion of these m lines $y = MP_j(s, t) + x/C(v_j, w_j)$, $j=1,...,m$, are the minimal transmission time for all values of σ and the intersection points along the lower portion separate the intervals.

Now the remaining problem is how to find the intersection points along the lower portion. This can be done in linear time by adding the lines $y = MP_j(s, t) + x/C(v_j, w_j)$ to the plane one by one and in the sequence of $j=m, m-1, ..., 1$. The line $y = MP_m(s, t) + x/C(v_m, w_m)$ is first added to the plane. Then, let us consider the situation of adding a line $y = MP_k(s, t) + x/C(v_k, w_k)$, $1 \leq k < m$, to the plane. The newly added line intersects the current lower portion at one point z (since the slopes of the lines are positive and decreasing in their order), which can be found by scanning the lower portion from right to left. Then, the point z is stored as a new intersection point and the intersection points on the right of z are discarded. Since each addition of a new line (except for the first line) generates exactly one intersection point, the total number of discarded intersection points is not greater than $m-1$. Consequently, the total time to find the point z (for all iterations) is not more than $O(m)$. It is not difficult to check that the time complexity of the algorithm is $O(mn^2)$.

References

[1] Y. L. Chen and Y. H. Chin, "The quickest path problem," *Computers and Operations Research*, vol. 17, 1989, pp. 153-161.

[2] Y. C. Hung and G. H. Chen, "On the quickest path problem," Tech. Rep., Department of Computer Science and Information Engineering, National Taiwan University, Taiwan, 1991.

Practical Adaptive Sorting

Vladimir Estivill-Castro   Derick Wood

Department of Computer Science
University of Waterloo
Waterloo, Ontario N2L 3G1
Canada

Abstract

We present a general constructive principle for the design of adaptive sorting algorithms that enables us to focus attention on the combinatorial properties of measures of presortedness rather than on the combinatorial properties of sorting algorithms. Using it, we obtain a practical adaptive sorting algorithm, optimal with respect to five important measures of presortedness and smoothly adaptive from $O(n)$ to $O(n \log n)$ time for other common measures. Moreover, we extend the proof techniques to analyze an adaptive variant of *Quicksort*; previous claims were based only on simulation results.

1 Introduction

Sorting algorithms that are optimal in the worst and expected cases are well known; however, few traditional algorithms take advantage of any order in an input sequence. Given that easy instances occur frequently, it is surprising that practical adaptive algorithms are uncommon; for example, the UNIX^{TM} *sort* does not profit from existing order in the input sequence. An adaptive sorting algorithm uses computational resources proportional to the amount of disorder in the sequence being sorted [11, page 224]. Recently, adaptive sorting algorithms have been the subject of intensive investigation [3, 5, 8, 9, 10, 12, 13]. Unfortunately, most of the proposed sorting algorithms have received limited acceptance because they are adaptive with respect to only one or two measures [1, 5, 6, 9, 12], they require complex data structures that have a significant overhead [2, 8, 10], or their adaptive behavior has eluded analysis [1, 3, 13].

We present a generic adaptive sorting algorithm that is optimal with respect to three common measures of presortedness and smoothly adaptive from $O(n)$ to $O(n \log n)$ comparisons with respect to other important measures. The algorithm is simple, practical, and does not require complex data structures. By a simple modification, optimality for two other important measures is achieved. Simulations show that our algorithm is efficient in terms of CPU time and its behavior on random sequences is competitive. It uses a divide and conquer scheme that shifts concern to combinatorial properties of measures of presortedness. Our results specify how much disorder, with respect to a measure, can be introduced during the division phase in order to obtain smooth adaptive behavior. Furthermore, we have used the same analytical techniques to analyze *Median Quicksort* [4], a variant of *Quicksort*, that uses the median as the pivot. Earlier claims about the adaptive behavior of variants of *Quicksort* [1, 3, 13] were founded on only empirical evidence. Although *Median Quicksort* is relevant only from the theoretical point of view it suggests a modification to the *sort* utility in UNIX. In this way we have obtained an implementation that is on average 20 to 100% faster for nearly sorted files and only 6% slower for random files.

2 Measures of presortedness

Informally, a measure of presortedness is an integer-valued function that is zero if there is no disorder. As the disorder grows, the value of the measure grows. Moreover, the value of the measure for a sequence depends only on the relative order of the elements in the sequence.

We now describe the most common measures of presortedness, many others can be found in the literature [8, 12]. An *inversion* is any pair of elements in a sequence that are in the wrong order. The total number of inversions in a sequence X is the measure Inv. We may consider that, in terms of the disorder it represents, an inversion pair of elements that are far apart is more significant than an inversion pair whose elements are closer. We define Dis as the largest distance determined by an inversion. Often local disorder is not as important as global disorder; for example, if books in a library are one slot away from their correct positions, we are still able to find them, since the index will get us close enough; however, a book very far away from its correct position is difficult to find. We define Max as the largest distance an element must travel to reach its sorted position. The number of operations required to rearrange a sequence into sorted order may be our first concern. We define Exc as the minimum number of exchanges required to sort a sequence. We may also consider that disorder is produced by inserting some records into the wrong positions. We define Rem as the minimum number of elements that must be removed to obtain a sorted subsequence. Ascending runs constitute sorted segments of the data. We define $Runs$ as the number of boundaries between runs.

Optimal adaptive sorting algorithms were introduced in a general setting by Mannila [10]. For a sequence X, $|X|$ denotes its length and for a set S, $\|S\|$ denotes its cardinality.

Definition 2.1 *Let M be a measure of presortedness and A be a sorting algorithm which uses $T_A(X)$ comparisons on input X. We say that A is* optimal *with respect to M (or M–optimal) if, for some $c > 0$, we have, for all sequences X,*

$$T_A(X) \leq c \cdot \max\{|X|, \log(\|below(X, M)\|)\},$$

where $below(X, M) = \{Y | Y$ is a permutation of $\{1, 2, ..., |X|\}$ and $M(Y) \leq M(X)\}$.

3 The generic sorting algorithm

In this section we describe *Generic Sort*, a generic sorting algorithm. We show that, under relatively weak conditions, we obtain a worst-case optimal sorting algorithm that is also smoothly adaptive. The structure of *Generic Sort* should not be surprising, it uses divide-and-conquer and balancing to ensure $O(n \log n)$ worst-case performance. What is novel, however, is that we can establish adaptability with respect to a measure of presortedness M by ensuring that the method of division, *the division protocol*, satisfies three requirements. First, division should take linear time in the worst case, second, the sizes of the sequences it gives should be almost the same, and, third, it should not introduce too much disorder. We formalize what is meant by too much disorder in the theorem below.

Generic Sort(X)
If X is sorted, then terminate. Otherwise, if X is "small",
  then sort using *Insertion Sort*.
Otherwise (if X is large and not sorted):
  apply a division protocol to obtain at least two disjoint sequences from X;
  recursively sort them using *Generic Sort*;
  combine the sorted sequences to give X in sorted order.

If a sequence cannot be divided into smaller sequences or it is short enough to be sorted by *Insertion Sort*, then it is considered "small".

Generic Sort leaves us with two problems. What are reasonable division protocols and what is meant by too much disorder? Three example division protocols are:

- *Straight division.* Divide $X = \langle x_1, \ldots, x_n \rangle$ into $X_L = X_{1..\lfloor X \rfloor/2}$ and $X_R = X_{1+\lfloor X \rfloor/2..\lfloor X \rfloor}$.

- *Odd-even division.* Divide X into the subsequence X_{even} of elements in even positions and the subsequence X_{odd} of elements in odd positions.

- *Median division.* Divide X into the sequence of all elements smaller than the median of X and the sequence of all elements larger than the median (denoted by $X_<$ and $X_>$ respectively).

Observe that each of these division protocols satisfies the linear time and equal size requirements. The notion of too much disorder is made precise in the main theorem of the paper.

Theorem 3.1 *Let M be a measure of presortedness, D and s be constants, $0 < D < 2$ and $s > 1$, and DP be a linear time division protocol that divides a sequence into s sequences of almost equal sizes. Then,*

1. *Generic Sort is worst case optimal; that is, on a sequence of length n, it takes $O(n \log n)$ time, and*

2. *if there is an $n_0 \in N$ such that, for all sequences X with $|X| > n_0$, DP satisfies*

$$\sum_{j=1}^{s} M(j\text{-th subsequence}) \leq D \lfloor s/2 \rfloor M(X), \tag{1}$$

then Generic Sort takes $O(|X|(1+\log[M(X)+1]))$ time in the worst case; that is, it is adaptive to the measure M.

Moreover, $D < 2$ is necessary.

Proof: We first establish the adaptive bound and then prove, by counterexample, that $D < 2$ in necessary.

Let $a > 0$ be a constant such that *Generic Sort* takes at most an time to test if a sequence of length n is sorted or to sort a "small" sequence (that is, a sequence of length at most n_0). We also assume that discovering that a sequence of length n is not sorted, splitting it into s subsequences, and merging s sorted subsequences to give the final solution takes at most an time. Let q $(0 < q < 2)$ be such that

$$2^{1-q/2} \geq 1 + D/2 \tag{2}$$

and let $d \geq a/q$. We prove by induction that if $T(n,k)$ is the maximum number of comparisons performed by *Generic Sort* on a sequence X of length n with measure $M(X) = k$, then

$$T(n,k) \leq 2dn(1 + \log[k+1]). \tag{3}$$

Basis: If the sequence is "small", then, by the assumption for a, $T(n,k) \leq an \leq 2an/q \leq 2dn$; thus, $T(n,k)$ satisfies inequality (3).

Induction hypothesis: Assume that, for all $n' < n$, if $0 \leq k' \leq \max_{|X|=n'}\{M(X)\}$, then $T(n',k') \leq 2dn'(1 + \log[k'+1])$.

Induction Step: Consider a sequence X of length n. If X is sorted or "small", then $T(n,k) \leq an \leq 2dn$ as required. Otherwise *Generic-Sort* divides X is into s subsequences $X_1, X_2, \ldots, X_s$ with $\sum_{j=1}^{s} M(X_j) \leq D \lfloor s/2 \rfloor M(X)$. Let $M(X) = k$ and $M(X_j) = k_j$, for $j = 1, \ldots, s$, in which case

$$\sum_{j=1}^{s} k_j \leq D \lfloor s/2 \rfloor k. \tag{4}$$

Now, by definition and the induction hypothesis,

$$T(n,k) \;\leq\; an + \sum_{j=1}^{s} T(n/s, k_j)$$

$$\leq\; an + 2dn \left(\sum_{j=1}^{s} \log \left[(k_j + 1)^{1/s} \right] + \sum_{j=1}^{s} \frac{1}{s} \right)$$

$$\leq\; an + 2dn \left(1 + \log \left[\prod_{j=1}^{s} (k_j + 1) \right]^{1/s} \right).$$

Since, the geometric mean is no larger than the arithmetic mean, we find that

$$T(n,k) \;\leq\; an + 2dn \left(1 + \log \left[\frac{\sum_{j=1}^{s} (k_j + 1)}{s} \right] \right)$$

$$\leq\; an + 2dn \log \left[2 + \frac{\sum_{j=1}^{s} k_j}{s/2} \right]$$

$$\leq\; qdn + 2dn \log[2 + Dk].$$

Now, $2^{1-q/2} \geq 1 + D/2 = 2 - (2 - D)/2 \geq 2 - \frac{k}{k+1}(2 - D)$, for all $k \geq 1$; therefore, (2) implies that $kD + 2 \leq (k+1)2^{1-q/2}$, for all $k \geq 1$. Hence,

$$T(n,k) \;\leq\; qdn + 2dn \log[2 + Dk]$$

$$\leq\; qdn + 2dn \log[(k + 1)2^{1-q/2}]$$

$$=\; 2dn[1 + \log(k + 1)].$$

We now demonstrate that $D < 2$ is necessary, completing the proof of the theorem. Consider the following variant of *Merge Sort*:

Straight Merge Sort(X);
if not *sorted*(X)
then *Straight Merge Sort*$(X_{1..|X|/2})$;
    Straight Merge Sort$(X_{1+|X|/2..|X|})$;
    Merge$(X_{1..|X|/2}, X_{1+|X|/2..|X|})$;

The straight division protocol takes linear time, and because

$$Dis(X_{1..|X|/2}) \leq Dis(X) \text{ and } Dis(X_{1+|X|/2..|X|}) \leq Dis(X)$$

we have

$$Dis(X_{1..|X|/2}) + Dis(X_{1+|X|/2..|X|}) \leq 2Dis(X).$$

This bound is tight because, if $W_0 = \langle 2, 1, 4, 3, \ldots \rangle$, then $Dis(W_0) = 1$, $Dis((W_0)_{1..|W|/2}) = 1$, and $Dis((W_0)_{1+|W|/2..|W|}) = 1$. Assume that Theorem 3.1 holds when $D = 2$. This implies that *Straight Merge Sort* should take $O(|W_0|[1 + \log 2]) = O(|W_0|)$ time. But clearly, *Straight Merge Sort* takes $\Omega(|W_0| \log |W_0|)$ comparisons to sort W_0. Thus, $D < 2$ is necessary for Theorem 3.1 to hold. □

3.1 Applications

For the measures *Inv* and *Rem* it is not difficult to prove that, for all X,

$$Inv(X_{1..|X|/2}) + Inv(X_{1+|X|/2..|X|}) \leq Inv(X)$$

and

$$Rem(X_{1..|X|/2}) + Rem(X_{1+|X|/2..|X|}) \leq Rem(X).$$

Thus, by Theorem 3.1, *Straight Merge Sort* is adaptive for *Inv* and *Rem*. It is easy to see that

$$Runs(X_{1..|X|/2}) + Runs(X_{1+|X|/2..|X|}) \overset{!}{\leq} Runs(X).$$

Since $\log \|below(X, Runs)\| = \Omega(|X| \log[1 + Runs(X)])$ [10], Theorem 3.1 implies that *Straight Merge Sort* is optimal with respect to *Runs*.

To obtain an algorithm that is adaptive with respect to *Dis* use the odd-even division protocol. Since we have proved [5] that $Dis(X_{odd}) \leq Dis(X)/2$ and $Dis(X_{even}) \leq Dis(X)/2$ we have immediately that

$$Dis(X_{even}) + Dis(X_{odd}) \leq Dis(X).$$

Moreover, it is easy to prove that, for any sequence X,

$$Inv(X_{even}) + Inv(X_{odd}) \leq Inv(X),$$

$$Max(X_{even}) + Max(X_{odd}) \leq Max(X),$$

and

$$Rem(X_{even}) + Rem(X_{odd}) \leq Rem(X).$$

Thus, the following modified version of *Merge Sort*:

Odd-even Merge Sort(X);
if not *sorted*(X)
then *Odd-even Merge Sort*(X_{even});
       Odd-even Merge Sort(X_{odd});
       Merge(X_{even}, X_{odd});

takes fewer comparisons than the minimum of $6n(\log[Inv(X) + 1] + 1)$, $6n(\log[Dis(X) + 1] + 1)$, $6n(\log[Rem(X) + 1] + 1)$ and $6n(\log[Max(X) + 1] + 1)$. Moreover, since, for all X, $Rem(X) \leq 2Exc(X)$ [8], *Odd-even Merge Sort* takes less than $6n(\log[Exc(X) + 1] + 2)$ comparisons. In other words, if *Odd-even Merge Sort* is given a sequence that is nearly sorted with respect to any of the above measures, it will adapt its time requirements accordingly and for *Dis* and *Max* it is optimal[5].

As a final application of Theorem 3.1 we combine the two previous algorithms and obtain an algorithm that is adaptive with respect to every measure mentioned above and optimal with respect to *Runs*, *Dis* and *Max*. We merely combine the division protocols to give:

Odd-even Straight Merge Sort(X);
if not *sorted*(X)
then *O-E S M Sort*(X_{even_L});
        O-E S M Sort(X_{odd_L});
        O-E S M Sort(X_{even_L});
        O-E S M Sort(X_{odd_R});
        Merge($X_{even_L}, X_{odd_L}, X_{even_R}, X_{odd_R}$);

By Theorem 3.1, the algorithm is smoothly adaptive for *Rem* and *Exc*.

Harris [6] has shown that *Natural Merge Sort* when implemented using linked lists, as suggested by Knuth [7, Sec. 5.2.4, Ex. 12, Sec 5.2, Ex. 12], is a competitive (with respect to comparisons and data movements) adaptive sorting algorithm that behaves well on random sequences. We have compared the CPU time of *Natural Merge Sort* and *Odd-even Straight Merge Sort* with other algorithms for nearly sorted sequences and have found the timings competitive. Note that *Natural Merge Sort* is optimal with respect to *Runs*. We have compared a linked list implementation of *Odd-even Straight Merge Sort* with *Natural Merge Sort*. Some of our results are presented in Tables

$\lvert X \rvert$	Algorithm	Percentage of disorder					
		0	4	8	12	16	20
500	*Natural Mergesort*	1.00	5.12	6.13	6.28	6.99	7.02
	O-E S M Sort	1.00	5.33	6.54	7.35	7.77	8.43
1000	*Natural Mergesort*	1.00	6.00	6.94	7.21	8.00	8.00
	O-E S M Sort	1.00	6.71	7.91	8.82	9.43	9.98
2000	*Natural Mergesort*	1.00	6.93	8.01	8.24	8.96	9.07
	O-E S M Sort	1.00	8.02	9.39	10.30	10.94	11.35

Table 1: *Comparisons*/$\lvert X \rvert$ for *Rem*-nearly sorted sequences

$\lvert X \rvert$	Algorithm	Percentage of disorder						
		1	2	4	8	12	16	20
500	*Natural Mergesort*	5.54	5.76	5.96	6.08	6.17	6.27	6.33
	O-E S M Sort	2.00	4.74	4.94	5.29	5.44	5.62	5.76
1000	*Natural Mergesort*	6.05	6.45	6.57	6.79	6.94	7.00	7.08
	O-E S M Sort	2.00	5.27	5.75	6.11	6.25	6.38	6.47
2000	*Natural Mergesort*	6.55	7.10	7.31	7.51	7.67	7.76	7.83
	O-E S M Sort	2.00	6.16	6.43	6.79	7.01	7.15	7.21

Table 2: *Comparisons*/$\lvert X \rvert$ for *Max*-nearly sorted sequences

1, 2 and 3. *Natural Merge Sort* and *Odd-even Straight Merge Sort* perform the same number of exchanges and data movements. The tables display the average number of comparisons performed by an algorithm for the same set of 50 permutations with the corresponding percentage of disorder. The percentage of disorder in Table 1 is given by $Rem(X)/\lvert X \rvert$ and permutations were generated as suggested by Cook and Kim [1]. The percentage of disorder in Table 2 is given by $Max(X)/\lvert X \rvert$. Table 3 summarizes the results for random sequences. As expected, *Odd-even Straight Merge Sort* is a competitive algorithm that guarantees good performance for random sequences. It is adaptive with respect to every measure presented above, performing a few more comparisons for sequences that are nearly sorted with respect to *Rem*, but is faster for sequences with local disorder.

The only disadvantage of *Odd-even Straight Merge Sort* is that it is not adaptive for sequences in descending sorted order, but then again neither is *Natural Merge Sort*. However, if we test for both ascending and descending sorted order and we modify merging to take this into account, the algorithm becomes adaptive with respect to $min\{M(X), M(Reverse(X))\}$.

If optimality with respect to *Rem* and *Exc* is desired, we need to extend the division protocol of *Odd-even Straight Merge Sort*. Use Cook and Kim's [1] linear time algorithm to extract a sorted subsequence from X leaving a subsequence of at most $2Rem(X)$ elements to be sorted. This can be combined with the test for sortedness.

4   Median Quicksort

The goal of sorting is to reduce the disorder in a given sequence to zero. The spirit of our approach is a local optimization that, at each recursive step, controls the amount of disorder introduced.

Algorithm	$\lvert X \rvert$		
	500	1000	2000
Natural Mergesort	8.49	9.29	10.22
O-E S M Sort	11.22	12.87	14.63

Table 3: *Comparisons*/$\lvert X \rvert$ for random sequences

UNIX utility	Sorted Sequence	Random Sequence
sort	983.76 ± 15.66	1692.15 ± 40.91
vsort	375.86 ± 4.51	1744.89 ± 38.33

Table 4: 99 % confidence intervals for the expected CPU time with $|X| = 1,000,000$.

UNIX	$Exc(X)/|X|$			
utility	0.2	0.4	0.6	0.8
sort	1423.21 ± 20.72	1424.15 ± 12.51	1439.22 ± 25.30	1439.60 ± 13.08
vsort	1448.38 ± 17.61	1451.64 ± 17.21	1469.23 ± 23.97	1470.53 ± 13.05

Table 5: 99% confidence intervals for the expected CPU time with $|X| = 1,000,000$.

In this section we discuss *Median Quicksort*, a variant of *Quicksort*. *Median Quicksort* uses the median division protocol. Since the median can be computed in linear time in the worst case, *Median Quicksort* takes $O(n)$ comparisons in the best case and takes $O(n \log n)$ comparisons in the worst case. Because we can guarantee only that D is asymptotically 2, Theorem 3.1 does not apply directly.

Median Quicksort is based on exchanges; thus, we would like to know if it is adaptive with respect to *Exc*. To show that *Median Quicksort* takes $\Omega(n(\log[Exc(X) + 1] + 1))$ comparisons is not difficult. Let $k \in N$, $2 \le k \le n/2$; then,

$$W_1 = \langle 2, 1, 4, 3, 6, 5, \ldots 2\lfloor k/2 \rfloor, 2\lfloor k/2 \rfloor - 1, 2\lfloor k/2 \rfloor + 1, 2\lfloor k/2 \rfloor + 2, \ldots, n \rangle$$

has $Exc(W_1) = \Omega(k)$ and *Median Quicksort* takes $\Omega(n \log k)$ time to sort it. However, to obtain a matching upper bound on the number of comparisons performed by the algorithm, we cannot apply Theorem 3.1 blindly since, for example, let n be odd and

$$A = \langle n, n-1, \ldots, \tfrac{n+1}{2} + 2 \rangle, \quad B = \langle \tfrac{n+1}{2}, \tfrac{n+1}{1} - 1, \ldots, 3 \rangle, \quad \text{and} \quad W_2 = \langle 1, \tfrac{n+1}{2} + 1 \rangle A \langle 2 \rangle B.$$

Now, $Exc(W_2) = (n-1)/2$, the pivot is $(n+1)/2$, and the first partition divides W_2 into

$$(W_2)_< = \langle 1, 3, 4, \tfrac{n+1}{2} - 1, 2 \rangle$$

and

$$(W_2)_> = \langle \tfrac{n+1}{2} + 2, \tfrac{n+1}{2} + 3, \ldots, n, \tfrac{n+1}{2} + 1 \rangle.$$

Therefore, $Exc((W_2)_<) + Exc((W_2)_>) = n - 4$. Although Theorem 3.1 allows $D \ge 2$ for finitely many n, it is still insufficient for *Median Quicksort* because there is no constant $D < 2$ such that $n - 4 \le D(n-1)/2$, for infinitely many n. Thus, we have shown that there is no $D < 2$ such that $Exc(X_<) + Exc(X_>) \le D Exc(X)$, for all X. However, using more sophisticated techniques, we have been able to prove [4] a similar theorem, namely,

Theorem 4.1 *If $T_{EQ}(X)$ is the number of comparison performed by* Median Quicksort *on input X, then $T_{EQ} = \Theta(|X|(\log[Exc(X) + 1] + 1))$.*

The *sort* utility in UNIX is based on *Quicksort*. We modified it to give *vsort*, that is equivalent to *sort*, but the inner *Quicksort* only continues recursively on sequences that are not sorted. We tested *vsort* and *sort* on sequences of distinct numbers. Both *vsort* and *sort* are sensitive to disorder measured by *Exc*. Moreover, *vsort* is at most 6% slower than *sort* on random files; however, for almost sorted files *vsort* turns out to be much faster than *sort*. Table 4 presents the contrast in the behavior of the two sorting utilities. The overhead in a random file is so small because the average length of the first run in a random sequence is about two [7]; thus, *vsort* quickly discovers that unsorted sequences require sorting. For nearly sorted sequences, where $Exc(X)/|X| \ge 0.1$ Table 5 shows that the adaptive behavior is absorbed by the overhead needed to test if a sequence is sorted. Table 6 shows that significant savings are obtained if the sequence is almost sorted.

UNIX	$Exc(X)/|X|$			
utility	0.00001	0.0001	0.001	0.01
sort	1005.90 ± 15.04	1023.20 ± 13.38	1222.35 ± 16.15	1264.80 ± 24.01
vsort	451.23 ± 15.08	830.77 ± 18.72	1098.55 ± 27.39	1210.11 ± 22.34

Table 6: 99 % confidence intervals for the expected CPU time with $|X| = 1,000,000$.

Acknowledgement

This work was carried out under a Natural Sciences and Engineering Research Council of Canada Grant No.A-5692 and under an Information Technology Research Centre grant.

References

[1] C.R. Cook and D.J. Kim. Best sorting algorithms for nearly sorted lists. *Communications of the ACM*, 23:620–624, 1980.

[2] E.W. Dijkstra. Smoothsort, an alternative to sorting in situ. *Science of Computer Programming*, 1:223–233, 1982.

[3] P.G. Dromey. Exploiting partial order with Quicksort. *Software — Practice and Experience*, 14(6):509–518, 1984.

[4] V. Estivill-Castro and D. Wood. A generic adaptive sorting algorithm. *Computer Journal.* To appear.

[5] V. Estivill-Castro and D. Wood. A new measure of presortedness. *Information and Computation*, 83:111–119, 1989.

[6] J. D. Harris. Sorting unsorted and partially sorted lists using the natural merge sort. *Software — Practice and Experience*, 11:1339–1340, 1981.

[7] D.E. Knuth. *The Art of Computer Programming, Vol.3: Sorting and Searching.* Addison-Wesley Publishing Co., Reading, Mass., 1973.

[8] C. Levcopoulos and O. Petersson. Heapsort — adapted for presorted files. In F. Dehne, J.R. Sack, and N. Santoro, editors, *Proceedings of the Workshop on Algorithms and Data Structures*, pages 499–509. Springer-Verlag Lecture Notes in Computer Science 382, 1989.

[9] C. Levcopoulos and O. Petersson. Splitsort—an adaptive sorting algorithm. Technical report, Department of Computer Science, Lund University, 1989.

[10] H. Mannila. Measures of presortedness and optimal sorting algorithms. *IEEE Transactions on Computers*, C-34:318–325, 1985.

[11] K. Mehlhorn. *Data Structures and Algorithms, Vol 1: Sorting and Searching.* EATCS Monographs on Theoretical Computer Science. Springer-Verlag, Berlin/Heidelberg, 1984.

[12] S.S. Skiena. Encroaching lists as a measure of presortedness. *BIT*, 28:755–784, 1988.

[13] R.L. Wainwright. A class of sorting algorithms based on Quicksort. *Communications of the ACM*, 28:396–402, 85.

LOWER BOUNDS FOR ALGEBRAIC COMPUTATION TREES
OF FUNCTIONS WITH FINITE DOMAINS

Nader H. Bshouty

Department of Computer Science, University of Calgary
Calgary, Alberta, CANADA. E-mail: bshouty@cpsc.ucalgary.ca

Abstract : In this paper we study the complexity of rational functions and multirational functions. These include 1) functions containing the absolute value, max and min functions, 2) data structure functions such as sort, insert and merge 3) integer functions such as the gcd (greater common divisor), modulo, bitwise 'and' and 4) polynomial functions such as the gcd and modulo of two polynomials.

We prove tight lower bounds for the above functions over a **finite input domain** in a RAM that uses arithmetic operations and that has unlimited power for answering YES/NO questions.

1. INTRODUCTION

Many tight bounds are known for functions when the domain of the input is infinite. For example, the complexity of sorting n integers using arithmetic operations and comparisons is $\Omega(n \log n)$ [PS, Y] and the complexity of computing the rational function $x_1^k + \cdots + x_n^k$ over the integers is $\Omega(n \log k)$, [B, Y]. But few results are known when

(1) The domain of the input elements is finite.
(2) The input elements are from an arbitrary field with arbitrary order.
(3) The RAM has unlimited power for answering YES/NO questions.
(4) The functions contain the operations $\{| \ |, \max, \min, ...\}$.
In this paper we prove the following:

1. Data structure functions

Result 1. (Sort). Let $S = \{s_1, \cdots, s_N\}$ be $N = n^{\Omega(n)}$ elements from an arbitrary field with arbitrary order. The complexity of sorting n elements from S is

$$\Omega(n \log n).$$

Result 2. (Merge).

Let $S = \{s_1, \cdots, s_N\}$ be $N = (nk)^{\Omega(nk)}$ elements from an arbitrary field with arbitrary order. The complexity of merging n sorted sequences of k elements from S is

$$\Omega\left(\frac{\log (nk)!}{(k!)^n}\right).$$

Result 3. (Insert). Let $S = \{s_1, \cdots, s_N\}$ be $N = n^{\Omega(n)}$ elements from an arbitrary field with arbitrary order. The complexity of inserting an element into n sorted elements is

$$\Omega(\log n).$$

2. Multirational functions

Result 4. (Rational function). Let f be a rational function over a field F. Suppose that the complexity of computing f over F is t (in the straight line model). Then for any subset D of F with $2^{\Omega(t)}$ elements, the complexity of computing f over the domain D is t (in the RAM model).

We remind the reader that our RAM model has unlimited power for answering YES/NO questions.

Result 5. (Multirational functions). Let

$$f(x) = \begin{cases} f_1(x) & \text{for } x \in S_1 \\ f_2(x) & \text{for } x \in S_2 \\ \vdots \\ f_m(x) & \text{for } x \in S_m \end{cases}$$

where $f_1, \cdots, f_m$ are rational functions. Let $\mu(f_i)$ be the complexity of computing f_i by a straight line algorithm. If $S_1, \cdots, S_m$ are sets with positive measure then there exists a domain with $O(m^2 2^{max_i \mu(f_i)})$ elements where the complexity of f is

$$\left\lceil \log\left(\sum_{i=1}^{k} 2^{\mu(f_i)}\right) \right\rceil.$$

Result 5 gives the exact complexity for functions that contain $\{+, -, \times, /, | \ |,$ $\max, \min, \cdots\}$. For example, the complexity of computing $|x_1| + \cdots + |x_n|$ is $2n - 1$ and the complexity of computing the functions $|x - y|, \max(x, y)$ and $(|x| + x)y$ is 5.

3. Integer functions

Result 6. (Modulu) . The complexity of computing $b \bmod a$ where $1 \leq a \leq b \leq N$ is

$$\Omega(\log N).$$

Result 7. (GCD) . The complexity of computing $GCD(a, b)$ where $1 \leq a \leq b \leq N$ is

$$\Omega(\log N).$$

4. Polynomial functions

Result 8. (GCD of polynomials). The complexity of computing $GCD(f,g)$ where $0 \leq \deg f \leq \deg g < n$ is

$$\Omega(n).$$

All of the above bounds are tight. In the paper general techniques are found that give lower bounds for many other functions.

2. THE RAM MODEL

We now describe the model of computation. Since our RAM does not contain indirect addressing we can investigate the complexity of a function in the algebraic computation tree. The algebraic computation tree is defined as follows. Let F be a field and τ be an integer. A computation τ-tree with r inputs that computes a function $f : A \to B$ where $A \subseteq F^r$ and $B \subseteq F^s$ is a tree with labeled vertices. The label of a vertex v is denoted by f_v. The tree $\mathbf{T}$ has four types of vertices:

(1) *Input vertices:* Each of the first r levels of $\mathbf{T}$ has exactly one vertex. The vertex in level i is labeled by x_i. These are the input vertices $\mathbf{x} = (x_1, \cdots, x_r)$.

(2) *Computation vertices:* Each computation vertex v is labeled with a binary operation $f_v = g_1 \circ g_2$, and has one child where $g_1, g_2 \in F \cup \{f_\mu | \mu \text{ is an ancestor of } v \text{ in } \mathbf{T}\}$ and $\circ \in \{+, -, \times, /\}$.

(3) *Question vertices:* Each question vertex v is labeled with $P_1, P_2, \cdots, P_{\zeta-1}$ where $\zeta \leq \tau$ is the number of its children, $P_i \subseteq A$ for $1 \leq i \leq \zeta - 1$ and $P_j \cap P_k = \emptyset$ for $1 \leq j < k \leq \zeta - 1$.

(4) *Output vertices:* The output vertices are the leaves of $\mathbf{T}$. Each leaf v of $\mathbf{T}$ is labeled $(f_{u_1}, \cdots, f_{u_s})$ where u_i are ancestors of v in $\mathbf{T}$.

The computation begins at the root of the tree with an input $\mathbf{x}$. When it arrives at a computation vertex v, the function f_v is evaluated, and then the computation proceeds to the only child of v. When the computation arrives at a question vertex labeled with $P_1, P_2, \cdots, P_{\zeta-1}$, it proceeds to i-th child if $\mathbf{x} \notin P_1, \cdots, \mathbf{x} \notin P_{i-1}, \mathbf{x} \in P_i$ and proceeds to ζ-th child if $\mathbf{x} \notin P_1 \cup \cdots \cup P_{\zeta-1}$. The computation terminates at a leaf v and returns the value $(f_{u_1}(\mathbf{x}), \cdots, f_{u_s}(\mathbf{x}))$.

we say that the computation τ-tree $\mathbf{T}$ *computes* f if for every $\mathbf{x} \in A$ the computation of the tree for the input $\mathbf{x}$ terminates at some leaf v and returns the value $(f_{u_1}(\mathbf{x}), \cdots, f_{u_s}(\mathbf{x})) = f(\mathbf{x})$.

Let v_0 be the root of $\mathbf{T}$ and $v_1, \cdots, v_T$ be its leaves. We define $\mathbf{L}_{1,\tau}(v_0, v_i)$ for $1 \leq i \leq T$ to be the number of arithmetic operations used in the path from v_0 to v_i, and $\mathbf{L}_{2,\tau}(v_0, v_i)$ to be the number of question vertices in this path. We also define

$$\mathbf{L}_\tau(v_0, v_i) = \mathbf{L}_{1,\tau}(v_0, v_i) + \mathbf{L}_{2,\tau}(v_0, v_i),$$

$$\mathbf{L}_\tau(\mathbf{T}) = \max_{1 \leq i \leq T} \mathbf{L}(v_0, v_i),$$

and
$$\mathbf{L}_r(f) = \min\{\mathbf{L}_r(\mathbf{T}) | \mathbf{T} \text{ computes } f : \mathbf{A} \to \mathbf{B}\}.$$

We say that $\mathbf{T}$ is a *minimal computation τ-tree for f* if $\mathbf{L}_r(f) = \mathbf{L}_r(\mathbf{T})$.

When there are no question vertices in the computation tree $\mathbf{T}$ we call $\mathbf{T}$ a *straight line algorithm*. In this case $\mathbf{T}$ can compute only functions $f \in F(x_1, \cdots, x_r)^s$ where $F(x_1, \cdots, x_r)$ is the field of all rational functions in the indeterminates $x_1, \cdots, x_r$ over the field F. For $f \in F(x_1, \cdots, x_r)^s$, $\mu(f)$ (resp. $\mu^*(f)$) denotes the number of arithmetic operations (resp. non-scalar multiplications/divisions) needed to compute f by a straight line algorithm. Obviously, if $\mathbf{T}$ is a computation τ-tree then every path that begins in the root v_0 and ends in a leaf v_i is a straight line algorithm that computes f in some domain Q_i.

A trivial upper bound is given by the following:

Theorem 1 . Let
$$f(x) = \begin{cases} f_1(x) & \text{if } x \in P_1 \\ \vdots & \vdots \\ f_M(x) & \text{if } x \in P_M \end{cases}.$$

where $f_1, \cdots, f_M \in F(x_1, \cdots, x_r)^s$. Then
$$\mathbf{L}_r(f) \leq \lceil \log_r M \rceil + \max_{1 \leq i \leq M} \mathbf{L}_r(f_i)$$

Notice that every function $f : \mathbf{A} \to \mathbf{B}$ with $|\mathbf{B}| \leq \tau$ can be computed in a computation τ-tree by one question vertex.

The paper is organized as follows. Section 3 includes some basic definitions and preliminary results. In section 4 we prove lower bounds for some functions with finite domains.

3. BASIC DEFINITIONS AND PRELIMINARY RESULTS

In this section we introduce some notation and prove the major lemmas and theorems needed to prove our results.

Throughout the paper F is a field, $F[x_1, \cdots, x_r]$ is the ring of multivariate polynomials in the indeterminates $x_1, \cdots, x_r$ with coefficients in F and $F(x_1, \cdots, x_r)$ is the field of rational functions in the indeterminates $x_1, \cdots, x_r$ with coefficients in F. For a set $\mathbf{A}$ the notation $|\mathbf{A}|$ is the cardinality of $\mathbf{A}$, while for a real number r the notation $|r|$ is the absolute value of r. The power set of $\mathbf{A}$ is $\mathbf{P}(\mathbf{A})$, $\log a$ is $\log_2 a$, $\mathbf{R}$ is the field of reals, $\mathbf{C}$ is the field of complex numbers and $\mathbf{Z}$ is the ring of integers.

We first start by studying the behavior of the roots of rational functions in finite domains.

Lemma 1. [S] . Let $\mathbf{S}_i = \{s_{i,1}, \cdots, s_{i,n}\} \subseteq F$ where $|\mathbf{S}_i| = n$, $i = 1, \cdots, r$. Let $g \in F[x_1, \cdots, x_r]$, $g \not\equiv 0$. If g has Mn^{r-1} roots in $\mathbf{S} = \mathbf{S}_1 \times \mathbf{S}_2 \times \cdots \times \mathbf{S}_r$ then $\deg g \geq M$.

Definition 1 . For a vector of rational functions $(f_1, \cdots, f_s) \in F(x_1, \cdots, x_r)^s$ we define

$$maxdeg(f_1, \cdots, f_s) = \max_{1 \le i \le s} maxdeg(f_i),$$

where for $f_{i,1}, f_{i,2} \in F[x_1, \cdots, x_r]$,

$$maxdeg\left(\frac{f_{i,1}}{f_{i,2}}\right) = \max\left(deg\left(\frac{f_{i,1}}{gcd(f_{i,1}, f_{i,2})}\right), deg\left(\frac{f_{i,2}}{gcd(f_{i,1}, f_{i,2})}\right)\right).$$

Using lemma 1, we have

Lemma 2 . Let $S_i = \{s_{i,1}, \cdots, s_{i,n}\} \subseteq F$ where $|S_i| = n$, $i = 1, \cdots, r$. For two vectors of rational functions $f, g \in F(x_1, \cdots, x_r)^s$, if $f \not\equiv g$ then the equation $f = g$ has at most

$$(maxdeg\ f + maxdeg\ g)n^{r-1}$$

solutions in $S = S_1 \times \cdots \times S_r$.

Lemma 3. [St1] . Let $f \in F(x_1, \cdots, x_r)^s$. Then

$$\mu^*(f) \ge \lceil \log(maxdeg\ f) \rceil .$$

Definition 2. Let $S_i = \{s_{i,1}, \cdots, s_{i,n}\} \subseteq F$ where $|S_i| = n$, $i = 1, \cdots, r$. Let $f : A \to B$ be a function where $A \subseteq S_1 \times \cdots \times S_r$ and $B \subseteq F^s$. We denote by M_f an integer such that there exists an integer d and distinct functions $f_1, \cdots, f_{M_f} \in F(x_1, \cdots, x_r)^s$ with maxdeg less than or equal to d where

$$|\{x \in A | f(x) = f_i(x)\}| \ge M_f(M_f^{1/\log r} + 3d)n^{r-1}.$$

Theorem 2. We have

$$\mathbf{L}_r(f) \ge \lceil \log_r M_f \rceil .$$

Proof. Let T be a computation r-tree that computes $f : A \to B$. Let $v_1, \cdots, v_T$ be the leaves of T. Every leaf v_i defines a set $Q_i \subseteq A$ which is the set of all inputs $(x_1, \cdots, x_r) \in A$ that terminate in the computation at the leaf v_i, and defines a function $g_i(x_1, \cdots, x_r) \in F(x_1, \cdots, x_r)^s$, $1 \le i \le T$. Obviously, $g_i(x) = f(x)$ for $x \in Q_i$, $\cup_{i=1}^T Q_i = A$ and $Q_i \cap Q_j = \emptyset$, $1 \le i < j \le T$. We assume (w.l.o.g) that

$$g_1, \cdots, g_t \in \{f_1, \cdots, f_{M_f}\} \quad \text{and} \quad g_{t+1}, \cdots, g_T \notin \{f_1, \cdots, f_{M_f}\}. \tag{1}$$

If $t \ge M_f$ then there exists a path in T that contains at least $\lceil \log_r M_f \rceil$ question vertices, therefore $t < M_f$. Hence, from (1) there exists f_{x_i} (w.l.o.g.) $= f_1$ such that $f_1 \notin \{g_1, \cdots, g_t\}$. For $1 \le i \le t$, let $\psi(g_i)$ be an integer such that $g_i = f_{\psi(g_i)}$. Then $\psi(g_i) \ne 1$ for $1 \le i \le t$.

Let $P_1 = \{x \in A | f(x) = f_1(x)\}$. For $x \in Q_i \cap P_1$, $f(x) = g_i(x) = f_{\psi(g_i)}(x)$ and $f(x) = f_1(x)$, which implies that $f_{\psi(g_i)}(x) = f_1(x)$ and $x \in \{x | f_1(x) = f_{\psi(g_i)}(x)\} \cap P_1$. Hence

$$Q_i \cap P_1 \subseteq \{x | f_1(x) = f_{\psi(g_i)}(x)\} \cap P_1.$$

Since $\psi(g_i) \ne 1$, by lemma 2, and since $t < M_f$ we have

$$|(\cup_{i=1}^t Q_i) \cap P_1| = |\cup_{i=1}^t (Q_i \cap P_1)| \le |\cup_{i=1}^t \{x | f_1(x) = f_{\psi(g_i)}(x)\} \cap P_1|$$

$$\leq |\cup_{i=2}^{t} \{x | f_1(x) = f_i(x)\} \cap P_1|$$

$$\leq M_f(2d)n^{r-1}. \tag{2}$$

Now since $|P_1| \geq M_f(M_f^{1/\log r} + 3d)n^{r-1}$ we have $\cup_{i=1}^{T} Q_i = \mathbf{A} \subseteq P_1$. Hence by (2) we have

$$|(\cup_{i=t+1}^{T} Q_i) \cap P_1| \geq M_f(M_f^{1/\log r} + d)n^{r-1}. \tag{3}$$

If $T - t \geq M_f$ then there exists a path in $\mathbf{T}$ that contains at least $\lceil \log_r M_f \rceil$ question vertices. Therefore $T - t \leq M_f$ and by (3) there exists Q_η for $t + 1 \leq \eta \leq T$ such that $|Q_\eta \cap P_1| \geq (M_f^{1/\log r} + d)n^{r-1}$. It follows that there exists $(M_f^{1/\log r} + d)n^{r-1}$ elements in $\mathbf{A} \subseteq \mathbf{S}_1 \times \cdots \times \mathbf{S}_r$ that satisfy the equation $g_\eta(x) = f_1(x)$. Since $g_\eta(x) \not\equiv f_1(x)$ and by lemma 2 the equation $g_\eta(x) = f_1(x)$ has at most

$$(maxdeg\ g_\eta(x) + d)n^{r-1}$$

solutions in $\mathbf{S}$, we have $maxdeg\ g_\eta(x) \geq M_f^{1/\log r}$. By lemma 3 computing g_η requires at least $\lceil \log_r M_f \rceil$ non-scalar multiplications/divisions. $\blacksquare$

Theorem 3. Let $\mathbf{S}_i = \{s_{i,1}, \cdots, s_{i,n}\} \subseteq F$ where $|\mathbf{S}_i| = n$ for $i = 1, \cdots, r$. Let $f : \mathbf{A} \to \mathbf{B}$ be a function where $\mathbf{A} \subseteq \mathbf{S}_1 \times \cdots \times \mathbf{S}_r$ and $\mathbf{B} \subseteq F^s$. Let $f_1 \in F(x_1, \cdots, x_r)^s$. If

$$|\{x \in \mathbf{A} | f(x) = f_1(x)\}| > \tau^{\mathbf{L}_r(f)}(2^{\mathbf{L}_r(f)} + maxdeg\ f_1)n^{r-1}$$

then every minimal computation tree $\mathbf{T}$ for f has a leaf with the label f_1.

Proof. Let $\mathbf{T}$ be a minimal computation τ-tree that computes $f : \mathbf{A} \to \mathbf{B}$. Let v_i, Q_i and g_i for $i = 1, \cdots, T$ be as in the proof of theorem 2. Assume that $f_1 \notin \{g_1, \cdots, g_T\}$. If $T > \tau^{\mathbf{L}_r(f)}$ then there exists a path with $\mathbf{L}_r(f) + 1$ question vertices. This is a contradiction, therefore

$$T \leq \tau^{\mathbf{L}_r(f)}. \tag{4}$$

Let $P_1 = \{x \in \mathbf{A} | f(x) = f_1(x)\}$. Since $\cup_{i=1}^{T} Q_i = \mathbf{A}$, we have $P_1 = (\cup_{i=1}^{T} Q_i) \cap P_1$ and therefore

$$|\cup_{i=1}^{T} (Q_i \cap P_1)| > \tau^{\mathbf{L}_r(f)}(2^{\mathbf{L}_r(f)} + maxdeg\ f_1)n^{r-1}.$$

By (4) there exists η such that

$$|Q_\eta \cap P_1| > (2^{\mathbf{L}_r(f)} + maxdeg\ f_1)n^{r-1}.$$

As in the proof of theorem 2, it follows that $maxdeg\ g_\eta > 2^{\mathbf{L}_r(f)}$ and therefore computing g_η requires at least $\mathbf{L}_r(f) + 1$ non-scalar multiplications/divisions. Again we have a contradiction and the result follows. $\blacksquare$

Definition 3. Let $(m_1, \cdots, m_k)$ be such that $m_1 \leq \cdots \leq m_k$. Let $\mathbf{T}$ be a τ-tree with k leaves such that each leaf is labeled by one of $\{m_1, \cdots, m_k\}$ and each m_i is in one leaf. Denote by $v(m_i)$ the leaf that is labeled by m_i and by $h(v(m_i))$ the depth of the leaf $v(m_i)$ (the root is in depth 0). We define $\omega(\mathbf{T})$, the *weight* of $\mathbf{T}$ by

$$\omega(\mathbf{T}) = \max_{1 \leq i \leq k} h(v(m_i)) + m_i,$$

and define

$$\Delta_\tau(m_1,\cdots,m_k) = \min_{\mathbf{T}} \ \omega(\mathbf{T})$$

where the minimum is taken over all the τ-trees with k leaves that are labeled by $m_1,\cdots,m_k$. If $\omega(\mathbf{T}) = \Delta_\tau(m_1,\cdots,m_k)$, we then say that $\mathbf{T}$ is a *minimal τ-tree for* $(m_1,\cdots,m_k)$.

In [G] it is proved that

Lemma 4. We have

$$\Delta_\tau(m_1,\cdots,m_k) = \left\lceil \log_\tau(\sum_{i=1}^{k} \tau_i^m) \right\rceil .$$

Theorem 4. Let $f_1,\cdots,f_{M_f}, \mathbf{S}_1,\cdots,\mathbf{S}_r$ be as in definition 2. If

$$|\{x \in \mathbf{A}|f(x) = f_i(x)\}| > \tau^{\mathbf{L}_\tau(f)}(2^{\mathbf{L}_\tau(f)} + maxdeg\ f_i)n^{r-1}, i = 1,\cdots,M_f$$

then

$$\mathbf{L}_\tau(f) \geq \Delta_\tau(\mu(f_1),\cdots,\mu(f_{M_f})) = \left\lceil \log_\tau(\sum_{i=1}^{M_f} \tau^{\mu(f_i)}) \right\rceil \geq \log_\tau M_f + \min_{1 \leq i \leq M_f} \mu(f_i).$$

Proof. Let $\mathbf{T}$ be any minimal computation tree for f. By theorem 3, $f_1,\cdots,f_{M_f}$ are in the leaves of $\mathbf{T}$. If the other leaves of $\mathbf{T}$ contain the functions $g_1,\cdots,g_q$ then, obviously, we have

$$\mathbf{L}_\tau(f) \geq \Delta_\tau(\mu(f_1),\cdots,\mu(f_{M_f}),\mu(g_1),\cdots,\mu(g_q)) \geq \Delta_\tau(\mu(f_1),\cdots,\mu(f_{M_f})). \quad \blacksquare$$

4. RESULTS

Example 1. Rational functions

Result 1. Let $\mathbf{S}_i = \{s_{i,1},\cdots,s_{i,n}\} \subseteq F$ where $|\mathbf{S}_i| = n$ for $i = 1,\cdots,r$. Let $\mathbf{S} = \mathbf{S}_1 \times \cdots \times \mathbf{S}_r$ and $f : \mathbf{S} \to F^s$

$$f(x_1,\cdots,x_r) = (f_1(x_1,\cdots,x_r),\cdots,f_s(x_1,\cdots,x_r))$$

where $f_i \in F(x_1,\cdots,x_r)$. Then for sufficiently large n we have

$$\mathbf{L}_\tau(f) \geq \mu(f).$$

Proof. By theorem 3, $f_1 = f$ and for sufficiently large n we have

$$|\{x \in \mathbf{A}|f(x) = f_1(x)\}| = |\mathbf{S}| = n^r > \tau^{\mathbf{L}_\tau(f)}(2^{\mathbf{L}_\tau(f)} + maxdeg\ f_1)n^{r-1}.$$

Therefore f is in some leaf v of the tree. This follows the result because the path from the root to the leaf v is a straight line algorithm that computes f and then the depth of the tree is greater than or equal to the length of this path. $\quad \blacksquare$

Example 2. Multirational functions

Definition 3.1 . Let $f : \mathbf{R}^r \to \mathbf{R}^s$ be a function. We call f *multirational function* if there exists a set $\{P_i\}_{i=1,\cdots,M}$ such that $\cup_{i=1}^M P_i = \mathbf{R}^r$ and

$$
f(x) = \begin{cases} f_1(x) & \text{if } x \in P_1 \\ \vdots & \vdots \\ f_M(x) & \text{if } x \in P_M \end{cases}
$$

where $f_1(x), \cdots, f_M(x) \in \mathbf{R}(x_1, \cdots, x_r)^s$. We denote the set of all multirational functions by $\mathbf{R}^*(x_1, \cdots, x_r)^s$ or simply $\mathbf{R}^*$.

It can be easily shown that if $f_i(x_1, \cdots, x_r) \in \mathbf{R}^*$ for $i = 1, \cdots, r'$ and $g(x_1, \cdots, x_{r'}) \in \mathbf{R}^*$ then $g(f_1, \cdots, f_{r'}) \in \mathbf{R}^*$.

Our main result for multirational functions is

Result 2 . There exists a finite set $\mathbf{S} \subseteq \mathbf{R}^r$ such that for $f : \mathbf{S} \to \mathbf{R}^s$

$$
\mathbf{L}_\tau(f) \geq \Delta_\tau(\mu(f_i))_{i \in I \subseteq \{1,\cdots,M\}}
$$

where I is the set of all integers i such that P_i contains an open set in $\mathbf{R}^r$.

Proof. Assume that each of $P_1, \cdots, P_k$ contains an open set. Then there exist sets $\mathbf{S}_j^{P_i} = \{s_{1,i,j}, \cdots, s_{B,i,j}\}$ for $j = 1, \cdots, r$ and $i = 1, \cdots, k$ such that $| \cup_{i=1}^k \{s_{1,i,j}, \cdots, s_{B,i,j}\}| = kB$ where B is arbitrary and $\mathbf{S}_1^{P_i} \times \cdots \times \mathbf{S}_k^{P_i} \subseteq P_i$.
Let

$$
\mathbf{S} = (\cup_{i=1}^k \mathbf{S}_1^{P_i}) \times \cdots \times (\cup_{i=1}^k \mathbf{S}_k^{P_i}),
$$

and let $\mathbf{L}$ denote $\mathbf{L}_\tau(f)$. For sufficiently large B, we have

$$
|\{x | f(x) = f_i(x)\}| = |\mathbf{S}_1^{P_i} \times \cdots \times \mathbf{S}_k^{P_i}| = B^k
$$

$$
\geq \tau^{\mathbf{L}}(2^{\mathbf{L}} + \max_{1 \leq i \leq k} maxdeg\ (f_i))k^{k-1}B^{k-1},
$$

so the result follows by theorem 4. ∎

We now give an example. Let

$$
f(x, y) = (|x - y|, \max(x, y), (|x| + x)y).
$$

Then

$$
f(x, y) = \begin{cases} (x - y, x, 2xy) & \text{if } x \geq 0, x \geq y \\ (y - x, y, 2xy) & \text{if } x \geq 0, x < y \\ (x - y, x, 0) & \text{if } x < 0, x \geq y \\ (y - x, y, 0) & \text{if } x < 0, x < y \end{cases}
$$

By result 4 and lemma 4 there exists a sufficiently large domain $\mathbf{S}$ such that

$$
\mathbf{L}_2(f(x, y)) = \Delta_2(1, 1, 3, 3) = \lceil \log_2(2^1 + 2^1 + 2^3 + 2^3) \rceil = 5.
$$

Example 3. Merge

Result 3 . Let $\mathbf{S} = \{s_1, \cdots, s_N\} \subseteq F$. Define the order $s_1 < \cdots < s_N$ on F. Let

$$
A = \{(x_{1,1}, \cdots, x_{1,n_1}, \cdots, x_{f,1}, \cdots, x_{f,n_f}) \in \mathbf{S}^n | n_1 + \cdots + n_f = n;
$$

$$x_{i,j} \text{ distinct } ; x_{i,j} < x_{i,k}, i = 1, \cdots, f, 1 \le j < k \le n_i\}.$$

Define

$$Merge_{n_1,\cdots,n_f}(x_{1,1}, \cdots, x_{1,n_1}, \cdots, x_{f,1}, \cdots, x_{f,n_f}) = (y_1, \cdots, y_n),$$

where $\{x_{1,1}, \cdots, x_{1,n_1}, \cdots, x_{f,1}, \cdots, x_{f,n_f}\} = \{y_1, \cdots, y_n\}$ and $y_1 < \cdots < y_n$. Then for sufficiently large N we have

$$\mathbf{L}_\tau(Merge_{n_1,\cdots,n_f}) \ge \log_\tau \binom{n}{n_1, \cdots, n_f},$$

and every minimal computation τ-tree $\mathbf{T}$ that computes $Merge_{n_1,\cdots,n_f}$ has all

$$\{f_\phi\}_{\phi \in \mathbf{S}_{n_1,\cdots,n_f}}$$

in its leaves where

$$\mathbf{S}_{n_1,\cdots,n_f} = \left\{ \phi \in \mathbf{S}_n | \phi(i) < \phi(j) \text{ for } \sum_{i=1}^{k-1} n_i < i < j \le \sum_{i=1}^{k} n_i, k = 1, \cdots, f \right\},$$

$\mathbf{S}_n$ is the symmetric permutations group of order n and

$$f_\phi(x_1, \cdots, x_n) = (x_{\phi^{-1}(1)}, \cdots, x_{\phi^{-1}(n)}).$$

For $n_i = \lambda_i n$ when $i = 1, \cdots, f$ we obtain

$$\mathbf{L}_\tau(Merge_{n_1,\cdots,n_f}) \ge H_\tau(\lambda_1, \cdots, \lambda_f)n$$

where

$$H_\tau(\lambda_1, \cdots, \lambda_f) = -\sum_{i=1}^{k} \lambda_i \log_\tau \lambda_i.$$

These results were first proved by N. Friedman [F] when the domain is $\mathbf{Z}$, the ring of integers. See also [PS] and [DD] for models with indirect addressing.

Proof. Let $P_\phi = \{(y_{\phi(1)}, \cdots, y_{\phi(n)}) | y_1 < \cdots < y_n\}$ where $\phi \in \mathbf{S}_{n_1,\cdots,n_f}$. Then $f_\phi(x) = Merge_{n_1,\cdots,n_f}(x)$ for $x \in P_\phi$, and $\cup_{\phi \in \mathbf{S}_{n_1,\cdots,n_f}} P_\phi = \mathbf{A}$. By theorem 1 we have

$$\mathbf{L}_\tau(Merge_{n_1,\cdots,n_f}) \le \log_\tau \binom{n}{n_1, \cdots, n_f}. \tag{5}$$

Also,

$$|\mathbf{S}_{n_1,\cdots,n_f}| = \binom{n}{n_1, \cdots, n_f}$$

For $N \ge \left(n! \binom{n}{n_1,\cdots,n_f}\right)^2$ and for every ϕ we have

$$|P_\phi| = \binom{N}{n} \ge \binom{n}{n_1, \cdots, n_f} \left(\binom{n}{n_1, \cdots, n_f}^{\frac{1}{\log_\tau}} + \right) N^{n-1},$$

so by theorems 3 and 4 and by equation (5) the results follow. ∎

The proof for *Sort* and *Insert* is similar.

Example 4. gcd in integers

Result 4. Let $S = \{1, \cdots, N\}$ and let $gcd : S^2 \to S$ where $gcd(a, b)$ is the greatest common divisor of a and b. Then for sufficiently large N we have

$$\mathbf{L}_\tau(gcd) \geq \frac{\log N}{1 + 3 \log \tau} = O(\log_\tau N).$$

Proof . Let $f_i(x) = t$ for $t = 1, \cdots, M$. It is known that $gcd(a, b) = w$ for

$$\frac{6}{\pi^2} \left(\frac{N}{w} \right)^2 + O \left(\frac{N}{w} \frac{\log N}{w} \right)$$

elements in S^2. For $M = N^{\log \tau / (1 + 3 \log \tau)}$ the result follows. ∎

Example 5. gcd of polynomials

Result 5. Let F be a finite field and let $F_n = F_n^*[x]$ be the set of all monic polynomials of rank less than $n + 1$. Let $gcd : F_n \times F_n \to F_n$ by $gcd(f, g)$ being the greatest common divisor (monic polynomials). Then

$$\mathbf{L}_\tau(gcd) \geq \frac{2 \log |F|}{1 + 3 \log \tau} n - o(n) = O(n \log_\tau |F|).$$

Sketch of Proof. We need the following:

Proposition 5.1. We have

$$T = |\{(f, g) \in F_n \times F_n | gcd(f, g) = 1\}| \geq |F|^{2n - o(n)}.$$

Obviously, $gcd(f, g) = h$ for $f = f'h$, $g = g'h$ and $gcd(f', g') = 1$. Therefore

$$N_h = |\{(f, g) \in F_n^2 | gcd(f, g) = h\}| \geq |F|^{2n - deg\ h - o(n)}.$$

Let $H_h = h$ where $h \in F_m$ and $m = n^{(2 \log |F|)/(1 + 3 \log \tau)}$. Then $gcd(f, g) = H_h$ for at least $|F|^{2n - deg\ h - o(n)}$ elements in $F_n \times F_n$, which implies the result. ∎

References

[AHU] A. V. Aho, J. E. Hopcroft, J. D. Ullman. *The design and Analysis of Computer Algorithms*, Addison Wesley, 1974.

[B] M. Ben-Or, Lower bound for algebraic computation trees, In *Proc. 15th ACM Symp. on Theory of Computing*, pp. 80-86, May 1983.

[Bs1] N. H. Bshouty, Lower bounds for the complexity of functions in random access machines. In preparation.

[Bs2] N. H. Bshouty, Euclidean GCD algorithm is not optimal. I. Upper bound. In preparation.

[Bs3] N. H. Bshouty, Euclidean GCD algorithm is not optimal. I. Lower bound. In preparation.

[BMST] N. H. Bshouty, Y. Mansour, B. Schieber, P. Tiwari, The complexity of approximating the square root. In preparation.

[BS] W. Baur, V. Strassen, The complexity of partial derivatives, *Theoretical Computer Science* **22**, 317-330, (1983).

[DD] E. Dittert, M. O'Donnell, Lower bounds for sorting with realistic instruction sets, *IEE Transactions on Computers* 34(4), 311-317, (1985).

[F] N. Friedman, Some results on the effect of arithmetics on comparison problem, In *Proc. IEEE Symp. on Foundation of Computer Science*, pp. 139-143, (1972).

[G] M. C. Golumbic, Combinatorial merging, *IEEE Trans. Comp.* **25**, 11, 1164-1167, (1976).

[IM] O. H. Ibarra, S. Moran, Some independence results in complexity theory, *Intern. J. Computer Math.* **17**, 113-122, (1985).

[KB] M. Kaminski, N. H. Bshouty, Multiplicative complexity of polynomials multiplication over finite fields, *J. of ACM*, **36**, 1, pp. 150-170, (1989).

[MST] Y. Mansour, B. Schieber, P. Tiwari, Lower bounds for integer greatest common divisor computation. In *Proc. 29th IEEE Symp. on Foundation of Computer Science*, pp. 54-63, October (1982).

[PS] W. Paul, J. Simon, Decision trees and random access machines, In *Monographie de L'Enseigment Mathematique*, No. 30, pp 331-340, (1981).

[Sc] C. P. Schnorr, An extension of strassen's degree bound, *SIAM J. Comute*, **10**, 371-382, (1981).

[S] J. T. Schwartz, Fast probabilistic algorithms for verification of polynomial identities, *J. of ACM*, **27**, 701-717, (1980).

[St1] V. Strassen, Die Berechnungskomplexitadotdott von elementarsymmetrischen Funktionen und von Interpolationskoeffizienten, *Numer. Math.* **20**, 238-251, (1973).

[St2] V. Strassen, The computational complexity of continued fractions. *SIAM J. of Computing*, **12**(1), 1-27, (1983).

[Y] A. Yao, Lower bounds for Algebraic Computation Trees with Integer Inputs, *Proc. 30th IEEE Symp. on Foundations of Computer Science*, 1989.

APPROXIMATION ALGORITHMS FOR THE BANDWIDTH MINIMIZATION PROBLEM FOR A LARGE CLASS OF TREES

James Haralambides   Fillia Makedon
Computer Science Program, The University of Texas at Dallas
Richardson, TX 75083-0688

Abstract. We present approximation algorithms for the Bandwidth Minimization Problem (BMP) for cases of special trees. The BMP has many different applications and has been studied for both graphs and matrices. The problem has important applications in large distributed processing systems and databases as well as communication theory. The technique presented here is used to provide a communication protocol for maximum throughput and concurrency control. We study the problem on a tree network model having the following property: For any node of the tree, if more than one subtree is present, then the difference of the depths of the subtrees is bounded. We call these trees *special height balanced trees*. If this difference is a constant on the size of the depth d of the tree, then an O(log d) algorithm is presented. For any depth difference F(d), where F(d) << d, the approximation factor becomes O(F(d)log d).

1. Introduction

The Bandwidth Minimization Problem (BMP) has been initially motivated by applications to sparse matrices [6], [7], [8]. The BMP for a real symmetric matrix M is to find a symmetric permutation of M, so that the maximum value of $|i - j|$ taken over all nonzero entries $M_{i,j}$ is a minimum.

Let G = (V,E) be a finite undirected graph. We call a *linear layout of G*, a one to one function $L : V \rightarrow \{1,...,|V|\}$. The BMP for a graph G is to label its vertices v_i, with distinct integers $f(v_i)$, so that the quantity $\max\{ |f(v_i) - f(v_j)| : (v_i,v_j) \in E \}$, taken over all linear layouts of G, is minimized. The BMP is NP-hard [1], even for trees with maximum vertex degree 3 [2]. It is NP-complete, if for an input graph G and an integer k as part of the input, we have to decide whether bandwidth(G) $\leq$ k. There is a linear time algorithm to recognize graphs with bandwidth 2 [3], and a dynamic programming algorithm to recognize graphs with fixed bandwidth k, for k $\geq$ 2 [4], [5].

There are no known approximation algorithms even in the case of general trees [9], [10]. A lower bound in the bandwidth of any graph G = (V,E) is given by $B_{lb} \geq \max(v,d)/2d$, where max(v,d) denotes the number of vertices v' that are within distance d of vertex v, taken over all possible pairs (v,d) of the graph.

In this paper we investigate the special case of trees called *h(k) trees*. A tree T is an *h(k) tree* whenever:

    a) k is constant in terms of the depth d(T) of T,

    b) if a node v of T has more than one subtree, then for any two such subtrees T_i, T_j,
        $|d(T_i) - d(T_j)| \leq k$. An h(2) tree is shown in Figure 1.1.

Figure 1.1 An h(2) tree

We construct approximation algorithms which are used for reducing communication complexity on tree networks. We restrict ourselves to cases where the graph describing the network is an h(k) tree. We use the linear layout of the tree network to provide a communication protocol for the nodes of the network. The distance between nodes in the linear layout will introduce a certain priority, as this will be directly related to the speed of the communication between the nodes. In other words, short distance in the linear layout establishes fast communication due to higher priority, while long distance a slower one. Furthermore, relative placement in the linear layout is used to establish priorities between network nodes in the same hierarchy level and thus result in an efficient control over concurrent activities.

In Section 2 we construct an approximation algorithm for binary h(0) trees. In Section 3 we extend the approximation algorithm devised in Section 2, for binary h(1) trees. In Section 4 we generalize to more general special height balanced trees and we conclude with Section 5.

2. Binary h(0) Trees

From the definition of an h(k) tree, we can see that there is no depth difference between any of the subtrees of an h(0) tree. Therefore, all the leaves of an h(0) tree are in the last level.

2.1 Definitions

Let $T = (V,E)$ be a binary h(0) tree with root r and depth d. We say that a node v is at level i, if the distance between v and r is i. So, the root is at level 0, its children at level 1 and so on. It is obvious that we can have as many as d levels.

Consider the path P connecting the root to the leftmost leaf of the tree. This path has always length d + 1 (consists of d + 1 nodes) for an h(0) tree. Path P is the backbone structure for the linear layout of the tree. The leftmost leaf of the tree will be assigned number 1, while the root of the tree will be assigned number n = | V |. The rest of the nodes will be assigned numbers 2 to n - 1 and they will be placed in the same relative order that they appear going from the leftmost leaf to the root of the tree. All nodes other than the nodes of path P are to be placed in relation to the path nodes.

A *window* is defined as the space between two consecutive nodes of path P. The term space is used in relation to linear layout, where if two nodes are assigned numbers i, j, j > i, they define a space for the placement of j - i - 1 nodes and in positions assigned numbers i + 1 up to j - 1. Each node of the path will identify a window. We call such a node the *window node*. A window w is identified by node i of path P whenever node i is at level w. Furthermore, window w is the space provided between nodes i and j if i, j are nodes of path P at levels w and w - 1, respectively. A *position* p of a node u, already placed in a window identified by node v, is the distance, in a linear layout, of node u from node v. A node is called the *[w,p] node*, if it is placed in window w, position p. The definitions are illustrated in Figure 2.1.

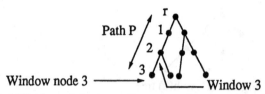

Figure 2.1 Windows 1-3 where placement of nodes takes place. Path P nodes r, 1,2,3 are considered placed and in the same relative order they appear.

The bandwidth achieved by our algorithm is represented by the maximum number of nodes placed in a single window as will be explained later. Furthermore, placement is defined in such a way, so that the following rule is true :

Rule 0 : *Tree nodes at level i can only be placed in window j, where j ≤ i.*

An edge connecting nodes placed in the same window is called an *internal* edge. Similarly, an edge connecting nodes placed in adjacent windows is called an *external* edge.

The idea of the algorithm is to place the tree nodes in the windows, as they are defined above, so that we minimize the number of nodes placed in a single window. A general rule that has to be followed is :

Rule 1 : *If a node is placed in window i, then its parent is placed in window i - jp, where 0 ≤ jp ≤ 1. Similarly, its children have to be placed in window i + jc, where 0 ≤ jc ≤ 1.*

This leads to the conclusion that we can only have internal and external edges in any layout produced using rule 1. We now state the following lemma :

Lemma 1. *If the maximum number of nodes placed in a window is k, then there exists a layout L, such that bandwidth(L) ≤ k + 1.*

Proof. Nodes are placed according to Rules 0, 1. Assume that we already have a placement that guarantees at most k nodes in a single window. We will show that by rearranging nodes placed in the windows, we can achieve a bandwidth of value at most k + 1. The basic idea is to place parent nodes in the same relative order as their respective children nodes.

We start at window d. All nodes placed here are nodes at level d of the tree (leaves). We move to window d - 1 and examine the placement of nodes in window d. We start with node [d,1]. If there is an external edge ([d,1],v), then node v becomes node [d-1,1]. Otherwise, we examine node [d,2] and so on, until all [d,_] nodes are examined. We then place the rest of the nodes in window d - 1 arbitrarily. A tree has the following property : Number of parents ≤ Number of their children. That allows an efficient placement of all nodes in window d - 1, as well as windows d - 2, d - 3 and so on, since we proceed in exactly the same way. Efficient placement means that no external edge will be stretched by more than k. This is true, since for any node [d,p] connected by an external edge to a node [d-1,q], a rearrangement of placed nodes will always produce q ≤ p (tree property and rule 1 are the major factors).

In addition, no internal edge is stretched by more than k, since we place at most k nodes in a window. For the same reason, no edge connecting two window nodes or a window node to any other node will be strehed by more than k. Since, we proved that no external edge is stretched by more than k either, the lemma is true. □

2.2 Placement Algorithm for the h(0) Tree

In this section we describe an algorithm which places tree nodes in windows, as defined above. This algorithm produces a linear layout L, such that the Bandwidth of the tree under L is within an O(log d) factor of the optimal bandwidth, where d is the depth of the tree.

2.2.1 Algorithm 1

Step 1: Identify the path connecting the root to the leftmost leaf (or any leaf for h(0) trees). This path will be the backbone structure for tree node placement.

Step 2: Compute $B = \max(\lceil n_i/2d_i \rceil) \leq B_{lb}$, where n_i is equal to the number of nodes of a sub-tree T_i, of tree T and d_i is equal to the depth of the subtree T_i. This value represents a lower bound on the bandwidth of the tree.

Step 3: Partition the leaves of the tree into disjoint sets of nodes so that:

    a) The number of leaves in a set is L, where $0 \leq L \leq 2B$.

    b) All of the L leaves have the same ancestor and, furthermore, this ancestor is the root of the subtree with leaves exactly these L leaves.

    c) No two neighbor subtrees have a total number of leaves less than 2B, otherwise combine these two neighbor subtrees to form a larger subtree. We call two subtrees *neighbor* subtrees if they are the left and right subtree of the same node.

Step 4: Define *subtree levels* on the subtrees introduced by Step 2. The notion of subtree levels follows the description of the algorithm.

Step 5: Merge levels of neighbor subtrees so that you get a single merged subtree. We call merged subtrees **m-trees** (the unmerged subtrees defined in Step 3 are trivial m-trees too). We continue merging neighbor m-trees, until we get a single m-tree. The levels on that final m-tree represent the windows of the layout.

In order to explain Step 4 we need to introduce the notion of *subtree levels*. A *subtree level* or *level* is defined as the set of nodes which are the same distance from the root of the subtree. For example, a tree with depth d has d levels. Levels play exactly the same role for subtrees, that windows do for the whole tree. The windows are the final form of levels, after all subtrees have their nodes placed. The purpose of levels or windows is to group nodes together. In other words, nodes that belong in the same level, will be placed closely together in the linear layout.

We observe that initially, for each subtree, going from the leaves to the root, the number of nodes in each level follow a nonincreasing sequence. This is not true for general trees. It is very important that the set of subtrees defined in Step 3 has this property.

We now give a more detailed description for Step 5 of Algorithm 1.

2.2.2 Procedure Merge

Assume that T_l, T_r are the left and right neighbor m-trees to be merged and k_l, k_r the maximum number of nodes placed in a single level of T_l, T_r, respectively. Without loss of generality, assume that $k_l = \max(k_l, k_r)$. Assume also that d is the subtree depth.

Step m1: Merge level d of T_r with level i of T_l. Level i is determined in the following way :

    1) The number of nodes in level i is less than 2B.

    2) The number of nodes in level i + 1 is either greater than or equal to 2B unless, of course, level i is the last level (i = d).

Condition 2 states that all levels j, where j > i, have more than 2B nodes. In the case that i is the last level (i = d) we simply merge level d of T_r to level d of T_l. Level i is the current level.

Step m2: If the number of nodes in the current level is greater than or equal to 2B, then current level = current level - 1. Otherwise, merge the next available level of T_r with the current level. Continue merging until either

    1) Level i has more than 2B nodes or

    2) both left and right subtree levels are the same distance from the common root of subtrees T_l and T_r.

Condition 1 states that we have obtained a level, for the resulting m-tree, with more than 2B nodes. Therefore we move to the next level. Condition 2 states that we have reached a point where we have exhausted all *extra* levels of T_r. Since i is generally less than d, we have to merge i levels of T_1 with d levels of T_r. This means that we have d - i *extra* subtree levels of T_r. This number of levels has to be combined in the way described above. In other words, possibly more than one subtree level of T_r has to be merged with the same subtree level of T_1. When all extra levels have been merged, we simply merge corresponding levels of T_1 and T_r (levels which are the same distance from the common root). Since we do not have any more extra levels, we are not able to obtain levels for the resulting m-tree containing more than 2B nodes, anyway.

Step m3: If the current level becomes level 1 then stop, otherwise goto Step m2.

Figure 2.2 provides an example of the application of Algorithm 1 on an h(0) tree. The example illustrates Steps 1-4 of the algorithm as well as the detailed application of procedure Merge (Step 5).

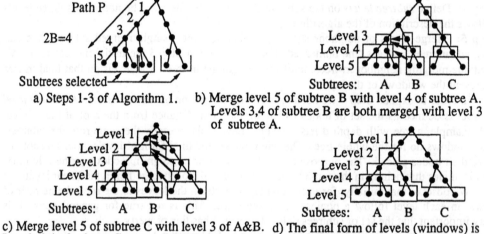

a) Steps 1-3 of Algorithm 1.   b) Merge level 5 of subtree B with level 4 of subtree A. Levels 3,4 of subtree B are both merged with level 3 of subtree A.

c) Merge level 5 of subtree C with level 3 of A&B. Levels 3,4 of subtree C are merged with level 2 of A&B. Similarly, levels 1,2of C are merged with level 1 of A&B.

d) The final form of levels (windows) is presented. All nodes in the same group are placed in the same window.

Figure 2.2 Algorithm 1

2.3 Analysis of Algorithm 1

The basic idea behind the algorithm is that we try to group nodes by placing them in the same level. The cardinality of the set of nodes per window (final form of levels) together with Lemma 1, provide the bound for the bandwidth of the graph. Therefore, in order to achieve a good lower bound, we try to place as few nodes per window (level) as possible.

The bandwidth B_i at the root of any subtree T_i has to be $B_i \leq B$, where $B_i = \lceil n_i/2d_i \rceil$ (n_i, d_i denote the number of nodes and the depth of T_i, respectively). So the number of nodes in T_i is $n_i \leq 2B_i d_i$. By having more than 2B nodes per level in procedure merge, we guarantee that all nodes of T_i can be placed in higher number levels than the level of their root. Of course, if $n_i < 2B_i d_i$, there will be some levels in the merged subtree with less than 2B nodes.

Algorithm 1 first fills up with $\geq 2B$ nodes level d (last level), then level d-1 and so on. It is important to note here that, since the number of level nodes follow a nonincreasing sequence from the leaves to the root, this property is maintained after the application of procedure Merge for all levels with $\leq 2B$ nodes. This property allows : a) the successful merging of all intermediate m-trees, b) the successful merging of extra subtree levels. The first fact is true, since we do not loose the property of the nonincreasing sequence after merging, for all levels with less than 2B nodes. The second fact is true, since merging of extra levels is done only for levels with less than 2B nodes. Furthermore, any extra level added for this purpose has less than 2B nodes, which means that we never exceed 4B nodes in any merging of extra levels.

Fact 1. The number of levels in the resulting m-tree will be $d + 1$, where d is the depth of T_l and T_r. This is true, since one of the two subtrees T_l and T_r always retains the number of levels that it has.

Lemma 2. *Procedure Merge ensures that all nodes of a subtree will be placed in levels with numbers greater than the level number of the root of the subtree.*

Proof. We are able to successfully apply the Merge procedure up to level 1 for any merged subtree. The total number of nodes in the merged subtree is $n \leq 2(d+1)B$, where d is the depth of its subtrees. We have more than 2Bd nodes up to the second level in the worst case. This means that the total number of unmerged nodes is less than $2(d + 1)B - 2Bd = 2B$. So, we are able to successfully place all these nodes in level 1. We can clearly see the important role that Fact 1 plays in the proof of Lemma 2.

We now consider the different cases which can occur in the merging of subtrees :

Case 1. *All subtrees are in serial order.* Serial order means that the right subtree is always a subtree with at most 2B leaves.

Lemma 3. *If all subtrees are in serial order, $B_{apx} \leq 4B$, where B_{apx} denotes the bandwidth of the approximation.*

Proof. By induction on the number k of subtrees.

Basis. For $k = 2$, it is obviously true.

Hypothesis. Assume it is true for k subtrees.

Induction Step. The left subtree is now a k-merged subtree, or in other words the result of merging of k subtrees. All levels below a certain level i have more than 2B nodes. Furthermore, these levels have less than 4B nodes by the inductive hypothesis. All subtree levels j, with $j < i + 1$, have less than 2B nodes and follow a nonincreasing sequence in the number of nodes, going towards the root. Assume that d is the number of tree levels. We merge level d of the right subtree with level i of the left subtree, as indicated in procedure Merge. We merge extra levels, if necessary. We know that no level, as a result of merging of extra levels, will have more than 4B nodes. Since we have at most 2B nodes per level in the right subtree, we can never have more than 4B nodes in a single level after the merging. $\square$

It is also clear that any serial subtree with at most 2B leaves, can never increase the maximum number of nodes in a level of an m-tree which has a maximum of more than 4B nodes in a single level (Merge procedure).

Case 2. *All subtrees are in parallel order* (parallel subtrees). We define parallel order recursively. T_0 is a parallel tree with one subtree having 2B leaves. T_1 is a parallel tree when both left and right subtrees are T_0 subtrees. More generally, T_i is a parallel tree when both left and right subtrees are T_{i-1} parallel trees.

We have at least 2B leaves for each pair of neighbor subtrees. The number of nodes for both those trees is at least 4B nodes (twice the number of leaves). Since the total number of tree nodes is at most 2Bd, we can have at most d subtrees in parallel order.

Lemma 4. *If all subtrees are in parallel order, $B_{apx} \leq 2B(\log d + 1) = 2B\log 2d$.*

Proof. By induction on the number k of parallel trees.

Basis. For $k = 2$, it is clearly true.

Hypothesis. Assume it is true for k subtrees in parallel order.

Induction Step. We have to prove the lemma for 2k subtrees in parallel order. Assume that the left subtree has k subtrees in parallel order. By the hypothesis, the left subtree T_L has $B_{L,apx} \leq 2B\log 2k$. Assume that the right subtree T_R has less than k subtrees in parallel order. Then, by the hypothesis $B_{R,apx} \leq 2B\log k$ (since the maximum degree of the parallel order is k/2). By merging T_L and T_R, we get at most $2B(\log k + 1)$, since in the worst case we add $2B\log k$ nodes to $2B - 1$ nodes. So, $B_{apx} \leq 2B(\log k + 1) = 2B\log 2k$. Assume now that the right subtree has k subtrees in parallel order. Then, in the worst case, we add $2B(\log 2k)$ nodes to $2B$ nodes to get a $B_{apx} \leq 2B(\log 2k) + 2B = 2B(\log 2k + 1) = 2B\log 4k$. In this case though, the number of subtrees in parallel is increased to 2k. Since d is the maximum value for k, Lemma 2 is true. □

Case 3. *Both serial and parallel order is present.*

Lemma 5. $B_{apx} \leq 2B(\log 2d)$. *In order to have* $B_{apx} > 2B\log k$, *we must have more than k subtrees involved in parallel order in the tree. If we have exactly k, then* $B_{apx} \leq 2B\log 2k$.

Proof. We will show that the bandwidth of the approximation depends only on the number of trees involved in parallel order. We will show that by induction in the number k of such trees.

Basis.

1) For k = 2, it is trivially true.

2) k = 4. In this case we have three possibilities.

   a) If all subtrees are serial, we get $B_{apx} \leq 4B = 2B\log (2 \times 2)$ (since we trivially have two trees in parallel).

   b) We have two trees in parallel, which is reduced to a).

   c) We have four trees involved in parallel order. This means that the tree contains four subtrees in parallel, plus a number of serial trees intermixed with the parallel subtrees in an arbitrary way. The result of merging the first two in parallel will be an m-tree with less than 4B nodes per level. Merging any subtree serially with that m-tree results in a new m-tree, with no more than 4B nodes per level (this is true because all serial subtrees have at most 2B nodes per level). The same idea applies to the second two subtrees in parallel, plus their corresponding serial trees. Merging those two m-trees now, might result in a subtree with at most 2B + 4B = 6B nodes in a single level (merging procedure). Furthermore, any subtree serial to the resulting m-tree will not increase the maximum number of nodes. So, $B_{apx} \leq 2B\log (2 \times 4)$ or $B_{apx} \leq 2B\log 2k$.

Hypothesis. Assume it is true for k.

Induction Step. We have to prove the lemma for 2k subtrees involved. Suppose that the left subtree has k subtrees involved in parallel order. Then, by the hypothesis, $B_{L,apx} \leq 2B\log 2k$. Consider now the right subtree. If it involves less than k subtrees in parallel, then by the hypothesis, $B_{R,apx} \leq 2B\log k$ (since the maximum degree of the parallel order is k/2). Merging these subtrees will result in $B_{apx} \leq 2B\log 2k$, since we have to add as many as $2B\log k$ nodes to as many as $2B - 1$ nodes, for a total of $B_{apx} \leq 2B\log k + 2B = 2B\log 2k$ (merging procedure). It becomes clear that we need more than k subtrees in parallel to exceed $2B\log 2k$. Since the total number of subtrees involved in parallel cannot be more than d, the lemma clearly follows. □

3. Binary h(1) Trees

In this section we investigate h(1) trees. We will show that an algorithm for h(1) trees can be generalized to apply to h(k) trees. A question that arises here is, what is the maximum depth difference between any two leaves of the tree. We will see later that this difference plays an important role in the value of the bandwidth of the approximation.

Lemma 6. *The maximum depth difference of any two leaves of an h(1) tree is d/2, where d is the depth of the tree.*

Proof. Consider the left and right subtrees of the tree. They have to have a depth difference of one, otherwise we can produce a worse depth difference tree by increasing the depth of one of the subtrees. Without loss of generality, assume that the right subtree is the shorter of the two. We observe that a recursive occurrence of this fact will produce the worst case depth difference. Furthermore, we notice that in order to increase the maximum depth difference of the leaves by one, we get a recursive decrease of the shortest subtree depth by two. Since for a depth difference increase by one we get a subtree depth decrease by two, it becomes clear that the maximum depth difference is d/2. Figure 3.1 illustrates this fact.

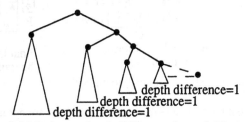

Figure 3.1 Maximum depth difference for an h(1) tree

3.1 Algorithm 2

Step 1: Partition the leaves of the tree into sets of at most 2B nodes each using a variation of the technique followed in Algorithm 1.

Step 2: Transform the h(1) tree into a h(0) tree, as explained later.

Step 3: Apply Algorithm 1 on the transformed tree.

The partition in Step 1 has to be slightly different, since not all leaves in an h(1) tree are in the same level. We select subtrees according to the following rule:

Rule 2. The number of nodes in the levels of selected subtrees must follow a nonicreasing sequence, going from the leaves to the root. Figure 3.2 shows examples of selected subtrees.

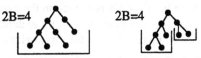

Figure 3.2 Subtrees selected by Rule 2

Assume that B is the bandwidth of the h(1) tree and B' the bandwidth of $h_T(0)$, the tree produced by the transformation. Then, by applying Algorithm 1 to $h_T(0)$, we get $B_{apx} = B'\log d'$, where d' is the depth of $h_T(0)$. Levels are defined in the same way as for Algorithm 1.

An informal description of the transformation procedure of an h(1) tree into an h(0) tree is given below:

Step t1: Find all subtrees with leaf depth exceeding the minimum leaf depth of the tree. Mark the levels of those subtrees as "unprocessed".

Step t2: Select all unprocessed consecutive pairs of levels which have maximum depth. Initially, these pairs consist of levels of depth d and d - 1.

Step t3: Combine the pairs of subtree levels selected in Step t2 into a single subtree level. The application of Step t3 reduces the tree depth by one.

Step t4: Mark all combined pairs as "processed". This ensures that the resulting level will not be considered for further processing.

Step t5: If the tree is transformed into an h(0) tree, then stop. Otherwise, go to Step t1.

The transformation is better illustrated in the example of Figure 3.3.

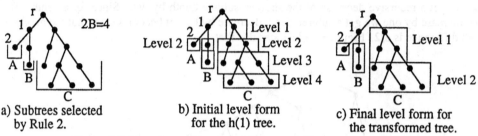

a) Subtrees selected   b) Initial level form   c) Final level form for
by Rule 2.   for the h(1) tree.   the transformed tree.

Figure 3.3 Transformation of an h(1) to an h(0) tree

Notice that the subtrees that have to have their levels combined are not necessarily the same with the ones defined in Step 1. They are generally larger subtrees. This is true for cases where the depth of the roots of subtrees, defined in Step 1 of Algorithm 2, is greater than the depth of the smallest depth leaf of the tree.

Since the maximum depth difference is d/2, combining pairs of consecutive levels is sufficient to transform an h(1) tree into an h(0) tree. Since we only need to combine pairs of levels, it is trivial to see that no level of the transformed tree contains more than $2 \times 2B = 4B$ nodes. Furthermore, the combination of pairs of levels will not destroy the property of nonincreasing sequence of the number of nodes per level, going from the leaves to the root.

Now, we need to compute the maximum change in the bandwidth of the original graph due to the transformation. Assume that subtree T_i has the maximum bandwidth B before the transformation. Assume also that d is the depth of T_i. We then have the following cases :

Case 1. T_i *is still the subtree with the maximum bandwidth after the transformation.*

Since the subtree having bandwidth B is an h(1) tree itself, it is also an h(0) tree for at least d/2 levels, going from the root to the leaves. Assume that d_i is the distance for which the lower bound of the bandwidth is maximum for T_i (lower bound inequality). Then $d_i \geq d/2$. Assume otherwise. Assume also that this distance is $x < d/2$, and the number of nodes in that distance is n_x. Then $2B = \lceil n_x/x \rceil$. So, we have $\lceil n_x/x \rceil$ nodes per level on the average. Since the number of nodes is nondecreasing, going from the root to the leaves, up to depth d/2, the number of nodes at distance $x + 1$ is at least n_x/x. Then, the bandwidth at distance $x + 1$ is $B' > \lceil \frac{n_x + n_x/x}{2(x+1)} \rceil = \lceil n_x/2x \rceil = B$, which means that it is increased, contradicting the assumption that it is maximum at distance d_i. This property is true for x up to d/2.

Now, assume that the bandwidth is maximum at distance $x > d/2$ or $x = d/2 + e$. Then, $B = \lceil \frac{n_i}{2(d/2 + e)} \rceil$. This means that the number of nodes up to distance x is less than $2(d/2 + e)B$. The number of the rest of the nodes of the subtree is less than $2(d/2 - e)B$. This is true, since the average number of nodes per level, for levels greater than x, has to be less than the average number of nodes per level, for levels less than or equal to x (an average of 2B nodes). Assume otherwise. Assume also that for a level $y > x$ the average number of nodes per level is greater than 2B. Then, the bandwidth computed at distance y from the root of T_i will be greater than B, which contradicts the original assumption that x is the distance where B obtains its maximum value. So, $B' < \lceil \frac{2(d/2 + e)B + 2(d/2 - e)B}{2(d/2)} \rceil$. That results in $B' < \frac{2dB}{d} = 2B$. So, in Case 1, the bandwidth is never increased by more than a factor of 2.

Case 2. T_j is now the subtree with the maximum bandwidth, where $T_j \neq T_i$. Assume B_j is the bandwidth of T_j. Then, by the same argument as in Case 1, we have $B'_j < 2B_j < 2B$. We can now state the following theorem:

Theorem 1. $B' \leq 2B$, *where B denotes the lower bound on the bandwidth of the h(1) tree and B' the lower bound on the bandwidth of* $h_T(0)$ *obtained by Step 2 of Algorithm 2.*

The bandwidth of $h_T(0)$ cannot be more than twice the bandwidth of the original tree, as shown in Cases 1 and 2 above. Since the transformed tree now simulates an h(0) tree, we can apply Algorithm 1.

Corollary 1. *Algorithm 2 results in an approximation for h(1) trees which is:* $B_{apx} \leq 4B\log d$ *(since the depth of the tranformed tree is now d/2).*

4. Generalization to a Larger Class of Trees

So far, we have showed that for a binary h(1) tree with depth d, $B_{apx} \leq 4B\log d$. We now show how the Algorithm 2 can be generalized for h(k) trees, where $k \geq 1$ and constant in terms of the depth d of the tree. In order to find the worst case depth difference between the leaves of an h(k) tree, we follow the same idea that was used for h(1) trees. In other words, recursively, the right subtree will have a depth difference of k with the left subtree. For the first level of the recursion, the right subtree has depth d - 1 - k. Generally, for the jth level of the recursion the right subtree will have depth d - j - jk. When this quantity becomes zero, j will be the maximum depth of the recursion. Furthermore, jk will represent the maximum depth difference between any two leaves of the tree. By solving the equation d - j - jk = 0, we obtain the minimum leaf depth of a depth d h(k) tree, which is j = d/(k+1) (the depth of the transformed tree). The maximum depth difference in a h(k) tree can be at most d - d/(k+1) = dk/(k+1).

We now need to compute the maximum change in the value of the bandwidth of the original tree due to the transformation of the tree into an h(0) tree. Observe that in order to be able to perform the transformation for a h(k) tree we have to combine *groups of k + 1 consecutive levels*. That results in $B' \leq \frac{n}{2d/(k+1)} = (k + 1)B$, where n is the number of nodes of the h(k) tree. So, finally the approximation value of the bandwidth of an h(k) tree is given by, $B_{apx} \leq 2(k + 1)B\log (d/(k+1)) = 2(k + 1)B(\log d - \log (k + 1))$ or $B_{apx} \leq O(\log d)B$.

Corollary 2. *The result of the algorithm, for trees with depth difference F(d) << d, will be* $B_{apx} \leq O(F(d)\log d)$.

Algorithms 1 and 2, applied to binary trees, are clearly applicable to all trees having this special height balance property, independent of the node degree. This class of trees is obviously quite large. In our h(k) trees we allow internal (nodes other than leaves) 2-degree nodes. This permits the study of a more general class of trees. If 2-degree nodes were not allowed (except for the root and nodes adjacent to the leaves of the tree), then all h(k) trees with n nodes would have depth d = O(log n) (balanced trees) and a bandwidth approximation of O(log n)B could be easily achievable, by simply applying a level algorithm (our algorithm would produce an O(loglog n)B factor). By allowing 2-degree nodes, the depth of the tree can grow up to O(n).

Another important observation is that the procedure Merge of Algorithm 1 can be modified so that we can obtain better results in our approximation. Recall that we merge the last level of the smaller bandwidth subtree with level i of the larger bandwidth subtree. Level i is determined as the level with less than 2B nodes (in the case of h(0) trees). All levels j, where j > i, have greater than or equal to 2B nodes. The better approach is to merge the last level with level i - p. The level i - p is determined as the level for which, the *average* number of nodes per level, for all levels j > i - p, is greater than or equal to 2B.

Lemma 7. *The approximation algorithm for specially height balanced trees takes $O(E)$ time, where E is the number of tree edges.*

Proof. We assume that the value of the lower bound is computed beforehand. The time needed to compute this value is $O(NE)$ or $O(N^2)$ (since $E = O(N)$), where N is the number of tree nodes (breadth first search for every tree node). Partition of the tree into subtrees with number of leaves less than or equal to 2B takes $O(E)$ time. For every node, we compute the number of leaves that the subtree with root this node has. This can be implemented using a recursive procedure and thus traversing the edges of the tree at most twice. It also takes $O(E)$ time to find which subtrees are neighbor subtrees (using a procedure similar to the technique for parenthesization). Merging of two levels can be done in $O(1)$ time using pointers for the current level containing less than 2B nodes. Therefore, the total time for merging cannot exceed the number of tree edges. The transformation procedure is simply a grouping of levels. That does not take more time than the time to visit all the subtree levels which is bounded by the number of tree edges.□

5. Conclusions

We have presented an $O(\log d)$ factor approximation for the Bandwidth Minimization Problem for a large class of trees. These trees have a special height balance property, namely, for any subtree the depth difference between any two of its leaves is constant in terms of the depth d of the tree. An extension of the depth difference constant to a function $F(d)$, where $F(d) \ll d$, results in a $O(F(d)\log d)$ factor of the approximation.

Our work presents a model for the establishment of communication priorities between nodes of a tree network. An open problem is the natural extension of the problem for more general structures, such as general trees, planar graphs and so on.

Acknowledgements

We wish to thank Professor F.T. Leighton for many valuable discussions and helpful comments.

References

[1] C.H. Papadimitriou, "The NP-completeness of the Bandwidth Minimization Problem", Computing, 16 (1976) pp. 263-270.

[2] M.R. Garey, D.S. Johnson, "Computers and Intractability: A Guide to the Theory of NP-completeness", W.H. Freeman and Company, San Francisco (1979).

[3] M.R. Garey, R.L. Graham, D.S. Johnson, and D.E. Knuth, "Complexity Results for Bandwidth Minimization", SIAM J. Appl. Math. 34 (1978), pp. 477-495.

[4] J.B. Saxe, "Dynamic Programming Algorithms for Recognizing Small Bandwidth Graphs in Polynomial Time", SIAM J. on Algebraic and Discrete Methods, December, 1980.

[5] E.M. Gurari and I.H. Sudborough, "Improved Dynamic Programming Algorithms for Bandwidth Minimization and the Min-Cut Linear Arrangement Problems", J. Algorithms, 5, (1984), pp. 531-546.

[6] E. Cuthill, J. McKee, "Reducing the Bandwidth of Sparse Symmetric Matrices", ACM National Conference Proc. 24, (1969), pp. 137-172.

[7] K.Y. Cheng, "Minimizing the Bandwidth of Sparse Symmetric Matrices", Computing 11, (1973), pp. 103-110.

[8] P.Z. Chinn, J. Chvatalova, A.K. Dewdney, N.E. Gibbs, "The Bandwidth Problem for Graphs and Matrices-A Survey", J. of Graph Theory, Vol. 6, (1982), pp. 223-254.

[9] J. Haralambides, F. Makedon and B. Monien, "Bandwidth Minimization: An Approximation Algorithm for Caterpillars", J. of Mathematical Systems Theory, to appear.

[10] J. Haralambides, F. Makedon and B. Monien, "Approximation Algorithms for the Bandwidth Minimization Problem for Caterpillar Graphs", Proc. of the 2nd Symposium of Parallel and Distributed Processing, 1990, pp. 301-307.

The Interpolation-Based Bintree and Its Application to Graphics

M. Aris Ouksel*
IDS Department (M/C 294), PoB 4348
The University of Illinois at Chicago
Chicago, IL 60680

Anan Yaagoub
EECS Department
Northwestern University
Evanston, IL 60208-3118

Abstract

A new structure for representing binary images, called the Interpolation-Based Bintree is introduced. This structure combines the features of some existing representations such as linear quadtrees, binary trees, and interpolation-based codes, to improve the performance of operations manipulating graphics images. The implementation of this method is performed on both randomly generated and actual images and is shown to be very simple and efficient. It is also shown to compare favorably with several popular techniques in both storage and processing requirement. Although this structure is mainly for binary images, it can also be utilized for a class of "color-coded" images, where the color-code has a nominal value, the difference between two codes has no meaning, and where areas of uniform code value are larger with respect to resolution.

1 Introduction

The problem of finding efficient encodings of images has been studied extensively due to the high economic value of compact representation in data transmission and data storage. We propose an encoding and a structure to represent a set of codes which provide a high level of compaction while at the same time allow flexible and efficient manipulations of images. Furthermore, this scheme is reversible in the sense that it operates without loss of information.

Many techniques have been devised and used in various domains such as computer graphics, image processing, computational geometry, geographic information systems, and robotics. These techniques are thoroughly surveyed in [11]. Basically, they can be classified into three categories. An image may be represented either as a tree, a string, or set of codes. Quadtrees [11], and Binary trees [7] are considered to be of the first type. Their main drawback is the additional space required by the tree internal nodes and the node pointers. On the other hand, the second type which in

---

*Research supported by NSF IRI-9010365.

particular includes Chain code [2], DF-expression [6], and Encoding Pixel Trees [12], represents structures that are very compact but whose processing of basic graphics operations is very time consuming. Finally the third type includes Linear quadtrees [3, 4, 5], and the Two dimensional run encoding [8] methods. Compared to tree structures, sets of codes require less space and yet are as efficient in terms of processing basic graphics operations. In this case, the time complexity is dependent on the cardinality of the set and thus, only reductions of this factor will result in performance improvements.

This work introduces a new structure which combines properties of bintrees [7] and interpolation based codes [10], called the "Interpolation-Based Bintree". This structure represents an image as a set of integer codes, where each code refers to a region of the binary image. The second section of the paper introduces the new method, discusses its properties by exhibiting how the various basic graphics operations are performed, and shows how rasters are converted to bincodes. In section three, we discuss practical aspects of the method. In particular, the number of bytes required by the representation of codes is explained. In section four the new technique is compared to linear quadtrees both analytically and then empirically on randomly generated and scanned images. Finally the conclusion discusses the results achieved and future work.

2 Interpolation-Based Bintree (IBB)

The bintree is a hierarchical representation of a $2^N \times 2^N$ binary array that is made of unit square pixels that can be black or white (we refer to N as the resolution parameter). As discussed in the literature, a bintree can be effectively used to describe the successive partitions of a $2^N \times 2^N$ array ($N \geq 1$) into halves, to separate a region from its background and to represent a set of pixels belonging to the same half (at any level of subdivision) as a single node. The bintree can be defined as a tree whose nodes are either leaves or have two sons. A node can be gray, white, or black and is, in general, stored as a record with 3 fields, two of which are pointers (to the left and right halves) and the third is a color identifier. Interpolation-Based Bintree encodes the nodes of a bintree, with the following characteristics:(i) Only black nodes are stored, (ii) Nodes are stored as integer numbers, (iii) The encoding used for each node incorporates adjacency properties in the four principal directions, (iv) The node representation implicitly encodes the path from the root to the node.

The Interpolation-Based Bintree (IBB) has several advantages over tree representations. Its space and time complexities depend only on the number of black nodes. Its representation is pointerless. Its application is versatile: the same structure can be used to handle a wide variety of operations very efficiently.

The structure has also several advantages over linear quadtrees. It requires less black nodes to represent regions. In the worst case, it requires the same number of nodes. Processing node codes is simple, since we are dealing with integers, and in most cases no need for bit manipulation. The performance is always at least as efficient as the best case achieved by any other structure. As a result of the previous points, the performance of the graphics operation algorithms is greatly improved.

2.1   Encoding Method

Encoding the nodes of a bintree is done by assigning a unique integer for each node, which we will call its "bincode". We assume a bintree of size $2N$ that contains 2^{2N} leaves and $2^{2N} - 1$ internal nodes representing an image in a $2^N \times 2^N$ screen. If the node at level l of a bintree corresponds to a block in the image at location (i, j) in the $2^N \times 2^N$ screen, then the bincode of that node is obtained as follows:

- First, i and j are converted to binary where $i = \sum_{k=0}^{N-1} i_k * 2^k$, and $j = \sum_{k=0}^{N-1} j_k * 2^k$

- Second, the level l is represented as a binary number consisting of l consecutive 1's followed by $2N - l$ zeros, we will refer to this number as s; $s = \sum_{k=2N-l}^{2N-1} 1 * 2^k = 2^{2N} - 2^{2N-l}$

- The bincode Q is given by: $Q = \sum_{k=0}^{N-1} i_k * 2^{4k+3} + \sum_{k=0}^{N-1} j_k * 2^{4k+1} + \sum_{k=0}^{2N-1} s_k * 2^{2k}$

As an example, consider the $2^2 \times 2^2$ image in Figure 1. To get the bincode of block AH which is at location $(0, 0)$ and of size 1×2 pixels, $i = 0 = (00)_2, j = (00)_2, l = 3, s = (1110)_2$. Applying the above encoding procedure, the value of Q obtained is $(01010100)_2 = 84$. As another example, block AG at position $(2, 2)$ and level $l = 2$, $i = (10)_2$, $j = (10)_2$, $s = (1100)_2$, $Q = (11110000)_2$ which is equal to 240. For the pixel AX at position $(2, 0)$ and level $l = 4$, $i = (10)_2$, $j = (00)_2$, $s = (1111)_2$, $Q = (11010101)_2 = 213$. Clearly, the bincode of the root node of a bintree, which corresponds to the whole screen, is equal to zero, since the (i, j) coordinates of the screen are $(0, 0)$, and the level of the root node is equal to 0.

Encoding a binary image of size $2^N \times 2^N$ thus requires $4N$ bits per node. As an example for a $2^2 \times 2^2$ image the codes will require 8 bits. (i.e. integer codes of nodes will range between 0 and

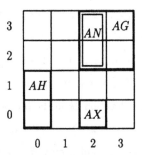

Figure 1: Blocks example

255). To encode a binary image represented by a bintree only the integer codes of the black nodes are stored. The encoding of the image given in Figure 2(a) is represented by $(87, 117, 124, 192)$, we refer to this list as the "image list". When a bincode can represent a subset of an image, we

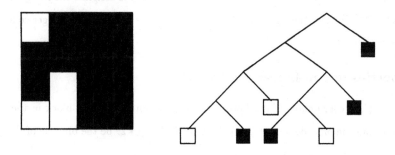

Figure 2: IBB example

call the subset an elementary block. From now on, we shall use the terms "node" of a bintree and "elementary block" interchangeably, unless otherwise stated.

Theorem 1 If A is the bincode of an internal node in the bintree, B and C are the bincodes of the right and left sons of A then: $B = A + 2^{2(2N-l-1)}$, and $C = A + 3 * 2^{2(2N-l-1)}$ where N is the resolution parameter, and l is the level of node A.

<u>Proof:</u> Assume that node A is at location (i_a, j_a). Two cases are distinguished, either A represents a square block or A represents a rectangle.

<u>Case 1:</u> If node A represents a rectangle then: $i_b = i_a$, $j_b = j_a$, $l_b = l + 1$, $i_c = i_a$, $j_c = j_a + w_a$, and $l_c = l + 1$ where w_a denotes the width of rectangle A, let s_a, s_b, and s_c denote the binary

representation of the levels of the nodes A, B, and C, respectively, as used in the IBB (i.e. for node A, s_a consists of l 1's followed by $2N - l$ 0's). $s_a = 2^{2N} - 2^{2N-l}$, $s_b = 2^{2N} - 2^{2N-l-1}$, and $s_c = 2^{2N} - 2^{2N-l-1}$. Bincode values of B and A differs only, in the values of s_a and s_b, $s_b - s_a = 2^{2N-l-1}$, since the $2N$ bits of s_a and s_b are located in different position in the bincodes A and B, (i.e. bit k of s_a is located at location $2k$ in the bincode of A). The real difference of A and B is equal to the difference $(s_b - s_a)^2 = 2^{2(2N-L-1)}$, it follows : $B = A + 2^{2(2N-L-1)}$. Bincode values of C and B differs in the values of j_c and j_b only. $j_c - j_b = j_a + w_a - j_a = w_a = 2N - \frac{l+1}{2}$. Since the kth bit of the coordinate j is located at position $4k + 1$ in the bincode.

$C - B = (j_c - j_b)^4 * 2^1 = 2 * 2^{2(2N-l-1)}$, and $C = B + 2 * 2^{2(2N-l-1)} = A + 3 * 2^{2(2N-l-1)}$

<u>Case 2:</u> If node A represent a square then: $i_b = i_a$, $j_b = j_a$, $l_b = l + 1$, $i_c = i_a + \frac{w_a}{2}$, $j_c = j_a$, and $l_c = l - 1$. The proof is the same as case 1. □

The above theorem provides a new recursive algorithm for encoding the nodes of a bintree. The root is assigned integer code 0, the left son of a node at level l is assigned the integer code of its father plus $2^{2(2N-l-1)}$ while the right son of a node at level l is assigned the integer code of its father plus $3 * 2^{2(2N-L-1)}$.

2.2   Properties of the Linear Bintrees

<u>1. Location:</u> The (i, j) coordinates of the lower left corner of an elementary block in the image can be obtained from the bincode of that block, let $Q = \sum_{k=0}^{4N-1} q_k * 2^k$ be the bincode of the block then:

$i = \sum_k q_k * 2^{k\,div\,4}$ where $0 \le k < 4N$ and $k \bmod 4 = 3$

$j = \sum_k q_k * 2^{k\,div\,4}$ where $0 \le k \le 4N - 1$ and $k \bmod 4 = 1$.

<u>2. Level Calculation:</u> The IBB binary representation of the level of an elementary block in a $2^N \times 2^N$ image, with bincode $Q = \sum_{k=0}^{4N-1} q_k * 2^k$, is given by $s = \sum_k q_k * 2^{k\,div\,2}$, where $k \in \{0, 1, ..., 4N - 1\}$ and $k \bmod 2 = 0$. If the level of the node is l then the above formula gives the binary representation which consist of l consecutive 1's followed by $2N - l$ 0's. The level can be computed from this representation, simply, by counting the number of consecutive 1's in that representation or equivalently by applying the following formula: $l = 2N - \log_2(2^{2N} - s)$

<u>3. Dimension:</u> A node in a bintree at level l represents a block of size $\frac{2^{2N}}{2^l}$ pixels in the $2^N \times 2^N$ screen. If l is an even number then the node represent a square block of side length $\frac{2^N}{2^{l/2}}$ pixels. On the other hand, if l is odd, it represents a rectangle of width equal to $\frac{2^N}{2^{(l+1)/2}}$ and height equal to twice the width. A node at level $2N$ represent an individual pixel.

4. Separation: The separation between two elementary blocks A and B is composed of the smallest distances between any points on the boundaries of the two elementary blocks in both the horizontal and vertical directions, and they are calculated by [9] :

$D_x(A, B) =\mid i_a - i_b \mid -s_w$, and $D_y(A, B) =\mid j_a - j_b \mid -s_l$ where s_w is the width of the leftmost of the two elementary blocks A and B, and s_l is the height of the lowermost of the two elementary blocks.

5. Adjacency: The general condition of adjacency for elementary blocks is defined [9], as follows:

$D_x(A, B) * D_y(A, B) = 0$, and $D_x(A, B) + D_y(A, B) < 0$.

6. Bincodes of the Corner Pixels of an Elementary Block: Given the bincode A of an arbitrary block in the image, the bincode of the pixels at the lower left and upper right corners denoted by B and C, respectively, can be calculated from A as described next.

Theorem 2 If A represents the bincode of an elementary block in the image then:

(i) $B = A + \frac{4^{2N-l}-1}{3}$, and (ii) $C = B + 2(B - A)$ where B and C denote the lower left and upper right pixels of block A, respectively.

Proof : let block A coordinates be (i, j) with level l, then pixel B is at location (i, j) with level $2N$, and pixel C is at location $(i + w_a - 1, J + h_a - 1)$ with level equal to $2N$, where w_a and h_a are the width and height of block A, respectively. The binary representation of the level as used in IBB is given by: $s_a = 2^{2N} - 2^{2N-l}$, $s_b = 2^{2N} - 1$, and $s_c = 2^{2N} - 1$. Bincode values of A and B differs in the value of s_a and s_b only : $s_a - s_b = 2^{2N-l} - 1 = \sum_{k=0}^{2N-l-1} 2^k$ Since the kth bits of s_a and s_b are at locations $2k$ in the bincode values A and B. $B - A = \sum_{k=0}^{2N-l-1} 2^{2k} = \frac{4^{2N-l}-1}{3} \Rightarrow B = A + \frac{4^{2N-l}-1}{3}$. To prove part (ii) of the theorem we assume that A represent the bincode of a square block, the proof when A represent a rectangle is the same. Bincodes B and C differ in the value of i_b and i_c, and j_b and j_c only. $i_c - i_b = w_a - 1 = 2^{N-\frac{l}{2}} - 1 = \sum_{k=0}^{N-\frac{l}{2}-1} 2^k$ $j_c - j_b = w_a - 1 = 2^{N-\frac{l}{2}} - 1 = \sum_{k=0}^{N-\frac{l}{2}-1} 2^k$ Since the kth bit of i is located at position $4k + 3$ in the bincode, and k^{th} bit of j is at position $4k + 1$; $C - B = \sum_{k=0}^{N-\frac{l}{2}-1} 2^{4k+3} + \sum_{k=0}^{N-\frac{l}{2}-1} 2^{4k+1} = 2 * \frac{4^{2N-l}}{3}$ $C = B + 2 * \frac{4^{2N-l}-1}{3} = B + 2(B - A)$ $\square$

7. Containment: One of the most important properties of the IBB method is the ordering of the bincodes for elementary blocks in the image. This ordering mechanism is stated in the following theorem where A and B denote the bincodes of two blocks in the image.

Theorem 3 Block A contains block B if and only if $A \leq B \leq C$, where C is the bincode of the upper right pixel of block A.

8. Merging and Decomposition: It follows from Theorem 1 that if two elementary blocks, at the same level l, with bincodes Q_A and Q_B where $(Q_A < Q_B)$ having difference $Q_B - Q_A$ equals

to $2^{2(2N-l)+1}$ where N is the resolution parameter, then both elementary blocks can be grouped together to represent a bigger elementary block at level $l - 1$ with bincode Q_C where $Q_C = Q_A - 2^{2(2N-l)}$.

2.3   Structure and Search

In IBB representation, a region is represented as a list of bincodes $R = \{Q_i, i = 1, 2, ..., NB\}$, where Q_i is the bincode of a black elementary block in region R, and NB is the total number of black elementary blocks in the bintree of region R. According to theorem 3, the bincode of any node is smaller than bincodes of all its sons (i.e. bincode of any elementary block is smaller than bincodes of all elementary blocks contained in it). If a given node, say bincode Q, belongs to a region R, then either Q belongs to the set R or Q is contained in the greatest bincode in R which is smaller than Q.

Let Q denote the bincode of an elementary block in an image. To determine whether Q belongs to the region of that image (i.e. Q represent an elementary block or not), a search of the image list for the greatest integer $Q\prime$, which is smaller than or equal to Q is made. A containment test to check whether $Q\prime$ contains Q or not is then performed. If $Q\prime$ contains Q, then Q represents a black node.

Since bincodes are integer numbers, a binary search on the sorted bincodes is used to check whether a given elementary block is black or white. The time complexity of the search is $O(\log_2 NB)$ where NB is the number of black nodes in the region.

2.4   Converting Rasters to bincodes

The raster-to-bincode algorithm processes the image by rows starting with the top row. The given binary image is assumed to be partitioned into rows, where the upper left pixel position is $(1,1)$ and the lower right pixel is at location $(2^N, 2^N)$. Clearly, no odd-numbered row can lead to merge of nodes. Thus, odd-numbered rows do not require as much processing as even-numbered rows. For an odd-numbered row, the set is constructed by processing the row from left to right adding the bincode of each pixel to the set. Even-numbered rows require more work since merging may also take place. In particular, a check for a possible merge with the processed codes must be performed at every pixel in the row. Once a merge occurs, we have to check if another merge is possible. In particular, for a pixel at odd position in the row, one merge only is possible. For pixel position $(a*2^i, b*2^j)$ where $a \bmod 2 = b \bmod 2 = 1$, a maximum of M merges is possible where:

$$M = \begin{cases} 2*i & \text{if } i \leq j \\ 2*j+1 & \text{otherwise} \end{cases}$$

Notes that we use the upper left corner of the image to be the origin, just for the purpose of scanning only. The bincode of a pixel at location (x, y), while scanning, should be produced from the position with respect to the lower right corner as the origin (i.e. producing the bincode from the location $(y - 1, 2^N - x)$ where N is the resolution parameter).

3 Practical Aspects of the Method

As seen earlier, to represent a $2^N \times 2^N$ image, the number of bits per IBB block code is $4N$. Therefore, for a 32-bit machine, the maximum picture size that can be represented without overflow is only 256×256 pixels. Larger picture sizes can be represented by storing the code not as an IBB code but as a pair $(code(i, j), level)$. This representation will reduce the number of bits needed to encode a block. In this case for a $2^N \times 2^N$ picture the number of bits is $(2N + \log_2(2N))$, where $2N$ bits are required to encode the (i, j) coordinate and $\log_2(2N)$ is required to encode the level. A picture of size $2^{10} \times 2^{10}$ requires only 25 bits. The suggested method is used only to store the pictures. To process them, the pair representation of the code has to be changed to an IBB code as described before. This conversion will result in some overhead.

4 Comparison and Testing

In this chapter, the best and worst case storage requirements of a random square image of size $2^m \times 2^m$ in a $2^n \times 2^n$ screen are investigated. The results obtained from empirically comparing IBB method with linear quadtree (LQ) for certain test cases are presented.

4.1 Analytical Comparison

This section deals with the storage requirements of the IBB representation for the special case in which a single square region of size $2^m \times 2^m$ is contained in $2^n \times 2^n$ image. The best and worst case IBB sizes are investigated. A similar analysis for quadtree representation is given in [1]. The complexity of operation algorithms depends on space efficiency. Thus significant reduction in space will result in an improvement in the performance of operations.

<u>Best Case</u> The best case occurs when the region can be represented by a single black node. This case occurs whenever the position (x, y) of the region is such that $x \bmod 2^m = y \bmod 2^m = 0$. Here

the $2^m \times 2^m$ region is represented by a single bincode. The best case for IBB representation is the same as for quadtree representation.

<u>Worst Case</u> Consider the case when the region is at position (x, y) such that :

$x \bmod 2^m = y \bmod 2^m = 1$, i.e. the region is shifted to the right and down one pixel from the best case position, as shown in Figure 3. In this case there are $2^m - 1$ blocks of size 1×1 along the top

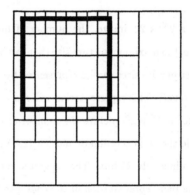

Figure 3: Worst case position

side of the region, also there are $2^{m-1} - 1$ blocks of size 2×2 along the left side of the region. Inside these two borders is a row containing $2^{m-2} - 1$ blocks of size 2×4; this filling in along the left and top sides continues until a single black block of size $(m-1) \times (m-1)$ occurs. Finally, $2^m + 1$ blocks of size 1×1 and $2^{m-1} - 1$ blocks of size 1×2 fill in the right and bottom borders of the region. Thus the number of black nodes is : $B = 2^m + 2^{m-1} + \sum_{i=0}^{m-1}(2^{m-i} + 2^{m-i-1} - 2) = 9 * 2^{m-1} - 2m - 3$. In contrast, a linear quadtree representation requires $3(2^{m+1} - m) - 5$ black node in the worst case. $\frac{\#of\ blocks\ required\ by\ IBB}{\#of\ blocks\ required\ by\ LQ} = \frac{9*2^{m-1}-2m-3}{3(2^{m+1}-m)-5} \approx 75\%$. Thus the worst case requirement of the number of blocks by IBB method is 75% of that of the LQ method. We conjecture that the gains are greater when the pattern is rectangular.

4.2 Empirical Comparisons

In this section the space required (in terms of number of blocks) by IBB method is empirically compared with the space required by the LQ representation. We define utilization percentage as the gain in terms of number of blocks required by the IBB structure when compared with the LQ method : $Utilization = \frac{\#\ of\ blocks\ by\ LQ\ -\ \#\ of\ blocks\ by\ IBB}{\#\ of\ blocks\ by\ LQ} * 100$ For this comparison some real images are used. These real images are scanned from real pictures. In Figure 4 a 256 × 256 image is shown. The number of blocks needed to represent the image by both IBB and LQ methods are

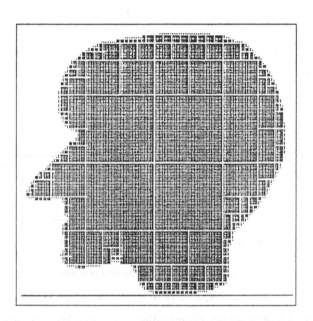

Figure 4: Scanned Image 256x256, Number of black pixels = 14742, Number of blocks required by IBB structure = 2532, Number of blocks required by LQ structure = 3498

also given. A utilization improvement of 27% was achieved using the IBB structure.

In addition to real images, randomly generated pixel arrays with controlled amount of black density has been tested using both methods. Figure 5 shows the utilization percentage in IBB over the LQ method for those pictures. One can observe from the plot that as the number of black pixels in the image increases the utilization increases as well. The graph shows that a peak of 25% utilization improvement is achieved when the pictures are 60% black. In general, real images occupy 35% to 60% of the screen, and in this range, the figure shows a gain varying between 20% and 25%. These empirical results confirm what has already been established analytically.

5   Conclusion and Further Work

The importance of space minimization in image representation and its direct effect on the time complexity of image processing algorithms make it imperative that we devise better and more

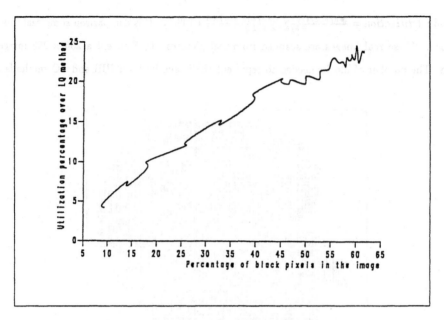

Figure 5: Utilization percentage of IBB over LQ

efficient structures. In this paper a new method (IBB) for image representation has been developed. Its properties have been studied and algorithms to operate on images represented by this method have been designed. The method and the algorithms have been tested on real scanned images. The comparison of the method over the most studied and used method in literature (the Linear Quadtree method) show improvement in space ranging from 20% to 25%. In addition, the worst case performance of IBB does not exceed the space utilization requirements of Linear Quadtree. Another feature of the above method not discussed as a part of this research is its extension to represent binary images in 3-D, and colored images.

References

[1] C. R. Dyer. The space efficiency of quadtrees. *Computer Graphics and Image Processing*, 19(4):335–348, 1982.

[2] H. Freeman. Computer processing of line-drawing images. *ACM Comput. Surv.*, 6(1):57–97, 1974.

[3] I. Gargantini. Detection of connectivity for regions represented by linear qaudtrees. *Computer and Mathematics with Applications*, 8(0):319–327, 1982.

[4] I. Gargantini. An effective way to represent quadtrees. *Commun. ACM*, 25(12):905–910, 1982.

[5] I. Gargantini. Translation, rotation, and superposition of linear quadtrees. *International Journal of Man-Machine Studies*, 18(3):253–263, 1983.

[6] E. Kawaguchi and T. Endo. On a method of binary picture representation and its application to data compression. *IEEE Transactions on Pattern Analysis and Machine Intelligence*, 2(1):27–35, 1980.

[7] K. Knowlton. Progressive transmission of gray-scale and binary pictures. In *Proceedings of IEEE 68*, July 1980. 885-896.

[8] J. P. Lauzon and L. Mark. Two dimensional run-encoding for quadtree. *Computer Graphics, Vision and Image Processing*, 30(1):56–69, 1985.

[9] S. Li and M. Loew. Adjacency detection using quadcodes. *Image Processing and Computer Vision*, 30, 1987.

[10] M. A. Ouksel. The interpolation-based grid file. In *Proc. 4th ACM SIGACT-SIGMOD-SIGART Symposium on Principles of Database Systems*, March 1985. pages 20-27, Portland, OR.

[11] H. Samet. The quadtree and related hierarchical data structures. *ACM Comput. Surv.*, 16(2):817–860, 1984.

[12] M. Tamminen. Encoding pixel trees. *Computer Graphics, Vision and Image Processing*, 28(1):44–57, 1984.

On the k-coloring of Intervals
(Extended Abstract)

Martin C. Carlisle   Errol L. Lloyd

Department of Computer and Information Sciences
University of Delaware
Newark, DE   19716

Abstract

The problem of coloring a set of n intervals (from the real line) with a set of k colors is studied.   In such a coloring, two intervals may have the same color if and only if those intervals do not overlap.   Two versions of the problem are considered. For the first, we provide an O(k+n) time algorithm for k-coloring a maximum cardinality subset of the intervals.   The best previous algorithm for this problem required time O(kn).   In the second version, we assume that each interval has a weight, and provide an O(knlogn) algorithm for k-coloring a set of intervals of maximum total weight.   The best previous algorithm for this problem required time O(n^{2}logn).   These results provide improved solutions to problems of local register allocation,   task scheduling, and the routing of nets on a chip.

1. Introduction

Over the past decade or so, a great deal of research has focussed on the tractability of various algorithmic problems concerning graphs.   A particularly popular topic has been graph coloring, where two related problems have been considered: 1) Given a graph G, what is the chromatic number of G? (or, stated as a decision problem: Given k colors, is G k-colorable?); and, 2) Given a graph G and k colors, find a maximum k-colorable subgraph of G.   Unfortunately, these problems are NP-complete [9] for arbitrary graphs.   Thus, attention has turned to identifying classes of graphs for which these problems are solvable in polynomial time. *Interval graphs* are one such class [6]. These are graphs for which there exists a set of n finite open intervals on the real line, such that the following two conditions hold:

1) there is a 1:1 correspondence between intervals and vertices, and,

2) two intervals overlap if and only if there is an edge between the vertices corresponding to those two intervals.

In this context,   there are O(n + e) algorithms[1] both for determining the chromatic number of an interval graph, and for the maximum k-coloring of an interval

---

[1]n and e are the number of vertices and edges, respectively, of G.

graph [11]. While these algorithms are asymptotically optimal for interval graphs as such, they may be quite unsatisfactory for applications involving "interval graphs". In most of these applications (some are discussed in section 4), the problem is typically presented not in the form of an interval graph, but rather as the underlying set of n intervals. In this context, the actual problem is to determine the chromatic number of, or a maximum k-coloring of, the set of intervals. In such colorings, overlapping intervals may not receive the same color. Often there is no need to explicitly construct the *interval graph* associated with the set of intervals. This is important since the number of edges in the interval graph may be quadratic in the number of intervals (consider n mutually overlapping intervals). It is well known for example, that the chromatic number of a set of *sorted intervals*[2] can be determined directly in time O(n), without making an explicit conversion to the interval graph representation.

In the next section, we give an O(k + n) algorithm for the maximum k-coloring of a set of n sorted intervals. This improves upon the best previous result [11] by a factor of k (i.e. they required O(kn) time). In section 3, we consider a weighted version of the problem. Here, a positive *weight* is associated with each interval, and the goal is to find a k-colorable set of intervals of maximum total weight. We give an O(knlogn) algorithm for finding such a coloring. The best previous result [1] required time O(n²logn). In section 4 we discuss several applications involving k-colorings of interval graphs. Finally, in section 5, we present some conclusions and discussion.

2. A linear algorithm for maximum (unweighted) k-coloring

In this section we present an O(k + n) algorithm for the maximum k-coloring of a set of n intervals. As noted above, we assume that the 2n endpoints of the intervals have been sorted. Thus, we denote the intervals by $I_1, I_2, ..., I_n$, and assume that the intervals are ordered by increasing value of their right endpoint. For interval I_i, we refer to i as the *index* of the interval. Since the ordering of the indices corresponds to the ordering of the right endpoints, we will often find it convenient to refer to indices in discussing the left to right ordering of intervals by right endpoint.

2.1 The algorithm

As noted in the introduction, the algorithms that we give will not explicitly construct the associated interval graph. Nonetheless, in explaining the motivation for, and the correctness of, these methods, we will sometimes find it convenient

---

2 We assume that the 2n endpoints of the intervals are sorted. This assumption follows quite naturally from many applications, such as those discussed in section 4.

to refer to that associated interval graph. This should present no problem, since the relationship between the intervals and the interval graph is clear. In this vein, we will make extensive use of the fact that interval graphs are *perfect*: the size of the largest clique is equal to the number of colors in a minimum coloring. Thus, a subgraph of an interval graph is k-colorable if and only if it contains no clique of size greater than k. In terms of the intervals themselves: a set of intervals is k-colorable if and only if not more than k of those intervals overlap at any single point.

The intuitive idea behind our algorithm for maximum k-coloring is to use a greedy approach. Intervals are considered for coloring (*processed*) in order of increasing right endpoint. Each interval I_i when processed, is either:

1) *discarded,* if there is no available color (that is, the inclusion of that interval in the colored subgraph would produce a k+1 clique), or,
2) *assigned* a color using a "best fit" principle.

To decide which color constitutes the "best fit" (if any), we consider for each color, the interval of largest index that has already been assigned that color. Such an interval is the *leader* for that color. The right endpoint of this interval is, in a certain sense, the right endpoint of that color. The interval being processed I_i, is assigned the color of the *best fit leader*. That is, the leader with greatest right endpoint no greater than the left endpoint of I_i. Note however that there is some difficulty in finding this best fit leader, since examining all colors would take time $O(k)$ per interval; whereas, in an amortized sense, our algorithm requires the use of time $O(1)$ per interval. Thus, we use the following method to determine the best fit leader without explicitly considering all k colors.

We begin by defining *adjacent(I_i)* to be the interval of greatest index that lies strictly to the left[3] of I_i. Clearly, as the algorithm executes, the best fit leader for I_i will be adjacent(I_i), if adjacent(I_i) is in fact a leader. In such a case, I_i will be assigned the same color as adjacent(I_i). But what if adjacent(I_i) is either not colored, or colored, but not a leader? In this case, how can we locate the best fit leader? We find this interval, or determine that there is no such interval, using the well known *union/find* operations on disjoint sets[10].

Here, each interval is initially in a set unto itself. Always, the *name of the set* is the interval in the set of least index (more to the point, this is also the interval in this set having the smallest right endpoint, and further, as we will show, is a leader). As the algorithm proceeds, these sets will of course grow, and will represent equivalence classes of intervals with respect to "best fits"[4]. In

---

[3] That is, the right endpoint of adjacent(I_i) is no greater than the left endpoint of I_i.

[4] Note that these are NOT sets of intervals of a given color.

particular, if an interval, I_j, is discarded, or is colored, but not a leader (an interval with right endpoint larger than that of I_j is assigned the same color as I_j), then the set containing I_j is unioned with the set containing the interval, I_{j-1}. This is done to indicate that no interval I_i having adjacent(I_i) = I_j, can be assigned the same color as I_j, and that the name of the set containing I_j is the new "best fit" for I_i. Thus, at any point in the algorithm, a set, except for the name, consists of discarded intervals, and intervals no longer at the right endpoint of the color to which they are assigned. The name of the set is either an interval that is a leader, or an interval that has not yet been processed (the latter is true only if the set is a singleton).

The complete algorithm is given as Algorithm 1.

2.2 The proofs of correctness and running time

In this section we prove the correctness of the algorithm and establish that it can be implemented in linear time. We begin with the proof of correctness.

Theorem 1: Algorithm 1 creates a maximum k-coloring.

We begin the proof by defining for each processed interval I_i, the *r-closest leader* to I_i to be I_j, the leader of greatest index, with $j \leq i$ (equivalently, right(I_j) $\leq$ right(I_i)). Since the r-closest leader to I_i may change as the algorithm proceeds, we have the following claim:

Lemma 1: As the algorithm proceeds, for each processed interval I_i, the name of the set containing I_i is the r-closest leader to I_i (at that point in the algorithm).

Proof: Since the lemma is trivially true prior to the execution of the main loop, we proceed inductively to the end of the ith iteration of the main loop. We consider how the sets may have changed since the end of the i-1st iteration. There are two possibilities:

Case 1: I_i was discarded (assigned "color" 0).

In this case, the only change to the sets in the ith iteration is that I_i is included in the set containing I_{i-1}. By the induction hypothesis, after the i-1st iteration, the name of that set is some I_h, the r-closest leader to I_{i-1}. After the ith iteration, I_i has been added to that set, and I_h is still the name of that set. Further, I_h is still a leader, and I_i is not a leader, since it did not get a real color. Thus, it follows from I_h being the r-closest leader to I_{i-1} that I_h is also the r-closest leader to I_i.

Case 2: color(I_i) was assigned color(I_j)

Here, the only change to the sets is that I_j is included in the set with I_{j-1}. Let I_h be the name of the set containing I_{j-1} after the i-1st iteration. By the induction hypothesis, I_h is the r-closest leader to I_{j-1}. After the ith iteration,

Algorithm 1. Maximum (unweighted) k-coloring of interval graphs

Input: An integer k, and a set of n intervals $I_1, I_2, ..., I_n$, sorted by right and left endpoints. The intervals are indexed in order of increasing right endpoint.

Output: A k-coloring of the intervals that maximizes the number of colored intervals. Each interval is assigned a value from 0 to k, where 1,2,...,k represent colors, and 0 represents no coloring.

Definitions:

$left(I_i)$ *and* $right(I_i)$: the left and right endpoints, respectively, of I_i.

$color(I_i)$: The color assigned to I_i. If I_i is not colored, then this is 0.

$I_{-k}, I_{-k+1}, ..., I_0$: These are dummy intervals that serve as the initial right endpoints of the colors (including the 0 "no color" color).

$adjacent(I_i)$: the interval whose right endpoint is the largest less than $left(I_i)$.

$find(I_i)$: returns the name of the set containing I_i.

$union(I_i, I_j)$: merges the sets with names I_i and I_j into a set named I_j.

Method:

```
for i ← 0 to k do                    (* setup & color the dummy intervals *)
    right(I_-i) ← -i;
    left(I_-i) ← -i-1;
    color(I_-i) ← k-i;
    create a singleton set containing I_-i;

for i ← 1 to n do                    (* setup adjacent, and the sets *)
    adjacent(I_i) ← max{j : right(I_j) ≤ left(I_i)};
    create a singleton set containing I_i;

for i ← 1 to n do                              (* the main loop *)
    I_j ← find(adjacent(I_i));                 (* this is I_i's "best fit" *)
    if j = -k
        then  color(I_i) ← 0;                  (* do not color I_i *)
              union(I_i, find(I_i-1));
        else color(I_i) ← color(I_j);
              union(I_j, find(I_j-1));
```

I_j is in that set, and I_h is still the name of that set. Further, I_j is not a leader since I_i is colored the same as I_j and lies strictly to the left of I_j. Also, since h $\neq$ j, and the only coloring change was to let color(I_i) = color (I_j), it follows that I_h is still a leader. Thus, it follows from I_h being the r-closest leader to I_{j-1}, that I_h is the r-closest leader to I_j. ∎

The proofs of the following lemmas are omitted due to space considerations.

Lemma 2: Interval I_j as found in the ith iteration is the best fit leader for I_i.

Lemma 3: As the algorithm proceeds, if interval I_j overlaps with g leaders, then the coloring of I_i produces a g+1-clique of colored intervals.

Now we proceed to complete the proof of Theorem 1.

Proof of Theorem 1: We begin with some notation and a definition. First, for $i \leq j$, let $I_{i \rightarrow j}$ represent intervals $I_i,...,I_j$, and let M be the set of all optimal colorings of $I_{1 \rightarrow n}$. Also, for a coloring C in M, a *subcoloring of C on $I_{1 \rightarrow i}$* is a coloring of $I_{1 \rightarrow i}$ such that every interval has the same color as in C, or has no color if it is not colored in C. We claim that for each i, the coloring C_i created after the ith iteration of the main loop in Algorithm 1 is a subcoloring of some element of M on $I_{1 \rightarrow i}$. Once this is established, the theorem follows when i = n.

Thus, we inductively assume that C_{i-1} is a subcoloring of some coloring in M for $I_{1 \rightarrow i-1}$ and consider C_i. There are three possibilities:

Case 1: I_i is not colored in C_i.

From Lemma 2 it follows that the best fit leader for I_i is L_k, and, since this interval has the least right endpoint among all of the leaders, it must be that all k of the other leaders overlap with I_i. From Lemma 3, the coloring of I_i would form a k+1-clique of colored intervals. Thus, since C_{i-1} was a subcoloring of some C* in M on $I_{1 \rightarrow i-1}$ then C_i must also be a subcoloring of C* on $I_{1 \rightarrow i}$ since C* cannot have colored I_i without also having created a k+1-clique of colored intervals.

Case 2: There is a C* in M such that C_{i-1} is a subcoloring of C* on $I_{1 \rightarrow i-1}$ and I_i is assigned different colors in C* and C_i.

We will construct a C' in M such that C_i is a subcoloring of C' on $I_{1 \rightarrow i}$. We begin by assuming that color(I_i) = 2 in C* and color(I_i) = 1 in C_i. Let I_m be the leftmost interval (i.e. interval of least index) of color 1 in C* that is not colored in C_{i-1} (note that m > i). If no such I_m exists, then C' is identical to C* except that color(I_i) = 1. Otherwise, C' is identical to C* except that: I_m, and all intervals of color 1 in C* that follow I_m, are assigned color 2; and, all intervals of color 2 in C* having a right endpoint of right(I_i) or greater, are assigned color 1. This is possible as by the "best fit" rule, the leader of color 2 in C_i must have an index no greater than that of the leader of color 1, otherwise I_i

would have been given color 2 by Algorithm 1. Since left(I_m) is larger than the right endpoint of color 1 (at the time that I_i was processed) I_m can be assigned color 2, which had a smaller or equal right endpoint. Thus, C_i is a subcoloring of C' on $I_{1 \to i}$. Further C' is an optimal coloring since it colors the same number of intervals as C* which is in M.

Case 3: There is a C* in M such that C_{i-1} is a subcoloring of C* on $I_{1 \to i-1}$, and I_i is not colored in C*.

Again we construct a C' in M such that C_i is a subcoloring of C' on $I_{1 \to i}$. Without loss of generality, let color(I_i) = 1 in C_i. Now, let I_m be the leftmost interval colored 1 in C* that is not in C_{i-1} (such an I_m must exist, otherwise we can add I_i to C*, an optimal coloring). Note that as Algorithm 1 colors intervals in order of increasing right endpoint, I_m has a larger right endpoint than I_i. Thus C' is identical to C*, except that I_m is not colored, and color(I_i) = 1. Thus, C' is an optimal legal coloring, and C_i is a subcoloring of C' on $I_{1 \to i}$.

Thus, Algorithm 1 produces an optimal coloring. ■

Next we consider the running time of Algorithm 1.

Theorem 2: The running time of Algorithm 1 is $O(k + n)$.

Proof: It is easy to see that the algorithm can be made to run in time $O(k + n)$, excluding the union/find operations, and leave the proof to the reader. To implement the union/find operations in a total time of $O(n)$, we utilize a method [7] for performing union/find operations in time $O(n)$ on sets where the possible unions are known in advance. Note that in Algorithm 1, each set is unioned only with the set containing the interval with the next smallest right endpoint. It follows from [7] that Algorithm 1 can be implemented in time $O(n)$. ■

3. An improved algorithm for weighted k-coloring

We now turn to the problem of finding a k-coloring of maximum total weight. Since interval graphs are perfect, such a k-coloring may be found by locating a maximum weight subgraph among all subgraphs having no clique of size greater than k. Using this approach, [11] gave a linear programming based solution to this problem. Later, an $O(n^2 \log n)$ algorithm that uses shortest paths to create a maximum weight k-colorable subgraph was given in [1]. In this section, we describe a solution that, like [1], uses shortest paths. Our method has a worst case running time of $O(kn \log n)$, thereby improving on prior results by a factor of n/k.

3.1 The weighted algorithm

Our approach is to construct a network for which a minimum weight flow of size k will provide a solution to weighted k-coloring of intervals. We begin with a brief description of that flow problem.

In the *minimum weight flow of size k* problem, we are given an integer k and a directed graph (a *network*) $G=(V,E,w,c)$, where V is a set of vertices, E a set of directed edges, and associated with each edge e is a positive *capacity* $c(e)$ and a nonnegative *weight* $w(e)$. Also, there are designated vertices s and t. The objective is to find a flow of size k from s to t that is of minimum weight among all such flows (see [4] for details). A polynomial time algorithm for finding such a flow is given in [4], and will be discussed later.

As noted above we will reduce maximum weighted k-coloring to finding a minimum-weight flow of size k. That reduction requires several steps, the first of which is a reduction to a *maximum* weight flow of size k problem. We begin with several definitions.

A *minimum clique subcover* of a graph is a minimum cardinality collection of cliques such that each edge of the graph appears in at least one clique. For interval graphs, it is straight-forward to find a minimum clique subcover in time $O(n)$. Thus, assume that a minimum clique subcover has been found. In that subcover, a *large clique* is a clique whose size exceeds k. It should be clear that a clique of size not exceeding k imposes no restrictions on a k-coloring. Further, if an interval does not appear in a large clique, then that interval will appear in every maximum weight k-coloring of the intervals. Thus, we assume that all such intervals have been removed from the set of intervals, and we concentrate on the large cliques. The *location* of a large clique is the leftmost point at which all of the intervals in the clique overlap. Finally, we let r represent the number of large cliques, and denote the large cliques in order of increasing location as $q_1,...,q_r$.

Next, we construct a network G, with nodes $s=v_0, v_1, ..., v_{r-1}, v_r=t$, and arcs (v_{i-1}, v_i) for $1 \leq i \leq r$. Each of these *clique-arcs* is given a weight of zero, and a capacity of k. Intuitively, clique-arc (v_{i-1}, v_i) represents large clique q_i. To complete G, we consider each I_i. That interval lies in some consecutive sequence of large cliques, $q_j, ..., q_k$. For that interval, we add to G an *interval-arc* (v_{j-1}, v_k) having a weight equal to the weight of I_i, and having a capacity of 1.

Lemma 4: The weight of a maximum weight flow of size k in G is equal to the weight of a maximum weight k-coloring of the n intervals.

Proof: Straight-forward and is omitted. ■

Corollary 1: Given a maximum weight flow of cost k for G, the intervals corresponding to the interval-arcs of flow 1 are exactly the intervals in some maximum weight k-coloring of the n intervals.

Recall however that the algorithm of [4] finds minimum weight flows of cost k, not maximum weight flows. Thus, we could modify G by negating the weight of each arc, and then finding a minimum weight flow of cost k. Unfortunately, that same algorithm of [4] also requires that all arc weights be non-negative. To get around this complication, we not only use the idea of negating all of the edge weights of G, but also use the notion of a *labelling* P of the vertices [4]. Here, each vertex, v, is assigned a label, P(v). Then, a new network D is constructed from G by using identical vertex and edge sets, and identical capacities, but where the weight of arc (u,v) is $w(u,v) = P(u)-P(v)-weight(u,v)$. If each such $w(u,v)$ is non-negative, then the algorithm of [4] can be applied to produce a minimum weight flow of cost k in D. From the results of [4] it follows that this flow can be used to produce a maximum weight flow of cost k in G, thereby (from Lemma 4) providing a maximum weight k-coloring of the intervals.

Obviously the key element in the above reduction is the construction of a labelling function P that yields all non-negative $w(u,v)$'s. It follows from [4] that such a labelling function exists if and only if there are no circuits of positive weight in G. Since G is acyclic, this is immediate, and the only difficulty is actually finding such a P. Thus, we define P(v) to be the length of the longest path in G from v to v_r. In Lemma 5 we show that this labelling function does indeed yield all non-negative $w(u,v)$'s.

The complete algorithm is given in Algorithm 2.

3.2 The proofs of correctness and running time

Since the introduction to the algorithm enumerated the steps in the reduction, the reader should be convinced of the correctness of the algorithm, provided we can establish that in D, each of the weights $w(u,v)$ is non-negative. Before giving that proof, we note that the correctness of the longest path computation itself is quite standard (G is acyclic), and is omitted.

Lemma 5: In network D, each $w(u,v)$ is non-negative.

Proof: By way of contradiction, consider an arc (u,v) such that $w(u,v) < 0$. From the construction of G (hence D) from the large cliques, it follows that $u < v$. That is, in the left to right ordering of the large cliques, the clique corresponding to u lies to the left of the clique corresponding to v. Also, since $w(u,v) < 0$, we have that $\Pi(u) - \Pi(v) - weight(u,v) < 0$. Recall though that $\Pi(u)$ is the length of the longest path in D from u to t. Analogously, for $\Pi(v)$. But then, $\Pi(u) < weight(u,v) + \Pi(v)$. But, this is a contradiction, since there is a path from u to t with weight $weight(u,v) + \Pi(v)$ using arc (u,v) and then the longest path from v to t. ■

Thus, from lemma 5 and the earlier discussion we have:

Theorem 3: Algorithm 2 finds a maximum weight k-coloring.

Theorem 4: The running time of Algorithm 2 is $O(kn\log n)$.
Proof: First, P can be computed in $O(n)$ time, since there are but $O(n)$ arcs and vertices in G, and the computation involving the *min* requires constant time. Second, it is obvious that D can then be constructed from G in linear time. Finally, it was shown in [4] that the minimum weight of size k network flow problem can be solved in time $O(\text{size-of-flow} \times \text{complexity-of-shortest-path})$. Here, we require a flow of size k, and Dijkstra's algorithm computes shortest paths in $O(e + n\log n)$ steps using Fibonacci heaps[5]. Thus, since there are $O(n)$ edges in D, the algorithm requires $O(kn\log n)$ operations to solve the flow problem, and overall. ∎

Algorithm 2. Maximum-weighted k-coloring of interval graphs.

Input: An integer k, and a set of n intervals, sorted by left and right endpoints. Each interval has a positive weight associated with it.

Output: A maximum weight k-coloring.

Method:

    find a minimum clique subcover of the intervals;
    let I* = {intervals not appearing in any large clique of the subcover};
    let r be the number of large cliques in that subcover;
    construct network G = (V,E,weight,capacity) from that minimum clique
        subcover, and the intervals that appear in a large clique;

    let P(v) = 0 for all vertices v;
    for i ← r to 1 step -1 do   (* find longest paths *)
        for each arc $(v,v_i) \in$ E do
            P(v) ←   min(P(v), weight(v,v_i) + P(v_i));

    for each arc (u,v) ∈ E do
        w(u,v) ←   P(u)-P(v)-weight(u,v);

    compute for network D = (V,E,w,capacity), the minimum cost flow of size k;

    for each interval-arc (u,v) ∈ E do
        if flow(u,v) > 0
            then include (u,v) in I*;

    k-color the intervals of I* using Algorithm 1;

Finally, we note that a similar approach to computing a maximum weight k-coloring is used in [1]. There, the algorithm of [4] was used in a direct fashion to locate a minimum weight set of intervals that could not be accommodated in a k-coloring. That approach required time $O(n^2 \log n)$ in the worst case since the flow is of size $O(n)$.

4. Improved results for applications

In this section we briefly mention three applications, each of which translates to finding a (weighted or unweighted) k-coloring of a set of intervals.

Register Allocation: We consider the problem of allocating a set of k registers to straight-line code within a single basic block (*local register allocation*). Here, each operand must reside in a register when the relevant operator is applied. The goal of is to minimize the number of spills of register values to main memory. This can be done in time $O(n \log n)$ using the well known method of [2]. However, by carefully modeling variable spans as intervals, this problem becomes that of finding a maximum k-coloring of a set of intervals. Thus, we provide an $O(k + n)$ algorithm for spill minimization in local register allocation.

Job Scheduling: We are given n *tasks* to be executed on k identical *processors*. *if* a task is executed, it must start precisely at it's given *start time*, and complete precisely at it's given *end time*. Further, each task has an associated *value*, and the goal is to schedule a set of tasks of maximum total value. It is easy to see that this is equivalent to finding a maximum weight k-coloring of a set of intervals with weights. This is the problem considered in [1], where an $O(n^2 \log n)$ algorithm was given. Our result improves the time to $O(kn\log n)$.

Routing of two point nets [8]: Here we are given a channel consisting of k horizontal tracks lying on a VLSI chip, along with a set of n two-point nets, where the terminals of the nets lie at fixed positions along the top or bottom of the channel. These nets are to be routed using two vertical and one horizontal wire segments, such that similarly oriented wires do not intersect. Since but one wire connects to each terminal, we need only be concerned with routing the horizontal segments. Since this is precisely the problem of maximum k-coloring a set of intervals, we provide an $O(k + n)$ solution.

5. Conclusions

In this paper we have provided improved algorithms for the k-coloring of a set of intervals in both the weighted and unweighted cases. For the weighted version, our Algorithm 2 improves over the best previous result [1] by a factor of n/k. Since n is likely to be much larger than k in practice, this is a considerable savings. Note that the running time becomes $O(kn\log n + e)$ if an interval *graph* is given, instead of the actual set of intervals. The extra $O(e)$ term arises from the need to convert the interval graph into such a set of intervals [3]. Note that even in this case, Algorithm 2 is an improvement over the $O(n^2\log n)$ algorithm.

For the unweighted version, our Algorithm 1 improves over the best previous algorithm [11] by a factor of k. Again in practice, this is likely to produce a significant savings. Further, the algorithm that we give is truly linear. This is in contrast to existing methods, which often claim to be linear by assuming that k is a fixed constant. Finally, note if an interval *graph* is given, then there is no asymptotic improvement over previous methods, since simply the time[5] to input that graph, ($O(n + e)$), dominates the running time.

References

1) Arkin, E.M. and E.B. Silverberg, "Scheduling jobs with fixed start and end times," Discrete Applied Mathematics 18 (1987), 1-8.

2) Belady, L.A., "A study of replacement algorithms for a virtual-storage computer," IBM Systems Journal 5 (1966).

3) Booth, K.S. and G.S. Leuker, "Testing for the consecutive ones property, interval graphs, and graph planarity using PQ-tree algorithms," J. Comp. and Sys. Sci. 13 (1976), 335-379.

4) Edmonds, J. and R.M. Karp, "Theoretical improvements in algorithmic efficiency for network flow problems," JACM 19 (1972), 248-264.

5) Fredman, M.L. and R.E. Tarjan, "Fibonacci heaps and their uses in improved network optimization algorithms," JACM 34 (1987), 596-615.

6) Golumbic, M.C., *Algorithmic Graph Theory and Perfect Graphs*, Academic Press, 1980.

7) Gabow, H.N. and R.E. Tarjan, "A linear-time algorithm for a special case of disjoint set union," J. Comp. and Sys. Sci. 30 (1985), 209-221.

8) Hashimoto, A. and J. Stevens, "Wire routing by optimizing channel assignment within large apertures," Proc. 8th IEEE Design Automation Workshop (1971), 155-169.

9) Karp, R.M., "Reducibility among combinatorial problems," in *Complexity of Computer Computations*, R.E. Miller and J.W. Thatcher, editors, Plenum Press, 1972.

10) Tarjan, R.E., "Efficiency of a good but not linear set union algorithm," JACM 22 (1975), 215-225.

11) Yannakakis, M. and F. Gavril, "The maximum k-colorable subgraph problem for chordal graphs," Information Processing Letters 24 (1987), 133-137.

---

[5] Note that $O(n + e)$ is also the time to convert the graph into a set of intervals.

Folding a Triangulated Simple Polygon: Structural and Algorithmic Results

Ali A. Kooshesh   Bernard M. E. Moret

Department of Computer Science
University of New Mexico
Albuquerque, NM 87131

(kooshesh@unmvax.cs.unm.edu and moret@cmell.cs.unm.edu)

ABSTRACT

We describe a linear-time algorithm that folds a triangulated simple polygon into a single triangle. Using this technique, we derive a particularly simple proof of Chvátal's art gallery theorem and improve or simplify a number of algorithms that deal with triangulated simple polygons. We describe two improved algorithms, both based on the degree sequence of the boundary vertices of the given triangulated simple polygon. The first is a linear-time algorithm that, using only the parity of the degree of each vertex, colors the vertices of a triangulated simple polygon using three colors. The second algorithm reconstructs the polygon and its triangulation from the degree sequence. We then show that our results extend to k-trees.

1   Introduction

We describe a linear-time algorithm that folds a triangulated simple polygon (here-after referred to as a TSP) into a single triangle. Using this technique, we can improve and simplify a number of algorithms that deal with triangulated simple polygons, as well as offer a structural characterization of various attributes of such polygons. Such characterizations include another simple proof of Chvátal's Watchman Theorem [3]. We describe two improved algorithms, both based on the degree sequence of the boundary vertices of the given triangulated simple polygon. The first is a linear-time algorithm that colors the vertices of a triangulated simple polygon using three colors; this algorithm, which only uses the parity of the degree of each vertex, improves on the $O(n \log n)$ algorithm of Avis and Toussaint [1]. The second algorithm reconstructs the triangulation from the degree sequence in linear time; Beyer *et al.* [2] gave a similar algorithm for maximal outerplanar graphs, but our approach is simpler and more intuitive. We then show that our results extend to k-trees.

2   Folding a TSP

We begin by introducing some terminology. The *dual tree* of a TSP is the tree formed by associating a vertex with each triangle and connecting two vertices exactly when their associated triangles share an edge. A *fan* is a sequence of adjacent triangles with a common apex, the *center* of the fan; the *base-path* of a

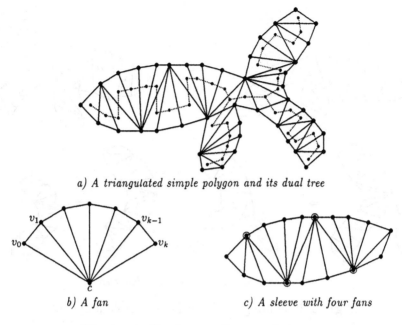

a) A triangulated simple polygon and its dual tree

b) A fan　　　　　　　*c) A sleeve with four fans*

Figure 1: Dual trees, fans, and sleeves

fan is the simple path $v_0, v_1, \ldots, v_k$ defined by the traversal of vertices adjacent to the center of the fan. Note that the degree of vertices v_1 through v_{k-1} must be exactly three; a fan in which neither v_0 nor v_k has degree three is called *maximal.* A *sleeve* is the union of adjacent maximal fans, the end-fans of which each have a vertex of degree two; the dual tree of a sleeve is a simple path. Figure 1 illustrates these concepts.

We fold a sleeve by folding one of its end-fans, thereby reducing the number of fans by one, and repeating the process until a single triangle results; we fold a TSP by folding subpolygons that form sleeves. More precisely, we proceed as follows. Let an end-fan of a sleeve have center c and base-path $v_0, v_1, \ldots, v_k$, where v_0 has degree two. We fold this fan by identifying vertex v_i with vertex v_{i+2}, for all i, $0 \le i \le k - 2$, where v_i has degree two; that is, we fold the fan along diagonals $\{c, v_1\}, \{c, v_2\}, \ldots, \{c, v_{k-1}\}$, in this order; this process is illustrated in Figure 2. The fan is thus folded into the triangle $cv_{k-1}v_k$, where, if k is even (respectively, odd), v_k represents the class of vertices with even (respectively, odd) index, while v_{k-1} represents the class of vertices with odd (respectively, even) index.

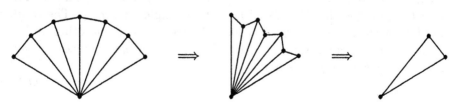

Figure 2: Folding a fan

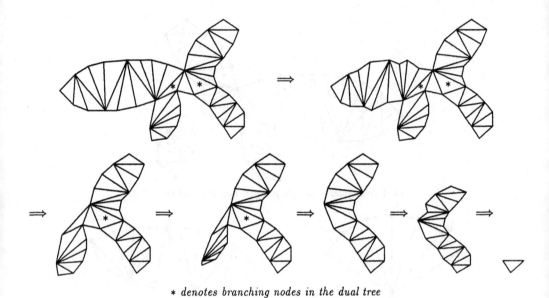

* denotes branching nodes in the dual tree

Figure 3: Folding a triangulated simple polygon

If the just folded fan was not the last fan left in the sleeve, we now fold along $\{c, v_k\}$, thereby reducing the sleeve by one fan. We then repeat this process until the entire sleeve is folded into one triangle. To fold a TSP, we effectively traverse its dual tree from its leaves (the dual tree need not be known, but it facilitates the description). When the search reaches a vertex, y, of degree three, we fold the sleeve, the dual tree of which is the simple path from the leaf to y. As a result of this folding, the degree of y becomes two; thus, after folding the sleeve, the dual tree contains one fewer vertex of degree three; repeating this process eventually folds the TSP into one triangle (see Figure 3).

Lemma 1 The folding algorithm just described partitions the vertex set of any TSP into three equivalence classes (induced by the relation "is identified with") in such a way that, for any three consecutive vertices, p_i, p_{i+1}, and p_{i+2} (indices are modulo n), selected on the boundary of the polygon, p_i and p_{i+2} are in the same equivalence class if and only if the degree of p_{i+1} is odd. □

Proof: That the relation "is identified with" on the vertex set of any TSP is an equivalence relation is immediate. Vertex p_{i+1} is the center of a fan with base-path $p_i = v_0, v_1, \ldots, v_k = p_{i+2}$. For $0 \le i < k$, if $\{v_i, v_{i+1}\}$ is a diagonal, we fold the section of the polygon that it cuts off into the triangle $v_i v_{i+1} p_{i+1}$. The result is a maximal fan in which v_0 and v_k both have degree two and the other vertices v_i, $1 \le i \le k - 1$ have degree three. Folding this fan identifies vertices v_0 and v_k if and only if the degree of p_{i+1} is odd.

Q.E.D.

Let $\{C_1, C_2, C_3\}$ be the partition induced by the relation "is identified with" on the vertex set of a TSP. Because we never fold an edge, but fold along edges, we have the immediate corollary.

Corollary 1 No two vertices of C_i, $1 \leq i \leq 3$, are adjacent. In particular, the vertex set of any triangulated simple polygon is three-colorable. □

This corollary allows us to give a particularly simple proof of a theorem of Chvàtal [3]; Fisk [4] also gave a simple proof based on colorability, but our folding technique allows us to reduce the problem of watching over the interior of a TSP to that of watching over the interior of a triangle.

Corollary 2 [Chvàtal's Watchman Theorem] Let $P = (V, E)$ be a simple polygon with $|V| = n$. There exists a subset $V' \subset V$, with $|V'| \leq \lfloor \frac{n}{3} \rfloor$, such that any point internal to P is visible from at least one vertex in V'. □

Proof: Fold the triangulated polygon into one triangle and choose the vertex that represents the equivalence class with fewest members. This class contains at most $\lfloor \frac{n}{3} \rfloor$ vertices. Any point interior to the polygon is in a triangle, and every triangle has one vertex in the chosen class; therefore, any interior point is visible from at least one vertex.

$Q.E.D.$

As we fold a triangle along an edge, we can only fold it in one way; indeed, no matter where we start the folding process, the resulting partition is unique.

Corollary 3 The partition of the vertices of the TSP induced by the folding procedure is unique. □

Proof: Assume, to the contrary, the existence of a different partition. Then there must exist vertices p_{i-1}, p_i, p_{i+1}, for some i, such that the folding procedure puts p_{i-1} and p_{i+1} in two different classes (implying that the degree of p_i is even), while the adversary puts them in the same class. But, since the length of the base-path of the fan centered at p_i is even, there must be two adjacent vertices in the same class, contradicting Corollary 1.

$Q.E.D.$

In fact, producing a three-coloring for a TSP is even simpler than folding the polygon: it suffices to know the parity of each vertex in order to produce a legal 2-coloring in linear time.

Corollary 4 Let T be a TSP given by its perimeter, $p_0, p_1, \ldots, p_n$. The following linear-time algorithm colors the vertex set of T using three colors.

$\text{Color}(p_0) \leftarrow 1; \text{Color}(p_1) \leftarrow 2$
for $i = 1$ to $n - 1$ do
    if $\text{odd}(\text{deg}(p_i))$
        then $\text{Color}(p_{i+1}) \leftarrow \text{Color}(p_{i-1})$
        else $\text{Color}(p_{i+1}) \leftarrow 6 - \text{Color}(p_{i-1}) - \text{Color}(p_i)$

Proof: We use induction on the number of vertices. The algorithm obviously colors the vertices of a triangle with three colors. Assume that we add vertex p, external to T, between vertices p_i and p_{i+1}, with edges $\{p, p_i\}$ and $\{p, p_{i+1}\}$. Although this addition changes the parity of p_i and p_{i+1}, still the algorithm assigns the same color to vertices p_{i+1} and p_{i+2}. Since the degree of p_{i+2} has not been changed, the algorithm proceeds as in the case of inductive hypothesis and thus produces a legal coloration.

$$Q.E.D.$$

This algorithm improves on the $O(n \log n)$ algorithm of Avis and Toussaint [1], both in its running time and in its simplicity.

Assume that $v_0, v_1, \ldots, v_k, v_{k+1}$ is a sequence of vertices on the boundary of a TSP colored by the preceding algorithm, such that vertices v_0 and v_{k+1} have been assigned color 1 and vertices $v_1, \ldots, v_k$ have been assigned alternately colors 2 and 3. It is easy to see that: if k equals 1, then the degree of v_1 is odd; if k equals 2, then the degrees of v_1 and v_2 are both even; and, if k exceeds 2, then the degrees of v_1 and v_k are both even while the degree of each v_i, $1 < i < k$, is odd. Also note that, if the degree of every vertex of a TSP is even, then the number of vertices must be divisible by three.

3 Finding the Branching Triangles

A triangle is *branching* if all three of its edges are diagonals of the triangulation. The branching triangles in a triangulation give rise to vertices of degree three in the dual tree; in other words, a TSP is composed of sleeves attached to branching triangles. Since reconstructing a sleeve is very simple, the identification of branching triangles (or, equivalently, the identification of branching nodes when reconstructing the dual tree of the triangulation) is the crucial part of an algorithm that reconstructs the TSP from its degree sequence. Beyer *et al.* [2] presented a linear-time reconstruction algorithm for maximal outerplanar graphs. We present below a linear-time version, based on folding, that walks the perimeter of the TSP and, on the basis of the degree sequence, identifies all branching triangles; in addition, our algorithm (with a very small modification) builds the dual tree in linear time from the degree sequence.

Our algorithm is based on balancing; it starts at a vertex of degree two (corresponding a leaf in the dual tree) and walks the perimeter until it encounters another vertex of degree two, recording on the way (in terms of degrees) what it sees of the (maximal) fans to which the vertices belong. On reaching the second vertex of degree two, it starts matching the information it has accumulated with what it encounters on the other side of the perimeter. If no branching triangle exists, the TSP is a simple sleeve and the degrees predicted from the information gathered on one side must exactly match the actual degrees of the vertices on the other side. When a mismatch is found (a vertex with actual degree larger than its predicted degree), it indicates the presence of a branching triangle; by keeping a stack of the vertices on the first side and popping the stack as matches are made

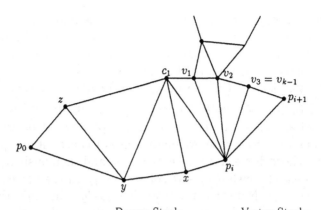

	Degree Stack	Vertex Stack
before processing x	$[3,3]$	$[y,y]$
after processing x	$[3,4]$	$[y,y,x]$
after processing p_i	$[3,5,3,3,3]$	$[y,y,x,p_i,p_i,p_i,p_i]$
after processing p_{i+1}	$[3,5,4,3]$	$[y,y,x,p_i,p_i,v_2,v_2]$

Figure 4: Reconstructing a TSP from its Degree Sequence

from the second side, we can identify the vertex on the first side that belongs to the branching triangle and thus reconstruct the TSP from its degree sequence.

When used for reconstruction, our algorithm uses a vertex-stack and a degree-stack. Let s_k^d denote the kth entry from the top of the degree stack and s_k^v the kth entry from the top of the vertex stack; our algorithm proceeds as follows. Let p_0 be a vertex of degree 2; we initialize the degree stack by pushing a 2 on it and call the procedure illustrated below to work on vertex p_0. (Refer to the accompanying illustration, Figure 4.)

`Reconstruct($p_{i-1}$)`
Label the next vertex of the polygon p_i.
Set p_{i-1} boundary-adjacent to p_i.

($d_i = 3$)　In this case, p_i (represented by vertex x in the figure) is on the base-path of some fan with center c_1 and s_1^d is the degree of c_1 in the sleeve p_0-p_i. Since p_i is diagonal-adjacent to c_1, we increment s_1^d by one and push a copy of p_i on the vertex-stack.

($d_i > 3$)　In this case, p_i (p_i itself in the figure) is the center of a fan. Thus p_i is also an end-vertex of the base-path of some other fan, say centered at c_1, such that c_1 lies on the left-chain and is diagonal-adjacent to p_i. To reflect this adjacency, we increment s_1^d by one. Then we push $d_i - 3$ threes on the degree-stack to account for vertices $v_{k-1}, \ldots, v_1$ (the vertices on the base path of p_i, excluding c_1), that are expected to be of degree three. Finally, we push $d_i - 2$ copies of p_i on the vertex-stack to be later identified with the vertices of its base-path.

$(d_i = 2)$ In this case, p_i (represented by p_{i+1} in the figure) is the last vertex on the base path of some fan. Let k be the smallest natural number such that $d_{i+k} > s_k^d$; if such a vertex does not exist, let $k = n - i$. For $j = 1, \ldots, k$, we do the following: (i) we label the next vertex p_{i+j}; (ii) we make p_{i+j-1} and p_{i+j} boundary-adjacent; (iii) we make p_{i+j} diagonal-adjacent to $s_n^v, \ldots, s_{n'+1}^v$, where $n' = \sum_{t=1}^{j-1}(s_t^d - 2)$ and $n = n' + s_j^d - 2$; and finally, (iv) we discard entries $s_k^d, \ldots, s_1^d$ and $s_n^v, \ldots, s_1^v$. If the stacks are empty, we set p_n and p_0 boundary-adjacent and stop. Otherwise, we increment s_1^d to account for $\{p_{i+k}, q\}$, where q is the vertex whose degree is represented by s_1^d and then push $d_{i+k} - s_k^d - 1$ threes on the degree-stack, push $d_{i+k} - s_k^d$ copies of p_{i+k} on the vertex-stack, and call Reconstruct(p_{i+k}). Note that the triangle $p_{i+k}s_1^v q$, where q is the vertex whose estimated degree is on the top of the degree-stack before the adjustments, is a branching triangle. Thus the algorithm identifies a branching triangle as it visits its second vertex.

4 Generalization to k-Trees

We extend our coloring procedure for TSPs by showing that linear time also suffices to color the more general k-trees [6], for each fixed k. A $k-$tree is recursively defined as follows.

1. The complete graph on k vertices (a k-clique) is a $k-$tree.

2. If G is a $k-$tree on n vertices, we construct a $k-$tree on $n + 1$ vertices by adding to G a vertex, v_{n+1}, and connecting it to all vertices of some k-clique in G. (By construction, G must contain at least one such clique.)

3. No other graph is a k-tree.

Hare *et al.* [5] have shown that a number of problems that are $\mathcal{NP}$-complete on general graphs become solvable in linear time on generalized series-parallel graphs, a family that includes k-trees, and gave some examples. We present a linear-time algorithm for coloring k-trees with the minimal number of colors. Our algorithm runs in time $O(k|V|)$—linear time for each fixed k—and colors the vertices of a $k-$tree using $k + 1$ colors (with the exception of the trivial k-tree consisting of a single k-clique, which it colors with k colors only); since a $k-$tree has cliques of size $k + 1$, the number of colors is minimal. Our algorithm takes advantage of the fact that any $k-$tree with at least $k + 1$ vertices has at least two vertices of degree k. With each vertex, $v \in V$, we associate a list, L_v, that is originally empty and a field, deg(v), that contains the degree of v. Our algorithm, using a stack, orders the vertices of G so as to allow each vertex to be colored in time $O(k)$—constant for each fixed k. In the description below, the operation Pop( ) removes and returns the top entry of the stack, and AdjList(v) is the adjacency list of vertex v in the input graph G.

procedure Order $(G = (V, E)$; stack; AdjList)

    stack $\leftarrow \phi$

    Let A be the set of $k + 1$ tuples $(v, v_1, \ldots, v_k)$ such that $\deg(v) = k$

        and $\{v, v_i\} \in E$ for $1 \leq i \leq k$.

    while stack contains fewer than $|V| - (k + 1)$ entries **do**

        Let $(v, v_1, \ldots, v_k)$ be a member of A

        Set $A \leftarrow A - \{(v, v_1, \ldots, v_k)\}$

        Push $((v, v_1, \ldots, v_k))$

        Set $L_{v_i} \leftarrow L_{v_i} \cup \{v\}$ for $1 \leq i \leq k$

        Set $\deg(v_i) \leftarrow \deg(v_i) - 1$ for $1 \leq i \leq k$

        for $1 \leq i \leq k$, **if** $\deg(v_i) = k$ **do**

            Let $\{v'_1, \ldots, v'_k\} = \text{AdjList}(v_i) - L_{v_i}$

            Set $A \leftarrow A \cup \{(v_i, v'_1, \ldots, v'_k)\}$

        endfor

    endwhile

    At this point, the $k + 1$ members of A form a complete graph on $k + 1$ vertices;

    color these $k + 1$ vertices using colors $1, \ldots, k + 1$.

endprocedure

procedure Assignment $(G = (V, E)$, stack)

    while stack is not empty **do**

        Set $(v, v_1, \ldots, v_k) \leftarrow \text{Pop}(\ )$

        Set $\text{Color}(v) \leftarrow \sum_{i=1}^{k+1} i - \sum_{i=1}^{k} \text{Color}(v_i)$

    endwhile

endprocedure

    Let s_i denote the ith entry of the stack from the bottom and define $G_i = G - \{s_1, s_2, \ldots, s_i\}$ so that, in particular, $G_0 = G$. It is easy to see that s_i in G_{i-1} has degree k. Thus, if G_{i-1} already has a legal coloration, then giving to s_i the color that is not been used by its neighbors results in a legal coloration of G_i. The fact that a k-tree always has at least two vertices of degree k guarantees that G_i can always be constructed from G_{i-1}.

    To see that the algorithm runs in linear time for each k, we need to explain how the set difference $\text{Adjlist}(v_i) - L_{v_i}$ is computed in time proportional to the number of members in $\text{AdjList}(v_i)$. We copy the members of $\text{AdjList}(v_i)$ into a lazy array; then, for each member of L_{v_i}, we mark, in constant time, its corresponding copy in the lazy array as "deleted." Now the k unmarked members can be found by a scan of the lazy array. Since we perform such operation at most once for each vertex, the total time spent for difference is proportional to the number of edges in G; but $E \in O(k|V|)$ for a k-tree, proving our claim. (Reconstruction of a k-tree from a degree sequence would pose no particular problem, if it were not for the fact that such a graph is, in general, not Hamiltonian, thereby preventing us from defining a natural sequence of its vertices.)

5 Conclusion

We have introduced the idea of folding triangulated simple polygons, which has led us to some simple characterizations of such polygons and then to particularly simple formulations of algorithms to color or reconstruct such polygons from their degree sequence. The same coloring strategy can be extended to the family of k-trees, yielding a new, linear-time algorithm for finding a minimal coloring for these graphs. Thus the folding paradigm is seen as a useful approach to several problems in computational geometry and algorithmic graph theory.

References

[1] D. Avis and G. T. Toussaint, "An efficient algorithm for decomposing a polygon into star-shaped pieces," *Pattern Recognition* **13** (1981), 395–398.

[2] T. Beyer, W. Jones, and S. Mitchell, "Linear algorithms for isomorphism of maximal outerplanar graphs," *J. ACM* **26** (1979), 603–610.

[3] V. Chvàtal, "A combinatorial theorem in plane geometry," *J. Combin. Theory Series B* **18** (1975), 39–41.

[4] J. Fisk, "A short proof of Chvàtal's watchman theorem," *J. Combin. Theory Series A* **24** (1978), 374.

[5] E. Hare, S. Hedetniemi, R. Laskar, K. Peters, and T. Wimer, "Linear-time computability of combinatorial problems on generalized series-parallel graphs," in *Discrete Algorithms and Complexity*, D.S. Johnson, T. Nishizeki, A. Nozaki, and H.S. Wilf, eds., Academic Press, New York (1986), 437–457.

[6] D.J. Rose, "On simple characterizations of k-trees," *Discrete Mathematics* **7** (1974), 317–322.

A Relationship Between Self-Organizing Lists and Binary Search Trees

Tony W. Lai   Derick Wood

Data Structuring Group
Department of Computer Science
University of Waterloo
Waterloo, Ontario N2L 3G1
CANADA

Abstract

We establish the following relationship between the move-to-front heuristic for lists and the move-to-root heuristic for trees. Suppose we have a list s and we access an element x using the move-to-front heuristic to obtain a list s'. If we insert s into an empty binary search tree to obtain T and insert s' into an empty binary search tree to obtain T', then we can obtain T' from T by accessing x using the move-to-root heuristic. We thus have a commutative diagram that relates the move-to-front and move-to-root heuristics.

Also, we show that there is no such commutative diagram relating the transposition heuristic for lists and the simple exchange heuristic for trees. But a new heuristic for trees, the conditional simple exchange heuristic, is related to the transposition heuristic by a commutative diagram. Furthermore, unlike the simple exchange heuristic, we show that the conditional simple exchange heuristic has an $O(\log n)$ asymptotic expected search time if the elements are accessed with independent and equal probabilities.

We conjecture that: if we are given an "oblivious" list heuristic that converges and we transform it into a binary search tree heuristic that results in a commutative diagram, then the tree heuristic also converges. The two examples of move-to-front and transposition support this conjecture.

1   Introduction

In this abstract, we investigate the relationship between self-organizing heuristics for sequential lists and self-organizing heuristics for binary search trees. Two of the simplest self-organizing heuristics for sequential lists are the transposition heuristic and the move-to-front heuristic of McCabe [6]. The transposition heuristic exchanges an accessed element with its predecessor in the list, unless the accessed element is at the front of the list. The move-to-front heuristic moves an accessed element to the front of the list without affecting the relative order of the other elements. If transpositions are used as a fundamental list reorganizing step, then the move-to-front heuristic transposes an accessed element until it reaches the front of the list.

Allen and Munro [1] proposed two self-organizing heuristics for binary search trees, the simple exchange heuristic and the move-to-root heuristic. The simple exchange heuristic promotes an accessed element once, unless the accessed element is at the root of the tree; the promotion operation is shown in Figure 1. The move-to-root heuristic promotes an accessed element until it reaches the root. Observe that the simple exchange and move-to-root heuristics are the binary tree analogs of the transposition and move-to-front heuristics, respectively, if transpositions are replaced by promotions. We call this type of correspondence an *operational correspondence*.

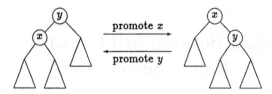

Figure 1. The promotion operation

Both the transposition heuristic and the move-to-front heuristic perform well if elements are accessed with fixed and independent probabilities. Rivest [7] proved that the expected search times of the transposition and move-to-front heuristics are within a constant factor of the expected search time of an optimal list. Surprisingly, while the move-to-root heuristic performs well, the simple exchange heuristic performs very poorly. Allen and Munro proved that the expected search time of the move-to-root heuristic is within a constant factor of the expected search time of an optimal tree if elements are accessed with fixed and independent probabilities, but they also proved that the expected search time of the simple exchange heuristic is $\Theta(\sqrt{n})$ if elements are accessed with independent and equal probabilities. Thus, the existence of operational correspondence between a tree heuristic and a list heuristic does not reveal much about the behavior of the tree heuristic.

Another correspondence exists, however, between the move-to-front heuristic and the move-to-root heuristic. There is a function T from the set of sequences to the set of binary trees such that, for any sequence s and element x of s, if s' is the sequence obtained after accessing x in s using the move-to-front heuristic, then $T(s')$ is the tree obtained after accessing x in the tree $T(s)$ using the move-to-root heuristic. We call this type of correspondence a *functional correspondence*. The existence of a functional correspondence between the move-to-front heuristic and the move-to-root heuristic implies that there is a simple commutative diagram relating the heuristics. We show that no functional correspondence exists between the transposition heuristic and the simple exchange heuristic.

Based on these results, we present a new heuristic for trees, the *conditional simple exchange heuristic*, that functionally corresponds to the transposition heuristic for lists. The conditional simple exchange performs at most one promotion during each access; we say that it has *constant linkage cost*. Yet, the conditional simple exchange has an expected search time of $O(\log n)$ if elements are accessed with independent and equal probabilities. However, the conditional simple exchange heuristic requires that a sequential list be explicitly stored. We therefore present a randomized version of the conditional simple exchange heuristic that requires only weight balance information.

Simulation results suggest that the asymptotic expected search times of the conditional simple exchange heuristic and the randomized conditional simple exchange heuristic are within a constant factor of an optimal tree if elements are accessed with fixed and independent probabilities. We thus conjecture that: if we are given an "oblivious" list heuristic[1] that has an optimal asymptotic expected search time and we transform it into a binary search tree heuristic that functionally corresponds to the list heuristic, then the asymptotic expected search time of the tree heuristic is within a constant factor of an optimal tree. The examples of the move-to-front heuristic and the transposition heuristic support our conjecture. If the conjecture is true, then it gives insight as to why the simple exchange heuristic performs poorly.

Some obvious open problems remain in the area of self-organizing heuristics for trees. A proof

---

[1]An oblivious heuristic has a fixed set $\pi_1, \pi_2, \ldots, \pi_n$ of permutations and it applies the permutation π_i to the list whenever an element in position i is accessed. In other words, the permutation that is applied on any access is determined solely by the position of the accessed element, not by its value or the previous accesses. Both the transposition and move-to-front heuristics are oblivious.

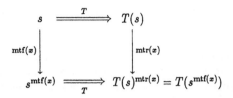

Figure 2. The correspondence between the move-to-front and move-to-root heuristics

or disproof of our conjecture is an open problem, along with the analyses and rates of convergence of the expected search times of the conditional simple exchange heuristic and the randomized conditional simple exchange heuristic.

As a final note, we mention that other self-organizing, constant linkage cost heuristics for binary search trees have been proposed. Cheetman et al. [2] devised the conditional rotation heuristic, which promotes an accessed node if the promotion reduces an estimate of the asymptotic expected search time. The notion of constant linkage cost is explored in much more detail in Lai [5].

2 The conditional simple exchange heuristic

Before proceeding, we first define some notation. Let s be some sequence of distinct elements of length n. We define $T(s)$ to be the tree obtained by inserting the elements of s into an empty binary search tree. We use $s^{\mathrm{mtf}(x)}$ to denote the sequence obtained after accessing x in s using the move-to-front heuristic, and $s^{\mathrm{trans}(x)}$ to denote the sequence obtained after accessing x in s using the transposition heuristic.

Let T be some binary search tree containing n distinct elements. $T^{\mathrm{mtr}(x)}$ denotes the tree obtained after accessing x in T using the move-to-root heuristic, and $T^{\mathrm{prom}(x)}$ denotes the tree obtained after promoting x in T.

We mentioned in Section 1 that there is a functional correspondence between the move-to-front heuristic and the move-to-root heuristic. Figure 2 depicts a commutative diagram of this correspondence. We state this correspondence more formally below[2].

Theorem 2.1 *For any sequence s and any element x of s, $T(s^{\mathrm{mtf}(x)}) = T(s)^{\mathrm{mtr}(x)}$.*

No such analog exists between the transposition heuristic for lists and the simple exchange heuristic for trees.

Theorem 2.2 *For any $n \geq 3$, there does not exist any function F mapping sequences of size n to trees of size n such that, for any sequence s and any element x of s, $F(s^{\mathrm{trans}(x)}) = F(s)^{\mathrm{prom}(x)}$.*

Proof: Because every tree of n nodes is reachable from any other tree of n nodes by some sequence of promotions, F must be surjective. Thus, there must exist some sequence s such that the root x of $F(s)$ has two children. Observe that x must be at the front of s. At least one child of x, say y, cannot be the successor of x. The first element of $s^{\mathrm{trans}(y)}$ must be x, so the root of $F(s^{\mathrm{trans}(y)})$ is x. However, since y is a child of x, we know that the root of $F(s)^{\mathrm{prom}(y)}$ is y, which implies that $F(s^{\mathrm{trans}(y)}) \neq F(s)^{\mathrm{prom}(y)}$. Since F is arbitrary, no function F exists such that, for any sequence s and any element x of s, $F(s^{\mathrm{trans}(x)}) = F(s)^{\mathrm{prom}(x)}$. □

Nevertheless, the transposition and simple exchange heuristics are weakly related as follows. Transposing an element x in a sequence s corresponds to promoting x in $T(s)$ only if x's parent in $T(s)$ is x's predecessor in s; otherwise, transposing x in s has no effect on $T(s)$.

---

[2]Most proofs are omitted in this abstract; they are to be found in the full paper[4]

Theorem 2.3 $T(s^{\text{trans}(x)}) = T(s)^{\text{prom}(x)}$ *if x's predecessor in s is x's parent in $T(s)$; otherwise,* $T(s^{\text{trans}(x)}) = T(s)$.

This suggests a new heuristic for trees, the *conditional simple exchange* heuristic. In the conditional simple exchange heuristic, we explicitly maintain a sequence s and use $T(s)$ as our binary search tree. The above lemma characterizes when a promotion is required to update $T(s)$ after a transposition in s; in particular, it implies that at most one promotion is necessary to update $T(s)$. Hence, the conditional simple exchange heuristic has constant linkage cost; that is, it performs no more than a constant number of pointer changes per access.

We claim that the expected cost of the conditional simple exchange heuristic is $O(\log n)$ if the elements are accessed with a uniform probability distribution. To prove this, we prove that each sequential list is equally probable.

Theorem 2.4 *If the probability of accessing any element is $1/n$, where n is the number of elements, then, under the transposition and conditional simple exchange heuristics, all sequences have equal asymptotic probability of appearing.*

Proof: Assume with loss of generality that we have n elements labeled $1, 2, \ldots, n$ that are accessed with probabilities $p_1, p_2, \ldots, p_n$, respectively. Let P be the set of all possible permutations of $\{1, 2, \ldots, n\}$. If $\pi = \langle x_1, x_2, \ldots, x_n \rangle$ is a permutation of $\{1, 2, \ldots, n\}$, then let $p(\pi) = \prod_{i=1}^{n} p_{x_i}^{n-i}$. Rivest [7] proved that the asymptotic probability of a sequence π appearing is $p(\pi)/\sum_{\sigma \in P} p(\sigma)$, although he expressed the result in a different form.

Therefore, to show that all lists have equal probability, it is sufficient to show that for any two permutations π and σ, $p(\pi) = p(\sigma)$. Since $p_1 = p_2 = \cdots = p_n = 1/n$, for any permutation $\pi = \langle x_1, x_2, \ldots, x_n \rangle$,

$$p(\pi) = \prod_{i=1}^{n} p_{x_i}^{n-i} = \prod_{i=1}^{n} \left(\frac{1}{n}\right)^{n-i} = \left(\frac{1}{n}\right)^{n(n-1)/2}.$$

Therefore, for any two permutations π and σ, we know that $p(\pi) = p(\sigma)$, which implies that every sequence is equally likely. $\square$

Corollary 2.5 *The expected search time in a tree of size n maintained using the conditional simple exchange heuristic is $O(\log n)$ for a uniform access probability distribution.*

An obvious question is whether the expected search time for the conditional simple exchange heuristic is optimal for nonuniform access probability distributions. Simulation results [4] suggest that the asymptotic expected search time is within a constant factor of an optimal tree. However, the conditional simple exchange heuristic appears to require $\Omega(n^2)$ accesses for its expected search time to converge to within a constant factor of its asymptotic search time, and is thus impractical. This is not surprising, considering that Gonnet et al. [3] proved that the transposition heuristic may take $\Omega(n^2)$ accesses to converge to within a factor of $1 + \epsilon$ of its asymptotic behavior.

3 The randomized conditional simple exchange heuristic

Before discussing the randomized conditional simple exchange heuristic, we define some more notation. We use $|T|$ to denote the number of internal nodes in a tree T, T_L to denote the left subtree of T, and T_R to denote the right subtree of T.

One undesirable aspect of the conditional simple exchange heuristic is that it uses a considerable amount of extra space to store the underlying sequence. This sequence is used as an oracle to decide whether the currently accessed element should be promoted or not. To reduce the space required, we use a randomized scheme; we use coin flips instead of an oracle to decide whether to perform a promotion or not.

We choose our randomized scheme to yield the same Markov chain as the conditional simple exchange scheme for the uniform access distribution. We define $P(T, x)$ to be the probability that an element x is the successor of its parent in a tree T, assuming that all sequences corresponding to T are equally probable. Our *randomized conditional simple exchange* heuristic is: if an element x is accessed in a tree T and x is not the root of T, then promote x with probability $P(T, x)$. Note that if x is at the root of T, then $P(T, x)$ is useless, so for convenience we define $P(T, x) = 1$ in this case.

Lemma 3.1   *1. If x is at the root of T, then $P(T, x) = 1$.*

2. If x is in T_L, then $P(T, x) = \frac{|T_L|}{|T|-1} P(T_L, x)$.

3. If x is in T_R, then $P(T, x) = \frac{|T_R|}{|T|-1} P(T_R, x)$.

Observe that we need only weight balance information to compute $P(T, x)$, and that we can determine $P(T, x)$ by inspecting only subtree weights on the root-to-x path. Although linear extra space is required to store the weight balance information, the information is more useful that the pointers required to store a sequence in the conditional simple exchange heuristic.

We claim that the expected search time of the randomized conditional simple exchange heuristic is $O(\log n)$ for a uniform access probability distribution. To prove this, we show that the asymptotic probability of any tree T appearing in the randomized conditional simple exchange heuristic is equal to the asymptotic probability of T appearing in the conditional simple exchange heuristic.

Theorem 3.2 *If elements are accessed with a uniform probability distribution, then for any tree, the asymptotic probabilities of that tree appearing under the conditional simple exchange heuristic and the randomized conditional simple exchange heuristic are equal.*

Corollary 3.3 *The expected search time of a tree of size n using the randomized conditional simple exchange heuristic is $O(\log n)$ for a uniform access probability distribution.*

Simulation results [4] suggest that the asymptotic expected search time of the randomized conditional simple exchange heuristic is within a constant factor of optimal for any access probability distribution. For some probability distributions, the heuristic converges faster than the conditional simple exchange heuristic, but the randomized conditional simple exchange heuristic still needs $\Omega(n^2)$ accesses to reach its asymptotic behavior for some distributions.

Unfortunately, the amortized search times of the conditional simple exchange and the randomized conditional simple exchange heuristics are $\Theta(n)$. To see this, observe that if we have a tree of height n, then the height of the tree is still n after accessing a deepest node x in the tree, regardless of whether we promote x or not.

Acknowledgements

This research was partially supported by Grant A-5692 from the Natural Sciences and Engineering Research Council of Canada and partially supported by a grant from the Information Technology Research Centre.

References

[1] B. Allen and I. Munro. Self-organizing binary search trees. *Journal of the ACM*, 25:526–535, 1978.

[2] R. P. Cheetham, B. J. Oommen, and D. T. H. Ng. Adaptive structuring of binary search trees using conditional rotations. Technical Report SCS-TR-126, Carleton University, October 1987.

[3] G. H. Gonnet, J. I. Munro, and H. Suwanda. Exegesis of self-organizing linear search. *SIAM Journal on Computing*, 10:613–637, 1981.

[4] T. W. Lai and D. Wood. Sequential search, binary search trees, and adaptivity. In preparation.

[5] T. W. H. Lai. *Efficient maintenance of binary search trees*. PhD thesis, University of Waterloo, 1990. In preparation.

[6] J. McCabe. On serial files with relocatable records. *Operations Research*, 13:609–618, 1965.

[7] R. L. Rivest. On self-organizing sequential search heuristics. *Communications of the ACM*, 19:63–67, 1976.

How Costly Can Red-Black Trees Be?

Helen Cameron   Derick Wood

Data Structuring Group
Department of Computer Science
University of Waterloo
Waterloo, Ontario N2L 3G1
CANADA

Abstract

We show that the internal path length of a red-black tree of size N is bounded above by $2N(\log N - \log \log N) + O(N)$ and that this is, asymptotically, tight. This result further affirms a conjecture that whenever trees of size N, in a class of height-balanced binary trees, have height bounded from above by $\alpha \log_2 N$, then the internal path length is bounded from above by $\alpha(\log_2 N - \log_2 \log_2 N) + O(N)$. We also prove that the asymptotic bound is tight for red-black trees. For this purpose, we introduce a class of red-black trees, the $C(k, h)$ trees, which achieve the bound when $k = h - 2 \log h + \epsilon$, where $|\epsilon| \leq 1/2$. This result solves the open problem of how bad red-black trees can be. In order to establish this result, we also prove that any red-black tree of a given height can be produced from a "skinniest" red-black tree of the same height by a series of simple insertions.

1 Introduction

The internal path length (IPL) of a search tree measures the average time taken to search the tree. Thus, it is a well-studied measure of performance for classes of search trees. Knuth [Knu73] examined the multiway trees that have the smallest and largest internal path length among all multiway trees with the same number of internal nodes. The binary trees with minimal IPL for their sizes are the perfect binary trees, which have external nodes on at most two adjacent levels. These binary trees are members of the class of AVL trees and the class of red-black trees; thus, the minimal IPL trees for each size have already been characterized for AVL and red-black trees. The 2,3 trees with minimal and maximal IPL are characterized by Miller et al [MPRS79].

Klein and Wood [KW90] derive an upper bound for the IPL of any AVL tree T of size N,

$$IPL(T) \leq 1.4404(\log_2 N - \log_2 \log_2 N) + O(N),$$

and present a family of AVL trees that achieve this bound. It is well known that the height of an AVL tree of size N is bounded above by $1.4404 \log_2 N$. We conjecture that, for any class C of height-balanced binary trees, if the height of a tree T in class C of size N is bounded from above by $\alpha \log_2 N$, then the IPL is bounded from above by

$$IPL(T) \leq \alpha(\log_2 N - \log_2 \log_2 N) + O(N).$$

In this paper, we further affirm the conjecture by proving such a bound for the red-black trees. The height of a red-black tree T of size N is bounded above by $2 \log_2 N$, and we show that

$$IPL(T) \leq 2(\log_2 N - \log_2 \log_2 N) + O(N).$$

In the course of deriving this bound, we prove that any red-black tree T is Skinny-reachable, where the Skinny trees are the red-black trees with the smallest sizes for their heights; that is, we show that there is a sequence of simple insertions that transform a Skinny tree of the same height as T into T. This result is similar in flavour to the results on iterative classes of trees of Ottmann and Wood [OW82]. Also, we introduce the $C(k,h)$ trees and prove that, by carefully choosing k as a function of h, the upper bound on the IPL is achieved by these trees. Although a subset of the $C(k,h)$ trees achieve the bound, we do not know whether these trees have maximal IPL for their size. The problem of characterizing maximal IPL red-black trees is still very much open. (The same problem remains open for AVL trees, too.)

2   An Upper Bound on the Internal Path Length

If a node has children, then it is *internal*; otherwise, it is *external*. A *binary search tree* T is a search tree in which each internal node has two children. The *maxheight* of a tree T is denoted by $maxht(T)$ and is the length of a longest root-to-external-node path. The *minheight* of a tree T, denoted by $minht(T)$, is the length of a shortest root-to-external-node path. Similarly, the maxheight of a node v in a tree T is the length of a longest path from node v to an external node that is a descendent of v, and the minheight of node v is the length of a shortest such path. The *weight* of a tree T, denoted by $wt(T)$, is the number of external nodes, and the *size* of T is the number of internal nodes. (The size of binary tree T is one less than its weight.) The *level* of a node in a tree T is the distance of the node from the root of tree T; the root is at level 0, its children are at level 1, and so on.

The class of trees in which we are interested are the red-black trees which were introduced by Guibas and Sedgewick [GS78]. The following definition is due to Olivié [Oli82], who called them half-balanced binary search trees. The trees were introduced by Bayer [Bay72], while Tarjan [Tar83] showed the two classes to be equivalent.

Definition 2.1 *A red-black tree is a binary search tree such that, for each node v in the tree, $maxht(v) \leq 2 \cdot minht(v)$; that is, a shortest path from v to an external node is at least one half as large as a longest such path.*

The *internal path length* of tree T is defined to be

$$IPL(T) = \sum_{v \text{ binary}} length(path(v)),$$

where $path(v)$ is the access path from the root of T to node v, and the length of the access path to a node on level i is $i + 1$. The *external path length* of tree T is defined to be

$$EPL(T) = \sum_{v \text{ external}} length(path(v)).$$

The external path length and the internal path length of a (binary) tree are related by the formula

$$EPL(T) = IPL(T) + 2 \cdot wt(T) - 1.$$

Using this relation and the definition of $EPL(T)$, we have

$$IPL(T) = (maxht(T) - 1)wt(T) + 1 - \sum_{i=1}^{wt(T)} (maxht(T) - l_i), \tag{1}$$

where l_i is the level on which the ith external node of T appears. Define the *area under* T, denoted by $U(T)$, as

$$U(T) = \sum_{i=1}^{wt(T)} (maxht(T) - l_i),$$

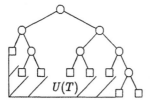

Figure 1: The "area" represented by $U(T)$

$$
\begin{array}{r}
Bin(\lceil h/2\rceil - 1) \\
Bin(\lceil (h-1)/2\rceil - 1) \\
Bin(\lceil (h-2)/2\rceil - 1) \\
\\
Bin(1) \\
Bin(1) \\
Bin(0) \\
Bin(0)
\end{array}
$$

Figure 2: The definition of $Skinny(h)$

the sum subtracted from the right side of Equation 1. The sum $U(T)$ is the nodeless "area" under the external nodes of tree T; see Figure 1. We can rewrite the equation for $IPL(T)$, Equation 1, using the definition of $U(T)$, to arrive at

$$IPL(T) = maxht(T) \cdot wt(T) + 1 - (U(T) + wt(T)).$$

Hence, if we derive a lower bound for $U(T) + wt(T)$, then we obtain an upper bound for $IPL(T)$. Let us now examine a family of red-black trees that, as we shall see, minimize $U(T) + wt(T)$ among the red-black trees of the same maxheight.

We begin by defining the skinniest trees of a given maxheight h, the $Skinny(h)$ trees; the definition is given in Figure 2. (Note: $Bin(h)$ is the complete binary tree of maxheight h.) In fact, there is more than one skinny tree of maxheight h; $Skinny(h)$ is a family of trees of maxheight h, each of which look like the tree displayed in Figure 2 with some sibling subtrees interchanged. Each $Skinny(h)$ tree has a "spine" (a longest root-to-external-node path) with pairs of complete binary trees hanging from the spine, starting with a pair of $Bin(0)$ trees at the bottom and increasing up to a $Bin(\lceil h/2\rceil - 1)$ tree as a child of the root. For convenience, we use $Skinny(h)$ to denote both the family of trees of maxheight h and individual trees in the family.

We will show that the $Skinny(h)$ trees minimize the value of $U(T) + wt(T)$ among all red-black trees T with maxheight h. As a first step, we obtain a lower bound for $U(Skinny(h)) + wt(Skinny(h))$.

Lemma 2.1 The weight of $Skinny(h)$ is given by

$$
wt(Skinny(h)) = \begin{cases} 2 \cdot 2^{h/2} - 1, & \text{if } h \text{ is even} \\ 3 \cdot 2^{(h-1)/2} - 1, & \text{if } h \text{ is odd} \end{cases}
$$

and this is the minimum weight among all red-black trees of maxheight h. The area under $Skinny(h)$

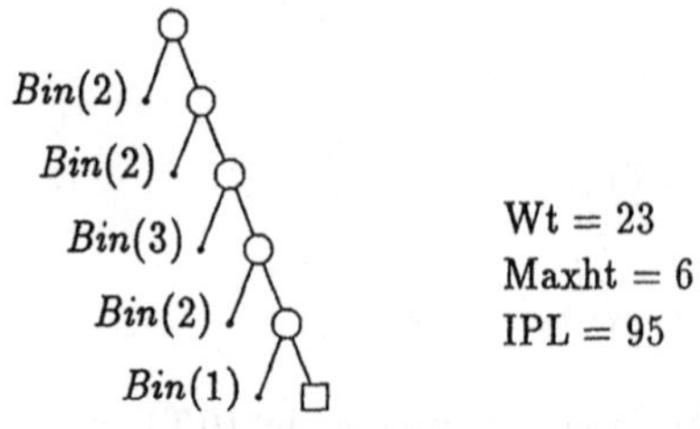

$$
\begin{array}{l}
Bin(2) \\
Bin(2) \\
Bin(3) \\
Bin(2) \\
Bin(1)
\end{array}
$$

Wt = 23
Maxht = 6
IPL = 95

Figure 3: A red-black tree with the same weight but larger IPL than $Skinny(7)$ (Note: $IPL(Skinny(7)) = 88$)

is given by

$$
U(Skinny(h)) = \begin{cases} (h-3)2^{h/2} + 3, & \text{if } h \text{ is even} \\ 3/2 \cdot (h-3)2^{(h-1)/2} + 3, & \text{if } h \text{ is odd.} \end{cases}
$$

Corollary 2.2 *If $h \geq 4$, then*

$$
U(Skinny(h)) + wt(Skinny(h)) \geq h2^{(h-1)/2}.
$$

Even though (as we will prove next) $Skinny(h)$ minimizes $U(T) + wt(T)$ among all red-black trees with maxheight h, $Skinny(h)$ does not necessarily have the maximum internal path length among all red-black trees of the same weight; see Figure 3.

We show that $Skinny(h)$ minimizes the value of $U(T) + wt(T)$ among all red-black trees T of maxheight h.

Definition 2.2 *The replacement of an external node in a binary tree by a new internal node with two external node children is called a* simple insertion. *That is, a simple insertion is the insertion of new node without any adjustments made to the structure of the tree to retain some desired property (for example, the red-black property).*

First, we show that any red-black tree of maxheight h can be produced from some tree in the family of $Skinny(h)$ trees by a series of simple insertions. Cameron and Wood [CW89] show that each intermediate tree produced by the series of simple insertions is also a red-black tree. Then we show that a series of simple insertions does not decrease the value of $U(T) + wt(T)$. Thus, we will conclude that $Skinny(h)$ minimizes $U(T) + wt(T)$ among all red-black trees of maxheight h.

Suppose T' is some red-black tree of maxheight h. Choose some longest root-to-external-node path P in T', and let it be the spine of T'; see Figure 4. Now choose the member T of $Skinny(h)$ the shape of whose spine matches that of the spine of T'. We want a sequence of simple insertions that changes $Skinny(h)$ tree T into tree T'. The sequence must transform each $Bin(\lceil (h-j+1)/2 \rceil - 1)$ subtree hanging from the node on level $j-1$ of the spine of $Skinny(h)$ tree T into the corresponding subtree T'_j hanging from the spine of T'. The following lemma tells us when a red-black subtree can be obtained from a complete binary tree by a sequence of simple insertions.

Lemma 2.3 *Let T be a red-black tree with $maxht(T) = h$ and $minht(T) = k \geq j$. There exists a sequence of simple insertions that can be applied to $Bin(j)$ to produce tree T.*

Proof: (Sketch) We examine the reverse sequence. We show that by starting at the level $h-1$, we can remove internal nodes (replace an internal node and its two external node children by an external node) one by one until we are left with $Bin(j)$. Reversing the order of removals, we obtain

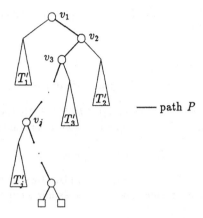

Figure 4: The path P in tree T' and the subtrees hanging from it

the desired sequence of simple insertions transforming $Bin(j)$ into tree T. □

Next, we must show that the subtree T'_j satisfies $minht(T'_j) \geq \lceil (h-j+1)/2 - 1 \rceil$ to prove that the $Bin(\lceil (h-j+1)/2 - 1\rceil)$ subtree hanging from the spine of $Skinny(h)$ tree T can be transformed into the corresponding subtree T'_j of tree T'. This relation holds since the node of the spine on level $j-1$ in tree T' must satisfy the red-black property and $maxht(T') = h$.

Thus, we obtain a sequence of simple insertions that transforms $Skinny(h)$ tree T into tree T' by catenating the sequences of insertions that transform each $Bin(i)$ subtree of $Skinny(h)$ tree T into the corresponding subtree of T'.

We now show that a sequence of simple insertions cannot decrease the value of $U(T) + wt(T)$.

Theorem 2.4 *Let T and T' be binary trees such that there is a sequence I of simple insertions that transforms T into T'. Then,*

$$U(T) + wt(T) \leq U(T') + wt(T').$$

Proof: By induction on the length of the sequence I.

In the induction step, we split a non-empty sequence I into a single simple insertion followed by a shorter sequence I'. The induction hypothesis applies to the shorter sequence I'. Thus, we need to show that a single simple insertion into a binary tree T_1, resulting in binary tree T_2, does not decrease the value of $U(T_1) + wt(T_1)$. This claim can be proved by examining two cases, either the insertion increased the maxheight of the tree, or it did not.

Suppose the insertion does not increase the maxheight of the tree. Since the insertion into T_1 replaced an external node u on some level $k < h$ by an internal node with two external node children, $U(T_1)$ and $U(T_2)$ differ only with respect to node u and its replacement. The contribution of u to $U(T_1)$ is $h-k$, whereas the contribution of u's children in T_2 to $U(T_2)$ is $2(h-k-1)$. Hence,

$$U(T_2) + wt(T_2) - U(T_1) - wt(T_1) = 2(h-k-1) - (h-k) + 1 \geq 0,$$

since $k < h$.

If the insertion increases the maxheight of T_1, the amount contributed to $U(T_1)$ by each external node increases by 1, except for the amount contributed by the replaced external node, which remains at 0. This one exception is made up for by the increase in weight. Therefore,

$$U(T_2) + wt(T_2) - (U(T_1) + wt(T_1)) = wt(T_1) \geq 0.$$

□

We can now prove that any member of $Skinny(h)$ has the minimum value for $U(T) + wt(T)$ among all red-black trees T of maxheight h.

Corollary 2.5 *For any red-black tree T of maxheight h,*

$$U(T) + wt(T) \geq U(Skinny(h)) + wt(Skinny(h)).$$

By Corollary 2.2, we have $U(Skinny(h)) + wt(Skinny(h)) \leq h2^{(h-1)/2}$. By Corollary 2.5, we have $U(T) + wt(T) \geq U(Skinny(h)) + wt(Skinny(h))$, for any red-black tree of maxheight h. Therefore,

$$IPL(T) \leq h \cdot wt(T) - h2^{(h-1)/2} + 1,$$

where T is a red-black tree of maxheight h. But there may be red-black trees of different maxheights with the same weight, so we need to discover which maxheight maximizes our bound.

Theorem 2.6 *Let T be a red-black tree of size N. Then,*

$$IPL(T) \leq 2N(\log N - \log \log N) + O(N).$$

Proof: By the above discussion, we have $IPL(T) \leq h(N+1) - h2^{(h-1)/2} + 1$. Let $f(x) = x(N+1) - x2^{(x-1)/2} + 1$. This function takes its extremal value at the zero of its first derivative:

$$\frac{df}{dx} = (N+1) - \left(2^{(x-1)/2} + \frac{1}{2} \cdot \ln 2 \cdot x2^{(x-1)/2}\right).$$

Consider the second derivative of $f(x)$:

$$f''(x) = -1/2 \cdot \ln 2 \cdot 2^{(x-1)/2}(2 + 1/2 \cdot \ln 2 \cdot x).$$

Clearly, $f''(x) < 0$, for $x > 0$. Thus, $f'(x)$ is a decreasing function for $x > 0$. But,

$$
\begin{aligned}
f'(0) &= (N+1) - (2^{-1/2} + 1/2 \cdot \ln 2 \cdot 0 \cdot 2^{-1/2}) \\
&\approx (N+1) - 0.7071 \\
&> 0, \quad \text{since } N \geq 0.
\end{aligned}
$$

Therefore, $f'(x)$ has exactly one zero at some point $x_0 > 0$. Furthermore, we have $f'(x) > 0$, for $0 < x < x_0$, and we have $f'(x) < 0$, for $x_0 < x$. Thus, the zero of $f'(x)$ is a maximum of $f(x)$.

Now, we wish to find an x satisfying

$$2^{(x-1)/2}\left(1 + \frac{\ln 2}{2}x\right) = (N+1).$$

Taking logarithms on both sides, we get

$$(x-1)/2 + \log x + O(1) = \log N + O(1).$$

Adding $\log \log N - \log x$ to both sides, we get

$$
\begin{aligned}
(x-1)/2 + \log \log N &= \log N + \log\left(\frac{\log N}{x}\right) + O(1) \\
&= \log N + \log\left(\frac{(x-1)/2 + \log x + O(1)}{x}\right) + O(1) \\
&= \log N + \log\left(\frac{1}{2} + \frac{\log x + O(1)}{x}\right) + O(1) \\
&= \log N + O(1).
\end{aligned}
$$

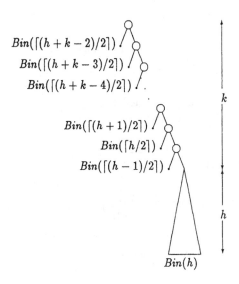

$Bin(\lceil(h+k-2)/2\rceil)$
$Bin(\lceil(h+k-3)/2\rceil)$
$Bin(\lceil(h+k-4)/2\rceil)$

$Bin(\lceil(h+1)/2\rceil)$
$Bin(\lceil h/2\rceil)$
$Bin(\lceil(h-1)/2\rceil)$

k

h

$Bin(h)$

Figure 5: A $C(k,h)$ tree

Therefore, $f(x)$ takes its maximum value at $x = 2(\log N - \log\log N) + O(1)$, and the value of $f(x)$ at that point is

$$[2(\log N - \log\log N) + O(1)](N+1)$$
$$- [2(\log N - \log\log N) + O(1)]2^{\log N - \log\log N + O(1)} + 1$$
$$= 2N(\log N - \log\log N) + 2(\log N - \log\log N) + O(1)(N+1)$$
$$- [2(\log N - \log\log N) + O(1)]\frac{N}{\log N}2^{O(1)} + 1$$
$$= 2N(\log N - \log\log N) + O(N).$$

$\square$

Having established an upper bound on the internal path length, we now prove that it is asymptotically tight. We present a class of red-black trees, some of which achieve the upper bound for the internal path length presented above. These are the $C(k,h)$ trees. Their definition is given in Figure 5.

Lemma 2.7 *The weight of a $C(k,h)$ tree is*

$$2^h + (2 + (h+k) \bmod 2)2^{\lfloor(h+k)/2\rfloor} - (2 + h \bmod 2)2^{\lfloor h/2\rfloor}.$$

Now we show that the $C(k,h)$ trees achieve the upper bound for the internal path length when k is chosen appropriately.

Theorem 2.8 *Let $k = h - 2\log h + \epsilon$, where $|\epsilon| \le \frac{1}{2}$, and let $C(k,h)$ have size N. Then, $IPL(C(k,h)) = 2N(\log N - \log\log N) + O(N)$.*

Proof: First, we show that $maxht(C(k,h)) = h + k = 2(\log N - \log\log N) + O(1)$.
Since $k = h - 2\log h + \epsilon$, we have

$$h + k = 2(h - \log h) + \epsilon$$
$$= 2\log\frac{2^h}{h} + \epsilon. \tag{2}$$

Now,

$$\begin{aligned} wt(C(k,h)) &= 2^h + (2 + (h+k) \bmod 2)2^{\lfloor (h+k)/2 \rfloor} - (2 + h \bmod 2)2^{\lfloor h/2 \rfloor} \\ &= 2^h + 2^{(h+k)/2 + 1 + \epsilon_1} - 2^{h/2 + 1 + \epsilon_2}, \end{aligned}$$

where

$$\epsilon_1 = \begin{cases} 0 & \text{if } (h+k) \bmod 2 = 0 \\ \log 3 - \frac{3}{2} \approx .08496 & \text{otherwise} \end{cases}$$

and

$$\epsilon_2 = \begin{cases} 0 & \text{if } h \bmod 2 = 0 \\ \log 3 - \frac{3}{2} \approx .08496 & \text{otherwise.} \end{cases}$$

Thus, we have

$$wt(C(k,h)) = 2^h + (\sqrt{2})^{h+k}(2^{1+\epsilon_1} - \frac{2^{1+\epsilon_2}}{(\sqrt{2})^k}). \tag{3}$$

¿From Equation (2), we get

$$(\sqrt{2})^{h+k} = (\sqrt{2})^{2\log \frac{2^h}{h} + \epsilon} = \frac{2^h}{h}2^{\epsilon/2}.$$

Substituting this into Equation 3, we have

$$\begin{aligned} wt(C(k,h)) &= 2^h \left(1 + \frac{2^{\epsilon/2}}{h}\left(2^{1+\epsilon_1} - \frac{2^{1+\epsilon_2}}{(\sqrt{2})^k}\right)\right) \tag{4} \\ &= (\sqrt{2})^{h+k}\left(\frac{h}{2^{\epsilon/2}} + \left(2^{1+\epsilon_1} - \frac{2^{1+\epsilon_2}}{(\sqrt{2})^k}\right)\right). \tag{5} \end{aligned}$$

Taking logarithms on both sides of Equation (5), we obtain

$$\log N + O(1) = \frac{h+k}{2} + \log\left(\frac{h}{2^{\epsilon/2}} + \left(2^{1+\epsilon_1} - \frac{2^{1+\epsilon_2}}{(\sqrt{2})^k}\right)\right) \tag{6}$$

and, from Equation (4), we get

$$\log N + O(1) = h + \log\left(1 + \frac{2^{\epsilon/2}}{h}\left(2^{1+\epsilon_1} - \frac{2^{1+\epsilon_2}}{(\sqrt{2})^k}\right)\right).$$

But,

$$2^{1+\epsilon_1} - \frac{2^{1+\epsilon_2}}{(\sqrt{2})^k} < 2^2$$

so

$$h = \log N + O(1).$$

Returning to Equation (6), we see that

$$\begin{aligned} \log\left(\frac{h}{2^{\epsilon/2}} + \left(2^{1+\epsilon_1} - \frac{2^{1+\epsilon_2}}{(\sqrt{2})^k}\right)\right) \\ = \log \frac{h}{2^{\epsilon/2}} + O(1) \\ = \log h - \frac{\epsilon}{2} + O(1) \\ = \log h + O(1) \\ = \log\log N + O(1), \quad \text{since } h = \log N + O(1). \end{aligned}$$

Substituting this into Equation (6), we have

$$\log N + O(1) = \frac{h+k}{2} + \log\log N + O(1),$$

or

$$h + k = 2(\log N - \log\log N) + O(1),$$

as required.

Now, we show that $U(C(k,h)) = O(N)$. Because $C(k,h)$ is $Skinny(h+k)$ with the area beneath some of the external nodes of $Skinny(h + k)$ completely filled in, we know that $U(C(k,h)) \leq U(Skinny(h + k))$. There are two cases to consider: $h + k$ is even and $h + k$ is odd.

- $h + k$ is even.

  Then,

  $$\begin{aligned}
  U(C(k,h)) &\leq U(Skinny(h + k)) \\
  &= (h + k - 3)2^{(h+k)/2} + 3 \\
  &= [2(\log N - \log\log N) + O(1) - 3]\frac{N}{\log N}2^{O(1)} + 3 \\
  &= 2^{O(1)}[2N - 2\frac{\log\log N}{\log N} + O(1)\frac{N}{\log N}] + 3 \\
  &= O(N).
  \end{aligned}$$

- $h + k$ is odd.

  Then,

  $$\begin{aligned}
  U(C(k,h)) &\leq U(Skinny(h + k)) \\
  &= \frac{3}{2}(h + k - 3)2^{(h+k-1)/2} + 3 \\
  &= \frac{3}{2}[2(\log N - \log\log N) + O(1) - 3]\frac{N}{\log N}\frac{2^{O(1)}}{2} + 3 \\
  &= 2^{O(1)}\frac{3}{4}[2N - 2\frac{\log\log N}{\log N} + O(1)\frac{N}{\log N}] + 3 \\
  &= O(N).
  \end{aligned}$$

In both cases, $U(C(k,h)) = O(N)$, and by Lemma 1,

$$\begin{aligned}
IPL(C(k,h)) &= (maxht(C(k,h)) - 1)(N + 1) + 1 - U(C(k,h)) \\
&= [2(\log N - \log\log N) + O(1)](N + 1) + 1 - O(N) \\
&= 2N(\log N - \log\log N) + O(N).
\end{aligned}$$

$\square$

Acknowledgements

This research was partially supported by Grant A-5692 from the Natural Sciences and Engineering Research Council of Canada and partially supported by a grant from the Information Technology Research Centre.

References

[Bay72]   R. Bayer. Symmetric binary B-trees: Data structure and maintenance algorithms. *Acta Informatica*, 1(4):290–306, 1972.

[CW89]   Helen Cameron and Derick Wood. The internal path length of red-black trees. Research Report CS-89-50, University of Waterloo, 1989.

[GS78]   L.J. Guibas and R. Sedgewick. A dichromatic framework for balanced trees. In *Proceedings of the 19th Annual IEEE Symposium on Foundations of Computer Science*, pages 8–21, 1978.

[Knu73]   Donald E. Knuth. *The Art of Computer Programming, Vol. 1: Fundamental Algorithms*. Addison-Wesley, Reading, MA, 1973.

[KW90]   Rolf Klein and Derick Wood. A tight upper bound for the path length of AVL trees. *Theoretical Computer Science*, 72:251–264, 1990.

[MPRS79] Raymond E. Miller, Nicholas Pippenger, Arnold L. Rosenberg, and Lawrence Snyder. Optimal 2-3-trees. *SIAM Journal on Computing*, 8(1):42–59, 1979.

[Oli82]   H.J. Olivié. A new class of balanced search trees: Half-balanced binary search trees. *RAIRO Informatique Théorique*, 16:51–71, 1982.

[OW82]   Th. Ottmann and D. Wood. A comparison of iterative and defined classes of search trees. *International Journal of Computer and Information Sciences*, 11(3):155–178, June 1982.

[Tar83]   Robert Endre Tarjan. Updating a balanced search tree in $O(1)$ rotations. *Information Processing Letters*, 16:253–257, 1983.

Balance in AVL Trees

Helen Cameron   Derick Wood

Data Structuring Group
Department of Computer Science
University of Waterloo
Waterloo, Ontario N2L 3G1
CANADA

Abstract

We characterize a family of AVL trees that have the maximum numbers of unbalanced nodes, nodes whose subtrees differ in height by one, for their heights and weights.

1 Introduction

In AVL trees, the heights of two subtrees rooted at sibling nodes can differ by at most one. (If the two sibling subtrees do not have the same height, then the parent of the two subtrees is said to be *unbalanced.*) This restriction keeps the search tree from being skewed too far from height $\lceil \log_2(N+1) \rceil$, the height of binary trees of size N with optimal comparison cost. For each size, there is an AVL tree that is comparison-cost optimal and also contains the fewest number of unbalanced nodes for AVL trees of that size, see [OPR+84]. However, characterizing pessimal comparison cost AVL trees seems to be a hard problem (see [KW90] and [KW89]). Perhaps the characterization of pessimally balanced AVL trees (that is, those with the largest numbers of unbalanced nodes for their sizes) will lead to new results on pessimal comparison cost AVL trees.

In [Knu73], it was shown that a balanced tree with N internal nodes never contains more than $(\phi - 1)N \approx 0.61803N$ unbalanced nodes and that Fibonacci AVL trees contain the most unbalanced nodes among all AVL trees with the same number of internal nodes. This result was duplicated in [KW87] using a more structural argument. The fringe analysis technique developed by [Yao78] was used by [Bro79] to derive bounds on the expected number of balanced nodes in AVL trees. An improvement of this result was derived in [Meh79] using the 1-2 brother trees of [OS76] and their close relationship with AVL trees (see [OW80]). A fringe analysis of AVL trees under random insertions and deletions was derived in [Meh82]. Using a larger tree collection than [Bro79], the following bounds were derived in [BYGZ89]:

$$0.56 + \frac{0.56}{N} \leq \frac{\bar{b}(N)}{N} \leq 0.79 - \frac{0.21}{N},$$

for $N \geq 20$, where $\bar{b}(N)$ is the expected number of balanced nodes in an AVL tree after the random insertion of N keys into an initially empty tree.

In this paper, we characterize a family of AVL trees, each with the maximum number of unbalanced nodes among all AVL trees of its size and height. We say that these trees are *locally pessimally balanced.* We must examine all the trees in this family with a given size to determine the heights of the AVL trees with the maximum number of unbalanced nodes for the given size.

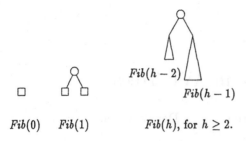

$Fib(0)$ $\qquad$ $Fib(1)$ $\qquad\qquad$ $Fib(h)$, for $h \geq 2$.

Figure 1: The recursive definition of Fibonacci AVL trees

2 Definitions

If a node has at least one child, it is *internal*; otherwise it is *external*. The *weight* of a tree, T, is denoted by $wt(T)$ and is defined as the number of external nodes. The *height* of a tree, T, is denoted by $ht(T)$ and is defined as the length of the longest root-to-leaf path. The *level* of a node p in tree T is its distance from the root of T; the root of T is at level 0, its children are at level 1, and so on.

Definition 2.1 *A complete binary tree of height h (a $Bin(h)$ tree) has external nodes only on level h. That is, in a $Bin(h)$ tree, level i contains 2^i binary internal nodes, for all i, $0 \leq i < h$, and level h contains 2^h external nodes.*

Definition 2.2 *A tree, T, has a complete binary prefix of height p (a $Bin(p)$ prefix), for some $1 \leq p \leq ht(T)$, if level i contains 2^i internal nodes, for $0 \leq i < p$.*

Every non-empty binary tree has at least a $Bin(1)$ prefix, because the root of a non-empty binary tree is binary.

Our characterization uses the definition of the *Fibonacci trees*, which are defined in Figure 1.

The Fibonacci numbers are defined by $f_0 = 0$, $f_1 = 1$, and $f_{i+2} = f_{i+1} + f_i$, for all $i \geq 0$. We also make use of the Fibonacci numbering system.

Theorem 2.1 ([Lek52]) *Every positive integer n has a unique representation $n = f_{k_1} + f_{k_2} + \ldots + f_{k_r}$, where $k_i \geq k_{i+1} + 2$, for $1 \leq i < r$, and $k_r \geq 2$.*

3 Characterizing Pessimally Balanced AVL Trees

Now we characterize a family of AVL trees that have the maximum numbers of unbalanced nodes for their weights and heights in the following theorem. The family is pictured in Figure 2.

Theorem 3.1 *Let w and h be integers such that $f_{h+2} \leq w \leq 2^h$. Then, there exists an AVL tree, T, of weight w and height h that contains the maximum number of unbalanced nodes for an AVL tree of weight w and height h, and AVL tree T is completely described by the following:*

1. *Levels $0, \ldots, p-1$ are completely binary, where p is the largest integer such that $2^{p-1} \cdot f_{h-p+3} \leq w$.*

2. *If $p < h$, then the 2^{p-1} subtrees rooted at level $p-1$ can be divided into the following groups:*

    (a) *Each of s nodes on level $p-1$ is the parent of two Fibonacci AVL trees of height $h-p$, where*
    $$\frac{w - 2^{p-1} \cdot f_{h-p+3} - f_{h-p}}{f_{h-p}} < s \leq \frac{w - 2^{p-1} \cdot f_{h-p+3}}{f_{h-p}}.$$

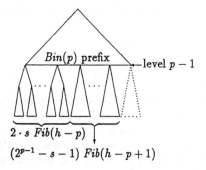

The form of AVL tree T, except for the rightmost subtree rooted at level $p - 1$.

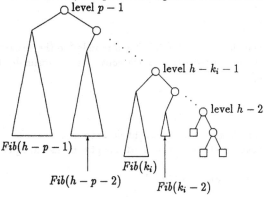

The rightmost subtree rooted at level $p - 1$.

Figure 2: An AVL tree T with height h and weight w that contains the maximum number of unbalanced nodes for an AVL tree of that height and weight

(b) *A further $2^{p-1} - s - 1$ nodes on level $p-1$ are the roots of Fibonacci AVL trees of height $h - p + 1$.*

(c) *Let $\sum_{i=1}^{r} f_{k_i}$ be the unique Fibonacci representation of*

$$w - 2^{p-1} \cdot f_{h-p+3} - s \cdot f_{h-p}.$$

The final subtree rooted at level $p-1$ consists of a chain of binary nodes of length $h-p+1$. Each node on the chain (except the last one) has a child that is the next node in the chain and one other child. (The last node in the chain has two external children.) The other child of the binary node on level j in tree T is the root of a Fibonacci AVL tree of height $h - j - 2$, except when $j = h - k_i - 1$. When $j = h - k_i - 1$, the other child is the root of a Fibonacci AVL tree of height k_i.

Proof: See [CW89]. □

Using the results of Theorem 3.1 and the fact that f_h is $\phi^h/\sqrt{5}$ rounded to the nearest integer, where $\phi = (1 + \sqrt{5})/2$, we have the following algorithm which constructs a pessimally balanced AVL tree of a given weight w and height h.

Construct(w, h)

```
{ Construct an AVL tree T of weight w and height h with the maximum
number of unbalanced nodes among all AVL trees of weight w and height h. }
```

```
{ Calculate the height of the binary prefix. }
```

$p = \lfloor (\log \sqrt{5}w - (h + 3) \log \phi + \log 2)/(\log 2 - \log \phi) \rfloor$
if $2^p \cdot f_{h-p+2} \le w$ **then** $p = p + 1$.
if $p = h$ **then**
    T is a $Bin(h)$ tree.
else begin

    ```
    { Fill levels 0 to p − 2 of tree T with binary internal nodes. }
    ```

    for $i = 0$ **to** $p - 2$ **do begin**
        Put 2^i binary internal nodes on level i.
    end

    ```
    { Now attach the appropriate subtrees on level p − 1. }
    ```

    $s = \lfloor (w - 2^{p-1} \cdot f_{h-p+3})/f_{h-p} \rfloor$
    Fill each of s of the 2^{p-1} empty places on level $p - 1$ with a subtree
    consising of a root with two $Fib(h - p)$ children.
    $ExtraWt = w - 2^{p-1} \cdot f_{h-p+3} - s \cdot f_{h-p}$
    if $ExtraWt = 0$ **then**
        Fill all remaining $2^{p-1} - s$ space on level $p - 1$ with $Fib(h - p + 1)$
        subtrees.
    else begin
        Fill all but one of the remaining $2^{p-1} - s$ spaces on level $p - 1$
        with $Fib(h - p + 1)$ subtrees.

        ```
        { Create the subtree to fill the one empty space on level p − 1. }
        ```

Make a chain of $h - p + 1$ binary internal nodes (one per level).
Give the bottom node of the chain two external node children.

{ So far, each node on the chain (except the bottom one) has only
one child. Now create the other child for each node, starting at
the root. The root of the chain is on level $p - 1$ of the whole
tree, and the two children of the bottom node are on level h. }

$prevk = h$
while $ExtraWt > 0$ do begin

    { Find the largest Fibonacci number no larger than $ExtraWt$. }

    $k = \lfloor \log(\sqrt{5} ExtraWt)/\log \phi \rfloor$
    if $f_{k+1} \leq ExtraWt$ then $k = k + 1$.
    for $i = 0$ to $k - 1$ do begin
        Give the node in the chain on level $h - i - 1$ a
        $Fib(i - 1)$ subtree as a child.
    end
    Give the node in the chain on level $h - k - 1$ a $Fib(k)$
    subtree as a child.
    $ExtraWt = ExtraWt - f_k$
end
for $i = k + 1$ to 1 do begin
    Give the node in the chain on level $h - i - 1$ a $Fib(i - 1)$
    subtree as a child.
end
    end
  end

In one of our pessimally balanced AVL trees, the two children of each of the nodes on levels
$0, \ldots, p - 2$ both reach all the way to level h; that is, the nodes on levels $0, \ldots, p - 2$ are balanced.
Therefore, to count the number of unbalanced nodes in such an AVL tree, we sum the number of
unbalanced nodes in the subtrees on levels $p - 1, \ldots, h$. Since most of these subtrees are Fibonacci
subtrees, we make use of the following theorem.

Theorem 3.2 *A Fibonacci tree of height h contains $f_{h+1} - 1$ unbalanced nodes.*

Corollary 3.3 *The maximum number of unbalanced nodes that an AVL tree of weight w and height
h can contain is*

$$2^{p-1} \cdot (f_{h-p+2} - 1) + s \cdot (f_{h-p-1} - 1) + \sum_{i=1}^{r}(f_{k_i-1} - 1),$$

where p is the largest integer such that $2^{p-1} \cdot f_{h-p+3} \leq w$, s is defined by

$$\frac{w - 2^{p-1} \cdot f_{h-p+3} - f_{h-p}}{f_{h-p}} < s \leq \frac{w - 2^{p-1} \cdot f_{h-p+3}}{f_{h-p}},$$

and $\sum_{i=1}^{r} f_{k_i}$ is the unique Fibonacci representation of

$$w - 2^{p-1} \cdot f_{h-p+3} - s \cdot f_{h-p}.$$

4 Conclusion

Although we have characterized AVL trees with the maximum numbers of unbalanced nodes for their heights and weights, there remain some unanswered questions.

The most obvious problem left open is the characterization of pessimally unbalanced AVL trees for a given weight. Experimental evidence suggests that the pessimally unbalanced AVL trees of a given weight have the maximum height for AVL trees of that weight. So far, we have not been able to prove this conjecture.

Also, the relationship between unbalanced AVL trees and comparison cost pessimal AVL trees remains an open problem.

Acknowledgements

This research was partially supported by Grant A-5692 from the Natural Sciences and Engineering Research Council of Canada and partially supported by a grant from the Information Technology Research Centre.

References

[Bro79]   M. Brown. A partial analysis of random height-balanced trees. *SIAM Journal on Computing*, 8(1):33–41, February 1979.

[BYGZ89] Ricardo A. Baeza-Yates, Gaston H. Gonnet, and Nivio Ziviani. Expected behaviour analysis of AVL trees. To appear, 1989.

[CW89]   Helen Cameron and Derick Wood. Unbalanced AVL trees and space pessimal brother trees. Research Report CS-89-20, University of Waterloo, 1989.

[Knu73]   Donald E. Knuth. *The Art of Computer Programming, Vol. 3: Sorting and Searching.* Addison-Wesley, Reading, MA, 1973.

[KW87]   Rolf Klein and Derick Wood. On the space cost of brother trees or: How unbalanced can an AVL tree be? See also Knuth, Vol. 3, page 470, Exercise 3, 1987.

[KW89]   Rolf Klein and Derick Wood. On the path length of binary trees. *Journal of the Association for Computing Machinery*, 36(2):280–289, 1989.

[KW90]   Rolf Klein and Derick Wood. A tight upper bound for the path length of AVL trees. *Theoretical Computer Science*, 72:251–264, 1990.

[Lek52]   C. G. Lekkerkerker. Voorstelling van natuurlijke getallen door een som van getallen van fibonacci. *Simon Stevin*, 29:190–195, 1952.

[Meh79]   K. Mehlhorn. A partial analysis of height-balanced trees. Report A 79/13, Universität des Saarlandes, Saarbrucken, West Germany, 1979.

[Meh82]   K. Mehlhorn. A partial analysis of height-balanced trees under random insertions and deletions. *SIAM Journal on Computing*, 11:748–760, 1982.

[OPR+84] Thomas Ottmann, D. Stott Parker, Arnold L. Rosenberg, Hans-Werner Six, and Derick Wood. Minimal-cost brother trees. *SIAM Journal on Computing*, 13(1):197–217, 1984.

[OS76]   Thomas Ottmann and Hans W. Six. Eine neueu Klasse von ausgeglichen Binärbäumen. *Angewandte Informatik*, 9:395–400, 1976.

[OW80]   T. Ottmann and D. Wood. 1-2 brother trees or AVL trees revisited. *The Computer Journal*, 23(3):248–255, August 1980.

[Yao78]   Andrew Chi-Chih Yao. On random 2-3 trees. *Acta Informatica*, 9:159–170, 1978.

A TIGHT LOWER BOUND FOR SELECTION IN
SORTED X+Y

Michel Cosnard   Afonso G. Ferreira[1]
LIP - IMAG / CNRS
Ecole Normale Supérieure de Lyon
69364 Lyon Cédex 07
e-mail: ferreira@lip.ens-lyon.fr

Abstract: The complexity of the problem of selecting the k-th element of a sorted matrix is known. In this note we show a lower bound for such a problem in sorted X+Y. This lower bound is tight since the upper bound for sorted matrices holds for sorted X+Y.

INTRODUCTION

Let A be a matrix such that the elements in each row and in each column respect some given order. We call A a matrix with sorted rows and columns or a *sorted matrix*, for short. Let $X = (x_1, x_2, \ldots x_n)$ and $Y = (y_1, y_2, \ldots y_n)$ be two vectors. The *Cartesian sum* X + Y is the n x n matrix where $a_{ij} = x_i + y_j$ can be computed in constant time. If X and Y are sorted, then X + Y is a special case of sorted matrices: *sorted X+Y*. The advantage of such sets is that they have n^2 elements but require only 2n space to be represented. Sorting, searching and selection in such data structures received considerable attention, due to their application in statistics, VLSI design, operations research and combinatorics ([CDF], [FJ2], [HPSS], [Lam], [LS], [MA]).

Searching
Despite being a problem only recently proposed in terms of sorted matrices and sorted X+Y, searching such structures for a given element has many reported applications. Both for sorted matrices and for X+Y, the time complexity of the searching problem is $\Theta(n)$ ([CDF],[LS]).

Sorting
The related problem of sorting has also been studied. It was shown that $\Theta(n^2 \log n)$ comparisons are both necessary and sufficient to build a sorted vector with all the elements of a sorted matrix. This sorting algorithm requires $O(n^2)$ space. On the other hand, if only $O(n)$ space is allowed then the generation of all the elements of X + Y in a sequential, sorted way, can be done in $O(n^2 \log n)$ time ([HPSS], [CDF]). Regarding sorting sorted X+Y, there is an algorithm that requires only $O(n^2)$ comparisons to sort

---

[1] On leave from the University of Sao Paulo, Brazil. Member of the BID/USP project.

the elements of sorted X+Y ([Lam]), which closes a question left open by the non-constructive proof of this fact proposed in [Fre].

Selection

Let *selection problem* stand for the problem of selecting the k-th smallest element of a given set. For X and Y unsorted, the time complexity of the selection problem is well characterized in $\Theta(n\log n)$, as well as for matrices with sorted column ([FJ1]). In [FJ2] the complexity of the selection problem in sorted matrices was proved to be $\Theta(k^{1/2})$. Notice that this result implies an upper bound of $O(k^{1/2})$ for the same problem on sorted X + Y. In this note we prove that this bound is tight by showing a family of sorted X+Y sets for which the selection problem requires at least $\Omega(k^{1/2})$ time.

THE LOWER BOUND

Selection has been the most studied problem in sorted matrices and X + Y. Recall that selecting the k-th smallest element in an unconstrained set has time complexity $\Theta(n)$ [BFPRT]. However, unlike selection in unconstrained sets, the lower bound for selection in sorted matrices depend asymptotically on the rank k of the element being selected. Examples of applications of the selection problem in sorted matrices can be found in [FJ2].

Since the number of total orders over a sorted X+Y matrix is less than the same number over a sorted matrix, one could be tempted to think that the selection problem on the former set would be easier than the same problem on the latter set. Notice that this is so for the problem of searching sorted multisets (sets of the form $X_1+X_2+...+X_m$) in comparison with the problem of searching sorted matrices ([CDF]). Unfortunately, however, we prove that the same lower bound proved for selection in sorted matrices holds also for sorted X+Y.

Let a vector D with q elements be given. The median of D refers to its (q/2)-th smallest element. We prove the proposed lower bound by deriving a family of sorted X+Y sets such that selecting the k-th element of such sets in time less than $O(k^{1/2})$ induces an algorithm to find the median of D in time less than $O(q)$. As D is a non sorted q-vector, computing its median takes $\Omega(q)$, which leads to a contradiction.

Let $D = \{\beta_i\}$, $0 \le \beta_i < M$; $i = 1,...,q$; for a given M.   (1)

Define X and Y as follows (remark that they are increasingly sorted) :

$$x_i = (i-1).M + \beta_i ; i = 1,...,n \qquad (2)$$

$$y_j = (j-q).M \; ; \; j = 1,\dots,n \tag{3}$$

Proposition 1. *Let X and Y be defined as above and* $A = X + Y = \{x_i + y_j \mid i,j = 1,2,\dots,n\}$. *Let U be the set of the q-th antidiagonal elements of* A : $U = \{u_i = x_i + y_j \mid i+j = q+1\}$. *Then* $u_i = \beta_i$ *(i.e.,* $U = D$).

Proof :

$$u_i = x_i + y_{q+1-i} = (i-1).M + \beta_i + (q+1-i-q).M =$$
$$= (i-1+1-i).M + \beta_i = \beta_i.$$

[]

Proposition 2. *Let U be defined as above. Let* $SU = \{x_i + y_j \mid i+j < q+1\}$ *be the set of the elements of A at left of U and* $BU = \{x_i + y_j \mid i+j > q+1\}$ *be the set of the elements of A at right of U. Let u be any element of U. Then :* 2.1. $\forall \, s \in SU, s < u.$

2.2. $\forall \, b \in BU, b > u.$

Proof :

(2.1) $s \in SU$

$\Rightarrow s = x_i + y_j \mid i+j < q+1$

$\Rightarrow s = (i-1).M + \beta_i + (j-q).M = (i+j-(q+1)).M + \beta_i$

$\Rightarrow s \le \beta_j - M$

$\Rightarrow s < 0$ by (1)

$\Rightarrow s < u$ by proposition 1

(2.2) Analogous to 2.1.

[]

In other words, proposition 1 states that $U = D$ separates A into two special sets : the triangle part at upper left of $X + Y$ (SU) with elements that are smaller than those of U and the triangle part below and at right of $X + Y$ (BU) that only contains elements larger than those of U. Furthermore the former order inside the set D is respected inside the set U.

Lemma *Let X and Y be two sorted vectors of n elements. If there exists an algorithm for selecting the p-th smallest element of X+Y in T(p) time then there exists an algorithm for finding the median of an unsorted set with q elements in time $O(T(q^2/2))$, $q \leq n$.*

Proof :

Let **Alg**(p,X,Y) be such an algorithm, and M,D,X and Y be as defined in (1) through (3).

We modify **Alg** to **Med**(D), , in the following way :

a) Each reference to X[i] in **Alg** is changed to (i-1).M + D[i] in **Med**.

b) Each reference to Y[j] in **Alg** is changed to (j-q).M in **Med**.

c) Each reference to p in **Alg** is changed to $(q/2 + (q^2-q)/2)$ $= q^2/2$ in **Med**.

Since the cardinality of SU is $(q^2-q)/2$ then, by proposition 2, the $(q^2/2)$-th smallest element of X + Y belongs to the set U. Moreover it is the median of U and hence (proposition 1) the median of D.

As the modifications a, b and c increase T(p) by only a constant factor, then the complexity of **Med**(D) is the complexity of selecting the $(q^2/2)$-th smallest element in X + Y ; i.e., $O(T((q^2/2))$.

◻

Theorem *Let X and Y be sorted vectors of length n. Then the selection problem in X + Y takes $\Omega(k^{1/2})$ time.*

Proof :

It follows immediately from the Lemma above and the obvious lower bound $(\Omega(q))$ for finding the median of non-sorted sets with q elements.

◻

This result was proved for sorted X + Y, then, as a consequence, we deduce a new proof for the lower bound of the selection problem in sorted matrices:

Corollary *The selection problem in sorted matrices takes $\Omega(k^{1/2})$ time.*

REFERENCES

[BFPRT] : M.Blum, R.W.Floyd, V.Pratt, R.L.Rivest and R.E.Tarjan, "Time bounds for selection", *JCSS*, 7 (1973), pp 448-461

[CDF] : M.Cosnard, J.Duprat and A.G.Ferreira, "The complexity of searching in X + Y and other multisets", *Information Processing Letters*, 34 (1990) 103-109

[Fre] : M.L.Fredman, "Two applications of a probabilistic search technique : sorting X + Y and building balanced search trees", in *Proc. 7-th Annual ACM Symp. on Theory of Computing*, (May 1975), ACM, 1975, pp 240-244

[FJ1] : G.N.Frederickson and D.B.Johnson, "The complexity of selection and ranking in X + Y and matrices with sorted columns", *JCSS* 24 (1982), pp 197-208

[FJ2] : G.N.Frederickson and D.B.Johnson, "Generalized selection and ranking : sorted matrices", *SIAM J. Comput.* 13 (1), Feb 1984, pp 197-208

[HPSS] : L.H.Harper, T.H.Payne, J.E.Savage and E.Straus, "Sorting X+Y", *Comm. ACM* 18 (6) (1975), pp 347-349

[Lam] : J.L.Lambert, Sorting the elements of X+Y with $O(n^2)$ comparisons, in *Proceedings of STACS 90*, Feb. 1990, Rouens, France

[LS] : N.Linial and M.Saks, "Searching ordered structures", *Journal of Algorithms* 6 (1985), pp 86-103

[MA] : A.Mirzaian and E.Arjomandi, "Selection in X+Y and matrices with sorted rows and columns", Inf. Proc. Letters 20 (1985), pp 13-17

GREEDY TRIANGULATION APPROXIMATES THE OPTIMUM AND CAN BE IMPLEMENTED IN LINEAR TIME IN THE AVERAGE CASE

Christos Levcopoulos   Andrzej Lingas

Department of Computer Science

Lund University, Box 118, 22100 Lund, Sweden

Abstract: Let S be a set of n points uniformly distributed in a unit square. We show that the expected value of the ratio between the length of the greedy triangulation of S and the minimum weight triangulation of S is constantly bounded. Our main result is an algorithm for constructing the greedy triangulation of S which runs in linear expected-time.

1. Introduction

Given a set S of n points in the plane, a *triangulation* of S is a maximal set of non-intersecting straight-line segments (diagonals) whose endpoints are in S. In numerical applications of triangulations, one of the proposed criteria of goodness involves the minimization of the total length of the diagonals in a triangulation [PS85]. A *minimum weight triangulation* of S (M(S) for short) is a triangulation of S that achieves the smallest total edge length. The complexity status of the problem of computing $M(S)$ has been open for at least a decade [A89,Ll77,PS85]. There is a known complicated polynomial-time heuristic for $M(S)$ yielding solutions within a logarithmic factor from the optimum [PH87]. The two most known, simple heuristics for $M(S)$ are the so called *greedy triangulation* and *Delaunay triangulation* ($GT(S)$ and $DT(S)$ for short, respectively) [A89,Ll77,PS85]. The former inserts a segment into the triangulation if it is a shortest among all segments between points in S not intersecting those previously inserted. The latter computes the straight-line dual of the Voronoi diagram of S completing it to a full triangulation if it is necessary. Neither approximates the optimum in the general case [Ki80,MZ79,Le87]. However, if S is convex, i.e. lies on its convex hull, the greedy triangulation yields a solution within a constant factor from the optimum [LL87]. Also, if S is uniformly distributed in a unit square then both heuristics yield solutions within a logarithmic factor from $M(S)$ *almost certainly*, i.e. with the probability $\geq 1 - cn^{-\alpha}$, $c > 0$, $\alpha > 1$ [Li86]. The above result on the Delaunay triangulation has been strengthened by showing that the expected length of $DT(S)$ is within a constant factor from the expected length of $M(S)$ [CL84]. In Section 3, we prove that the expected ratio between the length of $GT(S)$ and the length of $M(S)$ is $O(1)$. To derive this result we prove an important lemma saying that if a diagonal of S is crossed by an edge in $GT(S)$ then the length of the diagonal is at least proportional to the minimum distance between an endpoint of the edge in $GT(S)$ and a given endpoint of the diagonal.

While $DT(S)$ can be computed in time $O(n \log n)$, the most efficient, recent algorithm for $GT(S)$ runs in time $O(n^2)$ [LL90]. The algorithm uses a generalization of the algorithm from [AGSS87] for Voronoi diagram of a convex polygon.

There has been recently growing interest in finding practical algorithms for difficult planar optimization problems (see for instance the recent work due to D. Johnson on the traveling salesman problem [J90]). The practical value of such algorithms often can be confirmed by proving their efficiency on uniformly distributed input point sets.

If S is uniformly distributed in a square then $DT(S)$ can be computed in linear expected-time by using bucketing [BWY80] whereas the best known upper-bound on the expected-time performance of an algorithm for $GT(S)$ is $O(n \log^{1.5} n)$ [Li88].

In Section 4, we present an algorithm for $GT(S)$ that runs in linear expected-time if S is uniformly distributed in a unit square. Our algorithm combines the global approach of finding greedy edges based on Voronoi diagrams with barriers used in [Li88,Li89,LL90] with a dynamic local approach similar to that used in the linear expected-cost parallel algorithm for Voronoi diagrams in [LKL88].

2. Planar straight-line graphs and Voronoi diagrams with barriers

Planar point sets and simple polygons are special cases of the so called planar straight-line graphs (PSLG for short) [PS85]. A PSLG G is a pair (V, E) such that V is a set of points in the plane and E is a set of non-intersecting, open straight-line segments whose endpoints are in V. The points in V are called vertices of G, whereas the segments in E are called edges of G. If G has no edges, it is a *planar point set*. A *diagonal* of G is an open straight-line segment that neither intersects any edge of G nor includes any vertex of G and that has its endpoints in V. *Voronoi diagrams with barriers* for planar straight-line graphs are a natural generalization of standard Voronoi diagrams for planar point sets to include edges as visibility barriers [Li89].

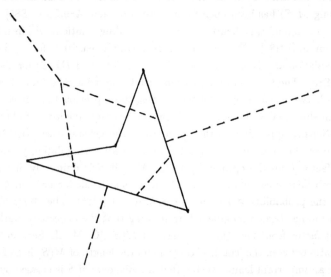

Fig. 1. The Voronoi diagram with barriers of a simple polygon

Definition 2.1: Let $G = (V, E)$ be a PSLG. For $v \in V$, the region $P(v)$ consists of all points p in the plane for which the shortest, open straight-line segment between p and a vertex of G that does not intersect any edge of G is (p, v). The minimal set of straight-line segments and half-lines that complements G to the partition of the plane into the regions $P(v)$, $v \in V$, is called the *Voronoi diagram with barriers of G* ($Vorb(G)$ for short). The maximal straight-line segments or half-lines on the boundaries of the regions $P(v)$, $v \in V$, that do not overlap with edges of G, are called edges of $Vorb(G)$. The endpoints of edges of $Vorb(G)$ are called vertices of $Vorb(G)$.

$Vorb(G)$ has several properties analogous to those of classical Voronoi diagrams (comp. [Li89]

with [PS85]). See also Fig. 1. Every edge of $Vorb(G)$ is a continuous part of the perpendicular bisector of a pair of vertices of G from which the edge is visible. Next, every vertex of $Vorb(G)$ is the common intersection of at least three edges of $Vorb(G)$ or residues inside an edge of G. For all $v \in V$, $P(v)$ is a collection of polygonal sub-regions separated by the edges incident to v. There are at most

$3n - 6$ edges in $Vorb(G)$ (see [Li89]). In [WS87], Wang and Schubert have presented an $O(n \log n)$-time algorithm for constructing the Voronoi diagram with barriers of G (called the bounded diagram of G in [WS87]).

In [Li89] the following characterization of a shortest diagonal of a PSLG has been given.

Fact 2.1 ([Li89], see also Remark 3.1 in [LL90]): A shortest diagonal of a PSLG $G = (V, E)$ either lies inside the union of the regions of its endpoints in $Vorb(G)$ (Case 1) or cuts off an empty triangular face from G and lies within at most four different regions in $Vorb(G)$, properly intersecting at most three of them (Case 2).

3. The expected length of the greedy triangulation

To prove that the expected ratio between $|GT(S)|$ and $|M(S)|$ is $O(1)$, we shall proceed as follows. First, we shall derive the key lemma which yields a lower bound on the length of a diagonal crossed by a greedy edge in terms of the minimum distance between a given endpoint of the diagonal and any endpoint of the edge (Lemma 3.1). Next, we shall introduce the notion of rough squares $SQI(s)$ of influence for sites s in S which will consist of a finite number of cells of the so called grid G_l around s. The parameter l defining the roughness of the grid will be determined by the distribution of other sites around s. Next, using the key lemma, we shall deduce that any greedy edge incident to s lies within $SQI(s)$ (Corollary 3.1). In the consecutive lemmas (Lemma 3.2, 3.3), we shall derive upper bounds on the expected size of $SQI(s)$ and the expected number of sites in $SQI(s)$. This all will enable us to estimate the expected total length of edges in $GT(S)$ incident to sites lying enough deep inside the unit square containing S (Lemma 3.4). The expected total length of the remaining edges will be estimated in Lemma 3.5. Combing the two above estimations, we shall obtain an upper bound on the expected length of $GT(S)$ which combined with the known $\Omega(\sqrt{(n)})$ bound on the length of any triangulation of S will yield the $O(1)$ bound on the expected ratio between $GT(S)$ and $M(S)$.
We start from the key lemma and its proof.

Lemma 3.1: Let S be a non-degenerate set of vertices (points) in the plane, i.e. no three vertices lie on the same line, and let v_1 and v_2 be two of the vertices in S. If there is some edge (v_1', v_2') in $GT(S)$ which crosses (v_1, v_2), then it holds that $|v_1, v_2| = \Omega(\min(|v_1, v_1'|, |v_1, v_2'|))$.
Proof: Let l be the line passing through v_1' and v_2'. For easier reference, we may assume w.l.o.g. that l is vertical, that v_1 lies to the left of l, and that $|v_1, v_1'| < |v_1, v_2'|$. Let s be the distance $|v_1, v_2|$. To prove the lemma, we hypothesize throughout the proof that $|v_1, v_1'| > 100s$, and we derive a contradiction from this hypothesis. In fact, probably any constant greater than 2 would suffice, but we use the large constant 100 to simplify the proof.
Let E' be the set of all edges in $GT(S)$ whose length is $\leq 99s$. From the definition of the GT we get that

(i) If there exist vertices v_3 and v_4 such that no edge in E' crosses the segment (v_3, v_4) and

(v_3, v_4) intersects (v_1', v_2'), then it holds that $|v_3, v_4| > 99s$ (because otherwise the edge (v_3, v_4) should be in E', which is impossible since we have assumed that (v_1', v_2') is in $GT(S)$).

To prove the lemma, it suffices to show that there are two vertices, v_3 and v_4, which do not satisfy (i).

To go on we need the following definition. A path in the plane is called *free* if it does not touch (i.e. neither intersects) any vertex of S nor any edge of E'. Let H be a path in the plane. H is called a *feasible* path if for each real r greater than zero there exists a free path H' whose length is not greater than r plus the length of H, and every point in H is within the distance r from some point of H'.

Let I be the intersection point of l with (v_1, v_2).

Proposition 3.1. If v_5, resp. v_6 are vertices to the left, resp. to the right of l, and then any feasible path connecting v_5, I and v_6 has length $> 99s$.

Proof of Proposition 3.1: Let H' be the shortest feasible path connecting v_5 to v_6, such that no vertices of S lie in any open region bounded by H and H' (if there is any such region).

A way to imagine H and H' is to think about the vertices in S and the edges in E' as being obstacles ("pins and walls") and about H as being a wire. Then H' has the shape of the wire which would be obtained if it would be "stretched" between v_6 and v_5 (without being able to cross any obstacle).

Suppose that H has length $\leq 99s$. Since both $|I, v_1'|$ and $|I, v_2'|$ are greater than $99s$, it follows that H' properly intersects (v_1', v_2') at an edge of length $\leq 99s$ connecting two vertices on either side of l, a contradiction to (i). Thus H cannot have length $\leq 99s$. Q.E.D.

Proposition 3.2. In E' there is an edge which crosses (v_1, I) and an edge which crosses (v_2, I).

Proof of Proposition 3.2: We prove the proposition for (v_1, I). The proof for (v_2, B) is symmetric. Suppose that there is no edge in E' intersecting (v_1, I). Since the edge (v_1, v_2) is not in E', there must be an edge in E' intersecting the segment (I, v_2). Let e_2 be the edge of E' with the leftmost intersection with (I, v_2), and let I_2 be that intersection. Next, let v_{e2} be the endpoint of e closest to I_2. Since e has length $\leq 99s$ and it does not intersect (v_1', v_2') both of its endpoints lie to the right of l. Thus, there is a feasible path from v_1 to v_{e2} of length $\leq 50.5s$ consisting of the segments (v_1, I_2), of length at most s, and (I_2, v_{e2}), of length at most $49.5s$, a contradiction to Proposition 3.1. Q.E.D.

By Proposition 3.2, we define e_2, I_2 and v_{e2} as in the proof of the proposition. Analogously we define e_1, I_1 and v_{e1} by substituting v_1 for v_2 and "rightmost" for "leftmost" in the definition. Let us consider the feasible path consisting of the segments $(v_{e1}, I_1), (I_1, I_2), (I_2, v_{e2})$. By the definition of v_{e1} and v_{e2} the length of these segments is not greater than $49.5s$, s and, again, $49.5s$ respectively. But since the path must be longer than $99s$ by Proposition 3.1, we conclude that both (v_{e1}, I_1) and (v_{e2}, I_2) must be longer than $48.5s$. Consequently, the distance of the other endpoint of e_1 to I_1 is between $48.5s$ and $50.5s$, and the analogous relation holds for e_2 and I_2. Thus e_1 and e_2 have length between $97s$ and $99s$, and they are almost parallel to l, i.e. almost vertical. More precisely, the euclidean distance from any endpoint of e_1 or e_2 to l is shorter than $2.5s$.

Let v_l, resp. v_r, be the uppermost endpoint of e_1, respectively e_2. By the above arguments, the length of both (v_l, I_1) and (v_r, I_2) is between $48.5s$ and $50.5s$. The difference between their x-coordinates is $\leq 5s$ and between their y-coordinates is $\leq 3s$. Let H be the feasible path consisting of the segments $(v_l, I_1), (I_1, I_2), (I_2, v_r)$. Let H' be the shortest feasible path such that every open region bounded by H' and H is empty (i.e. H' is obtained by "stretching" H). It is easily seen that there is a diagonal in H' of length $\leq 51.5s$ which intersects the segment (v_1', v_2'), a contradiction to the statement (i) above. Q.E.D.

Consider a set S of n points uniformly distributed in a unit square U. For $l = \frac{1}{2}\log\log n, ...,$ $\frac{1}{2}\log n$, let G_l be a grid that partitions U into $2^{\log n - 2l}$ equal squares $C_l(i,j)$, $i, j \in \{1, ..., 2^{\frac{1}{2}\log n - l}\}$. In the remainder of the paper we use a constant c, which should be any sufficiently large integer such that Corollary 3.1 would be correct. An integer which is sufficiently large can be derived from the proofs of Lemma 3.1 and Corollary 3.1. For $i, j \in \{1, ..., 2^{\frac{1}{2}\log n - l}\}$, let $SQ_l(i,j)$ be the smallest square that covers any square $C_l(i', j')$ where $i' \in \{i-c, i-c+1, ..., i+c\}$, $j' \in \{j-c, j-c+1, ..., j+c\}$. The term Q_l will denote the set of all the above squares $SQ_l(i,j)$. For a site s in S, the square $SQ_l(i,j)$ where s is in $C_l(i,j)$ will be denoted by $SQ_l(s)$. We define the *rough square of influence* of s, $SQI(s)$, as the square $SQ_l(s)$ such that:

a) each square $C_l(i,j)$ in $SQ_l(s)$ contains at least one site from S,

b) no rectangle $SQ_k(s)$, where $1 \leq k < l$, satisfies (a).

By convention, the term $\#SQI(s)$ will denote the number of points in $SQI(s) \cap S$. On the other hand, the term $| SQI(s) |$ will stand for the length of a side of $SQI(s)$.

The meaning of $SQI(s)$ is revealed in the following corollary from Lemma 3.1:

Corollary 3.1: Let s be a point in S for which $SQI(s)$ is well defined, such that c is sufficiently large. Any edge in $GT(S)$ incident to s has length bounded by $\frac{1}{2} | SQI(S) |$.

Proof: Suppose that there is a fragment e of an edge in $GT(S)$ incident to s such that e has length no less than $\frac{1}{2} | SQI(s) |$ and lies within $SQI(s)$. Then we can exhibit two sites a, b in $SQI(s)$ such that $|a, b| < 2 | SQI(s) | /c$, e intersects the segment (a, b) and both endpoints of s are sufficiently far from a and b to contradict Lemma 3.1. Q.E.D.

The purpose of the two following lemmas is to estimate the expected value of $| SQI(s) |$ and $\#SQI(s)$ respectively.

Lemma 3.2: Let s be a point in S for which $SQI(s)$ is well defined. The probability that $| SQI(s) | > \frac{1}{2^{\frac{1}{2}\log n - \frac{1}{2}l}}$ is $O(2^l 2^{-2^l})$.

Proof: It follows from the definition of $SQI(s)$ that at least one of the 23^l squares in $SQ_{l-1}(s)$ is empty. The length of a side of $SQ_{l-1}(s)$ is not less than $\frac{1}{2^{\frac{1}{2}\log n - \frac{1}{2}l+1}}$. Hence, the area of such an empty square is greater than $\frac{1}{d2^{\log n - l + 2}}$ for some positive constant d. The probability that a square of the above area is empty is less than $(1 - \frac{1}{d2^{\log n - l + 2}})^n$ which is $O(2^l 2^{-2^l})$. Consequently, the probability that there is a square in SQ_{l-1} with at least one empty square among its $(23)^2$ squares in G_{l-1} is $O(2^l 2^{-2^l})$. Q.E.D.

Lemma 3.3: Let s be a point in S for which $SQI(s)$ is well defined. The probability that $SQI(s)$ contains exactly m points in S is $\frac{m}{2^{\Omega(m)}}$.

Proof: The proof is similar to the proof of the preceding lemma, and analogous to the proof of Lemma 3.2 in [LKL88]. Q.E.D.

(1) We shall assume further that each square of the grid $G_{\frac{1}{2}\log\log n}$ contains a point in S. Let $Out(S)$ denote the squares in the eleven outer layers of $G_{\frac{1}{2}\log\log n}$, and let $Int(S)$ denote the remaining squares.

(2) We shall also assume further that the total number of points in $Out(S)$ is $O(\sqrt{n \log n})$.

Fact 3.1 (see p. 28 in [Li86]): The probability that the assumptions (1-2) hold is at least $1 - O(\frac{1}{n \log n})$.

Note that it follows from our assumption that for each s in $Int(S)$, $SQI(s)$ is well defined and belongs to Q_l where $l \leq \frac{1}{2} \log \log n$. This will help us to estimate the expected total length of edges in $GT(S)$ under (1-2) in the two following lemmas.

Lemma 3.4: Under (1-2), the expected total length of the edges in $GT(S)$ incident to points in $Int(S)$ is $O(\sqrt{n})$.

Sketch: Let $s \in Int(S)$. By Lemma 3.3, the expected number of points from S in $SQI(s)$ is $O(1)$. On the other hand, each edge in $GT(S)$ incident to s lies within $SQI(s)$ by Lemma 3.1. It follows that the expected number of edges in $GT(S)$ incident to s is $O(1)$. This combined with Lemma 3.2 yields an $O(\frac{1}{\sqrt{n}})$ bound on the expected total length of greedy edges incident to s. Q.E.D.

Lemma 3.5: Under (1-2), the expected total length of the edges in $GT(S)$ with both endpoints in $Out(S)$ is $O(\sqrt{n})$.

Sketch: Divide the outer layers of the grid $G_{\frac{1}{2} \log n}$ covering $Out(S)$ into vertical and horizontal strips of size $\frac{1}{\sqrt{n}} \times \theta(\log n)$ respectively. We can assume that each of the strips contains a point almost surely, i.e. with probability $\geq 1 - O(n^{-k})$, $k \geq 2$ (see Fact 5.1 in [LKL] for instance).

Then, by using an argumentation similar to that from the proof of Corollary 3.1, we can show that if a site s is located in a strip which is appropriately surrounded by strips covering a rectangle of size $(23 \frac{1}{\sqrt{n}}) \times \frac{23\theta(\log n)}{\sqrt{n}}$ centered at the strip than any greedy edge incident to s is of length $O(\log n / \sqrt{n})$. It follows that all edges in $GT(S)$ whose at least one endpoint is in the distance no less than $12/\sqrt{n}$ from the boundary of the unit square have length $O(\log n / \sqrt{n})$. The total length of the above edges is $O(\sqrt{n \log n} \log n / \sqrt{n})$, i.e. $O(\log^{1.5} n)$, by (2). It remains to consider edges with both endpoints in $Out(S)$ in the distance $\leq 12/\sqrt{n}$ from the unit square boundary. The number of such endpoints is $O(\sqrt{n})$ almost surely (see Fact 5.1 in [LKL88]). The subgraph of $GT(S)$ induced by the above points is planar. Thus, it contains $O(\sqrt{n})$ edges, each of length $O(1)$. Q.E.D.

Combining Lemma 3.4 with Lemma 3.5, we obtain the following theorem.

Theorem 3.1: Let S be a set of n points uniformly distributed in a unit square in the plane. The expected length of $GT(S)$ is $O(\sqrt{n})$.

Proof: By Lemmas 3.4, 3.5, the expected length of $GT(S)$ is $O(\sqrt{n})$ under (1-2). On the other hand, the assumptions (1-2) hold with the probability $1 - O(\frac{1}{n \log n})$ which yields the theorem. Q.E.D.

It is known that the expected length of any triangulation of S is $\Omega(\sqrt{n})$ with probability no less than $1 - \frac{1}{n}$ (see p. 254 in [Li88]). This combined with the above theorem, yields our first main result.

Theorem 3.2: Let S be a set of n points uniformly distributed in a unit square. The expected value of the ratio between $| GT(S) |$ and $| MWT(S) |$ is $O(1)$.

4. The linear expected-time algorithm

The idea of our algorithm for $GT(S)$ follows the proof of Theorem 3.1. For points in $Int(S)$, we use local tests for greedy edges based on rough squares of influence. For points in $Out(S)$, we use global tests based on Fact 2.1, maintaining Voronoi diagrams with barriers, and a global priority queue OPQ of candidate diagonals for greedy edges.

In the algorithm, the straight-line dual of $Vorb(G)$, called the generalized Delaunay triangulation of G [LL87,WS87], is denoted by $GDel(G)$.

Algorithm 4.1

Input: A set S of n points uniformly distributed in a unit square.

Output: A greedy triangulation T of S

begin

1. $T \leftarrow Q$;
2. Construct $Vorb(S)$ and its dual $GDel(S)$;
3. Insert all diagonals in $GDel(S) \cap (Out(S) \times Out(S))$ in the priority queue OPQ;
4. Insert all diagonals satisfying Case 2 in Fact 2.1 with both endpoints in $Out(S)$ in OPQ;
5. For all s in $Int(S)$, construct $SQI(s)$;
6. $IL \leftarrow Int(S)$;
7. *while* the list IL is not empty *do*

    begin

        pick s from IL;

        if there is a diagonal e of T incident to s that is not intersected by any shorter diagonal in $SQI(S)$ *then*

            begin

                $T \leftarrow T \cup \{e\}$;

                update $Vorb(T)$;

                augment IL by $Int(S) \cap K(e)$

            end

    end

8. *if* T is complete *then* *go to* E;
9. pick a shortest diagonal $e = (v, w)$ from OPQ;

    $T \leftarrow T \cup \{e\}$;

    update $Vorb(T)$;

    delete all diagonals in $(K(e) \cup \{v, w\}) \cap Out(S) \times (K(e) \cup \{v, w\}) \cap Out(S)$ from OPQ;

    insert all diagonals in $K(e) \cap Out(S) \times K(e) \cap Out(S))$ that are in $GDel(T)$ or satisfy Case 2 in Fact 2.1 with respect to T;

    augment IL by $K(e) \cap Int(S)$;

10. *if* T is not complete *then* *go to* 7

E: *end*

The correctness of Algorithm 4.1 follows from Lemma 3.1 and Fact 2.1.

In order to analyse the expected-time complexity of the algorithm, we need the following definitions and facts.

Definition 4.1 Let e be a shortest diagonal of a PSLG G that satisfies Case 2 in Fact 2.1. $K(e)$ denotes the set of vertices of G whose regions in $Vorb(G)$ share boundary edge with the part of the region of the apex v of the triangle in $Vorb(G)$ cut off by e from v.

In [IL90], by using a generalization of a linear-time algorithm for Voronoi diagram of a convex polygon from [AGSS87], it has been shown that for a PSLG, $Vorb(G)$ can be updated in linear time after insertion of its shortest diagonal. The following fact is a straight-forward generalization of Theorem 2 in [IL90] resulting from using the term $\#K(e)$ instead of the worst-case bound $O(n)$.

Fact 4.1: Let G be a PSLG, and let e be its shortest diagonal. Given $Vorb(G)$, $Vorb(G \cup \{e\})$ can be constructed in time $O(\#K(e))$.

The next fact (Lemma 3.1 in [Li88]) estimates the total expected value of $\#K(e)$'s. The term $|GT(S)|$ stands for the total length of $GT(S)$.

Fact 4.2: Let S be a set of n points uniformly distributed in a unit square. The expected value of $\sum_{e \in GT(S)} \#K(e)$ is $O(\sqrt{n} \mid GT(S) \mid)$.

The above fact combined with Theorem 3.1 yields the following corollary:

Corollary 4.1: The expected value of $\sum_{e \in GT(S)} \#K(e)$ is $O(\sqrt{n})$.

Tha last fact (see Theorem 2 in [IL90]) estimates the time complexity of testing whether a diagonal satisfies Case 2 in Fact 2.1.

Fact 4.3: Let e be a diagonal of a PSLG G, and let e_1, e_2 be two edges of G such that e_1, e_2, e form a triangle and no other edge of G incident to the common vertex of e_1, e_2 lies within the triangle. Given $Vorb(G)$, we can test whether e satisfies Case 2 in Fact 2.1 in constant time.

Complexity analysis of Algorithm 4.1

Step 2 takes $O(n \log n)$ time (see [PS85]).
Step 3 takes $O(n)$ time by Fact 3.1.
Step 4 takes also $O(n)$ time by Fact 3.1 and Fact 3.2.
Step 5: The construction of $QSI(s)$ can be done in linear expected-time similarly as the construction of rough rectangles of influence in the linear expected-cost, $\log n$-time algorithm for Voronoi diagrams in [LKL88].
Step 7: By Lemma 3.3, the expected time taken by the intersection tests is $O(1)$. The expected number of points inserted into IL (counting multiple insertions) is $O(n + \sum_{m=1}^{t} \#K(e_m))$, where e_m, $m = 1, \cdots, t$ are the edges of the resulting triangulation T. The updating of $Vorb(G)$ can be done also in time $O(n + \sum_{m=1}^{t} \#K(e_m))$ by Fact 4.1. The expected value of the latter term is $O(n)$ by Corollary 4.1. We conclude that the whole step takes linear expected-time.
Step 9 (sketch): The updating of $Vorb(G)$ and $GDel(T)$ can be done, similarly as in Step 7, in expected $o(n)$-time, by Fact 4.1, Corollary 4.1 and Fact 3.1.
There are at most four new candidate segments that could satisfy Case 2 in Fact 2.1 after an insertion of a shortest diagonal into T. Therefore, testing such segments totally takes expected $O(\sqrt{n \log n})$-time by Fact 3.1 and Fact 4.3. The most time-consuming in this step is updating OQP which totally takes $O(n + \log n \sum_{e \in T \cap (Out(S) \times Out(S))} \#K(e))$-time. In analogy to $Int(S)$ and $Out(S)$, consider $Out(Int(S))$ and $Int(Int(S))$. By repeating the argumentation for $Int(S)$,

each $SQI(s)$ for s in $Int(Int(S))$ is within $Int(S)$ with very high probability by Fact 3.1. It follows that each edge (v, w) in T where $v, w \in Out(S)$ is within $O(1)$ outer layers of $G_{\frac{1}{2} \log \log n}$. Now, reasoning analogously as in the proof of Fact 4.2, we show that the expected value of $O(\sum_{v, w \in Out(S)} \#K(v, w))$ is $O(\sqrt{\frac{n}{\log n}} \cdot \log n)$. Thus, the expected-time taken by Step 9 is $O(n + \sqrt{n} \log^{1.5} n)$. Summarizing, we obtain our second main result:

Theorem 4.1: Let S be a set of n points uniformly distributed in a unit square. Algorithm 4.1 constructs the greedy triangulation of S in linear expected-time.

References

[A89] A. Aggarwal, Research topics in computational geometry, *Bulletin of EATCS* 39 (October 1989), pp. 388-408.

[AGSS87] A. Aggarwal, L. Guibas, J. Saxe, P. Shor, A Linear Time Algorithm for Computing the Voronoi Diagram of a Convex Polygon, in: "Proc. of the 19th ACM Symposium on Theory of Computing, New York", pp. 39-45, 1987.

[BWY80] J.L. Bentley, B.W. Weide, A.C. Yao, *Optimal expected-time algorithms for closest point problems*, ACM Transactions on Mathematical Software 6, pp. 563-580.

[CL84] R.C. Chang and R.C.T Lee, *On the average length of Delaunay triangulations*, BIT 24, pp. 269-273.

[J90] D. Johnson, Local Optimization and the Traveling Salesman Problem, in "Proc. ICALP'90, Warwick", LNCS 443, Springer Verlag, pp. 446-462.

[Ki80] D.G. Kirkpatrick, *A Note on Delaunay and Optimal Triangulations*, IPL, Vol. 10, No. 3, pp. 127-131.

[Le87] C. Levcopoulos, An $\Omega(\sqrt{n})$ lower bound for non-optimality of the greedy triangulation, *Information Processing Letters* 25 (1987), pp. 247-251.

[LKL88] C. Levcopoulos, J. Katajainen and A. Lingas, An Optimal Expected-time Parallel Algorithm for Voronoi Diagrams, in "Proc. 1st Scandinavian Workshop on Algorithm Theory, Halmstad 88", LNCS 318, pp. 190-199.

[LL86] D.T. Lee and A. Lin, Generalized Delaunay Triangulation for Planar Graphs, *Discrete and Computational Geometry* 1(1986), Springer Verlag, pp. 201-217.

[LL87] C. Levcopoulos and A. Lingas, On approximation behavior of the greedy triangulation for convex polygons, *Algorithmica* 2, 1987, pp. 175-193.

[LL90] C. Levcopoulos and A. Lingas, Fast Algorithms for Greedy Triangulation, in "Proc. 2nd Scandinavian Workshop on Algorithm Theory, Bergen 90", LNCS 447, pp. 238-250.

[Li86] A. Lingas, The Greedy and Delaunay triangulations are not bad in the average case, *IPL* 22(86) pp. 25-31.

[Li88] A. Lingas, Greedy triangulation can be efficiently implemented in the average case, in "Proc. International Workshop WG'88, Amsterdam", LNCS 344, Springer Verlag, pp. 253-261.

[Li89] A. Lingas, Voronoi Diagrams with Barriers and their Applications, *Information Processing*

Letters 32(1989), pp. 191-198.

[Ll77] E.L. Lloyd, On Triangulations of a Set of Points in the Plane, in: "Proc. of the 18th Annual IEEE Conference on the Foundations of Computer Science, Providence",1977.

[MZ79] G. Manacher and A. Zobrist, Neither the greedy nor the Delaunay triangulation of a planar point set approximates the optimal triangulation, *Information Processing Letters* 9 (1979).

[PH87] D.A. Plaisted and J. Hong, A heuristic triangulation algorithm, *J. Algorithms* 8 (1987), pp. 405-437.

[PS85] F.P. Preparata and M.I. Shamos, "Computational Geometry, An Introduction", Texts and Monographs in Computer Science, Springer Verlag, New York, 1985.

[WS87] C. Wang and L. Schubert, An optimal algorithm for constructing the Delaunay triangulation of a set of line segments, in: "Proc of the 3rd ACM Symposium on Computational Geometry, Waterloo", pp. 223-232, 1987.

Generating Random Graphs Efficiently

Rajeev Raman

Computer Science Department
University of Rochester
Rochester, NY   14627
email: raman@cs.rochester.edu

Abstract

We consider the algorithmic complexity of generating labeled (directed and undirected) graphs under various distributions. We describe three natural optimality criteria for graph generating algorithms, and show algorithms that are optimal for many distributions.

1 Introduction

Many algorithms of practical interest turn out not to be amenable to precise analysis from a theoretical viewpoint. Typically these algorithms are heuristics that quickly give approximate solutions to problems that are difficult to solve exactly, like NP-complete problems. In such cases, the domain is either too complex to be analyzed formally, such as the Kernighan-Lin algorithm for the Euclidean TSP [7] or simulated annealing [11], or the performance guaranteed by the best analysis is a severe underestimation of the observed performance of the algorithm in practice, as in the greedy MIS algorithm. In both these situations, an empirical analysis of the performance of the algorithm is needed. Other uses of such analyses may include gaining some idea of how an algorithm may perform, prior to analyzing it theoretically. Since the output of the program may vary considerably with the input, the usual method is to run the algorithm on a large number of randomly generated test inputs, and to use statistical measures of the results obtained to judge performance. The importance of random graph generation in such a context is clear. Often the algorithm to be studied runs in time linear in the size of the graph, and almost always its run time is a polynomial of very small degree. It is clearly desirable that the time taken to *construct* an input to test the graph on should not exceed the time taken to actually run the test, and so the *efficient* generation of random graphs takes on significance.

Another fruitful area of application of the generation of random graphs arises in pure graph theory. Graph theorists sometimes attempt to catalog all the graphs of a given size and type. Such catalogs are used, among other uses, to settle conjectures by exhaustive enumeration or to come up with plausible conjectures. Such techniques are at their most useful in the study of *random graphs* where they have been used to obtain hints as to which way conjectures might be settled [16]. Again, due to the large number of graphs that need to be generated, the need for efficient generation is acute.

In this paper, we study ways of optimally generating random graphs with various properties. The notion of the optimality of a graph generating algorithm needs to be carefully defined: we have defined three natural ways in which such an algorithm may be considered optimal. To the best of our knowledge, this is the first such study of the algorithmic complexity of graph generation: all previous methods have either disregarded the complexity or have been content with polynomial-time generation (see [19] for a survey). We also consider some well-known types of random graphs, and exhibit efficient algorithms for these.

2 Preliminaries

2.1 Definitions and Notation

The *order* of a graph $G = (V, E)$ is the number of vertices in G, and is usually denoted by n. The *size* of a graph is the number of edges it has, and is usually denoted by m. In an undirected graph, the *degree* of a vertex is the number of edges incident upon it. In a directed graph, the *in-(out-)degree* of a vertex is defined to be the number of edges entering (leaving) the vertex. A *r-regular* graph is an undirected graph each of whose vertices has degree equal to r.

The probability of an event A is denoted by $Pr[A]$. If X is a discrete random variable with distribution D then we abbreviate $Pr[X = i]$ by $D[i]$, omitting mentioning the random variable. The expected value (average) of a discrete random variable X is denoted by $E(X)$. The uniform discrete distribution on the integers in the range $\{0, \ldots, k - 1\}$ is denoted by D_k. The binomial distribution with parameters z, p is denoted by $B(z, p)$, where

$$B(z, p)[i] = \begin{cases} \binom{z}{i} p^i (1 - p)^{z-i} & 0 \leq i \leq z \\ 0 & \text{otherwise} \end{cases}$$

We abbreviate "let x be the a value obtained by sampling distribution D" by "$x \sim D$". Logarithms are to the base 2 unless otherwise indicated.

Our model of computation based on the *uniform cost with logarithmic word size RAM* [1, 6]. The machine receives as input n, and after running a time polynomial in n outputs a graph of order n with the desired probability. We will assume that the machine can perform simple addressing and arithmetic operations on numbers with $O(\log n)$ bits each in constant time. We will assume that sampling once from D_k takes constant time, provided k is polynomial in n (*i.e.*, we are assuming the existence of a random integer generator). Having only a source of single random bits, it would be impossible to have a terminating algorithm that generated anything with probability not of the form $i/2^k$ for some integer k [10, 14]. We use the standard abbreviations for "uniformly at random" (u.a.r.) and "independent identically distributed" (i.i.d.).

2.2 Optimality Criteria

The operation of any algorithm A on input n can be represented by a tree, the leaves of which correspond to graphs. The branching factor of this tree will be finite and bounded by some polynomial in n. Let U_n be the set of graphs of order n that have a non-zero probability of being generated, and let $U = \cup_{i=0}^{\infty} U_i$. Denote the specified distribution on U_n by D_n. For any graph G, let $d_A(G)$ the random variable that represents the depth of a leaf labeled with G. For any random variable x let $\max\{x\}$ be the maximum value attained by it. Let $|G| = m + n$ be the size of the output. We have three notions of optimality:

Definition 1   *1. An algorithm A is called* optimal *if*

$$(\forall G \in U)[\max\{d_A(G)\} \text{ is } O(|G|)].$$

2. An algorithm A is called PA-optimal *(pointwise optimal on the average) if*

$$(\forall G \in U)[E(d_A(G)) \text{ is } O(|G|)].$$

3. *Let G be a random variable that is distributed according to D_n. An algorithm A is called A-optimal (optimal on the average) if*

$$(\forall G \in U_n)[E(d_A(G)) \text{ is } O(E(|G|))].$$

For optimality, the worst-case time taken by the algorithm to generate the graph should be asymptotically the same as the size of the output, while for PA-optimality, the expected time taken to generate any graph is asymptotically the same as its output size. However, all an A-optimal algorithm has to guarantee is that for each n, the expected running time of the algorithm on input n be asymptotically the same as the expected size of the output. Clearly, by definition, an algorithm is PA- and A- optimal if it is optimal, and is A-optimal if it is PA-optimal.

3 Procedures Used

3.1 Sampling the Binomial Distribution

The number of successes among z i.i.d. Bernoulli variables each with probability p of success is $B(z, p)$-distributed. This gives a simple method of generating such variables if p is rational. Let $p = r/s$. Then we sample D_s z times independently and return the number of times a number $< r$ was generated (this works within our model if s is small enough). A faster approach is given by the generator of Ahrens and Dieter [2] which generates these variates in $O(\log z)$ time. For more references we direct the reader to [13, 12].

3.2 Choosing Random Subsets

The procedure below (from [20]) chooses a random k-subset of the integers from 0 to $n - 1$ in $O(k)$ time using $O(n)$ space. It assumes an array $A[0..n-1]$ that is initialized such that location $A[i]$ contains

the value i. At the end, the locations $A[n - k], \ldots, A[n - 1]$ contain the desired random subset.

1. $i \leftarrow n$

2. $x \sim D_i$; swap $A[i]$ and $A[x]$;

3. $i \leftarrow i - 1$; if $i > n - k$ go to 2.

It is well known that any sequential RAM with an uninitialized memory can simulate one with an initialized memory with a constant factor increase in space and time, provided the initial value of each memory location in the initialized memory is computable in constant time from its address[1]. In our case, $A[j]$ would have contained the value j had it been initialized, so this trick can be used. Also, with this method, re-initializing the array takes $O(1)$ time, so we have:

Lemma 2 *Using $O(n)$ space, $m \geq 1$ random k subsets of the integers $\{0, \ldots, n-1\}$ can be chosen in $O(k)$ time each.*

By setting $k = n$ in the above algorithm and considering A as an ordered vector we obtain a random permutation of the integers $\{0, \ldots, n-1\}$, so:

Corollary 3 *Generating a random permutation of the integers $\{0, \ldots, n - 1\}$ takes $O(n)$ time.*

The space requirement can be restricted to $O(k)$ if we are willing to settle for an *expected* $O(k)$ running time. The approach taken in [15] achieves this bound, if $k \leq n/2$ (if not, the previous method is optimal). The idea is to keep generating random numbers in the range $\{0, \ldots, n-1\}$ until k distinct numbers are obtained. If k is as above, the expected number of trials required is $O(k)$. By using a hash table to store the partially generated subset, it is possible to check in $O(1)$ expected time whether or not a newly generated number is already present in the subset (note that since the set we store in the hash table is a subset of $\{0, \ldots, n-1\}$ that is generated u.a.r., the hash function $h(x) = x \bmod s$ where s is the size of the hash table would have this performance).

Lemma 4 *Choosing a random k subset of the integers $\{0, \ldots, n-1\}$ takes expected $O(k)$ time using $O(k)$ space.*

3.3 Computing "Pairing" Functions

Often, we will have to select an edge at random from a set of edges. For this purpose, it is extremely useful to have a bijection between all possible edges of a graph on the vertex set $\{0, \ldots, n-1\}$ and the integers in the range 0 through $\binom{n}{2} - 1$. Such mappings appear as "pairing" functions in the literature, but the complexity of computing these mappings is largely ignored. We present a bijection that can be computed in constant time on our model of computation (which corresponds roughly to using only integer operations in actual computers). The computation requires pre-computed tables of size $O(n)$.

Lemma 5 *There is a mapping that can be computed in $O(1)$ time on our model of computation.*

PROOF. We use the following mapping:

$$pair(s,t) = (n-1-s+t)(n-s+t)/2$$
$$+ (n-1-s)$$
$$unpair_s(z) = n-1-(z-(j)(j+1)/2)$$
$$unpair_t(z) = j - (z - (j)(j+1)/2),$$
$$\text{where } j = \lfloor (\sqrt{1+8z}-1)/2 \rfloor$$

Note that in our model directly computing $f(z) = \lfloor (\sqrt{1+8z}-1)/2 \rfloor$ is not permitted. We observe first that $y = \lfloor (\sqrt{1+8z}-1)/2 \rfloor$ implies that:

$$(\exists \delta)[0 \le \delta < 1 \wedge z = (y+\delta)(y+\delta+1)/2]$$

So, for a given y, the minimum integral value of z such that $f(z) = y$ is $y(y+1)/2$

and the largest such z is $(y+1)(y+2)/2-1$. For $1 \le z \le n$ we compute $f(z)$ directly using the above fact, and store the resulting values in a table.

For larger values of z, the above approach fails, since the table would be too large. We will directly compute the function $\sqrt{x}$ to within an additive $O(1)$ factor. After this, we will compute $f(z)$ to within $O(1)$ using the approximate value of $\sqrt{1+8z}$ and then use linear search to find the correct value of $f(z)$. To compute $\sqrt{x}$ to within an $O(1)$ additive factor, we use the following pre-computed tables: a table with $\lfloor \log x \rfloor$ computed for $1 \le x \le n$ and a table with $\lfloor \sqrt{x} \rfloor$ computed in *double* precision for $1 \le x \le n$. By double precision we mean that we store, for each x, numbers k_1 and k_2 such that $\lfloor (k_1 + k_2/n)^2 \rfloor = x$.

Using the tables for the log function, we first compute an approximate value for $\sqrt{x}$ as $y = 2^{\lfloor (\lfloor \log(\lceil x/n \rceil) \rfloor + \lfloor \log n \rfloor)/2 \rfloor}$. Now we compute $y' = \sqrt{\lfloor x/y \rfloor} \sqrt{y}$ using values from the double precision table that we precomputed. It is easy to show that the value y' is within $O(1)$ of the actual value of $\sqrt{y}$. The essential point is that $\sqrt{\lfloor x/y \rfloor}$ is within $O(x^{-1/2})$ of $\sqrt{x/y}$. $\square$

We would note that our mapping is perhaps a little complex to implement in practice, and for most applications the mapping $pair(s,t) = (s-1)n + t$ would be preferable. This mapping is not injective, and so we may be forced to reject some randomly integers since they would not correspond to legal edges. This would be a relatively infrequent occurrence, however.

4 Generation of Random Graphs

4.1 Graphs with Specified Number of Edges

The distribution $EN(n, m)$ (Edge Number) is such that all (undirected) graphs with order n and size m are equally likely to be generated. With the mapping of lemma

5, the problem reduces to selecting a random subset of size m of the set of integers 0 through $\binom{n}{2} - 1$. By lemma 2 and lemma 4 this can be done in expected $O(m)$ time using $O(m)$ space, or in $O(m)$ time using $O(n^2)$ space.

We have thus shown:

Theorem 6 *The distribution $EN(n,m)$ can be optimally generated using $O(n^2)$ space and PA-optimally generated using $O(m+n)$ space.*

4.2 Specified Edge Probability Graphs

The distribution $EP(n,p)$ (Edge Probability) is parametrized by a probability $p \in [0.0, 1.0]$ and the order n of the graph. Labeled undirected graphs of order n are generated in such a way that the probability of each possible edge being present is p independently of the other edges. The naive method consists of considering every possible edge in turn and adding it to the graph independently with probability p. This method takes $O(n^2)$ time, but as the expected number of edges is pm, it is non-optimal when p varies with n such that $p(n)$ is $o(1)$. Also, even when p is a constant, this algorithm is only A-optimal.

A better method depends on the fact that the number of edges in a $EP(n,p)$-distributed graph, k, is binomially distributed with parameters m and p. We mention that Tinhofer had a similar, if somewhat less efficient, variant of this idea [18]. This procedure consists of two stages. In the first, we sample the $B(m,p)$ distribution to obtain a value k for the number of edges in the graph. Using the efficient procedures mentioned above, we can do this in time $O(\log m) = O(\log n)$. In the second stage, we randomly generate a graph of order n and size k such that all graphs of order n and size k are equally likely to have been generated. From well-known properties of the binomial distribution it is easily seen that in any graph generated by the above procedure, the probability that any particular edge is present is p, independently of all other edges. From theorem 6 we can bound the (expected or deterministic) time complexity of the second phase by $O(m+n)$. Thus:

Theorem 7 *The distribution $EP(n,p)$ can be optimally generated using $O(n^2)$ space or PA-optimally using $O(m+n)$ space.*

Let $C(n)$, $E(n)$ and $Eu(n) = C(n) \cap E(n)$ be the uniform distributions over all labeled graphs with n vertices that are connected, have all vertex degrees even, and are Eulerian, respectively. Noting that $EP(n, \frac{1}{2})$ specifies that all labeled graphs on n vertices are equally likely, we obtain as a corollary:

Corollary 8 *$C(n)$ and $Eu(n)$ can be PA-optimally generated with $O(m+n)$ space, and $E(n)$ can be optimally generated with $O(n^2)$ space and PA-optimally with $O(m+n)$ space.*

PROOF. We generate $C(n)$ using a restarting procedure, *i.e.*, by generating graphs from $EP(n, \frac{1}{2})$ and testing to see if they are connected (such an approach was mentioned by Tinhofer). We note that the probability of generating an unconnected graph is less than $2^{-\Omega(n)}$. This is because the number of connected graphs of order n, c_n, obeys the following recurrence ([8]):

$$c_n = 2^{\binom{n}{2}} - \frac{1}{n} \sum_{k=1}^{n-1} k \binom{n}{k} 2^{\binom{n-k}{2}} c_k$$

Observing that $c_k < 2^{\binom{k}{2}}$ and that $\binom{n}{2} = \binom{n-k}{2} + \binom{k}{2} + k(n-k)$, it is easy to show that the latter term is asymptotically smaller by a factor of at least $2^{-n/2}$. Thus the expected cost to generate a graph G of size m is $T \leq 2^{-n/2}(O(n^2) + T) + (1 - 2^{-n/2})O(m+n)$, from which we obtain the PA-optimality of this restarting procedure.

The procedure for generating $E(n)$ depends on the 1-1 correspondence between all even degree graphs on n vertices and all graphs with $n-1$ vertices [8]: with each graph G on $n-1$ vertices associate the even-degree graph obtained by adding a new vertex v_n and joining all odd-degree vertices of G to v_n. The corollary follows.

For $Eu(n)$ we use a restarting procedure again. We generate a member of $E(n)$ as above and check to see if it is connected. Let G be a random element of $E(n)$ generated as above and let $G' = G - \{v_n\}$ be the graph generated from $EP(n-1, \frac{1}{2})$ in the above procedure. G will be unconnected only if either G' is unconnected or G' is an even degree graph, in which case v_n will be an isolated vertex. The probability that G' is not connected is at most $2^{-\Omega(n)}$, as argued above. The probability that G' is an even degree graph is exactly the fraction of all $n-1$ vertex labeled graphs that are even degree. From the 1-1 correspondence between between all even degree graphs on $n-1$ vertices and all graphs with $n-2$ vertices, we deduce that this probability is at most $\frac{2^{\binom{n-2}{2}}}{2^{\binom{n-1}{2}}}$ which is also of the order of $2^{-\Omega(n)}$. We thus observe that the restarting procedure has a probability $2^{-\Omega(n)}$ of failing on each iteration, giving us a PA-optimal algorithm for $Eu(n)$, by applying the above reasoning. $\square$

A similar approach can be taken towards generating labeled directed graphs with a specified number of edges.

4.3 Digraphs with Specified Outdegree

The distribution $DO(n, k)$ (Directed, Outdegree) specifies that all order n digraphs where each vertex has outdegree k are equally likely. Such graphs can be obtained by generating, for each vertex, a set of its successors of size k. If self-loops are allowed, lemma 2 directly gives us a $O(kn) = O(m + n)$ algorithm. If not, a variant of the method of lemma 2 needs to be used. If while generating the neighbors of vertex $v \in \{0, \ldots, n-1\}$, we know a position j such that $A[j] = v$, we can generate a random k-subset of $\{0, \ldots, n-1\} - v$ by swapping the contents of $A[j]$ and $A[n-1]$ before starting the selection. To find such a j efficiently, we can maintain an 'inverse' array $B[0 \ldots n-1]$ which has the property that $B[i] = j$ iff $A[j] = i$, and update it each time A is modified. Thus:

Theorem 9 *Given n and k, a graph distributed according to $DO(n, k)$ can be generated optimally.*

4.4 Graphs with Specified Degrees

A sequence of integers $d = (d_1, d_2, \ldots, d_n)$, $1 \leq d_i \leq n-1$ is called a *degree specification*. A degree specification is called *graphical* if there is a graph on the vertices $\{1, \ldots, n\}$ such that for all i, $d(i) = d_i$. The distribution $DS(d)$ (Degree Specification) states that all graphs with degree specification d are to be generated with equal probability (regular graphs form a special case of particular interest). Such graphs appear to be hard to generate u.a.r., and this problem, along with the related problem of exactly counting the numbers of such graphs, has remained open for several years. Tinhofer [18] gave a method for generating such graphs *non*-uniformly such that the *a posteriori* probability that the graph was generated can be obtained. His method runs in $O(n^4)$ time for simple generation and $O(n^5)$ time for generation with probabilities computed. Jerrum and Sinclair [9] describe a polynomial-time algorithm that generates such graphs with a distribution that can be made arbitrarily close to uniform, by increasing the running time appropriately. This algorithm only works for the set of *P-stable* degree specifications (which, however, includes all regular degree specifications as a special case) and is of doubtful practical utility since the running time to achieve any reasonable approximation is a polynomial of very high degree.

We present two practical algorithms that run quickly but do not guarantee uniform generation. By increasing the run time by a factor of n, the a posteriori probability that the graph was generated can be computed as well. While the first algorithm is optimal, the distribution that it generates may be undesirable since it produces with high probability graphs that are similar to a canonical graph. The second algorithm is a much more efficient implementation of Tinhofer's algorithm, and produces a distribution that may be better for some applications.

We now describe an optimal algorithm for generating a graph with degree specification d if one exists in $O(m+n)$ time. Define a *degree sequence* to be a degree specification sorted into non-decreasing order. The following claim (see [3]) is proved again here for completeness:

Claim 10 *Let* $d = (d_1, \ldots, d_n)$ *be a degree sequence. Then the degree sequence* $d' = (d_2 - 1, \ldots, d_{d_i+1} - 1, d_{d_i+2}, \ldots, d_n)$ *is graphical iff* d *is.*

PROOF. It is trivial to prove that if d' is graphical, then d is, so we will prove the other direction. Suppose d is graphical. Then there is a graph $G = (V, E)$ such that G has degrees specified by d. Let v be any vertex in G such that $d(v) = d_1$. If $(v, w) \in E$ is an edge and $(v, x) \notin E$ and $d(w) < d(x)$, then there is a graph $G' = (V, E')$ with the same degree sequence such that $(v, x) \in E'$ is an edge and $(v, w) \notin E'$ is not. To see this, note that since $d(w) < d(x)$, there is a vertex y such that $(x, y) \in E$ but $(w, y) \notin E$. Setting $E' = E - \{(v, w), (x, y)\} \cup \{(v, x), (w, y)\}$ we see that the above statement is true. Repeating this construction as often as necessary

we come to a point where for any vertex w that is a neighbor of v and for any vertex x that is not a neighbor of v, $d(w) \geq d(v)$. Deleting v from this graph gives a graph with degree sequence d', which proves the claim. $\square$

Let the *residual degree* r_i of a vertex i is the number of edges it needs to bring its degree up to d_i. The *residual degree sequence* of a graph is formed by arranging the residual vertex degrees in non-increasing order. Using the above claim, we have the following method of generating a canonical graph with degree specification d:

> Repeatedly join the vertex v with the largest residual degree, k, to the k vertices that have the k largest residual degrees.

Claim 11 *The above algorithm can be implemented to run in* $O(m+n)$ *time.*

PROOF. Suppose we have to store a set S variables $x_1, \ldots, x_k$, $x_i \in \{0, \ldots, n\}$ and perform the operations $max(S)$, which returns the index of a variable of maximum value and $dec(j,S)$, which decrements the value of x_j by 1 if it is non-zero. In [5] it is shown how to implement these operations in $O(1)$ time each.

The solution involves maintaining a list of lists. In the top-level list we keep as list headers each number in the range $\{0, \ldots, n\}$ that is the value of some variable in S. We keep this list of list headers sorted. With each of these headers we associate a list of the indices of variables with that value. Since the value of a variable is decreased only by $O(1)$ in each step, finding the list into which a variable must be inserted can be done in $O(1)$ time using linear search. $\square$

Now, starting with the canonical graph $G = (V, E)$ obtained above, we apply perturbations to the graph in a manner similar to Jerrum and Sinclair. Let $m = (\sum_{i=1}^{n} d_i)/2$ be the number of edges in the graph.

1. If the current graph G has degree specification d pick an edge (i, j) at random and delete it from E.

2. Otherwise, G has two vertices that currently have degree one less than they should. Pick one of these at random. Let this vertex be i. Pick an edge $(i, k) \notin E$ at random and add it to E. If now k has degree one more than it should, pick an edge $(k, l) \in E$ at random and delete it from E.

3. If $2m$ iterations have not been completed, go to 1.

4. If G does not have degree specification d, find the G' closest to G that has degree specification d and output it.

Theorem 12 *The above algorithm generates all graphs with degree specification d and runs in $O(m + n)$ time.*

PROOF. We will show that $2m$ such alterations suffice to transform the canonical graph $\bar{G}$ into any graph G with the required degree sequence. Note that $G' = \bar{G} \oplus G$ is an even-degree graph with at most $2m$ edges. G' can be broken up into disjoint Eulerian components. Consider an Euler tour on one of these components that alternates edges from $\bar{G}$ and G. It is clear that if the above perturbations convert $\bar{G}$ into a graph G with degree specification d then the algorithm must have performed an Euler tour on some Eulerian component of $\bar{G} \oplus G$. Since the number of edges in $\bar{G} \oplus G$ is at most $2m$, $2m$ iterations of steps 1-3 suffice to convert $\bar{G}$ into any graph with specification d.In case the graph at the end of the process does not have degree specification d, it is a simple matter to "complete" the Euler tour the algorithm was in, to give a graph with degree specification d. It is also $\square$

We now give an efficient implementation of an algorithm that is rather like Tinhofer's. We first permute the edges randomly. Then we consider each edge in turn

according to this permutation, adding it if the resulting residual degree sequence is graphical. It can be shown [3] that the residual degree sequence is graphical iff, for $1 \le k \le n$,

$$\sum_{i=1}^{k} r_i \le k(k-1) + \sum_{i=k+1}^{n} \min\{k, r_i\}. \quad (1)$$

Thus, we need the following operations on residual degree sequences: $test(e)$, which returns true if the residual degree sequence r' obtained by adding the edge e to the graph is graphical and false otherwise; and $add(e)$, which adds the edge e to the graph and updates the residual degree sequence from r to r'. A naive implementation would result in an $O(n^2)$ complexity for $test(e)$ and an $O(1)$ complexity for $add(e)$. Note that while $test(e)$ may be called $O(n^2)$ times, $add(e)$ will be called only $O(m)$ times, so often we can decreasing the complexity of $test(e)$ at the expense of increasing the complexity of $add(e)$ and still obtain an improved algorithm.

For any residual degree sequence $r = (r_1, \ldots, r_n)$, let $k_0(r) = \max\{i | r_i > i\}$. Let r be the current residual degree sequence, and let r be graphical (initially, $r = d$). Let n_k, $0 \le k \le n - 1$, be the number of times the number i appears in r. We let $N_k = \sum_{i=0}^{k} n_i$, for $0 \le k \le n - 1$ and $I_k = r_k + N_{k-1} - n + 1$, for $1 \le k \le n$. We now note that equation 1 may be restated as:

$$\text{for } 1 \le k \le n, S_k = \sum_{i=1}^{k} I_i \le 0. \quad (2)$$

Equation 2 need be checked only for $1 \le k \le K = k_0(r)$. This is because $I_k < 0$ for all $k > K$. We will show that the operations $dec(i)$, $inc(i)$ and $test()$ can be performed in $O(\log K)$ time, where $dec(i)$ and $inc(i)$ decrement or increment r_i and $test()$ tests if the current residual degree sequence is graphical or not. Clearly $add(e)$ and $test(e)$ above can be implemented using these primitives.

The effect of decreasing r_i from x to $x-1$ is to decrease I_i by 1, decrease I_{x+1} by 1 and increase I_x by 1. We keep the sums $S_1, S_2, \ldots, S_K$ at the leaves of a binary tree T with depth $\log K$ in the order above. We perform the following operations on these sums: $change(j, \delta)$ which sets S_i to $S_i + \delta$ for all $j \leq i \leq K$ and $max()$, which returns $\max\{S_1, \ldots, S_K\}$. We can perform each of these operations in $O(\log K)$ time, by storing at each internal node v of the tree the value of the maximum value M in the subtree rooted at v, as well as a quantity Δ that represents the sum of all values δ such that some previous operation $change(i, \delta)$ changed all values in the subtree rooted at v but did not change all values in the subtree rooted at v's parent. (I.e, the current value of S_i is obtained by adding to the value stored at the ith leaf the Δ values at all the ancestors of the ith leaf.) To implement $change(j, \delta)$, instead of directly changing the values $S_j, \ldots, S_K$, we split these up into at most $O(\log K)$ canonical subsets, each of which corresponds to a complete subtree of T, and add δ to the Δ values stored at the roots of these subtrees. This may cause $O(\log K)$ maximum values to change, but these values will be at children of nodes that are on the path from j to the root, and so percolating these values up can be done in $O(\log K)$ time.

These improvements give an algorithm runs in time $O(n^2 \log K)$ where $K = k_0(d)$ ($K = t$ for t-regular graphs):

Theorem 13 *Tinhofer's algorithm can be implemented to run in time $O(n^2 \log K)$ where $K = k_0(d)$.*

Remark In this algorithm as stated, the expected number of edges examined before the algorithm terminates is $\Theta(n^2)$, giving an expected running time of $\Theta(n^2 \log K)$. This is because if x edges are examined by the algorithm before the $m-1$st edge is chosen for inclusion, the unique edge that will satisfy the regularity test will be discovered

after examining $\frac{1}{2}(\binom{n}{2} - 1 + x)$ more edges on the average, for a total of $\Theta(n^2)$. This algorithm is thus not even within a $O(\log K)$ factor of A-optimality. To come closer to A-optimality, we suggest the following approach: we use the above algorithm until about m/n edges have been chosen. Suppose the residual degree specification is at this time is r'. We now make a recursive call to generate a graph with degree specification r'. Since it takes $O(n)$ time to initialize the data structures for a recursive call, the extra time taken would be $O(m)$. We conjecture that on the average, selecting $O(m/n)$ edges could be done by examining only $O(m/n)$ edges.

4.5 Labeled Trees

The distribution $LT(n)$ states that all free (unrooted) labeled trees of order n are equally probable. Cayley's formula states that there are n^{n-2} such trees. Prüfer proved an easily computable 1-1 correspondence between labeled trees of order n and sequences of integers between 1 and n of length $n - 2$. This suggests the following approach, used in [15]: generate a random sequence of $n - 2$ integers between 1 and n, and output the corresponding tree. This is the basis of both the algorithm given in [15] and our algorithm. The algorithm in [15] runs in time $O(n^2)$, though it can easily be made to run in time $O(n \log n)$. We describe an implementation that takes linear time.

Prüfer's method of obtaining a unique labeled tree with n vertices labeled $\{1, \ldots, n\}$ from a sequence P of $n-2$ numbers each in the range $\{1, \ldots, n\}$ is as follows (here we assume $n \geq 3$) :

1. Let E be the set of all the integers from 1 to n that do not appear in P.

2. Let k be the smallest integer in E, and m be the the first element in P. Add the edge (k, m) to the tree. Delete m

from the front of P, and k from E. If m does not appear elsewhere in the sequence, add m to E.

3. If P is now empty, there must be exactly 2 elements left in E. Call these n and o. Add (n, o) to the tree and quit.

In [15] the set E is represented by an unsorted array, and this implementation causes the running time to be $O(n^2)$. Using a heap instead would get the running time down to $O(n \log n)$. We can get a quicker algorithm, however. The observation is that in linear time, we can determine the operations that would be performed on the set E by this algorithm, which would be an intermixed sequence of commands of the form $insert(x)$ or $deletemin$ (the latter operation means to report the current minimum element in E and to delete it). This is because in $O(n)$ time we can determine the elements initially placed in E, as well as the last position any label occurs in the sequence (which is the point it is inserted into E), and this determines the position of the $insert$ operations with respect to the $deletemin$ operations. The problem of determining the answers to a sequence of such operations, when the operations are presented all at once, is the well-studied *off-line min* problem. In [1, 17] a simple algorithm is presented for this problem that takes time $O(n\alpha(n))$ to answer a sequence of n inserts and deletemins. (Here $\alpha(n)$ is a very slowly growing function such that $\alpha(n) \leq 3$ for all possible practical values of n.) Alternatively the more complex method of [6] achieves a true linear running time for solving this problem.

1. Generate the sequence $P = \{p_i\}_{i=1}^{n-2}$.

2. In linear time obtain $E0$, the set of all elements in $\{1, \ldots, n\}$ that do not appear in P, as well as the sequence $L = \{l_i\}_{i=1}^{n-2}$, where $l_i = 1$ if the value p_i does not reappear at some later point in P, and 0 otherwise.

3. Construct the sequence of operations O in the following way: for each $x \in E0$, put an operation $insert(x)$ before the first $deletemin$ operation. Thereafter, for $1 \leq i \leq n - 2$, do the following: append the ith deletemin to the sequence, followed by the operation $insert(p_i)$ if $l_i = 1$. Finally append two *deletemin* commands to O.

4. Solve the off-line min problem with operation sequence O.

5. Let a_i be the answer to the ith *deletemin* operation. Output the edges $(a_1, p_1), \ldots, (a_{n-2}, p_{n-2})$, (a_{n-1}, a_n).

Theorem 14 *The distribution $LT(n)$ can be optimally generated.*

4.6 Geometric Graphs

The parameters here are n, the order of the graph, and three real numbers X, Y and r. The distribution $GG(n, X, Y, r)$ is obtained as follows: drop n points at random in the rectangle $\{(x, y) | 0 \leq x < X, 0 \leq y < Y\}$ and join any pair of points that are less than r apart by an edge. This distribution was introduced in [11] as a natural distribution for examples to test heuristics for NP-complete problems like the TSP (which satisfy the triangle inequality) on. The straightforward method results in an $O(n^2)$ complexity independent of X, Y and r.

The geometric nature of this problem suggests techniques from computational geometry. Using the "circle" searching algorithm of [4] we can get a $O(n \log n + m)$ algorithm, which would be A-optimal whenever the values of X, Y and r are such that $E(|G|) = O(n \log n)$. We now describe a considerably simpler algorithm that is A-optimal for all values of X, Y and r.

We divide the $X \times Y$ rectangle into $m = \lceil X/r \rceil \cdot \lceil Y/r \rceil$ subrectangles with longer side at most r such that $R_{i,j} = \{(x, y) | ir \leq$

$x < \min\{(i+1)r, X\}, jr \leq y < \min\{(j+1)r, Y\}\}$, for $0 \leq i \leq \lceil X/r \rceil - 1, 0 \leq j \leq \lceil Y/r \rceil - 1$. We assign these rectangles numbers systematically, e.g., $\#(i,j) = j\lceil X/r \rceil + i$. Now we generate the n points, and for each point, determine the rectangle $R_{i,j}$ in which it lies. For each rectangle $R_{i,j}$ that already has has at least one point located inside it, we store $\#(i,j)$ in a hash table with $2n$ buckets using the hash function $f(k) = k \bmod 2n$, as well as a record with a list of points inside that square. The expected time to search in the hash table is clearly $O(1)$.

Now we consider the points one by one: for each point x, we obtain a list L_x of all the points in its rectangle as well as in its adjacent rectangles, by looking up the numbers of the adjacent squares in the hash table. Now in $O(|L_x|)$ time we determine the set A_x of all the points in L_x that are less than r away from x. The running time of this algorithm is:

$$T \leq c \sum_{x \in V} |L_x| + 1.$$

Since $E(|L_x|) = 9r^2n/XY$, we have by linearity of expectation,

$$E(T) \leq c \sum_{x \in V} E(|L_x|) + 1 \leq c(n + 9r^2n^2/XY).$$

However, since the expected size of the graph generated is $O(n + r^2n^2/XY)$, we have:

Theorem 15 *The above algorithm generates $GG(n, X, Y, r)$ A-optimally.*

We conjecture that the above algorithm could be modified to achieve PA-optimality.

5 Open Problems and Directions for Future Research

We now list some open problems:

1. Find a way (in our model) of choosing a random k-subset in $O(k)$ time

with $O(k)$ space. This would imply the optimality of the algorithms of theorems 6 and 7 even using linear space.

2. Find an optimal *uniform* generator for $DS(d)$, or at least a practical one. More concretely, is the modified algorithm of theorem 13 within a log factor of optimality?

3. Determine whether or not the algorithm of theorem 15 is PA-optimal.

4. Find optimal algorithms for *unlabeled* graphs and for other kinds of labeled graphs.

References

[1] A. V. Aho, J. E. Hopcroft, and J. D. Ullman. *The Design and Analysis of Computer Algorithms.* Addison-Wesley, Reading, Massachussetts, USA, 1974.

[2] J. A. Ahrens and U. Dieter. Computer methods for sampling from gamma, beta, poisson and binomial distributions. *Computing*, 12:223–246, 1974.

[3] J. G. Bondy and U. S. R. Murty. *Graph Theory and Applications.* North-Holland, 1976.

[4] B. Chazelle and H. Edelsbrunner. Optimal solutions to a class of point retreival problems. In *Proc. 12th International Colloquium on Automata, Lanuages and Programming (ICALP)*, 1985.

[5] P. Dietz and D. Sleator. Two algorithms for maintaining order in a list. In *Proc. 19th ACM STOC*, pages 365–372, 1987.

[6] H. N. Gabow and R. E. Tarjan. A linear-time algorithm for a special case

of disjoint set union. *Journal of Computer and System Sciences*, 30:209–221, 1985.

[7] M. R. Garey and D. S. Johnson. *Computers and Intractability*. W. H. Freeman and Company, 1979.

[8] F. Harary and E. M. Palmer. *Graphical Enumeration*. Academic Press, 1973.

[9] M. R. Jerrum and A. J. Sinclair. Fast uniform generation of regular graphs. Technical Report CSR 281-88, Department of Computer Science, University of Edinburgh, October 1988. To appear in *Theoretical Computer Science*.

[10] M. R. Jerrum, L. G. Valiant, and V. V. Vazirani. Random generation of combinatorial structures from a uniform distribution. *Theoretical Computer Science*, 48:169–188, 1986.

[11] D. S. Johnson, C. R. Aragon, L. A. McGeoch, and C. Schevon. Optimization by simulated annealing: an experimental evaluation (part I). Technical report, AT&T Bell Labs, 1987.

[12] V. Kachitvichyanukul and B. Schmeiser. Binomial random variate generation. *Communications of the ACM*, 31(2):216–222, February 1988.

[13] D. E. Knuth. *The Art of Computer Programming, Vol. 2: Seminumerical Algorithms*. Addison-Wesley, Reading, Massachussetts, USA, 1973.

[14] D. E. Knuth and A. C. Yao. The complexity of non-uniform random number generation. In J. F. Traub, editor, *Algorithms and Complexity: New Directions and Recent Results*. Academic Press, 1976.

[15] A. Ninjenhuis and H. S. Wilf. *Combinatorial Algorithms*. Academic Press, 1975.

[16] E. M. Palmer. *Graphical Evolution: An Introduction to the Theory of Random Graphs*. John Wiley, 1985.

[17] R. E. Tarjan. Efficiency of a good but not linear set union algorithm. *Journal of the ACM*, 1975.

[18] G. Tinhofer. On the generation of random graphs with given properties and known distributions. *Applied Computer Science (Munich)*, 13:265–297, 1979.

[19] G. Tinhofer. Generating graphs uniformly at random. *Computing, Supplementum*, 7:235–255, 1990.

[20] N. C. Wormald. Generating random regular graphs. *Journal of Algorithms*, 5:247–280, 1984.

LINEAR EXTENSIONS WITH BACKTRACKING

Ivan Rival   Siming Zhan

The University of Ottawa

Ottawa, Canada

A **linear extension** of an ordered set P is a totally ordered set $L = \{x_1 < x_2 < ...\}$ such that $x_i < x_j$ in P implies $x_i < x_j$ in L. Linear extensions arise in many applied contexts (e.g. scheduling and sorting) so it is not surprising that some theoretical problems turn out to be difficult. Among these three are particularly notable [5].

"How to construct an 'optimal' linear extension?" -- as in the design of a schedule to process a set of jobs.

The enumeration question -- "How many are there?" -- as in the probabilistic analysis of sorting algorithms.

"How many linear extensions are needed to realize the order?" Thus, if a and b are noncomparable elements then a realizer must have linear extensions L_1 and L_2 such that a<b in L_1 and b<a in L_2.

Except for a few tractable classes, ordered sets seem to have too many linear extensions either to, on the one hand, efficiently find an "optimal" one or, on the other, to count them all. Our aim in this paper is to present a natural class of linear extensions whose number is few, yet which, for certain broad classes is rich enough to guarantee realizers.

A common construction scheme is this. Take x_1 in minP, the minimals of P, and for $i \geq 1$, x_{i+1} in minP $-\{x_1,x_2,...,x_i\}$. Thus, at each step, any **accessible** element may be chosen, that is, one whose predecessors have already been chosen before. It is sensible to impose additional conditions, arising from particular problems, with a view to constructing an "optimal" linear extension from a smaller set of (feasible) linear extensions. A natural such condition involves "backtracking" and, indeed, there are already several such in circulation [1], [2], [3], [4].

We shall say that a linear extension L of P is a **backtracking linear extension** if it can be constructed by the following procedure: x_1 belongs to minP, and , for $i \geq 1$, x_{i+1} is lexicographically largest among the v(x)'s, where x belongs to minP - $\{x_1,x_2,...,x_i\}$ and

$$v(x) = (e^i_i(x), e^i_{i-1}(x),...,e^i_1(x))$$

where, for $1 \leq j \leq i$,

$$e^i_j(x) = \begin{cases} 1 & \text{if } x >- x_j \\ 0 & \text{otherwise} \end{cases}$$

(We write x >- y to mean x **covers** y, that is, whenever x > z ≥ y then y = z. We also say that y is a **lower cover** of x and x is an **upper cover** of y.)

Loosely speaking, the idea behind the construction is to choose the"next" element of the linear extension as "close as possible" to those already chosen -- a commonplace precept among "backtracking" algorithms. How close is "close"? Backtrack, starting from the most recent, until an accessible element is found, which covers (if possible and preferably) an element already chosen, starting from the most recently chosen. For instance, the ordered set $N = \{a<c, b<c, b<d\}$, illustrated in Figure 1, has precisely two backtracking linear extensions (and three non-backtracking linear extensions).

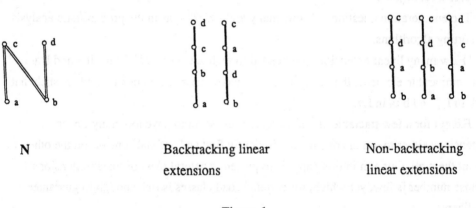

| N | Backtracking linear | Non-backtracking |
| | extensions | linear extensions |

Figure 1

After $x_1 = a$, $x_2 = b$, $v(c) = (1,1)$ and $v(d) = (1,0)$ so $x_3 = c$. After $x_1 = b$, $v(a) = (0)$ while $v(d) = (1)$ so $x_2 = d$. The ordered set $W = \{a<c, a<d, b<d, b<e\}$ illustrated in Figure 2 also has just two backtracking linear extensions.

W   Backtracking linear
extensions

Figure 2

Planar lattices constitute a familiar class of ordered sets for which special linear extensions have been studied. For instance, given a plane representation of a planar lattice the "left" linear extension, which is constructed, at each step, by "climbing as far to the left as it can", is itself a backtracking linear extension. The main point is that the two boundaries (left and right) of a face are traversed, without interruption, first the left boundary, short of the face's top, then the right boundary, through to the top. In particular, any planar lattice has at least two backtracking linear extensions, the left, and the right. And, as is well known, the intersection of the two is a **realizer** of the planar lattice, itself, that is, the intersection coincides precisely with the lattice's order.

In restricting the type of linear extension constructed we run the risk, of course, of overlooking the "optimal" ones -- for a given application area. Without entering into the details of applications, how might we ascertain that there are sufficiently many, of a particular type of linear extension? One sensible measure is that the intersection of all linear extensions, of the particular type, is a realizer of the order itself. That is, for our purposes, for each noncomparable pair of elements a and b, there exist backtracking linear extensions L_i and L_j, such that $a < b$ in L_i and $b < a$ in L_j.

Here is our first result.

THEOREM 1. If P is a W-free ordered set then, for each noncomparable pair of elements a and b in P, there is a backtracking linear extension L such that $a < b$ in L.

A **realizer** of an ordered set is a family of linear extensions whose intersection is the original order.

COROLLARY 2. Every W-free ordered set has a realizer consisting of backtracking linear extensions.

An ordered set is **W-free** as long as it contains no subdiagram isomorphic to the ordered set **W** (see Figure 2). The ordered set illustrated in Figure 3 is not **W**-free, for {c,a,d,b,e} isomorphic to **W**, is a subdiagram. It has just two backtracking linear extensions whose intersection includes $g < f$. On the other hand, with $g < f$ it is still not **W**-free and the intersection of its two backtracking linear extensions is a realizer (as is the case even for the ordered set **W** itself, cf. Figure 2).

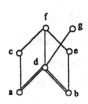

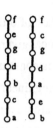

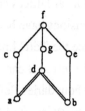

| P | Backtracking linear
extensions | The intersection
of its backtracking
linear extensions |

Figure 3

The enumeration of the backtracking linear extensions of an arbitrary ordered set P is unexpectedly simple. To this end let L(x), for $x \in P$, stand for the set of lower covers of x and define an equivalence relation θ on P by $a\theta b$ just if L(a)=L(b). Let $D_1, D_2, \dots$ be the θ-equivalence classes of P and let $d_1, d_2, \dots$ be their corresponding cardinalities.

THEOREM 3. For any ordered set

$$\text{\#backtracking linear extensions} = d_1!\, d_2! \dots$$

Thus, as each of the ordered sets **N** (Figure 1) and **W** (Figure 2) has just one element with more than one lower cover (two), each has just two backtracking linear extensions. The ordered set P illustrated in Figure 3 has, according to the formula of Theorem 3, precisely 2 backtracking linear extensions, and the intersection of these is not a realizer. On the other hand, the order $K_{m,n}$, say, with m minimals, and n maximals, each above every minimal, has m!n! different backtracking linear extensions. (In fact, every linear extension of $K_{m,n}$ is backtracking.)

Proof of Theorem 1. For an ordered set P and an element x set

$$L(x) = \{y \in P : x >\!- y\},$$

the set of lower covers of x;

$$U(x) = \{y \in P : y >\!- x\},$$

the set of upper covers of x;

$$u(x) = \{y \in P : x < y\},$$

the **up set** of x;

$$d(x) = \{y \in P : y < x\},$$

the **down set** of x.

We define a binary relation $a \, \Omega \, b$ on P just if, for any $x \succ a$, then $x > b$ (or, equivalently, $U(a)$ is contained in $u(b)$). This relation is transitive for, if $a \, \Omega \, b$ and $b \, \Omega \, c$ then, for any $x \succ a$, it follows that $x > b$ and, if $x \geq x' \succ b$ then, as $b \, \Omega \, c$, we have $x' > c$.

Now, to this binary relation we can associate an equivalence relation $a \, \Phi \, b$, just if $a \, \Omega \, b$ and $b \, \Omega \, a$. Let $[a]$ denote a Φ-equivalence class and $[P]$ the set of all Φ-equivalence classes. It is straightforward to verify that $[a] = [b]$ if and only if $u(a) = u(b)$ (if and only if $U(a) = U(b)$). Moreover, we may define an order $[a] \ll [b]$ on $[P]$ by $a \, \Omega \, b$.

For any element b in P we can inductively define a chain C with top element b, as follows. Put

$$e_0 = b \text{ and } C_0 = \{e_0\}.$$

For $i \geq 0$, choose e_{i+1} such that

$$[e_{i+1}] \text{ belongs to } \min\{[x] : x \in L(e_i)\}$$

until $L(e_i) = 0$. If $L(e_r) = 0$ then

$$C = C_r = \{e_0 > e_1 > ... > e_r\}.$$

For convenience though, we relabel the chain C from the bottom to top

$$C = \{a_r > a_{r-1} > ... > a_0\}$$

where $a_i = e_{r-i}$ and $a_r = b$.

Using this chain we construct "layers" for P.

$$L_0 = \{x \in P : x \not\geq a_0\},$$
$$L_i = \{x \in P : x \geq a_{i-1} \text{ but } x \not\geq a_i\},$$

for $1 \leq i \leq r$, and

$$L_{r+1} = \{x \in P : x \geq a_r\}.$$

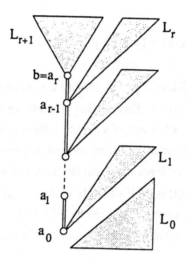

Figure 4

Here is the main idea of the proof. For any pair of noncomparable elements a and b in P, we construct a chain C with top b. Then construct layers with respect to this chain, whence a belongs to L_k, for some $k \leq r$ as a is noncomparable to b. Assuming that P is W-free, we show that there exists a backtracking linear extension L such that, for every element x in the layer L_i, $x < a_i$ in L, for $0 \leq i \leq r$. Hence $a < b$ in L.

Thus the matter is reduced to verifying this claim.

If the ordered set P is W-free, then there is a backtracking linear extension L such that for each $r \geq i \geq 0$ and x in L_i, $x < a_i$ in L and hence $a < b$ in L.

If this claim is false there exists k, $0 \leq k \leq r$, such that there is no backtracking linear extension L with $x < a_i$ for any $x \in L_i$ and $0 \leq i \leq k$. Let k be the smallest such value, that is, there exists L* such that $x < a_i$ (L*) for $x \in L_i$ and $0 \leq i \leq k-1$, but there exists no L such that $x < a_i$ for $x \in L_i$ and $0 \leq i \leq k$. We choose L* the linear extension which "climbs as far as it can" in L_k before a_k. By the assumption, there exists x* in L_k such that $a_k < x*$ (L*). Now L* = $\{x_1 < x_2 < ... x_{s-1} < x_s < ... < x_t < ...\}$ where $x_s = a_k$, $x_{s-1} \in L_k$, $x_t = x*$, and $s < t$. We may assume that $x* \in minP - \{x_1, x_2, ..., x_{s-1}\}$.

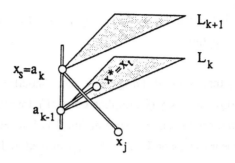

Figure 5

Why should we choose a_k before x^*? The only reason is that $v(a_k) > v(x^*)$ and a_k also belongs to $minP-\{x_1,x_2,...,x_{s-1}\}$. For any $x \in L_k - \{a_{k-1}\}$, a_k is noncomparable to x since $a_k \not< x$ according to the definition of layers and $a_k \not> x$ as $a_k \succ a_{k-1}$ and $x > a_{k-1}$. Since $v(a_k) > v(x^*)$ then $x^* \succ a_{k-1}$ as $a_k \succ a_{k-1}$, and there exists $x_j \in \bigcup(L_i : i < k)$, and hence $x_j < a_{k-1}$ (L*), such that $x_j \prec a_k$ but $x_j \not\prec x^*$ and x_j is such a largest element in L*. Since x^* and a_k are both in $minP-\{x_1,x_2,...,x_{s-1}\}$, then $x^* \not> x_j$. Otherwise there exists x_q, $x_j \leq x_q \prec x^*$ which contradicts $v(a_k) < v(x^*)$.

On the other hand, $x_j \not> x^*$, so x_j is noncomparable to x^*.

As a_{k-1} and x_j both belong to $L(a_k)$ why do we choose a_{k-1} in the chain C instead of x_j? The only reason is $[a_{k-1}] \in min\{ [x] : x \in L(a_k)\}$, that is, $[x_j] \not< [a_{k-1}]$. As $x^* \succ a_{k-1}$ and x^* is noncomparable to x_j, then $[x_j] \neq [a_{k-1}]$. So $U(x_j)$ is not contained in $u(a_{k-1})$, say $y \in U(x_j) - u(a_{k-1})$.

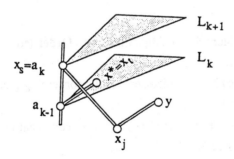

Figure 6

Now we only need to check that $\{x^*, a_{k-1}, a_k, x_j, y\}$ induces a subdiagram isomorphic to **W**. Since y does not belong to $u(a_{k-1})$, then $y \not\geq x^*$, or $y \not\geq a_k$ or $y \not\geq a_{k-1}$. Now $y \in U(x_j)$ so $y \not< a_k$ or $y \not< a_{k-1}$ or $y \not< x^*$ (as x^* is noncomparable to x_j). Therefore, we have x^* noncomparable to a_k, x_j, and to y, x^* noncomparable to a_{k-1}, y noncomparable to a_k, and a_{k-1} noncomparable to x_j. Hence, $\{x^*, a_{k-1}, a_k, x_j, y\}$ is isomorphic to **W**, a contradiction.

Proof of Theorem 3. Say that orders P and Q on the same underlying set are **consistent** if $x < y$ (P) implies $x \not> y$ (Q) and, $x < y$ (Q) implies $x \not> y$ (P), for every x, y.

In fact, it is enough to show that, given permutations L_i of the elements of D_i, there is a unique backtracking linear extension L of P which, restricted to D_i is consistent with L_i, for each i.

We may suppose that D_1 is so chosen that it contains some minimal elements of P. Vacuously, $D_1 = minP$. We construct a backtracking linear extension L as follows. Choose x_1 to be the first element in the permutation L_1 of D_1. Suppose $x_1 < x_2 < ... < x_t$ are chosen, consistent with each L_i so far considered. If x and y can both be now chosen for x_{t+1} in the backtracking linear extension then $L(x) = L(y)$ and hence any element that can be chosen for x_{t+1} must belong to the same equivalence class, say D_j. Since the chain $x_1 < x_2 < ... < x_t$ is consistent with L_j, if a_{jk} is the first element in L_j which does not belong to the chain $x_1 < x_2 < ... x_t$ then $x_{t+1} = a_{jk}$. Then, it is easy to see that the extended chain $x_1 < x_2 < ... x_t < x_{t+1}$ is the chain produced by backtracking and it is consistent with each L_i. Furthermore, the choice for x_{t+1} is unique.

By induction there is a unique backtracking linear extension L consistent with each L_i.

REFERENCES

[1] M. Habib (1985) Problem 4.2, in **Algorithms and Order** (ed. I. Rival), Kluwer Acad. Publ., Dordrecht, pp. 481.

[2] H. A. Kierstead (1986) NP-completeness results concerning greedy and super greedy linear extensions, **Order** 3, 123-134.

[3] H. A. Kierstead and W. T. Trotter (198) Super-greedy linear extensions of ordered sets, **Annals New York Acad. Sci.** , 262-271.

[4] H. A. Kierstead and W. T. Trotter (1989) The number of depth-first searches of an ordered set, **Order** 6, 295-303.

[5] I. Rival (1984) Linear extensions of finite ordered sets, **Annals Discrete Math.** 23, 355-370.

Storing Shortest Paths for a Polyhedron

Jindong Chen   *Yijie Han*

Department of Computer Science
University of Kentucky
Lexington, KY 40506

Abstract

We present a new scheme for storing shortest path information for a polyhedron. This scheme is obtained with a new observation on the properties of shortest path information of a polyhedron. Our scheme separates in a clear sense the problem of finding shortest paths and the problem of storing the shortest path information for retrieval. A tradeoff between time complexity $O(d \log n / \log d)$ and space complexity $O(n \log n / \log d)$ is obtained, where d is an adjustable parameter. When d tends to infinity space complexity of $o(n \log n)$ can be achieved at the expense of increased time complexity.

1 Introduction

The single source shortest path problem on the surface of a polyhedron has been studied by a number of researchers[CH][MMP][M1][M2][SS]. Recent result[CH] reveals that the single source shortest path problem can be solved in $O(n^2)$ time and $\Theta(n)$ space. Sharir and Schorr[SS] showed that by solving the single source shortest path problem for a convex polyhedron, the solution can be stored such that, for a query point $p = (f, c)$, where f is the face point p lies on and c is the position of p on f, the shortest distance from the source to p may be computed in $O(\log n)$ time and the edge sequence of the shortest path can be computed in $O(\log n + k)$ time, where k is the number of edges in the edge sequence. The information stored by Sharir and Schorr's algorithm is the subdivisions of the faces of the polyhedron. The subdivisions are, to a large degree, the immediate result of computing the shortest paths in their algorithm. Since their algorithm uses $O(n^2)$ space to compute $O(n^2)$ subdivisions, the solution is consequently stored using $O(n^2)$ space. Mount showed that the problem of storing shortest path information can be treated separately from the problem of computing the shortest paths. He showed that the shortest path information for a convex polyhedron can be stored in $O(n \log n)$ space while maintaining $O(\log n)$ time for a query of shortest distance and $O(\log n + k)$ time for a query of the edge sequence of the shortest path. What Mount observed is that the edges of the polyhedron, after certain processing, form a total order according to their "distance" from the source (we shall refer to this as the Mount order). The Mount order, in turn, can be used to mimic the shortest path edge sequences starting from the source point and extending outwards[M1]. Mount used these sequences to build a set of trees for storing the shortest path information.

For a nonconvex polyhedron no result on the space complexity better than $O(n^2)$ has been claimed. It is not clear whether Mount's scheme[M1] is extendible to nonconvex polyhedrons.

What remains unsolved is the question of whether the space complexity can be reduced further? In view of many known storing methods for various computational geometry problems, Mount[M1] and Mitchell, Mount and Papadimitriou[MMP] raised the open problem of whether space complexity of $O(n)$ can be achieved for storing shortest path information of a polyhedron?

In this paper we observe that the essential part of the shortest path information is the transformations represented by the notches in the planar layout of the polyhedron. Our observation leads to a fairly simple and clear interpretation of storing the transformations of the notches of the polyhedron (which need not be convex). When combined with the Mount order[M1] on the layout of a polyhedron, it provides a rather uniform scheme of storing the shortest path information in one tree which demonstrates the tradeoff between the space complexity (for storing the information) and the time complexity (for answering a query). Our scheme uses $O(n \log n / \log d)$ space for storing the shortest path information, $O(d \log n / \log d)$ time for processing a query of the shortest distance from the source point to the query point, $O(d \log n / \log d + k)$ time for computing the edge sequence of the shortest path, where k is the number of edges in the edge sequence of the shortest path and d is an adjustable parameter (which is the degree of the tree storing the shortest path information). For example, when d is a constant, our scheme yields the same result obtained by Mount[M1]. When $d = f(n)$ tends to infinity, the space used is $o(n \log n)$. When $d = n^\epsilon$, $0 < \epsilon \leq 1$, the space is reduced to $O(n)$ while the time is increased to $O(n^\epsilon)$.

For a simple exposition, the discussion of our scheme is aimed at a convex polyhedron. Our scheme is based on the techniques of coalescing and the Mount order and both can be trivially extended to the nonconvex case. We use a technique different from Mount's[M1] to handle the end region problem and our technique works for nonconvex polyhedron. Thus our scheme can be used for nonconvex polyhedron with time complexity $O(d \log n / \log d)$ and space complexity $O(n \log n / \log d)$.

The rest of the paper is organized as follows. In section two we explain the two layouts of a convex polyhedron, one is due to Sharir and Schorr[SS], the other is due to Chen and Han[Ch]. We note that Agarwal et al. discovered the layout independently[AAOS] shortly after we did. We also explain the Mount order of the edges of a polyhedron. This order is due to Mount[M1]. We give a simple scheme for storing shortest path information for a convex polyhedron in $O(n^2)$ space by using the two layouts. This scheme, although not efficient, provides an alternative approach to the problem. In section three we present our main result, namely the scheme of storing the shortest path information with stated space and time complexities. Conclusions are drawn in section four.

2 Layouts and the Mount Order

The planar layout of the surface of a convex polyhedron due to Sharir and Schorr is obtained by cutting all the ridge lines[SS]. Ridge lines are the loci of ridge points while a ridge point is a point for which there are more than one shortest paths from the source point. After cutting the ridge lines the surface of the polyhedron can be laid out on a plane. This layout is a star shaped polygon with the edges consisting of ridge lines. The vertices of the layout polygon are either vertices of the polyhedron or the Voronoi vertices on the ridge lines(after being transformed into the layout plane). If two ridge lines intersect each other at a vertex, they form a notch. An example of such a layout is illustrated in Fig. 1.

There is another layout of the surface of a polyhedron due to Chen and Han[CH], and Agarwal *et al.* [AAOS]. This layout is obtained by cutting the shortest paths from the source point to the vertices of the polyhedron. This layout is also a star shaped polygon with edges consisting of the shortest paths from the source point to vertices of the polyhedron. The vertices of the polygon are either the vertices of the polyhedron (after being transformed into the plane) or the images of the source point (there are $O(n)$ points which are images of the source point). Note that when a vertex of the polyhedron is also a ridge point, the shortest paths to this vertex form closed curves. A notch is formed in the layout when a shortest path to a vertex is cut. An example of such a layout is shown in Fig. 2. Recently Aronov and O'Rourke[AR] showed that such a layout of a convex polyhedron does not overlap.

We shall call the layout due to Sharir and Schorr outward layout (for shortest paths emanate from the center, *i.e.* the source point, outwards toward the destinations) and the layout due to Chen and Han inward layout (where a shortest path from the source to a destination going inward the interior of the layout polygon). The inward layout is called star unfolding by Agarwal *et al.* [AAOS].

In a layout the vertices of the polyhedron except the images of the source point (which can be a vertex of the polyhedron as well) can be arranged in a circular order. In the outward layout this circular order has been shown by Sharir and Schorr[SS] and Mount[M1]. The same circular order used in the outward layout can be used in the inward layout to order the vertices of the polyhedron. This is obvious because if we cut along the shortest paths to the vertices of the layout polygon in the outward layout (all these shortest paths are contained within the layout polygon) and then coalesce along the ridge lines of the layout polygon we obtain the inward layout. Observe that if we assume that the circular order in the outward layout is counter-clockwise then the circular order of the inward layout is clockwise.

For a convex polyhedron we can connect the adjacent vertices in the circular order by a straight line segment in the layouts. These line segments form a closed curve. This closed curve decomposes each layout polygon into two parts, one contains the source (we shall call it the arctic) while the other does not contain the source (we shall call it the antarctic). We shall call this closed curve the equator of the polyhedron with respect to the source point. Note that the equator is completely determined by the polyhedron and the source point. This equator can be used to devise an alternative scheme for storing the shortest path information for a convex polyhedron.

Consider the faces of the polyhedron. Each face could be cut by the equator into several regions. Each region is either in the arctic or in the antarctic. We associate each region with a transformation T which transforms the region to the right position on a layout. If the region is in the arctic, we associate it with a T which transforms it to the place on the outward layout. If the region is in the antarctic, we associate it with a T which transforms it to the place on the inward layout. If the information of the cutting of faces by the equator and the transformations associated with each cut region by the equator is stored, we can easily determine the shortest path for each query point on the surface of the polyhedron as follows. For a query point p on face f, first determine the region R point p lies on. If R is in the arctic we use the transformation T associated with R to transform R to the plane of outward layout, otherwise use T to transform R to the plane of inward layout. From the layouts we can determine the shortest distance and the orientation of the shortest path. This scheme requires $O(n^2)$ space to store the needed information. Note that we do not store the cutting of the faces by the ridge lines. We store the cutting of the faces by the equator. This scheme does not use less space than known schemes, it merely provides an alternative view to the problem of storing the shortest path information.

We now give a brief review of the ordering of the edges of the polyhedron obtained by Mount[M1], *i.e.* the Mount order. The first step in obtaining the ordering is to decompose each edge e of the polyhedron into two directed edges $\overleftarrow{e}$ and $\overrightarrow{e}$. For a shortest path $\overrightarrow{p}$ (which is a ray emanating from the source) crossing e, we say that $\overrightarrow{p}$ crosses edge $\overrightarrow{e}$ if the angle formed from $\overrightarrow{p}$ to $\overrightarrow{e}$ is less than π, otherwise we say that $\overrightarrow{p}$ crosses $\overleftarrow{e}$. With this convention the shortest paths on the outward layout always cross the edges from the left to the right. To obtain the total order of the (directed) edges Mount also split certain directed edges in order to break the possible spirals formed in ordering the edges. For a detailed description the readers are referred to Mount[M1].

For our purpose we use the result that the edges can be ordered on the outward layout, as to how to order the edges is not intimately related to our storing scheme. In the rest of the paper we simply assume that the (directed) edges (those that are present in the outward layout) form a total order in the outward layout.

3 A Scheme for Storing Shortest Path Information

We shall use the outward layout and the Mount order to store shortest path information. Recall that the outward layout is a polygon. The vertices of the layout polygon are vertices of the polyhedron and the vertices of the Voronoi diagram. There are a total of $O(n)$ vertices. We connect each of these vertices with the source by the shortest paths to the source. We thus obtain $O(n)$ ordered "triangles" by the circular order as shown in Fig. 3.

Note that the inward layout can be obtained by first cutting off these triangles from the outward layout and then coalescing them. This coalescing process can be viewed as transformations which associate each triangle with a transformation matrix. By the circular order of the triangles, the coalescing process can proceed in the following manner. Take the first triangle, coalesce it with the second triangle, then coalesce them with the third triangle, then coalesce with the fourth triangle, and so on.

Now consider two adjacent triangles T_1 and T_2. They can be related by a transformation matrix which coalesce T_1 with T_2. Take an edge $\vec{e}$ of the polyhedron and observe how $\vec{e}$ is laid out on the outward layout. $\vec{e}$ could traverse between the arctic and the antarctic (which is separated by the equator). For a subsegment e of $\vec{e}$ which is laid out in the arctic, e is continuous (we use the word *continuous* to mean that the edge is not broken by notches, a *noncontinuous* edge or a *broken* edge is an edge going through some notches). For a subsegment e' laid out in the antarctic, e' is broken up by the edges of the layout polygon. However, we can coalesce the triangles to obtain a continuous e'. (In fact certain parts of e' could still be missing because they are not present in the outward layout, this is a consequence of decomposing the edges into directed edges and forming the total order[M1]. These missing parts can be viewed, at least conceptually, as present. This phenomenon of missing parts does not affect the correctness of our scheme.)

We have essentially outlined a technique by which we can use transformation matrices to coalesce certain triangles to obtain a continuous edge of the polyhedron. Suppose M_1, M_2, $\cdots$, M_k are the transformation matrices used to obtain the continuous edge $\vec{e}$. For a point p on $\vec{e}$ we can use binary testing to find out on which triangle p lies. This is done by first transforming the tail of $\vec{e}$ from the polyhedron onto the outward layout, then by multiplying the transformed point p by transformation matrices M_1 through $M_{\lfloor k/2 \rfloor}$ to see whether p lies to the left, right or on the last triangle T coalesced. If p is on T then we are done because the triangle gives the distance of the shortest path and also the orientation of the shortest path which can be used to find out the edge sequence passed by the shortest path (it is actually done by transforming the orientation back to the polyhedron and then trace out the shortest path on the surface of the polyhedron). If p is to the left of T then we have overdone it, we should have multiplied fewer matrices. We undo what we have done and in the next step we will multiply p by transformation matrices M_1 through $M_{\lfloor k/4 \rfloor}$. If p is to the right of T then in the next step we will continue to multiply the transformed p by matrices $M_{\lfloor k/2 \rfloor+1}$ through $M_{\lfloor 3k/4 \rfloor}$. This process continues until we find the triangle p lies on. The matrix-to-matrix multiplications need not be done at the time of processing queries, they can be precomputed and stored, only to be used in the processing of queries.

The technique presented here would allow us to process the shortest path queries for points on a single edge of the polyhedron in $O(\log n)$ time using $O(n)$ storage. For different edges different sets of transformation matrices are needed to coalesce triangles. This is because different edges may have different patterns of entering and exiting the arctic and the antarctic. If we store different transformation matrices for each edge of the polyhedron using the above method we will end up with space complexity of $O(n^2)$. To reduce the space complexity we use Mount order.

Suppose edge $\vec{e_1} > \vec{e_2}$, i.e., $\vec{e_1}$ is "farther away" from the source than $\vec{e_2}$ in the Mount order. If transformation matrix M is not used to coalesce triangles for $\vec{e_1}$, then it is not used for $\vec{e_2}$. This situation is illustrated in Fig. 4. In general, if there are k consecutive transformation matrices the number of patterns of coalescing triangles is $2k$.

Example: 2 consecutive transformation matrices M_1, M_2 form 4 patterns of coalescing. The possible situations are as follows.

1). I, M_1, $M_1 M_2$, M_{1-2}.

2). I, M_2, M_1M_2, M_{1-2}.

I is the identity matrix. The value of M_{1-2} is equal to that of M_1M_2 although they represent different patterns. This example is illustrated in Fig. 4. $\square$

Note that we have to distinguish the pattern of M_{1-2} from the pattern of M_1M_2 because in the pattern represented by M_{1-2} we can not coalesce the first triangle with the second triangle by multiplying M_1 and then check whether the query point is to the left, right, or on the second triangle. For a query point on the edge represented by the pattern M_{1-2}, we have to coalesce the first triangle with the second triangle and the third triangle at the same time. In this case we say that the edge jumps through the second triangle.

We store transformation matrices into a tree. The transformation matrices associated with notches of the layout polygon are stored at the leaves of the tree from left to right by their circular order. Each leaf of the tree is associated with a notch of the outward layout polygon. A d-ary tree is used. Let a be an interior node of the tree. If the subtree rooted at a has k leaves we store $2k - 1$ transformation matrices at node a, each of them representing a pattern of coalescing the triangles which form the notches at the leaves of the subtree rooted at a. Note that we do not store the pattern of identity transformation. In addition, we store the information of edges jumping through the triangle between the notch at the rightmost leave of the subtree rooted at a and the notch at the leftmost leave of the subtree rooted at the immediate right sibling of a. Since there are $O(n)$ leaves in the tree which represent $O(n)$ notches in the outward layout, the tree has height $O(\log n/\log d)$. For each node a at level 0 of the tree (a is a leaf) we store one transformation matrix associated with the notch represented by a. For an interior node a at level i, we store $2d^i - 1$ matrices at a because the subtree rooted at a has d^i leaves and therefore it has at most $2d^i - 1$ patterns of coalescing represented by nonidentity transformation matrices. Since there are $O(n/d^i)$ nodes at level i, the total number of matrices stored at level i is $O(n)$. Therefore the total number of matrices stored in the tree is $O(n \log n/\log d)$.

For a query point on an edge of the polyhedron, we first use a transformation matrix associated with the tail of the edge to transform the tail into the plane of outward layout. We then use the tree to locate the triangle the query point lies on. At an interior node a, we test the transformations associated with the children of a one by one from the leftmost child of a to the rightmost child of a to find out which child of a should we continue the search. Since a has d children, it takes $O(d)$ tests to locate the child for the continuing search. Because the tree has $O(\log n/\log d)$ levels, the total number of tests for locating the triangle where p lies on is $O(d \log n/\log d)$. It remains to show that these tests can be done in $O(d \log n/\log d)$ time.

We describe in detail the data structure used to store the transformation matrices. We denote by $M_i^{j,k}$ the product of the matrices used to transform the i-th edge from the j-th triangle to the m-th triangle such that $m \leq k+1$ and m-th triangle is the largest indexed triangle edge i passes through (instead of jumping through). Call $[j, k+1]$ the range of the transformation. We also say that j-th notch(leaf) to the k-th notch(leaf) are covered by the transformation. For each $M_i^{j,k}$ we use an auxiliary matrix $N_i^{j,k}$ which is the product of the matrices from the m-th notch all the way to the k-th notch. When $m = k+1$, $N_i^{j,k} = I$. We call $M_i^{j,k}$ a boundary matrix if $M_i^{j,k} \neq I$ and $M_i^{j,k}$, $M_{i-1}^{j,k}$ represent different patterns of coalescing. Matrices stored at node a are those boundary matrices and their auxiliary matrices each has the range of transformation covering the leaves of the subtree rooted at a.. Boundary matrices and their auxiliary matrices stored at node a are ordered by their subscripts and placed into an array. $M_{i1}^{j,k}$ is stored before $M_{i2}^{j,k}$ if $i1 < i2$, $N_i^{j,k}$ is stored next to $M_i^{j,k}$. To facilitate searching on the tree we add two pointers to each boundary matrix stored in the tree. Let $M_i^{j,k}$ be a boundary matrix stored at node a. Let $M_{p_1}^{j,k_1}, M_{p_2}^{j,k_1}, ..., M_{p_q}^{j,k_1}$ be the boundary matrices stored at the leftmost child b of a, in that order. Let $M_{u_1}^{k+1,k_2}, M_{u_2}^{k+1,k_2}, ..., M_{u_v}^{k+1,k_2}$ be the boundary matrices stored at the immediate right sibling c of a, in that order. We use one pointer (the child pointer) for $M_i^{j,k}$ to point to $M_{p_t}^{j,k_1}$, where $M_{p_t}^{j,k_1}$ satisfies that $p_t \leq i < p_{t+1}$. In case $p_1 > i$ the pointer will point to $M_{p_1}^{j,k_1}$. The information provided by this pointer is the position among the matrices stored at b where M_i^{j,k_1} is to be inserted should we insert M_i^{j,k_1} into the matrices at b. Another pointer (the sibling pointer) points to the boundary matrix $M_{u_w}^{k+1,k_2}$ which satisfies $u_w \leq i < u_{w+1}$. In case $u_1 > i$ we let this pointer point to $M_{u_1}^{k+1,k_2}$. The information provided by this pointer is the position among the matrices stored at c where M_i^{k+1,k_2} would be inserted. We have yet to make an assumption in order to achieve $O(d \log n / \log d)$ time. We assume, for any two consecutive matrices $M_{i1}^{j,k}$ and $M_{i2}^{j,k}$ stored at a, that the number of matrices stored at c with indices between $i1$ and $i2$ (inclusive) (call it the number of matrices covered by $M_{i1}^{j,k}$ and $M_{i2}^{j,k}$) is no more than three. With this assumption we can trace the pointers in the tree to find the triangle the query point p lies on in time $O(d \log n / \log d)$. Assuming that the query point p is on edge $i3$ with $i1 < i3 < i2$ (the Mount order) and, the current node is a, the current matrix is $M_{i1}^{j,k}$, what is needed in moving from a to c is to find the index u_w satisfying $u_w \leq i3 < u_{w+1}$, among the indices of matrices at c which are between $i1$ and $i2$. Since there are no more than three such matrices the index u_w can be found in constant time.

To remove the assumption in the last paragraph we use the technique of padding. For each level of the tree we start from the rightmost node to the leftmost node. Assume that our assumption already holds for nodes at the same level and to the right of a. For two consecutive matrices $M_{i1}^{j,k}$ and $M_{i2}^{j,k}$ at a, let $u_1, u_2, ..., u_w$ be indices of matrices at c which are between $i1$ and $i2$, where c is the immediate right sibling of a. If $w > 3$ we pick every second indices from the sequence $u_1, u_2, ..., u_w$ (from the sequence $u_2, u_3, ..., u_w$ if $i1 = u_1$) and insert matrices $M_{u_2}^{j,k}, M_{u_4}^{j,k}, ..., (M_{u_3}^{j,k}, M_{u_5}^{j,k}, ..., $ if $i1 = p_1$) between $M_{i1}^{j,k}$ and $M_{i2}^{j,k}$ at node a. The same process is performed for all consecutive matrices at a. After this process any two consecutive matrices at a covers at most three matrices at c. Since each padding matrix is added for at least three existing matrices at c, the number of padding matrices added into the whole tree is no more than a constant multiple of the number of original matrices in the tree which is $O(n \log n / \log d)$.

Example: The two dimensional array shown in Fig. 5 gives the relation between edges and notches of an assumed outward layout. The x dimension is the notches and the y dimension is the edges. If the entry (i, j) is $-$, then the edge j is broken by notch i. Otherwise it is not broken by notch i. A $-$ between two $-$'s indicates that the triangle between the two notches is jumped through by the edge. The corresponding binary tree for storing shortest path information is also shown in Fig. 5. Note that auxiliary matrices are not shown in the figure although they are stored in the tree. $\square$

The scheme we explained above allows us to process queries with destination point

p lying on edges. To process a query of an arbitrary destination point on the surface of the polyhedron we have to first solve the end region problem.

We may assume that the faces of the polyhedron are triangles[CH][MMP][M1][M2]. For a triangle t on the outward layout we say t ends within face f if t intersects only one of the three edges of f. If t ends within f $t \cap f - \{\partial t \cup \partial f\}$ is called the end region of t, where ∂t and ∂f are the edges of t and f, respectively. If t intersects all three edges of f we say that t occupies f. If t has x end regions t must occupy $x - 1$ faces. Because a face f can be occupies by at most one triangle, the total number of end regions for a polyhedron is $O(n)$.

For a query point p not on an edge the shortest path to p must pass one of the three edges of the face f p lies on. If we test the query point using the coalescing patterns of these edges, we will have problem if there are triangles end within face f, for if we have coalesced to such a triangle we would have no way of knowing whether the query point is to the left or right of the triangle. We solve this problem by the following scheme. We cut end regions out from both the faces and the triangles and store them separately. Now each triangle t ends at an edge e. In constructing the search tree we treat edge e as if it jumps through triangle t.

Now for a query point p on face f we first test whether it is within an end region on face f. This can be done in $O(\log n)$ time using known point location techniques[LT]. If it is not in an end region we then test the query point by trying the coalescing pattern of each of the edges of f which are present in the outward layout (if the directed edge is not present, no shortest path crossing this edge exists), the edge which yields the shortest distance for point p is the edge the shortest path crosses.

We note that Mount[M1] handled the end region problem by making the ridge points the vertices of the polyhedron and introducing new edges to these ridge points. It is not clear whether his scheme is applicable to nonconvex polyhedrons because the introduced edges may intersect ridge hyperbolas.

We have proved the following theorem.

Theorem: The information for the single source shortest paths on the surface of a polyhedron can be stored in $O(n \log n / \log d)$ space which supports the processing of a query of shortest distance in $O(d \log n / \log d)$ time, and the processing of a query of shortest path in $O(d \log n / \log d + k)$ time, where k is the number of edges the shortest path passes through and $1 < d \leq n$ is an adjustable integer. $\square$

4 Conclusions

We have presented new schemes for storing shortest path information for a polyhedron. One scheme uses the equator and the other scheme uses the method of coalescing triangles. Both schemes provide new insight to the problem of storing the shortest path information. The question remains open whether simultaneous achievement of space complexity of $O(n)$ and time complexity of $O(\log n)$ is possible.

We note that the inward layout seems to be simpler than the outward layout for there is no edge jumping through triangles. We use the outward layout to store information because Mount order helps to cut the space complexity. It is of interest to us whether a total order on the inward layout similar to Mount order can be found to help the construction of a search tree from the inward layout.

References

[AAOS] P. Agarwal, B. Aronov, J. O'Rourke, and C. Schevon. Star unfolding of a polytope with applications. Proc. of the Scandanavian Workshop on Algorithm Theory. LNCS 447, 1990.

[AR] B. Aronov, J. O'Rourke. Nonoverlap of the star unfolding. manuscript.

[CH]. J. Chen and Y. Han. Shortest paths on a polyhedron. Proc. of 1990 ACM Symposium on Computational Geometry, 360-369.

[LT]. Lipton, R. and R. Tarjan. Applications of a planar separation theorem, SIAM J. Comput. 9(3) (1980), 478-487.

[MMP]. J. S. B. Mitchell, D. M. Mount, C. H. Papadimitriou. The discrete geodesic problem. SIAM J. Comput., Vol. 16, No. 4, 647-668(Aug. 1987).

[M1]. D. M. Mount. On finding shortest paths on convex polyhedra. Tech. Report 1496, Dept. of Computer Sci., Univ. of Maryland, Baltimore, MD, 1985.

[M2]. D. M. Mount. Storing the subdivision of a polyhedral surface. Proc. 2rd ACM Symposium on Computational Geometry, Yorktown Heights, NY, June 2-4, 1986.

[SS]. M. Sharir and A. Schorr. On shortest paths in polyhedral spaces. SIAM J. Comput., 15(1986), pp. 193-215.

178

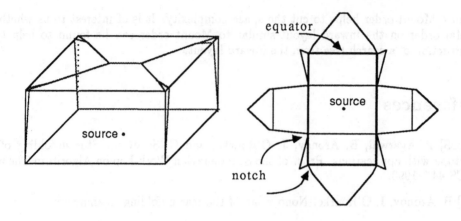

Fig. 1. A polygon and its outward layout

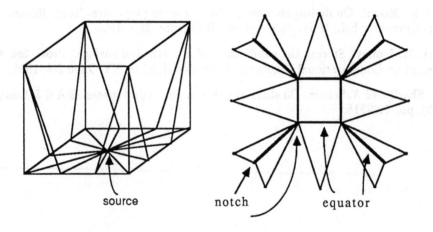

Fig. 2. A polygon and its inward layout

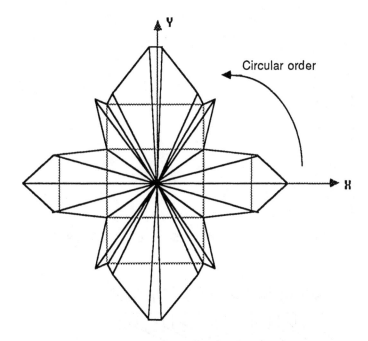

Fig. 3. Triangulation and the circular order

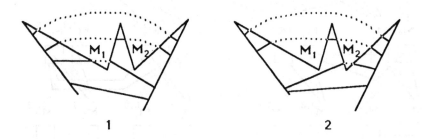

Fig. 4. Two situations of coalescing each has four patterns

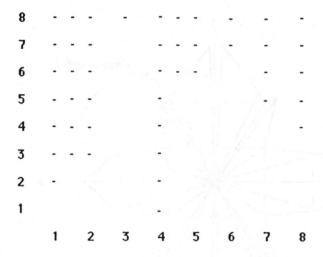

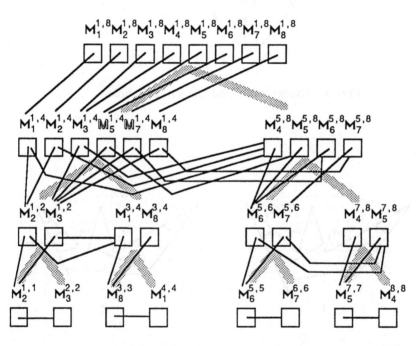

$M_5^{1,4}, M_7^{1,4}$ are padding matrices.

Fig. 5. Storing the coalescing patterns in the search tree

3. Databases and Information Systems

An Improved Join Dependency For Efficient Constraint Checking

K. P. Tan   T. C. Tan

Department of Information Systems and Computer Science
National University of Singapore
Lower Kent Ridge, Singapore 0511, Singapore

Abstract: In a relational database model, checking the contraints of join dependency involves examining a set of n tuples and solving m_1 constraint equalities. We derive a scheme called the (n,m)-JD in which the number of constraint equalities is reduced to m_2, by forming cyclic combinations of the (disjoint) elements of the partition and increasing the number of intersection operations to obtain the projections in the constraint equalities. The reduced set of constraint equalities results in less elementary checking operations and hence an overall increase in efficiency in the normalization effort. The relationship among (n,m)-JDs of various degrees and orders is also studied and formalised.

Keywords: Database design, join dependency, constraint checking.

1.   Introduction

The design of a database schema which does not contain any form of anomalies is a central problem in relational database design. *Normalization theory*, together with the technique of *non-loss decomposition*, has been devised as an aid to database design. Various normal forms have been introduced [Codd71] [Codd72] [Fagi77] [Nico78] [Delo78]. Rissanen introduced a data constraint known as the join dependency (JD) [Riss78], whose characteristics of lossless join decomposition leads to the formation of the fifth normal form [Fagi79]. Because of its importance, many papers have explored the properties and the complete axiomization of the JD, including [AhBU79], [BeVa81], [Gyss85] and [Scio82]. Checking whether a relation instance is in the fifth normal form requires checking it against the JD. This paper extends the modified JD concept proposed in [Tan84] and also gives the general expression which relates the number of projections involved in a JD to the number of disjoint sets of attributes in each cyclic component.

2.   Notations Used

Let U, the universe, be a finite set of attributes. In this paper, we denote attributes by small letters, and sets of attributes by capital letters. So $U = \{ a, b, c, ... \}$. Also, we shall write AB for $A \cup B$, where A and B are sets of attributes, and $abc...$ for $\{ a, b, c, ... \}$, where $a, b, c, ...$ are attributes. Let R be the set of relation schemes over U, and $X \subseteq U$. A tuple t over X is a mapping that associates with each attribute a of X a value of its corresponding domain. An instance r of R over X, denoted by $r(X)$, is then a set of tuples over X. Let $Y \subseteq X$. The projection of a tuple t onto Y, denoted by $t[Y]$, is obtained by restricting the attributes of t to Y. If r is an instance over X, the set obtained by projecting each tuple of r onto Y is said to be the projection of r onto Y, denoted $\pi_Y(r)$.

The join dependency is defined as follows [Maie83] [Ullm82]:

Let $R = X_1, X_2, ..., X_n$ be a set of n relation schemes over U, where $X_1, X_2, ..., X_n \subseteq U$. A relation $r(U)$ satisfies the n-JD, $*[X_1, X_2, \cdots X_n]$ if r decomposes losslessly onto n projections $X_1, X_2, ..., X_n$: $r = \pi_{X_1}(r) \bowtie \pi_{X_2}(r) \bowtie \cdots \bowtie \pi_{X_n}(r)$. That is, r is the natural join of its projections onto the X_i's.

In other words, if r contains tuples $t_1, t_2, ..., t_n$ such that $t_i(X_i \cap X_j) = t_j(X_i \cap X_j)$ for $1 \leq i, j \leq n$, then r must contain a tuple t such that $t(X_i) = t_i(X_i)$ for $1 \leq i \leq n$.

We also define the operation $\oplus_n$ as follows: for integers $i, i' \leq n$, $i \oplus_n i' = \begin{cases} i + i' & \text{if } i + i' \leq n \\ i + i' - n & \text{otherwise} \end{cases}$

$\oplus$ is used in place of $\oplus_n$ when there is no ambiguity.

3. (n,m)-JD

We extend the discussion in [Tan84] to allow for the general case in which the cyclic component may have $(n-1)$ or less disjoint attribute sets, and compare the relationship between these variants. A new parameter m is installed in the new scheme for which we adopt the name (n,m)-JD. The (n,m)-JD is defined as follows:

Suppose R(U) is a relation over $X_1, X_2, ..., X_n$ in the universe U, where $X_1, X_2, ..., X_n \subseteq U$, and $U = \bigcup_{i=1}^{n} X_i$. Let U be partitioned into n disjoint sets $Y_1, Y_2, ..., Y_n$, where $U = \bigcup_{k=1}^{n} Y_k$ and $Y_j \cap Y_k = \phi$ for all $j \neq k$. In the sequel, we shall call n, the number of projections X_i, the *degree*, and m, the number of disjoint attribute sets in each X_i, the *order*.

If each X_i in the above relation R(U) is a union of m Y_k's in the cyclic form, where $\lfloor n/2 \rfloor < m \le n-1$, that is, $X_i = Y_j Y_{j\oplus 1} \cdots Y_{j\oplus(m-1)}$, then the (n,m)-JD, $*[X_1, X_2, ..., X_n]$ holds in R(U) iff whenever there are n tuples $t_1, t_2, \cdots t_n \in$ R such that $t_k[\bigcap_{i=k} X_i] = \cdots = t_{k\oplus(m-1)}[\bigcap_{i=k} X_i]$ for all k=1,...,n, then there exists a tuple $t \in$ R such that $t[X_i] = t_i[X_i]$ for all i=1,...,n.

In subsequent discussion, we shall assume that the degree is n and the order is m. Let t be a tuple. Then $t = y_1 y_2 \cdots y_k$, where each y_i is a set of attributes, or simply attribute-set, which is either unprimed or primed. We define $pos(y_i)$ to be the position of y_i in t and $\delta(t)$ to be the difference in the positions of two primed attribute-sets in t, that is, if $pos(y_i) > pos(y_j)$, y_i and y_j both primed, then $\delta(t) = pos(y_i) - pos(y_j)$.

Lemma 1. Let R(U) be a relation scheme. Let $X_1, X_2, ..., X_n \subseteq U$, and $X_i = Y_i Y_{i\oplus 1} \cdots Y_{i\oplus(m-1)}$, where each Y_j is a partition element of U. Then the natural join of $R(X_i)$ and $R(X_{i\oplus 1})$ contains a spurious tuple t with $\delta(t) = m$.

Lemma 2. After each natural join operation in $R(X_1) \bowtie R(X_2) \bowtie \cdots \bowtie R(X_n)$, the set of spurious tuples T generated has $\delta(t) \ge m$, for all $t \in$ T.

Theorem 1. Let R(U) be a relation scheme. Let $X_1, X_2, ..., X_n \subseteq U$, and $X_i = Y_i Y_{i\oplus 1} ..., Y_{i\oplus(m-1)}$, where each Y_j is a partition element of U. If $m > \lfloor n/2 \rfloor$, then the cyclic formations X_i's is a non-loss decomposition of R.

4. Examples

Let R(U) be a relation schema over 5 subsets X_1, X_2, X_3, X_4, X_5 in the universe U. Let U = $abcdefghijklm$ be partitioned into the following disjoint sets: $Y_1 = ab$, $Y_2 = cde$, $Y_3 = fgh$, $Y_4 = ij$, and $Y_5 = klm$. Let
$$X_1 = Y_1Y_2Y_3Y_4 \; ; \; X_2 = Y_2Y_3Y_4Y_5 \; ; \; X_3 = Y_3Y_4Y_5Y_1 \; ; \; X_4 = Y_4Y_5Y_1Y_2 \; ; \; X_5 = Y_5Y_1Y_2Y_3$$

According to the definition of 5-JD, all instances of R will obey JD if any set of 5 tuples t_1, t_2, t_3, t_4, t_5 is in an instance such that

$$t_1[X_1 \cap X_2] = t_2[X_1 \cap X_2] \; ; \quad t_2[X_2 \cap X_3] = t_3[X_2 \cap X_3] \; ; \quad t_3[X_3 \cap X_5] = t_5[X_3 \cap X_5]$$
$$t_1[X_1 \cap X_3] = t_3[X_1 \cap X_3] \; ; \quad t_2[X_2 \cap X_4] = t_4[X_2 \cap X_4] \; ; \quad t_4[X_4 \cap X_5] = t_5[X_4 \cap X_5]$$
$$t_1[X_1 \cap X_4] = t_4[X_1 \cap X_4] \; ; \quad t_2[X_2 \cap X_5] = t_5[X_2 \cap X_5]$$
$$t_1[X_1 \cap X_5] = t_5[X_1 \cap X_5] \; ; \quad t_3[X_3 \cap X_4] = t_4[X_3 \cap X_4]$$

In other words, the 5 tuples should satisfy the constraints:

$$t_1[Y_2Y_3Y_4] = t_2[Y_2Y_3Y_4] \;\cdots(1); \quad t_2[Y_3Y_4Y_5] = t_3[Y_3Y_4Y_5] \;\cdots(5); \quad t_3[Y_5Y_1Y_3] = t_5[Y_5Y_1Y_3] \;\cdots(9)$$
$$t_1[Y_3Y_4Y_1] = t_3[Y_3Y_4Y_1] \;\cdots(2); \quad t_2[Y_4Y_5Y_2] = t_4[Y_4Y_5Y_2] \;\cdots(6); \quad t_4[Y_5Y_1Y_2] = t_5[Y_5Y_1Y_2] \;\cdots(10)$$
$$t_1[Y_4Y_1Y_2] = t_4[Y_4Y_1Y_2] \;\cdots(3); \quad t_2[Y_5Y_2Y_3] = t_5[Y_5Y_2Y_3] \;\cdots(7)$$
$$t_1[Y_1Y_2Y_3] = t_5[Y_1Y_2Y_3] \;\cdots(4); \quad t_3[Y_4Y_5Y_1] = t_4[Y_4Y_5Y_1] \;\cdots(8)$$

then there exists a tuple t in the instance such that

$$t[Y_4] = t_1[Y_4] \, , \; t[Y_5] = t_2[Y_5] \, , \; t[Y_1] = t_3[Y_1] \, , \; t[Y_2] = t_4[Y_2] \, , \; t[Y_3] = t_5[Y_3]$$

It can be easily seen that the above example leads to some redundant checkings. For instance, equalities (1) and (5) yield $t_1[Y_3Y_4] = t_3[Y_3Y_4]$, while equalities (3) and (8) give rise to $t_1[Y_4Y_1] = t_3[Y_4Y_1]$, which leads to $t_1[Y_3Y_4Y_1] = t_3[Y_3Y_4Y_1]$, or equality (2). If we use the (n,m)-JD, with $n = 5$, $m = 4$, and three intersections on four sets X_i's, we obtain the following equalities:

$$t_1[Y_4] = t_2[Y_4] = t_3[Y_4] = t_4[Y_4] \;\cdots(11); \quad t_4[Y_2] = t_5[Y_2] = t_1[Y_2] = t_2[Y_2] \;\cdots(14)$$
$$t_2[Y_5] = t_3[Y_5] = t_4[Y_5] = t_5[Y_5] \;\cdots(12); \quad t_5[Y_3] = t_1[Y_3] = t_2[Y_3] = t_3[Y_3] \;\cdots(15)$$
$$t_3[Y_1] = t_4[Y_1] = t_5[Y_1] = t_1[Y_1] \;\cdots(13)$$

This new set of 5 equations is sufficient to ensure that equalities (1) to (10) are satisfied. Instead of testing the original set of equalities which requires 30 ($n(n-1)(n-2)/2$) checks on the Y_j's, this is performed on the new set of equalities with 15 checks ($n(n-2)$). Suppose we refer to the comparison of an attribute value for two tuples (eg. $t_i[a] = t_j[a]$) as an *elementary checking*, and we let k be the number of attributes in the universe U (which is 13 in this case), then the number of elementary checks reduces from 78 (6k) for the original set of equalities to 39 (3k) for the new one, a saving of 50%. Apart from the modification on the constraint equations, the new tuple generated from the (n,m)-JD is the same as that from the old n-JD.

5. Results

Table 1 summarizes the differences between the old n-JD and the new (n,m)-JD. In terms of elementary checkings, the ratio of the old n-JD against (n,m)-JD is $(n-1)(n-2)/(2(m-1)):1$, or, in the case where $m = n-1$, the ratio becomes $(n-1)/2:1$. This shows an improvement in efficiency of (n,m)-JD over the old n-JD.

Number of	Old n-JD				$(n,n-1)$-JD				(n,m)-JD
X_i's	3	4	5	n	3	4	5	n	n
Y_j's in each X_i	2	3	4	$n-1$	2	3	4	$n-1$	m
Constraint equations	3	6	10	$n(n-1)/2$	3	4	5	n	n
Y_j checks	3*1	6*2	10*3	$n(n-1)(n-2)/2$	3*1	8*1	15*1	$n(n-2)$	$n(m-1)$
Elementary checks	k	$3k$	$6k$	$(n-1)(n-2)k/2$	k	$2k$	$3k$	$(n-2)k$	$(m-1)k$

Table 1. Comparison of n-JD with (n,m)-JD

The example in section 4 presents the special case of the (n,m)-JD where $m = n-1$. In analyzing the relationship among the various cases, we adopt the notation ${}^n J^m$ as a measure of the "complexity" in checking the constraints for a given n and m. With the restriction of the value of m, given by $\lfloor n/2 \rfloor < m \le (n-1)$, it becomes immediate from the definition that if the number of X_i's is reduced by one to $n-1$, the complexity of the checking procedure would be equivalent to an $(n-1,m)$-JD, yielding the following relationship:
$$\frac{\partial\, {}^n J^m}{\partial X_i} = {}^{n-1}J^m$$

We now consider the case where the number of Y_j's is reduced by one. If $m = n-1$, it is impossible to obtain the cyclic formation for the X_i's since each X_i contains m Y_j's. The order m would have to be reduced by one. Using the same example, the following would result if Y_5 is eliminated: $X_1 = Y_1Y_2Y_3$, $X_2 = Y_2Y_3Y_4$, $X_3 = Y_3Y_4Y_1$, $X_4 = Y_4Y_1Y_2$.

The problem does not occur when $m < n-1$. Hence we have:
$$\frac{\partial\, {}^n J^m}{\partial Y_j} = \begin{cases} {}^{n-1}J^{m-1} & \text{if } m = n-1 \\ {}^{n-1}J^m & \text{if } m < n-1 \end{cases}$$

6. Conclusion

In this paper, the new (n,m)-JD is presented. Each subset X_i contains m disjoint sets in the cycle combination and $m-1$ intersections of X_i's are implied in each constraint equality. The time for checking the constraints is reduced by at most a factor of $(n-1)/2$ for each set of n tuples, in the case where $m = n-1$. The (n,m)-JD is also studied for various degrees and orders and the comparison is done by expressing their relationship in an algebraic form.

7. References

[AhBU79] Aho, A. V., Beeri, C. and Ullman, J. D., "The Theory of Joins in Relational Databases", *ACM TODS 4*, No. 3, Sept. 1979, pp. 297-314.

[BeVa81] Beeri, C. and Vardi, M., "On the Properties of Total Join Dependencies", H. Gallaire, J. Minker, and J. M. Nicolas (Ed), *Advances in Database Theory*, Vol. 1, Plenum Press, New York, 1981, pp. 25-71.

[Codd71] Codd, E. F., "Normalized Data Base Structure: A Brief Tutorial", *Proc. 1971 ACM SIGFIDET Workshop on Data Description, Access and Control*, San Diego, Ca., Nov. 11-12, 1971, E. F. Codd and A. L. Dean (Eds).

[Codd72] Codd, E. F., "Further Normalization of the Data Base Relational Model", *Data Base Systems*, R. Rustin (Ed), Courant Computer Science Symposium, Vol. 6, Prentice-Hall, Englewood Cliffs, N.J., 1972, pp. 33-64.

[Delo78] Delobel, C., "Normalization and Hierarchical Dependencies in the Relational Data Model", *ACM TODS 3*, No. 3, Sept. 1978, pp. 201-222.

[Fagi77] Fagin, R., "Multivalued Dependencies and a New Normal Form for Relational Databases", *ACM TODS 2*, No. 3, Sept. 1977, pp. 262-278. Also *IBM Research Report RJ1812*.

[Fagi79] Fagin, R., "Normal Forms and Relational Database Operators", *Proc. 1979 ACM SIGMOD Intl. Conf. on Management of Data*, Boston, Mass., May 1979. Also *IBM Research Report RJ2471*, Feb. 19, 1979.

[Gyss85] Gyssens, M., "Embedded Join Dependencies as a tool for decomposing Full Join Dependencies", *Proc. 4th ACM SIGACT-SIGMOD Symposium on Principles of Database Systems*, March 1985, pp. 205-214.

[Maie83] Maier, D., *The Theory of Relational Databases*, Computer Science Press, 1983.

[Nico78] Nicolas, J. M., "Mutual Dependencies and Some Results on Undecomposable Relations", *Proc. 4th Int. Conf. on Very Large Data Bases*, West Berlin, Germany, Sept. 1978, pp. 360-367.

[Riss78] Rissanen, J., "Theory of Joins for Relational Databases - A Tutorial Survey",*Proc. 7th Sym. on Math. Foundations of Comp. Sc.*, Lecture Notes in Computer Sc. 64, Winkowski (ed), Spring-Verlag, New York, 1978, pp. 537-551.

[Scio82] Sciore, E., "A Complete Axiomization of Full Join Dependencies", *J.ACM*, Vol.29, No.2, Apr. 1982, pp 373-393.

[Tan84] Tan, K. P., "A Less Costly Constraints Checking for Join Dependency", *Proc. of the 10th Intl. Conference on Very Large Data Bases*, Aug. 1984, pp. 63-68.

[Ullm82] Ullman, J. D., *Principles of Database Systems*, Computer Science Press, Potomac, Maryland, 1982.

On the Power of Query-Independent Compilation

Jiawei Han [†]

School of Computing Science
Simon Fraser University
Burnaby, B.C., Canada V5A 1S6
han@cs.sfu.ca

Abstract. *Recursive query processing techniques can be classified into three categories: interpretation, query-dependent compilation and query-independent compilation. Query-dependent compilation compiles IDB programs based on possible query instantiations into query-specific EDB programs, while query-independent compilation compiles IDB programs into query-independent and easily analyzable EDB expressions. Previous studies show that linear recursions can be query-independently compiled into highly regular forms. This study analyzes the power of query-independent compilation and shows that (i) query-independent compilation captures more binding information than other methods for irregular linear recursions; (ii) the compilation provides succinct information for the selection of efficient query processing methods; and (iii) it facilitates the constraint-based processing of complex queries. Finally, query-independent compilation can be applied to more complex recursions as well.*

1. Introduction

Recursive query processing techniques [1-3, 7, 10, 12, 14, 15] can be categorized into three approaches: *interpretation, query-dependent compilation*, and *query-independent compilation*. Although the boundaries of these approaches are somewhat fuzzy [2], they can be generally characterized as follows. *Interpretation* [5] refers to the approach which interleaves deductive reasoning (the IDB processing) with query processing (the EDB accessing). The query evaluation method in Prolog is a typical such example. The top-down evaluation with memorization such as the SLD-AL procedure and QSQ [15] can also be categorized into this approach. The compilation approach has a separate compilation phase which accesses only the intensional database and compiles IDB programs into efficiently executable forms. *Query-dependent compilation* precompiles IDB programs based on query instantiations and generates rewritten rules for each IDB predicate on different query forms. The Magic Sets method and the Alexander method [2] are typical examples of this approach. Finally, *query-independent compilation* precompiles IDB predicates and generates compiled forms which are to be used in query analysis and processing.

[†] The work was supported in part by the Natural Sciences and Engineering Research Council of Canada under Grant A-3723 and a research grant of Centre for Systems Science of Simon Fraser University.

This paper studies the power of the third approach, query-independent compilation, with the focus on linear recursions. The compilation method has been discussed in previous studies [8]. It demonstrates that a linear recursion can be compiled to either a bounded recursion or an n-chain recursion. Here we study the power of such a compilation method and show that query-independent compilation of linear recursions generates a highly-regular, compact set of compiled forms on which optimization and more detailed qualitative/quantitative query analysis, such as chain vector binding analysis and constraint analysis, can be performed to generate efficient processing plans for complex queries.

The paper is organized as follows. Section 2 discusses query-independent compilation of linear recursions. Section 3 demonstrates its first power: *the capture of sufficient bindings for irregular linear recursions*. Section 4 discusses its second power: *the usefulness in the selection of efficient query processing algorithms*. Section 5 is on its third power: *the constraint-based query evaluation*. We summarize our study in Section 6.

2. Query-Independent Compilation of Linear Recursions

Like many researchers, we assume that a *deductive database* consists of three portions: (i) an **extensional database (EDB)** (a set of data relations), (ii) an **intensional database (IDB)** (a set of deduction rules in *function-free* Horn-clause forms), and (iii) a set of **integrity constraints (IC's)**. We assume without loss of generality that the EDB and IDB predicates are disjoint, and all the rules are *rectified* [14]. A recursive rule is **linearly recursive** if the head predicate is the sole recursive predicate and appears exactly once in the body. A recursion is a **linear recursion** if it consists of one linear recursive rule and one or more nonrecursive (exit) rules.

As a notational convention, we use the upper case letters to denote predicates, with those starting with P, ..., T indicating IDB predicates and all the others EDB predicates, and we use the lower case letters to denote attribute vectors, with those starting with u, ..., z indicating variables, and all the others indicating constants. Moreover, a "?" mark is used in front of an inquired variable in a query.

In the compilation of a linear recursion with R, we consider that the *first expansion* of R is the recursive rule itself. The *k-th expansion* of R ($k > 1$) is the unification of the recursive definition of R on the $(k-1)$-th expansion of R. The *k-th expanded exit rule* is the rule generated by the unification of the nonrecursive (exit) definitions of R with the k-th expansion of R. The **compiled formula** of R represents the set of EDB formulas generated by all the expansions of R.

Example 1. We present three recursive predicates: spouse, ancestor and the same generation cousin as shown in Fig. 1.

In Fig. 1, $SG(x, y, z)$ indicates that x and y are the same generation cousins and their same generation common ancestor is z, and *Sibling* (x, y, z) indicates that x and y are siblings with a common parent z. The compiled formulas of the two recursions are in Fig. 2.

In Fig. 2, $\cup$ denotes disjunction, and the notation, $Parent^i(x_{i-1}, x_i)$, is defined as below.

$$Parent^i(x_{i-1}, x_i) = \begin{cases} true & \text{if } i = 0, \\ Parent^{i-1}(x_{i-2}, x_{i-1}), Parent(x_{i-1}, x_i) & \text{if } i > 0. \end{cases}$$

Based on this example, we formally define a chain and an n-chain recursion.

(1a) $Spouse\,(x,y) :\!- Spouse\,(y,x).$

(1b) $Spouse\,(x,y) :\!- EdbSpouse\,(x,y).$

(2a) $Ancestor\,(x,y) :\!- Ancestor\,(x,x_1), Parent\,(x_1,y).$

(2b) $Ancestor\,(x,y) :\!- Parent\,(x,y).$

(3a) $SG\,(x,y,z) :\!- Parent\,(x,x_1), Parent\,(y,y_1), SG\,(x_1,y_1,z).$

(3b) $SG\,(x,y,z) :\!- Sibling\,(x,y,z).$

Figure 1. Three typical linear recursions

(1c) $Spouse\,(x,y) = EdbSpouse\,(x,y) \cup EdbSpouse\,(y,x).$

(2c) $Ancestor\,(x_0,y) = \bigcup_{i=0}^{\infty}(Parent^i\,(x_{i-1},x_i), Parent\,(x_i,y)).$

(3c) $SG\,(x_0,y_0,z) = \bigcup_{i=0}^{\infty}(\,Parent^i\,(x_{i-1},x_i), Parent^i\,(y_{i-1},y_i), Sibling\,(x_i,y_i,z)).$

Figure 2. The compiled formulas of the three recursions

Definition. A **chain** of *length* k $(k > 1)$ is a sequence of k predicates with the following properties: (1) all k predicates have the same name, say P, and the l-th P of the chain is denoted as $P_{(l)}$, (2) there is at least one shared variable in every two consecutive predicates, and if i is the variable position in the first predicate, j the variable position in the second, and the two positions contain the shared variables, then (i,j) is an invariant of the chain, i.e., the i-th variable of $P_{(l)}$ is shared with the j-th variable of $P_{(l+1)}$ for every l where $1 \le l \le k-1$. Each predicate of the chain is called a chain *element*. A chain element may also be formed by a sequence of connected predicates (i.e., predicates having shared variables). A 0-length chain is defined as a tautology.

Definitions. A linear recursion is an **n-chain recursion** if for any positive integer K, there exists a k-th expansion of the recursion consisting of one chain (when $n = 1$) or n synchronous (of the same length) chains (when $n > 1$) each with the length greater than K, and possibly some other predicates which do not form a chain. It is a **single-chain recursion** when $n = 1$, or a **multi-chain recursion** otherwise. The recursive rule of an n-chain recursion is called an **n-chain recursive rule**. A recursion is **bounded** if it is equivalent to a set of nonrecursive rules.

Our study of the compilation of linear recursions [8] discloses an important property of linear recursions as below.

Theorem 1. *A linear recursion is compilable to a bounded recursion or an n-chain recursion.*

The variables in the head predicate of a recursion are called **distinguished variables.** Query-independent compilation of linear recursions not only identifies compiled chains but also characterizes the roles of distinguished variables. By compilation, distinguished variables of a linear recursion can be classified into three categories: *chain-variables, exit-variables* and *bounded-variables.* We refer the *near end* of the chain to the end of the chain linked to the exit expression (the body of the exit rule) at any expansion and the *far end* of the chain to the other end of the chain. A **chain-variable** is a distinguished variable always linked to the *far end* of the chain after a finite number of expansions. An **exit-variable** is the one always linked directly to the exit expression. A **bounded-variable** is the one which, after a finite number of expansions, is not linked (directly or indirectly) to a chain element nor an exit expression.

For example, in $SG(x,y,z)$ of Ex. 1, x and y are chain-variables for the two *Parent* chains respectively, and z is an exit-variable.

3. Benefit 1: Capture of Sufficient Bindings for Irregular Linear Recursions

The Magic Sets method [1-3, 14] applies a rule rewriting technique to rewrite a recursion into an equivalent, but more efficiently evaluable one for a query based on the analysis of binding propagation in a rule/goal graph [1, 13]. Binding propagation in a rule/goal graph captures sufficient bindings for queries on many kinds of recursions. However, the technique can only be used to propagate bindings to future expansions *via IDB subgoals*. For some kinds of recursions, binding information should be propagated among different expansions *via EDB subgoals* as well. Such propagation cannot be caught by the rule/goal graph analysis because the graph does not register sufficient information for the propagation. As a result, a rule/goal graph-based rule rewriting technique, such as the Magic rule rewriting, is unable to capture such kind of bindings and thus generates unnecessarily large Magic Sets for such recursions.

The query-independent compilation technique overcomes this difficulty based on the expansion regularity of linear recursions [8]. It compiles a linear recursion into a compiled formula which captures the bindings propagated via both IDB and EDB subgoals. Efficient query evaluation plans can be generated based on the analysis of such compiled formulas.

Example 2. We analyze the binding propagation of a query "$? - P(c_1, c, y)$." on a linear recursion defined by a rule set $\{(r_0), (r_1)\}$, where c_1 and c are constants, x's and y's are variables, and P is a recursive predicate defined by EDB predicates A, B and E.

$(r_0) \quad P(x_1, x, y) :- E(x_1, x, y).$

$(r_1) \quad P(x_1, x, y) :- A(x, y), P(x_2, x_1, y_1), B(x_2, y_1).$

We assume that the readers are familiar with binding propagation [13] and the Magic rule rewriting [2, 3]. Following the binding propagation rules [13], the bindings in the adorned goal node, P^{bbf}, are propagated to the subgoal P in the body of the recursive rule, resulting in an adorned subgoal node, P^{fbf}, which are in turn propagated to the subgoal P in the body of the recursive rule at the next expansion, resulting in P^{fff}. Obviously, P^{fff} cannot propagate any binding information to the body of the rule. The adorned rules, (r_1'), (r_{12}') and (r_{13}'), represent such binding propagation, where (r_1') is an adorned rule of (r_1) with respect to the adorned goal node P^{bbf}, (r_{12}') is an adorned rule *unifying directly* (without renaming variables or modifying adornments) with (r_1') at the second expansion, which is called the **unifying rule** at the second expansion. Similarly, (r_{13}') is the unifying rule at the third expansion.

$(r_1') \quad P^{bbf}(x_1, x, y) :- A^{bf}(x, y), P^{fbf}(x_2, x_1, y_1), B^{bb}(x_2, y_1).$

$(r_{12}') \quad P^{fbf}(x_2, x_1, y_1) :- A^{bf}(x_1, y_1), P^{fff}(x_3, x_2, y_2), B^{bb}(x_3, y_2).$

$(r_{13}') \quad P^{fff}(x_3, x_2, y_2) :- A^{ff}(x_2, y_2), P^{fff}(x_4, x_3, y_3), B^{bb}(x_4, y_3).$

Since there is no binding information which can be passed to P in the body of (r_{13}'), the Magic Set involves the entire relation A. Clearly, the binding propagation cannot reduce the set of data to be examined in the semi-naive evaluation.

We may reorder the subgoals in the body of the rule in search for better rewritten rules [14]. For example, (r_1) can be reordered into (rr_1) by switching P and B in the body.

(rr_1) $P(x_1,x,y):-A(x,y),B(x_2,y_1),P(x_2,x_1,y_1).$

By propagation of bindings using a rule/goal graph, the corresponding adorned rule of (rr_1) is (rr_1'), and its unifying rule at the second expansion is (rr_{12}').

(rr_1') $P^{bbf}(x_1,x,y):-A^{bf}(x,y),B^{ff}(x_2,y_1),P^{bbb}(x_2,x_1,y_1).$

(rr_{12}') $P^{bbb}(x_2,x_1,y_1):-A^{bb}(x_1,y_1),B^{ff}(x_3,y_2),P^{bbb}(x_3,x_2,y_2).$

The reordering avoids the generation of the uninstantiated subgoal P^{fff}. However, both (rr_1') and (rr_{12}') contain an uninstantiated subgoal B^{ff}. This implies that the derivation of the Magic Set will involve the iterative processing of an uninstantiated subgoal B, i.e., the entire data relation B.

There are total $3! = 6$ possible subgoal orderings in this example. Besides the above discussed two: (1) "A,P,B" (subgoal ordering), and (2) "A,B,P", we have four more choices: (3) "B,A,P", (4) "B,P,A", (5) "P,A,B" and (6) "P,B,A". It is easy to verify that all the remaining alternatives have similar binding propagation problems.

However, this does not imply that there exists no efficient binding propagation for this example. Fig. 3 shows the propagation of the binding "$x_1 = c_1$" in three rules, (r_1), (r_{12}), and (r_{13}), where (r_{12}) is the unifying rule of (r_1), and (r_{13}) is the unifying rule of (r_{12}). We can see that the bindings between different expansions can be propagated *via EDB subgoals*. First, query constant c_1 binds X_1, which binds Y_1 of the predicate $A(x_1,y_1)$ in (r_{12}). The binding is propagated back to the predicate $B(x_2,y_1)$ in (r_1), making x_2 bound. Then x_2 in the predicate $P(x_3,x_2,y_2)$ in (r_{12}) is bound. x_2 plays the same role in (r_{12}) and (r_{13}) as x_1 in (r_1) and (r_{12}), making x_3 of the predicate $P(x_4,x_3,y_3)$ in (r_{13}) bound. Future expansions have the similar binding propagations.

Notice that it is natural to view such binding propagation as propagation via EDB subgoals among different expansions, especially when examining the expanded rules. Such propagation can also be viewed as passing bindings back and forth among several expansions via IDB subgoals. For example, binding of y_1 in $A(x_1,y_1)$ of (r_{12}) is passed to the head predicate $P(x_2,x_1,y_1)$, which is then passed back to the recursive predicate $P(x_2,x_1,y_1)$ in the body of rule (r_1), then to $B(x_2,y_1)$, making x_2 bound. The binding of x_2 is then passed forward to the head predicate $P(x_2,x_1,y_1)$ in (r_{12}) making x_2 of $P(x_3,x_2,y_2)$ in the body of (r_{12}) bound, etc. The entire binding propagation process can be explained well according to this viewpoint.

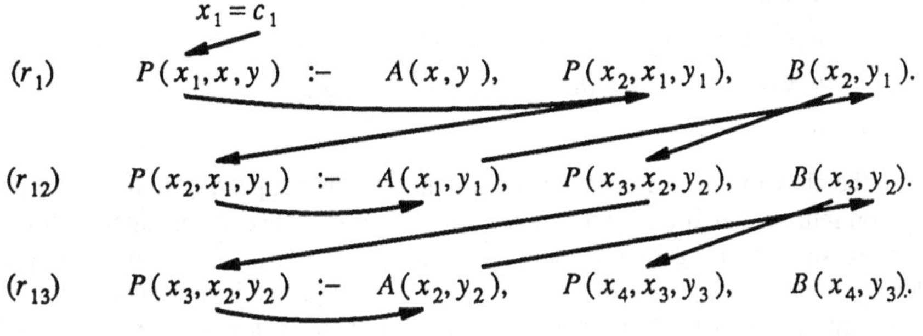

Figure 3. Propagation of binding "$x_1 = c_1$" in unifying rules

To make use of such binding propagation, we examine the second expanded rule (r_2), the rule obtained by unifying (r_1) and (r_{12}).

(r_2) $P(x_1, x, y) :- A(x, y), A(x_1, y_1), P(x_3, x_2, y_2), B(x_3, y_2), B(x_2, y_1).$

The subgoals of the second expanded rule (r_2) can be reordered by moving the last subgoal $B(x_2, y_1)$ to the front of the recursive subgoal P. Then the corresponding adorned rule becomes (r_2').

(r_2') $P^{bbf}(x_1, x, y) :- A^{bf}(x, y), A^{bf}(x_1, y_1), B^{fb}(x_2, y_1), P^{fbf}(x_3, x_2, y_2), B^{bb}(x_3, y_2).$

Similarly, the adorned rule for the third expansion should be (r_3').

(r_3') $P^{bbf}(x_1, x, y) :- A^{bf}(x, y), A^{bf}(x_1, y_1), B^{fb}(x_2, y_1), A^{bf}(x_2, y_2), B^{fb}(x_3, y_2),$
$$P^{fbf}(x_4, x_3, y_3), B^{bb}(x_4, y_3).$$

Since the bindings of the recursive subgoal P in the second and the third expansions share the same adornment, P^{fbf}, future expansions will have similar binding patterns.

Let "$AB(x_1, x_2) :- A(x_1, y_1), B(x_2, y_1).$". The compiled formula of the recursion can be derived as (r_c), which consists of a *well-formed AB*-chain [8]. Notice that the *AB*-chain is formed by connecting two EDB subgoals A and B in two consecutive expansions.

(r_c) $P(x_1, x, y) = E(x_1, x, y) \cup \bigcup_{i=0}^{\infty} (A(x, y), AB^i(x_i, x_{i+1}), E(x_{i+2}, x_{i+1}, y_{i+1}), B(x_{i+2}, y_{i+1})).$

We then examine the evaluation of the query, "$? - P(c_1, c, y).$". The compiled formula indicates that the query can be evaluated without using any uninstantiated subgoals since bindings can be propagated via a sequence of AB's. The answer to the query consists of two sets: the first is derived from $E(c_1, c, y)$, and the second from (r_c').

(r_c') $\bigcup_{i=0}^{\infty} (A(c, y), x_1 = c_1, AB^i(x_i, x_{i+1}), E(x_{i+2}, x_{i+1}, y_{i+1}), B(x_{i+2}, y_{i+1})).$

The formula (r_c') can be evaluated using a typical *partial* (i.e., query-relevant) transitive closure algorithm [14] by pushing the query constant "$x_1 = c_1$" into the *AB*-chain expression. An interesting alternative is to apply an *existence checking algorithm* [7] which verifies whether c_1 may derive any answer for the chain. Observe that (r_c') is the *logical and* of the expression $A(c, y)$ and the union of a sequence of the following expressions,

$E(x_2, c_1, y_1), B(x_2, y_1).$
$AB(c_1, x_2), E(x_3, x_2, y_2), B(x_3, y_2).$
$AB(c_1, x_2), AB(x_2, x_3), E(x_4, x_3, y_3), B(x_4, y_3).$
......

Since the above sequence does not contain any variable appearing in the query predicate, the evaluation returns *true* if *any* expression in the above sequence is evaluated to *true*, or *false* if *every* expression in the above sequence is evaluated to *false*. Therefore, the processing terminates as soon as one query expression in the above sequence is evaluated to true. That is, we first evaluate the first expression and terminate if there is any answer in the evaluation. Otherwise, evaluate the second one and terminate if there is any answer in the evaluation, etc. In the worst case, it evaluates the partial transitive closure of AB. Obviously, in most cases the evaluation terminates long before the partial transitive closure is completely computed. □

4. Benefit 2: Selection of Efficient Query Processing Methods

Query-independent compilation compiles complex linear recursions into highly regular compiled formulas, which benefits query processing in several ways. First, simple algorithms can be applied to simple kinds of recursions. Secondly, compilation saves the rule rewriting process of Magic Sets and extends the application domains of Counting to complex linear recursions. Thirdly, compilation provides important information for the analysis of complex recursive queries and generation of efficient processing plans.

4.1. Selection of simple processing methods

There are in general three kinds of methods, *transitive closure, Counting* and *Magic Sets* [1,2], in the evaluation of queries on function-free linear recursions.

After compiling a complex linear recursion into a bounded or an n-chain recursion, it is straightforward to select an appropriate query processing method. A bounded recursion requires only a nonrecursive query processing algorithm; a single-chain recursion may require a *partial* transitive closure algorithm; while a multi-chain recursion may require the Magic Sets or Counting method, depending on the complexity of data (e.g., cyclic vs. acyclic) and the type of queries (e.g., query closure vs. existence checking).

Interestingly, many application-oriented recursion problems, though in complex forms, can be compiled to single-chain or asynchronous chain recursions and processed by *partial* transitive closure algorithms [6, 11].

4.2. Derivation of Magic Sets without rule rewriting

The Magic Sets method is implemented by an interesting rule rewriting technique [1,3,14]. However, the number of Magic rules and modified rules generated by rule rewriting is exponential to the arity of the recursive predicate. A linear recursion with the recursive predicate of arity 10 may generate 1024 adorned rules and approximately the same number of Magic rules and modified rules. Although the arity of a recursion is often small, it could be large for some applications. For example, in a flight scheduling problem, the arity of the recursive predicate $flight(flight\_no\_list, departure\_port, arrival\_port, departure\_gate, arrival\_gate, departure\_time, arrival\_time, departure\_date, arrival\_date, fare)$ is 10. Moreover, the roles of variables in the recursive predicate are not clearly identified. Thus it is difficult to further optimize queries with complex instantiations and inquiries.

By query-independent compilation, multi-chain recursions can be evaluated using a method similar to Magic Sets but without Magic rule rewriting. The Magic Sets so-derived (i.e., *the relevant portions of the database being queried*) are the query-relevant transitive closures of the compiled chains on which semi-naive evaluation can be performed. By such compilation, the number of compiled chains generated is no more than the arity of the recursive predicate. Moreover, compilation provides an effective way to analyze complex queries.

Example 3. Suppose the recursion is SG of Ex. 1, and the query (q_1) is, "*find those in group A who have the same generation cousin(s) in China*", which contains two EDB predicates, GroupA and Country.

(q_1) $? - SG(?x, y, z), GroupA(x), Country(y, china)$.

Following the traditional binding propagation rules [13], x and z are free variables and y is a bound variable, Magic Sets may have to be derived by starting from a huge set, "$Country(y, china)$", i.e., everyone in China.

However, a simple quantitative analysis will disclose that the predicate "$GroupA(x)$", though not containing constants, provides more selective information than "$Country(y, china)$", and the processing should start at "$GroupA(x)$". After computing the recursion relevant to group A, "$Country(y, china)$" should then be used for selection.

Notice that it is difficult to work out an efficient processing plan without compilation even if we have the knowledge that "$GroupA(x)$" is highly selective and "$Country(y, china)$" is weakly selective. This is because instantiations may apply to the same or different chains of a recursion. For example, if both x and y were the chain-variables of the same chain, $Country(y, china)$, though weakly selective, should be pushed into the chain since it would sharpen the selection constant at the starting point. However, if x were a chain-variable and y were an exit-variable, the push of y-instantiation should be postponed until the Magic Sets for the chain related to $GroupA$ is computed but before the semi-naive evaluation. This is because y-instantiation, though weakly selective, would reduce the size of the initial set of the semi-naive evaluation. In our example, x and y are chain-variables of two separate chains, thus x-instantiation should, but y-instantiation should not be pushed into the iterative computation. $\square$

4.3. Smart Counting for different queries on complex linear recursions

The Counting method [1] is an efficient linear recursive query processing method. The worst case complexity for Counting is $O(ne)$ while that for Magic Sets is $O(e^2)$, where n and e are the number of nodes and the number of edges in the database graph respectively [14]. Notice that Counting may involve more sophisticated algorithms than Magic Sets at handling cyclic data.

Without compilation, Counting applies only to linear chain-rules [4]. Query-independent compilation makes it applicable to more complex linear recursions. Moreover, compilation facilitates the application of smarter Counting algorithms, such as the existence-checking Counting algorithm, in the processing of complex recursive queries [7].

Example 4. We examine the evaluation of the query, (q_1), on the recursion SG by Counting. We have known that the processing should start at $GroupA(x)$ and proceed to the other end of the chain before using the instantiation, "$Country(y, china)$". A careful examination may discover that the processing can be further optimized. Since there is only one inquired variable x in the query, it is only necessary to verify whether a specific value of x is the answer of the query. Therefore, an existence checking evaluation method can be adopted by following any specific source node x. The search terminates if it finds one instance of y and z satisfying the query (although there could be many such instances). Such an algorithm often performs better because many source nodes may terminate in their early search stage, and only those instantiated x's which do not have any answers to the query need to be searched exhaustively. $\square$

We elaborate this point further using a **quad-state variable binding analysis** approach [7]. There are two essential notions associated with a query, *instantiation* and *inquiry*. Therefore, there are four states associated to each variable in the query predicate as follows: (i) *b (bound): instantiated but not inquired*, (ii) *p (partially instantiated): both instantiated and inquired*, (iii) *f (free): inquired but not instantiated*, or (iv) *i (irrelevant to the query): neither instantiated nor inquired*.

An important task of query analysis is to select a (sub)-optimal processing plan for a recursive query. Our study [7] shows that there are four possible processing strategies for a recursive query: (i) **nonrecursive**, which uses only conventional nonrecursive processing algorithms; (ii) **total closure**, which derives the whole recursive relation; (iii) **query closure**, which derives a query-related closure, i.e., the portion of the closure derivable from the query constants; and (iv) **existence checking**, which checks the existence of answer(s) in the database for either a driver set or each driver in a driver set. (A *driver* is a source node in the processing of a chain). Furthermore, the arity (unary vs. binary) of the processing methods may strongly influence the efficiency of recursive query processing [2]. We distinguish *unary* algorithms from *binary* ones. A **unary algorithm** does not trace *driver* → *result* (i.e., *source* → *sink*) pairs in the processing while a **binary algorithm** does.

The total closure strategy should be applied only when the whole recursive relation is inquired. The nonrecursive strategy should be applied if the query is not relevant to any chain variable of a recursion.

In the case that a query is relevant to at least one chain, we provide the following algorithm selection table (proved in [7]) for the selection of binary vs. unary and query closure vs. existence checking algorithms. Notice that if there are more than one variable residing at the same end of a chain, these variables should be folded to one vector [7]. In Table 1, we assume that each state in the table is a folded (vector) state if there are more than one variable at the same end of a chain.

State and Direction	Processing Algorithm
$b \rightarrow$	Unary (U) or Binary (B) [†]
$p \mid f \rightarrow$	Binary (B)
$\rightarrow b \mid i$	Existence Checking (E)
$\rightarrow p \mid f$	Query Closure (Q)

[†] *Binary* in the case of multiple *driven* chains, and *Unary* otherwise.

Table 1. Selection of processing algorithms

Clearly, algorithm selection is determined by compiled chains, variable states (query instantiations and inquiries), and processing directions. The processing direction is determined by query information (highly selective vs. weakly selective), other EDB statistics (such as join selectivity, etc.), and the expected cost of an algorithm (e.g., existence checking usually costs less than deriving a query related closure). Thus a quantitative analysis should be performed in the query plan generation. Such an analysis can be relatively easily performed on the highly regular compiled chains.

Example 5. We demonstrate how a query plan can be generated for query (q_1) on the *SG* recursion using the quad-state variable binding analysis technique. Assume that the *Parent* chain linked to the variable x be A-chain and the other one be B-chain.

(q_1) $? - SG(?x, y, z), GroupA(x), Country(y, china).$

Since the query provides highly selective information at the A-chain only, the A-chain is the driving chain (i.e., processing starts at the far end of the A-chain), and the B-chain is a driven chain. The processing direction combination and the processing plan are presented in Table 2.

In the processing table, there are three variable vectors, *A-chain*, *B-chain* and *Exit-Vector*, and their associated vector states. For each chain, we present (i) the processing direction, ↑ for up-chain processing and ↓ for down-chain processing, (ii) the folded state of

Vector	A-chain	B-chain	Exit-Vector
Direction	↑	↓	—
State	p	b	i
Characteristic Vector	$p \rightarrow b$	$p \rightarrow b$	—
Algorithm	BE	BE	—

Table 2. The processing table for query (q_1)

the vector of the distinguished variable(s), (iii) the characteristic vector which indicates the processing direction and the states of both ends of the chain, and (iv) the algorithm selected.

Talbe 2 indicates that *A-chain* is in the state of "p", *B-chain* is in the state of "b", and *Exit-Vector* is in the state of "i". The two states of A-chain is "p" and "b" (since the state of the exit-variable "i" and that of another chain variable "b" are folded to "b"). Similarly, the two states of B-chain is "p" and "b". The processing should start at the A-chain (up-chain processing $p \rightarrow b$) using the BE (binary existence checking) algorithm and then step-down the B-chain using the BE algorithm. □

Such a smart Counting method is called the *multi-way Counting method* [7].

Notice that the existence checking evaluation is beneficial in Counting but may not be promising in the implementation of Magic Sets method. This is because the semi-naive evaluation does not trace the processing of each chain. In our example, as long as there is one person in Group A who does not have the same-generation cousin in China, the semi-naive evaluation must proceed to the end (i.e., find the whole Magic Sets and perform the complete semi-naive evaluation).

5. Benefit 3: Constraint-Based Query Evaluation

The third advantage of query-independent compilation is that it facilitates constraint-based query processing in deductive databases. Constraints can be classified into *query constraints* and *integrity constraints*. The former are the constraints enforced on query predicates while the latter are those reflecting the relationships among data in databases and/or the arguments of predicates in deduction rules. Constraints play an important role in reducing search space and producing knowledgeable answers.

By compilation of linear recursions into regular chain forms, it is easy to apply those constraints effectively. In the analysis of a query, the recursive predicate with uninstantiated variables is taken as the query predicate, and all the other predicates and instantiations are taken as query constraints. Following the popualr heuristic in database query processing, *pushing selection as deeply as possible into a relational expression* [4, 14], query constraints should be pushed as deeply as possible before the start of iterative processing. However, not all the query constraints can be pushed into the chain indiscriminately as shown in Ex. 5, where only the constraints associated with the start end of the chain should be pushed into the chain for initial processing. Therefore, it is important to distinguish which constraints belong to which end of the chain and take a more selective end as the starting point.

However, care should be taken for those constraints which are not associated with the start end. Although they can be used at the end of the iterative processing, *it is beneficial to use them during the iterative processing, when possible*. This can often be accomplished by the analysis of integrity constraints in the database.

Example 6. Suppose a query, *find John's ancestors who were born in the 19th century*, is posed to the database using the IDB predicate *Ancestor* defined in Ex. 2 (a single-chain recursion).

$?- Ancestor(john, ?y), Person(y, yr\_birth), yr\_birth \geq 1800, yr\_birth < 1900.$

Obviously, for the *Parent*-predicate, "*john*" is more selective than "*born in the 19th-century*". Thus the processing of the *Parent*-chain should start at the end where the constant "*john*" resides. Since John's ancestors reside at the other end of the chain, the query constraints "*Person(y, yr_birth), yr_birth \geq 1800, yr_birth < 1900*" cannot be easily pushed in. However, if there is an integrity constraint, *parents are older than their children*, that is, yr_birth of y is a monotonically decreasing function, the query constraints at the other end of the chain can be selectively pushed into the chain for iterative processing.

The general rule to push query constraints at the other end of the chain is that if a constraint can be used to block the growth or shrinkage of the values of the monotonic function, it or its transformed form can still be pushed into the chain for iterative processing. In our example, the constraint, $yr\_birth \geq 1800$, blocks the shrinkage of the values of the monotonic function, therefore it, together with the predicate, "*Person(y, yr_birth)*, $yr\_birth \geq 1800$", can be pushed into the chain during the iterative processing. However, the constraint, $yr\_birth < 1900$, cannot block the shrinkage of the values of the monotonic function, thus it should not be pushed into the chain during the iterative processing. This is obvious. Otherwise, John's parents may not be able to satisfy the constraint, and his grandparents and so on can never be generated. Thus this constraint can only be used at the end of the chain processing. □

In general, the monotonicty of an argument in the recursive predicate can be discovered based on the characteristics of data and rules. Such monotonic behavior is useful at constraint-based query processing. A detailed study of constraint-based deductive query evaluation is in [9].

Query-independent compilation greatly simplifies the constraint-based linear recursive query processing because of the elegance and simplicity of the highly regular compiled chains of linear recursions. Obviously, without compiling functional linear recursions into chain forms, it is difficult to fully explore various kinds of constraints in the processing.

6. Conclusions

We studied the power of query-independent compilation in the linear recursive query evaluation. Query-independent compilation facilitates the systematic development of efficient evaluation techniques for vairous kinds of linear recursive queries. This is because the compilation results in highly regular chain- or bounded- formulas, which not only captures the bindings which could be difficult to capture by other techniques but also provides precise chain connection information (in relational expression forms) for query optimization. Both qualitative and quantitative analyses can be performed on the compiled chains to determine the start end of the chain, the evaluation directions, the possible existence checking evaluation, the pushing of query constraints át the start end of a chain, and the possible pushing of other constraints into the chain for efficient evaluation. Query-independent compilation facilitates the derivation of flexible and efficient processing plans for complex recursive queries. Therefore, it is a promising technique in the processing of complex queries in deductive databases.

Many complex function-free recursions, which may contain single or multiple linear recursive rules, nonlinear recursive rules, mutually recursive rules and multiple-level recursions, can be compiled to highly regular compiled formulas consisting of single or asynchronous chains or other similar forms [6]. The query analysis techniques discussed here can be effectively applied to such recursions as well. It is important to study query-independent compilation of more complex recursions and extend our query analysis technique to the recursions which cannot be compiled into highly regular forms.

References

1. F. Bancilhon, D. Maier, Y. Sagiv and J. D. Ullman, Magic Sets and Other Strange Ways to Implement Logic Programs, *Proc. 5th ACM Symp. Principles of Database Systems,* Cambridge, MA, March 1986, 1–15.

2. F. Bancilhon and R. Ramakrishnan, An Amateur's Introduction to Recursive Query Processing Strategies, *Proc. 1986 ACM-SIGMOD Conf. Management of Data,* Washington, DC, May 1986, 16–52.

3. C. Beeri and R. Ramakrishnan, On the Power of Magic, *Proc. 6th ACM Symp. Principles of Database Systems,* San Diego, CA, March 1987, 269–283.

4. C. Beeri, P. Kanellakis, F. Bancilhon and R. Ramakrishnan, Bounds on the Propagation of Selection into Logic Programs, *Proc. 6th ACM Symp. Principles of Database Systems,* San Diego, CA, March 1987, 214–226.

5. H. Gallaire, J. Minker and J. Nicolas, Logic and Databases: A Deductive Approach, *ACM Comput. Surv.,* **16**(2), 1984, 153–185.

6. J. Han and W. Lu, Asynchronous Chain Recursions, *IEEE Trans. Knowledge and Data Engineering,* **1**(2), 1989, 185–195.

7. J. Han, Multi-Way Counting Method, *Information Systems,* **14**(3), 1989, 219–229.

8. J. Han, Compiling General Linear Recursions by Variable Connection Graph Analysis, *Computational Intelligence,* **5**(1), 1989, 12–31.

9. J. Han, Constraint-Based Reasoning in Deductive Databases, *Proc. 7th Int. Conf. Data Engineering,* Kobe, Japan, April 1991.

10. L. J. Henschen and S. Naqvi, On Compiling Queries in Recursive First-Order Databases, *J. ACM,* **31**(1), 1984, 47–85.

11. J. F. Naughton, One-Sided Recursions, *Proc. 6th ACM Symp. Principles of Database Systems,* San Diego, CA, March 1987, 340–348.

12. R. Ramakrishnan, Magic Templates: A Spellbinding Approach to Logic Programs, *Proc. Int. Conf. Logic Programming,* Seattle, WA, August 1988, 140–159.

13. J. D. Ullman, Implementation of Logical Query Languages for Databases, *ACM Trans. Database Syst.,* **10**(3), 1985, 289–321.

14. J. D. Ullman, *Principles of Database and Knowledge-Base Systems, Vol. 2,* Computer Science Press, Rockville, MD, 1989.

15. L. Vieille, Recursive Axioms in Deductive Databases: The Query/Subquery Approach, *Proc. 1st Int. Conf. Expert Database Systems,* Charleston, SC, April 1986, 179–193.

Parallel Transitive Closure Computation in Highly Scalable Multiprocessors

Anestis A. Toptsis
Dept. of Computer Science and Mathematics
York University, Atkinson College
Toronto, Ontario, M3J 1P3, Canada

ABSTRACT

Computation of transitive closure is a fundamental problem in the area of computer algorithms and among others a central issue in the process of integrating database and knowledgebase systems. Although a plethora of sequential transitive closure algorithms have been developed, parallel transitive closure algorithms are rather scarce. Moreover, the few existing parallel algorithms have severe limitations in terms of (a) *load balancing*, (b) *sufficient utilization of the allocated processors*, and (c) *inability to take advantage of highly scalable parallel architectures*. In this paper we present and analyze two parallel algorithms – PAR-TC and GPAR-TC – for the computation of the transitive closure of a binary database relation. Algorithm PAR-TC is a straightforward parallelization of an existing sequential algorithm [10,22,14]. In many cases, PAR-TC attains significant speedup over its sequential counterpart. In the worst case the speedup is marginal as this algorithm is also subject to the three limitations stated above. Nevertheless, algorithm GPAR-TC which is is a refinement of PAR-TC remedies all three limitations. In the worst case, GPAR-TC is at least as good as PAR-TC; and if a perfect hashing function is available for each value set of the two attributes of the input binary relation, then the speedup of GPAR-TC over the sequential algorithm is proportional to the number of processors available in the system. This last property makes algorithm GPAR-TC especially suitable for highly scalable parallel architectures.

1 Introduction

Recursive query evaluation is a capability of deductive data base systems that conventional data base systems do not support well, if at all [14]. Since every linear recursive query can be answered by the computation of a transitive closure possibly preceded and/or followed by operations already available in relational algebra [11], it is of interest to compute transitive closure efficiently. Finding transitive closure sequentially has received considerable attention [1,3,2,5,8,10,9,13,14,15,18,19,20, 21,22,24,25], etc. Naturally, it is desirable to take advantage of multiprocessors in performing the same task. Although by far outnumbered by their sequential counterparts, several parallel transitive closure algorithms have been proposed [23,4,17]. Three common and undesirable characteristics in all these algorithms are that (1) although a large number of processors is allocated by the algorithm, only a small number of the allocated processors is used at any given point during execution, (2) in case that the number of available processors in the system exceeds a certain limit, the additional processors are not allocated by the algorithm, and (3) the important issue of load balancing is either bypassed by making simplifying assumptions for equal data distribution [4,23], or not discussed at all [17].

   In this paper we present and analyze two parallel algorithms – PAR-TC and GPAR-TC – for the computation of the transitive closure of a binary database relation. Algorithm PAR-TC is a parallelization of the sequential algorithm Smart [10,22,14]. Algorithm Smart belongs to the category of logarithmic algorithms for the computation of the transitive closure. The algorithms in this category compute the transitive closure R^+ of a given relation R in $\Theta(log_2 D)$ iterations, where D is the depth of the transitive closure. Our analysis shows that PAR-TC encounters problems in load balancing, uses only a small fraction of the number of allocated processors during most of its execution, and in case that the number of processors exceeds a certain limit, the additional processors are not allocated at all. Algorithm GPAR-TC is a refinement of PAR-TC and it has the desirable properties of balancing the workload, using *all* the allocated processors during the entire course of its execution, and allocating *all* the processing available in the machine. The analysis shows that in the worst case GPAR-TC is equivalent to PAR-TC, while in the best case its performance improves as the size of the multiprocessor machine increases.

The organization of the paper is as follows. In Section 2, the sequential algorithm Smart is given as a reference. In Section 3, the parallel algorithm PAR-TC (parallel TC) is presented. In Section 4, we analyze the performance of algorithm PAR-TC, compare the algorithm to algorithm Smart, and point out the limitations of PAR-TC. Section 5 presents the parallel algorithm GPAR-TC (Group parallel TC). Section 6, is the performance analysis of GPAR-TC. Section 7 summarizes our findings and discusses future research directions.

2 Algorithm Smart

Algorithm SMART [10,22,14].
  for m = 1 to $\lceil log_2(D + 1) \rceil$ do
   1. $R^{2^m} := R^{2^{m-1}} \bowtie R^{2^{m-1}}$;
   2. $T = (R + R^2 + ... + R^{2^{m-1}}) \bowtie R^{2^m}$;
   3. $new\_E := R^{2^m} + T + old\_E$;
  end for.

In the above algorithm, "$\bowtie$" and "+" denote the relational join and union operations respectively. R, T, new_E, and old_E are binary (i.e. two-attribute) database relations. R is the input relation whose transitive closure is requested. T is an intermediate result relation. Relations new_E and old_E hold parts of the transitive closure during each iteration.

3 Algorithm PAR-TC

In this section the parallel algorithm PAR-TC is presented. PAR-TC is a parallelization of the sequential algorithm Smart given in the previous section.

Algorithm PAR-TC
for m = 1 to $\lceil log_2(D + 1) \rceil$ do
  for all P_i, $1 \leq i \leq 2^{m-1}$
    $R^{i+2^{m-1}} := R^i \bowtie R^{2^{m-1}}$;
  end for all
end for.

The "for all P_i" statement in algorithm PAR-TC means that processors P_1, P_2, ..., P_i perform the joins $R^i \bowtie R^{2^{m-1}}$, $i = 1, 2, ..., 2^{m-1}$ concurrently. That is, when m=1, processor P_1 performs $R \bowtie R$; when m=2 processors P_1 and P_2 work concurrently. Processor P_1 performs $R \bowtie R^2$ and processor P_2 performs $R^2 \bowtie R^2$; etc. In table 1, below, the joins performed in the first 4 iterations in algorithms Smart and PAR-TC, are shown.

From table 1, we can infer that during the m-th iteration, algorithm PAR-TC computes exactly what algorithm Smart computes in step (b) of the (m-1)-th iteration together with step (a) of the m-th iteration. For example, algorithm PAR-TC computes $R \bowtie R^2$ and $R^2 \bowtie R^2$ during iteration 2 and algorithm Smart computes $R \bowtie R^2$ during step (b) of iteration 1 and $R^2 \bowtie R^2$ during step (a) of iteration 2.

Convention: Hereafter, when we refer to the m-th iteration of the algorithms, we mean for algorithm PAR-TC the m-th iteration of this algorithm as shown in table 1 and for algorithm Smart step (b) of its (m-1)-th iteration together with step (a) of its m-th iteration. This setting of the meaning of the m-th iteration is fair, because this way both algorithms manipulate the same data volume and also generate the same tuples within the same iteration.

4 Performance analysis of algorithm PAR-TC

In this section we analyze the performance of algorithm PAR-TC, compare the algorithm to algorithm Smart, and point out the limitations of PAR-TC. The purpose of comparing the algorithms

Iteration	Smart	PAR-TC	No. Processors used
1	(a) $R \bowtie R$ (b) $R \bowtie R^2$	$R \bowtie R$ $R \bowtie R^2$	1
2	(a) $R^2 \bowtie R^2$ (b) $(R + R^2 + R^3) \bowtie R^4$	$R \bowtie R^2$ $R^2 \bowtie R^2$	2
3	(a) $R^4 \bowtie R^4$ (b) $(R + ... + R^7) \bowtie R^8$	$R \bowtie R^4$ $R^2 \bowtie R^4$ $R^3 \bowtie R^4$ $R^4 \bowtie R^4$	4
4	(a) $R^8 \bowtie R^8$ (b) $(R + ... + R^15) \bowtie R^16$	$R \bowtie R^8$ $R^2 \bowtie R^8$ $R^3 \bowtie R^8$ $R^4 \bowtie R^8$ $R^5 \bowtie R^8$ $R^6 \bowtie R^8$ $R^7 \bowtie R^8$ $R^8 \bowtie R^8$	8

Table 1: Algorithms Smart and PAR-TC at work

is to find the speedup obtained by algorithm PAR-TC over algorithm Smart. We find that in certain cases almost no speedup is obtained. These cases occur when the joins produce relations whose size is very different from the size of the joining relations.

In comparing the two algorithms, Smart and PAR-TC, the most important parameter is the cost incurred by performing joins. In the case of algorithm PAR-TC this cost is categorized into a) *communication* cost, which is roughly the cost incurred by initializing the local storage devices of the processors with the appropriate data, and b) *join* cost, which is the cost incurred by joining the relations in the individual processors. In the case of algorithm Smart there is only join cost. However, note that the join cost in algorithm Smart is in general significantly bigger that the join cost of algorithm PAR-TC. This is because in algorithm Smart a single processor handles the entire data volume involved in the joins, whereas in algorithm PAR-TC the data is scattered among many processors and, therefore, each processor has to handle a smaller data volume.

The analysis serves primarily to identifying the limitations of algorithm PAR-TC and also to establish a way for quantifying the join cost. As such, the analysis ignores the communication cost for algorithm PAR-TC. That is, we assume that the data is already available in the local storage device of each processor prior to start performing the joins. Of course this is not a realistic assumption and it also favors the parallel algorithm. A more complete analysis which also takes in account the communication cost, is presented when we do the analysis of algorithm GPAR-TC in section 6.

Clearly, the cost of joining a relation S with a relation T depends on the sizes of S and T. We denote these sizes by $|S|$ and $|T|$. There are mainly three methods to perform the join $S \bowtie T$. Nested loops join, merge-sort join and Hash-based join. Among these three methods Hash-based join in general performs the best [1]. This is because with this method the join operation can be carried out in linear time with respect to the size of the relations S and T [6,7,16]. That is, relations S and T can be joined in $\Theta(|S|+|T|)$ units of time. (Note, for nested loops and merge-sort, $\Theta(|S| \cdot |T|)$, and $\Theta(|S| \cdot log|S| + |T| \cdot log|T|)$ units of time are required respectively.)

After the above discussion, we assume that all joins performed in algorithms Smart and PAR-TC, are Hash-based joins. Now, we first compute the cost of joins during the m-th iteration of both algorithms and then we compute this cost over all k iterations, $k = \lceil log_2(D + 1) \rceil$.

$C_J(Smart)$: Join cost at m-th iteration of algorithm Smart: During the m-th iteration of algorithm

---

[1] This is also supported by results in [6,7,16].

Smart the joins $R^{2^{m-1}} \bowtie R^{2^{m-1}}$ and $(R + R^2 + \ldots + R^{2^{m-1}-1}) \bowtie R^{2^{m-1}}$ are performed. The cost of these joins is

$$C_J(Smart) = 2|R^{2^{m-1}}| + |R| + |R^2| + \ldots + |R^{2^{m-1}-1}| + |R^{2^{m-1}}| \qquad (1)$$

$C_J(PAR - TC)$: Join cost at m-th iteration of algorithm PAR-TC: During the m-th iteration of algorithm PAR-TC the joins $R \bowtie R^{2^{m-1}}$, $R^2 \bowtie R^{2^{m-1}}$, $\ldots$, $R^{2^{m-1}} \bowtie R^{2^{m-1}}$, are performed in parallel. The cost of these joins is

$$C_J(PAR - TC) = |R^{2^{m-1}}| + max\left[|R|, |R^2|, \ldots, |R^{2^{m-1}}|\right] \qquad (2)$$

The size $|R^i|$ of the relations R^i in expressions (1) and (2) above, depends on two parameters. One is the join selectivity (JS) and the other is $|R|$, the size of the initial relation R. The join selectivity of two relations S and T is expressed as $JS(S,T) = \frac{|S \bowtie T|}{|S| \cdot |T|}$. Therefore, $|S \bowtie T| = JS \cdot |S| \cdot |T|$. Assuming that JS is kept constant throughout the algorithm, we can derive $|R^i| = JS^{i-1} \cdot |R^i|$, for any $i \geq 1$. Equivalently, $|R^i| = A^{i-1} \cdot |R|$ (3), for any $i \geq 1$, where $A = JS \cdot |R|$. In expression (3), if $A = 1$ then $|R^i| = |R|$. That is, the size of any relation resulting from a join is the same as the size of the initial relation R. If $A > 1$, then the joins generate relations of bigger and bigger size. If $A < 1$, then the joins generate relations of smaller and smaller size. By looking at formula (2) (join cost for m-th iteration of algorithm PAR-TC) we observe the following. When $A = 1$, all processors which participate in the execution of the m-th iteration have to handle the same amount of data. That is, the work is equally distributed among all the active processors. This is a desirable property for any parallel algorithm, including algorithm PAR-TC. When $A > 1$, formula (2) becomes $C_J(PAR - TC) = 2 \cdot |R^{2^{m-1}}|$. That is, processor $P_{2^{m-1}}$ has to handle more data than what each of the processors $P_1, P_2, \ldots, P_{2^{m-1}-1}$ has. This is not a desirable property since the work is not equally distributed among all processors. Similar situation arises when $A < 1$. The analysis for the comparison of algorithm PAR-TC with Smart is split into two cases. In the first case we assume $A = 1$ and in the second case we assume $A \neq 1$.

Case I: $A = 1$.
When A=1, expressions (1) and (2) give the following join costs:
(1) $\Longrightarrow C_J(Smart) = (2 + 2^{m-1}) \cdot |R|$
(2) $\Longrightarrow C_J(PAR - TC) = 2 \cdot |R|$
Assuming that the algorithms perform k iterations, $k \geq 2$, the total join cost for k iterations of algorithm Smart is

$$total\_C_J(Smart) = |R| \cdot \sum_{m=1}^{k}(2 + 2^{m-1})$$

and the total cost for algorithm PAR-TC is

$$total\_C_J(PAR - TC) = 2 \cdot k \cdot |R|$$

We denote by S the *speedup* obtained by using algorithm PAR-TC instead of its sequential version, algorithm Smart.

$$S = \frac{total\_C_J(Smart)}{total\_C_J(PAR - TC)} = \frac{2k + 2^k - 1}{2k}$$

and 2^{k-1} processors used by algorithm PAR-TC.

Case II: $A \neq 1$.

• $A > 1$. In this case,

$$(1) \Longrightarrow C_J(Smart) = |R| \cdot (2 \cdot A^{2^{m-1}-1} + \frac{A^{2^{m-1}} - 1}{A - 1})$$

$$(2) \Longrightarrow C_J(PAR-TC) = 2 \cdot |R| \cdot A^{2^{m-1}-1}$$

Therefore, the total join cost for k iterations of algorithm Smart is

$$total\_C_J(Smart) = |R| \cdot \sum_{m=1}^{k} (2 \cdot A^{2^{m-1}-1} + \frac{A^{2^{m-1}}-1}{A-1})$$

and the total cost for algorithm PAR-TC is

$$total\_C_J(PAR-TC) = |R| \cdot \sum_{m=1}^{k} 2 \cdot A^{2^{m-1}-1}.$$

By dividing these costs we have the speedup S. For this case $(A > 1)$ it is $S > 1$ and it can be shown that $\lim_{A \to \infty} S = 1.5$. The meaning of this limit is that when the joins produce very large relations (i.e. A is very large) then the Smart algorithm (which runs on a uniprocessor machine) is only 1.5 times slower than the PAR-TC algorithm (which runs on a multiprocessor machine with 2^{k-1} processors. This poor performance of the PAR-TC algorithm is due to the fact that the work is not balanced among the processors used in algorithm PAR-TC within each iteration. Note, when A is very large, the processor which performs $R^{max} \bowtie R^{max}$ where max is the highest power of R computed so far, becomes the bottleneck. This is because due to $A \to \infty$, relation R^{max} is very large.

- $0 < A < 1$. In this case, the analysis is similar to the case $A > 1$ and it is not shown all over. An important point, however, is that in this case $\lim_{A \to 0} S = 1$ (less than in the $A > 1$ case). The meaning of this limit is that when the joins produce very small relations $(A \to 0)$ then the Smart algorithm (which runs on a uniprocessor machine) is as fast as the PAR-TC algorithm (which runs on a multiprocessor machine with 2^{k-1} processors). The reasons for which this happens are the same as in the $A > 1$ case.

Limitations of algorithm PAR-TC

The above discussion reveals the following major deficiencies of algorithm PAR-TC.

1. Within the m-th iteration of algorithm PAR-TC, the total amount of data handled is very unevenly distributed among the 2^{m-1} processors used in this iteration, when $A \neq 1$.

2. During the entire course of execution of algorithm PAR-TC, at least 50% of the available processors are idle most of the time. Note, assuming that algorithm PAR-TC terminates after k iterations, it uses 2^{k-1} processors at the k-th iteration. Therefore, a machine with at least 2^{m-1} processors is required. However, the algorithm uses only half of these processors in the (k-1)-th iteration, and even fewer processors in the earlier iterations. Therefore, while algorithm PAR-TC runs on a 2^{k-1}-processor machine, it only uses a rather small fraction of these processors during most of its execution.

3. Algorithm PAR-TC ignores the availability of additional computing power. In case that the algorithm terminates after k iterations and $2^{k-1} + z$ processors are available in the system, then z processors are useless as long as algorithm PAR-TC is concerned.

Algorithm GPAR-TC, presented next, overcomes all the above limitations.

5 Algorithm GPAR-TC

In this section algorithm GPAR-TC (Group PAR-TC) is presented and analyzed. Algorithm GPAR-TC is a refinement of PAR-TC and performs the same joins as algorithm PAR-TC but in a different way. This different way of performing the joins is an attempt to eliminate the three weaknesses of algorithm PAR-TC mentioned in the previous section 4. Algorithm GPAR-TC has the following characteristics.

1. Algorithm GPAR-TC uses all the available processors in the system and it does so in every one on its iterations. This eliminates weaknesses 2 and 3 mentioned in section 4.

2. In order to perform the joins $R \bowtie R^{2^{m-1}}$, $R^2 \bowtie R^{2^{m-1}}$, ..., $R^{2^{m-1}} \bowtie R^{2^{m-1}}$ in the m-th iteration of GPAR-TC, the available processors are partitioned into 2^{m-1} groups G_1, G_2, ..., $G_{2^{m-1}}$. Each group G_i consists of r_i processors and these r_i processors of group G_i are assigned the task of performing the join $R^i \bowtie R^{2^{m-1}}$. The number r_i of processors of group G_i is decided after taking in consideration the amount of data $D_i = |R^i| + |R^{2^{m-1}}|$ which is to be handled by group G_i. The bigger the D_i the more processors are allocated to group G_i. Specifically, for any two groups G_i and G_j, r_i and r_j are such that $\frac{D_i}{D_j} = \frac{r_i}{r_j}$. For example, if $D_i = 2 \cdot D_j$ and if group G_i consists of r_i processors, then group G_j consists of $\frac{r_i}{2}$ processors. Upon completion of the formation of the groups G_1, G_2, ..., $G_{2^{m-1}}$, each group G_i performs the join $R^i \bowtie R^{2^{m-1}}$ using a parallel join algorithm. Different groups may use different join algorithms in order to perform the joins faster. The basic idea behind the decision to have a group of processors rather than a single processor to perform a join and at the same time to allocate more processors to perform joins which involve larger amounts of data, is to achieve equal distribution of work among all the processors available in the system. This will eliminate weakness 1 mentioned in the previous section 4. We show later in the current section that if a Hash-based parallel join algorithm is used by all groups, then in the best case all processors of the system *process the same amount of data*, while in the worst case algorithm GPAR-TC coincides with algorithm PAR-TC.

Now we give a more formal description of algorithm GPAR-TC.

Algorithm GPAR-TC (We assume that $r \geq 2^{k-1}$ processors are available.)
for m=1 to k do
PHASE I /* Grouping phase */

1. Split the r available processors of the system into groups G_1, G_2, ..., $G_{2^{m-1}}$ such that

   (a) Group G_i consists of r_i processors, and

   (b) $\frac{|R| + |R^{2^{m-1}}|}{r_1} = \frac{|R^2| + |R^{2^{m-1}}|}{r_2} = ... = \frac{|R^{2^{m-1}}| + |R^{2^{m-1}}|}{r_{2^{m-1}}}$, and

   (c) $r_1 + r_2 + ... + r_{2^{m-1}} = r$

2. Designate group G_i to perform the join $R^i \bowtie R^{2^{m-1}}$. (This includes sending the required data to the processors of group G_i.)

PHASE II /* Join phase */

1. All groups G_i, i=1, ..., 2^{m-1}, perform $R^i \bowtie R^{2^{m-1}}$ concurrently. Each group may use a join algorithm of its choice.

end for.

6   Performance analysis of algorithm GPAR-TC

In this subsection we analyze algorithm GPAR-TC. The analysis takes in account both the join and the communication cost, as well as the important issue of data skew.

In analyzing algorithm GPAR-TC the cost of each of its iterations is categorized into *communication* cost and *join* cost. Communication cost is the cost incurred by initializing the local storage devices of the processors participating in each iteration of the algorithm with the appropriate data. This cost includes *synchronization* cost (signal the start and end of each iteration), processor *allocation* cost (decide which processors will do what) and *I/O* cost which is the cost incurred by sending the raw data to processors. Join cost is the cost incurred by performing the joins in the individual groups. This cost is dominated by the group which takes the longest to perform its assigned join. In our present analysis we take in account the join cost, and the I/O cost from the communication cost [2].

We mentioned in the description of algorithm GPAR-TC that each group is free to choose its own join strategy. However, again, in order to simplify our analysis we assume that all groups choose to perform their joins using the same Hash-based join algorithm [3]. In this algorithm, in order to join two relations S and T, hashing is used to distribute S and T into buckets S_i and T_i. Then each processor is assigned to join one or more pair (S_i, T_i) of buckets. An important issue which we must consider when S and T are split into buckets is the *data skew* [12]. In partitioning S and T into buckets, the hashing may not result to buckets of equal size. This happens when the joining attributes of S and T carry nondistinct values and/or a perfect hashing function cannot be found. Such data is referred to as skewed data [12]. A zero data skew means that all buckets will have approximately the same size (best case) whereas a nonzero data skew means that one bucket will be bigger than each of the remaining buckets. Thus, when the buckets are distributed among the processors, the processor which receives the largest bucket becomes the bottleneck in the computation since it will generally take more time to perform its corresponding join. The worst case occurs when both relations S and T each hashes into a single bucket. In such a case, the two buckets are sent to the same processor P and P performs $S \bowtie T$ while the remaining processors are idle. In such a case we say that the skew of S is equal to 1 and also the skew of T is equal to 1.

Now we discuss the cost incurred by running algorithm GPAR-TC. We denote by $C_J^{(m)}$ the join cost and by $C_{IO}^{(m)}$ the I/O cost in the m-th iteration of the algorithm. Assuming that a hash-based parallel join algorithm is used by all groups, $C_J^{(m)}$ is a linear function on the size of data joined. Let $max\_DS(G_i^{(m)})$ be the maximum data size handled by a processor within group G_i in the m-th iteration. Then

$$C_J^{(m)} = max\{max\_DS(G_i^{(m)})\} \qquad (1)$$

It can be shown that when the data skew is zero (**best case**) expression (1) above can be written as

$$C_J^{(m)} = \frac{|R| + |R^2| + |R^3| + \ldots + |R^{2^{m-1}}| + 2^{m-1} \cdot |R^{2^{m-1}}|}{r},$$

where r is the total number of available processors in the system. (Recall, in algorithm GPAR-TC we assume that $r \geq 2^{k-1}$). The enumerator on the right hand side of the above formula represents the entire data volume handled in the m-the iteration of algorithm GPAR-TC. Therefore, the meaning of the formula is that when there is no data skew then each of the r available processors has to handle the same amount of data when performing the join. This is a desirable property for any parallel algorithm including GPAR-TC. When the **worst case** occurs, that is, when both relations R^i and $R^{2^{m-1}}$ that are to be joined within group G_i hash each into a single bucket, the situation is as follows.

- When A = 1, $C_J^{(m)} = 2 \cdot |R|$. This means that a single processor within group G_i must handle the join assigned to that group while the remaining processors are idle. Note, in this case $C_J^{(m)}$ is identical to the join cost in algorithm PAR-TC when A=1.

- When $A > 1$, $C_J^{(m)} = 2 \cdot A^{2^{m-1}-1} \cdot |R|$. Again, note in this case $C_J^{(m)}$ is identical to to the join cost in algorithm PAR-TC when $A > 1$.

- When $0 < A < 1$, $C_J^{(m)} = (1 + A^{2^{m-1}-1}) \cdot |R|$. Again, in this case it is easy to see that $C_J^{(m)}$ is identical to the join cost in algorithm PAR-TC when $0 < A < 1$.

Collecting the above results over all k iterations, the total join cost is $C_J = \sum_{m=1}^{k} C_J^{(m)}$. Therefore, in summary we have:

Best case (data skew = 0):

---

[2] We maintain that the I/O cost is by far the largest component in the total communication cost. The other two components, processor synchronization and allocation cost, of the communication cost are not taken in account in our analysis for simplicity reasons.

[3] As it has been demonstrated in [6,7,16], hash-based is a very efficient join method.

- $A = 1$: $C_J = \frac{(2^{k+1}-1)\cdot|R|}{r}$

- $A > 1$: $C_J = \frac{|R|}{r}\cdot\sum_{m=1}^{k}\left(2^m - 1\cdot A^{2^{m-1}-1} + \frac{A^{2^{m-1}}-1}{A-1}\right)$

- $0 < A < 1$: Same as when $A > 1$.

Worst case (data skew = 1):

- $A = 1$: $C_J = 2\cdot k\cdot|R|$

- $A > 1$: $C_J = 2\cdot|R|\cdot\sum_{m=1}^{k} A^{2^{m-1}-1}$

- $0 < A < 1$: $C_J = |R|\cdot\left(k + \sum_{m=1}^{k} A^{2^{m-1}-1}\right)$

Now we must also compute the I/O cost. We assume that the distribution of data to all processors occurs in parallel. That is upon deciding to send say B blocks to each of the r processors of the system, then at time 0 (zero) the local storage devices of the r processors contain none of the B blocks and at time $B\cdot T_b$ the local storage devices of the r processors each contains all the B blocks. (T_b represents the time required to send one block from one processor to another processor.) Note, in the m-iteration, in the best case (skew = 0) each processor receives $(\frac{1}{r} - th$ of the total amount of data processed in the current iteration, whereas in the worst case (skew = 1) 2^{m-1} processors (one from each group) each receives $|R^i| + |R^{2^{m-1}}|$ amount of data. In other words, the I/O cost is the same as the join cost (since we also quantify the join cost with respect to the amount of data to be joined). Therefore,

$$Total\_cost = C_J + C_{IO} + 2\cdot C_J$$

After the above discussion, the speedup S of algorithm GPAR-TC over the Smart algorithm is:
Best case (data skew = 0) Speedup:

- $A = 1$: $S = r\cdot\frac{(2k + 2^k - 1)}{2\cdot(2^{k+1}-1)}$

- $A > 1$: $S = \dfrac{r\cdot\sum_{m=1}^{k}(2\cdot A^{2^{m-1}-1} + \frac{A^{2^{m-1}}-1}{A-1})}{2\cdot\sum_{m=1}^{k}(2^{m-1}\cdot A^{2^{m-1}-1} + \frac{A^{2^{m-1}}-1}{A-1})}$

- $0 < A < 1$: Same as when $A > 1$.

Worst case (data skew = 1) speedup:

- $A = 1 : S = \frac{S(PAR-TC)}{2}$, where S(PAR-TC) represents the speedup obtained in algorithm PAR-TC.

- $A > 1 : S = \frac{S(PAR-TC)}{2}$, where S(PAR-TC) represents the speedup obtained in algorithm PAR-TC.

- $0 < A < 1 : S = \frac{S(PAR-TC)}{2}$, where S(PAR-TC) represents the speedup obtained in algorithm PAR-TC.

Note, in all expressions in the best case above, r appears in the enumerator of the expressions and also $r \geq 2^{k-1}$. Therefore, the speedup obtained by algorithm GPAR-TC is certainly not less than the speedup obtained by algorithm PAR-TC. Moreover, the amount of obtained speedup is restricted only by the availability of processors. In case that more processors are added to the system, the performance of the GPAR-TC algorithm will improve.

7 Conclusion

We presented and analyzed two parallel algorithms - PAR-TC and GPAR-TC - for the computation of the transitive closure of a binary database relation. Algorithm PAR-TC is a parallelization of the sequential algorithm Smart [10,22,14]. The analysis showed that PAR-TC, like other existing parallel transitive closure algorithms, encounters problems in load balancing, uses only a small fraction of the number of allocated processors during most of its execution, and in case that the number of processors available exceeds a certain limit, the additional processors are not allocated at all. Algorithm GPAR-TC is a refinement of PAR-TC and it has the desirable properties of balancing the workload, using *all* the allocated processors during the entire course of its execution, and allocating *all* the processing available in the machine. The analysis shows that in the worst case GPAR-TC is equivalent to PAR-TC, while in the best case its performance improves as the size of the multiprocessor machine increases.

Although algorithm GPAR-TC has the desirable properties stated above, we believe that there is a lot more to be said. Our future research includes the following.

1. In some cases hash-based parallel join may not be the best algorithm to perform the join $R^i \bowtie R^{2^{m-1}}$ within group G_i. For example, it is stated in [12] that a nested loop parallel join algorithm may be useful when the relations to be joined are small. Therefore, it would desirable to establish a decision making policy for the join algorithm to be chosen by each group of processors.

2. Adapt algorithm GPAR-TC for the computation of the **restricted** closure. Computation of the restricted rather than the complete closure is agreed to be requested more often in "real-life" computations.

3. Algorithm GPAR-TC was presented assuming a generic parallel architecture. We believe that there are many issues to be discussed when the algorithm is to be tuned for particular architectures of different nature (e.g. shared vs distributed memory machines). Versions of the algorithm for several architectures and the results of comparing these versions is a topic deserving further investigation.

References

[1] Arlazarov, V. L., Dinic, E. A., Kronrod, M. A., and Faradzev, I. A. "On Economical Construction of the Transitive Closure of an Oriented Graph", *Soviet Math. Doklady*, 11, 1970, 1209-1210.

[2] Agrawal, R., Borgida A., and Jagadish, H., "Efficient management of transitive relationships in large data and knowledge bases", *ACM SIGMOD*, 1989, 253-262.

[3] Agrawal, R. and Jagadish, H.V. "Direct Algorithms For Computing the transitive closure Of Database Relations", *13-th VLDB*, Brighton, England, Sept. 1987.

[4] Agrawal, R. and Jagadish, H.V. "Multiprocessor Transitive Closure Algorithms", *Proc. Inter. Symp. on Databases in Parallel and Distributed Systems*, Austin, Texas, 1988, pp. 56-66.

[5] Baker, J.J. "A note on Multiplying Boolean Matrices", *CACM*, 1962, 102.

[6] Dewitt, D. J. and Gerber, R., "Multiprocessor Hash-Based Join Algorithms", *11-th VLDB*, 1985, pp. 151-164.

[7] Dewitt, D. J. et. al., "Implementation Techniques for Large Main Memory Database Systems", *ACM SIGMOD*, 1984.

[8] Bancilhon, F. and Ramakrishnan, R. "An Amateur's Introduction to Recursive Query Processing Strategies" *ACM SIGMOD*, 1986, 16-52.

[9] Ioannidis, Y.E. and ramble, R., "Efficient Transitive Closure of Relational Operators", *14-th VLDB*, Los Angeles, California, 1988, pp. 382-394.

[10] Ioannidis, Y.E., "On the Computation of the Transitive Closure of Relational Operators", *12-th VLDB*, Kyoto, Japan, 1986, pp. 403-411.

[11] Jagadish, H.V., Agrawal, R., and Ness, L. "A Study of Transitive Closure as a Recursion Mechanism" *ACM SIGMOD*, May 1987, 331-344.

[12] Lakshmi, M. S. and Yu, P. S., "Effect of Skew in Join Performance in Parallel Architectures", *Inter. Symp. on Databases in Parallel and Distributed Systems*, Austin Texas, December 1988.

[13] Lu, H., "New Strategies for Computing the Transitive Closure of a Database Relation", *13-th VLDB*, Brighton, England, 1987, pp. 267-247.

[14] Lu, H., Mikkilineni, K., and Richrardson, J.P., "Design and Evaluation of Algorithms to Compute the Transitive Closure of a Database Relation" *Proc. IEEE 3-rd Inter. Conf. Data Engineering*, Los Angeles, Feb. 1987, pp. 112-119.

[15] Naughton, J.F., Ramakrishnan, R., Sagiv, Y., and Ullman, J.D., "Efficient evaluation of right-, left-, and multi-linear rules", *ACM SIGMOD*, 1989, pp. 235-242.

[16] Qadah, G. Z. "The Equi-Join Operator on a Multiprocessor Machine: Algorithms and the Evaluatin of their Performance", *Database Machines, 4-th Inter. Workshop*, Spronger-Verlag, 1985, pp. 35-67.

[17] Guh, K.C., and Yu, C.T., "Evaluation of Transitive Closure in Distributed Database Systems", *IEEE Journal on Selected Areas in Communications*, 7, 1989, pp. 399-407.

[18] Schmitz, L., "An Improved Transitive Closure Algorithm", *Computing* 30, 1983, pp. 359-371.

[19] Schnorr, C.P. "An Algorithm for transitive closure with Linear Expected Time", *SIAM J. Computing* 7, 1978, pp. 127-133.

[20] Toptsis, A.A., Yu, C.T., and Nelson, P.C., "Computing the Transitive Closure of Symmetric Matrices", *Proc. Inter. Conf. on Computing and Information (ICCI '90)*, Niagara Falls, Canada, May 1990, pp. 149-154. (also in *Lecture Notes on Computer Science*, Springer-Verlag.)

[21] Toptsis, A.A., Yu, C.T., and Nelson, P.C., "Benchmarking two Types of Restricted Transitive Closure Algorithms", *Proc. COMPSAC '90*, Chicago, Illinois, Oct. 1990, pp. 375-381.

[22] Valduriez, P. and Boral, H., "Evaluation of Recursive Queries Using Join Indices" *Proc. 1-st Inter. Conf. on Expert Database Systems*, Charleston, 1986, pp. 197-208.

[23] Valduriez, P. and Khoshafian, S., "Transitive Closure of Transitevely Closed Relations", *Proc. 2-nd Inter. Conf. on Expert Database Systems*, 1988, pp. 177-185.

[24] Warren, H., Jr. "A Modification of Warshall's Algorithm for the transitive closure of Binary Relations". *CACM* 18, 1975, pp. 218-220.

[25] Warshall, S., "A Theorem on Boolean Matrices", *Journal of the ACM* 9, 1962, pp. 11-12.

METHODS AND TOOLS FOR INTEGRATING DATABASE SYSTEMS AND OBJECT-ORIENTED PROGRAMMING SYSTEMS

Bogdan Czejdo
Department of Mathematical Sciences
Loyola University
New Orleans, LA 70118

Malcolm Taylor
Department of Computer Science
University of Houston
Houston, TX 77204-3475

ABSTRACT

The object-oriented paradigm has gained rapid acceptance as the basis for the next generation of database systems. Yet many of the fundamental concepts behind the object-oriented approach are in conflict with the traditional ideas of database management. In this paper we investigate the similarities and differences between the relational database approach and the object-oriented programming language Smalltalk. We develop an object-oriented data model with abstract classes, and discuss the techniques for translating requests into a relational language.

1. INTRODUCTION

The object-oriented paradigm has had a dramatic impact on the design of many modern computing systems. Database management is one of several fields which have been influenced by this new approach [10]. Object-oriented data models are seen as providing greater power and flexibility than the traditional, record-oriented data models, and these features are necessary to various new application areas such as CAD and office systems. However, it seems that the object-oriented paradigm conflicts in some ways with the traditional goals of database management. In particular, the principle of encapsulation is contrary to the usual idea of providing a flexible data manipulation language for the definition of special-purpose application programs and ad hoc requests. Moreover, the idea of treating each object as a self-contained unit causes difficulties in representing associations between entities. Further, object-oriented languages generally manipulate one object at a time, in contrast to the set-oriented processing offered by the relational model. So far no generally-accepted high-level language has emerged for object-oriented database systems.

Object-oriented databases have their roots in semantic data models such as the E-R model [1] and SDM [5], some of which incorporate the database abstractions (generalization and aggregation) [9]. Languages for semantic data models (such as GORDAS [3]) provide a very good basis for the design of languages for object-oriented databases. A variety of theoretical approaches and implementations for object-oriented database languages have been proposed [10]. Shaw and Zdonik [7] propose an algebra synthesizing relational query concepts with object-oriented databases. The algebra supports access to relationships implied by the structure of the objects, as well as the definition and creation of new relationships between objects.

The GemStone system [6] is one of the leading object-oriented database implementations, and provides a language called OPAL which is used for data definition, data manipulation and general computation. It is based on the Smalltalk language [4], that is a popular object-oriented programming language and whose implementation is well understood by using a conceptual abstraction called the virtual machine. Using Smalltalk they avoid the problem of impedance mismatch [10] because the principal concepts of Smalltalk, such as object, message and class, were adopted for their system. To meet the requirements of a database system, several enhancements were included, such as support for a multi-user disk-based environment and a large object space.

In [2] we introduced an object-oriented data model based on Smalltalk, but without support for abstract classes. In this paper we investigate the similarities between object-oriented languages, with abstract classes, and relational databases. We show how a popular object-oriented language (Smalltalk) can be extended to serve as a view definition and query specification language. User requests are translated from an extended Smalltalk into a relational database language. The paper is organized as follows. In Section 2 we describe the object-oriented schema, and a subset of our language to operate on the underlying database. The creation of abstract objects and associated messages is described in Section 3. Section 4 discusses the translation of object-oriented requests into SQL expressions. A summary is given in Section 5.

2. OBJECT-ORIENTED MODEL

In this section we shall present an object-oriented data model, that is fully integrated with Smalltalk. This model includes typical object-oriented concepts such as object, object type, class, class instance, message and receiver. The main difference between this model and others is that class instances are sets of objects. For each class, maximal, minimal and starred object sets are defined. A maximal object set contains all objects of a given type. A minimal object set contains one object from a class instance. A starred object set is an arbitrary class instance.

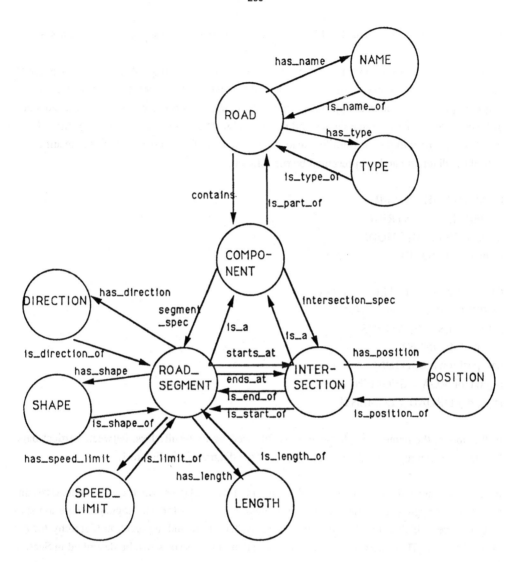

Figure 1. The object-oriented schema for 'Road' database

The basic model was introduced in [2]. In this paper we extend it to support abstract classes.

As an example, let us consider the Road database, adapted from [10] and whose object-oriented schema is shown in Figure 1. In the schema, and throughout this paper, the class names are always in upper-case; maximal object sets start with an upper-case letter, followed by a sequence of lower-case letters; message names and minimal object set names are all in lower-case. Messages are specified in the diagram by means of arrows from the receiver class to the result class. Part of the diagram can be represented by the following:

CLASS NAME   NAME
SUPERCLASS   STRING
MESSAGES & METHODS
is_name_of IROADI

CLASS NAME   INTERSECTION
SUPERCLASS   COMPONENT
MESSAGES & METHODS
is_a ICOMPONENTI
has_position IPOSITIONI
is_end_of IROAD_SEGMENTI
is_start_of IROAD_SEGMENTI

In the above, the name of each message is followed by its result class, between vertical bars. Similarly we can represent the remaining part of the diagram from Figure 1.

Among the classes defined in our model, there are abstract classes which can be subclasses, superclasses or aggregate classes. Among the messages defined for our language, there are special messages which define the subclass/superclass hierarchy and aggregation hierarchy for the abstract classes. These abstract classes and corresponding messages will be described in Section 3.

Our object-oriented query language is based on Smalltalk. The language requires several extensions to Smalltalk, however, in order to allow for database operations. A typical query consists of a class instance name, followed by a sequence of messages. A query can contain selection messages, which specify a subset of the current object set. A simple selection message is a keyword message (EQ, LT, GT, NE, etc.) that requires an argument that can be a constant or a query. GT and LT require one-element sets as the argument, and EQ and NE can accept any set as argument. Additionally, a query can contain an aggregate message. Aggregate messages perform operations such as COUNT, SUM, AVERAGE, MIN, MAX, etc., on the current object set to yield a set containing a single (aggregate) numerical value. We allow the usual set operations, i.e., UNION, INTERSECT and DIFFERENCE. A query may consist of several simpler queries linked by set operators. These set operations can be treated as binary messages.

The above-described messages are applied to the whole set of values for the current class instance. In order to perform grouping and aggregation operations, computations and complex selections, it is necessary to apply a sequence of messages to each element of a set individually. This can be performed by sending a block message that requires a Smalltalk-like block as an argument. The first block message, called group_by, allows for grouping and aggregation operations. For example, a valid query is (**Type EQ: #(highway)**) **is_type_of group_by: [road contains count]** which specifies the following:

Query 1

"For each highway, count the number of components"

There are some other situations where we need to apply operations to each element of the current object set individually. The 'compute' block message allows us to specify arithmetic operations to derive new values for each element of the current set. The arithmetic operators are defined on one-element sets. Also, it is helpful to select elements from the current object set using complex selection predicates similar to the approach of [7]. The 'select' block message allows such selections.

The result of any query is a set of objects. A query can thus be viewed as a compound message to compute such objects. To facilitate the expression of subsequent queries, it is often convenient to create a new message corresponding to the query. This task is performed by the message 'define_message', which is sent to the instance of class DATABASE that contains information about classes and messages. When the operator define-message is invoked, the new message is defined for each member of the class. For example, we can define a new message to determine the shapes of all road segments with a given speed limit. It can be specified by **database define_message: corresponds_to_shape for: SPEED_LIMIT as: [speed_limit* is_limit_of has_shape]**

A subclass automatically inherits the messages of its superclass, in the usual way for object-oriented systems. In case of multiple inheritance, it might happen that two superclasses have messages of the same name. We resolve this kind of conflict by explicitly specifying the superclass in the object-oriented query.

3. DEFINING ABSTRACT CLASSES

The object-oriented schema can be very complex, and might not contain classes that are helpful for the formulation of typical queries for a given user. Additionally, there exist queries, that correspond to multi-argument functions [8], which cannot be handled by previously-described messages. Therefore we allow the dynamic creation of abstract classes. There are many cases but, for the approach chosen in this paper, we discuss only three: creation of subclasses; creation of superclasses; and creation of aggregate classes.

For example, we might create an abstract subclass NORTH_ROAD_SEGMENTS from the class ROAD_SEGMENTS. It can be specified as **database define_subclass: NORTH_ROAD_SEGMENTS from: [ROAD_SEGMENTS] as: [(Direction EQ: #(north)) is_direction_of]**

In the definition of a subclass, the superclass name appears after the keyword 'from', and the query which materialises the subclass is given after the keyword 'as'. The new message is_a is created automatically for the new class. Additionally, it is possible to create a new message for ROAD_SEGMENTS, that would result in NORTH_ROAD_SEGMENTS, using a higher-order message 'inverse'.

To define a superclass, we need to specify the subclasses from which it is derived. For example, assuming that COMPONENT is not included in the schema, it can easily be created by **database define_superclass: COMPONENT from: [ROAD_SEGMENT, INTERSECTION]**

Similarly to the previous case, two new messages are created automatically, (namely road_segment_spec and intersection_spec) and others can be created explicitly by the user.

We can define an aggregate class by specifying the component classes and giving query expressions which determine the instances of the aggregate class. In general an aggregate class may be defined either as a Cartesian Product or as a subset of the Cartesian Product formed by including only related components. For example, let us consider a query

Query 2

"Determine the number of road segments in each direction for each road".

To answer this query, it is necessary to create first a complex class ROAD_DIRECTION that would be an aggregation of ROAD and DIRECTION. It can be specified as follows: **database define_aggregation: ROAD_DIRECTION from: [ROAD | DIRECTION] as: [road | road contains has_direction]**

We use the road minimal object set to restrict components in ROAD_DIRECTION to those that correspond to pairs of road and direction such that the road has indeed this direction. If the maximal object set were used, the aggregation would give us the full Cartesian product. The new messages has_road and has_direction are also created for the class ROAD_DIRECTION.

Having defined the class ROAD_DIRECTION, we can define a new message has_road_segment in the following way: **database define_message: has_road_segment for: ROAD_DIRECTION as: (road_direction* has_direction is_direction_of INTERSECT road_direction* has_road contains)** .

The part of the object-oriented schema, reflecting the changes caused by the above definitions, is shown in Figure 2. To specify query 2, we need to count the road segments for each road-direction object, as follows: **Road_Direction group_by: [road_direction has_road_segment count]**. The abstract class ROAD_DIRECTION can be used in a variety of other queries that might require new messages for ROAD and DIRECTION, that would result in ROAD_DIRECTION. It can be done using the higher-order message 'inverse'. One of the problems in the creation of abstract classes is to define links between the abstract class and external classes (i.e., those not participating in the aggregation). We allow the creation of these links by defining new messages.

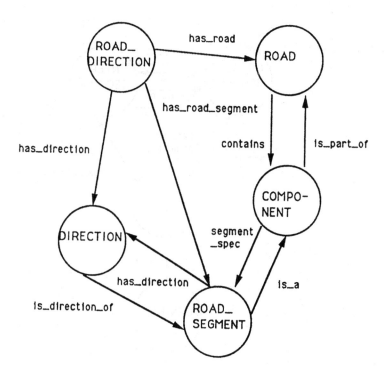

Figure 2. Creation of the aggregate class ROAD_DIRECTION

As another example of aggregation, let us assume that an end-user is interested in an abstract object composed of two road-segments and their intersection. The class containing such objects can be constructed as follows: **database define_aggregation: UNIT from: [ROAD_SEGMENT | INTERSECTION | ROAD_SEGMENT] as: [intersection is_end_of | intersection | intersection is_start_of]** A unit therefore comprises an intersection, one of its incoming segments, and one of its outgoing segments as shown in Figure 3. In this case ROAD_SEGMENT appears twice in the sequence of classes. Therefore, it is necessary to distinguish between two automatically-generated messages has_road_segment. To distinguish between these messages, we append an appropriate integer to each name. In addition, it is easy to define messages is_road_segment1_of and is_road_segment2_of by using the higher-order message 'inverse' for has_road_segment1 and has_road_segment2.

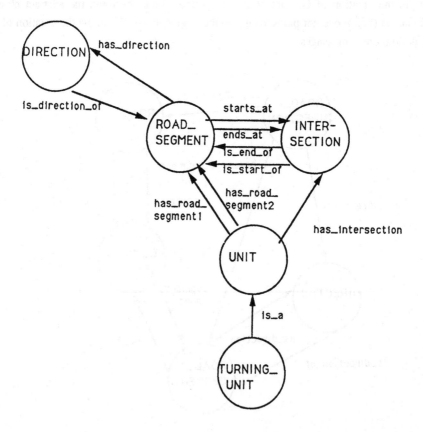

Figure 3. Creation of the aggregate class UNIT and the subclass TURNING_UNIT

In general, a given unit may or may not lie completely within one road. We can define a new message to give, for each road, the set of units that lie completely within it. **database define_message: contains_unit for: ROAD as: (road* contains is_road segment1_of**

INTERSECT road* contains is_road_segment2_of) A unit may be either straight (if its two road segments have the same direction) or a turning unit. The distinction between these two cases is significant if, for example, a user wishes to compute the time taken to travel the entire length of a given road. This time will depend on the time taken to traverse each road segment, and also on the delay imposed by each intersection. An intersection which lies on a turning unit may be expected to impose a longer delay than an intersection which lies on a straight unit. Hence we choose to define TURNING_UNIT as a subclass of UNIT. The definition is as follows: **database define_subclass: TURNING_UNIT from: [UNIT] as: [Unit select: [unit has_road_segment1 has_direction <> unit has_road_segment2 has_direction]]** .

When we define this subclass, the message is_a is automatically created to link the subclass to its superclass as is also shown in Figure 3. To provide the same link in the opposite direction, we define a new message turning_unit_spec as an inverse of is_a as follows: **database define_message: turning_unit_spec for: UNIT as: (unit* inverse_of: is_a)** .

Next we assume that an intersection on a straight unit imposes no additional delay, whereas one on a turning unit imposes a fixed delay of, say, 5. The time to travel the length of a road is therefore the sum of the times taken to traverse each of its segments, plus 5 times the number of turning units in the road. To define a new message to compute the time to traverse a road segment, we use the following: **database define_message: has_time for: ROAD_SEGMENT as: (road_segment* compute: [(road_segment has_length) * #(2) / (road_segment has_speed_limit)]**) .

Having defined this message, the time to travel the length of a road can be computed as follows: **database define_message: has_time for: ROAD as: (road* compute [(road contains has_time sum) + ((road contains_unit turning_unit_spec count) * #(5))]**) .

4. TRANSLATION OF REQUESTS INVOLVING ABSTRACT OBJECTS

In this section, we shall discuss the method of translation of database requests involving abstract objects into a relational language. The translation of simple requests without abstract objects has been described in [2]. A simple mapping of the object-oriented schema into binary relations was assumed, where each relation corresponds to a message. To allow for the same message name being used by different messages (with different receivers) we concatenate the receiver name with the message name to form a relation name, with a hyphen between. The attribute names are the receiver class and the result class. For example, some relations for the object-oriented schema shown in Figure 1 are listed below:

ROAD-HAS_NAME (road, name)

ROAD_SEGMENT-HAS_LENGTH (road_segment, length)

These relations should not be considered as stored relations, but rather as views defined on a database designed in a standard way. The same applies to views corresponding to the maximal object sets, e.g.,

ROAD (road)

Based on this mapping, we could define the translation of database requests into relational expressions.

The creation of an abstract class can be reflected in creation of relational views for each new message generated for the abstract class, and a view for the abstract class. In Section 3 we identified three distinguished cases: creation of a subclass, creation of a superclass and creation of an aggregate class.

Let us first consider the creation of a subclass. In the translation to SQL, we create a view for the message which is automatically generated. Since we are defining a subclass, the generated message is an 'is_a' message linking the new class to its superclass. In addition, in a very similar way a view is created for the maximal object set of the subclass. For example, let us consider the definition of NORTH_ROAD_SEGMENTS introduced in Section 3. The SQL statement defining the message is_a is as follows:

CREATE VIEW NORTH_ROAD_SEGMENT-IS_A (north_road_segment, road_segment) AS

    SELECT DIRECTION-IS_DIRECTION_OF.road_segment,

    DIRECTION-IS_DIRECTION_OF.road_segment

    FROM DIRECTION, DIRECTION-IS_DIRECTION_OF

    WHERE DIRECTION.direction = DIRECTION-IS_DIRECTION_OF.direction

    AND DIRECTION.direction = 'North'

This view usually will be omitted from queries because of the inheritance referred to in Section 2.

For a superclass definition, we create one new message corresponding to each subclass. The SQL expressions for defining new relational views are constructed in a straightforward way. Let us assume again that COMPONENT is not included in the schema. The definition of COMPONENT will be translated to two views corresponding to the messages road_segment_spec and intersection_spec.

For an abstract aggregate class definition we create one new message corresponding to each component in the aggregation. For example, let us consider the definition of ROAD_DIRECTION introduced in Section 3. The SQL statement defining the maximal object set for the aggregate class ROAD_DIRECTION is as follows:

CREATE VIEW ROAD_DIRECTION (road, direction) AS

    SELECT ROAD.road, ROAD_SEGMENT-HAS_DIRECTION.direction

    FROM ROAD, ROAD-CONTAINS, ROAD_SEGMENT-HAS_DIRECTION

    WHERE ROAD.road = ROAD-CONTAINS.road

    AND ROAD-CONTAINS.component =

    ROAD_SEGMENT-HAS_DIRECTION.road_segment

The SQL statement defining the messages has_road and has_direction are identical, and therefore they usually can be omitted. The new message 'has_road_segment' is translated into the following view:

CREATE VIEW
ROAD_DIRECTION-HAS_ROAD_SEGMENT (road, direction, road_segment) AS

    (SELECT ROAD_DIRECTION.road, ROAD_DIRECTION.direction,

    ROAD-CONTAINS.component

    FROM ROAD_DIRECTION, ROAD-CONTAINS

    WHERE ROAD_DIRECTION.road = ROAD-CONTAINS.road)

    INTERSECT

    (SELECT ROAD_DIRECTION.road, ROAD_DIRECTION.direction, DIRECTION-IS_DIRECTION_OF.road_segment

    FROM ROAD_DIRECTION, DIRECTION-IS_DIRECTION_OF

    WHERE ROAD_DIRECTION.direction = DIRECTION-IS_DIRECTION_OF.direction)

Query 2 can be translated as follows:

SELECT COUNT (ROAD_DIRECTION-HAS_ROAD_SEGMENT.road_segment)
FROM ROAD_DIRECTION-HAS_ROAD_SEGMENT
GROUP BY ROAD_DIRECTION-HAS_ROAD_SEGMENT.road,
ROAD_DIRECTION-HAS_ROAD_SEGMENT.direction

5. CONCLUSION

We have described an object-oriented data model with abstract classes, that allows uniform specification of database requests and application programs. Using this model, database requests can be represented by messages sent to instances of database classes. We defined object-oriented specification of new classes and messages. We also discussed the techniques for translating database requests involving abstract classes into a relational language.

This work has highlighted some of the differences and similarities between the relational data model and the object-oriented paradigm. Consequently we were able to identify correspondences between object-oriented requests and relational expressions, and thus alleviate the mismatch between the two approaches.

REFERENCES

[1]   P. Chen, "The entity-relationship model: towards a unified view of data", ACM TODS 1:1, 1976

[2]   B. Czejdo and M.C. Taylor, "Integrating database systems and Smalltalk", Symposium on Applied Computing, Kansas City, April 1991.

[3]   R. Elmasri et al, "The category concept: An extension to the entity-relationship model", Data and Knowledge Engineering 1, 1985.

[4]   A. Goldberg and D. Robson, "Smalltalk-80; the language and its implementation", Addison-Wesley, 1983.

[5]   M. Hammer and D. McLeod, "Database description with a semantic data model: SDM",ACM TODS 6:3, 1981.

[6]   D. Maier and J. Stein, "Development and implementation of an object-oriented DBMS", in Research directions in object-oriented programming, MIT Press, 1987.

[7]   G. Shaw and S. Zdonik, "A query algebra for object-oriented databases", International conference on data engineering, 1990.

[8]   D. Shipman, "The functional data model and the data language DAPLEX", ACM TODS 6:1, 1981.

[9]   J. Smith and D. Smith, "Database abstractions: aggregation and generalization", ACM TODS 2:2, 1977.

[10] S. Zdonik and D. Maier (eds.), "Readings in object-oriented database systems", Morgan-Kaufmann, 1990.

Incremental Database Design Revisited

Ke Wang   Li Yan Yuan

Department of Computing Science
University of Alberta
Edmonton, Canada T6G 2H1

Abstract

Three new classes of database schemes are defined. The class of weakly independent schemes is a generalization of independent schemes in a centralized environment. The classes of expansion-chased schemes and simple chase join bounded schemes are aimed at capturing the behaviour of the chase process by a static structure, i.e., derivation sequences of relation schemes. We first present a study on containment relationships among various classes of database schemes, which establishes the generality and desirability of these new classes. We then show that the new classes and the class of algebraic-maintainable schemes can be incrementally designed via a known scheme generating method.

1. INTRODUCTION

Three new classes of database schemes are proposed. A database scheme is said to be *weakly independent* if absence of explicit violation of functional dependencies in tuples of a state implies consistency. An explicit violation comes from two tuples, either within a single relation as in violation of local satisfaction or from different relations, that agree over all attributes of the left-hand side of some functional dependency and disagree over some attribute of the right-hand side of that same functional dependency. We will show that the class of weakly independent schemes properly contains all independent schemes and still enjoys the same desirable properties in terms of constraint enforcement and query answering. Weakly independent schemes are particularly useful in the case where the time for retrieving tuples from different relations is comparable to the time for retrieving tuples within a single relation. This is typical of a centralized environment, where independence is too strong a condition.

When a full chase process is used, it is very difficult to capture its behaviour by any static structure. On the other hand, an assertion about consistency or a query cannot be checked, in general, without carrying out the full chase process. A better understanding of chase process, preferably characterized by some static structure, is essential to consistency checking and query answering. This realization has once motivated Graham's path expressions [G]. Fortunately, many useful database schemes do not use the full power of chase process. Our other two classes of database schemes are aimed at characterizing the chase process by derivation sequences of relation schemes. In particular, we consider a restricted chase process which makes inferences using only original tuples in the state, not the newly inferred tuples nor missing values. This process was defined as the *expansion computation* in [W], in which each tuple is expanded by original tuples of the state. A database scheme is called *expansion-*

This work has been partially supported by the NSERC of Canada. The current address of Ke Wang: Department of Mathematical Science, University of Lethbridge, Lethbridge, Canada T1K 3M4.

chased if the expansion computation suffices to test consistency; a database scheme is called *simple chase join bounded (scj-bounded)* if the expansion computation produces all the total tuples in the representative instances. These two notions are incomparable in the sense that neither implies the other. As the name suggests, we shall show that scj-bounded schemes are exactly those schemes for which the X-total projection can be computed by a predetermined union of *simple chase join expressions* [AC,C] defined on the database schemes. For these two kinds of database schemes, the chase process and therefore consistency checking and query answering are completely characterized by derivation sequences of relation schemes. Identifying and designing these databases are therefore important to database applications.

We present a survey on relationships of database classes, which establishes both the generality and desirability of these new classes. We then consider design of these database schemes. Our tool is the notion of *extensibility* of database schemes [M]. The basic design idea is a set of rules of generating a new scheme in some class by making it *extensible* into some scheme already in that class. This scheme generating method was first proposed in [CH2] to design *bounded* schemes [MUV] and *constant-time-maintainable* schemes [GW], for which general test and design algorithms are unknown or very difficult to explore. To generalize these results, a condition under which this design method applies is defined based on the extensibility, rather than semantics, of the database classes. Then we show that the above newly defined classes as well as the class of *algebraic-maintainable* schemes of [CH1] satisfy this condition and therefore can be designed by the scheme generating method of [CH2].

2. PRELIMINARIES

2.1 Basics A detailed background is found in [Ma,U]. Let **R** be a collection $\{R_1,...,R_n\}$ of relation schemes. $\cup R$ is the abbreviation of unions $R_1\cup...\cup R_n$. A *(database) scheme*, denoted **(R,D)**, consists of a collection **R** of relation schemes and a finite set D of dependencies over $\cup R$ defined below. Very often, a database scheme refers to **R** alone if the set of dependencies D is not of interest. A *(database) state* over a database scheme **R**, usually denoted ρ, is collection of relations over elements of **R**, with $\rho(R_i)$ denoting the relation over R_i. It is also useful to treat a state as a set of tuples over elements of **R** and, therefore the phrase like "tuple v in ρ" should make sense.

An *functional dependency (fd)* over a set W of attributes is a statement of the form $X\rightarrow Y$, where X and Y are sets of attributes from W. Semantically, a relation $\rho(R_i)$ over R_i *satisfies* an fd $X\rightarrow Y$ over R_i if whenever there exists two tuples u and v in $\rho(R_i)$ such that u[X]=v[X], then u[Y]=v[Y]. A set of fd's F *(logically) implies* a set of fd's F´, denoted $F\models F'$, if whenever a relation r satisfies F, then r also satisfies F´. If $F\models G$ and $G\models F$, F is said to be *equivalent* to G, and we denote this by $F\equiv G$. F^+ is the set of all fd's implied by F. An fd $X\rightarrow Y$ is *embedded* in a relation scheme R_i if $R_i\supseteq XY$. F/R_i denotes the fd's of F that are embedded in R_i and F/R denotes the fd's of F that are embedded in elements of **R**.

2.2 Simple Chase Join Expressions Given a set of fd's F, a *derivation sequence* of some relation scheme $R_i\in R$ is a finite sequence of fd's $<Y_1\rightarrow Z_1,...,Y_n\rightarrow Z_n>$, $n\geq 0$, satisfying the following conditions:

(1) $Y_j\rightarrow Z_j\in F^+$, for all $1\leq j\leq n$, and (2) $Y_j\subseteq (R_i\cup(\bigcup_{k=1}^{j-1} Y_kZ_k))$ and $Z_j - (R_i\cup(\bigcup_{k=1}^{j-1} Y_kZ_k))\neq\emptyset$, for all $1\leq j\leq n$.

Essentially, a derivation sequence of R_i is a sequence of fd's used to derive new attributes starting with attributes in R_i by Armstrong's axioms. A derivation sequence *covers* attributes X if $(R_i\cup(\bigcup_{k=1}^{n} Y_kZ_k))\supseteq$

X. Given a derivation sequence $<Y_1 \to Z_1,...,Y_n \to Z_n>$ of R_i covering X, if each fd $Y_j \to Z_j$ is embedded in some relation scheme $R_{i_j} \in R$, then the *simple chase join expression (or scje)* [C] for the derivation sequence is defined as $\Pi_X(R_i * \Pi_{Y_1 Z_1}(R_{i_1}) * ... * \Pi_{Y_n Z_n}(R_{i_n}))$.

2.3 Chase and Representative Instances Given a state ρ over **R**, we define a tableau T_ρ over $\cup R$ and call it the *tableau for state* ρ: For each relation scheme $R_i \in R$ and for each tuple $t \in \rho(R_i)$, there is a row s in T_ρ corresponding to it. The row is the result of padding t as follows: $s[R_i]=t$; and $s[A]$, for all $A \in \cup R - R_i$, is a *null* that represents some unknown value and appears nowhere else in T_ρ. Let (R, Σ) be a database scheme and let ρ a state over **R**. State ρ is a *consistent state* of (R, Σ), or is *consistent* wrt Σ, if there exists a relation I over $\cup R$ satisfying Σ such that $\Pi_{R_i}(I) \supseteq \rho(R_i)$ for each R_i in **R** [H, M]. Constraint enforcement is to enforce consistency of database states.

We can test whether a database state ρ is consistent wrt a set F of fd's by applying the *chase process* [MMS] to T_ρ, the state tableau for ρ. In general, the chase process modifies a tableau T by applying the *fd-rules* to T as far as possible, until either a contradiction is found, or no rule can further modify the tableau.

A state ρ is consistent wrt a set F of fd's if and only if no contradiction is found in applying the chase process to the tableau T_ρ using fd-rules associated with fd's in F. If ρ is consistent wrt F, we shall denote by $CHASE_F(T_\rho)$ the final chased tableau and call it the *representative instance* of ρ wrt Σ [M,S]. Let T be a tableau over $\cup R$ that may contain nulls. Let $X \subseteq \cup R$. The *X-total projection* of T, denoted $\Pi_X^{\downarrow}(T)$, is defined as the set of tuples: $\{ t[X] \mid t \in T \text{ and } t[X] \text{ contains only constants} \}$.

Given a consistent state ρ, a query over attributes X is answered against the X-total projection of the representative instance of ρ [MUV].

2.4 Independence, Constant-time-maintainability, and Algebraic-maintainability These properties have been proposed to capture efficient constraint enforcement in the representative instance approach.

Graham and Yannakakis [GY], and Sagiv [S] defined and studied the notion of independent schemes. Let (R,F) be a database scheme, where F is a set of fd's over $\cup R$. A database scheme **R** is *independent* wrt F if every *locally satisfying* state ρ, i.e., $\rho(R_i)$ satisfies F^+/R_i for every $R_i \in R$, is consistent wrt F. More results on independent schemes can be found in [IIK].

Assume that the database state ρ is stored in a storage device that responds to the *requests* of the form $<R_j, \Psi>$ by returning, if it exists, an arbitrary tuple satisfying Ψ from the relation r_j over R_j, where $R_j \in R$, and Ψ is a Boolean combination of equalities of the form B=b, for some attribute $B \in R_j$ and constant b in the domain of B. Furthermore, every request $<R_j, \Psi>$ obeys the *no guess assumption* [GW] in the sense that the constants used in equalities of Ψ appear either in the inserted tuple or in some previously returned tuples. A database scheme **R** is said to be *constant-time-maintainable (ctm)* wrt a set D of dependencies if there exists an integer $k \geq 0$ such that, for all instance $<\rho, t>$, where ρ is a consistent state and t is a tuple over some relation scheme, there is some algorithm that determines whether $\rho \cup \{t\}$ is consistent by making no more than k requests [GW].

A database scheme **R** is *algebraic-maintainable* [CH1] wrt D if there is an algorithm which correctly determines whether an instance $<\rho, t>$ is consistent by examining the tuple t and the tuples generated from applying a predetermined sequence of expressions of the form $\sigma_{X=x}(E)$, where E is a *PJ-expression*, i.e., an expression involving only projection and join operations, and $\sigma_{X=x}(E)$ returns at most one tuple for any consistent state. These expressions $\sigma_{X=x}(E)$ are called *single-tuple conjunctive selections* in [CH1]. To capture the idea of no guess assumption, the constants used in the selection condition X=x must appear either in t, the tuple being inserted, or in tuples that have been returned by some previous expression in this sequence. When this is the case, the sequence is said to be *defined* on the instance <ρ,t>.

An inconsistent state is *minimal* if any proper substate of it is consistent. A database scheme is *bounded wrt consistency* by an integer k [GV] if the number of tuples in any minimal inconsistent state is no more than k. A database scheme is *bounded wrt dependencies* if the X-total projection of representative instances can be computed by a predetermined relational expression for every set X of attributes [MUV].

3. DATABASE CLASSES AND THEIR RELATIONSHIPS

In this section, we give results on the relationships among classes of database schemes in terms of their containments. We first define three new classes of database schemes. In Section 4, we will show that these classes can be designed incrementally via the scheme generating method of [CH2].

3.1 Weakly Independent Schemes One nice property of independent database schemes is the following: absence of explicit contradictory information within each relation implies that no contradictory information will be derived at all; that is, inferences on newly inferred tuples or missing values (or nulls) are not needed for testing consistency. Obviously, this property is important to efficiency of constraint enforcement. In the following, we will see that independent database schemes are not the most general schemes enjoying this property. This motivates us to define the following notions.

Let $(\mathbf{R},F)$ be a database scheme, where F is a set of fd's over $\cup \mathbf{R}$. A state ρ is said to *embedded-satisfy* F if for every pair R_i,R_j of relation schemes in $\mathbf{R}$, not necessarily distinct, $\Pi_{R_i \cap R_j}(\rho(R_i)) \cup \Pi_{R_i \cap R_j}(\rho(R_j))$ satisfies $F^+/R_i \cap R_j$. $\mathbf{R}$ is said to be *weakly independent* wrt F if every embedded-satisfying state is consistent wrt F. The notion of embedded-satisfying fd's excludes violation of fd's from tuples within a single relation as well as "across" different relations. If the R_i,R_j above are required to be the same, then this notion reduces to local satisfaction and the definition reduces to independent schemes. (This gives the name of "weakly independent schemes".) We will show that this class properly contains all independent schemes and still enjoys the same desirable properties in constraint enforcement and query answering. Independent schemes are highly desirable in a distributed environment where data transmissions between sites are supposed to be minimized. In a centralized case, however, localization of data is not a concern, and we believe that the time for retrieving tuples from different relations is comparable to the time for retrieving tuples within a single relation. In such a situation, checking embedded-satisfaction is no harder than checking local satisfaction, and the condition of being independent is too strong --- weakly independent schemes are just what we need. We will see in Section 4 that weakly independent schemes can be designed incrementally by the method of [CH2], while some extra constraints are needed for independent schemes.

Example 3.1: Consider the "City, Address, Zip" database $\mathbf{R} = \{R_1(CAZ), R_2(CZ)\}$ and $F = \{CA \rightarrow Z, Z \rightarrow C\}$. It is easy to see that $(\mathbf{R},F)$ is weakly independent, but not independent, because fd $Z \rightarrow C$ is embedded in both R_1 and R_2.□

Example 3.2: Consider a "Instructor, Course, Department" database scheme $\mathbf{R} = \{R_1(ID), R_2(IC),$ $R_3(CD)\}$ and $F = \{I \rightarrow D, I \rightarrow C, C \rightarrow I, C \rightarrow D\}$.

$\mathbf{R}$ is not weakly independent wrt F: The state $\rho=\{<i,d_1>,<i,c>,<c,d_2>\}$ is embedded-satisfying but is inconsistent wrt $F.\square$

3.2 Expansion-chased Schemes and Scj-bounded Schemes The chase process is not well statically structured in that its behaviour is not easy to be captured by any static structure. This fact makes consistency checking and query answering difficult in general. Fortunately, many useful databases, such as independent schemes, do not use the full power of chase process. In this section, we define two classes of databases for which the chase needed for testing consistency and answering query can be characterized by derivation sequences of relation schemes, respectively. .PP We first introduce the expansion computation of [W]. Let $(\mathbf{R},F)$ be a database scheme, where F is a set of fd's. Let ρ be a state over $\mathbf{R}$ and v a tuple over some R_i in $\mathbf{R}$. The *expansion computation* of v in ρ wrt F is defined as follows.

> Let v' be the row from augmenting tuple v out to $\cup\mathbf{R}$ with nulls. Repeatedly expand v' as follows until (i) no change can be made to v' any more or, (ii) some constant replaces another constant: If there is an fd $X\rightarrow Y$ in F^+/R_j for some R_j in $\mathbf{R}$, such that for some tuple u in $\rho(R_j)$, $v'[X]=u[X]$ and $v'[Y]\neq u[Y]$, then replace $v'[Y]$ by $u[Y]$.

We observe that (1) the sequence of fd's used in the expansion computation is a derivation sequence of R_i and (2) at most $|\cup\mathbf{R}|$ expansions are made before the computation exits. When the expansion computation of v in ρ exits from (i), v is said to be *expansible* in ρ (wrt F), and the final v' is called the *expansion* of v in ρ (wrt F); otherwise, v is *not expansible* in ρ (wrt F). A state ρ is said to be *conflict-free* (wrt F) if every tuple of ρ is expansible in ρ (wrt F). Let ρ be a conflict-free state. The *expansion* of ρ, denoted $\exp(\rho)$, is defined as the tableau over $\cup\mathbf{R}$: $\{v'|v'$ is the expansion of v in ρ wrt F, $v\in\rho\}$, where all nulls in $\exp(\rho)$ are unique. Obviously, computation of $\exp(\rho)$ is a strictly restricted (not full) chase process of T_ρ.

We say that a database scheme $(\mathbf{R},F)$ is *expansion-chased* if every conflict-free state is consistent wrt F. If a database scheme is expansion-chased, then consistency can be tested by expanding tuples of the state, one at a time, by the expansion computation, and hence the chase needed in this case is characterized by derivation sequences of relation schemes. In Subsection 3.3 we will show that the class of expansion-chased schemes properly contains the class of ctm schemes when only fd's appear.

We say that a database scheme $(\mathbf{R},F)$ is *simple chase join bounded (scj-bounded)* if for every consistent state ρ of $(\mathbf{R},F)$ and every subset $X\subseteq\cup\mathbf{R}$, $\Pi_X^{\downarrow}(CHASE_F(T_\rho))=\Pi_X^{\downarrow}(\exp(\rho))$, where $\exp(\rho)$ is the expansion of ρ wrt F. It will be shown that the class of scj-bounded schemes contains exactly those database schemes for which total projections of representative instances can be computed via a union of scje's. We now consider some examples.

Example 3.3: Let $(\mathbf{R},F)=(\{R_1(AB),R_2(BC),R_3(AC)\},\{A\rightarrow B,B\rightarrow C,A\rightarrow C\})$. In [W], we knew that $(\mathbf{R},F)$ is not ctm. We now show that $(\mathbf{R},F)$ is expansion-chased; that is, every inconsistent state is not conflict-free. Clearly, every state that is not locally satisfying is not conflict-free. We consider only locally satisfying state. From Example 1 in [CH2], a state is consistent wrt F if and only if it satisfies all fd's in F and the egd σ in Table 1. Let ρ be an inconsistent state of $(\mathbf{R},F)$ that is locally satisfying F. Then ρ violates σ, else ρ is consistent wrt F. That is, for some homomorphism h from T to ρ, ρ must contain $h(T)$ and $h(c_1)\neq h(c_2)$, where T is the tableau of σ. Note that ρ is not conflict-free, because expanding

$h(<a,b>)$ by $h(<b,c_1>)$ and then by $h(<a,c_2>)$ illustrates that $h(<a,b>)$ is not expansible in ρ. So we have shown that every inconsistent state is not conflict-free. By definition, $(\mathbf{R},F)$ is expansion-chased.□

251.if 87<65 .nr 52 65

A	B	C	Tag
a	b		R_1
a		c_1	R_2
	b	c_1	R_3
$c_1 =$			

Table 1: Egd σ: $T/c_1 = c_2$ for Example 3.3

The following two examples show that the class of expansion-chased schemes and the class of scj-bounded schemes are incomparable.

Example 3.4: We claim that the expansion-chased scheme in Example 3.3 is not scj-bounded. It is easy to verify that the state ρ in Table 2 is consistent. It is also easy to see that
$<a,b,c> \in \Pi^{\downarrow}_{ABC} (CHASE_F(T_\rho)) - \Pi^{\downarrow}_{ABC}(exp(\rho))$. Thus, $(\mathbf{R},F)$ is not scj-bounded.□

A B	B C	A C
<a, b>		<a´, c>
<a´, b>		

Table 2: State ρ for Example 3.4

Example 3.5: Let $R=\{R_1(AB),R_2(AC),R_3(AE),R_4(EB),R_5(EC),R_6(BCD),R_7(AD)\}$ and $F=\{A{\to}B,A{\to}C,A{\to}E,E{\to}A,E{\to}B,E{\to}C,BC{\to}D,D{\to}BC,A{\to}D,D{\to}A\}$. By a result in [CH1], $(\mathbf{R},F)$ is scj-bounded (since $\mathbf{R}$ is "key-equivalent" wrt F [CH1]). However, $(\mathbf{R},F)$ is not expansion-chased: The state ρ in Table 3 is conflict-free but is inconsistent.□

A B	A C	A E	E B	E C	B C D	A D
<a, b>	<a, c>	<a, e>	<e´, b>	<e´, c>		

Table 3: State ρ for Example 3.5

Now we show that scj-bounded schemes are exactly schemes for which the X-total projection can be computed by a union of scje's, therefore scj-bounded schemes are bounded wrt dependencies.

Lemma 3.1: A database scheme $(\mathbf{R},F)$ is scj-bounded if and only if X-total projections of representative instances can be computed via a union of scje's, for $X{\subseteq}\mathbf{R}$.

Proof: This follows essentially from one-to-one correspondence between the expansion computation and the way a total tuple is produced by a scje.□

3.3 Relations of Database Scheme Classes We now establish some relationships among some of the database scheme classes we introduced. This study is also aimed at establishing both the generality and desirability of the three newly defined classes. The following relationships follow from some previously known results.

Theorem 3.1:

(a) Every independent scheme is ctm, and there exists an independent scheme that is not ctm [GW].

(b) Every ctm scheme is algebraic-maintainable, and there exists an algebraic-maintainable scheme that is not ctm [CH1].

(c) When only embedded fd's appear, ctm schemes are scj-bounded [HW], and there exists a scj-bounded scj-bounded scheme that is not ctm [CH1].

(d) Every ctm scheme is bounded wrt consistency, and there exists a database scheme bounded wrt consistency that is not ctm [GW].

The following are more relationships to be proved.

Theorem 3.2:

(a) Every independent scheme is weakly independent, and there exists a weakly independent scheme that is not independent.

(b) Every weakly independent scheme is ctm, and there exists a ctm scheme that is not weakly independent. (Thus weakly independent schemes with embedded fd's are scj-bounded by Theorem 3.1(c).)

(c) Every ctm scheme with only fd's is expansion-chased, and there exists an expansion-chased scheme that is not ctm.

(d) Every expansion-chased scheme is bounded wrt consistency by the number of attributes plus 1.

(e) Every algebraic-maintainable scheme is bounded wrt consistency.

(f) When only fd's appear, a database scheme is weakly independent if and only if it is bounded wrt consistency by 2.

To prove Theorem 3.2, we need the following lemma.

Lemma 3.2 (Theorem 4.2.3 in [WG] or Theorem 3.3 in [W]): Let (R,F) be a database scheme with only fd's. (R,F) is ctm if and only if, for every instance $<\rho,t>$ of the maintenance problem of (R,F), $\rho \cup \{t\}$ is consistent if and only if t is expansible in ρ wrt F.

Proof of Theorem 3.2: For (a), it suffices to observe that every embedded-satisfying state is a locally satisfying state. Then it follows from definitions and Example 3.1.

Given any instance $<\rho,t>$ of the maintenance problem of (R,F), where t is a tuple over some R_i in R, we can check if $\rho \cup \{t\}$ is embedded-satisfying F by checking if $\rho(i,j)$ satisfies $F^+/R_j \cap R_i$, for every $R_j \in R$. This can be done by issuing, for every nontrivial fd $X \rightarrow Y$ in $F^+/R_j \cap R_i$, a request $<R_j, \wedge_{A \in X} A = t[A]>$ and verifying that the returned tuple, if it exists, has t[Y] as its Y values. Then (b) follows from Example 3.2.

We now show (c). Assume that (R,F) is ctm and that ρ is an inconsistent state of (R,F). Let ρ' be a substate of ρ such that ρ' is inconsistent and any proper substate of ρ' is consistent. For any t in ρ', $<\rho'-\{t\},t>$ is an instance of the maintenance problem of (R,F) (because $\rho'-\{t\}$ is consistent). Then (c) follows from Lemma 3.2 and Example 3.3.

Assume that scheme (R,F) is expansion-chased and that ρ is an inconsistent state of (R,F). Then ρ is not conflict-free. Further assume that some tuple t of ρ is not expansible in $\rho-\{t\}$. Since at most $|\cup R|$ tuples of ρ are used in the expansion computation of t in $\rho-\{t\}$, ρ contains an inconsistent substate of size at most $|\cup R|+1$. This shows (d).

Let scheme (R,D) be algebraic-maintainable. Let ρ be any inconsistent state that contains no proper inconsistent substate. Then <ρ-{t},t> is an instance of the maintenance problem of (R,D), where t∈ρ. From the algebraic-maintainability of (R,D), only a fixed number of tuples from ρ-{t} are examined in determining whether ρ is consistent wrt D (In this case every tuple of ρ-{t} must be examined because ρ is a "minimal" inconsistent state). Thus, every inconsistent state contains an inconsistent substate of size bounded by a fixed integer. This proves (e). □

4. INCREMENTAL SCHEME DESIGNS BY EXTENSIBILITY

We now consider designing database schemes proposed in the last section. A scheme generating methodology based on extensibility of database schemes [M] has been recently presented in [CH2]. Let (R,F₁) and (S,F₂) be two database schemes not necessarily over the same universe of attributes. We say that S *extends* R (wrt F₂), or R is *extensible into* S (wrt F₂), if for each R_i in R there exists $S'=\{S_{i_1},...,S_{i_k}\}\subseteq S$, k≥1, such that $R_i=S_{i_1}\cup...\cup S_{i_k}$ and $F_2 \models S'$ [CH2,M]. We will denote this by R≤S. The following lemma was proved in [CH2].

Lemma 4.1 (Corollary 2 in [CH2]): Let (R,F₁) and (S,F₂) be database schemes with only fd's, such that F₁=F₂, R≤S, and $\cup R \subseteq \cup S$. Then

(a) if (S,F₂) is bounded wrt dependencies, (R,F₁) is bounded wrt dependencies.

(b) if (S,F₂) is bounded wrt consistency, (R,F₁) is bounded wrt consistency.

(c) if (S,F₂) is ctm, (R,F₁) is ctm.

Based on this result, a set of formal rules for generating a new bounded (ctm) scheme (R,F₁) from a known bounded (ctm) scheme (S,F₂) was introduced in [CH2]. Each rule basically made some simple change, adding or deleting either a relation scheme or an fd, to scheme (S,F₂) so as to obtain a scheme (R,F₁) extensible into S. Then by Lemma 4.1, (R,F₁) is also bounded. Some sophisticated developments were also included to generate more database schemes. This technique is important particularly in the case where general tests and design algorithms are unknown or very difficult to explore. Since those rules were clearly described in [CH2] (i.e., Methodology 1 on pp. 494), we shall not restate them here. However, some working ideas can be illustrated by the following example.

Example 4.1 [CH2]: Let R = {R₁(ABC), R₂(ABE), R₃(AF), R₄(CFG), R₅(BCH), R₆(ABCF)},and F = {A → BC, B → AH, A → F, A → BE, B → AE, CF → G, B → C}. It is not easy to tell a priori whether (R,F) is ctm or bounded. However, this follows from Lemma 4.1 since R≤S, F≡G, and (S,G) is an independent database scheme, where (S,G) = ({AB, BE, AF, BC, BH, CFG}, {A → B, B → A, B → C, A → F, B → E, CF → G, B → H}). Now we want to add R₇(BCI) to R. Observe that (S′=S∪{BI},G) is independent [S]. Hence we can add R₇ to R and still have a ctm and bounded database scheme, since R∪{R₇}≤S′ and F≡G.□

A close inspection of [CH2] tells us the following important observation.

Observation: The soundness of the scheme generating rules in [CH2] (i.e., Lemmas 4-7 in [CH2]) is irrelevant to the concrete meaning of the database scheme class under consideration, provided that a result like Lemma 4.1 above holds for that class.

The reader should convince himself with this observation before proceeding further. Now we extend this scheme generating method to any class of database schemes based on only extensibility, like a result in a form of Lemma 4.1, not on the semantics of the class. We say that a class θ of database schemes is *extensibility-designable* if, for any two database schemes (R,F) and (S,G) with only fd's such that $R \leq S$, $\cup R \subseteq \cup S$ and $F \equiv G$, (S,G) is in θ implies (R,F) is in θ; that is, if extensibility into a scheme in class θ is a sufficient condition of being in class θ. Consequently, by the above observation the scheme generating method of [CH2] can be applied to any extensibility-designable class. The following theorem is our main results in this section.

Theorem 4.1: Assume only fd's appear. The following classes of database schemes are extensibility-designable.

(a) algebraic-maintainable schemes.

(b) weakly independent schemes.

(c) expansion-chased schemes.

(d) scj-bounded schemes.

Corollary 4.1: The scheme classes mentioned in Theorem 4.1 can be designed via the rules of [CH2].

To prove Theorem 4.1, we first need the following proposition, by which we need only consider database schemes with the same universe of attributes.

Proposition 4.1: Assume that only fd's appear. Let θ be a class of database schemes and let (R,F) be a database scheme. Assume further that, for any $R' \subseteq R$ such that F is defined over $\cup R'$, (R,F) is in θ implies (R',F) is in θ. Then class θ is extensibility-designable if and only if, for every two schemes (R,F) and (S,G) such that $R \leq S$, $\cup R = \cup S$ and $F \equiv G$, (S,G) is in θ implies (R,F) is in θ.

The proof of Proposition 4.1 is very much like that of Corollary 2 in [CH2], therefore we omit it here. In the following, we assume that there are two schemes (R,F_1) and (S,F_2) such that $\cup R = \cup S$, $F_1 \equiv F_2$, and $R \leq S$. Given any state ρ over R, σ shall denote the state over S obtained from ρ as follows: For each $S_i \in S$, $\sigma(S_i) = \cup \{\Pi_{S_i}(\rho(R_k)) \mid S_i \subseteq R_k, R_k \in R\}$. $\sigma(S_i)$ is empty for every S_i not contained in any relation scheme in R. Notice that every tuple t of σ originates from some tuple u of ρ in the sense that if t is in $\sigma(S_i)$ for some $S_i \in S$ then $t[S_i] = u[S_i]$. We borrow the following results from [CH2].

Lemma 4.2 (Lemma 1 in [CH2]): Let (R,F_1) and (S,F_2) be as specified above. Let ρ be a state over R and σ be the state over S defined from ρ. Then

(a) ρ is a consistent state of (R,F_1) if and only if σ is a consistent state of (S,F_2).

(b) If ρ is consistent, then for any $X \subseteq \cup R$, $\Pi_X^\downarrow(\mathrm{CHASE}_{F_1}(T_\rho)) = \Pi_X^\downarrow(\mathrm{CHASE}_{F_2}(T_\sigma))$.

Given $E(S)$, a relational expression over S, we shall denote by $E'(R)$ the relational expression over R obtained as follows: For each operand S_i in $E(S)$, if there is some R_1 in R such that $R_1 \supseteq S_i$, then substitute S_i in $E(S)$ by the expression $\cup \{\Pi_{S_i}(R_k) \mid S_i \subseteq R_k, R_k \in R\}$; else substitute S_i by the empty expression $\varnothing$ which we define to evaluate to the empty relation.

Lemma 4.3 (Proposition 2 in [CH2]): Let (R,F_1) and (S,F_2) be as specified above. Let $E(S)$ be a relational expression over S and let $E'(R)$ be the expression defined from $E(S)$. Then for any state ρ over R, $E'(\rho) = E(\sigma)$, where σ is the state over S defined from ρ.

The following lemma says that if $E(S)$ is a scje over S then $E'(R)$ is a union of scje's over R, provided that (R,F) and (S,G) are such that $F \equiv G$, $\cup R = \cup S$, and $R \leq S$.

Lemma 4.4: Let (R,F) and (S,G) be database schemes with only fd's, such that $F\equiv G$, $\cup R=\cup S$, and $R\leq S$. Assume $E(S)$ is a scje over S. Then for all consistent states over R, the nonempty expression $E'(R)$ defined from $E(S)$ is equivalent to a union of scje's over R.

Proof: Let $E(S)$ be a scje $\Pi_X(S_0*\Pi_{X_1Y_1}(S_1)*...*\Pi_{X_nY_n}(S_n))$, $n\geq 0$. Clearly, if $n=0$, $E'(R)$ is either empty or a union of scje's over R. We assume $n>0$. Let $R_1^i,...,R_{(i)}^i$ be the relation schemes of R that contain S_i, $0\leq i\leq n$, where (i) is an integer dependent on i. We also assume that (i)>0, for all $0\leq i\leq n$, because otherwise $E'(R)$ is empty. Let $\lambda_i=\Pi_{X_iY_i}(R_1^i)\cup...\cup\Pi_{X_iY_i}(R_{(i)}^i)$, for $1\leq i\leq n$, and let $\lambda=\lambda_1*...*\lambda_n$. We first show that for all consistent states ρ over R, $E'(R)=\Pi_X(R_1^0*\lambda)\cup...\cup\Pi_X(R_{(0)}^0*\lambda)$. By construction of $E'(R)$ and properties of relational expressions, we have the following equalities

$$E'(R) = \Pi_X \{ (\Pi_{S_0}(R_1^0) \cup ... \cup \Pi_{S_0}(R_{(0)}^0)) * \lambda_1 * ... * \lambda_n \}$$
$$= \Pi_X \{ (\Pi_{S_0}(R_1^0)*\lambda) \cup ... \cup (\Pi_{S_0}(R_{(0)}^0)*\lambda) \} = \Pi_X (\Pi_{S_0}(R_1^0)*\lambda) \cup ... \cup \Pi_X(\Pi_{S_0}(R_{(0)}^0)*\lambda) \}.$$

We claim $\Pi_X(R_{j_0}^0 * \lambda)(\rho) = \Pi_X(\Pi_{S_0}(R_{j_0}^0)*\lambda)(\rho)$, for $1\leq j_0\leq (0)$. Clearly, $\Pi_X(R_{j_0}^0 * \lambda) \subseteq \Pi_X(\Pi_{S_0}(R_{j_0}^0)*\lambda)$, for $1 \leq j_0 \leq (0)$. It is also easy to see that every tuple in $\Pi_X(\Pi_{S_0}(R_{j_0}^0)*\lambda)(\rho)$ is a tuple in $\Pi_X(R_{j_0}^0*\lambda)(\rho)$, for conflict-free state ρ. Substituting these equalities in the above last formula, we have $E'(R)=\Pi_X(R_1^0*\lambda)\cup...\cup\Pi_X(R_{(0)}^0*\lambda)$, as required.

The expression $\Pi_X(R_1^0*\lambda)\cup...\cup\Pi_X(R_{(0)}^0*\lambda)$ can be transformed equivalently into a union of scje's by moving ahead all joins over unions and then moving ahead all projections over unions. The lemma is proved. $\square$

The following is a key lemma of Theorem 4.1.

Lemma 4.5: Let (R,F_1) and (S,F_2) be database schemes such that $F_1\equiv F_2$, $R\leq S$, and $\cup R=\cup S$. If (S,F_2) is in θ, then (R,F_1) is in θ, where θ is any of the following classes.

(a) algebraic-maintainable schemes.

(b) weakly independent schemes.

(c) expansion-chased schemes.

(d) scj-bounded schemes.

Proof: In the following proofs, whenever a state ρ over R is specified, σ denotes the state over S defined from ρ as above.

We show (a). Let $<\rho,u>$ be an instance of the maintenance problem of (R,F_1), where u is a tuple over some R_l in R. Without loss of generality, we assume that $S_1,...,S_n$ are the relation schemes of S that are contained in R_l, for some $n\geq 1$ (note that $R\leq S$ implies $n>0$). Define $u_i = u[S_i]$, and $\sigma_i=\sigma_{i-1}\cup\{u_i\}$, for $1\leq i\leq n$, where $\sigma_0 = \sigma$. From Lemma 4.2, $\rho\cup\{u\}$ is consistent if and only if σ_n is consistent. In other words, $<\rho,u>$ is a yes-instance if and only if $<\sigma_i,u_{i+1}>$ is a yes-instance (of the maintenance problem of (S,F_2)) for all $0\leq i\leq n-1$. Since (S,F_2) is algebraic-maintainable, assuming $<\sigma_i,u_{i+1}>$ is an instance, there is a sequence $\Omega_i:\sigma_{X_1=x_1}(E_1(S)),...,\sigma_{X_{(i)}=x_{(i)}}(E_{(i)}(S))$ of single-tuple conjunctive selections defined on $<\sigma_i,u_{i+1}>$ such that examining the tuples returned by applying Ω_i to σ_i correctly determines whether $\sigma_i\cup\{u_{i+1}\}$ is consistent, where the sizes of expressions and integer (i) are all upper bounded by some integer independent of state size. In the following, we transform Ω_i into a sequence Ω'_i of single-tuple conjunctive selections defined on $<\rho,u>$. For each $1\leq j\leq (i)$, we define an expression $\theta_j(R)$ over R, such that $\theta_j(\rho)=E_j(\sigma_i)$, as follows: For each relation scheme S_p involved in $E_j(S)$, substitute S_p by an expression D_p over R given by $D_p=\cup\{\Pi_{S_p}(R_k)\mid R_k\supseteq S_p, R_k\in R\}$, if $S_p\notin\{S_1,...,S_i\}$, and

$$D_p=\cup\{\Pi_{S_p}(R_k)\mid R_k\supseteq S_p, R_k\in R\}\cup\{u_p\}, \text{ if } S_p\in\{S_1,...,S_i\}.$$

Clearly, both $S_p(\sigma_i)$ and $D_p(\rho)$ are equal to relation $\sigma_i(S_p)$, and therefore, $E_j(\sigma_i)=\theta_j(\rho)$.

However, $\theta_j(R)$ is not a PJ-expression because it contains union $\cup$ operations. By the distributivity of projections and joins over unions, we have $\theta_j(R)=E_1^j\cup...\cup E_{m_j}^j$, for some PJ-expressions $E_1^j,...,E_{m_j}^j$ over R. Therefore, the sequence $\sigma_{X_j=x_j}(E_1^j),...,\sigma_{X_j=x_j}(E_{m_j}^j)$ applied to ρ will return exactly the same tuples as $\sigma_{X_j=x_j}(E_j)$ applied to σ_i. Now let Ω'_i be the sequence obtained by concatenating these sequences for $1\leq j\leq(i)$. Then from the above discussion, we have

- the tuples returned by applying Ω_i to $<\sigma_i,u_{i+1}>$ can be returned by applying a sequence Ω'_i of single-tuple conjunctive selections defined on $<\rho,u>$;

- $<\rho,u>$ is a yes-instance if and only if for $i=1,...,n-1$, in that order, examining the tuples returned by applying Ω'_i to ρ evaluates to a "yes" answer.

Therefore, for every instance $<\rho,u>$, there is a sequence Ω of single-tuple conjunctive selections, which is the concatenation of the above sequences $\Omega'_1,...,\Omega'_{n-1}$, defined on $<\rho,u>$ such that examining the tuples returned by applying Ω to ρ correctly determines if $\rho\cup\{u\}$ is consistent. Furthermore, the sizes of expressions in Ω and the length of Ω are all upper bounded by an integer independent of state size. Hence, (R,F_1) is algebraic-maintainable.

We now show (b). Let ρ be an embedded-satisfying state of (R,F_1). Since $F_1\equiv F_2$ and every tuple of σ originates from some tuple of ρ, σ must be an embedded-satisfying state of (S,F_2). Then from hypothesis on (S,F_2), σ is consistent, and so is ρ from Lemma 4.2(a).

Now let ρ be a conflict-free state over R. By construction of σ, σ must also be conflict-free. (Otherwise, ρ is not conflict-free.) Therefore, by hypothesis on (S,F_2), σ is consistent, and so is ρ by Lemma 4.2(a). This shows (c).

For (d), let state ρ over R be consistent wrt F_1. By Lemma 4.2(b), we have

$$\Pi_X^{\downarrow}(CHASE_{F_2}(T_\sigma))=\Pi_X^{\downarrow}(CHASE_{F_1}(T_\rho)), \text{ for every } X\subseteq R.$$

Let $\Pi_X^{\downarrow}(CHASE_{F_2}(T_\sigma))=E(\sigma)$, for some union $E(S)$ of scje's over S. Let $E'(R)$ be the expression defined from $E(S)$ as in Lemma 4.3. Then from Lemma 4.3, $\Pi_X^{\downarrow}(CHASE_{F_1}(T_\rho))=E'(\rho)$, and by Lemma 4.4, $E'(R)$ is equivalent to a union of scje's over R. From Lemma 3.1, (R,F_1) is scj-bounded. $\square$

The above proofs of (a) and (d) are constructive in that they have actually constructed a sequence of expressions and a union of scje's for (R,F_1), respectively, provided that such a sequence and union for (S,F_2) are available.

Now we are ready to prove Theorem 4.1.

Proof of Theorem 4.1: First, it is easy to see that, for any $R'\subseteq R$ such that F is defined over $\cup R'$, (R,F) is in θ implies (R',F) is in θ, where θ is any of the classes mentioned in the theorem. Then the theorem follows from Lemma 4.5 and Proposition 4.1. $\square$

The reader may wonder if the class of independent schemes is also extensibility-designable. The following example and theorem show that this is true if and only if the scheme being extended does not violate independence in an "obvious way", i.e., if no fd is embedded in more than one relation scheme.

Example 4.2: Consider the two schemes (R,F) and (S,G) in Example 4.1, where $R = \{ABC, ABE, AF, CFG, BCH, ABCF\}$, $F = \{A \rightarrow BC, B \rightarrow AH, A \rightarrow F, A \rightarrow BE, B \rightarrow AE, CF \rightarrow G, B \rightarrow C\}$, $S = \{AB, BE, AF, BC, BH, CFG\}$, and $G = \{A \rightarrow B, B \rightarrow A, B \rightarrow C, A \rightarrow F, B \rightarrow E, CF \rightarrow G, B \rightarrow H\}$. We know from Example 4.1 that (S,G) is independent and that $\cup R=\cup S$, $R\leq S$ and $F\equiv G$. However, (R,F) is not independent because fd $B\rightarrow C$ is embedded in more than one relation scheme of R [GY,S]. $\square$

The above example shows that Lemma 4.5 does not hold for independent schemes. But that lemma does hold if some additional constraints are imposed. This is stated in the next theorem.

Theorem 4.2: If some nontrivial fd in F^+ is embedded in more than one relation scheme of **R**, then (**R**,F) is not independent; else, if there exists an independent scheme (S,G) such that $F \equiv G$, $R \leq S$, and $\cup R \subseteq \cup S$, then (**R**,F) is independent.

Proof: The first part of the theorem follows from a result in [GY]. When no nontrivial fd in F^+ is embedded in more than one relation scheme, independence coincides with weak independence. Then the second part follows from Lemma 4.5(b).□

References

[AC]   P. Atzeni and E.P.F. Chan, "Efficient optimization of simple chase join expressions," *ACM TODS, Vol. 14, No. 2 (1989)*, pp. 212-230

[C]   E.P.F. Chan, "Optimal computation of total projections with unions of simple chase join expressions," *ACM SIGMOD 1984*, pp. 149-163

[CH1]   E.P.F. Chan and H.J. Hernandez, "Independence-reducible database schemes," to appear in *JACM* (An extended abstract appeared under the same title in *ACM PODS 1988*, pp. 163-173)

[CH2]   E.P.F. Chan and H.J. Hernandez, "On generating database schemes bounded or constant-time-maintainable by extensibility," *Acta Informatica, 25, (1988)*, pp. 475-496

[G]   M.H. Graham, "Path expressions in databases," *ACM PODS 1983*, pp. 366-378

[GV]   M.H. Graham and M.Y. Vardi, "On the complexity and axiomatizability of consistent database states," *ACM PODS 1984*, pp. 281-289

[GW]   M.H. Graham and K. Wang, "Constant time maintenance or the triumph of fd's," *ACM PODS 1986*, pp. 121-141

[GY]   M.H. Graham and M. Yannakakis, "Independent database schemes," *JCSS, 28, 1, 1984*, pp. 121-141

[H]   P. Honeyman, "Test satisfaction of functional dependencies," *JACM, 29, 3, 1982*, pp. 668-677

[HW]   H.J. Hernandez and K. Wang, "On the boundedness of constant-time-maintainable database schemes," submitted to publication, 1989

[IIK]   M. Ito, M. Iwasaki and T. Kasam, "Some results on the representative instances in relational databases," *SIAM J. Comput., Vol. 14, No. 2, (May, 1985)*, pp. 334-353

[M]   A.O. Mendelzon, "Database states and their tableaux," *ACM TODS, Vol. 9, No. 2*, pp. 264-282

[Ma]   D. Maier, *The theory of relational databases*, CSP Inc., 1983

[MMS]   D. Maier, J.D. Ullman, Y. Sagiv, "Testing implication of data dependencies," *ACM TODS, Vol. 4, No. 4, (1979)*, pp. 455-469

[MUV]   D. Maier, J.D. Ullman, M.Y. Vardi, "On the foundations of the universal relation model," *ACM TODS, Vol. 9, No. 2, (1984)*, pp. 283-308

[S]   Y. Sagiv, "A characterization of globally consistent databases and their correct access pathes," *ACM TODS, Vol. 8, No., 2, (1983)*, pp. 266-286

[U]   J.D. Ullman, *Principles of database systems*, CSP, Inc., 1982

[W]   K. Wang, "Can constant-time-maintainability be more practically useful?" *ACM PODS 1989*, pp. 120-127

[WG]   K. Wang and M.H. Graham, "Constant-time-maintainability: a generalization of independence," submitted to publication, 1988 (See [GW] for an extended abstract)

Partial Document Ranking by Heuristic Methods

Dik Lun Lee
Wai Yee Peter Wong
Department of Computer and Information Science, Ohio State University
2036 Neil Ave, Columbus, Ohio 43210, U.S.A.

Abstract. In this paper, we study three methods for implementing the $tf \times idf$ ranking strategy with inverted files, where tf stands for term frequency and idf stands for inverse document frequency. The first one sorts the postings lists of the query terms by increasing length. It is the traditional sorting method used in the upperbound search algorithm. The second one sorts query terms based upon two parameters, namely the maximum tf of the postings list and the list length. The third one first requires each postings list to be sorted by decreasing tf value. It sorts disk pages, rather than postings lists, based upon three parameters, the maximum tf of the disk page, the length of the postings list and the number of document identifiers in the disk page. We show that the second and third methods are able to identify a large portion of top documents without using a large amount of disk page accesses. They outperform the first method by a large margin. The performance of these methods is demonstrated by experimental runs on four test collections made available with the SMART system.

1 Introduction

In most text retrieval systems, Boolean search strategies are used to distinguish documents that are to be retrieved from those that should be rejected. All retrieved documents satisfy the logical constraints of the Boolean query and are considered by the system to be equally relevant to the user's requests. However, their drawbacks are well-known [2,5,11,12]. It has been shown that the vector processing system without Boolean operators can be used to overcome the shortcomings of Boolean systems and improve retrieval performance [9,12].

In the vector processing system, a document D is represented as an V-dimensional vector, $< w_{t_1}, w_{t_2}, ..., w_{t_V} >$, where w_{t_i} specifies the relative importance of term t_i in the document and V is the size of the vocabulary (or dictionary). Similarly, a query Q can be represented as an n-dimensional vector, specifying the terms that the user is interested in. Both query and document terms can be weighted to distinguish terms that are more important for retrieval purposes from less important ones. The similarity between queries and documents can be computed in order to rank the retrieved documents in decreasing order of the query-document similarity. The user can then judge the relevance of the returned documents with respect to his information need. Based on the user's judgement, the system can modify the original query and perform another round of retrieval. This relevance feedback process can further improve the recall and precision of the retrieved results [8].

For the $tf \times idf$ ranking strategy, a document D is represented by $< w_{t_1}, w_{t_2}, ..., w_{t_V} >$, where $w_{t_i} = tf_D(t_i) \cdot idf(t_i)$. The value of $tf_D(t)$ represents the term frequency of the term t in document D (i.e., the number of occurrences of term t in document D). The function $idf(t)$ is set to $log_2(N/df(t))$, where N is the number of documents in a collection and $df(t)$ is the document frequency of term t (i.e., the number of documents in which term t is contained) [3,10]. Thus, a term has a high weight in a document if it occurs frequently in the document but infrequently in the rest of the collection. A query Q is represented by $< q_1, q_2, ..., q_V >$, where q_i is either 1 (specified) or 0 (not specified). The document score of document D with respect to query Q is computed by

$$\sum_{i=1}^{V} tf_D(t_i) \cdot idf(t_i) \cdot q_i.$$

Although the $tf \times idf$ ranking strategy is very simple conceptually, it has been shown to give good retrieval performance [3,8].

Various data structures have been used for implementing ranking strategies, such as inverted files [1,7], signature files [3,6,16] and search trees [4,14,15]. Here we concentrate on inverted files, which are used in most commercial text retrieval systems. Inverted files have fast response time, since only those postings lists specified in the query, which is usually a small portion of the whole file, are retrieved and processed. However, as the size of the queries increases after relevance feedback cycles, the processing cost becomes significant and needs to be reduced. Many optimization techniques on inverted file systems have been developed, and they mainly focus on the reduction of the amount of I/O, with the assumption that retrieval process is basically I/O bound [1,7,13].

In this paper, we investigate heuristic methods for implementing ranking strategies with inverted files. Although the $tf \times idf$ ranking function is used throughout this paper, the ideas of the heuristics can be applied to other ranking strategies such as those based on the Jacard and Dice functions, and the probabilistic model [9]. The organization of the paper is as follows. In Section 2, the upperbound search algorithm is studied in detail. Its weaknesses in implementing the $tf \times idf$ ranking strategy are demonstrated by experimental runs. The notion of retrieval accuracy is introduced. In Section 3, a simple search method is studied. It sorts query terms based upon two parameters, namely the maximum tf of the postings list and the list length. The performance of the first two methods is compared. In Section 4, a more complex search method is proposed. It requires postings lists to be sorted by decreasing tf value first, and then disk pages are sorted by three parameters, namely the maximum tf of the page, the list length and the number of document identifiers in the page. The amount of I/O operations and retrieval cost effectiveness are also studied. The objective of the proposed heuristic methods is to obtain a large portion of top documents fast with a relatively small number of disk accesses. The ability to achieve this objective is important when partial document ranking is implemented by retrieval systems. [1] In the last section, the merits of our methods are summaried. Throughout the rest of the paper, experimental runs are performed on four document collections made available with the SMART system, known as CACM, CISI, CRAN and MED.

2 The upperbound search algorithm

An optimization method known as the upperbound search algorithm has been studied extensively [1,3,4,6,7,13,15]. Given a query Q of k query terms, the algorithm first sorts Q by increasing length. [2] In this way, terms with high idf values (i.e., low df values) will be processed first. For simplicity, Q is represented by $(q_1, q_2, \ldots, q_k)$, in which $df(q_i) \leq df(q_j)$ for $i < j$. After a postings list is processed, partial document scores are sorted in descending order and the current top T documents are obtained. The upperbound of the $(T+1)$st document is then computed with the assumption that it contains all the remaining unsearched query terms. The retrieval process may stop if the upperbound of the $(T+1)$st document is smaller than the current score of the Tth document. This is because documents not in the current top T ranks cannot become one of the top documents even if the remaining unsearched lists are processed. If the search can be stopped early, the amount of disk access and CPU processing cost can be reduced substantially, since short lists are processed first and the unprocessed lists are long. Buckley et al. [1] study this optimization method for a number of ranking functions, and they find that little performance improvement can be expected if all the top documents are guaranteed to be returned. However, better improvement can be achieved if only some (not all) top documents are guaranteed to be returned. Due to the way postings lists are sorted, the upperbound search algorithm will be referred to as the L method in the paper.

We use Q_f to denote the final set of top documents obtained when all query terms are processed. To find out how fast the upperbound algorithm identifies the final document set and whether any saving can be obtained, checkpoints are taken to measure the number of documents in Q_f obtained at different points of the retrieval process. We use Q_j to denote the set of top documents obtained by processing the first j postings lists. The *retrieval accuracy* is defined as the percentage of documents in Q_j contained in Q_f

$$P_Q(j) = \frac{|Q_j \cap Q_f|}{|Q_f|} \cdot 100\%.$$

If $Q_j = \{2, 32, 45, 83, 149\}$ and $Q_f = \{14, 32, 45, 64, 83\}$, then $P_Q(j) = 3/5 \cdot 100\% = 60\%$. Definitely, $P_Q(k) = 100\%$. The values of $P_Q(j)$'s can serve as an indicator of the rate that documents in Q_f are identified. For instance, if $P_Q(j) = 80\%$, with $j = 0.4k$, it indicates that a large portion (80%) of the final solution Q_f is obtained after only a small amount of disk accesses (40%) has been performed. Due to the complexity of analyzing the retrieval accuracy of the L method mathematically, we will examine it by an experiment carried out on four test collections, which are made available with the SMART system. Some characteristics of the collections are given in Table 1.

The experiment is performed in the following manner. Ten queries are generated for each of the three different query sizes, namely 50, 100 and 200 terms, for each collection. Query terms in each query are randomly selected from respective dictionaries, and therefore they may not be related semantically. For each query, 10 equally spaced checkpoints are taken and the top 20 documents at each checkpoint are returned. In other words, $P_Q(j)$ is measured after every 10% of postings lists are processed. Finally, for each collection, we compute the average at each checkpoint for all the queries of the same size. The results are plotted as curves near the label L in Fig. 1.

---

[1] A partial document ranking is a ranking that includes some (not necessarily all) documents that are most similar to the query according to the similarity computation.

[2] The sorting requires the lengths of the postings lists to be kept in the inverted index, which can be accessed separately from the postings lists.

	CACM	CISI	CRAN	MED
Number of documents	3204	1460	1400	1033
Number of distinct terms	17137	7731	3763	6927
Maximum document frequency (df)	1316	659	860	359
Average df	6.87	19.98	19.74	7.69
Standard deviation of df	25.42	40.02	54.25	19.74
Maximum tf	59	82	27	25
Maximum idf	11.65	10.51	10.45	10.01

Table 1: Characteristics of the document collections.

For a point (h, v) on a curve in Fig. 1, it means that after $h\%$ of the terms in Q are processed, on the average, $v\%$ of the documents in Q_f are obtained. There are three curves shown for each collection, for 50-term ($\diamond$), 100-term ($\odot$) and 200-term ($\star$) queries. These curves are very close to one another, except for the queries in CACM. Moreover, they are basically monotonically increasing, which means that as more lists are processed, more documents in Q_f are revealed. However, the curves only show the average behavior. For an individual query, it is possible for the retrieval accuracy to decrease when more query terms have been processed. However, this is only a transient behavior that does not occur frequently. In Fig. 1, except the 100-term queries in CACM, the increment of $P_Q(j)$'s is rather slow for all queries in the four collections, and we get about 60% of the documents in Q_f after 90% of the terms in Q are processed. In most cases, all of the query terms must be processed in order to obtain all of the documents in Q_f. This indicates that the stopping criterion is hard to meet. No performance improvement is achieved by this method and the result is consistent with the study by Buckley et al. [1].

In the $tf \times idf$ ranking strategy, document scores are determined by both the tf and idf values. For typical document collections, the range of idf values is rather small since their values are compressed by the log function. Thus, idf is a secondary component for determining the weight of a term, when compared to tf, whose range is larger in general (see Table 1). However, the L method determines the processing order of query terms by sorting them according to their idf values alone, without taking tf values into account. This explains why the retrieval accuracy of the L method increases rather slowly and its inability to reduce the processing cost if all of the top documents are guaranteed to be retrieved.

In fact, the upperbound search algorithm is too conservative to yield any significant performance gain. First, it is highly unlikely for the $(T+1)$st document to get all the remaining unsearched terms. Second, the upperbound search method only focuses on the weight increment of the $(T+1)$st document, but the weights of all the current top documents have the same chance to be increased at the same time. Without taking these two factors into consideration, the algorithm makes it hard to meet the stopping criterion.

Two methods have been proposed to improve retrieval efficiency by relaxing the stopping criterion. The first one only guarantees a subset of top documents to be returned. The upperbound of the $(T+1)$st document is then compared with the current score of the Sth document, where $S < T$. With this relaxation, the chance to meet the stopping criterion is higher because of a larger difference in scores [1]. The second one applies probability on the upperbound computation [7,15]. The process may stop early if the probability for the upperbound of the $(T+1)$st document to exceed the current score of the Tth document is small. But we find that the probabilistic stopping criterion is still unlikely to be met because the score difference between the Tth and $(T+1)$st documents is usually very small. Figure 2 shows the document scores of the top 30 documents of one run on MED. There is no obvious gap between two consecutive scores. If there is one, its position is basically unpredictable. Thus, it is close to 100% chance that the $(T+1)$st document can become one of the top documents, except for the last few terms of the retrieval process. Moreover, the saving due to this method is still questionable since the cost of computing probabilities with a large number of terms could be very significant. Thus, the upperbound computation not only fails in producing any performance gain but also induces computation overhead.

Even though the $tf \times idf$ ranking strategy gives good retrieval effectiveness in general, it is known that not all the top documents returned are actually relevant to the query. In fact, ranking strategies alone are not the only way to control retrieval quality. Relevance feedback from the user could be more important in many circumstances. Effectiveness should not suffer greatly if the system can return a large portion of the top documents. To overcome the shortcomings of the L method, we will investigate two new search algorithms in the two next sections. The idea of the methods is based upon greedy algorithms, and their objective is to obtain a large portion of top documents fast without processing a large amount of I/O operations.

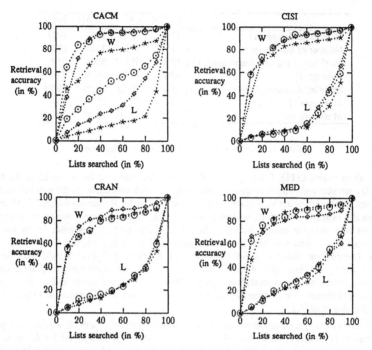

Figure 1: Average retrieval accuracy of the L method and W method: ◇ (50-term queries), ⊙ (100-term queries) and ∗ (200-term queries). Ten queries are tested for each query size.

3 The first new search method

To increase the chance of accumulating partial document scores fast, our first new search method takes two parameters into consideration, namely the maximum tf and the list length of the postings list. The query terms are then processed in descending order of the $tf_{max} \times idf$ values, where tf_{max} denotes the maximum tf of a list. In this case, the maximum tf value is stored in the inverted index for each postings list. A typical entry in the inverted file is like

$$\boxed{\text{term } t_i \mid tf_{max} \mid df} \longrightarrow \boxed{d_j, tf_x \mid d_k, tf_y \mid \cdots}$$

Since this algorithm processes postings lists which have a high potential of generating large increments of document scores, partial scores of top documents can be accumulated in a faster manner without using a large amount of I/O. This is an important property if partial document ranking is implemented by retrieval systems. However, this algorithm requires the maximum tf in each list to be stored in the inverted index, that will increase the overall storage overhead. Since two bytes are sufficient to store a term frequency, the additional storage overhead will not be significant. Since this method sorts postings lists by maximum weight, it is referred to as the W method in this paper.

An experiment to test the retrieval accuracy of the W method is carried out in a similar manner as described in Section 2. The results are plotted as curves near the label W in Fig. 1. In general, we find that, in all the test collections, more than 80% of the documents in Q_f are obtained only after 40% of the lists in Q are processed. Thus, the retrieval accuracy for the W method is high, demonstrating the superior performance of this search strategy. However, in Fig. 1, the retrieval accuracy is measured in terms of the number of postings lists processed, which is not a typical measure for database processing cost. In the following, we examine the performance of the L method and W method in terms of the amount of disk accesses, which is the dominating retrieval cost.

The problem of the W method is that it no longer processes shortest postings lists first as the L method does. Some long lists will be processed ahead of short lists. In fact, since the postings lists are sorted according to tf_{max} and idf, the longer is the postings list, the higher is the chance for it to contain a large tf value and thus be processed first. Therefore, we can expect the performance of the W method, when measured in terms of disk accesses, to be less than what Fig. 1 would have indicated.

	id	score		id	score		id	score
1	41	63.9	11	597	37.9	21	133	35.7
2	620	60.2	12	388	37.6	22	88	35.6
3	581	52.4	13	208	37.6	23	721	35.1
4	460	49.6	14	1025	37.6	24	197	34.9
5	390	48.2	15	902	37.4	25	594	34.8
6	77	45.1	16	240	37.0	26	603	34.7
7	697	40.9	17	137	36.7	27	573	33.7
8	505	40.1	18	272	36.6	28	608	33.2
9	344	40.1	19	457	36.5	29	837	33.2
10	681	38.2	20	463	35.8	30	120	33.2

Figure 2: Top 30 document scores of one run on MED.

The performance of the methods also depends on the page size, the basic unit of a disk access. In the extreme case, if the page size is large enough to hold the longest postings list, then the number of postings lists processed is the same as the number of disk accesses. Then, Fig. 1 correctly reflects the performance of the two methods in terms of disk accesses. However, when the page size is small, a postings list will occupy multiple disk pages. Since the W method may process some long postings lists first, it generates more disk accesses at the beginning of the processing than the L method does.

This property is again verified with experiments and the results are shown in Fig. 3. We assume that 4 bytes are used to represent a document identifier and 2 bytes a term frequency. We use P to represent the size of a disk page. Experiments are performed based upon 10 200-term queries for each of the four collections. The procedure of taking checkpoints is done in a similar manner as described in Section 2. The $\star$ curves correspond to the case where $P = 6$ bytes storing one document identifier per page. The $\odot$ curves correspond to the case where P equal to 120 bytes storing 20 document identifiers per page. The $\diamond$ curves correspond to the case where P equal to 240 bytes storing 40 document identifiers per page. The case where $P = 6$ bytes is practically impossible in reality, but it is included here as an extreme case for comparing the performance of the methods.

For $P = 6$ bytes, the W method in general generates a larger percentage of disk accesses than the L method for the same percentage of postings lists processed. In CISI, after 60% of the lists are retrieved, it almost accounts for 90% of the disk accesses for the W method, but only 5% for the L method. However, the difference between these two methods in terms of disk accesses narrow down as P increases. For P equal to 120 and 240 bytes, the differences of both methods in CACM and MED are relatively small, while the differences in CISI and CRAN are slightly larger. This can be explained from Table 1. In general, CISI and CRAN have longer term lists and their standard deviations of list lengths are larger as well, indicating a large variation in the lengths of the postings lists. In this case, the W method would very likely process many long postings lists, thus generating many disk accesses at the beginning of the search process. If the standard deviation is small, then the number of disk accesses generated will be more or less proportional to the number of postings lists retrieved. The best case is when P is larger than the maximum length of the postings lists; the gain in terms of retrieval accuracy for the W method over the L method is tremendous (see Fig. 1). The worst case is when the page size is so small that only one document identifier can be stored. The cost effectiveness of these two methods can be measured by the retrieval accuracy obtained for a certain amount of disk page accesses. We concentrate on the performance where 50% to 80% of top documents are obtained.

The cost effectiveness of both methods is shown in Fig. 4, in which the retrieval accuracy is measured after every 10% of total disk accesses, rather than every 10% of postings lists, are performed. In this figure, only the performance of 200-term queries is shown. Once again, the $\star$ curves correspond to $P = 6$ bytes, the $\odot$ curves $P= 120$ bytes and the $\diamond$ curves $P = 240$ bytes. Those curves nearest to the label L are the results of the L method and those nearest to the label W are the results of the W method. It can be seen that the W method still performs better than the L method in terms of retrieval accuracy in all collections, with all three different page sizes. For example, in CISI with $P = 120$ bytes, it takes about 10% of the total disk accesses to obtain 50% of the documents in Q_f by the W method, but it takes about 70% of the total disk accesses to obtain the same number of top documents by the L method. The saving is 60% of disk accesses by the W method. If more top documents in Q_f are required, say 80%, it takes about 45% of the total disk accesses by the W method, but about 95% by the L method. The saving is 50% of disk accesses by the W method. Generally, as the page size increases, the retrieval accuracy of the W method increases, while that of the L method decreases. Therefore, the performance gain of the W method is more significant when $P = 240$ bytes. It also indicates that when the page size

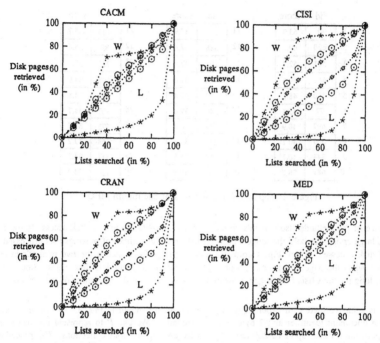

Figure 3: Average disk accesses of the L method and the W method. The curves correspond to the 200-term queries: $\star$ (P=6 bytes), $\odot$ (P=120 bytes) and $\diamond$ (P = 240 bytes).

decreases to the limiting case with P = 6 bytes, the retrieval accuracy of the W method is still better than that of the L method. Thus, the W method outperforms the L method by a large margin for most practical purposes.

4 The second new search algorithm

In the W method, postings lists are sorted by decreasing order of $tf_{max} \times idf$ values. When a postings list of high $tf_{max} \times idf$ is retrieved, many disk pages with low term weights are retrieved and processed at the same time, but they contribute little to find the top documents. Thus, processing the query Q list by list is not the best way to achieve high retrieval accuracy. To further utilize the idea of greediness, the following search method is investigated.

In this new method, a postings list is no longer viewed as a single item, but rather a sequence of individual disk pages. The disk pages of each postings list are sorted by decreasing tf values. In other words, for a given term, documents with high tf values are at the beginning of the list, and those with low tf's are put at the end. This organization allows disk pages of high term weights to be processed before those of low term weights. Thus, this method may process the first page of term t_i, and then the first page of term t_j, and then the first page of t_k, and then the second page of term t_i, and so on. The sorting requirement will definitely incur additional processing overhead. However, if updates are done in batch and are infrequent compared to retrieval, the overall performance of the retrieval system will not be degraded. Furthermore, we find that the number of document identifiers in a page can also affect the retrieval accuracy, so the disk pages are ordered for processing by the following function:

$$tf_{max} \times idf \times I^c,$$

where I is the number of document identifiers in a disk page, and c is a constant between 0 and 1 and its function is discussed below.

The idea of processing the heaviest pages first is to accumulate partial document scores fast. However, the weight itself is found not to be the only factor for fast weight accumulation, especially for those top documents whose weights are based upon the combination of many terms. For example, a page having one identifier with a maximum weight of 31 may not have a higher potential to accumulate weights than a page having 20 identifiers with a maximum weight of 29.

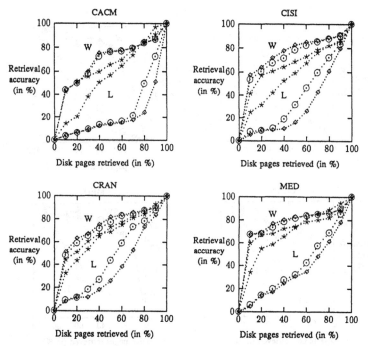

Figure 4: Average retrieval accuracy of the L method and W method with respect to disk accesses. The curves correspond to the 200-term queries: $\star$ (P=6 bytes), $\odot$ (P=120 bytes) and $\diamond$ (P = 240 bytes).

First of all, the weight difference between these two pages is small. Moreover, the former only increments the weight of one document, while the latter increments the weights of 20 documents. In this case, it is more reasonable to process the disk page with maximum weight of 29 first. According to the Zipf's law, most of the terms appear only infrequently in most document bases [9]. Many disk pages are only partially filled with document identifiers, so the above situation should be taken into account for determining the processing order. However, the significance of $tf_{max} \times idf$ should still be much higher than that of I; thus a power c, where $0 < c < 1$, is used to restrict the significance of I. Since this method requires the documents of each postings list to be sorted by decreasing tf value, it is referred to as the SW method in this paper.

In Fig. 5, the cost effectiveness of the L method, W method and SW method is compared. We only study the cases where P = 120 bytes and P = 240 bytes, because P = 6 bytes is not a realistic parameter. The procedure of taking checkpoints is similar to the one discussed in Section 3. Each curve corresponds to the average performance of 30 queries in each collection. For P = 120 bytes, c is set to 0.5. In other words, we take a square root of I in the formula. As P is increased to 240 bytes, with the maximum tf in each postings list unchanged, c is accordingly reduced to 0.4 to restrict the significance of I to the processing order. The value of c is used to allow some lighter postings lists to be processed ahead some heavier ones, but at the same time to avoid processing some long postings lists with very small weights before those with much higher weights. The optimal value of c for a certain page size requires further investigation. We find that in CACM and MED, the retrieval accuracy of the W method and SW method is basically the same for the first 30% of disk accesses, and the SW method performs better afterwards. In CISI and CRAN, the SW method obtains about 5-10% more top documents than the W method does at most checkpoints, demonstrating the performance improvement by the SW method over the W method.

In order to realize the advantage of partial document ranking, the system must be able to tell when to stop the search for a desired retrieval accuracy. If it fails to do so, we may have searched more postings lists than necessary, incurring unnecessary disk accesses, or stopped too soon, resulting in a lower accuracy than the user's specification. Therefore, it is desirable to have a system that estimates the number of top documents obtained at different points of retrieval and allows the user to specify the condition for termination. This can be done in a number of ways. For instance, the values of $P_Q(j)$'s can be determined by carefully calibrating the retrieval system. This method is simple and produce good estimations for a stable database, but may not work very well when the parameters of the database change frequently.

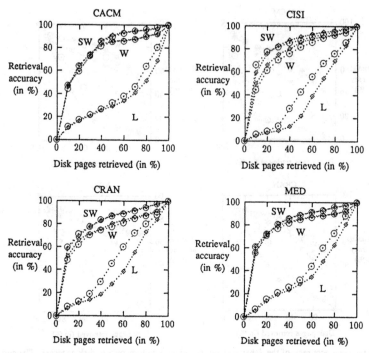

Figure 5: Average retrieval accuracy of the L method, W method and SW method with respect to disk accesses. The curves correspond to 30 queries: $\odot$ (P=120 bytes) and $\diamond$ (P = 240 bytes).

Alternatively, a analytical model can be developed based upon the distribution functions of the tf values and df values, and the search strategy. This method should be able to predict the $P_Q(j)$'s of *ad hoc* queries more accurately. Various approaches are being investigated and some results have been reported [17].

5 Conclusion

Ranking strategies alone are not the only way to control retrieval quality. Relevance feedback from the user is important as well. Effectiveness should not suffer greatly if the system is able to return a large portion of the top documents. The major contribution of this paper is to suggest search methods which are able to return a large portion of top documents while consuming only a small fraction of the total disk accesses required to obtain Q_f.

In this paper, we propose heuristic search methods for implementing the $tf \times idf$ ranking strategy with inverted files. Three methods are investigated. The first method is called the L method that sorts postings lists by increasing length. This is the traditional sorting method used in the upperbound search algorithm. The second method is called the W method that sorts postings lists by decreasing $tf_{max} \times idf$. The third method is called the SW method that requires the postings lists to be sorted by decreasing tf, and it sorts all disk pages by decreasing $tf_{max} \times idf \times I^c$. Based upon the experimental results on the four test collections made available with the SMART system, the SW methods performs better than the W method, in terms of the retrieval accuracy for a given number of disk accesses, and they both in turn outperform the L method by a large margin.

In order to implement a partial ranking of documents, an estimation method is needed to give the number of top documents obtained at different points of retrieval. A statistical model could be developed based upon the distributions of tf and idf values and the search strategy. Estimations can also be done by carefully calibrating the retrieval system. We find that the latter is good enough to give meaningful indications to the user for practical purposes.

References

[1] C. Buckley & A. F. Lewit, "Optimization of inverted vector searches," *Proceedings of the ACM SIGIR Conference*, 1985, 97–110.

[2] W. S. Cooper, "Getting beyond Boole," *Information Processing and Management*, Vol. 24, No. 3, 1988, 243–248.

[3] W. B. Croft & P. Savino, "Implementing ranking strategies using text signatures," *ACM Trans. Office Info. Syst.*, Vol. 6, No. 1, January 1988, 42–62.

[4] K. Fukunaga & P. M. Narendra, "A branch and bound algorithms for computing k-nearest neighbors," *IEEE Trans. on Computers*, Vol. C-24, No. 7, July 1975, 750–753.

[5] M. E. Maron & T. Radecki, "Trends in research on information retrieval-the potential for improvements in conventional boolean retrieval systems," *Information Processing and Management*, Vol. 24, No. 3, 1988, 219–227.

[6] K. C. Mohan & P. Willett, "Nearest neighbor searching in serial files using text signatures," *Journal of Info. Science*, Vol. 11, 1985, 31–39.

[7] S. A. Perry & P. Willett, "A review of the use of inverted files for best match searching in information retrieval systems," *Journal of Info. Science*, Vol. 6, 1983, 59–66.

[8] G. Salton, *Automatic Information Organization and Retrieval*. McGraw-Hill Book Co., New York, 1968.

[9] G. Salton, *Automatic Text Processing*. Addison-Wesley Publishing Co., Reading, MA, 1989.

[10] G. Salton, "Another look at automatic text-retrieval systems," *Commun. ACM*, Vol. 29, No. 7, July 1986, 648–656.

[11] G. Salton, E. A. Fox & H. Wu, "Extended boolean information retrieval," *Commun. ACM*, Vol. 26, No. 12, December 1983, 1022–1036.

[12] G. Salton & M. J. McGill, *Introduction to Modern Information Retrieval*. McGraw-Hill Book Co., New York, 1983.

[13] A. F. Smeaton & C. J. van Rijsbergen, "The nearest neighbour problem in information retrieval. An algorithm using upperbounds," *ACM SIGIR Forum*, Vol. 16, 1981, 83–87.

[14] M. Stewart & P. Willett, "Nearest neighbour searching in binary search trees: Simulation of a multiprocessor system," *Journal of Documentation*, Vol. 43, No. 2, June 1987, 93–111.

[15] S. F. Weiss, "A probabilistic algorithm for nearest neighbour searching," in *Information Retrieval Research*, R. N. Oddy, S. E. Robertson, C. J. van Rijsbergen & P. W. Williams, eds., Butterworths, London, UK, 1981, 325–333.

[16] W. Y. P. Wong & D. L. Lee, "Signature file methods for implementing a ranking strategy," *Information Processing and Management*, Vol. 26, No. 5, 1990, 641–653.

[17] W. Y. P. Wong & D. L. Lee, "A heuristic method for document ranking," *Proceedings of The Second International Symposium on Database Systems for Advanced Applications*, Tokyo, Japan, April 2-4, 1991.

Context Inheritance and Content Inheritance in an Object-Oriented Data Model

Li Yu   Sylvia L. Osborn

Department of Computer Science, The University of Western Ontario
London Ontario, Canada N6A 5B7, {lili,sylvia}@csd.uwo.ca

Abstract

One of the common features of existing object-oriented database systems is the support of an inheritance hierarchy, which allows the user to create new classes incrementally from existing, less specialized classes. However, the traditional inheritance notion seems to suffer from several limitations: (1) susceptiveness to incomprehensible conceptual semantics, (2) susceptiveness to class space pollution, and (3) rigorousness of the overriding mechanism that restricts objects to present only a single view of their behaviors. Herein we describe a new object-oriented data model, with focus on its new notion of the *dual inheritance* which captures the "KIND-OF" semantics in *context inheritance* and the "REUSE-OF" semantics in *content inheritance*. With these new notions, the model exhibits an attractive flexibility in ameliorating the above problems.

1   Introduction

Object-oriented databases (OODBs) are currently the subject of a great deal of database research. Many OODBs have been proposed and implemented, such as GEMSTONE [14], VISION [5], VBASE [1], IRIS [6], ORION [3], ENCORE [8], and O2 [10, 11]. One of the common features of these OODBs is the support of an inheritance hierarchy which allows the user to create new classes incrementally from existing, less specialized classes. Although the one-hierarchy inheritance notion is simple and easy to use, it appears to have several potential problems: (1) susceptiveness to incomprehensible conceptual semantics, (2) susceptiveness to class space pollution, and (3) rigorousness of the overriding mechanism that restricts objects to present only a single view of their behaviors.

The first problem arises when users try to take advantage of the code reusability implied by the inheritance hierarchy. For example, it is very easy for a user to make a new class GORILLA a subclass of an existing class BEAR simply because they "run" and "eat" in a similar manner. However, the specialization relationship between GORILLA and BEAR is conceptually incorrect. In database systems, this often means that when a query is issued against the class BEAR, you will see some gorillas as well because a GORILLA "is a" BEAR. Similarly, you might see some cats and dogs when you query against class PERSON if the creators of CAT and DOG have chosen PERSON's behaviors to personalize cats and dogs. Another consequence is that unexpected security violations might happen. For example, instances of BNR-RESEARCHER would be retrieved by a query against IBM-RESEARCHER if BNR-RESEARCHER were made a subclass of IBM-RESEARCHER simply for code reuse reasons.

One solution might be to move BEAR's behaviors to its superclass, say, ANIMAL and then let GORILLA inherit from ANIMAL. This is usually unrealistic both at the modeling level and at the implementation level. At the modeling level, the behavior "run" and "eat" of BEAR may not be general enough to be inherited by the majority animals. At the implementation level, moving "run" and "eat" from BEAR into ANIMAL means overwriting the behaviors "run" and "eat" attached to ANIMAL (if any) and re-implementing new "run" and "eat" in ANIMAL because they now rely on ANIMAL's representation.

Another solution might be to create a new class, say BEAR-OR-GORILLA, that has the desired "eat" and "run" behaviors and then let both BEAR and GORILLA inherit from the new class. However, because this kind of new class would have no direct instances, it is an example of the second problem we pointed out — class space pollution. If every time we encounter this situation we create a new class, very soon we will find our class hierarchy being polluted with many meaningless classes. In addition, frequent schema change could be very costly.

The third problem, the problem of a single view of object behaviors, refers to the overriding mechanism assumed by the inheritance hierarchy. In existing OODBs, if a class implements a method, then it overrides any implementations for the methods with the same name in the class's superclasses. Consider the following five classes: PROJECT-MANAGER is-a SYSTEM-ANALYST is-a PROGRAMMER is-a EMPLOYEE is-a PERSON, where "X is-a Y" means "X is a subclass of Y". Each of the five classes has a distinct implementation to support a behavior named "Introduce yourself". When the message "Introduce yourself" is sent to an instance of PROJECT-MANAGER, say *Mike*, we can only see *Mike* introducing himself as a "project manager" because the implementation invoked is the one designed for PROJECT-MANAGER (due to the overriding mechanism). In many situations, we would like a receiver to show a multiple view of the same behavior, such as the request "Introduce *Mike* as a person and forget about other details!". In most existing object-oriented systems, this requires a change in the message. For instance, the extended Smalltalk [4] uses the message of the form `class-name.method-name` to select a method implemented in `class-name`. The main problem with this kind of approach in OODBs is that polymorphism may not be properly supported in the case where a message is sent a set of receivers. For example, if we send "PROGRAMMER.Introduce yourself" to a set of PERSONs, those in the set who are only employees or persons would not be able to respond to this message. We will suggest a different way to achieve the same purpose without loss of the support for polymorphism.

This paper focuses on a new notion called *dual inheritance* introduced in an object-oriented data model called the KBO model, which was originally motivated to study "Knowhow-Bearing-Objects" [19]. A **knowhow** is a unique fragment of executable code crafted in an arbitrary general-purpose programming language. The *dual inheritance* notion allows KBO objects to be organized along two independent lattices, and captures the "KIND-OF" semantics in *context inheritance* and the "REUSE-OF" semantics in *content inheritance*. The model exhibits a flexibility in ameliorating the problems described above. In the next section, we introduce the basic concepts related to the dual inheritance notion. Section 3 provides a set-theoretic semantics for both context inheritance and content inheritance, and demonstrates the modeling power of the dual inheritance through an example. Section 4 defines the structures of objects and classes and Section 5 shows how to validate user-specified interclass relationships. Section 6 presents the message-sending mechanisms that support a multiple view of object behaviors. Finally, Section 7 compares our approach with related work and draws some conclusions.

2 Modeling Concepts

The data model has several underlying domains defined as follows:
- Let $\mathcal{C}$ be a countably infinite set of symbols called *class names*, and let $\mathcal{A}$ be a countably infinite set of symbols called *attribute labels*, where $\mathcal{C} \cap \mathcal{A} = \emptyset$.
- Let $\mathcal{O}$ be the *object universe*, a countably infinite set of real-world objects. Let $\mathcal{I}$ be a countably infinite set of *object-identities*, such that there exists a bijection *oid* from $\mathcal{O}$ onto $\mathcal{I}$. In other words, for each $o \in \mathcal{O}$ there is a unique $oid(o) \in \mathcal{I}$ that identifies o.

• Let $\mathcal{K}$ be a countably infinite set of *knowhows* such that there exists an injection bb from $\mathcal{K}$ into $\mathcal{O}$, which associates each knowhow $k \in \mathcal{K}$ with a unique "biological bearer" $bb(k) \in \mathcal{O}$ (i.e., object $bb(k)$ is created by k's implementor). Each knowhow $k \in \mathcal{K}$ has a *formal output specification*, $output(k) = c$ where $c \in \mathcal{C}$ and a *formal input specification*, $input(k) = \{(L_1, c_1), \ldots, (L_n, c_n)\}$ where $L_i \in \mathcal{A}$ and $c_i \in \mathcal{C}$ for $1 \leq i \leq n$ and $\forall i, j \in [1..n] : i \neq j \implies L_i \neq L_j$.

• Let $\mathcal{K}^* = \mathcal{K} \cup \{\phi_\perp, \phi_\top\}$, where $\phi_\perp$ is the *empty knowhow* and $\phi_\top$ is the *virtual knowhow*, such that there exists a surjection kh from $\mathcal{O}$ onto $\mathcal{K}^*$ which associates every object $o \in \mathcal{O}$ with a knowhow $kh(o) \in \mathcal{K}^*$.

Two comments should be made here. First, the nature of the function oid indicates that the KBO model supports a strong object-identity semantics — every object is a true first-class object. Many existing systems do not have object-identities for atomic objects and procedure objects (if procedures are treated as objects). Second, the introduction of the *knowhow* concept enables us to encapsulate the implementation of a "knowhow", because all we see is an executable reference (the knowhow) which identifies a computation that **knows how** to do things (e.g., "run" and "eat"); how the computation is implemented is a pure secret kept by its implementor. The primary motive for pursuing this point of view is that: (1) a multi-language framework can be assumed for "knowhow" implementations, and (2) a "knowhow" implementation can be changed or maintained without affecting database applications.

In the KBO model, because of the existence of the knowhow assignment kh, the world is viewed as composed of *Knowhow-Bearing-Objects*. Conventional "data" become objects bearing the empty knowhow, and conventional "processes" become objects bearing a non-empty knowhow. Because of the immutability of object-identity, a "data" object can become a "process" object by gaining a non-empty knowhow, and, similarly, a "process" object can become a "data" object by losing its non-empty knowhow. Consequently, objects not only represent a fact (by their values) but also can be invoked to exhibit a "knowhow" (by activating their knowhows). The position we are taking in the KBO model is that the knowledge about *how to do things* and the knowledge about *what things are* can be **seamlessly** modeled and manipulated.

Like any other data models, the KBO model provides several high-level abstractions which allow complex relationships to be categorized and viewed in comprehensible ways. The first abstraction categorizes objects into classes:

Axiom 1: *INSTANCE-OF (Classification).* There exists a binary relation $\textcircled{i}$ over $\mathcal{O} \times \mathcal{C}$ called *INSTANCE-OF* such that $\forall o \in \mathcal{O}, \exists c \in \mathcal{C} : o \textcircled{i} c$, where o is called an *instance* of class c. ∎

This axiom states that every object in the object universe is an instance of at least one class. The next abstraction captures the idea that objects can also be categorized by what owns them (or what they vitalize) — an object only exhibits its "knowhow" for its owner-classes.

Axiom 2: *BEHAVIOR-OF (Vitalization).* There exists a binary relation $\textcircled{b}$ over $\mathcal{O} \times \mathcal{C}$ called *BEHAVIOR-OF* such that $\forall o \in \mathcal{O}, \exists c \in \mathcal{C} : o \textcircled{b} c$, where o is called a *behavior* of class c. ∎

This axiom states that every object in the object universe is also owned as a behavior by least one class. Based on the above axioms, we introduce other two abstractions.

Definition 1: *KIND-OF (Generalization).* The "KIND-OF" abstraction $\textcircled{k}$ is a binary relation over $\mathcal{C} \times \mathcal{C}$. For any two classes $(c_1, c_2) \in \mathcal{C} \times \mathcal{C}$, $c_1 \textcircled{k} c_2$ if and only if both (1) and (2) hold:

$\quad$ (1) $\quad \forall o \in \mathcal{O} : o \textcircled{i} c_1 \implies o \textcircled{i} c_2$

$\quad$ (2) $\quad c_1 \neq c_2 \implies \exists o \in \mathcal{O} : o \textcircled{i} c_2 \land \neg(o \textcircled{i} c_1)$

When $c_1 \textcircled{k} c_2$, we call c_1 a *kind* or a *subclass* of c_2 and c_2 a *superclass* of c_1. ∎

Intuitively, any instance of a subclass is semantically a valid instance of any its superclasses. From the viewpoint of conceptual modeling, a class c_1 is a kind of class c_2 if and only if every instance of c_1 is *semantically necessarily* an instance of c_2. For example, COMPUTER-JOURNAL is a kind of JOURNAL, but NEWSPAPER is not a kind of JOURNAL even though they may be the same structurally (e.g., both of them are composed of two attributes, Name and Publisher).

Definition 2: *REUSE-OF (Re-utilization).* The "REUSE-OF" abstraction $\textcircled{r}$ is a binary relation over $\mathcal{C} \times \mathcal{C}$. For any two classes $(c_1, c_2) \in \mathcal{C} \times \mathcal{C}$, $c_1 \textcircled{r} c_2$ if and only if both (1) and (2) hold:

(1) $\forall o \in \mathcal{O} : o \textcircled{b} c_2 \Longrightarrow (o \textcircled{b} c_1 \vee (\neg(o \textcircled{b} c_1) \wedge (\exists o' \in \mathcal{O} : o' \textcircled{b} c_1 \wedge kh(o') = kh(o))))$

(2) $c_1 \neq c_2 \Longrightarrow \exists o \in \mathcal{O} : o \textcircled{b} c_1 \wedge \neg(\exists x \in \mathcal{O} : x \textcircled{b} c_2 \wedge kh(x) = kh(o))$

When $c_1 \textcircled{r} c_2$, we call c_1 a *reuse* or a *demandclass* of c_2 and c_2 a *supplyclass* of c_1. ∎

Intuitively, almost any behavior of a supplyclass will be inherited by all its demandclasses, except that if a behavior of the supplyclass is given a new value (renamed) in a demandclass then the original behavior will not be inherited by that demandclass. Notice that this definition is almost an inverse analogy of that of KIND-OF.

An interesting property of the REUSE-OF abstraction is that there is no explicit "overriding" of inherited behaviors (more precisely, their knowhows). The intuition here is that, since c_1 reuses c_2 as a whole (i.e., c_2's representation is utilized by c_1 as a whole), any behaviors of c_2 should be invocable on c_1's instances at the user's discretion because c_1 *does* have the representation they depend on. However, the "overriding" effect can still be achieved (at the user's discretion) by value-based message-sendings (described later in Section 6).

The following definition characterizes classes in the KBO model as two sets of objects.

Definition 3: *Interfaces and Populations.* Any class $c \in \mathcal{C}$ has an *interface*, denoted $\overset{*}{\Sigma}(c)$, and an *population*, denoted $\overset{*}{\Omega}(c)$, such that $\overset{*}{\Sigma}(c) = \{o|\, o \textcircled{b} c\,\}$ and $\overset{*}{\Omega}(c) = \{o|\, o \textcircled{i} c\,\}$. ∎

We also need to distinguish the difference between *direct* and *indirect* abstractions.

Definition 4: *Direct Abstractions*

- An object o is a *direct instance* of a class c, denoted $o \textcircled{i}_d c$, if and only if $o \textcircled{i} c$ and there is no class c' such that $c' \textcircled{k} c$ and $o \textcircled{i} c'$.
- An object o is a *direct behavior* of a class c, denoted $o \textcircled{b}_d c$, if and only if $o \textcircled{b} c$ and there is no class c' such that $c \textcircled{r} c'$ and $o \textcircled{b} c'$.
- Let $c_1, c_2 \in \mathcal{C}$ be any two classes, $c_1 \neq c_2$. Then, class c_1 is a *direct subclass* of class c_2, denoted $c_1 \textcircled{k}_d c_2$, if and only if $c_1 \textcircled{k} c_2$ and there is no class c such that $c_1 \textcircled{k} c$ and $c \textcircled{k} c_2$.
- Let $c_1, c_2 \in \mathcal{C}$ be any two classes, $c_1 \neq c_2$. Then, class c_1 is a *direct demandclass* of class c_2, denoted $c_1 \textcircled{r}_d c_2$, if and only if $c_1 \textcircled{r} c_2$ and there is no class c such that $c_1 \textcircled{r} c$ and $c \textcircled{r} c_2$. ∎

With the notion of direct abstractions, we formulate some important constraints:

Axiom 3: *Unique Direct Instance Axiom.* No object is a direct instance of two different classes. That is, $\forall o \in \mathcal{O}, \forall c_1, c_2 \in \mathcal{C} : o \textcircled{i}_d c_1 \wedge o \textcircled{i}_d c_2 \Longrightarrow c_1 = c_2$. ∎

Axiom 4: *Unique Direct Behavior Axiom.* No behavior is a direct behavior of two different classes. That is, $\forall o \in \mathcal{O}, \forall c_1, c_2 \in \mathcal{C} : o \textcircled{b}_d c_1 \wedge o \textcircled{b}_d c_2 \Longrightarrow c_1 = c_2$. ∎

3 Semantics of the Dual Lattice

This section attempts to provide a clean, set-theoretic semantics for *dual lattice schemas* (i.e., every schema has two lattices on one set of classes). We first define the notion of formal input space. For this definition, we let ARG denote the set of all possible legal actual arguments taken by any knowhow in $\mathcal{K}$. To simplify our formal discussion, we also let *Receiver* be a special label, manifesting the fact that there is always an "extra argument" — the receiver, for any knowhow.

Definition 5: *Formal Input Space* The formal input space $\mathcal{FIS}$ is a set of *formal input sources* defined as $\mathcal{FIS} = \{(L, c)|\, (L, c) \in input(k) \wedge k \in \mathcal{K}\} \cup \{(Receiver, c)|\, c \in \mathcal{C}\}$ such that $\forall arg \in ARG, \exists o \in \mathcal{O}, \exists (label, type) \in \mathcal{FIS} : arg = (label, o) \wedge o \textcircled{i} type$. ∎

A comment is in order here. In our model, the activation of a knowhow k follows the message passing paradigm [7]. As such, the activation of k depends on not only the input arguments specified in $input(k)$ but also the internal state of a receiver object. (Section 6 will elaborate this aspect.) Therefore, assuming that every class will have some behaviors (in order to be usable), instances of any class in $\mathcal{C}$ can receive some messages (and thus activate some knowhows). This fact is reflected by letting $\{(Receiver, c)|\ c \in \mathcal{C}\}$ be a subset of $\mathcal{FIS}$. In practice, the label $Receiver$ is not used because receivers will have an explicit place in our message-sending operation.

The following theorems show that the notion of subclass/superclass is based on context inclusion, whereas the notion of demandclass/supplyclass is based on content inclusion. Their proofs are straightforward.

Theorem 1: (Context Inheritance). *For any* $x \in \mathcal{C}$, *let its context be* $\mathbf{context}(x) = \{(l, t)|\ (l, t) \in \mathcal{FIS} \wedge \overset{*}{\Omega}(x) \subseteq \overset{*}{\Omega}(t)\ \}$. *Then, a class c is a kind of a class c' if and only if the context of c is a superset of the context of c'. That is,* $\forall c, c' \in \mathcal{C} : c \textcircled{k} c' \iff \mathbf{context}(c) \supset \mathbf{context}(c')$. ∎

This theorem implies that an instance of a subclass can always be used in any context in which an instance of a superclass was expected to be an actual input source or a receiver.

Theorem 2: (Content Inheritance). *For any* $x \in \mathcal{C}$, *let its content be* $\mathbf{content}(x) = \{kh(b)|\ b \textcircled{b} x\ \}$. *Then, a class c is a reuse of a class c' if and only if the content of c is a superset of the content of c'. That is,* $\forall c, c' \in \mathcal{C} : c \textcircled{r} c' \iff \mathbf{content}(c) \supset \mathbf{content}(c')$. ∎

This theorem implies a code-revision rule: If class y is a reuse of class x, then whenever class x's knowhows are revised (by their implementors), class y's knowhows are automatically revised. Also notice that the content of a class includes implicitly the private representation of the class, because implementations (code) tend to depend on the representation.

The $\textcircled{k}$ and $\textcircled{r}$ partial orderings can be considered to be a complete lattice over classes, when the greatest class OBJECT and the smallest class COMMON are introduced.

Definition 6: *Classes OBJECT and COMMON.* There exist two special classes OBJECT and COMMON in $\mathcal{C}$, such that

(1) $\forall o \in \mathcal{O}, \forall c \in \mathcal{C} : o \textcircled{i} \text{OBJECT} \wedge (o \textcircled{b} \text{OBJECT} \implies o \textcircled{b} c)$

(2) $\forall o \in \mathcal{O}, \forall c \in \mathcal{C} : o \textcircled{b} \text{COMMON} \wedge (o \textcircled{i} \text{COMMON} \implies o \textcircled{i} c)$

∎

Theorem 3: *The set of all classes $\mathcal{C}$ is a lattice (a directed acyclic graph) both under the KIND-OF relation $\textcircled{k}$ and under the REUSE-OF relation $\textcircled{r}$.* ∎

As such, the population of OBJECT is the set union of the populations of all classes and the population of COMMON is the set intersection of the populations of all classes. Notice that COMMON's population is not empty: it has three model-defined objects *null*, *same* and *fail*. They have special semantics when used as an invoker or a receiver in message-sendings (roughly, as the nullifier, the identity, and the complainant). Due to the space limit, we will not provide further details of their properties.

With the KBO model abstractions, any two classes in a database schema can be connected in three different manners: (i) when c_1 semantically specializes c_2 and also shares the knowhows of c_2, we have both $c_1 \textcircled{k} c_2$ and $c_1 \textcircled{r} c_2$; (ii) when c_1 semantically specializes c_2 without sharing the knowhows of c_2, we have $c_1 \textcircled{k} c_2$ but not $c_1 \textcircled{r} c_2$; and (iii) when c_1 shares the knowhows of c_2 without making a public semantic commitment to c_2, we have $c_1 \textcircled{r} c_2$ but not $c_1 \textcircled{k} c_2$. The following example illustrates these three cases.

Example 1: Consider the database schema shown in Figure 1. The schema contains five classes: PET, LOG, GUINEA-PIG, BIRD, DOG, and CAT (for simplicity, classes OBJECT and COMMON are omitted from the schema). Assume that b_1 ("run") and b_2 ("eat") of PET were created by PET's designer mainly with caged pets in mind. In this database schema, GUINEA-PIG and BIRD are connected with PET in the manner of case (i), because their instances are usually caged pets. CAT and DOG are connected with PET in the manner of case (ii), because their instances are usually not caged pets; they still "run" and "eat", but probably in very different ways. CAT is connected with DOG in the manner of case (iii), because CAT's designer likes the way DOG runs (e.g., with total freedom) and the way DOG eats (e.g., beside the kitchen table). CAT is

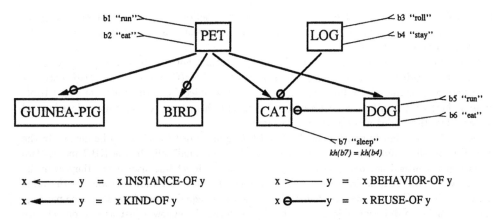

Figure 1: An Example of Dual Inheritance

also connected with LOG in the manner of case (iii), because CAT's designer thinks "cats sleep like a log" and "cats roll like a log". Notice that, although CAT is a reuse of LOG, behavior b_4 is excluded from CAT's interface because b_4 is renamed in behavior b_7 of CAT (in fact, b_7 is a revalued behavior defined in the next section); obviously CAT's designer does not like b_4's descriptor "stay" but prefers "sleep" for CAT. The (snapshot) interfaces of all the classes in this example can be easily derived as follows:

$$\overset{*}{\Sigma}(\text{PET}) = \{b_1, b_2\} \qquad \overset{*}{\Sigma}(\text{GUINEA-PIG}) = \{b_1, b_2\} \qquad \overset{*}{\Sigma}(\text{BIRD}) = \{b_1, b_2\}$$
$$\overset{*}{\Sigma}(\text{LOG}) = \{b_3, b_4\} \qquad \overset{*}{\Sigma}(\text{CAT}) = \{b_3, b_5, b_6, b_7\} \qquad \overset{*}{\Sigma}(\text{DOG}) = \{b_5, b_6\}$$

According to the context inheritance theorem, GUINEA-PIG, BIRD, CAT, and DOG all have **context**(PET) included in their contexts. But the context of CAT does not include the context of LOG or DOG. ∎

The idea demonstrated here can be easily generalized to much more complicated applications.

4   Objects and Classes

Definition 7: *Objects.* A KBO object $o \in \mathcal{O}$ is a quadruple $o = (i, c, v, g)$ where $i \in \mathcal{I}$ is the object-identity of o such that $i = oid(o)$, $c \in \mathcal{C}$ is the class of o such that $o \;\textcircled{i}_d\; c$, v is the value of o (for simplicity, let v be an atomic value[1] in the sense of [9]), and $g = (\omega, \xi, \wp)$ is the *vigor* of o where (1) $\omega \in \mathcal{C}$ is the *owner* of o such that $o \;\textcircled{i}_d\; \omega$; (2) ξ is the *signature* of o's knowhow, $\xi = (\; input(kh(o)), output(kh(o)) \;)$; (3) $\wp \in \mathcal{K}^*$ is the knowhow of o, i.e., $kh(o) = \wp$, such that if $\omega = \text{COMMON}$ then $\wp = \phi_\perp$. If $bb(\wp) = o$ then $\wp$ is called the *inherent knowhow* of o. When $input(\wp) = \{(L_1, c_1), \ldots, (L_n, c_n)\}$ and $output(\wp) = c_{out}$, we usually write ξ as $(A_1, c_1) \times \ldots \times (A_n, c_n) \longrightarrow c_{out}$. When $input(\wp) = \{\}$, we write ξ as $() \longrightarrow c_{out}$. Furthermore, we call o a *hollow object* when $\omega = \text{COMMON}$, and *solid object* otherwise. ∎

Notice that all objects, whether solid or hollow, are classified based on their values rather than their signatures. As such, the value of an object can be viewed as a description of the purpose and features of the object's knowhow. For instance, a solid object x with a TEXT value "Introduce the manager" is capable of achieving "Introduce the manager" when $kh(x)$ is activated, and a solid object y with a sequence value < "walk in", "find a seat", "order", "eat and chat", "pay

---

[1]For the purpose of this paper, we do not need structured values to make our point. However, we do have a precise semantics for structured values (aggregate, set, sequence, etc.) in the KBO model [19].

bill", "tips", "leave" > is capable of achieving a series of actions in a restaurant when $kh(y)$ is activated. Since the traditional message selectors are now treated as object values, they can be more descriptive and intuitive.

For technical purposes, we introduce the following notation. For any object $o = (i, c, v, (\omega, \xi, \wp))$, let $class(o) = c$, $value(o) = v$, $owner(o) = \omega$, $sig(o) = \xi$, and $obj(i) = o$. Obviously, $obj(oid(o)) = o$. Furthermore, for the sake of brevity, when o is a hollow object, we usually denote o as a triple (i, c, v) as long as it results in no confusion. Throughout this paper, we often use values instead of object-identities to denote objects in our examples.

We also let the identity test (denoted $\equiv$) and the equality test (denoted $=$) be defined in the sense of Khoshafian and Copeland's "identical" and "deep-equal" [9]. In the KBO model, two objects being identical not only means they are the same object but also means they bear the same knowhow. As such, the identity of an object in effect identifies a knowhow whereas the value of an object is in effect the message name. Two objects are equal if they have the same message name but might be different objects (i.e., bearing different knowhows) just as two objects are traditionally considered equal if they have the same value but may not necessarily be the same object.

Example 2: Assume classes PHONE, PERSON, and EMERGENCY-CENTRE are user-defined classes. In the following, o_1, o_2, o_3, o_4, and o_5 are KBO objects (o_3, o_4, o_5 are solid):

$o_1 = (i_1, \text{INT}, 911)$

$o_2 = (i_2, \text{TEXT}, \text{``Go see doctor''})$

$o_3 = (i_3, \text{TEXT}, \text{``Eat''}, (\text{PERSON}, () \longrightarrow \text{PERSON}, kh_3))$

$o_4 = (i_4, \text{INT}, 911, (\text{PHONE}, () \longrightarrow \text{EMERGENCY-CENTRE}, kh_4))$

$o_5 = (i_5, \text{TEXT}, \text{``Do you belong to this age group?''}, (\text{PERSON}, (\text{Age1}, \text{INT}) \times (\text{Age2}, \text{INT}) \longrightarrow \text{BOOL}, kh_5))$

∎

Definition 8: *Vacuous, Virtual, and Revalued Behaviors.* An object o is a *vacuous behavior* if and only if o is solid and $kh(o) = \phi_\perp$. An object o is a *virtual behavior* if and only if o is solid and $kh(o) = \phi_\top$. An object o is a *revalued behavior* if and only if o is solid and $kh(o) \neq bb(kh(o))$. ∎

Vacuous behaviors are useful for disregarding inherited behaviors in value-based message-sendings. Virtual behaviors are useful for simulating non-existent knowhows of the most general version of a concept. Real knowhows of the virtual behaviors of a class may be provided in its subclasses. As such, virtual behaviors often play the role of specifying a generic protocol for subclasses to obey. Revalued behaviors provide a great flexibility for a class to reuse behaviors from other classes without using their values (knowhow descriptors or message values). The example presented in Figure 1 has demonstrated the usefulness of revalued behaviors.

In the following, we define a KBO class. Because we do not discuss constructed values in this paper, a concept called "template" [19] will not be described here.

Definition 9: *Classes.* A KBO class is a quintuple (c, $L_k(c)$, $L_r(c)$, $\Omega(c)$, $\Sigma(c)$) where (1) $c \in \mathcal{C}$ is the class name; (2) $L_k(c)$ is a total ordering, $(\{x \mid c \; ⓚ_d \; x\}, \succ_k)$, of direct superclasses; (3) $L_r(c)$ is a total ordering, $(\{x \mid c \; ⓡ_d \; x\}, \succ_r)$, of direct supplyclasses; (4) $\Omega(c) \subset \mathcal{O}$ is the local population of c, $\Omega(c) = \{o \mid o \; ⓘ_d \; c \}$; (5) $\Sigma(c) \subset \mathcal{O}$ is the local interface of c, $\Sigma(c) = \{o \mid o \; ⓑ_d \; c \}$, such that $\forall x, y \in \Sigma(c) : x \not\equiv y \Longrightarrow value(x) \neq value(y)$. ∎

Notice that the total orderings $\succ_k$ and $\succ_r$ can be system-generated, user-defined, rule-based, etc.

Since a class inherits all the behaviors of each supplyclass (except those that are revalued), its interface may contain some equivalent behaviors. That is, some of them may have the same value but different object-identities. In our message-sendings, if an object receives a message (an invoker) which is not identical to any behavior in $\overset{*}{\Sigma}(c)$ but is equal to more than one behavior in $\overset{*}{\Sigma}(c)$, then the object would be confused, not knowing which knowhow to invoke. We refer to this situation as "behavior equality ambiguity". In order to resolve the behavior equality ambiguity, we introduce the notion of perspectives.

Definition 10: *Perspectives.* For any $c \in C$, its *perspective* $\overset{\circ}{\Sigma}(c)$ is a set of objects defined as

$$\overset{\circ}{\Sigma}(c) = \Sigma(c) \cup \{o \mid \exists c_1 \in L_r(c) : o \in \overset{\circ}{\Sigma}(c_1) \wedge o \in \overset{*}{\Sigma}(c) \wedge$$

$$\forall c_2 \in L_r(c) : c_2 \succ_r c_1 \Longrightarrow \neg(\exists x \in \overset{\circ}{\Sigma}(c_2) : x \in \overset{*}{\Sigma}(c) \wedge value(o) = value(x)) \}$$

■

Notice that this definition is recursively defined: to generate c's perspective, one has to generate the perspectives of all the classes in $L_r(c)$, and so on. Also, all the original behaviors which have been revalued are excluded from the perspective. It can be easily proved that the perspective of a class is unambiguous in terms of behavior equality.

5 Class Harmonization and Class Accommodation

Class harmonization and class accommodation are introduced mainly for validating (statically) the database schemas, so as to ensure the possibility of a multiple view of object behaviors (and of polymorphism when a message is sent to a set of receivers). Class harmonization is based only on the external interfaces of two classes, rather than including their structures (representations). Notice that class harmonization is not intended to provide conformance rules (such as those in [13]) for static type checking of invocation expressions.

Definition 11: *Class Harmonization.* For any two classes $c_1, c_2 \in C$, c_1 *harmonizes* with c_2 (written $c_1 \sqsubseteq_k c_2$) if for any $x \in \overset{\circ}{\Sigma}(c_2)$, $kh(x) \neq \phi_\perp$, $sig(x) = (A_1, c_{a_1}) \times \ldots \times (A_n, c_{a_n}) \longrightarrow c_a$, there is $y \in \overset{\circ}{\Sigma}(c_1)$, $sig(y) = (B_1, c_{b_1}) \times \ldots \times (B_m, c_{b_m}) \longrightarrow c_b$, such that: (1) $value(y) = value(x)$; (2) $\{B_1, ..., B_m\} = \{A_1, ..., A_n\}$; (3) $c_a \circledast c_b$; (4) $\forall i \in [1..n], \forall j \in [1..m] : A_i = B_j \Longrightarrow c_{b_i} \circledast c_{a_j}$. ■

In other words, c_1 must provide at least all the values of c_2's behaviors which are not vacuous behaviors; for each behavior of c_2, the corresponding behavior in c_1 must have the same number of formal input sources with the same labels; the result class of c_2's behavior must be a subclass of the result class of the corresponding behavior in c_1; and, the types of the formal input sources of c_1's behavior must be subclasses of the types of the formal input sources of the corresponding behavior in c_2. Condition 3 guarantees that if $kh(x)$ can be invoked on a receiver of c_1 then its result can still understand the messages which are intended to be sent to the result of invoking $kh(y)$. Conditions 3 and 4 indicate that class harmonization is neither *covariant* nor *contravariant* in the sense of [13]. This is mainly because our message-sendings support a multiple view of object behaviors. Harmonization based on contravariance simply does not work if we wish to support this feature. For example, let MANAGER be a kind and a reuse of EMPLOYEE; let b_1 be a behavior of EMPLOYEE, $value(b_1) = $ "make a friend" and $sig(b_1) = $ (Stranger,MANAGER) $\longrightarrow$ EMPLOYEE; let b_2 be a behavior of MANAGER, $value(b_2) = $ "make a friend" and $sig(b_2) = $ (Stranger,EMPLOYEE) $\longrightarrow$ MANAGER; let (Stranger,*Lee*) be an actual input source where *Lee* is an instance of EMPLOYEE; let *John* be an instance of MANAGER. Then, we can successfully send b_2 to *John* with (Stranger,*Lee*) as the actual input source. But we cannot send b_1 to *John* with (Stranger,*Lee*) as the actual input source, because there is a type violation — *Lee* is not an instance of MANAGER. Furthermore, neither covariance nor contravariance can guarantee what condition 3 can.

Definition 12: *Sound KIND-OF Relationships.* For any $c_1, c_2 \in C$, c_1 has a *sound KIND-OF relationship* with c_2 if and only if $c_1 \circledast c_2$ and $c_1 \sqsubseteq_k c_2$. ■

Every KIND-OF relationship in the application database schema should be validated to be sound.

Definition 13: *Class Accommodation.* For any two classes $c_1, c_2 \in C$, c_1 *accommodates* c_2 (written $c_1 \sqsubseteq_r c_2$) if the following hold: (1) there exists *no* class $c \in C$ such that $c \succ_r c_2$ in $L_r(c_1)$ and $c_2 \odot c$ or such that $c_2 \succ_r c$ in $L_r(c_1)$ and $c \odot c_2$; (2) if $\exists b \in \overset{\circ}{\Sigma}(c_1)$, $\exists b' \in \overset{*}{\Sigma}(c_2)$, $kh(b) = kh(b')$, then (i) for every formal input source (A, c_A) in $input(kh(b'))$ there must be a formal input source (B, c_B) in $input(kh(b))$ such that $B = A$ and $c_B \circledast c_A$, and (ii) $output(kh(b')) \circledast output(kh(b))$.

■

Condition 1 requires that the local ordering of $L_r(c_1)$ must be maintained. This constraint is violated when $L_r(c_1)$ contains x before y, and x is somehow a supplyclass of y. Condition 2 ensures that if a revalued behavior also changed the signature of the original behavior, then the new signature should be compatible with the original one.

Definition 14: *Sound REUSE-OF Relationships.* For any $c_1, c_2 \in C$, c_1 has a *sound REUSE-OF relationship* with c_2 if and only if $c_1 \odot c_2$ and $c_1 \sqsubseteq_r c_2$. ■

Every REUSE-OF relationship in the database schema should be validated to be sound.

6 Message-Sendings

The simplest query which can be expressed in the KBO Object Algebra [19] is a message-sending where a message is sent to a specific object.

Definition 15: *Syntax of Message-Sendings.* A *message-sending* has the form

$$\frac{Invoker}{Blackboard} \rightsquigarrow Receiver$$

where an object called *Invoker* is sent (by the end-user) to another object called *Receiver*. The actual input sources needed by the invoker may be provided in an argument-container called *Blackboard*, which is a set of *(label,input-source)* pairs, each with a distinct label. If no actual input sources are to be supplied on the Blackboard, then the message-sending can be simply denoted by *Invoker* $\rightsquigarrow$ *Receiver*. A message-sending always returns an object called *Response* which is the result of the message-sending. ■

Example 3: The following query is a simple message-sending:

$$\frac{\text{``Do you belong to this age group?''}}{Age1:\ 15,\ Age2:\ 30} \rightsquigarrow Mike \Rightarrow \textbf{True}$$

where the invoker is a TEXT object with value *"Do you belong to this age group?"*, the receiver is a PERSON object with the handle *Mike*, and the blackboard shows two labeled actual input sources, 15 with label *Age1* and 30 with label *Age2*. The message-sending produces an object with value **True** as the response, meaning that the person *Mike* is older than 15 and younger than 30. ■

For the following definition we need some notation. We use the symbol ℓ to denote a blackboard, and the set of *(label,input-source)* pairs appearing on blackboard ℓ is denoted as $args(\ell)$. For instance, if ℓ is the blackboard in the above query, then $args(\ell) = \{(Age1, 15), (Age2, 30)\}$. Now, the identity-based message-sending primitive, written $\rightsquigarrow$, is defined as follows.

Definition 16: *Semantics of Identity-Based Message-Sendings.* For any $s, o \in \mathcal{O}$:

$$\frac{s}{\ell} \rightsquigarrow o \triangleq \begin{cases} Impl_x(o, A_1: a_1, \ldots, A_n: a_n) & \text{if } \exists x \in \overset{*}{\Sigma}(class(o)) : x \equiv s \ \wedge \\ & sig(x) = (A_1, c_1) \times \ldots \times (A_n, c_n) \longrightarrow c_r \ \wedge \\ & \{(A_1, a_1), \ldots, (A_n, a_n)\} \subseteq args(\ell) \ \wedge \\ & a_i \textcircled{i} c_i \text{ for } 1 \leq i \leq n \\[2mm] \frac{s}{\ell} \overset{=}{\rightsquigarrow} o & \text{otherwise} \end{cases}$$

where $Impl_x = kh(x)$ and $kh(x) \neq \phi_\perp$ and $kh(x) \neq \phi_\top$. ■

Intuitively, when a message-sending $\frac{s}{\ell} \rightsquigarrow o$ occurs, the receiver o will first try to search for a behavior in its class's interface which is *identical* to the invoker s and, if successful, invoke (execute) the behavior's knowhow. However, if the receiver fails to find an identical behavior in its class's interface, the message-sending becomes a value-based message-sending, which is defined as follows:

Definition 17: *Semantics of Value-Based Message-Sendings.* For any $s, o \in \mathcal{O}$:

$$\frac{s}{\ell} \overset{=}{\leadsto} o \triangleq \begin{cases} Impl_x(o, A_1: a_1, \ldots, A_n: a_n) & \text{if } \exists x \in \overset{\circ}{\Sigma}(class(o)) : x = s \land \\ & sig(x) = (A_1, c_1) \times \ldots \times (A_n, c_n) \longrightarrow c_r \land \\ & \{(A_1, a_1), \ldots, (A_n, a_n)\} \subseteq args(\ell) \land \\ & a_j \ \textcircled{i} \ c_j \text{ for } 1 \leq j \leq n \\ \\ fail & \text{otherwise} \end{cases}$$

where $Impl_x = kh(x)$ and $kh(x) \neq \phi_\perp$ and $kh(x) \neq \phi_\top$. ∎

Here, the function-like notation $Impl_x(o, A_1: a_1, \ldots, A_n: a_n)$ needs an explanation. This notation is intended to capture the intuition regarding the implementation identified by $kh(x)$: the implementation $Impl_x$ is executed with the knowledge of the internal representation of the receiver o, plus a set of labeled actual input sources (i.e., $A_1: a_1, \ldots, A_n: a_n$). In other words, the receiver o performs a "knowhow" that depends on both the actual input sources and o's internal state which reflects the history of previous message-sendings on the receiver. As such, the internal state (i.e., all private attributes) encapsulated in o is directly visible to the encapsulated implementation $Impl_x$. For example, if $Impl_x$ was implemented in C++ [18], the notation $Impl_x(o, A_1: a_1, \ldots, A_n: a_n)$ would correspond to the C++ expression o.Impl_x(a_1, ..., a_n) . Notice that we use labeled arguments while C++ uses positioned arguments.

Example 4: Consider the KBO schema shown in Figure 2, where class PROJECT-MANAGER has five equivalent behaviors with different knowhows (but with the same value "Introduce yourself"). It can be easily observed that $\overset{*}{\Sigma}$ (PROJECT-MANAGER) $= \{b_1, b_2, b_3, b_4, b_5\}$ and $\overset{\circ}{\Sigma}$(PROJECT-MANAGER) $= \{b_5\}$. Now, let *Mike* be an instance of PROJECT-MANAGER. Then, the query *"Introduce yourself"* $\leadsto$ *Mike* will introduce *Mike* as a project-manager, because here *"Introduce yourself"* is a brand new object (i.e., created on-the-fly) and none of $b_1, ..., b_5$ is identical to this new object. However, the queries $b_1 \leadsto Mike, b_2 \leadsto Mike, b_3 \leadsto Mike, b_4 \leadsto Mike$ will introduce *Mike* as a person, employee, programmer, and system-analyst, respectively. Notice that the invokers $b_1, ..., b_4$ can be either reached by a (persistent) object handle or obtained by using other query expressions. If $b_1, ..., b_5$ are annotated, say, with an attribute TimeNeeded, we can even issue queries like "Please introduce *Mike* to me as briefly as possible". This kind of query is called *associative invocation* in our model (see [19]). ∎

It should be observed that this approach is different from the **super** mechanism in Smalltalk [7] and the `class-name.method-name` mechanism in the extended Smalltalk [4]. Our approach supports polymorphism in the sense that if there is no behavior in the receiver's class that is identical to the invoker, then an equivalent behavior in the receiver's class will be invoked. Moreover, our message-sending operator $\leadsto$ takes into account associative invocations because its left-hand-side operand can be obtained associatively from other query expressions.

7 Comparison and Conclusion

This work results from our on-going research on the seamless modeling of data and behaviors in object-oriented databases. There have been several attempts to separate inheritance and subclassing (or subtyping) in programming systems, such as CommonObjects [16, 17], Exemplar-based Smalltalk [12], POOL-I [2], and OROS [15] (OROS is a software development environment). The major differences between our dual inheritance and their approaches are: (1) Our approach was mainly motivated by how the knowhow-bearing entities should be organized and queried in

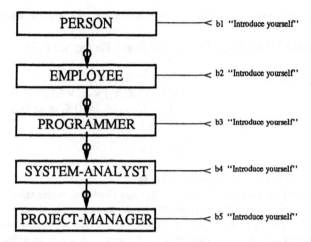

Figure 2: An Example of Equivalent Behaviors with Different Knowhows

database systems, while their approaches were motivated by how to reuse code without interfering with the conceptual generalization hierarchy in programming systems; (2) all behaviors in our approach are true first-class objects with their selectors as values; (3) the interface concept in our approach is object-identity-based, thus different from that of others; (4) our approach supports revalued behaviors; (5) our approach supports a multiple view of object behaviors; (6) none of other approaches has a lattice semantics for the separated inheritance. In other approaches the inheritance concept was separated in such a way that inheritance was degraded to an implementation-level concept: it was considered only as a practical means for code sharing between classes (or exemplars). We, on the other hand, have promoted the "reuse" concept from the implementation-level to the modeling-level by using it as an (almost) "inverse classification" of (knowhow-bearing) objects. For example, in the schema shown in Figure 2, if we query "Find all behaviors of PROJECT-MANAGER", we will see five objects: b_1, b_2, b_3, b_4, b_5. Therefore, it results in a natural model for querying classes both about instances and about behaviors. This feature is very useful, especially if many behaviors are annotated with special purpose attributes.

Finally, we should point out that our dual inheritance notion has a well-defined semantics while most other approaches do not. For instance, subtyping relationships in CommonObjects may not form a lattice because transitivity is not guaranteed. The approach of Exemplar-based Smalltalk seems to be aimed to separate "class variables" and "class methods" from "instance variables" and "instance methods". The approach of POOL-I uses inheritance among classes and subtyping among types. In contrast, our approach is based only on classes, and is thus closer to real-world analogies (e.g., "cats sleep like a log"). A weakness of our approach is that static type checking is difficult to perform unless invokers in KBO message-sendings are expressed as constants (literals). However, the KBO model itself was mainly intended to support interactive database applications with a large portion of behaviors, where the flexibility to manipulate behaviors is often more important.

In conclusion, the dual inheritance notion proposed in this paper provides the users with a maximum behavior reusability, a natural multiple view invocation flexibility, and an "inverse hierarchy" of behaviors that can be queried against. Because of the space limit, many features in the KBO model (such as "parcel objects" with constructed values as well as their behavioral semantics in message-sendings) are omitted. We would also expect the final shape of some ideas in the KBO model to differ from their preliminary forms in this paper.

References

[1] Andrews, T. and Harris C. Combining Languages and Database Advances in an Object-Oriented Development Environment. In *Proc. OOPSLA'87*, Oct. 1987, 430-440.

[2] America, P., and Linden, F.V.D. A Parallel Object-oriented Language with Inheritance and Subtyping. In *Proc. OOPSLA'90*, Oct. 1990, 161-168.

[3] Banerjee, J. et al. Data Model Issues for Object- Oriented Applications. *ACM Trans. on Office Info. Syst. 5*, 1 (Jan. 1987), 3-26.

[4] Borning, A.H., and Ingalls, D.H. Multiple Inheritance in Smalltalk-80. In *Proc. of the AAAI '82 Conference*, Pittsburgh, 1982.

[5] Caruso, M. and Sciore, E. The VISION Object-Oriented Database System. In *Proc. Intl. Workshop on Database Programming Languages*, Roscoff France, 1987.

[6] Fishman, D.H., et al. IRIS: An Object-Oriented Database Management System. *ACM Trans. Office Info. Syst. 5*, 1 (Jan. 1987), 48-69.

[7] Goldberg, A. and Robson, D. Smalltalk-80: The Language and its Implementation. Addison-Wesley Publishing Company, 1983.

[8] Hornick, M.F., and Zdonik, S.B. A Shared, Segmented Memory System for an Object-oriented Database. *ACM Trans. Office Info. Syst. 5*, 1 (Jan. 1987), 71-95.

[9] Khoshafian, S.N., and Copeland, G.P. Object Identity. In *Proc. OOPSLA '86*, Sept. 1986, 406-416.

[10] Lecluse, C., Richard, P., and Velez, F. O2, an Object-Oriented Data Model. In *Proc. 1988 ACM-SIGMOD Conference*, 424-433.

[11] Lecluse, C., and Richard, P. The O_2 Database Programming Language. In *Proc. Intl. Conf. on Very Large Data Bases*, 1989, 411-422.

[12] LaLonde, W.R., Thomas, D.A., and Pugh, J.R. An Exemplar Based Smalltalk. In *Proc. of OOPSLA'86 Conference*, Sep. 1986, 322-230.

[13] Moss, J.E.B. and Wolf, A.L. Toward Principles of Inheritance and Subtyping in Programming Languages. *Tech. Rep. 88-95*, Dept. of Computer and Information Science, Univ. of Massachusetts, Nov. 1988.

[14] Maier, D., et al. Development of an object-oriented DBMS. In *Proc. 1986 Conference on Object-Oriented Programming Systems, Languages, and Applications*, 472-482, Spet. 1986.

[15] Rosenblatt, W.R., Wileden, J.C., and Wolf, A.L. OROS: Towards a Type Model for Software Environments, In *Proc. OOPLSA'89*, Oct. 1989, 297-304.

[16] Snyder, A. Object-oriented Programming for Common Lisp. *Tech. Rep. ATC-85-1*, Hewlett-Pachard Company, July 1985.

[17] Snyder, A. Encapsulation and Inheritance in Object-Oriented Programming Langauges. In *Proc. of the OOPSLA'86 Conference*, Sep. 1986, 38-45.

[18] Stroustrp, B. The C++ Programming Langauge. Addison-Wesley Publishing Company. 1886.

[19] Yu, L. The Knowhow-Bearing-Object Model: Towards a Unified View of Data, Behaviors, and Invokers in Object-Oriented Database Systems. Ph.D. Thesis Proposal, Department of Computer Science, The University of Western Ontario, 1990.

GRAPHICAL SPECIFICATION OF RECURSIVE QUERIES

Bogdan D. Czejdo and Ralph P. Tucci
Department of Mathematical Sciences
Loyola University
New Orleans, Louisiana 70118

David W. Embley
Department of Computer Science
Brigham Young University
Provo, Utah 84602

ABSTRACT

We describe an OR database model and transformation operators on this model. A graphical query language based on these operators allows the user to specify conveniently a subclass of recursive queries.

1.   INTRODUCTION

The logical organization of data in a database system is usually complex and often difficult for users to comprehend. Moreover, database application programs tend to be complicated, as shown in [1]. Since graphical display can enhance users' understanding of complex objects, graphical aids such as semantic model diagrams can provide valuable assistance. The Entity-Relationship (ER) model [4] is the most popular of the semantic models. A graphical query language can be defined for the ER model to make it easier to formulate queries [3]. Using a graphical interface, users start with a given diagram which represents the database. Every user operation transforms an ER diagram to another ER diagram, and every diagram represents a meaningful user query.

The basic version of our graphical ER query language has been shown to be relationally complete [3] which means it is as powerful as Codd's relational algebra. Moreover, the language has been extended to include computations [5]. The language has also been augmented to operate on an extended ER model that includes generalization and specialization [6]. The language, however, still requires several extensions. The purpose of this paper is to extend the language to allow recursive query specifications [2].

The paper is organized as follows. In Section 2 we describe a variant of the ER model. In Section 3 we present a formal description of the model and and the basic query operations for this model. In Section 4 we present two examples of recursive queries illustrating new features of the graphical query language. In Section 5 we describe the translation of the graphical query language to SQL. In Section 6 we provide a summary of the results.

2. THE OBJECT-RELATIONSHIP MODEL

We use a semantic data model called the Object-Relationship (OR) model, which is based on the Entity-Relationship (ER) model and its extensions. Our OR model views the world as consisting of objects and relationships among those objects. Objects and relationships are classified into object sets and relationship sets respectively. The OR model differs from the original ER model in that it treats attributes as objects, and because it allows a richer set of relationships types among the objects. Figure 1 shows an OR model diagram, which describes a PART database.

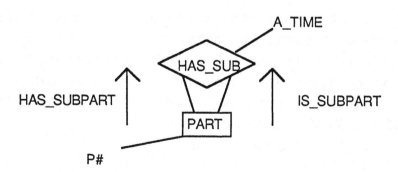

Figure 1

An object exists in the real world and is distinguished from other objects. An object set is a set of objects that have some common properties. In the OR model there are two different kinds of object sets, lexical and non-lexical. An object in a lexical object set is represented by a string; an object in a non-lexical object set is represented by a surrogate value. Lexical objects can be displayed or printed; non-lexical objects cannot be displayed or printed. Lexical object sets are represented in a diagram by the object set name; non-lexical object sets are represented by a box enclosing the object set name. For example, in Figure 1, PART is a non-lexical object set, and P# and A_TIME are lexical object sets.

A relationship is a meaningful connection among objects. A collection of relationships pertaining to the same object sets can constitute a relationship set. In Figure 1, HAS_SUB is a relationship set that connects object set PART with itself. Relationship sets might not be labeled; for example, in Figure 1, the line between object sets PART and P# is a relationship set, but it has no label.

Some relationships require roles, which define the direction of a relationship. For example, in figure 1, we have two roles, HAS_SUBPART and IS_SUBPART. For the sake of simplicity we suppress all labels on the edges in the remaining diagrams when they are not ambiguous. We can easily define an operator to do this.

3 A FORMAL DESCRIPTION OF THE OR MODEL

In this section we present a formal model that defines both a schema for the OR model and a graphical representation of the schema. The formal model is a 4-tuple (O, R, L, ORL) where O is a set of object descriptors, R is a set of relationship descriptors, L is a set of role descriptors, and ORL is a set of triples of these descriptors. An object descriptor is a tuple (NAME, DISPLAY, TYPE, CONDITION, VIEW) described as follows:

(1)   NAME is the name of the object set.

(2)   DISPLAY is the state of the icon for the object set with the values DISPLAYED, NOT-DISPLAYED, SELECTED.

(3)   TYPE is the type of the object set which can take on the values LEXICAL and NON-LEXICAL.

(4)   CONDITION specifies any restrictions on the object set.

(5)   VIEW specifies whether the object is virtual (computed) or not virtual. If the object is virtual, then VIEW is the set of information necessary to produce the view; i. e., a subset of the formal model and the operators and their arguments that have been applied to create this view. If the object is not virtual, then VIEW is the empty set.

A relationship descriptor is a tuple (NAME, DISPLAY, VIEW, LABEL), where the first three components are defined as for the object descriptor. The LABEL is either SHOWN or NOT-SHOWN, depending on whether we want to label the relationship set or not. If LABEL is SHOWN, then we display the relationship set icon together with lines connecting it to the appropriate object set icons. If LABEL is NOT-SHOWN, then we represent the relationship only by the lines connecting the appropriate object set icons.

A role descriptor is a tuple (NAME, LABEL), where NAME and LABEL are defined in a manner similar to that in the previous paragraphs. The fourth component **ORL** of the formal model is a set of triples (O, R, L), where O is an object set descriptor, R is a relationship set descriptor, and L is a role descriptor. As an example, in Figure 1, the first component **O** of the formal model is as follows:

O = {(PART, DISPLAYED, NON-LEXICAL, $\emptyset$, $\emptyset$),

   (P#, DISPLAYED, LEXICAL, $\emptyset$, $\emptyset$),

   (A_TIME, DISPLAYED, LEXICAL, $\emptyset$, $\emptyset$)}

The other components can be described similarly.

For the OR model we define transformation operators where each operator transforms a particular OR model instance into another OR model instance and thus a particular OR diagram into another OR diagram.

3.1 Restrict(O, e).   Restrict restricts the elements of the object set O to those that satisfy boolean expression e.

   O.CONDITION := O.CONDITION U {e};

3.2 Select (O).   Select marks the lexical object set O.

   O.DISPLAY := SELECTED;

The name of the selected object set would be underlined on the screen.

3.3 Delete(W). Delete hides the object W. If W is an object set, then the deletion of W also causes the relationship sets in which W participates to be hidden.

> W.DISPLAY := NOT-DISPLAYED ;
> For each R related to W do
>> R.DISPLAY := NOT-DISPLAYED;
>> If U is a LEXICAL object set related to W by R then
>>> U.DISPLAY := NOT-DISPLAYED;

If W is a relationship set, then the deletion of W is defined simply.

> W.DISPLAY := NOT-DISPLAYED;

3.4 Closure(R, O). Closure generates the transitive closure R+ for a recursive relationship set R for an object set O. For example, assume the PART database described in Figure 1 represents automobile parts. For the relationship set HAS_SUB, the closure HAS_SUB+ of HAS_SUB with respect to the first two attributes would be

HAS_SUB		
|car	body	0|
|car	engine	10|
|body	frame	0|
|body	doors	1|
|body	hood	2|

HAS_SUB+	
|car	body|
|car	engine|
|body	frame|
|body	doors|
|body	hood|
|car	frame|
|car	doors|
|car	hood|

This operator applied to the diagram in Figure 1 would produce the diagram in Figure 2.

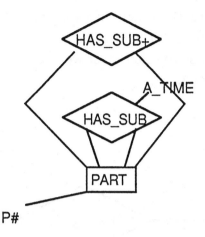

Figure 2

The formal definition of the operator is as follows.

Create a new relationship set descriptor S with

S.NAME := add-plus (R.NAME);{

{For example, if R.NAME = HAS_SUB, then

add-plus (R.NAME) := HAS_SUB+}

S.DISPLAY := DISPLAYED;

S.LABEL := R.LABEL;

S.VIEW := appropriate VIEW information

R := R U {S}; {Add the new relationship set S to the set of existing relationship descriptors}

ORL := ORL U {(O, S, L_1), (O, S, L_2)} {Add the new ORL triples to the set of existing ORL triples, where L_1, L_2 are roles of the initial relationship R}

3.5 Duplicate(O). Duplicating O creates a new object set O' that is identical to O. If O is related through a relationship R to an object set Z, Z ≠ O, then there are two cases to consider. If Z is NON-LEXICAL, then a new relationship R' is created which relates O' and Z; if Z is LEXICAL, then a new object set Z' is created and a new relationship R' is created which connects O' and Z'. On the other hand, if R is a recursive relationship on the object set O then the duplicate operator also creates a relationship set R' between O and O' and a recursive relationship set R" on O'. (We say that R connects O with itself, that R" connects O' with itself, and that R' connects O and O'.). We assume that

R is a binary relationship set; if not, then we can extend the definition below accordingly. As an example, let us consider the diagram in Figure 2 with the SUB_PART relationship set deleted. After we apply the Duplicate operator we get the diagram in Figure 3.

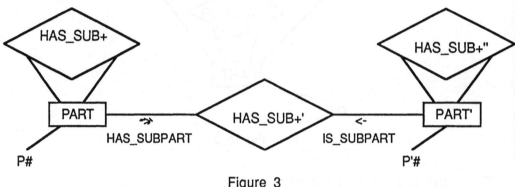

Figure 3

The formal definition of the operator is as follows.

Create a new object set descriptor T with

    T.NAME :=prime (O.NAME); {For example, if O.NAME = PART,
                                     then prime (O.NAME) := PART'}

    T.DISPLAY := DISPLAYED;

    T.TYPE := O.TYPE;

    T.CONDITION := $\emptyset$;

    T.VIEW := $\emptyset$

O := O U {T};   {Add the new object set T to the set of existing object descriptors}

For each relationship R connecting T with itself do

    Create new relationship set descriptors S_1, S_2 with

        S_1.NAME := prime (R.NAME);

        S_2.NAME := double-prime (R.NAME);

        For J := 1 to 2 do

            S_J.DISPLAY := DISPLAYED;

            S_J.LABEL := R.LABEL;

            S_J.VIEW := $\emptyset$;

        R := R U {S_1, S_2}; {Add the new relationship tuples S_1, S_2, to the set of existing relationship descriptors.}

    ORL := ORL U {(T, S_1, L_1), (T, S_2, L_2), (O, S_1, L_1),

$$(O, S_2, L_2)\}$$

{Add the new ORL triples to the set of existing ORL triples, where L_1, L_2 are roles of the initial relationship R.}

The case where R is a relationship set connecting T with an object set other than T itself is handled similarly.

3.6 Compute (O, N, f, SOR). Compute creates a new object set named N, attaches it by a new relationship set to object set O, and specifies that the objects in N are to be computed by f (for each element of O) over the OR submodel SOR. As an example, let us assume the diagram in Figure 4.

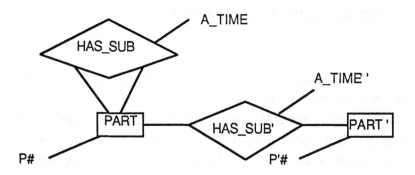

Figure 4

When the Compute operation is applied for O = PART, N = SUB_TIME, and f = SUM (A_TIME') and SOR consists of PART, HAS_SUB', PART', and A_TIME', the diagram in Figure 5 is created.

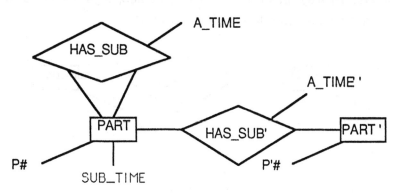

Figure 5

The formal definition of the operator is as follows.

Create a new object set descriptor T with

        T.NAME := N;

        T.DISPLAY := DISPLAYED;

        T.TYPE := LEXICAL;

        T.CONDITION := Ø;

        T.VIEW := appropriate VIEW information;

O := O U {T};

The new relationship set R is defined similarly.

4. GRAPHICAL QUERY SPECIFICATION

We now give two queries and show how to specify them graphically. Each query begins with the diagram in Figure 1.

SAMPLE QUERY #1. Find part numbers of all subparts of part 12345.

Step 1. Choose Closure; point at HAS_SUB and PART. This operation generates the transitive closure HAS_SUB+ of the relationship set HAS_SUB and the result is shown in Figure 2.

Step 2. Choose Delete; point at HAS_SUB.

Step 3. Choose Duplicate; point at PART.

Step 4. Choose Delete; point at HAS_SUB+ and HAS_SUB+".

Step 5. Choose Select, point at PART and specify the remaining part of the condition '=12345'.

Step 6. Choose Display; point at P'#. After this step, Figure 1 is transformed to Figure 6, which represents the original query #1.

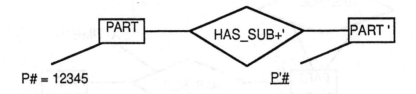

Figure 6

SAMPLE QUERY #2. Find total assembly time for the part CAR.

Step 1. Choose Duplicate; point at PART.

Step 2. Choose Delete; point at HAS_SUB". After step 1 and 2, Figure 1 is transformed to Figure 4.

Step 3. Choose Compute, point at PART, specify the name of a new object set SUB_TIME, specify a computation formula SUM(A_TIME), and select as the submodel the icons labeled PART, HAS_SUB', PART', and A_TIME'. Step 3 generates a new object set SUB_TIME related to PART as shown in Figure 5.

Step 4. Choose Delete; point at PART'.

Step 5. Choose Closure; point at HAS_SUB and PART.

Step 6. Choose Delete; point at HAS_SUB.

Step 7. Choose Duplicate; point at PART. After this step, there are two object sets PARTs, and three relationship sets HAS_SUB+. Except for the object sets SUB_TIME and SUB_TIME', the resulting picture is the same as that in Figure 3.

Step 8. Choose Delete; point at HAS_SUB+ and HAS_SUB+".

Step 9. Choose Compute, point at PART, specify name of a new object set TOTAL_SUB_TIME and specify a computation formula SUM(SUB_TIME'), and select as the submodel the icons labeled PART, HAS_SUB+', PART', and SUB_TIME'.

Step 10. Choose Delete; point at PART'.

Step 11. Choose Compute, point at PART, specify name of a new object set TOTAL_TIME , specify a computation formula TOTAL_SUB_TIME + SUB_TIME, and select as the submodel the icons labeled PART and TOTAL_SUB_TIME.

Step 12. Choose Select, point at PART and specify the remaining part of the condition '=12345'.

Step 13. Choose Display; point at TOTAL_TIME. After this step the diagram is transformed to Figure 7.

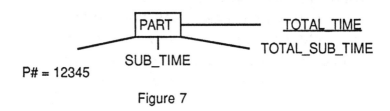

Figure 7

5. TRANSLATION OF THE GRAPHICAL QUERY LANGUAGE TO SQL

In this section we describe the translation of the graphical requests into an extended version of SQL which supports transitive closure. To facilitate such translation it is first necessary to define a mapping of the initial state of the model into the underlying relational schema. Here we are using a simple mapping of the initial state of the model into binary relations. Each relationship set descriptor corresponds to a single binary relation scheme.

As an example let us consider the parts database of Figure 1. The initial state of the model can be mapped into the following relational schema.

HAS_SUB (PART, PART')
P#-PART (P#, PART)
PART (PART)
P#   (P#)

These relations should not be considered as stored relations but rather as views defined on a relational database designed in a standard way.

For the given mapping it is possible to generate SQL expressions from any state of the formal model, which was described for non-recursive queries in [5]. In the case of recursive virtual objects, it is necessary to generate an SQL view containing a transitive_closure operator.

Using these rules the SQL expression for query #1 in section 4 is as follows:

```
CREATE VIEW HAS_SUB+ (PART, PART')
      AS SELECT PART, PART'
      FROM transitive_closure(HAS_SUB)
SELECT P#-PART'.P#
      FROM P#_PART, HAS_SUB+, P#_PART'
      WHERE P#-PART.P# = 12345
            AND P#-PART.PART = HAS_SUB+.PART
            AND HAS_SUB+.PART' = P#-PART'.PART
```

The SQL expression for query #2 can be derived similarly.

6. SUMMARY

We have described an OR model as a set of object sets and relationship set. For the OR model we have defined transformation operators. The most crucial for recursive queries are the Duplicate and Closure operators. Duplicate allows us to break a recursive loop when necessary, and Closure allows us to specify transitive closure. Using these operators, we have described a graphical query language which allows the user to specify a subclass of recursive queries.

REFERENCES

[1] M. P. Atkinson & O. P. Buneman, "Types and Persistence in Database Programming Languages", ACM Computing Surveys, Vol. 19, No. 2, 1987, 105-190.
[2] R. Agrawal, "Alpha: An Extension of Relational Algebra to Express a Class of Recursive Queries", IEEE Transactions on Software Engineering, Volume 14, Number 7, July 1988, 879-885.
[3] D. M. Campbell, D. W. Embley & B. Czejdo, "Graphical Query Formulation for an Entity-Relationship Model", Data & Knowledge Engineering, Volume 2, Number 1, June 1987, 89-121.
[4] P. P. Chen, "The Entity-Relationship Model: Toward a Unified View of Data", ACM Transaction on Database Systems, Volume 1, Number 1, January 1976, 9-36.
[5] B. Czejdo & D. W. Embley, "An Approach to Computation Specification for an Entity-Relationship Query Language", Proceedings of the Sixth International Conference on Entity-Relationship Approach, New York, New York, November 1987, 307-321.
[6] B. Czejdo, R. Elmasri, M. Rusinkiewicz & D. W. Embley, "An Algebraic Language for Graphical Query Formulation Using an Extended Entity-Relationship Model", ACM Fifteenth Annual Computer Science Conference, February 1987, 154-161.

On Designing Relational Database Schemes for Efficient Query Processing

Michio NAKANISHI[†], Yoshiki KATSUYAMA[††],
Minoru ITO[†] and Akihiro HASHIMOTO[†]

[†] Faculty of Engineering Science, Osaka University,
Toyonaka, Osaka 560, Japan
[††] Faculty of Economics, Shiga University,
Hikone, Shiga 522, Japan

Abstract

In relational databases, operations including joins sometimes become a cause of performance problems. We study scheme transformations to reduce the number of joins used by a class of routine database activities whose access patterns are fixed. Two scheme operations, merge and copy, are defined to transform relation schemes. The former merges two relation schemes into one, and the latter copies a functional dependency of a relation scheme to its tightly related relation scheme. Necessary and sufficient conditions are shown for applying these operations to a database scheme such that no new anomalies occur. From the necessity of the conditions, the database scheme obtained by exhaustive applications of these operations as long as the conditions hold, is optimal in the sense that further application of one of the scheme operations to the database scheme would cause anomalies. It is also proved that the resulting view of a retrieval on the original database scheme is equivalent to that of the corresponding retrieval on the new database scheme.

1. Introduction

Recently, several network operating systems and multiple access relational databases have been developed, and personal computers and work stations have been connected by LAN. This led to the emergence of on-line systems which use relational databases. Since normalizing a database scheme to third normal form (3NF) generates a lot of relation schemes, queries tend to require time consuming join operations. It is often said by experienced database designers that "normalization to 3NF is sometimes undesirable because it causes performance problems." In this paper, only functional dependencies (FDs) are considered as integrity constraints.

Our goal is to speed up the retrieval time in a class of routine database activities. In contrast to the studies which speed up join operations using hardware, we are going to reduce the number of joins. We introduce two operations on a database scheme, which transform relation schemes as if relations on the schemes were joined. One is to merge two schemes into one, and the other is to copy an FD. Since the commands or programs needed to perform the routine (database) activities must be changed according to the modified the database scheme, we define how to systematically translate insertion, deletion, update, and retrieval operations, respectively, for the modified database.

We assume that a database scheme and a class of routine activities are given. Each routine activity has a fixed access pattern, that is, each query in a routine activity uses fixed relation schemes and the operation of each query is one of the four operations: insertion, deletion, update, and retrieval. We also assume that non-routine activities only refer to the database but never modify it. The scheme transformation may impair the processing efficiency of non-routine database activities, however, non-routine database activities are not so frequently used, and thus we take no account of them.

In general, two scheme operations, merge and copy, cause anomalies because transformed relation schemes are not in 3NF. By considering the access patterns, one is able to design non-3NF database scheme which is free from anomalies under a particular condition. We show necessary and sufficient conditions for applying the scheme operations, which will not cause new anomalies. In the new database scheme obtained by applying the scheme operations, the number of joins are reduced and retrieval operations can be done more efficiently than in the original database scheme. The necessity of the conditions means that the database scheme obtained by applying one of the scheme operations, merge or copy, would cause anomalies, unless the conditions are satisfied. Thus the database scheme obtained by applying the scheme operations exhaustively is optimal in the sense that further application of one of the scheme operations to the database scheme would cause anomalies. It is also shown that the resulting view of a retrieval in the original database scheme is equivalent to that of the corresponding retrieval in the new database scheme obtained by applying the scheme operations.

2. Basic Concepts

For the sake of brevity, we assume that readers are familiar with the basic concepts of relational databases as in [1][2]. We denote a relation scheme by $\langle R, F \rangle$, where R is a set of attributes and F is a set of FDs on R. A relation r on $\langle R, F \rangle$ is a relation defined on R that satisfies all FDs in F. The closure of F, written F^+, is the set of FDs logically implied by F.

A sequence of relation schemes $\mathbf{R}$: $\langle R_1, F_1 \rangle, \cdots, \langle R_n, F_n \rangle$ is called a database scheme. A database $\mathbf{D}$ on $\mathbf{R}$ is a sequence of relations $r_1, \cdots, r_n$ such that r_i is a relation on $\langle R_i, F_i \rangle$ for $1 \leq i \leq n$. A relation in a database is called a base relation.

There are two types of queries, one which does not modify a database and one which does modify a database. The former operation is called retrieval. The latter is one of the three operations: insertion, deletion, and update, which are defined as follows:

1. An insertion of a tuple τ on $R_{i_1} \cup \cdots \cup R_{i_p}$ to a database $\mathbf{D}$: $r_1, \cdots, r_n$ is to replace r_{i_q} with $r_{i_q} \cup \{\tau[R_{i_q}]\}$ for $1 \leq q \leq p$, where $\tau[R_{i_q}]$ denotes the R_{i_q} values of τ. Note that if $r_{i_q} \cup \{\tau[R_{i_q}]\}$ does not satisfy F_{i_q}, then the insertion is rejected.

2. A deletion of a tuple τ on $R_{i_1} \cup \cdots \cup R_{i_p}$ from a database $\mathbf{D}$: $r_1, \cdots, r_n$ is to replace r_{i_q} with $r_{i_q} - \{\tau[R_{i_q}]\}$ for $1 \leq q \leq p$. Note that $r_{i_q} - \{\tau[R_{i_q}]\}$ satisfies F_{i_q}.

3. An update which replaces a tuple τ with a tuple τ' on $R_{i_1} \cup \cdots \cup R_{i_p}$ for a database $\mathbf{D}$: $r_1, \cdots, r_n$ is to replace r_{i_q} with $(r_{i_q} - \{\tau[R_{i_q}]\}) \cup \{\tau'[R_{i_q}]\}$ for $1 \leq q \leq p$. Note that if $(r_{i_q} - \{\tau[R_{i_q}]\}) \cup \{\tau'[R_{i_q}]\}$ does not satisfy F_{i_q}, then the update is rejected.

We say a query Q *uses* R_{i_q} if Q is performed to a tuple τ on $R_{i_1} \cup \cdots \cup R_{i_p}$ in a database $D{:}r_1, \cdots, r_n$, for $1 \leq q \leq p$.

For each modification operation there can be an anomaly. In this paper we assume that undefined value is not admitted in a database. Let X, Y and Z be subsets of R. Let r be a base relation on a relation scheme $\langle R, F \rangle$.

- An insertion anomaly in $\langle R, F \rangle$ occurs if the following conditions hold.
  1. There is an FD: $X \rightarrow Y \in F$ with $X \cup Y \subset R$, where $X \cup Y \subset R$ means that $X \cup Y$ is a proper subset of R.
  2. There is a request to insert the $X \cup Y$ values to r.
  3. The $R - (X \cup Y)$ values of the tuple to be inserted are undefined.
- A deletion anomaly in $\langle R, F \rangle$ occurs if the following conditions hold.
  1. There is an FD: $X \rightarrow Y \in F$ with $X \cup Y \subset R$.
  2. There is a request to delete the $X \cup Y$ values of a tuple τ from r.
  3. If τ is deleted, then the $R - (X \cup Y)$ values of τ are also lost.
- An update anomaly in $\langle R, F \rangle$ occurs if the following conditions hold.
  1. There is an FD: $X \rightarrow Y \in F$.
  2. There is a request to update the Y values of a tuple τ in r.
  3. There are a number of tuples τ' such that $\tau[X] = \tau'[X]$, and updating τ causes another update of τ' to keep F.
- A complex anomaly in $\langle R, F \rangle$ occurs if the following conditions hold.
  1. There are two FDs, $X \rightarrow Y \in F$ and $Y \rightarrow Z \in F$.
  2. There is a request to update the Y values of a tuple τ with respect to the relationship on FD: $X \rightarrow Y$ However, the $Y \cup Z$ values of τ with respect to the relationship on FD: $Y \rightarrow Z$ are requested to remain unchanged.
  3. The Z values corresponding to the new Y values are not given.
  4. There is no tuple τ' in r such that $\tau[Y] = \tau'[Y]$.

By the definition of update, an update operation is executed by deleting an old tuple followed by inserting a new tuple. If the four conditions above hold, a deletion anomaly occurs when τ is deleted and an insertion anomaly occurs when the corresponding new tuple is inserted. Thus this type of anomaly is called complex anomaly.

The following example illustrates these anomalies.

Example 1 : Consider a COURSE-INSTRUCTOR relation in Figure.1. A diagram of the dependencies within this relation appears in Figure.2. A glance at the relation reveals that there is data redundancy. We will encounter anomalies when we want to insert, delete or update the data, as follows:

1. *Insertion anomaly* : Assume that we want to add a new relationship between 'Baker' and '$A203$'. We can not insert a tuple until at least one *course* is assigned to 'Baker'. However a request to add a relationship between 'language' and 'Wilson' does not cause an insertion anomaly, because the 'Wilson's instructor-location '$A101$' can be obtained.

2. *Deletion anomaly* : Assume that we want to remove a relationship between 'Algorithm' and 'Wilson'. If we attempt to delete the tuple τ_3 from the relation, we will also lose the relationship between 'Wilson' and '$A101$'. However, a request to delete a relationship between 'Compiler' and 'Kemp' does not cause a deletion anomaly, because the relationship between 'Kemp' and '$A105$' would not be lost.

	course	instructor	instructor-location
τ_1 :	Automata	Kemp	A105
τ_2 :	Compiler	Kemp	A105
τ_3 :	Algorithm	Wilson	A101

Figure 1: COURSE-INSTRUCTOR relation

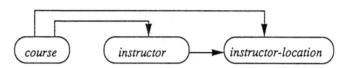

Figure 2: Diagram of dependencies for Figure 1

3. *Update anomaly* : Assume that we want to update Kemp's *instructor-location* from 'A105' to 'A101'. Since 'A105' occurs multiple times in the relation, any update of the *instructor-location* requires searching the entire relation to locate the desired tuples and then updating each tuple accordingly.

4. *Complex anomaly* : Assume that we want to replace the *instructor* of the 'Algorithm' by 'Baker'. but to keep the relationship between 'Wilson' and 'A101'. Updating a tuple τ_3 is executed by deleting τ_3 followed by inserting a new tuple τ_3' which contains 'Algorithm' and 'Baker'. Thus, a deletion anomaly occurs when we delete τ_3 because the relationship between 'Wilson' and 'A101' will be lost. An insertion anomaly also occurs when we insert τ_3' containing a relation between 'Algorithm' and 'Baker', because the *instructor-location* value is undefined. □

In this paper, we assume that a database scheme and the routine activities on it are given, and that the following conditions are satisfied for the routine activities.

1. Each routine activity contains a fixed set of queries $\{Q_1, Q_2, ..., Q_m\}$, and each query Q_i uses a fixed set of relation schemes in **R**, that is, schemes used as operands of Q_i are fixed. Furthermore, each operation of the query is fixed and modification is one of the three operations: insertion, deletion and update.

2. There may be a number of non-routine activities characterized by ad-hoc queries, that is, scheme used in queries are not fixed. These non-routine activities only retrieve data from a database but never modify it.

3. Merging relation schemes

A merge operation is defined as follows:

Definition 1: Let $\langle R_1, F_1 \rangle$ and $\langle R_2, F_2 \rangle$ be relation schemes in **R** such that $R_1 \cap R_2 \to R_2$ is in F_2^+. By merging $\langle R_1, F_1 \rangle$ and $\langle R_2, F_2 \rangle$, we mean that $\langle R_1, F_1 \rangle$ and $\langle R_2, F_2 \rangle$ are replaced with $\langle R_1 \cup R_2, F_1 \cup F_2 \rangle$ in **R**. Let r_1 and r_2 be base relations on $\langle R_1, F_1 \rangle$ and $\langle R_2, F_2 \rangle$, respectively. Let $S_{12} = \langle R_1 \cup R_2, F_1 \cup F_2 \rangle$. Then the base relation r_{12} on S_{12}

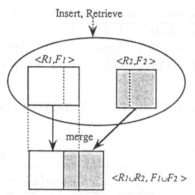

Figure 3: Merging schemes

is defined by $r_{12} = r_1 \bowtie r_2$, where $\bowtie$ denotes the join operator. Figure.3 illustrates the merge operation. □

By modifying the database scheme, each routine database activity must be translated accordingly. We require that if r_i is changed to r_i' by a query, then r_{12} should be changed to r_{12}' such that $r_i' = \pi_{R_i}(r_{12}')$ by a translated query, where $i = 1$ or $i = 2$, and $\pi_X(r)$ denotes the projection of a relation r onto a set of attributes X. In order to satisfy the requirement, $\langle R_1, F_1 \rangle$ and $\langle R_2, F_2 \rangle$ must satisfy some conditions, as will be given in Theorem 1.

Definition 2: Let r_1 and r_2 be base relations on $\langle R_1, F_1 \rangle$ and $\langle R_2, F_2 \rangle$, respectively. Let r_{12} be a base relation on $\langle R_1 \cup R_2, F_1 \cup F_2 \rangle$. Then the query is translated as follows:

• Insertion: Consider an insertion of a tuple τ on $R_{i_1} \cup \cdots \cup R_{i_p}$ to a database $\mathbf{D}:r_1, \cdots, r_n$. There are three cases to be considered.

1. If $i_q = 1$ for some q and $i_{q'} \neq 2$ for all q', then the insertion is translated to selecting a tuple τ_{12} in r_{12} such that $\tau_{12}[R_1 \cap R_2] = \tau[R_1 \cap R_2]$ followed by inserting to r_{12} a tuple τ_{12}' such that $\tau_{12}'[R_1] = \tau[R_1]$ and $\tau_{12}'[R_2] = \tau_{12}[R_2]$. Note that in order to avoid undefined values, the insertion is translated to first selecting such a tuple τ_{12} from r_{12}.

2. If $i_q \neq 1$ for all q and $i_{q'} = 2$ for some q', then the insertion is not applicable to r_{12}, because the R_1 values of τ can not be determined.

3. If $i_q = 1$ and $i_{q'} = 2$ for some q and q', then $\tau[R_1]$ and $\tau[R_2]$ are inserted to r_1 and r_2, respectively, and there is no insertion to one of r_1 or r_2 without the other in the original database. The insertion is translated to inserting a tuple $\tau[R_1 \cup R_2]$ to r_{12}.

• Deletion: Consider a deletion of a tuple τ on $R_{i_1} \cup \cdots \cup R_{i_p}$ from a database $\mathbf{D}:r_1, \cdots, r_n$. There are three cases to be considered.

1. If $i_q = 1$ for some q and $i_{q'} \neq 2$ for all q', then the deletion is translated to deleting *all* tuples τ_{12} such that $\tau_{12}[R_1] = \tau[R_1]$ from r_{12}. Note that in order to keep equality $r_i = \pi_{R_i}(r_{12})$, we must delete all such tuples τ_{12} from r_{12}.

2. If $i_q \neq 1$ for all q and $i_{q'} = 2$ for some q', then the deletion is translated to the deletion of all tuples τ_{12} such that $\tau_{12}[R_2] = \tau[R_2]$ from r_{12}.

3. If $i_q = 1$ and $i_{q'} = 2$ for some q and q', then $\tau[R_1]$ and $\tau[R_2]$ are deleted from r_1 and r_2, respectively, in the original database. The deletion is translated to deleting all tuples τ_{12} from r_{12} such that $\tau_{12}[R_1] = \tau[R_1]$ or $\tau_{12}[R_2] = \tau[R_2]$.

• Update: Consider an update of a tuple τ on $R_{i_1} \cup \cdots \cup R_{i_p}$ from a database $\mathbf{D}:r_1, \cdots, r_n$. There are three cases to be considered.

1. If $i_q = 1$ for some q and $i_{q'} \neq 2$ for all q', then the update is translated to updating all tuples τ_{12} in r_{12} such that $\tau_{12}[R_1] = \tau[R_1]$.

2. If $i_q \neq 1$ for all q and $i_{q'} = 2$ for some q', then the the update is translated to updating all tuples τ_{12} in r_{12} such that $\tau_{12}[R_2] = \tau[R_2]$.

3. If $i_q = 1$ and $i_{q'} = 2$ for some q and q', then tuples $\tau[R_1]$ of r_1 and $\tau[R_2]$ of r_2 are updated in the original database. The update is translated to updating all tuples τ_{12} in r_{12} such that $\tau_{12}[R_1] = \tau[R_1]$ or $\tau_{12}[R_2] = \tau[R_2]$.

• Retrieval

The retrieval from the join of r_1 and r_2 is translated to the retrieval from r_{12}. Other retrievals from r_1 or r_2 are translated to the retrievals by replacing r_1 and r_2 with $\pi_{R_1}(r_{12})$ and $\pi_{R_2}(r_{12})$, respectively. □

The following theorem shows a necessary and sufficient condition for applying a merge operation to a database scheme such that no new anomalies occur in the modified database.

Theorem 1: Let $S_1 = \langle R_1, F_1 \rangle$ and $S_2 = \langle R_2, F_2 \rangle$ be relation schemes such that $R_1 \cap R_2 \rightarrow R_2$ is in F_2^+. Merging S_1 and S_2 does not cause any new anomalies if and only if all the queries that use S_1 or S_2 satisfy the following conditions.

Condition 1: There is no deletion from r_1 and there is no deletion from r_2.
Condition 2: Every insertion that uses R_1 or R_2 includes the $R_1 \cup R_2$ values in its tuple, that is, the insertion is always performed to both of r_1 and r_2, and there is no insertion to one of r_1 or r_2 without the other.
Condition 3: The $R_1 \cap R_2$ values in r_1 are not updated.
Condition 4: No update is performed to r_2.

Proof: Let $S_{12} = \langle R_1 \cup R_2, F_1 \cup F_2 \rangle$. Let r_{12} be a base relation on S_{12}.

Assume that Conditions 1 to 4 hold. Then there are only two possible modification operations as follows:

(1) Insertion of a tuple τ on $R_1 \cup R_2$. The insertion is translated to inserting a tuple $\tau[R_1 \cup R_2]$ and thus no new insertion anomaly occurs.

(2) Update of $R_1 - R_2$ values of a tuple τ in r_1. The update is translated to updating all tuples τ_{12} in r_{12}, such $\tau_{12}[R_1] = \tau$. Note that the $R_1 \cap R_2$ vales of r_1 remain unchanged.

Since there are only two possible operations listed above in the original database, we have $\pi_{R_1 \cap R_2}(r_1) = \pi_{R_1 \cap R_2}(r_2)$. Thus the number of tuples in r_{12} is not less than the number of tuples in r_1. On the other hand, by $R_1 \cap R_2 \rightarrow R_2 \in F_2^+$, the number of tuples in r_{12} is not more than the number of tuples in r_1. Thus for each tuple τ in r_1, there is exactly one tuple τ' in r_{12} such that $\tau'[R_1] = \tau$. Hence the update to r_{12} does not differ from the update to r_1 as far as anomalies are concerned. That is, no new update anomaly occurs in r_{12}.

Conversely, if at least one of Conditions 1 to 4 does not hold, then new anomalies would be encountered in r_{12}. This is proved as follows:

(1) Assume that Condition 1 does not hold. Then there exist three cases of deletion.

Consider a deletion of a tuple τ from r_1. Consider the case where r_1 has just one tuple and thus r_{12} also has just one tuple. Since there is no duplication of the $R_2 - R_1$ values of in r_{12}, by deleting τ_{12} from r_{12}, the $R_2 - R_1$ values of τ_{12} would be lost, which means that a new deletion anomaly is encountered.

Consider a deletion of a tuple τ from r_2. The deletion must be translated to deleting all tuples τ_{12} in r_{12} such that $\tau_{12}[R_2] = \tau$. However, the $R_1 - R_2$ values of τ_{12} would be lost by the deletion in the case where there is only one tuple in r_{12}. This means that a new deletion anomaly is encountered.

Consider a deletion of tuples τ_1 and τ_2 from r_1 and r_2,respectively. The deletion must be translated to deleting all tuples τ_{12} in r_{12} such that $\tau_{12}[R_1] = \tau_1$ or $\tau_{12}[R_2] = \tau_2$. The R_1 values of τ_{12} would be lost by the deletion in the case where there are multiple tuples τ_{12} such that $\tau_{12}[R_1] \neq \tau_1$ and $\tau_{12}[R_2] = \tau_2$. This means that a new deletion anomaly is encountered.

(2) Assume that Condition 2 does not hold. Then there are two possible insertions.

Consider an insertion of a tuple τ to r_1. The insertion must be translated to inserting a tuple τ_{12} such that $\tau_{12}[R_1] = \tau$ to r_{12}. Consider the case where r_1 is empty, thus r_{12} is also empty. Since there is no tuple τ'_{12} in r_{12} such that $\tau'_{12}[R_1 \cap R_2] = \tau[R_1 \cap R_2]$, we can not determine the $R_2 - R_1$ values of τ_{12}, that is, a new insertion anomaly is encountered in r_{12}.

Consider an insertion of a tuple τ to r_2. The insertion cannot be translated by Definition 2. We cannot help encountering an insertion anomaly to insert to r_{12} a tuple τ_{12} such that $\tau_{12}[R_2] = \tau$.

(3) Assume that Condition 3 does not hold. Then there exists an update of the $R_1 \cap R_2$ values of a tuple τ in r_1. The update must be translated to updating all tuples τ_{12} such that $\tau_{12}[R_1] = \tau$ in r_{12}. Let r'_1 and r'_{12} be the resulting relations of r_1 and r_2, respectively. Since the $R_1 \cap R_2$ values of r_{12} must be changed by the update, it causes $\pi_{R_2}(r'_{12}) \neq r'_2$, which means a new complex anomaly is encountered.

(4) Assume that Condition 4 does not hold. Then there exists an update of the R_2 values.

Consider an update of the $R_2 - R_1$ values of a tuple τ in r_2. The update must be translated to updating all tuples τ_{12} in r_{12} such that $\tau_{12}[R_2] = \tau$. There is a case that r_{12} has tuples τ_{12} and τ'_{12} such that $\tau_{12}[R_2] = \tau'_{12}[R_2]$, thus an update anomaly is encountered.

Consider an update of the $R_1 \cap R_2$ values of a tuple in r_2. It can be shown similarly as in (3) that the update causes a new complex anomaly. □

When Conditions 1 to 4 are satisfied, $\pi_{R_1}(r_{12}) = r_1$ and $\pi_{R_2}(r_{12}) = r_2$ are satisfied by the proof of sufficiency. Assume that base relations, r_1 and r_2, are modified to r'_1 and r'_2 by a query Q,respectively. Then Q is translated to Q' for the merged scheme S_{12} such that $\pi_{R_1}(r'_{12}) = r'_1$ and $\pi_{R_2}(r'_{12}) = r'_2$, where r'_{12} denotes the modified base relation of r_{12} by Q'. Therefore the resulting view of a retrieval in the original database scheme is

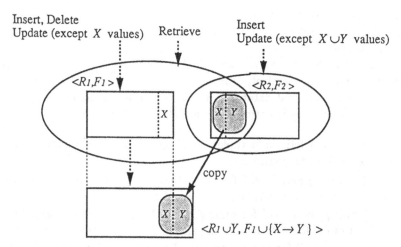

Figure 4: Copying a functional dependency

equivalent to the view of the corresponding retrieval in the new database scheme obtained by applying the merge operations.

Since retrievals which use either r_1 and r_2 are translated by replacing each occurrence of r_1 and r_2 by $\pi_{R_1}[r_{12}]$ and $\pi_{R_2}[r_{12}]$, respectively, their efficiency may be impaired because projection is required for each base relation. However, the efficiency of retrievals from the join of r_1 and r_2 is improved, because a join is eliminated by using r_{12}. Since join is, in general, a more time consuming than projection, merging two schemes is potentially useful.

4. Copying a Functional Dependency

A copy operation is defined as follows:

Definition 3: Let $\langle R_1, F_1 \rangle$ and $\langle R_2, F_2 \rangle$ be relation schemes in **R** such that $X \subseteq R_1 \cap R_2$ and $X \rightarrow Y \in F_2$. By copying the FD to $\langle R_1, F_1 \rangle$, we mean that $\langle R_1, F_1 \rangle$ is replaced with $\langle R_1 \cup Y, F_1 \cup \{X \rightarrow Y\} \rangle$ in **R**. Note that $\langle R_2, F_2 \rangle$ remains unchanged by the copy operation. Let r_1 and r_2 be base relations on $\langle R_1, F_1 \rangle$ and $\langle R_2, F_2 \rangle$, respectively. Let $S_{12} = \langle R_1 \cup Y, F_1 \cup \{X \rightarrow Y\} \rangle$. Then the base relation r_{12} on S_{12} is defined by $r_{12} = r_1 \bowtie \pi_{X \cup Y}(r_2)$. Figure.4 illustrates the copy operation. □

By modifying the database scheme, each routine database activity must be translated accordingly.

Definition 4: Let r_1 and r_2 be base relations on $\langle R_1, F_1 \rangle$ and $\langle R_2, F_2 \rangle$, respectively. Let r_{12} be a base relation on $\langle R_1 \cup Y, F_1 \cup \{X \rightarrow Y\} \rangle$. Then queries are translated as follows:

• Insertion: Consider an insertion of a tuple τ on $R_{i_1} \cup \cdots \cup R_{i_p}$ to a database $\mathbf{D}{:}r_1, \cdots, r_n$. There are three cases to be considered.

1. If $i_q = 1$ for some q and $i_{q'} \neq 2$ for all q', then the insertion is translated to selecting a tuple τ_2 in r_2 such that $\tau_2[X] = \tau[X]$, followed by inserting to r_{12} a tuple τ_{12} such

that $\tau_{12}[R_1] = \tau[R_1]$ and $\tau_{12}[R_2] = \tau_2$.

2. If $i_q \neq 1$ for all q and $i_{q'} = 2$ for some q', then the insertion is executed as usual. (It needs no translation.)

3. If $i_q = 1$ and $i_{q'} = 2$ for some q and q', then tuples $\tau[R_1]$ and $\tau[R_2]$ are inserted to both of r_1 and r_2, respectively, and there is no insertion to one of r_1 or r_2 without the other, in the original database. The insertion is translated to inserting a tuple $\tau[R_2]$ to r_2 followed by inserting a tuple $\tau[R_1 \cup Y]$ to r_{12}.

• Deletion: Consider a deletion of a tuple τ on $R_{i_1} \cup \cdots \cup R_{i_p}$ from a database $\mathbf{D}: r_1, \cdots, r_n$. There are three cases to be considered.

1. If $i_q = 1$ for some q and $i_{q'} \neq 2$ for all q', then the deletion is translated to deleting all tuples τ_{12} from r_{12} such that $\tau_{12}[R_1] = \tau[R_1]$.

2. If $i_q \neq 1$ for all q and $i_{q'} = 2$ for some q', then the deletion is translated to deleting a tuple $\tau[R_2]$ from r_2 followed by deleting all tuples τ_{12} such that $\tau_{12}[X \cup Y] = \tau[X \cup Y]$.

3. If $i_q = 1$ and $i_{q'} = 2$ for some q and q', then $\tau[R_1]$ and $\tau[R_2]$ are deleted from r_1 and r_2, respectively, in the original database. The deletion is translated to deleting $\tau[R_2]$ from r_2 followed by deleting all tuples τ_{12} from r_{12} such that $\tau_{12}[R_1] = \tau[R_1]$ or $\tau_{12}[X \cup Y] = \tau[X \cup Y]$.

• Update: Consider an update of a tuple τ on $R_{i_1} \cup \cdots \cup R_{i_p}$ for a database $\mathbf{D}: r_1, \cdots, r_n$. There are three cases to be considered.

1. If $i_q = 1$ for some q and $i_{q'} \neq 2$ for all q', then the update is translated to updating all tuples τ_{12} in r_{12} such that $\tau_{12}[R_1] = \tau[R_1]$.

2. If $i_q \neq 1$ for all q and $i_{q'} = 2$ for some q', then the update is translated to updating a tuple $\tau[R_2]$ in r_2 followed by updating all tuples τ_{12} such that $\tau_{12}[X \cup Y] = \tau[X \cup Y]$.

3. If $i_q = 1$ and $i_{q'} = 2$ for some q and q', then tuples $\tau[R_1]$ in r_1 and $\tau[R_2]$ in r_2 are updated, in the original database. The update is translated to updating a tuple $\tau[R_2]$ in r_2, followed by updating all tuples τ_{12} in r_{12} such that $\tau_{12}[R_1] = \tau[R_1]$ or $\tau_{12}[X \cup Y] = \tau[X \cup Y]$.

4. Retrieval

Retrieval from the join of r_1 and r_2 is translated to a retrieval from r_{12}. Retrieval from r_1 is translated to a retrieval by replacing r_1 with $\pi_{R_1}(r_{12})$. Retrieval from r_2 needs not be translated. □

The following theorem shows a necessary and sufficient condition for applying copy operation to a database scheme such that no new anomalies occur in the modified database.

Theorem 2: Let $S_1 = \langle R_1, F_1 \rangle$ and $S_2 = \langle R_2, F_2 \rangle$ be relation schemes and let $X \to Y$ be an FD in F_2 such that $X \subseteq R_1 \cap R_2$. Copying an FD: $X \to Y$ to S_1 does not cause any new anomalies if and only if all the queries that use S_1 and S_2 satisfy the following conditions.

Condition 5: There is no deletion from r_2.

Condition 6: (1) Whenever a tuple τ is inserted to r_1, the X values of τ must already exist in the projection of r_2 onto X, that is, $\tau[X] \in \pi_X(r_2)$, or (2) Every insertion that uses R_1 or R_2 includes the $R_1 \cup R_2$ values in its tuple.

Condition 7: The X values in r_1 are not updated.

Condition 8: The $X \cup Y$ values in r_2 are not updated.

Proof: Let $S_{12} = \langle R_1 \cup Y, F_1 \cup \{X \rightarrow Y\}\rangle$. Let r_{12} be a base relation on S_{12}.

Assume that Conditions 5 to 8 hold. Then, there are six possible modification operations:

(1) Consider an insertion of a tuple τ to r_1. By Condition 6, we can construct a tuple τ_{12} on $R_1 \cup Y$ such that $\tau_{12}[R_1] = \tau$ and $\tau_{12}[X \cup Y] \in \pi_{XUY}(r_2)$. Then inserting τ to r_1 is translated to inserting τ_{12} to r_{12}. Thus, no insertion anomaly occurs in r_{12}.

(2) Consider an insertion of a tuple τ on $R_1 \cup R_2$. The insertion is translated to inserting a tuple $\tau[R_2]$ to r_2 followed by inserting a tuple $\tau[R_1 \cup Y]$ to r_{12}. Thus no insertion anomaly occurs.

(3) Consider an insertion of a tuple τ to r_2. The insertion needs no translation, and thus no new insertion anomaly occurs.

(4) Consider a deletion of a tuple τ from from r_1. Conditions 6 implies $\pi_X(r_1) \subseteq \pi_X(r_2)$. Thus the number of tuples in r_{12} is not less than the number of tuples in r_1. On the other hand, by the fact that $X \rightarrow Y \in F_2$ and $X \subseteq R_1 \cap R_2$, the number of tuples in r_{12} is not more than the number of tuples in r_1. Thus for each tuple τ in r_1, there is exactly one tuple τ_{12} in r_{12} such that $\tau_{12}[R_1] = \tau$. Hence the deletion is translated to deleting the corresponding tuple τ_{12} such that $\tau_{12}[R_1] = \tau$ from r_{12}. Since the Y values of τ_{12} are the copy from r_2 and $\tau_{12}[X \cup Y] \in \pi_{XUY}(r_2)$ holds, the $X \cup Y$ values are not lost from the database. Thus no deletion anomaly occurs in r_{12}.

(5) Consider an update of the $R_1 - X$ values of a tuple τ in r_1. From the one to one correspondence shown in (4), the update is translated to updating the corresponding tuple τ_{12} in r_{12} such that $\tau_{12}[R_1] = \tau$. Hence, the update to r_{12} does not differ from the update to r_1, as far as anomalies are concerned. That is, no new update anomaly occurs in r_{12}.

(6) Consider an update of the $R_2 - (X \cup Y)$ values of a tuple τ in r_2. Since the update needs no translation, no new anomaly occurs.

Conversely, if at least one of Conditions 5 to 8 does not hold, then new anomalies would be encountered in r_{12}. This proved as follows:

(1) Assume that Condition 5 does not hold. Then there exists a deletion of a tuple τ from r_2. The deletion must be translated to deleting τ from r_2 followed by deleting a tuple τ_{12} in r_{12} such that $\tau_{12}[X \cup Y] = \tau[X \cup Y]$. However, the $R_1 - X$ values of τ_{12} is lost by the deletion. This means that a new deletion anomaly is encountered.

(2) Assume that Condition 6 does not hold. Then there exists an insertion of a tuple τ to r_1 such that $\tau[X] \notin \pi_X(r_2)$. The insertion must be translated to inserting a tuple τ_{12} such that $\tau_{12}[R_1] = \tau$ to r_{12}, however, the Y values of τ_{12} is undefined. This means that a new insertion anomaly is encountered.

(3) Assume that Condition 7 does not hold. Then there exists an update of the X values of a tuple τ_1 in r_1. The update must be translated to updating a tuple τ_{12} in r_{12} such that $\tau_{12}[R_1] = \tau_1$. The update of a tuple τ_1 such that $\tau_1[X] \notin \pi_X(r_2)$ is translated to updating the X values of the corresponding tuple τ_{12} in r_{12}, which introduces a new complex anomaly.

(4) Assume that Condition 8 does not hold. Then there exists an update of the $X \cup Y$ values of a tuple τ_2 in r_2.

Consider the update of the X values of a tuple τ_2 in r_2. The update must be translated to updating a tuple τ_2 followed by updating all tuples τ_{12} such that $\tau_{12}[X \cup Y] = \tau_2[X \cup Y]$ in r_{12}. The update of τ_{12} causes $\pi_{R_1}(r_{12}) \neq r_1$, which is a type of a new complex anomaly.

Consider an updating both of the X and Y values in r_2. The update introduces a new complex anomaly as shown just above.

Consider an update of the Y values of a tuple τ_2 in r_2. The update must be translated to updating all tuples τ_{12} in r_{12} such that $\tau_{12}[X \cup Y] = \tau_2[X \cup Y]$. Consider the case where r_{12} has a number of tuples τ_{12} such that $\tau_{12}[X \cup Y] = \tau_2[X \cup Y]$, then a new update anomaly is encountered. □

When Conditions 5 to 8 are satisfied, $\pi_{R_1}(r_{12}) = r_1$ and $\pi_{X \cup Y}(r_{12}) \subseteq \pi_{X \cup Y}(r_2)$ are satisfied by the proof of sufficiency. Assume that base relations, r_1 and r_2, are modified to r_1' and r_2' by a query Q, respectively. The query Q is translated to Q' for S_{12} such that $\pi_{R_1}(r_{12}'') = r_1'$ and $r_2'' = r_2'$, where r_{12}'' and r_2'' denote the modified base relations of r_{12} and r_2, respectively, by Q'. Therefore the resulting view of a retrieval in the original database scheme is equivalent to the view of the corresponding retrieval in the new database scheme obtained by applying the copy operations.

5. Examples

Let us consider a sales management system at an enterprise. There are two main activities called Sales and Reservation.

Example 2: Consider the Sales activity. When a customer comes into the store and gives a clerk an order, the clerk checks the product inventory. If the requested product is on hand, the clerk puts a sales record into a base relation on SALES. Consider the following two schemes. For simplicity, in the following examples only attribute names are put in angle brackets ⟨ ⟩, and FDs are explained by statements.

- SALES:⟨ sales♯, division-code, sales-date, cancel-date, product♯, selling-price, quantity, customer-phone♯ ⟩
- CUSTOMER:⟨ customer-phone♯, customer-name ⟩

When a product is sold, a tuple on SALES∪CUSTOMER is inserted, that is, a tuple τ_1 is inserted to a base relation on SALES and a tuple τ_2 is inserted to a base relation on CUSTOMER such that $\tau_1[customer\text{-}phone♯] = \tau_2[customer\text{-}phone♯]$. Tuples in both base relations are not deleted. The values of customer-phone♯ and customer-name are not updated. The customer-name in CUSTOMER is always referred to with the SALES data. Therefore, merge operation can be applied here and the following new SALES can be obtained and used in place of old two schemes.

- SALES:⟨ sales♯, division-code, sales-date, cancel-date, product♯, selling-price, quantity, customer-phone♯, customer-name ⟩

The efficiency of the retrieval operation can be improve by using the new SALES. □

Example 3: Consider the Reservation activity. A salesman reserves products which he/she wants to sell, then goes the rounds of his/her customers to sell those reserved products. After the salesman comes back, he/she puts his/her sales data into a base relation on SALES and cancels all his/her reservation. Two schemes, RESERVATION and ORGANIZATION, are mainly involved in the Reservation.

- RESERVATION:⟨ *reserve‡, reserve-date, product‡, reserve-quantity, salesman-name, division-code* ⟩
- ORGANIZATION:⟨ *division-code, division-phone‡, department-name* ⟩

There is no deletion from the base relation on ORGANIZATION. Neither of the values of *division-code* nor *division-phone‡* are updated in a base relations on RESERVATION and a base relation on ORGANIZATION. When inserting a tuple to the base relation on RESERVATION, *division-code* of the tuple always exists in the base relation on ORGANIZATION. The retrievals of reservation always returns *division-phone‡*. Therefore, by copying FD: *division-code → division-phone‡* to RESERVATION, the following new RESERVATION is obtained.

- RESERVATION:⟨ *reserve‡, reserve-date, product‡, reserve-quantity, salesman-name, division-code, division-phone‡* ⟩

The insertion of a reservation data is translated to selecting from ORGANIZATION followed by an insertion to the new RESERVATION. The retrieval of reservation is translated to use the new RESERVATION and its efficiency is improved.   □

6.   Conclusions

We introduced two scheme operations, merge and copy, to design a more efficient database scheme suitable for a class of routine activities. We also showed the database scheme obtained by exhaustive applications of the scheme operations is optimal in the sense that further application of one of the scheme operations to the database scheme would cause anomalies. We are planning a project based on this scheme transformation strategy. In the project, we will evaluate the performance of queries which use joins. We will compare the performance between the three types of physical database structure: (1) database with indexing which is supported by many database management systems to make join operations faster, (2) database using scheme transformation shown in this paper and (3) original database which uses no indexing and has not been transformed. The evaluation will also show the trade-off of loss in modification operations and gain in retrieval operations.

References

[1] C.J.Date : "An Introduction to Database Systems"(Third Edition), Addison-Wesley (1981)
[2] D.Maier : "The Theory of Relational Databases", Computer Science Press (1983).
[3] J.Martin : "Managing the Data-Base Environment", Prentice-Hall (1983)
[4] F.McFadden, J.Hoffer : "Data Base Management"(Second Edition), The Benjamin/ Cummings Publishing (1988).

THE MEAN VALUE APPROACH TO PERFORMANCE EVALUATION OF TIME-STAMP ORDERING ALGORITHMS

M. El-Toweissy
Old Dominion University
Norfolk, VA23529
e-mail: eltow_m @cs.odu.edu

N. El-Makky, M. Abougabal, S. Fouad
Alexandria University
Alexandria, Egypt
e-mail: alex@egfrcuvx.bitnet.bitnet

Abstract

The diversity of available concurrency control algorithms in database systems necessitates the development of quantitative methods for evaluating their performance. This paper proposes an analytical model to analyze the performance of Time-stamp Ordering algorithms. In particular, Time-stamp Ordering employing blocking and restarts, both with and without Thomas Write Rule. The modeling approach is promising since it has the potential of providing useful insights to DBMS designers and at the same time very inexpensive to use. Moreover, the results obtained are extensive and closely track those of simulation.

1 Introduction

The proliferation of concurrency control algorithms (CCAs) in DBMSs has motivated considerable research on the performance evaluation of the various algorithms [1,4,7-9,13-18]. However, due to the complexity of the issues affecting the performance of CCAs, most existing studies use different approaches and make different assumptions. The performance studies are informative, but the results that have emerged instead of being definitive have been very contradictory. For example, studies by Shum and Spirakis [16], suggest that a Two-Phase Locking (2PL) algorithm using blocking and restarts instead of pure restarts is preferable from a performance view point, but studies by Chesnais et al. [4], claim that pure restarts may lead to better performance. Optimistic algorithms outperformed locking in [7], whereas the opposite is reported in [13]. The results by Lin and Nolte [12] contradict those obtained by Galler [8]. Hence, there is a persistent need for a unified approach which can be used to fairly select, from the field of candidates, the CCA that best suits a specific environment.

A successful attempt towards achieving this goal has been taken by Tay et al. [17,18], who used a mean value analytical approach to analyze the performance of variants of the 2PL algorithm. Following the same route, and knowing that the performance evaluation of Time-stamp Ordering (T/O) algorithms has mostly been carried out using simulation, our work in [5,6] and this paper is devoted to analyzing the performance of these algorithms in a unified manner.

The paper is organized as follows: Section 2 summarizes the T/O algorithm using blocking and restarts, *both with and without Thomas* Write Rule (TWR), Section 3 portrays the proposed model, Section 4 shows the application of the model to the CCAs under investigation, and Section 5 presents some parametric studies. Finally, the paper concludes in Section 6.

2 Time-stamp Ordering (T/O) Algorithms

In T/O, the transaction manager, TM, assigns a unique time-stamp, $ts(T_i)$, to each transaction T_i. TM attaches $ts(T_i)$ to each operation, O, issued by T_i [2,3,12]. Using the basic T/O algorithm [2,3,12], the concurrency control manager (CCM) records the largest time-stamp of any processed Read or Write operation on data item X, these are denoted $Rts(X)$ and $Wts(X)$, respectively. The CCM rejects an operation, and hence aborts the issuing transaction, only if the time-stamp of the operation is smaller than the recorded time-stamp of a conflicting operation. The aborted transaction is undone then restarted with a new and larger time-stamp.

Two-Phase Commit (2PC) is incorporated to prevent undoing of aborted transactions. This takes place by time-stamping Prewrites and accepting and rejecting Prewrites instead of Writes. When the transaction is committed, the corresponding Writes are applied.

To implement the incorporation of 2PC using **blocking and restarts**, the CCM blocks Reads, Writes and Prewrites. Let $min - Pts(X)$ be the minimum time-stamp of any buffered $Prewrite(X)$ and $min - Rts(X)$ be the minimum time-stamp of any blocked $Read(X)$ and define $min - Wts(X)$ analogously. Now, the operation of the CCM is as follows: Let R be a $Read(X)$, if $ts(R) < Wts(X)$, R is rejected; however, if $ts(R) > Wts(X)$, then R is output only if $ts(R) < min - Pts(X)$, else it is blocked; let P be a $Prewrite(X)$; if $ts(P) < Rts(X)$ or $ts(P) < Wts(X)$, then P is rejected and the transaction issuing it is restarted, else P is buffered; let W be a $Write(X)$, W is never rejected; if $ts(W) > min - Pts(X)$ or $ts(W) > min - Rts(X)$ then W is blocked, else it is output; when W is output, the corresponding P is unbuffered, if this causes $min - Pts(X)$ to increase, the blocked Ws and Rs are tested to see if any can now be output, this causes $min - Rts(X)$ to increase and makes some Ws ready, so blocked Ws are retested and so forth. If **TWR** [2] is applied, W is blocked when $ts(W) > min - Rts(X)$, and P is only rejected when $ts(P) < Rts(X)$. The rules for the read-write synchronization remain unchanged.

3 The Proposed Model

The model uses a flow diagram to chart the progress of a fixed number of transactions in a centralized database system (Figure 1), and a set of equations derived with the help of this flow diagram [5,6,17,18]. Each node in the flow diagram represents a stage of a transaction, while the flow diagram as a whole represents the system in steady state. In deriving the equations only the steady state average values of the variables are used, thus avoiding the detailed dynamics involving instantaneous values of the variables. (Due to space limitations, cf. [5,6] for detailed derivations of the model equations).

Model presentation

The database is a collection of data granules. A granule may be a file, a page, or a record. The number of data granules (the database size), is denoted D.

The system processes transactions which may be either queries or updates. Other transaction classes may also be considered (for example, transactions that read and write). The ratio of updates to the total number of transactions is a fixed value, denoted b. (For the time being, and without loss of generality, the term transaction will be used to denote a query or an update in order to clearly present the concept of the model. Later, as the model is used to analyze the various CCAs, the processing of queries and updates will be shown for each variant).

Each transaction makes a sequence of $k + 2$ independent requests, where the first request (the $0th$) is to start, the last request (the $(k + 1)st$) to terminate, and the ith request, for $1 \leq i \leq k$, is to access a data granule. Transactions access the data granules with a uniform access pattern. This, in general, does not impose any restriction on the model because it has been shown in [17] that a system with nonuniform access and light workload is equivalent to a system with uniform access and heavier workload.

The time between the ith and the $(i + 1)st$ requests, the interrequest time, is a random variable assumed to be uniformly distributed on $[0, 2T]$, thus the average interrequest time is T. Unlike the exponential distribution (the favored distribution in performance analysis of computer systems), the choice of the uniform distribution imposes a limit of $2T$ on the interrequest time. However, this assumption is taken to prove that within the framework of the mean value approach, it is not required that the distribution of the granule processing time be exponential (cf. [17,18,9]).

The flow diagram in Figure 1 shows the basic components of the system described above. A node E_i, for $0 \leq i \leq k$, denotes the stage of a transaction which is processing its ith data granule, and a node B_i, for $0 \leq i \leq k - 1$, denotes a stage of a transaction which is blocked due to its $(i + 1)st$ request. The state of the system is denoted by the vector $[N_0, \ldots, N_k, W_0, \ldots, W_{k-1}]$, where N_i is the number of transactions in stage E_i, for $0 \leq i \leq k$, and W_i is the number of transactions in stage B_i, for $0 \leq i \leq k - 1$. As shown in Figure 1, transactions progress from stage to stage. The flow rate, th, denotes the throughput of the system, while the rate of blocking and the rate of abort for transactions in stage E_i are denoted b_i and a_i, respectively.

When a transaction terminates, it returns to the user at the terminal, who sends another transaction after some time lapse. It is assumed that there are always some transactions in the system queue such that whenever a transaction leaves the system (finished or aborted), a new transaction immediately enters, and the multiprogramming level, N is kept constant. This treatment of restarts is termed fake restarts [1]. Fake restarts simplifies the analysis of transaction processing systems, and has in general been used in analytical studies [17,18].

In order to obtain a unified framework for the performance evaluation of CCAs, the work here concentrates on the throughput, th, and abort rate, a, as the principal performance measures [17,18]. The model also adopts the approach in [17,18] to separate data contention from hardware resource contention, in other words, hardware contention is modeled by a function that describes how the interrequest time T is affected by the effective load of the system.

As the analysis proceeds, the basic model will be changed in various ways. With this model of the transaction processing system (and its modifications), the task of performance evaluation is to obtain solution for throughput, block and abort rates, and the state vector, given system parameters of N, k, T and D.

Having portrayed the basic model, the performance analysis of the required algorithms may now commence.

4 Analysis of the T/O Algorithm Using Blocking and Restarts

Employing this algorithm, a request may be allowed (granted), blocked or rejected. Figure 2 shows the diagram of a system applying this algorithm to synchronize queries and updates.

System equations

Following the equation derivation procedures for the basic model and its extensions detailed in [5,6], the set of equations for the T/O algorithms using blocking and restarts are as outlined below. Note that, all notations used are given in Tabel 1.

State vector equations

$$N_{Q,i} = N_{Q,0} \prod_{j=0}^{i-1}(1 - P_{a,Q,j}) \qquad i = 1, \ldots, kq \tag{1}$$

$$W_{Q,i} = \frac{R_{Q,i}}{T_Q} P_{b,Q,i} N_{Q,0} \prod_{j=0}^{i-1}(1 - P_{a,Q,j}) \qquad i = 1, \ldots, kq - 1 \tag{2}$$

and

$$W_{Q,0} = \frac{R_{Q,0}}{T_Q} P_{b,Q,0} N_{Q,0} \tag{3}$$

$$N_{P,i} = N_{P,0} \prod_{j=0}^{i-1}(1 - P_{a,P,j}) \qquad i = 1, \ldots, ku \tag{4}$$

$$N_{W,i} = \frac{T_W}{T_P} N_{P,0} \prod_{j=0}^{ku-1}(1 - P_{a,P,j}) = N_W \qquad i = 1, \ldots, ku \tag{5}$$

$$W_{W,i} = \frac{R_{W,i}}{T_W} P_{b,W,i} N_W = \frac{R_{W,i}}{T_W} P_{b,W,i} N_{P,0} \prod_{j=0}^{ku-1}(1 - P_{a,P,j}) \qquad i = 0, \ldots, ku - 1 \tag{6}$$

where

$$N_{Q,0} = \frac{N_Q}{\left(1 + \sum_{i=1}^{kq}(\prod_{j=0}^{i-1}(1 - P_{a,Q,j})) + \frac{1}{T_Q}(\sum_{i=1}^{kq-1}(R_{Q,i} P_{b,Q,i} \prod_{j=0}^{i-1}(1 - P_{a,Q,j}) + R_{Q,0} P_{b,Q,0})))\right)} \tag{7}$$

and

$$N_{P,0} = \frac{N_U}{\left(1 + \sum_{i=1}^{ku}(\prod_{j=0}^{i-1}(1 - P_{a,P,j})) + \frac{\prod_{j=0}^{ku-1}(1-P_{a,P,j})}{T_P}((ku+1)T_W + \sum_{i=1}^{kq-1}(R_{W,i} P_{b,W,i})))\right)} \tag{8}$$

Throughput

$$th = th_Q + th_U \tag{9}$$

where

$$th_Q = \frac{N_Q kq}{T_Q} \tag{10}$$

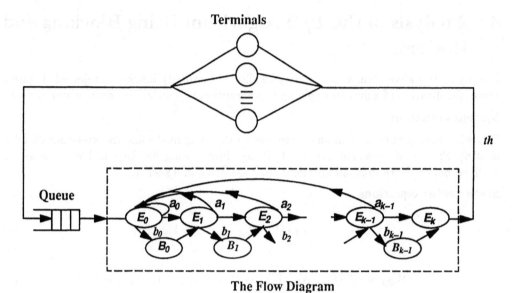

The Flow Diagram

Figure 1: The Flow Diagram in an Interactive System

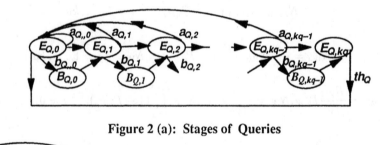

Figure 2 (a): Stages of Queries

Precommit Phase | Commit Phase

Figure 2 (b): Stages of Updates

**Figure 2: The Flow Diagram for Systems Employing
the T/O Blocking and Restarts Algorithm**

Parameter	Meaning
N_Q, N_U	number of queries, updates, respectively
th_Q, th_U	throughput of queries, updates, respectively
a_Q, a_U	abort rate of queries, updates, respectively
$N_{Y,i}, W_{Y,i}$	number of transactions in stage $E_{Y,i}$, blocked stage $B_{Y,i}$, respectively
$R_{Y,i}$	average waiting time in blocked stage $B_{Y,i}$
$c_{Y,i}$	rate of entering (or leaving) stage $E_{Y,i}$
$a_{Y,i}, b_{Y,i}$	abort, blocking rate upon leaving stage $E_{Y,i}$, respectively
$P_{a,Y,i}, P_{b,Y,i}$	probabilities of abort, blocking upon leaving stage $E_{Y,i}$, respectively

$Y = Q$ (for Queries), $Y = P$ (for Prewrites), $Y = W$ (for Writes)

Table 1: **Summary of Notations**

and

$$th_U = \frac{N_W ku}{T_W} = \frac{N_W}{T_W} \tag{11}$$

Abort rate

$$a = a_Q + a_U \tag{12}$$

where

$$a_Q = \sum_{j=0}^{kq-1} a_{Q,i} = \frac{1}{T_Q} \sum_{j=0}^{kq-1} P_{a,Q,j} N_{Q,j} \tag{13}$$

and

$$a_U = \sum_{j=0}^{ku-1} a_{P,i} = \frac{1}{T_P} \sum_{j=0}^{ku-1} P_{a,P,j} N_{P,j} \tag{14}$$

By finding $N_{Q,0}$ and $N_{P,0}$, the above set of equations can be solved for the throughput, abort rate and the state vector of the system. However, $N_{Q,0}$ and $N_{P,0}$ are expressed in terms of the input parameters and the probabilities of abort $P_{a,Q,i}$ and $P_{a,P,i}$, blocking $P_{b,Q,i}$ and $P_{b,W,i}$, and the waiting times $R_{Q,i}$ and $R_{W,i}$, for $0 \le i \le k-1$. Therefore the key to evaluating $N_{Q,0}$ and $N_{P,0}$ is to derive expressions for these probabilities of abort, probabilities of blocking, and the waiting times. These expressions, as shown in our work in [5,6] are not independent of the above set of equations, which means that the model will end up with a set of equations having more variables than equations. Hence, we resort to iteration to solve this problem. (Due to space limitation, cf. [5,6] for detailed derivations).

5 Performance Studies

This section presents various parametric studies based on solving the proposed analytical model for the algorithms previously analyzed. The performance indices used are the overall, queries and updates throughput, denoted by th, th_Q and th_U, respectively, and overall, queries and updates abort rate, denoted by a, a_Q and a_U, respectively. (Note that, unless otherwise specified, all the Figures shown are for the T/O algorithm using blocking, restarts and TWR with the following parameter values: $D = 1000$, $N = 40$, $kq = ku = 10$ and $T_Q = T_P = T_W = 1$).

5.1 Effect of varying the transaction size

This study investigates the effect of varying the query size, kq, and the update size, ku, on the performance of systems employing the T/O algorithm with blocking, restarts and TWR. Figure 3 shows the results obtained.

Following these results, the major observations, for all portions of updates, are:

1. as kq or ku increases, th decreases, while the change in a tracks that of a_U; the first part of this conclusion is mainly due to the increase in the time spent by the transaction in the system as its size increases and not as a direct result of the increase in the overall abort rate, since this latter may decrease as the transaction size increases as can be seen in Figure 3(b); the second part is attributed to the fact that the probability of abortion of updates is much greater than that of queries (queries may not be aborted except after the Writes that may cause its abortion are applied and their corresponding Prewrites are unbuffered, in other words, updates spend more time to be granted their Write requests);

2. as ku increases, th_Q decreases even though a_Q decreases; this indicates the existence of another factor that attributes to the decrease in th_Q; this factor is blocking; as shown in Figure 3(g), the increase in ku leads to a significant increase in the waiting time in blocked stages, consequently transactions spend more time in the system before they leave, thus leading to this interesting result.

5.2 Effect of varying the multiprogramming level

This study concentrates on how the changes in N affect the performance of systems employing the T/O algorithm using blocking, restarts and TWR. The study is carried out under both, relatively high and low conflict situation ($D = 250$ and $D = 1000$ granules, respectively). Figures 4 and 5 show the obtained results.

From the figures it can be observed that, as N increases, the following behavior occurs:

1. **in the low conflict situation:** the values of all the indices increase;

2. **in the high conflict situation:** updates throughput increases then drops for *query dominant systems*, while queries throughput increases then drops for *update dominant systems*; this behavior is similar to *thrashing* due to resource contention in (paging) operating systems; however, the interrequest time is constant in the figures, so that changes in N do not affect the the rate of execution of each transaction, the thrashing observed here is rather due to the effect of *data contention* (too many transactions accessing some shared data); Intuitively, beyond the thrashing point, fewer and fewer transactions make it to the last stage and consequently the throughput drops; it is to be noted that, the drop in the throughput for one transaction class is accompanied by the increase in the throughput in the other transaction class for the same N, this accounts for the monotonic increase in the overall throughput.

5.3 Effect of varying the update transaction ratio

Using Figures 3 through 5, as b increases, the updates throughput, th_U, increases whereas the queries throughput, th_Q, decreases. The overall throughput, $th = th_U + th_Q$, may therefore have a minimum. Similarly, as b increases, there are less queries, so the queries

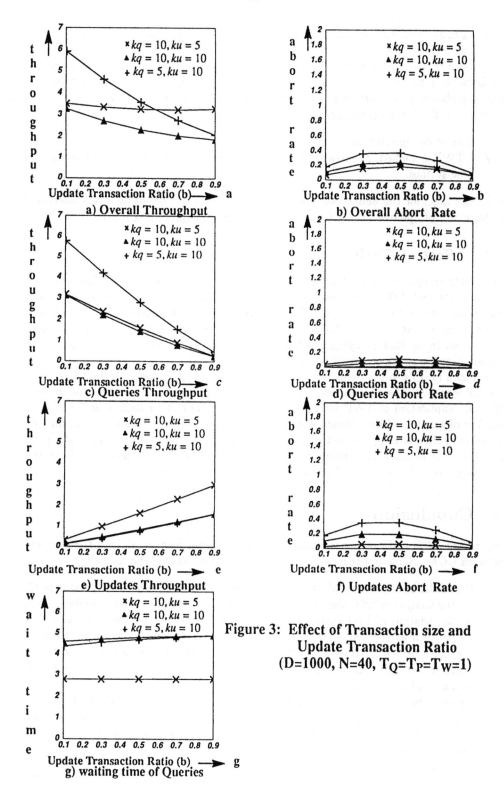

a) Overall Throughput

b) Overall Abort Rate

c) Queries Throughput

d) Queries Abort Rate

e) Updates Throughput

f) Updates Abort Rate

g) waiting time of Queries

Figure 3: Effect of Transaction size and
Update Transaction Ratio
(D=1000, N=40, $T_Q=T_P=T_W=1$)

abort rate, a_Q, and the updates abort rate, a_U, both increase then eventually decrease. The overall abort rate may therefore reach a maximum.

The above result indicates that, by replacing some updates in the system by queries, the performance may get worse. This could be explained as follows: although updates have a higher probability of abortion per request, there are two situations in which updates as a class may suffer less restarts. These situations are:

1. if $ku < kq$, updates have less requests;
2. if TWR is applied, updates are only aborted due to conflicts with reads hav ing greater time-stamps.

It follows that, for the above two situations, there exists two opposing forces affecting the performance of updates. These forces combine to give the preceding result.

5.4 Effect of TWR

This study compares the T/O algorithm using blocking and restarts with that using blocking, restarts and TWR. The results are shown in Figure 6. The figure yields to a very interesting observation; the application of TWR marginally improves the overall performance despite that it reduces the conflicts between the Write requests to zero. (Moreover, it is shown in [5] that applying TWR may even degrade the performance when the contention over hardware resources is high).

The reason for this result stems from the following argument: in general, the CC problem is divided into two subproblems, read-write synchronization and write-write synchronization [2]. The application of TWR reduces the write-write conflict to zero, thus increasing the number of granted Writes. Hence, the Prewrites that are otherwise unbuffered, due to the abortion of their issuing transactions, remain in the system and their corresponding Writes are eventually granted. As a result, the read-write conflicts increase, therefore there are two opposing forces the coupling of which leads to the preceding result.

6 Conclusions

Our work in [5,6] and this paper aimed at finding a unified framework for a fair comparison between CCAs. Some of the most important conclusions include the following:

1. the modeling approach and its associated modeling technique has been used in [9,17,18] for the analysis of 2PL algorithms; in [5,6] and this paper, we used a similar technique for the analysis of T/O algorithms; the approach could be also used to evaluate other CCAs such as the wound-wait and wait-die [3]; moreover, it could be extended for the performance analyses of CCAs in distributed DBMSs; hence, it could be safely claimed that this modeling approach comprises a unified approach for the performance evaluation of a wide range of CCAs;

2. The results obtained are extensive and closely track those obtained using simulation. From these results it is concluded that, data contention may cause thrashing, thus limiting the throughput. Increasing the transaction size always degrades the performance therefore arguing strongly for short transactions. Besides, replacing some updates in the workload by queries may degrade performance. It is also concluded that, the

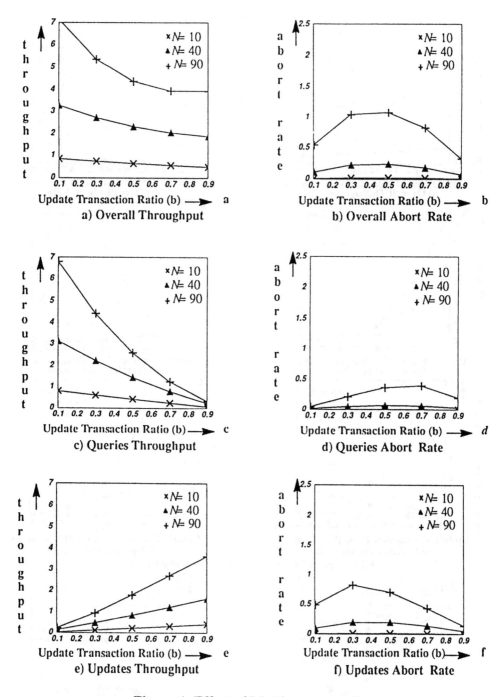

Figure 4: Effect of Multiprogramming Level
(Low Conflict (D = 1000))

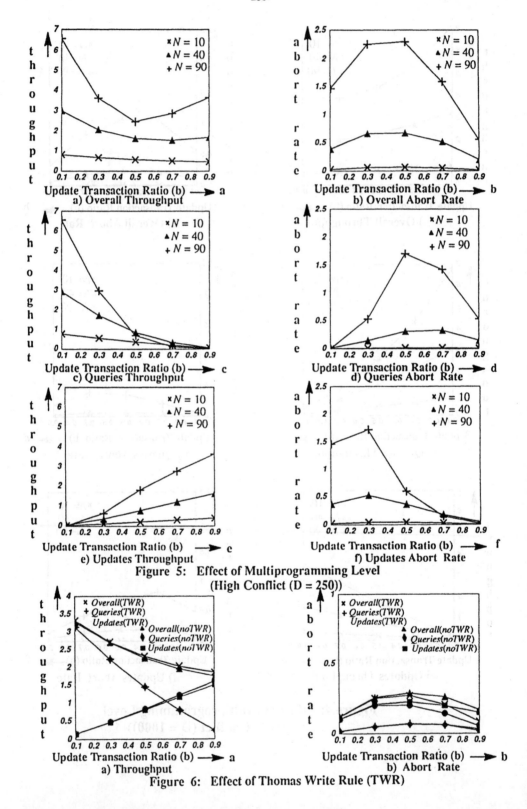

Figure 5: Effect of Multiprogramming Level
(High Conflict (D = 250))

Figure 6: Effect of Thomas Write Rule (TWR)

application of TWR has marginal effects on the overall performance even though it reduces the conflicts between write operations to zero.

References

[1] R. Agrawal, M. Carey, and M. Livny, " Concurrency control performance modeling : alternatives and implications," ACM TODS, vol. 12, no. 4, pp. 609-654, Dec. 1987.

[2] P. Bernstein and N. Goodman, "Concurrency control in distributed database systems," ACM Computing Surveys, vol. 13, no. 2, pp. 185-222, June 1981.

[3] P. Bernstein, N. Goodman and V. Hadzilacos, Concurrency control and recovery in database systems, Addison Wesley Pub., 1987.

[4] A. Chesnais, E. Gelenbe and I. Mitrani, "On the modeling of parallel access to shared data," Comm. ACM, vol. 26, no 3, pp. 196-202, Mar. 1983.

[5] M. El-Toweissy, A unified approach for performance evaluation of concurrency control algorithms in database systems, M.Sc. thesis, Computer Sc. Dept., Fac. of Eng., Alexandria Univ., Egypt, July 1989.

[6] M. El-Toweissy, M. Abougabal, N. El-Makky and H. Abdel-Wahab, "Performance evaluation of time-stamp ordering concurrency control algorithms in database systems: the pure restarts case," Techincal Report, TR-90-40, Old Dominion University, Sept. 1990.

[7] P. Franaszek and J. Robinson, "Limitations of concurrency in transaction processing," ACM TODS, vol. 10, no. 1, pp. 1-28, Mar. 1985.

[8] B. Galler, Concurrency control performance issues, Ph.D. dissertation, Computer Science Dept., Univ. of Toronto, Ontario , Sept. 1982.

[9] M. Hsu and B. Zhang, "The mean value approach to performance evaluation of cautious waiting," Technical Report TR-05-88, Harvard Univ., Aug. 1987.

[10] L. Kleinrock, Queuing systems, vol. 2, Wiley Interscience Pub., New York, 1976.

[11] H. Kobayashi, Modeling and analysis : An introduction to system performance evaluation methodology, Addison Wesley pub., 1978.

[12] W. Lin and J. Nolte, "Basic time-stamp, Multiple version time-stamp and two-phase locking," Proc. 9th Int. Conf. on Very Large Databases, pp. 109-119, Oct. 1983.

[13] D. Menasce and T. Nakanishi, "Optimistic versus pessimistic concurrency control mechanisms in database management systems," Inform. Sys., vol. 7, no. 1, pp. 13-27, 1982.

[14] C. Orji, L. Lilien and J. Hyziak, "A performance analysis of an optimistic and a basic time-stamp ordering concurrency control algorithm for centralized database systems," Proc. 4th Int. Conf. on Data Eng., pp. 64-73, Feb. 1988.

[15] K. Sevcik, "Comparison of concurrency control methods using analytic models," Proc. of the IFIP, North Holand, pp.298-307, 1983.

[16] A. Shum and P. Spirakis, "Performance analysis of concurrency control methods in database systems," Performance '81, North Holand, pp.1-19, 1981.

[17] Y.C. Tay, R. Suri and N. Goodman, "A mean value performance model for locking in databases : The no-waiting case," J. ACM, vol. 32, no. 3, pp. 618-651, July 1985.

[18] Y.C. Tay, R. Suri and N. Goodman, "Locking performance in centralized databases," ACM TODS, vol. 10, no. 4, pp. 415-462, Dec. 1985.

A Backend Text Retrieval Machine
for Signature-based Document Ranking

Budi Yuwono
Dik Lun Lee
Department of Computer and Information Science
Ohio State University
Columbus, Ohio 43210

Abstract

We discuss key issues of implementing a ranking strategy based on signature files. The main contribution of our method is the ability to represent term frequencies and obtain inverse document frequencies without explicitly storing them. This reduces the storage overhead significantly but without increasing the processing time. We then describe the design of a hardware signature processor for implementing the ranking strategy.

1 Introduction

As electronic document exchange becomes common among computer users, full-text database systems have become a necessity for managing large amounts of electronic documents. The most important function for full-text retrieval systems is to select and retrieve documents from a document collection. Statistical document ranking methods have been studied extensively and they have been shown to be much more effective than simple Boolean retrieval systems.

This paper will discuss major issues in the implementation of signature-based document ranking strategy. By considering the implementation details, we demonstrate the feasibility and superiority of hardware approaches for signature-based document ranking. We present the design of a hardware processor for supporting document ranking with signature files.

The design approach that we take is to improve retrieval speed by simplifying the system's components, such that system expansion will not increase system cost substantially while keeping the performance stable. In this section, some basic concepts on document ranking will be discussed briefly, followed by an overview of the signature file method and the problems with implementing document ranking with signature files. In section 2, we describe previous work which implemented various document ranking methods on signature file. Finally, section 3 describes the hardware design of our text retrieval machine and, in particular, the way that we obtain the term frequencies and inverse document frequencies and compute the document scores.

1.1 Document Ranking Methods

Traditional document retrieval systems are mostly based on Boolean retrieval, where documents which satisfy the boolean constraints of keywords specified in the query are retrieved. It has been shown that Boolean systems are difficult to use and have low recall and precision [2].

Document ranking is a method devised to enhance the effectiveness of text retrieval (i.e., to improve the chance of getting the desired documents). There are many methods proposed for representing documents for retrieval purpose. A commonly used method is based on the statistical properties of the documents.

In the vector space model, a document is represented as a vector $< w_{t_1}, w_{t_2}, ..., w_{t_v} >$, where w_{t_i} stands for the weight (or importance) of term t_i in the document and v is the size of the vocabulary for the document collection [10]. The weight of a term in a document is typically the product of two factors, namely, the term frequency (tf) which is the number of occurrences of the term in the document, and the inverse document frequency (idf) which is equal to $\log(nd/df)$ where nd is the number of documents in the document collection and df, the document frequency, is the number of documents containing the term. tf indicates the importance of a term within a document, whereas idf indicates the term's ability to distinguish a document from documents in the rest of the collection. This ranking method is often referred to as the $tf \times idf$ method. It is simple but has been shown to be effective. It is therefore adopted in this paper.

A query Q is likewise represented as $< q_1, q_2, ..., q_v >$ where q_i represents the weight of a query term. For simplicity, we assume q_i is either 1 when term t_i is specified in the query and 0 when it isn't. Documents are ranked by their similarity to the query:

$$\text{document weight} = \sum_{i=1}^{v} w_{t_i} \times q_i.$$

Documents with the highest weights (e.g., the top 20 documents) are then retrieved.

Document ranking is time consuming. It requires the idf of each term and the tf for each term in each document to be stored. The computation and disk accesses required are much more than a typical Boolean query, especially when the number of query terms is large. A number of studies have been performed on various implementation methods for document ranking. In this paper, we focus on those based on signature files.

1.2 Signature Based Text Retrieval

Signature-based text retrieval is a method that uses a signature file for keyword search. Signatures can be obtained in a number of ways [4]. In the concatenate codeword method, the signature file is a concatenation of binary signatures or codewords of all non common words in the original documents. Word encoding is done through some hashing function. Using superimposed coding, space can be reduced further by superimposing a number of word signatures into one signature. In a query, the query term is hashed into a query signature, which is matched against each signature in the signature file. **Figure 1** illustrates an example in which keywords in a text block are hashed into word signatures which are then superimposed to form the block signature. The query terms are similarly hashed and superimposed to generate a query signature, which is then matched against the block signatures.

Three possible outcomes of a match are illustrated in the figure. The first and second cases show a match between the query signature and the block signature when, for each bit in the query signature set, the corresponding bit in the block signature is also set. The second case shows that a conjunctive query of more than one query term can be matched in one comparison. The third case is a mismatch when some of the bits in the block signature are zero when the corresponding positions in the query signature are set. The fourth case is a false drop. False drops are text blocks which the signature file identifies as containing the query terms (i.e., a match) but indeed they don't. They are mainly caused by the information loss when word signatures are superimposed. They can be eliminated by further comparing the query terms with the text blocks but the performance will be degraded. This is a unique problem of the signature file approach, and much work has been done on minimizing the false drop probability [5,9]. Owing to its simplicity and low storage overhead, superimposed coding is widely studied in the literature and is adopted in this paper.

The advantage of signature-based text retrieval method over the conventional inverted file method is its moderate storage overhead — 10-20% for signature files compared to over 100% for inverted files.

```
text block  [  · · · text · · · · · · database · · ·  ]
```

```
word signatures:
                    text   001 000 110 010
                database   000 010 101 001
      block signature (∨)   001 010 111 011


      Queries              Query Signatures    Results
      1) database          000 010 101 001     ← match
      2) database ∧ text   001 010 111 011     ← match
      3) retrieval         010 001 000 011     ← no match
      4) information       001 000 111 000     ← false drop
```

Figure 1: Signature generation and comparison based on superimposed coding

A signature file is typically used for supporting Boolean queries. It performs best when the query is a conjunctive query. As for retrieval speed, the method is much faster than full-text scanning but slower than inverted file. In other words, it is a compromise between inverted file and full-text scanning methods.

Recent studies have been performed on the implementation of document ranking with signature file [3,12,15]. The objective is to be able to support document ranking at the same low storage overhead and simplicity of the signature file. However, it is difficult to represent term frequencies in a signature. Further, since we have to know exactly which query term exists in the text block, a query signature must be generated for each query term and matched against the block signature individually, thus increasing the processing time.

2   Previous Work

Although signature files have been studied very extensively, they are studied under the context of Boolean queries (in particular, conjunctive queries). Recently, there is an increasing amount of work on implementing document ranking methods using the signature file. In this section, we review some of the major efforts.

Stanfill and Kahle at The Thinking Machine Corporation have designed a system based on the signature file and run on the Connection Machine [12]. The signature file is partitioned across all the processors and the query signatures are sent to the processors for comparison. The weight of a document is based on the number of signature blocks of the document that contain the query term. This scheme is easy to implement on the Connection Machine. The weakness of their technique is that the ranking method is very primitive. The scheme only approximates the term frequency and, without normalizing the score with the length of the document. Thus, it favors long documents. Further, the ranking formula doesn't make use of the inverse document frequency. Owing to the simplification of ranking scheme, the effectiveness of the retrieval is degraded [11].

Croft and Savino studied several alternatives for implementing document ranking using signature files [3]. The alternatives have different levels of retrieval effectiveness. Each level is defined according to the inherent restriction imposed by the signature file organization used. Both a sequential file organization and a bit sliced organization are considered.

Croft and Savino suggest a document ranking strategy with a reasonable effectiveness based on the $tf \times idf$ method. In their technique an index file containing terms and their associated inverse document frequency (idf) is maintained. The term frequency (tf) for each query term is approximated by the number of block signatures that contain the query signature divided by the total number of block signatures within each document. This approach is much better than that of Stanfill and Kahle's method in terms of retrieval effectiveness. By using a simple signature file organization, the physical storage overhead and the disk seek time are reasonable. The major drawback of this approach is that the storage overhead required for the index file is large and the term frequencies are still an approximation.

Wong and Lee proposed a technique that uses a bitmap as a signature file [15]. Conceptually each document is encoded as a bit vector of v bits, where v is the vocabulary size of the document collection, with one bit set for each term in the document. As in Croft's technique, it maintains an index file containing the terms and their associated idf values. In addition, each entry in the index file also contains the bit position in the signature that is to be set for the term. This unique mapping between terms and signatures does not cause any false drop as superimposed coding does.

To encode the term frequencies, terms in a document are grouped according to their term frequencies and a subsignature is generated for each group. The subsignatures are then stored separately into the corresponding tf groups, each of which contains subsignatures for a particular term frequency. With the above signature file organization, the tf of a term is immediately known from the group in which it is stored.

Wong and Lee also suggested a way to compress the signature and divide the signature into tr (term range) groups so that disk accesses can be reduced. By storing the signature file in separate blocks for each tf and tr combination, expansion of the index file as new terms are introduced does not require any changes in the current structure; all it takes is simply adding another range group.

This technique gives a solution for obtaining the exact term frequency with modest storage requirement. The signature organization which divides the logical signature file into tf groups on one axis and tr groups on the other makes it possible to minimize storage even further, by not storing groups that contain all zeros.

However, the physical organization of the signature file is very complex, thus requiring some storage overhead for maintaining block pointers. Moreover, as the collection grows the signature blocks may expand arbitrarily and can no longer be stored in contiguous disk regions. Altogether these would degrade the performance as long disk accesses time are incurred. Finally, as with Croft and Savino's technique, the amount of storage taken up by the index file is considerable.

As far as implementation is concerned, the techniques described above are mainly software oriented. Stanfill and Kahle's technique is very straight-forward, where the only computation needed is addition. Thus, it can be implemented merely using simple 1-bit processors in the Connection Machine. However, the cost of a Connection Machine is significant and many hardware features in the machine (such as the hypercube communication network) are not utilized at all [13]. The technique proposed by Wong and Lee heavily relies on software, both system software, for its complex physical storage management tasks, and application software for index table lookup, signature block selection and weight computation. In that respect, Croft's technique lies somewhere between the two techniques.

3 A Signature Search Engine

Owing to the simplicity of signature files, a number of hardware signature processors have been proposed for searching signature files [1,6,14]. The rationale behind hardware signature processors has been provided by Lee [8]. However, all of the designs deal only with Boolean queries; none of them can handle document ranking.

In this section, we describe the design of our search engine which supports document ranking. We first describe the overall architecture of the machine, followed by the organization of the signature file and the design of a signature. Then, we discuss how we implement the exact $tf \times idf$ ranking strategy without explicitly representing tf and idf values. Finally, we describe the hardware design of the signature processor, which is the heart of the search engine.

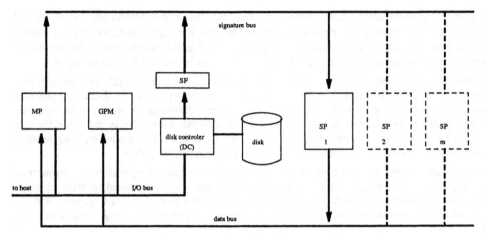

Figure 2: Architecture of the Signature-Based Text Retrieval Machine

3.1 Machine Architecture

Each disk in the architecture is attached to one search module. As shown in **Figure 2**, a single search module consists of one microprocessor (MP), one general purpose memory (GPM) unit, one disk controller (DC) with a signature formatter (SF) connected to its output channel, and a number of signature processors (SP) arranged in parallel. MP, GPM and DC are connected to the host computer through an I/O bus. A signature bus is used for transferring signatures from MP and/or SF to SPs. The third bus, a data bus, is used for transferring data from SPs to MP and GPM.

Query signatures are sent by the host to MP, which in turn distributes them to SPs. It is clear that the number of query signatures (thus query terms) is at most as many as the number of SPs in the module. Access to the signature file on the disk is performed by DC as requested by MP. SF is used for formatting the serial bit stream output from DC into a parallel format.

Computation of term frequencies (tf) and document frequencies (df) is performed by SPs, each of which has its own local memory. This computation process proceeds at the same rate as the disk's data transfer rate. The details of SP design will be discussed later in this section.

Upon completion of a search operation, MP sends a signal to the host, and allows the host to get the document scores through direct access to GPM. At this point, the document scores are stored in GPM ordered by document IDs. The host can then sort the scores and request the high ranked documents, which can be done by sending the desired document IDs directly to DC.

Since all files are stored in plain sequential manner, a straight forward disk management is possible. That is, DC needs only to remember the starting address of the signature file and document files physical locations.

3.2 Signature and Signature File Design

The signatures are stored in a sequential manner. Like Wong and Lee's design [15], term frequencies are represented by partitioning. However, instead of storing signatures generated from a document into different term frequency groups, we maintain a simple sequential organization. The process is depicted in **Figure 3**. First, the terms of a document are separated into groups according to their term frequencies. Then signatures are generated for each group and are stored *sequentially* into a signature segment in increasing term frequency order. In other words, a segment contains signatures generated from one document. Segments are again stored sequentially to form the signature file.

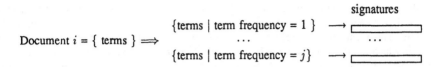

$$\text{Document } i = \{ \text{ terms } \} \implies \begin{array}{l} \{\text{terms} \mid \text{term frequency} = 1 \} \\ \qquad \cdots \\ \{\text{terms} \mid \text{term frequency} = j\} \end{array}$$

Figure 3: Generation of signatures for a document

It is clear that the size of a signature segment does not only depend on the size of the document it represents, but on the distribution of the term frequencies. A signature is divided into 3 fields:

1. **Segment start bit**

   This takes only one bit, and is set only in the first signature of each segment, indicating the document boundary. This field is used for various logical operations in the signature processor (SP), namely incrementing the document counter, enabling the document frequency counter, and resetting the term frequency counter. Details on these mechanisms will be given later.

2. **Term frequency increment field**

   This field contains a value to be added to a term frequency register (which is reset at the beginning of a segment) to get the term frequency (tf) of the terms represented by the superimposed code in the signature. In the current design, only the increment from the previous term frequency of the previous signature is encoded to reduce the number of bits required for this field. However, if the term frequency distribution is very wide and sparse, it is desirable to encode the actual values instead of the increment.

3. **Superimposed codeword**

   Terms in a document that have the same number of occurrences (tf) are encoded using superimposed coding. The superimposition is done incrementally, one term after another. When the number of bits set reaches one half of the signature length, the superimposition stops and the signature is done. If at this point there are terms of the same term frequency remaining, then the superimposition is repeated and another signature is produced. The term frequency increment bits of these subsequent signatures are set to zero, meaning that the term frequencies of these signatures are the same as the previous one. It has been shown that keeping the number of bits set close to one half of the signature length can reduce the false drop probability [9].

3.3 Document Ranking Implementation

As SP searches through the signatures, the term frequency (tf) of each document term can be obtained from the **term frequency increment** field of the signature when a **hit** (signature match) occurs. At the same time the tf value together with the ID of the document where the hit occurs is stored in SP's local memory. These can be done easily in hardware, which will be given later.

The inverse document frequency (idf) of a query term is more difficult to found. Unlike previous designs which use a global index to store the idf for each term [3,15], we obtain df, the document frequency, dynamically as SP searches through the signature file. With df and nd, we can then compute the idf for the query term.

Usually, nd and df are for the whole document collection. nd, the total number of documents, is rather static and thus can be stored in each signature processor and updated as documents are inserted into or deleted from the database. However, df, the number of documents containing the query term, cannot be obtained locally in each signature processor. The local document frequencies in the signature processors must be sent to the MP which then sums up the values to obtain the global document frequency, thus increasing the communication overhead. For modularity reason, local approximations of nd and df are used in our design, meaning their computations are only concerned with the particular disk attached to the search module. This means that the values may be different from one module to another when multiple disks, each of which is attached to a module, are used. The only drawback of the scheme is that when the topic in question is not evenly distributed across the disks, documents in the disk with relatively low df will get higher scores. However, when the database is large and when documents are inserted on the disk uniformly (e.g., in a round-robin manner), we can safely assume that the distribution of hit documents is uniform across the disks.

nd is a fixed variable memorized by MP, which is changed when new documents are added. But df for each query term is computed by counting the number of signature segments whose signatures match the term. This operation is done by SP's document frequency counter.

The next step is to compute the binary logarithm and multiply nd with tfs. Since they are too complicated to implement on SPs, these operations are performed by MP which has direct accesses to all local memory units and counters in SPs. As shown in **Figure 2** data communications from these units to MP are made possible through the data bus. First, MP gets the contents of SP's local memory units and the counters, one SP at a time. These values are stored into GPM. Next, it computes the idf of each query term and multiplies the corresponding tfs with idf. The latter step produces tables of **tf x idf**, one table for each query term. Finally, the $tf \times idf$ values are summed across the tables document-wise to get the document scores and ranks.

Of course the above operations could have been done in parallel by the SPs, which would speed up the process. However, that would make the SPs very expensive to implement, especially when the number of SPs in a module is necessarily large. From the application stand point, it is more important to have more SPs, which can facilitate more query terms, at reasonable cost than to have only a few of them with relatively faster processing speed. Besides, if all the data are in the main memory, GPM in this case, the sequential processing delay is not very significant and can be pipelined with the search operations in the SPs.

As a final note, let us compare the technique with the more popular approach which uses a lookup table for obtaining the $idfs$. While the latter approach can give the exact idf immediately, it requires a very large amount of storage (i.e., as many words as the number of unique terms in the whole document collection) and disk accesses. Our approach of counting the hits when the signature file is being searched does not require any storage overhead or any additional processing time.

3.4 SP Logic Design

The schematic diagram of the signature processor (SP) is shown in **Figure 4**. A signature coming in through the signature bus is buffered by a **signature register**. The signature is then gated by SP's system clock and made available to the other devices.

The tf value of the current signature is kept in the **term frequency register**. This register is reset when a **start bit** is detected, and incremented by the value obtained from the **term frequency increment** field of each signature.

A **signature comparator** is used for matching the signature against the query signature (which was set by MP before the search operation begins). When a match occurs (a **hit** signal is detected) the content of the **term frequency register** together with the content of the **document counter** is written to the **term frequency table**. The latter is advanced when a **start bit** is detected. At the same time, the **hit** signal also advances the **document frequency counter**. The latter operation is only performed when the **document frequency counter switch** is on. The main component of the switch is a T-flip-flop that is toggled on by a **block start bit** and toggled off by a **hit** signal. This signal prevents the document frequency counter from incrementing more than once when a document contains multiple occurrences of a query term. In the case of multiple occurrences, the last match overrides the previous one(s), thus the highest tf value retained. This is desirable for we prefer high retrieval recall. The search operation

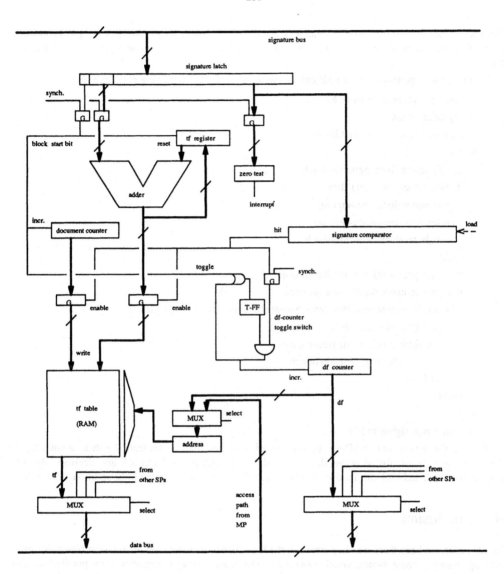

Figure 4: Logic design of the signature processor unit

terminates when a zero signature is detected. Finally, three multiplexors (MUXs) are put in place to allow direct access by MP to the term frequency table and the document frequency counter, via the data bus.

The operations performed by an SP can be summarized by the following pseudocode:

```
receive QuerySignature from MP
set signature-mask
while (not end of signature file) do
begin
    get Signature from signature-latch
    if (block-start-bit is set) then
        increment document-counter
        reset term-frequency-register
        toggle on document-hit-switch
    endif
    (term-freq-register) = (term-freq-register) + tf-increment
    if signature-mask results in a hit then
        write (document-counter, term-freq-register) into term-freq-table
        if document-hit-switch is on then
            increment document-freq-counter
            toggle off document-hit-switch
        endif
    endif
end
send interrupt signal to MP
```

Clearly, the search time in SP can be overlapped with the data transfer from the disk. Assuming the database is evenly distributed across the disks and the operations in SP and MP are pipelined, the time it takes to search and rank all the documents is the time to search a signature file partition from a disk.

4 Conclusion

In this paper, we have discussed key issues in the hardware implementation of signature based document ranking strategy. These issues, which essentially arise from hardware limitations, are parallelism, simplicity and modularity. Motivated by the need for a faster response time and lowering hardware cost, special purpose hardware, such as backend search engines, has become a feasible and attractive solution. With a simple design, this special hardware can be built cost effectively.

The hardware signature processor we proposed implements the $tf \times idf$ ranking method on signature file with little storage or processing overhead. The ideas of partitioning terms in a document according to term frequencies and computing the inverse document frequencies without storing them in a separate dictionary can applied to a software implementation as well. The former has already been exploited by Wong and Lee [15], but we maintain a sequential file structure which can greatly reduce implementation costs, especially in a hardware implementation.

There are clearly some design choices in the hardware design. For instance, the final computation of the document scores is done on the microprocessor (MP) now, but if hardware cost permits, it can be computed within the signature processors (SPs), and the sorting of the document scores can then be done in a distributed manner as in the Connection Machine. Further, associative memory [7] can be used to store and sort the document scores. These are cost/speed tradeoffs, but they will not affect the basic architecture.

5 References

[1] S.R. Ahuja and C.S. Roberts, "An associative/parallel processor for partial match retrieval using superimposed codes," presented at Proc. 7th Annual Symp. Comput. Arch., France, May 1980.

[2] D.C. Blair and M.E. Maron, "An evaluation of retrieval effectiveness for a full-text document-retrieval system," *Communications of ACM*, 28, no. 3, pp. 289–299, Mar. 1985.

[3] W.B. Croft and P. Savino, "Implementing ranking strategies using text signatures," *ACM Transactions on Office Information Systems*, 6, no. 1, pp. 42–62, Jan. 1988.

[4] C. Faloutsos, "Access methods for text," *ACM Computing Surveys*, 17, no. 1, pp. 49–74, Mar. 1985.

[5] C. Faloutsos and S. Christodoulakis, "Description and performance analysis of signature file methods for office filing," *ACM Transactions on Office Information Systems*, 5, no. 3, pp. 237–257, July 1987.

[6] D.L. Lee, "A word-parallel, bit-serial signature processor for superimposed coding," presented at Proceedings of the Second International Conference on Data Engineering, Los Angeles, Feb. 1986.

[7] D.L. Lee and C.W. Leng, "Design and Performance Evaluation of an Associative Memory with Distributed Control," presented at Journal of Parallel and Distributed Computing, Sep. 1990.

[8] D.L. Lee and F.H. Lochovsky, "Text retrieval machines," in *Office Automation*, D.C. Tsichritzis, Ed. New York, N.Y.: Springer-Verlag, pp. 339–375, 1985.

[9] C.W. Leng and D.L. Lee, Optimal weight assignment for signature generation, submitted for publication, 1990..

[10] G. Salton, *Automatic Text Processing: the transformation, analysis, and retrieval of information by computer.* Reading, MA, Addison-Wesley, 1989.

[11] G. Salton and C. Buckley, "Parallel text search methods," *Communications of ACM*, 31, no. 2, pp. 202–215, Feb. 1988.

[12] C. Stanfill and B. Kahle, "Parallel free-text search on the connection machine system," *Communications of ACM*, 29, no. 12, pp. 1229–1239, Dec. 1986.

[13] H. Stone, "Parallel querying of large databases: A case study," *IEEE Computer*, 20, no. 10, pp. 11–21, October 1987.

[14] N. Tavakoli and H. Modaress-Razavi, "An architecture for parallel search of large, full-text databases," presented at Proc. International Conference on Database, Parallel Architectures, and Their Applications (PARBASE-90), Miami, FL, Mar. 1990.

[15] W.Y.P. Wong and D.L. Lee, "Signature file methods for implementing a ranking strategy," *Information Processing and Management*, 26, no. 5, pp. 641–653, Oct. 1990.

4. Parallel Processing and Systems

Partitioning and Scheduling of Parallel Functional Programs using Complexity Information

Piyush Maheshwari [*]

Department of Computer Science
University of Manchester
Manchester M13 9PL, U.K.

This paper will discuss how to exploit parallelism efficiently by improving the granularity of functional programs on a multiprocessor. Asymptotic complexity analyses of a function, to estimate the computation time and also the communication involved in sending the arguments and receiving the results from the remote processor, are found to be quite useful. It is shown how some parallel programs can be run more efficiently with the prior information of time complexities (in big-O notation) and relative time complexities of its sub-expressions with the help of analytical reasoning and some practical examples on the larger-grain distributed multiprocessor machine LAGER. Ordered scheduling of the processes, determined by the priorities based on the relative time complexities, shows further improvement on the run-time dynamic load balancing methods and better utilisation of the resources.

Keywords: Functional programming, granularity, partitioning, scheduling, time and communication complexity functions.

1.0 Introduction

The programmers must tailor their applications to make the most efficient use of available computers – including those which are based on parallel processing. To exploit the power of multiprocessor architectures we must write parallel programs. The idea that the compiler will find the parallelism automatically (e.g. by strictness analysis) is plausible for simple programs but does not guarantee efficiency. There are many current research efforts in specifying parallel programs which differ in the size of the program unit (grain-size) that can be run in parallel, e.g., for a dataflow language Id [Arvind et al. 88] and for a single-assignment language Sisal [Sarkar 89] etc. There is also great interest in automatic parallelisation where sequential code is translated into parallel form by a software system. The automatic systems which are available, such as Pat [Appelbe et al. 89] and Ptool [Allen et al. 86], are able to improve the performance of many programs. However, many algorithms must be significantly modified to achieve efficient utilisation of parallel computers [Babb 84].

Functional (or applicative) languages have been a focus of interest for some time (especially since Backus' Turing Award Lecture [Backus 78]). Graph reduction is the most commonly used evaluation method to execute functional programs [Peyton-Jones 87]. It can be thought of as the graphical equivalent of reduction in the lambda calculus, and supports higher-order functions and normal-order evaluation in a very natural manner. A functional program should be thought of as an *expression* or a collection of *sub-expressions*, which can be executed by proper evaluation. A sub-expression which can be simplified, or reduced, using one of the conversion rules is called a *reducible expression* (or *redex*). The expression is said to be in *normal form* when it does not contain any redex. An expression may contain more than one redex to reduce. Operationally speaking, the Church-Rosser property states that if two arbitrary reduction sequences both terminate then they both yield the same result.

In the context of functional languages, the two important reduction orders are **applicative-order** reduction and **normal-order** reduction. If the *leftmost innermost redex* is reduced first, it is known as applicative-order reduction; otherwise if the *leftmost outermost redex* is reduced first, it is known as normal-order reduction. Loosely speaking, they correspond to eager and lazy evaluation respectively. Normal-order reduction guarantees to terminate if it happens at all. If an argument is not used in the body of a function, there is no need for its evaluation – normal-order reduction takes care of this and, hence, is essential for evaluating non-strict functions.

Functional programming languages are well-suited for parallel computation because they do not place artificial constraints on the evaluation order. Parallel execution is possible through concurrent graph reduction without adding any new language constructs or detailed program tuning. The absence of side-effects means that independent sub-expressions may be evaluated in any order, or in parallel (in fact, even concurrently with the function body, if exploiting vertical parallelism).

[*] Address in India: C/o Sri R.A. Maheshwari Advocate,   Najibabad 246 763 (U.P.)

2.0 How to improve performance - Larger Grain Computation

Optimal execution of parallel programs depends on partitioning the program into modules and scheduling those modules for the shortest execution time possible. Partitioning and scheduling are multiprocessor-dependent issues. Partitioning is necessary to ensure that the granularity of the parallel program is coarse enough for the target multiprocessor, without losing too much parallelism. Scheduling is necessary to achieve a good processor utilisation and to optimise inter-processor communication in the target multiprocessor. Data and task placement strategies are important to achieve a high degree of locality of reference.

The major factors that affect the performance of a parallel program are its *partition* or *grain-size*, *overheads due to communication* between computing agents and *how well the load is balanced* among the processors to keep them busy. Therefore, decomposing a program into a set of concurrent tasks that will run efficiently on all architectures is not easy. It is now believed that parallel machines built from closely coupled store/processor elements provide the most effective parallel structure [Watson et al. 87]. Parallel graph reduction machines such as ALICE [Cripps et al. 87], FLAGSHIP [Watson et al. 87] and GRIP [Peyton-Jones et al. 87] support mechanisms that automatically determine the dynamic allocation of processes to processors at run-time and contain general communication systems that allow an arbitrary pattern of communication to be realised.

2.1 Overheads of Parallel Execution

There are several overheads paid by parallel graph reduction machines against which the potential speed-up must be weighed:

Process Creation Cost: This involves building the *process descriptors* (*packets* in ALICE and FLAGSHIP) at either end of the rewrite process (i.e. before partitioning and after execution or suspension). The descriptors contain the information needed to execute a process. Similarly, after complete execution of a rewrite process, its descriptor must be removed and, if necessary, a value returned to the parent process that invoked it. The major components of this cost are the instruction executed and store accesses made to perform the actions.

Communication Cost: Communication costs between processors play a large role in the execution time of parallel programs. This may occur between tasks in order to provide synchronisation of share data. This may even involve accessing a shared variable or sending a message. In parallel graph reduction machines like ALICE, FLAGSHIP etc., one can view the computation as a single global graph manipulation, where sections of the graph are mapped on to physical processors. Communication need only occur when a particular operation overlaps the physical division of the global graph. Algorithm degradation can be severe due to communication costs both in terms of resource use and waiting delay.

Other Scheduling Costs: Every multiprocessor machine has its own scheduling (and non-scheduling) mechanisms. A cost is involved in the scheduling decision time, together with the accounting/ protection/ general context switching actions associated with a process change. In the FLAGSHIP machine, another cost is involved in scanning the packet to check that the conditions hold to allow the process to run to completion. This requires store accesses, tests etc. The different costs are also associated with a process suspension (saving state etc.), starting a new process (new stack etc.), re-starting a process (unsaving state) and some fixed penalty for remote access. If we move to a larger process size then some of these activities may involve more or less work but they should occur less often.

2.2 Granularity

An important issue in multiprocessor performance is the granularity of program execution. The *granularity of a parallel program* can be defined as the average size of a sequential unit of computation in the program, with no inter-processor synchronisations or communications. **Grain-size** is a measure of the complexity of primitive operations executed sequentially by a single processor (for example, the application of the fixed, primitive combinators in performing graph reductions).

The overheads of partitioning and scheduling begin to dominate when the **grain** of parallelism has become too fine, which suggests that we should aim for coarse-grain parallelism, even at the expense of some concurrency. On the other hand, if the grain becomes too coarse, each of these large grained tasks will take longer to execute, and the potential for exploiting parallelism will be reduced because each task may perform work serially that could actually be performed in parallel. In addition, we will probably incur greater process suspension penalties because of an increasing amount of state. So the major issue of partitioning is one of **granularity** i.e. how to choose an optimal grain-size for a particular host machine which can exploit useful parallelism. A program will execute efficiently if its average run-time granularity is large compared to the overhead of task creation, providing of course that enough parallelism has been preserved to achieve good load balancing.

2.3 Partitioning

The partition of a parallel program specifies the sequential units of computation in the program. For convenience, we call such a sequential unit of computation a *process*[1] (or *task*). A new (child) process can be created whenever a parent process discovers a strict application. But whether a fine-grained computation would prove worthwhile on a practical parallel machine when there is some administrative overhead cost associated with sparking, executing and completing a process, is debatable. In general, it is not possible to determine automatically when it is advantageous to send work to another processor. Although there are applications where a program can be partitioned into static process structures, generally the parallelism in functional programs is dynamic, and hence, most real problems have dynamic process creation. Partitioning can be performed at compile-time or postponed until run-time.

The target is to maximise (optimise) the grain-size, while still providing sufficient parallelism to exploit the machine's resources. Experience with graph reduction machine projects like ALICE and FLAGSHIP suggests that a process size should be of the order of a single user-defined function approximating to a single conditional, a single level of structure access or a single step of a recursion down a list. Generally, user-defined functions are more complex; breaking them down into smaller processes conflicts with the aims of the coarse-grained approach. Considering a single user-defined function as a process is the simplest approach to partitioning taken in the FLAGSHIP computational model and also in its extension to LAGER (Larger-Grain Graph Reduction) [Watson 88].

Another approach, a goal of this research, is to detect how long the evaluation of a sub-expression will take with the help of complexity analysis at compile-time, and if the overheads associated with the spawning of this sub-expression are not less than the time taken to perform that computation, there is no point in partitioning it for remote evaluation. The programs with complex data structures (like lists, trees etc.) generally have significant communication overheads. It is unreasonable to expect the machine to do this detection automatically, since it may require a considerable amount of mathematical expertise. It seems desirable, therefore, that the programmer should be allowed to *annotate* the program with complexity information. Large parallel machines are aimed at supporting real problems with large data sets – *asymptotic complexity analysis* should be favoured to detect an appropriate grain. In the cases where problems are small, it should be based on comparison of accurate run-time statistics.

2.4 Scheduling

The scheduling problem is to assign tasks in the partitioned program to various processors, so as to minimise the parallel execution time. The parallel execution time depends on processor utilisation and on the overhead of inter-processor communication. Several hardware dynamic scheduling techniques could be incorporated to find out the most optimal schedule for a program in a machine, which might be time consuming. The scheduling problem becomes more difficult when considering communication overheads with arbitrary data sizes. It also involves a trade-off between parallelism and these overheads. Parallelism dictates that processes should be assigned to different processors as much as possible. But the communication overhead is reduced when processes are assigned to the same processor. This trade-off has to be chosen carefully for optimal multiprocessor scheduling. Significant effort should be made in the direction of reducing the current scheduling overheads at the same time as increasing the grain-size.

In this paper, we will also show, with the help of some examples, that the overall parallel execution time of a parent process can be minimised if the compiler schedules the sub-processes in some particular order (priority) of their relative time complexities. This information of *relative complexity* can be supplied by the programmer or detected automatically by the compiler, if a sound and efficient automatic complexity analyser is developed.

3.0 Analysis of Optimal Parallelism

In this analysis, similar to [Goldberg 88], we are assuming that at any instant (during run-time scheduling), there are enough processors to share the newly generated parallel workload (sub-processes), while in a practical machine, it is possible that all processors are busy doing some work which might finish sooner or later. In this case, dynamic load balancing mechanisms play an important role in spawning these generated sub-processes to the processors as soon as they become free. Let us define some terms which we are going to use frequently in our analysis:

$T_{seq}(Exp)=$ Time taken if *Exp* is evaluated sequentially on one processor only,

---

1. Generally speaking, a process is a logical processor that executes code sequentially and has its own state and data. Processes are created either implicitly by their declaration or explicitly by some create construct.

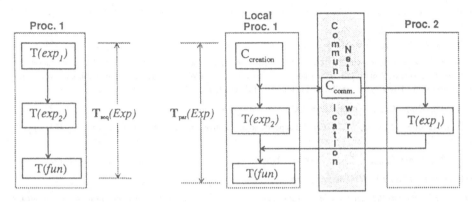

Figure 1 Evaluation of $Exp = fun (exp_1, exp_2)$

$T_{par}(Exp)$= Time taken if Exp is evaluated in parallel on many processors, assuming that there are enough processors for the needs of the program.

$T(exp)$ = Minimum (sequential or parallel) execution time of an expression exp.

$C_{creation}$ = Time spent by the local processor in creating (and spawning) a sub-process. It may vary from process to process, and actually depends on the implementation. For convenience, we assume it to be a constant for all processes.

C_{comm} = Cost of communication delay (latency) i.e. time elapsed between sending a message (sub-process) and receiving it on the remote processor. For simplicity, we assume that it will also incorporate the cost of receiving the return value of the completed process. We assume it to be a constant for the processes using atomic data. In the case of complex data structures, it will depend on the copying mechanisms used in the underlying architecture.

Parallel evaluation is better than sequential only if $T_{par}(Exp)$ is less than $T_{seq}(Exp)$.

Before it can be evaluated, a functional program must be compiled into a graph. The graph is then repeatedly transformed to a simpler form with the help of **reductions** until it reaches its *normal form*. These reductions may take place concurrently at different sites in the graph. A redex might be shared in the graph. The computational model must be able to deal with sharing and know when a combinator has all the arguments it requires for execution.

3.1 Function with two arguments

Let us assume that our expression, Exp, is an application of function, fun, to two strict arguments exp_1 and exp_2. We assume that a common sub-expression (if any) shared between exp_1 and exp_2 is computed to normal form beforehand (in fact this is taken care of by the static compiled code).

$$Exp = fun (exp_1, exp_2)$$

If it is computed sequentially then

$$T_{seq}(Exp) = T(exp_1) + T(exp_2) + T(fun) \quad \dots\dots\dots\dots\dots\dots\dots\dots\dots\dots\dots\dots\dots\dots\dots\dots\dots\dots\dots\dots\dots(1)[1]$$

If a sub-process exp_1 is sent to another remote processor for parallel evaluation, there will be some cost involved in creating it[2]. We have already defined this cost as $C_{creation}$. The second sub-process exp_2 will be kept by the first (local) processor and will start its evaluation only after exp_1 has been exported. There will also be some cost, C_{comm}, mainly due to the communication delay

---

1. It does not matter whether exp_1 or exp_2 is computed first in a functional program which has no side-effects.
2. In sequential evaluation, sub-processes are not created (so no cost is involved), instead they are evaluated on a first-come-first-served basis.

(and also little scheduling and unpacking costs – for simplicity let us assume that both of them have also been included in C_{comm}). So the execution time will be

$$T_{par}(Exp) = C_{creation} + \max(T(exp_2), C_{comm} + T(exp_1)) + T(fun) \quad \dots\dots\dots\dots\dots\dots\dots\dots\dots (2)$$

These two sequential and parallel execution time equations *(1 & 2)* are clear from Figure 1. Firstly, we concentrate on the parallel evaluation only. What if processor 1 keeps exp_1 instead of exp_2? Well, the execution time in this case, when $T(exp_2)$ and $T(exp_1)$ are swapped over in the parallel evaluation part of Figure 1, will be

$$T'_{par}(Exp) = C_{creation} + \max(T(exp_1), C_{comm} + T(exp_2)) + T(fun) \quad \dots\dots\dots\dots\dots\dots\dots\dots (3)$$

Which is better – $T_{par}(Exp)$ or $T'_{par}(Exp)$? It depends on the relative time complexities of exp_1 and exp_2. If $T(exp_2) \geq T(exp_1)$ then

$$T'_{par}(Exp) = C_{creation} + C_{comm} + T(exp_2) + T(fun) \quad \dots\dots\dots\dots\dots\dots\dots\dots\dots\dots\dots\dots from (3)$$

which shows $T'_{par}(Exp) \geq T_{par}(Exp)$ in every case.

⇒ *To minimise the parallel execution time of $Exp = fun(exp_1, exp_2)$, the least complex argument should be evaluated remotely.*

Now our next concern is under what conditions this parallel evaluation time $T_{par}(Exp)$ is better (less) than $T_{seq}(Exp)$.

$$T_{seq}(Exp) = T(exp_1) + T(exp_2) + T(fun)$$

$$T_{par}(Exp) = C_{creation} + \max(T(exp_2), C_{comm} + T(exp_1)) + T(fun)$$

$T_{par}(Exp) \leq T_{seq}(Exp)$ holds for the following two cases:

$$\text{i) } C_{comm} + T(exp_1) \leq T(exp_2) \text{ and } C_{creation} \leq T(exp_1) \quad \dots\dots\dots\dots\dots\dots\dots\dots cond. 1$$

or

$$\text{ii) } C_{comm} + T(exp_1) > T(exp_2) \text{ and } C_{creation} + C_{comm} \leq T(exp_2) \quad \dots\dots\dots\dots cond. 2$$

If the cost of creating a sub-process is greater than its actual execution time, it is not sensible at all to go for parallel execution. But if it is otherwise and we decide to go parallel by exporting the first sub-process, then it is worthwhile if it is evaluated before the second one is finished and the cost of creating the exported sub-process is not greater than the cost of executing the sub-process itself. The second condition is also self-explanatory – do not go parallel if the overheads (creation of sub-process and then communication) are more than your own (local) sub-process.

3.2 Function with multiple arguments

Here we will perform a similar analysis for the function, fun, with multiple arguments $exp_1, exp_2, \dots, exp_n$. Our expression Exp is $Exp = fun (exp_1, exp_2, \dots, exp_n)$. Sequential evaluation time will be equal to the sum of all the evaluations of sub-expressions $exp_1, exp_2, \dots, exp_n$ plus the time spent in function application after evaluating all the arguments. The ordering of exp_i is not very important in this case.

$$T (Exp) = T(exp_1) + T(exp_2) + \dots + T(exp_n) + T(fun)$$

$$\text{or} \quad = \sum_{i=1}^{n} T(exp_i) + T(fun) \quad \dots\dots\dots\dots\dots\dots\dots\dots\dots\dots (4)$$

Let us assume that *fun* is strict in all its arguments, and hence they can be evaluated in parallel. If they are all sent to remote processors in left to right order, then the parallel evaluation time equation will be

$$T_{par}(Exp) \quad = \max(C_{creation} + C_{comm} + T(exp_1), 2C_{creation} + C_{comm} + T(exp_2), \dots ,$$

$$nC_{creation} + C_{comm} + T(exp_n)) + T(fun) \quad \dots\dots\dots\dots\dots\dots\dots\dots (5)$$

It is quite obvious that the first sub-process is spawned after time $C_{creation}$, the second sub-process after $2C_{creation}$, and so on. The last sub-process exp_n is spawned to the processor n, and will start evaluation after $nC_{creation}$.

Our practical experience says that in order to minimise the parallel execution time (in this case of multiple sub-processes), spawning of these arguments should be done in *decreasing order* of their time complexities. We will show how this can be supported by theoretical reasoning. Consider, for example, for arguments exp_i and exp_j $(j > i)$, if $T(exp_i) \geq T(exp_j)$ then, from experience, exp_i should be spawned before exp_j. In this case, when exp_i is spawned before exp_j, the parallel evaluation time will be

$$T_{par}(Exp) = \max(\dots, iC_{creation} + C_{comm} + T(exp_i), \dots, jC_{creation} + C_{comm} + T(exp_j), \dots,$$

$$nC_{creation} + C_{comm} + T(exp_n)) + T(fun) \quad \dots\dots\dots\dots\dots\dots\dots\dots\dots\dots\dots (6)$$

or $\quad T_{par}(Exp) = \max(t_1, \dots, t_i, \dots, t_j \dots, t_n) + T(fun)$

where, for $1 \leq i \leq n$, $t_i = iC_{creation} + C_{comm} + T(exp_i)$ $\quad \dots\dots\dots\dots\dots\dots\dots\dots\dots\dots\dots (6.1)$

What will happen if we do the opposite? The parallel evaluation time, when exp_j is spawned before exp_i and they exchange positions, will be

$$T'_{par}(Exp) = \max(\dots, iC_{creation} + C_{comm} + T(exp_j), \dots, jC_{creation} + C_{comm} + T(exp_i), \dots,$$

$$nC_{creation} + C_{comm} + T(exp_n)) + T(fun) \quad \dots\dots\dots\dots\dots\dots\dots\dots\dots\dots (7)$$

or $\quad T'_{par}(Exp) = \max(t_1, \dots, \ell_i, \dots, \ell_j \dots, t_n) + T(fun) \dots\dots\dots\dots\dots\dots\dots\dots (7.1)$

where $\ell_i = iC_{creation} + C_{comm} + T(exp_j)$ and $\ell_j = jC_{creation} + C_{comm} + T(exp_i)$

Except for the associated spawning costs of exp_i and exp_j, other terms in equation (6) are the same as in equation (7). If we closely look at equations (6) and (7), we find that

$$\ell_j \geq \ell_i \text{ and } \ell_j \geq t_i \text{ and } \ell_j \geq t_j \text{ since } T(exp_i) \geq T(exp_j) \text{ and } j > i$$

or $\quad \max(\ell_i, \ell_j) \geq \max(t_i, t_j)$ for two arbitrary i and j.

This will be true in general (for $i < j$, $T(exp_i) \geq T(exp_j)$). From this we conclude that $T'_{par}(Exp)$ will always be greater than (or equal to) $T_{par}(Exp)$. So there is no benefit in spawning the complex sub-process after a simple one. The conclusion of all this is:

$\Rightarrow$ *The execution time is minimised when the arguments are spawned in decreasing order of their time complexities.*

Now we have to look again for the conditions under which parallel evaluation is better than sequential. Let us assume that the arguments are spawned off in decreasing order of their complexities, i.e. $T(exp_i) \geq T(exp_{i+1})$ for all $i < n$. Suppose that the mth process contributes towards the maximum time in equation (6), i.e.

$$mC_{creation} + C_{comm} + T(exp_m) \geq iC_{creation} + C_{comm} + T(exp_i) \text{ for all } i \leq n.$$

In this case, $\quad T_{par}(Exp) = mC_{creation} + C_{comm} + T(exp_m) + T(fun)$

and it will be less than $T_{seq}(Exp) = \sum_{i=1}^{n} T(exp_i) + T(fun)$ if and only if $mC_{creation} + C_{comm} \leq \sum_{\substack{i=1 \\ i \neq m}}^{n} T(exp_i)$

It means that the overhead costs associated with the most expensive branch (in parallel) should be less than the sum of the evaluation times of the rest of the sub-processes.

In the above analysis we have assumed that all the sub-processes have been spawned to remote processors. After $nC_{creation}$, the local processor will become free and might be idle for some time (unless it gets some work from any of the other processors). So to exploit parallelism in a better way, one of the strict arguments ($exp_1, exp_2, \dots, exp_n$) should be evaluated locally (an approach taken in the LAGER model), while the rest of the arguments should still be spawned off in decreasing order of complexities. A reasonable heuristic is that *if C_{comm} is very high compared to $nC_{creation}$ then the most complex argument should be kept for local evaluation – if not, then the least complex one should be kept for local evaluation.*

Limitations: This simple analysis considers the expressions whose subsequent computation threads are not interrupted by other factors. The analysis would be very different and difficult if we consider the cases where sharing of the results of sub-expressions occurs and affects the evaluation time of a suspended process waiting for its result to arrive. In a pure *lazy* functional language this might take place quite often where expressions are evaluated only once and according to the need. It is difficult, in general, to exploit parallelism in lazy programs.

Another limitation is that the analysis also needs exact estimations of time quantities mentioned in the above equations, which is not viable in general at compile-time. Even so, we have verified this analysis with various examples by changing the order of spawning of sub-processes based on their *relative time complexity* information. In the case of simple user-defined (non-recursive) functions it is easy to find out by counting and comparing the number of primitive operations in their respective function bodies. The cost of creation of a process is also estimated roughly by counting the number of machine operations needed. It depends on the number of arguments in the function.

The complexity analysis problem is undecidable in general, but there have been a few efforts to solve the problem for restricted cases [Wegbreit 75, Le Métayer 88, Rosendahl 89]. We have addressed the topic of how to obtain the complexity information in [Maheshwari 90], which also presents a survey of work done for the automisation of time complexity analyses.

4.0 Grain-size Control in LAGER

The LAGER model of computation is a packet-based graph reduction system with large packet rewrites [Watson 89, Wong 89]. A packet rewrite, which consists of several reductions, may be suspended if it has to wait for a remote data packet or has to activate an unevaluated argument. The whole computation is comprised of two different levels – the packet evaluation and the stack evaluation. A top-level active packet, an initial function supplied with a set of arguments, starts execution by creating an environment where the required function call is evaluated on the stack. Parallel processes are created (if necessary) in the form of packets with the help of special code inserted at compile-time. In a basic model of LAGER (a closely-coupled machine), the scheduling of these parallel packets (kept in a pool) is done dynamically at run-time, depending on the busyness of the machine – a parallel packet might be fetched back by the same processor if the rest of the machine is busy. Other processors looking for work *steal* these packets from the pool and evaluate them in parallel.

The execution time of a (parallel) program is the measurement of the maximum cycles among all the processors until the program terminates to its normal form. The grain-size of a rewrite is the total number of machine instructions executed during its evaluation. The control of parallelism is dynamic, as the model also introduces sequentiality in a rewrite by keeping its parallel (child) packet for local evaluation on the same stack. Or we can say, a rewrite self-adjusts its grain. It is difficult to measure how the grain-size of an individual rewrite changes when the program actually runs on a machine with a limited number of processors, though we can get some indication of it by the notion of average **granularity** of all the rewrites which occurred in a program.

Our example programs are written in the functional language HOPE[+] and the results shown are their various runs on two event-driven (original and enhanced [Wong 89]) simulators of LAGER. The compilation route from HOPE[+] to the target LAGER code is via FPM (Functional Programming Machine) code. It simply lifts all user-defined or higher-order functions on a first-come-first-served basis in the body of the (parent) strict function.

5.0 Examples and Results

We have discussed in [Maheshwari 90] how *divide-and-conquer* algorithms can be run efficiently using complexity information on LAGER. Here we present some other example programs. The results are presented in tables and graphs. A **Rewrite** is either a new creation of a packet (closure/process) or a re-activation of a suspended packet. For the readers who are very well aware of *processes*, it is actually the number of context-switchings in the whole machine. The number of **Instructions** gives the total number of machine instructions executed in the whole machine. Execution **Time** of a (parallel) program is the measurement of maximum cycles among all the processors until the program terminates to the normal form. Average **Granularity** = Instructions ÷ Rewrites. The last column **Idle** gives the average percentage (%) of time all the processors are idle.

5.1 Multiple Recursive Function

Version 1 (decreasing order of time complexities)

```
dec add3: num # num # num -> num;
--- add3(x, y, z) <= x + y + z;
dec fun: num -> num;
--- fun(n) <= if (n < 3) then 0 else add3(fun(n-1), fun(n-2), fun(n-3));
fun(20);
```

The function add3 is strict in all three arguments which implies that fun(n-1), fun(n-2) and fun(n-3) can be evaluated safely in parallel – but in what optimal order should they be spawned? In the above program, first fun(n-1) and then fun(n-2) are spawned for parallel evaluation. It is only then that fun(n-3) is evaluated locally. This is because of the static nature of compiler-code generation. If we change this order of scheduling at compile-time, the program's result will not be affected because of the commutativity and associativity of '+' in the definition of add3. The various runs (with different orders of static scheduling, made explicitly by hand) are made on the enhanced version of the event-driven LAGER simulator and the results are shown in the following table:

Processors	Rewrites	Instructions	Messages	Time	Speed-up	Granularity	Idle(%)
1	1	2138116	0	17447275	1.00	2138116	0.00
2	13	2138182	12	8728695	2.00	164475	0.03
4	1276	2145349	1248	4543499	3.84	1681	1.76
8	8062	2183950	7622	2699829	6.46	270	7.13
16	13809	2217687	13016	1546729	11.28	160	10.91
32	21400	2262043	20062	884149	19.73	105	13.05

Table 1 (Run of **Version 1** of Multiple Recursive Function on the enhanced LAGER)

Version 2 (Increasing order of time complexities)

```
--- fun(n) <= if (n < 3) then 0 else add3(fun(n-3), fun(n-2), fun(n-1));
fun(20);
```

Here firstly fun (n-3) and then fun (n-2) are put in the packet pool; fun (n-1) is kept for local evaluation. Here the sub-expressions are spawned in the increasing order of their time complexities. The following results also verify that this is the worst case:

Processors	Rewrites	Instructions	Messages	Time	Speed-up	Granularity	Idle(%)
1	1	2138116	0	17447275	1.00	2138116	0.00
2	828	2144253	1180	9167023	1.90	2589	2.04
4	4011	2166012	5046	5148916	3.39	540	5.86
8	14106	2233680	16758	3465431	5.03	158	13.38
16	24665	2306627	29378	2282677	7.64	93	20.07
32	32802	2364921	39804	1433797	12.17	72	26.71

Table 2 (Run of **Version 2** of Multiple Recursive Function on the enhanced LAGER)

Version 3 (an Intermediate case)

```
--- fun(n) <= if (n < 3) then 0 else add3(fun(n-2), fun(n-3), fun(n-1));
fun(20);
```

Here firstly fun (n-2) and then fun (n-3) are put in the packet pool; fun (n-1) is kept for local evaluation.

Processors	Rewrites	Instructions	Messages	Time	Speed-up	Granularity	Idle(%)
1	1	2138116	0	17447275	1.00	2138116	0.00
2	256	2140054	374	8874030	1.97	8359	0.78
4	2935	2158339	3628	4928529	3.54	735	4.16
8	11898	2218827	14030	3245052	5.38	186	11.77
16	17479	2256646	20396	1907121	9.15	129	16.17
32	27781	2328022	32946	1250785	13.95	83	23.23

Table 3 (Run of **Version 3** of Multiple Recursive Function on the enhanced LAGER)

The results of Table 1 support our argument of section 3.2 that in the case of functions with more than two arguments, the sub-processes should be spawned in decreasing order of their time complexities. We know intuitively (which can also be proven formally) that $T(\text{fun}(n-1)) \geq T(\text{fun}(n-2)) \geq T(\text{fun}(n-3))$ for any positive n in any version of the above programs. The improvement is due to better processor utilisation in the first version of the program. In this function fun of three arguments, there are three more intermediate cases of different orderings with results similar to Version 3.

5.2 Union of two lists

Here, we will discuss an interesting program which gives us the union of two lists. First of all, it is interesting to realise that our union program exploits a different kind of parallelism which is, in general, not clearly visible in the program written in a simple manner. Then, we present our reasoning, based on the complexity of the user-defined functions, about what should be executed remotely and what locally for better efficiency. The union program is as below:

```
dec union: list(num)#list(num)->list(num) ;
dec member: num#list(num)->truval ;
--- union(nil,ys)    <= ys ;
--- union(x::xs,ys) <= if member(x,ys) then union(xs,ys) else x::union(xs,ys) ;
```

```
--- member(_,nil)     <= false ;
--- member(x,l::ls)   <= if x=l then true else member(x,ls) ;
dec randnos: num -> list(num) ;
--- randnos(n) <= if (n = 0) then nil else ((n*27317) mod 3581)::randnos(n-1) ;
union(randnos(250),randnos(200))  ;
```

The second clause in the definition of `union` is the source of vertical parallelism. A simple compiler cannot detect the parallelism if written in this way. Both the instances of `union(xs,ys)` would be treated separately and they would be reached only after testing the boolean flag (`member(x,ys)`). Because `union(xs,ys)` appears in both the branches of if-then-else, it will definitely be computed. So it is quite clear from the definition of the `union` function, `member(x,ys)` and `union(xs,ys)` can be evaluated in parallel in any order with no side-effects. The vertical parallelism is exploited in this example because the child `member` function can be evaluated in parallel to the parent `union` function. If we write `union` as below:

```
--- union(nil,ys)    <= ys ;
--- union(x::xs,ys)  <= let is_member == member(x,ys) in
                        if is_member then union_of_rest
                        else x::union_of_rest where union_of_rest == union(xs,ys);
```

then, the compiler generates the code for `union(xs,ys)` (= `union_of_rest`) only once. Now, we need some annotation [Darlington et al. 89] to guide the compiler in which user-defined function should be built as a packet for remote evaluation – `member(x,ys)` or `union(xs,ys)`. Both user-defined functions are recursive (not primitive) and, hence, considered as equally potential candidates for larger-grain execution. In the LAGER scheme, one has to be kept in the main body of the function for local (sequential) evaluation. The following observations and systematic reasoning help us in choosing the right function for remote evaluation:

1. Sequential Time Complexity: The upperbound time complexity of the above program is computable by Rosendahl's automatic complexity analyser [Rosendahl 89]. Note that the time consumed by `member(x,l::ls)` is not fixed (constant) and is $O(m)$ (m is the length of list) in the worst-case, when the whole list is traversed.

The upperbound time complexity of `union(n,m)` = $4+19*n+12*n*m$ where n and m are the lengths (sizes) of two lists.

Asymptotic complexity of `union(n,m)` = $O(n*m)$,   when n and m are very large.

Observation: Of course, for very large n and m, both the lists contribute equally to the asymptotic complexity function, but it is clear from the definition of `union` that it terminates only when the first list becomes empty (`nil`). So, the first complexity *measure*, n, is dominating. Another important observation is that it also determines the amount of parallelism in the definition of the `union` function.

2. Relative Time Complexity: It is clear that, for large n, $T_{seq}(union(xs,ys)) > T_{seq}(member(x,ys))$ in the right hand side of the second clause of the `union` definition; `union(xs,ys)` calls `member(x,ys)` (n–1) times.

3. `member(x,ys)` as a packet for remote evaluation: In the case of two potentially parallel processes, the less complex process should be sent for remote evaluation, while the other should be evaluated locally to minimise the parallel evaluation time. So, from the above simple reasoning of relative complexity, we know that `member(x,ys)` should be built as a process for remote evaluation; and then `union(xs,ys)` should be done locally in the main body as a sequential thread to increase the granularity. The results have been verified experimentally.

If, alternatively, we annotate `union(xs,ys)` for remote evaluation on some processor, then the parallel execution time increases, not only because it is more complex in time compared with `member(x,ys)`, but also because of copying (and re-copying) both the list structures to that remote processor. The communication overheads of non-local copying of data structures (two lists) are more in this case, which obviously mars the performance of parallel execution. Network messages were increased tremendously and processors were idle for more time. We can see from the definition of the `union` function that the communication complexity $C_{comm}(union(xs,ys))$ is $O(n+m)$ when computed remotely, while $C_{comm}(member(x,ys))$ is only $O(m)$. Moreover, `member(x,ys)` returns only a boolean value, while `union(xs,ys)` returns a computed list after successful computation. In short, we can say that the copying overheads involved with `union(xs,ys)` are much more than that of `member(x,ys)`.

4. Results: The results of union of two random lists of length 250 and 200 have been shown in Figures 2 and 3 – using a page

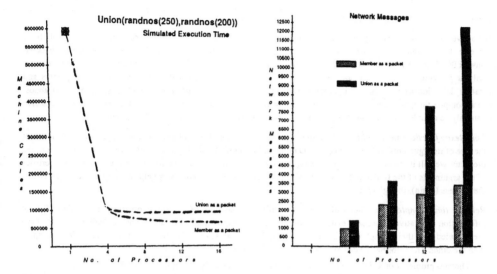

Figure 2 Execution Time and Network Messages of `union` function on the original LAGER

copying mechanism on the original LAGER simulator. Not only is the simulated time reduced (though slightly!), there is also a good saving in network messages. The first time-curve or message-bar in Figure 2 shows the results of a run when `member` was built as a packet; the second one shows the results when `union` was built as a packet. Figure 3 shows the improvements on the average granularity and cuts on the non-local accesses. As long as, there are any two huge lists, and passed to the parent `union` function, we conclude by saying that it is better to evaluate `member` remotely.

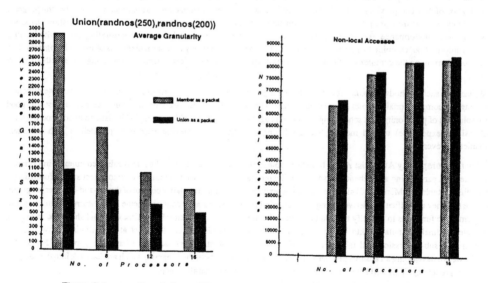

Figure 3 Average Granularity and Non-local Accesses of `union` function on the original LAGER

Another observation from the execution time curves is that the execution of this program is not efficient beyond 16 processors. So there is no point in engaging more processors, which unnecessarily increases the volume of traffic on the communication network without making an efficient use of resources. In a multiprogramming environment, these extra (beyond 16) processors can be used to do some other useful work for different programs. In the future, we are going to develop analysis to find out the optimal number of processors to run (efficiently) a given program with some input data.

6.0 Summary of the Requirements

In the above examples, we simply assume that the complexity function of each user-defined function is available from somewhere else. The derivation of such complexity functions is mechanisable to some extent, which we have discussed in detail in [Maheshwari 90]. The logic behind the method of partitioning and ordered scheduling to control the grain-size is based on a simple analysis presented in section 3, and requires exact estimations of sequential execution time of the process and communication delay incurred in sending it to the remote processor. Exact estimation of any of these quantities is almost impossible at compile-time, hence we have to compromise by asymptotic estimations. Especially, the grain-size of a recursive function can only be completely determined at run-time. In particular we require the following information:

- *Complexity functions in closed-form.* Traditionally, asymptotic complexity of a function is expressed by a function of the size of its arguments with the help of big-O notation, e.g. $O(n)$, $O(n^2)$, $O(\log_2 n)$,... etc., where 'n' is the size of the problem; we call it the *measure* of complexity. In a recursive function, the grain-size depends on the characteristics of the arguments of the function. So, in fact, this notion of asymptotic complexity helps us in determining the size of the process (grain), though crudely.

- *Relative time complexities.* This will decide the order of spawning of the sub-expressions at run-time. By the information of relative time complexities of two or more sub-expressions of a parent function here we mean to have the knowledge of their complexities in such a fashion that we can say confidently that one is more (or less) complex than the other. The information can also be obtained by *profiling*.

  The sub-problems of a divide-and-conquer algorithm are basically an application of the same (parent) function recursively on a reduced data size. The division of the input argument (complexity measure in this case) at run-time should be able to tell us which sub-problem is more complex than the other.

- *Communication overheads.* In programs using complex data structures, bad partitioning may ruin the whole gain of remote evaluation of some part of the program. Careful decisions should be taken, keeping the communication overheads in mind. Hence, the estimation of communication complexity is also essential in such programs. How a multiprocessor maintains the locality of data structures, a hard problem, will determine the volume of communication.

7.0 Conclusion

We have been able to point out that some parallel programs can be mapped in an optimal way on any multiprocessor with the information of time complexities of its sub-expressions and also communication complexities occurring between the program modules. Even without measuring the exact execution times of sub-processes or their creation or communication costs, we achieve an overall performance gain. In this paper, we have presented experimental results demonstrating how methods using complexity information, combined with run-time tests, can increase the efficiency of a particular class of parallel programs. The difficulty of determining the complexity of functions successfully in all cases restricts us from incorporating these methods in the compiler.

We can call such methods *heuristics* for optimal mapping of processes on a multiprocessor because of the extreme difficulty in knowing the computational complexity at compile-time. The encouraging results obtained in this research suggest that good quality solutions of partitioning and scheduling a parallel program can be expected from simple heuristic methods, and from the useful insight (experience) toward meeting the conflicting objectives of achieving maximum parallelism with minimum communication overhead.

Need for the Complexity Analysis: As we have been able to show in this paper, even the relative time complexity information is quite useful in partitioning and scheduling some parallel programs. We now need to find out how to detect such information at compile-time. [Rabhi and Manson 90] also use time complexity functions for granularity control of divide-and-conquer programs, but realise that they are difficult to derive. [King and Soper 90] report a granularity control scheme for concurrent logic programs using asymptotic functions to quantify the computation and communication in coalescing grains. Our goal should be to find the appropriate (optimal) granularity into which a program should be partitioned, i.e. to detect at compile-time, how long the evaluation of a sub-expression will take. Profiling estimates (run-time statistics) can lead to a better partition [Sarkar 89]. Presently, we are developing an abstract profiler to collect useful statistics about the program, which are fed back into the compiler after careful processing. This will help the compiler to produce an optimal parallel code.

References

[Allen et al. 86] R. Allen, K. Kennedy, and A. Porterfield. *PTOOL: A semi-automatic parallel programming assistant.* Proceedings of the International Conference on Parallel Processing, 164-170, 1986.

[Appelbe et al. 89] B. Appelbe, K. Smith, C.E. McDowell. *Start/Pat: A parallel-programming toolkit.* IEEE Software, 6(4):29-38, 1989.

[Arvind et al. 88] Arvind, D.E. Culler, G.K. Maa. *Assessing the benefits of grain parallelism in dataflow programs.* The International Journal of Supercomputer Applications, 2 (3):10-36, 1988.

[Babb 84] R.G. Babb. *Parallel processing with large-grain dataflow techniques.* IEEE Computer, 7:55-61, 1984.

[Backus 78] J. Backus. *Can programming be liberated from the von Neumann Style? A Functional Style and its Algebra of Programs.* Comm. ACM, Vol. 21, No. 8, pp. 613-641, August 1978.

[Cripps et al. 87] M.D. Cripps, J. Darlington, A.J. Field, P.G. Harrison, and M. Reeve. *The Design and Implementation of ALICE: A Parallel Graph Reduction Machine.* In Selected Reprints on Dataflow and Reduction Architectures, Shreekant Thakkar (Ed.), IEEE Computer Society Press, 1987.

[Darlington et al. 89] J. Darlington, M. Reeve, and S. Wright. *Declarative Languages and Program Transformation for Programming Parallel Systems: A Case Study.* Department of Computing, Imperial College, London 1989.

[Goldberg 88] B. Goldberg. *Multiprocessor Execution of Functional Programs.* Ph.D. Thesis, YALEU/DCS/RR-618, Department of Computer Science, Yale University, April 1988.

[King and Soper 90] A. King and P. Soper. *Granularity Control of Concurrent Logic Programs.* Technical Report CSTR-90-6, Department of Electronics and Computer Science, Southampton University, Southampton, March 1990.

[Le Métayer 88] D. Le Métayer. ACE: *An automatic complexity evaluator.* ACM Transactions on Programming Languages and Systems, Vol. 10, No. 2, pages 248-266, April 1988.

[Maheshwari 90] Piyush Maheshwari. *Controlling Parallelism in Functional Programs using Complexity Information.* Ph.D. Thesis, Department of Computer Science, University of Manchester, submitted October 1990.

[Peyton-Jones 87] S.L. Peyton-Jones. *The Implementation of Functional Programming Languages.* Prentice-Hall International, 1987.

[Peyton-Jones et al. 87] S.L. Peyton-Jones, C.D. Clack, J. Salkild, and M. Hardie. *GRIP – A High-performance Architecture for Parallel Graph Reduction.* Proceeding 1988 Conference on Functional Programming Languages and Computer Architecture, Springer-Verlag, LNCS 274, September 1987.

[Rabhi and Manson 90] F. Rabhi and G.A. Manson. *Using Complexity Functions to Control Parallelism in Functional Programs.* Technical Report CS-90-1, Department of Computer Science, University of Sheffield, Sheffield, 1990.

[Rosendahl 89] M. Rosendahl. *Automatic Complexity analysis.* In Proceedings Conference on Functional Programming Languages and Computer Architectures, London, ACM Press, September 1989.

[Sarkar 89] Vivek Sarkar. *Partitioning and Scheduling Parallel Programs for Multiprocessors.* Pitman, London and the MIT Press, Cambridge, Massachusetts, 1989. In the series, Research Monographs in Parallel and Distributed Computing.

[Watson 88] Ian Watson. *Lager - Interim Report.* Ref. No. FS/MU/IW/026-88. Department of Computer Science, University of Manchester, November 1988.

[Watson 89] Ian Watson. *Simulation of a Physical EDS Machine Architecture.* EDS Internal Report, Department of Computer Science, University of Manchester, October 1989.

[Watson et al. 87] I. Watson, J. Sargeant, P. Watson, and J.V. Woods. *Flagship Computational Models and Machine Architecture.* In ICL Technical Journal, Vol. 5, No. 3, May 1987.

[Wegbreit 75] B. Wegbreit. *Mechanical program analysis.* Comm. ACM, 18, 9:528-539, September, 1975.

[Wong 89] P.S. Wong. *Parallel Implementation Techniques for Efficient Declarative Systems.* Ph.D. Interim Report, Department of Computer Science, University of Manchester, November 1989.

SUBTREE AVAILABILITY IN BINARY TREE ARCHITECTURES

RAVI MITTAL

Department of Computer Science and Engineering
Indian Institute of Technology, Madras, 600 036, INDIA

BIJENDRA N. JAIN

Department of Computer Science and Engineering
Indian Institute of Technology, Delhi, 110 016, INDIA

RAKESH K. PATNEY

Department of Electrical Engineering
Indian Institute of Technology, Delhi, 110 016, INDIA

Abstract

In this paper we have studied fault tolerance of a full binary tree in terms of availability of non-faulty (full) subtrees. When an unaugmented full binary tree is faulty, then the computation can be carried out on the largest available non-faulty (full) binary subtree.

It is shown that the minimum number of faulty nodes required to destroy all subtrees of height h in a full binary tree of height n is given as $f_{bt}(n, h) = \lfloor (2^n-1)/(2^h-1) \rfloor$. It follows that the availability of a non-faulty subtree of height $h = n-w$, in an n level full binary tree containing u faulty nodes, can be ensured, where w is the smallest integer such that $u \leq 2^w$.

An algorithm which evaluates whether a given set of faulty nodes will destroy all subtrees of some specified height, is given. This algorithm can also evaluate the largest available non-faulty subtree in a faulty full binary tree. We also study the availability of a non-faulty subtree in some augmented binary tree architectures.

1. Introduction

A full binary tree is an efficient communication network, whose any two nodes exchange information in $O(\log N)$ time, where N is the total number nodes. The binary tree is expandable, and is thus considered to be an attractive and useful interconnection network [1-5]. However, its fault tolerance is low, since there exists only one path between any pair of nodes. Thus, in the presence of a single fault the tree may be disconnected.

To improve the fault tolerance of binary tree architectures, various networks based on augmentation of a full binary tree with redundant nodes (processors) and links, have been proposed [4-7]. In an augmented tree architecture, the rigid tree structure is maintained even in the presence of node faults. The redundant links and nodes are used to replace faulty nodes and links in the tree so as to maintain its binary tree topology.

The augmented binary tree architectures can be reconfigured only when the number of faults is limited. If the number of faulty nodes in an augmented binary tree is large then it will not be possible to reconfigure the faulty tree into a non-faulty full binary tree (of the same height). In which case, a largest non-faulty (full) binary subtree may be identified and used for computation. In this paper, we study availability of non-faulty binary subtrees in a full binary tree or an augmented tree architecture.

It is known that many of the basic algorithms for universal networks (such as n-cube, shuffle-exchange, binary tree, etc.) have the property that they can be formulated with the size of the network as a parameter of the algorithm. Thus, algorithms can invariably be executed efficiently on a subnetwork of the same topology with some slow-down factor [8]. For example, many fundamental algorithms designed for execution on a full binary tree of height n can be modified to run on a non-faulty subtree of height d, where d < n.

If a full binary tree contains faulty nodes/links then its non-faulty subtrees can be identified for possible use. The size of the largest possible non-faulty subtree depends on the number of faulty nodes and their locations in the network. In this paper we find out the size of the largest available non-faulty subtree when a full binary tree contains a given combination of faulty nodes. We also evaluate the minimum number of faulty nodes required to make all subtrees of a given height faulty. The binary tree considered here is rigid, i.e., interconnections between nodes are fixed. Also, the fault model assumes only permanent faults in nodes. Since the probability of a node failure is much higher than that of a link failure, only node failures have been considered in this study.

A *subtree* of height h, which originates from node j, is referred to as $ST_h(j)$. A subtree is considered to be faulty if it contains at least one faulty node. A *Fault set* is defined as a set whose elements correspond to indices of faulty nodes in the tree. If nodes of a fault set of a full binary tree of height n are such that they destroy all subtrees of height h then the fault set is known as *critical fault set* or CFS(n, h).

For given values of n and h, a *minimum critical fault set* MCFS(n, h) is defined as a critical fault set CFS(n, h) with minimum cardinality. Thus, $|MCFS(n, h)| = f_{bt}(n, h)$, where $f_{bt}(n, h)$ is defined as the minimum number of faulty nodes that destroy all subtrees of height h. Clearly, there may exist a number of minimum critical fault sets. Note that a critical fault set for a subtree of height h is also critical for subtrees of height greater than h, but it may or may not be critical for subtrees of height less than h. However, a minimum critical fault set for a subtree of height h is never a minimum critical fault set for a subtree of height larger than h. Such a minimum critical fault set will not be critical fault set for a subtree of height smaller than h.

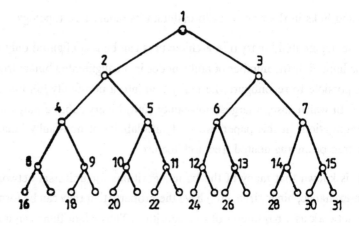

Figure 1. A Five level full binary tree

Example 1: Consider a five level full binary tree shown in Figure 1. A fault set $\{3, 4, 6, 7, 11\}$ is critical for subtrees of height three. However, the fault set $\{3, 4, 10, 12, 20\}$ is not critical because the subtree $ST_3(7)$ is non-faulty. Both fault sets are critical for subtrees of height 4. Further, a MCFS(5, 3) = $\{4, 5, 6, 7\}$. Another MCFS$\{5, 3\}$ = $\{4, 20, 12, 31\}$.

The rest of this paper is organized as follows: In section 2, we show that $f_{bt}(n, h)$ is computable and is equal to $\lfloor (2^n-1)/(2^h-1) \rfloor$. An algorithm which finds out whether a given fault set is critical for subtrees of some height h, is given in Section 3. In Section 4, we show that the cardinality of minimum critical fault set can be increased by augmentation of a full binary tree with redundant nodes and links. The cardinality of minimum critical fault sets for Hayes's binary tree [4], and RAE-tree [5] are also evaluated in this section.

2. Minimum critical fault set

Let the number of faulty processors in a full binary tree of height n be u. The number of nodes in a full binary tree of height n and a subtree of height h are represented as N and H, respectively. Obviously, $N = 2^n-1$ and $H = 2^h-1$. By definition of $f_{bt}(n, h)$, if $u < f_{bt}(n, h)$ then there exists at least one non-faulty subtree of height h. On the other hand, if $u > N-H$ then there does not exist any non-faulty subtree of height h. The following theorem determines the value of $f_{bt}(n, h)$.

Theorem 1: For a full binary tree of height n, the minimum number of faulty nodes required to destroy all (full) subtrees of height h is given by

$$f_{bt}(n, h) = \lfloor (2^n-1)/(2^h-1) \rfloor.$$

Proof: The proof follows in two parts. The first part shows that there exists a set of $\lfloor (2^n-1)/(2^h-1) \rfloor$ nodes which when faulty destroy all subtrees of height h. In the second part, we show that $\lfloor (2^n-1)/(2^h-1) \rfloor$ is the minimum number of faulty nodes required. Let n = m*h + k, where m = $\lfloor n/h \rfloor$ and k is an integer.

a). Consider a set of nodes {j: j at level i, where i = n-h+1, n-2*h+1, ..., n-m*h+1}. We show that if all of these nodes are faulty then there does not exist any non-faulty binary subtree of height h. This set of faulty nodes is then a CFS(n, h). To show this, consider a subtree of height h rooted at any level b, $1 \le b \le$ n-h+1. Clearly, such a binary tree of height h must include one or more nodes at level n-x*h+1, where x is largest integer such that (n-x*h+1) $\ge$ b. But, these nodes are assumed to be faulty. Thus, no non-faulty subtree of height h is available. Now, the number of nodes in CFS(n, h) can be found by adding nodes at each level i and is given as

$$|CFS(n, h)| = 2^{n-h} + 2^{n-2*h} + ... + 2^{n-m*h} \tag{1}$$

The right side of relationship (1) can be simplified as in following steps.

$$
\begin{aligned}
|CFS(n, h)| &= 2^{n-h}\{1+2^{-h}+2^{-2*h}+...+2^{-(m-1)*h}\}, \\
&= (2^n - 2^{n-m*h})/(2^h-1), \\
&= (2^n-1 -(2^k-1))/(2^h-1), \quad \text{where } k = n - m*h \\
&= \lfloor (2^n -1)/(2^h-1) \rfloor.
\end{aligned}
$$

The last equality follows from the fact that $(2^n-1-(2^k-1))/(2^h-1)$ is an integer, $0 \le (2^k-1)/(2^h-1) < 1$, and number of nodes is always an integer. Therefore, $f_{bt}(n, h) \le \lfloor (2^n-1)/(2^h-1) \rfloor$.

b). The number of nodes in a subtree of height h is $2^h -1$. It can be trivially shown that the maximum number of node-disjoint subtrees of height h in an n-level full tree is $\lfloor (2^n-1)/(2^h-1) \rfloor$. Since each subtree can be destroyed if it contains at least one faulty node, the minimum number of faulty nodes required to destroy all subtrees of height h, is $\lfloor (2^n-1)/(2^h-1) \rfloor$. Therefore, $f_{bt}(n, h) \ge \lfloor (2^n-1)/(2^h-1) \rfloor$.

From parts (a) and (b), $f_{bt}(n, h) = \lfloor (2^n-1)/(2^h-1) \rfloor$. $\qquad\qquad$ □

Example 2. Let n = 6, h = 3. Then, a minimum critical fault set is {1, 8, 14, 18, 20, 25, 44, 52, 61} as illustrated in Figure 2.

The following is a direct consequence of Theorem 1 and the fact that if the cardinality of a fault set is less than $f_{bt}(n, h)$, then there exists a non-faulty subtree of height h.

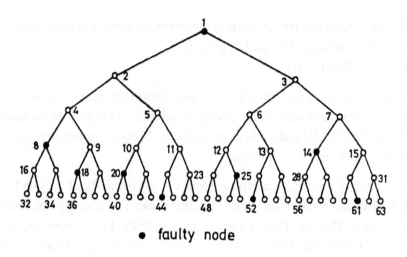

● faulty node

Figure 2. A MCFS(6, 3) = {1, 8, 14, 18, 20, 25, 44, 52, 61}

Corollary 1: Let the number of faulty nodes in an n-level full binary tree be u. Then there exists a non-faulty subtree of height h = n-w, where w is the smallest integer such that $u \leq 2^w$.

For example, if n = 20 and u = 13, then w = 4. Hence, there exists at least one non-faulty subtree of height 16.

3. Obtaining non-faulty subtrees

As stated earlier, a fault-set, for given values of n and h, is critical if it destroys all subtrees of height h. If the cardinality, u, of a fault set, FS, is less than $f_{bt}(n, h)$ hen the fault set is not critical. However, if $f_{bt}(n, h) \leq u \leq N-H$ then the fault set may be critical depending on locations of its faulty nodes. For a given height of a subtree, it can be evaluated whether or not a fault set is critical. The algorithm, **CHECK** (given below), may be used to evaluate whether a given fault set is a critical or not. Also, by repeatedly executing this algorithm for different values of h, it is possible to find out the largest non-faulty subtree.

In the following algorithm, a node j is said to be marked if $ST_h(j)$ contains at least one faulty node. Otherwise, it is unmarked. After executing this algorithm, each unmarked node corresponds to a non-faulty subtree of height h.

Algorithm **CHECK** /* *This algorithm finds out whether a given fault set is a critical* */
    begin
        for each node x, such that $x \in \{FS\}$ **do**
            begin
                mark node x;
                for i := 1 to h-1 **do**
                    if $(\lfloor x/2^i \rfloor \geq 1)$ **then** mark node $\lfloor x/2^i \rfloor$;
                if (any node at level i, $1 \leq i \leq$ n-h+1, is unmarked) **then**
                    FS is non-critical
                else fault set FS is critical;
            end;
    end;

The time required to mark ancestors of nodes of fault set FS is $h|FS|$. The time taken to find unmarked nodes is $2^{n-h+1}-1$. Hence, the total time required to execute the above algorithm is $h|FS| + 2^{n-h+1}-1$.

A non-faulty subtree of the largest size can be obtained by executing the algorithm CHECK starting with h = n-1. If no node is found unmarked, then the algorithm is executed for lower values of h, till an unmarked node is found.

4. Improvements in subtree availability

The availability of a non-faulty subtree of a given height is increased significantly if the cardinality of a minimum critical fault set is increased. The latter can be achieved by introducing some redundancy in the tree. For given values of n and h, there exist many MCFS(n, h). Consider an augmentation of a full binary tree with redundant nodes such that w number of nodes ($w \geq 1$) from each minimum critical fault set are replaced by redundant non-faulty nodes. Then, the minimum number of faulty nodes required to make all subtrees of height h faulty becomes $f'(n, h) = f_{bt}(n, h) + w$. The value of w depends upon the architecture of an augmented tree. This ensures availability of at least one non-faulty subtree of height h if the number of faulty nodes is less than $f'(n, h)$. Further, this technique increases the possibility of finding a non-faulty subtree even when the tree contains $f'(n, h)$ or more faulty nodes, unless the faults belong to a critical fault set.

Before determining the increase in the cardinality of a minimum critical fault set for some known augmented binary trees, the characteristics of minimum critical fault sets are discussed in the following subsection.

4.1 Characteristics of Minimum Critical Fault Sets

We also define *critical levels*. For given values of n and h, the ith critical level is defined as a level CL_i, where $CL_i = n+1- i*h$, $1 \le i \le m$, where $m = \lfloor n/h \rfloor$.

The value of m indicates the number of critical levels in a full binary tree and a subtree of height n and h, respectively. The only critical level in the tree of Example 1 is $CL_1 = 3$.

Lemma 1: Consider a full binary tree of height n and subtrees of height h, such that $n \ge 2h-1$, and $h \ge 2$. Each minimum critical fault set contains at least one node at level $CL_1 = n-h+1$.

Proof (by contradiction): Assume that an MCFS(n, h) does not contain a faulty node at level CL_1. The number of node disjoint subtrees of height h starting from CL_1 is 2^{n-h}. To make each of these subtrees faulty, at least 2^{n-h} faulty nodes are required. Since faulty nodes are assumed to be not at level CL_1, these nodes must lie at levels below CL_1, i.e. at CL_1+1, CL_1+2, ...CL_1+h-1.

It can be shown that the number of node disjoint subtrees which can be constructed from nodes at levels 1 through CL_1 is $\lfloor (2^{n-h+1}-1)/(2^h-1) \rfloor$. All of these subtrees can be faulty if each of these subtrees contains at least one faulty node. Hence, the minimum number of faulty nodes F required to destroy all subtrees in the entire tree is given as

$$F = 2^{n-h} + \lfloor (2^{n-h+1} -1)/(2^h-1) \rfloor.$$

If $n = 2h-1$, then $F = 2^{n-h} + 1 > f_{bt}(n, h)$, since $f_{bt}(2h-1, h) = 2^{n-h}$, which contradicts Theorem 1. But, if $n > 2h-1$, then F can be rewritten as (since 2^{n-h} is an integer):

$$F = \lfloor 2^{n-h} + (2^{n-h+1} -1)/(2^h-1) \rfloor,$$
$$= \lfloor (2^n-1)/(2^h-1) + (2^{n-h})/(2^h-1) \rfloor,$$
$$\ge \lfloor (2^n-1)/(2^h-1) \rfloor + \lfloor (2^{n-h})/(2^h-1) \rfloor > f_{bt}(n, h),$$

which again contradicts Theorem 1.

Hence, each minimum critical fault set contains at least one faulty node at CL_1. ☐

Lemma 2: If $n \ge 2h$, then each minimum critical fault set MCFS(n, h) contains at least one faulty node from each *critical level* CL_i, $1 \le i \le m-1$, $m = \lfloor n/h \rfloor$.

Proof (by contradiction): Let CL_i does not contain any faulty node. Then, the number of node disjoint subtrees which can be constructed from nodes at level CL_i and from nodes at levels below CL_i, is

$$= 2^{n-i*h} \lfloor (2^{i*h}-1)/(2^h-1) \rfloor,$$
$$= \lfloor (2^n-2^{n-i*h})/(2^h-1) \rfloor.$$

Similarly, the number of node disjoint subtrees which can be constructed from nodes at CL_i and levels above CL_i, is

$$= \lfloor (2^{n+1-i*h}-1)/(2^h-1) \rfloor.$$

Since there exists no faulty node at CL_i, all (node disjoint) subtrees can be faulty if each subtree contains one faulty node. Hence, minimum number of faulty nodes, F, required to make all subtrees faulty is given as

$$\begin{aligned}
F &= \lfloor (2^n-2^{n-i*h})/(2^h-1) \rfloor + \lfloor (2^{n+1-i*h}-1)/(2^h-1) \rfloor, \\
&\geq \lfloor (2^n-1)/(2^h-1) \rfloor - \lfloor (2^{n-i*h}-1)/(2^h-1) \rfloor + \lfloor (2^{n+1-i*h}-1)/(2^h-1) \rfloor, \\
&= f_{bt}(n, h) + k,
\end{aligned}$$

where $k = \lfloor (2^{n+1-i*h}-1)/(2^h-1) \rfloor - \lfloor (2^{n-i*h}-1)/(2^h-1) \rfloor$. Since $k \geq 1$, for all i, $1 \leq i \leq m-1$, the above contradicts Theorem 1. $\square$

Lemma 3: Each minimum critical fault set contains at least one node from level b, $CL_m \leq b \leq h$, where $m = \lfloor n/h \rfloor$.

Proof: Consider the following two cases:

a). n = m*h: For this case $CL_m = 1$. The subtree of height h rooted at node 1 can become faulty only if there exists at least one faulty node at level b, $1 \leq b \leq h$.

b). n = m*h + k, where $1 \leq k < h$: Let an MCFS(n, h) not contain a faulty node at level b, $CL_m \leq b \leq h$. Then the number of node disjoint subtrees which can be constructed from nodes at level CL_m and those below, is

$$\begin{aligned}
&= 2^{n-m*h} \lfloor (2^{m*h}-1)/(2^h-1) \rfloor, \\
&= \lfloor (2^n-2^{n-m*h})/(2^h-1) \rfloor.
\end{aligned}$$

A subtree of height h rooted at node 1 can be faulty only if it contains a faulty node at any level 1 through h. Because of the assumption above, it must be at a level 1 through CL_m-1. Hence, the total number of faulty nodes required is

$$\begin{aligned}
&= \lfloor (2^n-2^{n-m*h})/(2^h-1) \rfloor + 1 \\
&\geq \lfloor (2^n-1)/(2^h-1) \rfloor + \lfloor (1-2^{n-m*h})/(2^h-1) \rfloor + 1 \\
&> f_{bt}(n, h).
\end{aligned}$$

The latter is true since $\lfloor (1-2^{n-m*h})/(2^h-1) \rfloor = 0$. This contradicts Theorem 1

Therefore, each minimum critical fault set contains at least one node from a level b, $CL_m \leq b \leq h$. $\square$

The above results lead to the following Theorem.

Theorem 2: For a full binary tree of height n and subtrees of height h, $n \geq 2h-1$, each minimum critical fault set contains

    i)   at least one faulty node at each level CL_i, $1 \leq i \leq m-1$, where $m = \lfloor n/h \rfloor$, and

    ii)   at least one node that lies at level b, $CL_m \leq b \leq h$.   □

For a full binary tree of height n and subtrees of height h, the cardinality of a minimum critical fault set can be increased by augmenting the full binary tree with redundant nodes which can be used to replace some of the faulty nodes from each MCFS(n, h). We, now, evaluate the cardinality of a minimum critical fault set (from the viewpoint of availability of non-faulty subtrees) for RAE-tree [5], AB-tree [6] and Hayes's binary tree [4].

4.2 AB-tree and RAE-tree

The AB-tree [6] and RAE-tree [5] are functionally the same but topologically different. In the presence of one faulty node at each level, an n-level AB-tree (or RAE-tree) can be configured into an n-level non-faulty full binary tree. A minimum critical fault set for an n-level AB-tree corresponds to the minimum critical fault set for an n-level full binary tree where the faulty nodes are restricted to fewest number of levels. The following Theorem evaluates the minimum number of faulty nodes, $f_{AB}(n, h)$ required in an AB-tree to make all subtrees (of height h) faulty.

Theorem 3: Consider an AB-tree of height n and subtrees of height h. The minimum number of faulty nodes, $f_{AB}(n, h)$, required to destroy all subtrees of height h is given as $f_{AB}(n, h) = f_{bt}(n, h) + m$, where $m = \lfloor n/h \rfloor$.

Proof: The proof consists of two parts. The first part shows that there exists a set of $f_{bt}(n, h) + m$ faulty nodes which destroys all subtrees of height h. In the second part, we show that at least $f_{bt}(n, h) + m$ faulty nodes are required to destroy all subtrees of height h.

a). Consider the set of nodes {j: j at level CL_i, for i = 1, 2, ..., m} $\cup$ { i':i' at levels CL_i, for i = 1, 2,.., m}. It can be observed that if all these nodes are faulty then all subtrees of height h become faulty (Figure 3 for n = 5 and h = 3). Hence, $f_{AB}(n, h) \leq f_{bt}(n, h) + m$.

b). From Theorem 2, each MCFS(n, h) for a full binary tree contains at least one node at each level CL_i, $1 \leq i \leq m-1$, and a node at a level b, $CL_m \leq b \leq h$. Hence, one faulty node at each of these levels can be replaced by a non-faulty node at the same level. Thus, $f_{AB}(n, h) \geq f_{bt}(n, h) + m$.

    Hence, $f_{AB}(n, h) = f_{bt}(n, h) + m$.   □

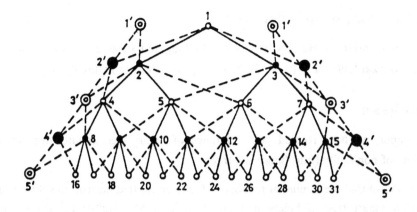

Figure 3. A five level AB-tree with fault set {2', 2, 3, 4', 8-15}

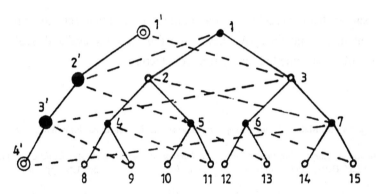

Figure 4. A four level Hayes's tree with fault set {1, 2', 3', 4, 5, 6, 7}

4.3 Hayes's binary tree architecture

Hayes's binary tree [4] of height n consists of an n-level full binary tree augmented with n redundant nodes and $2^{m+1}+2m-3$ redundant links. In the presence of a single faulty node, an n-level Hayes's tree can be reconfigured into a tree which is isomorphic to an n-level full binary tree. In this tree, there exists one redundant node at each level of the tree. Note that the redundant node at a level can replace one node at that level. However, due to fewer number of redundant links (as compared to that in the AB-tree), the Hayes's tree cannot be reconfigured into a full binary tree of the same height if there is one faulty node at each level.

Theorem 4: The cardinality of a minimum critical fault set, $f_{ht}(n, h)$, for Hayes's binary tree is given by $f_{ht}(n, h) = f_{bt}(n, h) + m$, where $m = \lfloor n/h \rfloor$.

Proof : The proof is similar to that Theorem 3. ☐

Example 3: Consider a Hayes's tree of height four and subtrees of height two. Then, a minimum critical fault set is $\{1, 2', 3', 4, 5, 6, 7\}$, as shown in Figure 4.

5. Conclusion

In this paper, we have studied fault tolerance of binary tree architectures in terms of availability of non-faulty (full) binary subtrees.

It is shown that the minimum number of faulty nodes that destroy all subtrees of height h in a full binary tree of height n is equal to $f_{bt}(n, h) = \lfloor (2^n - 1)/(2^h - 1) \rfloor$. Further, an algorithm, CHECK, is developed which determines whether or not a given fault set destroys all subtrees of a given height. This algorithm can be used to compute the largest non-faulty subtree in a binary tree containing faults.

We have shown that the cardinality of a minimum critical fault set can be increased by adding redundant nodes and links. We have used this to study availability of non-faulty subtrees in some of the augmented binary tree architectures.

References

[1]   G. J. Liopovski and M. Malek, *Parallel Computing: Theory and Comparisons*, John Wiley & Sons, 1987.

[2]   E. Horowitz and A. Zorat, *The Binary Tree as an Interconnection Network: Applications to Multiprocessor Systems and VLSI*, IEEE Transactions on Computers, Vol. C-30, No. 4, April 1981, pp. 247-253.

[3]   S. W. Song, *A Highly Concurrent Tree Machine for Data Base Applications*, Proceedings of the 1980 International Conference on Parallel Processing, pp. 259-268.

[4]   J. P. Hayes, *A Graph Model for Fault-tolerant Computing Systems*, IEEE Transactions on Computers, Vol. C-25, No. 9, September 1976, pp. 875-884.

[5]   C. S. Raghavendra, A. Avizienis and M. D. Ercegovac, *Fault Tolerance in Binary Tree Architectures*, IEEE Transactions on Computers, Vol. C-33, No. 6, June 1984, pp. 568-572.

[6]   B. N. Jain, R. Mittal, and R. K. Patney, *Fault Tolerant Analysis and Algorithms for a proposed Augmented Binary Tree*, Proceedings of the 9th International Conference on Distributed Computing Systems, Newport Beach, June 1989, pp. 524-529.

[7]   A. S. M. Hassan and V. K. Agarwal, *A Modular Approach to Fault-Tolerant Binary Tree Architectures*, Digest of Papers of the Fifteenth Symposium on Fault Tolerant Computing, June 1985, pp. 344-349.

[8]   B. Becker and H. U. Simon, *How Robust is the n-Cube?*, Proceedings of the 27th Annual IEEE Symposium Foundations Computer Sci., October 1986, pp. 274-282.

[9]   R. Mittal, *Augmented binary tree architectures and their fault tolerance*, Ph.D. Thesis, Department of Electrical Engineering, Indian Institute of Technology, New Delhi, August 1990.

An Optimal Parallel Algorithm for the Vertical Segment Visibility Reporting Problem

Ip-Wang Chan †   Donald K. Friesen ‡

† Department of Information Systems and Computer Science
National University of Singapore, Lower Kent Ridge Road, Singapore 0511
(e-mail: chaniw@nusdiscs)
‡ Department of Computer Science, Texas A&M University, College Station, TX 77843

Abstract

In this paper, we present a parallel algorithm for solving the all-pairs vertical segment visibility reporting (SVR) problem. Given a set $S = \{S_0, S_1, \ldots, S_{n-1}\}$ of disjoint vertical segments in the plane, the SVR problem asks for the determination and reporting of all the distinct visibility pairs. Our algorithm solves the SVR problem in $O(\log n)$ time using $O(n)$ space and $O(n)$ processors on a CREW PRAM (Concurrent Read Exclusive Write Parallel Random Access Machine) computational model.

1. Introduction

Suppose we are given a set $S = \{S_0, S_1, \ldots, S_{n-1}\}$ of vertical segments in the plane. For any two segments S_i, S_j in S, where $0 <= i < j < n$, we say S_i, S_j form a *visibility pair* (denoted by $< i, j >$) if there exists a horizontal line intersecting S_i, S_j but not any other segment, say S_k, in S that lies between S_i and S_j. For example, in Figure 1 the set of unique visibility pairs is given by $\{< 0, 1 >, < 0, 2 >, < 0, 4 >, < 1, 4 >, < 2, 3 >, < 2, 4 >, < 3, 4 >\}$. The all-pairs segment visibility reporting (SVR) problem can be stated as follows. Given a set $S = \{S_0, S_1, \ldots, S_{n-1}\}$ of disjoint vertical segments in the plane, determine and report all the distinct visibility pairs. The SVR problem has application in VLSI circuit layouts. The problem arises in the compaction of stick diagrams where all components are bounded by orthogonal segments, and it is necessary to determine the *visibility pairs* from among all pairs of vertical (or horizontal) segments [3].

Some sequential results have been reported in Lodi and Pagli [3] for solving the SVR problem. Given any arbitrary set $S = \{S_0, S_1, \ldots, S_{n-1}\}$ of vertical segments, the algorithm reviewed in Lodi and Pagli [3] solves the SVR problem in optimal sequential time $O(n \log n)$. Using the notion of *information transfer* across any chip, Lodi and Pagli [3] derive a lower bound to the area-time complexity of the SVR problem of $\Omega(n^2 \log^2 n)$. In this paper, we show that the SVR problem can

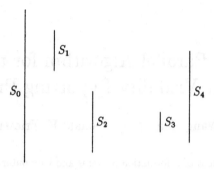

Figure 1: A set of $S = \{S_0, S_1, \ldots, S_4\}$ of five vertical segments

be solved in $O(\log n)$ time and $O(n)$ space using $O(n)$ processors on a CREW PRAM. Our result is optimal to within a factor of constant with respect to the processor-time complexity.

This paper is organized as follows. In section 2, we describe some basic observations and discuss informally our techniques for solving the SVR problem. In section 3, we present an algorithm called Solve-SVR for solving the SVR problem using the CREW PRAM as the basic computational model. A CREW PRAM is a shared memory parallel random access machine which allows concurrent reads but no two processors can simultaneously write into the same memory location. In section 4 we examine the run-time performance of algorithm Solve-SVR in the worst case. A brief summary of our work with recommendation for future research is given in section 5.

2. Some Observations and Informal Discussion

Let S be a given set of disjoint vertical segments in the plane. Imagine that there are two observers, possibly at infinity of the plane, in such a way that one is at the left side and the other at the right side of the plane. For the two observers, their "view" is one-dimensional in the sense that they each "see" a segment only when the horizontal line that exists between the observer and the segment does not intersect any other segment in S. For convenience we denote by "left (similarly, right) visibility window" of S the view as seen by the left (right) observer. For any given set S of line segments, one simple way to construct its two visibility windows is to imagine that each segment endpoint p in S sends out two horizontal rays, one to the left and the other to the right, of p. A ray will stop whenever it hits upon a segment on its way. Horizontal rays that reach a particular visibility window of S (or equivalently, an observer) will naturally induce a partitioning of the window (which can be represented as a vertical real line) into consecutive intervals. It is true that within any single interval on a window, only one segment, if any, can be seen. An interval may contain no visible segment. The same segment may be "visible" in a number of non-consecutive intervals pertaining to a specific window. One way to represent a visibility window is to project those segment endpoints whose horizontal rays reach the visibility window onto that window. These projected segment endpoints will constitute a linearly ordered list and act just like interval endpoints.

The SVR problem can be solved using the method of divide-and-conquer. The original input set A is divided into two subproblems B and C of equal size, where all segments in B have smaller x-coordinates than segments in C. Recursively each subproblem is solved in parallel. That is, on return subproblem B (similarly, C) will have determined its visibility pairs and the left as well as right visibility window of B (C), denoted by $W_{B,l}$ and $W_{B,r}$ ($W_{C,l}$ and $W_{C,r}$) respectively, will have been properly determined. The solution for set A is then obtained by combining the subproblems B and C. Thus it is essential to show how all the visibility pairs in A but not in B or C can be determined and also how the left as well as right visibility windows of A can be constructed during the marriage of subproblems B and C. On a CREW PRAM, the subproblem division step is done in a natural manner with the presorting of the input vertical segments into non-decreasing order of their x-coordinates. Thus initially each segment, say S_k, constitutes a subproblem of its own. The left and right visibility windows of S_k will each be comprised of three intervals, two of which are unbounded. In each window, the upper (similarly, lower) projected segment endpoint will carry a label k (∞) as its current visibility index. During the combination of a subproblem pair B and C into A, only those segments whose labels appear on either the right window of B (that is, $W_{B,r}$) or the left window of C (that is, $W_{C,l}$) will need to be examined. We represent each window of a subproblem in the form of a linearly ordered list consisting of all the segment endpoints inside the subproblem projected onto the window. Each window interval carries an indicator known as the "visibility index" showing which segment, if any, is visible across that particular interval. If a window interval contains no visible segment, its corresponding visibility index will be assigned a symbol of ∞.

For convenience, we let all projected segment endpoints that are contained in a left (similarly, right) window be repesented by circles (triangles). Denote by M the resultant list formed by merging the right window of B (that is, $W_{B,r}$) with the left window of C (that is, $W_{C,l}$). Figure 2 shows how the four windows within a given hypothetical subproblem pair B and C can be represented. By the method of divide-and-conquer, elements within each window in Figure 2 will have properly computed their corresponding visibility indices (shown in parentheses) with respect to the subproblem to which the window belongs. To identify the visibility pairs in A formed by merging subproblems B and C, one only needs to perform the following operations. On the combined list M, each element a (circle or triangle) locates the first element t which is immediately above a from the opposite window. For convenience, we refer to element t as the target point of a. By checking the visibility index of element a against the index of t, the pair of segments which are visible through the interval $[a, b)$ on M, where b denotes the point which is immediately below a on M, is readily identifiable. It should be noted that element b can be from either B or C. Also it is possible that the same visibility pair may be detected in more than one contiguous or

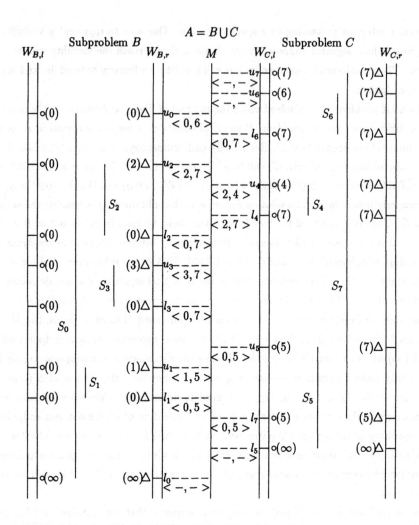

Figure 2: Visibility pairs determination for elements in subproblem $A = B \cup C$ (Note: (i) denotes the visibility index i and $< i, j >$ denotes the visibility pair for segments S_i and S_j)

non-contiguous interval on M.

One way to avoid reporting the same visibility pair by a group of contiguous elements in M is to specify that each element a on M compares the visibility pair it generates for its own interval with the visibility pair computed by the nearest neighbor above a on M. If the two visibility pairs happen to be the same, then there will be no need for a to report the duplicate pair it finds in M. On the merged list M, it is possible that some elements have no target elements. These elements will never form any visibility pair on M and hence do not take part in any visibility pair checking. For instance, points u_6 and u_7 in Figure 2 have no target point on M. Thus the interval $[u_7, u_6)$ and $[u_6, u_0)$ are each assigned the symbol $< -, - >$, indicating that no visibility pair occurs in the interval. On M, if either an element or its target has a visibility index of ∞, then the element cannot generate any visibility pair in M. In Figure 2 points l_0 and l_5 do not form any visibility pair on M, as indicated by the symbol $< -, - >$ in their corresponding intervals.

After forming the visibility pair by appropriate elements on the merged list M, the left and right windows from the combined problem are to be constructed as described below. The left window of A, $W_{A,l}$, is formed by merging the two window lists $W_{B,l}$ and $W_{C,l}$. On the combined list $W_{A,l}$, each circle locates its target element immediately above it on $W_{A,l}$. The computing of the visibility index by individual elements on $W_{A,l}$ can be done as follows.

1. If an element has no target on $W_{A,l}$, then its visibility index will be the same as before.

2. Hereafter let t denote the target of element a if t exists. If both a and t have a visibility index of ∞, then the visibility index for a on $W_{A,l}$ will also be ∞.

3. If the visibility index of a is ∞ but the visibility index for t is, say i ($\neq \infty$), then the visibility index for element a on $W_{A,l}$ will be set equal to i.

4. Suppose the visibility indices for a and t are i and j respectively, where $i \neq j \neq \infty$. Then if $i < j$, the resulting index for a on $W_{A,l}$ will be set equal to i.

The construction of $W_{A,r}$ is similar to that of $W_{A,l}$. It is formed by merging the window lists $W_{B,r}$ and $W_{C,r}$. The computing of the visibility index for individual elements on $W_{A,r}$ follows the procedure described above with the exception that in condition 4, if $i < j$, then the resulting index for a on $W_{A,r}$ will be set to j.

At first sight, it may appear that even though the above method of visibility pairs determination affords a way to discern all those same visibility pairs that are formed at contiguous intervals on the merged list M, identical visibility pairs that are formed at separate, non-contiguous intervals will still need to be identified. It will be shown in the sequel that if visibility pairs are to be determined through the endpoints of each segment, there can be at most $3n - 5$ such pairs. Each top endpoint of a segment, say S_k, can generate at most two visibility pairs of the form $< k, \cdot >$ and $< \cdot, k >$ respectively. The two pairs are such that one is to the left and the other to the right of S_k. Each bottom endpoint of a segment, say S_l, can yield only one visibility pair of the form $< i, j >$, where $i \neq j \neq l$. For example, in Figure 2, after solving the subproblem, the upper segment endpoints

328

u_1, u_2 and u_3 will have found the visibility pairs $< 0, 1 >, < 0, 2 >$ and $< 0, 3 >$ respectively to their left. On the merged list M, the same endpoints u_i, where $i = 1, 2, 3$, will discern the visibility pairs $< 1, 5 >$, $< 2, 7 >$ and $< 3, 7 >$ respectively to their right. After this, even though the projection of endpoint $u_i, i = 1, 2, 3$, may appear in the windows of the combined subproblem $A = B \bigcup C$ or later on in some other subproblems, the same endpoints will not generate visibility pairs involving segment $S_i, i = 1, 2, 3$, within the windows of those subproblems. The reason is that after forming its left (similarly, right) visibility pair, when projected onto the left (right) window of the combined subproblem within which the left (right) visibility pair is found, the same top endpoint will take on a different visibility index.

To show that the lower endpoint of each segment can produce at most one visibility pair, one first observes that in any segment, say S_k, the visibility pair that can be formed by the lower endpoint l_k of S_k will never have S_k as its component. The only situation in which l_k will form a visibility pair of the form $< i, j >$, where $i \neq j \neq k$, is when there exist two segments S_i and S_j with S_i to the left and S_j to the right of S_k such that the left and right horizontal rays from l_k hit S_i and S_j respectively without interruption by any other segment. After forming the pair $< i, j >$, even though l_k may still be present in the window of the combined subproblem A within which the pair $< i, j >$ is found, point i_k will not generate any additional visibility pair when A is combined with another subproblem during subsequent processing. The reason is that on the left and right windows of A, l_k will acquire a visibility index other than ∞ or k. Moreover, it can be seen that the visibility indices of the projected bottom point l_k and the endpoint (top or bottom), say p, which is immediately above l_k on the same window of A are always the same. For illustration, let the visibility index for both points l_k and p be h. Suppose later on subproblem A is merged with another subproblem, say D on its left. Let point q be the target of l_k on the list M formed by merging the right window of D with the left window of A. Assume that on the right window of D the visibility index computed for q is g. Then on M, two cases may arise. In case (a), q is in between p and l_k. After checking with point p, q will find $< g, h >$ as its visibility pair on M. Similarly after checking with q, l_k will discover the same pair (see Figure 3 (a)). In case (b), point q is above both p and l_k on M. Upon checking with q, both p and l_k will find the same visibility pair $< g, h >$ (see Figure 3 (b)). To avoid reporting the same visibility pairs by adjacent projected endpoints on a merged M, we delay the reporting process till the end of the cascading merge procedure. We assign to each lower endpoint, say l_k, a storage location called VP in the global memory. Initially VP is given a null symbol $< -, - >$. Whenever l_k locates its visibility pair during the cascading merge step, it stores the pair label in its own VP variable. After that, even though l_k may encounter other visibility pairs, the VP variable of l_k will never have to be changed. This is because after forming its visibility pair, each l_k will only generate duplicate copies of visibility pairs for segments in some other subproblems. It is clear that in both cases (a) and (b) in Figure 3, point l_k must have generated its visibility pair and hence l_k will never erroneously store its duplicate visibility pair $< g, h >$ in its VP variable. It is easy to see that the same rationale applies when l_k is a member of the right window of A. Thus in general we know

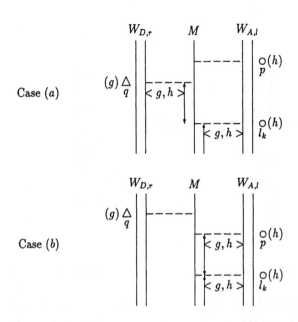

Figure 3: On M there is no need for point l_k to report its visibility pair $< g, h >$ since point q and p form the same visibility pair in cases (a) and (b) respectively (Note: in both cases point q represents the target of l_k on M)

that the lower endpoint of each segment can generate at most one visibility pair.

From the above observations that each top endpoint of a segment can give rise to at most two visibility pairs for the segment and each bottom endpoint can yield at most one visibility pair, it can be shown that there can be at most $3n - 5$ visibility pairs for a given set of n segments if the pairs are to be determined through the endpoints of each segment.

Figure 4 shows a specific case where $3n - 5$ visibility pairs actually occur within a set of n segments. In Figure 4, segments S_0 and S_{n-1} represent the leftmost and rightmost segments respectively. Let u_0, u_{n-1} (similarly, l_0, l_{n-1}) be the upper (lower) endpoints of segments S_0, S_{n-1} respectively. The top (similarly, bottom) endpoints of the $n - 2$ segments in between S_0 and S_{n-1} are all below (above) either u_0 or u_{n-1} (l_0 or l_{n-1}). These $n - 2$ segments can generate at most $3(\dot{n} - 2) = 3n - 6$ visibility pairs. The lower endpoints of S_0 and S_{n-1} can never generate any visibility pair. The upper endpoints of S_0 and S_{n-1} can generate a total of at most one additional pair. Thus there can be at most $3n - 5$ visibility pairs in a given set of n segments. It should be noted that out of these $3n - 5$ pairs, some of them may be identical. Different bottom or top endpoints may generate the same visibility pairs. Since reporting of the same visibility pairs more than once is totally undesirable, we delay the reporting process till the end of the cascading merge procedure. Instead we assign to each top endpoint, say u_k, two storage locations called VP1 and VP2 in their global memory. Initially both VP1 and VP2 are given the null symbol $< -,- >$. Each time a visibility pair is found for u_k, it is to replace the null symbol inside either VP1 or

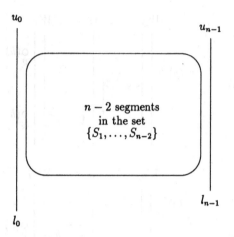

u_0

u_{n-1}

$n - 2$ segments
in the set
$\{S_1, \ldots, S_{n-2}\}$

l_{n-1}

l_0

Figure 4: There are at most $3n - 5$ visibility pairs in a given set of n vertical segments

VP2. Similarly each lower endpoint, say l_k, will store the visibility pair it finds, if any, in the global location VP. At the end of the subproblem merge procedure, all the visibility pairs in the form of $< i, j >$ in the locations VP, VP1 and VP2 will be encoded by concatenating the indices i and j given that they are of the same length (appending leading zeros if necessary). Null symbols of the form $< -, - >$ will be replaced by an arbitrary big number, say ∞. These transformed pairs are at most $3n - 5$ in quantity and can be sorted into nondecreasing order. Those pairs with the same encoded labels as their nearest lower neighbors represent duplicates and will be ignored during the actual reporting.

Using the method of divide-and-conquer, the merging of the two ordered window lists can be done using the cascading merge procedure described in [2]. The computing of the visibility indices by individual elements on a combined list is carried out only when the list (or equivalently, its corresponding tree node) becomes external or full. The parallel procedure presented in [2] performs the cascading merge operations on a set of $O(n)$ elements in $O(\log n)$ time using $O(n)$ processors and $O(n)$ space on a CREW PRAM computational model.

3. Algorithm for solving the SVR Problem

Based on the observations and informal discussions presented in the previous section, an algorithm known as Solve-SVR can be constructed for solving the SVR problem. A description of Solve-SVR is given below.

Algorithm Solve-SVR

Input: A set $S = \{S_0, \ldots, S_{n-1}\}$ of vertical segments in the plane. Each segment $S_i, i = 0, \ldots, n-1$, is represented by its associated top endpoint u_i and bottom endpoint l_i.

Output: A set of unique visibility pairs in the form of $< i, j >$ contained in S, where i and j denote segment indices with $0 \le i < j < n$.

Step 1. Preprocessing: The set of $2n$ endpoints, half of which are top endpoints and the other half bottom endpoints, are sorted into nondecreasing x-values. This presorting step corresponds to the division step in the method of divide-and-conquer.

Step 2. Initialization: At the beginning, each segment makes up a subproblem of its own. The top and bottom endpoints of a segment constitute a list ordered according to the y-values. Each segment endpoint, say a, maintains two working variables, LVI_a and RVI_a, for storing the visibility index on the left and right windows respectively of a subproblem containing the segment. Initially, each upper (similarly, lower) endpoint u_i (l_i), where $i = 0, \ldots, n-1$, will set its own LVI_i and RVI_i to i (∞) respectively. To facilitate the reporting of visibility pairs at a later stage, each top segment endpoint will be assigned two contiguous locations called VP1 and VP2 in the global memory for storing the visibility pairs found during the execution of algorithm Solve-SVR. Similarly, each bottom endpoint will maintain a global variable called VP for keeping the visibility pair found during the cascading merge step. Initially the VP1 and VP2 (similarly, VP) variables associated with each top (bottom) endpoint are (is) given a null symbol $< -, - >$, showing that no visibility pair has been detected.

Step 3. Subproblem merge: The technique of cascading merge introduced in [1] is applied to combine adjacent subproblem in pairs. Initially each subproblem consisting of a single segment is assigned to a leaf node of a complete binary tree so that for any two segments S_i, S_j in S, S_i is to the left of S_j on the x-coordinate if $i < j$ for $0 \le i < j < n$. The entire cascading merge process will be composed of $3 \log 2n$ stages. During each stage, if an internal tree node is nonempty but not full, the node will merge the two ordered lists, one from each of its two immediate sons to form its own list, and propagate a selected sample of the elements in its own list just formed to its parent. The size of the sample to be made depends on the stage the tree node is in. A tree node becomes full whenever it possesses all the descendents in its subtree. Once a tree node becomes full, the node will stop communicating with its parent or descendents. In a parallel environment, all internal nodes at the same level of the tree will become full at the same time. Whenever a tree node A (or eqivalently, subproblem) becomes full, individual endpoints within the combined list in the node will locate their corresponding target element on the same list using the ranking information computed when the elements were still at the two child nodes of A. For any endpoint a in A, let t denote its target. The determination of visibility pairs by individual elements in A can be done according to the following cases:

Case 1 If a does not have a target, then no visibility pair can be formed by a in A.

Case 2 Endpoint a has a target t and a is from tree node B which represents the left son of A. By definition t must be from tree node C which is the right son of A. Let i denote the right visibility index of a, RVI_a, computed at B. Also let j denote the left visibility index of t, LVI_t, computed at C. If one or both i and j is equal to ∞, no visibility pair exists for a in A. A null symbol $< -, - >$ is given to a. Otherwise the pair $< i, j >$ constitutes a visibility pair for a in A.

Case 3 Endpoint a has a target t and a is from tree node C. The situation is symmetrical to case 2. Let j be the left visibility index of a, LVI_a, computed at C. Let i denote the right visibility index of t, RVI_t, computed at B. If one or.both of i and j is equal to ∞, no visibility pairs exists for a in A. A null pair symbol $< -, - >$ is assigned to a. Otherwise the pair $< i, j >$ makes up a visibility pair for a in A.

After the checking and detecting of visibility pairs by individual elements in the combined node list A, in parallel each element a that has detected its visibility pair in A checks its pair label against the visibility pair label computed by its neighbor which is immediately above it on the list. It should be noted that the neighbor being sought may or may not be the target point of a. If either one of the two pair labels is $< -, - >$, the pair is to be ignored. If both pair labels are identical, the pair formed by a is to be ignored since the pair represents a duplicate and hence cannot be the correct visibility pair being computed.

Step 4. Visibility index updating: The computing of the visibility indices for the left and right windows by individual elements a in A can be carried out as follow. Again let t denote the target point of a. Three cases can be distinguished.

Case 1 If a does not have a target point in A, then the current values of LVI_a and RVI_a are correct for a with respect to A.

Case 2 Suppose a has a target and a is from tree node B which is the left son of A. If the right visibility index of t, RVI_t in C, is $j (\neq \infty)$, then RVI_a in A will be set equal to j. Otherwise no change will be needed for RVI_a.

Case 3 Suppose a has a target and a is from tree node C which is the right son of A. If the left visibility index of t, LVI_t in B, is $i (\neq \infty)$, then LVI_a in A will be set equal to i. Otherwise no change will be made for LVI_a.

Step 5. Visibility pair reporting: The cascading merge procedure terminates when all the input segment endpoints have moved up to the root node of the binary tree and all the visibility pairs (at most two for each top point and one for each bottom endpoint) have been properly determined. In parallel each input endpoint transforms its associated visibility pair label in the form of $< i, j >$, where $i \neq j$, into an integer formed by concatenating i and j, assuming that i and j both have the same number of significant digits (appending leading zeros to either i or j if necessary). Dummy pair labels in the form of $< -, - >$ will be coded into an arbitrarily big number, say ∞. Simultaneously all the coded visibility pair labels in the memory locations VP, VP1 and VP2 are sorted into nondecreasing order. Only the first or leftmost visibility pair in each group of identical pairs will need to be reported.

Step 6. Termination: Algorithm Solve-SVR terminates when all the distinct visibility pairs contained in the original input set S have been reported.

4. Analysis of Algorithm Solve-SVR

Theorem 1 *Given n vertical segments in the plane, algorithm Solve-SVR correctly solves the segment visibility reporting problem in $O(\log n)$ time and $O(n)$ space using $O(n)$ processors on a CREW PRAM model of computation.*

Proof: To show that algorithm Solve-SVR correctly solves the SVR problem, one only needs to show that the algorithm reports, for each top endpoint of a segment, at most two visibility pairs (one to the left and one to the right) for the segment. Also for each bottom endpoint in the input set S, the algorithm outputs at most one visibility pair. It can be seen that during the combination of a pair of adjacent subproblems B and C to form A, each possible visibility pair in the form $< i, j >$, where $0 \leq i < j < n$, that can be formed in A must have its first visibility index i come from the right window of B and the index j from the left window of C. Thus by merging elements in the left window list of B with those in the right window list of C, no visibility pair candidates in A will be left out during the subsequent checking and reporting. After the determination of visibility pairs by individual elements in A, each top endpoint that has formed its left (similarly, right) pair will never produce another left (right) pair later on during the execution of the algorithm. Similarly a bottom endpoint that has identified its visibility pair will never generate another pair as the algorithm proceeds. The above condition is safeguarded as seen by the updating of the variables VP1 and VP2 by individual top endpoints and the variable VP by individual bottom endpoints in Step 4. After forming all its associated visibility pairs, the same top endpoint of a segment will never have to change its associated variables VP1 and VP2 in the global memory. Similarly after detecting its visibility pair, the same bottom endpoint of a segment will not change the contents of its memory location VP.

The presorting and postsorting in steps 1 and 5 respectively can be accomplished in $O(\log n)$ time using the parallel merge sorting routine presented by Cole [2]. The sorting scheme in [2] sorts a set of n given items in $O(\log n)$ time and $O(n)$ space using $O(n)$ processors on a CREW PRAM. Step 2 takes only $O(1)$ parallel time for initialization. The cascading merge procedure described in [1] for combining subproblems in pairs in step 3 requires $O(\log n)$ time and $O(n)$ space using $O(n)$ processors on a CREW PRAM. Whenever an internal tree node list A becomes full, the location of targets by individual elements in A takes only constant parallel time using the ranking information computed at the two child nodes of A. The elimination of duplicate visibility pairs in contiguous intervals on a merged list M in A can be done in constant time. The same is also true for updating the visibility indices by individual elements in A. After the postsorting of the coded visibility pairs, deletion of duplicate pairs from reporting needs no more than a constant amount of parallel time. Thus algorithm Solve-SVR solves the SVR problem within the time, space and processor bounds as claimed in theorem 1. $\square$

5. Conclusion

In this paper, we have found that the all-pairs vertical segment visibility reporting (SVR) problem can be solved in $O(\log n)$ time using $O(n)$ space and $O(n)$ processors on a CREW PRAM. Our algorithm for the SVR problem is optimal to within a factor of constant. The idea of visibility pairs used in the present study assumes that all the input segments in the plane are in the vertical position and that each segment endpoint sends out two horizontal rays (one to the left and the other to the right of the endpoint). When some or all input segments are not vertical or the rays from each endpoint are not horizontal, a different concept of visibility pairs will need to be employed. In such a case, it would be of interest to examine how difficult it is to solve the SVR problem under the less restrictive notion of segment visibility.

References

[1] Atallah, M. J., Cole, R., and Goodrich, M. T. Cascading divide-and-conquer: A technique for designing parallel algorithms. *SIAM Journal on Computing,* **18**, 3, (June 1989), 499–532.

[2] Cole, R. Parallel merge sort. *SIAM Journal on Computing,* **17**, 4 (Aug. 1988), 770–785.

[3] Lodi, E., and Pagli, L. A VLSI solution to the vertical segment visibility problem. *IEEE Trans. Comput.,* **C-35**, 10 (Oct. 1986), 923–928.

A Fault-Tolerant Binary Tree Architecture [1]

Siu-Cheung Chau
Dept. of Mathematics and Computer Science, University of Lethbridge,
Lethbridge, Alberta, T1K 3M4, Canada

Arthur L. Liestman
School of Computing Science, Simon Fraser University
Burnaby, British Columbia, V5A 1S6, Canada

Abstract

A new fault-tolerant binary tree architecture is proposed. The approach, employing redundant processors, is suitable for use in long-life unmaintained applications. In our proposed scheme, processors connected as n level full binary tree, are backed up by k spare processors so that the fault-tolerant binary tree can tolerate any set of k faults. This new scheme is compared to previously proposed fault-tolerant binary tree architectures. In particular, we show that the new scheme can achieve the same level of reliability as other proposed scheme while using significantly fewer spares.

1. Introduction

Multi-computers connected in various architectures are now commercially available and are being used for a variety of applications. Some of the most commonly used architectures are the binary hypercube, binary tree, cube-connected cycles, mesh, and multistage interconnection networks. All of these architectures have the major drawback that a single processor or edge failure may render the entire network unusable if the algorithm running on the network requires that the topology of the network does not change. The failure of a single processor or the failure of a link between two processors would destroy the topology of these architectures. Thus, some form of fault-tolerance must be incorporated into these architectures in order to make the network of processors more reliable. We will concentrate on the binary tree architecture in this paper. In this section, we review various schemes which have been proposed for fault-tolerance in binary trees. In Section 2, we propose a new scheme for binary trees. In Section 3, we describe how to calculate the reliability of the proposed scheme. In Section 4, we compare both the reliability and hardware costs of our proposed scheme with those of previous schemes.

Raghavendra, Avizienis and Ercegovac [11] proposed a level oriented scheme which uses one spare processor per level of the binary tree. This scheme uses a structure which is very similar to the optimal one fault-tolerant binary tree constructed by Kwan and Toida [9]. Instead of using direct connections between the spares and the other active processors, they use two decoupling networks as switches to provide the appropriate connections. The lower levels of a large tree will have many nodes. In order to increase the reliability of the lower levels, this level oriented scheme can be applied to modules consisting of $k=2^i$ nodes of a given level. A single spare is provided for each module and the switches in the decoupling networks are controlled centrally through a host computer that uses the binary tree.

---

[1]This research was supported by the National Sciences and Engineering Research Council of Canada under Grant numbers A-1734 and 46197

Hassan and Agarwal [7] also proposed a modular scheme for fault-tolerant binary trees. Their approach uses fault-tolerant modules as building blocks to construct a complete binary tree. Each fault-tolerant module consists of four processors, three active and one spare. Soft-configurable switches provide connections between the active processors, the spare, and the rest of the tree. A distributed approach to reconfiguration is used in that the soft-configurable switches can be set locally in each module when failure occurs.

Both the level oriented scheme (with or without modules at the lower level) and the modular approach can only provide one spare per level (or module). Thus, the reliability that can be achieved by these schemes is insufficient for systems requiring a very high reliability. Singh [12] suggested an improvement to Hassan and Agarwal's modular scheme by allowing the sharing of spares across module boundaries and allowing more than one spare per module. He showed that his scheme is best suited for binary trees having 31 to 255 nodes.

For larger binary trees, Howells and Agarwal [8] devised a modular scheme that allows more than one spare per module. Each module in their scheme is a subtree. For example, a 10-level binary tree may be split into one 5-level subtree containing the root and 32 5-level subtrees. Each non-root subtree is a fault-tolerant module with its own spares. Each spare in a module may replace any active processor in the entire module. Each spare is connected to every processor in the subtree through direct links to each processor, soft-configurable switches, and three buses. Two of these buses are used to connect to the children of the processor being replaced and the last bus is used to connect to the parent. This technique cannot be used for the subtree containing the root node since its leaf nodes must be connected to the root nodes of the other fault-tolerant non-root subtrees. Fortunately, the subtree containing the root node can employ other schemes to provide fault-tolerance. Besides improving reliability, both Singh's and Howells and Agarwal's schemes also improve the yield for binary trees implemented in a single chip.

Lowrie and Fuchs [10] also proposed a subtree oriented fault-tolerance (SOFT) scheme which they show to be better than the schemes of Raghavendra, Avizienis and Ercegovac and of Hassan and Agarwal. In their scheme, up to 2^t spares, where $0 \leq t \leq n-2$, are connected to the leaf nodes of an n-level binary tree. The number of connections between a spare and the leaf nodes depends on t. An extra link is also used to connect the two children of a non-leaf node together. When a node becomes faulty, one of its children, s, will take over its task through the use of soft-configurable switches. The task of s will be taken over in turn by one of its children. This process is repeated until a spare takes over the task of a leaf node. The subtree oriented fault-tolerance scheme can also be extended to an m-ary tree.

Dutt and Hayes [6] introduced covering relations and graphs as fundamental parameters in the design of k-fault-tolerant trees. They showed that if the covering graph in each level of a non-homogeneous tree is acyclic, there exists a covering sequence for any set of k faults. With this approach, they came up with near optimal designs of a k-fault-tolerant non-homogeneous tree with arbitrary k. Their scheme can also be applied to k-fault-tolerant homogeneous trees.

2. Using Switching Networks to Construct Fault-Tolerant Binary Trees

2.1. Switching Network

In constructing fault-tolerant Binary Tree networks, we will require a switching network with n incoming and $n+k$ outgoing links as shown in Figure 2-1. In particular, let $\alpha_1, \alpha_2, \ldots, \alpha_n$ be a sequence such that $1 \leq \alpha_1 < \alpha_2 < \ldots < \alpha_n \leq n+k$. We want a switching network which allows the n incoming links to be connected to any such sequence $\alpha_1, \alpha_2, \ldots, \alpha_n$ of outgoing links so that incoming link i is connected to outgoing link α_i. The detailed design of two such switching networks is described in Chau and Liestman's [5] paper.

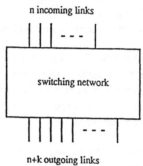

n incoming links

switching network

n+k outgoing links

Figure 2-1: A switching network with n incoming links
and $n+k$ outgoing links

A switching network can be implemented using a group of decoupling networks. The group of decoupling networks maps n incoming links (numbered 1 to n) to $n+k$ outgoing links (numbered 1 to $n+k$). Each outgoing link is connected to a processor. The use of decoupling networks has previously been proposed for other fault-tolerant multi-computer network architectures [11, 1, 3, 4, 5]. Figure 2-2 shows the connections for a group of 3 decoupling networks arranged in three levels.

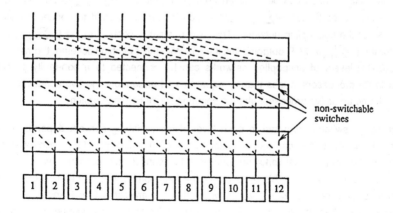

non-switchable switches

Figure 2-2: 3 decoupling networks arranged in 3 levels

The levels of each group of decoupling networks are numbered from 0 to $l-1$ with level 0 connecting to the outgoing links and level $l-1$ connecting to the incoming links. Each level contains at most $n+k-1$ switches numbered from 1 to $n+k-1$. The jth switch of level i may be connected to the jth or the $(j+2^i)^{th}$ switch of level $i-1$. The jth switch on level 0 can connect to either the jth outgoing link or the $(j+1)^{st}$ outgoing link. Initially, every switch j on level $i > 0$ is set to connect to switch j on level $i-1$. Switch j on level 0 is initially set to connect to outgoing link j. With this design, $l=\lceil \log_2(k+1)\rceil$ levels of decoupling networks are required to incorporate k spares.

In describing the construction of fault-tolerant binary trees, we use the term **active processors** to denote all the processors that participate in the execution of tasks. At any given time, n processors are active. We denote the active processors as $\alpha_1,\dots,\alpha_n$ with $\alpha_1 < \alpha_2 < \dots < \alpha_n$ such that α_1 is the number of the lowest numbered active processor and α_n is the number of the highest numbered active processor. In particular, $\alpha_i=j$ indicates that processor j is the ith active processor.

Consider one such l level decoupling network connected to n active processors and k spares. Initially $\alpha_i=i$ for $1 \le i \le n$. When the first active processor fails, the switch in level 0 that is connected to the failed processor and all the switches to the right of it are switched one position to the right. However, when subsequent failures occur, each remaining active processor and the spares used to replace the failed processors must determine which switches to use.

Suppose $\alpha_i=j$, the ith incoming link of the decoupling network should be connected to the jth outgoing link, that is, to the jth processor. In level $l-1$, the highest level, the ith switch connects to the ith incoming link. If $j-i \ge 2^{l-1}$, switch i will have to connect to the $(i+2^{l-1})^{th}$ switch of level $l-2$. Otherwise, no change is required and it remains connected to the ith switch of level $l-1$. Let $j-i=\sum_{m=0}^{l-1}a_m2^m$ where a_m is either 0 or 1 and $l=\lceil \log_2(k+1)\rceil$. If $j-i \ge 2^{l-1}$, $a_{l-1}=1$. Otherwise, $a_{l-1}=0$. For level $l-2$, the switch used in the connection from incoming link i to processor j depends on whether the switch used in level $l-1$ is switched or not. This information can be obtained from the value of a_{l-1}. If $a_{l-1}=1$, the $(i+2^{l-1})^{th}$ switch is used. Otherwise, the ith one is used. That is, the switch used in level $l-2$ is the $(i+a_{l-1}2^{l-1})^{th}$ switch. This switch is switched to connect to the $(i+a_{l-1}2^{l-1}+2^{l-2})^{th}$ switch in level $l-3$ if $(j-i)-a_{l-1}2^{l-1} \ge 2^{l-2}$. That is, if $a_{l-2}=1$. Otherwise, switching is not necessary. Hence, the switches used in the connection and the status of the switches used can be obtained from the equation $j-i=\sum_{m=0}^{l-1}a_m2^m$ with $a_l=0$ to simplify the formulas below. In particular, $i+\sum_{m=u+1}^{l}a_m2^m$ switch in level u is used to connect incoming link i to outgoing link j of the decoupling network. This switch is set to connect to the $(i+\sum_{m=u}^{l}a_m2^m)^{th}$ switch of level $u-1$ (or the $(i+\sum_{m=u}^{l}a_m2^m)^{th}$ outgoing link if $u=0$). With this switching scheme, the n incoming links of the $l=\lceil \log_2(k+1)\rceil$ levels of decoupling networks can be connected to n non-faulty processors if the number of faulty processors is less than or equal to k. Furthermore, no two connections between an incoming link and an active processor share a common link or common switch.

The number of switches required in each level of the switching network depends on n and k. If processor $n+k$, the last spare, can be connected to the nth incoming link of the decoupling networks, the switches in the decoupling networks are sufficient to connect any incoming link i, $1 \le i \le n$, to any outgoing link j, $i \le j \le i+k$. With this observation, the total number of switches in a group of decoupling network can be obtained. Let $k=\sum_{m=0}^{l-1}a_m2^m$, where the a_m's are either 0 or 1 and $a_{l-1}=1$. The level $l-1$ decoupling network has n switches which are connected to the n incoming links to the group of decoupling networks. The nth switch can connect to either the nth switch or the $n+2^{l-1}$ switch in level $l-2$. Thus, the number of switches in level $l-2$ is $n+a_{l-1}2^{l-1}$. The last switch $(n+a_{l-1}2^{l-1})$ in level $l-2$ is not required to connect to the $n+2^{l-1}+2^{l-2}$ switch in level $l-3$ when $a_{l-2}=0$. In this case, not all of the switches have to be switchable (see figure 2-2). Hence, for level l–3, the number of switches is $n+\sum_{m=l-2}^{l-1} a_m 2^m$. Similarly, for level i, the number of switches is $n+\sum_{m=i+1}^{l-1} a_m 2^m$. With this number of switches, the nth incoming link is able to connect to the last spare processor since $k=\sum_{m=0}^{l-1} a_m 2^m$. Thus, for a switching network with $l=\lceil \log_2 k+1 \rceil$ levels, the total number of switches is $nl+\sum_{m=1}^{l-1} ma_m 2^m$.

2.2. A New Fault-Tolerant Scheme for Binary Trees

A fault-tolerant binary tree can be constructed by using switching networks to connect the processors together to form a binary tree. Three groups of switching networks are used to connect the processors together. The first group is used to connect each processor to its parent. The second, and the third group are used to connect the processors to their left and right children, respectively. For a binary tree with d levels, we number the initially active processors in level order from 1 to 2^d–1 and the spare processors from 2^d to 2^d–1+k. That is, the processors are numbered from left to right in each level from the root down. For a d-level binary tree, the first group of switching networks has 2^d–1 incoming links and the processors are connected to its out-going links. For the second and third groups, only 2^{d-1}–1 incoming links are necessary and only the first 2^{d-1}–1+k processors are connected to the out-going links. The ith incoming link of the second group (which connects a processor to its left child,) is connected to incoming link $2i$ of the first group. The ith incoming link of the third group (which connects a processor to its right child,) is connected to incoming link $2i$+1 of the first group. Finally, the first incoming link of the first group is connected to an external link that provides input to or accepts output from the root of the tree. The connections between the three switching networks, and those between the switching networks and the processors for a 3-level binary tree with 1 spare are shown in Figure 2-3. Furthermore, the scheme can also be extended to m-ary trees [2].

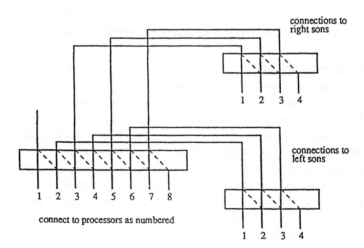

Figure 2-3: A fault-tolerant 3-level binary tree with 1 spare

When a processor fails, each of the three groups of decoupling networks must be reconfigured to remove the faulty processor, activate a spare processor and reassign tasks among the active processors. The reconfiguring process for a fault-tolerant binary tree is the same as described earlier except that all three switching networks used in the connection must be reconfigured simultaneously.

As an example of the reconfiguration process, consider a fault-tolerant 3-level binary tree with 2 spares. The initial configuration is shown in Figure 2-4. If processor 3 fails, the links that connect processor 3 in level 0 of the decoupling networks and all the links to the right of them are switched to the right. Processor 3 is disconnected from the incoming communication link to the three decoupling networks. Processor i takes over the task of processor $i-1$, for $i=4, \ldots, 8$. Figure 2-5 shows the connections in the binary tree after processor 3 has failed.

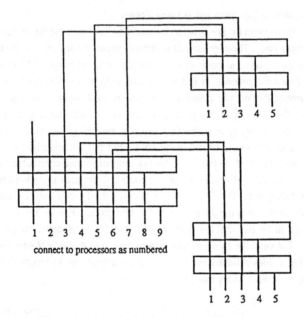

Figure 2-4: A 2-fault-tolerant 3-level binary tree

3. Estimation of the Reliability of the Scheme

Consider a fault-tolerant binary tree network constructed using switching networks which contains n active processors and k spares. In our reliability analysis, we consider only processor failure. We do not consider the failures in the switches and the links. However, if we assume that a failed switch is one that cannot be switched but it still provide connection between two links, a switch failure can be considered as processor failures. Because with this assumption, a switch failure can only make a few processor not being able to connected to the incoming links. Similarly, link failures can also be considered as processor failures. Other types of failures, such as fault-detection failures and recovery failures, are accounted for by the coverage factor [13] which is defined to be the probability that a failure is detected and the recovery is successful. If reconfiguration fails due to one of these failure types, the entire system is considered to be unreconfigurable.

Let c be the coverage factor, k the number of spares processors in the network, d the level of the binary tree, $n=2^d-1$ the number of active processors in the network, r the reliability of a single processor, and R_k the reliability of a fault-tolerant binary tree network with k spare processors. We assume that $r=e^{-\lambda t}$ where λ is a constant representing the failure rate of a processor over time t, expressed in millions of hours (see [13]).

The reliability of a non-redundant network R_0 is r^n. For $k=1$, the probability that the spare is needed is

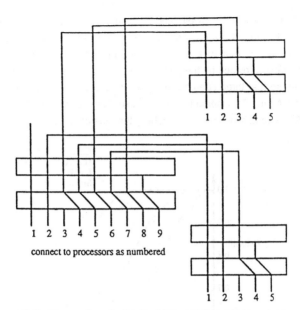

1 2 3 4 5

1 2 3 4 5 6 7 8 9
connect to processors as numbered

1 2 3 4 5

Figure 2-5: Connections in the fault-tolerant 3-level binary tree
with 2 spares after processor 3 has become faulty

equal to the probability that an initially active processor has failed which is $\binom{n}{1}r^{n-i}(1-r)$. The probability that a particular spare processor is reliable and can be switched successfully is rc. Thus, the additional reliability with one spare is $rc\binom{n}{1}r^{n-1}(1-r)$ and the reliability R_1 is $R_1 = r^n+\binom{n}{1}r^n(1-r)c = R_0+\binom{n}{1}r^n(1-r)c$. For $k=2$, the second spare is only used when there are exactly two faulty processors among the n initial active processors and the first spare. The probability that this occurs is $\binom{n-1}{2}r^{n-1}(1-r)^2c$. Thus, the reliability with two spares is $R_2 = R_1+\binom{n+1}{2}r^n(1-r)^2c^2$.

For arbitrary k,

$$R_k = R_{k-1}+\binom{n+k-1}{k}r^n(1-r)^k c^k = \sum_{i=0}^{k}\binom{n+i-1}{i}r^n(1-r)^i c^i.$$

4. Comparison with Previous Schemes

In Figures 4-1 and 4-2, the system reliabilities of an 8-level full binary tree using Singh's scheme, Howells and Agarwal's scheme, Lowrie and Fuchs's SOFT scheme and our scheme are plotted for $\lambda=0.1$ with $c=1$ and $c=0.95$, respectively. The number of spares used by each scheme is slightly different. For Lowrie and Fuchs's scheme, 64 spares (the maximum allowable) are used. Since the only accurate reliability equation given in their paper is for a 4-level tree, the reliability values used in the figures are approximate and have been obtained by averaging the upper and lower bounds that they give for their scheme. The lower bound, given in their paper, is the reliability of a modular tree where each module has three active processors and one spare. The upper bound is the reliability of a modular tree where each module has three active processors and two spares. This upper bound (suggested by Howells and Agarwal [8]), is justified because at most two failures can be tolerated for a node and its two children. With Singh's scheme, 127 spares are used which gives one spare to each module. This number is the smallest possible number of spares for his scheme and is already twice as many spares as used by

Lowrie and Fuchs's scheme. For Howells and Agarwal's scheme, 48 spares are used. The entire 8-level binary tree is split into a 4-level subtree containing the root and sixteen 4-level non-root subtrees. The subtree containing the root is assumed to be implemented using Lowrie and Fuchs's SOFT approach with the spares provided by the non-root subtrees. The 48 spares are divided equally among the sixteen subtrees so that three spares are allocated to each non-root subtree. With this number of spares, Howells and Agarwal's scheme is more reliable than the other two schemes. With our scheme, 25 spares are sufficient to achieve a higher reliability than the other schemes.

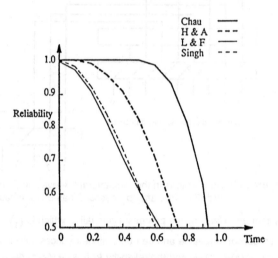

Figure 4-1: System reliabilities of the four schemes for an 8-level binary tree using $c=1$

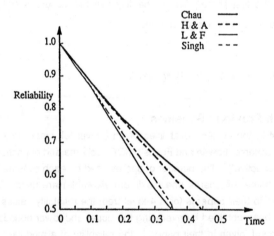

Figure 4-2: System reliabilities of the four schemes for an 8-level binary tree using $c=0.95$

For the range of t shown in Figures 4-1 and 4-2, our curves always lie above the curves of the other schemes even though our scheme uses fewer spares. At various points in the range $1 < t \le 2$ there are crossover points where the reliability of the new scheme drops below that of the other schemes. This must occur eventually since the other schemes use many more spares than our scheme. However, our scheme can achieve a higher level of reliability than the other schemes using only a fraction of the spares that are used when $t \leq 1$. Intuitively, our scheme is more reliable since it treats the entire binary tree as a single fault-tolerant module, that is a system with only k spares can tolerate any k faults in the binary tree. Thus, it is more flexible in its use of spares than the other schemes and is optimal in terms of the number of processor failures that a network can tolerate.

We have also calculated the reliabilities obtained by our scheme and by Howells and Agarwal's scheme for an 8-level binary tree with $c=0.95$ and $c=1$ when both schemes use 48 spares (approximately 20% of the number of active processors). In this comparison, our scheme achieves a higher reliability over the range $0 < t \leq 2.5$. The same result is obtained when we compare our scheme and that of Lowrie and Fuchs's (with 64 spares each) and when comparing our scheme with Singh's (with 127 spares each).

The hardware requirements of the different schemes are discussed in terms of two measurements - the number of spares and the number of switches. A clear comparison can be made with the number of spares required since the hardware required for a spare processor is the same for all the schemes. The complexity of the switches used by various schemes differs considerably and, thus, simply counting them is not sufficient. For example, the switches used in our scheme are simpler than those used in either Lowrie and Fuchs's scheme or in Howells and Agarwal's scheme.

In order to construct a d-level fault-tolerant binary tree, three groups of switching networks are required. The first one has 2^d-1 incoming links and 2^d+k-1 outgoing links. The other two have $2^{d-1}-1$ incoming links and $2^{d-1}+k-1$ outgoing links. Let $l=\lceil \log_2(k+1) \rceil$ and $k=\sum_{i=0}^{l-1} ia_i 2^i$, where the a_i's are either 0 or 1. From the calculations given in Section 2.1, the total number of switches required for our scheme is $2l(2^{d-1}-1)+l(2^d-1)+3\sum_{i=1}^{l-1} ia_i 2^i$. That is, $2l(n-3/2)+3\sum_{i=1}^{l-1} ia_i 2^i$ switches.

		No. of Spares		No. of Switches		Reliability	
d	n	L & F	Chau	L & F	Chau	L & F	Chau
4	15	4	2	154	94	0.9941	0.9957
5	31	8	3	318	192	0.9883	0.9956
6	63	16	4	646	529	0.9757	0.9893
7	127	32	6	1302	1051	0.9525	0.9828
8	255	64	8	2614	2630	0.9082	0.9195
9	511	128	13	5238	5224	0.8322	0.8377
10	1023	256	23	10486	12535	0.7160	0.7392
11	2047	512	42	20982	29290	0.5796	0.5803
12	4095	1024	82	41974	67023	0.4730	0.4978

Table 4-1: Hardware requirements for Lowrie and Fuch's SOFT scheme and our scheme to achieve the same level of reliability at $t=0.2$

In Table 4-1, the number of spares and switches required for our scheme to obtain approximately the

		No. of Spares		No. of Switches		Reliability	
d	n	Singh	Chau	Singh	Chau	Singh	Chau
4	15	7	2	144	94	0.9948	0.9957
5	31	15	3	304	192	0.9901	0.9956
6	63	31	4	624	529	0.9807	0.9893
7	127	63	6	1264	1051	0.9622	0.9828
8	255	127	9	2544	2632	0.9261	0.9608
9	511	255	14	5104	5232	0.8581	0.8965
10	1023	511	23	10224	12535	0.7366	0.7392
11	2047	1023	42	20464	29290	0.5427	0.5803
12	4095	2047	78	40944	66919	0.2947	0.3282

Table 4-2: Hardware requirements for Singh's scheme and our scheme to achieve the same level of reliability at t=0.2

same level of reliability as Lowrie and Fuchs's scheme is shown for $4 \leq d \leq 12$, with t=0.2 and c=1. Similarly, Tables 4-2 and 4-3 compare our scheme to Singh's scheme and to Howells and Agarwal's scheme, respectively. It can be seen that for $4 \leq d \leq 12$, our scheme uses only a fraction of the spares used by the other schemes. For $d \geq 8$, our scheme uses roughly 10% of the spares required by the other schemes and this percentage decreases as d increases. For smaller values of d, the percentage is somewhat higher but the improvement is still significant. For $d \leq 10$, the number of switches required is roughly the same as the other schemes. The number of switches does increase more rapidly for our scheme than Lowrie and Fuch's scheme, and Singh's scheme when $d \geq 10$. However, the savings in the number of spares when $d \geq 10$ should offset this increase. For Howells and Agarwal's scheme, the number of switches increases even more rapidly than our scheme for $d \geq 10$. Thus, the hardware requirement for our scheme is no more than for the other proposed schemes for $4 \leq d \leq 12$.

Table 4-4 lists the number of spares required for our scheme to achieve a reliability of at least 0.98 at time t=0.4 for $4 \leq d \leq 11$. It also lists the same values for Howells and Agarwal's scheme to achieve a reliability of at least 0.98. If a reliability of 0.98 is not achievable, the reliability of having 100% spares for the sub-trees are listed. The values in Table 4-1, Table 4-2, and Table 4-4 show that our scheme can achieve higher reliability for a longer period of time when d is large. Thus, it is more suitable for long-life unmaintained systems than the other proposed schemes for binary trees with a large d.

Finally, the reliability of our scheme and Dutt and Hayes's [6] scheme should be approximately the same for both scheme is optimal in terms of the number of spares required to tolerate any set of k faults. Since, no switch design is given in Dutt and Hayes's [6] paper, the only parameter that we can compare is the number of extra links required in both schemes. In our scheme, the number of extra links is equal to the number of switches for each switch induces one additional links. Thus, the total number of extra link is at most $2\log_2(k+1)(n+k)$. For Dutt and Hayes's scheme, at least $nk+k(k+1)/2$ extra links are required. That is, the extra links required in our scheme has a growth rate of $O(n\log_2 k)$ and Dutt and Hayes's scheme has a growth rate of $O(nk)$. Hence, our scheme always uses less extra links for $k \geq 7$

		No. of Spares		No. of Switches		Reliability	
d	n	H & A	Chau	H & A	Chau	H & A	Chau
4	15	4	2	103	94	0.9897	0.9957
5	31	8	3	206	192	0.9795	0.9956
6	63	8	3	398	384	0.9195	0.9580
7	127	16	4	796	1041	0.8445	0.8803
8	255	48	11	2492	2642	0.9881	0.9926
9	511	96	17	4984	6349	0.9765	0.9800
10	1023	224	32	17912	14856	0.9883	0.9920
11	2047	448	55	35824	29460	0.9757	0.9818
12	4095	960	101	136688	67367	0.9757	0.9767

Table 4-3: Hardware requirements for Howell and Agarwal's scheme and our scheme to achieve the same level of reliability at $r=0.2$

		No. of Spares		No. of Switches		Reliability	
d	n	H & A	Chau	H & A	Chau	H & A	Chau
4	15	8	3	123	96	0.9931	0.9954
5	31	16	4	246	273	0.9862	0.9887
6	63	24	6	606	539	0.9875	0.9816
7	127	112	10	2044	1360	0.9771	0.9805
8	255	240	18	8060	3285	0.9771	0.9879
9	511	480	31	16120	6479	0.9551	0.9843
10	1023	992	56	64760	15168	0.9551	0.9840
11	2047	1984	103	129520	34609	0.9098	0.9812

Table 4-4: Hardware requirements for Howell and Agarwal's scheme and our scheme to achieve a reliability of at least 0.98 at $r=0.4$

and for even smaller k when n is large.

5. Summary and Related Results

We have described a new method to construct a fault-tolerant binary tree architecture which is suitable for long-life unmaintained systems and it can also be extended to m-ary trees. Our scheme considers only processor failures. In particular, our scheme with k spare processors can tolerate any set of k processor failures. Thus, we are able to obtain high reliability while using few spare processors. Our scheme compares favorably with previously proposed schemes. Furthermore, the same approach can also be applied to other multi-computer networks such as binary hypercubes [3], cube-connected cycles [1] and multistage interconnection networks [4].

References

[1]   Chau, S.-C.
        Fault-Tolerance in Multi-Computer Networks.
        PhD thesis, Simon Fraser University, August, 1989.

[2]   Chau, S.-C. and A. L. Liestman.
        A Fault-Tolerant Binary Tree Architecture.
        Technical Report 88-8, Simon Fraser University, December, 1988.

[3]   Chau, S.-C. and A. L Liestman.
        A Proposal for a Fault-Tolerant Binary Hypercube Architecture.
        In *Digests of Papers of the 19th International Symposium on Fault-Tolerant Computing*, pages
            323-330. The Computer Society, IEEE, June, 1989.

[4]   Chau, S.-C. and A. L. Liestman.
        Fault-Tolerant for Multistage Interconnection Networks.
        Technical Report 89-1, Simon Fraser University, March, 1989.

[5]   Chau, S.-C. and A. L. Liestman.
        A General Scheme for Fault-Tolerance in Multi-Computer Networks.
        September, 1989
        Submitted to the IEEE Transactions on Computers.

[6]   S. Dutt and J. P. Hayes.
        Design and Reconfiguration Strategies for Near-Optimal k-Fault Tolerant Tree Architectures.
        In *Digests of Papers of the 18th International Symposium on Fault-Tolerant Computing*, pages
            328-333. The Computer Society, IEEE, 1988.

[7]   A. S. M. Hassan and V. K. Agarwal.
        A Fault-Tolerant Modular Architecture for Binary Trees.
        IEEE Transactions on Computers c-35(4):356-361, April, 1986.

[8]   M. Howells and V. K. Agarwal.
        A Reconfigurating Scheme for Yield Enhancement of Large Area Binary Tree Architectures.
        IEEE Transactions on Computers c-37(4):463-468, April, 1988.

[9]   C. L. Kwan and S. Toida.
        Optimal fault-tolerant realizations of hierarchical tree systems.
        In *Digests of Papers of the 11th International Symposium on Fault-Tolerant Computing*, pages
            176-178. he Computer Society, IEEE, 1981.

[10]   Mathew B. Lowrie and W. Kent Fuchs.
        Reconfigurable Tree Architectures Using Subtree Oriented Fault Tolerance.
        IEEE Transactions on Computers c-36(10):1172-1182, October, 1987.

[11]   C. S. Raghavendra, A. Avizienis and M. D. Ercegovac.
        Fault Tolerance in Binary Tree Architecture.
        IEEE Transactions on Computers c-33(6):568-572, June, 1984.

[12]   Adit D. Singh.
        A Reconfigurable Modular Fault Tolerant Binary Tree Architecture.
        In *Digests of Papers of the 18th International Symposium on Fault-Tolerant Computing*, pages
            298-304. The Computer Society, IEEE, 1987.

[13]   D. P. Siewiorek and R. S. Swarz.
        The Theory and Practice of Reliable System Design.
        Digital Press, Bedford, MA, 1982.

Unordered Tree Contraction

Lih–Hsing Hsu and Jones J. J. Wang

Department of Information and Computer Science, National Chiao Tung University

Hsinchu, Taiwan, Republic of China

FAX: 886–35–721490, E–mail: lhhsu@twnctu01.bitnet

Abstract

The tree contraction problem is for reducing a rooted tree to its root by a sequence of independent vertex removals. All of the previous research works are concentrated on ordered rooted tree whereas in this paper we are going to discuss the case of unordered rooted tree.

1. Introduction

The tree contraction problem is for reducing a rooted tree to its root by a sequence of independent vertex removals. All of the previous research works are concentrated on ordered rooted tree whereas in this paper we are going to discuss the case of unordered rooted tree. As a model for parallel computations, we choose the parallel random access machine (P–RAM) without writing conflicts. The processors are unit–cost RAMs that can access a common memory. Any subset of the processors can simultaneously read the same memory location. However, no two distinct processors can attempt to write simultaneously into the same location (CREW). By an optimal parallel algorithm for a given problem, we mean one that satisfies: $pt = O (n)$, where p is the number of processors used, t is the parallel computation time and where p is close to n.

The idea of ordered rooted tree contraction was proposed by Abrahamson, Daddoun, Kirkpatrick and Przytycka [1] and Gibbons and Rytter [5]. Usually, the ordered rooted tree contraction is composed of two separated parts. First, the ordered rooted tree is transformed into a binary rooted tree. Second, a sequence of "independent" executions of two fundamental operations, namely Prune(v) and Bypass (v), are performed. Here Prune(v) means that the leaf v is removed from the current tree; and Bypass(v) means that the non–root node v with exactly one child x is removed from the current tree and then the parent w of v becomes the new parent of x. By "independent", we mean that the parent of v can not be bypassed when v is pruned or bypassed. With this restriction, the ordered rooted tree contractions are ensured to be local and executable in parallel. Usually, the pair of operations, Prune(v) followed by Bypass(parent(v)) where v is any leaf, form a conceptual unit, cut (v), in execution. This unit usually called cutting. In order to execute cutting independently all leaves are labelled by 1 to n from left to right consecutively where n is the number of leaves. Now we may parallelly apply the cut(v) for every leaf which is a left–child and labelled by an odd number; then apply the cut(v) for every leaf which is a right–child and labelled by an odd number. After the above process the number of leaves is reduced to $n/2$.

Thus, we may recursively apply the above process $log\ n$ times and reduce the binary rooted tree to its root. Hence the above tree contraction takes $O(\ log\ n\ )$ time with n processors. However we can slightly modify the above algorithm so that it takes $O(\ log\ n\ )$ time with $n/\ log\ n$ processors. In this paper, we generalize the rooted ordered tree contraction into the unordered rooted tree contraction.

2. Unordered tree contraction

Let us consider a rather abstract problem. We use $\mathcal{T}$ to denote the set of all unordered rooted trees. Let f: $\mathcal{T} \to \mathcal{Z}$ be a function from $\mathcal{T}$ into another set $\mathcal{Z}$. Suppose that we are interested in writing a parallel algorithm to compute f. We say that a function f from $\mathcal{T}$ into $\mathcal{Z}$ is *contractible* if it satisfies the following conditions: (1) Every unordered rooted tree falls into exactly one of a finite set, say $S = \{S_1, S_2, ..., S_k\}$. We use $S(T)$ to denote the set S_i to which the unordered rooted tree T belong. With this notation, we may extend the function f into another function F where $F(T) = (S(T), f(T))$. (2) Given any unordered rooted tree T, let $T_1, T_2, ..., T_r$ be the children of T and let $t_i = |\{j|\ S(T_j) = S_i,\ j = 1, 2, ..., r\}|;\ i = 1, 2, ..., k$. Then $S(T)$ can be written as $S(T) = S(t_1, t_2, ..., t_k)$. (3) $f(T)$ can be written as $f(T) = f(g(T), h(T))$ where $g(T) = g(f(T_1), f(T_2), ..., f(T_r))$ is a symmetric function on r variables. For example, $g(x_1, x_2, ..., x_r) = \Sigma (x_i^2 - log\ x_i)$. Moreover $h(T)$ can be written as $h(T) = h(t_1, t_2, ..., t_k)$.

If f is contractible, we may transform an unordered rooted tree into a binary rooted tree. We can attach a proper accumulator for every node on the tree to keep the information of S and f. Again, we may attach a proper guess function at every node. Then, we can use all these information and correctly calculate F(T) using the ordered tree contraction sequence. However, if we restrict our time to be $O(log\ n)$, then the function f must be very good. That is to say all the composite functions while we perform the cutting process take constant time. With the above observation, there are several combinatorial problems solved by using our unordered rooted tree contraction. In the following, we give some examples.

3. Several examples

A *series-parallel network* (*network*, in short) N defined on a set Y of *type* $t \in \{L, S, P\}$ (which respectively means *leaf, series* and *parallel*), is recursively defined as follows:
(1) N is a network of type L if $|Y| = 1$.
(2) N is a network either of type S or of type P if $|Y| > 1$ and there exist $k \geq 2$ *child subnetworks* $N_1, N_2, ..., N_k$ such that each N_i is defined on a set Y_i of type t_i with $t_i \neq t$ and $\{Y_i\}$ forms a partition of Y.

Usually, every network is represented by a tree structure as in Figure 1. Every node together with all of its descendants forms a *subnetwork* of N. The subnetwork of N formed by a child of the root is called a child subnetwork of N. The *leaf node* is labelled by y if it is a subnetwork of type L defined on $\{y\}$. Every *internal node* is labelled by S or P according to the type of the subnetwork it represents. The definition of the network is very natural because all boolean functions are of the form, with the series connection implementing logical–and and with the parallel connection implementing logical–or. Note that the order of every subtree of a given tree is immaterial because different orders of the subtrees will lead to the same logically boolean functions.

Every network is represented by a series–parallel graph (s.p. graph, in short). An *s.p. graph* is an edge–labelled graph with two distinct vertices. We can recursively represent a network by an s.p. graph as follows:

(1) Every network N defined on $Y = \{y\}$ of type L is represented by an edge–labelled graph G[N] with only one edge labelled by y and two vertices as distinct vertices.

(2) Let N be a network of type S with $N_1, N_2, ..., N_k$ as the child subnetworks of N and $G[N_i]$ be an s.p. graph that represents N_i with distinct vertices $\{a_i, b_i\}$ for every i. We identify b_i with a_{i+1} for every $1 \leq i \leq k-1$. The resultant graph G[N] with distinct vertices $\{a_1, b_k\}$ represents the network N.

(3) Let N be a network of type P with $N_1, N_2, ..., N_k$ as the child subnetworks of N and $G[N_i]$ be an s.p. graph that represents N_i with distinct vertices $\{a_i, b_i\}$ for every i. We identify all a_i to get a new vertex a and identify all b_i to get a new vertex b. The resultant graph G[N] with distinct vertices $\{a, b\}$ represents the network N.

However, such graph representation for a network is not unique because the order of its subnetworks and the order of the two distinct vertices are fixed in each graph representation. Thus, several parameters [6,7,8] such as the maximum independent number among all graph representations for a network can be solved by the unordered tree contraction.

Reference
1. K. Abrahamson, N. Dadoun, D. G. Kirpatrick and T.Przytycka, A simple parallel tree contraction algorithm, *J. Algorithms* 10 (1989), 287–302.
2. I. Bar–On and U. Vishkin, Optimal parallel generation of a compution tree form, *ACM Trans. Programm. Lang. System* 7, No. 2 (1985), 348–357.
3. M. W. Bern, E. L. Lawler and A. L. Wong, Linear–time computation of optimal subgraphs of decomposable graphs, *J. Algorithms* 8 (1987), 216–235.
4. F. Y. Chin, J. Lam and I. Chan, Efficient parallel algorithms for some graph problems, *Commun. ACM* 25, No. 9 (1982), 659–665.
5. A. Gibbons and W. Rytter, Optimal parallel algorithms for dynamic expression and context–free recognition, *Inform. and Comput.* 81 (1989), 32–45.
6. L. H. Hsu and S. Y. Wang, Maximum independent number for series–parallel networks, to appear at *Networks*.
7. L. H. Hsu and S. Y. Wang, Maximum matching for series–parallel networks, submitted to *Discrete Applied Math.*.
8. L. H. Hsu, Y. C. Chang and T. Y. Ho, Double Euler trail on series–parallel networks, submitted to *Discrete Applied Math.*.
9. X. He and Y. Yesha, Binary tree algebraic computation and parallel algorithms for simple graphs, *J. Algorithms* 9 (1988), 92–113.
10. G. L. Miller and J. H. Reif, Parallel tree contraction and its application, *in* "26th IEEE Symp. on Foundations of Comput. Sci., 1985," 478–489.

Conflict–Free Sorting Algorithms under Single–Channel and Multi–Channel Broadcast Communication Models***

Chang–Biau Yang*, R. C. T. Lee** and Wen–Tsuen Chen**

* Department of Applied Mathematics, National Sun Yat–sen University
Kaohsiung, Taiwan 80424, Republic of China.

** Department of Computer Science, National Tsing Hua University
Hsinchu, Taiwan 30043, Republic of China.

*** This research work was partially supported by the National Science Council of the Republic of China under contract NSC77–0408–E007–04.

Abstract

In this paper, we shall first propose an optimal conflict–free parallel sorting algorithm under the single–channel broadcast communication model. The time complexity of this algorithm is $O((n/p)\log(n/p)+n)$ if p processors are used to sort n data elements. We then apply our single–channel sorting algorithm to improve the multi–channel sorting algorithm proposed by Marberg and Gafni. Since there is a constraint for the Marberg and Gafni's algorithm, we shall propose another conflict–free multi–channel sorting algorithm without this constraint. The time complexity of this algorithm is $O((n/p)\log(n/p)+(n/k)\log^2 k)$ if there are n data elements to be sorted by using p processors with k channels.

Section 1 Introduction

For designing parallel algorithms, the broadcast communication model [4, 5, 8, 9, 12, 14, 15, 17, 18] has attracted attentions from researchers recently. In this model, there is one or more than one shared communication channel. It is called a **single–channel broadcast communication system** if only one shared channel is used and called a **multi–channel broadcast communication system** if more than one shared channel is used. In a multi–channel broadcast communication system, each channel can be dynamically switched among processors. Each processor in a broadcast communication multiprocessor system can communicate with others only through the shared channels. Whenever a processor broadcasts messages in one channel, any other processor can hear the messages via this channel. If more than one processor attempts to use the same channel to broadcast messages simultaneously, a **broadcast conflict** occurs in this channel. When a conflict occurs in a channel, we have to use a conflict resolution scheme to resolve the conflict. An algorithm is **conflict–free** if there is no conflict during the execution of the algorithm. Of course, a conflict–free algorithm has better performance because no resolution time is needed.

Parallel sorting algorithms have been studied and designed by many researchers. For complete reviews of this subject, see [3, 16]. Some researchers [5, 8, 9, 12] have used the broadcast communication model to solve the sorting problem.

Both Levitan's sorting algorithm [8] and Dechter and Kleinrock's [5] sorting algorithm have the problem of broadcast conflicts. Willard [19] proved that the lower bound of the average time for any algorithm to resolve a broadcast conflict in a p–processor broadcast communication multiprocessor system is $\Omega(\log\log p)$. In other word, it is impossible that there exists a mechanism to resolve a broadcast conflict in a constant time. Thus, it is preferred to design an algorithm without any broadcast conflicts, which is a conflict–free algorithm.

Marberg and Gafni [9] first proposed a conflict–free sorting algorithm under the multi–channel broadcast communication model. The time required for their algorithm to sort n numbers with p processors and k channels, $n{\geq}p{\geq}k$, is $O((n/k)\log(n/k))$ with the constraint $n{\geq}k^2(k{-}1)$.

In this paper, based upon the concept of enumeration sorting [11], we first propose an optimal conflict–free sorting algorithm under the single–channel model. The time required for this algorithm is $O((n/p)\log(n/p)+n)$ if there are n data elements to be sorted and p processors are incorporated in the broadcast communication multiprocessor system. Our algorithm is better than those proposed by previous researchers [5, 8, 12]. Based upon our single–channel sorting algorithm, we also propose an improvement of Marberg and Gafni's multi–channel sorting algorithm.

We then propose a conflict–free multi–channel sorting algorithm, which is based upon the concepts of bitonic sorting [1, 13] and block sorting [2, 10]. In this algorithm, we propose a simple channel schedule to avoid broadcast conflicts. The time required for this algorithm is $O((n/p)\log(n/p)+(n/k)\log^2 k)$. For this algorithm, we use the same model used by Marberg and Gafni [9]. Our algorithm does not have the constraint $n{\geq}k^2(k{-}1)$, which is needed in Marberg and Gafni's algorithm.

Section 2 A Conflict–Free Single–Channel Sorting Algorithm

In this section, we shall propose an optimal conflict–free sorting algorithm under the single–channel broadcast communication model. First, we define the rank of an element in a set of numbers. Let S be a set of numbers and i belong to S. The **rank** of i, denoted as rank(i), is defined as the number of elements in S which are smaller than i. For example, consider S={10, 16, 2, 20, 5}. The ranks of all elements in S are as follows: rank(10)=2, rank(16)=3, rank(2)=0, rank(20)=4 and rank(5)=1.

In the following, we shall apply the idea of enumeration sorting [11] to sort n data elements by using p processors, $p{\leq}n$, under the single–channel broadcast communication model. We assume that p divides n. If it is not this case, we only add some dummy data elements with values being positive infinite to fulfill our assumption. These processors are numbered by 1, 2, ... and p. Each processor stores n/p data elements and reserves the storage for storing the ranks of these data. We assume that all data are mutually distinct; otherwise, each data element would be replaced by a 3–tuple consisting of itself, the identifier of the processor storing it and the index of the storage storing it. Our algorithm first computes the ranks of all data elements and then reports the sorted sequence by the increasing order of the ranks.

Algorithm Single–Channel–Sorting

Step 1: Each processor sorts its local data into an ascending list and computes the rank of each data elements with respect to the set of data elements stored in this processor.

Step 2: i=1. Repeat the following substeps p times.

    Step 2.1: Processor i broadcasts all data elements stored in it in the ascending sequence. All other processors temporarily store the broadcast data in their local memory.

    Step 2.2: All processors except processor i apply the **two–way ranking** scheme to update the ranks of the data elements stored in them.

    Step 2.3: i <— i+1.

Step 3: Report the sorted sequence according to the ranks of these n data elements.

In the above algorithm, only the two–way ranking scheme used in step 2.2 has to be designed. Suppose that there are two sorted lists $a_1 < a_2 < ... < a_m$ and $b_1 < b_2 < ... < b_m$ and one ranking list $r_1, r_2, ..., r_m$ associated with the first list such that r_i is the rank of a_i with respect to the first list. That is, $r_i = i-1$, $1 \leq i \leq m$. We assume that the data of these two sorted lists are all distinct. We apply the concept of the two–way merging algorithm [6] to find the position of the second list where a_i is bounded. If $b_j < a_i < b_{j+1}$, $1 \leq j \leq m-1$ and $1 \leq i \leq m$, then r_i is replaced by r_i+j. For the boundary condition that $a_i > b_m$, we substitute r_i with r_i+m. After the two–way ranking, r_i will be the rank of a_i with respect to these two lists. For example, consider two sorted lists A=(2, 5, 10, 16, 20) and B=(6, 7, 12, 13, 14), and a ranking list R=(0, 1, 2, 3, 4) associated with list A. After performing the two–way ranking, the ranking list R will become R'=(0, 1, 4, 8, 9). The time required for this two–way ranking scheme is O(m).

The total time required for our algorithm is $O((n/p)\log(n/p)+n)$, which can be easily calculated from the time complexity for each step as follows:

    Step 1: $O((n/p)\log(n/p))$.

    Step 2: $O((n/p)+(n/p)) \cdot p = O(n)$.

    Step 3: O(n).

In the following, we shall prove that the above sorting algorithm is optimal under the single–channel broadcast communication model. To prove the following lemmas, we need a definition. For two data elements x and y in a set, y is the **predecessor** of x if rank(y)=rank(x)−1.

[Lemma 2.1] Let a_1, a_2, ..., a_n be a sorted sequence where $a_1 \leq a_2 \leq ... \leq a_n$. Suppose that these n data elements are stored in p processors arbitrarily. The number of data elements stored in processor i is n_i, $1 \leq i \leq p$. Let n_j be the maximum among all n_i's, $1 \leq i \leq p$. If $n_j < n/2$, there exists one case such that for each data element a_k, $2 \leq k \leq n$, its predecessor, a_{k-1}, is not stored in the same processor with a_k.

PROOF: To prove this lemma, we need only to generate one such case. We rearrange the sorted sequence into a new sequence as $a_1 a_3 a_5 ... a_{n-1} a_2 a_4 ... a_n$ (Without losing generality, we assume that n is even.). We store the n data elements into the p processors according to the rearranged sequence. At step i, $1 \leq i \leq p$, we store the first n_i data elements of the rearranged sequence into processor i and then delete these n_i data elements from the sequence. After doing this, we claim that a_k and a_{k-1}, $2 \leq k \leq n$, would not be stored in the same processor. Two cases should be considered as follows.

Case 1: k is odd. If both a_k and a_{k-1} are stored in processor i, $1 \leq i \leq p$, then the subsequence $a_k a_{k+2} ... a_{n-1} a_2 a_4 ... a_{k-1}$ would be stored in processor i. The length of this subsequence is $n/2$. This is impossible since $n_i < n/2$. Thus, processor i can not store both a_k and a_{k-1}.

Case 2: k is even. For this case, it is similar to case 1.

By both these case, our claim is correct. Therefore, the proof is complete.

Q. E. D.

Dechter and Kleinrock [5] have proved that the lower bound of number of broadcasts is $\Omega(n)$ when p processors are used to sort n data elements under the single–channel broadcast communication model and these n data elements are divided and stored in the p processors evenly. We shall give a more general lower bound for this problem and prove it as follows.

[Lemma 2.2] In the single–channel broadcast communication model, the time required for an algorithm using p processors, $p \geq 1$, to sort n data elements is $\Omega(n)$ under the assumption that the data are preloaded into the processors and each data element is loaded into only one processor.

PROOF: If the sorted data need to be reported, the time required for reporting is $\Omega(n)$ since only one channel is available to report the sorted data. In the following, we assume that data do not need to be reported.

To determine the final position of one data element in the entire sorted sequence, we must compare it at least with its predecessor (except the smallest data element). Suppose that n_i data elements are preloaded into processor i. Here, $\sum_{i=1}^{p} n_i = n$. Let n_j be the maximum among all n_i's, $1 \leq i \leq p$. We have to consider two cases as follows.

Case 1: $n_j \geq n/2$. For each data element in processor j, either processor j compares this data element with its predecessor or broadcasts this data element to other processors to perform the comparison. Thus, processor j must read each data element stored in it at least once. The time required for processor j to read the data elements stored in it is at least $\Omega(n/2) = \Omega(n)$. Therefore, the time required for sorting is $\Omega(n)$.

Case 2: $n_j < n/2$. Let a_1, a_2, ..., a_n be the sorted sequence of these n data element where $a_1 \leq a_2 \leq ... \leq a_n$. Without losing generality, it is assumed that n is even. Consider the following n/2 data elements: a_2, a_4, a_6, ..., a_n. For each data element a_k where $2 \leq k \leq n$ and k is even, by Lemma 2.1, there exists one such case that a_{k-1} (the predecessor of a_k) would not be stored in the same processor with a_k. In order to compare each pair of a_k and a_{k-1}, either a_k or a_{k-1} must be broadcast. At least n/2 successful broadcasts are required if we want to compare a_2, a_4, ..., a_n with their predecessors respectively. Thus, the time required for sorting at least $\Omega(n)$ since only one channel is available.

By both these two cases, this lemma is true.   Q. E. D.

Under any parallel computation model, the time required for an algorithm using p processors, $p \geq 1$, to sort n data elements is at least $\Omega((n\log n)/p)$ since the lower bound for a sequential sorting algorithm to sort n data elements is $\Omega(n\log n)$ [6]. Combining with Lemma 2.2, we obtain that under the single–channel broadcast communication model, the lower bound for an algorithm using p processors, $p \geq 1$, to sort n data elements is $\Omega(n + (n\log n)/p)$.

[Theorem 2.3] Under the single–channel broadcast communication model, Algorithm Single–Channel–Sorting is optimal under the assumption that the data are preloaded into the processors and each data element is loaded into only one processor.

PROOF: The time complexity of Algorithm Single–Channel–Sorting is $O((n/p)\log(n/p) + n)$. We have to consider two cases as follows.

Case 1: $n \geq (n\log n)/p$.   In this case, $n \geq (n/p)\log(n/p)$. Then $n + (n\log n)/p = \Omega(n)$ and $n + (n/p)\log(n/p) = O(n)$.

Case 2: $n \leq (n\log n)/p$.   In this case, $p \leq \log n$.   Then $n + (n\log n)/p = \Omega((n\log n)/p)$ and $n + (n/p)\log(n/p) = O((n\log n)/p)$.

For both these cases, the time complexity of Algorithm Single–Channel–Sorting achieves the lower bound of any sorting algorithm under this model. The proof is complete.

Q. E. D.

Section 3 An Improvement of Marberg and Gafni's Sorting Algorithm

In this section, we shall propose an improvement of Marberg and Gafni's sorting algorithm [9]. Marberg and Gafni applied the column sort [7] to the multi–channel broadcast communication model and designed the first conflict–free sorting algorithm in this model. Their sorting algorithm uses p processors with k channels to sort n data elements where $n \geq p \geq k$. In their algorithm, they needed to sort the data stored in a group of processors which share one broadcast channel. In a group of processors, they only chose one of these processors to perform the sorting. In other words, all the data in one group of processors are sent to one of these processors to be sorted. The time required for their algorithm to sort n data elements by using p processors with k channels, $n \geq p \geq k$, is $O((n/k)\log(n/k))$ with the constraint $n \geq k^2(k-1)$. The constraint $n \geq k^2(k-1)$ is induced because of the use of Leighton's column sort.

There are two problems for Marberg and Gafni's sorting algorithm as follows. (1). Using more processors can not reduce the required time. The time required for the algorithm depends only on n and k, not on p. (2). There is a serious constraint: $n \geq k^2(k-1)$.

For the first problem, we can easily improve Marberg and Gafni's algorithm by applying Algorithm Single—Channel—Sorting. In our improvement, we use Algorithm Single—Channel—Sorting to perform the sorting of a groups of processors which share one channel. Since no processor is idle when Algorithm Single—Channel—Sorting is executed, the time complexity can be reduced. The time required for our improvement algorithm is $O((n/p)\log(n/p)+n/k)$ since there are n/p data elements in each processor and n/k data elements in each group.

For the second problem, we shall propose a new algorithm which does not have the serious constraint $n \geq k^2(k-1)$ in the next section.

Section 4 A Conflict—Free Multi—Channel Sorting Algorithm

In Marberg and Gafni's sorting algorithm [9], there is a constraint $n \geq k^2(k-1)$. In the following, we shall present a conflict—free multi—channel sorting algorithm which will work without this constraint.

In our multi—channel sorting algorithm, we assume that p processors with k channels are used in the multi—channel broadcast system and there are n data elements to be sorted, where $n \geq p \geq k$. These p processors are divided into 2k groups and each group consists of p/2k processors. We first apply our single—channel sorting algorithm to sort the data in every two groups by using one channel in parallel. Then, we use the famous bitonic sorting [1, 13] as our basic parallel sorting algorithm. When we perform the sorting, we view each group as a data element and replace each comparison—exchange operation by one merging—splitting of two groups. This is the spirit of blocking sorting [2, 10]. We give a simple channel schedule such that the merging—splitting of every two groups can be performed in parallel without any conflicts. Our multi—channel sorting algorithm is as follows.

Algorithm Multi—Channel—Sorting

Assumption: p processors with k communication channels are used to sort n data elements. p divides n, 2k divides p and $k=2^{m-1}$ where m is a positive integer. The p processors are divided into 2k groups with equal sizes. These 2k groups are numbered by 0,1,2,...,2k−1. Each processor is numbered by a pair of indices (i,j) where $0 \leq i \leq 2k-1$ and $0 \leq j \leq \frac{p}{2k} - 1$. The first index is the group index and the second index is the processor index within that group. These k channels are also numbered by 0,1,2,...,k−1.

Initialization: Each processor stores n/p data elements.

Final: Each processor stores a sorted sequence with n/p data elements. All data in processor (i,j) are smaller than those in processor (u,v) if i<u, or i=u and j<v.

Step 1: For each group i, $0 \le i \le k-1$, the processors of group i share channel i to sort the data stored in the processors of group i by using Algorithm Single–Channel–Sorting. After sorting, each processor stores a sorted sequence with n/p data elements and all data stored in processor (i,j) are smaller than those stored in processor (i,j+1) for $0 \le i \le k-1$, $0 \le j < \frac{p}{2k} - 2$.

Step 2: The processors of group i+k, $0 \le i \le k-1$, share channel i to sort the data stored in the processors of group i+k as do in step 1.

Step 3: Viewing each group as a data element, use bitonic sorting as the basic parallel sorting algorithm. Each comparison–exchange of two data elements is replaced by a merging–splitting of two groups which is performed by using one channel.

In the above algorithm, only step 3 has to be designed more detailedly. Our first problem is: How do we perform the merging–splitting of two groups under the broadcast communication model? Note that this must be done by using one broadcast channel and in a conflict–free fashion. We can perform the two–way merging algorithm [6] to merge the data in two groups by using one channel in a conflict–free fashion. Then, we can split the sorted data into the processors of these two groups. The time for this merging–splitting procedure is O(m) if there are totally m data elements to be merged and split.

Our multi–channel sorting algorithm is based upon bitonic sorting [1, 13]. Thus, we can use the same decision to overcome the second problem: Which two groups should be merged and split? Our third problem is how to select one channel for performing the merging–splitting of two groups. We shall also use the shuffle scheme proposed by Stone [13].

Assume that there are n data elements to be sorted in bitonic sorting. Stone used a shuffle scheme to choose two data elements to be compared for a comparison–exchange step. A **stage** consists of some parallel comparison–exchange steps. The jth stage consists of j parallel comparison–exchange steps. After the jth stage is completed, $n/(2^j)$ sorted sequences, each of length 2^j, are found. Naturally, the n data elements will be sorted after the (logn)th stage is completed. Thus, the total parallel comparison–exchange steps required for bitonic sorting is $O(\log^2 n)$. Assume that $n = 2^m$, where m is a positive number. An index i with the binary representation $i_{m-1} i_{m-2} \ldots i_0$ will become $i_{m-2} \ldots i_0 i_{m-1}$ after one left rotation, or say one **shuffle**. At the beginning of the jth stage, all indices are shuffled m−j times. For the subsequent j steps, each consists of one comparison–exchange followed by one shuffle. When a comparison–exchange is performed, the two data elements with their current indices (after several shuffles) differing only in the leftmost bit are compared. For example, consider that n=8. At the beginning of the second stage, 4=100 and 6=110. They become 001 and 101 respectively after one shuffle. At the first comparison–exchange step of the second stage, the data in positions 4 and 6 are compared since their current indices 001 and 101 differ only in the leftmost bit.

Here, we use the group indices instead of position indices used by Stone. When two groups are merged, the current group indices (after several shuffles) of these two groups must differ only in the leftmost bit. We remove the leftmost bit from these two indices to obtain a channel index, which is the index of the channel that we use to merge these two groups. Fig. 1 shows an example with

group number	channel usage										
	stage 1	stage 2		stage 3			stage 4			
0	0	0	0	0	0	0	0	0	0	0
1	0	4	0	2	4	0	1	2	4	0
2	1	0	1	4	0	1	2	4	0	1
3	1	4	1	6	4	1	3	6	4	1
4	2	1	2	0	1	2	4	0	1	2
5	2	5	2	2	5	2	5	2	5	2
6	3	1	3	4	1	3	6	4	1	3
7	3	5	3	6	5	3	7	6	5	3
8	4	2	4	1	2	4	0	1	2	4
9	4	6	4	3	6	4	1	3	6	4
10	5	2	5	5	2	5	2	5	2	5
11	5	6	5	7	6	5	3	7	6	5
12	6	3	6	1	3	6	4	1	3	6
13	6	7	6	3	7	6	5	3	7	6
14	7	3	7	5	3	7	6	5	3	7
15	7	7	7	7	7	7	7	7	7	7

Fig. 1   The channel schedule for Algorithm Multi–Channel–Sorting with 16 groups. For each step, the two groups which use the same channel will be merged and split.

sixteen groups and eight channels for the channel schedule. Our algorithm under this simple channel schedule is conflict–free since only two groups share one channel and these two groups are merged and split without any conflicts.

In the following, we shall calculate the complexity for Algorithm Multi–Channel–Sorting. The time required for step 1 or step 2 is $O(n/p)\log(n/p)+n/(2k)=O((n/p)\log(n/p)+n/k)$ since there are $n/2k$ data elements in each group to be sorted and there are n/p data elements in each processor to be sorted. The time required for step 3 is $O((n/2k)\log^2(2k))=O((n/k)\log^2 k)$ since each merging–splitting step requires $O(n/2k)$ time and the bitonic sorting requires $O(\log^2(2k))$ parallel merging–splitting steps. Thus, the total time required for Algorithm Multi–Channel–Sorting is $O((n/p)\log(n/p)+(n/k)\log^2 k)$.

In Algorithm Multi–Channel–Sorting, we assume that $n\geq p\geq k$, p divides n, 2k divides p and $k=2^{m-1}$ where m is a positive integer. We shall modify the algorithm to work correctly even if all constraints except $n\geq p\geq k$ are removed.

(1). If $2^{m-1}<k<2^m$ where m is a positive integer, we shall use k' to replace k where $k'=2^{m-1}$. If $k=2^{m-1}$ where m is a positive integer, let k'=k.

(2). If p can not divide n, we add (n'–n) dummy data elements with the infinite positive value such that n' is the smallest number satisfying that p can divide n'.

(3). If $p\geq 2k'$ and 2k' can not divides p, we still partition these p processors into 2k' groups evenly such that the difference of numbers of processors in different groups is at most one.

(4). If $k'\leq p<2k'$, let $k''=k'/2$ and k' be replaced by k''.

With the above modification, the time complexity for our algorithm remains unchanged. Our algorithm uses the same broadcast communication model as used by Marberg and Gafni [9]. Their sorting algorithm requires $O((n/k)\log(n/k))$ time with a serious constraint $n\geq k^2(k-1)$. Our algorithm does not have the constraint $n\geq k^2(k-1)$. We only assume that $n\geq p\geq k$.

Section 5 Concluding Remarks

In this paper, we proposed some conflict–free sorting algorithms under the broadcast communication model. We first proposed a conflict–free single–channel sorting algorithm based upon enumeration sorting [11]. The time required for this algorithm is $O((n/p)\log(n/p)+n)$ if p processors are used to sort n data elements. We also proved that this algorithm is optimal under the single–channel broadcast communication model. Then, we applied this algorithm to improve the multi–channel sorting algorithm proposed by Marberg and Gafni [9]. The time complexity of their algorithm is $O((n/k)\log(n/k))$ if the algorithm sorts n data elements by using p processors with k channels, where $n\geq p\geq k$ and $n\geq k^2(k-1)$. The improved algorithm proposed by us requires $O((n/p)\log(n/p)+n/k)$ time. We also designed a new conflict–free multi–channel sorting algorithm without the constraint $n\geq k^2(k-1)$ which is required in Marberg and Gafni's algorithm. This algorithm mixes the concepts of our single–channel sorting algorithm, Batcher's bitonic sorting algorithm [1, 13] and merging and splitting for block sorting algorithm [2, 10]. The time complexity of this algorithm is $O((n/p)\log(n/p)+(n/k)\log^2 k)$ if there are n data elements to be sorted with p processors and k channels, $n\geq p\geq k$.

For sorting algorithms under the multi–channel broadcast communication model, we have not found a lower bound of the time complexity yet. Intuitively, we believe that our new algorithm under the multi–channel broadcast communication model is not optimal. We are presently working on a better sorting algorithm under the multi–channel broadcast communication model.

REFERENCES

[1] K. E. Batcher, "Sorting Networks and Their Applications," Proc. AFIPS 1968 Spring Joint Computer Conf., Atlantic City, New Jersey. Vol. 32, 1968, pp. 307–314.

[2] G. Baudet and D. Stevenson, "Optimal Sorting Algorithms for Parallel Computers," IEEE Trans. Comput., Vol. C–27, No. 1, Jan. 1978, pp. 84–87.

[3] D. Bitton, D. J. DeWitt, D. K. Hsiao and J. Menon, "A Taxonomy of Parallel Sorting," Computing Surveys, Vol. 16, No. 3, Sept., pp. 287–318.

[4] S. H. Bokhari, "Max: An Algorithm for Finding Maximum in an Array Processor with a Global Bus," Proc. 1981 Int. Conf. Parallel Processing, 1981, pp. 302–303.

[5] R. Dechter and L. Kleinrock, "Broadcast Communications and Distributed Algorithms," IEEE Trans. Comput., Vol. C–35, No. 3, Mar. 1986, pp. 210–219.

[6] D. E. Knuth, The Art of Computer Programming: Sorting and Searching, Vol. 3, Addison, Wesley Publishing Company Inc., Reading, Massachusetts, 1973.

[7] T. Leighton "Tight Bounds on the Complexity of Parallel Sorting," IEEE Trans. Comput., Vol. C–34, No. 4, April 1985, pp. 344–354.

[8] S. Levitan, "Algorithms for Broadcast Protocol Multiprocessor," Proc. 3rd Int. Conf. Distributed Computing Systems, 1982, pp. 666–671.

[9] J. M. Marberg and E. Gafni, "Sorting and Selection in Multi–Channel Broadcast Networks," Proc. 1985 Int. Conf. Parallel Processing, 1985, pp. 846–850.

[10] J. Menon, "A Study of Sort Algorithms for Multiprocessor Database Machines," Proc. 12th Int. Conf. Very Large Data Bases, Kyoto, Japan, 1986, pp. 197–206.

[11] F. P. Preparata, "New Parallel Sorting Schemes", IEEE Trans. Comput., Vol. C–27, No. 7, July 1978, pp. 669–673.

[12] K. V. S. Ramarao, "Distributed Sorting on Local Area Networks," IEEE Trans. Comput., Vol C–37, No. 2, Feb. 1988, pp. 239–243.

[13] H. S. Stone, "Parallel Processing with the Perfect Shuffle," IEEE Trans. Comput., Vol. C–20, No. 2, Feb. 1971, pp. 153–161.

[14] C. Y. Tang and S. C. Wu, "Parallel Graph Algorithms under Broadcast Communication Model," Proc. Int. Computer Symp. 1988, Taipei, Taiwan, R. O. C., pp. 759–763.

[15] C. Y. Tang and M. J. Chiu, "Distributed Sorting on the Serially Connected Local Area Networks," Proc. 1989 Singapore Int. Conf. Networks, Singapore, pp. 458–462.

[16] S. S. Tseng, Parallel Sorting Algorithms, Ph. D. Dissertation, Institute of Computer Engineering, National Chiao Tung University, Hsinchu, Taiwan, Republic of China.

[17] C. B. Yang, R. C. T. Lee and W. T. Chen, "Finding Minimum Spanning Trees Based upon Single–Channel Broadcast Communications," Proc. Int. Computer Symp. 1988, Taipei, Taiwan, R. O. C., pp. 1451–1456.

[18] C. B. Yang, R. C. T. Lee and W. T. Chen, "Parallel Graph Algorithms Based upon Broadcast Communications," IEEE Trans. Comput., Vol C–39, No. 12, Dec. 1990, pp. 1468–1472.

[19] D. E. Willard, "Log–Logarithmic Protocols for Resolving Ethernet and Semaphore Conflicts," Proc. 16th Annual ACM Symp. on Theory of Computing, 1984, pp.512–521

Parallel Routing and Sorting on the Pancake Network

K. Qiu   H. Meijer   S.G. Akl

Department of Computing and Information Science

Queen's University, Kingston, Canada

Abstract

The pancake graph along with the star graph were proposed in 1986 [1] as attractive alternatives to the hypercube topology for interconnecting processors in a parallel computer. In this paper, we study some of their topological properties. We then present parallel routing schemes for both networks. Finally, we present an efficient algorithm for sorting K numbers on a pancake interconnection network with $n!$ nodes, where $K \geq n!$, and each node holds at most $N = \lceil K/n! \rceil$ numbers; the algorithm runs in $O(N\log N(n\log n) + Nn^3\log n)$ time, which is $O(n^3\log n)$ when $K = n!$.

1. Introduction

The star and pancake networks are attractive alternatives to the popular n-cube. They compare favorably with the n-cube in many aspects. Each has a rich structure, several symmetry properties, and a small diameter, as well as many desirable fault tolerance characteristics [1,2].

Given a set of generators for a finite group G, the *Cayley graph* with respect to G is defined as follows. The vertices of the graph correspond to the elements of the group G, and there is an edge (a, b) for $a, b \in G$ if and only if there is a generator g such that $ag = b$ [1].

Let G be a permutation group and V_n be the set of all permutations of symbols 1, 2, ..., n. A *star interconnection network* on n symbols, $S_n = (V_{S_n}, E_{S_n})$, is a Cayley graph of $n!$ nodes where $V_{S_n} = V_n$ and generators $g_i = i23 \cdots (i-1)1(i+1) \cdots n$, $2 \leq i \leq n$. Fig. 1 shows S_4. Each node in S_n is connected to $n-1$ nodes which can be obtained by interchanging the first symbol of the node with the ith symbol, $2 \leq i \leq n$. We call these $n-1$ connections *dimensions*. S_n is also called an n-star.

A *pancake interconnection network* on n symbols, $P_n = (V_{P_n}, E_{P_n})$, is a Cayley graph of $n!$ nodes where $V_{P_n} = V_n$ and generators $h_i = i(i-1) \cdots 321(i+1)(i+2) \cdots n$, $2 \leq i \leq n$. Fig. 2

This work is supported by the Natural Sciences and Engineering Research Council of Canada (grants A-0282 and A-3336), and by the School of Graduate Studies and Research, Queen's University, Canada.

shows P_4. Each node in P_n is connected to $n-1$ nodes which can be obtained by flipping (thus the name *pancake*) the first i symbols, $2 \leq i \leq n$. Therefore, a node in P_n is also connected to its $n-1$ neighbors through dimensions i, $2 \leq i \leq n$. P_n is also called an n-*pancake*. Clearly, $h_i = g_i$ for $i \leq 3$, and $S_n = P_n$, for $n \leq 3$.

In this paper, we present a number of results in connection with these two networks. The paper is organized as follows. Section 2 discusses several topological and embedding properties of both networks. A parallel scheme for routing on P_n is discussed in Section 3. The parallel routing scheme is then used in Section 4 to obtain a sorting algorithm for that network. The time complexity is improved in Section 5 to obtain an efficient sorting algorithm on P_n. Our conclusions are offered in Section 6.

2. Topological Properties of Star and Pancake Networks

Definition 1. $S_i(a_{i+1}a_{i+2} \cdots a_n)$ is a sub-graph in S_n induced by all the nodes with the same last $n-i$ symbols $a_{i+1}a_{i+2} \cdots a_n$, $1 \leq i \leq n$. $P_i(a_{i+1}a_{i+2} \cdots a_n)$ is defined similarly.

It is easy to see that $S_i(a_{i+1}a_{i+2} \cdots a_n)$ is an i-star and $P_i(a_{i+1}a_{i+2} \cdots a_n)$ is an i-pancake. In particular, S_n can be decomposed into n $(n-1)$-stars: $S_{n-1}(i)$, $1 \leq i \leq n$. For example, S_4 in Fig. 1 contains four 3-stars, namely $S_3(1)$, $S_3(2)$, $S_3(3)$, and $S_3(4)$, by fixing the last symbol at 1, 2, 3, and 4, respectively. P_n can also be decomposed similarly.

An embedding of graph $G=(V_G, E_G)$ into $H=(V_H, E_H)$ is a one-to-one function $f: \quad V_G \rightarrow V_H$. Let $d(x, y)$ denote the shortest distance between vertices x and y in graph $G(V, E)$. The *edge dilation* of edge (x, y) is $d(f(x), f(y))$. The *dilation cost* of the embedding f is defined as $\max_{(x,y) \in E_G} (d(f(x), f(y)))$ [5].

Proposition 1. S_n (P_n) can be embedded into P_n (S_n) with dilation cost $O(n)$.

Proof: For any arbitrary embedding, the statement is true simply because P_n (S_n) has a diameter $\Theta(n)$ [1,2]. □

Definition 2. A function f from V_n to V_n is said to be *edge preserving* on S_n if $(u, v) \in E_{S_n}$ implies $(f(u), f(v)) \in E_{S_n}$. An edge preserving function on P_n is defined similarly.

For example, the identity function $f(a_1 a_2 \cdots a_n) = (a_1 a_2 \cdots a_n)$ is edge preserving on both S_n and P_n, while the function $f(a_1 a_2 \cdots a_n) = (a_1 a_{n-1} a_{n-2} \cdots a_2 a_n)$ is edge preserving on S_n. Since S_n and P_n have the same vertex set, an edge preserving function on S_n or P_n can be used as an embedding from S_n to P_n or vice versa.

Proposition 2. Let f be a function on V_n which is edge preserving on S_n, then the embedding of S_n into P_n using f has dilation 4, for $n \geq 4$.

Proof: For any edge $(u, v) \in S_n$, $f(u), f(v) \in V_n$. Since f is edge preserving, there exists a generator g_i for S_n such that $f(u)g_i = f(v)$. Now, consider $f(u)$ and $f(v)$ as nodes in P_n, known to differ in their 1st and i^{th} positions. But we can show that each generator g_i of S_n can be realized (simulated) by at most 4 operators h_j of P_n. Indeed, $g_i = h_i$ for $i = 2, 3$. If $i \geq 4$, let w be $w_1 w_2 \cdots w_n$; then $w g_i = (((w h_{i-1}) h_{i-2}) h_{i-1}) h_i$. Therefore, $d(f(u), f(v)) \leq 4$ in P_n. $\square$

Proposition 3: The embedding of P_n into S_n using any edge preserving function on P_n has a dilation $\Theta(n)$, for $n \geq 4$.

Proof: The proposition is true because $\Theta(n)$ steps are needed in S_n to realize one step h_i in P_n, for $i = \Theta(n)$. $\square$

In a permutation $m_1 * m_2$, $*$ is used to denote any permutation of $n-2$ symbols in $\{1, 2, ..., n\}$-$\{m_1, m_2\}$. The $*$ in permutations $m_1 *$ and $* m_2$ can be defined similarly. Also, for a node $v \in V_n$, let $v(i)$ be the ith symbol in v, with $v(1)$ being the leftmost one. Clearly, for any node $v \in V_n$, since $\{v(1), v(2), ..., v(n)\} = \{1, 2, ..., n\}$, we have

$$\{u(1) \mid (u, v) \in E_{S_n}\} \cup \{v(1)\} = \{1, 2, ..., n\},$$
$$\{u(1) \mid (u, v) \in E_{P_n}\} \cup \{v(1)\} = \{1, 2, ..., n\}.$$

Proposition 4. Both S_n and P_n can be decomposed into $(n-1)!$ vertex disjoint paths of length n.

Proof: For any permutation $i_1 i_2 \cdots i_n$ and a vertex v_1 with $v_1(1) = i_1$, there is a path $v_1, v_2, v_3, ..., v_n$ such that $v_j(1) = i_j, j = 2, 3, ..., n$. We call v_1 the *starting point* of the path. The length of the path is n, the number of vertices on the path. If we define $(n-1)!$ distinct starting points of the form $i_1 *$ for some fixed i_1, $1 \leq i_1 \leq n$, and a fixed permutation $i_1 i_2 \cdots i_n$ of n symbols, then we get $(n-1)!$ paths of length n. Two paths generated by two distinct starting points $i_1 a_2 a_3 \cdots a_n$ and $i_1 b_2 b_3 \cdots b_n$ are vertex disjoint. Suppose that the two paths are not vertex disjoint, and let $v = i_j *$ be the vertex on both paths with the smallest index j, $j > 1$. On one of these paths v is connected to u with $u(1) = i_{j-1}$. On the other path v is connected to w with $w(1) = i_{j-1}$. Thus we conclude that $u = w$, which contradicts our assumption if $j > 2$. If $j = 2$, that implies that the two starting points are the same, also a contradiction. $\square$

Henceforth, whenever a path with starting point $i_1 a_2 \cdots a_n$ and permutation $i_1 i_2 i_3 \cdots i_n$ is considered, we will assume that $i_2 < i_3 < \cdots < i_n$. For example, P_4 in Fig. 2 can be decomposed into 6 vertex disjoint paths of length 4 in which all starting points are of the form $2*$.

path 1:	2134,	1234,	3214,	4123	path 2:	2143,	1243,	3421,	4321
path 3:	2314,	1324,	3124,	4213	path 4:	2341,	1432,	3412,	4312
path 5:	2413,	1423,	3241,	4231	path 6:	2431,	1342,	3142,	4132

3. Routing on the Pancake Network

In this section, we consider a scheme for routing data in the pancake network. The routing scheme involves a certain ordering on the processors. We begin by defining this ordering.

3.1. Ordering Nodes and Paths

Let $p_{a_1a_2\cdots a_n}$ denote the processor in S_n or P_n associated with the vertex $V = a_1a_2 \cdots a_n$. The ordering, $<$, on the processors is defined as follows: $p_{a_1a_2\cdots a_ia_{i+1}\cdots a_n} < p_{b_1b_2\cdots b_ib_{i+1}\cdots b_n}$ if there exists i, $1 \leq i \leq n$, such that $a_j = b_j$ for $j > i$, and $a_i < b_i$. In other words, the processors are ordered in reversed lexicographic order (lexicographic order if we read from right to left).

Definition 3. In P_n, the *rank* of a node u is the number of nodes v such that $v < u$, i.e. rank $(u) = |\{v \mid v < u\}|$. The rank of a node in S_n is defined similarly.

Consider the following routing problem for the pancake (the same problem can also be defined for the star network): Route all the elements of $P_{n-1}(i)$ to $P_{n-1}(i+1)$ such that if node v is ranked m^{th} in $P_{n-1}(i)$, then its content is routed to a node u in $P_{n-1}(i+1)$ which is also ranked m^{th} in $P_{n-1}(i+1)$, $1 \leq i \leq n-1$; the routing is to use only the processors in $P_{n-1}(i)$ and $P_{n-1}(i+1)$. We can view this routing as copying the contents of the processors in $P_{n-1}(i)$ to the processors in $P_{n-1}(i+1)$ while keeping the correct ordering.

In the following discussion, "routing node a to node b" is used as a short for "routing the content of node a to node b". The same should be understood when we talk about "routing a path to another path".

If keeping the correct ordering is ignored, the routing can be done easily using Proposition 4 as follows. Note that $(n-2)!$ nodes of the form $(i+1)*i$ in $P_{n-1}(i)$ define $(n-2)!$ paths of length $n-1$, $(n-2)!$ nodes of the form $i*(i+1)$ in $P_{n-1}(i+1)$ also define $(n-2)!$ paths of length $n-1$. We can route the path in $P_{n-1}(i)$ with starting point $(i+1)a_2 \cdots a_{n-1}i$ to the path in $P_{n-1}(i+1)$ with starting point $ia_{n-1} \cdots a_2(i+1)$ in $O(n)$ time in a pipelined fashion: in one step, the content of $(i+1)a_2 \cdots a_{n-1}i$ goes to $ia_{n-1} \cdots a_2(i+1)$, it then follows the path defined by the starting point $ia_{n-1} \cdots a_2(i+1)$; meanwhile, the contents stored in the path headed by $(i+1)a_2 \cdots a_{n-1}i$ move synchronously along the same route as that of their starting point. All $(n-2)!$ paths are routed in parallel without conflict in $O(n)$ time.

We now consider the routing that requires keeping the correct ordering. Nodes $(i+1)a_2a_3 \cdots a_{n-1}i$ in $P_{n-1}(i)$ and $ia_2a_3 \cdots a_{n-1}(i+1)$ in $P_{n-1}(i+1)$ have the same rank in their respective sub-pancakes, where $a_2a_3 \cdots a_{n-1}$ is any permutation on symbols in $\{1, 2, ..., n\}$ - $\{i, i+1\}$. Let the paths defined by these two starting points be

$$u_1, u_2, u_3, ..., u_{n-1}$$
$$v_1, v_2, v_3, ..., v_{n-1}$$

with $u_1 = (i+1)a_2 \cdots a_{n-1}i$ and $v_1 = ia_2 \cdots a_{n-1}(i+1)$. It follows that u_j and v_j have the same rank in their respective sub-pancakes, $2 \leq j \leq n-1$, since v_j can be obtained from u_j by interchanging i with $i+1$. Thus if two starting points as shown above in $P_{n-1}(i)$ and $P_{n-1}(i+1)$ have the same rank, then the two paths defined by the two starting points correspond to each other in the sense that u_j has the same rank as v_j, $1 \leq j \leq n-1$, in their respective $(n-1)$-pancakes. For example, path 3412, 1432, 4132 in $P_3(2)$ of P_4 corresponds to path 2413, 1423, 4123 in $P_3(3)$ of P_4. So our task is to route the path headed by $(i+1)a_2a_3 \cdots a_{n-1}i$ in $P_{n-1}(i)$ to its corresponding path in $P_{n-1}(i+1)$ headed by $ia_2a_3 \cdots a_{n-1}(i+1)$ for all possible permutations $a_2a_3 \cdots a_{n-1}$. Since all non-starting nodes on the path follow the same route as their starting point, it suffices to show how to route the starting points to their correct positions. Once the starting point $(i+1)a_2a_3 \cdots a_{n-1}i$ gets to $ia_2a_3 \cdots a_{n-1}(i+1)$, it keeps going along the path defined by $ia_2a_3 \cdots a_{n-1}(i+1)$ until the entire path headed by it completely enters the path headed by $ia_2a_3 \cdots a_{n-1}(i+1)$. Note that the two paths are now in opposite directions: the content of u_j is in v_{n-j}. This can be corrected easily in $O(n)$ time such that the content of u_i is routed to v_i, $1 \le i \le n-1$. Whenever we say path u_1, u_2, ..., u_{n-1} is routed to a path v_1, v_2, ..., v_{n-1} we mean that the content of u_j is routed to v_j, $1 \le i \le n-1$.

3.2. Conflict-Free Routing

Node $(i+1)a_2a_3 \cdots a_{n-1}i$ in $P_{n-1}(i)$ can reach node $ia_2a_3 \cdots a_{n-1}(i+1)$ in $P_{n-1}(i+1)$ in four steps (Proposition 2); Similarly, starting point $(i+1)a_{n-1} \cdots a_3a_2i$ in $P_{n-1}(i)$ can also go to its corresponding starting point $ia_{n-1} \cdots a_3a_2(i+1)$ in $P_{n-1}(i+1)$ in four steps:

$$
\begin{array}{ll}
(i+1)a_2a_3 \cdots a_{n-1}i & (i+1)a_{n-1} \cdots a_3a_2i \\
a_{n-1} \cdots a_3a_2(i+1)i & a_2a_3 \cdots a_{n-1}(i+1)i \\
a_2a_3 \cdots a_{n-1}(i+1)i & a_{n-1} \cdots a_3a_2(i+1)i \\
(i+1)a_{n-1} \cdots a_3a_2i & (i+1)a_2a_3 \cdots a_{n-1}i \\
ia_2a_3 \cdots a_{n-1}(i+1) & ia_{n-1} \cdots a_3a_2(i+1)
\end{array}
$$

As we can see, both starting points $(i+1)a_2a_3 \cdots a_{n-1}i$ and $(i+1)a_{n-1} \cdots a_3a_2i$ go through nodes $a_{n-1} \cdots a_3a_2(i+1)i$ and $a_2a_3 \cdots a_{n-1}(i+1)i$; we refer to this as a *routing conflict*. Note that no other starting point will use those two nodes as intermediate nodes in the routing. Another routing conflict occurs when starting point $(i+1)a_2a_3 \cdots a_{n-1}i$ goes through starting point $(i+1)a_{n-1} \cdots a_3a_2i$, and vice versa. We call two starting points $(i+1)a_2a_3 \cdots a_{n-1}i$ and $(i+1)a_{n-1} \cdots a_3a_2i$ a *conjugate pair*. To avoid these routing conflicts, our strategy is to group starting points into $(n-2)!/2$ conjugate pairs and route one starting point from a pair at a time since two starting points from two different pairs will not interfere with each other.

Lemma 1. In $(i+1)a_2a_3 \cdots a_{n-1}i$, if $a_2 < a_{n-1}$, then the path in $P_{n-1}(i)$ of length $n-1$ headed by the starting point $(i+1)a_2a_3 \cdots a_{n-1}i$ does not contain any node of the form $*(i+1)i$.

Proof: Let the path in $P_{n-1}(i)$ headed by the starting point $v_1 = (i+1)a_2a_3 \cdots a_{n-1}i$ be v_1, v_2, v_3, ..., v_{n-1}. Since $a_2 < a_{n-1}$, $a_{n-1} \ne \min \{i+1, a_2, ..., a_{n-1}\}$. But $v_2(1) = \min \{i+1, a_2, ..., a_{n-1}\}$, so $v_2(1) \ne a_{n-1}$. Therefore, in v_2, $i+1$ is in the position originally occupied by $v_2(1)$ in $v_1 = (i+1)a_2a_3 \cdots a_{n-1}i$, and this position is not $n-1$. Thus by the construction of the path, $i+1$ can never go to position $n-1$ in the path. □

We call the path headed by a starting point u of the form $(i+1)^*i$ such that $u(2) < u(n-1)$ an *active path*, and u an *active starting point*. Active paths and starting points in $P_{n-1}(i+1)$ are defined similarly. In each conjugate pair, exactly one starting point is active. By Lemma 1, nodes of the form $*(i+1)i$ do not belong to any active path, and we know from Proposition 7 that all active paths are vertex disjoint. Therefore if we first route all these $(n-2)!/2$ active paths in parallel, no conflict will occur. For the rest of the $(n-2)!/2$ paths, they can be routed to their corresponding paths in $P_{n-1}(i+1)$ as follows. Node $(i+1)a_2a_3 \cdots a_{n-1}i$ with $a_2 > a_{n-1}$ first goes to node $ia_{n-1} \cdots a_3a_2(i+1)$ in one step; thus the whole path is routed to the path headed by $ia_{n-1} \cdots a_3a_2(i+1)$ in $O(n)$ time. Node $ia_{n-1} \cdots a_3a_2(i+1)$ is now active and can be sent to its correct position $(i+1)a_{n-1} \cdots a_3a_2i$ in $P_{n-1}(i)$ in four steps as before (note that we are routing from $P_{n-1}(i+1)$ to $P_{n-1}(i)$, which can be done in the same manner as for those active starting points in $P_{n-1}(i)$). The whole path therefore is routed in $O(n)$ time. Finally in one more step, $(i+1)a_{n-1} \cdots a_2i$ goes to node $ia_2a_3 \cdots a_{n-1}(i+1)$ which is the node in $P_{n-1}(i+1)$ corresponding to $(i+1)a_2a_3 \cdots a_{n-1}i$. The above discussion shows that:

Theorem 1. The contents of $P_{n-1}(i)$ can be routed to the processors in $P_{n-1}(i+1)$, or vice versa, in $O(n)$ time using only these two sub-pancakes while keeping the correct ordering, $1 \leq i \leq n-1$. □

We give an example to demonstrate the routing scheme. Suppose that we want to route $P_4(2)$ to $P_4(3)$ in P_5 while keeping the correct ordering. $P_4(2)$ and $P_4(3)$ are as shown in Fig. 3 in which active paths are depicted by solid thick lines and other paths by dotted lines; starting points are indicated by circles. Unrelated connections are not shown. The three conjugate pairs in $P_4(2)$ are

(31452, 35412), (31542, 34512), (34152, 35142).

Three active starting points are 31452, 31542, and 34152. They are routed to three active paths in $P_4(3)$ in the first phase of the routing:

$$31452 \rightarrow 54132 \rightarrow 14532 \rightarrow 35412 \rightarrow 21453$$
$$31542 \rightarrow 45132 \rightarrow 15432 \rightarrow 34512 \rightarrow 21543$$
$$34152 \rightarrow 51432 \rightarrow 41532 \rightarrow 35142 \rightarrow 24153$$

Therefore, the contents of the path 31452, 13452, 43152, 51342, are routed to path 21453, 12453, 42153, 51243. In the second phase, take starting point 34512 for example, path 34512, 15432, 45132, 54132 is routed to active path 21543, 12543, 45213, 54213 in $P_4(3)$ by following the direct connection between 34512 and 21543. It is in an active path now. This active path is routed back to an active path in $P_4(2)$ while keeping the correct ordering as done in the phase 1, so path 34512, 15432, 45132, 54132 is in path 31542, 13542, 45312, 54312. Then finally it is routed to path 24513, 15423, 45123, 54123, which corresponds to the original path 34512, 15432, 45132, 54132, by the direct link between 31542 and 24513.

4. Sorting on the Pancake Network

Given K numbers, $K \geq n!$, and a fixed ordering $<$ on $n!$ processors in S_n or P_n in which each processor holds $N = \lceil K/n! \rceil$ numbers, the problem of sorting on the network is to arrange the numbers such that all numbers within a processor are sorted into non-decreasing order, and for processors p and q, if x is in p, y is in q, and $p < q$, then $x \leq y$. The sequential lower bound of $\Omega(K \log K) = \Omega(Nn! \log(Nn!))$ for sorting K numbers implies a lower bound of $\Omega(N \log(Nn!))$ on the number of parallel steps needed to sort on both S_n and P_n. Sorting on S_n has been considered in [7] in which an $O(N \log Nn \log n + Nn^3 \log n)$ algorithm is given. To our knowledge, no sorting algorithm has been designed for the n-pancake. In this section, we use the routing scheme developed in Section 3.2 to obtain a sorting algorithm on P_n by simulating the S_n sorting algorithm. The time complexity for our P_n sorting algorithm is $O(N \log Nn \log n + Nn^4 \log n)$.

The sorting algorithm on S_n is outlined below by considering an example in which each processor holds one elements. The ordering of the processors is defined as before (reversed lexicographic order). The algorithm works by simulating a sorting algorithm for the mesh-connected computer. Consider sorting on S_4; the processors are arranged in a mesh shown in Fig. 4(a). Note that if we exchange the 1st symbol with the last one in each node, we get Fig. 4(b) in which each column is connected to form a linear array by the definition of S_n. The rows in Fig. 4(a) are S_{n-1}'s and they are sorted recursively. It is shown in [7] that sorting on S_n is reduced, in this way, to sorting on the columns, or contiguous segments within the columns. Thus, to sort each column in Fig. 4(a), we first apply a transformation (called TR in [7]) which sends the element in $a_1 a_2 \cdots a_n$ to $a_n a_2 \ldots a_{n-1} a_1$; this yields Fig. 4(b). The *odd-even transposition sort* (see, for example, [3] or [6]) is then applied to each linear array (column) in Fig. 4(b). In the case where each processor holds $N > 1$ elements, the algorithm is essentially the same except that: (i) when recursion ends at a 1-star, S_1, N elements in the node are sorted in $O(N \log N)$ time sequentially within the processor, and (ii) performing one column sort becomes now performing N column sorts.

In order to simulate the algorithm, the only question that needs to be addressed is how to sort the columns in Fig. 4(a), as if they are the nodes of P_n, the rest of the algorithm being the same. Note that all the processors in the same column in Fig. 4(a) have the same rank in their respective sub-pancakes. (Thus, the transformation TR shows that the contents of $S_{n-1}(i)$ can be copied to $S_{n-1}(i+1)$ while keeping the correct ordering in S_n in constant time, $1 \leq i \leq n-1$.) Therefore, each step in the odd-even transposition sort using a linear array can be realized on P_n by routing $P_{n-1}(i)$ to $P_{n-1}(i+1)$, for $i = 1, 3, \cdots$, or $i = 2, 4, \cdots$, depending on which stage the transposition sort is in, while keeping the correct ordering as described before. This can be done in $O(n)$ time. That is, we can simulate the sorting algorithm for S_n, as given in [11], in $O(n)*O(n^3 \log n) = O(n^4 \log n)$ time on P_n in the case $N = 1$. In general, sorting on P_n has the time complexity $O(N \log N(n \log n) + Nn^4 \log n)$ The result of this section is summarized as follows:

K numbers, $K \geq n!$, can be sorted on P_n in $O(N\log N(n\log n) + Nn^4\log n)$ time, with each processor holding at most $N = \lceil K/n! \rceil$ numbers.

5. An Improved Sorting Algorithm on the Pancake Network

In this section we improve upon the complexity of the sorting algorithm on P_n developed in Section 4. The improved time complexity for sorting on P_n is $O(N\log N(n\log n) + Nn^3\log n)$, i.e. the same as that for sorting on S_n. The algorithm depends on a new routing scheme which is described below. This routing scheme applies to both networks; we therefore use X_n to mean either S_n or P_n.

Consider the following problem: Given $X_{n-1}(i)$, $X_{n-1}(j)$, with $i \neq j$, it is required to send the contents of the processors in $X_{n-1}(i)$ to the processors in $X_{n-1}(j)$ such that the contents of any two different processors in $X_{n-1}(i)$ are sent to two different processors in $X_{n-1}(j)$. We can view this problem as copying the contents of $X_{n-1}(i)$ to $X_{n-1}(j)$ in arbitrary order. This can be accomplished in 3 steps as follows. In the first step, those $(n-2)!$ nodes of the form $j*i$ in $X_{n-1}(i)$ send their contents to $(n-2)!$ nodes of the form $i*j$ in $X_{n-1}(j)$ through dimension n. At the same time, the remaining $(n-1)! - (n-2)!$ nodes in $X_{n-1}(i)$ of the form $k*i$, $k \neq i$, j, send their contents (also through dimension n) to the nodes of the form $i*k$ in $X_{n-1}(k)$. In one more step, the latter send their contents to the nodes of the form $j*k$, and from there, in another step through dimension n, the contents are sent to $k*j$ in $X_{n-1}(j)$. This algorithm is given below as procedure COPY.

Procedure COPY (i, j)

  1. do in parallel for all nodes $*i$

      send content to neighbor along dimension n

  2. do in parallel for all nodes $i*k, k \neq j$

      send content to neighbor v with $v(1) = j$

  3. do in parallel for all nodes $j*k, k \neq i$

      send content to neighbor along dimension n

End COPY

Lemma 2. The mapping defined by procedure COPY is a bijection between the nodes of $X_{n-1}(i)$ and $X_{n-1}(j)$.

Proof: For the case of star network, it is easy to see from the algorithm that node $ajbi$ in $S_{n-1}(i)$ is mapped to node $aibj$ in $S_{n-1}(j)$, where a and b are permutations of symbols in $\{1, 2, ..., n\} - \{i, j\}$, such that the set of symbols in a are different from the set of symbols in b, and $|a| + |b| = n - 2$, where $|a|$ and $|b|$ are the number of symbols in a and b, respectively. Note that either a or b could be empty, but not both. Therefore the mapping is a bijection.

The proof for the pancake case is similar, except that node $ajbi$ in $P_{n-1}(i)$ is mapped to node $ai\bar{b}j$ in $P_{n-1}(j)$, where $\bar{b} = b_k b_{k-1} \cdots b_1$ if $b = b_1 b_2 \cdots b_k$. $\square$

For an n-star, clearly, when $|i-j| = 1$, COPY corresponds to the transformation TR described in Section 4.

Lemma 3. The contents of $X_{n-1}(i)$ can be copied to processors in $X_{n-1}(j)$, $i \neq j$, in a bijective way in $O(1)$ time. □

We now extend this result as follows. Let I: i_1, i_2, ..., i_l and J: j_1, j_2, ..., j_l be two sequences from $\{1, 2, ..., n\}$ such that no two elements of I are equal, no two elements of J are equal, and $\{i_1, i_2, ..., i_l\} \cap \{j_1, j_2, ..., j_l\} = \varnothing$. It is desired to send the contents of $X_{n-1}(i_1)$, $X_{n-1}(i_2)$, ..., $X_{n-1}(i_l)$ to $X_{n-1}(j_1)$, $X_{n-1}(j_2)$, ..., $X_{n-1}(j_l)$ such that the contents of $X_{n-1}(i_m)$ are to be sent to $X_{n-1}(j_m)$, for $1 \leq m \leq l$. This task can also be achieved in $O(1)$ time by the following algorithm:

> **Procedure GROUP_COPY** (I, J)
>> **do in parallel** for $1 \leq m \leq l$
>>> Modified_COPY (i_m, j_m)
>
> **End GROUP_COPY**

where Modified_COPY is the same as COPY except that all "send contents" are replaced by "exchange contents". This operation means that the contents of $X_{n-1}(j_m)$ are sent to $X_{n-1}(i_m)$ at the same time as the contents of $X_{n-1}(i_m)$ are being sent to $X_{n-1}(j_m)$, $1 \leq m \leq l$. It can be shown easily that the given conditions imply that no conflict will occur.

As described in Section 4, to implement the odd-even transposition sort on the columns as in Fig. 4(a) in P_n, we need to route the contents of $P_{n-1}(i)$ to the nodes in $P_{n-1}(i+1)$ while keeping the correct ordering, for $i = 1, 3, \cdots$, or $i = 2, 4, \cdots$, depending on which stage the transposition sort is in. This routing is done in $O(n)$ time in Section 3. The following routing scheme does the same in $O(1)$ time using GROUP_COPY. The two sequences will be I: $1, 3, 5, \cdots$, J: $2, 4, 6, \cdots$ or I: $2, 4, 6, \cdots$, J: $3, 5, 7, \cdots$ for the odd and even stages of the sort, respectively. As pointed out in Section 3, node $a(i+1)bi$ in $P_{n-1}(i)$ has the same rank as that of node $aib(i+1)$ in $P_{n-1}(i+1)$. From Lemma 2, the content of the node $a(i+1)bi$ is sent to the node $aib(i+1)$ by COPY or GROUP_COPY in S_n in $O(1)$ time. In P_n, it is sent to $ai\bar{b}(i+1)$ instead, and $ai\bar{b}(i+1)$ does not have the same rank in $P_{n-1}(i+1)$ as that of $a(i+1)bi$ in $P_{n-1}(i)$ unless $|b| \leq 1$. But it can be seen easily that the following nodes form a cycle in $P_{n-1}(i+1)$:

$$ai\bar{b}(i+1), \ b\bar{i}\bar{a}(i+1), \ \bar{b}\bar{i}\bar{a}(i+1), \ aib(i+1), \ \bar{a}\,ib(i+1), \ \bar{b}ia(i+1), \ bia(i+1), \ \bar{a}\,i\bar{b}(i+1).$$

The length of the cycle is 8 if $|a| > 1$ and $|b| > 1$, and less than 8 otherwise. Thus if we first apply GROUP_COPY (I, J) to copy the contents of $P_{n-1}(i)$ to $P_{n-1}(i+1)$, for $i = 1, 3, \cdots$ or $i = 2, 4, \cdots$, then the content of node $a(i+1)bi$ can be routed to its correct node in $P_{n-1}(i+1)$ in constant time for all a and b using the cycle.

Theorem 2. The contents of $P_{n-1}(i)$ can be copied to the nodes in $P_{n-1}(i+1)$, or vice versa, while keeping the correct ordering, in $O(1)$ time, $1 \leq i \leq n-1$. □

The following example illustrates the procedure. Consider copying the contents of $P_5(3)$ to the nodes of $P_5(4)$ in P_6. Nodes

$$214653, 654213, 564213, 214563, 124563, 564123, 654123, 124653$$

are copied to

$$213564, 653124, 563124, 213654, 123654, 563214, 653214, 123564$$

which form a cycle. In constant time, they can all be routed to their corresponding nodes

$$213654, 653214, 563214, 213564, 123564, 563124, 653124, 123654.$$

If we use the result in this section to simulate the sorting algorithm in [7] on P_n, we have

Theorem 3. K numbers, $K \geq n!$, can be sorted on P_n in $O(N\log N(n\log n) + Nn^3\log n)$ time with each processor holding at most $N = \lceil K/n! \rceil$ numbers. $\square$

6. Conclusion

In this paper, we have studied the topological and embedding properties of S_n and P_n. We also presented several parallel routing schemes on S_n and P_n. One parallel routing algorithm is used to obtain a sorting algorithm on P_n with time complexity $O(N\log Nn\log n + Nn^4\log n)$ for sorting K numbers with $N = \lceil K/n! \rceil$. Using a new routing algorithm, this result is further improved to $O(N\log Nn\log n + Nn^3\log n)$, thus matching the complexity of sorting on S_n. Our routing schemes may also find other applications in the design of parallel algorithms for the star and pancake interconnection networks.

References

[1] S.B. Akers and B. Krishnamurthy, "A Group Theoretic Model for Symmetric Interconnection Networks," *IEEE Trans. on Compu.* Vol. 38, No. 4, 1989, pp. 555-566.

[2] S.B. Akers, D. Harel, and B. Krishnamurthy, "The Star Graph: An Attractive Alternative to the n-cube," *Proc. International Conference on Parallel Processing,* 1987, pp. 393-400.

[3] S.G. Akl, *Parallel Sorting Algorithms*, Academic Press, Orlando, Florida, 1985.

[4] S.G. Akl, *The Design and Analysis of Parallel Algorithms*, Prentice Hall, Englewood Cliffs, New Jersey, 1989.

[5] J.W. Hong, K. Mehlhorn, and A.L. Rosenberg, "Cost Trade-offs in Graph Embeddings, with Applications," *J. ACM*, Vol. 30, No. 4, October 1983.

[6] D.E. Knuth, *The Art of Computer Programming*, Vol. 3, Addison-Wesley, Reading, Massachusetts, 1973.

[7] A. Menn and A.K. Somani, "An Efficient Sorting Algorithm for the Star Graph Interconnection Network," *Proc. International Conference on Parallel Processing,* August, 1990.

[8] K. Qiu, H. Meijer, and S.G. Akl, "Decomposing a Star Graph into Disjoint Cycles", *Proc. 2nd Canadian Conference on Computational Geometry,* Ottawa, Canada, August 1990, pp. 70-73.

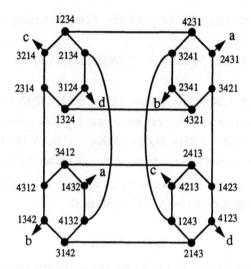

Figure 1. A 4-Star

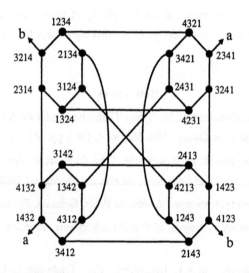

Figure 2. A 4-Pancake

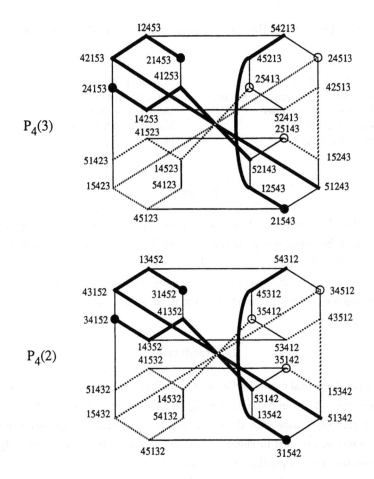

$P_4(3)$

$P_4(2)$

Figure 3. Routing From $P_4(2)$ To $P_4(3)$

4321	3421	4231	2431	3241	2341		1324	1423	1234	1432	1243	1342
4312	3412	4132	1432	3142	1342		2314	2413	2134	2431	2143	2341
4213	2413	4123	1423	2143	1243		3214	3412	3124	3421	3142	3241
3214	2314	3124	1324	2134	1234		4213	4312	4123	4321	4132	4231
		(a)							(b)			

Figure 4. Sorting on S_4

Practical Parallel Algorithms for Chordal Graphs

Extended Abstract

Eric S. Kirsch
Department of Computer Science
University of Tennessee
Knoxville, TN 37996
kirsch@cs.utk.edu

Jean R. S. Blair[†]
Department of Computer Science
University of Tennessee
Knoxville, TN 37996
blair@cs.utk.edu

Abstract

Until recently, a large majority of theoretical work in parallel algorithms has ignored communication costs and other realities of parallel computing. This paper attempts to address this issue by developing parallel algorithms that not only are efficient using standard theoretical analysis techniques, but also require a minimal amount of communication. The specific parallel algorithms developed here include one to find the set of maximal cliques and one to find a perfect elimination ordering of a choral graph.

1. Introduction

Most previous theoretical results pertaining to parallel algorithms have focused on proving the corresponding problem to be in NC, i.e., striving for poly-logarithmic running time while letting the number of processors grow with the problem size. This approach ignores communication costs which are incurred on real machines. Thus, these algorithms are not necessarily the most practical or even the fastest algorithms for existing machines. Recent results have focused on the communication delay involved in parallel processing. For example, in [7], communication delay is used as an integral part the analysis of the time complexity of parallel algorithms. This leads to the conclusion that algorithms which require no communication are superior algorithms since they can be run on any number of processors without incurring communication delay.

In this extended abstract, new parallel algorithms are presented to solve two problems on chordal graphs: finding the set of maximal cliques and finding a perfect elimination ordering(PEO). These new algorithms have several advantages. First, during the maximal clique algorithm, each processor performs its work without use of shared memory or communication. Previously developed algorithms use shared memory to communicate intermediate results to other processors. This means that these algorithms will incur a communication delay and require processors to operate synchronously. During the maximal clique algorithm presented here, each processor can perform its work without any knowledge of results from other processors, thus, avoiding any communication delays. Second, the partitioning of data for both algorithms is simple while, in other parallel

[†]Portions of this research were performed at the Mathematical Sciences Section of Oak Ridge National Laboratory and partially supported by the Applied Mathematics Science Research Program, Office of Energy Research, U.S. Department of Energy under contract DE-AC05-840R21400 with Martin Marietta Energy Systems Inc.

algorithms, the data requirements are often generated dynamically, making shared memory or communication a requirement. Third, while the algorithms can run on shared memory machines, the algorithms are designed for distributed memory machines, taking into consideration synchronization and communication costs. Fourth, the algorithms exhibit good scalability. That is, as processors are added, equal speed-up is achieved. Since we define *work* to be the running time of the algorithm times the number of processors, this means that on a parallel machine with a fixed number of processors (the only kind in existence) these new algorithms will run faster when the size of the problem exceeds the number of processors. Fifth, the work performed by the algorithms here is less than or comparable to the work performed by algorithms presented elsewhere for sparse graphs. Since one of the prime uses for the algorithms presented here is found in the solution to sparse matrices, the algorithms presented here are of practical importance. Previous algorithms make no use of the fact that the graphs corresponding to these matrices are also sparse.

The remainder of the paper is organized as follows. Section 2 presents some definitions and a basic version of the maximal clique algorithm. Section 3 gives a fast version of the maximal clique algorithm, and section 4 presents the PEO algorithm. Concluding remarks are in section 5.

2. The Basic Maximal Clique Algorithm

In this section, we present a basic version of a practical algorithm to find all maximal cliques for chordal graphs. We will develop the algorithm further in the next section. We begin with some definitions.

An undirected graph $G = (V, E)$, is *chordal* if every cycle of length 4 or greater has an edge between vertices that are not consecutive in the cycle. Chordal graphs have important applications in sparse matrix computation[8, 9] and in acyclic database schemes[1]. A *clique* is a set of vertices whose induced subgraph is complete. A clique is *maximal* if there is no clique that properly contains it. We use the term $adj(v)$ to refer to the set $\{u|(u,v) \in E\}$. We let $d_v = |adj(v)|$ and c_v be the number of maximal cliques to which vertex v belongs.

For the maximal clique algorithm, the data will be maintained as n adjacency lists, where $n = |V|$. The ith adjacency list is a list of vertices to which v_i is adjacent. We assume an implicit (arbitrary but consistent) ordering of these $v_1, v_2, ...v_n$ and that all adjacency lists adhere to this ordering. (That is, for each adjacency list, if v_i and v_j are both in the list and $i < j$, then v_i appears before v_j in the list).

Each processor will develop the set of maximal cliques for a single vertex p. To do this, each processor needs to have the adjacency vectors for each $u \in adj(p)$. This distribution of data can be accomplished using a direct access, concurrent read file. The time required for this operation on a distributed memory parallel processor will be limited by the number of I/O processors but will be at most $O(nd)$. For a shared memory machine, n processors could read the appropriate adjacency vectors in $O(d)$ time.

The key idea that we will use to develop maximal cliques is that if a vertex p is adjacent to a vertex v, then p and v are in a maximal clique together. As the algorithm proceeds, processor p will maintain a *Candidate Clique List*(CCL_p) for vertex p. Initially, we have one *Candidate Clique*(CC), the adjacency vector for p; upon termination, CCL_p will contain all maximal cliques(MC) to which p belongs. During processing, CCL_p is revised by considering each $v \in adj(p)$ as a *refinement vertex*(rv) in turn. Given an rv, each $CC_i \in CCL_p$ is checked to see if it contains rv. When rv is contained in CC_i, we check to see if rv is adjacent to each $v \in CC_i$. If it is, we continue to assume that this CC_i is correct. If it is not, we create two new CCs to replace CC_i. The first will contain rv and all $v \in CC_i$ such that $v \in adj(rv)$. The second will be $CC_i - \{rv\}$. It is important to note that as we make these refinements it is possible to develop candidate cliques that cannot lead to a maximal clique. For example, if CC_i is a subset of CC_j, then CC_i cannot lead to a maximal clique since the refinement process can only remove corresponding vertices from CC_i and CC_j and no vertices can be added.

While we will expand upon the algorithm described above, we will prove the correctness of this basic approach and then later prove that we can add additional steps to reduce the time complexity without violating its correctness. We begin by defining a few terms. Consider each candidate clique CC_i prior to refinement by rv. Let the prefix P_i of CC_i be the set of vertices in CC_i that have already been used to refine the CCL_p. Let the suffix S_i be the remaining set of vertices in CC_i. Note that rv may or may not be in S_i.

The following theorem shows that every maximal clique to which p belongs is in CCL_p at the completion of the algorithm.

Theorem 1 *A processor p using the above algorithm will halt with CCL_p containing every maximal clique to which vertex p belongs.*

Proof: Let $R = \{v_1, v_2, ..., v_x\}$ be the set of vertices that have been used to refine CCL_p and $\{M_1, M_2, ..., M_c\}$ be the set of maximal cliques for G. Let us define an equivalence relationship Λ on the set of maximal cliques defining classes $\lambda_1, \lambda_2, ...\lambda_l$ such that for each class λ_i defined by Λ, both M_a and M_b are in λ_i, if and only if $M_a \cap R = M_b \cap R$. Obviously, since one more rv is added to R after each refinement, these classes may change as the algorithm progresses. We also let $N_i = \bigcup_{M_a \in \lambda_i} M_a$. We will show, using induction on the number of refinements, that each equivalence class λ_i will be represented in CCL_p by a CC_i which consists of a prefix $P_i = N_i \cap R$, and a suffix $S_i = N_i - R$. We will also show that, after each refinement, $\bigcup_{\lambda_i \in \Lambda} \lambda_i = \{M_1, M_2, ..., M_c\}$ and $\bigcap_{\lambda_i \in \Lambda} \lambda_i = \emptyset$. Now, after n refinements, R contains all n vertices and it is not possible that $M_a \cap R = M_b \cap R, a \neq b$. Therefore, each class λ_i contains one unique maximal clique and there is a $CC_i \in CCL_p$ for each maximal clique.

It remains to be shown that each equivalence class λ_i is represented by a $CC_i = P_i \cup S_i$ where $P_i = N_i \cap R$ and $S_i = N_i - R$ and that $\bigcup_{\lambda_i \in \Lambda} \lambda_i = \{M_1, M_2, ..., M_c\}$ and $\bigcap_{\lambda_i \in \Lambda} \lambda_i = \emptyset$. We will use induction on the number of vertices used as the refinement vertex. The base case is the starting condition of one $CC_1 = adj(p)$, and Λ defines one class λ_1 which contains all maximal cliques. Obviously, $\bigcup_{\lambda_i \in \Lambda} \lambda_i = \{M_1, M_2, ..., M_c\}$ and $\bigcap_{\lambda_i \in \Lambda} \lambda_i = \emptyset$. $R = \emptyset$, so $N_1 \cap R = \emptyset = P_1$. Now, p is in a maximal clique with a vertex v if and only if $v \in adj(p)$, so $N_1 = adj(p)$ is correct. It is also true that $CC_1 - P_1 = S_1 = adj(p) = N_1 - R$.

Now, assume that after $k - 1$ refinements the above conditions are true, and consider the kth refinement by vertex rv. Consider a CC_i that defines a class λ_i such that $rv \notin CC_i$ before refinement by rv. It must be true that no $M_a \in \lambda_i$ contains rv and therefore N_i does not contain rv. Thus, after refinement by rv, $N_i \cap R$ is the same as is the prefix. Thus, $P_i = N_i \cap R$. $N_i - R$ also remains the same and since no $M_a \in \lambda_i$ contained rv, S_i remains the same and $S_i = N_i - R$. CC_i is the same after refinement by rv and correctly defines the same class λ_i.

Now, consider a CC_i that defines a class λ_i which does contain rv. There are two possibilities. First, $\forall u \in S_i$, $u \in adj(rv)$. In this case, CC_i does not split and defines the same class. Consider any maximal clique $M_a \in \lambda_i$. Since rv is adjacent to all $u \in CC_i$, it must be true that any M_a represented by CC_i must contain rv. Thus, it is still true that $P_i = N_i \cap R$. Since S_i has been reduced by only rv which is now R, it is still true that $S_i = N_i - R$. Again, CC_i is the same after refinement by rv and correctly defines the same class λ_i.

For the second possibility, suppose that rv is not adjacent to some set of vertices L in the suffix of CC_i defining the class λ_i. After refinement by rv, we will have two new candidate cliques $CC_r = CC_i - L$ and $CC_s = CC_i - \{rv\}$. We also refine the class λ_i into two classes: $\lambda_r = \{M_a | M_a \in \lambda_i$ and $rv \in M_a\}$ and $\lambda_s = \{M_a | M_a \in \lambda_i$ and $rv \notin M_a\}$. Obviously, $\lambda_r \cup \lambda_s = \lambda_i$ and $\lambda_r \cap \lambda_s = \emptyset$. Now, $rv \in N_r$ for λ_r and, since P_r also contains rv, $P_r = N_r \cup R$. Also, since any M_a which contains rv cannot contain any $u \in L$, N_r does not contain any $u \in L$ and $S_r = N_r - R$. For λ_s, $rv \notin N_s$ and $rv \notin P_s$. Therefore, $P_s = N_s \cap R$. Now, since the only element added to R is rv and no $M_a \in \lambda_s$ can contain rv, $N_s = N_i - \{rv\}$ and $S_s = S_i - \{rv\}$. Thus, $S_s = N_s - R$.

Since each CC_i either defines the same class after refinement or breaks into CC_r and CC_s such that $\lambda_r \cup \lambda_s = \lambda_i$ and $\lambda_r \cap \lambda_s = \emptyset$, after every refinement, it is true that $\bigcup_{\lambda_i \in \Lambda} \lambda_i = \{M_1, M_2, ..., M_c\}$ and $\bigcap_{\lambda_i \in \Lambda} \lambda_i = \emptyset$. Thus, after n refinements, each λ_i represents just one maximal clique and is represented by $CC_i \in CCL_p$. □

Theorem 1 shows that upon completion of the algorithm, there exists a $CC_i \in CCL_p$ for each maximal clique containing p. It should also be clear that at that point each $CC_i \in CCL_p$ represents a clique containing p. Removal of non-maximal cliques from CCL_p at this point is straight forward.

3. A Fast Maximal Clique Algorithm

Theorem 1 in the preceding section showed that our basic algorithm correctly develops the set of maximal cliques to which a vertex p belongs. To do this, the algorithm essentially scans CCL_p for each vertex in $adj(p)$. Unfortunately, the number of candidate cliques in CCL_p may become large, thereby making the running time of the algorithm expensive. The next results examine some possibilities for removing candidate cliques from CCL_p whenever it becomes clear that they cannot lead to a maximal clique. When we determine that a CC_i can not lead to a maximal clique we say it "can be removed from CCL_p". We define a CC_i to be a *Maximal Candidate Clique* (MCC_i) if P_i is the prefix of at least 1 maximal clique. The following easy to prove properties greatly reduce the possible size of CCL_p.

Lemma 1 *If CC_i and CC_j are two distinct candidate cliques in CCL_p, then*

(i) $P_i \neq P_j$, *and*

(ii) *if $CC_i \subset CC_j$ then CC_i cannot represent a maximal clique and can be removed from CCL_p.*

Consider a modified version of our algorithm that removes candidate cliques as soon as they become subsets of other candidate cliques. We have the following result.

Lemma 2 *Using the modified algorithm, every candidate clique $CC_i \in CCL_p$ is either MCC_i or has the form $CC_i = \{\bigcap_{x=1}^{k} P_{j_x}\} \cup \{\bigcup_{x=1}^{k} S_{j_x}\}$ for some set $\{CC_{j_1}, CC_{j_2}, ... CC_{j_k}\}$, $k \geq 2$.*

Proof (sketch): To prove this, we consider what possible forms CC_i might take on during the modified algorithm and show that each possible form either: (1) guarantees that CC_i is an MCC_i, (2) won't happen because subset candidate cliques are removed, or (3) has the form described in the statement of this lemma. □

The following lemmas (proofs omitted) show that the modified algorithm will never have more than $O(d_p^2)$ candidate cliques in CCL_p.

Lemma 3 *A vertex p can belong to at most d_p maximal cliques.*

Lemma 4 *There are never more than d_p MCCs in CCL_p for a vertex p.*

Lemma 5 *There can be no more than $O(d_p^2)$ candidate cliques in CCL_p for vertex p that are not MCCs.*

Although the modified version of our algorithm has a time complexity that is substantially less than that of our basic algorithm, it is still too expensive. In order to remove the candidate cliques which become subsets, after each refinement each $CC_i \in CCL_p$ must be checked to see if it is a subset of another CC_j. Thus, to allow $O(d_p^2)$ candidate cliques in CCL_p slows the algorithm considerably. However, using the fact that G is chordal, we can detect more candidate cliques that can be removed from the CCL_p during the processing.

Let CC_i be of the form, $CC_i = \{\bigcap_{x=1}^{k} P_{j_x}\} \cup \{\bigcup_{x=1}^{k} S_{j_x}\}$ for some set $\{CC_{j_1}, CC_{j_2}, ... CC_{j_k}\}$, $k \geq 2$, of candidate cliques in CCL_p. That is, the prefix of CC_i is contained in the prefixes of all the candidate cliques in the set, and S_i is the union of the suffixes of all the candidate cliques in the set. We call CC_i the **child** of each CC_{j_x}, $1 \leq x \leq k$, and each such CC_{j_x} the **parent** of CC_i.

Theorem 2 *Suppose CC_{p_1} and CC_{p_2} are distinct parents of CC_i. If there is another candidate clique CC_g such that $P_{p_1} \subset P_g$ and $P_{p_2} \subset P_g$, then CC_i can be removed from CCL_p.*

Proof: It must be true that $P_{p_1} \neq P_{p_2}$ by Lemma 1. It must also be true that $S_{p_1} \neq S_{p_2}$. Otherwise, there would be another candidate clique $CC_s = P_{p_1} \cup P_{p_2} \cup S_{p_1}$ which implies that both CC_{p_1} and CC_{p_2} would be removed from CCL_p. Since $P_{p_1} \subset P_g$ and $P_{p_2} \subset P_g$ it must be true that all $v \in P_{p_1}$ are adjacent to all $u \in P_{p_2}$. Let us consider $u \in P_{p_1}, u \notin P_{p_2}$, $v \in P_{p_2}, v \notin P_{p_1}$ $w \in S_{p_1}, w \notin S_{p_2}$ and $x \in S_{p_2}, x \notin S_{p_1}$. There are two possibilities. First, these vertices might imply a chordless cycle: $u \to v \to x \to w \to u$. Since there cannot be a cordless cycle in our chordal graph, we can remove CC_i. The other possibility is that u is adjacent to all $x \in S_{p_1}, x \notin S_{p_2}$ (and v is adjacent to all $w \in S_{p_2}, w \notin S_{p_1}$). But this implies the existence of a $CC_k = P_i \cup \{u\} \cup S_i$ and CC_i can be removed. $\square$

The fact that parent candidate cliques CC_{p_1} and CC_{p_2} both have prefixes which are subsets of a single prefix is necessary to ensure that all $v \in P_{p_1}$ and all $u \in P_{p_2}$ are adjacent. Thus, for any arrangement of cliques where a CC_i has two parents and those two parents have a common ancestor, CC_i can be removed. This property gives us the final modification to our basic maximal clique algorithm. We will call the basic algorithm with the two modifications incorporated (removal of subset candidate cliques and removal of candidate cliques that have parents that have prefixes where elements in these prefixes are adjacent) the maximal clique algorithm. We can show:

Lemma 6 *Given a set of $MCCs$, there must be at least $O(d_p)$ refinement vertices for there to be $O(d_p)$ candidate cliques in CCL_p.*

Corollary 1 *There are at most $O(d_p)$ candidate cliques in CCL_p during the maximal clique algorithm.*

We are now ready to formally present the algorithm for finding maximal cliques.

Algorithm: AlgMaxCl.

Input: A Chordal Graph G.

Output: The set of maximal cliques for G.

Method: Initially, each processor p is given the adjacency list for p and the adjacency list for each $v \in adj(p)$. The processor for vertex p will maintain a candidate clique list (CCL_p). Each $CC_i \in CCL_p$ is refined by each vertex $rv \in adj(p)$. After each refinement, each $CC_i \in CCL_p$ is checked to determine if it is a subset of another CC_j or if it violates the chordality of G according to Theorem 2, and thus can be removed. After n refinements, each $CC_i \in CCL$ is a maximal clique. Details are given in Figure 1.

Using our previous results, it is easy to show:

Theorem 3 *A processor/vertex p using AlgMaxCl correctly develops the set of maximal cliques to which p belongs.*

Theorem 4 *The running time for AlgMaxCl on processor/vertex p is $O(d_p^4)$*

Proof(sketch): The loop of statement 2 will be executed d times. The loops in statements 2(a), 2(c), 2(c)(i), 2(d), and 2(d)(i) are each executed $|CCL_p|$ times. We need to show that $|CCL_p| \in O(d_p)$. This follows from the fact all candidate cliques which have the form described in Theorem 2 are removed by the algorithm. To see this, note that any parents of a CC_i, which can be removed according to Theorem 2 must have at least two parents CC_{p_1} and CC_{p_2} which will be elements of $Parents_i$. When $Parents_{p_1}$ is unioned with $Grandpars_i$ and then $Grandpars_i$ is intersected with $Parents_{p_2}$ the intersection will be the parent(s) that CC_{p_1} and CC_{p_2} share. Thus, if the intersection is non-empty, CC_i will be removed. Therefore, all candidate cliques which can be removed according to Theorem 2 are removed by AlgMaxCl. Thus, by Corollary 1, $CCL_p \in O(d_p)$.

Each of the set operations in steps 2(a)(i)(A), 2(a)(i)(B), 2(c)(i)(A), 2(C)(i)(B), 2(d)(i)(A), and 2(d)(i)(B) require d_p time. Thus, the running time of AlgMaxCl on each processor $p \in O(d_p^4)$. $\square$

Corollary 2 *The work performed by a group of processors to find the maximal cliques for graph G with n vertices is $O(nd^4)$, where $d = max(d_p)$*

1. $CCL_p \leftarrow adj(p)$
2. for each $rv \in adj(p)$
   (a) for each $CC_i \in CCL_p$
      (i) if $rv \in CC_i$
         (A) $result \leftarrow CC_i \cap adj(rv)$ (is rv adjacent to all $u \in S_i$?)
         (B) if $result \neq CC_i$ (rv not adjacent to all $u \in S_i$)
            $CCL_p \leftarrow CCL_p \cup result$
            $CC_i \leftarrow CC_i - \{v\}$
   (b) for each $CC_i \in CCL_p$
      (i) $Parsuffix_i, Parents_i, Grandpars_i \leftarrow \emptyset$
   (c) for each $CC_i \in CCL_p$ (determine if CC_i is subset)
      (i) for each $CC_j \in CCL_p, i \neq j$ (and determine parents of CC_i)
         (A) if $CC_i \subset CC_j$
            $CCL_p \leftarrow CCL_p - CC_i$ (remove CC_i from list)
         (B) else if $P_i \subset P_j$ and $P_i \neq \emptyset$
            $Parents_i \leftarrow Parents_i \cup \{j\}$ (add CC_j to parent list)
            $Parsuffix_i \leftarrow Parsuffix_i \cup S_j$
   (d) for each $CC_i \in CCL_p$
      (i) for each $CC_j \in CCL_p, i \neq j$
         (A) if $CC_j \in Parents_i$ (CC_i meets
            and $Grandpars_i \cap Parents_j \neq \emptyset$ conditions
            and $S_i \subseteq Parsuffix_i$ of Lemma 2)
            remove CC_i from CCL_p
         (B) else $Grandpars_i \leftarrow Grandpars_i \cup Parents_j$

Figure 1: Details of AlgMaxCl

4. The PEO Algorithm

In this section, we will look at an algorithm to develop a Perfect Elimination Ordering (PEO) for a chordal graph. A *PEO* is an ordering of the vertices of a chordal graph G such that each vertex v_i is simplicial on the induced subgraph $G - \{v_j | j < i\}$. A vertex v is *simplicial* if $adj(v)$ is a clique.

The PEO algorithm presented here works with the information developed during the maximal clique algorithm, but requires no information transfer to update each processor. That is, to begin it only needs a list of its Maximal Cliques (MCL_p), which it can initialize to CCL_p from the previous algorithm. Thus, each processor may begin its work on the PEO as soon as it completes its work on the maximal cliques. That is, it is not necessary for all processors p to have completed before a processor starts on its portion of the PEO algorithm. The algorithm is based on the following widely accepted lemma.

Lemma 7 *Any simplicial vertex is a member of exactly one maximal clique.*

A consequence of Lemma 7 is that we can find a PEO from the maximal cliques that have already been found. It is possible to determine if a vertex is simplicial by determining when it is a member of exactly one clique. If each vertex that becomes simplicial is removed from all processors' set of maximal cliques, and as maximal cliques become subsets of other maximal cliques they too are removed, then it can be determined when a vertex is a member of one maximal clique and is, therefore, simplicial.

1. $timestamp \leftarrow 0$
2. while $|MCL| > 1$
   (a) receive(wait) simplicial vertex message($v, rtimestamp$)
   (b) find $MC_i \in MCL$ such that $v \in MC_i$
   (c) $MC_i \leftarrow MC_i - \{v\}$
   (d) for each $MC_j \in MCL, i \neq j$
       if $MC_i \subset MC_j$ then
           $MCL \leftarrow MCL - MC_i$
   (e) if $rtimestamp > timestamp$ then
       $timestamp \leftarrow rtimetamp$
3. $timestamp \leftarrow timestamp + 1$
4. send msg($p,timestamp$) to all $v \in$ final MC and to host

Figure 2: Details of processor AlgPEO

Any vertex v which is simplicial in the original graph (of which there must be at least 2) will end AlgMaxCl with $|MCL_v| = 1$. These processors will send messages to all $p \in MC_v$, where MC_v is the maximal clique to which v belonged, indicating that v is simplicial. Included in this simplicial message will be a timestamp. Thus, a simplicial message from a vetex v means that v is simplicial on the induced subgraph $G - \{x|$ has timestamp less than $v\}$. Vertices which are simplicial on the original graph will send simplicial messages with a timestamp of 1.

Each $p \in MC_v$ will, in turn, remove v from MC_v in CCL_p. Now, because the induced subgraph of any chordal graph is chordal, it must be true that there are at least two new vertices/processors p for which $|MCL_p| = 1$. These processors now send simplicial messages with a timestamp equal the largest timestamp received plus 1. This process continues until all p have sent their simplicial messages. A host processor will collect the simplicial messages in order of these timestamps. The PEO algorithm, AlgPEO, is as follows.

Algorithm: AlgPEO

Input: For each processor p, a list of all maximal cliques containing p and a count of the number of cliques in that list.

Output: A PEO on the host processor.

Method: Each processor p will receive messages from simplicial vertices and remove these vertices from the appropriate maximal clique. When some $MC_j \subseteq MC_i$ for MC_j, $MC_i \in MCL_p$ then MC_j is removed. When $|MCL_p| = 1$ then a simplicial message is sent to all vertices in the final clique and the host processor. Each processor will also keep track of the largest timestamp that it receives and will send its simplicial message with a timestamp equal to the largest timestamp that it received plus 1. The details of the vertex processor algorithm are given in Figure 2.
The host processor will maintain a set of lists, one for each possible timestamp. Then, when it receives a simplicial message from vertex p, it places p in the list corresponding to the appropriate timestamp. The details of the host processor algorithm are given in Figure 3.

Theorem 5 *Given the set of maximal cliques for a chordal graph G, a group of n processors using AlgPEO will correctly develop a PEO on a host processor.*

Proof: To prove this we need to show that a vertex p is simplicial on the graph $G - \{x|x$ has timestamp less than $p\}$ and that p will send a message when it is simplicial.

We use induction on the timestamp to prove the first part. The base case is vertices which are simplicial on the original graph which send a message with a timestamp of 1. Obviously they are

1. $msgcount \leftarrow 0$
2. while $msgcount < n$
   (a) receive(wait) simplicial msg($v, timestamp$)
   (b) add v to $PEO_{timestamp}$
   (c) $msgcount \leftarrow msgcount + 1$

Figure 3: Details of Host AlgPEO

simplicial on $G - \{x | x$ has timestamp less than $p\}$. For the induction step, assume true for vertices that send a message with timestamp $k - 1$. If p is going to send a message with $timestamp = k$ then it must be true that $adj(p) \cap \{x | x$ has timestamp less than $p\}$ have sent messages to p which made $|MCL_p| = 1$. All vertices of this subset were simplicial by the induction hypothesis and since $|MCL_p| = 1$, p is simplicial.

For the second part of the proof, we again use induction on the timestamp. For the base case, a processor p which is simplicial on the original graph must have an $|MCL_p| = 1$ and thus will never enter the while loop of step 2. These processors will send their simplicial message when simplicial. For the induction step, assume true for all processors which send messages with $timestamp = k - 1$. If a processor p is simplicial on the graph $G - \{x | x$ has timestamp less than $k\}$, then it must be true that $adj(p) \cap \{x | x$ has timestamp less than $k\}$, which we'll call T, have all sent messages to p by the induction hypothesis. It must be true that $adj(p) - T \subseteq MC_p$ else it would contradict the fact that p is simplicial. Thus all $MC_i \in MCL_p$ have been removed except one. Consequently, $|MCL_p| = 1$, the while loop in step 2 will terminate, and p will correctly send its simplicial message. $\square$

Theorem 6 *The time complexity of the AlgPEO on the vertex processors is $O(d^2c)$ plus some possible wait time, where $d = max(d_p)$ and $c = max(c_p)$ in G.*

Proof: The loop of step 2 can be executed a maximum of d_p times before $|MCL_p| = 1$, since only d_p elements make up the MCs. The set operations of steps 2(b) and 2(d) may require d_p time. Step 2(b) may also require that each $MC \in MCL_p$ be checked and so may require c_p checks. Step 2(d) will require at most $c_p - 1$ checks. All other steps take constant time. Thus the AlgPEO has a running time of $O(d^2c)$ plus whatever wait time is incurred at step 2(a). $\square$

The following theorem will be proven for synchronous distributed memory models. Order of magnitude results will hold for any reasonable asynchronous model of computation.

Theorem 7 *The overall time complexity of AlgPEO, including message wait time is $O(d^2C)$ where C is the total number of maximal cliques in G and $d = max(d_p)$.*

Proof (sketch): To see this, we can look at the combined elimination sequence (for all processors) as a sequence of removed cliques. The first clique would be removed at time 1 the second at time 2 (or earlier) etc. Thus we would have C clique removals. If our actual elimination sequence removed several cliques at once, then the time to remove the cliques is less than C.

Now after each removal of a clique, some number of vertices become simplicial. Let v be one of the vertices that is about to become simplicial. Using our worst case model, v can only have two cliques remaining: the clique that was just removed and the one in which it will be simplicial. In order to determine that v is simplicial, it's processor will have to receive, at most, d_p messages and use, at most, $2d_p$ steps to remove each of those vertices from one of its two remaining maximal cliques. Each processor corresponding to a simplicial vertex then sends, at most, d_p messages. Thus we have C clique removals each of which may require $O(d^2)$ steps for a time complexity of $O(d^2C)$. □

5. Conclusions

The new parallel algorithms presented here have several practical advantages over results presented elsewhere. One advantage is a faster or comparable running time for sparse graphs. Specific comparisons to some other work are difficult because problems are approached in different orders. In [6], maximal cliques are found in $O(n^4log^4n)$, and in [3], maximal cliques are found in $O(n^3log^2n)$. The algorithms in this paper are approached differently and therefore the running time is based on the degree of each vertex. The work performed by the maximal clique algorithm in this paper is $O(nd^4)$ which is obviously better for sparse graphs. The algorithm to find a PEO presented in [6] requires $O(n^2log^2n)$ work to find a PEO using the set of maximal cliques. The algorithm in this paper requires $O(nd^2c)$ work, again a significant reduction for sparse graphs. The algorithms also achieve equal speedup as processors are added (up to n).

Comparisons to the work in [5] are complicated by the fact that a PEO is found before finding maximal cliques. However, assuming that we are finding both, the algorithm in [5] will take $O((n+m)log^2n)$ work on a CRCW PRAM. If we assume that we have a sparse graph with $d_v \leq log\ n\ \forall v \in G$ and we also take away the power of the concurrent read (adding $O(log\ n)$ to the time complexity of [5]) then we have $O(nlog^4n)$ work in [5] and $O(nlog^4n)$ work for the algorithms presented here. However, in [5] (and in all of the other above mentioned work) communication delays are not considered, while they are included in the analysis included here.

Future work in this area will be in three directions. First, we want to examine the possibility of using some sort of data structure other than a list to hold the candidate cliques. The hope is that this data structure would enable us to refine the list and determine non-maximal cliques in $O(d^2)$ time rather than $O(d^3)$. Second, we wish to explore the possibility of developing portions of a PEO on a single processor from the data structure used for developing maximal cliques. Third, we want to examine the possibility of developing a clique tree simultaneous with the development of a PEO with no increase in running time.

References

[1] C. Beeri, R. Fagin, D. Maier and M. Yannakakis, "On the desirability of acyclic database schemes," *Journal of the Association for Computing Machinery* vol. 30, no. 3, pp. 205-212, 1974.

[2] M. C. Golumbic, *Algorithmic Graph Theory and Perfect Graphs*, Academic Press, London, 1980.

[3] C. Ho and R. C. T. Lee, "Efficient parallel algorithms for finding maximal cliques, clique trees, and minimum coloring on chordal graphs," *Information Processing Letters* Vol. 28, pp. 301-309, 1988.

[4] C. Ho and R. C. Lee, "Counting clique trees and perfect elimination schemes in parallel," *Information Processing Letters* Vol. 31, pp. 61-68, 1989.

[5] P. N. Klein, "Efficient parallel algorithms for chordal graphs," *Symposium on Foundations of Computer Science*, pp. 150-161, October 1988.

[6] J. Naor, M. Naor, A. A. Schaffer, "Fast parallel algorithms for chordal graphs," *Proceedings 19th Annual ACM Symposium on Theory of Computing*, pp. 355-364, 1987.

[7] C. Papadimitriou and M. Yannakakis "Towards an Architecture Independent Analysis of Parallel Algorithms," *SIAM Journal of Computing* Vol. 19, pp. 322-328, April 1990.

[8] D. J. Rose, "Triangulated Graphs and the Elimination Process," *Journal of Mathematical Analysis and Applications*, Vol. 32, pp. 597-609, 1970.

[9] D. J. Rose, "A graph-theoretic study of the numerical solution of sparse positive definite systems of linear equations," in *Graph Theory and Computing*, ed. R. Read, pp. 183-217, Academic Press, New York, 1973.

Logarithmic Time NC Algorithms for Comparability Graphs and Circle Graphs

Lin Chen

Department of Computer and Information Science

The Ohio State University

Columbus, OH 43210

USA

1 Introduction

In this paper, we present fast parallel solutions to some problems on comparability graphs and circle graphs. Our primary goal here is to obtain parallel algorithms which run as fast as possible. Our secondary goal is to use as few processors as possible. We show that a maximum weighted clique and minimum coloring of a comparability graph, and a maximum weighted independent set and a minimum clique cover of a permutation graph can be computed in $O(\log n)$ time with $O(n^3)$ processors. The class of permutation graphs is properly contained in that of comparability graphs. The above four problems were previously known to be solvable in $O(\log^2 n)$ time with $O(n^3)$ processors on a proper subclass of permutation graphs called cographs [1][2]. Our algorithms are superior to those by [1][2] in that our algorithms are faster, more efficient, and more general since they work for a much larger class of graphs. We further show that a maximum weighted clique of a circle graph can be computed in $O(\log n)$ time using $O(n^4)$ processors. Previously, it was shown that the problem can be solved in $O(\log n)$ time with $O(n^{4+\epsilon})$ processors for a constant $\epsilon > 0$ [22]. Our algorithm has a better processor bound while achieving the same time bound. It is easy to see that all the problems studied here are in NC^1, where NC^k is the class of problems solvable in $O(\log^k n)$ time using $O(n^{O(1)})$ processors.

The next section introduces many definitions and terminologies. It also describes a parallel procedure on rooted trees which is a useful tool for designing parallel graph algorithms. Section 3 shows that a maximum weighted clique and a minimum coloring of a comparability graph can be computed in $O(\log n)$ time using $O(n^3)$ processors. Section 4 further shows that, when restricted to permutation graphs, computing a maximum weighted independent set and a minimum clique cover can be done within the same resource bounds. Section 5 extends an algorithm on permutation graphs to that on circle graphs. Finally, Section 6 concludes this paper.

2 Preliminaries

Throughout this paper, all the graphs are simple graphs, *i.e.*, graphs which contain neither self loops nor parallel edges. A *clique* of a graph is a subset of its vertex set which induces a complete subgraph. A *maximum cardinality clique* is a clique of the maximum cardinality. If each vertex is associated with a number called *weight*, then the weight of a clique is the summation of the weights of the vertices in the clique. A *maximum weighted clique* is a clique of the maximum weight. An *independent set* of a graph is a subset of its vertex such that no two vertices in the subset are adjacent. A *maximum cardinality independent set* and a *maximum weighted independent set* of a graph are defined analogously. If there is no mention of 'cardinality' or 'weighted', then the former is implied. A *clique cover* of a graph is a family of disjoint subsets of its vertex set such that the union of the subsets equals the vertex set and each subset is a clique. A *minimum clique cover* of a graph is a clique cover of the minimum cardinality. The *chromatic number* of a graph is the minimum number of colors required to color the graph in such a way that in the resulting graph no two adjacent vertices have the same color. The *minimum coloring* problem on a graph is to color the graph using the minimum number of colors in that way.

$G' = (V', E')$ is called the *complement graph*, or simply *complement*, of $G = (V, E)$ if:

1. $V' = V$; and

2. $(v_i, v_j) \in E'$ if and only if $(v_i, v_j) \notin E$.

A graph is a *comparability graph* if it can be transitively oriented, *i.e.*, if we can assign a direction to each of its edges so that in the resulting directed graph the existence of directed edges (v_i, v_j) and (v_j, v_k) implies that of (v_i, v_k). A graph is a *permutation graph* if there exists a pair (P, Q) of permutations of the vertex set such that there is an edge between vertices x and y iff x precedes y in P and y precedes x in Q. A permutation graph is sometimes represented by a *permutation diagram* as follows: We use two columns to represent a pair (P, Q) of permutations of the vertex set. The left, and right columns consist of the vertices in the order given by P and Q, respectively. Two elements representing the same vertex in two columns are connected by a line. There is an edge between vertices x and y in the permutation graph if and only if the two corresponding lines cross in the permutation diagram. We give a permutation graph and its permutation diagram in Figure 1. Permutation graphs have been characterized as comparability graphs whose complements are also comparability graphs [21].

Graphs which do not contain a path linking four vertices (a P_4) as its induced subgraph are called *cographs*. They are a proper subclass of permutation graphs [6, 15]. The class of comparability graphs is a proper subclass of perfect graphs [12]. Lovász [17] showed the following:

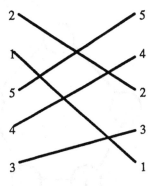
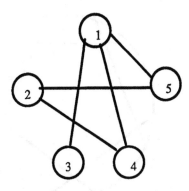

Figure 1: A permutation graph and its permutation diagram

Theorem 1 (Lovász) *For any undirected graph, the following two statements are equivalent:*

1. *For each induced subgraph, the size of the maximum independent set equals that of the minimum clique cover;*

2. *For each induced subgraph, the size of the maximum clique equals the chromatic number.*

A graph satisfying either of the two properties in the above theorem is called a *perfect graph*.

A graph is a *circle graph* if it is an intersection graph of a set of chords on a circle. In other words, $G = (V, E)$ is a circle graph if there exist a set of chords on a circle and a bijection $f: V \longrightarrow$ the set of chords such that $(v_i, v_j) \in E$ iff $f(v_i)$ and $f(v_j)$ intersect. The set of chords is an *intersection representation* of the circle graph. A circle graph and its intersection representation is shown in Figure 2.

The *level number of a vertex in a directed acyclic graph* is defined to be the length of the longest directed path from a vertex whose in-degree is 0 to the vertex. We denote by $l(v)$ the level number of vertex v. As a special case, the level number of a vertex in a rooted tree is the distance between the vertex and the root.

The model of computation used in this paper is concurrent read concurrent write (CRCW) parallel random access machine (P-RAM). Write conflicts are resolved in an arbitrary way. That is to say, our algorithms always give correct answers no matter which processor succeeds in writing in case of concurrent write. Algorithms which run in polylogarithmic time with polynomial number of processors are called NC algorithms. If a problem can be solved by an NC algorithm, then the problem is said to be in NC.

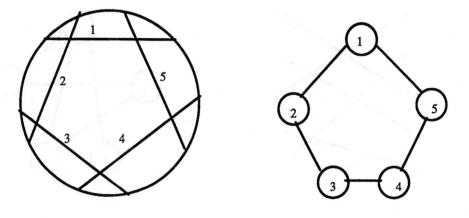

Figure 2: A circle graph and its intersection representation

In other words, NC is the class of problems solvable in $O(\log^{O(1)} n)$ time with $O(n^{O(1)})$ processors.

Before describing our algorithms for comparability graphs and circle graphs, we first give an efficient parallel procedure for computing a heaviest path in a weighted rooted tree by constructing an Euler tour as in Tarjan and Vishkin [24].

Given a rooted tree T, we construct an Euler tour as follows:

> For each vertex v in T with weight w, create a d-node[1] (down) and a u-node (up) having values w and $-w$, respectively. If v has k ($k > 1$) children, create $k - 1$ t-nodes (turn) each having value 0. If v has at least one child, then connect its d-node to the d-node of its first child; otherwise, connect its d-node to its u-node. If v has more than one child, then connect its ith t-node to the d-node of its $(i + 1)$st child, for all its t-nodes. If v is the ith child of its parent, connect its u-node to another node in the following way: if v is the last child of its parent, then connect its u-node to the u-node of its parent; otherwise, connect its u-node to the ith t-node of its parent.

Next, compute the prefix sums along the Euler tour using the well known pointer jumping technique [3]. The sum of a d-node gives the weight of path from the root to the corresponding vertex. The heaviest path can then be obtained easily. The procedure can be done in $O(\log n)$ time with $O(n)$ processors. If we set the weight of the root to 0 and set the weight of every other vertex to 1, the above procedure computes the level number of each vertex of the given tree.

To help understand the procedure described above, we give an example rooted tree in Figure 3 and the Euler tour constructed in Figure 4.

---

[1] To avoid confusion, we use 'nodes' to refer to the vertices constructed.

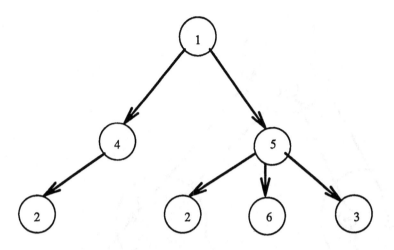

Figure 3: An example rooted tree

3 Comparability Graphs

Helmbold and Mayr [13] showed that computing a maximum weighted clique and minimum coloring of a comparability graph can be done in $O(\log^3 n)$ time with $O(n^4)$ processors. Their algorithm used a procedure for computing a maximal independent set [16][18] as a subroutine. Processor complexity can be reduced to $O(n^3)$ if a more efficient parallel algorithm for computing a maximal independent set by Goldberg and Spencer [10] is used. Further reduction in processor bound seems possible if we use $O(\log^4 n)$ time and invoke another procedure for computing a maximal independent set [11]; however, we are interested in quick algorithms in this paper. Recently, Novick [20] showed that a comparability graph can be transitively oriented in $O(\log n)$ time with $O(n^3)$ processors on an Arbitrary CRCW PRAM. A maximum weighted clique can be obtained from the transitive orientation by computing the heaviest (directed) path. Each path corresponds to a clique. We can show the relation between the paths and the cliques as follows. Suppose G is a comparability graph and $\vec{G}$ is the corresponding transitively oriented graph. If $v_1, \ldots, v_l$ is a directed path in $\vec{G}$, then each (v_i, v_j) is a directed edge in $\vec{G}$, for $0 < i < j \leq l$. Consequently, $v_1, \ldots, v_l$ form a clique in G. Conversely, suppose $v_1, \ldots, v_l$ form a clique in G. Sort these vertices in nondecreasing order according to their in-degrees in $\vec{G}$. Denote the result by $v_{k_1}, \ldots, v_{k_l}$. Since v_1, $\ldots, v_l$ form a clique in G, either $(v_{k_i}, v_{k_{i+1}})$ or $(v_{k_{i+1}}, v_{k_i})$ is a directed edge in $\vec{G}$. The in-degree of v_{k_i} is less than that of $v_{k_{i+1}}$ if and only if $(v_{k_i}, v_{k_{i+1}})$ is in $\vec{G}$. It follows that $v_{k_1}, \ldots, v_{k_l}$ is a directed path in $\vec{G}$. Note that $\vec{G}$ is acyclic since G does not contain self loops. It is not difficult to see that computing a heaviest path can be done in $O(\log n)$ time using no more than $O(n^3)$ processors, but this step is not trivial either. Here we briefly describe a method. First remove the directed edges in $\vec{G}$ implied by transitivity

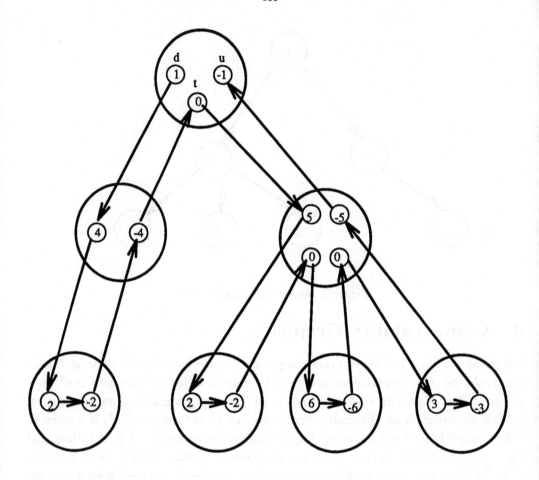

Figure 4: Euler tour construction

as described in Chen and Yesha [4][5]. This can be done in $O(T)$ time with $O(n^3/T)$ processors, for any T, $0 < T \leq n^3$. For each vertex v whose in-degree is 0, get a rooted tree whose vertices are those reachable from v and compute the heaviest path of the tree using the procedure described in Section 2. Hence we have the following theorem.

Theorem 2 *A maximum weighted clique of a comparability graph can be computed in $O(\log n)$ time with $O(n^3)$ processors on an Arbitrary CRCW PRAM.*

Recall that the class of comparability graphs is a proper subclass of perfect graphs, so the chromatic number c of a comparability graph equals the size of its maximum clique, by definition of perfect graphs. Next we show how to obtain the coloring using c colors. The procedure is very simple. First, compute the level numbers of all the vertices. Second, for each vertex v, assign color l to v if v is at level l.

Lemma 3 *The above procedure for computing a minimum coloring is correct.*

Proof. To justify the correctness of the procedure, we only need to show that if two vertices are at the same level of $\vec{G}$, then they are not adjacent in G. Assume the contrary, *i.e.*, there exist two vertices v and v' at the same level of $\vec{G}$ and v and v' are adjacent in G. Then either (v, v') or (v', v) is a directed edge in $\vec{G}$. Consequently, either $l(v) < l(v')$ or $l(v') < l(v)$, by definition of level number. This contradicts the assumption that v and v' are at the same level of $\vec{G}$. It follows that the procedure for computing a minimum coloring is correct. □

Level numbers of the vertices in $\vec{G}$ can be computed in a way similar to computing the heaviest path described above. We first remove the directed edges implied by transitivity in $\vec{G}$. For each vertex v whose in-degree in 0, get a rooted tree whose vertices are those reachable from v and compute the level numbers of the vertices in the tree. Observe that a vertex v may appear in several trees and may have different level numbers. The maximum of these level numbers is the level number of v in $\vec{G}$. It can be seen easily that all these can be done in $O(\log n)$ time using no more than $O(n^3)$ processors. Thus we have the following theorem.

Theorem 4 *A minimum coloring of a comparability graph can be computed in $O(\log n)$ time with $O(n^3)$ processors.*

4 Permutation Graphs

Since the class of permutation graphs is a proper subclass of comparability graphs, the following result follows easily from Theorem 2 and Theorem 4.

Corollary 5 *A maximum weighted clique and a minimum coloring of a permutation graph can be computed in $O(\log n)$ time using $O(n^3)$ processors.*

Some additional results can be obtained for permutation graphs. Following we give a procedure for finding a maximum weighted independent set in a permutation graph.

1. Obtain the complement of the input permutation graph.

2. Find a maximum weighted clique in the resulting graph.

The first step can be trivially parallelized. Since the input graph is a permutation graph, the complement is also a permutation graph. By Corollary 5, the second step can be done in $O(\log n)$ time using $O(n^3)$ processors. We can easily verify the following statements:

1. A subset of the vertex set of a graph is a clique if and only if it is an independent set of the complement graph;

2. A subset of the vertex set of a weighted graph is a maximum weighted clique if and only if it is a maximum weighted independent set of the complement graph.

Therefore, the above procedure correctly finds a maximum weighted independent set. The complexity bounds are dominated by the second step which takes $O(\log n)$ time and $O(n^3)$ processors by Corollary 5. Hence we have the following theorem.

Theorem 6 *A maximum weighted independent set of a permutation graph can be computed in $O(\log n)$ time using $O(n^3)$ processors.*

Following we give a procedure for computing a minimum clique cover of a permutation graph.

1. Obtain the complement of the input permutation graph.

2. Compute the minimum coloring and get the color sets of the resulting graph.

It can be readily seen that each color set of a graph corresponds to a clique of the complement graph and that all the color sets form a minimum clique cover. Therefore, the above procedure correctly computes a minimum clique cover. The resource requirements are dominated by the second step, which can be done in $O(\log n)$ time with $O(n^3)$ processors by Corollary 5. Thus we have the following theorem.

Theorem 7 *A minimum clique cover of a permutation graph can be computed in $O(\log n)$ time using $O(n^3)$ processors.*

Recently, Adhar and Peng [1][2] showed that the above problems on cographs, a proper subclass of permutation graphs, can all be solved in $O(\log^2 n)$ time using $O(n^3)$ a CRCW PRAM processors. Our algorithms are superior to theirs in that our algorithms are faster and work for a much larger class of graphs even though they use the same number of processors. Rhee, Dhall and Lakshmivarahan [22] showed that a maximum weighted clique of a permutation graph can be computed in $O(\log n)$ time with $O(n^{3+\epsilon})$ processors, for a constant $\epsilon > 0$. Our algorithm compares favorably with theirs in that our algorithm uses fewer processors and works for comparability graphs, a proper superclass of permutation graphs.

5 Circle Graphs

The class of circle graphs was introduced in Even and Itai [7]. Each circle graph can be modeled by a set of chords on a circle such that there is an edge between two vertices if and only if the corresponding two chords intersect. The set of chords is the intersection representation of the circle graph.

To see that the class of permutation graphs is contained in the class of circle graphs, we construct an intersection representation for a circle graph from a permutation graph. Recall that for any permutation graph, there exist two permutations of its vertex set such that there is an edge between v_i and v_j if and only if v_i precedes v_j in one permutation and v_j precedes v_i in the other. We embed one permutation of vertex set on the left half circle and the other permutation of vertex set on the right half circle. For each vertex, construct a chord which connects the vertex on the left half circle and the vertex on the right half circle. The resulting set of chords constitutes an intersection representation of a circle graph. Therefore, each permutation graph is a circle graph.

Circle graphs can also be modeled by a set of intervals such that there is an edge between two vertices if and only if the two corresponding intervals overlap. The set of intervals is the overlap representation of the circle graph.

The equivalence of these two models of circle graphs has been shown by Gavril [9]. An efficient algorithm for recognizing circle graphs has been given by Gabor, Hsu and Supowit [8]. We first show how to construct a set of intervals from a set of chords on a circle.

Choose a point p on the circle which is not an endpoint of any chord. Cut the circle at p and put the 'circle' on a line. Now a chord with endpoints e_i and e_j corresponds to an interval (e_i, e_j). It is easy to see that two chords intersect if and only if two corresponding intervals overlap.

Conversely, from a set of intervals, we can construct an equivalent set of chords as follows. Wrap a set of intervals around a circle which is large enough so that those intervals do not cover the entire circle. Then draw a chord between the two endpoints of each interval.

It can be readily seen that the transformation between the two models can be done in linear sequential time, or in $O(T)$ time with $O(n/T)$ processors on an EREW PRAM for any T, $0 < T \leq n$.

In light of the transformation between the two models, we are free to choose either of them in designing algorithms on the circle graphs.

We reduce the maximum clique problem on circle graphs to the problem on permutation graphs, a smaller class of graphs. This idea was due to Gavril [9]. Hsu [14] obtained a faster sequential algorithm for computing a maximum weighted clique. Rotem and Urrutia [23], and Masuda, Nakajima, Kashiwabara, and Fujisawa [19] both gave efficient sequential algorithms for computing maximum cliques in the cardinality case. For each vertex v_i of a circle graph G, denote by G_i the subgraph induced by v_i and its neighbors.

We compute the maximum weighted clique for each G_i, $0 < i \leq n$. Then select the maximum of the n maximum weighted cliques. Observe that if C is a maximum weighted clique of G, then C is also a maximum weighted clique of G_i, for each $v_i \in C$. Hence there exists an i, $0 < i \leq n$, such that the maximum weighted clique of G_i coincides with that of G. So the method of computation is correct.

We now show that each G_i is a permutation graph. Let G_i' be the graph induced by the neighbors of v_i. Since each induced subgraph of a circle graph is a circle graph, G_i is a circle graph. So there exists a set of chords on a circle representing G_i. Let c_i be the chord corresponding to v_i. The chord cuts the circle into two circular arcs. For any other chord, the two endpoints are on two circular arcs. Hence the chords other than c_i denote a permutation diagram for G_i'. It follows that G_i' is a permutation graph. Connecting a new vertex to every vertex of a permutation graph generates another permutation graph. Therefore, G_i is a permutation graph. From the above discussion we have the following theorem.

Theorem 8 *A maximum weighted clique of a circle graph can be computed in $O(\log n)$ time using $O(n^4)$ processors.*

The problem was shown to be in NC by Rhee, Dhall and Lakshmivarahan [22]. Their algorithm runs in $O(\log n)$ time with $O(n^{4+\epsilon})$ processors on a CRCW PRAM, for a constant $\epsilon > 0$. So we have obtained an improved processor bound.

6 Conclusion

We have given logarithmic time parallel algorithms for solving the maximum weighted clique and the minimum coloring problems on comparability graphs, the maximum weighted independent set and the minimum clique cover problems on permutation graphs, and the maximum weighted clique problem on circle problems. Our algorithms are more efficient than the previous ones. A number of questions are still open. An interesting one is whether the problems studied here can be solved using fewer processors without time penalty. It seems likely that there will be a positive answer to this question.

References

[1] G. S. Adhar and S. Peng. Parallel algorithms for cographs recognition and applications. In F. Dehne, J.-R. Sack, and N. Santoro, editors, *Proc. Workshop on Algorithms and Data Structures (Carleton University, Ottawa, Ontario, Canada, August 17-19), Lecture Notes in Computer Science, Vol. 382*, pages 335–351. Springer-Verlag, 1989.

[2] G. S. Adhar and S. Peng. Parallel algorithms for cographs and parity graphs with applications. *J. Algorithms*, 11(2):252–284, June 1990.

[3] S. G. Akl. *The Design and Analysis of Parallel Algorithms*. Prentice Hall, Englewood Cliffs, N.J., 1989.

[4] L. Chen and Y. Yesha. Parallel testing for the consecutive ones property and transformable convex bipartite graphs and finding a maximum matching. In *Proc. 27th Ann. Allerton Conf. on Communication, Control, and Computing (Monticello, Illinois, Sept. 27–29)*, pages 756–765. University of Illinois at Urbana-Champaign, 1989.

[5] L. Chen and Y. Yesha. Parallel recognition of the consecutive ones property with applications. *J. Algorithms*, 12(3), September 1991. (scheduled)

[6] D. G. Corneil, H. Lerchs, and L. Stewart Burlingham. Complement reducible graphs. *Discrete Applied Mathematics*, 3(3):163–174, 1981.

[7] S. Even and A. Itai. Queues, stacks and graphs. In Z. Kohavi and A. Paz, editors, *Theory of Machines and Computations*, pages 71–86. Academic Press, New York, 1971.

[8] C. P. Gabor, W.-L. Hsu, and K. J. Supowit. Recognizing circle graphs in polynomial time. In *Proc. 26th Ann. Symp. on Foundations of Computer Science*, pages 106–116. IEEE Computer Society, 1985.

[9] F. Gavril. Algorithms for a maximum clique and a minimum independent set of a circle graph. *Networks*, 3:261–273, 1973.

[10] M. Goldberg and T. Spencer. A new parallel algorithm for the maximal independent set problem. In *Proc. 28th Ann. Symp. on Foundations of Computer Science*, pages 161–165. IEEE Computer Society, 1987.

[11] M. Goldberg and T. Spencer. Constructing a maximal independent set in parallel. *SIAM J. on Discr. Math.*, 2(3):322–328, August 1989.

[12] M. C. Golumbic. *Algorithmic Graph Theory and Perfect Graphs*. Computer Science and Applied Mathematics. Academic Press, New York, 1980.

[13] D. Helmbold and E. Mayr. Perfect graphs and parallel algorithms. In *Proc. International Conference on Parallel Processing*, pages 853–860, 1986.

[14] W.-L. Hsu. Maximum weight clique algorithms for circular-arc graphs and circle graphs. *SIAM Journal on Computing*, 14:224–231, 1985.

[15] D. S. Johnson. The NP-completeness column: an ongoing guide. *J. Algorithms*, 6:434–451, 1985.

[16] R. M. Karp and A. Wigderson. A fast parallel algorithm for the maximal independent set problem. *Journal of the ACM*, 32(4):762–773, 1985.

[17] L. Lovász. A characterization of perfect graphs. *J. Combin. Theory B*, 13:95–98, 1972.

[18] M. Luby. A simple parallel algorithm for the maximal independent set problem. In *Proc. 17th Annual Symposium on Theory of Computing (Providence, RI)*, pages 1–10. Association for Computing Machinery, 1985.

[19] S. Masuda, K. Nakajima, T. Kashiwabara, and T. Fujisawa. Efficient algorithms for finding maximum cliques of an overlap graph. *Networks*, 20:157–171, 1990.

[20] M. B. Novick. Logarithmic time parallel algorithms for comparability and interval graphs. Technical Report TR89-1015, Cornell University, June 1989.

[21] A. Pnueli, A. Lempel, and S. Even. Transitive orientation of graphs and identification of permutation graphs. *Canad. J. Math.*, 23:160–175, 1971.

[22] C. Rhee, S. K. Dhall, and S. Lakshmivarahan. An NC algorithm for finding a maximum weight clique on a circle graph. In *Proc. 27th Ann. Allerton Conf. on Communication, Control, and Computing (Monticello, Illinois, Sept. 27–29)*, pages 776–777. University of Illinois at Urbana-Champaign, 1989.

[23] D. Rotem and J. Urrutia. Finding maximum cliques in circle graphs. *Networks*, 11(3):269–278, 1981.

[24] R. E. Tarjan and U. Vishkin. An efficient parallel biconnectivity algorithm. *SIAM Journal on Computing*, 14(4):862–874, November 1985.

Compact Hypercubes: Properties and Recognition

Alfred J. Boals, Ajay K. Gupta*
Jahangir A. Hashmi, Naveed A. Sherwani*
Department of Computer Science
Western Michigan University
Kalamazoo, MI 49008

Abstract

The binary hypercube, although a versatile multiprocessor network, has a draw back: its size must be a power of two. In order to alleviate this draw back, we define the concept of an n-node Compact Hypercube CH(n) which deals with the problem of computation with incomplete hypercubes. We show how to construct a hypercube like structure for any number n that can be easily upgraded to a complete hypercube. This concept allows the algorithms to work efficiently even if hypercubes are incomplete. Development of algorithms on compact hypercubes further allow us to efficiently execute several algorithms concurrently on a complete hypercube.

In this paper, we restrict our investigation to the graph properties and recognition algorithms for compact hypercubes. We show that compact hypercubes exhibit many properties which are common with complete hypercubes. We also present results on efficient representation and counting of compact hypercubes within a complete hypercube.

1 Introduction

The hypercube has emerged as one of the most effective and popular topology for parallel machines. The popularity of this architecture for parallel computation may be attributed to its regular structure and its rich interconnection topology. Hypercubes also allow simple and efficient algorithms, such as node to node communication and broadcasting, which are basic building blocks for development of other parallel algorithms. Several hypercube based machines (e.g; Intel IPSc and NCUBE) are commercially available.

Hypercube topology requires that the number of nodes in a network must be a power of 2. Furthermore, in the development of parallel algorithms it is usually assumed that the hypercube is *complete*. For example in the case of hypercube interconnection architecture if a problem requires 11 nodes, a complete 16 node hypercube is assumed available. However, in practice, due to budgetary constraints or node failures, it may not be possible to have a complete architecture. This frequently happens while upgrading an existing architecture to the next dimension. For example, when upgrading a 32 node hypercube an additional 32 nodes are needed before any algorithm requiring nodes in the range of 33-64 may be run. Thus, for any value of n we need to construct a hypercube-like network so that it is upgradable to the next dimension at a time when the remaining nodes become available.

*Research Supported in part by fellowships from the Faculty Research and Creative Activities Support Fund WMU-FRCASF 90-15 and WMU-FRCASF 89-225274, and by the National Science Foundation under grant USE-90-52346.

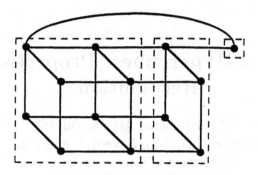

Figure 1: Example of a 13-node Compact Hypercube

We define the concept of Compact Hypercube of m nodes ($CH(m)$) that can be easily upgraded to a complete hypercube. This concept allows the algorithms to work efficiently even if hypercubes are incomplete. We next give the definition of a compact set which facilitates the definition of $CH(m)$. An n-dimensional hypercube Q_n has 2^n nodes and every node in Q_n is labeled as $b_{n-1}b_{n-2}\ldots b_0$ where $b_s \in \{0,1\}$ for $0 \le s \le n-1$. A node with label $b_{n-1}\ldots b_0$ is connected to n nodes having labels $b_{n-1}\ldots b_{s+1}\bar{b}_s b_{s-1}\ldots b_0$, for $0 \le s \le n-1$.

Definition 1 *A set of nodes S in a hypercube Q_n is called a* compact set *if*

i) $|S| \le 1$ *or*

ii) *For a positive integer k such that $2^{k-1} \le |S| < 2^k$, there exists a k-dimensional hypercube Q_k with S as a subset of its nodes. In addition, Q_k contains two disjoint $(k-1)$-dimensional hypercubes Q_{k-1}^0, Q_{k-1}^1 such that the node set V^0 of Q_{k-1}^0 is a subset of S and $S - V^0$ is a compact set in Q_{k-1}^1.*

Given a compact set S, the *compact hypercube* is defined to be a subgraph of a hypercube which is induced by the set S. (Recall that an induced graph on a set S of nodes in a graph G is the graph whose node set is S and whose edge set consists of those edges in G having both ends in S.) Figure 1 shows an example of a compact hypercube with 13 nodes. It is important to note that compact hypercubes are a generalization of hypercubes in the sense that they are defined for any arbitrary number of nodes.

In order to use a new architecture for development of parallel algorithms, one needs to investigate the underlying graph properties of the proposed architecture. Several properties such as diameter, connectivity, and maximum degree, influence the maximum routing distance, stability under node failure and ease of fabrication due to limited number of I/O ports per processor. Other properties such as colorability, domination number, circumference may also play an important role in algorithm development. In order to evaluate the effectiveness of compact hypercubes as a parallel architecture, we need to investigate the graph properties and compare them with other existing architectures.

In this paper, we investigate several graph theoretic properties of compact hypercubes. We show that compact hypercubes compare very well with hypercubes in these properties. The problem of counting different compact hypercubes in a hypercube is considered and we give an efficient algorithm for this computation. We also describe an efficient algorithm to recognize a compact hypercube in a hypercube. This algorithm is critical for task allocation and scheduling algorithms using compact hypercubes. Furthermore, this is crucial for the development of efficient algorithms on the compact hypercubes.

Another scheme of working with m nodes in Q_n appeared in [20]. The computation problem with incomplete hypercubes has been considered in [17]. The author describes a topology for connecting arbitrary m nodes in a hypercube fashion and it is shown that routing and broadcast algorithms may be done in an analogous manner to that of a complete hypercube. The architecture defined by the schemes in [20, 17] results in a compact hypercube. It is important to note that these scheme lead to a fixed compact hypercube whereas our scheme defines all possible compact hypercubes of m nodes. In [14], it is shown how to reconfigure a hypercube in case some nodes are faulty. This is accomplished via embedding of complete hypercube into the one with faults. The problem of routing in presence of faults has been investigated in [15]. Since faults are considered with some probability, the algorithms are probablistic. Several other paper consider routing, allocation and broadcasting problems on a faulty or 'injured' hypercube [7, 13, 16, 18].

The rest of the paper is organized as follows. Section 2 describes the properties of compact hypercubes and compares them with the ones of a hypercube. In Section 3, we consider the problem of recognizing a compact hypercube in a hypercube and present an efficient algorithm to recognize compact hypercubes.

2 Properties of Compact Hypercubes

In this section we investigate the properties of compact hypercubes. In particular, graph theoretic properties which are crucial in evaluating a parallel architecture. Graph theoretic properties of hypercubes have been extensively studied [12]. We show that compact hypercubes exhibit many properties which are common with hypercubes. We also describe an algorithm which computes the number of different compact hypercubes that exist in a hypercube. Counting the number of different compact hypercubes is important in task allocation problems where a hypercube machine is to be utilized for a number of algorithms running on compact hypercubes and thus different compact hypercubes are to be allocated dynamically to different tasks. We first briefly give the definitions and notations of the properties considered in this section and then describe these properties for compact hypercubes. For a more detailed definitions, reader is referred to standard text books in graph theory, such as [5, 2].

1. e = number of edges.

2. δ = minimum node degree, and Δ = maximum node degree.

3. κ (resp., λ) = node (resp. edge) connectivity number; i.e, minimum number of nodes (resp. edges) required to disconnect a graph.

4. ω = maximum clique size.

5. χ_0 (resp. χ_1) = node (resp. edge) chromatic number.

6. d = diameter; i.e., the distance between two nodes in the graph which are furthest apart. We call $[u, v]$ as a *diametrical pair*, if distance between u and v is equal to the diameter of the graph.

7. α_0 (resp. α_1) = node (resp. edge) covering number; i.e., the minimum number of nodes (resp. edges) required to cover all the edges (resp. nodes) of a graph.

8. β_0 = node independence number; i.e., the size of the maximum set of nodes in a graph such that no two of which share an edge.

9. β_1 = edge independence number (the matching number); i.e., the size of the maximum set of edges in a graph such that no two edges in the set are incident on the same node.

10. g = girth; i.e., the length of the shortest cycle in the graph.

11. c = circumference; i.e., the length of the longest cycle in the graph.

12. θ_0 (resp. θ_1) = node (resp. edge) clique number; i.e., the minimum number of cliques which contain all the nodes (resp. edges) of a graph.

Let CH_m be a compact hypercube of m nodes. We now compute the above stated properties of $CH(m)$. Observe that when m is a power of two, $CH(m)$ is equivalent to a hypercube $Q_{\log m}$. Let k be the smallest integer such that Q_k contains CH_m as a subgraph and let $m = b_{k-1}b_{k-2}\ldots b_0$ with $b_{k-1} = 1$. We thus have $k = \lceil \log m \rceil$.

Lemma 1 *The number of edges e in a compact hypercube $CH(m)$ is*

$$\sum_{j=0}^{k-1} j b_j 2^{j-1} + \sum_{j=0}^{k-2}(b_{j+1}\sum_{i=0}^{j} b_i 2^i).$$

Proof: Intuitively, the number of edges in $CH(m)$ is the maximum number of edges in an induced subgraph of Q_k having m nodes. The first term in the formula counts the number of edges in the disjoint hypercubes Q_j's that are contained in $CH(m)$. The second term counts number of edges that connect a hypercube Q_j with a hypercube Q_i, for all possible pairs j and i. An induction argument proves the formula for e and we omit it from the extended abstract. ∎

Lemma 2 *Let $[u, v]$ be a diametrical pair of $CH(m)$. Then, there exists a partition of Q_k into Q_{k-1}^0 and Q_{k-1}^1 such that*

1. *node u is a node of Q_{k-1}^0 and node v is a node of Q_{k-1}^1, and*

2. *distance between u and v is k.*

In other words, the diameter d of $CH(m)$ is $k = \lceil \log m \rceil$.

Proof: We only sketch the proof here. The detailed proof will appear in the full paper. The proof is based on the following two observations about hypercubes Q_k: 1) the diameter of Q_k is k, and 2) For every node x of Q_k, there exists a unique node y such that $[x, y]$ is a diametrical pair of Q_k.

We now proceed by induction on k. It is easy to see that the lemma holds for $k = 1$ and thus $m = 2$. Assume that the lemma is true for $p < k$. We now show that it holds for $p = k$. By the definition of compact hypercubes, there exists a partition Q_{k-1}^0 and Q_{k-1}^1 of Q_k such that Q_k^0 is contained in $CH(m)$ and $CH(m) - Q_{k-1}^0$ is contained in Q_{k-1}^1. For a diametrical pair $[u, v]$ of $CH(m)$, we first show that both u and v do not belong to either Q_{k-1}^0 or $Q_{k-1}^1 \cap CH(m)$. If u and v both belong to Q_{k-1}^0, then we know that $[u, v]$ must be a diametrical pair of Q_{k-1}^0 and thus the distance between u and v is exactly $k - 1$. This implies that any diametrical pair of Q_{k-1}^0 must be a diametrical pair of $CH(m)$ and hence we can choose u and v such that v is adjacent to a node v' in $CH(m) - Q_{k-1}^0 = Q_{k-1}^1 \cap CH(m)$. Now it can be seen that the shortest distance between u and v' is at least k since any path of length less than k implies distance between u and v to be less than $k - 1$ which is a contradiction. The argument that both u and v do not belong to $Q_{k-1}^1 \cap CH(m)$ is along the similar lines. We next need to show that the distance between u and v can not be more than k given that condition 1 of the lemma holds. This is easily shown by the fact that every node in $CH(m) \cap Q_{k-1}^1$ is adjacent to a node of Q_{k-1}^0 and that the diameter of Q_{k-1}^0 is $k - 1$. Hence, the diameter of $CH(m)$ is k and the lemma follows. ∎

It is well known that a hypercube Q_k contains a hamiltonian cycle. We can easily show that compact hypercube $CH(m)$ contains a hamiltonian cycle when m is an even integer and it contains a hamiltonian path when m is an odd number. Combining this with the observation that

Parameter	Compact Hypercube $CH(m)$	Hypercube $Q_{\lceil \log m \rceil}$
diameter	$\lceil \log m \rceil$	$\lceil \log m \rceil$
min node degree	$\sum b_j + i - 1$	$\lceil \log m \rceil$
	(i is smallest integer such that $b_i = 1$)	
max node degree	$\lceil \log m \rceil$	$\lceil \log m \rceil$
node connectivity κ	$1 \leq \kappa \leq \lceil \log m \rceil$	$\lceil \log m \rceil$
edge connectivity λ	$1 \leq \lambda \leq \lceil \log m \rceil$	$\lceil \log m \rceil$
max clique size	2	2
node chromatic number	2	2
edge chromatic number	$\lceil \log m \rceil$	$\lceil \log m \rceil$
covering number	$\lceil \frac{m}{2} \rceil$	$2^{\lceil \log m \rceil - 1}$
independence number	$\lceil \frac{m}{2} \rceil$	$2^{\lceil \log m \rceil - 1}$
girth	4 (for $m > 3$)	4
circumference	$2\lfloor \frac{m}{2} \rfloor$	$2^{\lceil \log m \rceil}$
node clique number	$\lceil \frac{m}{2} \rceil$	$2^{\lceil \log m \rceil - 1}$
edge clique number	$e = \#$ of edges	$\#$ of edges

Table 1: Comparison of Compact Hypercubes and Hypercubes

the $CH(m)$ is a bipartite graph, all the other properties of $CH(m)$ can be obtained somewhat easily. We tabulate these properties in Table 1. In order to compare these properties with the ones of a hypercube, we also list the properties of hypercube $Q_{\lceil \log m \rceil}$ in the same table. As we can see from the table, compact hypercubes retain almost all properties of a hypercube. However, we must note that the draw backs with compact hypercubes are lack of symmetry and regularity. Experience has shown that these draw backs can be overcome and many algorithms designed for hypercubes can be easily modified to run on compact hypercubes [3, 17, 19, 20].

We now consider the problem of counting different compact hypercubes $CH(m)$'s in a hypercube Q_n, for $m < 2^n$. Note that the problem is to count different and not disjoint compact hypercubes. The number of disjoint $CH(m)$ in Q_n is simply $\lfloor 2^n/m \rfloor$. It is well known that there are $2^{k-l} k!/(k-l)! \, l!$ different hypercubes Q_l's in a hypercube Q_k of k dimension, for $k > l$. We use this fact along with reduction Lemmas 3 and 4 to compute the number of different $CH(m)$'s in Q_n. Let N_m^n denote the number of $CH(m)$'s in Q_n. Let M_l^k be the number of Q_l's in Q_k and thus $M_l^k = 2^{k-l} k!/(k-l)! \, l!$. Since compact hypercubes are equivalent to hypercubes when m is a power of two, say $m = 2^l$ with $l < n$, we have $N_m^n = M_l^n$.

Lemma 3 If $m = 2^n - p$ for a positive integer p such that $0 < p \leq 2^{n-1}$, then $N_m^n = N_p^n$.

Proof: Omitted. ∎

Lemma 4 If $m < 2^{n-1}$, then $N_m^n = N_m^{n-1} \times M_{n-1}^n$.

Proof: Omitted. ∎

We can now give an algorithm to compute the number of compact hypercubes by using Lemmas 3 and 4 recursively. Since the algorithm is rather straight forward, we illustrate it with an example that counts different 10-node compact hypercubes in the hypercube Q_4 of 16 nodes. Using our notation, we are interested in computing the value of N_{10}^4. Using Lemma 3, we have $N_{10}^4 = N_6^4$. Lemma 4 can now be applied to compute the value of N_6^4 and thus $N_6^4 = N_6^3 \times M_3^4$. Since $N_6^3 = N_2^3$ by applying Lemma 3, we have reduced the problem to counting 2-node compact hypercubes in a 2^3-node hypercube which is equivalent to counting 2-node hypercubes in a 2^3

node hypercube and thus $N_2^3 = M_1^3$. The total count of 10 node compact hypercubes in Q_4 is therefore given by $N_{10}^4 = M_1^3 \times M_3^4 = 12 \times 8 = 96$.

In concluding this section, we note that compact hypercubes can be recursively partitioned. More precisely, compact hypercube $CH(m)$ can be easily partitioned into two compact hypercubes $CH(\lfloor \frac{m}{2} \rfloor)$ and $CH(\lceil \frac{m}{2} \rceil)$. This property should yield 'divide-and-conquer' type of algorithms to be designed somewhat easily on compact hypercubes.

3 Recognition of Compact Hypercubes

Given a hypercube Q_n and a description of nodes that have already been allocated to perform certain tasks. The hypercube recognition problem is to find 2^k free nodes forming a hypercube in Q_n, for any given $k < n$. This problem is of critical importance in task allocation and scheduling algorithms [1, 6]. The exponential number of subcubes in a hypercube makes this problem computationally difficult. Furthermore, the dynamic nature of allocating and deallocating tasks to nodes in a hypercube algorithm leads to fragmentation of the hypercube, i.e., a total of 2^k free nodes may be available but they may not form a hypercube. An allocation strategy minimizing fragmentation heavily depends on an efficient recognition algorithm.

In this section we investigate the recognition problem of a compact hypercube $CH(m)$ in a hypercube Q_n, for $m < 2^n$. We present an efficient algorithm for recognizing compact hypercubes. The algorithm uses the idea of decomposition of compact hypercube into several smaller complete hypercubes. Using existing algorithms, these subcubes can be recognized while ensuring that the subcubes together form a compact hypercube. Let us first briefly outline the basic strategy, viz., the Buddy Strategy, for recognizing subcubes in a hypercube which is crucial for our algorithm.

The basic idea in the Buddy strategy is to recognize subcubes inorder to allocate a task, and to merge them to get a bigger subcube at the time of deallocation. (This minimizes fragmentation.) Although the Buddy strategy is efficient, it recognizes only 2^{n-k} Q_k's in a Q_n. Recall that there are $2^{n-k} n!/(n-k)! k!$ different Q_k's in a Q_n. The strategy uses a height n complete binary tree representation of subcubes in a hypercube. This tree is called the Buddy tree. Every leaf of the Buddy tree represents a node of the hypercube and stores a binary value, 0 (resp. 1) indicates that the node is free (resp. allocated). A node at level k represents a subcube of dimension $(n-k)$ and its binary value is 0 if the binary value of all its descendents is zero. In order to recognize a free subcube of dimension $n-k$, we only need to search the nodes of the tree at level k. Recently, this strategy has been extended to recognize all possible different subcubes [1].

We now briefly describe the recognition algorithm for compact hypercube $CH(m)$ in Q_n. Let $m = b_{k-1}b_{k-2} \ldots b_0$ with $b_{k-1} = 1$. From the definition of $CH(m)$, it is clear that for every $b_i = 1$, $CH(m)$ contains Q_i. Thus, we need to recognize $\sum b_i$ subcubes. However, the selection of Q_{k-1} restricts us to recognize the remaining subcubes in a complement of Q_{k-1} since all Q_i's together should form $CH(m)$. Based on this observation, every time a subcube is selected the search for smaller subcubes is restricted to its complement.

In order to identify a subcube in Q_n using Buddy tree, an address is associated with each node of the tree. The address is of the form $a_{n-1}a_{n-2} \ldots a_0$ where $a_i \in \{0, 1, *\}$. The $*$ denotes a wild card character that could be either 0 or 1. The root of the Buddy tree identifies the whole hypercube Q_n and has address $*^n$. The left child has address $0*^{n-1}$ identifying a subcube Q_{n-1}. Similarly right child has address $1*^{n-1}$. In general, if a node v at level k has address $a_{n-1}a_{n-2} \ldots a_0$, then the left child of v has address $a_{n-1} \ldots a_{n-k+1}0a_{n-k-1} \ldots a_0$ and the right child has address $a_{n-1} \ldots a_{n-k+1}1a_{n-k-1} \ldots a_0$. Note that the address of v has only rightmost $(n-k+1)$ bits as $*$'s.

The algorithm starts by recognizing Q_{k-1} by searching level $n-k+1$ of the buddy tree and returns the address of the node. If the search fails at level $n-k+1$, then we search level $n-k+i+1$ and find 2^i $(k-i-1)$-dimensional subcubes that form a $(k-1)$-dimensional hypercube. This can be guaranteed by requiring that the leftmost $n - k + i + 1$ bits of the addresses of the nodes at level $n - k + i + 1$ form at least a hypercube of dimension i.

Lemma 5 *If there exists a free $(k-1)$-dimensional hypercube in Q_n, the strategy described above recognizes Q_{k-1}.*

Proof: Omitted. ∎

Once, a Q_{k-1} has been recognized having address $a_{n-1} \ldots a_0$. This address contains $n - k + 1$ bits which are 0 or 1. Let us define the complement of this hypercube by inverting a single bit out of the $n - k + 1$ bits having 0 or 1 in the address. The $CH(m) - Q_{k-1}$ is now found recursively by systematically searching all complements of Q_{k-1}.

Theorem 1 *If there exists a free $CH(m)$ in a Q_n, then the above algorithm ensures recognition of $CH(m)$.*

Proof: Omitted. ∎

4 Conclusions

In this paper, we have investigated the graph properties of compact hypercubes. We have presented combinatorial results on efficient representation and counting of compact hypercubes. We have also presented an efficient algorithm which recognizes compact hypercubes within a complete hypercube. This recognition algorithm is fundamental to task allocation problems and to development of efficient algorithms on compact hypercubes. Obviously, our work is simply a start if compact hypercubes are to be shown as an effective parallel interconnection network. There remains a number of issues that need be investigated for compact hypercubes. For example, complete hypercubes have been shown to efficiently simulate various other architectures, such as meshes, butterflies, and rings. In [4], authors have shown that compact hypercubes also simulate trees and meshes very efficiently. Naturally, simulations of other popular architectures such as shuffle-exchange and pyramids still remain open problems. In [21], authors have shown that fully normal algorithms on compact hypercubes achieve a close to linear speed up over a wide range of the size of the architecture. Hence, design of other classes of parallel algorithms on compact hypercubes remain to be investigated.

References

[1] S. Al-Bassam, H. El-Rewini, B. Bose, and T. Lewis, "Efficient Serial and Parallel Subcube recognition in Hypercube," To appear in the Procceedings of the *First Great Lakes Computer Science Conference*, 1989.

[2] M. Behzad, G. Chartrand, and L. Lesniak-Foster, "Graphs and Digraphs," Prindle, Weber and Schmidt, Boston, 1979.

[3] A. J. Boals, A. K. Gupta, N. A. Sherwani, K. Williams, "Load Balancing and List Ranking on Compact Hypercubes," manuscript, 1990.

[4] A. Boals, A. Gupta, and N. Sherwani, "On Optimal Embeddings into Incomplete Hypercubes," to appear in the *Proceedings of the Fifth International Parallel Processing Symposium*, 1991.

[5] J. A. Bondy and U. S. R. Murthy, "Graph Theory with Applications," MacMillan Press Ltd., 1976.

[6] M. Chen and K. G,. Shin, "Processor Allocation in an N-cube Multiprocessor using Gray Codes," *IEEE Transactions on Computer,* Vol C-36, No. 12, pp 1396-1407, 1987.

[7] M. Chen and K. G. Shin, "Message Routing in a Injured Hypercube," in the *Proceedings of the Third Conference on Hypercube Concurrent Computers and Applications,* 1988, pp. 312-317.

[8] S. Foldes, "A Characterization of Hypercubes," *Discrete Math.,* 17, pp. 155-159, 1977.

[9] M. R. Garey and R. L. Graham, "On Cubical Graphs," *J. Combin. Theory,* B18, pp. 84-95, 1975.

[10] A. Gupta and S. Hambrusch, "Multiple Network Embeddings into Hypercubes". In the *Proceedings of the Fifth Distributed Memory Conference,* April 1990.

[11] A. K. Gupta, A. J. Boals, N. A. Sherwani, and S. E. Hambrusch, "A Lower Bound on Embedding Large Hypercubes into Small Hypercubes". To appear in *Congressus Numerentium,* 1991.

[12] F. Harary, J. P. Hayes and H-J. Wu, "A Survey of the Theory of Hypercube Graphs," *Comput. Math. Applic,* Vol. 15, No. 4, pp. 277-289, 1988.

[13] J. M. Gordon and Q. F. Stout, "Hypercube Message Routing in the Presence of Faults," in the *Proceedings of the Third Conference on Hypercube Concurrent Computers and Applications,* 1988, pp. 318-327.

[14] J. Hastad, T Leighton and M. Newman, "Reconfiguring a Hypercube in the Presence of Faults," in *Proceedings of the Nineteenth Annual ACM Symposium on Theory of Computing,* May 1987, pp. 274-284.

[15] J. Hastad, T Leighton and M. Newman, "Fast Computation Using Faulty Hypercubes," in *Proceedings of the Twenty First Annual ACM Symposium on Theory of Computing,* May 1989, pp. 251-263.

[16] D. D. Kandlur and K. G. Shin, "Hypercube Management in the presence of Node Failures ," in the *Proceedings of the Third Conference on Hypercube Concurrent Computers and Applications,* 1988, pp. 328-336.

[17] H. P. Katseff, "Incomplete Hypercubes," *IEEE Transactions on Computers,* vol. 37, no. 5, May 1988, pp. 604-608.

[18] T. C. Lee and J. P. Hayes, "Routing and Broadcasting in Faulty Hypercubes Computers," in the *Proceedings of the Third Conference on Hypercube Concurrent Computers and Applications,* 1988, pp. 346-354.

[19] V. Prabhalla and N. Sherwani, "Parallel Single Row Routing on Compact Hypercubes," Technical Report, Dept. of Computer Science, Western Michigan University, 1990.

[20] P. K. Srimani and B. P. Sinha, "Message Broadcasting in Point-To-Point Computer Networks," in the *Proceedings of the International Symposium of Circuits and Systems, 1988,* pp. 189-192.

[21] V. Prabhalla and N. Sherwani, "Fully Normal Algorithms for Incomplete Hypercubes," to appear in the *Proceedings of the International Parallel Processing Symposium, 1991.*

Increasing Communication Bandwidth on Hypercube

Zhiyong Liu   Jia-Huai You

Department of Computing Science, University of Alberta

Edmonton, Alberta, Canada T6G 2H1

Abstract

We present an interconnection network, called *Syncube*, which is a new implementation scheme of hypercube. The hardware complexity of syncube is $O(Nlog_2N)$. Communication is much faster through syncube than that through a traditional hypercube with the same hardware complexity. We will give algorithm which can make full use of the connections and can realize $log_2 N$ permutations simultaneously so that communication bandwidth is fully increased.

Key words: Parallel and distributed processing, interconnection network, hypercube, complexity, permutations, communication bandwidth.

1 Introduction

Among various point-to-point interconnection schemes, hypercube topology has received much research interest [8, 3, 2]. Because of its powerful connectivity and flexible partitionality, hypercube is a promising topology for parallel and distributed processing systems.

Although hypercube topology has merits over some multistage interconnection networks (MINs), the conventional design of hypercube networks and their routing algorithms have some limitations. Suppose that there are N processing elements (PEs) in the system, and $n = \log_2 N$. Here we claim that in previously proposed schemes, the time length of a "cycle" increases with $O(\log_2 N)$, or more hardware is needed and thus the hardware complexity is no longer $O(N \log_2 N)$; it becomes $O(N(\log_2 N)^2)$.

Usually, the delay of message transmission is measured by "cycles". However, if we look at inside of a "router" (here by "router" we mean the functional unit used for routing in a node), we will find that the actual *time length* of the delay will be $\log_2 N$ times longer or the hardware complexity will be $\log_2 N$ times more complicated.

It has been noticed by McCrosky [7] that the time length to move all messages one step in Hillis's algorithm increases with $O(\log_2 N)$. This means a factor of $O(\log_2 N)$ longer time length of a "cycle" (step).

In Borodin-Hopcroft's algorithm [1], for a permutation of size N, conceptually as many as $\log_2 N$ message packets may arrive at one node at a time, and as many as $\log_2 N$ packets may be sent out from a node. So, all the $\log_2 N$ packets in a node can move one step in one "cycle". But if we want the $\log_2 N$ packets to be sent from $\log_2 N$ input ports to $\log_2 N$ corresponding output ports at a time, we will need full connectivity among them. As a result, the hardware complexity of the entire system will be $O(N(\log_2 N)^2)$. If we want them to be sent out one at a time, then a $\log_2 N$ times longer "cycle" is needed.

A hypercube structure is proposed in [7] to combine the advantages of all-directions-moves of Borodin and Hopcroft's algorithm and the heavier message load of Hillis's algorithm. In fact, similar analysis can be applied to the algorithm in [7], because in a node the incoming $\log_2 N$ messages are still released to the deliverable or forwardable buffers one at a time.

It is worthy noticing that there are $N \log_2 N$ links in hypercube because each node has $\log_2 N$ links, and there are only N messages traveling in hypercube if the hypercube is used to handle one permutation of size N at a time. So the utilization rate of the links is only $1/\log_2 N$, the communication bandwidth in such systems is very limited.

We will develop in this paper a new structure, called *Syncube, (Synchronized Hyper-*

cube) and corresponding algorithms for hypercube connected topology. The hardware complexity of syncube remains to be $O(N \log_2 N)$ because $n \times n$ crossbar has not been used; the time length of a "cycle" will not increase as any function of n, it only depends on the technological advance of the hardware; and all the dimensional links can be fully used at any time.

This paper is organized as follows: we will describe the structure of syncube in Section 2; an algorithm will be given to realize arbitrary permutations in Section 3; conclusion remarks will be given in Section 4.

2 Structure of the Syncube

A normal hypercube of size N has N nodes. There is a link between node i and node j $(0 \le i, j \le N - 1)$ if and only if the binary representations of i and j differ in exactly one bit position k $(0 \le k \le n - 1)$, and we call this link the kth dimensional link. We also call an n-dimensional hypercube an n-cube for abbreviation.

In an n-cube, if node A is connected by the ith dimensional link to node B, we say node A is the ith *imagery node* of node B, and denote it as $IMG^{(i)}(A) = B$. Of course, if $IMG^{(i)}(A) = B$, we also have $IMG^{(i)}(B) = A$.

A *Syncube* is just an implementation of hypercube topology, so the connections among the nodes in a syncube is the same as in a hypercube. A node in a syncube consists of a *PE module* and a *router*. The function of the router is to route the messages. A router in node S, $0 \le S \le N - 1$, has n registers numbered $R_0, R_1, \cdots, R_{n-1}$. Register R_i, $0 \le i \le n - 1$, is connected to R_j in the same router and to R_j in the router in node $IMG^{(i)}(S)$, where $j = i + 1 \bmod n$. The conceptual structure of the router of node S is shown in Figure 1.

From the structure of the router we can see that a node in syncube can simultaneously send out as many as n messages and accept as many as n messages. Obviously, the hardware complexity of the system is $O(N \log_2 N)$.

In the following we will give a routing algorithm for syncube, and make an analysis

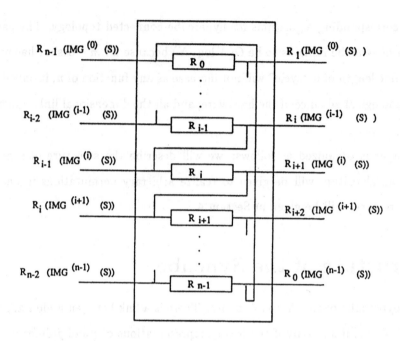

Figure 1: The Structure of a Router in Node S

of the passability of permutations through syncube. We have developed in [6] a routing algorithm for ordinary hypercube and given a sufficient condition for the passability of permutations through hypercube. The routing algorithm and passable condition here are special cases of the corresponding ones in [6] for the special structure — syncube.

In the following discussion, when we talk about one permutation of size N, we say a conflict occurs if a node is to hold more than one message; when we talk about simultaneous transmission of n permutations of size N, we say a conflict occurs if a node is to hold more than n messages. Our goal is to develop routing algorithms which will not cause any conflict in the routing procedure, so that buffer is not necessary, and the "cycle" will depend only on hardware technology.

We will use $\{\}$ to denote a set, and use $()$ to denote an ordered set.

A *subscript mapping scheme* $M(n-1, n-2, \cdots, 0) = (v_{n-1}, v_{n-2}, \cdots, v_0)$ is a mapping such that $(v_{n-1}, v_{n-2}, \cdots, v_0)$ is a permutation of $(n-1, n-2, \cdots, 0)$. A subscript mapping scheme is called *shift mapping* if $v_i = k \pm i \bmod n$, where $0 \le k \le n-1$.

The purpose of a subscript mapping scheme is to give an order in which the n dimensional links are used by the routing algorithm *for one permutation.*

With the definitions above, we now give a routing scheme for syncube, namely, *SMVDT-Routing (Shift-Mapping-Virtual-Destination-Tag-Routing).*

Let D be the destination address, and S be the address of the current node. Let $R_i(S)$ be the register R_i in node S, and "$R_i \Longrightarrow R_j$" means that message in R_i is sent to R_j. More precisely, given a shift mapping scheme $M(n-1, n-2, \cdots, 0) = (v_{n-1}, v_{n-2}, \cdots, v_0)$, where $v_i = k \pm i \bmod n$, SMVDT-Routing is as follows (at the beginning, the message on node S, $0 \leq S \leq N-1$, is put in R_k):

Algorithm SMVDT-Routing;

    BEGIN

        /* For the N packets on the N nodes do the following parallelly */

        FOR $i := 0$ TO $n - 1$ DO

            IF $s_{v_i} \neq d_{v_i}$

                THEN $R_{v_i}(S) \Longrightarrow R_{v_{i+1}}(IMG^{(v_i)}(S))$

                ELSE $R_{v_i}(S) \Longrightarrow R_{v_{i+1}}(S)$;

    END;

3   Passing Arbitrary Permutations on Syncube

In this section, we present an algorithm which can realize n arbitrary permutations simultaneously through syncube. We will first give a sufficient condition whose satisfaction by a permutation ensures that the premutation can be realized by our SMVDT-Routing in n steps (i.e. "one pass" through the syncube).

Let $(i : j)$ denote the set of integers from i to j. For example, $(0 : 5)$ denotes $(0, 1, 2, 3, 4, 5)$ while $(5 : 0)$ denotes $(5, 4, 3, 2, 1, 0)$.

A *Complete Residue System modulo m (CRS* $(\bmod m))$ is a set of integers which contains exactly one representative of each residue class $(\bmod m)$.

We define our *Virtual Module* operation $VMOD^{(l)}_{(k_1, k_2, \cdots, k_l)}(B)$ for an integer B.

The result of virtual modulo operation is an integer obtained from dropping the bits on dimensions $k_1, k_2, \cdots, k_l$ in the binary representation of B. For example, with $B = 100111$, $VMOD^{(1)}_{(1)}(B) = 10011$, and $VMOD^{(2)}_{(1,3)}(B) = 1011$.

We will refer to a message as a "number" which is the destination address of the message. We consider the destination addresses of the messages a permutation $(D_0, D_1, \cdots, D_{N-1})$. If all the messages can be sent to their destinations by SMVDT-Routing in $\log_2 N$ steps without any conflict, we say that $(D_0, D_1, \cdots, D_{N-1})$ is a *syncube passable* permutation.

Definition 1 $O(k) - subcube(d_1, d_2, \cdots, d_k)s$ $(1 \leq k \leq n)$ *of an n-cube are the hypercubes obtained by eliminating all the links in the n-cube on the $d_1 th, d_2 th, \cdots, d_k th$ dimensions, where $0 \leq d_1, d_2, \cdots\cdots, d_k \leq n - 1$.*

Let $Numbset^{(l)}_{(v_{n-1}:v_{n-l})}$, $1 \leq l \leq n - 1$, be the set which consists of all the numbers residing on an $O(l) - subcube(v_{n-1} : v_{n-l})$ of the syncube.

We have the following theorem for the passability of permutations on syncube.

Theorem 1 *Given a permutation $(D_0, D_1, \cdots, D_{N-1})$, if there exists a shift mapping scheme $M(n - 1, n - 2, \cdots, 0) = (v_{n-1}, v_{n-2}, \cdots, v_0)$, where $v_i = k \pm i \mod n$, such that $\forall O(l) - subcube(v_{n-1} : v_{n-l})$, $1 \leq l \leq n - 1$, we have*

$$\left\{ VMOD^{(l)}_{(v_{n-1}:v_{n-l})}(D) \mid D \in Numbset^{(l)}_{(v_{n-1}:v_{n-l})} \right\}$$

is a CRS (mod 2^{n-l}), then the permutation is syncube passable by SMVDT-Routing.

This condition is a special case of Theorem 1 in [6], we omit its proof here.

Let $P_0 = (D_{0,0}, D_{0,1}, \cdots, D_{0,N-1})$, $P_1 = (D_{1,0}, D_{1,1}, \cdots, D_{1,N-1})$, $\cdots$, and $P_{n-1} = (D_{n-1,0}, D_{n-1,1}, \cdots, D_{n-1,N-1})$ be n permutations. The following theorem gives a condition for the n permutations to be passable simultaneously through syncube by SMVDT-Routing.

Theorem 2 *Given* n *permutations* $P_0, P_1, \cdots, P_{n-1}$, *if there exist* n *shift mapping schemes* $M_0(n-1, n-2, \cdots, 0) = (v_{0,n-1}, v_{0,n-2}, \cdots, v_{0,0})$, $M_1(n-1, n-2, \cdots, 0) = (v_{1,n-1}, v_{1,n-2}, \cdots, v_{1,0})$, $\cdots$, $M_{n-1}(n-1, n-2, \cdots, 0) = (v_{n-1,n-1}, v_{n-1,n-2}, \cdots, v_{n-1,0})$, *where* $v_{j,i} = j \pm i \bmod n$, $0 \leq j, i \leq n-1$, *such that*

$$\forall\ O(l) - subcube(v_{j,n-1} : v_{j,n-l}),\ 0 \leq j \leq n-1,\ and\ 1 \leq l \leq n-1,$$

we have

$$\left\{ VMOD^{(l)}_{(v_{j,n-1} : v_{j,n-l})}(D_j) \mid D_j \in Numbset^{(l)}_{(v_{j,n-1} : v_{j,n-l})} \right\}$$

is a CRS $(\bmod\ 2^{n-l})$, *then the* n *permutations can be realized in* $\log_2 N$ *steps simultaneously on syncube by SMVDT-Routing under the* n *shift mapping schemes* $M_0, M_1, \cdots, M_{n-1}$.

Proof:

From the theorem we can see that $\forall\ i, j, k,\ 0 \leq i, j, k \leq n-1$, and $j \neq k$, we have $v_{j,i} \neq v_{k,i}$. So, according to Algorithm SMVDT-Routing, different permutations P_j and P_k use different registers $R_{v_{j,i}}$ and $R_{v_{k,i}}$ in any node at any step, each node hold n messages at any step, no conflict occurs.

According to Theorem 1, each one of the n permutations is realized in $\log_2 N$ steps by SMVDT-Routing.

Q.E.D.

Algorithms have been given for realization of arbitrary permutations on MINs [9, 4]. The basic idea in these algorithms is to partition the inputs at each stage into disjoint groups such that each pair of inputs will be put in different outputs which belong to different groups. Based on the same idea, we will give an algorithm which partitions the n permutations simultaneously without any conflict. From Theorem 2 we know if we can partition the n permutations simultaneously such that they satisfies the condition given by the theorem, they will be simultaneously passable on syncube.

Definition 2 *The* Virtual Address (VAD) *of a node* B *under a subscript mapping* scheme $M(n - 1, n - 2, \cdots, 0) = (v_{n-1}, v_{n-2}, \cdots, v_0)$ is:

$$VAD(B) = \sum_{i=0}^{n-1} b_{v_i} * 2^i.$$

Intuitively, the *virtual address* of a node is just the address obtained from its real address with the bits being reordered according to the given subscript mapping scheme. Under a shift mapping scheme, it is simply the result from circular shift of the real address. For example, with the real address of a node being $s_4 s_3 s_2 s_1 s_0 = 10011$ and the subscript mapping scheme being $(2, 1, 0, 4, 3)$, the virtual address of the node is then 01110 $(= s_2 s_1 s_0 s_4 s_3)$.

Initially, the n permutations are put in the $n \times N$ registers of the N nodes: P_j is put in R_{n-1-j}s. Then we arrange the n permutations independently such that The *virtual addresses* under subscript mapping scheme M_j of P_j on the two $O(1) - subcube(v_{j,n-1})$s constitute two $CRSs$ (mod 2^{n-1}), then arrange every two $O(1) - subcube(v_{j,n-1})$s such that the numbers (their virtual addresses under subscript mapping scheme M_j) of P_j on the two subcubes constitute four $CRSs$ (mod 2^{n-2}), etc., until all the $N/2$ $O(n - 1) - subcube(v_{j,n-1} : v_{j,1})$s constitute $N/2$ $CRSs$ (mod 2). What should be noticed is that although we have n permutations on the N nodes, no conflict will occur at any time. This is because, due to the connection scheme of the n registers in each node, $P_j, 0 \leq j \leq n-1$, only uses $R_{j'}$s and the links on dimension j' of each node in step k, where $j' = n - 1 - (j + k) \bmod n$. We call this $SMCRS - Partition$ (Simultaneous Complete Residue Set Partition). After the $SMCRS$-Partition procedure (it takes $n-1$ steps), the n permutations become n simultaneously passable permutations under the n shift mapping schemes. They will be realized by SMVDT-Routing under the n shift mapping schemes in $\log_2 N$ steps simultaneously.

In the above procedure, each permutation on one step uses only the links on one dimension, this is shown in Figure 2 for $n = 3$.

From Figure 2 we can see that all the dimensional links are busy in any step, so communication bandwidth is fully increased, and $\log_2 N$ permutations are realized in

Permut. # \ Dimens. # \ Cycle #	0	1	2	3	4
0	2	1	0	1	2
1	1	0	2	0	1
2	0	2	1	2	0

Figure 2: Transmission Scheme for $n = 3$

$2 \log_2 N - 1$ steps simultaneously. Because n messages are sent out (and are received) by the n registers in each node simultaneously, the time length of a cycle (step) does not increase with n. But because we have well-designed orders for the use of the n links and the n registers, $n \times n$ crossbar is not used in the network, so hardware complexity of the network remains to be $O(N \log_2 N)$.

An example is given for the realization of three permutations of size eight in Figure 3. In the figure, $P_0 = (6, 2, 7, 5, 0, 4, 1, 3)$, $P_1 = (7, 3, 5, 0, 2, 1, 6, 4)$, and $P_2 = (1, 0, 4, 5, 6, 3, 2, 7)$. The three numbers on each node are shown in the three boxes which represent the three registers R_0, R_1, and R_2 from the left to the right. Figure 4 shows the registers used by P_0 at each step.

Note that if we realize the n permutations just by simulating a Benes network using hypercube, we can only have the following two cases:

1. it takes $n \times (2n - 1)$ steps, if the links on the n dimensions are used sequentially as in some conventional hypercube connected systems.

2. it takes $3n - 2$ steps, even if an $n \times n$ crossbar is used in each node, and we have to use two hypercubes and let them work in a pipelined manner.

Syncube has merits over traditional (MINs).

The set of permutations passable in $\log_2 N$ steps through syncube is largely greater than that passable in the same steps through MINs. This will be reported in a separate paper.

Syncube has another advantage in that it can benefit localized communications.

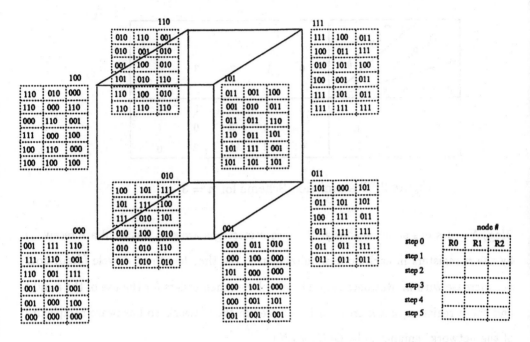

Figure 3: Simultaneous Realization of Three Permutations

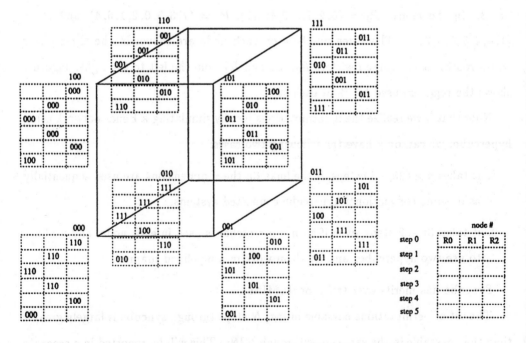

Figure 4: Transmission Procedure of P_0

Let's consider the frequently used permutations given in [5]. A large number of permutations are permutations within segments. They are frequently used in algorithms of "divide and conquer" style. These permutations are realized in the same number of steps on MINs as the permutations which are not within segments. When a permutation is within segments, it is obvious that there is locality in the communication. Because syncube structure retains the flexible partitionality of hypercube topology, permutations within segments of different sizes can be realized in different steps. This feature can make the average time spent for communication even shorter.

As an example, it is simple to see that, a cyclic shift within segments of size 2^{n-j} can be realized in $n - j$ steps on syncube. In an algorithm, if the cyclic shifts will occur within $2^1, 2^2, \cdots, 2^n$ evenly, the average delay for the communication will be $\frac{1}{2} \times \log_2 N$ steps.

4   Conclusions

We have presented syncube structure for the implementation of hypercube and routing algorithms. Hardware complexity of syncube remains to be $O(N \log_2 N)$ while the time length of a "step" does not increase with any function of the size of the network. Also, n permutations can be realized simultaneously by keeping all the links busy all the time. This makes the bandwidth of communication fully increased.

With limited additional links, syncube may realize all kinds of the frequently used permutations in $\log_2 N$ steps. This issue is worth further investigation.

Acknowledgement: This work is partly supported by the NSERC of Canada under the Grant OGP9225 and a central research fund from University of Alberta.

References

[1] A. Borodin and J. E. Hopcroft. Routing, merging and sorting on parallel models

of computation. In *Proc. of the 14th Annual Symposium on Theory of Computing*, pages 338–344, May 1982.

[2] M. T. Heath, editor. *Hypercube Multiprocessors 1987*. SIAM, Philadelphia, 1987.

[3] W. D. Hillis. *The Connection Machine*. MIT Press, Cambridge, MA, 1985.

[4] K.Y. Lee. On the rearrangeability of $2(\log_2 N) - 1$ stage permutation networks. *IEEE Trans. on Computers*, C-34(5):412–425, May 1985.

[5] J. Lenfant. Parallel permutations of data: A Benes network control algorithm for frequently used permutations. *IEEE Trans. on Computers*, C-27(7):637–647, July 1978.

[6] Z. Liu and J. You. Routing algorithms for hypercube. Technical Report 90-26, Department of Computing Science, University of Alberta, Edmonton, Alberta, Canada T6G 2H1, 1990.

[7] C. McCrosky. Message passing in synchronous hypercubes. Technical Report 86-4, Department of Computational Science, University of Saskatchewan, Saskatoon, Canada, 1986, (to appear in Computer System Science and Engineering).

[8] C. Seitz. The Cosmic Cube. *Communications of the ACM*, 28(1):22–33, Jan. 1985.

[9] A. Waksman. A permutation network. *Journal of the ACM*, 15(1):159–163, Jan. 1968.

PROGRAMMING A PARALLEL SORT USING DISTRIBUTED PROCEDURE CALLS

Daniel Herman

IRISA/INRIA, 35042 Rennes Cedex, FRANCE, Daniel.Herman@irisa.fr

Laurent Trilling

IMAG-LGI, 38041 Grenoble Cedex, FRANCE, trilling@imag.imag.fr

Abstract Our goal is to illustrate the interest of a new control structure, namely Distributed Procedure Call (DPC), to express parallel algorithms. As an application, we construct from a parallel sort program oriented to a shared memory implementation, a program oriented to a distributed implementation and using DPCs. Futhermore, we derive a program from it to be loaded on each processor of an hypercube supposing that processors communicate via DPCs of elementary procedures.

1. Notion of Distributed Procedure Call

We introduce this notion with an example. Let us consider the following procedure:

```
proc MinMax = (int a, int b) pair : (min(a, b), max(a, b))
```

We consider that a procedure such as MinMax, which has exactly the same number of parameters and results, can be called in a so called distributed manner. This is done by the mean of **partial calls** issued from different processes. Each partial call provides a parameter. A group of partial calls providing all actual parameters of such a procedure is called a **Distributed Procedure Call** (DPC). If a partial call, belonging to a DPC, provides the ith parameter, its results is the ith component of the call of the procedure.

The syntax of a partial call providing the first actual parameter is p(a, -, …, -), the second p(-, b, -, …, -) and so on. For example, the expression (MinMax(4, -), MinMax(-, 3)) expresses that two processes make partial calls which compose a DPC. The value of this expression is (3, 4). Accordingly, the value of the expression (MinMax(4, -) + 1, MinMax(-, 3) + 2) is (4, 5).

It is clear that some conditions are required so that a group of partial calls compose a DPC [HERMAN 90]. Intuitively, the set of the processes issuing them must be the set of all the participants of a **collateral** expression (as it is in the preceding examples).

2. A distributed expression of a sorting algorithm

The sorting algorithm that we consider is presented via an example where integers (t0,..., t7) = (1, 5, 7, 0, 4, 3, 6, 2) have to be sorted.

Step 1 : sort all the first (resp. second) elements of each pair. We get (t0',..., t7') = (1, 0, 4, 2, 6, 3, 7, 5) where (t0', t2', ...) (resp. (t1', t3', ...)) is the sorted array deduced from (t0, t2, ...) (resp. (t1, t3, ...)).

Step 2 : sort all the elements belonging to the external (resp. internal) pairs of each quadruplet. We get $(t0'', ..., t7'') = (1, 0, 3, 2, 5, 4, 7, 6)$ where $(t0'', t3'', t4'', t7'')$ (resp. $(t1'', t2'', t5'', t6'')$) is the sorted array deduced from $(t0', t3', t4', t7')$ (resp. $(t1', t2', t5', t6')$).

Step 3 : sort locally each pair. We get $(r0, r1, ..., r7) = (0, 1, ..., 7)$.

This algoritm can be represented by a sorting network à la BATCHER [BATCHER 68]. Our objective is to represent such a network as a program expressing the independence of the comparisons and which does not use a shared memory. Then, the problem is to construct N (with $N = 2^P$) procedures SE_0^N, ..., SE_{N-1}^N (SE is for Sorted Element) such that

$$(SE_0^N(t_0), ..., SE_{N-1}^N(t_{N-1})) = (r_0, ..., r_{N-1})$$

These procedures can be deduced easily from distributively callable procedures $SP_0^M, ..., SP_{M-1}^M$ (where $M = N/2$) such that

$$(SP_0^M(t_0, t_1), ..., SP_{M-1}^M(t_{N-2}, t_{N-1})) = ((r_0, r_1) ..., (r_{N-2}, r_{N-1}))$$

since

$$(SP_0^M(t_0, -), SP_0^M(-, t_1) ..., SP_{M-1}^M(t_{N-2}, -), SP_{M-1}^M(-, t_{N-1}))$$

$$= (r_0, r_1, ..., r_{N-2}, r_{N-1})$$

Procedures $SP_0^M, ..., SP_{M-1}^M$ can be recursively defined and proven correct accordingly to the algorithm. For that purpose, more general procedures SP_i^m have to be defined such that if $k = M/m$ and (l, r) is the pair numbered i/k of an array t of m elements numbered from 0 to $m-1$ then $SP_i^m(l, r)$ delivers the pair numbered i/k of the sorted array deduced from t. From these definitions, it can be easily noticed than these procedures are interconnected according to a "butterfly" scheme. Then, it is possible to derive from these procedures the procedures $PSP_i(l, r)$ (for Program for Sorted Pair on processor i) which can be installed on each processor of a hypercube. The exchanges between processors are expressed by using elementary distributively callable procedures.

3. Conclusion

Our goal was to show the practical convenience of rigourously deriving a distributed program(SP_i^m) using DPCs from an initial shared memory oriented specification. Furthermore, we transform this last program into another distributed program running on a hypercube (PSP_i). Even if developments may appear rather technical, we still believe that each step is easily understandable.

Firstly, it is noteworthy to underline the fact that the final program as well as initial specification are recursively expressed. For us, it appears to be a higher level of expression as it also is for sequential programs. It is not so common for distibuted programs. It may be worthwhile to remark that our sorting algorithm is close to BATCHER's odd-even sort and that odd-even sort has not been considered for implementation on a hypercube. It is BATCHER's bitonic sort which is well-known to be suited for that.

A second point, in the same line of reasonning, concerns the fonctional aspects of the program. These aspects appear clearly as the main problem is in designing the procedures SP_i^m

from elementary ones(MinMax). From our wiewpoint, the main benefit seems to be a better understanding. To be conscious of this improvement, one can see how similar algorithms to the one given in section 2 are presented in [BATCHER 68, AKL 85]. These presentations clearly illustrate the underlying ideas of these algorithms, but they cannot be exactly considered as programs giving the full possibilities of asynchronism.

DPCs may be seen as an intermediary concurrent control structure between a rather well-structured but too weak one(collateral expression) and more powerful but too primitive ones(like semaphores or monitors). To the authors's knowledge, there is little related work. If some authors, like[FRANCEZ 86] , propose a general framework in which DPCs could be modelized, they do not focus on them. The original idea of this extension of procedure call is due to J.P.BANATRE[BANATRE 81]. He and his colleagues propose similar, nevertheless somewhat different, linguistic constructions [BANATRE 89] to be embedded into a concurrent object oriented language for system programming. Apart from their work, one can cite [QUINIOU 88] which describes embedding DPCs into PROLOG for OR-processes communication and applies the resulting facilities to program the heuristic search algorithm A^*.

References

[AKL 85] S.G. AKL, *Parallel Sorting Algorithms*, Academic Press (1985).

[BANATRE 81] J.P. BANATRE, *Contribution à l'étude d'outils de construction de programmes parallèles et fiables*, Thèse, Université de Rennes (1981).

[BANATRE 89] J.P. BANATRE, M. BENVENISTE, *Multiprocedures: generalized procedures for concurrent programming*, 3rd workshop on Large Grain Parallelism, Software Engineering Institut, CMU (1989).

[BATCHER 68] K. BATCHER, *Sorting Networks and their Applications*, AFIPS Spring Joint Computing Conference **32** 307-14 (1968).

[FRANCEZ 86] N. FRANCEZ, B. HALPERN, G. TAUBENFELD, *Script: A communication abstraction mechanism and its verification*, Science of Computer Programming, (6):35-88 (1986).

[HERMAN 90] D. HERMAN, L. TRILLING, *Programmation d'un tri parallèle à l'aide d'une architecture de processus définie récursivement*, Rapport de recherche IRISA, to appear.

[QUINIOU 89] R. QUINIOU, L. TRILLING, *Collective predicates for expressing control of OR-parallelism in PROLOG*, 3rd Conference on Artificial Intelligence: Methodology, Systems and aplication, Varna, T. O'SHEA, V. SGUREV(eds), 159-167 North-Holland (1988).

A Note on Off-line Permutation Routing on a Mesh-Connected Processor Array

Danny Krizanc

Department of Computer Science

University of Rochester

Rochester, NY 14627

1 Introduction

The mesh-connected array is the basis for a number of proposed and implemented parallel computers due to its simplicity and the regularity of its interconnection pattern which makes it ideal for VLSI implementation. The performance of an algorithm on a packet-switched mesh depends on the mesh's ability to realize the communication patterns between processors arising from the algorithm. Often it is the case that these communication patterns are permutations of the processors which are known at the time of the algorithm's design. This leads naturally to the problem of off-line routing of permutations on the mesh, i.e., given a fixed permutation of the processors, each processor being the origin and destination of one packet, find paths connecting the origin-destination pairs and a schedule of when packets cross the edges of their path, which minimizes the time required to realize the permutation. At the same time we are interested in minimizing the number of packets a single processor must store between steps of the routing.

Our model of the $n \times n$ mesh is sometimes referred to as the MIMD model. It consists of n^2 processors with the interconnections between them defined by the two dimensional grid without wraparound edges. Edges are assumed to be bidirectional and a processor can send (and receive) a single packet along each of its edges in single time step.

There is an obvious lower bound of $2n - 2$ steps for our problem since in the worst case a permutation may have a packet originating in the top left corner processor and destined for the bottom right corner processor. Lieghton, Makedon and Tollis [3] gave an algorithm for on-line permutation routing (and therefore for off-line as well) which achieves this bound. However, in their algorithm the processors must store a large number of packets between communication steps. (The number is constant but estimated to be in excess of 500.) As a corollary to one of their theorems, Annexstein and Blaumslag [1] show how to off-line route in $3n$ steps with at most 1 packet per processor. In this note we extend this result by showing that by allowing only a slight increase in the amount of storage required a great improvement in the time can be made. In particular, by allowing at most 2 packets per processor per step any permutation can be off-line routed in $2.5n$ steps and by allowing 4 packets per processor per step any permutation can be off-line routed in $2.25n + 3$ steps.

2   Off-line Routing

Our results require the following lemmas which are of interest in their own right. We assume that $n = 4k$, for some k, whenever it is convenient in the discussion below.

Lemma 1 *On an n processor linear array, any permutation can be routed (on- or off-line) in n steps with at most 1 packet per processor per time step.*

Proof. We use the well known reduction of routing to sorting by destination. It is easy to show that odd-even transposition sort sorts a sequence on a linear array in n steps (see [2]).

Lemma 2 *On an n processor linear array, 2 permutations can be simultaneously routed (on- or off-line) in $n + 1$ steps with at most 2 packets per processor per time step.*

Proof. Again we use the well known reduction of routing to sorting by destination and show how to sort 2 sequences in $n + 1$ steps. During odd steps of odd-even transposition sort, packets are compared and exchanged along odd edges of the array, and during the even steps along even edges. To perform 2 sorts simultaneously, start a second sort after the first step of the first sort using the odd edges while the first sort uses the even edges and vice versa. The second sort completes after $n + 1$ steps. On each step, processors send and receive 2 packets and thus exactly 2 packets reside at each processor between steps. □

Lemma 3 *On an $n \times n$ mesh, 2 permutations can be simultaneously routed off-line in $3n$ steps with at most 2 packets per processor per time step.*

Proof. Recall how Annexstein and Blaumslag [1] perform off-line permutation routing on the mesh. They show that any permutation can be realized by first performing a permutation of each of the rows, followed by a permutation of the columns and finishing with another permutation of the rows. (The three permutations are calculated off-line.) We observe that a second permutation may be simultaneously routed by first performing a permutation of each of the columns (while the first permutation is being routed in the rows) followed by permutations in the rows and then again in the columns. Using lemma 1 the above can be performed in $3n$ steps with at most 2 packets per processor between steps. □

Lemma 4 *On an $n \times n$ mesh, 4 permutations can be simultaneously routed off-line in $3n + 3$ steps with at most 4 packets per processor per time step.*

Proof. Analogous to lemma 3, we send 2 permutations first by row, then by column and finally by row and send the other 2 permutations first by column, then by row and finally by column. Using lemma 2, the routing is completed in $3n + 3$ steps with at most 4 packets per processor between steps. □

We are now ready to show our main results.

Theorem 1 *On an $n \times n$ mesh, any permutation can be off-line routed in $2.5n$ steps with at most 2 packets per processor per time step.*

Proof. Divide the mesh into 4 $n/2 \times n/2$ submeshes in the natural fashion (i.e., into quadrants). Imagine the submeshes as forming a 2×2 mesh. Our algorithm consists of 3 phases. In the first phase, packets move either 0 or $n/2$ steps in their row so as to be in their correct column of the 2×2 mesh. After this phase each processor contains 0, 1, or 2 packets. During the second phase we route within the submeshes. If a packet's destination is within the submesh it goes there. If its destination is within the other submesh in the column of submeshes, it goes to the image of its final destination if the two submeshes were overlaid. Any processor is now the intermediate destination of 0, 1 or 2 packets. It is easy to see that the $2-to-2$ mapping thus defined can be completed to form 2 permutations which may be routed off-line using lemma 3. During the last phase, packets travel either 0 or $n/2$ steps to their final destination. The storage requirements of the algorithm are the same as those of the algorithm for lemma 3. $\square$

Theorem 2 *On an $n \times n$ mesh, any permutation can be off-line routed in $2.25n + 3$ steps with at most 4 packets per processor per time step.*

Proof. The proof is analogous to theorem 1. Divide the mesh into 16 $n/4 \times n/4$ submeshes with the submeshes forming a 4×4 mesh. First we correct the column submesh by moving 0, $n/4$, $n/2$ or $3n/4$ steps. The second phase consists of a $4-to-4$ mapping which is realized using lemma 4. During the last phase, packets must travel 0, $n/4$, $n/2$ or $3n/4$ steps to their final destination. By sending those that must go furthest first, this can be achieved in $3n/4$ steps. The storage requirements are the same as those of the algorithm in lemma 4. $\square$

3 Discussion

It should be noted that the above algorithms are very easy to implement requiring only $O(\log n)$ bit headers and the ability to check a flag, subtract 1, and test if a value equals 0. The question of whether every permutation can be routed (on- or off-line) in $2n - 2$ steps using a small amount of storage (say less than 10 packets) remains open.

References

[1] F. ANNEXSTEIN AND M. BLAUMSLAG, *A Unified Approach to Off-Line Permutation Routing on Parallel Networks*, Symp. on Parallel Algorithms and Architectures, 1990, pp. 398-406.

[2] T. LEIGHTON, C. E. LEISERSON, B. MAGGS, S. PLOTKIN AND J. WEIN, *Lecture Notes for Theory of Parallel and VLSI Computation*, MIT/LCS/Research Seminar Series 1, 1988.

[3] T. LEIGHTON, F. MAKEDON AND I. TOLLIS, *A $2n - 2$ Step Algorithm for Routing in an $n \times n$ Array with Constant Size Queues*, Symp. on Parallel Algorithms and Architectures, 1989, pp. 328-335.

A FULLY-PIPELINED SOLUTIONS CONSTRUCTOR
FOR DYNAMIC PROGRAMMING PROBLEMS

Jean Frédéric MYOUPO

L.R.I, Bat. 490, Université Paris-Sud et URA 410 CNRS
91405 Orsay, France

Fax: (33) 1.69.41.65.86, e-mail myoupo@lri.lri.fr.

Abstract: The problem of designing modular linear systolic arrays for dynamic programming was raised in [9]. An attempt to solve this problem appeared in [8]. Unfortunately, the size of the local memory of each processor and the time delay between two consecutive processors of this array (in [8]) are still depending on n as in [9]. Moreover, these two arrays (in [8, 9]) are partially pipelined. Some elements have to be initially stored in the array. However, the difference between these two linear arrays is that the one in [8] is faster and more easy to handle than in [9]. In this paper we discuss a way of designing fully - pipelined modular linear systolic arrays for dynamic programming. The algorithm we obtain requires n^2+1 processors (or simply cells) and $6n^2-n-3$ time steps for its execution: each cell has a local memory of size 1 and the time delay between two consecutive cells of the array is constant. As far as the author knows, It is the only fully-pipelined modular linear systolic array algorithm for dynamic programming appearing in the literature for the moment.

Key Words: Design of Algorithms, Parallel Algorithms, Linear Systolic Arrays, Modular Arrays, Complexity, Dynamic Programming.

1- Introduction

Recently, systolic arrays have received much attention [5], because they have simple control and timing, local interconnection between processors and modular designs. In practice, linear arrays are more attractive than two-dimensional arrays. This is due to the fact that they have bounded I/O requirements [5]. In wafer containing faulty cells, a large percentage of non-faulty cells can be efficiently reconfigured into a linear array [6]. Synchronization between cells in a linear array can be achieved by a simple global clock whose rate is independent of the size of the array [2].There have been many efforts to formalize the synthesis of systolic arrays from algorithm descriptions, but only very regular algorithms in the form of systems of uniform recursive equations can be successfully treated (In a typical application, such arrays would be attached as a peripheral device to a host computer which would insert input values and extract output values from them). However, in practical application there are certain classes of algorithms which are slightly irregular.

Dynamic Programming is one of the several widely used problem-solving techniques in Computer Science and Operation Research [1]. Parallel algorithms for this problem have been studied in [1, 3, 4, 7, 8, 9, 10]. Linear arrays for the dynamic programming problems appeared in [8, 9]. The array in [9] uses n cells and requires $2n^2+2n-2$ time steps for its execution. Three of the channels of this array have their time delays (between two consecutive cells) depending on n: That is $2n+2$, $2n+3$ and $2n+4$ time steps respectively. In [8], a faster linear array algorithm is derived from [9] using a geometric approach. It requires n cells and n^2+2n-1 time steps for its execution, which is faster than the one in [9].

Furthermore, only two of its channels have their time delays (between two consecutive cells) as functions of n: That is n+1 and n+3 time steps respectively. unfortunately these two linear systolic algorithms are not modular since the time delay between 2 consecutive cells and the size of the memory (in each cell) in each of them depend on the size of the problem. That is n.

In this paper we derive a fully pipelined modular version of the algorithm in [8]. It requires n^2+1 cells and $6n^2-n-3$ time steps for its execution. Each cell has a local memory of size 1 and the time delay between two consecutive cells of the array is constant.

The rest of this paper is organized as follows: In section 2, we set the dynamic programming problem and describe the linear array model. Next, in section 3, we give a sketch of the proof of correctness of the algorithm. The conclusion follows in section 4.

2-Dynamic Programming and Linear array Model

The dynamic programming problem is to solve the following recurrence:
Given $w(i, j)$, $1 \le i < j \le n$ and $c(i, i+1)$, $1 \le i < n$, compute

$$c(i, j) = w(i, j) + \min_{i < k < j}(c(i, k) + c(k, j)) \text{ for } 1 \le i < j \le n.$$

This scheme can be used to solve many combinatorial optimization problems. Its essential feature is that the optimal solution to a problem is written as a recurrence relation in optimal solutions of subproblems. In this paper, we will restrict our attention on the construction of an optimal binary search tree which is a well-known example of dynamic programming:

$$c(i,j) = w(i, j) + \min_{i < k < j}(c(i, k) + c(k, j)), \quad 1 \le i < j \le n+1. \tag{1}$$

2.1 Geometric Approach

The operations of the systolic array we design here is the result of the projection of the space-time diagram of equation (1) on the space axis. This projection is such that the trajectories of an element $c(i, j)$ become simple pieces of lines, each of which has a defined slope, in the plane whose axes are cell's axis and time axis. Then we have to determine the resulting timing function, $t_0(c(i, j))$, which gives for any $c(i, j)$ its final computation date, and the task allocation function, $s_0(c(i, j))$, which assigns to a cell of the array the computation of $c(i, j)$. If we know the slopes of the different paths on which the different elements $c(i, j)$ are going to travel, then the dates and the cells of the different intersections of the trajectories of the elements $c(i, j)$ can be easily defined.

Concretely, consider the plane whose axes are cell's axis and time axis. The trajectory of a token travelling in the array through a channel with a time delay r between 2 consecutive cells , is a line of slope r. For example, let $t_0(ci, j))$ be the time at which $c(i, j)$ is completely computed, $t(c(i, j))$ the time at which $c(i, j)$ reaches the cell numbered s and r the time delay through the channel in which $c(i, j)$ is travelling. Then the equation of the trajectory of $c(i, j)$ in the plane defined above is $t(c(i, j)) = rs + t_0(c(i, j))$ (the origin of the plane is transferred to $(s_0(c(i, j)), t_0(ci, j))$. Then we first have to define slopes which can give efficient arrays. After we have defined suitable task allocation and timing functions, the method consists of drawing these different trajectories of the elements $c(i, j)$ in the plane (whose axes are cell's axis and time axis). At some suitable intersections of these lines the elements $c(i, j)$ are computed.

2.2 Linear Array Model

We compute the recurrence (1) on a linear array of n^2+1 cells. Each cell has a local memory of size 1. Our array contains six data channels, H_f, H_s, V_f, V'_f, V_s and W, three control channels, H_c, V_c and W_c as shown in Figure 1.

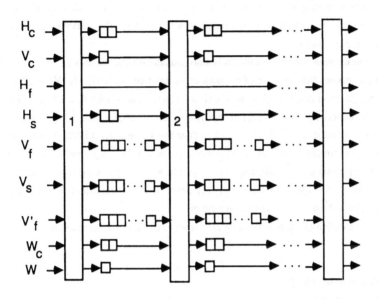

Figure 1.

Tokens travelling in the fast channel H_f are transferred in the slow channel H_s at some time. The tokens travelling in V_f are transferred in V'_f at some time; after V'_f, they are transferred in V_s at some time and after V_s they are transferred in V'_f at some time and vice-versa. The tokens travelling in H_c, V_c W_c and W stay in the same channels as they traverse the array.

The tokens travelling in H_f, H_s, V_f, V'_f, V_s, H_c, V_c, W_c and W encounter a delay (between two consecutive cells) of 1, 3, 6 , 6, 8 , 3 , 3 , 2 and 1 clock cycles respectively.

Set $\partial=j-i$ and let $c(i, j)$ be the contents of the location 1 of the cell $\mu=\partial-1+(n-1)(n-i)$, that is initialized to 0; then

$$c(i, j)=\min(H_f(\mu)+V_s(\mu), V_f(\mu)+H_s(\mu)) \qquad (2)$$

or

$$c(i, j)=\min(c(i, j), H_f(\mu)+V_s(\mu), V_f(\mu)+H_s(\mu) \qquad (3)$$

where $H_f(\mu)$, $V_f(\mu)$, $H_s(\mu)$ and $V_s(\mu)$ are the cell's input tokens in H_f, V_f, H_s and V_s respectively. Let $c(i, j)$ be the contents of the only location in the cell μ. The operation of a cell $\mu(1\leq\mu\leq n^2+1)$ in any clock cycle is the following:

Step 1. If there is a control token in its input channel V_c, then it changes the contents of its input channels H_s and V'_f to that of its input channels H_f and V_f respectively.

Step 2. If there is a control token in its input channel W_c and an input token in V'_f, then the token in V'_f is transferred in V_s.

Step 3. If there are data in its input channels H_f, H_s, V_f and V_s then:

    i)- If $c(i, j)=0$, then (2) is performed.

    ii)- If $c(i, j)\neq 0$ then (3) is performed.

Step 4. If there is a control token in its input channel H_c and a token in its input channel W, then $c(i, j)=W(\mu)+c(i, j)$, and it changes the contents of its input channels H_f and V_f to the updated value of $c(i, j)$. $W(\mu)$ is its input token in the channel W.

Step 5. If there is a token in its input channel V_s then it is automatically transferred in V'_f.

Remark 1. Step 3 supposes the presence of the data in its input channels H_f, H_s, V_f and V_s: This means that at a partial computation point of $c(i, j)$, there exists integers k and k' with $i<k$, $k'<j$ such that $c(i, j)=\min(c(i, k)+c(k, j), c(i, k')+c(k', j))$ (using (2)) or $c(i, j)=\min(c(i, j), c(i, k)+c(k, j), c(i, k')+c(k', j))$ (using (3)). If $k=k'$, then $c(i, k)$ must arrive in cell $\mu=j-i-1$ in channels H_f and H_s and $c(k, j)$ must arrive in the same cell in V_f and V_s: consequently, when $c(i, k)$ and $c(k, j)$ reach cell μ, they meet the control token travelling in V_c. In the exprssion $c(i, j)=\min(c(i, k)+c(k, j), c(i, k')+c(k', j))$ or $c(i, j)=\min(c(i, j), c(i, k)+c(k, j), c(i, k')+c(k', j))$, $c(i, k)$, $c(k, j)$, $ci, k')$ and $c(k', j)$ arrive in cell μ respectively in channels H_f, V_s, H_s and V_f. This completes the description of the algorithm.

Remark 2. The only location of the memory of a cell is set to 0 initially. consequently $c(i, j)=0$ initially.

2.3 Method of Evaluation of c(i, j)

Here, we describe the way we compute an element $c(i, j)$ which is supposed to be computed in cell μ:

a)- If $j-i-1=0$, then there does not exist an integer k such that $i<k<j$. So, the value of $c(i, j)$ in this case is $w(i, j)$.

b)- If $j-i-1>0$, then in general, there exists $j-i-1$ integers k_p, $1\leq p\leq j-i-1$, such that $i<k_p<j$ for all p. The set of these integers k_p is ordered in the following way: $k_1<k_2<k_3...<k_{j-i-1}$.

i) j-i-1 is even: Then the evaluation of $c(i, j)$ is the following: Let t^0 be the time at which the first partial computation of $c(i, j)$ starts. At time t^0, $c(i,j)$ is zero, then (2) is performed in this way:

$c(i, j)=\min(c(i, i+(j-i-1)/2)+c(i+(j-i-1)/2, j), c(i, i+((j-i-1)/2)+1)+c(i+((j-i-1)/2)+1, j))$.

Next, the partial computations of $c(i, j)$ accur every other time using (3) in this order: At time t^0+2, $c(i, j)=\min(c(i, j), c(i, i+((j-i-1)/2)-1)+c(i+((j-i-1)/2)-1, j), c(i, i+((j-i-1)/2)+2)+c(i+((j-i-1)/2)+2, j))$. At time t^0+4, $c(i, j)=\min(c(i, j), c(i, i+((j-i-1)/2)-2)+c(i+((j-i-1)/2)-2, j), c(i, i+((j-i-1)/2)+3)+c(i+((j-i-1)/2)+3, j))$. At time t^0+6, $c(i, j)=\min(c(i, j), c(i, i+((j-i-1)/2)-3)+c(i+((j-i-1)/2)-3, j), c(i, i+((j-i-1)/2)+4)+c(i+((j-i-1)/2)+4, j))$. .... At time $t^0+j-i-3$, $c(i, j)=\min(c(i, j), c(i, i+1)+c(i+1, j), c(i, j-1)+c(j-1, j))$. At time $j-i-1$, the control token in H_c arrives in cell μ, then $c(i, j)=w(i, j)+c(i, j)$.

Example 1: Set $n=8$, $i=1$ and $j=8$; Then we have 6 integers less than 8 and greater than 1: 2, 3, 4, 5, 6, 7. At time t^0, $c(1, 8)=\min(c(1, 4)+c(4, 8), c(1, 5)+c(5, 8))$. At time t^0+2, $c(1, 8)=\min(c(1, 8), c(1, 3)+c(3, 8))$, $c(1, 6)+c(6, 8))$. At time t^0+4, $c(1, 8)=\min(c(1, 8), c(1, 2)+c(2, 8), c(1, 7)+c(7, 8))$. At t^0+6, the control token in H_c arrives in cell μ, then $c(1, 8)=w(1, 8)+c(1, 8)$.

ii) j-i-1 odd: then there exists an integer k_m in the set of the integers k_p, $1 \leq p \leq j-i-1$, such that the number of elements k_p less than j and the number of elements k_p greater than i are equal. Let t^0 be the time at which the first partial computation of c(i, j) starts. At time t^0, c(i, j) is zero, then (2) is performed in this way:

c(i, j)=min(c(i, k_m)+c(k_m, j), c(i, k_m, c(k_m), j). This means that c(i, k_m) and c(k_m, j) meet the control token travelling in V_c in cell μ.

Next, the partial computations of c(i, j) accur every other time using (3) in this order: At time t^0+2 c(i, j)=min(c(i, j), c(i, (k_m-1)+c(k_m-1, j), c(i, k_m+1)+c(k_m+1, j)). At time t^0+4 c(i, j)min=(c(i, j), c(i, k_m-2)+c(k_m-2, j), c(i, k_m+2)+c(k_m+2, j)). At time t^0+6 c(i, j)=min(c(i, j), c(i, k_m-3)+c(k_m-3, j), c(i, k_m+3)+c(k_m+3, j)). . . . .At time t^0+j-i-3, c(i, j)=min(c(i, j), c(i, i+1)+c(i+1, j), c(i, j-1)+c(j-1, j)). At time j-i-1, the control token in H_c arrives in cell μ, then c(i, j)=w(i, j)+c(i, j).

Example 2: Set n=7, i=1 and j=7; then k_m=4. At time t^0, c(1, 7)=min(c(1, 4)+c(4, 7), c(1, 4)+c(4, 7)). At time t^0+2, c(1, 7)=min(c(1, 7), c(1, 3)+c(3, 7), c(1, 5)+c(5, 7)). At time time t^0+4, c(1, 7)=min(c(1, 7), c(1, 2)+c(2, 7), c(1, 6)+c(6, 7)). At t^0+6, the control token in H_c arrives in cell μ, then c(1, 7)=w(1, 7)+c(1, 7).

The linear array algorithm is the following:

At the input cell:

a). Insert w(i, j) in W at time 5n(n-i)+2(j-i-1)+1.

b). Insert a control token relative to c(i, j) in H_c at time (3n+2)(n-i)+1.

c). Insert a control token in V_c at time (4n+1)p, for all $p \geq 0$.

d). Insert a control token relative to c(i, j) in W_c at time (3n+2)(n-i)+3n(j-i+1)-2+(3n+2)p, for all $p \geq 0$.

e). Extract c(i,j) from the last cell through the channel H_s at time 3n(2n-i-1)+5n-2j+4.

This completes the description of the algorithm.

2.4 Timing and Task Allocation Functions

As in [8, 9] its effect is the following: Let ∂=j-i. Let c(i, j) be the token in the location 1 of the cell μ=j-i-1+(n-1)(n-i)=∂+(n-1)(n-i). The way we project the space-time diagram on the space lead us to define the timing and the task allocation functions as follows: The element c(i, j) is computed and is ready in cell μ at time (6n-1)(n-i)+3(j-i-1)+1. The cell μ then starts transmitting c(i, j) in both H_f and V_f. c(i, j) travels in H_f for an additional ∂ clock cycles and is transferred into H_s at cell $\mu+\partial$. It remains in H_s till eternity. c(i, j) travels in V_f for an additional $6n\partial$ clock cycles before being transferred into V'_f at cell $\mu+\partial n$. It remains in V'_f from $\mu+\partial n$ to $\mu+\partial n+n-1$. From $\mu+\partial n+n-1$, it is transferred in V_s till cell $\mu+\partial n+n$ and its travel continues in the same way as from cell $\mu+\partial n$ to cell $\mu+\partial n+n$, in a cyclic manner. That is from cell $\mu+\partial n+n$ the path of c(i, j) from $\mu+\partial n$ to $\mu+\partial n+n$ (through V'_f and V_s) is repeated periodically.

Remark 3. The geometric interpretation of our algorithm is the following: c(i, j), which is computed and is ready in cell μ, has 2 paths which lead it to cell n^2+1: the first is a line of slope 1 from μ to $\mu+\partial$ and the second is a line of slope 6 from μ to $\mu+\partial n+n-1$. From the cell numbered $\mu+\partial$, the first path changes to a line of slope 3 till cell n^2+1. From cell $\mu+\partial n+n-1$ the second changes to a line of slope 8 till it reaches cell $\mu+\partial n+n$. And from $\mu+\partial n+n$, the part of the second path from $\mu+\partial n$ to $\mu+\partial n+n$ (through V'_f and V_s) is repeated periodically till cell n^2+1. The method consists of drawing these different trajectories of the elements c(i, j) in the plane (whose axes are cell's axis and time axis). At the intersection of these lines, (2) or (3) is performed. In figure 2, we have drawn the different paths of tokens travelling in

H_C, V_C and W_C. We have not drawn all the trajectories of the elements $c(i, j)$ (dashed lines), because they could make these figures unreadable. However one can easily verify on them that for n=4, the elements $c(i, j)$ are correctly computed. The linear algorithms in [8, 9] and the one of this paper share the same geometric configuration. consequently the proof of correctness of the algorithm presented here is the same as in [8, 9]. The elements $c(i, j)$ are extracted from the last cell numbered n^2+1 of the array through the channel H_S. The channel V'_f is used to avoid averlappings of trajectories of some elements $c(i,j)$.

Theorem 1: A problem of dynamic programming of size n can be solved in time $6n^2-n-3$ on an array of n^2+1 cells.

Proof. $c(1, 2)$ is the last element to be extracted from the cell n^2+1. Its computation is completed at time $(6n-1)(n-1)+1$ in cell n^2-2n+2. It travels in H_f for 1 ($\partial=1$) time step to reach the cell n^2-2n+3 where it is transferred in H_S. It travels in H_S for $3(n^2+1-n^2-2n-3)=3(2n-2)$ time steps to reach the last cell of the array numbered n^2+1. consequently it is extracted from the array at time $(6n-1)(n-1)+2+3(2n-2)=6n^2-n-3$.

Example 3: Suppose n=4 and consider the computation of $c(1, 5)$. We know that
$c(1, 5)=w(1, 5)+\min(c(1, 2)+c(2, 5), c(1, 3)+c(3, 5), c(1, 4)+c(4, 5))$.

From Figure 2, $c(1, 3)$ and $c(3, 5)$ are ready in cell 10 and 4 at times 73 and 27 respectively. $c(1, 3)$ then flows through H_f for an additional 2($\partial=2$) clock cycles and reaches cell 12 ($\mu+\partial=12$) at time 75. $c(3, 5)$ flows through V_f for an additional 48 ($6\partial n=48$) clock cycles and reaches cell 12 at the same time. From the step c) of the algorithm, the control token inserted in V_C at time 51, reaches cell 12 at time 75. So, at time 75, $c(3, 5)$ is on both V_f and V_S and $c(1, 3)$ is on both H_f and H_S. According to the operation of a cell in any clock cycle, since $c(1, 5)=0$, then (2) is performed; that is
$c(1, 5)=\min(c(1, 3)+c(3, 5), c(1, 3)+c(3, 5))$.

From Figure 2 again, $c(2, 5)$ is ready at time 53 in cell 8. It travels on V_f from cell 8 and arrives in cell 12 at time 77. $c(1, 2)$ is ready in cell 9 at time 70. It travels for an additional 1 clock cycle on H_f till it reaches cell 10 ($\mu=1$) at time 71. It is then transferred into H_S. It travels in H_S for an additional 6 clock cycles till it reaches cell 12 at time 77. So at time 77, $c(1, 2)$ and $c(2, 5)$ arrive in H_S and V_f respectively in cell 12.

$c(1, 4)$ is ready in cell 11 at time 76. It travels on H_f for an additional 1 clock cycle and reaches cell 12 at time 77. The case of $c(4, 5)$ is more interesting: it is ready in cell 0 at time 1. It then flows through V_f for an additional 24 ($6\partial n=24$) clock cycles and reaches cell 4 at time 25. From the step c) of the algorithm, the control token inserted in V_C at time 17, reaches cell 4 at the same time . So, at time 25, $c(4, 5)$ is transferred in V'_f. From cell 4, it travels in V'_f for 18 ($6\partial n-6=18$) clock cycles to reach cell 7 at time 43. From the step d) of the algorithm, the control token inserted in W_C at time 22, reaches cell 7 at the same time. So, at time, 43 $c(4, 5)$ is transferred in V_S. It travels in V_S for 8 clock cycles and reaches cell 8 at time 51 where it is automatically transferred in V'_f. From cell 8, the trajectory of $c(4, 5)$ from cell 4 to cell 8 (through V'_f and V_S), is repeated till cell 12, that is , $c(4, 5)$ arrives in cell 12 at time 77 in V_S. So at time 77, $c1, 2)$, $c(2, 5)$, $c(1, 4)$ and $c(4, 5)$ are respectively in channels H_S, V_f, H_f and V_S of cell 12. Since $c(1, 5)\neq0$, (3) is performed; that is
$c(1, 5)=\min(c(1, 5), c(1, 2)+c(2, 5), c(1, 4)+c(4, 5))$.
At time 79, the control token travelling in H_C inserted at time 43 and $w(1, 5)$ inserted at time 67 arrive in cell 12. Then $c(1, 5)=w(1, 5)+c(1, 5)$.

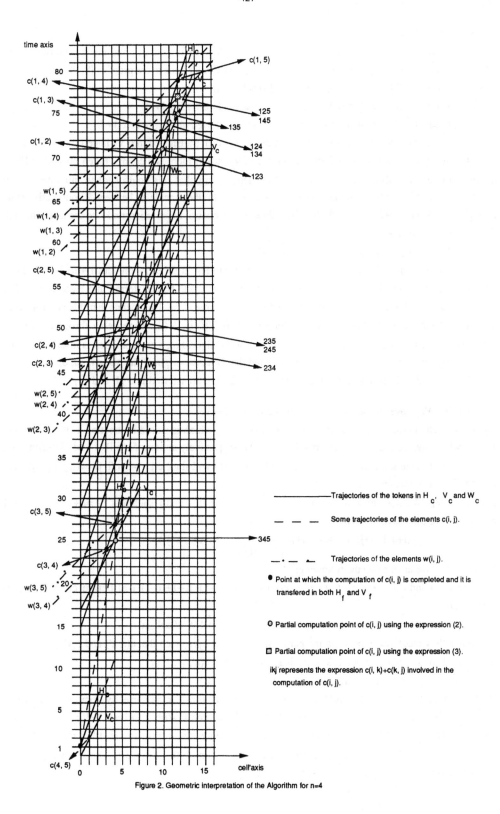

Figure 2. Geometric interpretation of the Algorithm for n=4

3. Proof of Correctness

The approach here is geometric. We consider the plane defined above and the trajectories of the different elements travelling in the array. Our proof is along similar lines to the proof in [8, 9]:

Lemma: Let $\partial=j-i$, $1\leq i<j\leq n+1$ and $\mu=j-i-1+(n-1)(n-i)$.

1)- $c(i, j)$ is transferred into H_f and V_f in cell μ at time $(6n-1)(n-i)+3(\partial-1)+1$.

2)- a) $c(i, j)$ travels in H_f for ∂ clock cycles and is then transferred into H_S in cell $\mu+\partial$.

   b) $c(i, j)$ travels in V_f for $6(\partial+1)n-6$ clock cycles and is then transferred into V_S in cell $\mu+(\partial+1)n-1$.

Proof. 1)- $c(i,j)$ will be transferred into H_f and V_f only if there is a control token present in H_C at the input of cell μ at time $(6n-1)(n-i)+3(j-i-1)+1$. This means that this control token must have been inserted into H_C of cell 0 at time $(6n-1)(n-i)+3(j-i-1)+1-3(\mu-1)$ (the time delay between 2 consecutive cells through H_C is 3) i.e $(3n+2)(n-i)+1$. By b) of the algorithm, a control token is inserted into the array through H_C at time $(3n+2)(n-i)+1$.

2)- We will prove a); the proof of b) is similar.

   a) By 1) of the lemma, $c(i, j)$ is transferred into H_f at time $t1=(6n-1)(n-i)+3(j-i-1)+1$. In ∂ additional clock cycles, it will reach cell $\mu+\partial$. In order for $c(i, j)$ to be transferred into H_S at cell $\mu+\partial$, it must meet a control token in V_C at the input of cell $\mu+\partial$ at time $t1+\partial$. This means that this control token must have been inserted into the array at time $t2=t1+\partial-2(\mu+\partial-1)$ (the time delay through V_C is 2). Substituting $\partial=j-i$, $t2$ reduces to $(4n+1)(n-i)$. From c) of the algorithm, a control token is inserted into the array through V_C at time $(4n+1)p$, $p\geq 0$. Keep in mind that here, the origin of the plane is $(0, 0)$.

Theorem 2: $c(i, j)=w(i, j)+\min(c(i, k)+c(k, j))$ when it is transferred into H_f and V_f.
$$i<k<j$$

Proof. We prove this as in [8, 9], by induction on $\partial=j-i$.

Basis: $\partial=1$. The correct value of $c(i, j)$ when $\partial=1$ is $w(i, j)$ which is stored in location 1 of cell $\mu=+(n-1)(n-i)$: $w(i, j)$ and a control token inserted in W and H_C respectively at times $5n(n-i)+1$ and $(3n+2)(n-i)+1$, arrive in cell μ at the same time. That is at time $(6n-1)(n-i)+1$ and since $c(i, j)=0$, $c(i, j)=w(i, j)+c(i, j)=w(i, j)$. So $w(i, j)$ gets transferred into H_f and V_f.

Inductive step: We have to show that the theorem holds for all i' and j' such that $j'-i'=\partial+1$. Let $i'=i+a-1$ and $j'=a+j$. We then have to prove that

$$c(i+a-1, a+j)=w(i+a-1, a+j)+\min(c(i+a-1, k)+c(k, a+j)).$$
$$i+a-1<k<a+j$$

To prove this, we must show the following:

i)- $c(i+a-1, k)$ and $c(k, a+j)$ meet at cell $\mu'=\partial+(n-1)(n-i-a+1)=\mu+1+(n-1)(1-a)$ before $c(i+a-1, a+j)$ is transferred.

ii)-When they meet, $w(a+i-1, a+j)$ is not yet in the input channel W of cell μ'.

iii)- When they meet, there exists an integer k', with $i+a-1<k'<j+a$, such that $c(i, k')$ and $c(k', j)$ also meet in cell μ'. then $c(i, j)=\min(c(i+a-1, k)+c(k, j+a), c(i+a-1, k')+c(k', j+a))$ or $c(i, j)=\min(c(i, j), c(i+a-1, k)+c(k, j+a), c(i+a-1, k')+c(k', j+a))$.

i)-By the inductive hypothesis and part 1) of the lemma, $c(i+a-1, k)$ is correctly computed when it is transferred into H_f and V_f at cell $k-i-a+(n-1)(n-i-a+1)$ at time $t1=(6n-1)(n-i-a+1)+3(k-i-a)+1$. It then travels in H_f for an additional $(k-i-a+1)$ clock cycles. Subsequently, it travels in H_S till it reaches cell μ'. Let $t2$ be the time taken to reach cell μ' after the transfer. Then $t2=(k-i-a+1)+3(\mu'-2k+2i+2a-2-(n-1)(n-i-a+1))$, which can be simplified to $2i+3j+5a-5k-2$; then

$$t1+t2=(6n-1)(n-i-a+1)-2k+2a-i+3j-1. \qquad (4)$$

By the inductive hypothesis again, $c(k, a+j)$ is correctly computed in cell $a+j-k+(n-1)(n-k)$ when it is transferred into Hf and Vf at time $t3=(6n-1)(n-k)+3(a+j-k-1)+1$. It then travels in Vf till it reaches cell μ'. Let $t4$ be this travel time. So $t4=6(\mu'-a-j+k-(n-1)(n-k))$.

$t3+t4=(6n-1)(n-k)+3(a+j-k-1)+1+6(\mu'-a-j+k-(n-1)(n-k))$

$\qquad =6n(n-i-a)-2k+3a+3j-2+5n$

$\qquad =6n(n-i-a)+6n-2k+2a-i+3j-1-(n-i-a+1)$

$\qquad =(6n-1)(n-i-a+1)-2k+2a-i+3j-1$, which is the same as (4).

We next show that (4) is less than the time at which $c(i+a-1, a+j)$ is transferred into Hf and Vf. By 1) of the above lemma, this time is $(6n-1)(n-i-a+1)+3(j-i)+1$. We then have to show that

$$(6n-1)(n-i-a+1)-2k+2a-i+3j-1<(6n-1)(n-i-a+1)+3(j-i)+1.$$

Which reduces to showing that

$$-2k+2a-i+3j-1<3j-3i+1.$$

This last inequality reduces to $k>i+a-1$. Which is true by the definition of k

ii)- We must show that when $c(i+a-1, k)$ and $c(k, j+a)$ meet in μ', $w(i+a-1, j+a)$ is not yet in the input of μ'. $w(i+a-1, j+a)$ is inserted in the array at time $t5=(6n+1)(n-i-a+1)+j-i+1$. It then travels for $2\mu'$ clock cycles to reach the cell μ'. Let $t6$ be this travel time, then $t6=2(j-i+(n-i-a+1)(n-1))$. Then $w(i+a-1, j+a)$ arrives in cell μ' at time $t7=t5+t6=(6n+1)(n-i-a+1)+j-i+1+2(j-i+(n-i-a+1)(n-1))=(6n-1)(n-i-a+1)+3(j-i)+1$. Which is the time at which $c(i+a-1, j+a)$ is ready in cell μ'. This proves ii) according to 1) of the lemma.

iii)- It is proved as in i)-.

4. Conclusion

In this paper, we have presented a fully-pipelined modular linear systolic algorithm for dynamic programming; we have used geometric considerations to design this array. It that is more interesting than those in [8,9] since it is modular (see TABLE I for the comparison of the 3 arrays). It runs in $6n^2-n-3$ time steps on an array of n^2+1 processors.

ACKNOWLEDGEMENTS. I am grateful to Professor M. Tchuente for introducing me in the area of parallel algorithms.

References

[1]   K. Q. Brown: "Dynamic programming in computer science", CMU Tech. Report (February 1979).

[2]   A. L. Fischer and H. T. Kung:"Synchronizing large VLSI processor arrays", *Proc. Tenth Annual IEEE/ACM Symposium on Computer Architecture,* June 1983, PP. 54-58.

[3]   L. J. Guibas, H. T. Kung and C. D. Thompson:"Direct VLSI implementation of   combinatorial algorithms", *Proc. Conf. very Large Scale Integration: Architecture, Design, Fabrication,* California Institute of Technology (January 1979), PP. 509-525.

[4]   D. E. Knuth:" *The Art of computer Programming*", Vol. 3 Sorting and Searching, Addison-Wesley (1973).

[5]   H. T. Kung: "Why systolic architecture?", *IEEE Computer* 15 (1) January, 1980, PP. 37-46.

[6]   F. T. Leighton and C. E. Leiserson:"Wafer-scale integration of systolic arrays", *Proc. Twenty third Symp. Foundations of Computer Science*, November 1982, PP. 297-311.

[7]   B. Louka and M. Tchuente:"Dynamic programming on two-dimensional systolic arrays", *Inform. Process. Lett.* 29, (1988), PP. 97-104.

[8]   J. F. Myoupo:" Dynamic programming on linear systolic arrays", *Proc. 28th Annu. Allerton Conf. Contr., Commun., Comput.* PP. 254-261, Oct. 1990.

[9]   I. V. Ramakrishnan and P. J. Varman:" Dynamic programming and transitive closure on linear pipelines", *Proc. Int. Conf. Parallel Processing*, St. Charles, August 1984.

[10]   F. L. Van Scoy:"The parallel recognition of classes of graphs", *IEEE-TC, Vol. C-29, No.7* (July 1980), PP. 563-570.

TABLE I

Comparison of Linear Algorithms for Dynamic Programming

Characteristics of the array		This paper	Method in [8]	Method in [9]
Number of Cells		n^2+1	n	n
Time of Execution		$6n^2-n-3$	n^2+2n-1	$2n^2+2n-2$
Time Delay between two	V_f	6	$n+1$	$2n+2$
Consecutive	V_s	8	$n+3$	$2n+4$
Cells through the Channel...	V_c	2	2	$2n+3$
Size of the memory of each cell		1	$n+1$	n
		Fully Pipelined	Partially Pipelined	

On the Fault-Tolerance of Quasi-Minimal Cayley Networks (Extended Abstract)

Marc Baumslag
Graduate Center
City University of New York
33 W 42 Street
New York, NY, 10036

Abstract

In this paper, we study the fault-tolerance of a large class of networks, whose underlying communication topology is a *quasi-minimal Cayley graph*, by studying their *connectivity*. Many "benchmark" parallel networks are included in this class, such as hypercube networks, butterfly networks, cube-connected cycles networks, double ring networks and star networks. Our main result is a proof that all quasi-minimal Cayley graphs have connectivity equal to their degree. This theorem generalizes results of Godsil [Go] and Akers and Krishnamurthy [AK]. We employ a proof technique which differs substantially from previous ones used to study the connectivity of highly symmetric graphs and, in particular, our method constitutes a more *constructive* approach to the problem. Based on our results, we are also led to suggest a *hierarchical* method for the *packaging* of a parallel network that provides the network with a high degree of fault-tolerance.

1. Introduction

Our motivation for this work proceeds from two independent sources. The first is in the study of fault-tolerance of parallel networks. A basic and commonly used measure of the fault-tolerance of a parallel network is the *connectivity*[1] of its underlying communication graph. The class of *quasi-minimal Cayley graphs* contains many important commonly encountered network topologies. Akers and Krishnamurthy [AK] showed that a certain subclass of these graphs have optimal connectivity, *i.e.*, they have connectivity equal to

---

[1] All formal definitions appear imminently.

their degree. This paper extends their results to the *entire* class of quasi-minimal Cayley graphs. In addition, our results suggest a new method for the packaging of a parallel network which provides a high degree of fault-tolerance.

The second motivation arises from the theoretical study of the connectivity of "symmetric" graphs. This problem has been studied by several authors in recent years (see, for example, [Go,Gr,Ha,Im,Ma,Wa1,Wa2]). Much of the effort has gone into determining which vertex-transitive graphs are optimally connected. The most general result known prior to this paper was proved by Godsil [Go]. He showed that every Cayley graph with a minimal generating set possesses optimal connectivity[2]. In this paper, we extend Godsils' result (in the case of finite groups) by showing that every Cayley graph equipped with a *quasi-minimal* generating set has optimal connectivity. Our proof techniques are constructive, based on the connectivity of smaller vertex-transitive graphs, and thus differ markedly from previous ones.

The remainder of the paper is organized as follows. Section 2 introduces definitions and preliminary results. Section 3 proves the main theorem of the paper and Section 4 discusses the application of our results to fault-tolerance in parallel networks.

2. Preliminary definitions and results

For any terms not found here, we refer the reader to any standard text on group theory (*e.g.*, see [Ro]) and graph theory (*e.g.*, see [Bo]). All graphs in this paper are finite, undirected and without self-loops. If Γ is a regular graph, then $\rho(\Gamma)$ denotes the degree of the graph. Let S be a generating set[3] for a finite group[4] G. The **Cayley graph of G with respect to S**, denoted by $\Gamma(G, S)$, has vertex set $V(\Gamma) = G$ and there is an edge between g and h if gh^{-1} or $hg^{-1} \in S$. From this definition we see that $\rho(\Gamma(G, S)) = |S \cup S^{-1}|$, where $S^{-1} = \{s^{-1} : s \in S\}$.

S is a **minimal** generating set for G if S generates G but no proper subset of S does. S is a **quasi-minimal** generating set for G if there exists an ordering of S, say $s_1, s_2, \cdots, s_k$, such that $s_i \notin \langle s_1, s_2, \cdots, s_{i-1} \rangle$ for $2 \leq i \leq k$. Every minimal generating set for a group G is obviously quasi-minimal but not vice-versa. For example, consider the set of permutations

$$S = \{(1, 2), (1, 2, 3), \cdots, (1, 2, 3, \cdots, n)\}$$

for any $n \geq 2$, which generates the symmetric group on n symbols. This is clearly a quasi-minimal generating set for all n but contains a subset of size 2, namely $\{(1, 2), (1, 2, \cdots, n)\}$, which also generates the group (see [CM]).

The **connectivity** of a finite graph is the minimum number of vertices that must be removed in order to disconnect the graph. We denote the connectivity of Γ by $\kappa(\Gamma)$. The

---

[2]He proved this result for infinite as well as finite groups. Our results pertain only to the finite case.

[3]S is a **generating set** for the group G if every element of G can be expressed as a product of elements in S.

[4]All groups in this paper are finite.

following equivalent formulation of the notion of connectivity (see [Bo]) is utilized in this paper:

> Γ has connectivity $\kappa(\Gamma)$ if and only if for any pair of vertices x, y and for any subset of vertices $A \subset V(\Gamma) - \{x, y\}$ of size $\kappa(\Gamma) - 1$, there exists a path in Γ between x and y that does not pass through any vertices of A. That is, there is a path between x and y that avoids A.

We sometimes call A the **avoidance set**. In the case that $\rho(\Gamma) = \kappa(\Gamma)$, Γ is said to have **optimal connectivity**.

A graph Γ is **vertex-transitive** if, for an arbitrary pair of vertices, x and y, there exists an automorphism of Γ that maps x to y. We now introduce a method for constructing vertex-transitive graphs due to Sabidussi [Sa] (also, see [Ya]) which performs a central role in this paper. Let G be a group generated by S and suppose that H is a non-trivial subgroup of G. The **left-coset graph**[5], denoted by $\Gamma(G/H)$, has a vertex set consisting of the set of *left* cosets[6] of H in G and an edge set composed of all pairs of distinct cosets, $(g_1 H, g_2 H)$, for which there exists an $s \in S$ such that

$$g_1 h_1 s = g_2 h_2$$

for some $h_1, h_2 \in H$. A key property of left-coset graphs is found in the following theorem.

Theorem 1 (Theorem 2, [Sa]) *If H is a subgroup of G then the left-coset graph $\Gamma(G/H)$ is vertex transitive.*

Since all cosets in this paper are *left* cosets we simply use the word "coset" to mean "left coset".

The connectivity of vertex-transitive graphs has been studied in general in [Gr, Wa1, Wa2]. In particular, Watkins showed the following lower bound on the connectivity of an arbitrary vertex-transitive graph:

Theorem 2 (Theorem 3, [Wa2]) *If Γ is a vertex-transitive graph then*

$$\kappa(\Gamma) \geq 2/3(\rho(\Gamma) + 1).$$

For vertex-transitive graphs of small degree, Watkins [Wa2] infers 2 important corollaries to this theorem:

Corollary 1 *Any vertex-transitive graph Γ having $\kappa(\Gamma) = 2$ is a polygon.*

Corollary 2 *If Γ is a vertex-transitive graph with $\rho(\Gamma) = 2$, 4 or 6, then $\kappa(\Gamma) = \rho(\Gamma)$.*

---

[5]In [Ya], this graph is called a **group-coset graph**.
[6]A left coset is a set of the form $gH = \{gh : h \in H\}$ for some $g \in G$.

3.   Proof of the main theorem

In this section we prove the following theorem.

Theorem 3 *Every Cayley graph of a finite group with a quasi-minimal generating set has optimal connectivity.*

Throughout the proof we assume that $S_H = \{s_1, s_2, \cdots, s_k\}$ is a quasi-minimal generating set for the subgroup H of G and $S = S_H \cup \{s\}$, where $s \notin H$, generates G. Hence, S is a quasi-minimal generating set for G. Suppose there are k_1 elements of order 2 and k_2 elements of order greater than 2 in S_H. For convenience, we write $\Gamma(G) = \Gamma(G, S)$, $\Gamma(H) = \Gamma(H, S_H)$ and note some simple facts:

- $\rho(\Gamma(H)) = k_1 + 2k_2$.

- $|H| \geq 2^k$ since S_H is a quasi-minimal generating set for H.

- $\Gamma(G)$ consists of $|G|/|H|$ isomorphic copies of $\Gamma(H)$ connected by edges all of which are labeled by s (these are sometimes termed s-edges).

- If s is of order 2 then $\rho(\Gamma(G)) = \rho(\Gamma(H)) + 1$, otherwise $\rho(\Gamma(G)) = \rho(\Gamma(H)) + 2$.

We now investigate the graph-theoretic structure of the left-coset graph $\Gamma(G/H)$. Notice that all of the edges between cosets arise from s-edges since, by definition of a quasi-minimal generating set, edges arising from the other generators lie inside H. The next lemma counts the number of edges of $\Gamma(G)$ that "collapse" in order to form a single edge of $\Gamma(G/H)$.

Lemma 1 *The number of edges in $\Gamma(G)$ that collapse to form each edge of $\Gamma(G/H)$ is a fixed constant.*

Proof. Without loss of generality, we may restrict ourselves to the edges emanating from H since Cayley graphs are vertex-transitive. Let

$$K = \{h \in H : hs = sh' \text{ for some } h' \in H\}.$$

Then it is evident that $K = sHs^{-1} \cap H$ and thus K is a subgroup of H. Notice that the edge (H, sH) of $\Gamma(G/H)$ is formed by collapsing precisely $|K|$ edges of $\Gamma(G)$.

We now show that the set of s-edges emanating from each coset of K in H collapses to form a *distinct* edge of $\Gamma(G/H)$. Choose 2 distinct cosets of K in H, say $r_1K \neq r_2K$ (for some $r_1, r_2 \in H$) and consider the cosets (of H in G) in which these sets of group elements end up after multiplication by s:

$$r_1Ks = r_1sH'$$
$$r_2Ks = r_2sH'$$

for some $H' \subseteq H$.

CLAIM: $r_1 s$ and $r_2 s$ are in distinct cosets of H in G.

Suppose the claim is false. Then there exists an $h \in H$ such that

$$(r_2 s)^{-1} r_1 s = h$$

and hence

$$r_2^{-1} r_1 s = sh.$$

This implies that $r_2^{-1} r_1 \in K$, i.e., r_1 and r_2 are in the same coset modulo K, contradicting the choice of r_1 and r_2.

This lemma shows that $\Gamma(G/H)$ is formed in a very regular fashion from $\Gamma(G)$. Let d_e denote the index of K in H and let d_i denote the size of K. The degree of $\Gamma(G/H)$ is at least d_e and the number of edges in $\Gamma(G)$ that collapse to form a single edge of $\Gamma(G/H)$ is at least d_i. In the sequel, we refer to d_i as the **internal degree** of $\Gamma(G/H)$ and d_e as the **external degree** of $\Gamma(G/H)$. Since S is quasi-minimal, it is evident that

$$|H| = d_i d_e \geq 2^k. \tag{1}$$

We prove that $\Gamma(G)$ has optimal connectivity by induction on the number of generators.

INDUCTIVE HYPOTHESIS: $\Gamma(H)$ has optimal connectivity.

The basis of this induction is the case when $k \leq 6$. We omit the basis case from the proof (it is quite similar to the inductive step, involving a more careful analysis of the left coset graphs that arise) for lack of space.

Choose an arbitrary vertex x in $\Gamma(G)$ and suppose A is a subset of vertices of $\Gamma(G)$ such that $e, x \notin A$ (e denotes the identity of G) and either $|A| = k_1 + 2k_2 + 1$ or $|A| = k_1 + 2k_2$, depending on whether s is of order greater than 2 or equal to 2, respectively (we handle both cases simultaneously). The proof proceeds by constructing a path from e to x that avoids A. This is clearly sufficient because of the vertex-transitivity of $\Gamma(G)$. To do this, we use the connectivity of $\Gamma(H)$ together with the connectivity of the vertex-transitive graph $\Gamma(G/H)$, implied by Theorem 2. Intuitively, because of (1), either the internal degree or the external degree must be "large" and in either case this provides us with the freedom to find a path of the required type. The proof splits into several cases.

CASE 0: $|G : H| = 2$.

If there are exactly 2 cosets then the Cayley graph $\Gamma(G)$ consists of 2 copies of $\Gamma(H)$ connected by either one or two perfect matchings (depending on whether s is of order 2 or greater than 2, respectively). Suppose $x \in H$ and s is of order 2 (the other 3 cases are handled similarly). If there are at most $\rho(\Gamma(H)) - 1$ members of A in H then by the connectivity of $\Gamma(H)$ there is a path (in $\Gamma(H)$) between e and x avoiding A. If all of A lies in H, then we can find a path (in the second coset) between s and xs that avoids A and hence a path between e and x that avoids A.

CASE 1: The purpose of case 1 is to reduce the problem to the case in which there are at most $k_1 + 2k_2 - 1$ vertices of A in any given coset. This provides us with "mobility" inside each coset since $\Gamma(H)$ has connectivity $k_1 + 2k_2$ by the inductive hypothesis. Thus, for case 1, we may assume A lies in at most 2 distinct cosets. (Otherwise, we can immediately assert that there are at most $k_1 + 2k_2 - 1$ vertices in each coset.) Let $A = A_1 \cup \{a\}$ where A_1 is contained in a single coset and a is a vertex in an arbitrary coset.

CASE 1A: $\Gamma(G/H)$ is a polygon.

Using the fact that A resides in at most 2 cosets, we first show that there exists some coset, say yH, such that

1. There is a path between e and y avoiding A.

2. $yH \cap A = \emptyset$.

If s has order 2 then $|A| = \rho(\Gamma(H)) = k_1 + 2k_2$. If A is a subset of H then clearly, $y = s$ satisfies the assertion. Similarly, if A does not intersect H then $y = e$ satisifies the assertion. If A is not a subset of H then there are at most $k_1 + 2k_2 - 1$ members of A in each coset since $|A| = k_1 + 2k_2$.

On the other hand, suppose that s is of order greater than 2. Let H contain $\rho(\Gamma(H))$ members of A. Then, there is some neighbor, say v, of e (either s or s^{-1}) that is not an element of A and the coset vH contains at most 1 member of A. If there are no members of A in vH then $v = y$ satisfies the assertion; otherwise, there is some vertex in vH (which we can reach using the connectivity of $\Gamma(H)$) adjacent to an element of a coset yH that does not intersect A. (This follows since there are at least $|H|/2$ vertices of vH that are adjacent to a coset $yH \neq H$.)

By a similar argument, there must exist at least one coset, say wH, such that

1. There is a path between x and w avoiding A.

2. $wH \cap A = \emptyset$.

Note that yH may equal wH. Now, if either A resides completely in a single coset or both A' and a lie between yH and wH on the same side of the polygon then there is obviously a path between e and x avoiding A. If A' and a are on opposite sides of the polygon, then, we find a path between yH and wH on the side containing a. The single vertex a is easily avoided since there are at least 2 distinct edges between adjacent cosets.

CASE 1B: $\Gamma(G/H)$ is not a polygon.

If $\Gamma(G/H)$ is not a polygon, by Corollary 1 we infer that $\kappa(\Gamma(G/H)) \geq 3$. As before, there exists some coset, say yH, such that $yH \cap A = \emptyset$ and there is a path between e and y avoiding A; similarly, there exists some coset, say zH, such that $zH \cap A = \emptyset$ and there is a path between e and y that avoids A. Since $\kappa(\Gamma(G/H)) \geq 3$, there exists a path in $\Gamma(G/H)$ between yH and zH avoiding the 2 cosets that contain A. This path can easily be converted to a path between y and z in $\Gamma(G)$ since each coset is a connected subgraph of $\Gamma(G)$ and there are no members of A in any of the cosets along this path. Hence, there is a path between e and x in $\Gamma(G)$ avoiding A.

CASE 2: We are now free to assume that no coset contains more than $k_1 + 2k_2 - 1$ vertices of A and thus, for any 2 vertices (that are not members of A) in a fixed coset, there is a path between them that avoids A. Notice that this path does not leave the given coset.

CASE 2A: For all $a \in A$, $a \notin H \cup xH$.

If $x \in H$, we can find a path between e and x in $\Gamma(H)$ avoiding A by simply using the connectivity of H. Thus, suppose $x \notin H$. We find a path between e and x that avoids A by first finding a path from *some* vertex in H to *some* vertex in xH avoiding A. This is sufficient since a path of this type can easily be extended to a path of the required type using the connectivity of $\Gamma(H)$.

Recall from equation (1) that $d_i d_e \geq 2^k$. By using the connectivity of $\Gamma(G/H)$ implied by Theorem 2, we can avoid at least

$$\Delta := \frac{2}{3} d_e - \frac{1}{3} \tag{2}$$

cosets completely, and hence we can avoid any Δ vertices in A. We now take into account the internal degree of $\Gamma(G/H)$. Recall that each edge of $\Gamma(G/H)$ is composed of at least d_i parallel edges in $\Gamma(G)$. Thus, a path in $\Gamma(G/H)$ can be converted to a path in $\Gamma(G)$ that avoids an arbitrary $d_i - 1$ vertices by using the connectivity of $\Gamma(H)$ inside each coset. Hence, the total number of vertices that can be avoided is at least

$$\Delta + d_i - 1. \tag{3}$$

We now determine the minimum value of this expression subject to the constraint given by equation (1). To simplify the exposition, we rename our variables: Put $X = d_e, Y = d_i$ and $c = 2^k$. Now, substitute for Y in terms of X and c in (3) (using equation (1)) and let

$$f(X) = \frac{2}{3} X + \frac{c}{X} - \frac{4}{3}. \tag{4}$$

By differentiating f, we see that

$$f'(X) = \frac{2}{3} - \frac{c}{X^2}, \tag{5}$$

and thus we infer that $f(X)$ acheives a minimum when

$$X_{\min} = \sqrt{\frac{3c}{2}}. \tag{6}$$

(This is a minimum since $f''(X_{\min}) > 0$.) By substituting (6) into (4) and simplifying, we have that the minimum value of f is

$$\frac{2\sqrt{2}}{\sqrt{3}} \sqrt{c} - \frac{4}{3}. \tag{7}$$

Thus, we conclude that we can avoid at least

$$\left\lceil \frac{2\sqrt{2}}{\sqrt{3}} 2^{\frac{k}{2}} - \frac{4}{3} \right\rceil \tag{8}$$

members of A (since this quantity must be an integer). In order to avoid all members of A it suffices to have

$$\left\lceil \frac{2\sqrt{2}}{\sqrt{3}} 2^{\frac{k}{2}} - \frac{4}{3} \right\rceil \geq k_1 + 2k_2 + 1. \tag{9}$$

By checking the validity of this equation when $k = 7$ and noting that the function on the left hand side is increasing faster than that on the right hand side, we infer that we can find a path between e and x avoiding A when $k \geq 7$

CASE 2B: When some members of A are in either H or xH (*i.e.*, the initial or final cosets) then the paths found in the preceding case may have an endpoint at one of these vertices. Thus, we need to find a path between H and xH that does not start or end at a member of A and avoids all of the members of A that are outside of the cosets H and xH.

Firstly, we show that without loss of generality, we may assume that H and xH are not adjacent in $\Gamma(G/H)$. Suppose, to the contrary, that H and xH are adjacent in $\Gamma(G/H)$. Either we can find a path from e to x directly by using the d_i edges that connect H and xH or all of these edges have (at least) one of their endvertices in A. In the latter case, we consider all of the s-edges of vertices in H that do not have either of their endvertices in A. Let C denote the set of these endvertices not in H. The size of this set is at least $\Phi := 2^k - (2k+1)$ and must comprise at least $\lceil \Phi/d_i \rceil$ distinct cosets. If any member $c \in C$ is in a coset not adjacent to xH then we have reduced the problem to finding a path between c and x where c and x are not in adjacent cosets, as desired. On the other hand, suppose all members of C are in cosets that are adjacent to xH. In this case, there are at least Φ edges in $\Gamma(G)$ that can be used to get to xH from vertices in C. At least one of these edges must have both of its endvertices outside of A since $\Phi > 0$ (as long as $k \geq 3$). Hence, we can reach xH from H via a single intermediate coset. Once inside xH we can find a path to x using the connectivity of $\Gamma(H)$.

s is of order 2. If s is of order 2 then we can reduce the problem to case 2a as follows. Let B denote the subset of A that lies in H. Replace A by $A' = (A - B) \cup C$ where C is the set of vertices $\{hs : h \in B\}$, *i.e.*, the set of all s-neighbors of vertices in B. Since s is of order 2, it is sufficient to avoid A' in order to avoid A. Note that $|A'| = |A|$ and H does not contain any members of A' and thus the problem reduces to the case 2a. Now assume that the order of s is at least 3.

s is of order greater than 2.

CASE 2B(I): $d_i = 1$.

Let B denote the subset of A inside $H \cup xH$. Form a new set A' consisting of $A - B$ together with all of the neighbors of B that are not in $H \cup xH$. Clearly, a path which avoids A' also avoids A. The maximum possible size of A' is

$$2(2k+1) = 4k + 2$$

since each member of A is adjacent to at most 2 distinct cosets. Since $d_i = 1$ we see that $\Delta = 2^{k+1}/3 - 1/3$. In order to avoid A' it suffices to have

$$\left\lceil \frac{2^{k+1}}{3} - \frac{1}{3} \right\rceil \geq 4k + 2. \tag{10}$$

As long as k is at least 6 this inequality is satisfied.

CASE 2B(II): $d_i \geq 2$.

Unlike case 2b(i), the total number of vertices that we need to avoid in this case is at most $|A|$ although some of them must be avoided as complete cosets. Recall from case 2a that we can avoid at least Δ vertices lying between H and xH by completely avoiding the cosets in which they reside.

Let B be the set of vertices of A that are in $H \cup xH$. We assume $|B| \leq k_1 + 2k_2$ without loss of generality. This follows since $|B| > k_1 + 2k_2$ implies that all members of A are in $H \cup xH$. In this case, unless $|G : H| = 2$ (see case 0), both H and xH have an adjacent reachable coset that does not intersect A.

We say that a subset $B' \subset B$ saturates an edge (H, vH) of $\Gamma(G/H)$ if for each edge (h, vh') of $\Gamma(G)$ that collapses to form (H, vH), we have $h \in B'$. For each subset B' of B that saturates an edge of $\Gamma(G/H)$ we replace B' by the neighbors of B' in $\Gamma(G/H)$. Note that this consists of at most 2 cosets. We avoid these vertices by completely avoiding the cosets in which they reside. The maximum number of cosets we need to avoid is

$$\frac{2(k_1 + 2k_2)}{d_i}$$

and hence it suffices to have

$$\Delta = \frac{2}{3}d_e - \frac{1}{3} \geq \frac{2(k_1 + 2k_2)}{d_i}. \tag{11}$$

An easy calculation shows that if k is at least 4, then for each value of $d_i \geq 2$ this inequality is satisfied.

Remark. Notice that the method for avoiding A is constructive, provided we have an algorithm for finding paths in $\Gamma(G/H)$ and $\Gamma(H)$ that avoid a given set of vertices.

4. Implications for fault-tolerant routing in parallel networks

In this section, we consider parallel networks that consist of a set of **processing elements** (PEs), each having a processor and a local memory, connected via a fixed interconnection network. This type of network is modelled by a graph in which vertices represent PEs and edges represent bi-directional communication links between pairs of PEs.

A primary function of a parallel network is its ability to facilitate communication between its PEs[7]. However, as the number of PEs in a network increases, the chance of failure of some of the components[8] becomes quite large. This implies the need for a redundancy in the choice of possible communication paths. In graph-theoretic terms this redundancy corresponds to the connectivity of the underlying communication graph of the network: If the graph has connectivity κ, then the failure[9] of any $\kappa - 1$ PEs does not preclude any other pair of PEs from communicating. This represents a *worst-case* approach to the problem which clearly cannot be overcome except by improving or adding hardware. For example, a family of bounded degree networks can tolerate only a constant number of faults *independent* of the size of the network. However, if we slightly relax the assumption of a worst-case distribution of faults then we can often tolerate a much larger number of faults. The next theorem provides a quantitative measure of this for networks that have an underlying topology of a quasi-minimal Cayley graph. This class includes many familiar parallel networks including star networks and pancake networks [AK], hypercube networks, cube-connected cycles networks, butterfly networks, torioidal mesh networks, and various ring networks.

Theorem 4 *Let $\Gamma(G, S)$ be a quasi-minimal Cayley graph as defined in the proof of Theorem 1. Let x and y represent 2 PEs in a network having $\Gamma(G, S)$ as its underlying topology and suppose $\mathcal{F}$ is a set of faulty PEs such that*

- $|\mathcal{F}| \leq \kappa(\Gamma(G/H)) + d_i - 2.$

- *There are no faulty PEs in the left cosets containing x and y.*

Then there is a path in the network between x and y avoiding $\mathcal{F}$.

Proof. This is simply a restatement of the observation made in the proof of case 2a, Theorem 3. (See equation (2).)

We illustrate this approach to fault-tolerance by considering two examples. Let us first consider the **butterfly network**, a commonly studied parallel network in the literature, defined as follows. The order-n version, denoted by $\mathcal{B}_n$, has a vertex set consisting of the set of pairs

$$\langle \ell; B \rangle$$

where ℓ is an integer between 0 and $n-1$ and B is an n-bit integer. (Thus, there are $n2^n$ vertices in $\mathcal{B}_n$.) The set of all vertices with a fixed first component is called a **level** of the butterfly. The set of all vertices with a fixed second component is called a **column**. There is an edge between $\langle \ell_1; B_1 \rangle$ and $\langle \ell_2; B_2 \rangle$ when either $B_1 = B_2$ and $(\ell_1 - \ell_2) \bmod n = 1$ or $(\ell_1 - \ell_2) \bmod n = 1$ and B_2 differs from B_1 in the ℓ_1-th bit. In [ABR], the authors

---

[7]We assume a store-and-forward regimen for the movement of messages through the network.
[8]We only consider *processor* failures.
[9]If a PE fails then we assume that data cannot be routed though it.

proved that this network is in fact a Cayley graph of the wreath product[10] of Z_2 by Z_n, denoted by $Z_2\, wr\, Z_n$ (see [ABR] for details). The generating set involved is of size 2 and is quasi-minimal. Each column is a left coset of the subgroup isomorphic to Z_n contained in $Z_2\, wr\, Z_n$. Now form the left coset graph by factoring out by this subgroup. This graph is isomorphic to the n-dimensional hypercube with external degree equal to n and internal degree equal to 2. The connectivity of the hypercube is well-known to be n and thus (using Theorem 4) we can find a path between 2 vertices in distinct columns avoiding any $(n-1)+1 = n$ vertices as long as they are not in the columns containing the source and destination.

Remark. The above discussion suggests a fault-tolerant and modular way of packaging the butterfly network; namely, we fabricate each column as a single unit, say on a single chip, and then appropriately connect the chips to form the topology of the butterfly. It now follows from the above discussion that in the event of failure of any n chips (assuming total failure of a chip in this case), the remainder of the network can continue to communicate.

As a final example (representing the opposite extreme in comparison to the butterfly network), we consider an arbitrary quasi-minimal Cayley graph of an *abelian* group[11], denoted by G. This class of graphs generalizes the interconnection pattern of mesh-type networks (such as the toroidal mesh and the hypercube). Let H be the subgroup of G generated by all of the generators except the last one, which we denote by s. Assume, for the sake of simplicity, that the order of s is greater than 2. The graph $\Gamma(G/H)$ is easily seen to be an ℓ-vertex ring where ℓ is the order of s. Thus, the external degree in this case is 2 and the internal degree is $|H|$. Hence, appealing to Theorem 4, we obtain a method for routing around faults in such networks by recursively reducing the problem to routing around faults in ring networks.

5.   Acknowledgments

Thanks to Mahesh Ghirkar for helpful comments. Also, thanks to Stephen Ahearn and Victor Yodaiken for their input during this research.

6.   References

[AK] S.B. Akers and B. Krishnamurthy (1987): On group graphs and their fault tolerance. *IEEE Trans. Comp.*, C-36, 885-888.

[ABR] F. Annexstein, M. Baumslag, A.L. Rosenberg (1990): Group action graphs and parallel architectures. *Siam J. Computing*, Vol. 19, No. 3, 544-569.

[Bo] B. Bollobas (1978): Extremal graph theory, Academic Press.

---

[10] Z_k represents a cyclic group of order k.

[11] An abelian group is one in which all elements commute.

[CM] H.S.M. Coxeter, W.O.J. Moser (1972): Generators and Relations for Discrete Groups, 3rd ed., Springer-Verlag, Berlin.

[Go] C.D. Godsil (1981): Connectivity of minimal Cayley graphs. *Arch. Math.*, Vol. 37, 473-476.

[Gr] A.C. Green (1975): Structure of vertex-transitive graphs. *Journal of Combinatorial Theory*, Series B 18, 1-11.

[Ha] Y.O. Hamidoune (1984): On the connectivity of Cayley digraphs. *European J. of Combinatorics* 5, 309-312.

[Im] W. Imrich (1979): On the connectivity of Cayley graphs. *Journal of Combinatorial Theory*, Series B 26, 323-326.

[Ma] W. Mader (1971): Eine Eigenschaft der Atome endlicher Graphen. *Arch. Math. (Basel)* 22, 333-336.

[Ro] D.J.S. Robinson (1980): A Course in the Theory of Groups, Springer-Verlag.

[Sa] G. Sabidussi (1964): Vertex-transitive graphs. *Monatsh. Math.* 63, 124-127.

[Wa1] M.E. Watkins (1969): Some classes of hypoconnected vertex-transitive graphs. *Recent Progress in Combinatorics; Proceedings of the Third Waterloo Conference on Combinatorics*, Edited by W.T. Tutte & C.St.J.A. Nash-Williams, Academic Press, New York.

[Wa2] M.E. Watkins (1970): Connectivity of transitive graphs. *Journal of Combinatorial Theory*, 8, 23-29.

[Ya] H.P. Yap (1986): Some Topics in Graph Theory, London Mathematical Society Lecture Note Series 108, Cambridge University Press.

Some Fast Parallel Algorithms for Parentheses Matching

Sajal K. Das,[1] Calvin C.-Y. Chen,[1] Gene Lewis,[1] and Sushil Prasad[2]

Abstract

The *parentheses matching* problem is to determine the mate of each parenthesis in a balanced string of n parentheses. In this paper, we present three novel and elegant parallel algorithms for this problem on parallel random-access machine (PRAM) models. Each of our algorithms has *polylog*-time complexity and two of them are cost-optimal.

1 Introduction

Parentheses matching is an integral subproblem of parsing and evaluating arithmetic expressions, which is an important area of research in parallel computing. Therefore, several parallel algorithms have been proposed for parentheses matching. (A stack-based, optimal sequential algorithm runs in $O(n)$ time.) An optimal parallel algorithm on a CREW PRAM model was first proposed by Bar-On and Vishkin [BV85], which requires $O(\log n)$ time using $O(n/\log n)$ processors. This algorithm builds a binary search tree to compute the nesting level of each parenthesis, and performs concurrent search on this tree to find the mates of the parentheses. Tsang, et al [TLC89] proposed the first optimal parallel algorithm on an EREW PRAM model, which requires $O(\log n)$ time employing $n/\log n$ processors. This algorithm also builds a binary tree, and then recursively assigns unique identifiers to each parenthesis which are in turn used to find the mates. Though this algorithm is cost-optimal, the strategy involves pipelining and tedious assignment of identifiers. Further references related to parallel parentheses matching include [CD90a, DP89, LP89, RD90].

In this paper, we present two EREW PRAM algorithms − one requiring $O(\log n)$ time and the other $O(\log^2 n)$ time − and an $O(\log n)$-time CREW algorithm for parentheses matching. Our algorithms utilize $O(n/\log n)$ processors and $O(n)$ space, are considerably simpler than the existing ones, and provide new insights into this important problem. Furthermore, they do not use pipelining as in [TLC89] nor complicated data structures as in [DP89]; and their time complexity and correctness proofs are easily seen. Algorithm I for the EREW PRAM model is based on a divide-and-conquer strategy, exploiting a novel characterization of a balanced string of parentheses. Compared to existing parallel algorithms for parentheses matching, Algorithm I is very simple and elegant though not cost-optimal. Algorithm II for the CREW model is based on building a binary tree, and it involves an encoding scheme for *representative* unmatched parentheses. Algorithm III on the EREW model is a combination of several existing approaches. In this relatively simple and adaptive algorithm, a 'virtual' copying/matching tree is produced and stored in a distributed fashion among the various processors. With the help of an *extended prefix-sum* algorithm, the use of cumbersome data structures is avoided and greater simplicity is achieved in less space. Both the Algorithms II and III are cost-optimal.

2 Preliminaries

We introduce the terminology and notations used in this paper. Without loss of generality, we assume that the input string consisting of left and right parentheses has length $n = 2^k$.

---

[1]Center for Research in Parallel and Distributed Computing, Department of Computer Science, University of North Texas, P.O. Box 13886, Denton, TX 76203-3886.

[2]Department of Mathematics and Computer Science, Georgia State University, Atlanta, GA 30303.

Furthermore, let the input string be in an array INPUT[1 .. n] such that INPUT[i] = 0 (or 1) if the ith parenthesis is a left (or right) parenthesis. The output of an algorithm is available in an array MATCH[1 .. n], such that MATCH[i] = j if and only if the parentheses at positions i and j are mates. An algorithm whose time complexity is a polynomial in the logarithm (all logarithms are assumed to be in base two) of input-size is called a *polylog*-time algorithm. Suppose an array of $i_1 + i_2 + ... + i_l$ elements is divided into l disjoint segments, $(x_{11}, x_{12}, ..., x_{1i_1})$, $(x_{21}, x_{22}, ..., x_{2i_2})$, ..., $(x_{l1}, x_{l2}, ..., x_{li_i})$, where each segment has contiguous indices and the first element in each segment can be identified. Then the *extended prefix-sum* problem is defined as one which computes all the sums $x_{m1} + x_{m2} + ... + x_{mk}$, for $1 \leq k \leq i_m$ and $1 \leq m \leq l$.

Our model of computation is a parallel random access machine (PRAM), consisting of p processors, $\{P_1, P_2, ..., P_p\}$, and a global shared memory. All processors can access any *cell* in the shared memory in constant time; also simple arithmetic or logical operations can be performed in unit time. In the EREW (exclusive-read and exclusive-write) variant of the PRAM model, more than one processor is not allowed to simultaneously read from or write into a memory cell. In the CREW (concurrent-read and exclusive-write) variant, simultaneous reads but not simultaneous writes are allowed. The *speedup* of a parallel algorithm running on p processors is the ratio between the time (T_1) required by the fastest known sequential algorithm to the time (T_p) required by the parallel algorithm. If the speedup is $O(p)$, then the algorithm is said to achieve *optimal* speedup or is simply called optimal. Thus a parallel algorithm is *cost-optimal* if $pT_p = O(T_1)$.

3   Algorithm I

Our first algorithm is based on the following two easily proved observations concerning a *balanced* input string.

Lemma 1: The mate of a parenthesis at an odd position in a balanced input string lies at an even position (and vice versa).

Lemma 2: If a balanced string does not have a left parenthesis at an even position (or, equivalently, a right parenthesis at an odd position), then the mate of any left parenthesis in the string lies immediately to its right.

By induction, we can show that any string satisfying Lemma 2 is of the form

$$( ) ( ) ( ) ... ( ) \qquad \qquad \textbf{[F]}$$

Algorithm I is now formulated by using a divide-and-conquer approach. By Lemma 1, the set of left parentheses at odd positions have their mates in the set of right parentheses at even positions. These parentheses can be matched independent of the matching between the set of left parentheses at even positions and the set of right parentheses at odd positions. Thus, the input string can be partitioned into two substrings — the first substring containing the left and right parentheses at, respectively, odd and even positions; and the second substring containing the left and right parentheses, respectively, at even and odd positions. If this partitioning fails to split the input string (i.e., if one of the substrings is empty), then by Lemma 2, it will have the form **F** if the input string is balanced. In this case, all the mates can easily be found in parallel. Otherwise, the partitioning scheme can be repeatedly applied to the substrings until the form **F** is obtained.

Consider the example in Figure 1 with input length $n = 16$, illustrating Algorithm I. Let the symbols $(_i$ and $)_j$ denote a left and a right parenthesis at the ith and jth positions, respectively.

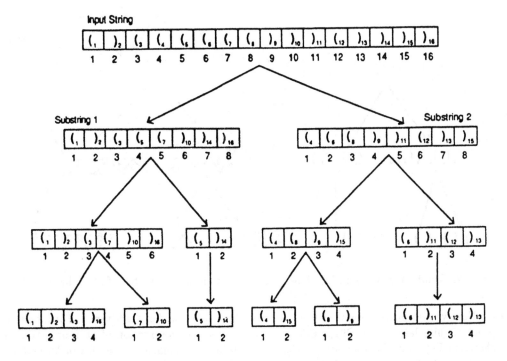

Figure 1. Illustration of Algorithm I

In three partitioning steps, the input string in Figure 1 is converted into form F. The two substrings generated by a partition can be stored in the same array as the parent string by packing those parentheses belonging to the left substring at the beginning of the array followed by those belonging to the right substring. The segmented parallel prefix algorithm [Ma79, Sc80] can be used for packing. Algorithm I can now be precisely stated as follows.

Step A.   **for** $i = 1$ **to** $k - 1$ **do**

  (i) If a left parenthesis is at an odd position in its substring, then mark it by a 0, else by a 1. Similarly, mark a right parenthesis at an even position in its substring by a 0, and at an odd position by a 1. //Those marked by 0's belong to the left partition.//

  (ii) Use segmented parallel prefix algorithm to determine the new index of each parenthesis in its partition.

  (iii) Move each parenthesis to its new position. **endfor**

Step B. (i) Check if the input string has been converted to form **F**.

         If not then the input string is unbalanced and **Exit.**

    (ii) Match the parentheses, and store the results in array MATCH.

Since each substep of Algorithm I can be implemented in $O(\log n)$ time using $\frac{n}{\log n}$ processors on an EREW PRAM, and there are $\log n - 1$ iterations, Algorithm I requires $O(\log^2 n)$ time employing $\frac{n}{\log n}$ processors. The space required is clearly $O(n)$.

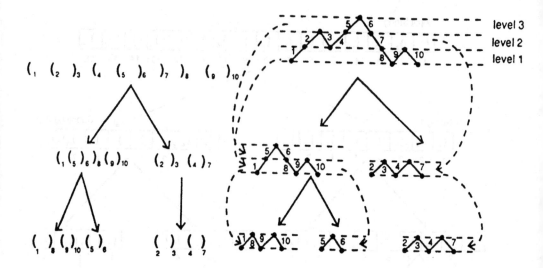

Figure 2. Graphical representation showing the reduction in the number of levels by partitioning

Now we informally show that $k - 1$ iterations are sufficient for Algorithm I. For a rigorous proof of this claim, see [LD91]. Consider the graphical representation of an input string as shown in Figure 2. It is apparent that the parentheses belonging to a level can be matched independent of any other level. The level of a left parenthesis at a position i is given by the difference in the number of left and right parentheses in the substring INPUT[1 .. i]. The level of a right parenthesis at position j is one more than the difference in the number of left and right parentheses in INPUT[1 .. j]. It is also clear that the partitioning scheme places the parentheses belonging to the odd levels in the left partition and those belonging to the even levels in the right partition. This phenomenon is illustrated in Figure 3. Thus, if a string has l levels, its left partition would have $\lceil \frac{l}{2} \rceil$ levels while its right partition would have $\lfloor \frac{l}{2} \rfloor$ levels. Furthermore, since the maximum number of levels in a balanced string of $n = 2^k$ parentheses is 2^{k-1} (in a string of 2^{k-1} left parentheses followed by 2^{k-1} right parentheses), the number of levels in the left and right partitions of a string cannot exceed 2^{k-2}. Subsequent $(k - 2)$ repeated partitionings of the substrings would reduce the number of levels in any substring to $2^0 = 1$, thus converting the input string to form F.

Furthermore, it can be shown that the average number of such steps required is also $\Theta(\log n)$. Interested readers may obtain a proof by using a result on the average height of planted plane trees [BKR72].

4   Algorithm II

While Algorithm I was cost-wise non-optimal, Algorithm II is a cost-optimal algorithm on the CREW PRAM. It requires $O(\log n)$ time and uses $n/\log n$ processors.

Initially, each processor is assigned a $\log n$-size substring. It scans its substring sequentially, finds possible local matches, and carries over for the next phase the remaining unmatched parentheses which contains zero or more right parentheses followed by zero or more left parentheses. Figure 3 shows an example, also depicting the mates of the leftmost left and the rightmost right parentheses of each substring held at a processor. We call these two parentheses in the un-

input

$$\underbrace{(_1 \ (_2 \ (_3 \ (_4}_{P_1} \quad \underbrace{)_5 \ (_6 \ (_7 \ (_8}_{P_2} \quad \underbrace{(_9 \ )_{10} \ (_{11} \ )_{12}}_{P_3} \quad \underbrace{)_{13} \ )_{14} \ (_{15} \ (_{16}}_{P_4} \quad \underbrace{)_{17} \ (_{18} \ (_{19} \ (_{20}}_{P_5} \quad \underbrace{)_{21} \ (_{22} \ )_{23} \ )_{24}}_{P_6} \quad \underbrace{)_{25} \ )_{26} \ )_{27} \ (_{28}}_{P_7} \quad \underbrace{)_{29} \ )_{30} \ )_{31} \ )_{32}}_{P_8}$$

9, 10 matched
11, 12 matched

resulting substrings

$$(_1^{32} \ (_2 \ (_3 \ (_4^4 \quad)_5^{27} \ (_6 \ (_7 \ (_8 \quad -- \quad -- \quad)_{13}^{7} \ )_{14}^{26} \ (_{15} \ (_{16} \quad)_{17}^{16} \ (_{18} \ (_{19} \ (_{20}^{25} \quad)_{21}^{19} \ )_{24} \quad)_{25} \ )_{26}^{6} \ )_{27}^{29} \ (_{28} \quad)_{29} \ )_{30} \ )_{31} \ )_{32}^1$$

Figure 3. Initial phase of Algorithm II

matched substring at a processor its **representative** parentheses. As in Figure 3, if the mates of all the representative parentheses are found by some method, then the mates of the rest of the parentheses in a substring can also be determined as follows in an additional $O(\log n)$ time using $n/\log n$ processors [BV85]. Each processor marks the mate of its left-representative-parenthesis. Next, the mate of the ith left parenthesis following the left-representative-parenthesis is found as the ith right parenthesis to the left of the mate of the left-representative-parenthesis. A processor, however, discontinues this matching process when it encounters a marked right parenthesis. Naturally, Algorithm II finds the mates of only the representative parentheses. We will use an encoding scheme for the unmatched substring at a processor. For example, a substring of six parentheses $)_5 \ )_6 \ (_{11} \ (_{14} \ (_{15} \ (_{16}$ will be encoded as $2)_6 \ (_{11}4$. Figure 4 uses such an encoding of the unmatched substrings of Figure 3, and shows a merging process along a full binary tree explained below.

The basic idea is to successively 'merge' the contents of the nodes at a level to obtain the contents of the nodes at the next higher level. Thus, the mates of some of the representative parentheses are determined. As a next step, starting at the root (highest level), the mates are found at a parent node and extended to the parentheses at its children. Eventually, the mates of all the parentheses at level 0 (leaf-level) are found. Figure 4 denotes the matching information by superscripts of the parentheses. A superscript $\downarrow< i, j >$ of a left parenthesis denotes that its mate is the jth unmatched right parenthesis to the left of $)_i$, and that this mate is found while going down the merge tree. Likewise, superscript $\downarrow< i, j >$ on a right parenthesis denotes that its mate is the jth unmatched left parenthesis to the right of $(_i$. The superscript $\uparrow< i, j >$ has similar meaning except that the mate is found while traversing up the merge tree. Consider the merger of the first and the second leaves (from left-to-right) at level 0, namely the merger of $(_14$ with $1)_5 \ (_63$. It results in matching the third left parenthesis following $(_1$ with $)_5$, which is denoted by the superscript $\downarrow< 1, 3 >$ on $)_5$. The three unmatched left parentheses of the leaf 1, denoted as $(_13$, followed by the three left parentheses of leaf 2, namely $(_63$, form the content of the parent node at level 1a. Contents of other nodes at level 1a are similarly obtained. Next the contents of the nodes at level 1a are encoded to obtain those of nodes at level 1b.

Now assuming that the mates (i.e., the superscripts) of all the parentheses at level 1b are found by continued merger process down to the root and subsequent traversal up the merge tree, let us see how these superscripts are extended to the parentheses of level 1a. The first node at level 1b is now $(_16$ with a superscript $\uparrow< 32, 0 >$, denoting that $)_{32}$ is the mate of $(_1$. This is simply copied as the superscript of $(_1$ at the first node of level 1a. Furthermore, the mate of $(_6$ is found to be $)_{27}$ by examining the last node, $3)_{27} \ 3)_{32}$, of level 1a and comparing the number of left and right parentheses. This is denoted by the superscript $\uparrow< 27, 0 >$ over $(_6$. Likewise, the mates of the parentheses at the second node of level 1b, $2)_{14} \ (_{15}2$, are extended to those at the second node at level 1a. However, a simple calculation is required for this purpose. According to its superscript, the mate of $)_{14}$ is the fourth parenthesis following $(_1$. But after examining the

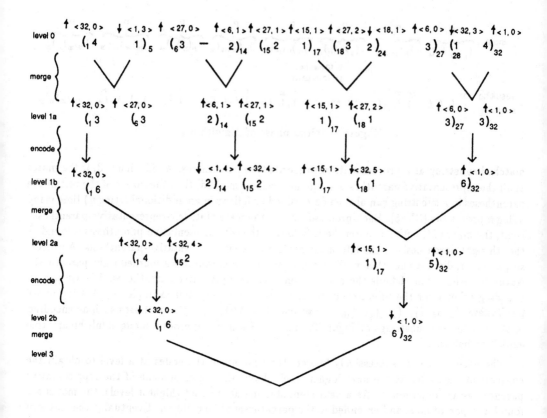

Figure 4. Merge tree corresponding to the example in Figure 3

node containing $(_1$ at level 1a, the mate of $)_{14}$ is more accurately found as the first unmatched parenthesis following $(_6$. Thus, the superscript of $)_{14}$ is $\uparrow< 6, 1 >$. The superscript $\uparrow< 32, 4 >$ of $(_{15}$ at level 1b is similarly updated to $\uparrow< 27, 1 >$ at level 1a. The superscripts of the parentheses at level 0 is obtained by simply copying those from level 1a to level 0. These superscripts of the representative parentheses at level 0 enable the determination of their mates in $O(1)$ time from the unmatched substrings held at individual processors.

We now precisely describe Algorithm II. For the sake of simplicity, we use $p = 2^q$ processors, where $q = \lceil \log \lceil \frac{n}{k} \rceil \rceil$, assuming input length $n = 2^k$.

Step A. (i) Assign processor P_i to sequentially process the substring

$$\text{INPUT}[((i-1)k+1) .. (ik)], \text{ for } i = 1, 2, ..., 2^q.$$

(ii) Encode the unmatched substring remaining at P_i using its representative

parentheses to form the ith leaf of the merge tree for Step B.

Step B. (i) Processor P_i merges nodes i and $i + 1$ of level 0, for $i = 1, 3, 5, ..., 2^q - 1$,

to produce the contents of the parent node at level 1a.

(ii) P_i encodes the contents of the ith node at level 1a, for $i = 1, 2, ..., 2^q - 1$, to produce the contents of the ith node at level 1b.

(iii) Call Step B recursively on the nodes of level 1b, with processor P_i assigned to its ith node, for $1 \le i \le 2^{q-1}$. This recursion continues until the qth level when the content of root is calculated. If root is non-empty, declare input string unbalanced and **Exit**. Else, determine the superscript of the two parentheses at level $q - 1$.

(iv) Processor P_i extends the superscripts of the parentheses at the ith node at level 1b to those parentheses at the ith node of level 1a, for $1 \le i \le 2^{q-1}$.

(v) P_i copies the superscripts of the parentheses at the ith node of level 1a to the parentheses at leaves $2i - 1$ and $2i$, for $1 \le i \le 2^{q-1}$.

Step C. Processor P_i examines the leaf i, for $1 \le i \le 2^q$, and uses the superscripts of its constituent representative parentheses to mark their mates in array MATCH.

We note that extending superscripts from level 1b to level 1a might require concurrent-read – for example, determining the superscript of $(_{15}$ and $(_{18}$ at the second and third nodes of level 1a in Figure 4 both require reading the content of the last node of level 1a. The time complexity of Algorithm II is clearly seen to be $O(\log n)$ using $O(n/\log n)$ processors on the CREW PRAM model. The total space requirement is $O(n)$. Note the similarity between Algorithm II and the recursive solution of the parallel prefix algorithm [LF80]. The concurrent read can be eliminated by carrying over all the unmatched representative parentheses along the merge tree (by removing Step B(ii)) as shown in [DP89] while maintaining the same time and processor complexity but at the expense of memory space.

5 Algorithm III

This is an adaptive, cost-optimal, privatized EREW match/copy algorithm, using p processors, with time and space complexities $O(\frac{n}{p} + \log p)$ and $O(n + p \log p)$, respectively. The following notations and concepts permit a succinct description.

(a) In a string α of parentheses, the *inmates* are those that have a mate in α, the *unmates* those that that do not. For any α, the unmates have the form ...)...)...)...)...(...(...(..., where there are $r_{[\alpha]}$ right and $l_{[\alpha]}$ left unmates, and the rightmost right and leftmost left unmates (if any) are $)_{r_\alpha}$ and $(_{l_\alpha}$ respectively. For a left unmate $(_i$ of α, if $u = 1+$ the number of left unmates of α to the right of $(_i$, we write $(_i^u$, and likewise for $)_i^u$.

(b) If $U[\alpha]$ is the string of unmates of α then $U[\alpha\beta] = U[\alpha] * U[\beta]$, concatenation with deletion of mated pairs, is associative. Given a factorization $\alpha = \alpha_1\alpha_2...\alpha_p$, with p a power of 2, the *unmates tree* M_α has leaves (at level 0) $U[\alpha_1]$, $U[\alpha_2]$, ..., $U[\alpha_p]$, level 1 nodes $U[\alpha_1\alpha_2]$, $U[\alpha_3\alpha_4]$, ... level 2 nodes $U[\alpha_1\alpha_2\alpha_3\alpha_4]$, $U[\alpha_5\alpha_6\alpha_7\alpha_8]$, ... up to the root $U[\alpha]$. Thus M_α has p leaves, $2p-1$ nodes, and $(\log p) + 1$ levels.

(c) The *matching tree*, $\bar{M}_\alpha$, is an encoded form of M_α. The leaf $U[\alpha_i]$ encodes as $r_{[\alpha_i]})_{r_{\alpha_i}}(_{l_{\alpha_i}} l_{[\alpha_i]}$, or $r_{[\alpha_i]})_{r_i}(_{l_i} l_{[\alpha_i]}$, and if $\bar{d})_{\bar{i}}(_i d \bullet \bar{e})_{\bar{j}}(_j e = \bar{d})_{\bar{i}}\bar{e} - d)_{\bar{j}}(_j e$ for $\bar{e} \geq d$, and $\bar{d})_{\bar{i}}(_i d - \bar{e}(_j e$ for $d \geq \bar{e}$, where $(_i 0$ and $)_i 0$ are empty, then the operation $\bullet$ is associative, and $\bar{M}_\alpha$ is the analogue of M_α, having a typical node of the form $\bar{d}_1)_{j_1}^{\bar{u}_1} ... \bar{d}_s)_{j_s}^{\bar{u}_s}(_{j_s}^{u_s} d_s ... (_{j_1}^{u_1}$, where we have added the labels $u_i = d_1 + ... + d_i$, $\bar{u}_{\bar{i}} = \bar{d}_1 + ... + \bar{d}_{\bar{i}}$. (A symbol $\bar{d})_{\bar{i}}^{\bar{u}}$ or $(_i^u d$ is called a *representative record*.)

(d) If ν is a node in a binary tree, with left and right children ν' and ν'', we speak of the *clause* (ν, ν', ν''), or clause ν. We use the standard numbering, e.g. [1] for the root, [2] and [3] for its children (left to right), etc. The *span* of node ν of M_α, written as $span[\nu]$, is the concatenation of the leaves of the subtree with root ν. The (r, l) numbers of ν are $(r_{[span[\nu]]}, l_{[span[\nu]]})$, written (r_ν, l_ν). For a clause (ν, ν', ν''), we have $(r_\nu, l_\nu) = (r_{\nu'}, l_{\nu'}) + (r_{\nu''}, l_{\nu''}) - (m_\nu, m_\nu)$, where $m_\nu = min\{l_{\nu'}, r_{\nu''}\}$ is the number of parentheses matched at clause ν. (If $\nu = [j]$, we write m_j for $m_{[j]}$.)

The Algorithm

Given a balanced parentheses string α of length n and p processors such that n and p are powers of 2. As working data structures, we use "matching arrays" LMATCH and RMATCH, each of size $n/2$; storage and duplication arrays *no_of_spaces* and *lastpos*, each of size $p - 1$; an array *list* of size $p \log p$; and variables *current_node*, *r_rep*, *l_rep*, *r_value*, *l_value*, *r_temp*, and *l_temp* in the private memory of each processor P_i. The algorithm proceeds in stages, the details of which are available in [CD90a].

Stage A: Local Operations and Initialization. The input is divided into p domains, and each processor first performs local matching and then left packing of the unmates within the domain assigned to it. The possible left and right representatives in the ith domain, $)_{r_i}$ and $(_{l_i}$, are located, labeled and stored in the *r_rep* and *l_rep* cells of P_i. Other private cells are also initialized. This stage requires $O(n/p)$ time and uses $O(n)$ space.

Stage B: Prefix Sums Calculation and Duplication. Find m_j, store it in *no_of_spaces*[j], and compute $m_1 + m_2 + ... + m_j$, which is stored in *lastpos*[j]. Now, for processor P_i at a child-node (at level h) of clause $[j]$, compute P_i's copy of *lastpos*[j] and store in *list*[hp + i], using extended prefix sums, where $j = \frac{p}{2^{h+1}} + \lfloor \frac{i}{2^{h+1}} \rfloor$. Since extended prefix sums can be computed in $O(\frac{n}{p} + \log p)$ time [CD90a], this stage has $O(\frac{n}{p} + \log p)$ time and $O(p \log p)$ space complexities.

Stage C: Match/Copy Processing. Each P_i, acting independently, shepherds its encoded unmates symbol $\bar{d})_{\bar{i}}^{\bar{u}}$ ($(_{l_i}^u d$ up the root path of the ith leaf in $\bar{M}_\alpha$. As chunks of the unmate blocks are matched at right or left siblings of the current node, they are copied into LMATCH and RMATCH, and the remaining diminished blocks are reencoded by an updated symbol. This continues until a level at which all the unmates from the ith local domain have been matched. To carry out this process, P_i must know the current clause $[j]$, the (r, l) numbers of the child-nodes at $[j]$, the number m_j of unmates matched at $[j]$, the matching array index $lastpos[j]$, and the current encoded symbol $\bar{d})^{\bar{u}}_{r_i}$ ($^u_{l_i}d$, residing in P_i's private cells, $\bar{d})^{\bar{u}}_{r_i}$ in r_rep, $(^u_{l_i}d$ in l_rep. In greater detail: starting at level 0, the algorithm makes a parallel, level-by-level sweep up the matching tree, performing (r, l) exchanges between paired processors at sibling-nodes, copying matched portions of representative records into the matching arrays, updating the record labels for the remaining unmatched unmates, and computing the (r, l) numbers of the current parent node.

(r, l) Exchange: For each clause (ν, ν', ν''), with ν' and ν'' at level h, processors P_i at ν' and P_{i+2^h} at ν'' exchange (r, l) numbers, storing the sibling numbers in their r_temp and l_temp cells.

Matching and Copying: At clause $(\nu, \nu', \nu'') = ([j], [2j], [2j + 1])$ we consider the operations on left interior unmates, the right case being similar. Processor P_i consults its *current_node* cell, sees $[2j]$, hence knows it is at a left sibling. In its cell l_rep it finds $(^u_{l_i,l'_i}d$, and computes $m_j = min\{l_{[2j]}, r_{[2j+1]}\}$, obtaining $l_{[2j]}$ from l_value and $r_{[2j+1]}$ from r_temp. There are now three cases: (i) $m_j \geq u$. Here all d left unmates match, so $(^u_{l_i}d$ is copied into LMATCH$[m_1 + ... + m_{j-1} + u] = $ LMATCH$[lastpos[j] - (m_j - u)]$, leaving a gap of $d - 1$ cells to be filled in later. (ii) $u > m_j > u - d$. This is a partial match. The leftmost matched parenthesis of the d-block — call it $(^{m_j}_{l_{i,h}}$, where h is the level of ν' — is then made/designated an "honorary" representative. Since $(_{l_i}$ is left-packed in cell l'_i, therefore $(_{l_{i,h}}$ is stored in cell $l'_i + u - m_j$, and so can be retrieved in constant time. Its record $(^{m_j}_{l_{i,h},l'_i+u-m_j}m_j - (u - d)$ is then created and copied into LMATCH$[lastpos[j]]$, leaving a gap of $m_j - (u-d) - 1$ cells, and the record of $(_{l_i}$ is updated to $(^{u-m_j+l_{\nu''}}_{l_i,l'_i}u - m_j$. (iii) $u - d \geq m_j$. No unmate of $(^u_{l_i,l'_i}d$ is matched, so processor P_i updates the record to the form $(^{u-m_j+l_{\nu''}}_{l_i,l'_i}d$.

Because these operations take constant time, this entire stage requires $O(\log p)$ time and uses $O(n)$ space.

Stage D: Filling in the Gaps. The goal of the copying by the processors active at a clause $[j]$, is to fill the target intervals LMATCH$[m_1 + ... + m_{j-1} : m_1 + ... + m_j]$ with the left unmates matched at clause $[j]$. But to finish the job, the gaps must be filled in. This is easily done by a parallel scan, as follows. In LMATCH and RMATCH, let P_i initially scan the cells of index $i\frac{n}{2p}$. The processors scan from higher to lower indexed cells, filling gaps as they go, subject to the following rules: (i) the first non-empty cell scanned is marked, (ii) a processor halts when it scans a marked cell, or just before falling off the end of the array, or after it has completed processing its $(\frac{3}{2}\frac{n}{p} - 1)$st scanned cell. It is easy to see that this procedure fills the gaps exactly once, in time $O(n/p)$.

Stage E: Matching. At this point, every matched pair of unmates $(^u_i$ and $)^u_i$ at clause $[j]$ have been copied into cells LMATCH$[m_1 + ... + m_{j-1} + u]$ and RMATCH$[m_1 + ... + m_{j-1} + u]$, respectively. So now parallel matching is immediate, and requires $O(n/p)$ time and $O(n)$ space.

An Example: Let $n = 16$ and $p = 4$, and consider the input string

$$\alpha = (_1 (_2 (_3 (_4)_5 (_6)_7 (_8)_9)_{10} (_{11} (_{12})_{13})_{14})_{15})_{16} .$$

The matching tree, whose leaves are the encoded forms of the local unmate strings, is shown in Figure 5. In this figure, $[j]$ is the jth node in the standard numbering, a symbol $\bar{d}\,{}^{\bar{u}}_{\bar{i}}$ $(^u_i d$ at a node encodes the parentheses represented by $)_{\bar{i}}$ and by $(_i$ that are unmatched in the span of the given node. The (r, l) exchanges are indicated by (r, l)-labeled arrows joining the processors at a node, which are drawn above their representative records at the node. Recall that the

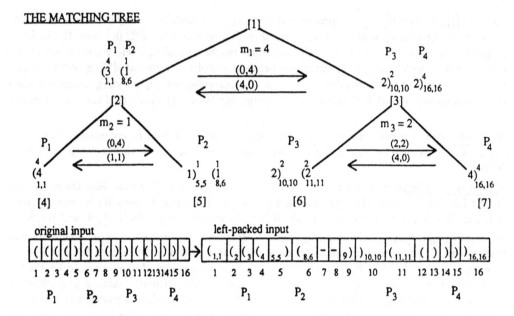

Figure 5. Matching tree and packing, illustrating Algorithm III

elements of the tree do not simultaneously exist in any memory structure, instead they arise one level at a time in the private memories of the processors. Figure 5 also depicts the packing after the initial local matching. During left packing, the representative parentheses (in boldface) are labeled with their original and left-packed indices, the nonrepresentatives with their original indices only. The rest of Algorithm III is traced in Figure 6.

The following lemma summarizes the complexity of the preceding algorithm.

Lemma 3: Algorithm III requires $O(\frac{n}{p} + \log p)$ time and $O(n + p \log p)$ space, employing p processors on the EREW PRAM model. Thus, for $p \leq n/\log n$, the algorithm achieves optimal speedup and its space complexity is $O(n)$.

6   Conclusion

We have presented three polylog-time parallel algorithms for matching parentheses. Algorithms I and III require respectively $O(\log^2 n)$ and $O(\log n)$ time on an EREW PRAM, while Algorithm II runs in $O(\log n)$ time on the CREW model, each employing $\frac{n}{\log n}$ processors. Thus, Algorithms II and III are cost-optimal. All of our algorithms are simple, elegant, and amenable for easy implementation. The continued innovation of such new, parallel algorithms for the parentheses matching problem thus points to the richness of the structure in this important problem which has applications in parsing and expression evaluation. Recently, we have applied parentheses matching algorithm III to designing cost-optimal parallel algorithms for breadth-first traversal of trees and sorting a special class of integers [CD90b].

CALCULATION OF TARGET INDICES AND DUPLICATES

Here we have calculated the m_j, the $m_1 + \ldots + m_j$ and the duplicates for the level 0 and level 1 processors (shown with the nodes at which they are active). For clarity, the entries are displayed in algebraic form rather than as the unrevealing sequence of numbers obtained by setting $m_1 = 4$, $m_2 = 1$, $m_3 = 2$.

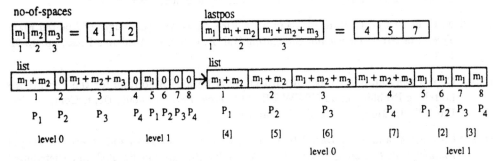

THE MATCH/COPY PHASE

We display the matching arrays after the level 0 and the level 1 processing and briefly trace the actions of the processors, underscoring cells containing honorary representatives and showing which processor filled which cell

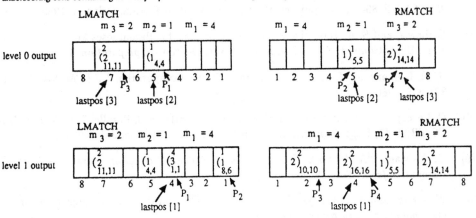

FILLING IN THE GAPS

Since $\frac{n}{2p} = \frac{16}{8} = 2$, the $\frac{n}{2p}$ spacing of the initially scanned cells leads to an initial scanning picture

Fill-in yields:

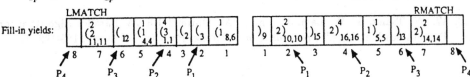

THE MATCHING

Recall that $(_6$ and $)_7$ were matched during the local matching. Now P_4 matches $(_{11}$ with $)_{14}$, P_3 matches $(_{12}$ with $)_{13}$ and $(_4$ with $)_5$, and so on -- all in parallel. So the final MATCH array is:

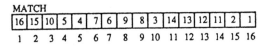

MATCH

16	15	10	5	4	7	6	9	8	3	14	13	12	11	2	1
1	2	3	4	5	6	7	8	9	10	11	12	13	14	15	16

Figure 6. Detailed tracing of Algorithm III

References

[BV85]   I. Bar-On and U. Vishkin, "Optimal Generation of a Computation Tree Form," *ACM Trans. Program. Lang. Syst.*, Vol. 7, No. 2, pp. 659-663, 1985.

[BKR72] N. G. de Bruijn, D. E. Knuth, and S. O. Rice, "The Average Height of Planted Plane Trees," in *Graph theory and Computing* (Ed. R. C. Reid), Academic Press, pp. 15-22, 1972.

[CD90a] C.-Y. Chen and S. K. Das, "A Cost-Optimal Parallel Algorithm for the Parentheses Matching Problem on an EREW PRAM," *Tech. Rep.* N-90-005, Dept. Comput. Sci., Univ. North Texas, Denton, TX, May 1990.

[CD90b] C.-Y. Chen and S. K. Das, "Breadth-First Traversal of Trees and Integer Sorting in Parallel," *Tech. Rep.* CRPDC-90-4, Center for Research in Parallel and Distributed Computing, Dept. Comput. Sci., Univ. North Texas, Denton, TX, Nov. 1990.

[DP89]   N. Deo and S. Prasad, "Two EREW Algorithms for Parentheses Matching," *Tech. Rep.* CS-TR-89-18, Comput.Sci. Dept., Univ. Central Florida, Orlando, 1989.

[LD91]   G. Lewis, and S. K. Das, "Fast Parallel Algorithms for Parentheses Matching," *Tech. Rep.*, Dept. Comput. Sci., Univ. North Texas, Denton, *in preparation*, 1991.

[LF80]   R. E. Ladner and M. J. Fischer, "Parallel Prefix Computation," *JACM*, Vol. 27, pp. 831-838, 1980.

[LP89]   C. Levcopoulos and P. Petersson, "Matching Parentheses in Parallel," *Tech. Rep.* LU-CS-TR:89-47, Dept. Comput. Sci., Lund Univ, Lund, Sweden, July 1989.

[Ma79]   G. A. Mago, "A Network of Computers to Execute Reduction Languages," *Int. J. Comput. Inform. Sci.*, 1979.

[RD90]   W. Rytter and K. Diks, "On Optimal Parallel Computations for Sequences of Brackets," *manuscript*, 14 pages, 1990.

[Sc80]   J. T. Schwartz, "Ultracomputers," *ACM Trans. Program. Lang. Syst.*, Vol. 2, pp. 484-521, Oct. 1980.

[TLC89] W. W. Tsang, T. W. Lam, F. Chin, "An Optimal EREW Parallel Algorithm for Parentheses Matching," *Proc. Int. Conf. Parallel Process.*, Vol. 3, pp. 185-192, 1989.

A Simple Optimal Parallel Algorithm to Solve the

Lowest Common Ancestor Problem

R. Lin
Department of Computer Science
SUNY at Geneseo
Geneseo, NY 14454

S. Olariu
Department of Computer Science
Old Dominion University
Norfolk, VA 23529-0162

Abstract The problem of computing the lowest common ancestors of all pairs of nodes in a rooted tree is central in a large number of practical applications. The purpose of this note is to propose a very simple cost-optimal parallel algorithm to solve the lowest common ancestor problem. More precisely, with an n-node rooted tree as input, our algorithm runs in $O(\log n)$ time using $O(\frac{n^2}{\log n})$ processors in the EREW-PRAM model.

Key Words: ordered trees, list ranking, Euler tour, lowest common ancestors, parallel algorithms, EREW-PRAM.

1. Introduction and background

The problem of finding *lowest common ancestor* (*lca*, for short) information for nodes in a rooted, ordered tree is a recurring theme in a large number of seemingly unrelated problems including detecting negative cycles in sparse networks [6], computing dominators in reducible flow graphs [2], finding a set of fundamental cycles in a network [5], testing planarity, biconnectivity [5,7,10,11], to mention just a few.

It does not come as a surprise, therefore, that the lowest common ancestor problem has received considerable attention in the literature [2,4-11]. In particular, Tsin and Chin [11] propose a parallel algorithm that runs in $O(\frac{n}{k}\log n)$ time using nk processors ($k>0$) in the CREW-PRAM model (for a discussion on the PRAM family the interested reader is directed to [12]). Later, Tsin [10] proposed two algorithms to solve the same problem running in $O(\frac{n^2}{p}\log n)$ and $O(\frac{n^2}{p}+\log n)$ time using p (p>0) processors in the CREW-PRAM model. Recently, Schieber and Vishkin [8] proposed a preprocessing algorithm that allows k lca queries to be answered in $O(\log n)$ time using $\frac{n+k}{\log n}$ processors, provided read conflicts are allowed. Specifically, after $O(\log n)$ preprocessing time with $\frac{n}{\log n}$ processors, they can answer n^2 lca queries in constant CREW time using n^2 processors; by using the standard simulation of an EREW-PRAM their complexity is $O(\log n)$ with $O(n^2)$ EREW processors being, thus, suboptimal.

The purpose of this note is to propose a very simple optimal parallel algorithm that computes the lowest common ancestor information for all pairs of nodes in a rooted, ordered, tree. Central to our algorithm is the result contained in Lemma 1 which shows how the lowest common ancestors are computed when the preorder numbering of the nodes is available. Specifically, our algorithm runs in $O(\log n)$ time using $O(\frac{n^2}{\log n})$ processors in the EREW-PRAM model. Since there are $O(n^2)$ distinct pairs of nodes in an n-node tree, it is easy to see that our algorithm is cost-optimal.

2. The algorithm

Let T be a rooted, ordered tree with n nodes. For convenience, we assume that the tree is stored in an unordered array, every node having a parent pointer along with a doubly linked list of children. It is easy to see [1] that such a representation can be obtained efficiently starting with other, more primitive, representations.

The problem of *list ranking* is to determine in parallel the rank of every element in a given linked list, that is, the number of elements following it in the list. List ranking has turned out to be one of the fundamental techniques in parallel processing, playing a crucial role in a vast array of important parallel algorithms [1,3,9]. In particular, Cole and Vishkin [3] have showed that list ranking can be done optimally in $O(\log n)$ time using $O(\frac{n}{\log n})$

processors in the EREW-PRAM model.

The well-known *Euler-tour technique* developed in [9] allows one to obtain a preorder numbering of the nodes of an ordered tree T by reducing the problem to list ranking. To make our presentation self-contained, we shall present now the details of a variant of this technique. To begin, we replace every node u in T with $d(u)$ children by $d(u)+1$ copies of u, namely $u^1, u^2, ..., u^{d(u)+1}$. Next, letting $w_1, w_2, ..., w_{d(u)}$ stand for the children of u in T, with w_i $(1 \le i \le d(u))$ having d_i children, set for all $i=1,2,...,d(u)$:

- $\text{link}(u^i) \leftarrow w_i^1$,

- $\text{link}(w_i^{d_i+1}) \leftarrow u^{i+1}$.

Finally, set:

- $\text{link}(u^{d(u)+1}) \leftarrow p(u)$.

(here, $p(u)$ is the corresponding copy of the parent of u in T).

Assuming that the root of T has t children, what results is a linked list starting at $\text{root}(T)^1$ and ending at $\text{root}(T)^{t+1}$ with every edge of T traversed exactly once in each direction. Therefore, the total length of the resulting linked list is $2n-2$. It is worth noting that the linked list can be obtained in $O(\log n)$ time using roughly $\dfrac{d(u)}{\log n}$ processors associated with every node in T. Clearly, this translates into a total number of

$$O(\sum_{u \in T} \frac{d(u)}{\log n}) = O(\frac{n}{\log n}) \text{ processors.}$$

To obtain a *preorder* numbering of the nodes in T we only need assign a weight of $+1$ to every u^1 and a weight of 0 to all the others, and compute the weighted rank of every element of the linked list. Since the list has a total length of $O(n)$, this numbering can be obtained in $O(\log n)$ time using $O(\dfrac{n}{\log n})$ processors by using the list ranking algorithm in [3].

For later reference, every node u in T records the interval $[l(u),r(u)]$ with $l(u)$ and $r(u)$ standing for the weighted ranks of u^1 and $u^{d(u)+1}$, respectively. For simplicity, we shall assume, without loss of generality, that the nodes of T are denoted by their preorder number.

In this notation, it is immediate that [l(u),r(u)] denotes all the nodes contained in the sub-tree T_u of T rooted at u. To simplify the notation, we shall let lca(x,y) stand for the lowest common ancestor of nodes x and y.

Let u be an arbitrary node in T with children w_1, w_2, ..., $w_{d(u)}$. The following result is central to our algorithm.

Lemma 1. lca(x,y)=u if, and only if, x (resp. y) coincides with u and y (resp. x) belongs to T_u, or $x \in [l(w_i),r(w_i)]$ and $y \in [l(w_j),r(w_j)]$ ($1 \le i \ne j \le d(u)$).

Proof. First if x and u coincide then, obviously, lca(x,y)=u if, and only if, y belongs to T_u. On the other hand, if neither x nor y is u, then lca(x,y)=u if, and only if, x and y are in distinct subtrees of T_u. The conclusion follows. □

To store the lowest common ancestor information for pairs of nodes in T we shall use a matrix L[1..n,1..n] that we initialize to 0: note that this can be done in O(log n) time using $O(\frac{n^2}{\log n})$ processors in the obvious way. Note that Lemma 1 suggests the following simple algorithm to compute lca(x,y) for all pairs x, y of nodes in T.

Procedure Find-lca(T);
 {Input: a rooted, ordered tree T;
  Output: the matrix L[1..n,1..n] containing lowest common ancestor
        information for all nodes in T}
 1. **begin**
 2.   compute a preorder numbering of all nodes in T;
 3.   **for** all nodes u of T **do in parallel begin**
 4.   compute [l(u),r(u)];
 5.   store [l(w_i),r(w_i)] for all children w_i of u
 6.   **for** all $v \in [l(u),r(u)]$ **do in parallel**
 7.   L[u,v] ← u;
 8.   **for** all $x \in [l(w_i),r(w_i)]$ and $y \in [l(w_j),r(w_j)]$ ($1 \le i < j \le d(u)$) **do in parallel**
 9.   L[x,y] ← u
 10.   **end** {for}
 11.   return(L)
 12. **end**;

Theorem 1. With a rooted, ordered tree T with n nodes as input procedure Find-lca correctly computes the lowest common ancestor of every pair of nodes in T in O(log n) time using $O(\frac{n^2}{\log n})$ processors in the EREW-PRAM model.

Proof. The correctness follows directly from Lemma 1. To argue about the complexity, we note that by our previous discussion lines 4 and 5 can be performed altogether in $O(\log n)$ time using $O(\frac{n}{\log n})$ processors by using the Euler tour technique.

The processors are assigned to the nodes of T in two stages. Initially, we assign to every node u with d(u) children $\lceil \frac{d(u)}{\log n} \rceil$ processors. Note that, altogether, the number of processors allocated to all the nodes in T is $\sum_{u \in T} \lceil \frac{d(u)}{\log n} \rceil \leq \sum_{u \in T} (\frac{d(u)}{\log n} + 1) \leq \lceil \frac{\sum_{u \in T} d(u)}{\log n} \rceil + n \leq$

$\lceil \frac{\sum_{u \in T} d(u)}{\log n} \rceil = \lceil \frac{n-1}{\log n} \rceil + n \in O(\frac{n^2}{\log n}).$

Next, let $\#_i(v)$ stand for $\sum_{i<j \leq d(u)} [r(w_i)-l(w_i)+1]*[r(w_j)-l(w_j)+1]$ Since for all i $(1 \leq i \leq d(u)-1)$, $l(w_{i+1})=1 + r(w_i)$, we can write

$\#_i(u) = [r(w_i)-l(w_i)+1]* \sum_{1<j \leq d(u)} [r(w_j)-l(w_j)+1] = [r(w_i)-l(w_i)+1]*[r(w_{d(u)})-l(w_{i+1})+1].$

To compute all the values $\#_i(u)$ $(1 \leq i \leq d(u)-1)$, we use the $\lceil \frac{d(u)}{\log n} \rceil$ processors $P_1(u)$, $P_2(u)$, ... ,$P_{\lceil \frac{d(u)}{\log n} \rceil}(u)$ allocated to node u. First, we broadcast $r(w_{d(u)})$ to all these processors in $O(\log \frac{d(u)}{\log n}) \subseteq O(\log n)$ time. Next, every processor is responsible for computing, roughly, log n of the $\#_i(u)$'s. Therefore, the total running time is $O(\log n)$. Once this computation has been performed, every node of T releases all its processors.

In the second stage, assign to each node u of T exactly $\sum_{i=1}^{d(u)-1} \lceil \frac{\#_i(u)}{\log n} \rceil$ processors. It is easy to confirm that

$$\sum_{u \in T} \sum_{i=1}^{d(u)-1} \#_i(u) = \frac{n(n-1)}{2}.$$

[To see this, observe that for every node u of T, $\sum_{i=1}^{d(u)-1} \#_i(u)$ counts the number of pairs of nodes in distinct subtrees of T_u. Consequently, $\sum\limits_{u\in T}\sum\limits_{i=1}^{d(u)-1}$ #$_i(u)$ stands for the number of

pairs of nodes in T which is exactly $\dfrac{n(n-1)}{2}$.]

It follows that the total number of processors assigned to all the nodes of T in this

second stage is

$$\sum_{u\in T}\sum_{i=1}^{d(u)-1}\lceil\frac{\#_i(u)}{\log n}\rceil \leq \sum_{u\in T}\sum_{i=1}^{d(u)-1}(\frac{\#_i(u)}{\log n}+1) = \sum_{u\in T}\frac{\sum\limits_{i=1}^{d(u)-1}\#_i(u)}{\log n} + (n-1) = \frac{n(n-1)}{2\log n} + (n-1) \in$$

$O(\dfrac{n^2}{\log n})$ processors.

With this processor assignment, lines 6-7 take $O(\log n)$ time using the first

$\lceil\dfrac{r(v)-l(v)}{\log n}\rceil$ of the processors allocated to every node u of T.

To perform the computation specified in lines 8-9 of the procedure we proceed as fol-

lows. For all 1 $(1\leq i\leq d(u)-1)$ $\lceil\dfrac{\#_i(u)}{\log n}\rceil$ processors are responsible for writing a "u" in the

$\#_i(u) = [r(w_i-l(w_i) +1] * [r(w_{d(u)})-l(w_{i+1}) +1]$ entries of the *rectangular* submatrix

$L[l(w_i)..r(w_i),l(w_{i+1})..r(w_{d(u)})]$.

Obviously, this takes $O(\log n)$ time. Consequently, the entire computation takes

$O(\log n)$ time using at most $O(\dfrac{n^2}{\log n})$ processors. Since no read/write conflicts arise, the

computation can be carried out in the EREW-PRAM model.

This completes the proof of Theorem 1. □

References

1. K. Abrahamson, N. Dadoun, D. G. Kirkpatrick, and T. Przytycka, A simple parallel tree contraction algorithm, *Journal of Algorithms*, 10 (1989) 287-302.

2. A. V. Aho, J. E. Hopcroft, and J. D. Ullman, On finding Lowest Common Ancestors in Trees, *SIAM Journal on Computing*, 5, (1976) 115-132.

3. R. Cole and U. Vishkin, Approximate parallel scheduling. Part I: The basic technique

with applications to optimal parallel list ranking in logarithmic time, *SIAM Journal on Computing*, 17, (1988) 128-142.

4. D. Harel and R. E. Tarjan, Fast algorithms for finding nearest common ancestors, *SIAM Journal on Computing*, 13, (1984) 338-355.

5. J. JaJa and J. Simon, Parallel Algorithms in Graphs Theory: Planarity Testing, *SIAM Journal on Computing*, 11, (1982) 314-328.

6. D. Maier, An efficient method for storing ancestor information in trees, *SIAM Journal on Computing*, 8, (1979) 559-618.

7. C. D. Savage and J. JaJa, Fast, efficient parallel algorithms for some graph problems, *SIAM Journal on Computing*, 10, (1981) 682-691.

8. B. Schieber and U. Vishkin, On finding lowest common ancestors: simplification and parallellization, *SIAM Journal on Computing*, 17 (1988) 1253-1262.

9. R. E. Tarjan and U. Vishkin, An efficient parallel biconnectivity algorithm, *SIAM Journal on Computing*, 14 (1985) 862-874.

10. Y. H. Tsin, Finding lowest common ancestors in parallel, *IEEE Trans. on Computers*, 35 (1986), 764-769.

11. Y. H. Tsin and F. Y. Chin, Efficient Parallel Algorithms for a class of Graph Theoretic Problems, *SIAM Journal on Computing*, 13, (1984) 580-599.

12. U. Vishkin, Synchronous parallel computation - a survey, TR. 71, Department of Computer Science, Courant Institute, NYU, 1983.

Extended Cycle Shrinking: A Restructuring Method For Parallel Compilation

S.Biswas   A.Sanyal   L.M.Tewari

Department of Computer Science and Engineering
Indian Institute of Technology, Bombay 400076, INDIA

Abstract

An important part of a parallelizing compiler is the restructuring phase, which extracts parallelism from a sequential program. We consider an important restructuring transformation, called cycle shrinking [1], which partitions the iteration space of a loop so that the iterations within each partition can be executed in parallel. We propose a new cycle shrinking transformation, called extended cycle shrinking, which is an improvement over the existing methods. We present the conditions under which our method can be applied, and give an algorithm which performs this transformation. Further, we present results to show that our method always leads to a minimal number of partitions, whereas the earlier methods do not. Thus our algorithm is, in this sense, optimal.

1   Introduction And Basic Definitions

In this paper, we shall be concerned with indexed statements only. Let $S_i(I_1, \ldots, I_n)$ represent an indexed statement surrounded by n loops, where I_j represents the index of the jth loop (with lower bound 1 and upper bound N_j). Such a statement has $\prod_{1 \leq j \leq n} N_j$ different instances, one for each value of each of I_j. The order of execution is given by the relation $<$ where $S_i < S_j$ means S_i precedes S_j in execution order. If $S_i(i_1, \ldots, i_n)$ represents an instance of the statement S_i, then $OUT(S_i(i_1, \ldots, i_n))$ and $IN(S_i(i_1, \ldots, i_n))$ denote the set of variable instances defined and used respectively by this statement instance. Two statements $S_i(I_1, \ldots, I_n)$ and $S_j(I_1, \ldots, I_n)$ are involved in a dependence $S_i \delta S_j$ iff there exist index values $(i_1, \ldots, i_n)$ and $(j_1, \ldots, j_n)$, such that $S_i(i_1, \ldots, i_n) < S_j(j_1, \ldots, j_n)$, and
$OUT(S_i(i_1, \ldots, i_n)) \cap IN(S_j(j_1, \ldots, j_n)) \neq \phi$ (flow dependence), or
$IN(S_i(i_1, \ldots, i_n)) \cap OUT(S_j(j_1, \ldots, j_n)) \neq \phi$ (anti dependence), or
$OUT(S_i(i_1, \ldots, i_n)) \cap OUT(S_j(j_1, \ldots, j_n)) \neq \phi$ (output dependence).
In all three cases $S_i(I_1, \ldots, I_n)$ is called the dependence source and $S_j(I_1, \ldots, I_n)$ is called the dependence sink. Note that the dependence $S_i \delta S_j$ could have several different instances.

A program data dependence graph is a directed graph G(V,E), with a set of nodes $V = S_1, \ldots, S_n$ corresponding to statements in the program, and a set of arcs $E = \{(S_i, S_j) | S_i, S_j \in V \text{ and } S_i \delta S_j\}$.

The data dependence graph is used to determine whether loops can be parallelized. A loop whose iterations can execute in parallel is called a DOALL loop.

DO I = 1, N

S_1 :   A [I+5] = B [I] - 1

S_2 :   B [I+4] = A [I] + C [I]

ENDO

(a)

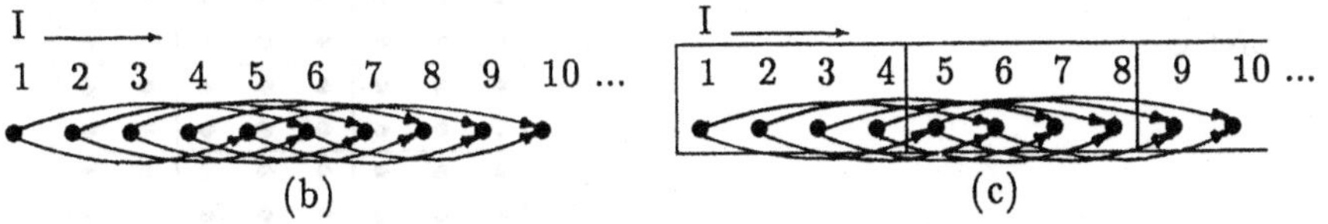

Figure 1: (a) Loop with dependence cycle (b) Dependences shown in iteration space. The top arrows represent dependence instances from S_1 to S_2 and the the bottom arrows from S_2 to S_1. (c) Parts which can be executed in parallel

The body of a loop which does not contain any dependence cycles, can be parallelized using well known transformations such as node splitting. However, if there are cycles of dependences in the body of the loop, then a straightforward parallelization cannot be done, especially if the dependences involved in the cycle are flow dependences [2]. In such cases cycle shrinking can be used.

2   Cycle Shrinking

Loops which contain cycles of data dependences can be parallelized partially, if the gaps between the dependences are known. The method was first discussed in [1]. We now provide a brief description of the method.

Consider the loop shown in Figure 1. Clearly, there is a cycle of dependence between the statements S_1 and S_2. However, since a value generated by S_1 in a particular iteration is used five iterations later by S_2, and similarly a value generated by S_2 is used four iterations later by S_1, we can partition the iteration space into groups of four iterations so that the following important condition is satisfied. There is an ordering of the groups of the partition such that the data items used in iterations of group j are defined in the iterations of groups 1 to $j - 1$. Under such a condition, if all the iterations of groups 1 to $j - 1$ are already done, then the iterations of the group j can be done in parallel. We call such a partition of the iteration space a legal partition and the notion is formalized below.

Definition 2.1 *Consider a partition $P = \{p_1, \ldots, p_m\}$ of the iteration space, i.e. each p_i is a group of iterations such that $p_i \cap p_j$ is empty if $i \neq j$, and $\bigcup_{1 \leq i \leq m} p_i = \mathcal{N}$ (we denote the entire iteration space $N_1 \times N_2 \times, \ldots, N_n$ as $\mathcal{N}$). P is a legal partition, if for any i, the sources of the dependences corresponding to the sinks in p_i are confined to the groups $\{p_j | j < i\}$.*

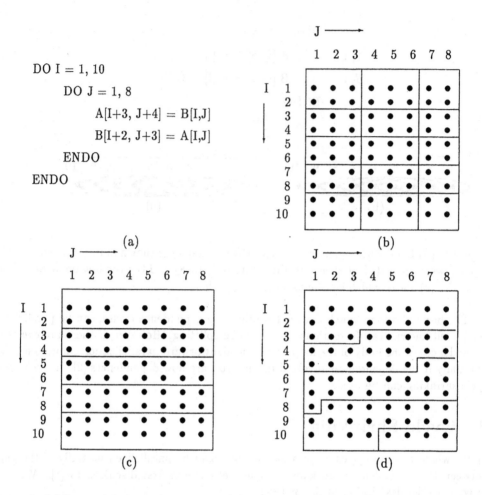

Figure 2: (a) Loop with dependence cycle (b) Partition in simple shrinking (c) Partition in selective shrinking (d) Partition in true distance shrinking

The minimum distance between the source and sink of a dependence, over all dependence instances (four in the example) is called the dependence distance. Figure 1 shows the iteration space of the loop and the iterations which can be done in parallel.

For multiply nested loops, the notion of dependence distance has been extended to a vector, each element of the vector corresponding to a particular loop index. The idea of cycle shrinking has then been extended in three ways. In the case of simple shrinking, the method in the single nested loop case is applied separately at each nest level. In selective shrinking, the outermost level with a positive dependence distance is selected, and simple shrinking is applied at this level. All the inner levels are converted to DOALLs. In the case of true distance shrinking, the partitions of the iterations are created on the basis of true distances; the true distance being the actual number of iterations between the source and sink of dependences, considering the loop bounds at each nest level.

Figure 2 shows an example of a loop, and parts which can be done in parallel in each of the three methods.

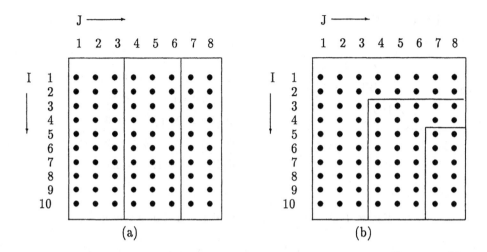

Figure 3: (a) A different partition of the loop in Figure 2(a). (b) Partition created in extended cycle shrinking.

However, a greater degree of parallelism can be achieved in the same example, if we partition the iteration space as shown in Figure 3(a). This reduces the number of groups from $\lceil 10/2 \rceil$ to $\lceil 8/3 \rceil$. It may also be observed that, for this example, $\lceil 8/3 \rceil$ is the minimum number of groups in any legal partition.

This improvement over Polychronopoulos' scheme cannot be done in a straightforward manner because it requires the values of the loop bounds to be known at compile time.

As we shall show in Section 4, selective shrinking and true distance shrinking methods do not always partition the iteration space in a minimal way. The extension proposed in the next section manages to do this.

3 Extended Cycle Shrinking

Our extension to cycle shrinking is based on the observation that, for the loop considered above, the iteration space can be partitioned in the manner shown in Figure 3(b). Notice that this partition is also legal and therefore each of the groups in the partition can be done in parallel. Further, the number of groups in this partition is $min(\lceil 10/2 \rceil, \lceil 8/3 \rceil) = 3$. The transformed loop is shown in Figure 6. As can be seen from the examples, the notion of dependence distance is central to cycle shrinking. As our notion of dependence distance differs from [1], we now formally define this concept.

3.1 Dependence distance

The dependence distance is a measure of the gap between the definition and the use of a data. Consider a pair of statements enclosed in a loop. Since there may be more than one dependence instance between these statements, we associate a dependence distance vector with each dependence instance. After we collect such dependence vectors for all dependence instances in a loop, we summarize this information to obtain the dependence distance vector for the entire loop.

```
        DO I = 1, N
            DO J = 4, M
S₁:             A[I+2, J-3] = B[I,J]
S₂:             B[I+3, J-2] = A[I,J]
            ENDO
        ENDO
```

δ_1: any instance of a dependence between S_1 and S_2

δ_2: any instance of a dependence between S_2 and S_1

$\Phi_1(\delta_1) = 2$, $\Phi_2(\delta_1) = -3$,

$\Phi_1(\delta_2) = 3$, $\Phi_2(\delta_2) = -2$,

$\Phi(L) = <\Phi_1(L), \Phi_2(L)> = <2, -2>$

Figure 4: A loop and its dependence distance vector

Definition 3.1 *Consider a n-nested loop with indices $I_1, I_2 \ldots, I_n$. Let $S_1(i_1, \ldots, i_n)$ (source) and $S_2(j_1, \ldots, j_n)$ (sink) be two statement instances with a dependence δ between them. Then the rth distance $(1 \le r \le n)$ of δ, denoted by $\Phi_r(\delta)$, is given by $\Phi_r(\delta) = j_r - i_r$.*

Notice that $\Phi_r(\delta)$ could be positive ,negative or 0.

The vector $\Phi(\delta) = <\Phi_1(\delta), \Phi_2(\delta), \ldots, \Phi_n(\delta)>$ is called the dependence distance vector for the dependence instance δ.

We now extend the notion of dependence vector to the loop L. Let δ_i denote a dependence instance in L. Then the rth component of the loop dependence vector $\Phi_r(L)$ is defined by

$$\Phi_r(L) = \begin{cases} 0, & \textit{if there exists some dependence instance } \delta_i \\ & \textit{for which } \Phi_r(\delta_i) = 0, \textit{ or there exist two} \\ & \textit{dependence instances } \delta_i \textit{ and } \delta j \textit{ such that} \\ & \Phi_r(\delta_i) \textit{ and } \Phi_r(\delta_j) \textit{ have opposite signs,} \\ min\{|\Phi_r(\delta_i)|\}, & \textit{if } sign(\Phi_r(\delta_i)) \textit{ is positive for all } (\delta_i), \textit{ and} \\ -min\{|\Phi_r(\delta_i)|\} & \textit{otherwise.} \end{cases}$$

The vector $\Phi(L) = <\Phi_1(L), \Phi_2(L), \ldots, \Phi_n(L)>$ is called the dependence distance vector for the loop L. When the loop L being referred to is clear from the context, we shall write Φ instead of $\Phi(L)$.

Our definition of dependence distance can be explained by considering the kind of parallelization that we intend to achieve. For a particular loop index, if the distance of every dependence instance is positive, then we take the minimum of these distances. On the other hand, if every distance is negative then we take the minimum distance ignoring the sign, but also retain the sign information. The reason for retaining the sign information is that it decides the manner in which the iteration space should be partitioned, as can be seen from the example in Figure 4.

Clearly, from the dependences shown in the iteration space in Figure 5(a), the previous method of partitioning would be illegal. For instance, the iterations (1,6) and (4,4), which form the source and sink of a dependence, would belong to the same group of the partition. We get around this problem by partitioning the iteration space in the manner shown in Figure 5(b).

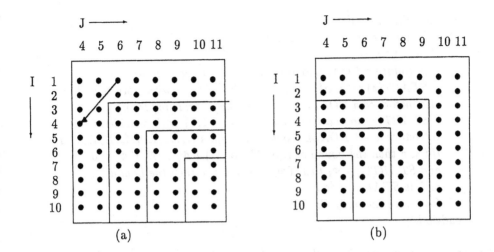

Figure 5: (a) An illegal partition of the loop in Figure 5 (b) A legal partition

It is now easy to see why the dependence distance at a particular index is summarized to 0 when there are two instances, one having a positive distance at this index and the other a negative distance. In such a case, the iterations at this index have to be done serially.

Finally, note that our notion of dependence distance differs from that of [1] in the following respects. Firstly, it takes care of cases where different dependence instances between a pair of statements do not have the same distance. Second, the definition is general enough to handle cycles of anti or output dependence along with flow dependence.

3.2 Algorithm for Extended Cycle Shrinking

We now give the algorithm which will do this transformation.

Input: A n-nested loop L with bounds $N_1, N_2, \ldots, N_n$, body B, and
its dependence distance vector $\Phi(L)$.
Output: A parallelized loop.

1. Introduce an outer serial loop. The loop index k increases from
1 to $min\{\lceil N_i/\Phi_i \rceil \mid 1 \leq i \leq n\}$ with a stride of 1. The body of the loop
is defined by steps 2 and 3.
2. Introduce a DOALL loop with the index i ranging from 1 to n
with stride 1. The body of this loop is given by 2.1.
   2.1 Introduce the statement
      if $\Phi_i \geq 0$ then $START(i) = 1 + (k - 1) * \Phi_i$
      else $START(i) = N_i + (k - 1) * \Phi_i$.
3. Within a PARBEGIN-PAREND construct introduce parallel
statements, each statement being defined by an iteration of the
while loop in step 3.1.

3.1 Start with the index I_1.

  While there are any more indices I_r with $\Phi_r \neq 0$ do
    if $\Phi_r > 0$ then
      introduce a DOALL loop with index I_r ranging from
        $START(r)$ to $min\{START(r) + \Phi_r - 1, N_r\}$ with a stride of 1
    else introduce a DOALL loop with index I_r ranging from
        $START(r)$ to $max\{START(r) + \Phi_r + 1, 1\}$ with a stride of -1;
    Introduce $n - 1$ DOALL loops with indices $I_1, \ldots, I_{r-1}, I_r, I_{r+1}, \ldots, I_n$
    If $i < r$ then the bound of I_i is $START(i) + \Phi_i$ to N_i if $\Phi_i > 0$
    and $START(i) + \Phi_i$ to 1 if $\Phi_i < 0$. If $i > r$ then the bound
    of I_i is $START(i)$ to N_i;
    Introduce the body B;
  endwhile

Our algorithm would transform the loop of Fig. 2. into the loop shown in Figure 6.

It is important to note that, inside the transformed loop, the statements of the body B of the original loop can be executed in parallel. We have not shown this explicitly in the algorithm.

4 Performance Analysis

In this section we first establish the correctness of our algorithm and then prove that it always partitions the iteration space into a minimal number of groups. To keep our proofs simple, we assume that the dependence distance at each index is positive. Consider the group of iterations in the iteration space of the original loop, covered by the kth iteration of the DO loop of step 1. It can be shown that this group, denoted by p_k, is given by $p_k = \bigcup_{1 \leq i \leq n} p_k^i$, where

$$p_k^i = \{\mathbf{X}_{1 \leq j \leq n} I_j \mid \text{ where } I_j = \begin{cases} \{k\Phi_j + 1 \ldots N_j\}, & \text{if } j < i, \\ \{(k-1)\Phi_j + 1 \ldots k\Phi_j\}, & \text{if } j = i, \\ \{(k-1)\Phi_j + 1 \ldots N_j\}, & \text{if } j > i. \end{cases} \tag{1}$$

The notation $\{m \ldots n\}$ denotes the set $\{i \mid m \leq i \leq n\}$, and $\mathbf{X}$ denotes the cross product of sets.

Lemma 4.1 shows that the algorithm divides the iteration space of the original loop into legal partitions.

Lemma 4.1 The partition $P = \{p_k \mid 1 \leq k \leq min\{\lceil N_i/\Phi_i \rceil\}\}$, where p_k is given by equation 1, is a legal partition.

Proof Outline: We first prove that P is a partition of $\mathcal{N}$. It is easy to see that the p_k's are disjoint. To show that $\bigcup p_k = \mathcal{N}$ we use lemma 4.2. Let $k = min\{\lceil N_i/\Phi_i \rceil \mid 1 \leq i \leq n\}$, and assume that this minimum corresponds to the index j. Then $s_k = 0$, because $m_j = 0$.

Consider the group p_k. Let $(x_1, \ldots, x_n)$ be the sink of a dependence in p_k. The closest dependence source for this sink is $(x_1 - \Phi_1, \ldots, x_n - \Phi_n)$. We show that this source cannot belong to p_k; in particular, it belongs to the group p_{k-1}.

```
DO K = 1, min(⌈ 10 / 2 ⌉, ⌈ 8 / 3 ⌉)
   DOALL M = 1, 2
      IF Φ_M ≥ 0 THEN START(M) = 1 + (K − 1) * Φ_M
      ELSE START(M) = N_M − (K − 1) * Φ_M
   ENDOALL
   PARBEGIN
      DOALL I= START(1), min(START(1)+1,10)
         DOALL J= 1,8
            A[I+3,J+4] = B[I,J]
            B[I+2,J+3] = A[I,J]
         ENDOALL
      ENDOALL
      DOALL J= START(2), min(START(2)+2,8)
         DOALL I= START(1)+2, 10
            A[I+3,J+4] = B[I,J]
            B[I+2,J+3] = A[I,J]
         ENDOALL
      ENDOALL
   PAREND
ENDO
```

Figure 6: Transformed loop after extended cycle shrinking for the example in Figure 2(a)

Without any loss of generality assume that $(x_1, \ldots, x_n)$ is in p_k^i for some i. Then, from equation 1, it is easy to see that $(x_1 − \Phi_1, \ldots, x_n − \Phi_n)$ is in p_{k-1}^i.

The partition P is therefore legal.

Lemma 4.2 *The number of iterations remaining after k groups have been removed from the iteration space is given by*

$$s_k = \prod_{1 \leq i \leq n} m_i$$

where $m_i = (N_i − k\Phi_i)$, if $N_i > k\Phi_i$ and 0 otherwise.

Proof Outline: We prove this lemma by an induction on k. For $k = 1$ the size of p_1^i, from equation 1, is $(N_1 − \Phi_1)(N_2 − \Phi_2) \ldots (N_{i-1} − \Phi_{i-1})\Phi_i N_{i+1} \ldots N_n$, if $N_i > \Phi_i$ for all i and $N_1 N_2 \ldots N_n$ otherwise. Therefore

$$s_1 = N_1 N_2 \ldots N_n − \sum_{1 \leq i \leq n} (\prod_{1 \leq j \leq i-1} (N_j − \Phi_j))\Phi_i(\prod_{i+1 \leq j \leq n} N_j)$$

and 0 otherwise. It can be shown after rearranging the terms of the right hand side, that this is the same as $\prod_{1 \leq i \leq n}(N_i − \Phi_i)$.

Assume that the lemma holds for k=r. Then $s_{r+1} = s_r − p_r$. Substituting for the value s_r from the induction hypothesis, and p_r from equation 1, $s_r − p_r$ simplifies to $\prod_{1 \leq i \leq n}(N_i − (k + 1)\Phi_i)$ if $N_i > (k + 1)\Phi_i$ for all i, and 0 otherwise.

Lemma 4.3 *For a multiply nested loop, the partition produced by the algorithm is a minimal legal partition.*

Proof Outline: We have already shown that the partition created by our algorithm is legal. For minimality, consider the situation after k-1 groups have been created by our algorithm (i.e. after completion of k-1 iterations of the outer serial loop). The next group p_k created by the algorithm is maximal in the sense that any iteration contained in the remaining iteration space $\mathcal{N} - \bigcup_{1 \leq i < k} p_i$ is a dependence sink whose source belongs to $\bigcup_{1 \leq i < k} p_i$. We can then show by induction that this property holds for all k between 1 and $min\{\lceil N_i/\Phi_i \rceil \mid 1 \leq i \leq n\}$. The resultant partition is therefore minimal.

We now give an example which shows the worst case behaviour of selective shrinking and true distance shrinking. Consider a loop of nest level 3 with $N_1 = N_2 = N_3 = 50$ and $\Phi = < 2, 3, 5 >$. Then the number of groups created by both selective and true distance shrinking is 25, whereas extended cycle shrinking creates only 10 groups. It is not difficult to see that selective shrinking performs worst when $\lceil N_1/\Phi_1 \rceil \geq \lceil N_i/\Phi_i \rceil$ for all i, and true distance shrinking performs worst when $\lceil N_1/\Phi_1 \rceil \geq \lceil N_2/\Phi_2 \rceil \geq \lceil N_3/\Phi_3 \rceil \ldots \geq \lceil N_n/\Phi_n \rceil$.

5 Conclusions

We have presented a new transformation for nested loops having dependence cycles so that the iteration space gets partitioned into groups, and the iterations within each group can be done in parallel. Our algorithm is an improvement over the existing ones in more than one ways. Firstly, our algorithm always creates a minimal number of groups without assuming any information about the loop bounds. Secondly, our method is general enough to handle dependence cycles involving all three types of dependences, whereas, it appears to us that the existing methods handle cycles of flow dependences only. However none of the cycle shrinking methods (including ours) are applicable for loops containing dependences whose distances are not determinable at compile time.

References

[1] C.D.Polychronopoulos, "Compiler Optimizations for Enhancing Parallelism and Their Impact on Architecture Design", IEEE Transaction on Computers, Vol 37, No. 8, August 1988.

[2] J.R.Allen and K.Kennedy, "Automatic Translation of FORTRAN Programs to Vector Form", ACM Trans. Programming Lang. Syst., Vol 9, October 1987.

Sequential and Distributed Algorithms for the All Pairs Quickest Path Problem[*]

J.B. Rosen[†]   Guo-Liang Xue[‡]

1. Introduction

We have a network $N = (V, A, c, l)$, where $G = (V, A)$ is a simple digraph with n nodes and e arcs, $c(u, v) > 0$ is the *capacity* for an arc $(u, v) \in A$, $l(u, v) \geq 0$ is the *lead time* for an arc $(u, v) \in A$. The quickest path problem considered is that of finding a path to send a given amount of data from one node to another in shortest possible time. We assume that the r distinct capacity values of the given network are $c_1 < c_2 < \cdots < c_r$.

For a $v_1 - v_k$ path $p = (v_1, v_2, \ldots, v_k)$, the *lead time* and *capacity* of path p are $l(p) = \sum_{i=1}^{k-1} l(v_i, v_{i+1})$ and $c(p) = \min_{1 \leq i \leq k-1} c(v_i, v_{i+1})$, respectively. The *total transmission time* to send $\sigma \, (> 0)$ units of data from v_1 to v_k through path p is $T(\sigma, p) = l(p) + \dfrac{\sigma}{c(p)}$. A *quickest path* to send σ units of data is one which has minimum total transmission time.

This quickest path problem model was proposed by Chen and Chin [1]. It is a nontrivial generalization of the shortest path problem model. Two extreme cases of the quickest path problem are the *largest capacity path problem* and the *shortest lead time path problem*.

In this paper, we study algorithms for the all pairs quickest path problem for all σ values. In section 2, we present a Floyd like $O(rn^3 + r^2n^2)$ sequential algorithm. In section 3, the sequential algorithm is parallelized to run on a hypercube multiprocessor. With $p \, (\leq n^2)$ processors, the theoretical speedup of our parallel algorithm can be as high as p, for sufficiently large n. The scaled speedup of our parallel algorithm is also shown to be very good. Experimental computations are carried out on a 64-processor NCUBE hypercube.

2. A Sequential Algorithm for the All Pairs Problem

For any positive number w, define $N(w) = (V, A(w), c, l)$ to be a subnetwork of N, where $(u, v) \in A(w)$ if and only $(u, v) \in A$ and $c(u, v) \geq w$. For any pair of nodes u and v in $N(w)$, the shortest $u - v$ path in $N(w)$ with respect to the weight function l will be called the *shortest $u - v$ path in $N(w)$*.

---

[*] This is a summary of results. The complete paper is available as a Technical Report of the Computer Science Department at the University of Minnesota. The authors of this paper are listed according to alphabetical order.

[†] Computer Science Department, University of Minnesota, Minneapolis, MN 55455, USA. E-mail: rosen@cs.umn.edu.

[‡] Computer Science Department, University of Minnesota, Minneapolis, MN 55455, USA. E-mail: xue@cs.umn.edu. Institute of Operations Research, Qufu Normal University, Qufu, Shandong, PRC.

Theorem 2.1. (Rosen, Sun, Xue[8]) Let p_j be a shortest $s - t$ path in $N(c_j)$, $j = 1, ..., r$. Let

$$l(p_l) + \sigma/c(p_l) = \min_{1 \le j \le r} \{l(p_j) + \sigma/c(p_j)\} . \tag{2.1}$$

Then p_l is a quickest $s - t$ path in N to send σ units of data. $\square$

Using this theorem, we can modify Floyd's all pairs shortest path algorithm to compute the all pairs shortest paths in each $N(c_k)$. In particular, the lead time and capacity from i to j in $N(c_k)$ are stored in $L[i, j, k]$ and $C[i, j, k]$, respectively. Given any pair of nodes i and j, and a positive σ, the total transmission time to send σ units of data from i to j is given by

$$f(i, j, \sigma) = \min_{\substack{1 \le k \le r \\ C[i,j,k] > 0}} \{L[i, j, k] + \sigma/C[i, j, k]\} , \tag{2.2}$$

and a quickest path is the shortest path in $N(c_k)$, where k is the largest index which takes the minimum in (2.2). Note that $f(i, j, \sigma)$ is a piecewise linear concave function of σ. The number of linear pieces is no more than r. Therefore the time complexity of this sequential algorithm is $O(rn^3 + r^2 n^2)$.

3. Distributed Algorithm and Implementation

Since our quickest path algorithm makes use of the all pairs shortest path algorithm. Techniques used in parallel shortest path algorithms [2-7] might be used to parallelize our quickest path algorithm. In particular, an analog of the rectangle partition of [4] is used to derive a hypercube implementation of the quickest path algorithm. With $p(\le n^2)$ processors, the theoretical speedup of our algorithm is

$$\frac{p}{1 + O(\frac{\sqrt{p}\log_2 p}{n + r}) T_{send} + O(\frac{p\log_2 p}{nr(n + r)}) T_{start}} , \tag{3.1}$$

where T_{start} is the start up time and T_{send} is the time to transfer a unit packet. We can easily see that for any given number p of processors and any given efficiency $eff < 1$, our parallel algorithm can achieve a efficiency of eff with p processors on the all pairs quickest path problem provided $n + r = O(\frac{eff}{1 - eff}\sqrt{p}\log_2 p)$. This shows that our parallel algorithm has very good scaled speedup [5].

The parallel algorithm was coded in FORTRAN and implemented on an NCUBE/7 hypercube with 64 processors with randomly generated test problems. Because of the limited local memory, the largest problem we could solve on a single processor is $n = 64$ and $r = 5$. With this problem size, a speedup of nearly 30 was achieved by using all 64 processors. To measure scaled speedup, we make use of all the local memories. To be specific, we double the number of nodes n in the network whenever we double the number of processors. In this way, problems of size $n = 512$ and $r = 5$ were solved using all 64 processors. The results with $r = 5$ are illustrated in Table 3.1.

From Table 3.1, it is clear that for any fixed value of n, the speedup increases as the number of processors increases (provided that n is suitably large). Also, for fixed p, the speedup increases as n increases and then finally approaches p (if there is enough local memory for large n). For fixed value of

n	p=1	p=2	p=4	p=8	p=16	p=32	p=64
16	1.62	0.97	0.75	0.49	0.46	0.53	0.62
32	11.72	6.15	3.41	2.03	1.39	1.19	1.16
64	89.34	45.48	23.33	12.48	6.98	4.43	3.21
128	—	—	178.29	91.29	47.28	25.70	14.77
256	—	—	—	—	357.05	183.69	95.97
512	—	—	—	—	—	—	716.79

Table 3.1. Time (secs) used with $r=5$ and different n and p.

r, the time complexity of our parallel algorithm is approximately $O(n^3/p)$. Therefore the time used must be quadrupled each time p and n are both doubled. Looking at the diagonal elements of the table, we find that the time used is no more than quadrupled each time p and n are doubled. This confirms our analysis that the parallel algorithm scales well.

Acknowledgment

This research was supported in part by the Air Force Office of Scientific Research grand AFOSR-87-0127 and a University of Minnesota Graduate School Doctoral Dissertation Fellowship. Thanks are due to Professors S. Sahni and V. Kumar for providing useful references.

References

[1]   Chen, Y.L. and Chin, Y.H., The Quickest Path Problem, *Computers and Operations Research*, Vol. 17 (1990), 153-161.

[2]   Deo, N. and Pang, C., Shortest Path Algorithms: Taxonomy and Annotation, *Networks*, Vol. 14(1984), 244-253.

[3]   Deo, N., Pang, C.Y. and Lord, R.E., Two Parallel Algorithms for Shortest Path Problems, *Proceedings of ICPP*(1980), 244-253.

[4]   Jenq, J. and Sahni, S., All Pairs Shortest Paths on a Hypercube Multiprocessor, *Proceedings of ICPP*(1987), 713-716.

[5]   Kumar, V. and Singh, V., Scalability of Parallel Algorithms for the All Pairs Shortest Path Problem: A Summary of Results, *Proceedings of ICPP*(1990), 136-140.

[6]   Paige, R.C. and Kruskal, C.P., Parallel Algorithms for Shortest Path Problems, *Proceedings of ICPP*(1985), 14-20.

[7]   Quinn, M.J. and Deo, N., Parallel Graph Algorithms, *Computing Surveys*, Vol. 16(1984), 319-348.

[8]   Rosen, J.B., Sun, S.-Z., Xue, G.-L., The Quickest Path Problem and the Enumeration of Quickest Paths, to appear in *Computers and Operations Research*.

An Efficient Approximation Algorithm for Hypercube Scheduling*

A. Boals, A. Gupta, J. Hashmi, and N. Sherwani
Department of Computer Science
Western Michigan University, Kalamazoo, MI 49008

Abstract

Given a set of m tasks, where each task has an execution time and a subcube requirement, the Hypercube Scheduling Problem (HSP) is to find an assignment of tasks which minimizes the total completion time. The general HSP is known to be NP-hard. In this paper, we present a $O(m \log m)$ time algorithm for HSP when all the m tasks have the same execution time. We also present a polynomial time approximation algorithm which generates a solution within $\frac{2}{(1+\frac{1}{2^n})}$ of the optimal solution for the general HSP, where n is the hypercube dimension.

1 INTRODUCTION

Hypercube is currently considered the most popular parallel architecture. This is partly due to good underlying graph properties of hypercubes. Hypercubes of dimension n have 2^n nodes, n-diameter, n-connectivity and the maximum degree of a node is also n. These properties allow hypercubes to be used in a versatile manner for a wide range of applications. Several practical algorithms have been implemented on hypercubes demonstrating its efficiency and flexibility. One of the important problems in parallel algorithm design is to develop an efficient schedule of the interacting tasks of an algorithm. This problem is usually referred to as the minimum completion time (schedule length) multiprocessor scheduling problem (MSP), and it has been studied extensively by a number of researchers [1, 2, 6, 8, 9, 11]. In this paper, we consider various solutions to the MSP for hypercube multiprocessors. Before giving the details of our results, let us first define the problem precisely.

Let x_i be a task which is to be scheduled on a hypercube and let $MD(x_i)$ be the minimum subcube size on which x_i may execute. Let $X = \{x_1, x_2, x_3, \ldots, x_m\}$ be the set of tasks to be scheduled on an n-dimensional hypercube. Let $T(x_i)$ be the execution time of x_i on a subcube of dimension $MD(x_i)$. We assume that all the tasks are scalable and $\psi(x_i, d_i)$ is the speedup function which gives the speedup for the task x_i when it uses a subcube of dimension d_i. A task is said to be scalable, if the subcube requirement of the task can be changed dynamically and often increasing the subcube size the execution time of the task decreases [2]. For simplicity we assume that $\psi(x_i, d_i) < \psi(x_i, d_i + 1)$, $1 \leq i \leq m$. An schedule $S = \{x_{\pi(1)}, x_{\pi(2)}, x_{\pi(3)}, \ldots, x_{\pi(m)}\}$ is a sequence of tasks $x_i \in X$ arranged in the order of their starting times on the hypercube. Let $T_0(S)$ be the time at which the first task $x_i \in X$ starts and $f_{x_i}(S)$ is the finish time of task x_i according to the

---

*Research Supported in part by fellowships from the Faculty Research and Creative Activities Support Fund WMU-FRCASF 90-15 and WMU-FRCASF 89-225274, and by the National Science Foundation under grant USE-90-52346.

TABLE I

Problem No.	Number of Processors	Task Processing Times	Complexity
1.	arbitrary	equal	$O(n)$
2.	Fixed > 2	$t_i = 1$ or 2	NP-hard
3.	arbitrary	arbitrary	NP-hard

schedule S. The completion time of a schedule S is defined as $F(S) = \max\{f_{x_i}(S) | \forall x_i \in X\}$ is the latest time when any task $x_i \in X$ finishes. Given a set of tasks, the hypercube task scheduling problem (HSP) is to find S which minimizes $F(S)$.

It is well known that MSP is computationally hard; i.e., NP-hard. Hence it is easy to see HSP is also a NP-hard problem. In fact, scheduling hypercube multiprocessors is further complicated due to subcube recognition and fragmentation problems. In case of scheduling a single task requiring a subcube of dimension d_i on a hypercube, in which several tasks are already executing, one not only finds the required number of free processors but makes sure that they should also form a subcube of dimension d_i [3, 4, 5]. The problem of fragmentation of hypercube arises due to dynamic nature of allocation and deallocation of subcubes. In a fragmented hypercube one may have sufficient number of nodes but they may not form a subcube [7]. In order to develop a schedule that minimizes completion time, we have to consider several factors such as subcube size and task execution time. In addition, a good schedule should minimize fragmentation. To the best of our knowledge, this is the first attempt to find an approximation algorithm for the HSP.

In this paper, we present a $O(m \log m)$ time algorithm for the Hypercube Scheduling Problem when all the tasks have the same execution time. We also present a polynomial time approximation algorithm which generates a solution within $\frac{2}{1+\frac{1}{2^n}}$ of the optimal solution for the general HSP.

In the next section we prove the NP-completeness of the HSP. In Section 3, we consider the restricted subproblems of the HSP. We show that when all the tasks have same dimension the HSP problem still remains NP-hard, but when all the tasks have the same execution time then we show that there exist a polynomial time solution to the HSP. We then present the main result of this paper, an efficient approximation algorithm. In Section 4, we show that our algorithm provides near optimal solution.

2 NP-Completeness of the HSP

The minimum completion time (schedule length) multiprocessor scheduling problem (MSP) is known to be difficult to solve and is generally intractable; it is well known that some relaxed or simplified subproblems (constructed from the original scheduling problem by imposing a variety of restricting conditions) still fall into the class of NP-hard problems [1, 8]. The difficulty of scheduling varies with the inclusion or exclusion of pre-emption, the number of processors, and attributes of tasks such as the uniformity of the task processing times. Almost all problems relaxed or simplified by imposing some restricting conditions are known to be NP-hard. These results are summarized in Table I.

Theorem 1 *The Hypercube Scheduling Problem (HSP) is NP-hard, and remains so if all the tasks need same size subcubes to execute.*

Proof: It can be easily shown that if all tasks need same size subcubes to execute, then the HSP reduces to multiprocessor scheduling Problem 3 in Table I above. The main idea is to view the

TABLE II

Problem No.	Task Dimension	Task Processing Times	Complexity	Reference
1.	equal	equal	$O(n)$	Coffman [1]
2.	equal	1 or 2	NP-hard	Garey [10]
3.	equal	arbitrary	NP-Hard	Graham [11]
4.	arbitrary	equal	polynomial	This paper
5.	arbitrary	arbitrary	NP-hard	This paper

hypercube Q_n as composed of 2^n processors and then use the proof of Problem 3. We omit the details. ∎

In Section 3 we show that if every task has the same execution time then the HSP can be solved in polynomial time, and in particular $O(m \log m)$ time for m task scheduling. In Table II we have summarized all the relaxed subproblems of the HSP.

In this section, we have shown the NP-completeness of the HSP problem. In the next section, we give a polynomial time algorithm for relaxed subproblems of HSP.

3 Task Scheduling With Relaxed Parameters

An optimal schedule must take into consideration both the subcube dimension required and the execution time of each task. However, as we have shown in the previous section optimizing both parameters is an NP-hard problem. In many situations, one may not have a general HSP but a restricted version of HSP. For example, if several users are running the same application then the subcube dimension required by each user in this type of multi-user environment would be same, but, execution time may vary for each user. In this section, we consider two special cases of hypercube task scheduling. First we consider the case when all the tasks have same execution times. We show that this restricted version of HSP is not NP-hard by presenting an algorithm which finds an optimal schedule in polynomial time. Next we consider the case when all the tasks have same subcube dimensions. In this case, the HSP reduces to p identical processors minimum finish time problem. This restricted version of HSP remains NP-hard, but there exists an approximation algorithm which finds the near optimal schedule [9].

3.1 Fixed Execution Time

In this section we consider the hypercube scheduling problem when all the tasks have the same execution times, that is, $T(x_i) = c$ for some constant c and $x_i \in X$. In this case the only criteria for selecting a task is dimension of the subcube required. Selecting tasks arbitrarily may result in an internal fragmentation which we define below.

Definition 1 Internal Fragmentation: *If at any instance a task x_i which requiring a subcube of size d_i is to be scheduled and there are at least 2^{d_i} processors available but they do not form a subcube of dimension d_i, then the hypercube is said to be internally fragmented.*

In the case of HSP an efficient ordering of tasks is very critical because an arbitrary ordering would produce fragmentation which may increase the total completion time. Thus, an algorithm which will minimizes the internal fragmentation can guarantee an optimal solution for the HSP when all the jobs have same execution time.

Algorithm, *Find-Seq*, given below guarantees that as long as there are enough tasks available the hypercube would never be fragmented. The basic idea behind *Find-Seq* is to find sets of tasks such that the total processor requirements for every set is 2^n.

Algorithm Find-Seq (SQ, n)

> (⋆ *This algorithm takes a sequence SQ as the input and returns*
> *an integer q such that sum of first q elements of SQ in 2^n ⋆*)

begin Find-Seq
   $q \leftarrow 1$
   while $(a_1 \neq 2^n)$ **do** {
      select minimum value of i such that
         $\exists j$ and $a_i = a_j = 2^p$, $1 \le i < j \le r, p \le n$.
      if no such i exists then declare failure, exit.
        (⋆ *all a_i's are distinct* ⋆)
      else { (⋆ a_i *found* ⋆)
         $q \leftarrow q + 1$
         $a_i = a_i + a_j$
         delete a_j from SQ
      }
   }
   return (q)
end Find-Seq

In order to prove the correctness of the above algorithm, we show that *Find-Seq* can always find sequence of tasks such that the total processor requirement is 2^n.

Theorem 2 *Given a sequence $SQ = a_1, a_2, \ldots, a_r$ such that $\forall a_i = 2^{d_i}, a_i \ge a_{i+1}, d_i \le n$, and $N = 2^{d_1} + 2^{d_2} + \ldots + 2^{d_r}$, algorithm* Find-Seq *finds an integer q, such that $SQ_1 = a_1, a_2, \ldots, a_q$ such that $\sum_{i=1}^{q} a_i = 2^n$ provided that $N \ge 2^n$.*

Proof: When algorithm *Find-Seq* terminates successfully it returns a value q, $1 \le q \le r$ such that $\sum_{i=1}^{q} a_i = 2^n$, $a_i \in SQ$.

If Algorithm *Find-Seq* fails then all d_i's are distinct *i.e* $d_1 > d_2 > d_3 \ldots$. Clearly $N \le 2^{d_1+1} - 1$. Since $d_1 < n$ we have $N \le 2^{d_1+1} - 1 < 2^n$, which contradicts the assumption that $N \ge 2^n$. ∎

Lemma 1 *Let $X = \{x_1, x_2, x_3, \ldots, x_m\}$ be a set of tasks and Y be a sequence which represents a permutation of the tasks of X arranged in the descending order of dimensions. Then, Y gives the order of tasks for schedule S_{max} such that $F(S_{max}) = F(OPT)$.*

Proof: Let us assume that the execution time of each task is k. At the beginning, the hypercube can be fully loaded, (*i.e.* no processors are idle). *Find-Seq* is called to find a set of tasks such that entire hypercube could be allocated. After k time units all of these tasks will complete so *Find-Seq* is called again with the remaining tasks. The above process will be repeated until there are not enough tasks available to fully load the hypercube. All the processors of the hypercube remained allocated until the last cycle, in which some of the processors may not be allocated. It is clear that we can not reduce the fragmentation produced in the last cycle.

As the hypercube was fully loaded all the times, except the last cycle in which there are not enough tasks available, we conclude that it is not possible to find a better schedule. ∎

From the above lemma it is clear that executing the tasks in the descending order of dimension will result in a minimum completion time. Next we show that executing the tasks in the ascending order of dimension will also result in a minimum completion time.

Lemma 2 *Let $X = \{x_1, x_2, x_3, \ldots, x_m\}$ be a set of tasks and Z be a sequence which represents a permutation of tasks of X arranged in the ascending order of dimensions. Then, Z gives the order of tasks for schedule S_{min} such that $F(S_{min}) = F(OPT)$.*

Proof: Argument is similar to Lemma 1 and hence omitted. ∎

From the above two lemmas we conclude Theorem 3.

Theorem 3 *Let $X = \{x_1, x_2, x_3, \ldots, x_m\}$ be a set of tasks, let S_{max} be schedule obtained from a sequence of tasks of X arranged in the descending order of dimension and let S_{min} be the schedule obtained from a sequence of tasks of X arranged in the ascending order of dimension then $F(S_{max}) = F(S_{min}) = F(OPT)$.*

Proof: Follows from Lemmas 1 and 2. ∎

From Theorem 3 we can see that an optimal schedule can be found either by arranging the tasks in the descending order of dimension or an ascending order of dimension. Such a schedule can be found in only $O(m \log m)$ time, where m is the number of tasks.

3.2 Fixed Subcube Dimension

When all the tasks have same subcube dimensions, the HSP problem reduces to the minimum finish time schedule on n identical processors. Obtaining minimum finish time schedule on $p, p \geq 2$ identical processors is NP-hard. In [9], Graham has given an approximation algorithm *LPT* (Longest Processing Time) that finds a schedule with finish time very close to that of an optimal schedule.

The *LPT* is a list scheduling algorithm, it uses a list of tasks and builds a feasible schedule. The tasks are sorted into descending order by dimension. Whenever a processor becomes free, it allocates that processor to the next largest task among the tasks which are not allocated. The *LPT* algorithm guarantees a solution within $(\frac{4}{3} - \frac{1}{3p})$ of the optimal solution. The *LPT* algorithm can be implemented in time $O(m \log m + m \log p)$ where p is the number of processors and m is the number of tasks.

4 Task Scheduling with Arbitrary Execution Time and Subcube Dimension

We have already seen in Section 2 that the problem of finding a minimum completion time schedule is NP-hard when both the execution time and subcube dimension are arbitrary. In this section we give an efficient approximation algorithm to find a minimum completion time schedule and prove that it produces a schedule S with the guarantee that $F(S) \leq \frac{2F(OPT)}{(1+\frac{1}{2^r})}$.

When both subcube dimension and execution time are arbitrary, algorithm *Find-Seq* can be used to produce an schedule S in which there would not be any internal fragmentation. However, consider a scenario in which a task x_i with large execution time is scheduled towards the end in S. In this situation, the total completion time of S is greater than the optimal schedule. Furthermore, many processors may be idle towards the end of S due to the internal fragmentation. One way to resolve this problem is to schedule these types of tasks earlier in the schedule, but this may lead to internal fragmentation resulting in an overall increase in the total completion time. Hence, we need to device another strategy to solve this problem.

Another way to resolve this problem is to increase the subcube dimension requirement for those tasks before starting the scheduling. This forces the problematic tasks to appear earlier in the schedule resulting in no internal fragmentation.

Almost all practical algorithms developed for running on the hypercube systems are scalable and often increasing the number of processors assigned to a task leads to execution time decrease.

In this section, we assume that all the tasks $x_i \in X$ are scalable and we also assume that $\psi(x_i, d_i) < \psi(x_i, d_i + 1)$. We now present an algorithm, *Schedule*, which dynamically increases the size of subcube assigned to a task in the hope that the overall completion time would decrease. In fact, if the completion time decreases our algorithm changes the task assignment leading to a near optimal solution. The basic idea behind *Schedule* is to first find the average processing load per processor and then to decrease the execution time of all tasks having execution time higher than the average by increasing their minimum subcube requirement.

If X is to be scheduled on an n-dimension hypercube then the average load for each processor is $AVG(S) = \dfrac{1}{2^n} \displaystyle\sum_{i=1}^{m} \dfrac{T(x_i).2^{d_i}}{\psi(x_i, d_i)}$ where d_i is the size of the subcube currently allocated to x_i.

Schedule uses the maximum dimension first strategy of Section 3.1 and hence there is no internal fragmentation. Algorithm *Schedule* is given on the next page, the discussion and detail follow.

Algorithm Schedule accepts the set of tasks X as the input and returns a sequence S which is a permutation of X. Executing jobs in the order given by S results in a near optimal solution. At Step 1, *Schedule* finds the average load per processor assuming that each task will execute on $MD(x_i)$ size subcube. Before starting scheduling, at Step 2, the execution time of all the longer tasks, *i.e.* tasks having $\dfrac{T(x_i).2^{MD(x_i)}}{\psi(x_i, MD(x_i))}$ greater than the average load per processor, is reduced by increasing their minimum dimension $MD(x_i)$. At the next step, *Schedule* selects enough tasks to keep all the processors busy *i.e.* minimize internal fragmentation. At Step 5, *Schedule* finds the task on the current schedule which has largest speedup function. At the next step we check whether increasing the size of the subcube currently assigned to the selected task will help reduce the completion time of the schedule developed so far. A new schedule is produced at Step 7 by simply increasing $D_s(x_i)$ for the task with the maximum speedup, all the tasks having $D_s(x_i)$ greater than this task are also included in the new schedule. If there are more processors available then more tasks are included in this new schedule. If the completion time of this new schedule is smaller than the completion time of the old schedule then it is accepted as the current schedule otherwise the changes are rejected. Step 8 is the only terminating point of the algorithm, if all the tasks are scheduled at that step then *Schedule* returns the current sequence as the valid schedule, otherwise it moves the schedule time to the next time any task will finish and when some processors become available.

In order to show that the algorithm *Schedule* produces a schedule S (a permutation of the tasks in X) whose completion time is within $\dfrac{2}{(1+\frac{1}{2^n})}$ of the optimal completion time. We first prove two lemmas which establish lower and upper bounds on $F(S)$, the completion time of S. Lemma relationship between the average load computed in Step 1 of *Schedule*. Finally, by using Lemmas 3, 4, 5 and 6, we establish the near optimality result of *Schedule*.

Lemma 3 *For every schedule S produced by the algorithm* **Schedule**, *$F(S) \geq AVG(S)$.*

Proof: We need to consider two cases; first all tasks have the same execution time, second they have different execution times. In the first case, if $\displaystyle\sum_{i=1}^{m} 2^{d_i} = 2^n$ then we have $F(S) = AVG(S)$, otherwise $F(S) > AVG(S)$, where m is the number of tasks and n is the hypercube dimension. In the second case, tasks have different execution times and hence let us consider a situation in which we have only two tasks, a and b. Let the execution time of a be greater than that of b. The average time of a and b is less than the execution time of a. Hence in this case we can conclude that $F(S) > AVG(S)$. The lemma now follows. ∎

A task with large execution time and scheduled towards the end of the schedule can increase the total completion time of the schedule. We now show how this effects the completion time. Let w be the execution time of a task with the maximum execution time among all the tasks finishing precisely at $F(S)$ *i.e.* $w = \max\{\dfrac{T(x_i).2^{D_s(x_i)}}{\psi(x_i, D_s(x_i))} | \forall x_i \in S \text{ and } f_{x_i}(S) = F(S)\}$. The effect of such a task on the total completion time can be seen from the next lemma.

Algorithm Schedule (X)
(⋆ *Schedule takes the set of tasks 'X' as input and returns a near optimal Schedule 'S'* ⋆)
begin Schedule
1. (⋆ *find the average load per processor* ⋆)
$$\text{AVG} \leftarrow \frac{1}{2^n}\sum_{i=1}^{m} T(x_i)2^{MD(x_i)}; \quad \forall x_i \in X$$
2. (⋆ *increase subcube size for all the tasks with execution time more than the average* ⋆)
for all $x_i \in X$ and $\frac{T(x_i)}{\psi(x_i, MD(x_i))} > \text{AVG}$ **do** {
    while ($\frac{T(x_i)2^{MD(x_i)}}{\psi(x_i, MD(x_i))} > \text{AVG}$ and $MD(x_i) \neq n$) $MD(x_i) \leftarrow MD(x_i) + 1$
}
3. (⋆ *initialize S:Schedule, t:current time . . .*⋆)
$S \leftarrow \emptyset$, t $\leftarrow 0$, p $\leftarrow$n, $f_{x_i}(S) \leftarrow$ t, $D_S(x_i) \leftarrow MD(x_i)\forall x_i \in X.$
repeat
4. (⋆ *pick tasks with the maximum dimension first criteria* ⋆)
    while ($\sum_{x_i \in S, f_{x_i}(S) > t} 2^{MD(x_i)} < 2^p$ and $|S| \neq m$)**do** {
        $S \leftarrow S + x_i$ such that $D_S(x_i) \geq D_S(x_j)$; $\forall x_i, x_j \in X$ and $x_i \notin S$
    }
5. (⋆ *find a task from S which gives maximum speedup* ⋆)
    $B \leftarrow x_i$ such that $\frac{T(x_i)2^{D_S(x_i)+1}}{\psi(x_i, D_S(x_i)+1)} \geq \frac{T(x_j)2^{D_S(x_j)+1}}{\psi(x_j, D_S(x_j)+1)}$; $x_i, x_j \in S$, and $f_{x_i}(S), f_{x_j}(S) >$ t
    $L \leftarrow f_B(S)$
6. (⋆ *check if x_i can directly affect the completion time* ⋆)
    if $F(S) \neq L$ **then** skip 7
7. (⋆ *make new schedule in which the subcube size for the task with max. speedup is* ⋆)
    (⋆ *increased. If new schedule reduces the completion time then accept it, else reject.* ⋆)
    $S' \leftarrow \{x_i | x_i \in S$ and $D_S(x_i) > D_S(B)\}$
    if ($\sum_{x_i \in S'} 2^{D_S(x_i)} + 2^{D_S(B)+1}) \leq 2^p$) **then** {
        $S' \leftarrow S' + \{B\}$; $D_S(B) \leftarrow D_S(B) + 1$
        while ($\sum_{x_i \in S'} 2^{D_S(x_i)} < 2^p$ and $|S| \neq m$) **do** {
            a $\leftarrow \{x_i | x_i \in S, x_i \notin S', D_S(x_i) \geq D_S(x_j), \forall x_i, x_j \in S \}$
            $S' \leftarrow S' + \{ a \}$
        }
        if $F(S') < F(S)$ **then** $S \leftarrow S'$ (⋆ *accept the new schedule* ⋆)
    }
8. (⋆ *if more tasks to be scheduled then move to the next open slot in the schedule* ⋆)
    if $|S| \neq m$ **then** { (⋆ *there are more tasks to be scheduled* ⋆)
        t $\leftarrow \min\{f_{x_i}(S)|x_i \in S$ and $f_{x_i}(S) > $ t $\}$
        p $\leftarrow \log_2(2^n - \sum_{x_i \in S, f_{x_i}(S) > t} 2^{D_S(x_i)})$
    }
until ($|S| \neq m$)
return schedule S
end Schedule

Lemma 4 *If S is a schedule produced by algorithm* **Schedule** *and w is the execution time of the task x_w with maximum execution time among all the tasks finishing exactly at F(S) then* $F(S) \leq AVG(S) + w(1 - \frac{1}{2^n})$.

Proof: Let y be the time at which the task x_w starts according to the schedule S, then we know that $y \geq w$. Let $\overline{AVG}(S)$ be the average of all the tasks starting before time y, then $F(S) - w \leq \overline{AVG}(S)$ and $\overline{AVG}(S) \leq AVG(S) - \frac{w}{2^n}$. From the above two relations we can see that $F(S) - w \leq AVG(S) - \frac{w}{2^n}$ which implies that $F(s) \leq AVG(S) + w(1 - \frac{1}{2^n})$. ∎

Now, we use the above lemma to derive a relation between the completion time of a schedule and the average load per processor in that schedule.

Lemma 5 *If S is a schedule produced by algorithm* **Schedule** *then $F(S) \leq \frac{2AVG(S)}{(1+\frac{1}{2^n})}$.*

Proof: In Step 2 of the algorithm Schedule we make sure that either the execution time of all the tasks is less than the average time or we have allocated the entire hypercube, Q_n, to a task. In the second case it is guaranteed that such a task is executed before any smaller tasks, therefore it can not have the property $f_S(x_i) = F(S)$. Therefore $AVG(S) - \frac{w}{2^n} \geq w$ or $w \leq \frac{AVG(S)}{1+\frac{1}{2^n}}$. Using this in the result of Lemma 3, we get $F(S) \leq \frac{2AVG(S)}{(1+\frac{1}{2^n})}$. ∎

The above lemma gives a relation between the total completion time of a schedule and the average load per processor in that schedule. We want to build a relationship between the completion time of a schedule S and the completion time of the optimal schedule. Next, we show that the average load per processor in a schedule produced by algorithm *Schedule* is less than or equal to the average load per processor in an optimal schedule.

Lemma 6 *If S is a schedule produced by algorithm* **Schedule** *and $F(S) \neq F(OPT)$, then $AVG(S) \leq AVG(OPT)$.*

Proof: The completion time of a schedule S can not be less than the completion time of an optimal schedule, therefore, $F(S) > F(OPT)$. The total amount of work done by the hypercube during the optimal schedule is same as the total amount of work done by the hypercube during the schedule S. It means that during the schedule S some of the processors were idle for more time than the processors in the optimal schedule. This implies that there is less fragmentation in the optimal schedule and processors are heavily utilized. Thus we conclude that the average load per processor in the optimal schedule is greater than the average load per processor in the schedule S. ∎

Using the above lemmas now we give the upper bound for the algorithm *Schedule*.

Theorem 4 *If S is a schedule produced by algorithm* **Schedule** *then $F(S) \leq \frac{2F(OPT)}{(1+\frac{1}{2^n})}$.*

Proof: From Lemmas 2 and 4 we can give the relation between the the final finish time of schedule S, $F(S)$, and the average time for the optimal solution *i.e.* $F(S) \leq \frac{2AVG(OPT)}{(1+\frac{1}{2^n})}$. Lemma 1 can also be applied to the optimal schedule because even for the optimal schedule $F(OPT) \not< AVG(OPT)$, therefore $F(OPT) \geq AVG(OPT)$. Combining the above results we get $F(S) \leq \frac{2F(OPT)}{(1+\frac{1}{2^n})}$. ∎

The above theorem gives the upper bound for the algorithm *Schedule*. In the worst case when n is very large the algorithm will produce an schedule S twice as much as the completion time of the optimal schedule *i.e.* $F(S) \leq 2F(OPT)$.

Let us consider an example as shown in Figure 1. Figure 1(a) shows the minimum subcube dimension $MD(x_i)$ and the execution time $T(x_i)$ for task x_i. The speedup function ψ is given in Figure 1(b), *e.g.* $\psi(3,4) = 2.4$. Tasks x_3, x_4, and x_5 have execution time greater than the average (which is 7.41), thus these tasks are scaled-up such that there execution time would be less than the average. Thus we have, $MD(3) = 2$, $MD(4) = 2$, and $MD(5) = 3$. First x_3, x_4, and x_5 are selected, as shown in 2(a), among these x_3 has the maximum speedup thus $D(x_3)$ is incremented. After one iteration x_3 and x_5 are scheduled, as shown in Figure 2(b). For the next partial schedule x_2, x_4, and x_7 are selected, x_4 has maximum speedup thus its dimension is increased, as shown in Figure 2(c). The same process is repeated for each partial schedule until all the tasks are included in the schedule Figure 2(d) shows the final schedule.

Our experimental results show that algorithm *Schedule* produces schedules with completion times very close to the completion times of the optimal schedule. In the next section we present some experimental results.

5 Conclusions

In this paper, we investigated the HSP problem. We have presented a polynomial algorithm for the HSP problem when all the tasks have the same execution times. We have also presented an approximation algorithm, *Schedule*, which guarantees a solution within $\frac{2}{(1+\frac{1}{2^m})}$ of the optimal solution. Algorithm *Schedule* can be implemented in $O(m^2 \log m)$ time, where m is the number of tasks to be scheduled.

References

[1] E. G. Coffman, "Computer and Job-Shop Scheduling Theory," *New York Wiley, 1976.*

[2] K. P. Belkhale and P. Banerjee, "Approximation Algorithm For The Partitionable Independent Task Scheduling Problem," *Proceedings of The 1990 International Conference on Parallel Processing,* 1990, Vol. I, pp. 72-75.

[3] M. Chen and K. G. Shin, "Processor Allocation in an n-cube Multiprocessor Using Gray Codes," *IEEE Transactions on Computers,* vol. C-36, no. 12, Dec. 1987, pp. 1396-1407.

[4] S. Al-Bassam, H. El-Rewini, B. Bose, and T. Lewis, "Efficient Serial and Parallel Subcube Recognition in Hypercubes," to appear in *The Proceedings of the First Great Lakes Computer Science Conference, August 1990.*

[5] Abdullah Al-Dhelaan and Bella Bose, "A new strategy for processor allocation in an n-cube multiprocessor," 8th *Annual International Phoenix Conf. on Computers and communications,* March 1989, pp. 114-118.

[6] Win-Tsung Lo, S. K. Tripathi and D. Gosal, "Task Allocation on the Hypercube Multiprocessor," *1990 International Conference on Parallel Processing,* vol I, pp. 573-574.

[7] M. Chen and K. G. Shin, "Message Routing in a Injured Hypercube," in the *Proceedings of the Third Conference on Hypercube Concurrent Computers and Applications,* 1988, pp. 312-317.

[8] J. K. Lenstra and A. H. G. R. Kan, "Complexity of Scheduling Under Precedence Constraints," *Oper. Res., Jan 1978,* vol 26, pp. 22-35.

[9] R. L. Graham, "Bounds on Multiprocessing Timing Anomalies," *SIAM Journal of Applied Math.,* vol. 17, pp. 263-269, 1969.

[10] K. P. Garey and D. S. Johnson, "Computers and Intractability, A Guide to the Theory of NP-Completeness," *W. H. Freeman and Company, N. Y.,* 1979.

[11] R. L. Graham, E. L. Lawler, J. K. Lensta, and A. H. G. Rinnooy Kan, "Optimization and Approximation in Deterministic Sequencing and Scheduling: A Survey," *Annals of Discrete MAthematics,* vol. 5, pp. 287-326, 1979.

Tasks

	1	2	3	4	5	6	7
Min. Dim.	0	1	1	1	2	1	1
Exec Time	4	4	10.5	7.8	12	6	5

(a) Set of tasks with execution times &
dimension requirements.

Tasks

		1	2	3	4	5	6	7
Dimension	0	1	*	*	*	*	*	*
	1	2.0	1	1	1	*	1	1
	2	2.3	1.6	1.5	1.3	1	2.0	2.5
	3	2.7	2.0	1.9	1.8	2.4	2.4	2.8
	4	2.9	2.3	2.4	2.4	2.8	2.7	3.2

(b) Speedup functions

Figure 1: An example of HSP with 7 tasks

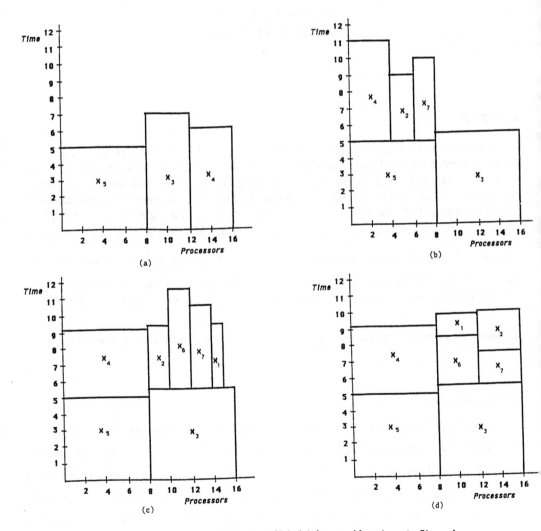

Figure 2: Several steps of algorithm {Schedule} on problem shown in Figure 1.

An Optimal Parallel Algorithm to Reconstruct a Binary Tree from its Traversals

Stephan Olariu   Michael Overstreet   Zhaofang Wen
Department of Computer Science
Old Dominion University
Norfolk, VA 23529-0162
USA

Abstract

We consider the following problem. For a binary tree $T = (V, E)$ where $V = \{1, 2, ..., n\}$, given its inorder traversal and either its preorder traversal or it postorder traversal, reconstruct the binary tree. We present a new parallel algorithm for this problem. Our algorithm requires $O(n)$ space. The main idea of our algorithm is to reduce the reconstruction process to parallel merging. With the best results for parallel merging, our algorithm can be implemented in $O(\log n)$ time using $O(\frac{n}{\log n})$ processors on the EREW PRAM, or in $O(\log\log n)$ time using $O(\frac{n}{\log\log n})$ processors on the CREW PRAM. Consequently, an ordered tree can be reconstructed from its preorder and postorder traversals. Our results improve the best previous results for this problem in literature either in cost or in the model of computation.

Keywords: Algorithms, Binary trees, Ordered trees, PRAM, Parallel algorithms, Traversals.

1. Introduction

We study the problem of reconstructing binary trees from their traversals. It is well-known that a binary tree can be reconstructed from its inorder traversal along with either its preorder traversal or its postorder traversal [8]. Recently, sequential solutions to this classical problem have been reported in [1,4]. Especially, the algorithm in [1] takes $O(n)$ time and space. Parallel solutions to this problem can be found in [3,9]. In particular, the algorithm in [9] runs in $O(\log n)$ time using $O(n)$ processors on the CREW PRAM; and the solution in [3] takes $O(\log\log n)$ using $O(\frac{n}{\log\log n})$ processors on the CRCW PRAM.

In this paper, we present a new parallel algorithm for this problem. Our algorithm requires $O(n)$ space. The main idea of our algorithm is to reduce the reconstruction process to parallel merging. With the best results for parallel merging, our reconstruction algorithm can be implemented in $O(\log n)$ time using $O(\frac{n}{\log n})$ processors on the EREW PRAM, or in $O(\log\log n)$ time using $O(\frac{n}{\log\log n})$ processors on the CREW PRAM. Our algorithm thus improves the results in [3,9].

As pointed out in [3], optimal parallel algorithms that runs in $O(\log\log n)$ time usually needs to be implemented on the CRCW PRAM. The only known exception is Kruskal's parallel merging algorithm which runs in $O(\log\log n)$ time using $O(\frac{n}{\log\log n})$ processors on the CREW PRAM. Our result gives another example for designing doubly logarithmic time parallel algorithm on CREW PRAM.

2. Preliminaries

Many methods can be used to generate traversals for a binary tree. Here, we are interested in one the them, known as the *Euler tour technique* [10]. This powerful technique was proposed by Tarjan and Vishkin for designing efficient parallel algorithms on trees. Specifically, this technique reduces the computation of various kinds of information about the tree structure to the computation on a linked list [10]. To make this paper self–contained, the Euler tour technique for binary trees is described next:

The Euler tour technique: let T be a binary tree. Every node v of T is split into three copies v_1, v_2, v_3, all having the same node label[1] as v. For each of the resulting nodes, we define a *next* field as follows. If v has no left child then $v_1.next = v_2$. If v has no right child then $v_2.next = v_3$. If w is the left child of v then $v_1.next = w_1$, and $w_3.next = v_2$. If w is the right child of v then $v_2.next = w_1$ and $w_3.next = v_3$. What results is a list, called an *Euler path*, which starts at $root_1$ and ends at $root_3$ and traverses each edge of T exactly once in each direction. In other words, let $\Omega(T)$ denote the Euler path of a binary tree T. The Euler path of a binary tree with left subtree T_1 and right subtree T_2 can be expressed as $root_1\ \Omega(T_1)\ root_2\ \Omega(T_2)\ root_3$.

When no confusion is possible, we let *Euler path* also stand for the sequence of node labels induced by an Euler path.

Obviously, an Euler path of a tree contains three copies of each node label in the tree. An interesting property of the Euler path of a tree T is that keeping only the first copy of each

---

1. *For simplicity, we assume in this paper the nodes of the binary tree are labeled by integers 1, 2, ..., n.*

label results in a preorder traversal of T; keeping only the second copy of each label gives an inorder traversal of T; keeping the third copy of each label yields a postorder traversal of T [10].

For convenience, we define a *preorder–inorder Euler path* to be a sequence of labels obtained by deleting the third copy of each label in an Euler path. Similarly, an *inorder–postorder Euler path* is a sequence of labels obtained by deleting the first copy of each label in an Euler path. It is known that a binary tree can be reconstructed from its inorder traversal along with either its preorder traversal or postorder traversal [8]. It follows that a binary tree is completely determined by its preorder–inorder Euler path or its inorder–postorder Euler path.

For example, Figure 1 features a binary tree along with the associated Euler path, Preorder–inorder Euler path, preorder traversal, and inorder traversal.

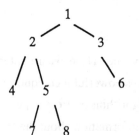

Euler path: 1 2 4 4 2 5 7 7 7 5 8 8 8 5 2 1 3 3 6 6 6 3 1

Preorder–inorder Euler path: 1 2 4 4 2 5 7 7 5 8 8 1 3 3 6 6

Preorder traversal: 1 2 4 5 7 8 3 6

Inorder traversal: 4 2 7 8 1 3 6

Figure 1. a binary tree, its various Euler paths and traversals

Lemma 1. A sequence of labels $b_1, b_2, ..., b_{2n}$ represents a preorder–inorder Euler path (respectively, the inorder–postorder Euler path) of an n–node binary tree T *if, and only if,* the following conditions hold:

  (1) there are exactly two copies of each label in the sequence, and

  (2) there exist no integers i, j, k, m with $1 \le i < j < k < m \le 2n$ such that $(b_i = b_k)$ and $(b_j = b_m)$.

Proof. We prove the statement for the case of a preorder–inorder Euler path (the case of an inorder–postorder Euler path follows by a mirror argument).

Let $\Psi(T)$ denote the preorder–inorder Euler path of a tree T. By definition, the preorder–inorder Euler path of a tree with left subtree T_1 and right subtree T_2 can be expressed as $root_1\ \Psi(T_1)\ root_2\ \Psi(T_2)$. Thus, the "only if" part of the lemma is obvious.

The "if" part will be proved by induction on n. When $n = 1$ the lemma is obviously true. Assume the lemma is true for $n < l$. When $n = l$, let b_t be the second copy of b_1, i.e. $b_t = b_1$. By condition (2) and the induction hypothesis, $b_2, ..., b_{t-1}$ and $b_{t+1}, ..., b_{2n}$ can both be seen as preorder–inorder Euler paths. Let T_1 and T_2 be the binary trees induced by $b_2, ..., b_{t-1}$ and $b_{t+1}, ..., b_{2n}$ respectively. The tree rooted at b_1 with left subtree T_1 and right subtree T_2 is the tree determined by $b_1, b_2, ..., b_{2n}$. ∎

Let $b_1, b_2, ..., b_{2n}$ be a preorder–inorder Euler path with $2n$ labels. For any pair of duplicate labels b_i and b_j $(1 \le i < j \le n)$, we call b_i "the first copy of its duplicate label" and b_j "the second copy of its duplicate label."

Corollary 1. Let $c_1, c_2, ..., c_n$ and $d_1, d_2, ..., d_n$ be the inorder and the preorder traversals of a binary tree. There do not exist integers $i_1, i_2, j_1, j_2, k_1, k_2$, such that $(1 \le i_1 < j_1 < k_1 \le n)$, $(1 \le k_2 < i_2 < j_2 \le n)$ and $(c_{i_1} = d_{i_2}) \wedge (c_{j_1} = d_{j_2}) \wedge (c_{k_1} = d_{k_2})$.

Proof. Assume there exist integers $i_1, i_2, j_1, j_2, k_1, k_2$, such that $(1 \le i_1 < j_1 < k_1 \le n)$, $(1 \le k_2 < i_2 < j_2 \le n)$ and $(c_{i_1} = d_{i_2}) \wedge (c_{j_1} = d_{j_2}) \wedge (c_{k_1} = d_{k_2})$. Then in the according preorder–inorder Euler path, we can find $... c_{i_1} ... c_{j_1} ... c_{k_1} ... d_{k_2} ... d_{i_2} ... d_{j_2} ...$ contradicting the condition (2) of Lemma 1. ∎

2. The Algorithm

In this section, we develop an optimal parallel algorithm to reconstruct a binary tree from its preorder and inorder traversals. Before we present our parallel algoirthm, we need the following sequential algorithms, an algorithm to generate the preorder–inorder Euler path from the preorder and inorder traversals of a binary tree, and an algorithm to reconstruct a binary tree from its preorder–inorder Euler path.

The algorithm to reconstruct the tree from its preorder–inorder Euler path is as follows:

```
Procedure EulerPath-to-Tree;
Input: a preorder–inorder Euler path b₁, b₂, ..., b₂ₙ ;
Output: A binary tree with root node r and set of nodes, S;
begin
    S:= { b | b is the second copy of its duplicate label in b₁, b₂, ..., b₂ₙ}
    r:= the second copy of b₁;
    for each label bᵢ (2 ≤ i ≤ 2n) do
        if (bᵢ is the second copy of its duplicate) then
            if (bᵢ₋₁ is the second copy of its duplicate label) then
                leftchild(bᵢ):= bᵢ₋₁ ;
            if (bᵢ₊₁ is the first copy of its duplicate label) then
                a:= the second copy of label bᵢ₊₁ ;
                rightchild(bᵢ):= a;
end.
```

Lemma 2. Given a preorder–inorder Euler path with $2n$ labels, procedure *EulerPath–to–Tree* correctly reconstruct the corresponding binary tree. If each label is associated with the position of the other copy of the label in the preorder–inorder Euler path, the binary tree can be reconstructed in $O(n)$ time.

Proof. The correctness of the algorithm follows directly from the proof of Lemma 1. Under the condition that each label remembers the position of its duplicate, computing the set S takes $O(n)$ time; each iteration of the for loop takes $O(1)$ time. Consequently, the entire procedure takes $O(n)$ time. ∎

Next, we show how to generate a preorder–inorder Euler path given a preorder and inorder traversal of a binary tree T. The details are as follows:

Procedure Traversals–to–EulerPath;
Input: sequence of labels, $c_1, c_2, ..., c_n$ as a preorder traversal of a tree, and another sequence of labels $d_1, d_2, ..., d_n$ as an inorder traversal of the same tree;
Output: a preorder–inorder Euler path induced by the traversals, $b_1, b_2, ..., b_{2n}$, in which each label is associated with the position of the other copy of the label.
begin
    $Stack := \Phi$;
    $j := k := 1$;
    for $i := 1$ **to** $2n$ **do**
        if (d_k matches the label on the top of *Stack*) **then**
            $b_i := d_k$;
            $k := k + 1$;
            $\alpha := $ **pop** *Stack*;
            α and d_k remembers each other's position in the sequence $b_1, b_2, ..., b_i$
        else
            $b_i := c_j$;
            push c_j onto Stack;
            $j := j + 1$;
    return$(b_1, b_2, ..., b_{2n})$
end.

The correctness and the time complexity of this procedure are established by the following result.

Lemma 3. Given the preorder and the inorder traversals of an n–node binary tree T, Procedure Traversals–to–EulerPath computes in $O(n)$ time the preorder–inorder Euler path of

T, such that every label remembers the position of its duplicate in the preorder–inorder Euler path.

Proof. We prove the correctness of the procedure by induction on n. When $n=1$, the algorithm is obviously correct. Assume that the algorithm is correct for $n < l$. Consider the case when $n = l$. Without loss of generality, assume $d_q = c_1$. By the definitions of inorder and preorder traversals, c_1 is root of T, and the left subtree of T has preorder traversal $c_2, ..., c_q$ and inorder traversal $d_1, ..., d_{q-1}$; the right subtree of T has preorder traversal $c_{q+1}, ..., c_k$ and inorder traversal $d_{q+1}, ..., d_k$. By the induction hypothesis, consuming subsequences $c_2, ..., c_q$ and d_1, ..., d_{q-1} the algorithm computes $b_2, b_2, ..., b_{2q-2}$ as the preorder–inorder Euler path of the left subtree, with c_1 left on the top of Stack. After matching d_q with the top of Stack, the algorithm computes $b_{2q}, b_2, ..., b_k$ as the preorder–inorder Euler path of the right subtree by consuming subsequences $c_{q+1}, ..., c_k$ and $d_{q+1}, ..., d_k$. From the statements above, we see that the output sequence $b_1, b_2, ..., b_{2n}$ satisfies both conditions of Lemma 1. Deleting the second copies of the duplicate labels in $b_1, b_2, ..., b_{2n}$ results in $c_1, c_2..., c_n$. Also, deleting the first copies of the duplicate labels in $b_1, b_2, ..., b_{2n}$ results in $d_1, d_2..., d_n$. It follows that $b_1, b_2, ..., b_{2n}$ is the preorder–inorder Euler path of the tree. By the use of Stack in the algorithm, we ensure that each label in the output sequence remembers the position of its duplicate. The algorithm runs in $O(n)$ time, since each iteration of the for loop has $O(1)$ time. ∎

Combining Lemma 2 and Lemma 3, we have the following lemma.

Lemma 4. An n-node binary tree can be reconstructed from its preorder and inorder traversals in $O(n)$ time with $O(n)$ extra space. ∎

We are now in a position to present our parallel solution to the problem of reconstructing an n-node binary tree from its preorder and inorder traversals. Our parallel algorithm is developed based on the two sequential algorithms described above. That is, we first show that given a preorder–inorder Euler path in which every label remembers the position of its duplicate in the path, the corresponding binary tree can be reconstructed in $O(1)$ time using $O(n)$ processors on the EREW PRAM. We then show that computing the preorder–inorder Euler path from the preorder and inorder traversals can be reduced to parallel merging.

Lemma 5. Given a preorder–inorder Euler path with $2n$ labels such that each label is associated with the position of its duplicate in the preorder–inorder Euler path, the corresponding binary tree can be reconstructed in $O(1)$ time using n processors on the EREW PRAM.

Proof. Simply parallelize procedure EulerPath-to-Tree. ∎

We now discuss how to compute the preorder–inorder Euler path from a preorder traversal $c_1, c_2, ..., c_n$ and an inorder traversal $d_1, d_2, ..., d_n$. For simplicity, we assume that $c_1, c_2, ..., c_n$ is $1, 2, ..., n$, and $d_1, d_2, ..., d_n$ is a permutation of $1, 2, ..., n$ (the case where $c_1, c_2, ..., c_n$ is a permutation of $1, 2, ...n$ can be reduced to this case easily). We compute the preorder–inorder Euler path from sequences $c_1, c_2, ..., c_n$, and $d_1, d_2, ..., d_n$ by merging according to some order as we are about to explain. We will define such an order that both sequences $c_1, c_2, ..., c_n$ and $d_1, d_2, ..., d_n$ are already sorted.

Construct a sequence of triples $(1, j_1, c_1), (1, j_2, c_2), ..., (1, j_n, c_n)$ such that $d_{j_i} = c_i (i = 1, 2, ..., n)$ and another sequence of triples $(2, 1, d_1), (2, 2, d_2), ..., (2, n, d_n)$. Denote $\Pi = \{ (1, j_1, c_1), (1, j_2, c_2), ..., (1, j_n, c_n), (2, 1, d_1), (2, 2, d_2), ..., (2, n, d_n) \}$. Define a binary relation $\ll$ on Π as follows: for arbitrary triples (α, β, γ) and $(\alpha', \beta', \gamma')$ in Π we have

Rule 1. $((a = 1) \wedge (a' = 1)) \rightarrow (((\alpha, \beta, \gamma) \ll (\alpha', \beta', \gamma')) \leftrightarrow (\gamma < \gamma'))$;

Rule 2. $((a = 2) \wedge (a' = 2)) \rightarrow (((\alpha, \beta, \gamma) \ll (\alpha', \beta', \gamma')) \leftrightarrow (\beta < \beta'))$;

Rule 3. $(a = 1) \wedge (a' = 2)) \rightarrow (((\alpha, \beta, \gamma) \ll (\alpha', \beta', \gamma')) \leftrightarrow ((\beta < \beta') \vee (\gamma \leq \gamma')))$;

Rule 4. $((a = 2) \wedge (a' = 1)) \rightarrow (((\alpha, \beta, \gamma) \ll (\alpha', \beta', \gamma')) \leftrightarrow ((\beta < \beta') \wedge (\gamma < \gamma')))$.

It is easy to confirm that the binary relation $\ll$ is total on Π. In addition, it turns out that $\ll$ is transitive (refer to the Appendix for the proof), and so $\ll$ is a linear order on Π.

By Rules 1 and 2, we can see that according to $\ll$ both sequences $(1, j_1, c_1), (1, j_2, c_2), ..., (1, j_n, c_n)$ and $(2, 1, d_1), (2, 2, d_2), ..., (2, n, d_n)$ are already sorted. Merging these two sequences we obtain a sorted sequence of triples $(\alpha_1, \beta_1, \gamma_1), (\alpha_2, \beta_2, \gamma_2), ..., (\alpha_{2n}, \beta_{2n}, \gamma_{2n})$. We claim that $\gamma_1, \gamma_2, ..., \gamma_{2n}$ is the preorder–inorder Euler path of the tree determined by the traversals. The correctness of the claim relies on the following facts:

(a) There are exactly two copies of each label in $\gamma_1, \gamma_2, ..., \gamma_{2n}$ (satisfying the condition 1 of Lemma 1); the first copy is from the preorder traversal and the second copy is from the inorder traversal;

(b) There do not exist integers $1 \leq i < j < k < m \leq 2n$ such that $(\gamma_i = \gamma_k)$ and $(\gamma_j = \gamma_m)$ (satisfying the condition 1 of Lemma 1);

(c) Deleting the second copies of the duplicate labels in $\gamma_1, \gamma_2, ..., \gamma_{2n}$ results in $c_1, c_2, ..., c_n$, and deleting the first copies of the duplicate labels in $\gamma_1, \gamma_2, ..., \gamma_{2n}$ gives $d_1, d_2, ..., d_n$.

Fact (a) follows directly from Rule 3 and the construction of the triples in Π. By the definition of $\ll$ both sequences $(1, j_1, c_1), (1, j_2, c_2), ..., (1, j_n, c_n)$ and $(2, 1, d_1), (2, 2, d_2), ..., (2, n, d_n)$ are already sorted, so fact (c) is also true. The proof of fact (b) is given below:

Proof of (b). (by contradiction)

(1) $(\gamma_i = \gamma_k) \wedge (\gamma_j = \gamma_m)$ where $1 \le i < j < k < m \le 2n$ [Assumption]

(2) $(\alpha_i, \beta_i, \gamma_i) \ll (\alpha_j, \beta_j, \gamma_j) \ll (\alpha_k, \beta_k, \gamma_k) \ll (\alpha_m, \beta_m, \gamma_m)$ [by $1 \le i < j < k < m \le 2n$ in (1)]

(3) $(\alpha_i = 1) \wedge (\alpha_j = 1) \wedge (\alpha_k = 2) \wedge (\alpha_m = 2)$ [by (1), (2), Rule 3 and the construction of the triples]

(4) $(\beta_i = \beta_k) \wedge (\beta_j = \beta_m)$ [by (1) and the construction of the triples]

(5) $(\beta_j < \beta_k) \vee (\gamma_j \le \gamma_k)$ [by $(\alpha_j = 1) \wedge (\alpha_k = 2)$ in (3), $(\alpha_j, \beta_j, \gamma_j) \ll (\alpha_k, \beta_k, \gamma_k)$ in (2) and Rule 3]

(6) $(\beta_m < \beta_k) \vee (\gamma_m \le \gamma_k)$ [replacing β_j, γ_j in (5) with β_m, γ_m respectively, by (1) and (4)]

(7) $(\beta_k < \beta_m)$ [by $(\alpha_k, \beta_k, \gamma_k) \ll (\alpha_m, \beta_m, \gamma_m)$ in (2), $(\alpha_k = 2) \wedge (\alpha_m = 2)$ in (3) and Rule 2]

(8) $(\gamma_m \le \gamma_k)$ [by (6) and (7)]

(9) $(\gamma_i < \gamma_j)$ [by $(\alpha_i, \beta_i, \gamma_i) \ll (\alpha_j, \beta_j, \gamma_j)$ in (2), $(\alpha_i = 1) \wedge (\alpha_j = 1)$ in (3) and rule 1]

(10) $(\gamma_k < \gamma_m)$ [by (1) and (9)]

(11) Contradiction   [(8) and (10)]
∎

Since $d_1, d_2, ..., d_n$ is a permutation of $1, 2, ..., n$, we define an array $J[1..n]$ such that $J[d_i] := i$ $(i = 1, 2, ..., n)$. For every c_i $(i = 1, 2, ..., n)$ determining the subscript j_i with $d_{j_i} = c_i$ can be implemented by letting $j_i = J[c_i]$. Consequently, constructing the sequences $(1, j_1, c_1), (1, j_2, c_2), ..., (1, j_n, c_n)$ and $(2, 1, d_1), (2, 2, d_2), ..., (2, n, d_n)$ can be implemented in $O(1)$ time using n processors on the EREW PRAM. Therefore, we have successfully reduced the problem to parallel merging.

Using the optimal algorithms in [2,7], merging sequences $(1, j_1, c_1), (1, j_2, c_2), ..., (1, j_n, c_n)$ and $(2, 1, d_1), (2, 2, d_2), ..., (2, n, d_n)$ according to $\ll$ can be done in $O(\log n)$ time using

$O(\frac{n}{\log n})$ processors on the EREW PRAM [2], or in O(loglogn) time using $O(\frac{n}{\log\log n})$ processors on the CREW PRAM [7]. Summarizing the discussion above along with Lemma 5, we have the following.

Theorem 1. For a binary tree $T = (V, E)$ where $V = \{1, 2, ..., n\}$, given its inorder and preorder traversals, the binary tree can be reconstructed using o(n) space, in O(logn) time using $O(\frac{n}{\log n})$ processors on the EREW PRAM, or in O(loglogn) time using $O(\frac{n}{\log\log n})$ processors on the CREW PRAM. ∎

In case the inorder traversal and the postorder traversal is given, the binary tree can be reconstructed similarly.

3. Conclusion

We have shown how to reconstruct a binary tree from its inorder traversal along with either its preorder traversal or its postorder traversal. The most interesting part of our parallel solution is to reduce the problem to parallel merging. With the best results for parallel merging, our reconstruction algorithm can be implemented in O(logn) time using $O(\frac{n}{\log n})$ processors on the EREW PRAM, or in O(loglogn) time using $O(\frac{n}{\log\log n})$ processors on the CREW PRAM.

As shown in [8], an ordered tree can be represented by a binary tree whose preorder traversal is the same as that of the ordered tree, while the inorder traversal of the binary tree is the same as the postorder traversal of the ordered tree. Therefore, our algorithm can be applied with the same complexity to reconstruct an ordered tree from its preorder and inorder traversals.

References

[1]   A. Anderson, S. Carlsson, "Construction of a tree from its traversals in optimal time and space," *Information Processing Letters*, 34 (1990) pp. 21–25

[2]   R. J. Anderson, E. W. Mayr and M. K. Warmuth, "Parallel approximation algorithms for bin packing," *Information and Computation*, 82, October, 1989, pp. 262–277.

[3]   O. Berkman, Z. Galil, B. Schieber and U. Vishkin, "Highly Parallelizable Problems," in Proceedings of the *IEEE Symposium on Foundation of Computer Science*, 1989.

[4]   G. H. Chen , M. S. Yu and L. T. Liu, "Two algorithms for constructing a binary tree from its traversals," *Information Processing Letters*, 28 (1988) pp. 297–299.

[5]   R. Cole, "Parallel Merge sort," in *Proceedings of the 27th Annual IEEE Symposium on the Foundations of Computer Science*, 1986, pp. 511–516.

[6]   R. Cole and U. Vishkin, "Approximate and exact parallel scheduling with applications to list, tree and graph," *Proc. 27th Annual Symp. on Foundations of Computer Science*, 1986, pp. 487–491.

[7]   C. Kruskal, "Searching, merging and sorting in parallel computation," *IEEE Transactions on Computers* C–32, 10 (October), pp.942–946.

[8]   D. E. Knuth, The Art of Computer Programming, Vol. 1, Fundamental Algorithms, Second Edition, Addison–Wesley, Reading, Mass., 1973.

[9]   F. Springsteel, I. Stojmenovic, "Parallel general prefix computations with geometric, algebraic and other applications," In Proceedings of International Conference on Fundamentals of Computation Theory, Szeged, Hungary, August 1989, 424–433, Springer–Verlag.

[10] R. E. Tarjan and U. Vishkin, "Finding biconnected and computing tree functions in logarithmic parallel time," in *Proceedings of the 25th Annual Symposium on Foundations of Computer Science, 1984*, pp. 12–22.

[11] U. Vishkin, "Synchronous parallel computation," a Survey, *TR 71*, Dept. of Computer Science, Courant Institute, NYU, 1983.

Appendix

The property of the binary relation $\ll$ defined in Section 3 is given in this appendix. For completeness, we repeat the definition of $\ll$ before we give the proof. Let T be an n–node binary tree and let $c_1, c_2, ..., c_n$ and $d_1, d_2, ..., d_n$ be the preorder and inorder traversals of T, respectively. Construct a sequence of triples $(1, j_1, c_1), (1, j_2, c_2), ..., (1, j_n, c_n)$ such that $d_{j_i} = c_i$ $(i = 1, 2, ..., n)$ and another sequence of triples $(2, 1, d_1), (2, 2, d_2), ..., (2, n, d_n)$. Denote $\Pi = \{ (1, j_1, c_1), (1, j_2, c_2), ..., (1, j_n, c_n), (2, 1, d_1), (2, 2, d_2), ..., (2, n, d_n) \}$. We define a binary relation $\ll$ on Π as follows: for arbitrary triples (α, β, γ) and $(\alpha', \beta', \gamma')$ in Π we have

Rule 1. $((a = 1) \wedge (a' = 1)) \rightarrow (((a, \beta, \gamma) \ll (a', \beta', \gamma')) \leftrightarrow (\gamma < \gamma'))$;

Rule 2. $((a = 2) \wedge (a' = 2)) \rightarrow (((a, \beta, \gamma) \ll (a', \beta', \gamma')) \leftrightarrow (\beta < \beta'))$;

Rule 3. $(a = 1) \wedge (a' = 2)) \rightarrow (((a, \beta, \gamma) \ll (a', \beta', \gamma')) \leftrightarrow ((\beta < \beta') \vee (\gamma \le \gamma')))$;

Rule 4. $((a = 2) \wedge (a' = 1)) \rightarrow (((a, \beta, \gamma) \ll (a', \beta', \gamma')) \leftrightarrow ((\beta < \beta') \wedge (\gamma < \gamma')))$.

We note that Rules 1–4 above imply that the binary relation $\ll$ is total on Π. We propose to show that, in fact, $\ll$ is a linear order. For this purpose, we only need to justify that $\ll$ is transitive. We shall present our arguments in the form of a case–by–case analysis. Let $(\alpha, \beta, \gamma), (\alpha', \beta', \gamma')$ and $(\alpha'', \beta'', \gamma'')$ be arbitrary triples in Π satisfying:

$(\alpha, \beta, \gamma) \ll (\alpha', \beta', \gamma')$ and $(\alpha', \beta', \gamma') \ll (\alpha'', \beta'', \gamma'')$

Case 1. $\alpha = \alpha''$

    Subcase 1.1. $\alpha = \alpha' = \alpha'' = 1$.

        By Rule 1 and the assumption, we have $\gamma < \gamma'$ and $\gamma' < \gamma''$ and therefore $\gamma < \gamma''$. The conclusion follows by Rule 1.

    Subcase 1.2. $\alpha = \alpha'' = 1$ and $\alpha' = 2$.

        By Rule 3,

$$(\beta < \beta') \vee (\gamma \le \gamma') \qquad \text{(a)}$$

        By Rule 4,

$$(\beta' < \beta'') \wedge (\gamma' < \gamma'') \qquad \text{(b)}$$

        If $\gamma < \gamma''$ then conclusion follows immediately from Rule 1. Therefore, we assume

$$\gamma'' < \gamma \qquad \text{(c)}$$

        Note that (a), (b) and (c) combined imply that $(\gamma' < \gamma'' < \gamma) \wedge (\beta < \beta' < \beta'')$ which is contradicting Corollary 1.

    Subcase 1.3. $\alpha = \alpha' = \alpha'' = 2$.

        By Rule 2, we have $\beta < \beta'$ and $\beta' < \beta''$ and therefore $\beta < \beta''$. The conclusion follows by Rule 2.

    Subcase 1.4. $\alpha = 2$, $\alpha' = 1$ and $\alpha'' = 2$.

        by Rule 4,

$$(\beta < \beta') \wedge (\gamma < \gamma') \qquad \text{(d)}$$

        by Rule 3,

$(\beta' < \beta")\vee(\gamma' \leq \gamma")$ \hfill (e)

If $\beta < \beta"$ then conclusion follows instantly from Rule 2. We may assume, therefore,

$\beta" < \beta$ \hfill (f)

But now, (d), (e) and (f) combined imply that $(\gamma < \gamma' < \gamma")\wedge(\beta" < \beta < \beta')$ which contradicts Corollary 1.

Case 2. $\alpha \neq \alpha"$

Subcase 2.1. $\alpha = \alpha' = 1$ and $\alpha" = 2$.

By Rule 1,

$\gamma < \gamma'$ \hfill (g)

by Rule 3,

$(\beta' < \beta")\vee(\gamma' \leq \gamma")$ \hfill (h)

Note that if $(\beta < \beta")\vee(\gamma \leq \gamma")$ then by Rule 3, we have $(\alpha, \beta, \gamma) \ll (\alpha", \beta", \gamma")$. Therefore, we may assume that

$(\beta" < \beta)\wedge(\gamma" < \gamma)$ \hfill (i)

But now, (g), (h) and (i) combined imply $(\gamma" < \gamma < \gamma')\wedge(\beta' < \beta" < \beta)$ contradicting Corollary 1.

Subcase 2.2. $\alpha = 1$, and $\alpha' = \alpha" = 2$.

By Rule 3,

$(\beta < \beta')\vee(\gamma \leq \gamma').$ \hfill (j)

By Rule 2,

$\beta' < \beta"$ \hfill (k)

Note that if $(\beta < \beta")\vee(\gamma \leq \gamma")$ then the conclusion follows by Rule 3. Therefore, we may assume

$(\beta" < \beta)\wedge(\gamma" < \gamma)$ \hfill (l)

However, by (j), (k) and (l) we have $(\gamma" < \gamma < \gamma')\wedge(\beta' < \beta" < \beta)$ contradicting Corollary 1.

Subcase 2.3. $\alpha = 2$, and $\alpha' = \alpha" = 1$.

By Rule 4,

$(\beta < \beta')\wedge(\gamma < \gamma')$ \hfill (m)

by rule 1,

$\gamma' < \gamma"$ \hfill (n)

If $(\beta < \beta")\wedge(\gamma < \gamma")$ then by Rule 4 the conclusion follows. Therefore, we may assume

$(\beta" < \beta)\vee(\gamma" \leq \gamma)$ \hfill (o)

Note that by (m), (n) and (o) combined, we have $(\gamma < \gamma' < \gamma")\wedge(\beta" < \beta < \beta')$ contradicting Corollary 1.

Subcase 2.3. $\alpha = \alpha' = 2$ and $\alpha" = 1$.

By Rule 2,

$\beta < \beta'$ \hfill (p)

by Rule 4,

$(\beta' < \beta")\wedge(\gamma' < \gamma")$ \hfill (q)

Note that if $\gamma < \gamma"$ then (p) and (q) combined give $(\alpha, \beta, \gamma) \ll (\alpha", \beta", \gamma")$ by Rule 4. Thus, we may assume $\gamma" < \gamma$. But now (p) and (q) imply $(\gamma' < \gamma" < \gamma)\wedge(\beta < \beta' < \beta")$ contradicting to Corollary 1.

■

AN EFFICIENT MULTIPROCESSOR ARCHITECTURE FOR IMAGE PROCESSING IN VLSI *

Hee Yong Youn
Department of Computer Sciences
University of North Texas
Denton, Texas 76203-3886
youn@ponder.csci.unt.edu

Abstract

Image processing generally requires to manipulate a large number of data of small granularity. In this paper a multiprocessor architecture which allows an efficient image processing in VLSI is proposed. The proposed network is as efficient as hypercube using $O(n^{1/2}log\ n)$ less chip area when n is the number of nodes in the network. The effectiveness of the proposed design is verified by studying some important image processing algorithms developed for hypercube network. The proposed architecture is also simple and modular, and thus it is relatively easier to develop efficient fault tolerance designs.

1   Introduction

Processor arrays of regular interconnection topology allow a high performance computation by concurrently processing data and transferring the result through interconnection lines. This system is very effective for a class of problems where a large number of data are required to be manipulated. Image processing such as image transformation and template matching[1] is one of the typical examples of these problems. Here the two-dimensional image data can be distributed and concurrently processed in each processing element(PE) of the array.

The size of data assigned to each PE for image processing is usually small, while the total amount of data is very large. Therefore, a large size processor array with PEs of small granularity seems to be an appropriate structure for

---

*This work was supported in part by NSF Grant MIP-9009643.

image processing. Also, the required interconnection topology is regular and simple. This nature of image processing problems makes VLSI processor arrays to be the most effective and practical system for solving them.

For the efficient parallel processing, especially for image processing, several multiprocessor architectures and corresponding parallel algorithms have been proposed in the literature[2-4]. Among them, the hypercube network[2] has been recognized as one of the most efficient architectures. Recently, Ranka and Sahni[5] developed a scheme which can transform a gray scale $N \times N$ image in $O(logN)$ time using an N^2 node hypercube network, while a uniprocessor system requires $O(2^N)$ time. However, the main drawback of the hypercube network is that it is inefficient to be implemented in VLSI. This is because the number of interconnection edges of hypercube network grows exponentially ($O(n2^n)$) along the number of nodes in the network(n). Note that n is usually very large for image processing, and thus the chip area and maximum edge length overhead due to the complex interconnection will be significant. This results in the VLSI implementation of hypercube network to be very inefficient. Furthermore, fault tolerance[6] design is essential for multiprocessor systems in VLSI environment to achieve a practical level of yield and reliability. By the same reason, it is relatively difficult to devise efficient fault tolerance schemes for hypercube network.

In this paper, a multiprocessor architecture is proposed for efficiently processing image data in VLSI environment. Our design is at least as efficient as hypercube using $O(n^{1/2}log\ n)$ less chip area. The proposed architecture is constructed by connecting some basic modules where the basic module is a Cube-Connected Cycle(CCC)[7]. We call it $MCCC$(Modular CCC). CCC network allows an efficient VLSI implementation mainly due to its degree boundness as three, while a flexible communication between nodes is still allowed. As a result, many efficient layout and fault tolerance schemes[8-11] could have been developed for it.

The rest of the paper is organized as follows. The proposed $MCCC$ architecture is introduced in Section 2, along with the consideration of some VLSI implementation issues. Section 3 analyzes and compares the efficiency of $MCCC$ with hypercube for two important image processing problems such as image shrink (expansion) and one-dimensional convolution. The paper is concluded in Section 4.

2   The Proposed $MCCC$ Architecture

In this section the proposed Modular Cube-Connected Cycle($MCCC$) architecture is introduced. Two important VLSI implementation issues – chip area and maximum edge length – are then investigated along with hypercube architecture.

2.1   The Modular Cube-Connected Cycles Network

The proposed $MCCC(m, h)$ network can be described as follows.

- An $MCCC(m, h)$ network is composed of m modules and each module contains 2^h cycles of h PEs. The total number of PEs in the network (n) is, thus, $n = mh \cdot 2^h$. Note that each module is equivalent to a CCC(h,h)[7]. Figure 1 depicts an $MCCC(4, 4)$ network, where each circle represents a PE.

- Two adjacent modules are connected or disconnected through a linear array of switches ('SW' in Figure 1). Observe that the switch structure is very simple and a single line(bit) is enough to control the switches. Note that a cycle of length h, $2h$, ..., mh PEs can be constructed by appropriately setting the switches.

- For a $PE(l, p)$ and $SW(l, p')$, $l(= 0, 1, ..., 2^h - 1)$, $p(= 0, 1, ..., mh - 1)$, and $p'(= 0, 1, ..., m - 1)$ denote the cycle, position of the PE, and position of the switch in the cycle, respectively.

We next study two important issues related to the VLSI implementation.

2.2   VLSI Implementation Issues

Here the $MCCC$ network is analyzed in terms of area efficiency and maximum edge length.

2.2.1 Area Efficiency

Each PE in the proposed $MCCC$ network has a constant number of edges of three for any size network. This property allows us to efficiently lay out the network in VLSI[8,9]. The area efficiency of $MCCC$ network is as follows.

Theorem 2.1: The layout of $MCCC$ network is optimal and it is $O(n^{3/2}/\log n)$.

Proof: Krishnan and Hayes[9] developed an efficient layout scheme for processor arrays, and showed that an optimal layout of a CCC network of $x = h \cdot 2^h$ nodes is $O(x^2/h^2)$. The proposed $MCCC$ network is constructed by combining m CCC modules side by side, and thus the layout based on [9] is also optimal. Recall that there is $n = m \cdot x = mh \cdot 2^h$ nodes in the $MCCC$ network. Then area is bounded by $O(m \cdot (x^2/h^2)) = O(m \cdot x \cdot (x/h^2)) = O(n \cdot (2^h/h))$. Here, without loss of generality, assume that $MCCC$ network is a square shape. Then $mh = 2^h = n^{1/2}$, and $h = (1/2)\log n$. Finally, the bound becomes $O(n^{3/2}/\log n)$. $\square$

The area of an n node hypercube network has proven to be $\Omega(n^2)$. Therefore the proposed $MCCC$ network is at least $O(n^{1/2}\log n)$ times more area efficient than hypercube.

2.2.2 Maximum Edge Length

$MCCC$ network also displays a much shorter maximum edge length than hypercube as shown next.

Theorem 2.2: The maximum edge length of $MCCC$ network is $\Theta(n/\log n)$.

Proof: Using again Krishnan and Hayes' layout, the maximum edge length of a x node CCC network is $\Theta(x/\log x)$. Note that the longest edge in an $MCCC(m, h)$ occurs when all modules are connected to form the largest cycle. For example, the edges between the pairs of two nodes at the top and bottom in Figure 1 are the longest ones. Consequently, the maximum edge length of an $MCCC(m, h)$ is $\Theta(m \cdot (x/\log x)) = \Theta(n/\log x) = \Theta(n/(\log h + h)) = \Theta(n/\log n)$ (because $\log h \ll h$). $\square$

The maximum edge length of an n node hypercube network is $\Omega(n)$. This is because one side of a rectangle of area n^2 is minimal when it is a square shape, and it is n. Thus the maximum edge length of $MCCC$ is $\Omega(log\ n)$ shorter than that of hypercube.

The structural simplicity of the proposed $MCCC$ network – modularity and degree boundness – also allows that efficient fault tolerance schemes[10,11] can be more easily found than hypercube network. We next present how the proposed $MCCC$ network can efficiently process image data by considering two basic algorithms – image shrink and one-dimensional convolution.

3 Image Processing Using $MCCC$

In this section we analyze the efficiency of $MCCC$ network by solving some important image processing problems such as image transformation and convolution using the network. We also compare it with hypercube network.

3.1 Image Shrink and Expansion

Ranka and Sahni[5] have recently proposed an efficient $O(log\ n)$ image shrink algorithm for a gray scale $N \times N$ image using an N^2 node hypercube. Employing a similar strategy, we show how the problem can be solved using an $MCCC(m, h) = MCCC(N/log\ N, log\ N)$ network. Note that the number of nodes(n) in this network is $(N/logN)logN \cdot 2^{logN} = N \times N$. Also it is a square shape because $m \cdot h = N/log\ N \cdot log\ N = N = 2^{log\ N} = 2^h$. Each PE in this $MCCC(N/logN, logN)$ network contains a pixel data, as a node in the hypercube of same size does. The basic operation in the image transformation is shift, and it is defined next.

3.1.1 Shift Operation

$SHIFT(PE(l, p), i, W)$ circularly shifts the content of a register of $PE(l, p)$ by i PEs clockwise in a window of size W, if i is positive. For a negative i, a counterclockwise shift is assumed. The clockwise shift replaces the content of $PE(l, m)$ by $PE(l, (m + i)mod\ W)$ since the operation includes the nodes – $PE(l, m)$, $PE(l, (m + 1)mod\ W)$, $PE(l, (m + 2)mod\ W)$, ..., $PE(l, (m + W - 1)mod\ W)$.

3.1.2 Shrink Operation

Assume a two-dimensional image data I[0..N-1,0..N-1] and let $B[i,j]$ be a block of pixels of size $M \times M$: { $[u,v]$: max {$(u-i), (v-j)$} $\leq M$}, $0 \leq i,j < N$. Here assume $M = 2^k \leq N$, and (i,j) denotes the pixel at the lower left corner as shown in Figure 2. Also assume the center pixel is at $(i+(M/2), j+(M/2))$. The shrink operation using the proposed $MCCC$ network needs two main steps for finding and distributing the minimum pixel value of the $M \times M$ image block. The two main steps – Vertical Shrink(VS) and Horizontal Shrink(HS) – are presented next. In what follows, it is assumed that each PE has three registers A, B and I and the register I contains its pixel value. Also the links between two PEs are unidirectional. Figure 3 illustrates how a block of image is shrunk by VS and HS operation.

[**Vertical Shrinking** $VS[u,v]$] – This operation is defined as

$$VS[u,v] = min[u, y \bmod N], \quad j \leq y \leq (j+M-1)$$

for any (u,v) in $B[i,j]$ and $0 \leq i,j < N$.

Here PEs $(u,v), (u, (v+1) \bmod M), ..., (u, (v+M-1) \bmod M)$ form a cycle by properly setting the switches. In this step, the minimum value among these PEs for each $u(0 \leq u < M)$ is obtained. After $logM$ iterations of shift and comparison, every PE in a cycle get the same minimum value. Since there exist M such cycles in an $MCCC$, there exist M minimum values at the completion of this step. We denote them to $m[0], m[1], ..., m[M-1]$. VS procedure is shown in Figure 4.

VS operation takes $logM$ steps where each step is composed of shift and comparison operation. Therefore, the computation time in terms of T_t(transfer time) and T_c(comparison time) is

$$(2^0 + 2^1 + ... + 2^{(k-1)}) \times T_t + k \times T_c = (2^k - 1) \times T_t + k \times T_c$$

$$= (M-1) \times T_t + logM \times T_c$$

The difference in the time complexity between our design and hypercube arises from the shift operation. VS operation in our design requires circular shifts of size 2^i, $(0 \leq i \leq (k-1))$, while the hypercube architecture provides a direct connection between the PEs whose distance is 2^i by the gray code definition.

Those PEs involved in the VS operation perform the shift operations indirectly, in other words messages are passed through PEs to get their destination PEs. However, as explained below, this indirect transfer time becomes equivalent with the direct transfer time in hypercube due to its shorter edges in VLSI implementation.

[Horizontal Shrink $HS[u, v]$] – The horizontal shrink is defined as

$$HS[u, v] = min(x, v), i \leq x \leq (i + M - 1)$$

for any (u, v) in $VS[u, v]$ and $0 \leq i, j < N$.

This operation is for computing and distributing $min(m[0], m[1], ..., m[M - 1])$, and as a result every PE in the block get the same minimum value. The following is the HS algorithm and it is composed of two stages.

HS Algorithm:

1. Stage 1;

   (a) Send $m[u]$ from $PE(u, v)$ to $PE(u + 1, v)$.

   (b) At $PE(u + 1, v)$, compute $x = min(m[u], m[u + 1])$.

   (c) Send x from $PE(u + 1, v)$ to $PE(u, v)$ and $PE(u + 1, v + 1)$.

   (d) Send x from $PE(u, v)$ to $PE(u, v + 1)$.

   (e) Repeat steps (a)-(d) $logM$ times until the topmost PEs in the block find the minimum value.

2. Stage 2; Vertical propagation of the same minimum value in each vertical line.

Here each stage utilizes direct connections between PEs, and the basic connections used in Stage 1 are depicted in Figure 5. For each iteration in Stage 1, $3T_t + Tc$ time is required. Since there are $logM$ such iterations, the topmost PEs find the minimum value in $(3T_t + Tc) \times logM$ time. The propagation time of Stage 2 is $T_t \times logM$. Thus it takes $(4T_t + Tc) \times logM$ time to complete the HS operation. Note that the image shrink operation can be used for expansion by finding maximum value instead of minimum. The following table compares the time complexity of the two basic step of both architectures in terms of T_t and T_c.

Table I. Computation time comparison with [5] for shrink operation.

Procedure	$MCCC$	MIMD hypercube[5]
VS	$(M-1)T_t + logN \times T_c$	$(T_t + T_c)logN$
HS	$(4T_t + T_c)logN$	$(T_t + T_c)logN$

$MCCC$ network requires $O(M)$ (or $O(N)$ because $M \leq N$) unit transfer operations while hypercube does $O(log N)$ operations. However, recall that the maximum edge length of $MCCC$ network is $\Omega(log n)$ shorter than hypercube. Signal propagation time in VLSI circuit roughly grows quadratically with length. Therefore the actual VS operation time ratio of the two networks is $O(N/log^3 N)$, and they are comparable for practical sizes of N. Note that, if the maximum edge length of hypercube was $O(n^2)$ (not the lower bound value used above), then the ratio becomes $O(1/log^2 N)$ even with the assumption of linear propagation time with length. This estimation shows that the VS operation using $MCCC$ network takes at least as comparable time as hypercube. We can observe the same relation for HS operation. Consequently, the image shrink operation using $MCCC$ network can be said to be more efficient than hypercube because it uses less chip area. We next consider one-dimensional convolution problem.

3.2   One-Dimensional Convolution

Image template matching problem requires the solution of the following two-dimensional convolution($C2D$) of two image arrays, $A[0..N-1, 0..N-1]$ and $T[0..M-1, 0..M-1]$.

$$C2D[i,j] = \sum_{u=0}^{M-1}\sum_{v=0}^{M-1} A[(i+u)mod\ N, (j+v)mod\ N] \times T[u,v]$$

where I is an $N \times N$ image matrix and T is an $M \times M$ template, and $0 \leq i, j < N$. One-dimensional convolution($C1D$) is a basic step to compute $C2D$. In this section, we present how the proposed $MCCC$ network can efficiently compute $C1D$ by employing the same strategies proposed for hypercube[12]. Given two input arrays, $A[0..N-1]$ and $T[0..N-1]$, the $C1D$ is defined as;

$$C1D = \sum_{v=0}^{M-1} A[(i+v) mod \ N] \times T[v], \quad 0 \le i < N$$

When we assume that each PE can contain only one pixel value, a pair register A and B are employed to keep the pixel values required to compute $C1D$. Also, we need another register T, which stores the template value. The $C1D$ algorithm consists of two stages. The first stage obtains appropriate pairing of pixels for A and B registers in each PE. The second stage actually computes $C1D$ using the results of the first stage. When M is the size of the template T, the first stage computes paired values in $O(log M)$ time. Observe that the pairing operation takes two different sizes of circular shift operation of size M and N. The size M shift is done inside the loop while the size N shift occurs outside.

To compute the $C1D$ algorithm, switches between modules must be controlled to form cycles of different lengths during the execution. Table II compares the computation time for $C1D$ using $MCCC$ network with hypercube[12]. Observe that a same relation as for the image shrink operation is obtained.

Table II. Computation time comparison with [12] for $C1D$.

Stage	$MCCC$	MIMD hypercube[12]
1	$(2M-1)T_t$	$(2log M + 1)T_t$
2	$(2M)T_t$	$(2M)T_t$

4 Conclusion

We have presented an architecture which can be an efficient alternative of hypercube architecture in VLSI environment. The proposed modular cube-connected cycle architecture requires much less chip area and the maximum edge length is shorter than hypercube for a fixed size network. Structure of the $MCCC$ network is also simple and modular. Consequently efficient fault tolerance designs can be easily found. Case studies of some typical image processing problems clearly verify the effectiveness of the proposed $MCCC$ architecture. It is expected to be more significant for the problems which need to manipulate a large number of data of small granularity, and thus the VLSI implementation is very effective. Other important parallel algorithms on $MCCC$ are under investigation.

References

[1] R.J. Offen, "VLSI Image Processing," Reading, 1985, NcGraw-Hill, New York.

[2] T.E. Chan and Y. Saad, "Multigrid Algorithms on Hypercube Multiprocessor," IEEE Trans. Comput. vol. c-35, pp. 969-977, Nov. 1986.

[3] V.K. Prasanna Kumar and V. Krishnan, "Efficient Image Template Matching on SIMD Hypercube Machines," in Proc. Int'l Conference on Parallel Processing, pp. 756-771, Aug. 1987.

[4] J.H. Baek and K.A. Teague, "Parallel Edge Detection on the Hypercube," in Proc. Fourth Conference on Hypercubes, Concurrent Computers, and Applications, pp. 983-986, March 1989.

[5] S. Ranka and S. Sahni, "Hypercube Algorithms for Image Transformations," in Proc. Int'l Conference on Parallel Processing, pp. III 24-31, Aug. 1989.

[6] W.R. Moore, "A Review of Fault-Tolerant Techniques for the Enhancement of Integrated Circuit Yield," Proc. IEEE, vol. 74, pp.684-698, May 1986.

[7] F.P. Preparata and J. Vuillemin, "The Cube-Connected Cycles: A versatile network for parallel computation," Commun. ACM, vol. 24, pp. 300-309, May 1981.

[8] J.J. Shen and I. Koren, "Yield Enhancement Designs for WSI Cube-Connected Cycles," in Proc. Int'l Conf. Wafer Scale Integration, pp. 289-298, Jan. 1989.

[9] M.S. Krishnan and J.P. Hayes, "An Array Layout Methodology for VLSI Circuits," IEEE Trans. Comput. vol. c-35, pp. 1055-1067, Dec. 1986.

[10] P. Banerjee, S.Y. Kuo and W.K. Fuchs, "Reconfigurable Cube-Connected Cycles Architectures," in Proc. 16th Int'l Symp. Fault-Tolerant Computing., pp. 286-291, June 1986.

[11] H.Y. Youn et al., "An Efficient Reconfiguration Scheme for WSI of Cube-Connected Cycles with Bounded Channel Width," in Proc. 1989 Int'l Workshop on Defect and Fault Tolerance in VLSI Systems, Oct. 1989.

[12] S. Ranka and S. Sahni, "Image Template Matching on MIMD Hypercube Multicomputers," in Proc. Int'l Conference on Parallel Processing, Vol III. pp. 92-99, Aug. 1988.

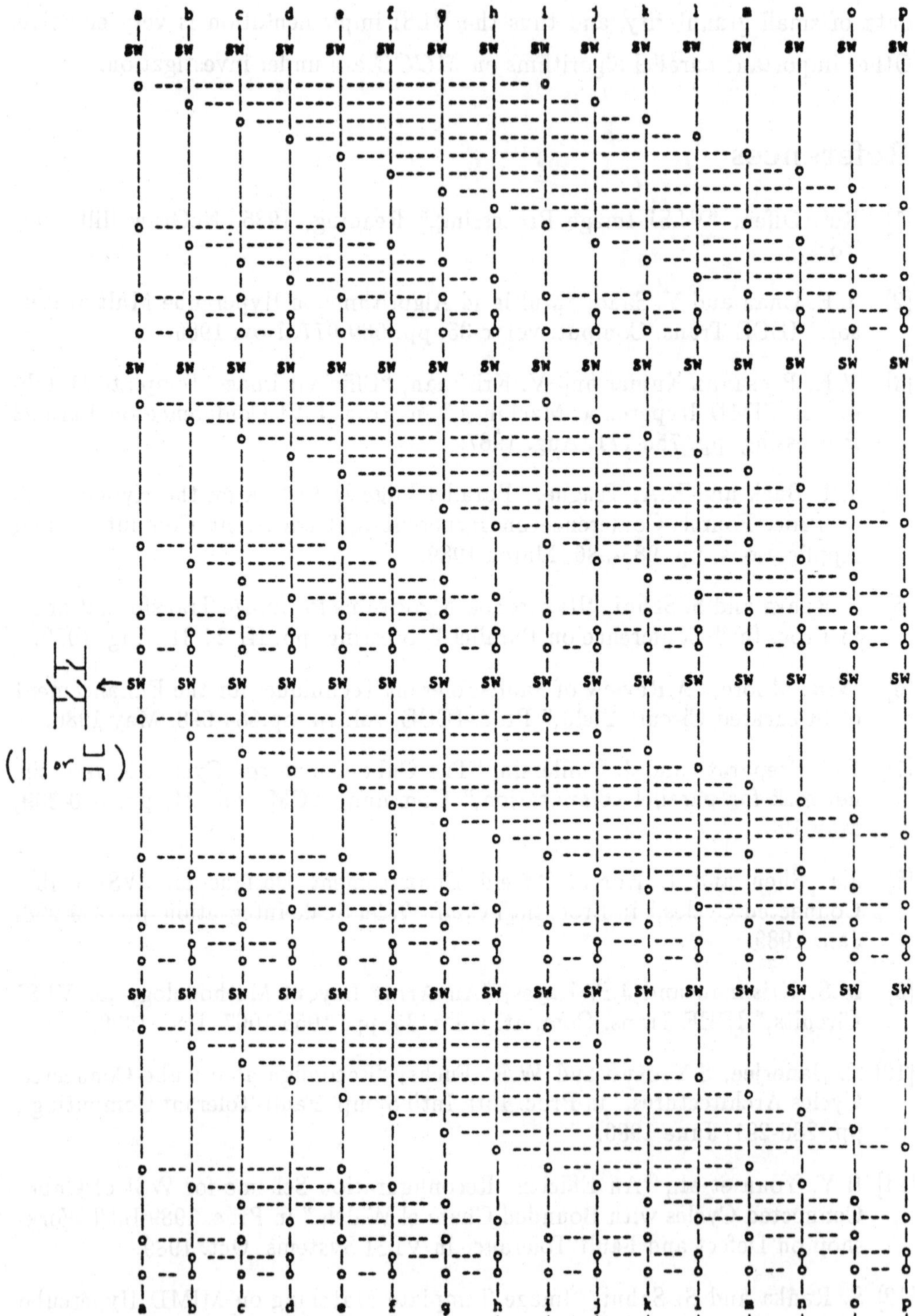

Figure 1. An MCCC(4,4) network

```
. . . (i-1,j+M)   (i,j+M)    (i+1,j+M)   . . .   (i+M,j+M)   (i+M+1,j+M)  . .
                  +-------------------------------------------+
. . . (i-1,j+M-1)|(i,j+M-1)  (i+1,j+M-1) . . .  (i+M,j+M-1)|(i+M+1,j+M-1) . .
. . .      .     |    .          .        . . .      .     |     .          . .
. . .      .     |    .          .        . . .      .     |     .          . .

. . .      .     |    .          .        . . .      .     |     .          . .

. . .      .     |    .          .        . . .      .     |     .          . .
. . . (i-1,j+1)  |(i,j+1)    (i+1,j+1)   . . .  (i+M,j+1)  |(i+M+1,j+1)    . .
. . . (i-1,j)    |(i,j)      (i+1,j)     . . .  (i+M,j)    |(i+M+1,j)      . .
                  +-------------------------------------------+
. . . (i-1,j-1)   (i,j-1)    (i+1,j-1)   . . .  (i+M,j-1)   (i+M+1,j-1)   . .
. . .      .          .          .        . . .      .           .          . .
```

Figure 2. B[i,j] of size M x M

```
B = +-----------------+      VS = +-----------------+      HS = +-----------------+
    | 5 4 3 3 3 3 2 2 |           | 4 4 3 3 3 3 2 2 |           | 2 2 2 2 2 2 2 2 |
    | 4 5 4 4 3 3 2 2 |           | 4 4 3 3 3 3 2 2 |           | 2 2 2 2 2 2 2 2 |
    | 4 4 4 4 3 4 2 2 |           | 4 4 3 3 3 3 2 2 |           | 2 2 2 2 2 2 2 2 |
    | 5 4 4 5 3 3 4 2 |           | 4 4 3 3 3 3 2 2 |           | 2 2 2 2 2 2 2 2 |
    | 5 5 4 4 4 3 2 2 |           | 4 4 3 3 3 3 2 2 |           | 2 2 2 2 2 2 2 2 |
    | 6 5 4 3 4 4 2 2 |           | 4 4 3 3 3 3 2 2 |           | 2 2 2 2 2 2 2 2 |
    | 4 6 5 3 4 4 3 2 |           | 4 4 3 3 3 3 2 2 |           | 2 2 2 2 2 2 2 2 |
    | 5 4 4 7 3 5 6 3 |           | 4 4 3 3 3 3 2 2 |           | 2 2 2 2 2 2 2 2 |
    +-----------------+           +-----------------+           +-----------------+
```

Figure 3. Image shrinking by VS and HS

```
procedure VS;
begin
        A(u,v) := I(u,v);         {0 <= u,v < M}
        for i := 0 to k-1 do      { M = 2**k }
        begin
                B(u,v) := A(u,v);
                SHIFT(B(u,v), -2**i, M);  {counter-clockwise circular}
                A(u,v) := min{A(u,v), B(u,v)};
        end;
end;
```

Figure 4. Vertical Shifting Procedure

```
o (u,v+1)
|
|             o (u+1,v+1)
|             |
|             |
o-------o (u+1,v)
(u,v)
```

Figure 5. Connections for
Stage 1 operation

5. Distributed Computing and Systems

GENERALIZED FAULT TOLERANCE PROPERTIES

OF STAR GRAPHS

Pradip K Srimani
Department of Computer Science
Colorado State University
Ft. Collins, CO 80523
srimani@CS.ColoState.Edu

Abstract

Recently an attractive interconnection topology has been proposed which compares very favorably with the well known n-cubes in terms of degree, diameter, fault tolerance and resilience. In this paper we investigate further fault tolerance properties of star graphs using the generalized measure of fault tolerance as introduced recently to study n-cubes. Star graphs are found again to compare favorably with n-cubes even using this generalized measure of fault tolerance.

I. Introduction

The underlying topology of any multiple processor system is, in general, modeled as an undirected graph where the nodes represent the processing elements and the arcs (edges) represent the bidirectional communication channels. Design features for an efficient interconnection topology include properties like low degree, regularity, small diameter, high connectivity, efficient routing algorithms, high fault-tolerance, low fault diameter etc. Since more and more processors must work concurrently these days in a multiple processor environment, the criterion of high fault tolerance and strong resilience [3], [4] (we'll define those terms precisely later in the paper) has become increasingly important. Until very recently, one of the most efficient symmetric interconnection networks has been the well known binary n-cubes or the hypercubes. Extensive research has been done to investigate the different desirable characteristics of the n-cubes.

Recently, a new interconnection topology, called the star graphs, has been reported in the literature [1] - [4]. It seems to be a very attractive alternative for the n-cubes in terms of various desirable properties of an interconnection structure. It has been shown that not only the star graphs can accomodate more processors with less interconnection and less communication delays, but these star graphs are also optimally fault tolerant and strongly resilient [3] like the more popular n-cubes. That is, the star graphs enjoy most of the desirable features of the n-cubes at a considerably less cost. Thus, it is of interest to further investigate the properties of these graphs as well as to design schemes to map parallel algorithms on this structure in order to make them a truly viable alternative for the n-cubes.

In order to develop deterministic measures of fault tolerance, people have mainly used the graph theoretic concept of connectivity. It has been shown in [3] that a star graph G can tolerate up to $\kappa(G)$ processor failures and upto $\lambda(G)$ link failures just like the n-cubes where $\kappa(G)$ and $\lambda(G)$ represent the vertex connectivity and edge connectivity of the underlying symmetric graph G. It has also been shown in [2], [3], that in the presence of this maximum number of tolerable faults, the fault diameter of a star graph increases at best by 3 over its fault free diameter and this fault diameter is better than the fault diameter of the n-cube of comparable size.

In a recent paper [5], the author has shown that this measure of fault tolerance in terms of the vertex connectivity of the graph suffers from several inherent drawbacks and this measure is too restrictive under the assumption of uniform distribution of faults. He has generalized the measure by introducing the concept of restricted connectivity i.e., by restricting the faulty sets to some subsets of the system components. Using this new model, the author in [5] has shown that the n-cubes can tolerate up to 2n-3 processor failures provided that, for each node (processor), all the immediately adjacent nodes do not fail simultaneously and in this situation the fault diameter of the n-cube does increase at best by 6.

Our purpose in the present paper is to investigate the star graphs in this model of generalized fault tolerance. We prove that under similar conditions, i.e., when the adjacent vertices of a node don't all fail simultaneously, the star graphs can sustain up to 2n-5 processor failures and the fault diameter increases only by a constant, i.e., the star graphs are also strongly resilient under the new measure. In section II we discuss the necessary background material and terminology while section III describes our main results. Section IV concludes the paper and presents some open problems related to star graphs.

II. Notation, Terminology and Background

In this section we define few terminologies and discuss the background information necessary for our subsequent discussion. Graph theoretic terms not defined here can be found in [6] and the complete details about the properties of star graphs can be found in [1] - [3]. A star graph, S_n, of order n, is defined to be a symmetric graph $G = (V, E)$ where V is the set of n! vertices each representing a distinct permutation of n symbols and E = set of (n-1)n!/2 symmetric edges such that two permutations (nodes) are connected by an edge iff one can be reached from the other by interchanging its first symbol with any other. Figure 1 shows star graphs of order 3 and 4. The diameter of S_n is given by $\lfloor 3(n-1)/2 \rfloor$ and an efficient routing algorithm exists to compute the minimal path given any two arbitrary points in a star graph [2]. Let A(G:v) or simply A(v) (when G is understood from the context) denote the set of vertices adjacent to vertex v in graph G. For any subset $X \subset V$, A(X) is defined as $\bigcup_{v \in X} A(v) - X$.

Then $|A(S_n:v)| = n-1 = d(v)$ for all $v \in S_n$, where d(v) denotes the degree of vertex v. The diameter of S_n will be denoted by k_n. The vertex connectivity $\kappa(G)$ of a graph G is defined to be the least $|X|$ for a subset $X \subset G$ such that G - X is disconnected. It has been shown in [3] that the vertex connectivity of the star graph S_n is n-1 and S_n is optimally fault tolerant or (n-2) fault tolerant in the sense that whenever an arbitrary set of (n-2) or fewer vertices are removed the remaining graph is still connected. S_n is also strongly resilient [4] under tolerable number of faults ($\leq$ n-2), in the sense that the fault diameter is upperbounded by k_n, the fault free diameter of S_n.

Author in [5] has pointed out that use of vertex connectivity of the underlying graph as the only measure of fault tolerance of the interconnection network has at least two potential disadvantages : 1) we don't get an idea about the nature of damage done to the network when $\kappa(G)$ nodes are disconnected, and 2) it is implicitly assumed that any subset of system components is equally likely to be faulty at the same time which may not be true in real life applications. Author in [5] has emphasized and elaborated on the second point with respect to the n-cubes. Let us illustrate the point with respect to the star graphs and then introduce the generalization in the fault tolerance measure as proposed in [5]. Note that each minimum cut in S_n is of size n-1 and also the fact that a subset of (n-

1) vertices can be a cut when, and only when, these vertices represent the entire adjacency set of any vertex in S_n. Thus, out of all possible $\left[\begin{array}{c} n! \\ n-1 \end{array}\right]$ vertex subsets of size n-1, only n! are minimum cuts of the star graph S_n (we'll prove this rigorously in the next section). Assuming that every fault set is equiprobable, the probability that an arbitrary fault set of size n-1 will disconnect the the remaining network is very small and gets smaller as n grows large. This motivates one to define the restricted connectivity or the R-vertex-connectivity [5] $\kappa'(G|Y:R)$ of a graph G as the minimum cardinality $|Y|$ of vertices such that G-Y is disconnected and Y is restricted to a given set of subsets of V [5]. For a given S_n, we define, as in [5], $R = \{X \subset V \mid$ for any $v \in V$, $A(v) \notin X\}$, and $\kappa'(S_n) = \kappa(G|Y:R)$. Hence a star graph S_n can tolerate up to $\kappa' - 1$ processor failures provided that for any node in the graph all of its adjacent nodes do not fail simultaneously. Author in [5] has computed this κ' for n-cubes to be 2n-2. We compute the same for the star graphs in the next section and also establish a few more related results to show that star graphs compare favorably with n-cubes even with respect to this generalized measure of fault tolerance.

III. Main Results

We will assume $n \geq 3$ in order to avoid trivial cases. We use $V(S_n)$ to indicate the vertex set and $E(S_n)$ to indicate the edge set of S_n.

Lemma 1 : For an arbitrary edge (u,v) in $E(S_n)$, we have $\{A(u) - v\} \cap \{A(v) - u\} = \varnothing$.

Proof : Let the first symbol in u and v be Y and X respectively. For all vertices in A(v) - u, the symbol Y is in the same position as in v, say j. Now Y is in the first position of u and vertices in A(u) are generated by exchanging Y with any other symbols in u. To bring Y to the j-th position will lead to vertex v. Thus the vertices in A(u) - {v} can't have Y in j-th position. Hence the result.

Corollary : For any arbitrary u, v $\in S_n$, $|A(v) \cap A(u)| \leq 1$.

Lemma 2 : Consider two edges (u,v) and (v,w) in $E(S_n)$. We have $\{A(u) - v\} \cap \{A(w) - v\} = \varnothing$.

Proof : Use similar arguments as in proof of lemma 1.

Corollary : If we define $Q(e) = \{A(u) - v\} \cup \{A(v) - u\}$ for any edge e = (u,v) in S_n, then $|Q(e)| = 2n-4$.

Theorem : $\kappa'(S_n) = 2n - 4$.

Proof : Let F be an arbitrary subset of $V(S_n)$ such that $|F| = 2n - 5$ and for any vertex $v \in V(S_n)$, $A(v) \not\subset F$. Let (u,v) be an arbitrary edge in $E(S_n)$. Define $Z = \{A(v) - u\} \cup \{A(u) - v\}$. Clearly $|Z| = 2n-4$ [lemma 1]. Also Z belongs to the set R as defined in the preceding section, i.e., Z is an allowed fault set and the graph S_n - Z is clearly disconnected. Hence $\kappa'(S_n) \leq 2n-4$.

To show the equality, we prove that S_n - F is always connected. By looking at the $f = |F|$ permutations (corresponding to the faulty nodes), there must be at least one symbol X that does *not* appear *more than once* in the first position (since $f < 2n-2$). Additionally, there must be a position i $(2 \leq i \leq n)$ where X does not appear more than once. Consider those vertices of S_n having X in the i-th position; call them X_i vertices. There are (n-1)! of them and they form a subgraph isomorphic to S_{n-1}; call it S_{n-1}^*. So $|S_{n-1}^* \cap F| = 1$ and hence S_{n-1}^* - F is connected. Now consider all those vertices of S_n that have X in the first position; call those X_1 vertices. All of these X_1 vertices excepting one are faultfree and none of them are in S_{n-1}^*. Also each X_1 vertex is connected to a unique vertex in S_{n-1}^* and each vertex in S_n, other than the X_1 and X_i vertices, are connected to a unique X_1 vertex. All we need to show is that each nonfaulty vertex in S_n - S_{n-1}^* is connected to some nonfaulty vertex in S_{n-1}^* (S_{n-1}^*-F is connected). Consider an arbitrary nonfaulty vertex u (non X_1 vertex) in S_n - S_{n-1}^*. Let X_1^u and X_i^u be the corresponding X_1 and X_i vertices (note that for a given u, X_1^u and X_i^u are unique).

Case 1 : If both X_1^u and X_i^u are nonfaulty, we are done.

Case 2 : Assume X_i^u is faulty and X_1^u is nonfaulty. Let $RA(X_1^u) = A(X_1^u) - X_1^u$ for any X_1 vertex X_1^u. Then $|RA(X_1^u)| = n-2$ and $|RA(X_1^u) - F| \geq 1$ since $u \in RA(X_1^u)$ is faultfree by assumption. Consider the set $A(RA(X_1^u) - F)$: this set does not have any X_1 or any X_i vertex and also $|A(RA(X_1^u) - F| = (n-2)(n-2-i)$ where $i = |RA(X_1^u) \cap F|$ and $0 \leq i$ n-3 [see lemma 2]. Since X_i^u is faulty, one X_1 vertex is faulty, i of $RA(X_1^u)$ are faulty and $|F| = 2n-5$, we can write

$$| A(RA(X_1^u) - F) - F | \geq (n-2)(n-2-i) - (2n-5) + (i+2)$$

$$= (n-2)^2 - i(n-3) - (2n-5) + 2 \geq 2$$

Thus the vertex u is connected to non faulty vertices, say v and w, by a distance of at most 3. Both X_1^v and X_1^w can't be faulty and neither of X_i^v and X_i^w is faulty. Hence u is connected to a nonfaulty vertex in S_{n-1}^* by a path length of at most 5.

Case 3 : Assume X_i^u is fault free and X_1^u is faulty. Again consider the set $A(u) - X_1^u$. Then $|\{A(u) - X_1^u\} - F| = i \geq 1$, by assumption of the nature of the faults. Consider any nonfaulty vertex v in $A(u) - X_1^u$. X_1^v must be faultfree (only one X_1 vertex can be faulty). If Xsupy is fault free, we are done. If not, there are two subcases : **Subcase a) :** $i > 1$. Select another nonfaulty vertex v from $A(u) - X_1^u$. Now both X_1^v and X_i^v must be nonfaulty and we are done. **Subcase b) :** consider the set $\{A(v) - X_1^v - u\} - F$. If this set is nonnull, choose any w from it; otherwise, $|RA(X_1^v) - v| \geq 1$ (since there are only $2n-7$ non-$(X_1$ or $X_i)$ faults, $n-3$ of them are already accounted for and $|RA(X_1^v) - v| = n-2$). Consider any $w \in \{RA(X_1^v) - v\} - F$. We have $d(u,w) = 4$. X_1^w can't be faulty and neither can X_i^w and hence u is connected to a nonfaulty vertex in S_{n-1}^* by a path of length at most 6.

Case 4 : Assume both X_1^u and X_i^u are faulty. Consider any nonfaulty vertex $v \in \{A(u) - X_1^u\}$; there must be at least one. X_1^v or X_i^v can't be faulty and hence u is connected to S_{n-1}^* by a path of length at most 3.

It is apparent from this proof that the diameter of $S_n - F$ is $\leq k_n + 15$ since the diameter of $S_{n-1}^* - F$ is $k_n + 3$ [3]. Note that we strongly suspect that this bound is very loose; we have not considered myriad of edges in S_n. Also we have not used the fact that S_{n-1}^* contains only one fault. Although our method shows the strong resilience of the star graphs under this generalized fault tolerance measure, we believe that the diameter of the faulty graph will be much less.

Hence, we have shown that when not all the adjacent nodes of a single node fail simultaneously, a star graph S_n can tolerate up to $2n-5$ processor failures. We have shown that even under the assumption of restricted faulty sets $S_n - F$ is disconnected when $|F| = 2n-4$. As was initially asked in [5] of n-cubes, we want to ask a similar question : what happens in a star graph S_n when an arbitrary set of $2n-4$ processors fail at the same time ? Also, can we determine efficiently whether $S_n - F$ is disconnected when $|F| \leq 2n-4$? This question can be answered by using any one of the existing graph search algorithms [5], but the complexity is of the order of the number of edges in the graph. In our case the number of edges in the S_n is $n!(n-1)/2$. We attempt to design an algorithm which is polynomial in n, the order of the star graph. This was done for the n-cubes in [5].

Lemma 3 : Let x be an arbitrary vertex in S_n and assume $F = A(x) \cup \{x\}$. Then $S_n - F$ is connected.

Proof : In order to prove the lemma we show that given two nonfaulty vertices u and v $\notin$ F, there always exists a path that avoids F. Without loss of generality, assume that the vertex x represents a permutation that is at a distance k_n from the vertex y representing the identity permutation. Thus $d(x) = k_n$. Hence for any vertex x_i, adjacent to x, we must have $d(x_i) = k_n - 1$. Now if $d(u) < k_n$, no vertex on the minimal path from u to y can belong to F (the routing algorithm of [2] ensures that every move on the minimal path reduces the distance by one). Assume $d(u) = k_n$. The minimal path from u to y can't contain x. If $A(u) \cap A(x) = \varnothing$, we are done; otherwise $|A(u) \cap A(x)| = 1$ (see lemma 1) and $A(u) \cap A(x) = x_i$, say. In this case we claim that there is another adjacent vertex of u which is also on a minimal path from u to y. There are two possibilities : 1) the permutation of u starts with A (identity permutation is ABCD...Z) and therefore each adjacent vertex of u is on a minimal path from u to y, 2) the permutation of u starts with anything other than A and there must be more than one cycle in permutation (u) and hence u has more than one adjacent vertex that can lead minimally to y. We can similarly argue for the vertex v and hence there is always a path from u to v that avoids F.

Lemma 4 : Let $F \subset V(S_n)$ such that $|F| = n-1$. Then S_n-F is disconnected iff F contains A(v) for some v in S_n. Also when S_n-F is disconnected, it contains two components : one isolated vertex and the rest of the graph.

Proof : Readily follows from theorem 1 and lemma 3.

Theorem 2 : Let F be a subset of $V(S_n)$ such that $|F| = 2n-4$ and there does not exist a vertex $v \in S_n$ such that $A(v) \subset F$. Then S_n-F is disconnected iff there does exist an edge e such that $Q(e) = F$.

Proof : The proof is very much similar to that of theorem 1; we have to modify arguments at few places to show that there always exists a path between two nonfaulty vertices when there does not exist an edge e with $Q(e) = F$.

Now to compute if S_n-F is disconnected when arbitrary F with $|F| \le 2n-4$ is given, we can design the following algorithm which is similar to algorithm 1 of [5] designed for the same purpose for n-cubes.

Step_0 : If $|F| < n-1$ then S_n-F is connected. Stop

Step_1 : If $|F| \le 2n-4$, then if there exist a vertex v such that $v \notin$ and $A(v) \subset$ F then S_n-F is disconnected. Stop.

Step_2 : If $|F| < 2n-4$, then S_n-F is connected. Stop

Step_3 : If $|F| = 2n-4$ and there exists an edge e such that $Q(e) = F$ then S_n-F is disconnected; otherwise S_n is connected. Stop.

Step_1 takes $O(n.|F|)^2$ computation steps [5]. We show that Step_3 can also be computed in $O(n^2)$ steps for star graphs just like the n-cubes [5].

Lemma 5 : For any edge e $\in$ S_n, the vertices in $Q(e)$ can be divided into two equal groups such that each vertex in the same group has the same last symbol.

Proof : It follows from the simple observation that for edge (u,v) the last symbol in each of the vertices in $A(u)$ - {v} must be the same.

Lemma 6 : Consider an arbitrary subset $X \subset A(v)$ - {u} for any edge (u,v) in S_n. Collect in a set Y the symbols in position i, $2 \leq i \leq n$ from all vertices in X. Then $|Y| \leq 2$.

Proof : Obvious.

A simple operation MIN is defined on 3 arbitrary permutations u, v, and w as follows. Use u_i to denote i-th symbol in u, $1 \leq i \leq n$.

1) Set i = 1.
2) Check u_i, v_i and w_i. If they are same, set i = i+1 and go to step 2). If they are all different, return "MIN(u, v, w) undefined". If two of them are equal and the third is different, say u_i, then MIN(u,v,w) is obtained by interchanging the symbol u_i with u_1 in u.

Lemma 7 : Consider any arbitrary x, y, z $\in$ $A(v)$ - {u} for an edge (u,v) in S_n. Then v = MIN (x, y, z).

Proof : Obvious.

We can now describe an $O(n^2)$ implementation of Step_3 of our original algorithm.

1) See if the given set F can be divided into two sets F_1 and F_2 such that vertices in each set has the same last symbol. If not, return NO. This can be done in $O(|F|)$ steps.
2) Choose any 3 arbitrary vertices u, v, w from F_1. Compute x_1 = MIN (u, v, w). If it is undefined, then return NO. Otherwise check if x_1 is adjacent to each vertex in F_1. If not, return NO. This step can be done in $O(n^3)$ steps.
3) Repeat step 2) with F_2. Call the relevant vertex x_2.

4) Check if x_1 and x_2 are adjacent. If not, return NO; otherwise return YES.

It is easy to show that this implementation has a complexity of $O(n^3)$ and therefore our original algorithm is $O(n^4)$.

IV. Conclusion

We have used the generalized measure of fault tolerance as introduced in [5] to investigate the star graphs. We have shown that, just like n-cubes, the star graphs are also strongly resilient, where the adjacent sets of vertices are considered forbidden faulty sets. Although we have computed the fault tolerant diameter of the star graphs under the stated assumptions, we suspect that our bound is not tight; our main objective in the present paper is to prove the result on the restricted connectivity of star graphs.

V. References

[1] S. B. Akers and B. Krishnamurthy, " A group theoretic model for symmetric interconnection networks", **Proceedings of Intl. Conf. on Parallel Processing**, pp. 216-213, 1986.

[2] S. B. Akers, D. Harel and B. Krishnamurthy, " The star graph : an attractive alternative to the n-cube", **Proceedings of Intl. Conf. on Parallel Processing**, pp. 393-400, 1987.

[3] S. B. Akers and B. Krishnamurthy, "The fault tolerance of star graphs", **Proceedings of 2nd Intl. Conf. on Supercomputing**, 1987.

[4] M. S. Krishnamurthy and B. Krishnamurthy, "Fault diameter of interconnection networks", **Journal of Comput. Math. Appl.**, Vol. 13, pp. 577-582, 1987.

[5] A. -H. Esfahanian, "Generalized measures of fault tolerance with application of N-cube networks", **IEEE Trans. Comput.**, Vol. 38, pp. 1586-1591, Nov. 1989.

[6] F. Harary, Graph Theory, **Addison-Wesley**, Reading, MA, 1972.

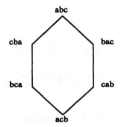

Figure 1(a) : The 3-Star

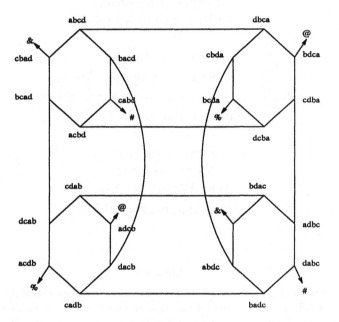

Figure 1(b) : The 4-Star

Figure 1: Star Graphs of order 3 and 4

A Formal Description of the IC* Model of Parallel Computation

B. Gopinath *
Department of Computer Science
Rutgers University
New Brunswick, NJ 08903

Ambuj K. Singh *
Department of Computer Science
University of California at Santa Barbara
Santa Barbara, CA 93106

Prem Uppaluru *
Fluent Machines
1881 Worcester Road
Framingham, MA 01701

Abstract

Formal semantics for a new model for parallel computation called IC* is defined. This model differs widely from existing parallel models and is suitable for describing hardware and communication protocols with real time properties. Its interesting features are the absence of interleaving assumptions and a high-level predicate-based specification and programming language. In this paper, the semantics of IC* is given by first describing the basic idea of a behavior and later building on this definition to obtain three increasingly complex models of computation. Finally, the IC* model is compared with some existing formalisms.

1   Introduction

Because of increased computing capacity and the raw speed of parallel hardware, parallel computing offers great potential for designing, verifying, and implementing large and complex software systems. However, the limited experience with parallel computing has demonstrated that programming parallel hardware is extremely difficult. Straightforward extensions to sequential computing such as vector processing, shared variables, message passing and remote procedure calls have either not delivered the expected performance or proved too complex to program [3]. Consequently, fundamental changes are needed

---

*This work was done while the authors were at Bellcore.

in our approach to problem solving and in our models of computation in order to fully exploit the potential of parallel computing. We need to break away from conventional computational paradigms in which the notions of processes, synchronization, mutual exclusion, coordination, message exchange or shared data are the primitive concepts and look for inherently parallel models of computation in which properties of systems and their behavior can be expressed in precise mathematical logic without any of the implementational concerns. Such models should also permit easy expression of conventional notions of processes, synchronization etc., but not enforce them.

The IC* model of parallel computation [4, 9] is one such model. It has been useful in specifying and implementing complex protocols and in specifying and modeling of communication systems [7, 8]. It differs from other existing models of parallel computation in a number of ways, the foremost being that it does not model parallelism by a non-deterministic interleaving of *actions*. The interleaving model, besides being unnatural, usually relies on some fairness in order to model parallelism adequately. In IC*, parallelism is modeled by the simultaneous enforcement of global properties through dynamic composition of local properties. These local properties may be specified in a causal or a non-causal way, thus permitting an elegant integration of prescriptive and declarative specifications. The focus on the properties of systems rather than on the primitive units of computation permits a wide spectrum of choices to the designer in tailoring a language to a specific domain. The designer can select the set of primitive functions and predicates best suited to the specification of properties in an application domain. For example, a hardware description language may use functions and predicates on boolean vectors and a database language may use relational calculus.

In IC*, conflicts are avoided and simultaneity is permitted by specifying some degree of nondeterminism in the enforcement of global properties. By clearly identifying at every step, the set of properties that have to be maintained and the set of entities that are free to change, the model allows precise and flexible specification of global consistency at every step. Though an interleaving of actions can be modeled in IC*, it is an exception, complete parallelism is the rule.

The unit of specification in IC* is an *invariant*. The local properties of the system can be specified either causally or non-causally through the use of *differential* and *static* invariants. Global properties of the system are defined via the conjunction of properties resulting from the differential and static invariants. Typically, in existing models of computation, a unit of computation identifies the set of entities that are permitted to change by specifying the changes either through an assignment of new values to variables or through a substitution of old symbols by new ones. In IC*, the set of entities that are permitted to change is dynamically derived from precise composition of properties resulting from the invariants. Such a composition allows independently specified systems to be dynamically integrated into a more complex system.

Another departure from existing models of computation is the decision to deal with time explicitly. This is because the IC* model is targeted towards describing real time properties of communication protocols and timing in hardware circuits. We assume a tight-coupling and specify the system using a global reference clock and shared variables. As a result, modeling conflicting activities such as *collision detect* on Ethernet or multiple circuits driving a bus line is simple in IC*.

Yet another another novel feature of the IC* model is the concept of static invariants. First and foremost, this concept provides modeling of an ideal *wire* as in the hardware. It also forms a basis for constructing complex systems from simpler, independently specified subsystems. By specifying a precise notion of composition, static invariants provide a gluing mechanism that has the potential for enhancing module reuse in software systems. In addition, static invariants can also be used as integrity constraints.

In this paper we present a formal semantics for the IC* model [14]. Our approach is layered: first, we formulate the notion of a *behavior* and later, we build on this definition and present three successive computational models each of which is a generalization of the previous one. Rest of the paper is organized into four sections. The first section defines the notions of static and differential invariants and defines the concept of a *behavior* of a system. The second section describes the three models of computation. The third section compares the IC* model of computation with some existing models of computation: event-based model [13], and UNITY [6], and some logics for real time [10, 11, 12]. The last section concludes with an informal discussion of assumptions and intuitions underlying the design of the IC* model.

2   Basic Definitions

In this section we present the basic constructs of IC*. These include the modeling of time, state variables, interpretations, static and differential invariants, and behaviors. We discuss them successively next.

As stated earlier, we model time explicitly in order to describe real time properties of communication protocols and timing in hardware circuits. This modeling is achieved through a global integer variable t that is initially 0 and increments by 1 at each computation step.

In order to allow past and future references to a variable's values, we model a program variable (store) as a function from integers to the type of the variable. For example, a *natural* variable v is modeled as a function called v with domain integers and range naturals. Thus, $v(5)$ represents the value of the variable v at time 5. An unknown value is represented by the special symbol $\bot$. Thus, $v(10) = \bot$ represents that the value of the variable v at time 10 is unknown. We assume that a predicate with argument $\bot$ evaluates to false and a function with argument $\bot$ evaluates to $\bot$. For any variable v and any time i, the entity $v(i)$ is called a *term*. Next we define an *interpretation*.

Definition: An *interpretation* is an assignment of values to all the terms in the system.
□

As an example, consider a system with only one variable v. A possible interpretation then is given by $v(0) = 5$ and $v(i) = \bot$ for all $i \neq 0$.

Notation: We use symbols π, π_0, π_i, etc. to denote individual interpretations and symbol Π to denote a sequence of interpretations $\pi_0, \pi_1, \ldots$, one for every time. Symbol $\tau|_i$ denotes the value of the term τ at time i as defined by interpretation π_i. Similarly, for any expression E, the symbol $E|_i$ denotes the value of the expression E at time i under interpretation π_i.
□

Example: Assume a system with a single variable v and let interpretation π_3 be defined as follows:

$v(0) = 1, v(1) = 2, v(2) = 3, v(3) = 4$, and $v(4) = v(5) = v(6) = \cdots = \bot$

Then, using the above notation we can assert the following:

$v(1)|_3 = 2, v(t)|_3 = v(3)|_3 = 4$, and $(v(t) = v(t-1) + 1)|_3 = true$

As computation progresses, an increasing number of terms may get defined. For example, assume that at time 0, $v(0)$ equals 7 and all other terms are unknown. What about the terms at time 1? It is clear that $v(0)$ should still be 7. However, the other terms may be different. For example, $v(1)$ may now be 13. (It is also possible for some *future* term, say $v(5)$, to get defined at this time.) In order to formalize this requirement, we introduce the notion of a *consistent* interpretation sequence.

Definition: An interpretation sequence Π is *consistent* iff the following two conditions hold for all terms $v(j)$:

- $v(j)|_i \neq \perp \Rightarrow v(j)|_i = v(j)|_{i+1}$, and

- $j \leq i \Rightarrow v(j)|_i = v(j)|_{i+1}$.

The first requirement states that terms committed to a non-$\perp$ value are not changed and the second requirement states that terms in the *past* are not modified. □

The basic constructs for writing specifications or programs in IC* are static and differential invariants. We discuss them next. A static invariant is akin to a safety property and expresses a constraint that is always maintained. Syntactically, it is a predicate in which variable t (representing time) occurs freely. As an example, consider the static invariant $v(t + 1) = w(t)$. It expresses the requirement that at all times the **v**-values lag behind the **w**-values by one unit of time and thus models a unit-delay wire with end points v and w. Static invariants are useful for describing integrity constraints and interconnection between modules, hardware and software.

A differential invariant is akin to a progress property and expresses causal relationships. It represents the driving force behind the sphere of computation as opposed to a static invariant which decides the shape of the sphere of computation. A differential invariant has two parts: a *cause* predicate, that determines when it will be triggered and an *effect* predicate, that expresses the constraints on the *next* state if it is triggered. It is written as a tuple $\langle cause\ predicate,\ effect\ predicate \rangle$. As in static invariants, the only variable occurring free in the cause and effect predicates is t, the variable modeling time. As an example, consider the differential invariant $\langle v(t) = w(t),\ u(t) \rangle$. It expresses the requirement that whenever variables **v** and **w** have the same value, at the next time boolean variable **u** will be true. The cause predicate of a differential invariant is evaluated at the current time whereas the effect predicate is evaluated at the next time.

Notation: We use symbols $\delta, \delta_0, \delta_i$, etc. to denote sets of invariants – static and differential, and symbol Δ to denote a sequence of invariant sets $\delta_0, \delta_1, \ldots$, one for every time. For any set of invariants δ, symbols $S(\delta)$ and $D(\delta)$ denote respectively the set of static and differential invariants in δ. □

As in an assignment statement of an ordinary programming language, where only those variables that appear on the left hand side of the assignment change as a result of the assignment, the IC* model also has a syntactic restriction on what can change from one state to next. This requirement is stated in terms of the *difference set* [14] and only the terms in the difference set are allowed to change from one state to the next.

The difference set is dynamically determined by the set of triggered differential invariants and the static invariants. It is computed by the closure of all the terms that are mentioned in static invariants and the effect predicates of triggered differential invariants as follows.

- Every term occurring in the effect of a triggered differential invariant belongs to the difference set.

- Every term co-occurring with a term in the difference set in a static invariant belongs to the difference set.

- No other term belongs to the difference set.

As an example, assume that at $t = 5$, the set of invariants consist of a differential invariant $\langle true, v(t) > 0 \rangle$ and a static invariant $w(t + 2) > 0$. Then, by definition, the difference set at time 5 is the set $\{v(6)\}$. (Note that the effect predicate is evaluated at time $t = 6$.) The term $v(6)$ is in this set as it appears in the effect of a differential invariant whose cause is true and the term $w(7)$ is not in the set as it does not appear with the term $v(6)$ in a static invariant. Now, if the above static invariant is modified to $w(t + 2) > v(t + 1)$, then the difference set becomes $\{v(6), w(7)\}$. As before, the term $v(6)$ is in this set because it appears in the effect of a differential invariant whose cause is true; however, now the term $w(7)$ is also in this set because both the terms $v(6)$ and $w(7)$ occur in the same static invariant. The difference set at time i is denoted $diff_i$.

There is one kind of a change that is not characterized by the difference set. Consider a system with a variable $\mathbf{v}$ and assume that the terms $v(5)$ and $v(6)$ are assigned the values 10 and $\bot$, respectively under some interpretation at time 5. Further, suppose that the value of the variable does not change at time 6. Then, this means that the value of the term $v(6)$ under the interpretation at time 6 should be the old value, i.e., 10. Thus, though the value of the term $v(6)$ has changed from $\bot$ to 10 under the new interpretation, the new value is merely a copy of the old value. Such changes in which $v(i+1)|_{i+1}$ equals $v(i)|_i$ are called *trivial* changes and are not characterized by the difference set.

Next, we define the notion of a behavior. This definition serves as a building block for the computational models presented in the next section.

Definition: A *behavior* is a tuple (Π, Δ) where Π is a consistent interpretation sequence and Δ is a sequence of invariant sets such that the following three conditions hold.

- The static invariants hold at all times, i.e., $(\forall i, \phi \ : \ \phi \in S(\delta_i) \ : \ \phi|_i)$.

- If the cause ϕ of a differential invariant $\langle \phi, \psi \rangle$ is true in the current state i, then the effect ψ is true in the next state, i.e., $(\forall i, \phi, \psi \ : \ \langle \phi, \psi \rangle \in D(\delta_i) \ : \ \phi|_i \Rightarrow \psi|_{i+1})$.

- If the value of the term $v(i + 1)$, changes non-trivially between time i and $i + 1$ then $v(i + 1)$ belongs to the difference set at time i, i.e.,
  $(\forall i, v :: v(i+1)|_{i+1} \neq v(i)|_i \ \Rightarrow \ v(i+1) \in diff_i)$.
  Furthermore, if the value of a term $v(j)$ at time $i + 1$, where $j > i + 1$, is different from the corresponding value at time i then $v(j)$ belongs to the difference set at time i, i.e., $(\forall i, j, v \ : \ j > i + 1 : v(j)|_{i+1} \neq v(j)|_i \ \Rightarrow \ v(j) \in diff_i)$.

□

Example: Consider a hardware system consisting of three elements: a nondeterministic signal source that chooses an integer value at random with an output port u, a comparator that compares successive input values at its input port v and outputs a 1 at its output port w iff the two values are the same, and a unit-delay wire that connects output port u of the nondeterministic signal source to the input port v of the comparator.

The signal source can be modeled by the differential invariant $\langle true, u(t) \neq \bot \rangle$, the comparator can be modeled by the differential invariant $\langle v(t) = v(t - 1), \ w(t - 1) \rangle$, (for example, if $v(5) = v(4)$ at time 5 then $w(5)$ will be true at time 6, and hence, from the consistency condition, will also be true at time 5), and the wire can be modeled by the static invariant $v(t+1) = u(t)$. The system can then be described by a set HS consisting of the above three invariants.

Let Δ be a sequence of invariant sets such that each element of the sequence consists of HS. Let Π be a sequence of interpretations for the above system given by the following table. (All the terms not mentioned in the table are undefined, i.e., evaluate to $\perp$.)

π_0 : $\quad u(0) = 4$
$\qquad v(0) = 5$
$\qquad w(0) = false$
π_1 : $\quad u(0) = 4, u(1) = 11$
$\qquad v(0) = 5, v(1) = 4$
$\qquad w(0) = false, w(1) = false$
π_2 : $\quad u(0) = 4, u(1) = 11, u(2) = 11$
$\qquad v(0) = 5, v(1) = 4, v(2) = 11$
$\qquad w(0) = false, w(1) = false, w(2) = false$
π_3 : $\quad u(0) = 4, u(1) = 11, u(2) = 11, u(3) = 15$
$\qquad v(0) = 5, v(1) = 4, v(2) = 11, v(3) = 11$
$\qquad w(0) = false, w(1) = false, w(2) = false, w(3) = true$
$\cdots$
$\cdots$

The pair (Π, Δ) constitutes a behavior of the abovementioned system as all the conditions of the definition are satisfied.

3 Three Models of Computation

Recollect from the previous section that a behavior is a tuple consisting of a sequence of interpretations and a sequence of invariant sets. So far, we have not discussed how behaviors, i.e., the above mentioned sequences, are generated. We do so here by presenting three different mechanisms. Though these mechanisms vary in power and complexity, the basic theme remains the same; in each we first define a *program* and then define an *execution* of the program with the help of behaviors defined in the previous section. The semantics of a program is then given by the set of its executions.

In the first computational model, described in subsection 3.1, the set of invariants is fixed initially and does not change after that. In the second computational model, described in subsection 3.2, the set of invariants may change with time. We also allow a dynamic binding of some constants. The final computational model, described in subsection 3.3, is a generalization of the second computational model; in it the set of invariants is imparted some structure by a tree-based organization.

3.1 Computational Model 0

This is a simplest possible computational model in which the set of invariants does not change with time. Accordingly, a program is defined by a set of invariants and an initial interpretation.

Definition: A *program* is a tuple $\langle \pi_{init}, \delta \rangle$ where π_{init} is an interpretation and δ is an invariant set. $\qquad\qquad\square$

Next, the notion of an *execution* of a program is defined by using the definition of a behavior presented in the previous section.

Definition: A tuple $\langle \Pi, \Delta \rangle$ is an *execution* of a program $\langle \pi_{init}, \delta \rangle$ iff the following three conditions hold.

- The initial interpretations are identical, i.e., $\pi_{init} = \pi_0$.

- All the invariant sets in Δ are identical to δ, i.e., $(\forall i :: \delta_i = \delta)$.

- The tuple $\langle \Pi, \Delta \rangle$ is a behavior.

$\square$

Based on the above definition, we define the semantics of a program to be the set of all its executions. The example of a hardware system presented earlier falls under this computational model.

3.2 Computational Model 1

The previous computational model is useful for systems whose behavior is fixed over time. There are instances when the assumption of fixed behavior does not apply well. As an example, consider a protocol for transferring data over a message-passing network. It essentially consists of three phases: the connect phase, the transmission phase, and the disconnect phase. In order to describe this system adequately, we require a set of invariants for each of the three phases; initially, the first set of invariants is active and upon the completion of each phase, the next set of invariants is triggered. As another example, consider a concurrent program in which processes are created and destroyed dynamically. In this system, the set of invariants changes with the creation and deletion of processes.

In order at describe the above systems, we extend the previous computational model in two ways: first, the set of invariants is determined dynamically and generated through a set of *rules*, and second, some special constants that are bound dynamically are introduced. A *rule* identifies a set of invariants and defines when this set will be added to and removed from the *current* set of invariants.

Definition: A *rule* is a triple $\langle \phi, \delta, \psi \rangle$, where ϕ and ψ are predicates and δ is an invariant set.

$\square$

Predicate ϕ, called the *addition condition*, determines when the invariant set δ will be added to the current set of invariants and predicate ψ, called the *removal condition*, determines when δ will be removed from the current set of invariants. Once a set of invariant becomes active, we evaluate its removal condition and store it along with the invariant. Such a tuple consisting of a predicate and an invariant set is called an *activation*. As a program executes, some new activations (from the rules) may get added because of their addition conditions becoming true and some current activations may get removed because of their removal conditions becoming true. The addition of activations is modeled by a function called *grow* and the removal of activations is modeled by a function called *prune*. (Their definitions appear in [14] and are skipped for brevity.) The main difference of this model with the previous model is that now instead of the current set of invariants we have the current set of activations. However, given a set of activations a, it is quite straightforward to obtain the set of invariants that are contained within; this set is called $inv(a)$.

As stated earlier, some special constants for dynamic binding are also introduced in this model. There is such a special constant for t, the variable modeling time, and for each program variable. The dynamic binding of these special constants is performed only when a rule gets activated and the corresponding activation gets added to the current set of activations. This binding is achieved by a function called *compile* defined in [14]. For brevity, we do not discuss this aspect any further.

A program in this computational model consists of an initial interpretation, an initial set of activations, and a set of rules for dynamic generation of invariant sets.

Definition: A *program* is a triple $\langle \pi_{init}, a_{init}, r \rangle$ where π_{init} is an interpretation, a_{init} is a set of activations, and r is a set of rules. □

Next, we define the notion of an *execution* of a program.

Definition: A tuple $\langle \Pi, A \rangle$, where Π is a sequence, $\pi_0, \pi_1, \ldots$, of interpretations and A is a sequence $a_0, a_1, \ldots$, of activation sets, is an *execution* of a program $\langle \pi_{init}, a_{init}, r \rangle$ iff the following three conditions hold.

- The initial activation sets are identical, i.e, $a_{init} = a_0$, and the initial interpretations are identical, i.e., $\pi_{init} = \pi_0$.

- The activation set a_{i+1} is obtained by the correct removal and addition of activations from the activation set a_i, i.e.,
$(\forall i, \delta, \phi :: \langle \delta, \phi \rangle \in a_{i+1} \Leftrightarrow (\langle \delta, \phi \rangle \in prune(a_i, \pi_i) \vee \langle \delta, \phi \rangle \in grow(r, \pi_i)))$.

- The tuple $\langle \Pi, \Delta \rangle$ is a behavior, where Δ is defined to be the sequence $inv(a_0), inv(a_1), .$ of invariant sets.

□

As before, we define the semantics of a program to be the set of all its executions.

3.3 Computational Model 2

This computational model is obtained by a further generalization of the previous one. Observe that in the previous computational model there is no structure to the set of rules defined by a program. In some applications, it is natural to organize the rules in the form of a tree and ensure that a rule gets activated only if its parent is active. This computational model is based on this generalization. For brevity, we skip the rest of the details and refer the reader to [14].

4 Related Work

In this section we compare IC* to two other computational models – UNITY by Chandy and Misra [6], an event-based model by Lam and Shankar [13]. Later, we also compare IC* to some existing logics for reasoning about time [10, 11, 12]. These comparisons are in subsections 4.1, 4.2, and 4.3 respectively.

4.1 UNITY

IC* and UNITY share an important concept – that of absence of any notion of processes. They are both based on the thesis that the process notion complicates the specification and clutters up the design and that mapping programs onto hardware should be the last step in the design process. Whereas UNITY achieves this by defining a program to be set of assignment statements, IC* achieves this by defining a program to be a set of static and differential invariants. They both eschew control flow.

The *always* section of a UNITY program is a restricted form of the static invariants in IC*. Both the *always* section and the static invariants are useful for describing interconnections and postponing certain implementations to a later stage. We show later how an *always* section can be translated into a set of static invariants.

The IC* model differs from UNITY in two important ways – first, IC* does not model parallelism by a non-deterministic interleaving, and second, IC* explicitly models time. Both of these decisions have repercussions in the design process. Since IC* models time explicitly, two different modules can use the same global time for coordination. As a result, some of the typical synchronization problems in distributed systems can be solved trivially.

We end the comparison by illustrating how a program in UNITY can be translated into an equivalent program in *Computational Model 0*. Consider the following simple UNITY program which implements x as a random value.

> **declare integer:** x;   **boolean:** $b, sign$
> **always** $sign = x \geq 0$
> **initially** $x, b, sign = 0, true, true$
> **assign**
> $\qquad x := x - 1 \quad$ **if** b
> $\qquad\|\; x := x + 1 \quad$ **if** $\neg b$
> $\qquad\|\; b := \neg b$
> **end**

In order to translate this program, we introduce three function symbols, x, b, and $sign$. The weak fairness of UNITY is modeled by introducing a function $fair$ with domain naturals and range $\{0, 1, 2\}$ where $0, 1$, and 2 refer to the three assignment statements in the above UNITY program. This function has a value at every time indicating the statement chosen for execution; the value of the function at time i is denoted $fair(i)$. The constraint of weak fairness is introduced by adding the following fourth condition to the definition of an *execution* in Section 3.1.

$$(\forall i, id \;:\; id \in \{0, 1, 2\} \;:\; (\exists j \;:\; j > i \;:\; fair(j) = id))$$

The equivalent program in *Computational Model 0* is $\langle \pi_{init}, \delta \rangle$ where π_{init} and δ are defined as follows.

- The initial interpretation is derived from the *initially* section of the UNITY program and assigns values to the various terms as follows.

    - $x(0) = 0$, and $x(i) = \bot$ for all $i \neq 0$.
    - $b(0) = true$, and $b(i) = \bot$ for all $i \neq 0$.
    - $sign(0) = true$, and $sign(i) = \bot$ for all $i \neq 0$.

- The *always* section is transformed into a set consisting of the single static invariant
    $s \;::\; sign(t) \;=\; (x(t) \geq 0)$.

- Each assignment statement is transformed into a differential invariant. The differential invariants corresponding to the three statements are d_0, d_1, and d_2 respectively and defined as follows.

  - $d_0 = \langle (fair = 0) \wedge b(t), \quad x(t) = x(t-1) + 1 \rangle.$
  - $d_1 = \langle (fair = 1) \wedge \neg b(t), \quad x(t) = x(t-1) - 1 \rangle.$
  - $d_2 = \langle (fair = 2), \quad b(t) = \neg b(t-1) \rangle.$

- The initial set of invariants δ is defined as the set $\{s, d_0, d_1, d_2\}$

4.2 An event-based model

The event-based model by Lam and Shankar has much in common with UNITY and IC*. There is no notion of processes and a program is a collection of events. Each event specifies a predicate on variable values immediately before and after the event occurrence. As in UNITY, there is a non-deterministic fair choice at every step. Much of the earlier discussion about absence of control flow and modeling of parallelism by an interleaving of actions applies here too.

However, unlike UNITY, there is a notion of time in this model. There is a collection of local timers which may drift with respect to each other within some error bound and a collection of ideal timers which tick at a constant rate. The events can start and stop these timers and also check their values. These timers are useful in specifying and proving properties about time-dependent systems. By an appropriate choice of predicates and functions, it is possible to model these timers in IC*. A major difference is that in IC* it is possible to refer to values of state variables at any point in the past or in the future while in this model one can only refer to the values immediately before and after an event occurrence.

4.3 Logics for Reasoning About Time

There are two kinds of timing properties that are of special interest to designers of real time systems. The first kind of property specifies that some event does not happen before certain time elapses (e.g., a traffic light does not change from green to non-green in less that 20 seconds) and the second kind of property specifies an upper bound on the response time of a system (e.g., a traffic light will change to green within 50 seconds of a driver arriving at an intersection.) Both of these properties measure real time with respect to a particular event occurrence can be represented within Computational Model 1 through an appropriate definition of rules and binding of special constants. For example, the first requirement can be represented by a rule whose addition condition is $green(t) \wedge red(t-1)$, (i.e., the traffic light changes from red to green), invariant (static) is $t \leq @t + 20 \Rightarrow green(t)$ (here $@t$ is a special constant that is instantiated to the time when the rule is activated), and removal condition is $t > @t + 20$. Similarly, the second requirement can be modeled by a rule whose addition condition is arrival of the driver at the intersection, invariant (static) is $t \leq @t + 50 \vee green(t)$, and removal condition is $green(t)$.

Temporal logic as proposed initially by Pnueli [12] cannot be used for reasoning about quantitative notions of time. Recently, there have been a number of extensions to this logic in order to facilitate reasoning about real time. One such logic is a real time temporal interval logic proposed by Narayana and Aaby [11]. In essence, the authors combine the abstraction of intervals (defined in terms of events) with a quantitative notion of time. Though, it is possible to encode such intervals in IC* by using rules (Computation Model 1) and also nest them (Computation Model 2), IC* is perhaps not as abstract as the temporal logics. This is partly because IC* is meant to be a computational model and not only as a logic for specifying and verifying systems.

Another approach towards specifying and reasoning about real time systems is the Real Time Logic (RTL) of Jahanian and Mok [10]. As in IC*, the authors avoid the interleaving assumption and present an event-action model that allows the counting of event occurrences. Real time constraints are expressed using timing constraints on events. It is possible to translate specifications in RTL into equivalent specifications in IC* by using rules and special constants. (Computational Model 1)

5 Discussion

The IC* model of parallel computation is different from existing models of computation in several ways. Each of these differences result from deliberate decisions made to explore the potential of a fundamentally new way of thinking about parallel program design and implementation. The models and techniques used in the design of complex hardware, protocols and real time systems have guided the choices throughout the process of defining the model and deciding among alternatives. An explicit decision was made to come up with a model of computation general enough and expressive enough to describe a wide variety of complex systems. For a particular application domain, the model can then be specialized through domain specific-axioms.

Often, in the specification of a system, there is a trade-off between the static invariants and differential invariants depending on the priorities of high level abstraction and low level efficiency. Static invariants can elevate the expressive power, some times at the expense of efficiency. It is often possible to generate an equivalent specification with differential invariants with low computational overhead.

In this paper, we presented three mechanisms with varying power and complexity for generating the invariant sets. These mechanisms are intended to illustrate the flexibility built into the model and not meant to be a complete set. Differing domains of applications can choose different ways of generating the invariant sets. For example, a hardware description language may not require a dynamically varying invariant set unless there is a need to dynamically modify the hardware being described. On the other hand, a parallel programming language for building efficient parallel algorithms can very effectively use a language such as the one presented in Computational Models 2 or 3. These computational models can model dynamic creation and deletion of processes and communication channels in a very direct way through the use of activators and deactivators.

Acknowledgements The design of IC* has been the result of cooperative work among B. Gopinath, Prem Uppaluru, David Cohen, Sudhir Aggarwal, Linda Ness and Jane Cameron. We would like to thank Yves Caseau, Bob Horgan, and Linda Ness for reviewing the earlier drafts of this paper and suggesting improvements.

References

[1] Aggarwal, S., D. Barbara, and K. Z. Meth, "Specifying and Analyzing Protocols with SPANNER," Proceedings of the IEEE International Conference on Communications, Toronto, Canada, 1986.

[2] Aggarwal, S., D. Barbara, and K. Z. Meth, "SPANNER: A Tool for the Specification, Analysis, and Evaluation of Protocols," IEEE Transactions on Software Engineering, March 1988.

[3] Backus, J., "Can Programming Be Liberated from the Von Neumann Style? A Functional Style and Its Algebra of Programs," CACM 21:8, August 1978.

[4] Cameron, E. J., D. M. Cohen, B. Gopinath, W. M. Keese II, L. Ness, P. Uppaluru, and J. Vollaro, "The IC* Model of Parallel Computation and Programming Environment," IEEE Transactions on Software Engineering, March 1988.

[5] Chandy, C. M., "Concurrent Programming for the Masses," invited address, Third Annual ACM Symposium on Principles of Distributed Computing, Vancouver, Canada, 1984.

[6] Chandy, K. M. and J. Misra, Parallel Program Design: A Foundation, Reading, Mass.: Addison-Wesley 1988.

[7] Cohen, D. M. and E. J. Isganitis, "Automatic Generation of a Prototype of a New Protocol from its Specification," IEEE Global Telecommunications Conference, Houston, Texas, 1986.

[8] Cohen, D. M. and T. M. Guinther, "The IC* System for Protocol Development," Proceedings of SIGCOMM 1987, Stowe, Vermont, 1987.

[9] Cohen, D. M., M. L. Honig, W. M. Keese, P. Levin, J. Myers, P. Uppaluru, D. Slepian, and J. R. Vollaro, "IC*: An Environment for Specifying Complex Systems," IEEE Global Telecommunications Conference, Houston, Texas, 1986.

[10] Jahanian, F. and A. K. Mok, "Safety Analysis of Timing Properties in Real-Time Systems," IEEE Transactions on Software Engineering, Sept. 1986.

[11] Narayana, K. T., and A. A. Aaby, "Specification of Real-Time Systems in Real-Time Temporal Interval Logic", IEEE Conference on Real-Time Systems, 1988.

[12] Pnueli, A., "The Temporal Semantics of Concurrent Programs," Theoretical Computer Science, 13, 1981.

[13] Shankar, A. U., and S. S. Lam, "Time Dependent Distributed Systems: Proving Safety, Liveness, and Real-Time Properties," Distributed Computing, August 1987.

[14] Singh, A., and P. Uppaluru, "A Formal Description of the IC* Model of Parallel Computation," Bellcore Technical Memorandum TM-ARH-012977, 1988.

AN EFFICIENT ALGORITHM FOR QUIESCENCE DETECTION IN A DISTRIBUTED SYSTEM

Satyendra P. Rana
Department of Computer Science, Wayne State University
Detroit, Michigan 48202
(Internet: rana@cs.wayne.edu, Fax: (313) 577-6868)

Abstract:A message-efficient quiescence detection algorithm is presented that does not employ a pre-defined ring or tree structure among processes.
Keywords: quiescence detection, distributed algorithms, asynchronous communication.

1. Introduction

Consider a distributed system P of n processes. Each process has a distinct identity ($\leq$n) and it knows the identity of its neighbors. Communication is reliable, FIFO, and asynchronous with bounded delays such that maximum delay $\leq$ 2 * minimum delay. A process is either *active* or *passive*. The system P is said to be *quiescent* when all processes in P are passive and no messages (hereafter called *basic* messages) of P are in transit. Only an active process sends basic messages. An active process becomes passive when its local termination condition is satisfied. A passive process, when receives a basic message, becomes active again. The processes in P terminate only after P is quiescent. A detection computation is superimposed on P for detecting quiescent state of the system (for a comprehensive list of references on quiescence detection problem, see [1]). In this paper, we present a simple and message-efficient detection algorithm that does not rely upon the existence of a pre-defined ring or tree structure among processes.

2. The Detection Computation

The detection computation proposed below involves the propagation of a probe that carries a list *visited* to keep track of processes visited by it in its current round. Also, each process i maintains a list $activated_i$ which records the processes to which process i sent basic messages after the last visit of the probe. These lists are implemented by bit-vectors of size n.When process i receives the probe and finds a process both in *visited* and $activated_i$, it nullifies both lists and initiates a fresh round of the probe.

Let us define a *traversal sequence* for P rooted at r to be a sequence, say S, of integers 1 to n such that the first element in S is r and and each integer in the range 1..n appears at least once in S. We use variable NEXT to refer to the next process in a traversal sequence rooted at the initiator of the current round of the probe. A process always forwards the probe to NEXT until all processes join *visited* and quiescence is announced.

The detection computation is described as a collection of rules to be executed atomically and fairly. Initially all bits in all the lists are zeros. A predesignated process, say r, when passive for the first time starts the first round of the probe by setting rth bit in *visited* to 1 and sending *probe(visited)* to NEXT. The rules described below are followed by all processes- i denotes an arbitrary process:

R1: Process i, when sends a basic message to process j, sets jth bit in *activated$_i$* to 1.

R2: Process i, when receives a *probe(visited)*, becomes probe_holder.

R3: Process i, when passive and probe_holder, sets ith bit in *visited* to1. Further, if a bit is 1 in both *visited* and *activated$_i$*, i sets all except ith bit in *visited* to zero. Now, if all bits in *visited* are 1, i announces quiescence else it sets all bits in *activated$_i$* to zero, sends *probe(visited)* to NEXT, and ceases to be probe_holder.

A traversal sequence rooted at i is generated by a depth-first traversal of P starting at i and NEXT is the process which is next in the corresponding depth-first traversal order. The depth-first traversal order for this purpose is generated on the fly. Since the probe carries the list of processes visited by it in the current round, NEXT is taken as any neighbor who is not on list *visited*. If there is no such neighbor, NEXT is the neighbor from which the current probe was received for the first time (for details of such a scheme, see [2]).

2.1 Correctness arguments

<u>Quiescence is announced within finite time after its occurrence</u>

After quiescence, no more processes join *activated* lists. Since a process nullifies its *activated* list when forwarding the probe, within finite time after quiescence, all *activated* lists are nullified. The round initiated by the process that nullifies the last non-zero *activated* list cannot be aborted by any process, and thus, within finite time the above round will include all processes in the *visited* list and announce quiescence.

No false detection of quiescence

Consider the following invariant **I**: "For all i in *visited*, either process i is passive and no basic messages from i are in transit **or** there exists a pair j, k of processes such that j is in both *visited* and *activated$_k$* but k is not in *visited*". First, we show that **I** is preserved. Assume that at some instant, process i is active and in *visited* and there are no j, k such that j is both in *visited* and *activated$_k$* and k is not in *visited*. By rule 3, process i joins *visited* only when it is passive. Thus process i received a basic message from, say process r, after it joined list *visited*. If process r is also in *visited*, then it must have also received a basic message before sending a basic message to i. By repeating this argument, we get that there must be a process, say k, not in *visited* which sent a basic message to a process in *visited*, say j. Thus, j must be in *activated$_k$*.

If process j receives the probe from i directly, a basic message from i to j cannot be in transit because of FIFO assumption. However, a basic message from j to i may be in transit in which case i will be in *activated$_j$* and if the current round of the probe reaches j, it will be aborted at j. This shows that there cannot be any message in transit when all processes are in *visited*. Thus, **I** is preserved. Since a process announces quiescence only when all processes are in *visited*, the truth of **I** implies that P will be quiescent in the above state.

3. Concluding Remarks

We presented a distributed algorithm for quiescence detection. After its occurrence, quiescence is announced by the presented algorithm after zero delay in the best case and within at most two traversals in the worst case. In contrast, existing similar algorithms require either at least one traversal (for probe must return to its initiator) or at least two traversals (an extra round to take care of behind the back communication). The main advantage of the presented algorithm is its simplicity and message efficiency. A disadvantage is that bit vector sizes increase with the number of processes.

References

[1]. Mattern, F., "Algorithms for distributed termination detection", Distributed Computing, 2, pp. 161-175 (1987).

[2]. Sharma, M. B., Iyengar, S. S., and Mandyam, N.K., "An efficient distributed depth first search algorithm", Information Processing Letters, 32, pp. 183-186 (1989).

Interval Arithmetic for Computing Performance Guarantees in Client-Server Software

C.M. Woodside, S. Majumdar, J.E. Neilson
Telecommunications Research Institute of Ontario
Department of Systems and Computer Engineering, and
School of Computer Science
Carleton University
Ottawa K1S 5B6, Canada

Abstract

Performance analysis of client-server software systems through bounds on task throughputs is presented. The upper and lower bounds (performance guarantee) are both independent of any assumptions about the stochastic behavior of the client tasks, and make only weak assumptions on the server. The analytic expressions for the bounds however, are not in closed form. A new technique based on interval arithmetic is developed to compute numerical values for the bounds.

1 Introduction and Model

Client-server software structures are very common in distributed computer systems, for transaction processing, including database and other common services and for performing specialized computations. Remote procedure calls (RPCs) are widely used for this purpose and are explicitly supported for instance in SUNOS and in the Mach operating system [1]; server access via messages from the client to the server is used in other systems such as V [2]. The general architecture of a client-server system with R client tasks and a single server task is shown in Figure 1(a). The typical activities performed by the tasks during a client response cycle are displayed in Figure 1(b). The response cycle for a client task (say, client r) starts with task r sending a request message to the server; after sending a message the client must wait for the reply. The request joins a FIFO queue and is served with a server execution time $\tilde{s}_{1r}$, called the *phase 1 service time* for client r. The reply conveys the results to the client and allows it to continue but the server optionally executes a *phase 2* of duration $\tilde{s}_{2r}$ seconds for clean-up, data commits or other post-processing. The client executes its own program for a time $\tilde{c}_r$ and then repeats the cycle. The work rate of the system may be measured by the set of rates f_r at which the clients cycle and make requests to the server.

The throughputs f_r depend on the average execution time parameters c_r and s_{ir} (the means of the random variables $\tilde{c}_r$ and $\tilde{s}_{ir}$), on the network delays and also on the contention between clients, which depends on the shapes of the probability distributions of $\tilde{s}_{ir}$ and $\tilde{c}_r$. Server times $\tilde{s}_{ir}$ are i.i.d. with general, but increasing- failure-rate (IFR) distributions. Existing queueing theory does not solve this problem because of the second phase of service and the combination of different general service time distributions with FIFO queueing. Queueing approximations are possible and have been described in [3] and [4], but approximations always raise questions about the magnitude of errors. The approach of this paper is to find exact results which are independent of distributions, and of statistical independence assumptions on the clients, by finding bounds on the throughputs. We assume that each client and the server runs on a processor of its own, and that network contention effects are small enough to ignore, so that network delays can be included for modelling purposes in the client times $\tilde{c}_r$.

The upper bound found below is well-known but the lower bound is a new result. The importance of the lower bound is that it gives a performance guarantee. The contribution of this note is the expression for the lower bounds and a method of computation for them using interval arithmetic. Generalizations to many servers, and to second-level servers, are possible and are considered in [5]. The present paper covers the case of distinct service times to different clients, which is not considered elsewhere.

2 Bounds on Throughput

Only the first moments c_r, s_{1r} and s_{2r} for each of the R clients must be known for the following analysis. A well-known result for the upper bound of f_r is given by (see [3])

$$f_r \leq min[1/(c_r + s_{1r}), (\frac{1 - \sum_{m \neq r} f_m S_m}{S_r})] \qquad (1)$$

where the summation over m covers all clients except r and $S_i = s_{1i} + s_{2i}$ is the total mean service time for client i. The expected time C_r for a single

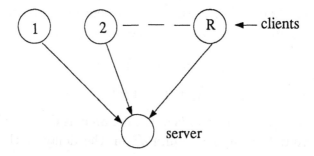

(a) The Client-Server Architecture

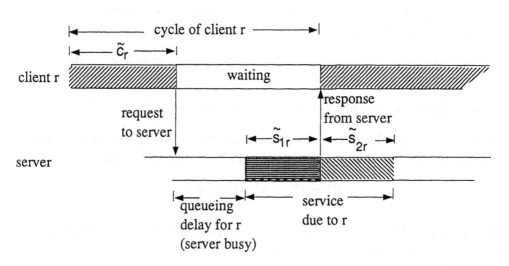

(b) A Response Cycle for Client r

Figure 1: **The Client-Server System**

response cycle of client r is the sum of two components: its own execution time c_r and the average delay d_r introduced at the server. Thus,

$$C_r = c_r + d_r \tag{2}$$

$$\text{and } f_r = 1/C_r$$

We seek the upper and lower bounds of C_r, denoted as C_r^+ and C_r^- respectively. For the upper bound, an upper bound d_r^+ on the delay at the server will be used:

$$C_r^+ = c_r + d_r^+ \tag{3}$$

The delay d_r^+ includes:

- l_r^+, the longest possible residual of a second phase (phase 2) left from a previous invocation of the server by any client,

- the service to each of the other clients queued ahead of client r at the server, and

- s_{1r}, client r's own phase 1 service at the server.

Let q_m^+ be an upper bound on the mean number of times client m can interfere with client r by appearing ahead of it (per visit of r to the server); then

$$d_r^+ = l_r^+ + \sum_{m \neq r} q_m^+ S_m + s_{1r} \tag{4}$$

Because of the IFR service distributions, the residual service times are bounded above by the mean service times. Thus:

$$l_r^+ = max[s_{21}, s_{22}, \ldots s_{2R}] \tag{5}$$

The bound q_m^+ is provided by the following theorem, proven in [6]:

Theorem [6]: The mean number of services q_m to client m that client r must wait for, per visit to a FIFO queue, is bounded above by:

$$q_m \leq q_m^+ = min[1, f_m/f_r] \tag{6}$$

A sketch of the proof is, that clearly for FIFO service $q_m \leq 1$ (the competitor cannot finish service and re-enter the queue ahead of r a second time); also, each visit of m can interfere with at most one visit of r. Thus if r visits the service center more often ($f_r > f_m$) then the relative frequency of contention is bounded by f_m/f_r.

By using inequalities 4, 5 and 6 we get:

$$d_r^+ = max[s_{21}, s_{22}, \ldots s_{2R}] + \sum_{m \neq r} min[1, f_m/f_r] \, S_m + s_{1r} \tag{7}$$

From equations 3 and 7 and noting that $f_r \geq 1/C_r^+$ we obtain:

$$f_r \geq 1/(c_r + s_{1r} + max[s_{21}, s_{22}, \ldots s_{2R}] + \sum_{m \neq r} min[1, f_m/f_r] \, S_m) \tag{8}$$

Both the upper as well as the lower bound on f_r are expressed in terms of the throughputs of the other client tasks in the system (see inequalities 1 and 8). Since the throughputs are all unknown it is hard to extract the bounds in a closed analytic form. A new technique based on interval arithmetic is used to obtain numeric values for both the upper and lower bounds on client task throughputs.

3 Interval Arithmetic for Computation of the Bounds

Interval arithmetic can be performed in a variety of ways (a recent survey is given in [7]). We have used the interval arithmetic capability available as a special feature of the BNR Prolog [8] language developed at Bell Northern Research; the language has been used in a variety of different problem areas and lends itself naturally to the computation of the bounds presented in the paper. The concept of interval arithmetic is centred around a data type called *interval* which is an object that represents a real number lying between an upper and lower bound. The bounds of the real number define its range which may vary during the lifetime of a computation. The interval arithmetic provided by BNR Prolog allows the expression of arithmetic relationships among intervals and offers a mechanism for solving sets of linear and nonlinear equations and inequalities.

Typically a set of equalities and inequalities may be specified as a set of Prolog sub-goals. The BNR Prolog interpreter evaluates each of these equalities (inequalities) and computes the range associated with each interval that satisfies the arithmetic relationship specified in each of these sub-goals. As a computation proceeds forward intervals can change their values only by *narrowing*. An interval is narrowed if its lower bound is raised or its upper bound is lowered or both. This may occur due to the evaluation of an arithmetic expression and the intervals are said to have been constrained by the Prolog sub-goal corresponding to the arithmetic expression. When required, BNR Prolog uses backtracking to undo the narrowing of an interval which is analogous to the unbinding of ordinary variables.

The interval arithmetic feature of BNR Prolog is explained further with the help of examples. Three Prolog programs are shown in Figure 2(a), Figure 2(c), and Figure 2(e). The predicate *range* in the programs is used to generate the bounded intervals _A and _B. The predicate *print_interval* is used to print the intervals _A and _B at the end of the computation. The upper and lower bounds obtained for each interval at the end of computation correspond to the lowest and highest values that satisfy the inequality. Consider Figure 2(a). Since the ranges specified for _A and _B already satisfy the inequality in the program no narrowing of intervals is performed (see Figure 2(b)). For satisfying the inequality in the program in Figure 2(c), the lower bound for _A is raised and the upper bound for _B is lowered (see Figure 2(d)). The constraint specified in the program of Figure 2(e) is inconsistent with the interval ranges of _A and _B. As a result the sub-goal corresponding to the inequality fails.

Now let us consider the use of this interval arithmetic capability for computing the bounds described earlier. As an example, the Prolog program for a system with two clients is shown in Figure 3. For any number of clients, there are two inequalities per client, based on (1) for the upper bound and (8) for the lower bound. Each of these is represented by a single sub-goal in the Prolog program. When the program is executed each inequality is evaluated and a set of upper and lower bounds (f_r^+, f_r^-) that satisfies the inequalities is obtained for each client task r. This set of upper and lower bounds form the corner points of a rectangular polytope in an R-dimensional throughput space $(f_1, f_2, \ldots f_R)$ and the feasible set of throughputs for the client tasks must lie inside this rectangular polytope.

3.1 Numerical Results

As an example, we considered four identical client tasks with equal phase-1 and phase-2 service times. Six cases, with different partitioning of the work between the client and the server, were solved with the results shown in Table 1. The ratio $\theta_r = f_r^+/f_r^-$ in the last column measures the tightness of the bounds, with a value of unity corresponding to equal upper and lower bounds. Table 1 indicates that tight bounds (as reflected by values of θ_r near unity) are obtained in two extreme situations: when most of the work in a response cycle is performed at the reference tasks and the server is lightly

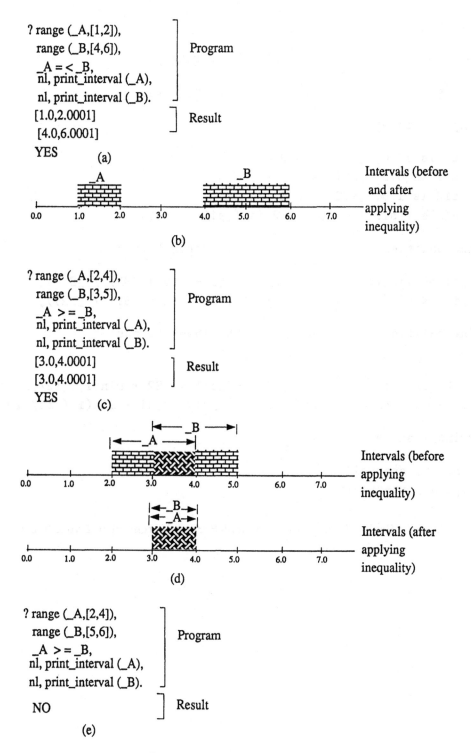

```
? range (_A,[1,2]),
  range (_B,[4,6]),
  _A = < _B,
  nl, print_interval (_A),
  nl, print_interval (_B).        Program

  [1.0,2.0001]
  [4.0,6.0001]                    Result

  YES
            (a)
```

(b)

Intervals (before and after applying inequality)

```
? range (_A,[2,4]),
  range (_B,[3,5]),
  _A > = _B,
  nl, print_interval (_A),
  nl, print_interval (_B).        Program

  [3.0,4.0001]
  [3.0,4.0001]                    Result

  YES
            (c)
```

Intervals (before applying inequality)

Intervals (after applying inequality)

(d)

```
? range (_A,[2,4]),
  range (_B,[5,6]),
  _A > = _B,
  nl, print_interval (_A),
  nl, print_interval (_B).        Program

            NO                    Result

            (e)
```

Figure 2: **Example of Interval Arithmetic**

```
userserver :-

%Create intervals for client task throughputs

   range(_f1, [0, 1.0]), range(_f2, [0, 1.0]),

%Input parameters

   _c1 is 10.0, _c2 is  5.0,
   _s11 is 0.5, _s21 is 0.6,
   _s12 is 1.0, _s22 is 0.5,
   _S1 is (_s11 + _s21), _S2 is (_s12 + _s22),

%Inequalities corresponding to the upper bounds

   _f1 =< min((1 / (_c1 + _s11)),((1 - _f2 * _S2) / _S1)),
   _f2 =< min((1 / (_c2 + _s12)),((1 - _f1 * _S1) / _S2)),

%Inequalities corresponding to the lower bounds


_f1 >= 1/(_c1 + max(_s21,_s22) + _s11 + _S2 * min(1,(_f2/_f1)))),
 _f2 >= 1/(_c2 + max(_s21,_s22) + _s12 + _S1 * min(1,(_f1/_f2)))),

%Print results

nl,print_interval(_f1),
nl,print_interval(_f2).
```

Figure 3: **Prolog Program for a Client-Server System with Two Clients**

loaded, or when most of the work in a response cycle is performed by the server.

The relationship between θ_r and the relative load at the client and server processors is explored further and the results are presented in Figure 4. The relative utilization α of the server processor with respect to the processor used by any client is an indicator of the relative load at the client and the server and is used as a variable factor in the investigation. The relationship of α with the system parameters is given by:

$$\alpha = \frac{f_r S_r R}{f_r c_r} = \frac{S_r R}{c_r}$$

A high value of α indicates that the client processor is lightly loaded in comparison to the server processor whereas a lower value of α indicates more activity at the client than at the server. c_r was fixed at 10 and the expected service times for the two phases of the server were made equal to one another. Thus given any value of α and R the expected execution times for the two phases of the server are given by:

$$s_{1r} = s_{2r} = \frac{10\alpha}{2R} \quad \text{(for all clients } r)$$

Results obtained with three different client populations $R = 2$, 4 and 8, and for a range of values of α from 0.2 to 5, are presented in Figure 4. For both large and small α, θ_r goes towards unity for any R, confirming the observation made from Table 1. For values of α near unity we have a balanced system, and $\theta_r > 1$, with larger values for larger R.

Analysis of other test cases (not included here because of limitations on space) indicate that the division of work between the two phases of a server also has an impact on the value of θ_r; the bounds become tighter as more and more work is performed in phase 1.

4   Summary

The development of an analytic expression for a lower bound (or guarantee) on performance for a client-server distributed system with servers having two phases and multiple classes of service is presented in this paper. However a closed form solution is intractable, so a novel technique based on interval arithmetic is developed for the computation of the bounds. The bounds are

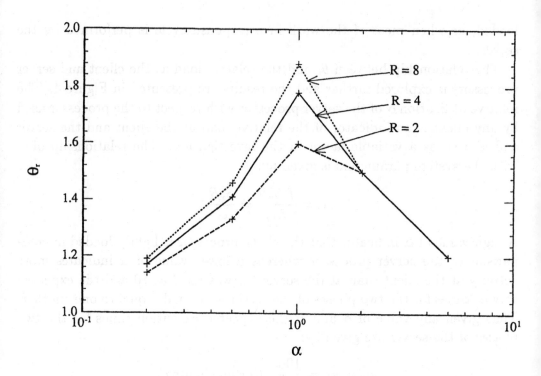

Figure 4: **The Relationship Between the Relative Utilization of the Server Processor and the Tightness of Bounds**

robust since they do not depend on any stochastic assumptions about the behavior of the system.

The computational complexity of the Prolog programs used for the computation of the performance bounds depends on the number of inequalities in the program. Intrinsically these computations appear to scale well, although our experience is limited. Other related BNR Prolog programs have scaled nearly linearly up to hundreds of inequalities [9]. Work is underway to further our understanding of the complexity of the bound computations. Research is also continuing in other directions. Software systems with more complex architectures than the client-server system but with only a single class of service are considered in [5]. Application of the interval arithmetic technique to obtain performance bounds for multiclass queueing network models is also under current investigation.

Table 1: **Tightness of Bounds for the Homogeneous Client-Server Architecture (4 clients)**

c_r	s_{1r}	s_{2r}	f_r^-	f_r^+	$\theta_r = f_r^+/f_r^-$
10.0	0.1	0.1	0.092592	0.09901	1.0693
8.0	1.1	1.1	0.059523	0.10990	1.8464
6.0	2.1	2.1	0.043859	0.059524	1.3572
4.0	3.1	3.1	0.034722	0.040323	1.1613
2.0	4.1	4.1	0.028735	0.030488	1.0610
0.2	5.0	5.0	0.024875	0.025001	1.0051

Acknowledgements

The support of the Telecommunications Research Institute of Ontario and of the Natural Sciences and Engineering Research Council of Canada are gratefully acknowledged, and also the donation of BNR Prolog to the university by Bell-Northern Research. Gerald Karam helped us to understand and use BNR Prolog.

References

[1] R.F. Rashid, "From RIG to Accent to Mach: the evolution of a network operating system," tech. rep., Computer Science Dept., Carnegie Mellon University, U.S.A., 1987.

[2] D.R. Cheriton, "The V kernel: A software base for distributed systems," *IEEE Software*, vol. 1, pp. 19–42, April 1984.

[3] C.M. Woodside, "Throughput calculation for basic stochastic rendezvous networks," *Performance Evaluation*, vol. 9, pp. 143–160, 1989.

[4] J.A. Rolia, "Performance estimates for systems with software servers: The lazy boss method," *Proceedings VIII SCCC International Conference on Computer Science*, pp. 25–43, July 1988.

[5] S. Majumdar, C.M. Woodside, J.E. Neilson, and D.C. Petriu, "Performance bounds for concurrent software with rendezvous," 1990. (Submitted for publication).

[6] S. Majumdar, C.M. Woodside, J.E. Neilson, and D.C. Petriu, "Robust box bounds: Performance guarantees without stochastic assumptions." (Submitted for publication).

[7] Special issue of IEEE Software on Interval Arithmetic, Sept. 1990.

[8] Computing Research Laboratory, Bell Northern Research Ltd., Ottawa, Canada, *BNR Prolog Reference Manual*, 1988.

[9] W. Older. Personal communication, Oct. 1990.

ENHANCED RELIABILITY IN
SCHEDULING CRITICAL TASKS FOR
HARD REAL-TIME DISTRIBUTED SYSTEMS

Ghasem S. Alijani
Computer Science Department
University of Wyoming
Laramie, WY 82071

Horst F. Wedde
Computer Science Department
Wayne State University
Detroit, MI 48202

Abstract

Hard real-time systems are characterized by the execution of tasks under strict time constraints. The importance of meeting a task execution deadline makes the scheduling scheme a central issue for the correctness and reliability of such systems. While reliability is one of the objectives, it cannot be guaranteed that any system be free from faults during its operational lifetime. Thus, in systems performing critical activities, measures that provide fault tolerance should be included [2].

This paper focuses on the design and evaluation of a highly reliable integrated system which consists of *local* and *global* task schedulers. Our approach to error detection and recovery problems is to utilize safety times associated with the scheduled tasks and combine local and global recovery techniques. This approach supports system level error detection and recovery for the local scheduler and affected tasks. The performance of the system in terms of the number of recovered tasks is evaluated and the results are presented.

I. Introduction

In distributed systems, every node consists a set of system programs, each of which performs a set of tasks. The system program responsible for task scheduling in this environment is referred as a distributed scheduler. Often, a distributed scheduler consists of both a *local* and a *global* scheduler. The local scheduler consists of strategies which utilize the time-slices of a single processor for execution of assigned tasks. On the other hand, the global scheduler imposes policies for scheduling tasks that must be transferred from one node to another.

Due to the need for load balancing [7, 10, 14], response time [5, 12, 13], and resource management [17, 19] in hard real-time processing, much research has been directed toward the global task scheduling problem, leaving local task scheduling to the traditional single-processor scheduling techniques [6]. However, the single-processor scheduling schemes lack the required flexibility in a dynamic environment. Further, it has been shown that constructing a scheduler with arbitrary arrival rates, computation and laxity requirements leads to an NP-complete problem [8, 9]. Therefore, there has been an increased interest in heuristic solutions to the local task scheduling problem. Mok and Dertouzos [16] have shown that local scheduling algorithms based on the Earlier-Due-Date (EDD) and Least-Laxity-First (LLF) sequencing may produce an optimal solution. In fact, many of the heuristic approaches in the literature realize this result.

In a guaranteeing procedure presented in [17], a newly arrived task is only considered guaranteed if it can be executed before its deadline and without jeopardizing other already scheduled tasks. Otherwise, the new task should be scheduled for remote execution. The locally guaranteed tasks are executed in the order of EDD next. Another heuristic local task scheduling method is presented by Liu et al. [15]. In their work, they defined a new method of guaranteeing a task deadline by utilizing imprecise results of periodic and iterative processes. Since the solution is dependent on iterative processes, the scheduler must be able to identify such processes. Thus, this method may not be suitable for scheduling sporadic tasks that could be critical to the system.

Biyabani et al. [4] designed an interesting heuristic approach that combines the concepts of deadline and criticalness in a hard real-time distributed environment for scheduling sporadic tasks. A task's criticalness is a metric of its relative importance. In this technique, if a task arrives at a node with an already full schedule, an attempt is made to remove enough lower priority tasks from the scheduler list to guarantee the new task. The authors found that this approach outperforms the general priority-only based and deadline-only based algorithms in terms of being able to handle a greater diversity of the system load. However, this method relies on surplus computation time of the system which may not be available during the entire operation. Considering the above discussion, we turn our attention to description of a multi-robotics system which has been designed to served local as well as remote clients on real-time basis.

II. System Specification

The objective system here consists of a communication subsystem and a set of application subsystems. Each application subsystem consists of a control station (node) and one or more mobile robots. The control stations are connected to each other via a communication subsystem and together they constitute a Local Area Network using a multicasting or a broadcasting protocol. Each control station is independent of the other stations and controls one or more robots that are able to communicate with the station directly.

During the operation, every station can be in one of two possible states that are referred to as a client state or a server state. A station is in the server state if it is utilizing its own resources to process local tasks and the tasks which are requested by remote stations. On the other hand, a station is in a client state when it is requesting services from one or more of the remote stations. Thus, every station should be provided with a set of appropriate processes that can be utilized when the station is functioning in either a client or a server state. The schematic form of these processes is shown in the following figure.

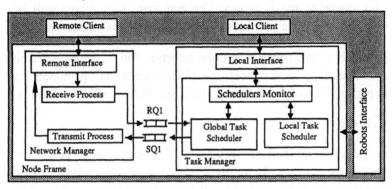

Figure 1: Internal Structure of a Control Station

As figure 1 shows, each node is composed of a network manager and a task manager. The network manager consists of an external interface and a set of processes for communicating with remote nodes and the task manager respectively. On the other hand, the task manager provides services to local clients and the network manager using the task schedulers (local and global) and its controlled robots.

Network Manager : The network manager is responsible for the receipt and transmission of messages over the shared network through the remote interface. The messages are sent to and received from the global scheduler using a **request** (RQ1) and a **service** (SQ1) queue respectively. The request queue may consist of requests for services from other nodes and responses from the remote nodes to requests made previously by the local node. The service queue contains messages that represent requests from the local node to other nodes and responses to requests received from remote nodes.

The remote interface consists of two primary **receive** and **transmit** processes. The receive process gets a message from the shared network and sends it to the global scheduler using the request queue. On the other hand, the transmit process retrieves a request/response from the service queue and sends it to the shared network media through the remote interface.

Task Manager : The primary process in each node is the task manager. It is responsible for communicating with the network manager, local robots and local clients. The messages from either the network manager or local client are presented to the task manager in the form of requested tasks using the request queues which are established between the task manager and network manager as well as between the internal interface and the task manager.

To handle different classes of local and remote tasks, the task manager is provided with a task scheduler which consists of a **local** and a **global** task scheduler. The local task scheduler is responsible for communicating with the local client through the internal interface and scheduling local and remote tasks using local resources. On the other hand, the global scheduler facilitates the process of a remote request/response by communicating with the network manager and the local task scheduler. Once a task is scheduled, the task manager sends a message to an appropriate local robot using the request queues which are established between the task manager and it robots. The response from robots will be stored and forwarded using the service queue between the robots and the task manager.

Since the emphasis of this paper is on error detection and recovery mechanisms, only an overview and an example of the local and global schedulers provided here. Detailed discussions and performance of our local and global schedulers can be found in [1].

Local Task Scheduler

The incentive for developing the local task scheduling scheme is to guarantee a maximum number of unpredictable critical tasks locally. Unfortunately, while a task's deadline is known at the arrival time, its computation time can only be estimated based on static characteristics or previously observed behavior. Using such an estimation for scheduling in hard real-time environment may cause a deadline failure. To alleviate this problem, we make use of the idea of *safety time*, a factor that is added to the worst-case computation time of each task whenever the deadline of the new task and the status of the already scheduled tasks allow. A three-phase local task scheduler was designed to schedule periodic and sporadic tasks accordingly. This local scheduler utilizes accumulated safety time and locally available resources provided by replication and relocation techniques [18]. The following is a brief description of task characteristics and each individual phase of the local scheduler.

We assume that at time t_1, the system contains a set of tasks, T, where each task, $T_i \in T$ can be characterized as follows:

$$T_i = (AT_i, WT_i, DT_i, CR_i, ST_i, STF_i)$$

where AT_i represents the arrival time of task T_i based on the local clock

WT_i is defined as worst-case computation time of T_i

DT_i is the deadline of the task T_i

CR_i is the criticalness of T_i, it may be considered as T_i's relative priority metric

ST_i is the starting time of the task T_i

STF_i is the safety time factor that must be added to WT_i .

The success of scheduling a new task depends on its deadline, its worst-case computation time and the current status of scheduled tasks. The current status of each scheduled task will be stored in a schedule list defined as S-LIST. To find an available time, AVT, for a new task a search must be conducted within a *window frame*. The size of the window, WS, can be defined in terms of the present time, t, and the deadline of the new task, $WS = DT_i - t$. The local scheduler maintains the S-LIST in which the tasks are ordered according to their start times. Therefore, the task with the Earliest-Start-Time will be executed next.

First Phase : In this phase all generated tasks (local or remote) are to be examined and possibly scheduled <u>without</u> using the STF associated with each scheduled task. This phase will activate the second phase of the local scheduler if a new critical task meets a preset threshold (to be explained in the second phase), and thus cannot be scheduled without further manipulation of the already scheduled tasks.

Second Phase : In this phase, the scheduler tries to guarantee a new task by manipulating the already scheduled tasks within a window frame and utilizing the accumulated safety times. A metric will be defined in order to decide whether a task is "critical enough" to activate the second and possibly the third phase of the scheduler. The scheduler compares a new task criticalness, CR_i , with a flexible threshold, TH, that will be set by the system as a parameter. If CR_i is greater than TH, then the new task is considered as a critical task. Otherwise, it will be classified as a non-critical task. Within the window frame, a *forward shifting* is performed to utilize the STFs and AVTs for scheduling the new critical task. If the provided time frame is greater than the WT_i, then the tasks will be scheduled. Otherwise the third phase of the local scheduler will be activated.

Third Phase : The critical tasks that are not processed by the second phase will be passed to the third phase for further consideration. Removal of one or more less critical tasks from the list is performed in order to provide a time slot for a new highly critical task. Combination of the threshold and window frame will provide the system with an efficient search scheme. In order to illustrate the effect of our local scheduler, we define three separate cases as follows:

Case-1 : In this case, the current scheduled tasks and S-LIST for a node at a given time are shown in figure 2 and 3 respectively.

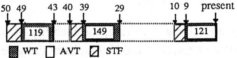

Figure 2 : Current schedule for case-1, before T_{162}

ID	AVT	WT	DT	CR	ST	STF
121	0	9	10	5	0	1
149	19	10	40	9	29	1
119	3	6	50	2	43	1

Figure 3 : Current S-LIST for case-1, before T_{162}

Now assume that a new task, $T_{162} = (162, 0, 15, 40, 5, ST, STF)$ arrives. The STF and ST can be calculated in phase one and the available time, AVT, is defined once a location for the new task in the schedule has been determined. Since there is enough available time in the schedule (see figure 2), the first phase can schedule T_{162}. Figure 4 shows the current schedule after including T_{162}.

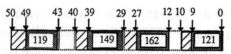

Figure 4 : Current schedule for case-1, after T_{162}

Case-2 : In this case, we assume that no task has been retrieved from the S-LIST and a new task, T_{132} = (132, 0, 5, 30, 9, ST, STF) arrives. The first phase will not be able to schedule this new task. But since T_{132} is a critical task (CR_{132} > TH) , the second phase will be activated. The effect of the second phase in scheduling the new task is shown in figure 5.

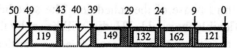

Figure 5: Current schedule for case-2, after T_{132}

Case-3 : The schedule and corresponding S-LIST resulting from adding T_{132} in case-2 is now considered the current situation while a new task arrives T_{103} = (103, 0, 10, 40, 8, ST, STF) arrives. Because of the deadline and criticalness of T_{103}, and the current status of the schedule, the first and second phases are not able to schedule the new task without further manipulation of the current scheduled tasks. Thus, the third phase will be activated to remove T_{162} and schedule T_{103}. The resulting schedule can be shown as following figure.

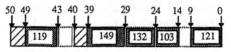

Figure 6: Current schedule for case-3, after T_{103}

III. Maintaining The Local Scheduler

Excluding failures of the underlying hardware, the inability of the local task scheduler to perform its associated functions can be caused by faults in the scheduler itself, errors created by a previously scheduled task, or external environment. For the system to provide reliable scheduling, it must be able to detect failures and provide a recovery mechanism to prevent the scheduled tasks from missing their deadlines. Since both detection and recovery processes add overhead to the system, the design strategy should embody a method that minimizes the cpu time for execution of these processes and reduces possibility of deadline failures.

Error Detection. Design of an errors detection technique must meet two objectives. First, an error should be detected before the execution time of the running task expires. Second, it should not add a significant overhead to the system. Combination of these two objectives may save the scheduled tasks from missing their deadlines. Our approach to this problem is based on asynchronous interprocess communication and the relationships between the scheduler monitor and the local scheduler.

When the monitor decides to send a task, T_i, to the local task scheduler, it sets a new timer, T_r, to the starting time, ST_i, of the task T_i. As the system continues its operation, the monitor will check the local scheduler every $ST_i + KT$ time units within the interval $[ST_i, ST_i + WT_i]$. Thus, the following inequality is held:

$$ST_i \leq ST_i + kT \leq ST_i + WT_i \qquad (1)$$

Where k indicates the number of check points where tests should be conducted and T is the length of each subinterval. Simplifying (1) we have:

$$0 \leq k \leq WT_i / T \qquad (2)$$

Now let $WT_i / T = C$ or $T = WT_i / C$, where C indicates the number of subintervals within $[ST_i, ST_i + WT_i]$. For instance if $C = 2$, then the number of check points is 3 ($k = 0$ task starts, $k = 1$, and $k = 2$ task terminates). Thus, the check points, CP, can be formulated as follows:

$$CP_{k+1} = ST_i + k\, WT_i / C \qquad \text{for } k = 0, 1, 2, ..., C \qquad (3)$$

For instance, assume that $C = 3$, $WT_i = 15$, and $ST_i = 3$ then the check points are: $CP_1 = 3$, $CP_2 = 8$, $CP_3 = 13$ and $CP_4 = 18$.

To make the error detection process complete, the local scheduler must respond to check points by sending signals to the monitor. The number of signals, NS, in conjunction with $k+1$ (check points counter) can be used to detect an error in efficient way. However, since the monitor and local scheduler communicate with each other asynchronously, there will be a constant delay between the time that the local scheduler sends a signal and the time that the monitor checks the value of NS. To solve this problem, we introduce a constant delay, d, and modify (3) as follows:

$$CP_{k+1} = ST_i + k\, WT_i / C + d \qquad (4)$$

Therefore, the local scheduler should send its very first signal at time ST_i (when the task starts) and sets NS=1. Accordingly, the monitor compares the value of NS with the value of $K+1$ at time $CP_{k+1} = ST_i + d$ (for $K = 0$). If these two values match, the system continue its operation. Otherwise, a failure occurred and a recovery process should take place.

Recovery Process

A failure in the local task scheduler means that tasks on the S_List cannot be scheduled until some form of recovery has take place. The recovery process involves restoring the affected elements to a consistent state and providing a copy of required system or application programs to resume the computation. Although this recovery procedure may takes a fixed amount of time and thus it can be determined in advance [11], it may still be impossible to complete the recovery in time for the next task to be scheduled by its required start time.

Our approach to the recovery problem is based on a combination of local and global recovery procedures. A local recovery procedure takes place when the local node utilizes the locally available resources to handle failures. On the other hand, global recovery procedures will be imposed when the local resources are tight. Thus, the local node may seek remote resource to handle errors.

Once an error is detected, the primary steps toward the recovery process is to save the current task from missing its deadline and restore the local scheduler to a consistent state to resume its computation. The success of these primary steps depends on the following factors.

- Remaining Execution Time (RET) of the current task, $RET_i = WT_i - PC_{k+1}$,
- Recovery Time (RT), the time that takes to recover the local scheduler and

- The accumulate safety and available times, $\sum_{j=1}^{n} STF_j + \sum_{j=1}^{n} AVT_j$ Where n is the size of window from the present time to the deadline of the current task. In other words, saving the current task from missing its deadline is dependent on a particular phase which the scheduler is functioning.

Since the local scheduler itself is the most critical task, it has to be recovered first. This can be done by restoring a locally available back up copy and providing the S_LIST that is available in the monitor. If the local copy is corrupted, then a request for a fresh copy of the local scheduler should be sent to one of the remote nodes. As stated earlier, it is impossible to determine how many tasks should be rescheduled (locally or remotely) unless the exact value of the RT is defined. Therefore, the following actions should be taken to determine the value of RT and at the same time any task that is effected by the recovery time should be rescheduled remotely.

1- As soon as an error is detected, the local node should reject any incoming task.

2- If $WT_i + TT \leq DT_i$, then the current task must be sent out onto the network through the remote scheduler. TT is the transmission time.

3- Use the STF_i and RET_i of T_i to recover the local scheduler.

4- If $RT > STF_i + RET_i$ send next task, T_{i+1} for remote scheduling, continue to recover the local scheduler using STF_{i+1} and RET_{i+1} .

If we can complete the recovery process by the deadline of T_{i+1}, then all the following tasks can be scheduled. Otherwise, we continue using the global recovery procedure and send tasks one at a time onto the network (repeat step 4) until the recovery of the local scheduler is completed. In this way, we minimize the amount of global scheduling while the value of RT is determined. Once the recovery time is determined, the following procedure can be applied to recover the current task (at this time there is a new current task, T_j).

Case-1 : The scheduler is operating in phase-1. In this case there may be enough available time and accumulated safety times to reschedule the current task locally. Thus, if the following relation is held, then the task can be rescheduled at the local node.

$$\sum_{k=1}^{n} AVT_k + \sum_{k=1}^{n} STF_k + RET_j \geq RT + WT_j \qquad (5)$$

Otherwise, we should determine the possibility of scheduling the task using one of the remote nodes. This can be established using the following test the transmission time, TT.

$$WT_j + TT \leq DT_j \qquad (6)$$

If the inequality (6) holds then there will be enough time to route the task to one of the remote node [3]. Otherwise it will miss its deadline.

Case-2 : In this case the scheduler is functioning in phase-2 and according to the status of the S_List, there may not be available times ($\sum_{k=1}^{n} AVT_k = 0$ in (5)) within the deadline of task. Therefore, the tests (5) and (6) can be conducted to determine where the task can be rescheduled.

Case-3 : Finally, this is the case in which the scheduler is operating in phase-3. Considering the status of S_LIST the terms $\sum_{k=1}^{n} AVT_k$ and $\sum_{k=1}^{n} STF_k$ in (5) must be set to zero and since $RET_j \geq RT + WT_j$ cannot be true, we conclude that if the scheduler is in phase-3 the current task cannot be rescheduled locally. However, still there is the possibility that the task can be rescheduled at one of the remote nodes. This possibility can be determined using (6).

IV. Experimental Results

Since the emphasis of this research is to determine the performance of the system in terms of the number of recovered tasks in presence of failures, an attempt was made to reflect this goal using a experimental model and monitoring the results. The major factors that have significant effect in evaluation of the model can be characterized as follows:

- Characteristics of scheduled tasks including criticalness, worst-case computation time and deadline,
- Generated Error Rate, GER,
- Check Points, CP_{k+1}, $k = 0,1,...,C$,
- Error Recovery Time, RT and
- The STF and the AVT, where their values can be derived from the S_LIST.

As these factors characterize the model, each individual factor has its own place in performance of the system. However, the most crucial factor is GER which as a system parameter determines the capability of the system in handling failures. In the first experiment the value of GER was selected randomly with range between 10 to 20 errors/time-unit. This number of errors was distributed among N_1 nodes where $| N_1 | = 1/3 | N |$. In this way, 2/3 of the nodes were always functioning normally (the total number of nodes is 18). The remaining factors were configured as follows:

- Criticalness, $1 \leq CR \leq 10$, worst case computation, $10 \leq WT \leq 50$ time units,
- Deadlines, $20 \leq DT \leq 100$ time units beyond the WT,
- Tasks Arrival Rate, $0 \leq TAR \leq 12$ tasks / time unit and number of check points , C =3.

It should be noted that since the recovery time may be larger than the deadline of the first task, the number of scheduled tasks that can be affected by the error recovery process may be greater than the number of generated errors. As figure 7 indicates, the system is capable of handling 80 % of the affected tasks if the scheduler is operating in phase-1. However, when the scheduler is in phase-2 about 60 % of tasks are recovered. Finally, when the scheduler moves to phase-3, since there is no AVTs, or STFs (see figure 5) only 10 percent of tasks can be recovered. Of course, in all these cases the local scheduler is successfully recovered. Overall this experiment shows that with the above range of generated failures, the system is capable of functioning in a steady state and recovering the local task scheduler. Further, in the average, 50 percent of affected tasks can be rescheduled successfully.

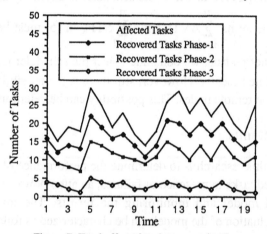

Figure 7: Total affected and recovered tasks

To verify our findings we conducted another test using a different approach. Instead of selecting the value of generated errors randomly, we used a first degree polynomial to present the changes in generated errors. As the results in figure 8 indicate, when the rate of errors increases linearly, the number of affected tasks grows in a quadratic form. Further, as the value of generated errors approaches 25 errors /time-unit, the number of recovered tasks degrades rapidly depending on the phase in which the scheduler is functioning. Indirectly, these results also show the effect of AVTs and SFTs. For instance, when the scheduler is in phase-3, none of the affected tasks can be recovered for the value of GER > 22, while in phase- 2 and 3 this value is about 32.

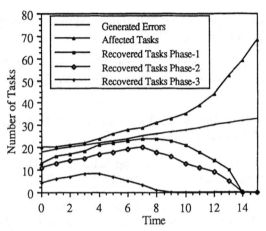

Figure 8: Error generated, affected and recovered tasks

V. Conclusion

For a system performing critical activities, it is essential to develop a highly reliable distributed task scheduling scheme that is able to achieve nearly continuous operation under hard real-time constraints. This research provides a new approach for error detection and recovery problems in a hard real-time environment. The combination of the local and global recovery described here provides support for automatic system level recovery for the local scheduler and affected tasks. The results of the experiments indicate that the system is capable of recovering the local scheduler and a significant portion of affected tasks.

References

[1] G.S. Alijani and H.F. Wedde, "A Three-Phase Scheduling Scheme in Hard Real-Time Environments", *Proc. of First Great Lakes Computer Science Conference*, October 1989.

[2] T. Anderson and J.C. Knight, "A Framework for Software Fault Tolerance in Real-Time Systems", *IEEE Transactions on Software Engineering, Vol.SE-9, No. 3*, May 1983.

[3] S. Balaji, et al., "Workload Redistribution for Fault Tolerance in a Hard Real-Time Distributed Computing System", *Proc. 19th Sym. on Fault-Tolerance Computing*, June 1989.

[4] S.R. Biyabani, J.A. Stankovic and K. Ramamritham, " The Integration of Deadline and Criticalness in Hard Real-Time Scheduling", *Proc. Real-Time Sys. Sym.* December 1988.

[5]   T.L. Casavant and J.G. Kuhl, "Effects of Response and Stability on Scheduling in Distributed Computing Systems", *IEEE Software Engineering, Vol. SE-14, No. 2*, February 1988.

[6]   F.G. Coffman and P.J. Denning, "Operating Systems Theory", *Prentice-Hall inc. Englewood Cliffs, New Jersey*, 1973.

[7]   D.L. Eager, E.D. Lazowska and J. Zahorjan, "Adaptive Load Sharing in Homogeneous Distributed Systems", *IEEE Transaction of Software Engineering, Vol. SE-12, No. 5*, May 1986.

[8]   M.R. Garey and D.S. Johnson, "Two-Processor Scheduling with Start-Time and Deadlines", *SIAM Journal, Comp., Vol. 6, No. 3*, 1977.

[9]   R.L. Graham et al., "Optimization and Approximation in Deterministic Sequencing and Scheduling: A Survey", *Ann. Discrete Math., Vol. 5*, 1979.

[10]   A. Hac and X. Jin, "Dynamic Load Balancing in a Distributed System using a Decentralized Algorithm", *International Conference on Distributed Computing Systems*, September 1987.

[11]   K.H. Kim, "An Approach to Experimental Evaluation of Real-Time Fault-Tolerant Distributed Computing Schemes", *IEEE Transactions on Software Engineering, Vol. SE-15, No. 6*, June 1989.

[12]   J.P. Lehoczky, L. Sha and J.K. Stronider, "Enhanced Aperiodic Responsiveness in Hard Real-Time Environments", *Proc. real-Time Sys. Sym*, December 1987.

[13]   D.W. Leinbaugh and M-R, Yamini, "Guaranteed Response Times in a Distributed Hard Real-Time Environment", *IEEE Transactions on Software Engineering, Vol. SE-12, No. 12*, December 1986.

[14]   F.C.H. Lin and R.M. Keller, "The Gradient Model Load Balancing Method", *IEEE Transactions on Software Engineering, Vol. SE-13, No. 1*, January 1987.

[15]   J.W.S. Liu, K-j Lin and S. Natarajan, "Scheduling Real-Time Periodic Jobs using Imprecise Results", *Proc. Real-Time Sys. Sym.* December 1987.

[16]   A.K. Mok and M.L. Dertouozs, "Multiprocessor Scheduling in a Hard Real-Time Environment", *Proc 7 th Texas Conference on Computing Systems*, November 1978.

[17]   J.A. Stankovic, K. Ramamritham and S. Cheng, "Evaluation of Flexible Task Scheduling Algorithm for Distributed Hard Real-Time Systems", *IEEE Transactions on Computers, Vol. c-34, No. 12*, December 1985.

[18]   H.F. Wedde and G.S. Alijani, " MELODY : A Distributed Adaptive File System for Handling Real-Time Tasks in Unpredictable Environments", *to appear in Journal of Real-Time Systems*.

A Design and Modeling Environment to Develop Real-time, Distributed Software Systems

Reda Ammar   Ping Zhang [1]

U155, Computer Science & Engineering Department

University of Connecticut

Storrs, CT 06268, USA

abstract

This paper presents the general structure of a design and modeling environment for real-time, parallel/distributed software systems. It is provided for the designer to cope with different modeling and analysis methods during the different design stages. It captures three trends of concerns in the design of a real-time, distributed system: functionality, performance and distributed aspects. An object-oriented database and a plan generator are two core components. The database is used to organize data so that they can be easily retrieved and easily reused for further study, reference and reporting. More significantly, it is used to integrate the dependencies and relationships between different modeling techniques and performance evaluation tools. The plan generator has a role of analyzing plan development, recommending plan modifications, suggesting plan modeling, and validating plans. It provides the ability to handle incomplete and uncertainty information, the ability to handle update propagation, and the ability to make more intelligent design decision.

1 Introduction

In the span of four decades, computing has become one of the most pervasive and powerful technologies for information management, communications, design, manufacturing, and scientific progress. Parallel and distributed computing [3] is a new class of computing that becomes essential to progress in science and engineering. As new high performance architectures and networks are being built, software technology becomes an increasingly central concern. Effective exploitation of the performance potential of emerging distributed systems poses a special challenge to software design which should be faced by developing a coherent design methodology supported with a powerful environment. Most of these previous research efforts concentrated only on the functionality of a software system in the design stage. Only a few considered the performance factor in the design stage, but they only considered the performance of sequential software systems. Our work focus on the functionality and the performance of parallel software systems since parallel and distributed computing is of prime interest for areas where execution time evaluation is important, even critical (e.g. real-time applications).

---

[1] This work was partially supported by the National Science Foundation and the Naval Underwater System Center through grant No. CCR 8701839 and by the University of Connecticut Research Foundation through grant No. 506-35-066.

This paper presents an advanced design and modeling environment for real-time, parallel/distributed software systems. First, a design methodology is developed based on the integration of a hierarchical performance modeling framework with the top-down design approach. Second, a knowledge-based system is designed to integrate different analysis and construction tools and provide a richer environment for the designer to cope with different modeling and analysis methods during the different stages of the design process. Various case studies will be used to show the feasibility of the design methodology and the usefulness of the environment.

2 The Hierarchical Design Methodology

Our previous research efforts supported by the Naval Underwater System Center produce a hierarchical modeling framework for a real time, parallel/distributed software design [2]. It has two dimensions of activities. Vertically, it consists of a set of levels at which the system varies; horizontally, it consists of a set of activities at each level.

2.1 The Vertical Structure

The vertical structure of the design is derived from a number of basic levels:

- System level
- Task (process) levels
- Module (procedure, algorithm) level
- Operation level

At the system level, the designer concentrates on the behavior of the complete system and its interconnection with the outside world. Only most general properties of the information are being processed. The performance model at this level will often be a queueing network [8].

The task level may be repeated iteratively depending on the system complexity and the intent of the designer. Performance analysis at the level will normally depend on a flow analysis [14] and architecture specification. The analysis will include both estimates of the mean, variance, and maximum of the response time for that process.

At the module level, the designer specifies a detailed software design for the particular algorithm of concern and the performance analysis to be carried out is thus very specific. This is based on the specific tasks to be performed and the detailed structure of the information being used by the module. The performance model at this level is the computation structure model [14].

At the operational level, the performance of the basic machine operations must be considered. The cost expressions associated with an abstract data type will have a number of parameters. These parameters depend upon the cost of the basic machine operations executed to carry out the computation and are strongly machine dependent [2, 3].

As can be seen from the above description, different models describe different aspects of the software being investigated at different levels. However, these models and their attributes are not completely independent. Therefore, it is important to capture the relationships among these models and integrate these relationships in a coherent form.

2.2 The Horizontal Structure

If the system design is viewed as a multi-level function, a generic view of design can be described as consisting of five activities of definition, structuring, partitioning, allocation, and analysis. Each of these five activities represents a separate component of the overall design process where interaction with a designer is necessary to allow the design to proceed in a methodological manner.

The structuring process [15] provides a method by which a specifiable level of the system can be configured into alternative organizations that are viable candidates for the particular architectures.

Following the structuring process, the partitioning process [10,13] can be approached for each structure. This process attempts to define the partition solutions in order of minimum resource utilization where the amount of resource required to meet the expected performance requirements of throughput and response time is determined.

The allocation process [7] consists of mapping a designer-selected partition into the specified hardware architecture such that the resource/performance requirements will be met. The goal in this mapping is to minimize the overall processing power used while meeting the performance requirements as constraints.

3 General Structure of the Environment

The hierarchical modeling framework captures three trends of concerns in the design of real-time, parallel/distributed software system. In the vertical structure, it considers the in top-down direction and the performance in bottom-up direction. In the horizontal structure, it considers the parallel/distributed aspect. One of our targets is to integrate those different trends to create a flexible environment to support the hierarchical modeling framework for real-time, distributed software design. The environment has three components as shown in Figure 1.

3.1 Project Organization

The first component is the Project Organization. The activities involved in this component include:

1. Specifying the functional requirements, performance requirements, and environment constraints of the project to be designed. The designer will define goals for the software. It consists of a top-down analysis of goals that iteratively decomposes high-level goals into detailed subgoals.

2. Characterizing the architecture properties, resource usage, system performance and software outline. During the characterizing phase, based upon its needs and characteristics, the component will provide the context for preliminary planing, that includes resource estimation, allocation information, software and hardware available, environmental characteristics of concern.

3. Refining the preliminary plan so that it can be stored in the object-oriented database. Information includes input data, data flow, control flow, precedence constraints, performance metrics, etc.

4. Formalizing and generalizing plan. The component will generalize the information that it has gathered either from the designer or from the feedback information. Then it will formalize the information to enhance the plan.

5. Enhancing and Feedback. The results from second component can be fed back to the organization to enhance the plan, change attributes and characteristics. It involves interaction between designer and knowledge base to improve planning, development, and assessment.

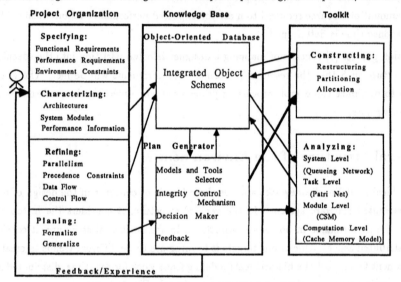

Figure 1 - Structure of the System

Efforts have been spent to design this part of the environment in a graphical form. A specification language is developed and implemented into the graphical interface GRAPE [4]. GRAPE supports five different performance models: queueing model, state model, computation structure model, data flow model, and statistical model. Each of these models is contained in a separate sub-system. However, these sub-systems are linked together to represent a multi-level hierarchical modeling. This allows the user to integrate the relationships between different performance models at different levels.

3.2 Knowledge Base

The second component (named hereon as the "knowledge base") is the core component. It has the role of monitoring and analyzing project development, packaging experience for reuse in the form of knowledge, tools, and supplying it to the Project Organization upon request. The construction and maintenance of the knowledge base serves as a foundation for reasoning about design plans.

3.2.1 Object-Oriented Database

During the design process, it is necessary to retain the structure of the overall system and the relation that each sub-system has to the whole system. The designer must be free to move from one level to another during the design process and the system must be able to track this movement. The designer will, at different points in the design, wish to modify portions of the system and track how these changes impact both the functional and performance of the complete system.

Due to the above reasons a database support system is needed to keep the design configuration information and provide facilities for accessing this information as needed during later stages of the design effort. More significantly, the database support system should be designed to:

- Identify the appropriate modeling and analytical techniques to evaluate different design alternatives at different levels.

- Record the different performance metrics at different levels and the role of each metric in the design process.

- Represent the interdependencies between different performance metrics used at different levels.

- Integrate these interdependencies into a system that is able to propagate any changes in a metric at a level to all upper levels.

We chose to use the object-oriented database system GemStone [6, 9] to implement the developed data model. GemStone supports modeling of complex objects and relationships. It organizes class of objects into an inheritance hierarchy. The developed scheme is a directed graph in which nodes denote objects, and edges identify relationships between objects. The graphic notation for the relationships is given in Figure 2-a. There are six relationships introduced here: **is instance of, is part of, is a, is member of, consists of,** and **depends on**. These relationships are defined as:

- **Is-instance-of** represents a relationship between an object class in a schema and an object in a database. For example, Peter is an instance of class Name.

- **Is-part-of** represents a relationship between component objects and a higher level aggregate object. For example, Name is a part of Person.

- **Is-a** represents a relationship between category objects and a higher level generic object. For example, a professor is a person.

- **Is-member-of** represents a relationship between member objects and a higher level set object.

- **Consists-of** represents a relationship between component objects and a higher level object. It is different with the is-part-of relationship. In this relationship, the component objects have a cross reference relationship each other.

- **Depends-on** represents a relationship between an object of a class and an object of another class. It is similar with the column dependency relationship in the relational data model. The changes in the object will change another object.

Figure 2-b shows the relationships and interdependencies between different performance models [4]. Performance information flows bottom up. The cost of any basic instruction which is analyzed in the cache memory model or statistical model will affect a node's cost in the module level. The module's time cost can be determined by using computation structure model. The service time of the queueing model could be influenced by the lower level modeling results. Finally, the whole system's response time could be determined by using queueing network model. The scheme shows the spreadsheet relationships between the different models at different levels.

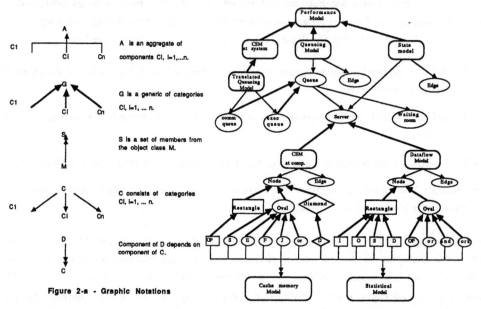

Figure 2-a - Graphic Notations

Figure 2-b - Relationships and Interdependencies between Performance Models

As the design progresses (advances to lower levels) more and more information is collected about the expected performance. This information should be propagated through the upper levels to either confirm or invalidate design decisions and specific assumptions that were made to establish the higher level performance boundaries. If it is shown that one or more of the higher level performance boundaries is incorrect, the designer must backtrack and re-evaluate the higher level design decisions in the light of the new information. If the re-evaluation does not require modification of the previously established design decisions then no corrective action is required. However if a serious mismatch is detected at some level the design process must back up to that level and all lower decisions must be re-evaluated.

Figure 2-c shows the integrated object scheme which represents the three trends of concerns during the design: The *horizontal arrow* in Figure 2-c shows the relationships between different phases which are interest of parallel/distributed consideration. The restructuring phase produces a set of alternative structures. Based on these structures the partitioning phase is used to produce a set of partitions. Then the allocation phase will map those partitions to a specified hardware architecture. In each of three phases performance analysis has been applied. The *down arrow* takes care of the functionality from top to bottom while the *up arrow* concerns the performance information from bottom to top (see Figure 2-b for detail).

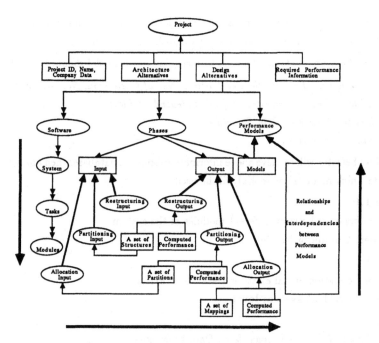

Figure 2-c - Integrated Object Scheme

3.2.2 Plan Generator

Plan Generator has a role of monitoring and analyzing plan development, recommending and justifying plan revisions, validating plans on the basis of current knowledge, recognizing violated assumptions, and maintaining consistency of knowledge.

Basically, it consists of following parts:

- Model/Tool Selector
- Integrity Control Mechanism
- Design Decision Maker
- Feedback Generator

Figure 3 shows the function of each part.

3.2.3 Model/Tool Selector:

The Model/Tool Selector consists of a set of rules that will be derived at each level of system definition to select the modeling technique which best represents the features of the system at that level. Also, at some level the constructing tools is needed when the design plan produces a product that can not meet the time and/or resource constraints. For example, if the system contains a large iterative loop which represents a bottleneck, the restructuring tool is used for loop unfolding [15]. Similarly if the degree of parallelism in the data flow graph is greater than the number of processors, then the restructuring tool is used to match this architecture constraints. It is also usual to find many partitioning and allocation methods that may lead to an acceptable solution. In this case, the Model/Tool Selector will have a policy to distinguish among them.

For example, the following facts can be used to recognize which model should be used:

- *Data Flow, Arrival Pattern, Service Pattern, No. of Customers, No. of Severs.*
- *Control Flow, Control Activation Signal, Independent Flow.*
- *Data Structure, State of Data Structure.*
- *Underlying Architectures*

The Model/Tool Selector will retrieve above information from the database, then apply the following rules to decide which model(s) or tool(s) will be used.

Rule 1.1
Data Flows exist between different modules of the system
→ Assert **Queueing Model**;

Rule 1.2
Control Activation Signal exists & Data Flows exists
→ Assert **CSM at system level**;

Rule 1.3
Only Control Activation Signal & no Data Flow exists
→ Assert **CSM at module level**;

Rule 1.4
State of Data Structure keeps changing & the State is the size { Birth-Death feature}
→ Assert **State Diagram Model**;

Rule 1.6
No sequenceness between the modules
→ Assert **Data Flow model**;

Rule 1.7
Architecture has cache memory
→ Assert **Cache memory model**;

The rule base is organized in a hierarchical form. Above rules are at the highest abstract level. The system is composed of rules that specify a situation and the conclusions that can be drawn in that situation. The procedure of working forward from the condition to the conclusion is called forward chaining and is the system's fundamental reasoning mechanism.

3.2.4 Integrity Control Mechanism

The hierarchical design methodology has two-dimensional consideration. Vertically, it has several levels. Along this dimension, design process goes top-down; and performance information flows bottom up. Horizontally, at each level, there are different phases. So the software system may be visualized via one or more views. It is necessary to keep the system consistent and maintain the multiple views. The integrity control will also

- verify assumptions;
- handle incomplete and uncertain information;
- update propagation hierarchically [6].

Assumptions are made in the early stage of the design when the data are lacking. Do they match the reality? We need to compare the assumptions to the measurements in the later stage. When assumptions prove to be incorrect, report the discrepancies. Also give feedback on how close the assumptions matched reality, and give insights into the mismatches.

The system accepts *uncertain information* with an associated confidence factor. The confidence factor is an informal measure of the extent to which the designer believes the information is true. Confidence factors are propagated with the inferences. The system that accept confidence factors have rules for combining and managing them. These confidence factors are presented with the conclusions.

Incomplete information is also handled by the system. When the system is missing a fact that it needs to derive a conclusion, it will first ask the user for the requisite information. If the user provides the information, the system continues. If the user does not have the information, the system may make some assumptions or use inference mechanism to derive the information. It may try to develop and continues along different lines of reasoning. If too much information is missing, the system will be unable to derive a conclusion for the problem at hand.

Update propagation is a very important issue in the knowledge base. The relationships and interdependencies between performance models (Figure 2-b) has implied that we need to define a complex update propagations that are automatically cascaded through the different design levels when conditions are satisfied. The trigger and alerters [6] will be adapted in the mechanism. Triggers have been used to cause changes in the database when certain conditions are satisfied, while alerters are used to report information when changes occur. A propagation channel will be specified by source trigger and target alerter when we design the object-oriented data schemes. Whenever modifying a object type with a trigger, all the object types along this channel will be modified.

3.2.5 Design Decision Maker

There can be many design alternatives to develop a software. The assessment of alternative design plans will be performed in terms of the design criteria, cost/performance, implementation techniques, etc. Decision maker will recommend the promising candidates and use appropriate problem-solving procedures to select a plan that meet certain specified goals and constraints.

The design alternatives are modeled as an AND/OR tree. A project may be decomposed into a set of sub-problems, each of which is necessary for the solution of the problem; this is represented in the design tree as an AND node. A problem may also be decomposed into a set of alternative solutions; these are represented in the design tree as OR nodes. In general, each component will itself be decomposed into a combination of AND and OR nodes. The problem is to search an appropriate solution among the nodes. A heuristic function is used to guide the search process in the most profitable direction, by suggesting which path to follow first when more than one is available.

3.2.6 Feedback

The environment is used in an interactive manner. Feedback information does not only report error message but also aid designer to improve previous designs by providing recommendations. For example, at some stages, it will give suggestions on how to select models/tools and how to modify plans. it will also give the designer feedback on how close the estimates matched reality. These information include:

- Rate Table about system behavior at different level for different plans;
- Report Facility for defects, violations, and bottleneck;
- Guidelines for modification, extension and enhancement.

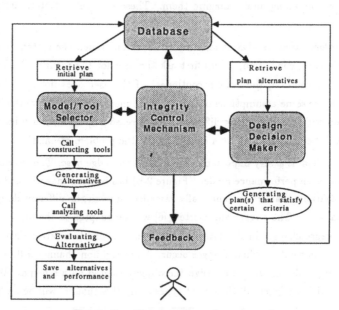

Figure 3 - The function of each part

3.3 The Toolkit

The third component is the toolkit which consists of basic tools for constructing and analyzing the real time, parallel/distributed software. The tools serve to augment and reinforce the hierarchical methodology and provide additional intellectual control over increasing complexity of design process. In this section, we give a brief description of the available tools in the environment.

A Restructuring Tool (RST) was developed to carry the developed software structuring techniques for parallel and distributed applications [15]. Through the user interface, the user can input all necessary information about his/her software system, issue a command to activate the options, and receive the structuring results. The software structuring phase provides alternatives solution structure for pipeline system and limited connectivity parallel system.

The set of software structures produced by the above tool are evaluated and ordered on the basis of clustering the modules into partition blocks, and determines the set of partitions which are most efficient in satisfying the real time requirements. In this respect, two Partitioning Tools were developed. The first is called PROSPECT [13] which supports the partitioning process for pipelined sequential organization. The second is EXPECT [10] which extends PROSPECT's activities to the parallel case.

One of the problems of the allocation process is to find the best allocation policy to distribute the given processing power. We developed an Allocation Tool called OPAS to apply different allocation methods to minimize the time cost of the computation [12]. OPAS can derive different statistics of the time cost distribution of the given computation. It can also determine the speed up of the computation and the efficiency of the used processors.

FAMAS [1] is a tool to construct probabilistic grammar models for the information to be processed by the software being designed. FAMAS can also integrate the constructed model with the computation model provided by the designer to derive the time cost function of the computation. COPES [2] realizes that there are two aspects of software performance; static and dynamic and both are important to provide a complete insight in software performance. Therefore COPES provides a unified approach to derive and measure both aspects. It can measures the execution time and trace the control flow and the software variables.

The capabilities of FAMAS and COPES were then expanded to cover parallel computations. We considered two different parallel architectures: shared memory architecture and data flow architecture. For shared memory architecture, we developed TCAS [14] and RTS [11]. TCAS uses analytical techniques to derive the time cost of parallel computations. Due to uncertainity during the communication between different processors, we used a simulation approach to overcome the problem. This simulation approach was implemented in RTS. Both TCAS and RTS are running together such that the designer can switch from the analytical mode to the simulation mode and vice versa.

All of the above tools are integrated into our system. The model/Tool selector will apply rules to select one of them to do the evaluation when it is necessary. They are the basis to provide certain degree of automation for the designer.

4 Conclusions

Manufacturers are generating new, more powerful hardware and networks at an alarming rate, and applications engineers are struggling to determine how these systems can or should be used effectively for particular needs. This paper describes an advanced design and modeling environment to build an efficient distributed software systems. This environment uses a graphical interface to interact with the designer, stores different design configurations and information in an object-oriented database and derives a design plan that can lead to the best structure of the software being constructed.

References

[1] Ammar, Reda A. and Simick, P.A., "FAMAS: Finite Algorithmic Modeling, Analysis, and Simulation Software Tool", IEEE 1988 International Conference on Systems, Man and Cybernetics, Beijing, China, August 1988.

[2] Ammar, Reda A. and Qin, B., "Time Cost Analysis of Parallel Computations in a Shared Memory Environment," ISMM International Conference on Mini and Microcomputers, from Micros to Supercomputers, Miami Beach, Florida, Dec. 14-16, 1988.

[3] Ammar, Reda A., et. al. "An Architecture Assessment Environment for the Design and Analysis of Massively Parallel Computations", 1989 IEEE Conference on Systems, Man and Cybernetics, Cambridge, MA, 1989.

[4] Ammar, Reda A. and Zhang, P., "Object-Oriented Database Support for Hierarchical Performance Modeling of Real-time, Distributed Software Systems", 1990 Symposium on Applied Computing, Fayetteville, Arkansas, April 5-6, 1990.

[5] Ammar, Reda A. and Pe, C., "Visualizing a Hierarchy of Performance Models for Software Systems", Tech. Rep. No. CSE-TR-90-3, Computer Science and Engineering Dept., University of Connecticut, 1990.

[6] Beshers, G.M., Demurjian, S.A., and Maryanski F.J., "Incorporating Propagation Semantics into an Object-Oriented Data Model", University of Connecticut Technical Report, No. CSE-TR-88-63, June, 1988.

[7] Chu, W.W., Holloway, L.J., Lau, M.T., and Efe, K. "Task Allocation in Distributed Data Processing," IEEE Computer, 1980

[8] Heidelberger, P. and Trivedi, K.S., "Queueing Network Models for Parallel Processing with Asynchronous Tasks" IEEE Trans. on Computers, Vol. C-31, No. 11, Nov. 1982.

[9] Maier, D. and Stein J., "Development and Implementation of an Object-Oriented DBMS", Research Directions in Object-Oriented Programming, edited by Bruce Shriver and Peter Wegner, MIT Press, 1987.

[10] Qian, Y., "Task Coalescence and Performance Evaluation for Parallel Software on Distributed, Real-Time Systems", Master's Thesis, Univ. of Connecticut, August, 1988.

[11] Qin, B., Sholl, H.A., Ammar, R.A., "RTS: a System to Simulate the Real Time Cost Behavior of Parallel Computations," Software Practice and Experience, October 1988.

[12] Qin, B., Sholl, H.A., Ammar, R. A., "OPAS: a Tool to Minimize the Time Costs of Parallel Computations through Optimal Processing Power Allocation", Software Practice & Experience, March 1990.

[13] Sholl, H.A. and Iyer, V., "PROSPECT: Prototype Software Performance Evaluation and Coalescence Tool", 2nd Int. Conf. on Computers and Applications, Beijing, 1987.

[14] Sholl, H.A., Ammar, Reda A., and Qin, Bin, "TCAS: A Time Cost Analysis System for Parallel Computations", ISMM International Conference on Mini and Microcomputers, From Micros to Supercomputers, Miami Beach, Florida, Dec. 14-16, 1988.

[15] Sholl, H.A. and Fergany, T.A., "Performance-Requirements-Based Software Loop Structuring for Real-Time Distributed Systems" ISMM International Conference on Mini and Microcomputers, From Micros to Supercomputers, Miami Beach, Florida, Dec. 14-16, 1988.

ON THE MANAGMENT OF REMOTE PROCEDURE CALL TRANSACTIONS

Wanlei Zhou

Brian Molinari

Department of Computer Science
The Australian National University
ACT 2601, Australia
e-mail: zhou@anucsd.anu.oz.au   Phone: (06)249-3786

ABSTRACT

This paper describes the problems arise in managing remote procedure call (RPC) transactions. The structures and constructions of RPC-based systems have been widely discussed, while how to maintain the RPC transactions by using these existing structures and constructions remains unclear. This paper presents a model for maintaining the single and parallel RPC transactions. Some properties of the model are also described.

Key Words: Distributed Computing; Remote Procedure Call (RPC); Transaction Management.

1. Introduction

Transaction management is a well established concept in database system research[10]. Two kinds of transactions are defined over an *object system* (a system with a collection of objects, and an object here can be a database file, an entry of the database file, or other proper things): the *atomic transaction* and the *non-atomic transaction*. An atomic transaction is defined as a sequence of operations which has the following two properties[2,5,11]:

(1). *Recoverability*. The overall effect of a transaction is all-or-nothing: either all of the object states changed by the transaction remain in their states before the transaction, or all changed to their final states.

(2). *Indivisibility*. The partial effects of a transaction is invisible to other transactions. That is, if the objects being modified by a transaction are observed over time by another transaction, then the later transaction will either always observe the initial states before the former transaction, or the final states after the former transaction.

A non-atomic transaction is similar to an atomic transaction except that the second property is no longer hold. Non-atomic transactions are needed when the duration of a transaction is long so that it is intolerable to wait for a transaction commits before the next transaction begins on the same data objects[3].

The needs for transaction-oriented RPC calls are obvious[12]. For example, in our distributed calendar application[13], a user usually issues a meeting which involves a group of people. Suppose that everybody in the group is a key person to the meeting, that is, if anybody cannot attend the meeting, then the meeting period must be re-arranged by the issuer. As we have known, the calendar database of those participants may locate on several different hosts. So, if anything goes wrong (such as the system failure of the related hosts or the time periods of some participants are already occupied and cannot be re-allocated) during the meeting arrangement call, which is a concurrent call of several RPCs, we need a method to rollback those calls that have been performed.

Existing RPC implementation or proposals usually do not deal with the transaction management of a RPC call or even a set of RPC calls because of the difficulties[7]. Almost all the existing RPC implementations use *at-most-once*[2] as the calling semantics. That is, when a return message is obtained, the user can have confidence that the remote procedure has been executed exactly once. Otherwise, an exception will be raised and the user does not know if the RPC is executed or not. For example, if the RPC request message is lost, the remote procedure will not be executed; while if the reply message from the remote procedure is lost, then the remote procedure does executed. But in both cases the client can only know that something is wrong between the client and server from the raised exception. It cannot tell if the remote procedure is or is not executed.

Liskov and her colleagues considered the atomicity of RPC from the viewpoint of programming languages. Concepts such as *guardians, actions*[5], *atomic data types*[8], and *promises*[6] are introduced to ensure the atomicity of some segments of a program. But a programmer has to incorporate into his program many "new" segments that deal with the atomicity of the RPC calls. In that case the programming is not so easy. They also do not consider the atomic transactions with server / client structure in usual RPC-oriented systems and applications.

We are not going to consider the full atomic RPC transaction within this paper. Instead, we only consider non-atomic transactions. So, from now on when we say transaction, we understand it means non-atomic transaction.

Two problems are to be dealt with in this paper:

- *Single RPC transaction management*: The transaction management of a single RPC call.
- *Parallel RPC transaction management*: The transaction management of a set of parallel RPC calls.

The remainder of this paper is organised as follows. Section 2 introduces the RPC transaction models used in our transaction management. Section 3 presents the design of a management system for single RPC transactions, and properties of the system are described. Based on that, Section 4 describes a system for managing a set of (parallel) RPC calls. Properties of the extended system are also described.

2. RPC Transaction Models

In this section we consider the RPC model from the viewpoint of a user process. Let

$P = \{ p \mid p$ is a remote procedure call $\}$ and $A = \{ a \mid a$ is an argument list of a RPC call $\}$.

After we made a RPC call, the call may return successfully or failed. We divide all errors of a call into two classes. The first class includes those errors by which we are definitely sure that the call is not performed. Whereas the second class includes those errors that we cannot tell whether the call is performed or not. So we abstract the *type* of a RPC call as a mapping

$c : P \times A \rightarrow \{OK, FL, US\}.$

OK means that everything is perfect during the RPC's execution and the RPC call is successful. *FL* means *accessing failure*. It means that the RPC is not executed. *US* means *unknown state*. That is, we do not know if the remote procedure has been executed or not.

We may have several strategies to deal with the case of receiving a *US* type. For example, a strategy might be:

- Query the system so that we are told if the RPC really happened.
- If it really happened, give us the result. Otherwise we can explicitly call it again.

But the strategy is not applicable because the query may last intolerably long. For example, if the links between the server and the client are down, the query will never have a correct result until a link is recovered. So we adopt the following strategy:

- We provide a *rollback* operation that will reverse the call if it happened and do nothing if it did not happen. The operation is defined as:

  $r : P \times A \rightarrow \{OK, FL, US\}.$

Set $\{OK, FL, US\}$ has the similar meaning as above. If no confusion will be caused, we may simplify a RPC call $c(p, a)$ into $c(p)$, and a rollback call $r(p, a)$ into $r(p)$.

The rollback operation is managed by the system. When a rollback operation is issued, the user can go back to his own work immediately instead of waiting for the result. The system will guarantee that the RPC will be rolled back. We have the following assumptions (their detail explanation can be found in [13]):

(1).   All RPC operations can be rolled back. And all r mappings are idempotent operations.

(2).   The First-In-First-Serve (FIFS) strategy is used to order all operations of a server (except parallel operations).

(3).   All orphaned calls[7] are exterminated before a host recovers from crash to normal operation.

(4).   When a RPC updates a data item, it locks the data item until the transaction the RPC belongs to finishes (commits of aborts). RPCs in other transactions that want to update the same data item will have FL returned.

Now we can describe our RPC transaction models. We define a *single RPC transaction* as $T = \{c(p, a)\}$. Where $c(p, a)$ is a RPC call. If there is no confusion, we also denote T as $T = \{c(p)\}$. The semantics of a single RPC transaction is that after issuing the transaction, $c(p)$ will be executed if everything is all right, or will be rolled back if something is wrong.

We define a *parallel RPC transaction* as $T = \{ c(p_1, a_1), \cdots, c(p_m, a_m)\}$. Where $c(p_i, a_i)$ $(1 = 1, 2, ..., m)$ is a RPC call, and $p_i : P$, $a_i : A$. If there is no confusion, we also denote T as $T = \{ c(p_1), \cdots, c(p_m)\}$. The semantics of a parallel RPC transaction is that after issuing the transaction, all $c(p_i)$ of T will be executed, or if any one of them fails, all executed RPCs will be rolled back. The execution of all $c(p_i)$ in T is in parallel. Some parallel primitives can be built for parallel execution of remote procedures[9]. Sequential executed transaction can be easily established from the parallel model.

3. Single RPC Transaction Management

3.1. The Manager

Each host in the network has a RPC transaction manager (RM) executing on it. Let each host be assigned a unique number and $\{1, 2, ..., N\}$ is the set of host numbers, the set of RMs in the network can be expressed as $\{RM_1, RM_2, ..., RM_N\}$. A RM consists of a managing server and three tables which are stored in the *stable storage*[4]. These tables are:

LET   *Local Executed RPC Table*. When a RPC is performed by a server in the host, it is reported to the RM and stored into LET. The function of LET table is to denote the executed RPCs and report them to the calling hosts. An entry of the table is defined as:

```
typedef struct let {
    char *rpc;    /* name of the finished RPC call */
    int   host_from;   /* client host number of the RPC call */
} LET;
```

UST   *Unknown State Table*. When a RPC call finds the return is *US*, then the RPC call is recorded by the RM into the UST. Combining the local UST table with related LET entries of other RMs, we can decide which entries in the UST are executed and which are not. The definition of a UST entry is:

```
typedef struct ust {
    char *rpc;    /* name of the unknown state RPC call */
    int   host_to;    /* destination / server host number */
    long time;    /* local timestamp when issuing the call */
} UST;
```

NRT   *Needed Rollback Table*. If the RM decided that a RPC is to be rolled back, it is put into the NRT. A NRT table entry is defined as:

```
typedef struct nrt {
    char *rpc;    /* name of the needed rollback RPC call */
```

```
} NRT;
```

We denote the tables on host j as LET_j, UST_j, and NRT_j, respectively.

3.2. Algorithms

The RM's algorithm is described in Algorithm 1, where LET, UST, and NRT tables and their counters are located in the stable storage. When the RM is first invoked, all these tables are set to empty and their counters are set to 0 by the initialisation function. Constant *MAXENTRIES* is defined as the maximum number of entries in each of these tables. The RM forks into five "forever running" concurrent processes when it is invoked.

```
LET *let_table[MAXENTRIES];     /* LET table */
int let_ct;                     /* count of LET table */
UST *ust_table[MAXENTRIES];     /* UST table */
int ust_ct;                     /* count of UST table */
NRT *nrt_table[MAXENTRIES];     /* NRT table */
int nrt_ct;                     /* count of NRT table */
Initialisation();                                            Algorithm 1
COBEGIN
   send_my_let(let_table);    /* periodically send out entries in LET */
   rollback_nrt(nrt_table);   /* periodically roll back entries in NRT */
   listen_extern_lets(ust_table, nrt_table);   /* receive & process LETs of other RMs */
   manage_rpc_calls(ust_table);   /* manage the RPC calls issued by its clients */
   listen_local_servers(let_table);   /* put executed RPC names into LET */
COEND
```

The first function *send_my_let()* periodically groups all entries in the LET table according to their *b.host_from* fields, and sends them out to that host. If the sending of a group of entries (called a LET *entry package*) is successful, those entries are deleted. The algorithm of the function is as follows:

```
send_my_let(let_table)
LET *let_table[];
{
   int j, k;
   LET *grp_let[MAXENTRIES];
   while (TRUE) {
     j = the first host number;                             Algorithm 2
     while (j != 0) {   /* loop until all host numbers are checked */
       /* group all let_table entries which have the same b.host_from=j field into grp_let table */
       /* k is the returned number of entries in grp_let */
       k = group(grp_let, j, let_table);
       if (k != 0) {
         /* send out the LET entry package grp_let if the sending is successful, delete these entries */
         if (send_out(grp_let, k) == SUCCESS)
           delete_let(grp_let, j, let_table);
       }
       j = next host number (if no next, j = 0);
     }
   }
}
```

Function *delete_let(grp_let, j, let_table)* deletes all the LET entries that belong to both *grp_let* and *let_table*. We denote the LET entry package obtained in Algorithm 2 as LET_i^j if the local host is i, and the remote host is j.

The second function periodically rolls back all entries in the NRT table. If a rollback is successful, the entry is deleted. Next is the algorithm of the function:

```
rollback_nrt(nrt_table)
NRT *nrt_table[];
{
   while (TRUE) {                                          Algorithm 3
     for all b ∈ NRT do {
       s = r(b);   /* roll back it */
       if (s == OK)   /* if rollback succeeds, delete b */
         delete b from NRT;
     }
   }
}
```

The third function is to listen to the sending of LET entry packages from other RMs and process them according to the local UST table. Suppose the local host is j and one of the remote hosts is k. If a RPC call issued by host j is performed by the destination host k, then the destination host k will finally send this message back through the LET entry package extracted from LET_k table (see Property 3.4 in Section 3.3 latter). Now host j will check into its own UST_j table against the received LET_k tables entries. Suppose we now received the LET entry package LET_k^j from host k. If any entry is found in both LET_k^j and UST_j, that means the call returns US and it is actually executed by host k. So it is put into the NRT_j table for rolling back. If a call returns US but it is not executed by the destination host, there will be no such entry in the received LET_k^j package. In that case, we need to find the largest issuing time T of all RPCs executed by host k and issued by j, by joining the UST_j table and LET_k^j table together. Then we can delete those entries in UST_j which $host\_to$ field is k and the issuing time plus the maximum delay time is larger than the largest issuing time T found above. The function is described in Algorithm 4:

```
listen_extern_lets(ust_table, nrt_table)
UST *ust_table[];
NRT *nrt_table[];
{
  LET *rcvd_let[MAXENTRIES], *b;
  UST *c;
  int k;
  long T;
  while (TRUE) {
    /* listen to the sending of LET entry packages. the process suspends until a sending comes */
    /* the first received package is put into rcvd_let */
    /* other sendings are suspended until the local host processes over the received package */
    /* k is the host number which sends the package */
    k = receive(rcvd_let);                                 Algorithm 4
    /* processing the executed RPCs on host k put them into NRT if they appear in local UST */
    for all b ∈ rcvd_let {
      if (b.rpc = c.rpc where c ∈ UST) {
        NRT += b.rpc;   /* += here means insert. */
        delete c from UST;
      }
    }
    /* processing other RPCs to host k and return US delete them from UST if they are not executed */
    /* T = largest time of executed RPC */
    T = max(c.t | c ∈ UST, b ∈ rcvd_let and b.rpc = c.rpc);
    for all c ∈ UST {
      if (c.t ≤ T + MAX_DELAY) and (c.host_to == k)
```

```
        delete c from UST;    /* delete entries whose RPCs are not executed */
    }
  }
}
```

The fourth function of RM manages single RPC transaction calls of its clients. If any client program wants to make a RPC call, it calls the *manage_rpc_calls()* function and hands the call to the function. The function makes the RPC call. If the call is successful or not executed, it simply returns these massage to the client program. If the call returns *US*, then a UST entry is created and stored into the local UST table.

```
manage_rpc_calls(ust_table)
UST *ust_table[];
{
  int k;
  long t;
  UST *b;
  while (TRUE) {
    /* listen to local RPC call p the process suspends until a call p comes */
    /* if more calls come, they are queued up until the processing of the current call is over */
    listen_call(p);
    s = c(p);    /* do the RPC call */
    k = the destination host number;                              Algorithm 5
    t = the time when issuing p;
    switch {
      case (s == OK):    /* The RPC executed and returns OK. */
        break;
      case (s == FL):    /* the RPC is not executed */
        break;
      case (s == US):    /* the RPC may or may not executed */
        initialise b;
        b.rpc = p; b.host_to = k; b.time = t;
        UST += b;
    }
    tell the client the RPC returns s;
  }
}
```

The fifth function is to listen to the local servers and log their executed RPC names into the local LET table. So, each server will report its work if it has performed a RPC call. Two phase protocol[1,4] can be used here to ensure that when a server reports its execution of a RPC, it will be executed even in the present of failures. Next is the algorithm:

```
listen_local_servers(let_table)
LET *let_table[];
{
  char *p;
  int h;
  LET *b;                                                         Algorithm 6
  while (TRUE) {
    /* listen to the report of executed RPC p. the process suspends until a report comes */
    /* if more reports come, they are queued until the processing of the current call is over */
    h = listen_server(p);    /* h is the reported client host number */
    initialise b;
    b.rpc = p; b.host_from = h;
    LET += b;
  }
}
```

3.3. Properties

Before describing and prove properties of the model, we make the following assumptions. It is easy to know these assumptions are mostly realistic.

(1). The life-cycle of system entities (hosts, links, and servers) is *work --> down_repair_restart --> work*. Without losing generality, we assume that the work time and down time (include repair and restart time) are finite and denote them as T_w and T_d, respectively.

(2). The maximum delay time of a RPC call is *MAX_DELAY*. That is, if a RPC call is issued at time t, then at time $t + MAX\_DELAY$, that call is either executed or will never be executed.

(3). The average time of making a RPC call is relatively long. Particularly, it needs at least the same time as the average time that a RM sends out one of its LET entry packages, as well as at least the same as the average time of a rollback call.

(4). The probability of a RPC call or a rollback call that returns *OK* is much larger than the probabilities that return *FL* and *US*. That is, in most cases a RPC call or a rollback call will be successful.

Following properties can be established for our single RPC transaction management model. We outline informal proofs here.

Property 3.1. If a RPC returns *OK*, it is executed and will not be rolled back.

*Proof:*By definition, the RPC is executed correctly when *OK* returns. Rollbacks are only performed in *rollback_nrt()* algorithm according to entries in NRT table. While entries in NRT table come from UST table by the working of algorithm *listen_extern_lets()*. According to algorithm *manage_rpc_calls()*, if a RPC call returns *OK*, it will not be put into the UST table, and so will not be put into the NRT table. So the property is true.

Property 3.2. If a RPC returns *FL*, it is not executed and will not be rolled back.

*Proof:*Similar as above.

Corollary 1. The time of sending out any entry in LET table is finite.

*Proof:*Algorithm 2 *send_my_let()* is responsible of sending out LET table entries. Because we grouped together all LET entries which have the same *host_from* field before sending them out, so ideally we can view the LET table as a circular table of N components, where N is the number of hosts in the system. Each component contains a LET entry package. Now, the function of Algorithm 2 is to circularly send out all entries, one LET entry package each time. If the time needed to send out a LET entry package is 1 time unit, then the time needed to have a circular sending is N units (we ignore the local processing time because they are very small compared to the communication time needed by the sending). That is, any entry of the LET table will be sent out in N time units if no failures occur. As we have assumed the maximum down time for a host is T_d, that means the time for sending out the LET entry package of a failed host is at most $T_w + N$. So, any LET entry will be sent out in finite time. From now on, we denote this time as SEND_LET_TIME.

Corollary 2. The size of any LET entry package is finite.

*Proof:*As we know, while we processing the LET table by using Algorithm 2, the RM will concurrently fill in LET by using Algorithm 6 (*listen_local_servers()*). Let us assume the time needed to send out a LET entry package is 1 time unit and the average numbers of RPCs performed in a host in a time unit is s. The worst case is that all the RPCs are called from one host i. As Corollary 1 tells us that the time to send out any entry of LET is N when no failures occur, so the maximum length of the LET entry package for host i is $s * N$. If host i fails, or the links to the host i fail, then no RPC calls from host i can be successful. That means the length of any LET entry packages for host i will not grow until the failures are recovered. Other cases are the same. So, the corollary holds.

Corollary 3. The time of rolling back all entries of NRT table is finite.

*Proof:*If we can prove that the speed of filling NRT table is less than the speed of deleting NRT table, the Corollary will hold. Rollback and delete NRT entries is the responsibility of algorithm *rollback_nrt().* While rolling back, the RM will concurrently fill in NRT by using function *listen_extern_lets()* from UST table. UST table is filled in by function *manage_rpc_calls()* when RPCs return *US*. From assumption 4, only a small portion of RPCs need rollback, and assumption 3 tells us that the speed of rolling back is at most the same as the speed of RPC calls. So, if on average there are s RPCs performed in a time unit, then the filling speed to NRT table is $s * p$, where p is the probability that a RPC fails and $p < 0.5$. While the rollback speed is also s with $s * q$ rollbacks return *OK* in a time unit, where $q > 0.5$. Because $s * p < s * q$, the corollary holds. We use ROLLBACK_NRT_TIME to denote this time.

Property 3.3. If a RPC returns *US*, it will eventually be rolled back if it is executed.

Proof: Suppose $US = c(p)$, and the client is on host i, the server is on host k, and the timestamp is t. According to function *manage_rpc_calls()*, an entry will be put into UST table. We denote it as d, and $d.rpc = p$, $d.host\_to = k$, and $d.time = t$. After a finite time period (at most SEND_LET_TIME long by Corollary 1), host k will send all the names of performed RPCs (that were issued by host i) to host i. Suppose now all RPCs from host i to host k are processed before the sending. If p has been executed, then there is a $b : B_k$, such that $b.rpc = d.rpc = a$, where B_k is the set of all entries in LET_k with host name fields equal to i (that is, the LET entry package from host k to host i). In that case, according to function *listen_extern_lets()*, p will be put into NRT table. After a while (at most ROLLBACK_NRT_TIME long according to Corollary 3), the RM_i will issue the rollback operation $r(p)$ in function *rollback_nrt()*. If p is not executed, there will be no such b in B_k. So, the second segment of function *listen_extern_let()* will delete d from UST table, and no rollback operation is needed.

Now suppose p is performed just after k sent out package B_k. In that case, b will be put into LET_k but not in B_k. Because the RPC returns *US*, d is put into UST_i. In function *listen_extern_lets()*, RM_i will find that $d.time > T + $ MAX_DELAY because of assumption 2. So, d will remain in the UST_i table. Eventually, MAX_DELAY time will pass and when host k sends the B_k next time, b will be there and will be rolled back as above.

Because the round time periods for function *send_my_let()* and function *rollback_nrt()* are finite, the MAX_DELAY time is finite, and the time between two neighbour *works* for system entities are finite, the above rollback operation will eventually take place.

Property 3.4. The LET, NRT, and UST tables will not grow indefinitely and any entry will be sent out or deleted eventually.

Proof: From Corollary 1 and 2, the finite host numbers in the system and the limited down time, it is easy to know that the assertion for LET table is true.

The UST table is filled in by function *manage_rpc_calls()*. It is easy to know that the average length of UST table is less than or equal to the average length of LET table. Because the UST contains only those RPC entries which return are *US*'s, while the LET contains the *OK* return entries. By assumption 4 the assertion holds. From the assumption that the down time of any system entity is definite, we know that all RPCs issued by a host will be acknowledged and checked in function *listen_extern_lets()*. So we can conclude that any entry in the table will be deleted eventually.

From Corollary 3, the speeds difference between NRT filling and rolling back, and the limited down time, it is easy to know that the assertion for NRT table is true.

4. Parallel RPC Transaction Management

4.1. Algorithms

The RPC manager and algorithms used by RMs in the network when processing parallel RPC transactions is almost the same as in processing single RPC transaction calls except the function *manage_rpc_calls()* is extended to include the parallel RPC transaction processing.

The extended function at first listens to a parallel RPC transaction call from the local host and processes them concurrently. If all of the RPCs returns *OK*, or there are error returns but no RPCs are performed in the parallel call, then it simply tells the client the result and exits (to listen to new parallel calls). If there are some error returns and there are some RPCs were performed in the parallel call, then a parallel rollback operation for all those performed RPCs is issued and their results are collected. If all rollback operations returns *OK*, then it tells the client that the transaction is failed but all performed RPCs are rolled back. If some of the rollback operations do not return *OK*, then they are put into the NRT table for further rolling back by the RM and the algorithm tells the client that the transaction failed and some rollbacks are to be performed by the RM. Next is the extended function:

```
manage_rpc_calls(ust_table)
UST *ust_table[];
{
  UST *b;
  while (TRUE) {
    /* listen to local RPC transaction calls. (suspends until a transaction call comes) */
    /* if more transaction calls come, they are queued up until current processing is over */
    listen_call(p₁, ..., pₘ);
    COBEGIN  /* concurrently execute the RPC calls within the transaction */
      retᵢ = c(pᵢ),
      kᵢ = the destination host number,
      tᵢ = the time when issuing c(pᵢ),  i = 1, 2, ..., m;
    COEND;
    S_US = {pᵢ | retᵢ == US};
    S_FL = {pᵢ | retᵢ == FL};
    S_OK = {pᵢ | retᵢ == OK};
    switch {
      case (S_US == S_FL == ∅):  /* all RPCs executed and returned OK */
        tell the client the transaction returns OK;                    Algorithm 7
        exit;
      case (S_FL ≠ ∅ and S_US == ∅):  /* error, but none RPCs are executed */
        ERR = FL; break;
      case (S_US ≠ ∅):  /* error, but some RPCs maybe executed */
        for each pᵢ ∈ S_US {
          b.rpc = pᵢ; b.host_to = kᵢ; b.time = tᵢ;
          UST += b;
        }
        ERR = US; break;
    }
    /* arrive here only when failures */
    if (S_OK == ∅) {  /* no RPC is executed */
      tell client: transaction returns ERR and none needs rollback;
      exit;
    } else {
      COBEGIN /* roll back */
        retᵢ = r(pᵢ),    pᵢ ∈ S_OK;
      COEND;
      R_US = {pᵢ | retᵢ == US};
      R_FL = {pᵢ | retᵢ == FL};
      if (R_US == R_FL == ∅) {  /* all rollbacks are OK */
        tell client: transaction returns ERR and all rollbacks are done;
        exit;
      }
      /* some rollbacks are not performed, log them into NRT */
```

```
        NRT += pᵢ,   pᵢ ∈ R_US ∪ R_FL;
        tell client: transaction returns ERR and some rollbacks are not done;
        exit;
    }  /* else */
  }  /* while */
}
```

4.2. Properties

It is evident that Property 3.4 of Section 3.3 holds for parallel RPC transactions. The following properties can be easily established:

Property 4.1. If a RPC transaction returns OK, all its RPCs are executed and will not be rolled back.

*Proof:*The only place for the system to return OK is when $S_{US} == S_{FL} == \emptyset$. In that case, all RPC are executed correctly, and nothing is put into UST table. So, they will not be rolled back.

Property 4.2. If a RPC transaction returns FL, any executed RPCs will be rolled back.

*Proof:*The ERR is assigned to FL when $S_{FL} \neq \emptyset$ and $S_{US} == \emptyset$. If $S_{OK} == \emptyset$ now, then the algorithm exits and no rollbacks are needed. Otherwise, the necessary rollbacks are performed. If all rollbacks return OK, the algorithm exits and all rollbacks are done. If any rollbacks fail, they are put into the NRT table and according to Property 3.4 of Section 3.3, they will be eventually rolled back.

Property 4.3. If a RPC transaction returns US, any executed RPCs will be rolled back.

*Proof:*The ERR is assigned to US when $S_{US} \neq \emptyset$. In that case, all those unknown state RPCs are put into the UST table. According to Property 3.4 of Section 3.3, those entries will be put into NRT table and rolled back eventually. Other situations are similar as above.

5. Remarks

The design of a RPC transaction manager is described in this paper. After the introduction of the problem and the RPC transaction models, we used two steps to solve the RPC transaction management problem. At first, a system for managing transactions of single RPC calls is developed. Algorithm and properties of the system are described. Then, by extending the single RPC transaction management system, the parallel RPC transaction management system is described.

Almost all transaction management approaches use two-phase protocol. It is easy to modify our model into two-phase paradigm. In that case, the system will be also able to deal with RPCs that are not capable of being rolled back. But the efficiency of two-phase model will be less than our model, mainly because the executability checking (checking if the RPC will return OK or not) will take much time, and the stable storage management in two-phase protocol is more complex than our model.

Our model is transparent to programmers. It can act as a run-time system within the programming environment. Programmers will not have too much burden to maintain the RPC transactions in their programs. They can use RPC transaction calls as usual RPC calls and the system will do all the job. We feel this is better than the language level implementation.

Several extensions of the model is possible. For example, one may want to explore the *nested RPC transaction* model, or extend the model to maintain the atomic RPC transactions.

References

1. Bernstein, P. A., Hadzilacos, V., and Goodman, N., *Concurrency Control and Recovery in Database Systems*, Addison-Wesley Publishing Company, 1987.

2. Coulouris, G. F. and Dollimore, J., *Distributed Systems: Concepts and Design,* Addison-Wesley Publishing Co. Inc., 1988.

3. Korth, H. F., Kim, W., and Bancilhon, F., "On Long-Duration CAD Transaction," *Information Sciences*, ACM, 1988.

4. Lampson, B. W., "Atomic Transactions," *Lecture Notes in Computer Science*, vol. 105, pp. 246-265, Springer-Verlag, 1981.

5. Liskov, B. and Sheifler, R., "Guardians and Actions: Linguistic Support for Robust, Distributed Programs," *ACM Transactions on Programming Languages and Systems*, vol. 5, no. 3, pp. 381-404, July 1983.

6. Liskov, B. and Shrira, L., "Promises: Linguistic Support for Efficient Asynchronous Procedure Calls in Distributed Systems," *Proceedings of the SIGPLAN '88 Conference on Programming Language Design and Implementation*, Atlanta, Georgia, June 1988.

7. Nelson, B. J., "Remote Procedure Call," Report CSL-81-9, Xerox Palo Alto Research Centre, May 1981.

8. Weihl, W. and Liskov, B., "Implementation of Resilient, Atomic Data Types," *ACM Transactions on Programming Languages and Systems*, vol. 7, no. 2, pp. 244-269, April 1985.

9. Zhou, W. and Molinari, B., "A Performance Evaluation Model for Programs Using Remote Procedure Calls," *Australian Computer Science Communications*, vol. 11, no. 1, pp. 98-109, February 1989.

10. Zhou, W., "Transaction Management: An Overview," *Internal Report, Department of Computer Science, The ANU*, January 1990.

11. Zhou, W., "On the Management of Remote Procedure Call Transactions," *Internal Report, Department of Computer Science, The ANU*, February 1990.

12. Zhou, W., "On The Rapid Prototyping of Distributed Information System Applications," *Proceedings of the International Conference on Computing and Information*, pp. 176-180, Niagara Falls, Ontario, Canada, May, 1990.

13. Zhou, W., "Computer-Aided Prototyping of Distributed Programs: A Case Study," *Australian Software Engineering Conference '90*, Sydney, Australia, May 1990.

Simple Atomic Snapshots
A Linear Complexity Solution With Unbounded Time-Stamps[1]

Lefteris M. Kirousis[2,3] Paul Spirakis[2,3,4] Philippas Tsigas[2,3]
E-addresses: ⟨lastname⟩@grpatvx1.bitnet

Abstract

Let $X_1, \ldots, X_c$ be variables shared by a number of processes which operate in a totally asynchronous and wait-free manner. An operation by a process is either a write on one of the variables or a read of the values of *all* variables. All operations are assumed to be atomic, i.e. an execution of any number of them (including reads) must be serializable in a way compatible with the values returned by the reads. We give a new protocol implementing such operations for the case of a single-reader and one writer per variable. Our construction uses time-stamps that may take values as large as the number of operations performed. The advantages of our construction over previous (bounded time-stamps) solutions are: (i) It has very simple semantics. (ii) The time complexity of an operation (i.e. the number of its sub-operations) and the space complexity of the construction (i.e. the number of subregisters used) are equal to the number of processes involved.

1 Introduction

Recently a number of constructions have been proposed for a shared, array-like variable (called a **composite register**) that comprises a number $X_1, \ldots, X_c$ of variables (the **components**), so that each X_k, $k = 1, \ldots, c$, can be written on by a set of processes (the **writers**) and the values of *all* components can be read in a single atomic operation by one or more processes (the **readers**). All operations (i.e. either writes on a component or multi-reads) are assumed to be executed in a totally asynchronous and wait-free manner [Afek et al., 1990], [Anderson, 1990]. The building blocks of these constructions are atomic, single-component variables called **subregisters**. A read or a write operation on the level of the composite register (a high-level operation) may have as sub-operations both reads and writes on the level of subregisters (low-level operations).

The importance of the problem of constructing composite registers is eloquently described in [Afek et al., 1990]: "... much of the difficulty in proving correctness of concurrent programs is due to the need to argue based on 'inconsistent' views of shared memory, obtained concurrently with other process's modifications. Verification of concurrent algorithms is thus complicated by the need for a 'non-interference' step [...]. By simplifying (or eliminating) the non-interference step, atomic snapshot memories can greatly simplify the design and verification of many concurrent algorithms."

A formalism for the problem can be found either in [Anderson, 1990] or in [Afek et al., 1990]. In [Lamport, 1986] one can find a formalism for the notion of atomic registers. We tried to keep our notation compatible with these formalisms. We assume that there is a precedence relation on operations which is a strict partial order (denoted by '→'). Semantically, $a \to b$ means that operation a ends before operation b starts. If two operations are incomparable under → they are

---

[1]This research was partially supported by the ESPRIT II Basic Research Actions Program of the EC under contract no. 3075 (project ALCOM).

[2]Department of Computer Science and Engineering, University of Patras, Patras 26110, Greece.
[3]Computer Technology Institute, P.O. Box 1122, Patras 26110, Greece.
[4]Courant Institute of Mathematical Sciences, NYU, U.S.A.

said to **overlap**. If $a \to b$ then for any sub-operations s and t of a and b, respectively, we have that $s \to t$.

A construction of a composite register comprises: (i) a descriprion of the set of the subregisters and their initial values and (ii) procedures (protocols) that describe a high-level operation in terms of its sub-operations on the subregisters. A protocol, apart from the shared variables (i.e. the subregisters) makes use of **local** variables as well (these cannot be shared by concurrent processes). The local variables are assumed to retain their values between invocations of the corresponding procedures, i.e. they are *static*. We adopt the convention to denote shared variables with capital letters and local variables with lower case letters. A **reading function** π_R for a subregister R is a function that assigns a write operation w to each read operation r on R, such that the value returned by r is the value written by w. If the value read by r is the initial value of the register, we assume that $\pi_R(r)$ is a write on R that precedes all other operations on R. Similarly, a reading function π_k for a component X_k of the composite register is a function that assigns to each high-level read r a high-level write w on X_k so that the value for X_k returned by r is written on X_k by w.

A **run** is an execution of an arbitrary number of operations according to the respective protocols. A run is **atomic** if the partial order $\to$ on its operations can be extended to a strict *total* order $\Rightarrow$ and if for each component X_k there is a reading function π_k such that for all high-level reads r: (i) $\pi_k(r) \Rightarrow r$ and (ii) there is no write w on X_k such that $\pi_k(r) \Rightarrow w \Rightarrow r$. A construction for a composite register is atomic if all its runs are atomic. We assume all subregisters to be atomic, therefore all operations on a subregister are totally ordered by $\to$. Thus we can assume that the reading function associated with each subregister will associate to each sub-read the value of the last sub-write preceding it by the relation $\to$. In this paper we assume that all high-level reads, as well as all writes on the same component, are linearly ordered by $\to$ (i.e., we assume that there is a single reader and one writer per component). Moreover, with each subregister we assume that there is associated a reading function such that a sub-read from the subregister reads the value of the last sub-write preceding it.

Both Afek et al. [1990] and Anderson [1990] give constructions for composite registers. All constructions by Anderson are recursive on the number of components and because at each recursive call the number of steps of an operation is at least doubled, the time complexity of the algorithms (i.e. the number of sub-operations of an operation) is exponential as a function of the number of components. Afek et al. give constructions with polynomial complexity, but in all cases both time and space complexity are at least quadratic (space complexity is the number of subregisters used in the construction). These algorithms are originally given with unbounded time-stamps, i.e. with the assumption that the subregisters can hold arbitrarily large integers and subsequently it is shown that bounded integers are sufficient. The complexities, however, of both bounded and unbounded versions of these constructions are the same and, moreover, the unbounded versions are not semantically much simpler than the bounded ones.

Kirousis, Spirakis, Tsigas [1990] improved the previous results showing how to construct composite registers for the single-reader case with *asymptotically* linear time and space complexity.

In this paper, we give a construction for the single-reader, one-writer per component case using unbounded time-stamps. However, we gain in semantic simplicity as well as in time and space complexity. Our construction has time and space complexity that are both *exactly equal* to the total number of proccesses. The size of the time-stamps we use is at most equal to the number of operations in a run, therefore it is enough to assume that the subregisters of our construction can hold a number of bits that is linear in the logarithm of the number of operations. Given the word-length that is achieved with today's technology, it seems that "unbounded" time-stamps in this sense is a fair price to pay for the semantic simplicity attained.

2 The Protocol

In order to prove the correctness of our construction, we first give an atomicity criterion.

Theorem 1 *In the case of a single-reader, one-writer per component, c-component, composite register a run is atomic if for each k, where $1 \le k \le c$, there exists a reading function π_k, whose domain is the set of high-level reads and whose range is a set of high-level writes to component k, such that the following four conditions hold.*

(F) Future *For any high-level read r and for any component k it is not the case that: $r \to \pi_k(r)$.*

(P) Past *For any high-level read r, for any component k and for any high-level write w to component k it is not the case that: $\pi_k(r) \to w \to r$.*

(N-O) New-Old Inversion *For all high-level reads r_1, r_2, and for any component k it is not the case that: $(r_1 \to r_2$ and $\pi_k(r_2) \to \pi_k(r_1))$.*

(C) Consistency *For any high-level read r, for all components k, l and for any high-level write w to component k it is not the case that: $\pi_k(r) \to w \to \pi_l(r)$.* $\square$

Intuitively, the theorem is true because any partial order can be extended to a total order satisfying certain given conditions, if it is true that the *partial* order satisfies all limitations induced onto it by the conditions on the total order. We omit the proof of the above theorem, since the proof does not offer much to the understanding of our construction.

2.1 Informal Description

The architecture of the construction is: for each component $k = 1, \ldots, c$ we introduce an atomic subregister $B[k]$ which is written on by the writer of the corresponding component and is read by all processes. We call these subregisters Buffers. A buffer holds an **array**$[1..c]$ of Records. The ith component of this array is a Record which holds a value corresponding to the ith component of the composite register and a tag attached to this value.

The reader and writer procedures are shown in Figure 1. The protocol's behaviour is:

• The writer of the ith component $(i = 1, \ldots, c)$ reads sequentially $B[1], \ldots, B[c]$. Thus, since each $B[i]$ is an **array**$[1..c]$, the writer obtains a matrix mw (writer's matrix) of dimension (c, c). Each column of this matrix corresponds to a component, and each entry of a column has a value and a tag written by a high-level write onto the component corresponding to this column. The writer now selects an entry with a maximum tag for each column $col = 1, \ldots, i-1, i+1, \ldots, c$ and stores its value and its tag into a local variable $b[col]$. On the other hand, for $col = i$ (i.e. the value of col corresponding to the component where this writer writes) the writer selects again from column i an entry with maximum tag, increments this tag by one and stores into $b[i]$ the value that it must write onto component i (say, this value is u) together with the incremented tag. Finally, the writer writes the array b into $B[i]$.

• The reader acts in the same way as the writer. First it reads sequentially $B[1], \ldots, B[c]$. Thus, the reader obtains a matrix mr (reader's matrix) of dimension (c, c). Next, the reader selects for each $col = 1, \ldots, c$ an entry with maximum tag and stores the corresponding value into $a[col]$. Finally, it returns the array a.

It is easy to check from the similarity of the reader's and writer's procedures that the writer of the ith component takes a snapshot of the other $c-1$ components and writes this snapshot appended with the value u onto $B[i]$.

Initially the subregisters $B[1], \ldots, B[c]$ hold the same arbitrary value. The local variables are arbitrarily initialized.

```
type Rtype = record val : valtype; tag : integer end;
var  B : array[1..c] of array[1..c] of Rtype;
     /* Shared variables declaration*/
```

```
procedure reader /*returns array[1..c] of valtype*/
var  mr : array[1..c] of array[1..c] of Rtype;
     a : array[1..c] of valtype;
     j, col, row : 1..c;
begin
     for j := 1 to c do mr[j] := B[j] od;
     for col := 1 to c do
```
select row such that $(\forall l : 1 \leq l \leq c)(mr[row][col].tag \geq mr[l][col].tag)$;
```
          a[col] := mr[row][col].val;
     od;
     return (a[1], ... , a[c]);
end
```

```
procedure writer /* writes u : valtype on component i*/
var  mw : array[1..c] of array[1..c] of Rtype;
     b : array[1..c] of Rtype;
     j, col, row : 1..c;
begin
     for j := 1 to c do mw[j] := B[j] od;
     for col := 1 to c do
```
select row such that $(\forall l : 1 \leq l \leq c)(mw[row][col].tag \geq mw[l][col].tag)$;
```
          b[col].val := mw[row][col].val;
          b[col].tag := mw[row][col].tag;
     od;
     b[i].tag := b[i].tag + 1;
     b[i].val := u;
     write [b[1], ... , b[c]] to B[i];
end
```

Figure 1: The formal protocol

2.2 Proof of Correctness

In this subsection we give the formal correctness proof of our protocol. The proof is given by a series of lemmas.

Lemma 1 *The prorocol satisfies condition (F).*

Proof Because $B[k]$ is atomic for $k = 1, \ldots, c$, it follows from the protocol that for all high-level reads r and for all $k = 1, \ldots, c$ the final step of $\pi_k(r)$ occurs before the final step of r.□

Lemma 2 *The protocol satisfies condition (P).*

Proof Assume, towards a contradiction, that there is a high-level read r, a component k of the composite register and a high-level write w to this component such that $\pi_k(r) \to w \to r$. Assume that the tag that $\pi_k(r)$ attaches to its value is α. Since $\pi_k(r) \to w$, w attaches to its value a tag β such that $\beta > \alpha$. Since $w \to r$, the reader will read a value from $B[k]$ written by a high-level write w_1 onto component k such that either $w \to w_1$ or $w_1 = w$. Thus, the reader will store in column k and row k of its matrix mr a value written by w_1 with tag greater than or equal to β. Therefore, it will not return the value written by $\pi_k(r)$, since this value has smaller tag than the tag of the value written by w_1, a contradiction.□

Lemma 3 *The protocol satisfies condition (N-0).*

Proof Assume, towards a contradiction, that there are two high-level reads r_1 and r_2 and a component k of the composite register such that: $r_1 \to r_2$ and $\pi_k(r_2) \to \pi_k(r_1)$. It is easy to see that the last sub-operation of $\pi_k(r_1)$ (which is its only sub-write) occurs before the last sub-operation of r_1. Because now $r_1 \to r_2$, we have that $\pi_k(r_2) \to \pi_k(r_1) \to r_2$, a contradiction.□

Lemma 4 *The protocol satisfies the condition (C).*

Proof Assume, towards a contradiction, that there is are two components k, l of the composite register high-level read r, and a high-level write w to component k such that $\pi_k(r) \to w \to \pi_l(r)$. By this hypothesis, the reader during r returns as value for component l a value written by the high-level write $\pi_l(r)$. This high-level write, at its last subwrite on $B[l]$, besides writing its "own" value with a tag on $B[l][l]$, it writes a value and a tag on $B[l][k]$ as well. This tag, since $w \to \pi_l(r)$, is greater than or equal to the tag that w attaches to its value on component k and, therefore (since $\pi_k(r) \to w$), it is strictly greater than the corresponding tag of $\pi_k(r)$. Now, since r reads $\pi_l(r)$, the tag that r has at its disposal for choosing a value for component k is greater than equal to the tag of $B[l][k]$, so r cannot read $\pi_k(r)$, a contradiction.□

From the above results and by Theorem 1 we have that:

Theorem 2 *A single-reader, c-component,1-writer per component composite register can be constructed using c atomic, $c+1$-reader, 1-writer, subregisters. The number of sub-operations for a read operation is c, while a write operation has $c+1$ sub-operations.*

Acknowledgment

We thank Andreas Veneris for many helpful comments on an earlier draft of this paper.

References

Y. Afek, H. Attiya, D. Dolev, E. Gafni, M. Merritt and N. Shavit (1990): Atomic snapshots of shared memory, *Proceedings of the 9th ACM Symposium on Principles of Distributed Computing, Quebec City, Quebec, Canada.*

J.H. Anderson (1990): Composite registers, *Proceedings of the 9th ACM Symposium on Principles of Distributed Computing, Quebec City, Quebec, Canada.*

L.M. Kirousis, P. Spirakis and Ph. Tsigas (1990): Reading Many Variables in One Atomic Operation: Solutions With Linear Complexity *Technical Report, November 1990, Computer Technology Institute, Patras*

L. Lamport (1986): On interprocess communication, part i: basic formalism, part ii: basic algorithms, *Distributed Computing* 1, 77-101.

A DISTRIBUTED SCHEDULING ALGORITHM FOR HETEROGENEOUS REAL-TIME SYSTEMS

Osman ZeinElDine Mohamed El-Toweissy Ravi Mukkamala
Department of Computer Science, Old Dominion University
Norfolk, Virginia 23529.

Abstract

Much of the previous work on load balancing and scheduling in distributed environments was concerned with homogeneous systems and homogeneous loads. Several of the results indicate that random policies are as effective as other more complex load allocation policies. In this paper, we investigate the effects of heterogeneity on scheduling algorithms for hard-real time systems. We propose a distributed scheduler specifically to handle heterogeneities in both nodes and node traffic. The performance of this algorithm is measured in terms of the percentage of jobs discarded. While a random task allocation is very sensitive to heterogeneities, our algorithm is shown to be robust to such non-uniformities in system components and load.

1. Introduction

Meeting deadline is of utmost importance for jobs in hard real-time systems. In these systems, when a job cannot be executed to completion prior to its deadline, it is either considered as having a zero value or as a discarded job with possible disastrous side-effects. Scheduling algorithms are assigned the responsibility of deriving job schedules so as to maximize the number of jobs that meet their deadline. Most of the literature in real-time systems deals with periodic deterministic tasks which may be prescheduled and executed cyclically [1,2,5,6]. The aperiodically arriving random tasks with deadlines have not been thoroughly investigated [3]. In addition, much of the studies in this area assume systems dedicated to real-time applications and working at extremely small loads (10% or less).

In a distributed real-time system, jobs with deadlines are received at each of the nodes in the system. Each node is generally capable of executing a job completely. These jobs are scheduled for execution at the nodes by a scheduler. A distributed scheduler is a distributed algorithm with cooperating agents at each node. Basically, the agents cooperate through exchange of local load information. The decision for scheduling a job, however, is taken by a local agent. Much of the current work in distributed scheduling assumes identical scheduling algorithms, homogeneous processing capabilities, and identical request arrival patterns at all nodes across the distributed system [7].

In this paper, we are interested in investigating the effects of heterogeneity and aperiodicity in distributed real-time systems on the performance of the overall system. We have designed a distributed scheduler specifically aimed at tolerating heterogeneities in distributed systems. Our algorithm is based on a tree-structured scheduler where the leaves of the tree represent the processing nodes of the distributed system, and the intermediate nodes represent controlling or server nodes. The server node is a guardian for nodes below it in the tree. The leaf nodes attempt to keep its guardian node informed of their load status. When a leaf node cannot meet the deadline of an arriving job, it transfers the job to its guardian (or server). The guardian then sends this job either to one of its other child nodes or to its guardian. We measure the performance of our algorithm in terms of percentage of discarded jobs. (A job may be discarded either by a leaf node or by one of the servers.) Since random scheduling is often hailed to be as effective as some other algorithms with more intelligence, we compare the performance of our algorithm with a random scheduler [4]. Even though a random algorithm is often effective in a homogeneous environment, our investigations found it to be unsuitable for heterogeneous environments.

This paper is organized as follows. Section 2 presents the model of the system adopted in this paper. Section 3 describes the proposed scheduling algorithm. Section 4 summarizes the results obtained from simulations of our algorithm and a random scheduler algorithm. Finally, Section 5 presents some conclusions from this study and proposes some future work.

2. The System Model

For the purposes of scheduling, the distributed system is modeled as a tree of nodes and is shown in Figure 1. (The choice of the hierarchical structure is influenced by our scheduling algorithm which can handle a system with hundreds of nodes. The choice of three levels in this paper is for ease of illustration.) The nodes at the lowest level (level 0) are the *processing* nodes while the nodes at the higher levels represent guardians or *servers*. A processing node is responsible for executing arriving jobs when they meet some specified criteria. The processing nodes are grouped into *clusters*, and each cluster is assigned a unique server. When a server receives a job, it tries to either redirect that job to a processing node within its cluster or to its guardian. It is to be noted that this hierarchical structure could be logical (i.e., some of the processing nodes may themselves assume the role of the servers).

In summary, there are four components in the system model: jobs, processing nodes, servers, and the communication subsystem. A job is characterized by its arrival time, execution time, deadline, and priority (if any). The specifications of a processing node include its speed factor, scheduling policy, external arrival rate (of jobs), and job mix (due to heterogeneity). A server is modeled by its speed and its node assignment policy. Finally, the communication subsystem is represented by the speeds of transmission and distances between different nodes (processing and servers) in the distributed system.

3. Proposed Scheduling Algorithm

We describe the algorithm in terms of the participation of the three major components: the processing node, the sever at level 1, and the server at level 2. The major execution steps involved at these three components are summarized in Figure 2.

3.1 General

First let us consider the actions at the processing node. When a job arrives (either from an external user or from the server) at a *processing node*, it is tested at the gateway. The local scheduling algorithm at the node decides whether or not to execute this job locally. This decision is based on pending jobs in the local queue (which are already guaranteed to be executed within their deadlines), the requirements of the new job, and the scheduling policies (e.g., FCFS, SJF, SDF, SSF etc. [8]). In case the local scheduler decides to execute it locally, it will insert it in the local processing queue, and thereby guaranteeing to execute the new job within its deadline. By definition, no other jobs already in the local queue will miss their deadlines after the new addition. In case the local scheduler cannot make a guarantee to the new job, it either sends the job to its server (if there is a possibility of completion), or discard the job (if there is no such chance of completion).

Let us now consider the actions at level-1 server. Upon arriving at a *server*, a job enters the server queue. First, the server attempts to choose a candidate processing node (within its cluster) that is most likely to meet the deadline of this job. This decision is based on the latest information provided by the processing node to the server regarding its status. This information includes the scheduling algorithm, current load and other status information at each of the processing nodes in its cluster. (The choice of the information content as well as its currency are critical for efficient scheduling. For lack of space, we omit this discussion here.) When more than one candidate node is available, a random selection is carried out among these nodes. (We found a substantial difference in performance between choosing the first candidate and the random selection.) If a server cannot find a candidate node for executing the job, it forwards the job to the level-2 server.

The level-2 server (or *top level server*) maintains information about all level-1 servers. Each server sends an abstract form of its information to the level-2 server. Once again, the information content as well as its currency are crucial for the performance of the algorithm. This server redirects an arriving job to one of the level-1 servers. The choice of candidate servers is dependent on the ability of these servers to redirect a job to one of the processing nodes in their cluster to meet the deadline of the job.

The rule for discarding a job is very simple. At any time, a job may be discarded if the processing node or the server at which the job exists finds that if the job is sent elsewhere it would never be executed before its deadline. This may be due to the jobs already in the processing queue, and/or the communication delay for navigation along the hierarchy.

3.2 Information Abstraction at Different Levels

The auxiliary information (about the load status) maintained at a processing node or a server is crucial to the performance of the scheduling algorithm. Besides the information content, its structure and its maintenance will dictate its utility and overhead on the system. To maximize the benefit and minimize the overhead, every level is assigned its own information structure. The information at the servers is periodically updated by nodes at the lower level. (The time interval for propagating the information to the servers is a parameter of the system.)

The jobs waiting to be executed at a processing node are classified according to the *local* scheduling algorithm (e.g., the classification would be on based priority if a priority scheduler is used.). Due to this dependency on the scheduling algorithm, we allow each processing node to choose its own local classification. Typically, the following attributes are maintained for each class:

- the average response time; (used for performance statistics)

- the likely end of execution (time) of the last job, including the one currently being served;

- the minimum slack among the jobs currently in the processing queue.

In addition, depending on the scheduling policy, we may have some other attributes.

The server maintains a copy of the information available at each of its child nodes including the scheduling policy. Since the information at a child node is dependent on the local scheduling policy, the server node should be capable of maintaining different types of data. Using this information, the server should be able to decide which processing nodes are eligible for executing a job and meet its deadline.

The information at level 2 server consists of an abstraction of the information available at each of the level-1 servers. Since each level-1 server may contain nodes with heterogeneous scheduling policies, level-2 server abstracts its information based on scheduling policies for each server. Thus, for a FCFS scheduling policy, it will contain abstracted status information from each of its child servers. This is repeated for other scheduling policies. Thus, the information at this level does not represent information at a processing node; rather it is a summary of information of a group of nodes in a cluster with the same scheduling policy.

4. Results

In order to evaluate the effectiveness of our scheduling algorithm, we have built a simulator and made a number of runs. The results presented in this paper concentrate on the sensitivity of our algorithm to four different parameters: the cluster size, the communication delay (between nodes), the frequency of propagation of load information (between levels), and the node heterogeneity. For lack of space, we have omitted other results such as the scheduler's sensitivity to heterogeneity in scheduling algorithms, heterogeneity in loads, and the effects of information structures. Accordingly, all the results reported here assume:

- FCFS scheduling policy at every node,

- the total number of processing nodes is 100,

- equal load at all nodes,

- communication delay between any nodes is the same.

The performance of the scheduler is measured in terms of the percentage of jobs discarded by the algorithm (at levels 0,1, 2). The rate of arrivals of jobs and their processing requirements are combinedly represented through a load factor. This load factor refers to the load on the overall system. Our load consists of jobs from three types of execution time constraints. The first type are short jobs with average execution of 10 units of time and with a slack of 25 units. (The actual values for a job are derived from an exponential distribution.) The second type of jobs have an average execution time of 50 units and a slack of 35 units. Long jobs have average execution times of 100 units and slacks of 300 units. In all our experiments, all these types have equal contribution to the overall load factor.

We now discuss our observations regarding the characteristics of the distributed scheduler in terms of the four selected parameters. In order to isolate the effect of one factor from others, the choice of parameters is made judiciously. For example, in studying the effects of cluster size (Figure 3), the updation period is chosen to be a medium value of 200 (stat=200), the communication delay is chosen to be small (com=5), and the nodes are assumed to be homogeneous (node: hom). Similarly, while studying the effects of the updation period (Figure 4), the cluster size is chosen to be 100 (cluster =100). Similar choices are made in the study of other two factors.

4.1 Effect of Cluster Size

Cluster size indicates the number of processing nodes being assigned to a level-1 server. In our study, we have considered three cluster sizes: 100, 50, and 10. A cluster of 100 nodes indicates a centralized server structure where all the processing nodes are under one level-1 server. In this case, level-2 server is absent. Similarly, in the case of cluster of 50 nodes, there are two level-1 servers, and one level-2 server. For 10-node cluster, we have 10 level-1 servers. In addition, we consider a completely decentralized case represented by the *random* policy. In this case, each processing node acts as its own server and randomly selects a destination node to execute a job which it cannot locally guarantee. We make the following observations (Figure 3).

- Both cluster sizes of 100 and 50 nodes have identical effect on performance.

- With cluster size of 10, the percentage of discarded jobs has increased. This difference is apparent at high loads.

- The random policy results in a significantly higher percentage of jobs being discarded.

From here, we conclude that our algorithm is robust to variations in cluster size. In addition, its performance is significantly superior to a random policy.

4.2 Effect of The Frequency of Updations

As is the case for all distributed algorithms, the currency of information at a node about the rest of the system plays a major role in performance. Hence, if the state of processing nodes vary rapidly, then the frequency of status information exchanges between the levels should also be high. In order to determine the sensitivity of the proposed algorithm to the period of updating statistics at the servers, we experimented with four time periods: 25, 100, 200 and 500 units. (These time units are the same as the execution time units of jobs.) The results are summarized in Figure 4. From here we make the following observations.

- Our algorithm is extremely sensitive to changes in period of information exchanges between servers and processing nodes.

- Even in the worst case of 500 units, the performance of our algorithm is significantly better than the random policy.

4.3 Effect of Communication Delay

Since processing nodes send jobs that cannot be executed locally to a server, communication delay is a major factor in reducing the number of jobs discarded due to deadline limitations. Here, we present results for four values of of communication delay: 0, 5, 10 and 20 units. (These units are the same as the execution time units of jobs.) The results are summarized in Figure 5. The communication delay of zero represents a closely coupled system with insignificant time of inter-node or inter-process communication. A higher communication delay implies lower slack for jobs that cannot be executed locally. It may be observed that

- When the communication delay is 0, 5, or 10, the number of discarded jobs with our algorithm (DSA) is relatively small and independent of this delay. In all these cases, the percentage of discarded jobs with DSA is much smaller than with random policy.

- When communication delay is 20, however, the percentage of discarded jobs is much higher. In fact, in this case the random policy has a better performance than our algorithm.

- The performance difference between random policy and our algorithm reduces with the increase in communication delay. When the communication delay is higher, this difference has vanished, and in fact the random policy has displayed better performance.

We attribute our observation to the selection of slacks for the input jobs. If a shortest job could not be executed at the processing node at which it originated, it has to go through two hops of communication (node to server, server to node), resulting in twice the delay for a single hop. Since the maximum value of the slack for jobs with short execution time has been taken to be 25 units of time (in our runs), any communication delay above 12 units will result in a non-local job being discarded with certainty. Thus, even though our algorithm is robust to variations in communication delay, there is an inherent relationship between the slack of an incoming job and the communication delay.

4.4 Effect of Node Heterogeneity

As mentioned in the introduction, a number of studies claim that sending a job randomly over the network would be almost as good as using a complex load balancing algorithm [4]. We conjecture that this claim is only valid under homogeneous nodes assumption and jobs with no time constraints. Since one of our major objectives has been to test this claim for jobs with time constraints over a set of heterogeneous nodes, experiments have been conducted under four conditions. For each of these conditions, we derive results for our algorithm (DSA) as well as the random policy. The results are summarized in Figure 6. The homogeneous case (denoted by *hom*) represents a system with all 100 nodes having the same unit speeds. (Since a job is only distinguished by its processing time requirements, we have considered only speed heterogeneities.) The three heterogeneous cases are represented by *het1, het2, het3*. The heterogeneities are described through a set of <# of nodes, speed factor> pairs. For example, *het1* relates to a system with 50 nodes with a speed factor of 0.5 and 50 nodes with a speed factor of 1.5. Thus the average speed of a processing node is still 1.0, which is the same as the homogeneous case. The other two heterogeneous cases may be similarly explained. Among the cases considered, the degree of heterogeneity is maximum for *het3*. From our results it may be observed that:

- With our algorithm, even though the increase in degree of heterogeneity resulted in an increase of discarded jobs, the increase is not so significant. Hence, our algorithm appears to be robust to node heterogeneities.

- The performance of the random policy is extremely sensitive to the node heterogeneity. As the heterogeneity is increased, the number of discarded jobs is also significantly increased.

With the increase in node heterogeneity, the number of nodes with slow speed also increase. Thus, using a random policy, if a slow speed node is selected randomly, then the job is more likely to be discarded. In our algorithm, since the server is aware of the heterogeneities, it can suitably avoid a low speed node when necessary. Even in this case, there is a tendency for high-speed nodes to be overloaded and low speed nodes to be under loaded. Hence, the difference in performance.

5. Conclusions

In this paper, a distributed algorithm has been proposed to help schedule jobs with time constraints over a network of heterogeneous nodes, each of which could have its own processing speed and job-scheduling policy. Several parametric studies have been conducted. From the results obtained it can be concluded that:

- the algorithm has a large improvement over the random selection in terms of the percentage of discarded jobs;

- the performance of the algorithm tends to be invariant with respect to node-speed heterogeneity;

- the algorithm efficiently utilizes the available information; this is evident from the sensitivity of our algorithm to the periodicity of update information.

- the performance of the algorithm is robust to variations in in the cluster size.

In summary, our algorithm is robust to several heterogeneities commonly observed in distributed systems. Our other results (not presented here) also indicate the robustness of this algorithm to heterogeneities in scheduling algorithms at local nodes. In future, we propose to extend this work to investigate the sensitivity of our algorithm to other heterogeneities in distributed systems. We also propose to test its viability in a non-real time system where response time or throughput is the performance measure.

ACKNOWLEDGEMENT

This research was sponsored in part by the NASA Langley Research Center under contracts NAG-1-1114 and NAG-1-1154.

References

[1] S. R. Biyabani, J.A. Stankovic, and K. Ramamritham, "The integration of deadline and criticalness in hard real-time scheduling," *Proc. Real-time Systems Symposium*, pp. 152-160, December 1988.

[2] J.-Y. Chuang and J.W.S. Liu, "Algorithms for scheduling periodic jobs to minimize average error," *Proc. Real-time Systems Symposium*, pp. 142-151, December 1988.

[3] D. W. Craig and C.M. Woodside, "The rejection rate for tasks with random arrivals, deadlines, and preemptive scheduling," *IEEE Trans. Software Engineering*, Vol. 16, No. 10, pp. 1198-1208, Oct. 1990.

[4] D. L. Eager, E.D. Lazowska, and J. Zahorjan, "Adaptive load sharing in homogeneous distributed systems," *IEEE Trans. Software Engineering*, Vol. SE-12, No. 5, pp. 662-675, May 1986.

[5] R. Rajkumar, L. Sha, and J.P. Lehoczky, "Real-time synchronization protocols for multiprocessors," *Proc. Real-time Systems Symposium*, pp. 259-269, December 1988.

[6] K.G. Shin, C.M. Krishna, and Y.-H. Lee, "Optimal resource control in periodic real-time environments," *Proc. Real-time Systems Symposium*, pp. 33-41, December 1988.

[7] J. Stankovic and K. Ramamritham, "Evaluation of a bidding algorithm for hard real-time distributed systems," *IEEE Trans. Computers*, Vol. C-34, No. 12, pp. 1130-1143, Dec. 1986.

[8] W. Zhao, K. Ramamritham, and J. Stankovic, "Scheduling tasks with resource requirements in hard-real time systems," *IEEE Trans. Software Engineering*, Vol. SE-13, No. 5, pp. 564-577, May 1987.

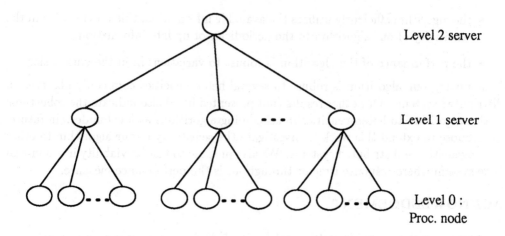

Figure 1 : System Model

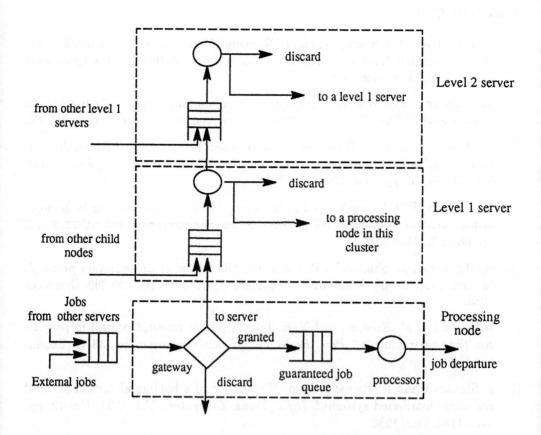

Figure 2 : Flow diagram of The Algorithm

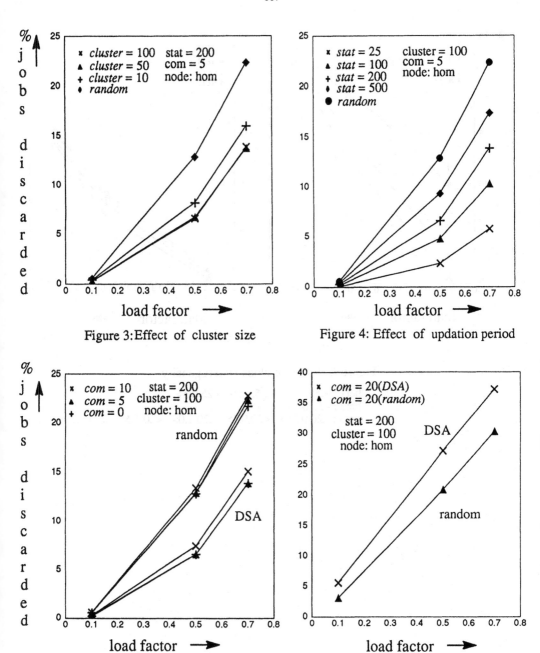

Figure 3:Effect of cluster size

Figure 4: Effect of updation period

Figure 5:Effect of communication delay

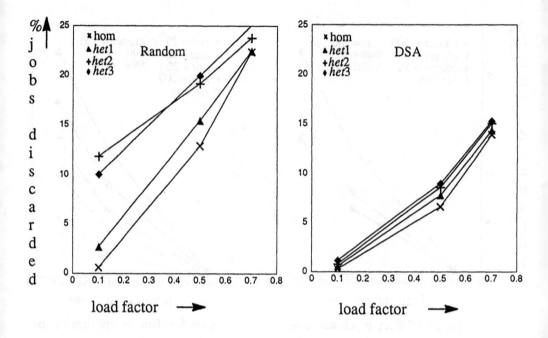

Figure 6: Effect of Node Heterogeneity

het1 : <50,1.0> , <25,1.5> , <25,0.5>
het2 : <50,0.5> , <50,1.5>
het3 : <20,0.25> , <20,0.5> , <20,1.0> , <20,1.5> , <20,1.75>

A distributed solution to the k-out of-M resources allocation problem

Michel RAYNAL
IRISA
Campus de Beaulieu
35042 Rennes-Cédex, FRANCE
raynal@irisa.fr

Abstract

We consider, in a distributed system, a set of M identical resources shared between n processes. Each of these resources can be used by at most one process at a given time (i.e. in mutual exclusion). In the k-out of-M resources allocation problem a process P_i can request at once any number k_i of these M resources ; this process remains blocked until it has got a set of k_i resources. A distributed algorithm, which generalizes the Ricart-Agrawala's mutual exclusion algorithm, is given for this problem ; a variant reducing the number of messages is also proposed. Finally this solution is extended to solve the generalized resources allocation problem in which a process request can concern several instances of different types of resources, each type being represented by some number of identical resources.

Index terms : k-out of-M resources allocation, distributed mutual exclusion, distributed synchronization, and-synchronization, permission-based algorithms.

1 The basic k-out of-M problem

We are interested in the management of a set of M identical resources shared by n processes $P_1, \ldots, P_i, \ldots, P_n$. At any time a resource can be used by at most one process, i.e. in mutual exclusion. On the other hand a process can request and use several of these resources at the same time. When a process wants to use any number k_i ($1 \leq k_i \leq M$) of these resources it requests them at once, and not one after the other, in order to avoid deadlock ; a process remains blocked until it has got the requested number of resources. After having used and released them it can make a new request for any number k_i' of these M resources. The k-out of-M problem lies in ensuring a correct management of these M resources, that is to say in the two following properties :

- safety property : the number of resources which are allocated to the processes at any time is always less than or equal to M. (Each resource being allocated to only one process at a time).

- liveness property : each request has to be satisfied within a finite time (under the hypothesis that the allocated resources are eventually released).

If we consider the case *M=1*, the *k*-out of-*M* problem reduces to the mutual exclusion one [10] ; if for any *i*, k_i is always equal to 1, the problem reduces to the multiple entries critical section one [1,2,9].

We consider the *k*-out of-*M* problem within the context of a distributed system composed of *n* sites ; we suppose one and only one process is associated to each site and we use the terms process and site without distinction. In such a system, the sites communicate only by exchanging messages along channels. These channels allow each process to send messages to each other ; they are reliable (no loss, no duplication, no spurious messages), and fifo (i.e. for each channel the delivery order of messages is the same as the sending one). Communication is asynchronous : transfer delays are finite but umpredictable.

2 Underlying ideas of the solution

In order to ensure the safety property a solution consists in giving a site P_i, that wants to use k_i resources, a consistent view of the number of resources used by the other sites. Let us call $used_i[j]$ the P_i's local view of the number of resources used by P_j. If $used_i[j]$ is greater than or equal to the number of resources actually used by P_j, then the test :

$$\sum_{1 \leq j \neq i \leq n} used_i[j] + k_i \leq M$$

is a consistent one ensuring safety. The management of these local variables has to be done accordingly.

One way to ensure liveness lies in putting a total order on the requests and serving them according to this order [5,11]. Such an order can easily be obtained by associating timestamps to requests (the timestamp attached to a request by a process has to be higher than any timestamp attached to a request received by this process ; timestamps can be generated using Lamport's rule [5]).

These two devices (over estimates of the number of resources used and total order on the requests) are combined to get the solution. Ricart-Agrawala's distributed mutual exclusion algorithm [12] is also based on these two principles. In this algorithm when a process P_i wants to enter the critical section it asks each other process the permission to enter ; it is only after having received the *(n-1)* permissions that a process can proceed (safety). Requests (asking the permissions) are timestamped and consequently totally ordered. This total order allows to ensure liveness : the sending of a permission by a requesting process is immediate or delayed according to the timestamps of the conflicting requests. As [9] we use this algorithm as a building block on which the solution to the *k*-out of-*M* problem is grafted. So the algorithm proposed belongs to the family of permission-based distributed algorithms [1,2,3,5,10,11,12,13].

3   The algorithm

Each site P_i is endowed with the following local context :

var boolean : $scdem_i$, ok_i, $prio_i$ **init** $false$;
   integer : h_i, $maxh_i$ **init** 0;
   $[1..n]$ **of integer** : $used_i$ **init** 0;
   set of $1..n$: $delayed_i$ **init** ϕ;
   integer: k_i;

The variable $scdem_i$ has the value $true$ when P_i is requesting resources ; ok_i is true when P_i has got the resources it was waiting for ; $maxh_i$ represents the highest logical clock value ever received by P_i ; it allows it to timestamp its requests with h_i [5,12]. When P_i wants to use resources, it does not know how many resources are actually used by the other sites P_j. Such a P_j can be using an arbitrary number of them comprised between O and M ; consequently before sending its timestamped request to each site P_j, the process P_i increments by M each variable $used_i[j]$ in order its value be greater than or equal to the actual value.

When P_i receives from some P_j a request message $req(h,j)$ ((h,j) is the timestamp of this request), it sends back a message $free(M)$ if it is not interested in the resources or if its request has not priority over P_j's one (i.e. it has a higher timestamp). In the contrary case (P_i's request has priority over P_j's one) P_i sends back P_j a message $free(M - k_i)$ (where k_i is the number of resources P_i is requesting or using) ; this message indicate to P_j it can use only $M - k_i$ resources from P_i's point of view ; moreover P_i memorises, by including j into the set $delayed_i$, it will have to send P_j a message $free(k_i)$ when it has finished to use these k_i resources. In the particular situation where P_i is such that $j \in delayed_i$ when it receives a request from P_j, it can send back $free(M)$ to P_j immediately : indeed in this case P_j knows the number of resources P_i is using (P_j learnt this number previously with the P_i's answer to its preceding request ; moreover the P_i's request had priority over P_j's one).

The behaviour of each P_i is defined by the 4 following statements. Each of these statements is presented as a procedure body triggered by some event ; they are atomic, except for the one including a $wait$ instruction. The order over the timestamps is defined as usual by

$$(h_i, i) < (h, j) \equiv (h_i < h \text{ or } (h_i = h \text{ and } i < j))$$

when requesting resources
begin $k_i :=$ *number of resources requested by* P_i;
      $scdem_i := true$;
      $ok_i := false$;
      $h_i := maxh_i + 1$;
      for $1 \leq j \neq i \leq n$ **do** $used_i[j] := used_i[j] + M$;
                         send $req(h_i, i)$ to P_j
                od;
      wait (ok_i);
end

when releasing the resources
begin $ok_i := false$;
      for $j \in delayed_i$ **do** send *free* (k_i) to P_j **od**;
      $delayed_i := \phi$;
end

when receiving $req(h, j)$ **from** P_j
begin $maxh_i := max(maxh_i, h)$;
      $prio_i := (scdem_i \text{ or } ok_i)$ and $(h_i, i) < (h, j)$;
      case not $prio_i$: send $free(M)$ to P_j
           $prio_i$: **if** $j \in delayed_i$ **then** send $free(M)$ to P_j (XX)
                else begin
                      if $k_i \neq M$ **then** send $free(M - k_i)$ to P_j **fi**;
                      $delayed_i := delayed_i \cup \{j\}$
                    end
              fi
      endcase
end

when receiving free (y) **from** P_j
begin $used_i[j] := used_i[j] - y$;
      if $scdem_i$ and $\sum_{x \neq i} used_i[x] + k_i \leq M$ **then** $scdem_i := false$;
                                      $ok_i := true$ **fi**
end

The number of messages per use of a set of resources lies between $2(n-1)$ and $3(n-1)$. The lower bound can be improved (cf. §5.1).

4 Proof

Proof of safety (respt. liveness) relies on the following propositions $P1$ and $P2$ (respt. $P4$).

4.1 Proposition $P1$

$$\forall i, j \; : \; used_i[j] \geq 0$$

The proof of this proposition is left to the reader.

4.2 Proposition $P2$

Let us consider the following situation. At a given time t the sites $i(1)$, ..., $i(g)$, ..., $i(m)$ have carried out requests and are either waiting or using resources. These requests are ordered by their timestamps in the following way :

$$(h_1, i(1)) < (h_2, i(2)) < \ldots < (h_g, i(g)) < \ldots < (h_m, i(m))$$

Moreover the site $i(y)$ is waiting for or using k_y resources ($i(m+1)$ to $i(n)$ are not requesting resources at time t).
If the condition allowing $i(g)$ to use the requested resources is true then the condition is also true or will eventually be true for every site $i(x)$ such that $1 \leq x < g$.
Proof
Let us examine the values the array $used_{i(g)}$ contain when $i(g)$ evaluates to true its condition and the values the array $used_{i(x)}$ contains or will eventually contain (the word "eventually" is used to take into account the arbitrary transit delays of the messages along channels). The values are determined by the answers (messages *free*) of the sites to the requests of respectively $i(g)$ and $i(x)$. The answer that some $i(y)$ has sent for $used_{i(g)}[i(y)]$, and has sent or will eventually send for $used_{i(x)}[i(y)]$, has involved (or will involve) the following values :

i) $1 \leq y \leq x - 1$:

$$used_{i(g)}[i(y)] = k_y$$
$$used_{i(x)}[i(y)] = k_y$$

ii) $x < y \leq n$:
    ii1) value for $i(x)$:
    the site $i(y)$ is now either requesting with a higher timestamp (if $x + 1 \leq y \leq m$) or not ($m + 1 \leq x \leq n$). In either case $i(y)$ might be requesting k_y' resources when

it received the request from $i(x)$, with a request timestamp lower than the $i(x)$ one. If it was the case we could have

$$used_{i(x)}[i(y)] = k'_y$$

but as the site $i(y)$ has released its k'_y resources at the time t, the variable will eventually contain :

$$used_{i(x)}[i(y)] = 0$$

We get also this value if $i(y)$ was not requesting when it receives the $i(x)$ request.

ii2) for $i(g)$ we have :

$$x \leq y \leq g - 1 : \quad used_{i(g)}[i(y)] = k_y$$

$g < y \leq n$: the same reasonning as previously can be applied.

So by summing the values in each of the two arrays we can conclude :

$$\textbf{if } (\sum_{y \neq g} used_{i(g)}[i(y)] + k_g)) \leq M$$

$$\textbf{then } (\sum_{y \neq x} used_{i(x)}[i(y)] + k_x)\text{is or will eventually be} \leq M$$

In other words if the condition is true for $i(g)$, it is also true or will eventually become true (it depends on messages speed) for any site that has priority over $i(g)$.

Remark

This proposition clearly illustrates how the algorithm works. Requests are virtually satisfied in their timestamp order. The actual order depends on the message delays. If $M=1$ actual and virtual orders are of course the same.

4.3 Safety $P3$

At most M resources can be used simultaneously (each resource being used by at most one process at a time).

Proof (by contradiction)

let us consider the situation depicted in proposition $P2$ and suppose :

- that $\sum_{y < x} k_y \leq M$ (the requests of the processes $i(1)$ to $i(x\text{-}1)$ are or will be granted)

- and that, although the site $i(h)$ ($x < h \leq g$) has evaluated its condition to true there are not enough resources to satisfy its request, i.e. : $\sum_{y \leq h} k_y > M$.

We have seen in *P2* first that when $i(h)$ evaluates to true its condition we have :

$$\sum_{y \neq h} used_{i(h)}[i(y)] + k_h \leq M$$

and second that the left part of this inequation cannot be less than $\sum_{y \leq h} k_y$ (as $i(1)$ to $i(x-1)$ have not released their resources). Hence the contradiction : $M > M$, proving safety.

4.4 Proposition $P4$

Let us consider the following situation. There are K not granted resources and the unsatisfied request owning the lowest timestamp has been issued by $i(x)$, asks for $k_x \leq K$ resources and remains unsatisfied. We proof this situation cannot last indefinitely. In other words resources are allocated each time it is possible according to the timestamps of requests.

Proof

Let us consider the situation depicted in proposition *P2* with $1 \leq x \leq g$ and with :

$$\sum_{y < x} k_y + K = M$$

The answers to the $i(x)$ request will eventually produce :

- $1 \leq y < x$: $used_{i(x)}[i(y)] = k_y$ after receiving the first *free* message from $i(y)$ $= 0$ after $i(y)$ released its resources.

- $x < y \leq n$: $used_{i(x)}[i(y)] = 0$.

So by summing we eventually obtain :

$$\sum_{y \neq x} used_{i(x)}[i(y)] + k_x \leq \sum_{y < x} k_y + k_x$$

as $k_x \leq K$ the condition for $i(x)$ will then be true.

4.5 Liveness $P5$

Each request will be satisfied within finite time.

Proof

Let us consider the unsatisfied request with the lowest timestamp. If there are enough resources not granted to satisfy it, proposition $P4$ applies. In the other case the requesting site will remain blocked until its condition becomes true. That request can be blocked only by requests endowed with a lower timestamp. When the sites that have issued these requests will release their resources, they will send *free* messages and as soon as enough *free* messages have been sent we are in the context of proposition $P4$. Consequently each request will be satisfied within a finite time.

5 Variants

5.1 Reducing the number of messages

It is possible to reduce the number of messages by taking into account the following fact. At the time P_i sends a request it knows already the number of resources used by some P_j if $used_i[j] \neq 0$; so it is no use to send P_j a request in that case (consequently the statement noted XX in the algorithm can be removed). But it is now necessary for P_i to send P_j a request when it is waiting for resources and it receives from P_j a message $free(y)$ such that $used_i[j]$ becomes 0 (in fact this value means either P_j dont use resources or P_i knows nothing about P_j). So an array $asked_i$ is used by each P_i to memorize the sites to which requests have been sent. (After P_i has sent its requests and is waiting, $used_i[j] = 0$ and $asked_i[j]$ to $true$ mean that P_j do not use resources from P_i's point of view ; $asked_i[j]$ to $false$ means P_i knows nothing about P_j and consequently has to ask P_j).

The modified algorithm is defined by the following behaviour for each P_i. The number of messages is now included between 0 and $3(n-1)$; however the waiting time of a site can now be greater than in the first version as request messages can be sent later.

```
when requesting resources
begin k_i := number of resources requested by P_i;
      h_i := maxh_i + 1;
      for 1 ≤ j ≠ i ≤ n do
          if used_i[j] = 0 then used_i[j] := M;
                                 asked_i[j] := true;
                                 send req(h_i, i) to P_j
                            else asked_i[j] := false
          fi         od;
      ok_i := ∑ used_i[j] + k_i ≤ M);
             j≠i
      scdem_i := not ok_i;
      wait (ok_i);
end

when releasing the resources
begin ok_i := false;
      for j ∈ delayed_i do send free(k_i) to P_j od;
      delayed_i := φ;
end

when receiving req(h, j) from P_j
begin maxh_i := max(maxh_i, h);
      prio_i := (scdem_i or ok_i) and ((h_i, i) < (h, j));
      case not prio_i : send free(M) to P_j
           prio_i :        begin
                           if k_i ≠ M then send free(M − k_i) to P_j fi;
                           delayed_i := delayed_i ∪ {j}
```

```
                        end
        endcase;
end

when receiving free(y) from Pⱼ
begin usedᵢ[j] := usedᵢ[j] − y;
        if scdemᵢ and usedᵢ[j] = 0 and not askedᵢ[j]
            then usedᵢ[j] := M;
                    send req(hᵢ, i) to Pⱼ;
                    askedᵢ[j] = true
        fi;
        if scdemᵢ and (∑ₓ≠ᵢ usedᵢ[x] + kᵢ ≤ M) then scdemᵢ := false;

                                        okᵢ := true    fi;
end
```

5.2 Adaptation to others topologies

A fully connected network has been implicitly assumed to carry *req* and *free* messages. The algorithm can be adapted to take into account a ring topology by using the principle described in §6.3. of [12], or a tree topology [8,14] or an arbitrary network [4].

6 A solution to the generalized AND-allocation

Now we consider there exist several types of resources : $R(1)$, ..., $R(p)$. Each type is represented by several identical resources : there is $M(\alpha)$ instances of the resource type $R(\alpha)$. A process P_i requests simultaneously all the resources it needs ; in the following demand for example :

$$demand((k_i(\alpha), R(\alpha)), (k_i(\beta), R(\beta)))\quad (Z)$$

the process P_i asks for $k_i(\alpha)$ resources of type $R(\alpha)$ and $k_i(\beta)$ resources of type $R(\beta)$. P_i remains blocked until it has obtained all the requested resources. This problem is a generalized AND-allocation one (several types of resources are requested and for a given type $R(\alpha)$ the request asks for $k_i(\alpha)$-out of-$M(\alpha)$ resources).

The preceding algorithm constitutes a basic building block to obtain a simple solution to this problem. Let us call $GR(\alpha)$ the set of sites which share the $M(\alpha)$ resources of type $R(\alpha)$; in such a set the sites have distinct identities. Giving a unique timestamp to each demand allow to solve all the conflicts in the same way whatever is (or are) the resource(s) concerned. So, for example, if P_i and P_j are in conflict to use resources of type $R(\alpha), R(\beta)$ and $R(\gamma)$, these three conflicts are solved in the same way : either in favour of P_i or P_j according to the two timestamps of their requests.

As an illustration, here is the program text relative to the demand by P_i described in line (Z) ; it concerns 2 types of resources. The text is obtained from the initial version (the other texts are obtained in the same way).

when requesting resources
begin

$k_i(\alpha) :=$ *number of resources of type* $R(\alpha)$ P_i *needs*;
$k_i(\beta) :=$ *number of resources of type* $R(\beta)$ P_i *needs*;
$h_i := max h_i + 1$;
$scdem_i(\alpha) := true$; $ok_i(\alpha) := false$;
$scdem_i(\beta) := true$; $ok_i(\beta) := false$;
for $x = \alpha, \beta$
  do %$used_i(x)$ *is the array relative to the resource type*
     $R(x)$; *its entries are the elements of* $GR(x)$%
     for $j \in GR(x), j \neq i$
       do $used_i(x)[j] := used_i(x)[j] + M(x)$;
          send $req(R(x), (h_i, i))$ **to** P_j
       od
  od;
wait $(ok_i(\alpha)$ **and** $ok_i(\beta))$;
end

Messages *req* and *free* take the resource type concerned as a parameter. Statements associated to the reception of these messages use the data structures associated to the type of resources defined by the corresponding parameter.

Remark

The drinking philosophers problem [3] is some kind of AND-allocation problem. Each philosopher (i.e. site or process) shares bottles with it neigbhours and can request any subset of these ones. However between two neigbhours philosophers sharing M bottles, neither philosopher can request k out of M of these bottles : his request must concern an a priori defined set of k bottles and not an arbitrary set of k of these M bottles (yet he may need distinct sets of bottles for different consecutive requests). A very interesting property of the Chandy-Misra's solution to the drinkers problem lies in using only bounded variables (there are no timestamps).

7 Conclusion

The proposed solutions to solve the basic and the generalized resources allocation problems are simple. They have been designed from a well-known building block, namely the Ricart-Agrawala's distributed mutual exclusion algorithm [12]. Other basic building blocks are possible : algorithms based on a travelling token [6,7,8], or algorithms using a more sophisticated permission-based protocols [11,13]. An interest on the proposed solution lies in its simplicity. The variant illustrated some tradeoff between response time and number of messages.

8 References

[1]   CARVALHO O.S.F., ROUCAIROL G. *Assertion decomposition and partial correctness of distributed algorithms.* In Distributed Computing, (Paker and Verjus Ed.), Academic Press, (1983), pp. 67-93.

[2]   CARVALHO O.S.F., ROUCAIROL G. *On the distribution of an assertion.* Proc. of the 2d ACM Sigact-Sigops Symposium on P.O.D.C., (August 1982), pp. 121-131.

[3]   CHANDY K.M., MISRA J. *The drinking philosophers problem.* ACM Transactions on Programming Languages and Systems, 6(4) :632-646, (1984).

[4]   HELARY J.M., PLOUZEAU N., RAYNAL M. *A distributed algorithm for mutual exclusion in an arbitrary network.* The Computer Journal, 31(4) : 289-295, (1988).

[5]   LAMPORT L. *Time, clocks and ordering of events in distributed systems.* communications of the ACM, 21(7) : 558-564, (1978).

[6]   LE LANN G. *Distributed systems : towards a formal approach.* IFIP congress, Toronto, (1977), pp. 155-160.

[7]   MARTIN A.J. *Distributed mutual exclusion on a ring of processes.* Science of Computer Programming, vol.5, (1985), pp. 265-276.

[8]   RAYMOND K. *A tree-based algorithm for distributed mutual exclusion.* ACM Transactions on Computer Systems, 7(1) : 61-77, (1989).

[9]   RAYMOND K. *A distributed algorithm for multiple entries to a critical section.* Inf. Processing Letters, vol.30, (1989), pp. 189-193.

[10]   RAYNAL M. *Algorithms for mutual exclusion.* MIT Press, (1986), 107 p.

[11]   RAYNAL M. *Distributed computations and networks : concepts, tools and algorithms.* MIT Press, (1988), 160 p.

[12]   RICART G., AGRAWALA A.K. *An optimal algorithm for mutual exclusion in computer networks.* Communication of the ACM, 24(1) : 9-17, (1981).

[13]   SANDERS B. *The information structure of distributed mutual exclusion algorithms.* ACM Transactions on Computer Systems, 5(3) : 284-299, (1987).

[14]   Van De SNEPSCHEUT J.L. *Fair mutual exclusion on a graph of processes.* Distributed Computing, 2 : 113-115, (1987).

Efficient Distributed Resource Scheduling for Adaptive Real-Time Operation Support[†]

Horst F. Wedde   Douglas C. Daniels   Dorota Huizinga

Computer Science Department
Wayne State University
Detroit, MI 48202

Abstract

In this paper we are concerned with real-time operating system services which provide for deadlock-free and starvation-free access to distributed resources that may be replicated or exist in different versions. We define and discuss novel distributed resource scheduling algorithms which provide the support for efficient real-time operations on replicated distributed files, realizing them in the manner of *distributed atomic real-time transactions*. After constructing a base line algorithm, called *Simultaneous Enqueuing*, we state formally its relevant properties: starvation-freeness and a minimal message overhead. We then enhance this algorithm by mechanisms which allow for promoting tasks ahead of resource competitors, e.g. because of an earlier deadline. This leads to the *Hurry-Up* version of Simultaneous Enqueuing. We performed a first series of simulation experiments under varying resource contention and with varying upper bounds for the task laxity, using *Partial Ordering resource scheduling* as a benchmark. The results are very favorable for the new algorithms which are implemented as part of the kernel services of the real-time version of the distributed operating system DRAGON SLAYER, designed to support its distributed and adaptive replicated file system MELODY.

0. Introduction

Background

Our research in the DRAGON SLAYER/ MELODY research project is concerned with distributed operating systems support for applications in military land vehicles of the 1990's. Such vehicles are to operate safely in an *unpredictable* and *hazardous environment*. Anticipating the hardware situation at that time we attempted to pay equal attention, and give equal relevance, to the following topics crucial in mission control computing:

Real-time responsiveness and predictability;
Reliability/ fault tolerance/dependability;

[†]This work was partially supported by IBM Endicott (Research Agreement No. 6073-86 and 9018-89), by the State of Michigan (IMR-89-146751), and by General Dynamics Land Systems (#DEY-605089).

Graceful degradation of services in case of node/ link failures;
Adaptability to internal or environmental changes;
Modularity;
Scalability;
Maintainability;
Real-time Transaction Processing.

Although *protection* and *security* are very important issues for military systems development they can be treated separately, in contrast to the listed topics as will be shown in the sequel. We therefore neglected them for the first development stages. We considered the other issues, and oriented our development accordingly, on three different levels (see fig.1): Hardware, operating system kernel services, file/ application system.

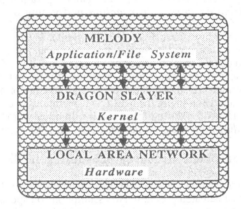

Figure 1: Design Levels for DRAGON SLAYER/MELODY

On each level we were led to specific design insights, requirements, and decisions.

Clearly there are design conflicts between different design topics, like optimization of real-time responsiveness and maximal reliability/ fault tolerance. As has been discussed in detail in [WeA88, WeA89 a - d] a feasible system design has to *integrate* and equally respect the requirements on **all** design levels listed in fig.1 . The result was the design and development of the distributed operating system DRAGON SLAYER and a novel adaptive distributed file system called MELODY. While the resource management strategy in DRAGON SLAYER allows for a very general form of *distributed object* management [WeKo89], in our real-time project we had focussed our efforts in the first place on reliable and predictable distributed file handling which constitutes the MELODY project. Specifically we had to observe the following:

In the application systems under study a major part of the processors are *dedicated* to perform specific tasks. *Thus in our model tasks would essentially not migrate, in contrast to the work in the SPRING project [HST89] but would have to be scheduled to run at the node where they arrive.* Instead files may be **replicated** or **relocated** to a node where they are frequently needed. By eliminating communication times for remote file access requests there might then be a better chance to meet all task deadlines.

For the MELODY file system we established the following guidelines:

F 1 In order to achieve *reliability* and *availability of information* multiple and mutually consistent copies of files should be maintained. This should be further enhanced by requesting that a minimum number of copies is available at any time, for information of crucial relevance (highest priority).

F 2 The *real-time responsiveness* of the system should be optimized by placing copies of a file at nodes at which they are most frequently used. If file information does not age to soon it should be determined by the system at what time a copy would have to be to be "refreshed". This would help to reduce the communication overhead, thus further enhancing the real-time performance of the system.

Distributed Transactions and MELODY

Operating system support for real-time transactions is provided through the services of the MELODY file system [WeA90, WeA89 a-c]. An update operation to a file in MELODY is, however, already a *distributed atomic transaction* performing on a number of file copies: Update requests from different sites require that the access to all affected copies be *logically simultaneous,* thus the atomicity. *Already on the file system level, we so find transaction-like operations which access data objects (file copies) at various remote sites.* Their management must not rely on any centralized control mechanism or on global information, due the required robustness for the highly vulnerable military application systems. While extensive simulation studies [WeA90,WeA89c] have demonstrated both the superior real-time performance and adaptivity of the MELODY system the actual scheduling of the MELODY operations under real-time constraints was just assumed to be done efficiently, during those studies. In other words: *the existence of efficient real-time resource scheduling algorithms on the DRAGON SLAYER kernel level was assumed.*

Distributed Real-Time Resource Scheduling in DRAGON SLAYER

Due to the unpredictable application environment distributed resource scheduling in the DRAGON SLAYER project was a sophisticated problem. No assumptions on speed, periodicity, priorities of jobs were to be made. In a first step a general resource scheduling algorithm was developed and implemented that **guaranteed** service to every request for a multiplicity of distributed resources in a *flexible* way [WeKo89]. *In this paper we report on a novel generation of such distributed resource scheduling algorithms which are particularly targeted to optimizing a timely treatment of distributed transaction requests and to minimizing, if not avoiding, deadline failures.* We approached this in two subsequent steps:

✳ We developed a distributed scheduling algorithm which *in its basic mode guarantees service requests for a number of distributed resources, with a minimal number of messages required.* This property is **indispensable** in the context of the real-time scheduling requirements.

✳ For appropriately dealing further with specific real-time features like static priorities or a classification into critical and *essentially* critical tasks, specific advanced mechanisms were added to the basic algorithm. These particularly allow to take care of the newly imposed constraints, under a minimal relaxation of the scheduling guarantee for tasks of lesser criticalness.

Previous and Related Work

Over the years, many approaches to distributed resource scheduling have been actively researched and reported on. One of the more familiar is based upon the **atomic broadcasts** [BJ87], [Cr90]. Broadcast atomicity guarantees that if one site receives a message then the same message is received at all sites which have been *targeted* to receive that message, i.e. atomic multicast. Furthermore, though there may be no way to determine which of two broadcasts was *transmitted* first, the order in which they are received is the same at all sites.

There are different mechanisms for achieving broadcast atomicity. One depends upon a single and therefore central server that orders the broadcasts and insures their reception in the same order at all sites, generally employing message acknowledgements. Another depends on synchronization mechanisms, (clocks) which are hardware dependent (dependent on the variance in message transmission times). In the baseline algorithm, the events are ordered by slot number. However, the baseline algorithm accomplishes this without resorting to a central service which would increase system vulnerability to total failure and which would set an upper bound on the level of system concurrency (parallelism). It also allows for a total global ordering of distributed events independent of the hardware, in a very loosely coupled environment in which all interaction between sites is limited to message passing without assumptions on the relative speeds at which messages are exchanged. Methods of synchronization which rely on accurate clocks which must periodically synchronize, have their own limitations and overheads. Depending on messaging granularity and the worst case wait for a single message pass, the quantity of synchronization messages generated might be very large and this messaging is necessary even when there is no scheduling activity. Moreover, when long haul networks are combined with local networks or when there are multiple busses with different characteristics, the message turnaround time can be vary greatly and this would all the more complicate a clock synchronization mechanism. With the baseline algorithm, the total ordering of distributed events is *negotiated* rather than time stamped, and these negotiations are conducted in a completely distributed fashion which does not rely on a central service.

In the context of Distributed Real-Time Databases, real-time transactions have rapidly become a focus of investigation through the past three years. An efficient algorithm for better and timely availability of data in partitioned networks is presented in [Lin88]. It is based on object replicas and modified consistency protocols with relaxed consistency requirements. Real-time scheduling algorithms are used in [SRL88a,b] for real-time concurrency control. Their application is restricted, however, to transactions accessing data at their originating site only. Another specialized study of a centralized form of real-time concurrency control can be found in [Ma88]. In addition, a few approaches have been published for measuring the performance of distributed real-time transactions [ChM89, HSTR89], in form of simulation studies.

There has long been known a distributed scheduling algorithm, both deadlock-free and starvation-free, which is based on a total ordering of a systems global resources [Hav68]. It is frequently referred to in real-time papers on task scheduling when relating to resource scheduling problems [SRL88a]. Basically, this protocol of scheduling by a fixed ordering of the resources, sometimes addressed as **Partial Ordering** algorithm, works as follows. A process wishing to access a set of resources will *lock* those resources according to the global ordering of the system resources. This simple protocol will guarantee deadlock and starvation freeness providing all processes agree on the partial ordering of the their needed resources. As more and more research is devoted to distributed systems and particularly to real-time distributed systems, the problems associated with distributed resource scheduling, in terms of locking (mutual exclusion) for reasons of consistency (concurrency control mechanisms) have often been *assumed* to be *somehow* handled, often by the partial ordering protocol [SRL88b, SRL89]. As this simple, and in some ways minimal, protocol is well known and often referenced, we have decided that it will serve well as a benchmark algorithm for comparison purposes. This protocol will be described in greater detail in the section in which the experimental framework and results are given.

Organization of the Paper

In section 1 we describe our novel resource scheduling algorithms as a 2-step development: First we introduce a base line algorithm, called *Simultaneous Enqueuing*. In the second step we enhance this algorithm by additional features (so-called *Hurry-up* features) which provide for higher flexibility and better real-time performance. In section 2 we report on a series of comparative simulation experiments in order to evaluate our algorithms. In a concluding section we summarize our findings and mention ongoing and future work.

1. The Construction of the Distributed Real-Time Resource Scheduling Algorithms

Simultaneous Enqueuing Method

Basic Mode of Operation

For the sake of simplicity of the following algorithm description we assume that no *loss of messages or site crashes occur. Messages are, as usual, assumed to have bounded delay.* The implementation in our labs, however, contains the necessary provisions for dealing with those problems. This is subject of a forthcoming paper.

In its basic, starvation-free mode of operation, Simultaneous Enqueuing scheduling amounts to a process requesting of each of its required resources that it be given a ticket. This ticket taking may be viewed as analogous to the situation of patrons being served at a retail counter in the order in which they obtain a ticket from a paper ticket dispenser, (also known as the **Baker's Algorithm**). In the case where a transaction will require that the process be served at more than one resource site, then the highest numbered, or worst case, ticket is selected and the process requests that the lower numbered tickets that it currently has obtained at other resources be exchanged for this higher numbered ticket. After these requests have been satisfied, the process holds identically numbered tickets for each resource. It is possible for a process to request that a ticket be exchanged for a number already held by another process. In this case, more than one process may be enqueued in the same *slot*, ordered by priority or some global tie breaking mechanism.. A stepwise description of the basic idea is as follows:

1. The process multicasts to all needed resources its request for a slot. It then waits for all resources to respond with the number of the slot into which the process was placed and a "go" or a "no-go".

2. If all resources have been granted a "go", then the process has won all resources and may GOTO step 5.

3. Not having received the needed "go" message from all required resources, the process now determines which is the largest slot number into which it was placed at any required resource. (It is always enqueued at the rear of a resource's list in the slot one greater than the old rear of the queue, e.g. in slot 1 in an empty list). Having determined this **Max Slot**, the process multicasts, its request that it be **moved** to its max slot at all needed resources at which it is enqueued in a *lower* slot.

4. Now, having had itself placed in the same slot all resources, the process waits for a "go" message from all required resources.

5. The process enters its critical section.

Those processes which were not immediately allowed to enter their critical sections must execute step 3 of the above simplified algorithm. Such processes, upon completing step 3 are said to be **scheduled.** They occupy the same slot in the queues at all required resources and will wait until they are have been informed that they are at the top (winning position) of all queues. Once a process has been scheduled, the rules of the game will insure that no other, newly arriving process, will be enqueued ahead of it as resources always place newly arriving requests at the end of their queues and also as a **move** request may amount to a *demotion* in the queues, but never to a *promotion* in the queues.

In this simply stated algorithm, which allows for a **multicast** capability, the messaging involved in the scheduling of a critical section involving n resources is one multicast and n responses for the first round (step 1) and one multicast and n responses for the second round, if the second round is needed (steps 3 and 4). Thus, the best case messaging for the scheduling of a critical section involving n resources is N + 1 messages and the worst case messaging is 2(N + 1) messages. The best case messaging is very good and occurs whenever there is no contention for resources. The worst case is also good in that it is still relatively low, constant and thus well bounded and only occurs when there is contention for resources. Moreover, as processes which require only one resource will always be in the same slot everywhere (because they occupy a slot in only one queue), the scheduler may skip any communication regarding actual slot numbers when scheduling processes requiring a single resource. A process requiring a single resource merely requests access to that resource and waits until it receives a "go" from that resource. Thus, for the single resource case, the messaging required to schedule a critical section is constant, always requiring N + 1 or exactly 2 messages.

This simple scheduler, or **Baseline Scheduler**, allows a process with complex resource requirements to wait for those resources *at the same time* or in all the queues at the same time. That is, access to the queues is not serialized, but rather, the process waits in all queues simultaneously. This **simultaneous enqueuing** method of scheduling allows for a **distributed first-come-first-serve** scheduling protocol which has some good behavioral characteristics in terms of minimizing the worst case scheduling wait for processes with complex resource requirements while at the same time remaining minimal, in terms of messaging overheads, when contention for resources is slight and when tasks have simple resource requirements.

Scheduling of waiting and privileged processes

Inevitably, if scheduling activity is ongoing at all times at some point in the network, then the slot numbers will grow in size, not being able to reset to small numbers, until some largest integer, or max-int is assigned to a slot. At this point, the local scheduler may be said to have *run out of numbers*. This leads to a sophisticated reset problem. Because of the finiteness of the counters, but also for avoiding *confusion* or even *starvation*, in the absence of assumptions on the (relative) speed of processes, one cannot start fresh with slot number 1 after running out of numbers at a particular site.

In order to deal with the eventual need to *reset* the local schedulers to small slot numbers, we introduce two new categories of processes. These are *waiting* and *privileged* processes. Waiting processes are those who have requested a slot from a resource that has run out of numbers. Such a process informs all of its required resources that it has become a waiting process. Such resources, those which have run out of numbers and those who have been informed that they have a reset waiting client, become **resetting resources.** Such a resource will enqueue all newly arriving processes requesting *regular* slots in a reset waiting list and inform such processes that they have become reset waiting processes. Thus, all newly arriving requests will be placed in the reset waiting process list to wait until **the local reset event** takes place. This local reset event takes place when the local *backlog of regularly scheduled processes* has been serviced, i.e. when all regularly scheduled processes have entered their critical sections. Eventually, all regularly scheduled processes will have entered their critical sections and the resetting resource will reset. A resource which has just reset, will inform its waiting clients of the slot that they occupy in the waiting list. Such processes become privileged processes at that resource. Eventually, waiting processes become privileged processes at all required resources. At this time, the max slot is determined (maximum of the waiting list slot number in which which the process had been enqueued) and the process requests of all required resources that it be placed within this slot in the regular slot queues at all required resources. At such a time, the process will occupy the same slot at all required resources and is thus scheduled as is in step 3 of the algorithm outlined above. A resource will always grant this slot request to a privileged client process even if this results in a process being placed at the front of the regular slot queue. In such a case, another process may have already been given a "go". Such a process is **called back.** A called back process will *return the "go"* if it has not already entered its critical section. Otherwise, a called back process would complete its critical section.

The formal correctness as far as starvation freeness and particularly those aspects which are concerned with the need to reset the local schedulers, is established through the following properties:

Property 1: The set of processes which *were* waiting for some resource R to reset cannot grow so long as R does not reset again.

Property 2: Once a process P has been enqueued in some slot list at a resource R, then so long as P does not request that it be removed from the list, then R will not reset until P has entered its critical section (by the rules of the game, resource R will clear its backlog of regularly scheduled processes).

Property 3: Only a finite number of privileged processes can be placed in the slot list, at some resource, ahead of some process P (from Property 1, the set of waiting processes will not grow until resource R resets and only waiting processes can become privileged processes).

Property 4: Once a process P has been successfully placed in the slot list of all its required resources, it will eventually enter its critical section (from Property 3).

Property 5: The total worst case *reset* wait for a process is finite.

Corollary: Processes will remove themselves from slot lists, do to reset waiting, a finite number of times.

Theorem 1: The algorithm is starvation free for all processes.

The proofs are omitted here, due to space limitations.

The *demotion* of a process at the very front of a resource's slot list by some privileged process is a special situation deserving some consideration. Should such a process be demoted by a privileged process requesting a lower numbered slot, or a privileged and higher *priority* process requesting the same slot, then it becomes possible for a process to become demoted although it had been informed by a resource manager that it may enter its critical section. Such a demoted process, one removed from the *winning* front position, will be *called back* . This calling back, which is a request to defer entry into a critical section, can be safely ignored by a process which has been given permission to enter its critical section at all of its other needed resources. Such a process, a winner, may ignore the call back and proceed with its critical section. Either way, whether it follows the called back process, or is allowed to go ahead of it, the privileged process will be enqueued at its requested slot at the front of the list. Of course, it too may be demoted by yet another privileged process being enqueued in front of it.

There is no danger of deadlock because of called back processes. This is because, either a process is prepared to *give back* all received "go" messages, or it has all needed "go" messages and may proceed with its critical section. Thus, such a process will either unblock wherever such a request is made, or it will proceed to its critical section and upon exit of critical section it will unblock everywhere.

Admittedly, it would have been simpler, if some easy, elegant, modular mechanism allowing for the resetting of the slot numbers could be found. We will give evidence that this is impossible. As it is, the message overhead it generates amount to one extra level of messaging plus some possible call backs and can be minimized if the maximum slot number available to the local schedulers is set large enough. The number of processes that must wait for the reset event at some resource could be made a very small fraction of all those scheduled at that resource. Moreover, there are other variations on this baseline scheduler which do not require any resetting. Finally, as the reset waiting processes are enqueued in the reset waiting list, first-come-first-serve, this FCFS protocol is preserved through the reset mechanism with there being at most one later arriving process that may be promoted ahead of a waiting process in any local slot queue. This occurs when a process which had arrived later than the privileged process cannot be called back because it has already entered its critical section.

Advanced Real-Time Resource Scheduling Features

The scheduler, as it has been so far offered, is starvation-free. As there is always a trade-off between scheduling in a starvation-free manner and scheduling according to processes priority, the scheduler may at times decide to select, from a subset of client processes, processes which may be allowed to proceed ahead of others in the slot lists. These promoted processes would be allowed to play the *Hurry-up* version of the scheduling game. More technically, we constructed this version of the Simultaneous Enqueuing Method in the following way:

When a resource becomes free, it looks to its complete list of clients to determine which task is most critical in terms of failure to meet its deadline. If this task's remaining *laxity* is below a certain level (*deadline_threshold*) then, provided that the task is *waiting for this resource*, it is scheduled to play the hurry-up game. If this task is not in the list of client tasks that are waiting for the resource then the resource manager will do nothing. If the most critical task in a resource client set is not in danger of failing to meet its deadline, i.e., its *Laxity* value is above the threshold, then the resource manager will select, randomly or according to other criteria, tasks from its waiting list as candidates for the hurry-up game. If a waiting list is empty then it waits. The selection criterion used in the simulations was **Earliest Deadline First.** (This simplification has been chosen for convenience only. The scheduling policy could be different and arbitrary at each node.)

After a winner has been found at a particular resource all losers of the Hurry-up game at that resource will return the slots that they currently occupy at other resources, and they will be enqueued in the waiting list of the resource at which they lost. The slot lists at resources are empty when the resource is busy. After the resource is freed, tasks will be scheduled to play the Hurry-up game. In other words, the Hurry-up mode of scheduling enforces that a set of promoted tasks will have a better chance to be scheduled as long as no client process is in danger of failing to meet its deadline. At that point, Hurry-up scheduling at that resource is suspended until the endangered process has been handled. Also, useless messaging is held to a minimum as tasks in the resource waiting list are kept from playing the game.

The Hurry-up scheduler tries to maximize its resource's utilization. As it becomes free, it attempts to schedule one of the tasks waiting for it. This selected task or tasks is given a slot in the resource's emptied slot list and started in the Simultaneous Enqueuing scheduling game. Should a client become a winner, then the resource will be utilized. Should the selected tasks be losers, the Hurry-up scheduler may select another task from its wait list for playing the game. Should all waiting tasks be eventually selected to play, and should they all lose, then the list of waiting clients will be exhausted, the resource is idled: its client tasks are waiting at other, busy resources.

Summarizing, the Hurry-up scheduler will attempt to promote processes which are not at the front of the regular scheduling queue. For instance suppose that a resource r has two client processes, p and q and that process p cannot execute because it is waiting for some other resources to become free. In this case, resource R might allow process q to play the Hurry-up game. Process q will either win the Hurry-up game, or at least one of its required resources will be either busy or made busy. Resource R may continue through its list of processes until a process which has one the game can be found or all of R's clients have become losers and are waiting at other, busy resources. How many processes to choose to play the Hurry-up game and in what order are local decisions made by resource R alone.

The following simplified pseudocode example should help clarify the Hurry-up scheduler's behavior. All three schedulers that we are comparing are purely message driven. Therefore, they are implemented as message handlers.

```
do forever {

                Receive_Message;

    if ( Message =='initial' ) {
      Enqueue(Task_Id , Client_List);

    /* The above line is omitted in hurry call. */

      if ( Resource_Busy or Least_Client_Laxity<Threshold ) {
            Enqueue(Task_Id,Wait_List);
            Send_Task('wait');
      }
      else
      {
            Enqueue(Task_Id,Hurry_List);
            if ( Largest_Slot >= Slot_Requested )
                  Largest_Slot <-- Largest_Slot+1;
            if ( Front_List(Task_Id) )
                  Send_Task(slot,'go');
            else
                  Send_Task(Largest_Slot,'no_go');
      }
    }

                /* Tasks that get a go are winners. */

    if ( Message == 'hurry' ) {

      /* The Code is the same as for 'initial' message except      */
```

```
        /* client is not placed in the client_list and a client      */
        /* with a deadline below threshold would not wait.            */

  }

  if ( Message == 'loser' ) {
    Dequeue(Task_Id , Hurry_List);
    if ( Empty(Hurry_List) and Empty(Wait_List) )
        Resource_Idled;
      else if ( not Empty(Wait_List) ) {
          Task_Id <-- Select_To_Play(Wait_List);
          Enqueue(Task_Id,Hurry_List);
          Largest_Slot <-- 1;
          Send_Task(Largest_slot,'go');
          }
          else if ( New_Front(Hurry_List) )
                  Send_Task(Front(Hurry_List),"go");

  /* When the loser was at the front of the Hurry_List          */
  /* the task in the slot behind is promoted to a winner.       */


  }

  if ( Message = 'release' ) {
    Dequeue(Task_Id , Client_List);
    if ( Least_Client_Laxity and not Empty(Wait_List) ) {
          Task_Id <-- Select_To_Play(Wait_List);
          Enqueue(Task_Id , Hurry_List);
          Largest_Slot <-- 1;
          Send_Task(1,'go');
      }
    }
  }

}
```

Figure 2: Pueudo-Code for Hurry-Up scheduling mode

Provided that only a finite number of such promotions are granted before the processes at the front of the list is allowed to proceed, the algorithm remains starvation-free.

We mention without proof that this enhanced algorithm is still compatible with scheduling using multiple priority queues. (More details, also about the Hurry-up algorithm, are to be found in a forthcoming paper.) Another common assumption about scheduling in the truly distributed environment is that critical sections are not preemptible. The use of multiple priority queues coupled with non-preemption of critical sections allows for scheduling with well bounded priority inversion. All that is required of a protocol is that, should a higher priority task request a resource locked by a lower priority task then the lower priority task would be *called back*. Recall that a task which has been called back is obliged to return the lock on a resource (release the resource) provided it has not yet been granted locks at *all* of its required resources (i.e. it is already in its second locking phase). Should a high priority task requiring n resources find them all locked by lower priority tasks, then the worst case wait will occur when none of the lower priority tasks are obliged to release their locks. In this case, the worst-case wait would be the longest critical section time among the n low priority processes, assuming full distribution of the tasks. Thus, priority inversion may be well bounded by the length of single critical section (see [SG89]).

2. Simulation and Performance Comparison

As our main interest is to investigate the real-time performance of the resource scheduling aspect of distributed task scheduling only, our primary concern is about the length of time from the point at which a process requests a set of resources, to the time at which the process is allowed to access those resources. It is this period of time, *the time that tasks are in competition for resources*, which mostly characterizes the performance of a given resource scheduling policy. In order to unambiguously determine the impact of resource scheduling on the deadline behavior of the tasks, we *neglect any further local task deadline scheduling. We assume instead in our simulation that after a task obtained all resources required for accessing the critical section, there is no other task preventing the given task from starting execution.* Consequently once a task has been granted access to its required resources it will immediately begin its critical section as though it runs alone on its node unless it has been determined that it can no longer meet its deadline. *What tasks do before they have requested mutually exclusive access to a set of resources and what tasks do after they have released such resources is likewise neglected.*

The model for our simulation testbed is based on further simplifying assumptions. *Each resource is unique, there is no replication of resources. Each resource requested by a process is remote. Each task will request multiple resources, and each requested resource will reside on a different remote node. There is only one critical section per task cycle.* These simplifying assumptions are aimed at the elimination of interaction which could mask the actual, underlying performance characteristics of the various **resource scheduling** policies we are comparing. The assumption the remoteness of resources is motivated by our research in application systems like military vehicles in which information that is generated or processed in one subsystem is used at other sites and subsystems on a frequent basis.

In our model, a task *starts* when it enters the resource competition phase. If at any point during this scheduling phase, it is determined that a task can no longer meet its deadline, the task is terminated. If a task successfully gains access (locks) to all required resources without being aborted then it has been *successfully scheduled*. Therefore, a task has a fixed amount of time *(laxity)* from the moment it requests resources in which to access those resources. If the task fails to gain access to all its required resources before its given laxity has elapsed, the task is said to have *failed to meet its deadline*.

The resources that a task is accessing in its critical section remain unavailable to other tasks for the duration of it's critical section *(critical_section_time)*. After the critical section is complete, the task releases the resources. It will be restarted, to enter another competition phase after a fixed amount of time *(next_start_time)*. **In this manner each task will attempt to repeatedly (but not necessarily *periodically*) access its *(only)* critical section within its process life cycle.**

Our model also assumes that *messages arrive safely and in the order in which they were sent.* In order to unambiguously determine the impact of resource scheduling on the deadline behavior of the tasks, we neglect any further local task deadline scheduling. The message system simulates varying message delays *(message-delay)*, however, thus adding to the realism of the model. Finally, our model assumes that all scheduling policies are amenable to scheduling with multiple priority queues.

In our first round of investigation, we wanted to evaluate our algorithms by comparing them to a well-known resource scheduling algorithm as a *benchmark*. This algorithm is based on a partial ordering of the resources [Hav68]. It allows tasks with overlapping distributed resource requirements to be scheduled in a deadlock free manner. Basically, a task wishing to access a resource is enqueued within a list at that resource. Upon arrival at the front of this queue, the resource is locked by the task, as a prerequisite to enter its critical section. Should there be a critical section within the critical section, *a critical section involving multiple resources*, then these resources are to be accessed in a particular order, namely, according to their partial ordering as reflected in some total ordering of the system resources. The situation in which tasks have critical sections where overlapping sets of shared resources are to be accessed, typically mutually exclusively, is common in transaction processing environments and particularly troublesome in distributed environments. As scheduling by a partial ordering is provenly both deadlock and starvation free in a fully distributed environment, and, as it is often referred to in the literature when the problem of distributed scheduling of complex critical sections arises [SRL88b, SRL89], we felt that it would serve as good benchmark for purposes of performance comparisons.- The other algorithms mentioned in the introduction [BJ87, Cr90] do not really compare to ours since they are based on *atomic broadcast* to be realized through central servers or clock synchronization. *Either measure is unrealistic, however, in our application context (see introduction).*

The second scheduling algorithm in our comparative simulation is the **Simultaneous Enqueuing** method proposed in this paper. The third algorithm is the **Hurry-up mode** of the Simultaneous Enqueuing method. We will report the results of *four sets of simulation runs*. In all four sets the three algorithms

Simultaneous Enqueuing
Hurry-Up Simultaneous Enqueuing
Partial Ordering Scheduling

were compared. The first and second series of simulation involved only **periodic** tasks and the third and fourth series of simulation involved only **aperiodic** tasks.

All tasks require between 2 and 5 resources for their critical section. These required resources were randomly selected from the set of system resources. For example, given that there are 20 system resources, then as the tasks are initially generated at the beginning of a run, a set of 2 to 5 unique numbers will be generated for each task, on the interval 1 to 20, to represent the tasks resource requirements. Other run parameters were randomly generated on the following intervals.

Laxity	40 to 80 units of time
Critical_Section_Time	3 to 10 units of time
Message_Delay	.1 to .2 units of time
Deadline_Threshold	15 units of time
Next_Start_Time	20 to 40 units of time

These characteristics were randomly generated for multiple populations of 15 tasks. For a single experiment, each of the three scheduling policies was given its chance to schedule 20 such populations for a period of 400 units of time. The total number of system resources was allowed to vary between each such set of runs. As the quantity of resources available in the system was increased, the contention between tasks for resources was decreased. We were most interested in finding that region where the various modes demonstrated their greatest comparative differences. Fig. 3 depicts total deadline failures as plotted against the number of resources.

In terms of the number of tasks that have not met their deadlines, the partial ordering mode was everywhere worse than both the regular and the hurry-up simultaneous enqueuing modes. This is to be expected as the worst case wait for a task using the partial ordering scheme is the **sum of the worst case waits** for each required resource whereas the worst case wait for simple simultaneous enqueuing is the **maximum of the worst case waits** for the required resources. These facts follow directly from the two protocols. Conceptually Simultaneous Enqueuing would seem superior in the matter of its waiting boundedness, and the deadline failure curve indicates this.

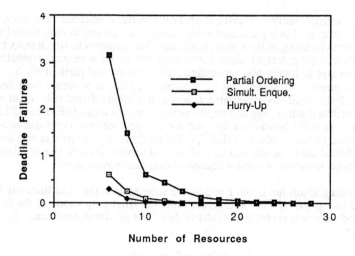

Number of Resources

Figure 3: Simulation 1

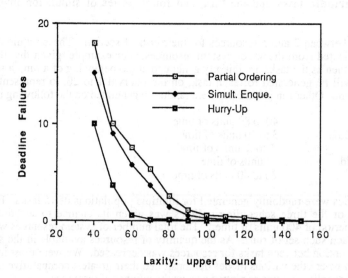

Laxity: upper bound

Figure 4: Simulation 2

For the **second series of simulation**, the *task laxity* ranges were allowed to vary while other parameters were held constant. The lower bound laxity was 40 units of time while the upper bound was allowed to vary. Again, deadline failures were expected to decline as the upper bound laxity was increased. The curves in fig.4 depict the increasing upper bound of laxity as plotted against deadline failures. In the first simulation, the scheduling environment was made more hospitable as the number of resources was increased and the contention over resources decreased. Similarly, during each successive experiment in the second series of simulation the tasks were generated with larger average laxities. As expected, as the tasks get more time during which they could be scheduled the number of deadline failures per run decreases. The Hurry-Up scheduler performed markedly better than the other two. The partial ordering scheduler was everywhere worse than both of the other modes. Again, the worst case wait of the partial ordering mode, previously mentioned to be the sum of the worst case waits at each queue, is causing it to fail to schedule all tasks within their deadlines long after the other two modes have begun to successfully do so.

Two other series of simulation were conducted in which only **aperiodic** tasks were scheduled. We were interested in determining the effects of both periodicity and the lack of it upon the behavior of the three different schedulers.

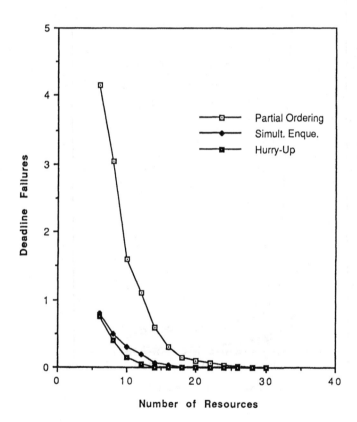

Figure 5: Simulation 3

In order to allow for aperiodicity, our basic model is altered only in that a task's Next_Start_Time is randomly generated on a fixed interval at the time the task either exits its critical section or is aborted because of expired laxity. The parameters for these runs are identical to those used in simulations 1 and 2. In Figure 5, deadline failures are plotted against the number of resources. The run parameters for simulation 3 are identical to those of simulation 1, the only difference between the simulations being task periodicity. Again, as the number of system resources is increased, the contention for them decreases and all three scheduling modes improve in terms of the average number of deadlines missed per run. The hurry-up scheduler does the best, scheduling all tasks in all runs with 14 resources. The regular, simultaneous enqueuing as able to schedule all tasks within their deadlines with 18 system resources and the partial ordering scheme requires 28 resources.

The run parameters for simulation 4 are identical to those for simulation 2, the only difference being that in simulation 2, all tasks are periodic and in simulation 4 they are aperiodic.

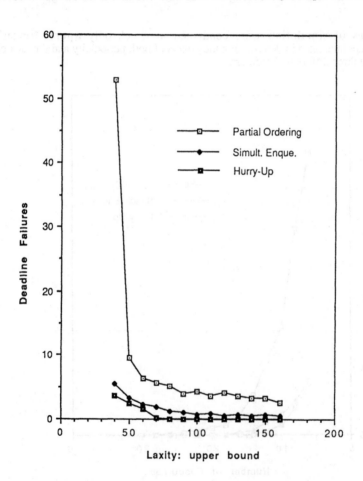

Figure 6: Simulation 4

In Figure 6, deadline failures are plotted against task laxity. The hurry-up scheduler does by far the best as the upper bound of task laxity is increased. Neither of the other modes was able to schedule without missing any deadlines though the simultaneous enqueuing method was markably superior to partial ordering.

Conclusion and Future Work

We defined and discussed distributed real-time resource scheduling algorithms for efficient support of distributed replicated file operations, thus realizing distributed atomic transaction management on the file system level. The algorithms consist of a base version *(Simultaneous Enqueuing)* and an enhanced version *(Hurry-Up)* which allows for including a variety of real-time scheduling policies. The algorithms are starvation-free, the base version has a provenly minimal message overhead.

The MELODY file system has been designed to ideally providing **local access** to needed file resources, achieved through file migration, replication, and change of of concurrency status [WeA90]. Its mechanisms are to be *adaptive* because typically aperiodic task patterns do not allow for any stable resource distribution scheme. Given this there seems to be no basis for a realistic analytic algorithm evaluation. Instead we did some steps towards a comprehensive distributed experimentation, with the focus on the deadline failure behavior of the studied algorithms. In this paper we have reported on a comparative evaluation through *simulation*. The message overhead as it influences the deadline behavior, was systematically investigated. This number was found reasonably low, given higher model sophistication compared to the base version, in simulation experiments designed for comparing the real-time performance of the Simultaneous Enqueuing and its Hurry-Up version with Partial Ordering resource scheduling as a benchmark. While these results show a very clear advantage for both of our algorithms these have the additional potential of including deadline-sensitive adaptivity measures. In this respect we successfully used the decreasing task laxity as a parameter for dynamically reconfiguring the Hurry-Up Simultaneous Enqueuing algorithm working under Earliest Deadline First.

Further simulation studies are under way in which our *resource scheduling* at each node is to be combined with the function of Local Task Schedulers, thus allowing for treating these two scheduling aspects *in an integrated way*.

The Hurry-Up Simultaneous Enqueuing algorithm is a kernel service in the real-time version of our distributed operating system DRAGON SLAYER, for supporting the functions of the adaptive distributed file system MELODY. At this time we are preparing distributed experiments and benchmark tests on target equipment for operating in hazardous environments (military vehicles) that are to more realistically explore the potential of the novel DRAGON SLAYER/ MELODY services.

References

[BJ87]   K.P. BIRMAN, T.A. JOSEPH, Reliable Communication in the Presence of Failures; *ACM Trans. on Computer Syst.* Vol. 5, No. 1, February 1987

[ChM89]   W.W. CHU, M. MERZBACHER, R. CHRISTENSON, Evaluating Data Error for a
           Concurrency Control Algorithm in Real-Time Distributed Database Systems;
           unpublished material, UCLA 1989

[Cr90]   F. CRISTIAN, Synchronous Atomic Broadcast for Redundant Broadcast Channels;
           Real-Time Systems, Vol. 2, No. 3, September 1990

[Hav68]   J. W. HAVENDER, "Avoiding Deadlock in Multitasking Systems," *IBM Systems
           Journal,* Vol.7, No.2, (1968) p. 74-84.

[HSTR89]   J. HUANG, J.A. STANKOVIC, D. TOWSLEY, K. RAMAMRITHAM,
           Experimental Evaluation of Real-Time Transaction Processing; Proc. of the 10th IEEE
           Real-Time Systems Symposium, Santa Monica, December 1989

[Lin88]   K.-J. LIN, M.-J. LIN, Enhancing Availability in Distributed Real-Time Databases;
           SIGMOD RECORD, Vol. 17 No. 1(1988)

[Ma88]   K. MARZULLO, Concurrency Control for Transactions with Priorities, Cornell
           University, unpublished material, 1988

[SG89]   L. SHA, J. GOODENOUGH, Real-Time Scheduling Theory and Ada; Proc. of the
           1989 Workshop on "Operating Systems for Mission Critical Computing" University
           of Maryland, College Park, Sept 1989

[SRL88a]   L. SHA, R. RAJKUMAR, J.P. LEHOCZKI, A Priority-Driven Approach to Real-
           Time Concurrency Control; Technical Report, Carnegie Mellon 1988

[SRL88b]   L. SHA, R. RAJKUMAR, J.P. LEHOCZKY, Real-Time Synchronization Protocols
           for Multiprocessors; Proc. IEEE Real-Time Systems Symposium, Huntsville,
           December 1988.

[SRL89]   L. SHA, R. RAJKUMAR, J.P. LEHOCZKI, An Experimental Investigation of
           Synchronization Protocols; Proc. IEEE Workshop on Real-Time Operating Systems
           and Software, Carnegie Mellon-Software Engineering Institute, Pittsburgh, PA, May
           1989.

[WeA90]   H.F. WEDDE, G.S. ALIJANI, D. HUIZINGA, G. KANG, B-K. KIM, *MELODY:*
           A Completely Decentralized Adaptive File System for Handling Real-Time Tasks in
           Unpredictable Environments; *Real-Time Systems* Vol. 2 No. 4(1990)

[WeA89a]   H.F. WEDDE, G.S. ALIJANI, D. BARAN, G. KANG, B-K. KIM, *DRAGON
           SLAYER/ MELODY:* Distributed Operating System Support for Mission Critical
           Computing; Proc. of the 1989 Workshop on "Operating Systems for Mission Critical
           Computing" University of Maryland, College Park, September 1989

[WeA89b]   H.F. WEDDE, G.S. ALIJANI, D. BARAN,W.G. BROWN, S. CHEN, G. KANG,
           B-K. KIM, Operating System Support for Adaptive Distributed Real-Time Systems in
           DRAGON SLAYER; *ACM Operating Systems Review* Vol. 23 No. 3 (July 1989),
           pp. 126 - 140

[WeA89c]   H.F. WEDDE, G.S. ALIJANI, D. BARAN, G. KANG, B-K. KIM, Real-Time
           Performance of a Completely Decentralized Adaptive File System; Proc. of the 10th
           IEEE Real-Time Systems Symposium, Santa Monica, December 1989

[WeA89d]   H.F. WEDDE, G.S. ALIJANI, D. BARAN, G. KANG, B-K. KIM, Adaptive Real-Time File Handling in Local Area Networks; 1989 EUROMICRO Workshop on Real Time, Como/ Italy, June 1989

[WeKo89]   H.F. WEDDE, B. KOREL, W.G. BROWN, S. CHEN, Transparent Distributed Object Management under Completely Decentralized Control; Proceedings of the 9th International IEEE Conference on Distributed Computing Systems, Newport Beach, June 1989

[WeA88]   H.F. WEDDE, G.S. ALIJANI, G. KANG, B-K. KIM, MELODY: A Distributed Real-Time Testbed for Adaptive Systems; Proc. of the 1988 International IEEE Symposium on Real-Time Systems; Huntsville, December 1988.

MAPPING OF FAULT-TOLERANT PERMUTATIONS

IN OMEGA INTERCONNECTION NETWORK

Uma Bhattacharya
Dept. of Computer Science & Tech.
Bengal Engineering College
Shibpur, Howrah - 711 103
West Bengal; INDIA

Swapan Bhattacharya
Dept. of Computer Science
University of Calcutta
92, A.P.C. Road
Calcutta - 700 009; INDIA

Abstract : *This paper presents a comprehensive treatment of the fault-tolerant characteristics of Omega interconnection network, which is a typical member of a class of non-redundant multistage interconnection networks characterised by the full-access property and unique-path property, in the presence of single faulty switching element in the network. A significant amount of research works has already been made in making a multistage interconnection network fault-tolerant by introducing redundancy in the network, which in its turn, increases the cost and complexity of the system. The extent to which an Omega network can be considered to be fault-tolerant in the presence of single faulty switching element and without the introduction of any redundancy, has been explored in this paper. Several claims, together with the corresponding proofs, have been made in this respect. In view of the unique-path property of this non-redundant network, every permutation is definitely not attainable in the presence of faults in the network; but, even a set of some fault-tolerant permutations, as discussed in this paper, may be of immense help in a distributed computing environment, which is characterised by the absence of any preference amongst all the possible permutations.*

1. Introduction

Multistage interconnection network [6], [9] plays a very important role in the distributed computing environment in providing programmable data paths between functional modules. Example of such an environment is a set of processor modules and a set of memory modules, interconnected by a multistage interconnection network (or simply MIN) which is usually segmented into several stages. Design and performance of a class of non-redundant MINs characterised by the unique-path property [1] and full-access property [11] have been studied in [10]. This paper deals with the Omega network [1] which is a typical member of such a class of multistage interconnection networks.

The reliabilty [4] of MINs is of immense importance for correct functioning of a distributed computing system. A MIN is said to be fault-tolerant [5] if under certain faults, it can establish a desired input-output performance. Methods for detection of faults in several MINs have been studied in [4], [5], [7]. A fault in a non-redundant network results in the loss of its full-access capability [1], [8], which can be revived by introducing redundancy in the MIN via additional links, switches or stages [3], thereby increasing the cost and complexity of the network. But, from the practical point of view, in a distributed computing environment characterised by the indistinguishability amongst the processors and memory modules, the primary objective of a MIN is to maintain the mapping of the set of inputs to the set of outputs through some permutation(s), which again do not have any preference amongst themselves.

2. Scope of the work

This paper deals with the fault-tolerant characteristics of Omega networks built from 2X2 switching elements (or, simply SEs).

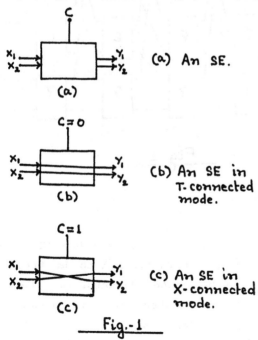

(a) An SE.

(b) An SE in T-connected mode.

(c) An SE in X-connected mode.

Fig.-1

Fig.-1 illustrates the basic form and the two allowed states of a 2X2 SE. The logical levels at the control input lines decide whether it is in its straight (T) connected mode or exchange (X) mode. Fig.-2 shows a multi-processor system with 16 processors interconnected by an Omega network. This network consists of n = $\log_2 N$ stages of 2X2 SEs for connecting N inputs to N outputs, with N/2 SEs in each stage.

A switching element in the network is represented by an ordered pair (r,s) where r is the stage number in which the element is located and s is the switch number in the same stage, $0 \leq r \leq n-1$ and $0 \leq s \leq N/2 - 1$. It may be observed from Fig.-2 that the pair of SEs (i,s), (i,s+N/4) in the ith stage of the network is connected to only one pair (i+1,2∗s) and (i+1,2∗s+1) of the next stage for all (i,s) satisfying the relations $0 \leq s \leq N/4$ and $0 \leq i < n-1$. This is described as *buddy property* in [12]. The pair of SEs in the ith stage is called the output buddies, and the pair of SEs in the (i+1)th stage is called the input buddies.

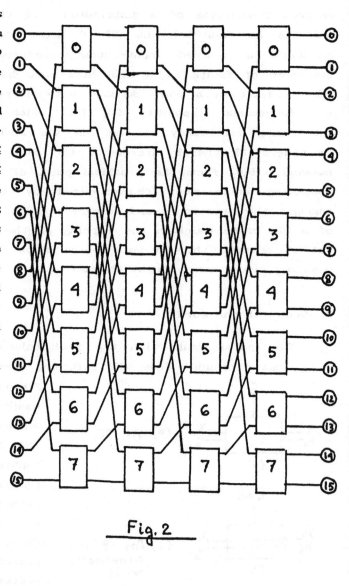

Fig. 2

The fault model used here is one in which only the SEs fail and the connecting links do not fail. A faulty switch is treated as unusable and no connections can be routed through it. Faults in the connecting links can be accomodated in this model by treating them as part of the switching elements.

A graph model of the Omega network can be constructed [12] with the SEs represented by nodes, and connecting links by directed arcs. When viewed from one of the SEs in the first/last stage, the graph takes the shape of a binary tree where the leaves are the SEs in the last/first stage. If the faulty SE exists in the first/last stage, the communication tree rooted on this element is completely destroyed so that no transfer of data is possible from/to the module connected to the faulty SE. In this paper, our discussions are restricted to the faults occurring at any stage excepting the first and the last one.

The following two properties of the Omega network have been used in the subsequent sections in the process of making several claims, together with the corresponding proofs, regarding the fault-tolerant characteristics of this non-redundant MIN.

(i) For a particular control setting of the Omega network, let the set of inputs $I = \langle i_0, i_1, \ldots, i_{N-1} \rangle$ be mapped to the set of outputs $O = \langle O_0, O_1, \ldots, O_{N-1} \rangle$ satisfying a specific permutation so that the input i_l is mapped to the output O_l where $l = 0, 1, \ldots, N-1$. If the specified control setting is complemented, then the set of inputs will be mapped to the set of outputs satisfying another permutation characterised by the property that now i_l will be mapped to O_l', $0 \leq l \leq N-1$ where O_l' is the $(N-1)$'s complement of O_l.

(ii) In the presence of a single faulty SE in stage-1, the number of elements in the set of unaffected outputs is the same as the number of elements in the set of affected outputs, and each element of the former is the $(N-1)$'s complement of the corresponding element of the later.

The research work discussed here establishes the fact that some fault-tolerant permutations [2] exist even in the presence of single faulty SE. In the subsequent sections it has been proved that at least two passes are required to map such permutations. For a particular permutation, the entire set of inputs is split into two subsets with $(N-4)$ and 4 elements respectively. The set of $(N-4)$ inputs is mapped in the first pass, and the set of the remaining 4 inputs is mapped in the second pass. None of these mapping involves the faulty SE. Selection criteria for splitting up the set of inputs has also been explored. Finally, it has been shown that there exists at least 2^n fault-tolerant permutations of the set of inputs to the set of outputs in the presence of a single faulty SE.

3. Fault-tolerant permutations in Omega network

In presence of a single faulty switching element (i,s), $1 \leq i \leq n-2$ and $0 \leq s \leq N/2 - 1$ (it is being assumed that the input stage $i = 0$ and the output stage $i = n-1$ are fault free), the number of affected inputs and outputs (i.e. the inputs and outputs which are connected to the faulty SE through some path) are 2^{i+1} and 2^{n-i} respectively, so that the total number of unaffected outputs are $2^n - 2^{n-i}$. In such a situation with one faulty SE, let the set of inputs I be partitioned into two disjoint subsets I_f and $I-I_f$, where I_f represents the set of affected inputs. Under such circumstances, there always exists a subset O_u of the set of outputs O such that O_u contains the affected outputs, i.e. the outputs which remain connected to all the inputs in I, in spite of the presence of the faulty SE in the network. In fact, the elements of the sets I_f and $O - O_u$ can be obtained as the leaves of the trees, generated by taking the faulty SE as a root and then proceeding towards the input side and output side respectively in the graph model of the network.

3.1 Characteristics of the Omega network in presence of single faulty switching element

Several claims, and the corresponding proofs, are being presented in this section in the process of discussing the characteristics of the Omega network in presence of single faulty switching element.

3.1.1 Lemma - 1 : In presence of single faulty SE, the number of affected inputs is less than or equal to the number of Unaffected outputs, and hence there exists some permutation mapping the set of inputs to the set of outputs.

Proof : If the number of elements in I_f and O_u be l and k respectively, then we have to prove that $l \leq k$, or in other words $2^{i+1} \leq 2^n - 2^{n-i}$; i.e. $n > i + 1$.

In view of the fact that i is the stage in which the faulty SE exists, and also that the faulty SE cannot exist in the first and the last stage (according to our basic premises), the minimum possible value of n (say, n_{min}) is related to i by the relation $n_{min} = i + 2$. Therefore, the requisite relationship $n > i+1$ is valid for any value of n. Hence, it is possible to map (i) the set of affected inputs to a subset of unaffected outputs, and (ii) the set of unaffected inputs to the subset of outputs containing the elements which are not used in (i).

This proves the Lemma-1.

3.1.2   Lemma - 2 :   It is not possible to map, in one pass, the set of inputs I to the set of outputs O in presence of single faulty SE.

Proof :   In presence of single faulty SE (i,s) in the Omega network, the two affected inputs of the set I_f which are on the two input lines of the faulty switch, will be blocked to reach their corresponding two affected outputs of the set $O - O_u$; and hence the set of inputs I cannot be propagated to the set of outputs in one pass.

This proves the Lemma - 2.

3.1.3   Lemma - 3 :   In presence of single faulty SE, the set of unaffected outputs O_u is the superset of the set containing the elements which are (N-1)'s complement of the elements present in the set $O - O_u$.

Proof :   In the presence of one faulty SE in stage-1, i.e. when $i = 1$, let $O_f = \langle O_0, O_1, O_2, \ldots, O_{(N/2)-1} \rangle$.

Then, in accordance with property #2 mentioned in section 2 $O_u = \langle O_0', O_1', O_2', \ldots, O_{(N/2)-1}' \rangle$ where O_i' represents the (N-1)'s complement of O_i , $0 \leq i \leq (N/2)-1$.

Again, $O = O_f \cup O_u$ ....(1)

Now, considering the binary tree structure originating from the faulty SE in stage-1, each child of this SE in stage-2 must be connected to the elements of two disjoint subsets of O_f. Considering a child of the SE $(1,i)$ to be faulty now and not the previous one, let O_{fn} and O_{un} represent the sets of the affected and unaffected outputs respectively.

Therefore, $O_{fn} \subset O_f$ ....(2)

Again, $O = O_{fn} \cup O_{un}$ .... (3)

Now, combining (1), (2) and (3), we get $O_{un} \supset O_u$.

Since O_u contains the elements which are the $(N-1)$'s complements of those of the set O_f and $O_f \supset O_{fn}$, the set O_{un} also contains the elements which are the $(N-1)$'s complements of those in set O_{fn}. So, in the presence of a faulty SE in stage-2, the set of unaffected outputs is the superset of the set containing the elements which are $(N-1)$'s complement of the elements present in the affected set. Again, due to the binary tree structure, starting from the SE in stage-2, the same inference can be drawn for stage-3, and so on for the subsequent stages also. This proves the Lemma.

3.2 Fault-tolerant mapping in Omega network

The assertion made in the section 3.1.2 reveal that all the inputs excepting the two affected and blocked ones, can be propagated to the outputs in one pass in the presence of single faulty SE. The affected inputs excepting the blocked two, will always be mapped to the unaffected outputs, since the propagation paths corresponding to these input-output combinations do not involve the faulty SEs in the stage i. Hence, the primary objective of the next pass is to map these two blocked inputs to two unaffected outputs, which, in turn, should be left unused in the first pass. Thus, in the first pass, two more inputs have to be left out of the mapping process, thereby allowing N-4 inputs to be mapped to N-4 outputs. Let us now formalise these discussions in terms of several claims, supported by the corresponding proofs.

3.2.1 **Lemma - 4** : In presence of a single faulty SE (i,s), if the two inputs $(i_1, i_2) \in I_f$ are blocked from reaching their corresponding outputs $(j_1, j_2) \in O - O_u$ respectively, then the inputs i_1, i_2 can be mapped to the unaffected outputs j_3 and j_4 under complemented control setting, where

$$j_3 = j_1' = (N-1)\text{'s complement of } j_1 \quad ....(1)$$

and $\qquad j_4 = j_2' = (N-1)\text{'s complement of } j_2 \quad ....(2)$

Proof : In accordance with the Lemma-3 of the Omega network mentioned under section 3.1.1,

$$j_3, j_4 \in O_u \qquad (3)$$

and by the property (i) under complemented control setting i_1 will be mapped to $(N-1)$'s complement of j_1 , which is j_3 by (1) ; and i_2 will be mapped to $(N-1)$'s complement of j_2 which is j_4 by (2).

Hence, using (3), we conclude that the Lemma-4 is proved.

3.2.2 **Lemma - 5** : In presence of a single faulty SE (i,s), let the inputs $i_1, i_2 \in I_f$ be blocked from reaching the corresponding outputs $j_1, j_2 \in O-O_u$, and also let $j_3, j_4 \in O_u$ be such that j_3 and j_4 are the $(N-1)$'s complement of j_1 and j_2 respectively. If i_3, i_4 be the inputs which are mapped to the outputs j_3, j_4 under normal control setting, then under the complemented control setting, the inputs i_3, i_4 will be mapped to the outputs j_1, j_2 respectively.

Proof : According to Lemma-4, under the complemented control setting, i_1 is mapped to j_3 and i_2 is mapped to j_4. Under normal control setting, i_3 is mapped to j_3 and i_4 is mapped to j_4. But, by the statement of this Lemma (i.e. Lemma-5),

$$j_3 = j_1' \text{ and } j_4 = j_2'$$

so that $\qquad j_3 = j_1 \text{ and } j_4 = j_2$

Hence, by the property (i) mentioned in section 2, under the complemented control setting, i_3 is mapped to j_1 and i_4 is mapped to j_2 ; and this proves the Lemma-5.

3.2.3 **Lemma - 6** : The four inputs i_1, i_2, i_3, i_4 as specified in Lemma-4 and Lemma-5 will be mapped to their respective destinations in one pass.

Proof : The pair of inputs (i_1, i_2) and (i_3, i_4) can be called dual to each other, in view of the fact that their destinations are interchanged under the complemented control setting with respect to those under normal control setting; and hence, the four inputs i_1, i_2, i_3, i_4 will be mapped to their respective destinations under the complemented control setting in one pass. This proves the Lemma-6.

3.3.4 Lemma - 7 : At least two passes are required to map a set of inputs to the set of outputs in presence of a single faulty SE.

Proof : According to Lemma-2, it is impossible to map, in one pass, the set of inputs to the set of outputs in presence of single faulty SE. However, under such situation, all the inputs, excepting the blocked ones i_1 and i_2, can be mapped to their destinations in one pass. Also, according to Lemma-6, the four inputs i_1, i_2, i_3, i_4 where (i_1, i_2) and (i_3, i_4) are dual to each other, can reach their respective destinations in one pass, under complemented control setting.

Hence, if (i) the remaining (N-4) inputs be mapped in the first pass under normal control setting, and (ii) the specified four inputs be mapped to their specified destinations in the second pass under the complemented control setting, then it is possible to map the permutation in two passes, in spite of the presence of the faulty SE (i, s). This proves Lemma-7.

3.2.5 Lemma - 8 : In presence of a single faulty SE, there exists at least 2^n permutations mapping the set of inputs to the set of outputs.

Proof : For n-stage Omega network, 2^n different control settings are possible, and this proves the presence of at least 2^n permutations mapping the set of inputs to the set of outputs in presence of single faulty SE.

4. Illustrative example

Considering the switching element (2,0) in the Omega network shown in Fig. 2, to be faulty, we have

I = { 0, 1, 2, 3, 4, 5, 6, 7, 8, 9, 10, 11, 12, 13, 14, 15 }

I_f = { 0, 2, 4, 6, 8, 10, 12, 14 }

O = { 0, 1, 2, 3, 4, 5, 6, 7, 8, 9, 10, 11, 12, 13, 14, 15 }

O_f = { 4, 5, 6, 7, 8, 9, 10, 11, 12, 13, 14, 15 }

Let the control setting for the 4-stage Omega network be c = XXXX, for which the inputs i_1 = 12 and i_2 = 14 and the corresponding outputs j_1 = 3 and j_2 = 1.

Therefore, j_3 = 12 and j_4 = 14 from which again, we get i_3 = 3, i_4 = 1 when c = XXXX.

In the presence of the faulty SE (2,0), the input-output permutation for each of the two control settings XXXX and TTTT are being mentioned below :

	c = XXXX			$\bar{c}$ = TTTT	
Input		Output	Input		Output
0	$\longrightarrow$	15	0		0
1		14	1	$\longrightarrow$	1
2	$\longrightarrow$	13	2		2
3		12	3	$\longrightarrow$	3
4	$\longrightarrow$	11	4		4
5	$\longrightarrow$	10	5		5
6	$\longrightarrow$	9	6		6
7	$\longrightarrow$	8	7		7
8	$\longrightarrow$	7	8		8
9	$\longrightarrow$	6	9		9
10	$\longrightarrow$	5	10		5
11	$\longrightarrow$	4	11		11
12		3	12	$\longrightarrow$	12
13	$\longrightarrow$	2	13		13
14		1	14	$\longrightarrow$	14
15	$\longrightarrow$	0	15		15

4. Conclusion

A comprehensive treatment of the fault-tolerant characteristics of Omega interconnection network in a distributed computing environment, with respect to the failure of a single switching element in the network, has been made in this paper. Several significant results in this aspect, have been established in the course of this presentation.

It may be noted that while exploring the fault-tolerant characteristics of the Omega network, no redundancy has been introduced in the network, and this is very significant from the point of view of cost and complexity. However, since in each of these networks, there exists a unique path from any particular input to any particular output, some of the permutations from the set of inputs to the set of outputs cannot be acchieved (without the introduction of redundancy) in the presence of faults in the network. It has been established that at least 2^n (where n is the number of stages in the network) permutations can still be mapped from the set of inputs to the set of outputs of an Omega network, in the presence of a single faulty switching element. However, the attainability of every permutation is not demanded for the fault-tolerant operation of a distributed cmputing system, which is characterised by the absence of any preference amongst all the possible permutations. It is from this point of view that the fault-tolerant permutations achieveable in the presence of one faulty switching element in an Omega network, have been explored in this paper.

REFERENCES

1. A. Verma and C.S. Raghavendra, "Fault-tolerant routing in multistage interconnection networks," IEEE Trans. Comput., vol 38 no. 3, pp. 385-393, Mar. 1989.

2. I. Gazit and M. Malek, "Fault tolerance capabilities in multistage network-based multicomputer systems," IEEE Trans. Comput., vol 37 no. 7, pp. 788-798, Jul. 1988.

3. G.B. Adams and H.J. Siegel, "The extra-stage cube : a fault-tolerant interconnection network for supersystems," IEEE Trans. Comput., vol c-31 no. 5, pp. 443-454, May 1982.

4. T. Feng and C. Wu, "Fault-diagnosis for a class of multistage interconnection networks," IEEE TRans. Comput., vol c-30 no. 10, pp. 743-758, Oct. 1981.

5. D.P. Agarawal, "Testing and fault-tolerance of multistage interconnection networks," IEEE Computer, vol 15, pp. 41-53, Apr. 1982.

6. T. Feng, "A survey of interconnection networks," IEEE Computer, vol 14, pp. 12-27, Dec. 1981.

7. C. Wu and T. Feng, "Fault diagnosis for a class of multistage shiffle/exchange networks," IEEE Trans. Comput., vol c-30, pp. 743-758, Oct. 1981.

8. J.P. Shen and J.P. Hayes, "Fault-tolerance of dynamic full-access interconnection networks," IEEE Trans. Comput., vol c-33 no. 3, pp. 241-248, Mar. 1984.

9. L. Bhuyan and D.P. Agarwal, "Design and performance of a general class of interconnection networks," Proc. 1982 Int. Conf. Parallel Process., Bellaire, Mi, pp. 2-9, Aug. 1982.

10. C. Wu and T. Feng, "On a class of multistage interconnection networks," IEEE Trans. Comput., vol c-29, pp. 694-702, Aug. 1980.

11. D.P. Agarwal and J.S. Leu, "Dynamic accessibility testing and path length optimization of multistage interconnection networks," Proc. 4th Int. Conf. Distributed Comput. Syst., pp. 266-277, May 1984.

12. D.P. Agarwal, "Graph theoretical analysis and design of multistage interconnection networks," IEEE Trans. Comput., vol c-32 no. 7, pp. 637-648, Jul. 1983.

———————— * ————————

6. Expert Systems, Artificial Intelligence

Artificial neural networks
for predicting silicon content in raw iron
from blast furnaces

Abhay B. Bulsari   Henrik Saxén

Värmeteknik, Kemisk–tekniska fakulteten, Åbo Akademi
SF 20500 Turku/Åbo, Finland
Telephone: 358 (21) 654 721, Telefax: 358 (21) 654 479
E–mail: abulsari@abo.fi, hsaxen@abo.fi

ABSTRACT : Artificial neural networks often perform better than conventional statistical methods for correlations. Prediction of silicon content in pig iron from blast furnaces has been rather difficult and inaccurate, when possible, and mathematical modelling of the process is still qualitatively inadequate for the purpose. This paper illustrates the feasibility of using a feed–forward neural network for predicting silicon content from actual industrial data. The eight inputs to the network were silicon contents of two previous tappings, and some operational parameters, and the output was the predicted silicon content of the next tapping. Levenberg–Marquardt method was used for training the network by minimising the sum of squares of the residuals. The output of each node was calculated by the logistic activation (sigmoid) function on the weighted sum of inputs to that node, with different gain values. It is shown therein that this technique results in better predictions compared to conventional statistical correlation methods.

1. Introduction

Neural networks offer interesting possibilities in chemical and metallurgical engineering. Various configurations and topologies of neural networks have been suggested [1]. The number of configurations and topologies being considered is proportionately large compared to the number of researchers working on them. Although back propagation has become popular on grounds of simplicity and its capability to learn sequentially from training instances, we have used the Levenberg–Marquardt method [2] for achieving the minimum of the sum of squares of errors. The Levenberg–Marquardt method is fast, reliable and easy to use when the number of weights is not very large, say less than 100.

There are several processes for which accurate mathematical modelling is difficult or too complicated. In such cases, neural networks can learn from the observation of the gross behaviour of the process to provide a kind of simulation model. It could save enormous amounts of model development effort, as well as effort for developing the simulation programs. Even CPU time for simulation can be saved in cases where the mathematical models are quite complicated or involve solution of a set of differential equations.

Artificial neural networks are new to chemical and metallurgical engineering, although there are already half a dozen journals devoted entirely to neural networks [3]. The major efforts known to us are on fault diagnosis in processes and process control. Bulsari and Saxén [4, 5] present two applications of feed–forward neural networks. The first paper deals with a system identification task for a chemical reactor with two reactions in series, and the second illustrates the implementation of a chemical reactor selection expert system in a feed–forward network.

2. The blast furnace operation

The blast furnace is a complex chemical reactor and an efficient heat exchanger which produces raw iron from iron ore. Iron ore and coke are fed into the furnace from the top and a blast of moist air is injected from tuyeres close to the bottom of the furnace. The air partially oxidises the coke to form carbon monoxide, which reduces the iron oxides to raw iron which trickles down to the bottom of the furnace. Carbon dioxide leaves the furnace from an exit near the top of the furnace. Limestone fuses with silica to form calcium silicate as slag. At irregular intervals, the molten raw iron, also called pig iron, is tapped out, along with the slag. The temperature inside the furnace varies from about 200°C to 1450°C. Typical blast furnaces, such as the one at Raahe in Finland have a volume of about 1000 m^3 and a hearth diameter of about 7 metres.

2.1. Silicon content in pig iron

Silicon exists in iron ore as well as in coke, to a smaller extent. This silicon exists in the form of oxide and silicates, a part of which get reduced in the highly reducing atmosphere of the blast furnace to silicon. The reduced silicon stays in the raw molten iron. Typical carbon content of pig iron is 4 % and silicon content is about 0.3 %. Silicon content in pig iron is an important quality parameter. The steel produced from pig iron should not have more than a certain maximum amount of silicon in it, depending on its end use. Moreover, as silicon content is an indicator of the thermal state of the process, its prognosis would be valuable.

Prediction of silicon content in pig iron has been a difficult problem for several reasons. Phenomenological models are not good enough to explain silicon reduction quantitatively. The residence time distributions are complex and change with time and operating conditions. Empirical models are not accurate, partly because of poor accuracy of measured industrial data. Some data, like silicon content of coke, which is required is often not measured at all. Artificial neural networks can sometimes perform better than conventional statistical methods, and that is the motivation for this investigative research.

3. Results

On the whole, the results of this work have been positive and very encouraging. The predictions were better than those obtained from conventional statistical methods.

The data is actual industrial data from Rautaruukki Oy (Raahe, Finland). It was collected from one week's operation of the blast furnace 2 resulting in 80 tappings. Since two previous silicon content data are required as inputs, we had a table of 78 instances. For most of the work presented in the following sections, first 50 were used as training instances and remaining 28 as test instances.

A correlation analysis was carried out to determine which parameters or operating conditions or indices were related to silicon content in the pig iron. All such parameters and operating conditions are not measured, so the ones which were available were considered. It was then decided that for the initial investigation, blast pressure (15 minute averages, 30 minutes earlier and 1 hour earlier), heat loss (1 hour average, 1 hour earlier and 7 hours earlier) blast volume (1 hour average, 5 hours earlier) and oil rate (1 hour average, 5 hours earlier) would be included as the inputs, besides values of silicon contents in percentages in the two previous tappings. The output would be the expected silicon content in the next tap.

3.1. The Levenberg–Marquardt method

The Levenberg–Marquardt method was used to calculate the weights in the neural networks which minimised the sum of squares of errors. Network training aims at achieving the least sum of squares of errors, the errors measured as the difference between the calculated output and the desired output. Back propagation by the generalised delta rule, a kind of a gradient descent method is one popular method [6] for such training. Many algorithms for least–squares optimisation use Taylor–series models [2] . The Levenberg–Marquardt method uses an interpolation between the approaches based on the maximum neighbourhood (a "trust region") in which the truncated Taylor series gives an adequate representation of the non–linear model.

The program ANNEX, developed in April 1990 [7] , was used for this work. The method has been used successfully [4, 5] and found to be efficient.

3.2. The network without hidden layers

The network without hidden layers is usually not good enough for getting a good performance after training, but it provides useful information. It indicates [4] to some extent the qualitative effect of each input variable on each output variable. With all the 78 instances, the SSQ (sum of squares of errors) was 0.4444 and none of the weights were negligible. The effects of blast pressure 30 minutes earlier, heat losses and oil rate were negative, and the effects of the blast pressure 60 minutes earlier and blast volume were positive. This neural network is not very useful since a linear discriminant analysis results in a SSQ of 0.4744, which also shows the same effects of the inputs. One may wonder what significant effects, if any, could these various inputs have on the silicon content in the succeeding tap. An autocorrelation analysis (with two previous values) resulted in a SSQ of 0.6276, which answers positively the usefulness of the other variables.

3.3. The network with one hidden layer

A hidden layer provides additional computational and correlational capacity to the network. First 50 instances of the 78 instances were used as training instances. Several values of NHID (number of nodes in the hidden layer) were considered.

An (8,3,1) network resulted in a SSQ of 0.0955 (rms error of 0.0437) whereas an (8,1) configuration (without hidden layers) resulted in a SSQ of 0.3243 with the same 50 instances. Two instances contribute about half of the total SSQ for the (8,3,1) network. They may be considered as outliers. Linear discriminant analysis of the same 50 instances results in a SSQ of 0.3321 (rms error of 0.0815). This indicates a significant improvement of the correlation by this versatile technique of feed-forward neural networks.

It is not uncommon to find low values of SSQ on the training instances and a bad performance on the untrained instances. Therefore, the remaining 28 instances were tested using the same values of weights which were obtained by training the (8,3,1) network with the first 50 instances. Out of those 28 test instances, 6 errors were 0.09 or larger. They could be inaccurate data, typical of measurements under industrial conditions. The largest was 0.11. Only 5 predictions showed a trend in the wrong direction, but one of them was required to correct the previous inaccurate prediction, and the resulting prediction was very close to the correct value.

Autocorrelation with one hidden layer (2,NHID,1) was not very impressive. (2,2,1) and (2,3,1) with all 78 instances results in a SSQ of 0.5824 and 0.5709 respectively.

3.4. The network with two hidden layers

On the whole, the results with 2 hidden layers (8,NHID,NHID,1) were not much better than those of other configurations including (8,3,1). It was much more difficult to arrive at a minimum in this case. There are evidently more local minima, and dozens of starting guesses were required. Convergence was very slow and the weights often reached their limits of -1000 and +1000. After 2100 iterations, the SSQ for (8,2,2,1) with 50 training instances was 0.19087, decreasing extremely slowly. (2,2,2,1) with 78 training instances resulted in a SSQ of 0.5534.

4. Conclusions

This work demonstrated that artificial neural networks can be used conveniently to predict the silicon content in pig iron tappings. The results obtained with (8,3,1) feed-forward network were better than the ones with conventional linear discriminant analysis or autocorrelation. Networks with two hidden layers did not perform much better than the ones with one hidden layer. This may be due to convergence on local minima far from the global minimum.

Acknowledgements : Rautaruukki Oy (Raahe, Finland) is gratefully acknowledged for its eager and fruitful collaboration with the AI research group at Institutionen för värmeteknik, Åbo Akademi.

References

1. Lippmann, R. P., "An introduction to computing with neural nets",
   IEEE ASSP Magazine, (April 1987) 4-22.

2. Marquardt, D. W., "An algorithm for least-squares estimation of nonlinear parameters",
   J. Soc. Indust. Appl. Math., 11 (June 1963) 431-441.

3. Chapnick, P., "Neural network update", *AI Expert*, 4 (December 1989) 5-6.

4. Bulsari, A. and H. Saxén, "Applicability of an artificial neural network as a simulator for a chemical process", The fifth International Symposium on Computer and Information Sciences, Nevsehir, Turkey, October–November 1990.

5. Bulsari, A. and H. Saxén, "Implementation of a chemical reactor selection expert system in a feed–forward neural network", sent to second Australian Conference on Neural Networks, Sydney, Australia, February 1991.

6. Jones, W. P. and J. Hoskins, "Back–Propagation: A generalized delta learning rule",
   Byte, (October 1987) 155-162.

7. Bulsari, A., B. Saxén and H. Saxén, "Programs for feedforward neural networks using the Levenberg–Marquardt method : Documentation and user's manual", Technical report 90-2, Värmeteknik, Åbo Akademi, 1990

A chemical reactor selection expert system created by training an artificial neural network

Abhay B. Bulsari, Björn Saxén and Henrik Saxén

Kemisk Tekniska Fakulteten, Åbo Akademi
SF 20500 Turku/Åbo, Finland
Tel: 358 (21) 654 721, 654 444
Fax: 358 (21) 654 479
E-mail: vt_ai@abo.fi

ABSTRACT

This work investigated the feasibility of using a feed-forward neural network for knowledge acquisition and storage, and subsequent use as a chemical reactor selection expert system. Feed–forward neural networks have the capability of learning heuristics from given examples.

Levenberg-Marquardt method was used to train the network by minimising the sum of squares of residuals. The output of each node was calculated by the logistic activation (sigmoid) function on the weighted sum of inputs to that node. It is shown therein that the number of hidden layers and the number of nodes in the hidden layers are critical, and increase in the number of hidden layers does not always improve the performance of the simulator network. It is possible in certain cases like this one to attribute meanings to the nodes in the hidden layer.

Redundancy in the outputs was considered by having separate output nodes for selecting batch and continuous operations, and for stirred-tank and tubular reactors. The network performance did not significantly change on excluding one of the outputs, although it was not possible to arrive at the converged solution equally easily when four outputs were considered.

This work demonstrated that a selection expert system can be created in a feed-forward neural network. In other words, neural networks can be used for knowledge acquisition and storage for selection expert systems, suitable for convenient retrieval and inferencing. Inspite of covering a wide range (several orders of magnitude) of inputs, the performance was found to be very good.

Keywords : neural networks, chemical reactor selection, knowledge acquisition

1. Introduction

Neural networks offer interesting possibilities for expert systems in chemical engineering. Artificial neural networks, also called connectionist models, parallel distributed models, neuromorphic systems or simply neural nets consist of many simple computational elements called nodes, or neurons each of which collects by weighted addition the signals from various other nodes which are connected to it directionally. This sum, the net input to the node, is processed by a function (usually a sigmoid or a step) resulting in the output or the activation of that node. In multilayer feedforward networks of the type considered in this paper (Fig. 1), there are a few layers (the input layer, the output layer, and possibly some hidden layers) across which all the nodes of each layer are connected to all the nodes in the layer above it, but there are no connections within the layer. A constant term, a bias, is usually added to each of the nodes.

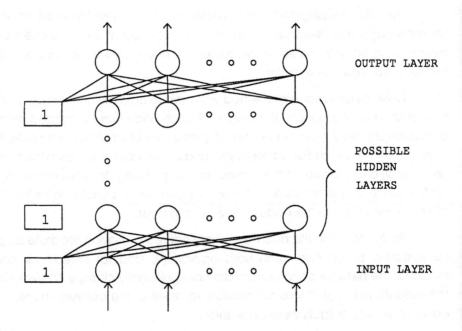

Figure 1. Feed–forward neural network

Various configurations and topologies of neural networks have been suggested [1] . The number of configurations and topologies being considered is proportionately large compared to the number of researchers working on them. Nevertheless, there are no clear guidelines on the number of hidden layers or number of nodes in hidden layers for optimal performance of the neural network. This work considers these questions alongwith a new application in chemical engineering, *viz.*, a neural network as a reactor selection expert system. Although back propagation has become popular on grounds of simplicity and its capability to learn sequentially from training instances, we have used the Levenberg-Marquardt method [2] for achieving the minimum of the sum of squares of errors. The Levenberg-Marquardt method is fast, reliable and easy to use when the number of weights is not very large, say less than 100. Different initial guesses have been used when one initial guess leads to a minimum which is suspectably a local minimum. It has been successfully used for a system identification task [3] .

2. Neural network applications in chemical engineering

Artificial neural networks (ANNs) have a good potential for knowledge acquisition, representation and storage, besides being capable of learning from data, called training instances.

There are several cases for which knowledge acquisition is difficult or too complicated. In such cases, neural networks can learn from a table of observations. It could save enormous amounts of knowledge engineering effort, as well as effort for developing the expert system. Even CPU time for inferencing can be saved in cases where the expert systems have large knowledge bases or involve several levels of inferencing.

Artificial neural networks are new to chemical engineering, although there are already half a dozen journals devoted entirely to neural networks [3] . The major efforts known to us are on fault diagnosis in processes and process control. In the earliest work, Hoskins and Himmelblau [4] consider a case of three reactors in series with six different faults that the neural network recognises / finds from the numerical process data on six variables. Venkatasubramanian and Chan [5] consider 13 faults and 18 causes in a fluidised catalytic cracking unit. The authors find that single hidden layer networks outperformed the two hidden layer networks in terms of efficiency as well as accuracy. This agrees with our work, where we also find that in most cases, a network with one hidden layer performs better than a network with two hidden layers in terms of accuracy and efficiency. A subsequent work [6] considers two chemical process systems, a reactor with controllers, and a reactor and a distillation column with controllers. It is mentioned therein that "several researchers have discounted the notion that hidden nodes and strengths of the connections possess special meaning", contrary to the conclusions of Touretzky and Pomerleau [7]. Watanabe *et al.* [8] present a two-stage multi-layer neural network for fault diagnosis in a chemical reactor considering five faults. Ungar *et al.* [9] look at two examples: fault diagnosis in a reactor with several sensors and valves with 12 possible faults; and a bioreactor control problem. Bhat *et al.* [10] present 3 examples: a reactor at steady state, a dynamic pH stirred tank, and interpretation of biosensor data. Bhat and McAvoy present the example of the dynamic pH stirred tank also in [11]. Ydstie [12] considers six examples to illlustrate adaptive forecasting using neural networks for dynamics and control of systems. Bulsari and Saxén [3] illustrate the applicability of neural networks as simulators through an example of a continuous stirred tank reactor with two reactions in series.

3. The reactor selection problem

To illustrate (or investigate) the feasibility of implementing a selection expert system in a feed-forward neural network, we wanted a system that was familiar to chemical engineers, and easy to understand for others as well, training instances could be provided easily, a system that had convenience of physical interpretation, where several orders of magnitude of inputs could be covered, and a system that was not very complicated and had few inputs and few outputs.

One system that satisfied the above criteria was selection of the type and mode of operation of a chemical reactor for a single homogeneous reaction. A few simple rules were used to create a table of 25 training instances. *e.g.*,

1. If the reaction is highly exothermic or highly endothermic, (say 15 kCal/gm mol), select a stirred tank reactor.

2. If the reaction mass is highly viscous (say 50 centipoise or more), select a stirred tank reactor.

3. If the reactor type is tubular, the mode of operation is continuous.

4. If r_0/r_1 is 1.6 or more, and the reaction mass is not very viscous, but the reaction is highly exothermic or endothermic, then prefer a stirred tank reactor, operated in batch mode.

r_0 is the rate of reaction under inlet conditions, and r_1 is the rate of reaction under exit conditions. If this ratio is large, a plug flow reactor (tubular) requires significantly less volume than a stirred tank reactor operated continuously. A stirred tank reactor operated in batch mode is similar to a plug flow reactor. The aim of the work is to investigate the feasibility of implementing a selection expert system in a neural network, hence the rules mentioned above are typical, and not necessarily the best set of rules for selecting reactors for single homogeneous reactions.

Redundancy was caused by having separate nodes for selecting batch and continuous operations, and for stirred-tank and tubular reactors, although they were mutually exclusive.

4. Results

4.1. The feedforward network

The feedforward neural network has an input layer which simply transmits the input variables without any processing to the next layer. The bias is a weighted unit input to each node, thus adding a constant term to the net input of the node. Two, one or no hidden layers are considered. Each node in the upper layers (hidden or output layers) receives weighted inputs from each of the nodes in the layer below it. These weighted inputs are added to get the net input of the node, and the output x_i (or the activation) is calculated by a logistic activation (sigmoid) function of the net input a_i as

$$a_i = \sum_{j=0}^{N} w_{ij} x_j$$

$$x_i = \frac{1}{1 + e^{-\beta a_i}}$$

where N is the number of nodes in a hidden layer or the number of output nodes and w_{i0} is the bias of node i. For the purposes of programming, the weights have been arranged sequentially as a one-dimensional array and not as a matrix. The number of nodes in each hidden layer is NHID, which has been assumed to be the same for every hidden layer. This assumption is not really necessary, but this study has considered relatively little regarding networks with 2 hidden layers. The numbering of the weights starts from the first node of the first hidden layer (if there is a hidden layer, else the output layer) to the bias node through the elements in the input layer. Next come the weights from the second node of the first hidden layer to the bias node through the elements in the input layer, and so on until the first hidden layer layer is covered. The second hidden layer is taken next, and finally the output layer. The program ANNEX was used [13] for this work.

4.2. The Levenberg-Marquardt method

The Levenberg-Marquardt method was used to calculate the weights in the neural networks which minimised the sum of squares of errors (SSQ). Network training aims at achieving the least sum of squares of errors, the errors measured as the difference between the calculated output and the desired output. Minimising the SSQ is not always the best way of training a neural network as pointed out in [3] , but for this application, it suffices. Back propagation by the generalised delta rule, a kind of a gradient descent method is one popular method [14] for such training. Most algorithms for least-squares optimisation problems use either steepest descent or Taylor-series models [2] . The Levenberg-Marquardt method uses an interpolation between the approaches based on the maximum neighbourhood (a "trust region") in which the truncated Taylor series gives an adequate representation of the non-linear model. The method has been found to be advantageous compared to other methods which use only one of the two approaches.

4.3. The network without hidden layers

The network configuration without hidden layers is (5,4). The five inputs are r_0, r_1, F, μ and $|\Delta H_{rxn}|$. r_0 is the rate of formation of the product in gm mol / m^3 under reactor inlet conditions, r_1 is the rate of formation of the product in gm mol / m^3 under reactor exit conditions, F is the production rate in gm mol / sec, μ is the viscosity of the reaction mixture in centipoises, and $|\Delta H_{rxn}|$ is the absolute value of the heat of reaction in kCals / gm mol. The 25 training instances fed to the neural network for learning span a fairly large range of magnitudes from 0.3 to 2140. The weights were constrained between -1000 and +1000.

For $\beta=1$, the 24 weights were found to be :

To: From	batch	continuous	stirred-tank	tubular
bias	-97.0	97.0	-846.	846.
r_0	1.97	-1.97	-4.28	4.28
r_1	-0.512	0.512	-25.6	25.7
F	-0.482	0.482	6.03	-6.03
μ	0.842	-0.842	10.1	-10.1
$|\Delta H_{rxn}|$	4.66	-4.66	48.6	-48.6

with a SSQ of 0.3225 (an average square error of 0.003225, or rms error of 0.0568), which can be considered somewhat high. The error was contributed exclusively by four training instances, in the last two variables. None of the errors were higher than 0.3, implying that the qualitative selection was correct. The errors were not symmetric, *i.e.*, the errors for the third output and fourth output were not exactly the same (varying by about 1 to 5 %) with opposite signs, since there were small differences in the weights also. From the signs of the weights, the selection procedure can be partly explained. The weights for "continuous" are simply the negative of the weights for "batch" which is a result of our training instances - if a selection is "batch", it is not continuous, and vice versa. Similarly, the weights for stirred tank and tubular reactors are of opposite signs. High values of F, μ and $|\Delta H_{rxn}|$ prefer a stirred tank reactor, as can be seen from the weights. Large biases tend to reduce the net input to reasonably low values.

The SSQ is fairly insensitive to a wide range of weights. This solution is difficult to arrive at since most initial guesses in its vicinity tend to converge to different solutions very distinct from this one. There are some (perhaps many) local minima, which result in different weights (different magnitudes, opposite signs) for the third and the fourth output variables, with SSQ of between 0.38 and 0.405.

When the redundancy was removed by excluding the first and the fourth output nodes (now nodes only for continuous and stirred tank), the minimum SSQ was found to be 0.1613, which is roughly half of the 0.3225. The individual errors were observed to be contributed by four training instances and were similar to the ones in the case of four output nodes (the weights were very similar.)

Nevertheless, it provides a model which satisfactorily explains qualitative relations between the variables.

The effect of changing the gain, β for (5,2) was studied, but its effects are still inconclusive. The variation of minimum SSQ with β is shown in Fig. 2. The lowest value of minimum SSQ was 0.08285 for $\beta = 38.2$. However, one can never be sure that the converged result is the global minimum. A negative β simply inverses the weights, leaving the minimum SSQ unaffected. It seems that much additional work will be required before the effects of the gain term are understood completely.

4.4. The network with one hidden layer

The networks with one hidden layer (5,NHID,4) were considered next. Fig. 1 shows a (5,3,4) network, having 34 interconnections. The networks with one hidden layer performed well when NHID was 3 or higher. SSQ for (5,1,2) was quite large. The configuration (5,2,2) learnt perfectly (SSQ was 1.79×10^{-11}.) The larger configurations (5, > 2, 2 or 4) could also learn perfectly. For example, the SSQ for (5,3,4) was 0.72×10^{-17}.

This exact fit can be understood when one considers the role of the nodes in the hidden layer. From the weights for (5,2,2), it was inferred that the first node selected the continuous mode, and preferred a tubular reactor when r_0 and r_1 were not very high compared to F, and μ and $|\Delta H_{rxn}|$ were not very high either. This is not what we had intended, but this is what the network gathered from the training instances. The word 'select' is stronger than 'prefer', and a selection is not overruled by another node's preference. The second node looks for high values of F, μ and $|\Delta H_{rxn}|$ (and r_1 not very high) to select a stirred tank reactor, and prefers batch operation. These were not our rules, but the training instances conform to these (5,2,2)'s indigenous rules. More training instances or more nodes in the hidden layer are therefore needed for further classification (bearing a better resemblance to our set of rules.)

The configuration (5,3,4) was considered next. There was little reason to have 4 outputs instead of 2, except for the interest in seeing if there were additional local minima, or any other side-effects of the redundancy. However, the convergence was rather straightforward, and the minimum SSQ was found to be 0.72×10^{-17}. The weights from the nodes in the hidden layer to the outputs were negatives of each other for prefering batch and continuous, and for stirred tank and tubular reactors. The classification task seemed to be a little more distributed between the three nodes in this case. The first node looked for high values of F, μ and $|\Delta H_{rxn}|$ (and r_1 not very high) and selected a stirred tank reactor (a weight of 105) and preferred a batch process (a weight of 53), similar to the second node in the (5,2,2). The second node looked for high values of F compared to r_1 and preferred a continuous operation (70) in a stirred tank reactor (76). The third node had the weakest influence, preferring a tubular reactor (35) in continuous mode (35), when r_0 was high compared to r_1. This also incorporates the rule that a tubular reactor is operated in continuous mode, almost synonymously. This is more similar to the set of rules we started with.

NHID > 3 only induces more redundancy in the hidden layer causing equally good fits to the training instances, but with a tendency of being less general. This develops an individualistic flavour, and effectively adds an extra rule (at a sub-symbolic level) for each additional node. Besides, the solutions for the weights are not unique.

Considering that the inputs can be positive numbers of any magnitudes, this accuracy is very good.

The networks with two hidden layers did not perform better. None of the converged results showed a reliable performance for (5,NHID,NHID,4) networks with NHID varied from 1 to 5 with a variety of initial guesses for the weights, presumably due to convergence on local minima far from the global minimum. One wonders if it is possible to use the back propagation method or one of its modifications, which are much slower compared to the Levenberg-Marquardt method used in this work, for this simple problem.

4.5. The network as an expert system

After training the network successfully, it was put to test as an expert system for selection of the reactor type and mode of operation. Table 1 shows the results of the test inputs, which were not in the training instances. The classification is correct for all the instances therein.

5. Conclusions

A selection expert system can be created by training a feed-forward neural network. In other words, artificial neural networks can be used for knowledge acquisition and storage for selection expert systems, suitable for convenient retrieval and inferencing. Inspite of covering several orders of magnitude of inputs, the performance of the networks (5,NHID,4), NHID > 1 was very good. Expert system development for realistic problems in this manner can now be

Table 1. Evaluation of the expert system.

r_0	r_1	F	μ	$|\Delta H|$	batch	continuous	stirred tank	tubular
20	10	50	20	8	0.102E-22	1.00	0.398E-30	1.00
300	120	200	10	11	0.697E-01	0.934	0.363E-13	1.00
100	15	30	0.5	1	0.694E-01	0.935	0.362E-13	1.00
120	60	500	2	20	1.00	0.177E-03	1.00	0.265E-19
22	8	49	10	19	1.00	0.411E-26	1.00	0.398E-30
40	10	100	100	2	1.00	0.120E-08	1.00	0.718E-09
100	40	50	500	8	1.00	0.507E-29	1.00	0.398E-30
12	11	100	8	10	0.398E-30	1.00	0.996	0.518E-02
10	9.5	100	8	10	0.398E-30	1.00	1.00	0.439E-20
200	12	180	20	15	1.00	0.940E-29	1.00	0.398E-30
800	40	640	40	3	1.00	0.520E-29	1.00	0.398E-30
40	10	200	11	5	0.398E-30	1.00	1.00	0.398E-30
120	40	580	18	14	0.398E-30	1.00	1.00	0.398E-30
0	0	0	0	0	0.398E-30	1.00	0.518E-17	1.00
20	10	90	150	20	1.00	0.628E-29	1.00	0.398E-30
100	15	30	75	18	1.00	0.208E-25	1.00	0.398E-30

considered. This was an example where neural networks can perform the learning task more efficiently than inductive learning. Inductive learning would have required conversion of the quantitative inputs to qualitative form, an additional step which could lead to questions of what is large, and what is not.

The network with one hidden layer performed better than the one with 2 hidden layers with 2 nodes each, and also better than the one without hidden layers when NHID was 2 or greater. The effect of the gain, β is still not understood. It is possible in certain cases like this one to attribute meanings to the nodes in the hidden layer, contrary to what is mentioned in [6].

References

1. Lippmann, R. P.,

    "An introduction to computing with neural nets",

    IEEE ASSP Magazine, (April 1987) 4-22.

2. Marquardt, D. W.,

   "An algorithm for least-squares estimation of nonlinear
      parameters",

   J. Soc. Indust. Appl. Math., 11 (June 1963) 431-441.

3. Bulsari, A. and H. Saxén,

   "Applicability of an artificial neural network as a simulator for a
      chemical process",

   The fifth International Symposium on Computer and Information Sciences,
      Nevsehir, Turkey (October 1990).

4. Hoskins, J. C. and D. M. Himmelblau,

   "Artificial neural network models of knowledge representation
      in chemical engineering",

   Computers and Chemical Engineering, 12 (1988) 881-890.

5. Venkatasubramanian, V. and K. Chan,

   "A neural network methodology for process fault diagnosis",

   AIChE Journal, 35 (1989) 1993-2002.

6. Venkatasubramanian, V., R. Vaidyanathan and Y. Yamamoto,

   "Process fault detection and diagnosis using neural networks
      I : Steady state processes",

   Computers and Chemical Engineering, 14 (1990) 699-712.

7. Touretzky, D. S. and D. A. Pomerleau,

   "What's hidden in the hidden layers ?",

   Byte, 14 (August 1989) 227-233.

8. Watanabe, K. *et al.*,

   "Incipient fault diagnosis of chemical processes via artificial
      neural networks",

   AIChE Journal, 35 (1989) 1803-1812.

9. Ungar, L. H., B. A. Powell and S. N. Kamens,

   "Adaptive networks for fault diagnosis and process control",

   Computers and Chemical Engineering, 14 (1990) 561-572.

10. Bhat, N. V., P. A. Minderman, Jr., T. McAvoy and N. S. Wang,

   "Modeling chemical process systems via neural computation",

   IEEE Control systems magazine, (April 1990) 24-30.

11. Bhat, N. and T. J. McAvoy,

   "Use of neural nets for dynamic modeling and control of chemical process systems",

   Computers and Chemical Engineering, 14 (1990) 573-582.

12. Ydstie, B. E.,

   "Forecasting and control using adaptive connectionist networks",

   Computers and Chemical Engineering, 14 (1990) 583-599.

13. Bulsari, A., B. Saxén and H. Saxén, "Programs for feedforward neural networks using the Levenberg–Marquardt method : Documentation and user's manual", Technical report 90-2, Värmeteknik, Åbo Akademi, 1990

14. Jones, W. P. and J. Hoskins,

   "Back-Propagation: A generalized delta learning rule",

   Byte, (October 1987) 155-162.

A Modeling Technique for Generating
Causal Explanations of Physical Systems

Rattikorn Hewett[*]

Department of Computer Science
Florida Atlantic University
Boca Raton, FL 33431.

ABSTRACT

This paper introduces an approach for physical system modeling that gives a basis for generating causal explanations of system behaviors. We explicitly represent knowledge about structures and functions of physical systems in two levels of abstraction: *domain* and *prime* models. Domain models explicitly represent the actual structures and processes that make up particular systems, whereas prime models explicitly represent the abstract normal and abnormal structures and processes underlying certain classes of physical systems with analogous behavior. Each domain model is viewed as an instance of a particular prime model and thus during the reasoning about the domain model, any causal behavior of a corresponding prime system model can be inherited. Our approach differs from other systems that generate causal explanation for tutorial purposes in two ways. First it generates a causal explanation of a particular physical system's behavior from general knowledge of causal mechanisms derived from appropriate physical principles rather than a specific causal knowledge about the particular system. Second, unlike the systems that generate causal explanation from qualitative simulation, our approach explicitly represents system structures and processes, instead of sets of qualitative constraints, and thus can directly generate causal explanations for behaviors of the system structures and processes with no additional interpretation required. This paper discusses the approach with an illustrated example and an ongoing research in extending this technique when dealing with multiple granularities. The limitations and other advantages of this approach are described.

1. Introduction

A system that explains dynamic physical system behavior can produce clearer explanations

* The author gratefully acknowledges Barbara Hayes-Roth, Adam Siever, M.D and Micheal Hewett for their supports and ideas. This research was supported by EPRI grant #RP2614-48 and performed at the Knowledge Systems Laboratory, Department of Computer Science, Stanford University. Thanks to Ed Feigenbaum for sponsoring the work within the Knowledge Systems Laboratory.

by providing qualitative causal explanation along with appropriate underlying physical principles. Much work has been done in mental models [3, 18] and qualitative physics [4, 7, 16] to qualitatively simulate the behavior of physical systems. However, the output of qualitative simulations needs to be interpreted for an understandable causal explanation [5, 15]. We introduce an approach for constructing models of physical systems and an algorithm that exploits these models to generate causal explanations underlying the system behaviors. Based on reasoning from first principles i.e. knowledge about system structures, functions and behaviors [4, 7, 8], we represent knowledge about physical systems at two levels of abstraction: *Prime Models* and *Domain Models*. Prime models explicitly represent the abstract structures and processes, both normal and abnormal, underlying classes of physical systems. Domain models explicitly represent the actual structures and processes that make up particular systems. Each domain model is viewed as an instance or a type of a particular prime model. For example, both the human respiratory system and circulatory system can be viewed as instances of a prime flow model, as can an ordinary water-delivery system. During reasoning about a domain model, any properties of the prime model may be instantiated. For example, an abstract causal relation, such as "a leak of a flow structure causes decreased outflow of the flow process that occurs in that structure," may be instantiated for the water-delivery system as, "a leak of the pipe causes decreased flow of water that flows out of that pipe." Unlike the systems such as STEAMER [15] and QUALEX [4] that generate causal explanation based on qualitative simulation, our approach can directly generate a causal explanation from the models rather than having to interpret results of the simulated behavior and map to corresponding structures and processes of the systems. This approach also has other advantages: it provides a building block capability for reasoning about more complex systems; it offers a compact representation for a potentially very large body of knowledge; and it makes the knowledge available for use in multiple tasks.

The remainder of the paper describes the modeling technique and how to use it to generate causal explanations. The approach is implemented in ICE [12], a blackboard system that reasons about human pulmonary system from first principles. We illustrate an example of causal explanation generated in ICE as a component of the Guardian system [10] which is a prototype system for monitoring medical intensive care patients. We explore an extension of how this technique can be applied when dealing with different granularities and conclude with a discussion on advantages and limitations of this work.

2. A Modeling Technique

A physical system comprises a set of structures organized to support a set of related processes. Domain models explicitly represent the actual structures and processes that make up particular systems.

Definition 2.1. A *domain model* D of any particular physical system is defined as a tuple (C, R) where C is a set of concepts representing system structures, processes and associated parameters; and R is a set of binary relations among elements in C.

Let $\mathbb{D}$ be a class of physical systems that have analogous normal behavior and C^* be a set of concepts representing abstract structures, processes and parameters of the systems of class $\mathbb{D}$. Let R^* be a set of binary relations among elements in C^* and $\leq$ denote a partial ordering relation, subtype, of a type hierarchy.

Definition 2.2. $D^* = (C^*, R^*)$ is defined to be an *abstract normal system* of class $\mathbb{D}$ if $\forall$ D $\in \mathbb{D}$ $\exists$ a subgraph D' of D and a projection π such that i) $\pi D^* = D'$ and ii) $\forall$ c $\in C^*$ and r $\in$ R^*, πc and πr are a concept and a relation in D' respectively, where type(πc) $\leq$ type(c) and type(πr) $\leq$ type(r). In other words, D^* represents the abstraction of the normal states of structures and processes underlying a certain class of physical systems.

Definition 2.3. A *prime model* P of a system class $\mathbb{D}$ is defined to be $D^* \cup$ abn(D^*), where $D^* = (C^*, R^*)$ is an abstract normal system of class $\mathbb{D}$ and abn(D^*) = (F, L) where F is a set of abstract faults and symptoms of systems of class $\mathbb{D}$; and L is a set of relations among elements in F and C^*. Prime models represent the abstraction of both the normal and abnormal behaviors of physical systems.

Examples of domain models include a respiratory system, a circulatory system, a traffic system and an irrigation system. They all behave analogously to a fluid flow system and so can be viewed as instances of the prime flow model. A diffusion system is another example of a prime system model whose domain models can be pulmonary exchange systems where O_2 diffuses from the air (in the lung) to the blood (in the pulmonary capillaries) and CO_2 diffuses from the blood to the air respectively.

Proposition 2.1. If D is a domain model of class $\mathbb{D}$ and P is a prime model of the same class then $\models_P \Rightarrow \models_D$ i.e. every proposition that is true for a prime model is also true for a domain model of the same class.

This simple proposition provides a basis for our reasoning mechanism. In general, reasoning about the domain model may entail instantiation of relevant properties of the corresponding prime model (see also [12]).

2.1. An Illustrated Scenario

Let us consider the typical situation of a post-operative patient whose respiration is assisted by a respirator, which controls various parameters including the patient's breathing rate and the volume of the inspired and expired air (minute volume). One important function of the respiration is to maintain normal levels of partial pressure of CO_2 in arterial blood ($PaCO_2$). A physician sets standard settings for these controls and orders a lab test for $PaCO_2$ which will take about 20 minutes. Observing that the patient's body is very cold, he knows immediately the result of the lab test. Having knowledge of human anatomy and physiology in mind (as shown diagrammatically in figure 1), he explains to his students as follows.

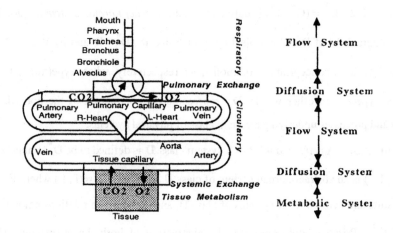

Figure 1. O_2 and CO_2 Transportation

Low body temperature slows down metabolic rate causing a decrease in O_2 consumption in the tissue metabolism. This causes a decrease in CO_2 produced in the tissues. Thus there is decreased CO_2 diffusion from the tissue to blood that flows through the vein, the right heart, the pulmonary artery and the pulmonary capillaries where gas exchange occurs. The amount of CO_2 that diffuses from the capillaries to the alveoli in the lung depends on the partial pressure difference of CO_2 in the two structures. The more CO_2 ventilated out from the alveoli the greater the partial pressure difference and so more CO_2 diffuses from the capillaries to the alveoli. In this case, the patient has a standard breathing rate and minute volume which results in normal ventilation of CO_2. However, there is a decrease of CO_2 in the capillaries, therefore there is a low amount of CO_2 remaining in the artery, *i.e. a condition of low $PaCO_2$ exists.*

To generate such an explanation, the system needs to have knowledge of human anatomy, physiology and some physical laws. We will proceed to see how we represent such knowledge.

2.1.1. Modeling

Our models are represented in a conceptual network [17] whose objects represent concepts (in **bold**) and links represent relations among them (in *italic*). Each link can have an associated reverse link. Domain models represent structures and processes that make up actual particular systems. Each domain model contains a symbolic representation for different concepts such as system components, processes that occur in the corresponding components, and the associated parameters. These concepts are related by appropriate type, part-whole, spatial and temporal relations. Figure 2 illustrates a part of a domain model for the human circulatory system. The model represents circulatory structures (e.g. **r-heart, vein**), circulatory processes (e.g. **deoxygenated-circulation, oxygenated- circulation**) and their relationships including type and part-whole relations (e.g. *includes*), process relations (e.g. *occurs-in*), temporal relations (e.g. *precedes*) and spatial relations (e.g. *continues*). As an example, the model in figure 2 represents the fact that: "*A circulatory system includes an oxygenated circulation process and a deoxygenated circulation process. Both processes are measured by blood flow which has O_2 and CO_2. An oxygenated circulation process includes a circulation process (O-PC) occurring in the pulmonary capillary, which precedes a circulation process (O-V) occurring in the pulmonary vein which precedes a circulation process (O-LH) occurring in the left heart and so on. The circulatory structure, pulmonary capillaries continue to the pulmonary vein which continues to the left heart and so on.*" Note that all the objects and links

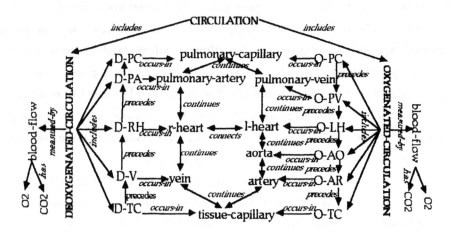

Figure 2. A Domain Model of Human Circulatory System

in the domain model shown in figure 2 correspond to sets of concepts C and relations R in the definition 2.1, respectively. C includes the circulatory structures, processes and parameters of interest. Thus C = { **r-heart, vein, artery,..., oxygenated-circulation, O-PC, O-V,..., blood-flow,...**} and R = { *includes, occurs-in, precedes,...*}.

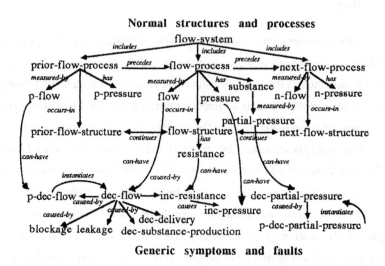

Figure 3. A Prime Flow Model

Many systems have analogous structures, common functions, behaviors and faults, and so are classified in the same class. Prime models explicitly represent the abstraction of both the normal and abnormal states of structures and processes underlying classes of physical systems. Figure 3 illustrates part of a prime flow model. The top part represents normal behavior in which an abstract **flow-process** *occurs-in* an abstract **flow-structure**. The **flow-process** exhibits abstract process relations: *isa* type-of-process (not shown here), *includes* component process (not shown here), *precedes* succeeding-process (**next-flow-process**) and *has* process-measurement (**substance, pressure**). The **flow-structure** exhibits generic structural relations: *isa* type-of-structure, *includes* component-structures, *continues* physically-connected-structures (not shown here). Just as a particular flow system may be viewed as an instance of the prime flow model, each of its constituent structures and processes may be viewed as an instance of the corresponding element of the prime model. For example, the respiratory system, which is a flow system, includes the mouth, which is a flow structure.

In addition to the abstraction of normal structure and behavior of the systems, prime models also abstract generic faults and the presenting symptoms of those faults. For example, for a prime flow model, given the generic symptom, decreased flow of a flow process (**dec-flow**), three potential underlying faults are: 1) blockage of a structure in which the faulty flow process occurs (**blockage**); 2) leakage of a structure in which the faulty flow process occurs (**leakage**); and 3) A decrease of flow in a flow process prior to the faulty flow process (**p-dec-flow**). The bottom part of figure 3 represents abstract faults and symptoms of flow systems. For each type of symptom, abstract faults exhibit relations: *isa* type-of-faults, *caused-by* type-of-fault, and *can-be-had-by* process-measurement.

Referring to definitions 2.2 and 2.3, D^* corresponds to an abstract normal flow system as shown in the top part of figure 3, where $C^* = \{$ **flow-structure**, **prior-flow-structure**,..., **flow-process**, **prior-flow-process**,..., **flow**, **pressure**,...$\}$ and $R^* = \{$ *occurs-in*, *precedes, measured-by,...*$\}$ and abn(D^*) corresponds to a set of abstract flow system faults and symptoms as shown in the bottom part of figure 3, where F = { **blockage, leakage**,..., **dec-flow, inc-resistance**,...} and L = { *causes, can-have,...*}.

2.1.2. Generating Causal Explanations of the System Behavior

Given a domain model and its corresponding prime model, by proposition 2.1 and standard graph operations, causal explanation of the behavior of the domain system model can be generated by the following algorithm.

Inputs: Any subgraph A and subgraph B of the given domain models representing instances of system behaviors at particular structures and processes. For example, subgraphs A and B may correspond to the system fault and symptom, respectively.

Output: Qualitative Causal Explanation of how subgraph A causes subgraph B.

Algorithm:

1. Retrieve a subgraph of the given models that matches or partially matches a given subgraph A by a *Graph Matching* operation.

2. Instantiate the resulting graph by a *Graph Instantiating* operation.

3. Compare the graph instantiated in step 2 to subgraph B. If it matches (i.e. the explanation reaches the given consequence to be explained), terminate, otherwise continue to step 4.

4. Using generic knowledge from the prime model, instantiate new generic causal behavior. From instances of the graph constructed in step 2, if there is an instance of an object in the prime model that has a *causes* link that has not been traversed, traverse *causes* link in the prime model to obtain the abstract causal behavior *x*, say by *Causal Search* operation.

5. Find an object in the domain model that has a context corresponding to an abstract object x found in step 4. This is done by *Context Search* operation. For example, x could be **p-dec-flow** (a decreased flow of a prior flow process) from a prime flow model. By the domain model of human circulatory system in figure 2, suppose a current process is **O-AO** (an oxygenated-circulation process that occurs in the **aorta**). *Context Search* infers **p-dec-flow** to be a decreased flow of **O-LH**, an oxygenated-circulation process in the l-heart which precedes **O-AO**.

6. Precede with step 2 using the context of the object found in step 5.

We will now give an example to show how ICE generates a causal explanation of the scenario described in section 2.1. The domain model considered is a model of the O_2 and CO_2 transportation system, which can be decomposed into five domain models: respiratory, circulatory, pulmonary exchange, tissue exchange and tissue metabolic systems. The conceptual view of the system structures and behaviors is shown in figure 1 where the rightmost column indicates the corresponding prime models of these domain models. Given the above five domain models and the three prime models: flow, diffusion and metabolism, ICE applies the above algorithm to generate a causal explanation of why a patient with cold body temperature and standard ventilation settings would have low $PaCO_2$.

The partial reasoning steps of ICE are shown in figure 4. Starting from the observation **low-body-temperature** which is internally represented as a subgraph (a process "tissue-metabolism" that *occurs* in "tissue" and *has* "dec-temperature") which corresponds to a subgraph A in the algorithm. By step 1, ICE matches the process and structure to corresponding objects in the tissue metabolism domain model (not shown here) and matches the "dec-temperature" to the abstract **dec-temperature** in the prime metabolic model. By step 2, ICE instantiates the graph instance of a process **tissue-metabolism-0** that *occurs* in structure **tissue-0** and *has* **dec-temperature-0**. This graph instance does not match with the subgraph representing **low-$PaCO_2$** (an oxygenated-circulatory process "O-AR" that *occurs* in "artery" and *has* "dec-partial-pressure"), which corresponds to a subgraph B in the algorithm, so proceed to step 4. **Dec-temperature-0** is an instance of an abstract **dec-temperature** in the prime metabolic model (not shown here), stating that in any metabolic process decreased temperature causes decreased metabolic rate. By step 4, ICE identifies the effect to be **dec-metabolic-rate** and by step 5, it identifies the corresponding context of the faulty process as tissue metabolism. Thus, the corresponding effect – a **dec-metabolic-rate** of **tissue-metabolism** that *occurs* in the **tissue** – is instantiated by step 2. Each graph instantiation in step 2 of the algorithm is enclosed by a square box in the figure. The causal generation continues by stepping through

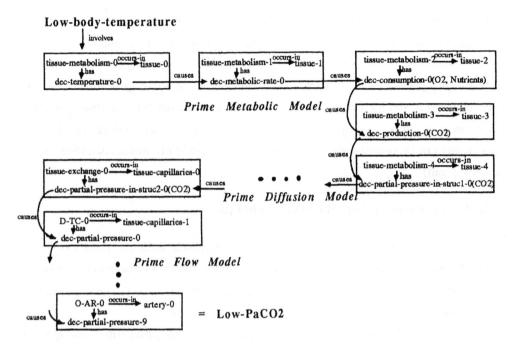

Figure 4. ICE's partial causal explanation of the scenario

relevant processes and structures of the domain models and instantiating causal effects from the corresponding prime models. However, it is usually undesirable and infeasible to enumerate all possible chains of causes underlying an observation. Therefore, the system must make judgments about which types of causal effects are more likely in the current context and use those judgments to prune the search. One approach is to construct a type hierarchy of fault classifications describing the likelihood of each fault causing certain effects (see [12]).

3. Generating Causal Explanation with Multiple Granularities

In many real-world applications we have to deal with large and complex systems. To be able to explain or reason about the physical system behavior at different levels of abstraction provides a powerful tool to enhance user understanding and thus is a desirable capability for any intelligent system.

3.1. Two Dimensions of Granularities - abstraction and aggregation

The idea of using different granularities is hardly new and has been implicit in many AI systems [1, 6]. Hobbs [14] explicitly defines and characterizes granularities and shows how they can be represented and used in the area of natural languages. Greer and McCalla [9] extend and refine Hobbs' notion and introduce two types of granularities: abstraction and aggregation.

Intuitively, abstraction maps from a specific concept to a more general concept whereas aggregation maps from subparts to a part that can be decomposed into such subparts. Greer and McCalla apply their work to the recognition of novice LISP programming strategies.

Applying granularities in physical systems differs from the above application in that they can be viewed in various perspectives, for examples, quantity, structure, function, granularity over time (e.g. a short-term dynamic system, a long-term equilibrium system), and ontology (e.g. liquid can be viewed under three ontologies: piece-of-stuff, molecular-collection and contained-stuff).

3.2. An Extension to our Modeling Technique

In section 2, we have established the notion of abstraction by defining a prime model as an abstract model of domain models which can be viewed as subtypes or instances of the prime model and thus they are classified in the same class. By replacing a subtype relation by a part-whole relation, we can establish the notion of an aggregated model.

Our modeling technique is capable of representing multiple granularities over quantity, structure and function. For example, we have shown in ICE how the respiratory model can be abstracted as a flow system or how the five models of respiratory, pulmonary exchange, circulatory, tissue exchange and tissue metabolism can be aggregated as an O_2 and CO_2 transportation system. Our modeling technique also supports using granularity over different ontology and time. For example, by specifying an appropriate role relation, a circulatory system can be abstracted as a flow system (contained-stuff ontology) or as an equilibrium system (molecular-collection ontology) in the role of mass and energy conservation. Currently ICE can instantiate causal behavior from both a prime flow model (long-term causal model) and a prime equilibrium model (short-term causal model - how a certain dynamic behavior reaches an equilibrium state) to reason about a circulatory system.

We have just begun to extend our research on model aggregation based on explicit part-whole relations. Consider an aggregation over system structures; ICE currently explains the effect of decreased flow of CO_2 in the expired air by stepping through each respiratory structure: alveolus, bronchiole, bronchus, trachea, throat and mouth. By realizing that these structures are part of an upper airway of the respiratory system, by aggregating these structures, ICE can shorten the chain of causal explanation. Structural aggregation (not present in the current system) can be implemented easily by augmenting the above algorithm to generate an intermediate level of a domain model that contains aggregated structures (by traversing part-whole relations in the domain model), before generating a causal explanation (see details in [13]). Functional and ontological aggregation are our ongoing research.

4. Advantages and Concluding Remarks

The proposed approach has several desirable properties. First, by modeling physical systems to explicitly represent conceptual structures, processes and causal behaviors, a qualitative causal explanation can be generated directly from the models without the need for interpretation. Second, by representing multiple domain models as instances of a particular prime model, it provides a compact representation of a potentially very large body of knowledge. Third, by including within a prime model abstract representations of both normal and abnormal mechanisms, it provides a basis for reasoning from first principles about individual domain models. This provides students with a better understanding of physical system behavior. For example, in our previous example, given a causal explanation generated by ICE, a student should be able to explain what would happen to the patient's PaCO2 if his temperature rises or if the nurse lower his breathing rate by using the same principle. Fourth, by representing both prime and domain models declaratively, it provides flexible use of models for various reasoning tasks. Though we have shown how to apply these models for explanation, we have also implemented a diagnostic task that employs the same models with similar reasoning operations [11]. Finally, by modularizing knowledge of different prime and domain systems, it provides building blocks for reasoning about more complex systems as illustrated in an earlier example.

Our approach differs from other systems that generate causal explanation for tutorial purposes in two ways. First it generates a causal explanation of a particular physical system's behavior from general knowledge of causal mechanisms derived from appropriate physical principles rather than a specific causal knowledge about the particular system. Second, unlike the systems that generate causal explanation from qualitative simulation, our approach explicitly represents system structures and processes, instead of sets of qualitative constraints, and thus can directly generate causal explanation for behaviors of the system structures and processes with no additional interpretation required.

5. Limitations and Future Work

In addition to the lack of knowledge, ICE has the following limitations. First, ICE is not interactive enough to allow a flexible user interface. It allows students to ask for explanation of the system behaviors that it predicts and can elaborate the explanation of the current step. Second, ICE currently does not have explicit justifications for its explanation. This is crucial information for use in ICE's control or when ICE is integrated in a dynamic environment. One approach to overcoming this limitation is to develop a language that can explicitly represent justifications. We have started investigating the use of this technique to deal with multiple granularities. Our ongoing research addresses these issues.

REFERENCES

[1] Clancey, W. J., 1985. Heuristic Classification. Artificial Intelligence 27:289-350.

[2] Davis, R., 1983. Reasoning from first principles in electronic trouble shooting. International Journal of Man-Machine Studies, 19:403-423.

[3] de Kleer, J. and J.S. Brown, 1981. Mental Models of Physical Mechanisms and Their Acquisition. In Anderson, (Ed.), Cognitive Skills and Their Acquisition, pp. 285-309, Erlbaum.

[4] de Kleer, J. and J.S. Brown, 1984. A Qualitative Physics based on Confluences. Artificial Intelligence, 24:7-84.

[5] Douglas, S., and Z. Liu, 1989. Generating Causal Explanation from a Cardio-Vascular Simulation. In Proceedings of the Eleventh International Joint Conference on Artificial Intelligence, Detroit.

[6] Falkenhainer, B. and K. Forbus, 1988. Setting up Large-scale qualitative models. In Proceedings of National Artificial Intelligence, August, 1988.

[7] Forbus, K., 1984. Qualitative Process Theory. Artificial Intelligence, 24, 1984.

[8] Genesereth, M., 1984. The use of design description in automated diagnosis. Artificial Intelligence, 24:411-436.

[9] Greer, J. and G. McCalla, 1989. A computational Framework for Granularity and its application to Educational Diagnosis. In Proceedings of the Eleventh International Joint Conference on Artificial Intelligence, Detroit.

[10] Hayes-Roth, B., R. Washington, R. Hewett, M. Hewett and A. Seiver, 1989. Intelligent real-time monitoring and control. In Proceedings of the Eleventh International Joint Conference on Artificial Intelligence, Detroit.

[11] Hewett, R., B. Hayes-Roth and A. Seiver, 1989. Using Prime Models in Model-Based Reasoning. In Proceedings of the Eleventh International Joint Conference on Artificial Intelligence Workshop on Model-Based Reasoning, Detroit.

[12] Hewett, R. and B. Hayes-Roth, 1990. Representing and Reasoning about Physical Systems using Prime Models. To appear in Sowa, Shapiro and Brachman (Eds.), Principles of Semantic Networks, Morgan Kaufmann Publishers, San Mateo, CA.

[13] Hewett, R., 1990. Aggregation in Model-based Reasoning using Prime Models: A Preliminary Report. Technical Report FAU-CS-90-01, Florida Atlantic University, Boca Raton, FL.

[14] Hobbs, J.R., 1985. Granularity. In Proceedings of the Ninth International Joint Conference on Artificial Intelligence, Los Angeles.

[15] Hollan, J.D., E.L. Hutchins and L.Weitzman, 1984. STEAMER: An Interactive Inspectable Simulation-Based Training System. The AI Magazine, Summer 1984, pp. 15-27.

[16] Kuipers, B., 1987. Qualitative simulation as causal explanation. IEEE Trans. Syst., Man., Cybern., 17(3):432-444.

[17] Sowa, J., 1984. Conceptual Structures: Information Processing in Mind and Machine. Addison-Wesley, Reading, MA.

[18] Williams, M.D., J.D. Hollan and A.L. Stevens, 1982. Human Reasoning About a Simple Physical System. In Gentner, D. and A.L. Steven (Eds.), Mental Models, pp. 131-154, Lawrence Erlbaum Associates, Publishers, Hillsdale, NJ.

PLANNING IN CONCEPTUAL NETWORKS[*]

Leixuan Yang

Department of Computer Science, University of Ottawa
Ottawa, Ontario, Canada K1N 6N5

Stan Szpakowicz[**]

Computer Science Department, University of the Witwatersrand
P.O. Wits, Johannesburg 2050, South Africa

In the classical planning problems, the world is in a particular state at any given instant. The effect of an action is to cause the world to move from one state to another. We are given a set of allowable actions, a set of possible initial states, and a set of acceptable goal states. Told that the world is currently in one of the possible initial states, we are then asked to find a sequence of allowable actions that, when executed, will leave the world in one of the acceptable goal states (Pednault 1986).

Two formal languages exist for planning problems: the situation calculus (McCarthy and Hayes 1969), and the STRIPS representation of actions (Fikes and Nilsson 1971). Both are domain-specific rather than general-purpose knowledge representation (KR) languages, so that it is difficult or inefficient to use them to represent other kinds of knowledge, for example, inheritance hierarchies. On the other hand, although "reasoning about actions and plans is seen as fundamental to the development of intelligent machines that are capable of dealing effectively with real-world problems" (Georgeff 1987), among the general-purpose KR languages, such as logic, frames, Conceptual Structures (Sowa 1984), only logic has been demonstrably useful in planning. The examples of systems that show how the logic can be used in planning include Green's problem solving system (1969), and Warren's WARPLAN (1974). In this paper, we show the possibility of representing actions for the classical planning problem in Conceptual Network. Conceptual Network (in short: CN) is an associational KR language, originally developed for a text analysis system (Szpakowicz 1990).

Our view of the world which underlies a CN representation is that there are a number of instances (objects) in the world. In every state, each instance has a particular *ontological status*, which is essentially its type. Instances are inter-related in a particular way. The effect of an action is to cause the world to change its state. Different world states are reflected by the different ontological status of the instances and the different relationships between those instances. Our work might offer a new way of approaching the planning problem.

There are four basic elements in CN: concepts, relations, structures and conditions. Knowledge is represented by a combination of these elements. *Concepts* represent a number of instances in the world. We use I(c) to denote the set of instances of concept c. Concept c1 is called a subclass of concept c2 (and c2 a superclass of c1) if and only if I(c1) is a subset of I(c2). The concepts are broadly classified into three groups: *objects, activities* and *properties*.

Relations capture the relationships that hold between concepts. If concepts c1 and c2 are related by relation R, and there is no restriction has been stated for this relation, then for any instance i1 of c1 there exists an instance i2 of c2 such that i1 can be related to i2 by R. *Structures* are used to represent *complex concepts*, composed of other concepts. The available structures are *individual, sequence, collection, tuple, union,* and *intersection*.

---

[*] This work was supported by the Natural Sciences and Engineering Research Council of Canada, and by Cognos Inc.
  The full version of this paper has been published as a report of the Dept. of Computer Science, Univ. of Ottawa (TR-91-03).

[**] On leave from the University of Ottawa.

Conditions represent contextual restrictions on the concepts involved in a relation. A condition attached to $R(c1, c2)$, where R is a relation between concepts $c1$ and $c2$, can be regarded as the description of a subclass $c11$ of $c1$ and a subclass $c22$ of $c2$; only $c11$ and $c22$ can be in the relation R. The condition is a logical expression built of *simple conditions*, each describing a number of instances of $c1$ or $c2$ by giving either their relationships to other instances or concepts which have them as instances. There are two kinds of conditions: *preconditions* and *postconditions*. A precondition attached to the relation $R(c1, c2)$ must be satisfied by instances $i1$ of $c1$ and $i2$ of $c2$ before $i1$ and $i2$ can be in this relation. A postcondition attached to $R(c1, c2)$ is treated as satisfied by $i1$ and $i2$ after $i1$ and $i2$ have entered this relation.

Let an instance i play a role in an action $\mathbf{A}$—the ontological status of i or its relation to other instances may be changed after $\mathbf{A}$. i is called a *related instance* of $\mathbf{A}$. The prerequisite of an action can be regarded as the prerequisites for its related instances. The prerequisite for an instance i is a restriction either on the ontological status of i or on the necessary relationships involving i. The first is called *ontological restriction*, the second — *relational restriction*. The effects of an action are considered as the effects on its related instances. The effect on an instance i indicates the change of the ontological status of i and/or the changes of its relationships with other instances.

An ontological restriction is represented as a condition of CN in the following form:

$\quad$ [this_slot is c1] $\hfill$ (1)

c1 is a concept. this_slot in a condition attached to relation R($c1$, $c2$) represents $c2$, this_frame represents $c1$.

Let (1) serve as a precondition of relation r($\mathbf{A}$, c), where $\mathbf{A}$ is an action and c is a concept. (1) describes a prerequisite for the ontological status of i_0, an instance of c, which is to play a role in $\mathbf{A}$. If (1) is a postcondition of $r(\mathbf{A}, c)$, it describes the effect of $\mathbf{A}$ on the ontological status of i_0 which has played a role in $\mathbf{A}$.

A relational restriction on i, a related instance of an action $\mathbf{A}$, restricts its relationships with other related instances of $\mathbf{A}$. A relational restriction is represented as a condition of CN in the following form:

$\quad$ [r1 of this_slot is r2 of this_frame] $\hfill$ (2)

Let (2) be a precondition of relation r($\mathbf{A}$, c), and i_0 an instance of c, which is to play a role in $\mathbf{A}$. (2) describes a prerequisite for the relationships of i_0 with another related instance of $\mathbf{A}$. If (2) is a postcondition, it describes the effect of $\mathbf{A}$ on the relationship of i_0 (which has played a role in $\mathbf{A}$) with other related instances of $\mathbf{A}$.

Generally speaking, an action can be applied to a state iff there exist instances which can play the required roles in the action. Suppose that a role in action $\mathbf{A}$ must be played by an instance of concept c. This may be represented by relation $r(\mathbf{A}, c)$. Let an instance i play the role r in an instance $a1$ of $\mathbf{A}$. This is denoted by $r(a1, i)$. If no precondition is attached to this relation, any instance of c can play the role r in an instance of $\mathbf{A}$. If an ontological restriction [*this_slot is c1*] is a precondition of this relation, an instance i can play the role r in an instance of $\mathbf{A}$ if and only if *instance_of(i, c)* & *instance_of(i, c1)*[***] . If the precondition contains a relational restriction [*r1 of this_slot is r2 of this_frame*], an instance i can play this role r in the instance $a1$ if and only if there exists an instance j such that *instance_of(i, c)* & $r2(a1, j)$ & $r1(i, j)$.

After an action, a new state will arise. It can be obtained by changing the indicated ontological status of the related instances and changing the indicated relationships between the related instances in the previous world state. All changes are indicated by the postconditions in the frame of the action. If a postcondition [*this_slot is c1*] is attached to the relation $r(\mathbf{A}, c)$, then after an instance $a1$ of $\mathbf{A}$, the ontological status of the instance i of c which

---

[***] *instance_of* relates an instance to its concept, that is, to the set it is an element of.

plays this role in *a1* must be changed to *c1*, i.e. *instance_of(i, c1)*. If a postcondition [*r1 of this_slot is r2 of this_frame*] is attached to the relation $r(\mathbf{A}, c)$, then after an instance *a1* of $\mathbf{A}$, *j* is the instance which is related to the instance *i* of *c* by *r1*, i.e. *r1(i, j)*, where *r(a1, i)* & *r2(a1, j)*.

If A is an action, and S', S'' are world states, applying A to state S' and achieving state S'' will be written as A(S', S''). The classical planning problem consists in finding, for a given initial state S_0 and a final state S_f, a sequence of actions A_1, A_2, ..., A_k such that

$$A_1(S_0, S_1), A_2(S_1, S_2), ..., A_k(S_{k-1}, S_f).$$

We use forward chaining in our system. We start from S_0, selecting an action A_i applicable to S_0, then reach a new state S_1 such that $A_i(S_0, S_1)$. For every new state we would repeat the same procedure of selecting, until the final state S_f would be reached. If no action could be applied to a state S_j, we would backtrack to the previous state S_{j-1} and select another action applicable to S_{j-1}.

Regarding the frame problem: at any instant, only a single description of the world is maintained, and updated to reflect the result of any particular action—this contrasts with the situation calculus approach. We record, the actions with their instantiation in order to be able to undo the changes when we backtrack.

Comparing our approach with STRIPS: after the execution of an action in STRIPS a new world description is obtained via the *delete* and *add* lists. In CN, it is obtained via the postconditions, which describe the changes of the relations between the instances of the world. We do not argue that CN offer a better solution for the planning problem. We do show, that although CN is a general-purpose KR formalism, it also can be used as a formalism for the planning problem. Having a formalism which is applicable to various AI problems may help design AI system. It is a disadvantage to have many formalisms in one problem-solving system. If we use CN, we can not only represent actions (as shown in this paper), but also inheritance hierarchies (Yang and Szpakowicz 1990).

References

Fikes, R. E. and N. J. Nilsson (1971) "STRIPS: a new approach to the application of theorem proving to problem solving". *Artificial Intelligence*, vol. 2, pp. 189-208.

Georgeff, M. P. (1987) "Planning". *Ann. Rev. Computer Science*, vol. 2, pp. 359-400.

Green, C. (1969) "Application of Theorem Proving to Problem Solving". *Proc 1st IJCAI*, pp. 219-239.

McCarthy, J. and P. J. Hayes (1969) "Some Philosophical Problems from the Standpoint of Artificial Intelligence". *Machine Intelligence*, vol. 4, pp. 463-502.

Pednault, E. P. D. (1986) "Formulating Multiagent, Dynamic-world Problems in the Classical Planning Framework". M. P. Georgeff and A. L. Lansky (eds.) *Reasoning about Actions and Plans: Proc of the 1986 workshop*, Morgan Kaufmann, pp. 47-82.

Sowa, J. F. (1984) *Conceptual Structures: Information Processing in Mind and Machine*. Addison-Wesley.

Szpakowicz, S. (1990) "Semi-Automatic Acquisition of Conceptual Structure from Technical Texts". *Int J of Man-Machine Studies*, vol. 33, pp. 385-397.

Warren, D. H. D. (1974) "WARPLAN: a system for generating plans". *DGL Memo 76*, University of Edinburgh.

Yang, L. and S. Szpakowicz (1990) "Inheritance in Conceptual Network", submitted for publication.

EMPIRICAL STUDY OF THE MEANING OF THE HEDGE "VERY"

Patricia Cerrito[1], Waldemar Karwowski[2], and Krzysztof Ostaszewski[1]
[1]Department of Mathematics
[2]Center for Industrial Ergonomics, Department of Industrial Engineering
University of Louisville
Louisville, KY 40292, U.S.A.
FAX: 1-502-588-7397
e-mail addresses: pbcerr01@ulkyvm, w0karw01@ulkyvm, kmosta01@ulkyvx

ABSTRACT

In an empirical study designed to test the meaning of the linguistic hedge VERY, and using statistical techniques, the concentration operator is shown to model the human perception in the context of load heaviness better than the shift operator and the fuzzy normalization operator.

INTRODUCTION

The theory of fuzzy sets developed by L.A. Zadeh [5,6] has been successfully applied to modeling all forms of human reasoning. In [8] Zadeh introduces the concept of a linguistic variable whose values are natural language words identified with certain fuzzy sets via a specified rule. The linguistic hedge VERY modifies the value of a linguistic variable in a manner resembling the natural language. Several models of this hedge have been proposed: the concentration operator, see Schmucker [4]; the horizontal shift operator, see: Hersh and Caramazza [1], Macvicar-Wheelen [3]; and fuzzy normalization operator, see Karwowski and Ostaszewski [2]. In this work we analyze the applicability of those operators in modification of the values of the linguistic variable *load heaviness*.

THE EXPERIMENT

To test the above models, nine subjects, all male, whose weights and heights were known and used to derive a composite strength parameter, lifted boxes with loads ranging from 10 to 65 pounds, in increments of 5 pounds. They were asked to lift each box repeatedly until they were certain that they could make a judgement about the box, as if the task was to be performed for an eight-hour work day. The subjects then filled out a questionnaire concerning each box. They were asked to assign a number between 0 and 10 which would best describe the degrees of membership to which each of the boxes belonged to the following four categories: HEAVY, VERY HEAVY, LIGHT, VERY LIGHT. The resulting numbers were normalized by dividing by 10.*

STATISTICAL ANALYSIS

We have regressed the membership function $f_{VH}(x)$ for the VERY HEAVY category against $f_H(x)$, the membership function for HEAVY to get:

$$f_{VH}(x) = .89 f_H(x) - .027 \text{ with a correlation of } R^2 = .859.$$

---

* The exact data from the experiment is available upon request from the authors.

If we also regress against the actual load heaviness (denoted here by $LOAD$), R^2 increases slightly to .867 with

$$f_{VH}(x) = .78 f_H(x) + .003(LOAD) - .09.$$

Both models are highly significant. The results clearly indicate that the fuzzy set-theoretical model claiming the existence of a relationship between membership function of HEAVY and VERY HEAVY is justified. Analogous analysis for the membership functions of LIGHT and VERY LIGHT produced

$$f_{VL}(x) = 1.39 f_L(x) + .004(LOAD) - .023 f_L(x)(LOAD) - .19 \text{ with } R^2 = .826.$$

The results indicate the existence of a relationship and the applicability of the fuzzy set-theoretic model of the hedge VERY.

In order to test the claim of the applicability of the concentration operator for the hedge VERY, we have also regressed the values of $f_{VH}(x)$ on the values of $(f_H(x))^2$. We obtained:

$$f_{VH}(x) = .909 \left(f_H(x)\right)^2 + .062 \text{ with } R^2 = .846,$$

indicating the applicability of the concentration operator in this setting. Similarly

$$f_{VL}(x) = .892 \left(f_L(x)\right)^2 + .02 \text{ with } R^2 = .79.$$

The results clearly indicate that the concentration operator is an excellent model for the hedge VERY.

Next we tested the applicability of the translation operator, as suggested by Hersh and Caramazza [1] and Macvicar-Wheelen [3]. The exact value of the appropriate shift is difficult to exhibit and may require additional studies. The best model obtained by us was:

$$f_{VH}(x) = .403 \left(f_{H1}(x)\right)^2 + .009(LOAD) - .179 \text{ with } R^2 = .657,$$

where $f_{H1}(x) = f_H(x - 5)$ represents the shifted HEAVY membership function. We have concluded that the shift operator is less applicable than the classical concentration operator.

Finally we have tested the fuzzy normalization operator of Karwowski and Ostaszewski [2]. This was done by introducing the modified functions $f_{H2}((x + 65)/2) = (f_H(x))^2$ and $f_{L2}(x/2) = (f_L(x))^2$. The results were

$$f_{VH}(x) = .574 f_{H2}(x) + .045 \text{ with } R^2 = .324,$$

and

$$\dot{f}_{VL}(x) = .54 f_{L2}(x) - .165 \text{ with } R^2 = .155.$$

The operator turns out to be the least appropriate of the three considered.

As the last conclusion of our statistical analysis we present below the graphical representations of the regression lines of load lifted heaviness versus the value of the membership function for LIGHT vs. VERY LIGHT and HEAVY vs. VERY HEAVY. They show the respective pairs of lines almost parallel stressing the underlying relationship between the values of the linguistic variable studied.

674

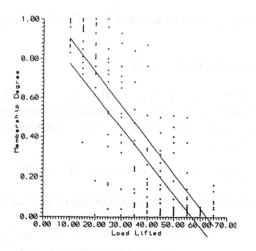

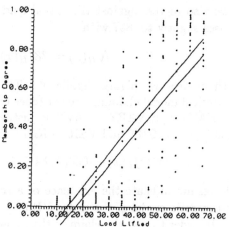

***** Light category
***** Very light category
    Light regression: y=-.017x+1.077
    v light regression:y=-.016x-0.941

***** Heavy category
***** Very heavy category
    Heavy regression: y= .016x-.236
    v heavy regression:y= .016x-.941

REFERENCES

[1] Hersch, H.M., and Caramazza, A., A fuzzy set approach to modifiers and vagueness in natural language, *Journal of Experimental Psychology: General* **105**(3)(1976), 254-276.

[2] Karwowski, W., and Ostaszewski, K., Linguistic hedges and fuzzy normalization operator, *Proceedings of the Third Congress of the International Fuzzy Systems Association*, Seattle, Washington, U.S.A., 1989, pp. 528-531.

[3] Macvicar-Wheelen, P.J., Fuzzy sets, the concept of height, and the hedge VERY, *IEEE Transactions on Systems, Man, and Cybernetics* vol. SMC-8, 6(1978), 507-511.

[4] Schmucker, K.J., *Fuzzy Sets, Natural Language, Computations, and Risk Analysis*, Computer Science Press, 1984.

[5] Zadeh, L.A., Calculus of fuzzy restrictions, in: *Fuzzy Sets and Their Applications to Cognitive and Decision Processes*, edited by L.A. Zadeh, K.S. Fu, K. Tanaka, and M. Shimura, Academic Press, New York, 1975.

[6] Zadeh, L.A., Fuzzy sets, *Information and Control* 8(1965), 338-353.

[7] Zadeh, L.A., Outline of a new approach to the analysis of complex systems and decision processes, *IEEE Transactions on Systems, Man, and Cybernetics* 3(1973), 28-44.

[8] Zadeh, L.A., The concept of a linguistic variable and its application to approximate reasoning, *Information Science*, part I: 8(1975), 199-249, part II: 8(1975), 301-357, part III: 9(1975), 43-80.

Kernel knowledge versus belt knowledge in default reasoning: a logical approach

M.A. Nait Abdallah

Department of Computer Science
University of Western Ontario
London, Ontario, Canada

Abstract

In this paper, we formalize in logic the dichotomy between *kernel* (or *hard*) *knowledge* versus *belt* (or *soft*) *knowledge* introduced by Popper and Lakatos in the philosophical logic of scientific discovery. The logic we obtain, *default ionic logic*, generalizes Reiter's default logic to a *continuous* and *monotonic* reasoning system. Default ionic logic gives a solution so some well-known non-monotonic reasoning problems: Lottery paradox, weak implication, disjunctive information, default transformation, normal versus non-normal defaults, the Yale shooting problem and several of its variants, Haugh's Assassin problem, Kautz's Vanishing car problem, and Haugh's Robot problem.

1 Introduction

In this paper we investigate the proof theory and model theory of default reasoning. We have as a goal a general theory for combining defaults, with the possibility of having *nested defaults*, and a logical tool for choosing among defaults for implementation purposes. We also would like to have a model theory for default reasoning that is a simple generalization of the usual Tarskian semantics for classical logic. The approach developed here is based on the novel notions of *default ion*, *partial model* and *regular model* of a *default logic program*. A preliminary report on this research was published in [6], where the notion of default ion was first introduced.

We recall that a *default* in the sense of Reiter [9] is an inference rule of the form $\dfrac{a \;:\; b}{c}$ where a is the requisite, b is the justification and c is the conclusion. For example, the statement "*Birds typically fly*" may be expressed as: $\dfrac{bird(x) \;:\; fly(x)}{fly(x)}$ or $\dfrac{:\; bird(x) \to fly(x)}{bird(x) \to fly(x)}$. The second default has no requisite (i.e. a requisite that is vacuously true.)

The calculus on extensions developed by Reiter [9] has yielded a kind of reasoning that has been called *non-monotonic*. This non-monotonicity is the source of some major problems for implementers and theoreticians alike. Indeed, given a default theory, it is extremely hard in general to construct its associated set(s) of "theorems" (called *extension(s)*), because what is provable both determines and is determined by what is not provable. Thus, in the general case, we are well beyond recursive or recursively enumerable sets, i.e. well beyond ordinary notions of computability.

We prefer the phrase "*reasoning with partial information*" to "*non-monotonic reasoning*" for naming the kind of reasoning we investigate in this paper. We shall attempt to justify this preference in this introduction. Our reasons will become clearer throughout the paper.

Several problems have been left open in Reiter's logic. For example,the applicability of *modus tollens*, a fundamental tool in resolution, is unclear. Thus L. Sombé [10] p 143 indicates, without any justification, that the contrapositive of default $\dfrac{u \;\; : \;\; v}{v}$ should be $\dfrac{\neg v \;\; : \;\; \neg u}{\neg u}$, but that such a contraposition operation is missing in default logic. On the other hand, Poole [8], encountering a similar problem, writes: *"Assume we have the following Theorist fragment:*

$$\textbf{default } \mathit{birds fly} \;\; : \;\; \mathit{bird(x)} \rightarrow \mathit{flies(x)}$$

... Using the default we can also explain ¬bird(b) from ¬flies(b). ... Theorist users have found that they needed a way to say "this default should not be applicable in this case" [8] p 15. He then proceeds to introduce an operational device he calls *constraints*, *"a very useful mechanism in practice"* [8]. These *constraints*, however, have no clear logical semantics.

The *Yale shooting problem* has also been a major challenge to default logic. In [2], Hanks and McDermott show that default logic, in its current form, does not allow to solve the following problem: *"After performing an action, things normally remain as they were. After loading a gun, the gun is loaded. After a man is shot with a loaded gun, he dies. After loading the gun, waiting and shooting Fred, is it the case that will Fred die?"* They show that the default logic formalization of this problem provides two extensions: one where Fred is alive, and one where he is dead. No choice is shown to be preferable. Etherington [1] dismisses this problem as one of *"inadequate axiomatic formalization, rather than inadequacies of non-monotonic reasoning"*, but he does not elaborate on what an adequate default logic formalization would be.

In Reiter's system, defaults are expressed by means of *proof rules*, and each time the problem under consideration is changed, the proof rules are also changed, and *stricto sensu* the logic is changed. Thus, in a way, each default theory (W, D) is a logic in itself, where the inference rules in D are (generally) non-computable. *Open defaults* are more like inference rule schemes because "variables" can be instantiated only in very specific places: in a default rule, variables are object variables belonging to the object language. This contrasts with an inference rule such as *modus ponens* $\dfrac{\alpha \; , \;\; \alpha \rightarrow \beta}{\beta}$, where α and β can just be any formulae; in other words, α and β are plain *metavariables* belonging to the *metalanguage*. *Closed defaults* work only for very specific values of their premisses, namely those *fixed* (constant) values given in their statement.

It is not clear whether these different *default logic* proof rules are instances of some universal proof rule. Classical logic, on the other hand, uses a small fixed number of proof rules, such as modus ponens. Is there an intrinsic reason why, in non-monotonic reasoning using defaults, we should have (potentially) infinitely many such proof rules?

So far, much of the theory of default reasoning has relied upon non-monotonic techniques. Abandoning *monotonicity*, however, entails a severe cost for the computer scientist. This cost has two aspects. From a logical point of view, the notion of deduction as we know it simply vanishes, and some algorithmic versions of it can only be retrieved in very special cases (e.g. normal defaults). From a semantic point of view, we are no better off. Since we are abandoning *monotonicity*, *continuity* in Scott's sense is also gone.

Non-continuity (in Scott's sense) in Reiter's system means that, in general, the final solution of a problem cannot be obtained as a limit of continuous process generating better and better approximations of this solution. This lack of continuity property creates problems in situations where the notion of continuity seems to be relevant. One such example is provided by the "Yale shooting problem" mentioned above, where for some unknown reason, the gun may get unloaded during the waiting period, an obvious "discontinuity", at least in the intuitive sense.

This absence of monotonicity and continuity in default reasoning may seem unsatisfactory, since after all, programs written in *classical* programming languages are nothing but formal specifications of *partial* (computable) *functions*, and both *monotonicity* and *Scott-continuity* are fundamental tools for studying these programs and partial functions.

Now the question is the following. Since default logic theories are formal specifications of *partial* (hopefully computable) *descriptions of the world*, can we use monotonicity and Scott-like continuity for studying at least some of these theories and partial descriptions? If the answer is yes, to what extent can this be done? Can we solve that way some of the aforementioned problems with Reiter's system? When continuity is not available, can we say something about *discontinuity*? (For example, in real function theory, we can in some cases isolate discontinuity points, and say something about the function in the neighborhood of those points.)

The question may seem unorthodox, even heretical, in the context of *non-monotonic reasoning*. But if there is a general *theory of computation* for computer science objects, then surely not everything that has proved so useful in the study of *function-oriented programming languages* should be thrown away when we want to deal with *knowledge-oriented programming languages*. Or should it? What is the precise link between the semantics of function-oriented programming languages and the semantics of knowledge-oriented programming languages?

In the research reported in this paper, we lay some preliminary foundations for studying and answering these questions.

2 Principles guiding our approach

The principles guiding our approach are as follows.

Logic *is* monotonic. The idea here is that the apparent non-monotonicity of default reasoning is due to some essential parameters of the reasoning being hidden. Their hiding is the sole cause of non-monotonicity. The display of these *hidden parameters* shows the obvious monotonicity of the logic involved.

We want to link non-monotonic reasoning to the rest of computation theory. Monotonicity, continuity and its counterpart, discontinuity, should be examined. Complete partial orders, and other bundle-theoretic structures [5] play a central role in computation theory. We want to elucidate the role of these structures in non-monotonic reasoning.

Classical logic theories are syntactic objects that specify *models* (of the world).

Default logic theories are syntactic objects that specify *partial models* (of the world).

Syntax should be clearly separated from the *semantics*, by providing a *proof theory* on the one hand, and a Tarskian *model theory* on the other hand. Tarski defines truth in terms of satisfaction, and satisfaction is a relation between (open) sentences and interpretations. We shall follow the same method in our framework. The only difference is that our interpretations are *partial* because we are dealing with partial descriptions of the world.

We attempt to *rehabilitate the classical point of view* that *reasoning amounts to establishing logical consequences* in the sense of the deductive system we have developed. The classical properties of deduction in predicate logic should be preserved, and no additional *operational* features, such as Poole's [8] *constraints* saying when modus tollens should not be applied to a default, should be needed.

In accordance with classical logic, we want a framework with as few proof rules as possible. These proof rules should be fixed once and for all. They should not change every time the problem is changed. Only the statements should change when the problem changes.

Defaults are not used simply as *tools* for approximating propositional (or first-order) theories.

Rather, we should be developing a logic on its own, where *defaults are considered as statements*, i.e. as first-class citizens, that should be studied on their own.

The rational (common sense) agent to be implemented is reasoning at the syntactic level (i.e., using the terminology of this paper, at the *default ionic logic* level) and not at the extension level (extension in the sense of Reiter).

The rational agent to be implemented attempts to reason about the (unknown) world. The syntactic theory he has about that unknown world specifies possibly more than one partial model. The agent may, or may not, be able to choose among those partial models. Each partial model can be mapped to a propositional (or predicate) logic theory. These theories correspond to Reiter's extensions.

We aim at a *general theory for combining defaults*, with the possibility of having *nested defaults*, and a *logical tool for choosing among defaults* for implementation purposes. It should be clear from the beginning that, in our approach, *we are not using defaults* in the usual sense (e.g. for building extensions), but *we are talking about defaults*. In other words, we are using defaults the way predicate formulae are used in predicate logic, i.e. as the basic building stones upon which we are going to build our proofs. In our framework, defaults are not auxiliary tools to build *extensions*, (which would then provide something like a semantics for the formulae) they are the basic building stones of the system. The semantics, on the other hand, is clearly separated from the syntax, and is given by a notion of *interpretation*.

The two central concepts of programming language theory are the notion of a *program* at the syntax level, and the notion of a *partial function* at the model-theoretic level. Programs are simply used to *specify* partial functions.

In the approach we are presenting in this paper, the two central concepts of default reasoning theory are the notion of a *default ionic formula* at the syntax level, and the notion of a *partial model* at the model-theoretic level. Default ionic formulae are used to *specify* partial models. The precise mathematical meaning of these terms is discussed in details in [7]. We shall limit ourselves here to analysing some foundational principles.

3 Default ions

The basic idea of our approach is the same as the one used by D. Scott when he made "*absence of information/termination*" into an element of the domain (of computation) called *bottom*. Essentially, we make Reiter's default

$$\frac{: n}{p}$$

into an element of a set of generalized formulae, called *ionic logic formulae*, and denote it by the formula:

$$(n, p)_\star$$

Default ion $(n, p)_\star$ should be read: If n is consistent with our beliefs (i.e. current logical scope), then infer (or assert) p. For the sake of having a shorter notation, default ion $(n, n)_\star$ will be sometimes abbreviated as $[n]$. The intuitive meaning of $[n] = (n, n)_\star$ is *If 'n' is consistent with the current context, then assert n*. In other words, we "weakly" assert n. Statements of the form $[n]$ will be called *weak statements* and they shall be read "*weakly n*". Symmetrically, statements from "usual" logic will be called *strong statements*.

The default

$$\frac{m : n}{p}$$

will be translated by the ionic formula

$$m \rightarrow (n, p)_\star$$

In the terminology of default logic, m is the prerequisite, n is the justification, and p is the conclusion.

As mentioned earlier, the introduction of default ions into propositional (or predicate) logic is inspired from Dana Scott's introduction of a *bottom element* into denotational semantics. With the bottom element, denotational semantics can discuss non-terminating computations and partial functions. The bottom element is used to fill-in the "holes" in the definition of a partial function.

Default ions in our theory play very much the same role: they are used to fill-in the "holes" in partially specified propositional (or predicate logic) theories. We use these ions to discuss *partial models* of the world. These partial models of the world we formalize by means of partial interpretations we call *default interpretations*.

A *default ion* is nothing but a statement labelled by its justification(s), if any. If the label is empty, i.e. there are no justifications, then we simply have a statement from classical propositional (or predicate) logic. If the label is non-empty, then we have indeed a default ion that attempts to fill some gap in our knowledge, in the case the justifications supporting that attempt do not fall apart in the current logical context. Our notion of justification is related to the notion of justification used in *truth maintenance systems*.

4   First-order predicate default ionic logic

We shall use the following alphabets: a set R of relation symbols, a set F of function symbols, a set V of object variables, and a set Ξ of *justification variables*. Elements of Ξ will be 0-ary relation variables; they will be denoted by $\gamma, \varphi, \ldots \in \Xi$. We shall also use the usual connectives plus the single ionic operator $(\ . \ , \ . \ )_\star$.

The definition of our logic displays a striking dissimilarity between our approach and Reiter's approach. In Reiter's logic, justifications lead an *underground life* controlling the actual value of the extensions associated with the given default theory. The way this control is performed is not explicit in the syntax of the logic. In our approach, justifications are first-class citizens, both syntactically and semantically, and the way they intervene in the reasoning is analyzed and displayed in detail.

The *terms* of first-order default ionic logic are defined as usual. The formulae are called (first-order) *default ionic formulae*. They are recursively defined as follows

- atoms : $r(t_1, \ldots, t_n)$, where $r \in R_n$, and t_i are terms

- closure under connectives : $\wedge, \vee, \neg, \rightarrow$

- closure under the ionic operator : For every *enumerated* set of formulae $\Phi = \{f_1, \ldots, f_n\}$ and formula g, the expression $(\Phi, g)_\star$ is a formula. For every justification variable $\gamma \in \Xi$, and formula g, the expression $(\gamma, g)_\star$ is a formula. Formulae of the form $(\Phi, g)_\star$ and $(\gamma, g)_\star$ thus constructed are called *default ions*. The intuitive meaning of *default ion* $(\{f_1, \ldots, f_n\}, g)_\star$ is as follows: *If all of the f_i are simultaneously consistent with the current set of beliefs (logical context), then one can assert g.*

- closure under existential and universal quantification over objects: If g is a formula, and if x is a variable, then $(\forall x g)$, and $(\exists x g)$ are also formulae.

- closure under existential and universal quantification over justifications: if g is a formula, and if γ is a justification variable, then $(\forall \gamma g)$, and $(\exists \gamma g)$ are also formulae.

The intuitive meaning of default ionic formula $\exists \gamma (\gamma, g)_\star$ is that g holds under some justification, or g has some justification. The statement "Statement g has no justification" could be expressed by the formula $\neg \exists \gamma (\gamma, g)_\star$.

Example

An example of ionic formula (here of nested default) is given by the following statement. *If supporters of sdi are not pacifists, and if it is consistent to believe that republicans typically support sdi, then infer that republicans, typically, are not pacifists.* In a (generalized) syntax a la Reiter, this would be expressed as follows.

$$\frac{\forall x (s(x) \to \neg p(x)) \; : \; \forall x \dfrac{r(x) \; : \; s(x)}{s(x)}}{\forall x \dfrac{r(x) \; : \; \neg p(x)}{\neg p(x)}}$$

In our syntax, this is expressed as:

$$\forall x (s(x) \to \neg p(x)) \to (\forall x (r(x) \to [s(x)]), \forall x (r(x) \to [\neg p(x)]))_\star$$

As one can see Reiter's syntax is more readable (especially if one omits universal quantifiers) but ours is more general.

4.1 Axioms and proof rules for first-order predicate default ionic logic (FDIL)

Axioms of our first-order logic are of two kinds: *axioms inherited from predicate logic*, and specific axioms dealing with *default ions*.

The set *Axioms* of *logical axioms* of first-order default ionic logic is the set of all formulae of the following forms. Our notations are as follows : a, b, c, f, g, h, k, j are arbitrary default ionic formulae, J, Γ and Δ are arbitrary finite sets of ionic formulae, and t are terms.

4.1.1 Axioms inherited from propositional default ionic logic

- $a \to (b \to a)$
- $a \to (b \to c) \to ((a \to b) \to (a \to c))$
- $(\neg a \to \neg b) \to (b \to a)$
- justification elimination : $j \wedge (j \wedge k, g)_\star \to (k, g)_\star$
- elementary transformations : 1. $(\Gamma, a \to b)_\star \to (a \to (\Gamma, b)_\star)$
  2. $(a \to (\Gamma, b)_\star) \to (\Gamma, a \to b)_\star$
  3. $(\Gamma, (\Gamma, a)_\star \to b)_\star \to (\Gamma, a \to b)_\star$
- $\vee$-intro in justification : $(\Gamma \cup \{j\}, g)_\star \wedge (\Gamma \cup \{k\}, g)_\star \to (\Gamma \cup \{j \vee k\}, g)_\star$
- $\wedge$-intro in conclusion : $(\Gamma, f)_\star \wedge (\Gamma, g)_\star \to (\Gamma, f \wedge g)_\star$
- Thinning : $(\Gamma, g)_\star \to (\Gamma \cup \Delta, g)_\star$
- Empty set of justifications : $(\emptyset, g)_\star \to g$
- Justification introduction : $g \to (\Gamma, g)_\star$
- Abstraction : 1. $(\Gamma, (\Delta, g)_\star)_\star \to (\Gamma \cup \Delta, g)_\star$
  2. $(\Gamma \cup \Delta, g)_\star \to (\Gamma, (\Delta, g)_\star)_\star$

4.1.2 Quantification logic axioms inherited from first-order logic

1. $\forall x(g \to f) \to (g \to \forall x f)$, where variable x has no free occurrence in g.

2. $\forall x \neg g \leftrightarrow \neg \exists x g$.

3. $\forall x g(x) \to g(t)$, if t is free for x in g.

4.1.3 Axioms that are specific to first-order default ions

- $\forall x(\Gamma, g)_\star \to (\Gamma, \forall x g)_\star$, if variable x does not occur free in Γ.

- $\forall \gamma(\gamma, g)_\star \to (\Delta, g)_\star$, if Δ is some justification variable, or justification set which contains no occurrence of justification variables.

4.1.4 Proof rules

- J-modus ponens : $\dfrac{(\Gamma \cup \{j\}, g)_\star \quad k \to j}{(\Gamma \cup \{k\}, g)_\star}$

- C-modus ponens : $\dfrac{(\Gamma, a \to b)_\star \quad (\Gamma, a)_\star}{(\Gamma, b)_\star}$

- I-modus ponens : $\dfrac{a \quad a \to b}{b}$

- generalization : $\dfrac{g}{(\forall x \ . \ g)}$

The meaning of most of these axioms and proof rules is intuitively obvious.

A *propositional default ionic logic* (PDIL) can be defined along the same lines [7].

5 Kernel knowledge versus belt knowledge

We want to formalize the "*common sense*" reasoning of some rational agent about the *actual world*. We assume that the actual world is unknown, or only partially known to the rational agent. From a model-theoretic point of view, this actual world corresponds to some *total model* $\mathcal{M}$ living in some *Cantor paradise*. (Cantor paradise is the conceptual universe where live all mathematical objects.)

The rational agent will have some *theory of the world*. He will use this theory to draw conclusions about the world, and also as a guide for possible actions. This theory will be given by a set of default ionic formulae, say Φ. Set Φ describes what the agent knows and/or believes about the world.

The set Φ will be satisfied (in the logical sense) by some set C of *partial models of the world*. The elements of C will be (according to our theory Φ) possible approximations of the total model $\mathcal{M}$ corresponding to the actual world.

From the point of view of an external observer, these two components Φ and C describe the rational agent's *knowledge of the world*.

Let us consider an example. When we say that *Tweety is a bird*, then we isolate among all possible partial models of the world, those that make this statement true; call that class of partial models C_0. Notice that "*Tweety is a bird*" is a "hard" statement, reflecting some hard fact. It will be represented by an ordinary formula. The statement "*Tweety flies if there is no information to the contrary*" is a "gap-filling" statement. We do not *know* for sure whether Tweety actually flies in the *actual world*. Such a statement will be represented using default ions. If we add this statement to our theory of the world, then our class of partial models C_0 is going to split into two *smaller* classes of "bigger" partial models:

1. a subclass C_{01} where Tweety is a bird, where there is no information to the contrary that he flies, and where Tweety actually flies.

2. a subclass C_{02} where Tweety is a bird, and where he cannot possibly fly (e.g. Tweety is a *coq au vin*).

Thus in the process of adding more and more information, we are getting better and better partial models, and there may be more than one partial model that corresponds to one given specification. This notion of getting "better and better partial models" is embedded in our notion of *extension ordering* between default interpretations. The extension ordering is a *partial ordering*. It corresponds to the partial ordering used in denotational semantics (a la Scott-Strachey) for *monotonicity* purposes.

We use Lakatos' approach [4] to the philosophy of knowledge to analyse our *knowledge of the world*. This analysis corresponds to our dichotomy between *ordinary* formulae and "*gap-filling*" formulae.

Following Lakatos, we analyse our *theory of the world*, i.e. the set Φ of default ionic formulae, into two part: the first part, called the *kernel*, corresponds to the statements we are sure about (e.g. analytic statements), or those we decide to make unfalsifiable by *fiat*. This first part will be expressed in default ionic logic by means of ordinary propositional logic, or predicate logic, formulae. In the previous example, *Tweety is a bird* is part of the *kernel* knowledge.

The second part, called the *belt*, corresponds to our *working hypotheses*; we must be willing to withdraw those in light of new incoming hard facts that contradict them. This second part will be expressed in default ionic logic by using *default ions*. In the previous example, *Tweety flies* is part of the *belt* knowledge.

The idea in default ionic logic is that *kernel knowledge* is given for granted, and what the agent is doing, is to try to extend this kernel knowledge he already has by making suitable conjectures.

This dichotomy between kernel knowledge and belt knowledge will also be present at the *partial model* level.

6 Model theory of the "kernel knowledge versus belt knowledge" paradigm

In his default logic [9], given a set S of first-order axioms and default rules, Reiter defines an *extension* as a set of possible beliefs about the world. Some of these beliefs may have to be abandoned and replaced by new ones, which gives rise to what has been called *non-monotonicity*. Other beliefs, however, should be held quite firmly, as they are not *revisable*: those are logical consequences of the predicate logic part of the axiom system S. In our view, there is, to some extent, a symmetry between *revisable beliefs* and *non-revisable beliefs*. Quite often this symmetry between the two kinds of beliefs, has been overlooked in favour of the revisable ones.

We use Lakatos's [4] approach to refine Reiter's notion of an extension into an object with two components: a *hard* part (the *kernel*), that cannot be revised (e.g. $1+1 = 2$ or "*Tweety is a bird*"), and a *soft* part (the *belt*), that can be revised and changed (e.g. "*Tweety flies*").

Both components will be given by a partial interpretation, and the full interpretation will be obtained by putting them together. The full interpretation will be called a *default interpretation*.

Roughly speaking, a given *strong statement* will be considered as being true under a given interpretation if and only if the *kernel component* of that interpretation contains enough information to force that statement to be true. A given *weak statement* will be considered as being true under the same interpretation if its justification part is acceptable under the given interpretation, and its "conclusion" part is true for the *belt* part of that interpretation.

The belt part is supported (in the intuitive sense) by a set of *signed justifications*. A justification has a positive sign if it is assumed to be acceptable, and a negative sign if it is assumed to be not acceptable. Since justifications are themselves (sets of) default ionic formulae, this set of signed justifications determines a class of default interpretations that are *possible extensions* of the *kernel component*. As an example, if we use Reiter's syntax, then default rule $\dfrac{: p \wedge \neg p}{q}$ never fires because its justification $p \wedge \neg p$ is always unacceptable. So, according to this default, no extension of the kernel part is acceptable. The class of default interpretations extending the kernel component and making justification $p \wedge \neg p$ acceptable (i.e. true) is empty. Default rule $\dfrac{: r \vee \neg r}{s}$ however, always fires because the justification is a tautology, and, thus, is always acceptable, and yields s. The class of default interpretations extending the kernel component and making $r \vee \neg r$ true is the class of all extensions of the kernel component. So, according to this default, any extension of the kernel part is acceptable. Thus, at least intuitively, the latter rule is equivalent to the statement s, whereas the former is equivalent to the void statement *True*.

Intuitively, the set of signed justifications describes the class of interpretations that are considered to be acceptable extensions of the kernel part of the interpretation, whereas the belt part specifies the extension of the kernel part that is actually taken by the interpretation.

More formally, a (propositional logic) *default interpretation* is a triple (i_0, J, i_1) (usually denoted by $i_0 \oplus (J, i_1)$) such that: (i) i_0 (the *kernel valuation*) and i_1 (the *belt valuation*) are partial mappings from the set of propositional symbols to the interpretive structure, (ii) the union of the graphs of i_0 and i_1 is a (total) classical propositional logic interpretation, (ii) J is a *stable* [7] set of default interpretations extending i_0. The example "*Tweety is a bird, birds typically fly*", if we use abbreviations $a = $ *Tweety is a bird*, $b = $ *Tweety flies*, can be represented by default ionic theory $\Phi = \{a \ , \ a \rightarrow (b, b)_* \}$. Some models of Φ are $\{\mathbf{T}a\} \oplus (\{+b\}, \mathbf{T}b)$ and $\{\mathbf{T}a\} \oplus (\{-b\}, \perp)$, where $\perp$ denotes the undefined valuation (cf. section 5).

Since we are using partial interpretations (called here *valuations*), it may be the case that a given expression cannot be evaluated, because the valuation used is not defined for all the occurrences of symbols of the expression. An example of such a situation is given by a formula with no occurrence of default ions, and whose propositional variables are evaluated only by the belt component of the interpretation, and such that the kernel component does not say anything about the truth values of these variables. There are several possible answers to this problem [7]. The solution we explore in this paper is to accept as a fact of life that not every statement g has a truth value under every interpretation defined on the propositional variables occurring in g. This leads us to the consideration of *partial models*.

As a result, the problem of definedness will play an important role in the framework described here. Indeed, there are two things our model theory must accomplish. First, since we are modelizing a *logic*, our model theory must allow us to *reason about truth of statements*. This is essentially accomplished by the *Beth tableau* technique which generalizes the usual *semantic tableau* technique to default ionic formulae. Second, since we must deal with partial interpretations, we must *reason about model construction*, and take into account the fact that a model may be less partial than another model, whereby allowing more statements to be assigned truth values. This notion of a model being *less partial* than another model is formalized by the notion of *extension ordering*.

Default ions are used to express "facts" that we are not so sure about, and different default ionic theories may express different degrees of certainty of knowing certain facts.

By *semantic scope*, we mean the set of all possibles models (and antimodels, i.e. interpretations but not models) a given formula is capable of talking about, i.e. in which that formula can be assigned a truth value. In classical propositional logic, this notion can be defined, but is of no particular importance. Indeed, the alphabet of the language being fixed, since all the interpretations are total, the semantic scope of any formula is simply the full set of interpretations, and thus plays no role in the logical meaning of this formula.

7 Applications to non-monotonic reasoning

The correct way to look at default ionic logic is to see it as a calculus on partial models of propositional (or predicate) logic. These models are specified by means of default ionic formulae. *Beth tableaux* are a constraint solving technique for building the partial models specified. To simplify computation and reasoning, these partial models will be chosen to be *minimal* in some formal sense formalizing the following intuition: *Apply as many defaults as you can*. This notion of minimality corresponds, at the semantic level, to the notion of *maximality* in Reiter's extensions.

The yield of our research is a a generalization of Reiter's framework [9] to a *monotonic* reasoning system, called *default ionic logic*. The model theory of our logic uses standard techniques and algebraic structures from the *denotational semantics of programming languages*. Our logic solves in a simple and straightforward way all of the problems left open in Reiter's logic that were discussed in the introduction of this paper [7]. In particular the Yale Shooting problem (and its variants) is given a *monotonic solution*.

The framework presented here is *continuous* in three ways. First, at the proof-theoretic level, default ionic logic is compact and thus, the inference mechanism is continuous. Second, the spaces Δ_∞ and ∇_∞ of denotations, which are here partial models, are both *continuous bundles*. Third, the approximation mechanism used for solving the Yale shooting problem and other problems is itself regular, and regularity is, in our framework, an approximation of continuity.

We define in [7] a restricted class of default ionic theories, called *default logic programs*. Model theory then gives a solution, in terms of *regular models* of default logic programs, to the following problems: Haugh's robot problem, Kautz's vanishing car problem, and several forms of the Yale shooting problem(frame problem for temporal projection, modified frame problem for temporal projection, Haugh's assassin problem, temporal projection problem).

The class of regular models decomposes into *continuous models* and $\sqsubseteq$-*minimal* discontinuous models. The solution given by model theory to Haugh's robot problem and Kautz's vanishing car problem is in terms of *minimal (discontinuous) models*. The solution given by model theory to some forms of the Yale shooting problem(frame problem for temporal projection, modified frame problem for temporal projection, Haugh's assassin problem, temporal projection problem), and some instances of the *specificity problem* is in terms of *continuous models*.

Intuitively, when everything goes fine (Fred is dead after being shot, the robot is immobile after having both its gears locked, etc.) the regular models we obtain are *continuous models*. On the other hand, when something goes wrong (Fred is still alive after the shooting, the robot is observed moving after having both its gears locked, etc.), then the regular models we obtain are *non-continuous models*.

These questions are discussed in details in [7].

To illustrate how our logic works, we now show how it handles *transitivity* and *contraposition* for statements of the form "*A's are typically B's*", e.g. "*Birds typically fly*".

There are infinitely many ways of combining two propositional letters a, b, the implication connective, and the default ionic operator, to obtain some kind of "weak implication". Some examples are: $a \to (b,b)_\star$, $(a \to b, a \to b)_\star$, $(a,a)_\star \to (b,b)_\star$, $(a,a)_\star \to b$, $(a \to (b,b)_\star, a \to (b,b)_\star)_\star$, $([a \to (b,b)_\star], [a \to (b,b)_\star])_\star$, etc... We concentrate on formulae $a \to (b,b)_\star$ and $(a \to b, a \to b)_\star$ which seem to express more adequately the notion of typicality. These also correspond in our syntax to Reiter's normal defaults $\dfrac{a : b}{b}$ and $\dfrac{: a \to b}{a \to b}$.

As we have mentioned earlier, the statement $a \to [b]$ should be read "a implies weakly b". If we take some liberties with our terminology, it can also be seen as stating a relation between a and b: "a weakly implies b". This yields our first notion of *weak implication*. Weak implication in this sense is *transitive* on the condition that we *concatenate* the justification prefixes, since:

$$
\begin{array}{lll}
1. & a \to (b,b)_\star & \\
2. & b \to (c,c)_\star & \\
3. & a & \\
4. & (b,b)_\star & \text{1,3 I-modus ponens} \\
5. & (b, b \to (c,c)_\star)_\star & \text{2, justification introduction} \\
6. & (b, (c,c)_\star)_\star & \text{2,5 C-modus ponens} \\
7. & a \to (b,(c,c)_\star)_\star & \text{3 through 6, deduction theorem}
\end{array}
$$

Whence $\{a \to [b], b \to [c]\} \vdash a \to (b, [c])_\star$. By the deduction theorem, we can conclude $(a \to [b]) \land (b \to [c]) \to (a \to (b, [c])_\star)$. Notice that the contrapositive of "weak implication" $(a \to [b])$ is $(\neg[b] \to \neg a)$, and not $(\neg b \to \neg[a])$ as suggested by L. Sombé [10].

A *second* notion of weak implication is given by $[a \to b]$ i.e. *"Weakly "a implies b""*. First notice that this second notion of weak implication is deductively stronger than the first one, since $[a \to b]$ entails $a \to [b]$ in the J-logic. Indeed,

$$
\begin{array}{lll}
1. & (a \to b, a \to b)_\star & \text{hypothesis} \\
2. & b \to (a \to b) & \text{axiom} \\
3. & (b, a \to b)_\star & \text{1,2 J-modus ponens} \\
4. & (b, a \to b)_\star \to (a \to (b,b)_\star) & \text{elem transf. 1} \\
5. & a \to (b,b)_\star & \text{3,4 I-modus ponens}
\end{array}
$$

The contrapositive of $[a \to b]$ is not clearly defined, but *modus tollens* reasoning can be performed in a straightforward manner, if we keep our justification prefix:

$$
\begin{array}{lll}
1. & (a \to b, a \to b)_\star & \text{alternative notation for } [a \to b] \\
2. & (a \to b) \to (\neg b \to \neg a) & \text{propositional calculus tautology} \\
3. & (a \to b, (a \to b) \to (\neg b \to \neg a))_\star & \text{justification introduction} \\
4. & (a \to b, \neg b \to \neg a)_\star & \text{1,3 C-modus ponens}
\end{array}
$$

Now if we add the additional hypothesis $\neg b$, then by the justification introduction axiom, we deduce $(a \to b, \neg a)_\star$. Therefore we have $\{[a \to b], \neg b\} \vdash (a \to b, \neg a)_\star$, i.e. $[a \to b]$ entails $\neg b \to (a \to b, \neg a)_\star$.

Now consider the following "modus tollens on defaults" problem: *Birds typically fly. Tweety does not fly. Is Tweety a bird?* Both of the two notions of weak implication defined above give a possible formalization of this problem in PDIL. Our abbreviations are : $a = $ *Tweety is a bird*, and $b = $ *Tweety flies*.

In the first case, we translate "If Tweety is a bird, then Tweety typically flies" as "*If Tweety is a bird, then weakly (Tweety flies)*". From this translation we can build a deduction that yields the conclusion $(b, \neg a)_*$, i.e. *If it is consistent to believe that Tweety flies, then Tweety is not a bird*. This conclusion does not bring much information about Tweety's being a bird or not, since we know as a fact that Tweety does not fly, and it is not acceptable to believe that he does.

In the second case, we translate "If Tweety is a bird, then Tweety typically flies" as "*Weakly (If Tweety is a bird, then Tweety flies)*". We obtain as a conclusion $(a \rightarrow b, \neg a)_*$, i.e. that: *If it is consistent to believe that "if Tweety is a bird then Tweety flies", then Tweety is not a bird*. Intuitively at least, this conclusion brings more information about Tweety than the one obtained from the previous formalization, since now it is acceptable to believe that Tweety is not a bird and that it does not fly. Indeed, it is consistent to believe that "*if Tweety is a bird, then Tweety flies*".

The model theory of PDIL confirms this state of affairs. The *first translation* of typicality yields *two* minimal models: one model $\mathbf{F}b \oplus (\{-b\}, \bot)$, where Tweety does not fly, and may or may not be a bird; and one model $\{\mathbf{F}b, \mathbf{F}a\}$, where Tweety does not fly, and is not a bird. Only in the second model do we have the guarantee that Tweety is not a bird. The *second translation* yields *one* single minimal model: $\mathbf{F}b \oplus (\{+a \rightarrow b\}, \mathbf{F}a)$, where Tweety is not a bird (weak knowledge) and does not fly (strong knowledge).

References

[1] Etherington D. *Reasoning from incomplete information*, Research notes in AI, Pitman, London (1987)

[2] Hanks S., and McDermott D. *Nonmonotonic logic and temporal projection*, Artificial Intelligence 33, (1987), pp. 379-412

[3] Konolige K. *On the relation between default and autoepistemic logic*, Artificial Intelligence 35, (1988), pp. 343-382

[4] Lakatos I. *Falsification and the methodology of scientific research programmes*, in Problems in the Philosophy of Science, Lakatos and Musgrave (eds.), North Holland, Amsterdam (1970), pp. 91-196

[5] Nait Abdallah M. A. *The local approach to programming language theory*, in Continuous Lattices and Their Applications, Hoffmann and Hofmann (eds.), Marcel Dekker, (1985), pp 219-236

[6] Nait Abdallah M. A. *An extended framework for default reasoning*, Springer LNCS 380 (1989), pp. 339-348

[7] Nait Abdallah M. A. *Default ionic logic: A continuous framework for reasoning with partial information* (1990), (University of Western Ontario)

[8] Poole D. *A logical framework for default reasoning*, U. of Waterloo report CS-87-59 (1987)

[9] Reiter R. *A logic for default reasoning*, Artificial Intelligence 13, (1980), pp. 81-132

[10] Sombé L. *Inférences non-classiques en intelligence artificielle* in Actes des Journees Nationales Intelligence Artificielle, D. Pastre ed., Teknea (1988) pp. 137-230

NEURAL NETWORK PROCESSING ELEMENTS AS A NEW GENERATION OF "FLIP-FLOPS"

Eugeniusz Eberbach

Jodrey School of Computer Science, Acadia University
Wolfville, Nova Scotia, Canada B0P 1X0
E-Mail: eugene@AcadiaU.CA, FAX: (902) 542 7224

Abstract

This paper deals with the problem of the relation between conventional computers and the neural networks approach. We concentrate our efforts on comparison of traditional computing elements "flip-flops" and their potential successors - neural network processing elements. We show that both flip-flops and artificial neurons exhibit very similar properties, although their goals, complexity and ways of computation are different. To compare flip-flops and neurons we use a universal theory for problem solving - the Calculus of Self-modifiable Algorithms.

1 Introduction

The new neural computing paradigm, according to many authors, may give the foundations of the sixth generation computers [16]. *Neural computers* are parallel computer architectures which emulate the organization and function of neurons and which provide means for pattern processing. *Neural Network Processing Element* is the basic element of neural computers.

Neural information processing, as might be expected, occupies a mid-point between conventional forms of processing (which we understand) and the brain (which we do not) [17]. Neurocomputing attempts to mimic the brain, in which a signal fired from a one neuron can trigger a cascade of thousands of other signals from one region to another and back [16]. The brain is believed to be a massively parallel "natural computer" composed of 10-100 billion brain cells (neurons), each neuron connected to about 10,000 others. A neuron consists of a cell body, branching extension (*dendrites*) for receiving input, and an *axon* that carries the neuron's output to the dendrites of other neurons. The junction between an axon and a dendrite is called a *synapse*. A neuron is believed to carry out a simple threshold calculation. It collects signals at its synapses and sums them. If the combined signal strength exceeds a certain threshold, the neuron sends out a signal [17].

Neural information processing exhibits many properties analogous to the human brain: association, generalization, parallel search, learning, fault tolerance, and flexibility. Compared to conventional computers which process information with a single complex central processing unit (CPU), neurocomputers process information by using a large number of simple processing elements called neurons.

According to [16], neural computers and digital computers are so different that they do not compete. Taken together, the two technologies promise a new age in computers, with digital machines doing calculations and neural machines serving as eyes and ears, able to match, listen and talk back. The main areas of neurocomputer applications are vision and image processing, speech and language understanding, associative learning, sensory-motor control and robotics, parallel distributed processing, and combinatorial optimization.

In the present paper we focus our attention on comparison of basic hardware elements in both models: conventional flip-flops and neural network processing elements. The comparison was possible due the Calculus of Self-modifiable Algorithms (CSA for short) [1,2,3,4], which has been designed as a general tool for problem solving. The Calculus of Self-modifiable Algorithms seems to be the missing element which joins neurocomputing with the rest of computer science. The CSA model is based on two concepts: a SMA-net and a self-modifiable algorithm itself. The SMA-net defines a mathematical environment for self-modifiable algorithms. Two special cases of the SMA-net are the Rule-Based and Logic net, and the Neural Network and Connectionist net. Self-modifiable algorithms are simply a mathematical abstraction of adaptive computer systems.

The basic elements of self-modifiable algorithms, i.e. *transits*, have the following form:

$$PRE \rightarrow ACT \rightarrow POST$$

These have a unique interpretation:

if precondition PRE, then action ACT, fi postcondition $POST$.

Such a structure is so universal that it can be interpreted either as production rules or clauses in a Rule-Based and Logic net [4], as neural networks processing elements in a Neural Network and Connectionist net [4]; or also, for instance, as state automata transition/output functions for flip-flops.

The flip-flops from conventional computing can be completely characterized by the following statement

if $INPUTS$ and $STATE$, then $TRANSITION$ and $OUTPUT$ $FUNCTIONS$, fi $OUTPUTS$ and NEW $STATE$.

On the other hand, the neural network processing elements can be described briefly using the same formalism as

if $INPUTS$ and $WEIGHTS$, then $LEARNING$ and $TRANSFER$ $FUNCTIONS$, fi $OUTPUTS$ and NEW $WEIGHTS$.

The first impression from these two statements is that both approaches are in fact equivalent, and after renaming neurocomputing-used terms: learning, transfer, and weights by state automaton transition, output, and states, we should return to conventional roots, i.e. flip-flops.

Fortunately, there are also the differences between both approaches. However, we would hesitate to say that they are completely different. Really, the transformation function of the neuron F(X,W)=(Y,W') with X as inputs, W as weights, Y as outputs, W' as updated weights, subsumes the transition and output functions of finite state automata F(X,S)=(Y,S'), where X are inputs, S are control states, Y outputs, S' updated control states. The above means that weights of formal neuron are analogues of the flip-flop control states and they fulfill similar functions, remembering history of the neuron computation. This result is not unexpected, because state automata were designed to model natural neurons. Only recently, the flip-flop model turned out to be insufficiently precise for this purpose, but a similar thing can happen with the present, so promising, neural network processing element after, say, 20 years.

The main differences depend on

- allowing inputs and outputs to take continuous and not only discrete values,

- allowing a larger number of inputs, outputs for the elementary computational element (massive parallelism)

- different purpose of computation.

From these three differences, the most important is likely the third one, i.e. the *different purpose of computation*. In the case of the state automaton F, X, S are given and there are calculated Y and S'. In the case of the formal neuron either F, X, Y are given and W and W' are calculated (supervised learning) or F, X are given and Y, W and W' are calculated (unsupervised learning or self-learning). This means that a formal neuron is like an adaptive flip-flop with changeable transition function. The process of learning depends on finding such appropriate transition functions for an adaptive "flip-flop" - neuron.

In section 2 we briefly present CSA. In section 3 we show how conventional flip-flops are interpreted in the CSA formalism. In section 4 neural network processing elements are presented as SMA transits. The above paper should be received as a trial of demythologizing very promising but still unknown neurocomputing and to connect it with the rest of computer science.

2 Calculus of Self-modifiable Algorithms

A Calculus of Self-modifiable Algorithms [1,2,3,4] is a universal theory for parallel and intelligent systems, integrating different styles of programming and applied in different domains of future generation computers. The scope of potential applications of CSA is very wide, including expert systems, machine learning, adaptive systems, pattern recognition, neurocomputing, fault tolerant systems, distributed and parallel computing, new computer architectures and languages [2,3].

To basic notions used in CSA belong: **EBA Formulas** (Extended Boolean Algebra Formulas), **SMA-net** and **Self-Modifiable Algorithm** itself.

The EBA-formulas are useful to deal with systems with incomplete information, and such systems are characteristic for AI and neurocomputing. Some basic elements of self-modifiable algorithms, i.e. control states, pre and postconditions in transits are predicates taking values in the extended Boolean algebra (EBA-formulas). EBA-formulas are in some extent similar to predicate calculus used in logic programming. The main differences depend that predicates can take three and not two values, namely: true, false and unknown; and that besides traditional disjunction, conjunction, and negation operators, there are two new "dynamic" operators performing *verification of matching* and *updating conditions*.

The SMA-net (from: Self-Modifiable Algorithm net) defines a mathematical environment for self-modifiable algorithms. Two special cases of SMA-net are an RBL-net (from: Rule-Based and Logic net) and an NNC-net (from: Neural Network and Connectionist net). The SMA-net provides the means for procedural and data abstraction, i.e. the way how to build the algorithm from lower-level elements using basic programming operators.

Elements of SMA-net consist of preconditions PRE, activity ACT and postcondition $POST$. We assume that an element of SMA-net $PRE \rightarrow ACT \rightarrow POST$ matches if its precondition is true. In other words, if EBA-formula in precondition has value 1, action ACT can be executed. If PRE is equal 0, ACT cannot be executed; and if PRE is unknown then there are two possibilities: either suspension or conditional execution with verification of PRE during or after execution. This has an analogy with the reasoning by default from logic programming. After correct termination of action ACT, $POST$ becomes true.

By a **SMA-net** we mean the following system:

$$(X, \{pre, act, post\}, \{ \uplus, \sqcup, \sqcap, \circ, \,, \Re, !\}, \{\bot, \top, \varepsilon, \gamma\}), \text{ where}$$

(a) X is a set, called a *universum* (domain) of the net. $X = \Phi \times (2^Z)^* \times \Phi^+$, where Φ are EBA-formulas, Z is a set of atomic activities. In other words, elements of X are triples in the form (ϕ_1, z, ϕ_2), where ϕ_1 is precondition, z is activity, and ϕ_2 is postcondition. Φ^+ means that ϕ_2 can contain recursion, i.e. $\phi_2 = \phi_{21}...\phi_{2p}$, where ϕ_{2i} and ϕ_{2i+1} can be connected by any of operators $\circ$, $,$, $\bullet$

(b) for every subset of $(2^X)^*$ $pre, act, post$ are the projection functions allowing to find precondition, activity, and postcondition, respectively,

(c) $\uplus, \sqcup, \sqcap, \circ, ,, \Re, !$ are the operators allowing to build higher-order elements, and
   $\uplus$ is a *nondeterministic choice*,
   $\sqcup$ is a *general choice*,
   $\sqcap$ is an *intersection*,
   $\circ$ is a *sequential composition*,
   $,$ is a *parallel composition*,
   $\Re$ is a *general recursion*,
   $!$ is a *skip operator*,

(d) $\bot, \top, \varepsilon, \gamma \in X$ are distinguished elements of X, and
   $\bot$ is *zero*, and $pre(\bot) = 0$
   $\top$ is *top*, and $pre(\top) = 1, act(\top) = (2^X)^*, post(\top) = 1$
   ε is a *sequential unity*, and $(\forall a \in (2^X)^*)$ $a \circ \varepsilon = \varepsilon \circ a = a$
   γ is a *parallel unity*, and $(\forall a \in (2^X)^*)$ $a, \gamma = a$. $\square$

As a special case of recursion $\Re$ operator there are distinguished different types of iteration operators. Let $*, ^{\circledast}, ^{\pm}, ^{\underline{\circledast}}$ be the following unary operators $(2^X)^* \to (2^X)^*$: $(\forall a \in (2^X)^*)$

$\{a\}^* = \{x\} \Re \{a \circ x \sqcup \varepsilon\}$

$\{a\}^{\circledast} = \{x\} \Re \{a \circ x \uplus \varepsilon\}$

$\{a\}^{\pm} = \{x\} \Re \{a, x \sqcup \gamma\}$

$\{a\}^{\underline{\circledast}} = \{x\} \Re \{a, x \uplus \gamma\}$, where

$*$ will be called a (sequential) **iteration**, $^{\circledast}$ - a **modifiable iteration**, $^{\pm}$ - a **partation** (from parallel iteration), $^{\underline{\circledast}}$ - a **modifiable partation**.$\square$

The complete definition of the SMA-net operators and their interpretations can be found in [4].

Self-modifiable algorithms are a mathematical model of processes (programs) with possibilities of modifications to its behavior. They describe a single (recursive or iterative) modifiable program or systems of cooperating modifiable programs. An articulation of a self-modifiable algorithm has been introduced in [1], and the current definition is based on [4]. Self-modifiable algorithms have many different roots, but undoubtedly their nearest analogue was a mathematical model of programs without self-modifiability, so-called Mazurkiewicz algorithm [12].

By a **self-modifiable algorithm** SMA over an SMA-net $(X, \{pre, act, post\}, \{\uplus, \sqcup, \sqcap, \circ, ,, \Re, !\}, \{\bot, \top, \varepsilon, \gamma\})$ we mean any pair:

$$SMA = (S, T), \text{ where}$$

S - is a nonempty set of **control states**. Control states have the form of EBA-formulas. S is dynamic, in the sense that during execution there are created new and destroyed existing control states. At the beginning $S = \{\sigma, \omega\}$, where σ is the **initial control state**, and ω is the **terminal control state** (goal) of the algorithm.

T - is a set of **transits** . $T = X \times R_\eta^\infty$, where X is the domain of the net, and R_η^∞ is the set of so called *beyond-real numbers* (in particular, real numbers). During execution of SMA new transits are created, some are modified and some destroyed. Transits consist of **data** D , **actions** A , and **modifications** M ($T = \{D, A, M\}$). The main criterion in the distinction between data, actions and modifications is a domain in which a given set operates. Actions A operate on data D exclusively. Modifications M are a generalization of actions and the essence of SMA , and they operate on data, actions and modifications. Every transit $t \in T$ has the form of a quadruple $t = (pre(t), act(t), post(t), cost(t))$, where $pre(t)$ and $post(t)$ are *precondition* and *postcondition* in the form of EBA-formulas, $act(t)$ denotes an *activity* (contents) of the transit, and $cost(t)$ is the transit weight in the form of a certain real (beyond-real) number. *pre* and *post* are responsible for pattern matching, i.e. for binding control states with appropriate transits, and *cost* is used as a criterion for adaptation and learning of SMA. The structure of transits is open in the sense that it is possible to extend it by adding new components as, for instance, generalizations of transits, specializations, domain, analogies, history, informal definition, etc. The design or work of SMA (design because SMA modifies itself) consists of 3 phases: *select, examine, and execute*, and is based on the optimization mechanism with the use of the costs of transits. □

REMARK 1 *Data can be simple (as for example integer or real numbers, characters, logical values) or they may be structured (as arrays, records, symbolic data (strings, trees), relations, etc.). Data are passive but they can change between particular control states. Actions are active and they operate exclusively on data D; and at the same time, they can be data themselves for modifications M. The set of actions can be identified with instructions of "classic" imperative programming languages. Modifications are active and operate upon data, actions and modifications. The foregoing means that modifications are applicable to actions and that there exist modifications applicable both to actions and to data. Modifications are simply a generalization of actions. They cause generation of new instructions and change old instructions (actions and modifications) of the algorithm. Analogues of modifications can be found in knowledge representation languages (see e.g. Lenat's RLL metarules [10], updating weight functions in neurocomputing [9,11], or compiler instructions transforming other instructions). A self-modifiable algorithm with the empty set of modifications (M = ∅) is simply a traditional algorithm (conventional program).*

REMARK 2 *One of the important components of transits is the* **cost**, *which represents the weight of a transit. The costs, represented by real numbers (more precisely* **beyond-real numbers** *[1]), can have different interpretations, such as, for instance, weights in the neuralcomputing sense, values of transits, time of execution, real cost of execution, probability, beliefs, Lenat's level of interestingness [10], penalty, subjective impression, payoff from the game theory, Holland's fitness from genetics [6], reward from psychology, a linear composition of all of the above factors, and so on. The beyond-real numbers are similar to complex numbers, and were introduced in order to specify the cost of iteration (recursion) with an unknown number of repetitions. The cost of iterated and non-iterated parts of the program are then represented by a beyond-real number, consisting of two ordered real numbers, respectively [1].*

REMARK 3 *In [4] two paradigms representing different classes of models described by a SMA-net have been presented. These are the* **Black-Box paradigm** *and the* **Total Equivalence paradigm**. *In the Black-Box paradigm two transits are equal if their pre- and postconditions are equal. The Total Equivalence paradigm requires additionally the equality of activities. Both approaches lead to different properties and laws of programming depending on paradigm chosen.*

The input-output behavior of self-modifiable algorithms is described as the solutions (the fixed points) of some sets of equations. These sets of equations can be built starting from the initial control state (forward equations) or from the terminal control state (backward equations). Their solutions contain redundant threads of transits; therefore they are optimized by removing operators connected with nondeterminism (for instance: by removing nondeterministic choice, modifiable iteration and modifiable partation). Optimization uses the costs of transits and operations as the main criterion to find the best algorithm to realize a given goal. The construction and solution of the SMA sets of equations, and their cost optimization is described elsewhere.

3 Conventional Computing

By *conventional computing* in the present paper we mean computers up to the fifth generation. We limit our discussion to the most popular electronic digital computers.

The basic (hardware) computing element of conventional computers, called *flip-flops* (triggers, latches), can be described as the following SMA transit

$$\textbf{if } (X = X_0) \wedge (S = S_0), \textbf{ then } F(X, S), \textbf{ fi } (Y = Y_0) \wedge (S' = S'_0),$$

where X is a set of inputs, Y is a set outputs, S is a set of current control states, and S' is a set of updated control states. F is a generalized transformation consisting of transition and output functions. If sets X, Y, S, S' are limited to discrete values (in particular, to two values, say, 0 and 1, or better three values: zero, one and unknown) then such basic computing elements are called triggers, latches, flip-flops, and they are elementary elements to build more complex units registers, counters, PLA's, memories RAM's, ROM's, control units, CPU's, i.e. *sequential circuits*. Sequential circuits remember their history of computation, which received an abstract form of control states (representing previous input and output signals). If sets of control states are infinite then such sequential circuits have the computational power of Turing machines. Complex sequential circuits are simply higher-order flip-flops, and they may realize sequential or parallel composition, choices, recursion, etc. The same may be said about their software, i.e. programming languages, because everything what is programmable in software is executed finally by hardware, and every hardware can be simulated by programs. There are no distinct and sharp boundary between hardware and software.

The name sequential circuits is traditional and, perhaps, misleading, because sequential circuits are at the same parallel devices, and they are used to build parallel computers, although undoubtedly flip-flops can be used for the design of sequential components.

If the set of control states is either empty or consists of one control state only (i.e., there are no changes of control states), then such subclass of sequential circuits is called *combinatorial circuits*, and is used to realize logic gates, multiplexers, encoders, ALU's. Combinatorial circuits can be described by Boolean algebra, or, more precisely, by the Extended Boolean Algebra, EBA-formulas, and transits.

We will omit the discussion of combinatorial circuits, treating them simply as a special case of sequential circuits.

All types of sequential circuits can be expressed using the same SMA-model.

PROPOSITION 1 Sequential Circuits *are a subclass of self-modifiable algorithms.*
PROOF. *Sequential Circuits are self-modifiable algorithms with the set of control states S represented by EBA-formulas over input/output/state signals, and transits in the form of flip-flops. Higher-order flip-flops form registers, memories, processors, computers. Data D are unity flip-flops with precondition the same as postcondition from the set of input/output/state signals, and the identity relation as the set of transforming functions. Actions A are represented by flip-flops*

performing transfer functions of inputs/state onto outputs/state. Modifications M are not widely used as the ready product in conventional computing. Mostly on the level of hardware design, or in the case of software (compiler instructions transforming other instructions, or metarules from expert systems). Modifications are flip-flops transfer functions updating either directly, or indirectly transfer functions of other flip-flops. The cost of flip-flops can be identified with states of flip-flops (but only for the atomic, lower level flip-flops). For the higher level-flip flops, the costs are the functions of states. The SMA optimization mechanism may be used to obtain stable state of computation (i.e. the minimum between cost difference), or in the process of hardware design. □

For illustration let's consider the work of typical flip-flops described in the CSA formalism. From 4 basic types of flip-flops: D,T,RS, and JK , we will present D and RS.

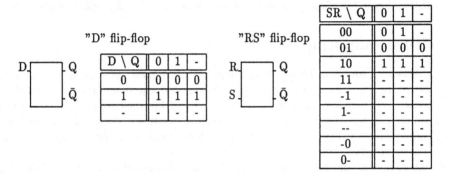

Figure 1: Examples of conventional flip-flops

For the "D" flip-flop, we have one data transit D with the cost equal Q, and for the "RS" flip-flop we have a parallel composition of data transits R, S (i.e. R and S are given in parallel) as the input of flip flop with the cost equal Q. All D, R, S, Q may take three possible values from the Extended Boolean algebra: 1 (true), 0 (false), and - (unknown). Unknown has the interpretaion as undefined (unstable) value of a signal, but not as "don't care" symbol from the switching theory.

Instead of $x = 1$, $x = 0$, and $x = -$, we will write shortly x, $\bar{x}$, and $\hat{x}$, respectively.

"D" flip-flop has exactly one action (its transition table) with precondition $D \wedge Q$ and postcondition Q. Activity of this action is described by the following 3 characteristic equations:

$Q = Q \circ D \sqcup (\bar{Q} \sqcup \hat{Q}) \circ D$ (to achieve $Q = 1$)

$\bar{Q} = \bar{Q} \circ \bar{D} \sqcup (Q \sqcup \hat{Q}) \circ \bar{D}$ (to achieve $Q = 0$)

$\hat{Q} = \hat{Q} \circ \hat{D} \sqcup (\bar{Q} \sqcup Q) \circ \hat{D}$ (to achieve $Q = -$)

Consider the solution of the first equation:

$Q = (\bar{Q} \sqcup \hat{Q}) \circ D \circ D^*$, which has the simple interpretation: to be in state $Q = 1$ starting

from $\bar{Q}$ or $\hat{Q}$ there is necessary to provide at least once signal $D = 1$ (i.e., $D \circ D^*$).

For the "RS" flip-flop, we will write only equation how to achieve $Q = 1$:

$Q = Q \circ ((\bar{S}, \bar{R}) \sqcup (S, \bar{R})) \sqcup (\bar{Q} \sqcup \hat{Q}) \circ (S, \bar{R})$

because $(\bar{S}, \bar{R}) \sqcup (S, \bar{R}) = \bar{R}$, we can write that

$Q = Q \circ \bar{R} \sqcup (\bar{Q} \sqcup \hat{Q}) \circ (S, \bar{R})$

with the solution

$$Q = (\bar{Q} \sqcup \hat{Q}) \circ (S , \bar{R}) \circ \bar{R}^*$$

This solution can be read: in order to be in state $Q = 1$ starting from $\bar{Q}$ or $\hat{Q}$ the input "RS" flip-flop should consist of $S = 1$ and $R = 0$ and next R should be kept 0 and S can be either 1

or 0 $((S , \bar{R}) \circ \bar{R}^*)$.

REMARK 4 *Note that due to the CSA theory the flip-flops are at the same parallel and sequential devices, what seems be a more natural interpretation compared to the traditional approach. Due to 3-values in Extended Boolean algebra, the nondeterministic behavior of "RS" flip-flop for both R and S equal 1 receives clear and natural description (value of Q becomes unknown, instead to say that such combination of input signals is disallowed. The disallowance is because the traditional model is simply too poor and not because the flip-flop will be destroyed).*

4 Neurocomputing

Neural Network Processing Elements or nodes used in neural net models are nonlinear, and typically analog [11]. The simplest node sums N weighted inputs and passes the result through a nonlinearity. The node is characterized by an internal threshold and the type of nonlinearity (hard limiters, threshold logic elements, and sigmoid functions). More complex nodes may include temporal integration or other types of time dependencies and more complex mathematical operations than summation.

In the literature (see for instance [16]) there are distinguished a *transfer function*, which defines the relation between the inputs and the output of a neuron, and a *learning function*, which processes a state of a neuron. The transformation F is universal in the sense that it subsumes the transfer function where W' is empty (for instance, the transfer function F can be of the form $f(\sum XW) = Y$, where f is a threshold function) and the learning function with empty Y (with F, for instance, of the form $W' = W + c\Delta Y$). Compared to a natural neuron, in our approach there is more than one output signal. This allows to use the same model for higher-order neurons, i.e. neural networks having more than one output signal.

A *neural network processing element* has 3 components: precondition PRE, activity ACT and postcondition $POST$. **Preconditon** consists of input signals X, weights W, an **activity** F(X,Y) performs different transformations on inputs and weights, and **postcondition** consists of outputs Y and updated weights W'. The uniform artificial neuron is presented in figure 2.

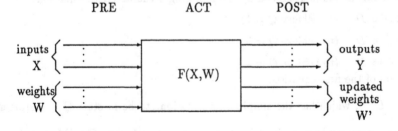

Figure 2: Neural Network Processing Element - Neuron

Using of EBA-formulas, the three steps of the formal neuron computation can be described as

if $(X = X_0) \wedge (W = W_0)$, **then** $F(X, W)$, **fi** $(Y = Y_0) \wedge (W' = W'_0)$.

Such neurons can be connected in higher-order neurons. Neural networks are just higher-order neurons.

Neural net models are specified by the net topology, node characteristics, and training or learning rules. These rules specify an initial set of weights and indicate how weights should be adapted during use to improve performance. A neural network that learns patterns, does so by adjusting the weights between neurons, analogous to synaptic weights. Through these adjustments a neural network exhibits properties of generalization and classification. There are three classes of transforming functions: **transfer function** calculating outputs on the basis of inputs and weights, **learning functions** updating weights, and **error functions** showing when learning can be terminated.

We can distinguish the following network models [17]: Hopfield/Kohonen associative memories [7], Single-Layer Perceptron [13], Delta Rule Single-Layer Perceptron, called also Widroff-Hoff [11], Back Propagation [14], Boltzmann Machine [14], Counter Propagation [18], Self-organizing Map [11], and Neocognitron [5].

All these types of neural networks can be described using the same SMA-model.

PROPOSITION 2 Neural Networks *are a subclass of self-modifiable algorithms, i.e. SMA over the Neural Network and Connectionist net.*

PROOF. *Neural Networks are the SMA over the NNC-net with the set of control states S represented by values of input/output/weight signals, and transits in the form of neurons. Data D are unity neurons with precondition the same as postcondition from the set of input/output/weight signals, and the identity relation as the set of transforming functions. Actions A are represented by neurons performing transfer functions of inputs/weights onto outputs. Modifications M are neurons performing learning and error functions, i.e. updating weights and checking the end of training. The cost of neurons is the neurocomputing error function, responsible for the termination of the learning process (weight modifications). The SMA optimization mechanism minimizes the error function to terminate the training phase.* $\square$

As the illustration of neural networks, we will present the classic and the oldest neural network model, namely *Single-Layer Perceptron* described in the CSA-like style. Note that Single-Layer Perceptron is a higher-order neuron, i.e. it consists of elementary neurons.

The **single-layer perceptron** [13] (threshold logic unit) is the classic example of neural networks, and very often is treated even as the definition of the formal neuron [9]. It classifies a set of continuous input data X into two disjoint classes $Y = \{1, -1\}$ after the process of learning - the convergence procedure for adjusting weights W. Rozenblatt [13] proved that if the inputs presented from the two classes are separable (if they fall on opposite sides of some hyperplane) then the process of learning terminates, i.e. procedure of weight updating converges.

By the **single-layer perceptron** we mean the following self-modifiable algorithm over the NNC-net

$$SMA = (S, T) \text{ , where}$$

$S = \{\sigma, \omega\}$
    start(σ): $(all\_input\_presented = 0) \vee \neg(a.cost = 0) \vee (all\_input\_presented = 1) \wedge$
    $(a.cost = 0)$
    /* a.cost denotes the cost of action a */
    /* a.cost, all_input_presented, etc. are the names of neuron signals */
    goal(ω): $(perceptron\_ready\_for\_classification = 1)$

$T = \{D = \{d\}, A = \{a\}, M = \{b, e, f, m\}\}$

datum(d)

      pre: $(x_0 = r_0) \wedge .... \wedge (x_{n-1} = r_{n-1}) \wedge (y = r_n) \wedge (w_0 = r_{n+1}) \wedge .... \wedge (w_n = r_{2n-1})$

      act: ϵ (empty activity)

      post: $(x_0 = r_0) \wedge .... \wedge (x_{n-1} = r_{n-1}) \wedge (y = r_n) \wedge (w_0 = r_{n+1}) \wedge .... \wedge (w_n = r_{2n+1})$

      cost: 1

action(a)

      pre: $(x_0 = r_0) \wedge .... \wedge (x_{n-1} = r_{n-1}) \wedge (y = r_n) \wedge (w_0 = r_{n+1}) \wedge .... \wedge (w_n = r_{2n-1})$

      act: $y' := f(\sum_{i=0}^{n-1} w_i x_i + w_n)$, $f(z) = 1$ if $z > 0$ or $f(z) = -1$ if $z < 0$

      post: $(y = r_n) \wedge (y' = f(\sum_{i=0}^{n-1} w_i x_i + w_n)$

      cost: 0

modification(b)

      pre: $(all\_input\_presented = 1) \vee (a.cost = 0)$

      act: present new continuous inputs $x_0, ..., x_{n-1}$ and the desired output y; if these were the last input values then $all\_input\_presented := 1$

      post: $(x_0 = r_0) \wedge .... \wedge (x_{n-1} = r_{n-1}) \wedge (y = r_n) \wedge (w_0 = r_{n+1}) \wedge .... \wedge (w_n = r_{2n-1})$

      cost: 1

modification(e)

      pre: $(all\_input\_presented = 1) \wedge \neg(a.cost = 0)$

      act: ϵ (empty activity)

      post: $(all\_input\_presented = 0) \wedge (a.cost = 0)$

      cost: 1

modification(f)

      pre: $(all\_input\_presented = 1) \wedge (a.cost = 0)$

      act: ϵ (empty activity)

      post: $(perceptron\_ready\_for\_classification = 1)$

      cost: 1

modification(m)

      pre: $(y = r_n) \wedge (y' = f(\sum_{i=0}^{n-1} w_i x_i + w_n)$

      act: $w_i := w_i + c(y - y')x_i$, $i = 0, 1, ..., n - 1$, $0 < c < 1$; if $y \neq y'$ then $a.cost := a.cost + 1$

      post: $(all\_input\_presented = 1) \vee \neg(a.cost = 0) \vee (all\_input\_presented = 1) \wedge (a.cost = 0)$

      cost: 1

The **select** phase of Single-Layer Perceptron learning depends on matching control states $(\sigma, \alpha, \beta, ...)$ with transits $(b, e, f, ...)$, which can be written in the form of the below equations:

$x(\sigma) = b \circ x(\alpha) \sqcup e \circ x(\sigma) \sqcup f \circ x(\omega)$

$x(\alpha) = d \circ x(\beta)$

$x(\beta) = a \circ x(\gamma)$

$x(\gamma) = m \circ x(\sigma)$

$x(\omega) = \varepsilon$

The **examine phase** depends on removing nondeterminism by the optimization, and in the case of deterministic perceptron algorithm is empty.

The last **execute phase** is equivalent to the following threads of transits:

$$((b \circ d \circ a \circ m)^* \circ e)^* \circ f$$

with the cost of learning equal to the following beyond-real number $1 + \eta 5$. The internal iteration $(b \circ d \circ a \circ m)^*$ performs classification and weight updating for successive input data. If modifications of weights were necessary then the whole process is repeated by the external iteration $((b \circ d \circ a \circ m)^* \circ e)^*$, otherwise is stopped ($f$ modification).

It can be formally proved that learning process is the solution (the least fixed point) of the set of equations from the select phase. The cost of learning is equal to $1 + \eta 5$ because during learning all transits have cost equal 1, and 5 of them are iterated (b, d, a, m, e) and only one f no. Beyond-real numbers are written in a similar form as complex numbers, i.e. as ordered pairs of real numbers (x,y) or in the form $x + \eta y$ with the "beyond-real factor" η. If we know the number of repetitions of iterations then η is replaced by such a number and cost is represented only by a single real number.

In other words, the process of learning (training) depends on finding the minimum for the classification algorithm ($a.cost = 0$). Such a minimum will be achieved if there is no weight modification. Note that learning is associated with action a performing classification by changing the weights - parameters of the classification function f, and it requires both action a working on d and modification m working on a (by changing w_i in a).

5 Conclusions

In this paper we have presented a non-conventional approach to neurocomputing, showing its links with conventional computing. Because neurocomputing is based on a non-conventional form of computing, as the natural consequence of this "double non-conventionality", we obtained links of neurocomputing with traditional computing. In spite of common beliefs, we showed that both conventional flip-flops and artificial neurons are based on similar concepts: states (weights), transition (updating) functions, and so on. There are also differences, due to massive parallelism, new technologies, and the different goal of computation (not outputs but states are calculated). However, they do not overshadow the similarities. This should not be understood as a criticism of neurocomputing, but rather as the theoretical possibility of evolution for neural network processing elements into some kind of new generation "flip-flops". This is the main result of our analysis. However, the open question remains when we will have standard artificial neurons able to replace the "D" or "JK" flip-flops in building blocks of future computers.

ACKNOWLEDGEMENTS

This paper is dedicated to the memory of Jan Just, my co-author of many papers on distributed computing.

The work of the author was partially supported by an operating grant from the Natural Sciences and Engineering Research Council of Canada, No. OGP0046501, and a general NSERC grant.

References

[1] Eberbach E., Algorithms with Possibilities of Selflearning and Selfmodification, Fundamenta Informaticae 6, 1 (1983), 1-44.

[2]   Eberbach E., Self-Modifiable Algorithms and Their Applications, Research Note RN/88/27, Department of Computer Science, University College London, (June 1988).

[3]   Eberbach E., Selected Aspects of the Calculus of Self-Modifiable Algorithms Theory, Proc. Intern. Conf. on Computing and Information ICCI'90, Niagara Falls, Canada, (1990), 57-61 (also in Lect. Notes in Computer Science 468, Springer-Verlag, 1991).

[4]   Eberbach E., CSA: Two Paradigms of the Language for Adaptive Expert Systems, Proc. of the 19th Annual ACM Computer Science Conference CSC'91, San Antonio, 1991.

[5]   Fukushima K., A Neural Network for Visual Pattern Recognition, IEEE Computer, March 1988, 65-75.

[6]   Holland J.H., Adaptation in Natural and Artificial Systems: An Introductory Analysis with Applications to Biology, Control and Artificial Intelligence, Univ. of Michigan Press, Ann Arbor, 1975.

[7]   Hopfield J.J., Neural Networks and Physical Systems with Emergent Collective Computational Abilities, Proc.Nat.Acad.Sci., vol.79, 1982, 2554-2558.

[8]   Jackson P., Introduction to Expert Systems, second edition, Addison-Wesley, 1990.

[9]   Kohonen T., An Introduction to Neural Computing, Neural Networks, vol.1, 1988, 3-16.

[10] Lenat D.B., Brown J.S., Why AM and EURISKO appear to work, Artificial Intelligence 23, (1984), 269-294.

[11] Lippmann R.P., An Introduction to Computing with Neural Nets, IEEE ASSP Magazine, April 1987, 4-22.

[12] Mazurkiewicz A., Iteratively Computable Relations, Bulletin of the Polish Academy of Sciences, Ser. Math. Astron. Phys., 20, 9, (1972), 799-803.

[13] Rosenblatt R., Principles of Neurodynamics, New York, Spartan Books, 1959.

[14] Rumelhart D.E., McClelland J.L., Parallel Distributed Processing: Explorations in the Microstructure of Cognition, MIT Press, Cambridge,Mass., vol. 1 & 2, 1986.

[15] Simpson P.K., A Survey of Artificial Neural Systems, Tech.Report, Unisys, San Diego Systems Engineering Center, March 1987.

[16] Souček B., Souček M., Neural and Massively Parallel Computers. The Sixth Generation, John Wiley & Sons, 1988.

[17] Treleaven P.C., Neurocomputers, Department of Computer Science, University College London, 1989.

[18] Wasserman P.D., Schwartz T., Neural Networks, Part2, IEEE EXPERT, vol.3, no.1, 1988, 10-15.

A Proof-Theoretic Framework
for Nonmonotonic Reasoning and Logic Programming

Li Yan Yuan, Jia-Huai You and *Chenghui Wang*

Department of Computing, Science University of Alberta
Edmonton, Alberta   Canada, T6G 2H1

Abstract

This paper proposes a general proof-theoretic framework, where negative literals in a query are proved by a new mechanism of negation-as-failure. This new mechanism handles nonground negative literals and thus guarantees that queries never *flounder*. We show how to derive proof procedures within this framework, which are always sound, for a number of semantics formalisms, including the GCWA (generalized closed world assumption) and the stable model semantics of logic programs. We also show a new proof procedure for the well-founded semantics which is "more complete" than the previous one in that the floundered queries can be safely pursued.

1. Introduction

A minimal model of a formula is a model of the formula such that no proper subset of the true atoms is also a model of that formula. In this paper, we deal with sets of clauses and Herbrand interpretations and models only. The GCWA proposed by Minker [7], which generalizes the closed world assumption of Reiter, says that a ground atom A is false with respect to a set of clauses under the GCWA iff it is false in every minimal model of the clauses. The extra condition for an atom to be false is very difficult to verify since it is completely semantic. Several attempts have been made to develop proof methods for this kind of formalisms; see, for example, [6, 9, 13]. However, all previous approaches work only for certain types of clauses with the restrictions such as function symbols free, stratified, or non-Horn but without negative literals in the body of a clause.

In the context of logic programming with negation, promising semantics formalisms, such as the well-founded and stable model semantics [4, 11] suffer from the lack of procedures that can handle nonground negative literals (cf. [10]). This problem has been called *floundered* query problem, which refers to the situation in SLDNF-resolution where a goal cannot be safely pursued if it contains nonground negative literals.

An important distinction between the GCWA and logic program semantics is that in the former a clause is a disjunction of literals while in the latter clause orientation is crucial in determining a program's meaning.

In this paper, we propose a general framework for proving queries under a number of semantics formalisms. First, we employ a new mechanism of negation-as-failure that can treat nonground negative literals. Our solution has some similarities with the idea of *constructive negation*. Przymusinski [8] provided an elegant theory for constructive negation and in particular, a nonfloundering procedure for stratified logic programs. Chan's procedures [1, 2] are based on the idea of *reversing* solutions and ours to be described in this paper is entirely based on *inference rules*.

With this mechanism, we show that proof procedures can be derived in this framework for all of the semantics mentioned earlier. Roughly, the idea is that we can use our new negation-as-failure procedure to prove negative literals using clauses of *negative* head (we therefore adopt a more explicit version of negation-as-failure than the SLDNF-resolution), and a new standard version of resolution to prove positive literals using clauses of *positive* head. We call this resolution *SL-Twin-Resolution*. For different semantics it only requires different formulations of these two sets of clauses, which can be derived from the given set of clauses, plus some mechanisms to ensure that the derivations possess certain properties. We show that these derived procedures are always sound.

In the next section, we explain in more details the floundered query problem and present our solution. Section 3 defines SL-Twin-Resolution. In Section 4, we show how to derive proof procedures for the GCWA and the logic program semantics.

2. The Floundered Query Problem and its Solution

The potential pitfall in pursuing a nonground negative literal in a goal can be explained by the following example.

Example 2.1. Let program Π be

$$P(x) \leftarrow \neg Q(y)$$
$$Q(z) \leftarrow L(w)$$
$$Q(a)$$
$$L(b).$$

and query $\leftarrow \neg P(x)$, from which we try to show that $\exists x \, \neg P(x)$ follows from *Semantics(Π)* where *Semantics(Π)* denotes the intended models of Π under a particular semantics. The query is actually transferred, by the first clause, to a universally qualified query—whether $\forall y \, Q(y)$ is true in *Semantics(Π)*. If this is resolved with $Q(a)$, we will then get a wrong answer, since what has been shown is an existential query. This is the reason why it is unsafe to pursue nonground negative literals. The common practice is to simply abort the proof. However, this universal query can again become an existential one, by the second clause (since the variable w, which does not appear in the head, is actually existentially qualified), which then resolves with $L(b)$ to yield a correct refutation.

2.1 Restricted Goals

The similarity with constructive negation is that we also need to handle equality and inequality. Unlike constructive negation, the only role that equality and inequality plays in our approach is to constrain the derivations.

We assume Clark's Equational Theory [3] and use $E(x_1, x_2)$ and $\neg E(x_1, x_2)$ to denote equality and inequality atoms respectively.

Definition 2.1. [1, 8] The inequality $\neg E(t_1, t_2)$ is *valid* if t_1 and t_2 cannot be unified. It is *satisfiable* if there exists a substitution θ for some variables in the inequality such that

$(\neg E(t_2, t_2))\theta$ is valid. Similarly, the equality $E(t_1, t_2)$ is *valid* if t_2 and t_2 are the same. It is *satisfiable* if t_1 and t_2 are unifiable. A conjunction of equalities and inequalities $L_1, ..., L_k$ is satisfiable if there exists a substitution θ such that $L_i\theta$ is valid for $i = 1, ..., k$. $\square$

Example 2.2. $\neg E(f(t), g(x))$ is valid, both $\neg E(f(x), f(g(t)))$ and $\neg E(x, g(t))$ are satisfiable, and $\neg E(f(g(t)), f(g(t)))$ is unsatisfiable. $\square$

A *restricted goal*, a goal for short, is a headless clause $\leftarrow L_1, ..., L_k, \neg E_1, ..., \neg E_q$, where the L_i are non-inequality literals and the $\neg E_j$ are inequalities. When $k = 0$ the goal is called a *pseudo-empty* clause. A computational rule R is a fixed rule that selects exactly one non-inequality literal from a non-pseudo-empty goal. Notationally, we will use underline to highlight a selected literal in a goal, if not explicitly mentioned. Also, by an *extended clause*, we mean a clause of the form: $L_0 \leftarrow L_1, ..., L_n$, where $n \geq 0$ and the L_i are all literals.

Definition 2.2. Let $\{ \leftarrow L_1, ..., \underline{L_m}, ..., L_q, \neg E_1, ..., \neg E_k \}$ be a goal, where L_m is the selected literal, and $\{ L \leftarrow B_1, ..., B_p, F_1, ..., F_j \}$ be an extended clause, where the F_i are all equalities or inequalities.

(1) A substitution θ is a *restricted unifier* of L_m and L if

    (a) θ is a unifier of L_m and L; and

    (b) the conjunction $(\neg E_1, ..., \neg E_k, F_1, ..., F_j)\theta$ is satisfiable.

(2) A substitution θ is a *restricted mgu* of L_m and L if θ is a restricted unifier of L_m and L, and for any restricted unifier σ of L_m and L, there exists a substitution α such that $L_m\theta\alpha = L_m\sigma = L\sigma$.

(3) Unifiability is now defined as: L_m and L are unifiable if there exists a restrict mgu of L_m and L. $\square$

Example 2.3. Let $\{ \leftarrow \underline{\neg Q(x)}, \neg E(x, a) \}$ be a goal and $\{ \neg Q(f(y)) \leftarrow \neg E(y, b) \}$ be an extended clause. Then $\{x/f(y)\}$ is a restricted mgu of $Q(x)$ and $Q(f(y))$. $\square$

For simplicity, in this paper we only consider programs without the equality predicate and goals possibly containing inequalities. As will become clear shortly, any derived goal may contain inequalities but not equalities.

2.2. Blocking Formulas

The formulation of blocking formula is based on the Clark's predicate completion semantics and can be used to derive negative conclusions from programs. Before presenting the definition of blocking formula, we first recall the normal form of a clause which has been used to define the predicate completion in [3].

Assume $P(x_1, ..., t, ..., x_n) \leftarrow L_1, ..., L_k$ is a clause, where t is a non-variable term. The clause can then be rewritten as $P(x_1, ..., x, ... x_n) \leftarrow L_1, ..., L_k, E(x, t)$. In addition, multiple occurrences of a variable in the head can be replaced by distinct variables and expressed in the body by equalities; for example, $P(x, x)$ can be written as $P(y, z) \leftarrow E(y, z)$. The normal form of a clause is one without non-variable term or multiple occurrences of variables in the head, which can be obtained by repeating the above processes. For example

$P(x, x, f(w), a) \leftarrow R(x, w)$ can be rewritten as

$$P(x, y, z, u) \leftarrow R(x, w), E(x, y), E(z, f(w)), E(u, a).$$

The normal form of a clause may contain existentially quantified variables. For example, $P(x) \leftarrow R(y)$ represents the statement that $P(x)$ if $\exists y R(y)$. It is such existential quantified variables that cause all the troubles in so called *unsafe* negation. Our solution is very simple but effective. For each normal form of a clause with some existentially quantified variables, a new normal form of the clause is obtained by replacing each existentially quantified variable with a new Skolem constant/function. For the above example we need consider one more clause, i.e., $P(x) \leftarrow R(g(x))$, where g is a new Skolem function. Note that we add one more clause without existentially quantified variables, not replace the original one. We will call a clause such as $P(x) \leftarrow R(g(x))$ a *Skolem clause* of $P(x) \leftarrow R(y)$. The Skolem functions are not subject to Clark's Equational Theory, their function symbols are disjoint to those in the underlying language.

Notation: We will use $P(x)$ (with x being bold) to denote an n-ary predicate where x is a list of n distinct variables.

Definition 2.3. Let Π be a program with all the clauses in the normal forms and Skolem clauses added. Assume

$$P(x) \leftarrow L_{11}, ..., L_{1k_1}$$

$$\cdots\cdots$$

$$P(x) \leftarrow L_{q1}, ..., L_{qk_q}$$

be the set of all normal form clauses in Π whose head is P, including those with Skolem functions. Then, a blocking formula of P is defined as an extended clause with a negative head:

$$\neg P(x) \leftarrow \neg L_{1S_1}, ..., \neg L_{qS_q},$$

where L_{iS_i} is a literal in the i'th definition clause of P. That is, the body of a blocking formula contains a negated literal from each definition clause of P. $\square$

Note that $\{ \neg P(x) \leftarrow truth \}$ is the blocking formula for P should P not be the head of any clause in the program.

Example 2.4. Consider the following program: $\{P(x) \leftarrow \neg R(y), P(f(x)) \leftarrow S(x)\}$. Then the set of all normal form clauses with P as the head is

$$P(x) \leftarrow \neg R(y)$$
$$P(x) \leftarrow \neg R(g(x))$$
$$P(x) \leftarrow S(z), E(x, f(z))$$
$$P(x) \leftarrow S(h(x)), E(x, f(h(x)))$$

Therefore, P has four blocking formulas, that is,

$$\neg P(x) \leftarrow R(y), R(g(x)), \neg S(z), \neg S(h(x))$$
$$\neg P(x) \leftarrow R(y), R(g(x)), \neg S(z), \neg E(x, f(h(x)))$$
$$\neg P(x) \leftarrow R(y), R(g(x)), \neg E(x, f(z)), \neg S(h(x))$$
$$\neg P(x) \leftarrow R(y), R(g(x)), \neg E(x, f(z)), \neg E(x, f(h(x))) \quad \square$$

The blocking formula is actually an explicit representation of negation-as-failure. The predicate completion takes the formula $P(x) \to L_{1S_1} \vee ... \vee L_{1S_q}$, while our blocking formula, on the other hand, takes its reverse direction. Let us now see how blocking formulas combined with Skolem clauses solve the floundering problem.

Example 2.5. Consider the program in Example 2.1 again. We then have two Skolem clauses: $\{P(x) \leftarrow \neg Q(g(x)), Q(z) \leftarrow L(h(x))\}$. Starting with the query

$$\leftarrow \neg P(x)$$

and by the only blocking formula of P, we derive

$$\leftarrow Q(y), Q(g(x))$$

and subsequently drive

$$\leftarrow L(w), Q(g(x))$$
$$\leftarrow Q(g(x))$$
$$\leftarrow L(w)$$

$\square$

This derivation resembles the case that a universally qualified query finally changes to existentially qualified and leads to a correct answer. On the other hand, the literal $Q(g(x))$ successfully blocked the rout that can wrongly prove $\forall y Q(y)$ by resolving with $Q(a)$.

2.3. Full Programs

Although clause orientation plays a crucial role in logic program semantics, the semantics such as the GCWA cannot treat clauses as oriented. For the stable model semantics, because of the possible existence of multiple stable models, clauses are no longer completely oriented, either. Therefore, the resolvents by unifying the subgoal with any literal in a clause should be considered. In order to take the linear resolution in the framework of the SLD-resolution, we define the full program from a given program Π by taking any literal as the head of the clause.

Definition 2.4. Let Π be a set of clauses. Then the full program of Π consists of extended clauses, denoted as $F(\Pi)$, defined as

$$F(\Pi) = \{ L_0 \leftarrow L_1, ..., L_n \mid \{ L_0, \neg L_1, ..., \neg L_n \} \in \Pi \}. \qquad \square$$

In the above definition a clause in Π is viewed as a set of literals without orientation. When Π is a set of oriented clauses, or a set of extended clauses, $F(\Pi)$ is also valid by simply treating those oriented clauses as non-oriented ones.

Given a set of extended clause Π, we will use $B(\Pi)$ to denote the set of blocking formulas of Π. We assume that the processes of normalization and adding Skolem clauses are automatically done in Π whenever we take blocking formulas $B(\Pi)$. Note that only predicates that appear positively in the head of some clause may have blocking formulas.

3. SL-Twin-Resolution

In the SLDNF-resolution, the given program is used to derive positive conclusions and negation-as-failure to derive negative conclusions. Since the intergration of the two are not considered, SLDNF-resolution is limited to one-model-semantics only. Because of the formulation of full program and its corresponding blocking formulas in our approach, these two types of derivations can be uniformly treated. We call this the *SL-Twin-resolution*.

In the SL-Twin-resolution, we are given two separate sets of oriented clause, Π_P and Π_N, where the head of a clause in Π_P is either positive negative and in Π_N strictly negative. Usually, Π_P is the given logic program and Π_N is the set of blocking formulas of Π. We will describe in the next section how to formulate Π_P and Π_N for different semantics. Thus, the SL-Twin-resolution can be considered as a generic resolution procedure with parameters which will determine its precise behaviors.

Definition 3.1. Let Π_P and Π_N be two sets of oriented clauses, $G = \{ \leftarrow L_1, ..., L_m, ..., L_k, \neg E_1, ..., \neg E_q \}$ be a goal, and $C = \{ A \leftarrow B_1, ..., B_p \}$ be a clause. A goal G' is said to be *P-derived* (resp. *N-derived*) from G and C using an mgu θ if

(1) L_m is the selected literal in G;

(2) θ is a restricted mgu of L_m and A; and

(3) G' is the goal $\{ \leftarrow (L_1, ..., B_1, ..., B_p, ..., L_k, \neg E_1, ..., \neg E_q)\theta \}$.

The $B_i\theta$ in G' is said to be a *P-descendant* (resp. an *N-descendant*) of L_m in G. Furthermore, any P-descendant (resp. N-descendant) of $L_j\theta$ in G' is a P-descendant (resp. an N-descendant) of L_j in G. □

Example 3.1. Consider the program in Example 2.4 and goal $\{ \leftarrow \neg P(x), \neg E(x, a) \}$. Then $\{ \leftarrow R(y), R(g(x)), \neg S(z), \neg S(h(x)), \neg E(x, a) \}$ is N-derived from the goal. □

Now we are ready to define a simpler version of SL-Twin-resolution.

Definition 3.2. Let Π_P and Π_N be two sets of oriented clauses, and G be a goal. A *nontight-SL-Twin-derivation* of $\Pi_P \cup \Pi_N \cup \{G\}$ is a (finite or infinite) sequence $G_0 = G$, $G_1, ..., G_n, ...$ of goals and a sequence $\theta_1, ..., \theta_n, ...$ of mgu's such that each goal G_{j+1} is either

(1) P-derived from G_j and C using θ_{j+1}, where C is a clause in Π_P; or

(2) N-derived from G_j and C using θ_{j+1}, where C is a clause in Π_P. □

Example 3.2. Consider program Π_P below

$$c_1 \quad b \leftarrow \neg a$$
$$c_2 \quad q \leftarrow a, \neg p$$
$$c_3 \quad p \leftarrow b, \neg q$$

Let $\Pi_N = B(\Pi_P)$. That is,

$$c_4 \quad \neg b \leftarrow a$$
$$c_5 \quad \neg q \leftarrow \neg a$$
$$c_6 \quad \neg q \leftarrow p$$
$$c_7 \quad \neg p \leftarrow \neg b$$
$$c_8 \quad \neg p \leftarrow q$$
$$c_9 \quad \neg a \leftarrow true$$

Then D_1 and D_2 below are two nontight-SL-Twin-derivations of $\Pi_P \cup \Pi_N \cup \{\leftarrow p\}$:

D_1 :			D_2 :		
G_0	$\leftarrow p$		G_0	$\leftarrow p$	
G_{11}	$\leftarrow \underline{b}, \neg q$	(P-derived from c_3)	G_{21}	$\leftarrow b, \neg \underline{q}$	(P-derived from c_3)
G_{12}	$\leftarrow \neg a, \neg \underline{q}$	(P-derived from c_1)	G_{22}	$\leftarrow b, \underline{p}$	(N-derived from c_6)
G_{13}	$\leftarrow \neg a$	(N-derived from c_5)	G_{23}	$\leftarrow b, \neg \underline{q}$	(P-derived from c_3)
G_{14}	$\square$	(N-derived from c_9)	G_{24}	$\leftarrow b, \underline{p}$	(N-derived from c_6)
				$\cdots$	

D_1 is a finite derivation that ends up with an empty clause, but D_2 is an infinite one. $\square$

The tight-derivation, proposed by Van Gelder [12], is a generalization of the SLDNF-resolution by adopting the loop checking technique to eliminate useless positive circulars in the program to obtain the finite failure whenever possible. The technique is crucial for semantics based on a notion of minimal models (all of the three semantics we consider in this paper are this kind of semantics). Similar to the tight-derivation, by adopting the loop checking technique, we are able to tighten the nontight-SL-Twin-derivation to obtain a complete resolution, whenever the completeness is possible.

Example 3.3. The following is obtained from the program in Example 3.2 by adding a meaningless clause $q \leftarrow q$.

c_1	$b \leftarrow \neg a$
c_2	$q \leftarrow a, \neg p$
c_3	$p \leftarrow b, \neg q$
c_3'	$q \leftarrow q$

Consider the following nontight-SL-Twin-derivation:

G_0	$\leftarrow \neg q$	
G_1	$\leftarrow \neg \underline{a}, \neg q$	(N-derived)
G_2	$\leftarrow \neg q$	(N-derived)
G_3	$\leftarrow \neg \underline{a}, \neg q$	(N-derived)
G_4	$\leftarrow \neg q$	(N-derived)
G_5	$\leftarrow \neg \underline{a}, \neg q$	(N-derived)
	$\cdots$	

G_5 is the same as G_3 and G_1, and the derivation is infinite. $\square$

The trouble in the above example was brought up by a meaningless clause $q \leftarrow q$. In fact, $\leftarrow \neg q$ should be true under the well-founded model semantics, but not the negation as finite failure semantics.

Definition 3.3. Let $G_0, ..., G_i, ..., G_j, ...$ be a nontight-SL-Twin-derivation, and L_j be a negative, non-inequality literal in G_j. Then L_j is said to be *N-reducible* if there exists a negative literal L_i in G_i, where $i < j$, such that L_j is an N-descendant of L_i and $L_j = (L_i) \theta_{i+1} ... \theta_j$. $\square$

An N-reducible literal is, in fact, the same as those atoms in the tight-SLD tree with common ancestors. The SL-Twin-derivation is a generalization of the nontight-SL-Twin derivation by eliminating all N-reducible literals.

It has been shown that when the logic implication semantics is concerned, the linear resolution is incomplete unless the goals with a unit subgoal, called a *merge*, are also used to derive new resolvents [5]. For the semantics with more than one model, we have to consider the merge resolvents, which can be implemented by recognizing so called *P-reducible* literals below.

Definition 3.4. Let $G_0, ..., G_i, ..., G_j, ...$ be a nontight-SL-Twin-derivation, and L_j be a non-inequality literal in G_j. Then L_j is said to be *P-reducible* if there exists a unit goal G_i, where G_i is $\{ \leftarrow L_i \}$ and where $i < j$, such that L_j is a P-descendant of L_i and $L_j = (\neg L_i) \theta_{i+1}... \theta_j$. $\square$

Definition 3.5. An SL-Twin-derivation is defined the same as a nontight-SL-Twin-derivation, except that all N-reducible (resp. P-reducible) literals are eliminated during the N-deriving (reps. P-deriving). $\square$

Example 3.4 The following is an SL-Twin-derivation for the program in Example 3.3 and goal $\{ \leftarrow \neg q \}$:

$$
\begin{array}{lll}
G_0 & \leftarrow \neg q & \\
G_1 & \leftarrow \neg a & \text{(N-derived)} \\
G_2 & \square & \text{(N-derived)}\square
\end{array}
$$

Given two sets Π_P and Π_N of oriented clauses, the SL-Twin-resolution is designed to derive all positive and negative conclusions from both Π_P and Π_N. The integration is automatically done by taking either P- or N-deriving for any selected literals whenever appropriate.

Definition 3.6. (*SL-Twin-refutation*) Let Π_P and Π_N be two sets of oriented clauses and G be a goal. Then an SL-Twin-refutation of $\Pi_P \cup \Pi_N \cup G$ is defined as a finite SL-Twin-derivation of $\Pi_P \cup \Pi_N \cup G$ that ends up with the pseudo-empty clause. $\square$

4. Proof Procedures for Various Semantics

We report our main findings in the following theorem.

Theorem 4.1. Let Π is finite set of clauses. $G = \{ \leftarrow Q \}$ be a goal, where Q denotes a conjunction of non-equality literals. If there exists an SL-Twin-refutation of $\Pi_P \cup \Pi_N \cup G$, then

(i) if Π is a logic program and $\Pi_P = \Pi$ and $\Pi_N = B(\Pi)$, then $\exists x Q$, where x is a list variables appearing in Q, is true in the well-founded model of Π;

(ii) if Π is a logic program and $\Pi_P = F(\Pi \cup B(\Pi))$ and $\Pi_N = B(\Pi)$, then $\exists x Q$ is true in every stable model of Π; and

(iii) if $\Pi_P = B(\Pi) \cup F(\Pi)$ and $\Pi_N = B(\Pi)$, then $\exists x Q$ is true in the GCWA semantics. $\square$

These results are summarized in the following table:

	Well–Founded Semantics	Stable Model Semantics	GCWA
Π_P	Π	$F(\Pi \cup B(\Pi))$	$B(\Pi) \cup F(\Pi)$
Π_N	$B(\Pi)$	$B(\Pi)$	$B(\Pi)$

Due to the semi-decidability of first order logic, we shall not enjoy the completeness of the resolution, as shown below.

Example 4.1. Consider program $\{ P(x) \leftarrow P(s(x)) \}$ and goal $\{ \leftarrow \neg P(x) \}$. There exists no SL-Twin-refutation of the given goal. However, $\neg P(x)$ is true in the well founded model semantics for all x concerned. $\square$

5. Conclusions

We showed in this paper how the unsafe negation problem in negation-as-failure could be tackled by the mechanism of blocking formulas combined with Skolem functions. We then showed how this result allowed us to formulate a a general proof-theoretic framework for nonmonotonic reasoning, i.e., a proof procedure with parameters. We demonstrated how to derive proof procedures for some specific semantics by supplying appropriate parameters. We showed that all these procedures are sound but may not be always complete.

The proposed framework is interesting enough to warrant further investigation. We claim that with appropriate parameters and control mechanism, proof procedures for other nonmonotonic reasoning formalisms can be derived.

References

1. Chan D., Constructive Negation based on the Completed Database, in *Proc. 5th Symposium/Conference on Logic Programming*, R. A. Kowalski and K. A. Bowen (ed.), MIT Press, 1988, 111-125.

2. Chan D., An Extension of Constructive Negation and its Application in Coroutining, in *Proc. North American Conference on Logic Programming*, E. Lust and R. Overbeek (ed.), MIT Press, 1989, 477-496.

3. Clark K., Negation as Failure, in *Logic and Databases*, H. Gallaire and J. Minker (ed.), Plenum Press, New York, 1978, 293-322.

4. Gelfond M. and V. Lifschitz, The Stable Model Semantics for Logic Programming, in *Proc. 5th Symposium/Conference on Logic Programming*, R. A. Kowalski and K. A. Bowen (ed.), MIT Press, 1988, 1070-1080.

5. Genesereth M. and N. Nilsson, *Logic Foundations of Artificial Intelligence*, Morgan Kaufman Publishers, Los Altos, 1987.

6. Henschen L. and H. Park, Compiling the GCWA in Indefinite Deductive Databases, in *Foundations of Deductive Databases and Logic Programming*, J. Minker (ed.), Morgan Kaufman Publishers, 1988, 395-438.

7. Minker J., On Indefinite Databases and the Closed-World Assumption, in *Proc. Sixth Conf. on Automated Deduction*, Springer-Verlag, New York, 7-9 June, 1982.

8. Przymusinski T. C., On Constructive Negation in Logic Programming, in *Proc. North American Conference on Logic Programming*, MIT Press, 1989.

9. Rajasekar A. and J. Minker, A Stratification Semantics for General Disjunctive Programs, in *Proc. North American Conference on Logic Programming*, E. Lust and R. Overbeek (ed.), MIT Press, 1989, 573-586.

10. Ross K., A Procedural Semantics for Well Founded Negation in Logic Programs, in *Proc. the 8th ACM PODS*, 1989 , 22-33.

11. Van Gelder A., K. Ross and J. Schlipf, Unfounded Sets and Well-founded Semantics for General Logic Programs, in *Proc. the 7th ACM PODS*, 1988, 221-230.

12. Van Gelder A., Negation as Failure Using Tight Derivations for General Logic Programs, in *Foundations of Deductive Databases and Logic Programming*, J. Minker (ed.), Morgan Kaufman Publishers, 1988, 149-176.

13. Yahya A. and L. Henschen, Deduction in Non-Horn Databases, *J. Automated Reasoning 1*, (1985), .

On Semantics, Syntactics and Fixpoints of General Programs
(Extended Abstract)

Li Yan Yuan
Department of Computing Science
University of Alberta
Edmonton, CANADA T6G 2H1

Abstract

In this paper, we extend the unified view of logic programs, characterized by van Emden and Kowalski, in terms of semantics, syntactics, and fixpoints into the context of general programs. We first propose a general model semantics which is a natural extension of the Herbrand model semantics. We have shown that any program has a unique least model. Then we show that the least model of a program is precisely the set of all minimally derived disjunctive facts from the program and reveal the relationship between semantics and syntactics of general programs. Finally we show that the least model of a program can also be characterized by the least fixpoint of the natural operator associated with general programs. Our unified view of general programs enhances the theoretical foundation of logic programming and deductive databases.

1. Introduction

There is currently considerable interest in knowledge and deductive database systems that are based on logic programming. A logic program, i.e., a set of Horn clauses, certainly enjoys many desirable properties that should be seriously considered while searching for an appropriate formalism. Among other things, there is the coincidence of semantics, syntactics[†], and fixpoints of logic programs. That is, a logic program has a unique minimal model, which is precisely the set of all ground facts that can be derived from the program, and this particular model is also characterized as the least fixpoint of a transformation associated with the program. It is this unified view of logic programs that plays a central role in the theory of logic programming [Ll89, vEK76].

However, logic programming does not seem to be expressive enough for knowledge and deductive database systems. In particular, we need to express negation and incomplete information. That is why general programs, i.e., indefinite programs with negation, have been proposed [Sh88]. The extension from logic programs into general programs, though indeed increases the expressive power, has brought many new challenges to us.

This work has been partially supported by the NSERC of Canada.
† By syntactics we mean proof theoretic perspective.

First, an indefinite program has more than one minimal models, and therefore, the least model no longer exists. The lack of the least model has stimulated intensive study on declarative semantics of general programs [Sh88, ABW88, VG88]. In terms of syntactics, due to incomplete information an indefinite program has a set of minimally derived disjunctive facts, instead of having a set of ground facts. The relationship between semantics and syntactics of a general program is not clear so far. In other words, we do not understand how the set of minimal models and the set of minimally derived disjunctive facts are related. Another difficulty in studying general programs is that the natural operator originally introduced by van Emden and Kowalski [vEK76] is non-monotonic in the presence of negation and disjunction and may not have least fixpoints. Consequently, the unified view of semantics, syntactics, and fixpoints fades out in the extension from logic programs to general programs, which weakens the theoretical foundation of logic programming.

In this paper we are trying to reestablish the unified view of general programs in terms of semantics, syntactics, and fixpoints.

First, we propose the general model semantics, which is a natural extension of the Herbrand model semantics by considering incomplete information. We have shown that any consistent general program has a unique least model. If a program is definite, its least model coincides with its unique minimal model.

Then we show that the least model of a general program is precisely the set of all minimally derived disjunctive facts of the program. We also reveal the relationship between the set of minimal models of a general program and the set of its minimally derived disjunctive facts.

We extend the natural T operator of van Emden and Kowalski into the context of general programs and show that the operator, though non-monotonic, has the least fixpoint which is computable by ordinal powers of the operator.

Finally, we show that the least fixpoint of the operator of a general program coincides with its unique least model, which provides a unified view of general programs in terms of semantics, syntactics, and fixpoints. We also demonstrate that the unified view of logic programs is just a special case of our unified view. This unified view enhances the study on the theoretical foundation of logic programming and deductive databases.

Recently, Lobo, Minker, and Rajasekar have independently proposed similar view of general programs [LMR89]. They proposed the minimal model-state of a general program and shows that the minimal model-state, which is unique, subsumes all logical consequences of the program. The minimal model-state of a program is also justified by a fixpoint semantics. In fact, it is easy to show that the minimal model-state of a program is exactly the same as our least general model of the program. However, our unified view is a direct extension of the unified view of van Emden and Kowalski. That is, our general model is defined based on the truth values of foumulas in a general model, which is a direct extension of the Herbrand model semantics, but the minimal model-state of a program is defined based on Herbrand model itself [LMR89]. Secondly, we have clearly characterized relationships between the Herbrand models and all the logical consequences of a program by the means of the general model semantics, which has remained unknown for quite long time. Another important contribution of this peper is that we have discussed properties of non-monotonic operators and shown that some non-monotonic operators may have the least fixpoint.

We believe that the main point of this paper is not just its particular results, but rather the *methodology* by which the relationship between the semantics and syntactics is examed and results are obtained. We do not consider general programs with negation in this paper. However the method developed in the paper may also be used to study the relationship between the semantics and syntactics of general programs with negation and we shall continue our study in this direction.

The rest of the paper is organized as follows. In Section 2 some preliminaries are recalled. The general model semantics is proposed in Section 3. Section 4 discusses the least fixpoints of some non-monotonic operators. The unified view of general programs is characterized in Section 5. Section 6 offers the conclusion.

2. Preliminaries

In this section we review some fundamental results and give the notations that are utilized in the paper.

2.1. Syntactics We consider here a first order language. Its atomic formulas (i.e., atoms) are denoted by A, B, C, and tuples of atoms by **u**, **v**, **w**. An atom is called *ground* if no variables occur in it. A literal is an atom A, called a *positive literal*, or its negation $\neg$ A, called a *negative literal*. A clause is a set of literals which may also be written as a formula of the form: $B_1 \wedge ... \wedge B_m \rightarrow A_1 \vee ... \vee A_n$, where the B_i and A_i are atoms. The disjunction $A_1 \vee ... \vee A_n$ is called *head* of the clause, while the conjunction $B_1 \wedge ... \wedge B_m$ is called *body* of the clause. A *general program*, or a *program* for short, is a finite set of clauses[†]. A substitution θ = (**t**/**x**) is defined as usual.

Let Π be a program and θ be a clause. θ is said to be *derivable* from Π, denoted as $\Pi \vdash \theta$, if and only if there is a finite "proof" of θ from Π, that is, θ can be derived from Π by applying a finite sequence of certain inference rules. Despite the semidecidability of the first order logic, a sound and complete procedure, such as the Robinson resolution, does exist for computing derivability. The set of all minimally derived disjunctive facts from a program Π, denoted as MDDF(Π), is defined [YH85] as

MDDF(Π) = { $\{A_1,..., A_n\}$ | A_i are ground atoms, $\Pi \vdash A_1 \vee ... \vee A_n$, and

$$\Pi \nvdash A_1 \vee ... \vee A_{i-1} \vee A_{i+1} \vee ... \vee A_n \text{ for each } i = 1,..., n\}.$$

---

† In this paper, we do not consider programs that may contain negation in the body.

2.2. Semantics The language of a program Π is the first order language determined by all and only the logical symbols occurring in Π. The *Herbrand base* of a program Π, denoted as H_Π, is defined as the set of all ground atoms in the language of Π. A *Herbrand interpretation* is a subset of the Herbrand base. The truth of a formula is defined as usual. A Herbrand interpretation **m** is a *model* of Π if each clause in Π is true in **m**. The models here are usually called *Herbrand models*. A *minimal model* of Π is a model of Π such that no proper subset of it is a model of Π. A program which has only one minimal model is *definite*, otherwise it is *indefinite*. We say a clause θ is a *logical implication* of a program Π if θ is true in every model of Π. It has been shown that θ is a logic implication of Π if and only if $\Pi \vdash \theta$.

2.3. Fixpoints Let L be a set with a partial order $\leq$. We use glb(X) and lub(X) to denote the greatest lower bound and least upper bound of a subset X of L. Then L is said to be a *complete lattice* if both glb(X) and lub(X) exist for every subset X of L. The top element lub(L) and bottom element glb(L) of the complete lattice L are denoted as $\top$ and $\bot$ respectively. A subset X of a complete lattice is *directed* if every finite subset of X has an upper bound in X. Let L be a complete lattice and T: $L \to L$ be a mapping. An element **a** in L is (1) a *pre-fixpoint* of T if $T(\mathbf{a}) \leq \mathbf{a}$; (2) a *fixpoint* of T if $T(\mathbf{a}) = \mathbf{a}$; and (3) the *least fixpoint* of T if **a** is a fixpoint and for all fixpoints **b** of T we have $\mathbf{a} \leq \mathbf{b}$. T is said to be (1) *monotonic* if $T(x) \leq T(y)$, whenever $x \leq y$; and (2) *continuous* if $T(\text{lub}(X)) = \text{lub}(T(X))$, for every directed subset X of L. T is monotonic if it is continuous, but the vise versa is not true.

We now define ordinal powers of a mapping. Intuitively, the ordinals are what we use to count with. The non-negative integers are the finite ordinals and ω is the first infinite ordinal, i.e., the set of all non-negative integers. Then come with $\omega + 1$, $\omega + 2$, ..., 2ω, $2\omega + 1$, ... [Ll89].

Definition 2.1. Let L be a complete lattice and T: $L \to L$ be a mapping. Then

$$T\!\uparrow\!0 = \bot$$
$$T\!\uparrow\!n = T(\,T\!\uparrow\!(n-1)\,)$$
$$T\!\uparrow\!\omega = \text{lub}\,\{\,T\!\uparrow\!n \mid n = 0, 1, 2, \ldots\,\}. \quad \square$$

The ordinal power $T\!\uparrow\!\alpha$ can be extended beyond ω, but we shall not need this.

The following proposition presents the well known results regarding fixpoints and monotonic operators.

Proposition 2.1 [Ll89]. Let L be a complete lattice and T: $L \to L$ be monotonic. Then

(1) T has a least fixpoint lfp(T) and $\text{lfp}(T) = \text{glb}\{\,x \mid T(x) = x\} = \text{glb}\{\,x \mid T(x) \leq x\}$;

(2) for any ordinal α, $T\!\uparrow\!\alpha \leq \text{lfp}(T)$;

(3) there exists an ordinal β such that $\gamma \geq \beta$ implies $T\!\uparrow\!\gamma = \text{lfp}(T)$; and

(4) if T is continuous then $\text{lfp}(T) = T\!\uparrow\!\omega$. $\quad \square$

Our interest in these concepts arises from the fact that the set of all Herbrand interpretations of a definite program forms a complete lattice and there is a continuous mapping associated with this lattice. In Section 4, we shall extend results in Proposition 2.1 into some non-monotonic operators.

2.4. Definite Programs

In this subsection we discuss the unified view of definite programs in terms of the semantics, syntactics, and fixpoint theory.

Let Π be a definite program. Then 2^{H_Π}, which is the set of all Herbrand interpretations of Π, is a complete lattice under the partial order of set inclusion $\subseteq$. The least upper bound of any set of Herbrand interpretations is the union of all the interpretations in the set. The greatest lower bound is the intersection.

One of nice properties enjoyed by definite programs is the model intersection property, as stated in the proposition below.

Proposition 2.2 [Ll89]. Let Π be a definite program and M be a non-empty set of Herbrand models of Π. Then $glb(M) = \cap_{m_i \in M} m_i$ is also a model of Π. $\square$

Now we define the mapping associated with definite programs.

Definition 2.2 [Ll89]. Let Π be a definite program and I be a Herbrand interpretation. A mapping $T_{\Pi_D} : 2^{H_\Pi} \to 2^{H_\Pi}$ is defined as follows. $T_{\Pi_D}(I) = \{ A \mid A \in H_\Pi, A_1 \wedge ... \wedge A_n \to A$ is a ground instance of a clause in Π, and $\{A_1, ..., A_n\} \subseteq I\}$.

Clearly, T_{Π_D} is monotonic. It has also been shown that T_{Π_D} is continuous [Ll89]. T_{Π_D} provides the link between the declarative and procedural semantics of a definite program Π. Next we present the major result in the theory of definite programs.

Proposition 2.3. Let Π be a definite program, T_{Π_D} be the mapping defined over the set of all Herbrand interpretations of Π, M_Π be the unique minimal model of Π, and $MDDF(\Pi)$ be the set of grand facts that can be derived from Π. Then

$$M_\Pi = MDDF(\Pi) = lfp(T_{\Pi_D}) = T_{\Pi_D} \uparrow \omega. \quad \square$$

This proposition, which is due to van Emden and Kowalski [vEK76], provides a clear characterization of a definite program in terms of its semantics, syntactics, and fixpoints. The major contribution of this paper is to extend this result into the context of general programs.

3. General Model Semantics

In this section we first define the general model semantics which is a natural extension of the Herbrand model semantics. Then we show that any program has exactly one least model in the context of general models. Finally, relationships among ordinary models, general models, and syntactics are analyzed.

Definition 3.1. Let H_Π be a Herbrand base. A *general interpretation* I is defined as a set of nonempty subsets of H_Π such that for any two distinct tuples **u** and **v** in I, **u** and **v** are not subsets of each other. $\square$

When for each $\mathbf{u} \in I$ $|\mathbf{u}| = 1$, a general interpretation reduces to an ordinary interpretation. The truth of a formula in a general interpretation is defined similarly as that in an ordinal interpretation[†]. Formally, we proceed by induction.

Definition 3.2. Let I be a general interpretation.

1. A formula S is true in I iff each of its closed instances is true in I, that is, for each x occurring free in S, and each variable -free term t, $S(t/x)$ is true in I.

2. A closed formula $\exists x \, S$ is true in I iff for some variable free terms $t_1, ..., t_n, n \geq 1$, the formula $S(t_1/x) \vee ... \vee S(t_n/x)$ is true in I.

3. A closed formula $\forall x \, S$ is true in I iff (by (1)!) S is true in I.

4. A closed formula $\neg A \vee S$ is true in I, where A is a ground atom, iff for each $\mathbf{u} = \{A, A_1, ..., A_n\}$ in I, $A_1 \vee ... \vee A_n \vee S$ is true in I.

5. A closed formula $S_1 \wedge ... \wedge S_n$ is true in I iff each of the S_i is true in I.

6. A disjunction of ground atoms $A_1 \vee ... \vee A_n$ is true in I iff there is a tuple $\mathbf{u}$ in I such that $\mathbf{u} \subseteq \{A_1, ..., A_n\}$.

7. A formula $\neg A$, where A is a ground atom, is true in I iff $A \notin \mathbf{u}$ for each $\mathbf{u}$ in I.

A general interpretation M is called a *general model* of a program Π if each clause in Π is true in M. $\square$

Obviously a model of a program Π is also its general model. Note that we do not distinguish a model $\mathbf{m}$ and a general model M if $M = \{ \{A\} \mid A \in \mathbf{m} \}$.

The following lemma describes the relationship between general models and logical implications.

Lemma 3.1. Let Π be a program and θ be a clause. Then θ is a logical implication of Π, i.e., $\Pi \vdash \theta$, if and only if θ is true in any general model of Π. $\square$

Example 3.1. Consider a program $\Pi = \{ A \vee B, A \rightarrow C \vee D \}$. Assume $I_1 = \{ \{A, B\}, \{B, C, D\} \}$ and $I_2 = \{\{A\}, \{B, C\}\}$. Then I_1 is a general model of Π. However I_2 is not. Since $\{A\}$ is in I_2, for $A \rightarrow C \vee D$ to be true in I_2 there should be a tuple $\mathbf{u}$ in I_2 such that $\mathbf{u} \subseteq \{C, D\}$, which is not the case. $\square$

An indefinite program has more than one minimal models, which indicates the existence of incomplete information. One of the main purposes of proposing general models is to represent such incomplete information in the model theoretic semantics of programs. Now we discuss the relationship between general models and ordinary models.

Definition 3.3. Let I be a general interpretation, $\mathbf{m} = \{A_1, ..., A_n\}$ be an ordinary interpretation. Then $\mathbf{m}$ is said to be contained in I, if

---

[†] Note that we have defined the truth of a first order sentence, which is more general than that of a program.

(1) each **u** in I contains some A_i in **m**, and

(2) for each A_i in **m** there exists a tuple $\mathbf{u}_i$ in I such that $\mathbf{u}_i \cap \mathbf{m} = \{A_i\}$. $\square$

C[I] is used to denote the set of all interpretations contained in I. Consider I_1 in Example 3.1. $\{A, C\}$ is contained in I_1, but $\{A, B\}$ is not. $C[I_1] = \{\ \{B\}, \{A, C\}, \{A, D\}\}$.

The following theorem reveals the relationship between general models and ordinary models.

Theorem 3.1. Let Π be a program and I be a general interpretation. Then I is a general model of Π if and only if each **m** in C[I] is a model of Π. $\square$

Consider Π, I_1 and I_2 in Example 3.1. We have $C[I_1] = \{\ \{B\}, \{A, C\}, \{A, D\}\ \}$ and $C[I_2]$ $= \{\ \{A, B\}, \{A, C\}\ \}$. Since interpretations $\{B\}$, $\{A, C\}$, and $\{A, D\}$ are Herbrand models of Π and $\{A, B\}$ is not, I_1 is a general model of Π and I_2 is not.

As indicated in the proceeding section, the set of all Herbrand interpretations forms a complete lattice under the partial order of set inclusion $\subseteq$. The minimal model of a definite program is also defined based on this partial order. Similarly we are going to define a partial order on the set of all general interpretations.

Definition 3.4. Let Π be a program and L be the set of all general interpretations of Π. Then a binary relation $\leq$ is defined on L as follows. Assume I_1 and I_2 are two general interpretations of Π in L. We say $I_1 \leq I_2$ if for each tuple $\mathbf{u}_1$ in I_1 there exists a tuple $\mathbf{u}_2$ in I_2 such that $\mathbf{u}_2 \subseteq \mathbf{u}_1$. $\square$

Example 3.2. Let $I_1 = \{\ \{A, B\}, \{B, C, D\}, \{A, C\}\ \}$ and $I_2 = \{\ \{A\}, \{B, C\}\ \}$. Though I_2 contains less tuples than I_1 does, we have $I_1 \leq I_2$ and $I_2 \nleq I_1$. $\square$

Clearly $\leq$ is a partial order on L, that is, it is reflexive, antisymmetric, and transitive. It is easy to check that the partial order $\subseteq$ defined over the set of all Herbrand interpretations is just a special case of the partial order $\leq$. That is, for two ordinal interpretations I_1 and I_2, $I_1 \subseteq I_2$ if and only if $I_1 \leq I_2$. We know that the set of all Herbrand interpretations under $\subseteq$ is a complete lattice. Similarly we have shown that L under $\leq$ is also a complete lattice.

Definition 3.5. Let X be a set of general interpretations. Then two general interpretations $\overline{X}$ and $\underline{X}$ are defined as follows[†].

(1) $\overline{X} = \cup_{I_i \in X} I_i$, and

(2) $\underline{X} = \{\ \mathbf{u}\ |\ \text{for every } I_i \text{ in X there exists a tuple } \mathbf{v} \in I_i \text{ such that } \mathbf{v} \subseteq \mathbf{u}\}$.

Example 3.3. Let $X = \{\ I_1, I_2, I_3\}$ be a set of general interpretations, where $I_1 = \{\ \{A, B\}, \{B, C\}\ \}$, $I_2 = \{\ \{A\}, \{B, C, D\}\ \}$, and $I_3 = \{\ \{A, D\}, \{C, D\}\ \}$. Then $\underline{X} = \{\ \{A\}, \{B, C\}, \{C, D\}\ \}$ and $\overline{X} = \{\ \{A, B, D\}, \{B, C, D\}\ \}$. $\square$

---

† Note that both $\overline{X}$ and $\underline{X}$, as general interpretations, shall not contain redundant tuples.

When X is the set of ordinal interpretations, $\overline{X}$ and $\underline{X}$ reduce to the union and intersection of all the interpretations in X respectively.

Theorem 3.2. The set of all general interpretations of a program Π under the binary relation $\leq$ forms a complete lattice. Furthermore, for any subset X of L, $lub(X) = \overline{X}$ and $glb(X) = \underline{X}$. $\square$

We now extend the model intersection property into the context of general models.

Theorem 3.3. Let Π be a program and M be a set of general models of Π. Then $glb(M) = \underline{M}$ is also a general model of Π. $\square$

Definition 3.6. Let Π be a program and M be a general interpretation of Π. M is said to be the least model of Π if (1) M is a general model of Π and (2) for any general model N of Π, we have $M \leq N$. $\square$

The least model is defined in the same way as one defined in the context of Herbrand models. Note that a program may not have a least model in the context of Herbrand models unless it is definite. However, Theorem 3.4 (1) below guarantees the existence of the least model of any program.

Theorem 3.4. Let Π be a program and MDDF(Π) is the set of all minimally derived disjunctive facts from Π. Then

(1) Π has one and exactly one least model,

(2) MDDF(Π) is the least model of Π. $\square$

Note that MDDF(Π) is defined in terms of the proof theoretics and the Robinson resolution provides a sound and complete procedure to compute MDDF(Π). Due to the semidecidability of first order logic, we may not be able to develop an effective procedure to compute MDDF(Π) for any Π. However, in many applications, such as deductive databases, an algorithm for MDDF does exist. Theorem 3.4 establishes the relationship between semantics and syntactics of general programs. That is, the least model, though defined in terms of the model theoretics, is precisely the set of minimally derived disjunctive facts defined in terms of the proof theoretics. The following theorem reveals the relationship between the set of minimally derived disjunctive facts and the set of minimal models of a program.

Theorem 3.5. Let Π be a program and M be a set of disjunctions of ground atoms. Then M is the set of minimally derived disjunctive fact from Π if and only if C[M] is the set of all minimal models of Π. $\square$

Consider I_1 in Example 3.1. $C[I_1]$ is the set of all three minimal models of Π. Therefore, I_1 is the set of minimally derived disjunctive facts from Π. By Definition 3.3, Theorem 3.4 and 3.5, the least model can also be extended into the context of logical sentences. That is, M is the least model of a logic sentence T if and only if C[M] is the set of all minimal models of T. With our natural extension of Herbrand models, any program can enjoy an elegant uniformity of the semantics and syntactics. That is, any program has a unique least model which is the set of all minimally derived disjunctions of ground atoms. Furthermore, the least model also contains the set of all minimal models of the program. Due to incomplete information, the extension from ordinary models into general models is natural and necessary.

The following theorem reveals the relationship between the least model and the generalized closed world assumption, i.e., GCWA, proposed by Riter and Minker [Mi82].

Theorem 3.6. Let Π be a program and M_Π be the least model of Π. Then a clause θ is true in Π under the GCWA if and only if θ is true in M_Π. $\square$

4. Fixpoints and Some Non-Monotonic Operators

It is well known that the monotonicity is a sufficient but not necessary condition for the existence of the least fixpoint. In this section, we show that some non-monotonic operators may also have the least fixpoint.

Definition 4.1. Let L be a complete lattice and T: $L \to L$ be a mapping. Then T is said to be

(1) *pseudo-monotonic* if $\mathrm{lub}(T(x), x) \leq \mathrm{lub}(T(y), y)$, whenever $x \leq y$, and

(2) *growing* if $T\!\uparrow\!\alpha \leq T\!\uparrow\!(\alpha + 1)$ for any ordinal α. $\square$

It is easy to show that T is both pseudo-monotonic and growing if T is monotonic. But the vise versa is not true. Furthermore, the pseudo-monotonicity and growingness do not imply each other.

Example 4.1. Let $L = \{A, B, C, D, E\}$. Assume we have $A \leq B, A \leq C, A \leq D, A \leq E, B \leq C, B \leq D, B \leq E, C \leq E$, and $D \leq E$, as shown in the Fig. Then L is a complete lattice under the partial order $\leq$, and $\top = E$ and $\bot = A$. Consider the following two mappings over L:

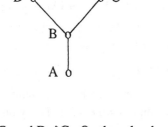

$T_1(A) = B, T_1(B) = A, T_1(C) = C, T_1(D) = D, T_1(E) = A$; and
$T_2(A) = B, T_2(B) = D, T_2(C) = C, T_2(D) = D, T_2(E) = A$.
The only difference between T_1 and T_2 is that $T_1(B) = A$ and $T_2(B) = D$. Then T_1 is pseudo-monotonic but T_2 is not, since we have $B \leq C$ but $\mathrm{lub}(T_2(B), B) = D, \mathrm{lub}(T_2(C), C) = C$, and $D \not\leq C$. On the other hand, T_2 is growing but T_1 is not. The reason becomes obvious if one observes that $T_1\!\uparrow\!0 = A, T_1\!\uparrow\!1 = B, T_1\!\uparrow\!2 = A$, and $B \not\leq A$. $\square$

The following lemma indicates that a pseudo-monotonic operator T has a least pre-fixpoint lpfp(T), that is, $T(\mathrm{lpfp}(T)) \leq \mathrm{lpfp}(T)$, and for any x in L such that $T(x) \leq x$, we have $\mathrm{lpfp}(T) \leq x$.

Lemma 4.1. Let L be a complete lattice and T: $L \to L$ be pseudo-monotonic. Then T has a least pre-fixpoint lpfp(T). Furthermore, $\mathrm{lpfp}(T) = \mathrm{glb}\{x \mid T(x) \leq x\}$. $\square$

A pseudo-monotonic mapping may not have a least fixpoint, though it has a least pre-fixpoint. Consider T_1 in Example 4.1. T_1 has two fixpoints, i.e., C and D, but has no least fixpoint. Let Π be a definite program and T_{Π_D} be the mapping. Since a Herbrand interpretation I is a model of Π if and only if I is a pre-fixpoint of T_{Π_D}, by Lemma 4.1, the existence of the least model of Π is guaranteed by the pseudo-monotonicity of T_{Π_D}. However, the existence of the least pre-fixpoint does not necessarily imply that the least pre-fixpoint can be computed by the ordinal powers of T_{Π_D}.

Theorem 4.1. Let L be a complete lattice and T: $L \rightarrow L$ be a mapping. If T is both pseudo-monotonic and growing then

(1) T has a least fixpoint lfp(T) and $lfp(T) = glb \{x \mid T(x) = x\} = glb \{x \mid T(x) \le x\}$;

(2) for any ordinal α, $T \uparrow \alpha \le lfp(T)$;

(3) there exists an ordinal β such that $\gamma \ge \beta$ implies $T \uparrow \gamma = lfp(T)$; and

(4) if $T'(x) = lub(T(x), x)$ is a continuous mapping defined over L then $lfp(T) = T \uparrow \omega$. $\quad\square$

Theorem 4.1 extends Proposition 2.1 into the context of some non-monotonic operators. Its application can be found in the next section.

5. Unified View of General Programs

In this section we extend the unified view of a definite program, characterized by van Emden and Kowalski, into the context of general programs. We start by defining an operator on the set of all general interpretations of a program, which is a complete lattice under $\le$.

Definition 5.1. Let I be a general interpretation and θ: $B_1 \wedge ... \wedge B_m \rightarrow A_1 \vee ... \vee A_n$, where $m + n \ge 1$, be a ground clause. A set **u** of ground atoms is called an *immediate consequence of I under* θ if for each B_i, $i = 1,..., m$, there exists a tuple $v_i = \{B_i, C_{i1}, ..., C_{iq_i}\}$, where $q_i \ge 0$, in I such that $\mathbf{u} = \{A_1, ..., A_n, C_{11}, ..., C_{1q_1}, ..., C_{m1}, ..., C_{mq_m}\}$. $\quad\square$

An immediate consequence of I under θ is a set of ground atoms that can be derived from I by applying θ once and only once.

Example 5.1. Let $I_1 = \{ \{A, B\} \}$, and $I_2 = \{ \{A\}, \{B, D\} \}$, and θ be $A \rightarrow C$. Then $\{B, C\}$ is an immediate consequence of I_1 under θ and $\{C\}$ is an immediate consequence of I_2 under θ. $\quad\square$

Now we define a mapping over the set of all general interpretations.

Definition 5.2. Let Π be a program, I be a general interpretation, and L be the set of all general interpretations of Π. A mapping T_Π: $L \rightarrow L$ is defined as follows. $T_\Pi(I)$ is the set of all immediate consequences of I under every ground instance θ of clauses in Π. That is,

$T_\Pi(I) = \{ \mathbf{u} \mid$ there exists a ground instance θ of a clause in Π such that
$\mathbf{u}$ is an immediate consequence of I under $\theta \}$. $\quad\square$

Example 5.2. Let $\Pi = \{ A \vee B, C \rightarrow A \vee D\}$ be a program, and $I_1 = \varnothing, I_2 = \{ \{A\} \}, I_3 = \{ \{A, B\} \}$, and $I_4 = \{ \{B\}, \{A, C\} \}$ be general interpretations. Then $T_\Pi(I_1) = \{ \{A, B\} \}, T_\Pi(I_2) = \{ \{A, B\} \}, T_\Pi(I_3) = \{ \{A, B\} \}$, and $T_\Pi(I_4) = \{ \{A, B\}, \{A, D\} \}$. $\square$

Note that in the above example, since $\{A, B\}$ is a clause in Π, $\{A, B\}$ is contained in $T_\Pi(I)$ for any general interpretation I. When Π is a definite program then T_Π reduces to T_{Π_D} defined in Section 2. In other words, T_{Π_D} is just a special version of T_Π in the context of definite programs and Herbrand interpretations. However, T_Π is not monotonic as shown in the following example, despite the fact that T_{Π_D} is monotonic.

Example 5.3. Let $\Pi = \{ A \rightarrow B \vee C\}, I_1 = \{ \{A, D\} \}$, and $I_2 = \{ \{D\} \}$. Then we have $I_1 \leq I_2$. However, $T_\Pi(I_1) = \{ \{B, C, D\} \}, T_\Pi(I_2) = \varnothing$, and , $\{ \{B, C, D\} \} \nleq \varnothing$. $\square$.

T_Π is non-monotonic, but the following theorem shows that is is pseudo-monotonic and growing.

Theorem 5.1. Let Π be a program, T_Π be the mapping defined above, and $T'_\Pi(I) = lub(T_\Pi(I), I)$ be a mapping defined on the set of all general interpretations of Π. Then

(1) T_Π is pseudo-monotonic;

(2) T_Π is growing; and

(3) T'_Π is continuous. $\square$

General interpretations which are general models can be characterized in terms of T_Π.

Theorem 5.2. Let Π be a program and I be a general interpretation of Π. Then I is a general model of Π if and only if $T_\Pi(I) \leq I$. $\square$

Consider Π and I_i, $i = 1, ..., 4$, in Example 5.2. We have $T_\Pi(I_2) \leq I_2$ and $T_\Pi(I_3) \leq I_3$, so both I_2 and I_3 are general models of Π. On the other hand, since $T_\Pi(I_1) = \{ \{A, B\} \} \nleq I_1 = \varnothing$ and $T_\Pi(I_4) = \{ \{A, B\}, \{A, D\} \} \nleq I_4 = \{ \{B\}, \{A, C\} \}$, neither I_1 nor I_4 is a general model of Π.

The existence of the unique least model of a general program, shown in Theorem 3.4 (1), is in fact implied by Lemma 4.1, Theorem 5.1 (1) and 5.2. The following theorem, which is an extension of Proposition 2.3 in the context of general programs, directly follows from Theorem 4.1, 5.1, and 5.2.

Theorem 5.3. Let Π be a general program, T_Π be the mapping defined above, M_Π be the unique least model of Π, and MDDF(Π) be the set of all minimally derived disjunctive facts from Π. Then

$$M_\Pi = \text{MDDF}(\Pi) = \text{lpf}(T_\Pi) = T_\Pi \uparrow \omega. \quad \square$$

Example 5.4. Consider Π in Example 5.2. The least model of Π is $\{ \{A, B\} \}$, and the only minimally derived fact is $A \vee B$. Furthermore, we have $T_\Pi \uparrow 0 = \varnothing, T_\Pi \uparrow 1 = T_\Pi(\varnothing) = \{ \{A, B\}$

}, and for any ordinal α such that $\alpha \geq 2$, $T_\Pi \uparrow \alpha = \{ \{A, B\} \} = \text{lfp}(T_\Pi)$. $\square$

Theorem 5.3 presents the major result in this section, which provides a fixpoint characterization of the least model of a general program. By extending the Herbrand model semantics into the general model semantics, we have reestablished the unified view of general programs in terms of semantics, syntactics, and fixpoints.

6. Conclusions

We have proposed the general model semantics and reestablish the unified view of general programs without negation. In the next step, we are going to investigate the declarative semantics of general programs with negation and try to establish the unified view of declarative meanings of the programs in terms of the semantics, syntactics, and fixpoints.

References

[ABW88] Apt, K.R., Blair, H.A., and Walker, A., Towards a Theory of Declarative Knowledge, in *Foundations of Deductive Databases and Logic Programming*, Minker, J. (editor), Morgan-Kaufman Pub., 1988, pp. 89-148.

[Ll89] Lloyed, J.W., *Foundations of Logic Programming*, 2nd Edition, Springer-Verlag, 1989.

[LMR89] Lobo, J., Minker, J., and Rajasekar, A., Extending the Semantics of Logic Programs to Disjunctive Logic Programs, Proc. the 6th International Conference on Logic Programming, 1988, pp. 255-267.

[Mi82] Minker, J., On Indefinite Databases and the Closed World Assumption, in Lecture Notes in Computer Science 138, Springer-Verlag, 1982 pp. 292-308.

[Sh88] Shepherdson, J.C, Negation in Logic Programming, in *Foundations of Deductive Databases and Logic Programming*, Minker, J. (editor), Morgan-Kaufman Pub., 1988, pp. 19-88.

[vEK76] van Emden, M.H. and Kowalski, R.A., The semantics of Predicate Logic as a Programming Language, JACM Vol. 23, 4, Oct. 1976, pp. 733-742.

[VG88] Van Gelder, A., Negation as Failure Using Tight Derivations for General Logic Programs, in *Foundations of Deductive Databases and Logic Programming*, Minker, J. (editor), Morgan-Kaufman Pub., 1988, pp 149-176.

[YH85] Yahya, A. and Henschen, L., Deduction in Non-Horn Databases, J. of Automated Reasoning, 1, 1985, 141-160.

A framework for variable-resolution vision

Anup Basu   Xiaobo Li[1]

Alberta Center for Machine Intelligence and Robotics
Department of Computing Science
University of Alberta
Edmonton, Alberta, Canada T6G 2H1

Abstract

The human visual system has a high resolution fovea and low resolution periphery.
We demonstrate here that a variable resolution Computer Vision system resembling
humans may indeed have several advantages over a uniform resolution system (as
are most presently existing equipment). Specifically, we look at the following problems to demonstrate our point: (a) stereo matching and gaze control, (b) obstacle
detection and navigation, (c) tracking a moving object, (d) character thinning.

1. Introduction

There has been significant research on multi-resolution vision in the recent past
[7] [11]. The theories developed have clearly demonstrated that various advantages
exist in such a visual system. However, one important concept has been generally
overlooked; a variable resolution imaging system such as the human eye can simplify
many visual tasks. This is the problem we address in this paper.

Consider the problem of vergence and matching in a stereo system [4] [8]. We would
like the left and right cameras to focus on the same object. Vergence makes various
problems in vision much simpler as noted by several authors [1]. [2], In the next
section it is shown how a two-stage matching process can make vergence simpler.
Gross peripheral match is first established then finer adjustments are made on the
fovea.

For the problem of detecting obstacles [12] low resolution peripheral vision helps in
reducing the number of operations substantially, thereby making real-time response
possible. The savings result from the reduction in the number of masks that need to
be matched per image pixel when resolution is decreased. Of course, the sensitivity
of the periphery in detecting small objects decreases. However, the response time

---

[1]This work is supported in part by the Canadian Natural Sciences and Engineering Research
Council under Grant OGP9198.

for identifying significantly large objects is reduced substantially. This problem is discussed in section 3.

In section 4 we discuss how the task of tracking a moving object or person is simplified by using both the high-resolution fovea and the low-resolution periphery at the same time. One way to track a contour would be to keep details on a small portion of the contour and have a low resolution outline of the remaining part. For example when we talk to a person who is moving around we focus on the face and have an outline of the remaining part of the body. On the other hand when a football player chases a receiver who is running with the ball, attention is placed on the legs (of the receiver).

Another interesting application of this new approach is in character thinning. The algorithm described in section 5 is a powerful tool for eliminating artifacts that are often generated during thinning. Experimental results demonstrate how masks based on variable resolution give much better results compared to existing techniques. We also show that the cost of our method is significantly lower than a comparable uniform resolution scheme.

2. Stereo Matching and Gaze Control

Consider a simple gaze control system (e.g. [4]). Fixing one camera (say left) on a desired object we would like to move the other (right) so that the fovea of both cameras fixate on the same object.

Fig. 1. A uniform resolution image

In Fig. 1, for example, we may wish to fixate on the small girl. A uniform resolution scheme for doing this is slow and unreliable in the presence of noise since small features are often lost.

Let us now consider the scene in Fig. 1 in variable resolution (Fig. 2).

Fig. 2. Variable resolution version of Fig. 1

In order to focus on the same object (or person) we use the following algorithm:

(a) generate variable resolution stereo images,

(b) fixing the fovea in one of the eyes move the fovea in the other,until a match is obtained with required precision.

The details of this method is described in [3]. It is shown that a variable resolution technique makes the matching function smooth, unlike the step function it resembles in uniform resolution. We have also established that this method does not involve correspondence of image features, and is thus very useful in real-time applications. Unfortunately we cannot describe the details of the algorithm here due to lack of space.

2.1 Elimination of redundant edges in the periphery

Replacing pixel values in a small neighborhood by a smoothed average reduces insignificant edges. The effect of smoothing at different scales on edge detection has been discussed by Witkin [13]. For example, the image of a building can generate edges which represent bricks at high resolution, however at lower resolution only the general outline of the building and doors/windows are detected. Since unnecessary details are eliminated in the periphery, stereo matching and tracking operations are simplified.

2.2 Accuracy of matching in the fovea

The periphery helps in speeding up the matching process, but the high resolution fovea is needed to increase the accuracy of the match. Consider Fig. 3(a). At lower resolution it is difficult to accurately locate (or fixate) on the girl in the picture. The same problem becomes much simpler in Fig. 3(b).

724

(a)

(b)

Fig. 3. High and low resolution outlines of Fig. 1

The reason for this happening is that some proportion of features in an image is always generated by the background and also certain parts of the outline corresponding to the object of interest may not appear (drop-outs). Let us consider this problem from a statistical point of view and examine how a high resolution fovea helps in the accuracy of the matching. First we need to define some notation:

p_1 : Proportion of actual contour (corresponding to object of interest).

p_2 : Proportion of random drop-ins due to background.

p_3 : Proportion of random drop-out of actual contour.

When the resolution is increased by a factor r, say, the proportion of the edges which are due to the actual contour decreases to p_1/r, assuming the window size remains the same (Fig. 4).

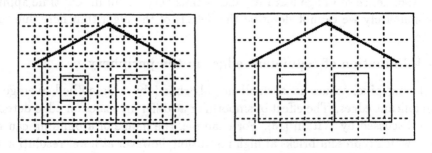

Fig. 4. Proportion of edges at high and low resolutions

We also assume that the object of interest may be small compared to the background (i.e. p_1 may be less than p_2). The proportion of background points also decreases to p_2/r. The random drop out of actual contour is assumed to remain the same. For the problem of stereo vergence we would like to match images between left and right eyes. Consider the matching function to be simply the correlation between features in the two images. This function will have the form

$$C^\theta(x,y) = C^\theta_{act}(x,y) + C^\theta_{ran}(x,y)$$

where, C_{act} : correlation due to actual match

C_{ran} : correlation due to random background match

θ : orientation of right camera with respect to left

(we consider only one degree of freedom, the pan angle)

The following notations are used for windows:

W_m: window at resolution m x m

W_{mr}: window at resolution mr x mr

As θ varies we would like to select the value θ^d the desired orientation of the right eye with respect to the left. In order to quickly and accurately obtain θ^d, $\sum_{x,y \in windows} C^\theta$ should have a high value corresponding to θ^d and low value outside. Let $p_4 = p_1(1 - p_3)$ in the following equations.

$$E^\theta_{act} = E\left(\frac{1}{m^2} \sum_{x,y \in W_m} C^\theta_{act}(x,y)\right) = \begin{cases} p_4 & \text{if } \theta = \theta^d \\ p_4^2 & \text{if } \theta \neq \theta^d \end{cases}$$

(A random match is assumed for $\theta \neq \theta^d$)

$$E^\theta_{ran} = E\left(\frac{1}{m^2} \sum_{x,y \in W_m} C^\theta_{ran}(x,y)\right) = p_2^2$$

$$E^\theta = E^\theta_{act} + E^\theta_{ran}$$

$$L = \frac{E^\theta(\theta \neq \theta^d)}{E^{\theta^d}} = \frac{p_4 + p_2^2}{p_4^2 + p_2^2} \quad (1)$$

$$R = \frac{E^\theta(\theta \neq \theta^d)}{E^{\theta^d}} = \frac{\frac{p_4}{r} + \frac{p_2^2}{r^2}}{(p_4^2 + p_2^2)/r} = \frac{rp_4 + p_2^2}{p_4^2 + p_2^2} \quad (2)$$

Fig. 5 shows how the matching function varies with θ at low and at high resolutions.

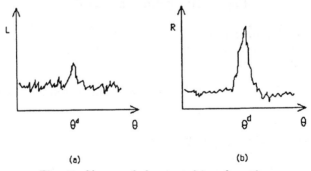

(a)　　　　　　　　　(b)

Fig. 5. Shape of the matching function

3. Obstacle Avoidance and Navigation

It is interesting to observe that humans focus on free spaces while moving around and use their peripheral vision to detect obstacles. For example, when we drive a car we try to focus on the obstacle free road in front of us, while the periphery is used to detect if other cars are moving unexpectedly or not. In a two-way road we never focus on a car that is moving the opposite way but instead concentrate on the clear road in front.

For detecting obstacles the existing algorithms all depend on matching masks to the image flow patterns. However, the size of an obstacle (as seen in the image) can vary considerably. If the maximum size of the obstacle in the image in $m \times m$ (say) then the total number of possible masks that need to be matched is $O(m^3)$. This follows from the fact that there are $O(\ell^2)$ possible positions where a mask of size $\ell \times \ell$ can be placed ($\ell = 2, ..., m$), within an $m \times m$ window (and $\sum_{\ell=1}^{m} \ell^2 = O(m^3)$). Thus the cost of obstacle detection by testing divergence of flow field ([9], [10]) is $O(m^3)$, when an $m \times m$ window is used. When the resolution is reduced by a factor r (say) the corresponding reduction in the number of masks to be matched is reduced by a factor $\frac{1}{r^3}$.

Consider Fig. 6 where we have a continuously changing resolution.

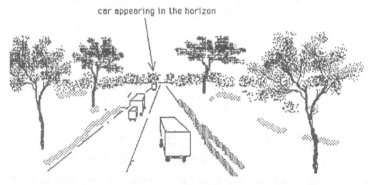

car appearing in the horizon

Fig. 6. Navigating on a road

Unexpected obstacles appear either:

- at the periphery at very low resolution, or

- at the horizon where it is very small (in terms of number of pixels) even at high resolution.

A system for visual navigation should:

(a) keep track of obstacles already in view, (this is the problem of tracking objects which we discuss in the next section.)

(b) detect new obstacles as they become visible.

The problem in (b) becomes computationally much easier with a variable resolution system. Obstacles need to be detected mostly in the periphery where the number of masks that need to be matched is small. Once an obstacle is detected the problem then is to keep track of it. Small masks for obstacle detection can be used in the fovea. This would detect obstacles which are small relative to the image and thus pick up things appearing in the horizon. The only problem occurs when the road slopes upward and the horizon appears abruptly. In such a situation even humans are slow in reacting.

4. Tracking

One important visual task is to keep track of an object or a person in motion. Examples include, chasing a burgler or following a car in front while driving. The problem of tracking does not necessitate keeping detailed information of the entire object of interest. We obtain details only on specific parts of the object or person being tracked. While talking to a person we keep details only of the face, whereas when we play tennis we concentrate our attention on the racquet and arm. Fig. 7 shows a possible representation of a person when the fovea is concentrated on the face and the peripheral resolution is continuously decreasing. If one now wishes to find out what type of shoe the person is wearing the fovea needs to be focussed on the feet instead.

Fig. 7. Outline as represented in continuously varying resolution

4.1 Accuracy of the reconstruction

We have shown how the accuracy of obtaining 3-d parameters vary with change in image resolution. Details are given in [3]. and cannot be included here due to lack of space.

4.2 Reduction in complexity

There are several ways of implementing a variable resolution system. One would be to have the resolution decrease continuously as we move away from the center of the image. Consider a straight line segment AB of length n (in terms of number of pixels) in uniform resolution. Two schemes for a variable resolution system are described below:

Scheme I:

1. The fovea is a $k \times k$ array (Region 1).

2. Resolution is reduced by a ratio 2:1 for a length k strip around the fovea (Region 2).

3. Resolution is reduced by a ratio L:1 for a length k strip around the Region $(L-1)$, (Region L), $(L = 3, \cdots)$.

Scheme II:

Similar to Scheme I, except that the resolution of Region L is reduced by a ratio 2:1 compared to the resolution of Region $(L-1)$. With respect to Scheme I, the length of line segment is lk, where

$$\sum_{i=1}^{\ell} ik = n \Rightarrow k\ell(\ell+1)/2 = n \Rightarrow \ell \approx \sqrt{\frac{2n}{k}}$$

$\Rightarrow$ length of segment AB in Scheme I is $O(\sqrt{nk})$

If we consider Scheme II, again the length of the line segment is lk, where

$$\sum_{i=1}^{\ell} 2^{(i-1)} k = n \Rightarrow k2^{\ell} = n \Rightarrow \ell = \log_2 n - \log_2 k$$

Thus, length of line segment AB in Scheme II is $O(k \log n)$.

5. Character thinning

Another application of variable resolution vision is in character thinning. The input is a binary image of a character. The pixels with value 1 form the character and the pixels with value 0 form the background. Most thinning algorithms use a 3×3 window to scan through all character pixels along the contour of the character in order to determine if each pixel should be eliminated from the character (value changed from 1 to 0). After several iterations, a skeleton of the character is obtained. Various thinning algorithms differ in the templates used and the order in which they are applied. Since the template is small, the algorithm has no way to obtain global knowledge of the entire character. Fig. 8 shows the results obtained by existing thinning algorithms on the letter "K". The character pixels (marked with "A") are deleted from the character, and a "valley" is formed. Several existing thinning algorithms [5] using 3 × 3 templates will generate a skeleton similar to that in Fig. 8(c).

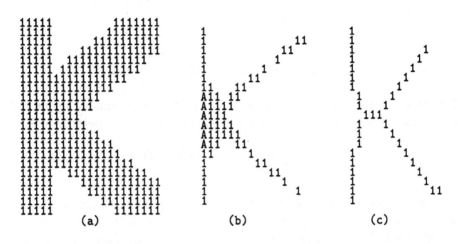

Fig. 8 Character "K" and some thinning results
(a) input, (b) after iteration 3, (c) after iteration 4
(d) the final skeleton of algorithm in [17]

In order to solve the above problem and similar problems in thinning some thinning algorithms [6] use templates larger than 3 × 3 to obtain knowledge of a larger neighborhood of the character pixel currently being considered. However, the computational complexity increases exponentially with increasing template size, as shown in the following table.

template size	number of comparisons	number of possible templates
3 × 3	9	2^9
5 × 5	25	2^{25}
7 × 7	49	2^{49}
9 × 9	81	2^{81}

We propose a variable resolution approach to thinning. This approach uses a set of templates. Some templates are 3 × 3 and some of them employ two resolution levels. A two-level template covering a 9 × 9 pixel region of the input image is shown in Fig. 9. This template is partitioned into 9 equal square-shaped parts. The center part is a regular 3 × 3 template, Each one of the eight peripheral parts also covers a 3 × 3 region.

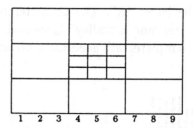

Fig. 9 A variable resolution template

Two binary values, X and Y, are generated from each peripheral region of 9 pixels. In our current experiment, a simple thresholding is used to determine X as

$$X = \begin{cases} 0 & \text{if there are} < 5 \text{ character pixels in this region} \\ 1 & \text{otherwise} \end{cases}$$

Binary variable Y is used to record some special pattern of the pixel arrangement in this 3×3 region. For example, a 3×3 region with three "1" pixels randomly arranged should be distinguished with three "1" pixels forming a straight line in this region. In this case, the periphery forms a straight line so the center pixel should not be deleted. Variable Y is set to 1 in such a situation. Other situations, such as a horizontal line or a corner, can also be represented. Fig. 10 gives a few examples of such templates.

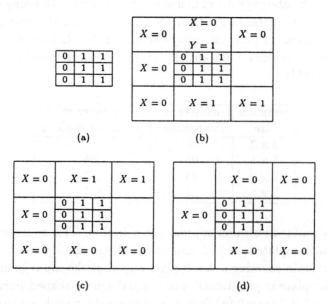

Fig. 10 Example templates
(a) a 3×3 template, (b), (c), and (d) are variable resolution templates.

Since at most two binary values are used for each peripheral region, at most $16 + 9$ bits are used for each large template. We take a contour following approach. During the thinning process, the set of templates will be used to match the neighborhood of each contour pixel following the contour of the character. The templates with only the center part of 3×3 high-resolution pixels are used first. When a match is found and certain templates (3×3) are identified a set of related variable resolution templates are applied. For example, when the template in Fig. 10(a) matches the neighborhood of a character pixel, the templates in Fig. 10(b) through Fig. 10(d) are used. These three larger templates specify that the character possibly has a long vertical stroke. If the neighborhood matches the template in Fig. 10(b) or (d), this character pixel should NOT be deleted.

Fig. 11 is the result of a thinning experiment using the proposed algorithm. Note that the straight vertical stroke is perserved, while a valley is formed when only 3×3 templates are used (Fig. 9). The experimental results demonstrate the advantages of a variable resolution scheme over existing methods.

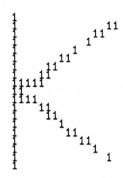

Fig. 11 The result skeleton of character "K" using
the variable resolution template approach

6. Conclusions

In this paper we studied how a variable resolution vision system can simplify several visual tasks. Specifically, we considered the problems of stereo matching, obstacle avoidance, tracking and character thinning. The theory has already been implemented for character thinning where it is shown to perform better than several existing algorithms. Presently we are working on practical experiments for the other applications.

References

[1] J. Aloimonos, A. Bandyopadhay, and I. Weiss. Active vision. *Proc. ICCV*, 35(54), 1987.

[2] D.H. Ballard. Animate vision. *Proc. IJCAI*, 1989.

[3] A. Basu and X. Li. Variable resolution vision. *Technical Report TR 90-14, Dept. of Comuting Science, University of Alberta*, 1990.

[4] C.M. Brown. Gaze controls with interactions and delays. *IEEE Trans. SMC-20*, 1, 1990.

[5] Y. Chen and W. Hsu. A modified fast parallel thinning algorithms for digital patterns. *Pattern Recongnition Letters*, 7(2):99–106, 1988.

[6] V. Govindan and A. Shivaprasad. A pattern adaptive thinning algorithm. *Pattern Recognition*, 20(6):623–637, 1987.

[7] A.D. Gross and A. Rosenfeld. Multiresolution object detection and delineation. *Computer Vision, Graphics and Image Processing*, 39:102–115, 1987.

[8] M. Jenkin and J.K. Tsotsos. Applying temporal constraints to the dynamic stereo problem. *Computer Vision, Graphics and Image Processing*, 33:16–32, 1986.

[9] D. Marr. *Vision*. W.H. Freeman: San Francisco, 1982.

[10] R. Nelson and J. Aloimonos. Using flow field divergence for obstacle avoidance in visual navigation. *IEEE Trans. PAMI*, 11:1102–1106, 1989.

[11] D. Terzopoulous. Multiresolution computational process for visual surface reconstruction. *Computer Vision, Graphics and Image Processing*, 24:52–96, 1983.

[12] W.B. Thompson and T.C. Pong. Detecting moving objects. *Proc. IEEE ICCV*, pages 201–208, 1987.

[13] A.P. Witkin. Scale space filtering: a new approach to multi-scale description. *S. Ullman and W. Richards (eds.), Image Understanding 1984, Ablex Publishing Co., Norwood, NJ*, 1984.

AN RMS FOR TEMPORAL REASONING WITH ABSTRACTION

V. Sundararajan, Hitesh N. Dholakia and N. Parameswaran
Artificial Intelligence and Robotics Laboratory,
Department of Computer Science and Engineering,
Indian Institute of Technology,
Madras 600 036, INDIA.

e-mail: parames@shiva.ernet.in

Abstract

This paper focuses on reasoning with action and time. A framework for representation of activities and time in the form of a dependency network is discussed. While in earlier works an RMS framework has been used for representing actions, our framework captures temporal knowledge also in the network in terms of relations between intervals. This framework thus enables integration of temporal reasoning along with causal reasoning among activities. An algorithm for truth propagation in such a network has been applied to a specific domain and an example illustrating its use in temporal and causal reasoning is provided. Abstraction of activities and states has been done by defining abstract temporal intervals and thus layering the knowledge into various levels. Some relational abstractions which are useful in describing the temporal relationships among activities and facts have also been defined.

Keywords:

Causal and Temporal Reasoning, Reason Maintenance Systems, Representation of Action and Time.

1 INTRODUCTION

Motivation

Reasoning about action and time is important in many areas of artificial intelligence, primarily in problem solving, planning and natural language processing, and an adequate representation of action and time is necessary for such reasoning. Reason Maintenance Systems (RMS) have come in to be used as subsystems for inferential problem solving [Doyle, 1979], [Petrie, 1987]. The advantages offered by RMS can be availed when we have to reason about a dynamically changing world. Actions, their preconditions and effects have been represented in an RMS framework to aid in reasoning about action and planning [Jaidev et al, 1990], [Kulkarni and Parameswaran, 1989]. The need for enhancing this framework arises when we have to perform temporal reasoning about activities in addition to causal reasoning. While we adopt an interval-based approach for dealing with time, the typical queries asked in a temporal reasoner leads us to abstractions over time intervals.

Problem statement

Given the description of a plan of activities and facts, we need to answer queries which will require causal and temporal reasoning about these activities and facts. This requires a scheme for representing actions, their preconditions and consequences and their temporal relations, and a reasoning algorithm that can be used as a basis for answering typical queries. Since actions take time, we should also be able to reason about what events can happen when some action is being performed.

Our approach

We use intervals as the basis for representing various actions and facts. The intervals can be related by any of Allen's thirteen primitive relations (or by abstract temporal relations defined later). We represent the actions, their preconditions and consequences in the form of a dependency network. The reasoner distinguishes three different types of nodes in the dependency network, namely relation nodes, action nodes and dummy nodes (introduced in our implementation). The changes arising as a result of performing an action, which are basically changes to time relations among the preconditions, the action and the consequences, can be captured in this network. We treat abstract activities or states as intervals which are temporal abstractions. The basis for the temporal reasoner is an algorithm for propagating truth in the dependency network.

Scope

Issues addressed in this paper relate to representation and reasoning with time and action in an RMS framework. A brief survey of related work is given in Sec. 2. The dependency network and how time can be captured in the network are discussed in Sec. 3. Various temporal abstractions which are useful for denoting abstract relationships among activities and facts are defined in Sec. 4. The concepts presented in these sections are used in a specific application domain in Sec. 5. Sec. 6 deals with limitation of this approach and scope for future work.

2 PREVIOUS WORK

Representation of activity knowledge has been addressed in [Sathi et al, 1985]. A layered approach for abstraction of knowledge represented in the form of a semantic network is discussed with emphasis on project management application. Abstraction of activities and states has been done using subactivity and substate relations. Sathi's representation is based on Brachmann's five layers of knowledge.

The concept of time has turned out to be a recurring problem in many application domains. Allen [Allen, 1983] introduced an interval-based temporal logic and defined thirteen primitive relations between intervals. He gave a reasoning algorithm based on relational constraint propagation. Koomen [Koomen, 1990] modified this algorithm for efficiency and suggested further abstract relations over temporal intervals. Allen also proposed a formalism for reasoning about actions based on this temporal logic [Allen, 1984]. A scheme for temporal as well as causal reasoning in an activity knowledge base is proposed in [Dholakia et al, 1990].

The technique of reason maintenance was first implemented in Doyle's Truth Maintenance System (TMS) [Doyle, 1979]. The purpose of the TMS is to provide explanations for belief or disbelief in assertions by means of attached justifications. Another important capability of the TMS is Dependency-Directed Backtracking (DDB). de Kleer proposed another implementation of the TMS in his Assumption-based Truth Maintenance System (ATMS) [de Kleer, 1986].

If actions are modeled in terms of dependencies over facts, the inherent advantages of an RMS can be utilized in reasoning with this knowledge. A scheme for representing actions in an ATMS is discussed in [Morris and Nado, 1986]. The use of an ATMS to reason about and maintain plan networks is described in Plan Network Maintenance System (PNMS) [Beetz and Lefkowitz, 1989]. A Reason Maintenance System (RMS) for planning and reasoning about actions is discussed in [Jaidev et al, 1990].

3 REPRESENTATION OF TIME IN RMS

An RMS consists of a dependency network and a mechanism for truth propagation. A dependency network is defined as a pair DN = (N,J) where N is a set of nodes and J is a set of justifications.

The conventional RMS does not represent actions. Actions can be naturally represented in terms of preconditions and consequents which can be easily captured by dependencies. When an action deletes its own precondition it leads to an odd loop in the network. Jaidev [Jaidev et al, 1990] has represented actions in an RMS framework in a way that overcomes this problem.

However this framework does not capture temporal knowledge. Actions do take time and require preconditions and consequents to follow specific temporal relations. For example, some actions produce their effects while they are executed completely, while some may produce consequents which start even while action is still going on. Similarly some facts occurred in the past may trigger some action and thus will form part of the preconditions for that action.

In this paper, we follow Allen's interval based approach to represent time. Intervals are related by thirteen primitive mutually exclusive relations: *before (:b)*, *meets (:m)*, *overlaps (:o)*, *starts (:s)*, *finishes (:f)*, *during* (*:d*) and their inverses (denoted by the suffix i e.g. *:oi* for *overlapped by*) and the *equal (:e)* relation. But to reason about actions we also need causal dependency relations. We have unified the interval based logic with RMS representation to reason with actions and time. We define three types of the nodes in RMS network as:

N = {A, R, D}

where A are action nodes, R are relation nodes and D nodes are dummy nodes to support actions non-monotonically.

D-nodes are similar to the non-deletion assumptions of [Morris and Nado, 1986]. The D-nodes partially solve the qualification problem i.e. the difficulty in enumerating all possible preconditions for an action to take place. The D-node justifies an action thus making it possible to retract the action even if all the preconditions stated are true. (This retraction is necessary if the action can not take place due to some reason which is not specified among its preconditions).

Conventionally an action's preconditions and consequents are specified in terms of facts or predicates. Facts are denoted by the corresponding intervals over which the facts hold in the temporal graph. So it is natural to represent intervals as nodes for the preconditions and consequents. Actions more generally require relations between intervals to be preconditions and may similarly result in consequents which are temporally related. This requires relation nodes also in the RMS network. We have found it sufficient to use relation nodes (R-nodes) only, because a relation inherently captures both the fact that the intervals exist and that they are related by some temporal relation. Since both actions and facts are denoted by intervals in the temporal graph, an action can also be represented as a precondition or consequent for some other action.

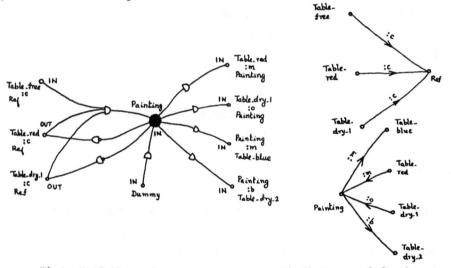

Fig.1a RMS Network   Fig.1b Temporal Graph

An example of representing action is given below. Suppose the action is to paint a table which is originally red, to blue. This requires the preconditions : (i) table should be free, (ii) table is red and (iii) table is dry. When the painting action starts, the table is no longer red in color (it will be partially blue and partially red). Also it will be no longer dry when the painting action is going on.

When painting is finished the table will be blue. But the table will be dry only after some time. The above example states that we have to use temporal relations to state preconditions and consequents. The temporal graphs before and after performing the action are shown in Fig 1b. The corresponding RMS representation is also shown in Fig 1a.

4 TEMPORAL ABSTRACTIONS

Once we have primitive relations over intervals, more complex relations can be defined to give more abstract relations which are often used in real life. "The diagnosis should *start before* the treatment": in this statement a more abstract relation *start before* is used. This relation states that the interval corresponding to diagnosis has a start point before the start point of the interval corresponding to treatment. Thus it can be defined as {*:o :di :fi :m :b*}. The following are some useful abstractions:

Within (:w)	{:d :s :f}
Started before (:sb)	{:o :di :fi :m :b}
Finished before (:fb)	{:o :d :m :b :s}
Later (:l)	{:sbi :e :si}
Disjoint (:dj)	{:b :a}
Intersects (:p)	{:o :fi :di :m}

One can extend the list of thirteen primitive relations by adding durational relations on intervals like longer than, shorter than, n times, etc.

Abstract Intervals

An abstract activity or state can be decomposed into sub activities or sub states. Each such subactivity or substate will correspond to an interval in the temporal network. Thus an interval corresponding to an abstract activity or state can be defined as a subgraph of the temporal network.

Thus, an abstract interval is defined by a pair:
$I_r = (I, R)$,
where I is a set of intervals $\{i_1,...,i_n\}$,
R is set of relations $\{r_1,...,r_m\}$ over the intervals $\{i_1,...,i_n\}$ and
I_j (:d :s :f) I_r for all j, j = 1,...,n.

Abstract intervals will be useful in containing the combinatorial growth, a discouraging feature typical of temporal reasoning [Allen, 1983]. The abstract interval somewhat resembles the reference interval of Allen. In our representation abstract intervals are not just intended to obtain computational efficiency but they serve as a means to represent various levels of abstraction in the knowledge base.

Representation of Abstract Intervals

The representation of abstract activity and state is done in the same way as at the lower level. An abstract relation between I_{r1} and I_{r2} is justified by all lower level intervals which define them. The abstract action node is justified by corresponding lower level actions. Thus we can form a network at this abstract level.

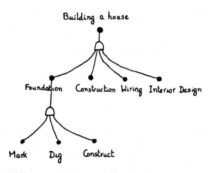

Fig.2 Abstraction over activities

Such a three layered representation of a plan is shown in Fig.2. *Building a house* is an abstract activity composed of subactivities like *foundation, construction, wiring, interior decoration*, etc. Each will correspond to an interval and will have temporal relations with other intervals forming a graph. This graph (actually a subgraph of the whole network) can be represented as an abstract node *Building a house* in the upper level temporal net.

Truth propagation at abstract levels

When a change is made in the lower level network of RMS this change is propagated. A change at lower level may cause changes at higher levels because all abstract nodes are dependent on lower level nodes. This propagation continues upto the highest level of abstraction.

If a change is made at an upper level of abstraction it can be propagated at that level or the layers above it. If one wants to infer the effects at a lower level, the status of all the intervals which define the abstract intervals involved in the change can be changed thus propagating the effect at lower levels.

5 AN APPLICATION

In real life problems, one has to reason about the past, the present and the future. We have chosen activities in a health center as our application domain. Temporal reasoning about activities is essential in this domain. A few typical queries which involve reasoning about time as well as actions are listed below:

What will happen if some *doctor is not free*?
If an *operation* can't take place what are the consequences?
When can a particular *consultation* take place?
What activities can go on when *operation* is going on?
Why is *treatment* not possible?

One can think of several temporal abstractions which pertain to a given domain of application. These temporal abstractions make use of the primitive relations as well as domain independent abstractions defined in section 5.1. Some of the abstractions useful for our domain along with the queries which make use of this are listed below (abstractions are mentioned in italics):

What is the *earliest* that one can meet the doctor?
How long will the operation last?
Can treatment of patient-1 *finish during* treatment of patient-2?
How often does a drug cause some reaction?

Many more such relations like *when, longest, started during* etc. involving two or more intervals or even the entire temporal graph can be defined.

Given a plan of activities, the actions along with their preconditions and consequences will form a network of dependency relations. One such net for hospital activities is shown in Fig. 3a (on the next page). The temporal graph is also shown in Fig. 3b (on the next page).

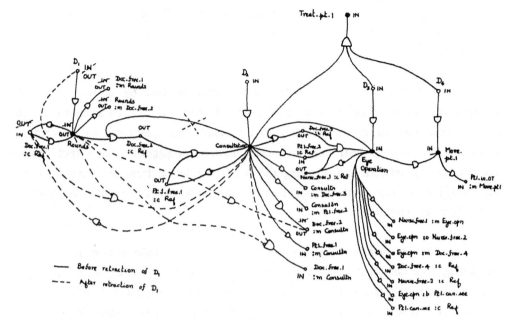

Fig. 3a Dependency network

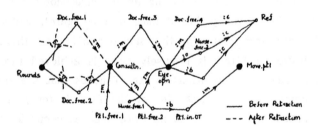

Fig. 3b Temporal graph

Only those relations that are asserted as preconditions and consequences of action intervals are shown. Other relations can be inferred through transitivity closure when required.

Consider the query: What will the temporal relation be between the first instance of *doctor free* and the action *consultation* if due to some reason the action *rounds* can not go on according to the plan? This query can be answered by retracting the D-node justifying the action *rounds*, propagating the effect through the dependency network and inferring the required relation from the temporal graph. The working of the truth propagation in the dependency network is described below with an example.

The action *rounds* will be made OUT. This will make *doctor free-1* to be continuing. We can find the consequent *doctor free-2* continuing as of the same type as *doctor free-1* continuing (Different instances of the same fact at different intervals of time are grouped to be of the same type). Also *doctor free-2* continuing is a precondition for the action *consultation*. Now the action *consultation* is justified through a new justification with *doctor free-1* continuing as its monotonic supporter and the action *rounds* as its nonmonotonic supporter (Newly added justifications are shown by dotted lines in the figure). Note that it is the first instance of *doctor free* continuing that should now become the precondition for the action *consultation* and this is precisely what is achieved through this newly added justification. Similar justifications for the R-nodes that are relations between the action node *consultation* and instances of the fact *doctor free* are added. As the action *consultation* was already IN no more changes occur in the network and the propagation stops. From the modified temporal network, we infer that the required relation is :*m*.

6 CONCLUSION

We have presented a framework to represent temporal and activity knowledge in an RMS network. Instead of representing preconditions and consequents of an action as intervals we have chosen to use relations between intervals as the nodes in the RMS. We have suggested a partial solution to the qualification problem in our representation. Abstract temporal intervals are proposed for representing knowledge at different levels of abstraction. An algorithm for truth propagation at a particular level has been proposed.

Our representation assumes that most of our temporal knowledge is relative and hence temporal reasoning is done based on relations between intervals only. In real life applications, one must also include a reference time line such as the real time line.

In a more complex and practical environment, the application described in this paper can be extended to a distributed hospital system for reasoning with complex activities over space and time.

ACKNOWLEDGEMENT

We are grateful to Dr. R. Nagarajan for his valuable suggestions during the discussions we had with him.

References

[Allen, 1983]
James F. Allen, Maintaining Knowledge about Temporal Intervals, Communications of the ACM, Vol. 26, pp. 832-843, 1983.

[Allen, 1984]
James F. Allen, Towards a General Theory of Action and Time, Artificial Intelligence, Vol. 23, pp. 123-154, 1984.

[Beetz and Lefkowitz, 1989]
Beetz M. and Lefkowitz S. L., Reasoning about Justified Events : A Unified Treatment of Temporal Projection, Planning Rationale and Domain Constraints (An Extended Abstract), MEMO-P-89-21, TA TRIUMPH-ADLER AG, Germany, 1989.

[de Kleer, 1986]
de Kleer J., An Assumption-based Truth Maintenance System, Artificial Intelligence 28, pp. 127-162, 1986.

[Dholakia et al, 1990]
Hitesh N. Dholakia, V. Sundararajan and N. Parameswaran, Truth Propagation in Activity Knowledge-base, Proc. of the Third KBCS Conference, Pune, India, 1990.

[Doyle, 1979]
Doyle J., A Truth Maintenance System, Artificial Intelligence, Vol. 12, pp. 231-272, 1979.

[Jaidev et al, 1990]
Jaidev, Tadepalli K. and Parameswaran N., A RMS Based Plan Representation, Proc. of the Third UNB Artificial Intelligence Workshop, Canada, 1990.

[Koomen, 1989]
Johannes A. G. M. Koomen, Reasoning about Recurrence, Doctoral Thesis, 1989.

[Kulkarni and Parameswaran, 1989]
Kulkarni D. and Parameswaran N., Action Representation for Planning using Truth Maintenance System, Proceedings of TENCON-89, The 4th IEEE region 10 International Conference, Bombay, pp. 995-998.

[Morris and Nado, 1986]
Morris P. H. and Nado R. A., Representing Actions with an Assumption-Based Truth Maintenance System, Proc. AAAI-86, 1986.

[Sathi et al, 1985]
Arvind Sathi, Mark S. Fox and Michael Greenberg, Representation of Activity Knowledge for Project Management, IEEE Transactions on Pattern Analysis and Machine Intelligence, Vol. PAMI-7, No. 5, Sep. 1985.

AUTHOR INDEX

This series reports new developments in computer science research and teaching – quickly, informally and at a high level. The type of material considered for publication includes preliminary drafts of original papers and monographs, technical reports of high quality and broad interest, advanced level lectures, reports of meetings, provided they are of exceptional interest and focused on a single topic. The timeliness of a manuscript is more important than its form which may be unfinished or tentative. If possible, a subject index should be included. Publication of Lecture Notes is intended as a service to the international computer science community, in that a commercial publisher, Springer-Verlag, can offer a wide distribution of documents which would otherwise have a restricted readership. Once published and copyrighted, they can be documented in the scientific literature.

Manuscripts

Manuscripts should be no less than 100 and preferably no more than 500 pages in length.
They are reproduced by a photographic process and therefore must be typed with extreme care. Symbols not on the typewriter should be inserted by hand in indelible black ink. Corrections to the typescript should be made by pasting in the new text or painting out errors with white correction fluid. Authors receive 75 free copies and are free to use the material in other publications. The typescript is reduced slightly in size during reproduction; best results will not be obtained unless the text on any one page is kept within the overall limit of 18 x 26.5 cm (7 x 10½ inches). On request, the publisher will supply special paper with the typing area outlined.
Manuscripts should be sent to Prof. G. Goos, GMD Forschungsstelle an der Universität Karlsruhe, Haid- und Neu-Str. 7, 7500 Karlsruhe 1, Germany, Prof. J. Hartmanis, Cornell University, Dept. of Computer Science, Ithaca, NY/USA 14853, or directly to Springer-Verlag Heidelberg.

Springer-Verlag, Heidelberger Platz 3, D-1000 Berlin 33
Springer-Verlag, Tiergartenstraße 17, D-6900 Heidelberg 1
Springer-Verlag, 175 Fifth Avenue, New York, NY 10010/USA
Springer-Verlag, 37-3, Hongo 3-chome, Bunkyo-ku, Tokyo 113, Japan

ISBN 3-540-54029-6
ISBN 0-387-54029-6